T0189154

More information about this subseries at http://www.springer.com/series/7407

Fritz Henglein · Sharon Shoham ·
Yakir Vizel (Eds.)

Verification, Model Checking, and Abstract Interpretation

22nd International Conference, VMCAI 2021
Copenhagen, Denmark, January 17–19, 2021
Proceedings

 Springer

Editors
Fritz Henglein
University of Copenhagen
Copenhagen, Denmark

Sharon Shoham
Tel Aviv University
Tel Aviv, Israel

Yakir Vizel
Technion
Haifa, Israel

ISSN 0302-9743   ISSN 1611-3349 (electronic)
Lecture Notes in Computer Science
ISBN 978-3-030-67066-5   ISBN 978-3-030-67067-2 (eBook)
https://doi.org/10.1007/978-3-030-67067-2

LNCS Sublibrary: SL1 – Theoretical Computer Science and General Issues

This Springer imprint is published by the registered company Springer Nature Switzerland AG
The registered company address is: Gewerbestrasse 11, 6330 Cham, Switzerland

Preface

Welcome to the proceedings of VMCAI 2021, the 22nd International Conference on Verification, Model Checking, and Abstract Interpretation.

Nonlocation. VMCAI 2021 was held January 17–19, 2021, jointly with the 48th ACM SIGPLAN Symposium on Principles of Programming Languages (POPL 2021). In contrast to previous years, VMCAI took place entirely online due to the COVID-19 pandemic, after originally being planned to be held at Hotel Scandic Copenhagen in Copenhagen, Denmark, colocated with POPL 2021.

Conference description. VMCAI provides a forum for researchers working on verification, model checking, and abstract interpretation and facilitates interaction, cross-fertilization, and advancement of hybrid methods that combine these and related areas.

The topics of the conference include program verification, model checking, abstract interpretation, program synthesis, static analysis, type systems, deductive methods, decision procedures, theorem proving, program certification, debugging techniques, program transformation, optimization, and hybrid and cyber-physical systems.

Focus on reproducibility of research sesults. For the second time, VMCAI 2021 included an optional artifact evaluation (AE) process for submitted papers. Reproducibility of results is of the utmost importance to the VMCAI community. Therefore, we encouraged all authors to submit an artifact for evaluation. An artifact is any additional material (software, data sets, machine-checkable proofs, etc.) that substantiates the claims made in a paper and ideally makes them fully replicable. The evaluation and archiving of artifacts improves replicability and traceability for the benefit of future research and the broader VMCAI community.

Paper selection. VMCAI 2021 received a total of 50 paper submissions, of which 2 were rejected without a full review for being out of scope and 1 was withdrawn during the reviewing period. After a rigorous review process, with each paper reviewed by at least three program committee members and a subsequent online discussion, the program committee eventually accepted 23 papers for publication in the proceedings and for presentation at the conference: 20 regular papers, 2 case studies, and 1 tool paper. The main selection criteria were quality, relevance, and originality.

Invited talks and papers. The conference program included three invited keynote presentations. They were by Bernd Finkbeiner (Universität des Saarlandes and CISPA Helmholtz Center for Information Security) on *Model Checking Algorithms for Hyperproperties*, by Laura Kovács (TU Wien) on *Algebra-Based Synthesis of Loops and their Invariants*, and by Bernhard Steffen (TU Dortmund) on *Generative Program Analysis and Beyond: The Power of Domain-Specific Languages*.

Each of the keynote presentations is accompanied by a paper the speakers were invited to contribute to these proceedings. David Schmidt (Kansas State University), who was jointly invited, elected to defer to and support Bernhard Steffen's invited talk and paper.

No winter school. In contrast to previous years there was no winter school preceding the conference. The organizers figured that the interactive spirit and intensity of a winter school would be too difficult to achieve in the purely online setting necessitated by COVID-19.

Artifact evaluation process. VMCAI 2021 continued the artifact evaluation process established by VMCAI 2020. The goals of artifact evaluation are: (1) to get more substantial evidence for the claims in the papers, (2) to simplify the replication of results in the paper, and (3) to reward authors who create artifacts. Artifacts are any additional material that substantiates the claims made in the paper. Examples of artifacts are software, tools, frameworks, data sets, test suites, and machine-checkable proofs.

Authors of submitted papers were encouraged to submit an artifact to the VMCAI 2021 artifact evaluation committee (AEC). We also encouraged the authors to make their artifacts publicly and permanently available. Artifacts had to be provided as `.zip` or `.tar.gz` files and had to contain all necessary software for artifact evaluation as well as a `README` file that describes the artifact and provides instructions on how to replicate the results. Artifact evaluation had to be possible in the VMCAI 2021 virtual machine, which ran Ubuntu 20.04 and was made publicly and permanently available on Zenodo[1].

All 22 submitted artifacts were evaluated in parallel with the papers. We assigned three members of the AEC to each artifact and assessed it in two phases. First, the reviewers tested whether the artifacts were working, e.g. there were no corrupted or missing files and the evaluation did not crash on simple examples. For those artifacts that did not work, we sent the issues to the authors. The authors' answers to the reviewers were distributed among the reviewers, and the authors were allowed to submit an updated artifact to fix issues found during the test phase. In the second phase, the assessment phase, the reviewers aimed at reproducing any experiments or activities and evaluated the artifact based on the following questions:

1. Is the artifact consistent with the paper and the claims made by the paper?
2. Are the results of the paper replicable through the artifact?
3. Is the artifact well documented?
4. Is the artifact easy to use?

21 of the 22 submitted artifacts passed this second phase. Of these, 12 artifacts also had their corresponding paper accepted, and were rewarded with the 'Functional' VMCAI artifact evaluation badge. Ten of these further consisted of artifacts that were made permanently and publicly available; they were awarded the 'Available' VMCAI artifact evaluation badge. Four of these were further considered remarkably well structured, well documented and easy to adapt to future experiments or comparisons, and received the 'Reusable' badge.

Acknowledgments. We would like to thank, first of all, the authors for submitting their papers and, in many cases, supporting artifacts to VMCAI 2021.

---

[1] https://zenodo.org/record/4017293.

The program committee and the artifact evaluation committee did a great job of reviewing: they contributed informed and detailed reports and engaged conscientiously in the discussions and, in 3 cases, shepherding that eventually led to the decisions which submissions to accept for presentation at the conference and for inclusion in the present proceedings.

We warmly thank the keynote speakers for their participation and contributions.

We also thank the organizational committee of POPL 2021, in particular POPL General Chair Andreas Podelski, for the umbrella organization they provided for the entire POPL 2021 conference week.

Special thanks go to Clowdr for providing an online conference platform that not only provided live audio/video transmission of the presentations, but also facilitated low-carbon interactive and social participation from around the world.

We thank Christine Reiss and her publication team at Springer for their support, and EasyChair for facilitating an efficient reviewing process.

The VMCAI steering committee and the previous year's PC co-chairs, Dirk Beyer and Damien Zufferey, have provided helpful advice, assistance, and support. Special thanks go to Andreas Podelski for his experienced supervision and support from initial planning to execution and finalization of VMCAI 2021.

Last but not least, we thank the sponsors, Amazon Web Services, Cadence, and Springer, for their financial contributions. They made it possible for students and others without the financial means to cover the registration fee to participate in VMCAI 2021.

November 2020

Fritz Henglein
Sharon Shoham
Yakir Vizel
Klaus von Gleissenthall
Troels Henriksen

Organization

Program Committee (PC)

Aws Albarghouthi	University of Wisconsin-Madison
Josh Berdine	Facebook
Dirk Beyer	LMU Munich
Nikolaj Bjørner	Microsoft
Roderick Bloem	Graz University of Technology
Ahmed Bouajjani	IRIF, University of Paris
Swarat Chaudhuri	University of Texas at Austin
Yu-Fang Chen	Academia Sinica
Hana Chockler	King's College London
Rayna Dimitrova	CISPA Helmholtz Center for Information Security
Dana Drachsler-Cohen	Technion
Cezara Drăgoi	Inria and ENS
Grigory Fedyukovich	Florida State University
Jean-Christophe Filliatre	CNRS
Orna Grumberg	Technion
Arie Gurfinkel	University of Waterloo
Fritz Henglein (Co-chair)	University of Copenhagen and Deon Digital
Guy Katz	The Hebrew University of Jerusalem
Rupak Majumdar	Max Planck Institute for Software Systems
Antoine Miné	Sorbonne Université
Jorge A. Navas	SRI International
Oded Padon	Stanford University
Corina S. Pasareanu	Carnegie Mellon University and NASA Ames Research Center and KBR
Azalea Raad	Imperial College London
Xavier Rival	Inria and CNRS and ENS and PSL University
Ilya Sergey	Yale-NUS College and National University of Singapore
Sharon Shoham (Co-chair)	Tel Aviv University
Alexander J. Summers	The University of British Columbia
Niki Vazou	IMDEA Software Institute
Michael Whalen	Amazon Web Services
James R. Wilcox	Certora and University of Washington
Yakir Vizel (Co-chair)	Technion
Lenore Zuck	University of Illinois at Chicago

Artifact Evaluation Committee (AEC)

Shaun Azzopardi	University of Gothenburg
Alexey Bakhirkin	MathWorks
Guillaume Bau	Nomadic Labs
Marek Chalupa	Masaryk University
Mingshuai Chen	RWTH Aachen
Yu-Ting Chen	Chalmers University of Technology
Julia Eisentraut	Technical University of Munich
Isabel Garcia	IMDEA Software Institute & Universidad Politécnica de Madrid
Miriam García Soto	IST Austria
Aman Goel	University of Michigan
Hari Govind V. K.	Unaffiliated
Daniel Hausmann	Friedrich-Alexander-Universität Erlangen-Nürnberg
Troels Henriksen (Co-chair)	University of Copenhagen
Nouraldin Jaber	Purdue University
Konstantinos Kallas	University of Pennsylvania
Bettina Könighofer	Technical University of Graz
Yunjeong Lee	National University of Singapore
Thomas Lemberger	Ludwig Maximilian University of Munich
Monal Narasimhamurthy	University of Colorado Boulder
Abdelraouf Ouadjaout	LIP6, Sorbonne Université
Tanja Schindler	University of Freiburg
Yoshiki Takashima	Carnegie Mellon University
Klaus v. Gleissenthall (Co-chair)	Vrije Universiteit Amsterdam
Joakim Öhman	IMDEA Software Institute

Steering Committee (SC)

Tino Cortesi	Università Ca' Foscari Venezia
Patrick Cousot	New York University
Ruzica Piskac	Yale University
Andreas Podelski	University of Freiburg
Lenore Zuck	University of Illinois at Chicago

Additional Reviewers

Shaull Almagor	Yotam Feldman
Mohamed Faouzi Atig	Karlheinz Friedberger
Jérôme Dohrau	Adam Geller
Masoud Ebrahimi	Shachar Itzhaky
Gidon Ernst	Jacques-Henri Jourdan

Sudeep Kanav
Jason Koenig
Konstantin Korovin
Yunjeong Lee
Thomas Lemberger
Makai Mann
Christoph Matheja
Dmitry Mordvinov

Andrei Paskevich
Wytse Oortwijn
Martin Spiessl
Divyesh Unadkat
Nico Weise
Philipp Wendler
Yoni Zohar

Contents

Decision Procedures

Invited Papers

Model Checking Algorithms
for Hyperproperties (Invited Paper)

Bernd Finkbeiner$^{(\boxtimes)}$ [iD]

CISPA Helmholtz Center for Information Security, Saarbrücken, Germany
finkbeiner@cispa.saarland

Abstract. Hyperproperties generalize trace properties by expressing relations between multiple computations. Hyperpropertes include policies from information-flow security, like observational determinism or noninterference, and many other system properties including promptness and knowledge. In this paper, we give an overview on the model checking problem for temporal hyperlogics. Our starting point is the model checking algorithm for HyperLTL, a reduction to Büchi automata emptiness. This basic construction can be extended with propositional quantification, resulting in an algorithm for HyperQPTL. It can also be extended with branching time, resulting in an algorithm for HyperCTL*. However, it is not possible to have both extensions at the same time: the model checking problem of HyperQCTL* is undecidable. An attractive compromise is offered by MPL[E], i.e., monadic path logic extended with the equal-level predicate. The expressiveness of MPL[E] falls strictly between that of HyperCTL* and HyperQCTL*. MPL[E] subsumes both HyperCTL* and HyperKCTL*, the extension of HyperCTL* with the knowledge operator. We show that the model checking problem for MPL[E] is still decidable.

1 Introduction

In recent years, the linear-time and branching-time temporal logics have been extended to allow for the specification of hyperproperties [3,5,7,8,11]. Hyperproperties are a generalization of trace properties. Instead of properties of individual computations, hyperproperties express *relations* between multiple computations [4]. This makes it possible to reason uniformly about system properties like information flow, promptness, and knowledge.

In model checking, hyperproperties have played a significant role even before these new logics became available. An early insight was that the verification of a given system against properties that refer to multiple traces can be reduced to the verification of a *modified* system against properties over individual traces. The idea is to self-compose the given system a sufficient number of times. The resulting traces contain in each position a tuple of observations, each resulting from a different computation of the system. With this principle, certain hyperproperties like observational determinism and noninterference can be verified using model checking algorithms for standard linear and branching-time logics [1,13,18].

© Springer Nature Switzerland AG 2021
F. Henglein et al. (Eds.): VMCAI 2021, LNCS 12597, pp. 3–16, 2021.
https://doi.org/10.1007/978-3-030-67067-2_1

The development of new logics specifically for hyperproperties considerably broadened the range of hyperproperties that can be checked automatically. HyperLTL is an extension of linear-time temporal logic (LTL) with quantifiers over trace variables, which allow the formula to refer to multiple traces at the same time. For example, *noninterference* [12] between a secret input h and a public output o can be specified in HyperLTL by requiring that all pairs of traces π and π' that have, in every step, the same inputs except for h (i.e., all inputs in $I \setminus \{h\}$ are equal on π and π') also have the same output o at all times:

$$\forall \pi. \forall \pi'. \ \mathbf{G} \ \big(\bigwedge_{i \in I \setminus \{h\}} i_\pi = i_{\pi'} \big) \ \Rightarrow \ \mathbf{G} \ (o_\pi = o_{\pi'})$$

By combining universal and existential quantification, HyperLTL can also express properties like *generalized noninterference* (GNI) [15], which requires that for every pair of traces π and π', there is a third trace π'' that agrees with π on h and with π' on o:

$$\forall \pi. \forall \pi'. \exists \pi''. \ \mathbf{G} \ (h_\pi = h_{\pi''}) \ \wedge \ \mathbf{G} \ (o_{\pi'} = o_{\pi''})$$

HyperLTL is the starting point of an entire hierarchy of *hyperlogics*, depicted in Fig. 1 and analyzed in detail in [5]. The hyperlogics are obtained from their classic counterparts with two principal extensions. The temporal logics LTL, QPTL, and CTL* are extended with quantifiers and variables over traces or paths, such that the formula can refer to multiple traces or paths at the same time; the first-order and second-order logics FO, S1S, MPL, and MSO are extended with the equal-level predicate E, which indicates that two points happen at the same time (albeit possibly on different computations of the system).

A key limitation of HyperLTL, as first pointed out by Bozzelli et al. [2], is that it is not possible to express promptness requirements, which say that there should exist a common deadline over all traces by which a certain eventuality is satisfied. Such properties can be expressed in FO$[<, E]$, monadic first-order logic of order extended with the equal-level predicate. FO$[<, E]$ is subsumed by the temporal logic HyperQPTL, which extends HyperLTL with quantification over propositions. The following HyperQPTL formula specifies the existence of a common deadline over all traces by which a certain predicate p must become true on all traces. The quantification over the proposition d, which expresses the common deadline, introduces a valuation of d that is *independent* of the choice of trace π:

$$\exists d. \forall \pi. \ \neg d \ \mathcal{U} \ (p_\pi \wedge \mathbf{F} \ d)$$

HyperQPTL captures the *ω-regular hyperproperties* [9]. Even more expressive is S1S$[E]$, monadic second order logic with one successor equipped with the equal-level predicate. While the model checking problem of HyperQPTL is still decidable, it becomes undecidable for S1S$[E]$. This is different from the case of trace properties, where S1S is equally expressive to QPTL, and both have decidable model checking problems.

Extending HyperLTL to branching time leads to the temporal logic Hyper-CTL* [3], which has the same syntax as HyperLTL, except that the quantifiers refer to paths, rather than traces, and that path quantifiers may occur in the scope of temporal modalities. HyperCTL* is subsumed by monadic path logic equipped with the equal-level predicate (MPL[E]), which is a second-order logic where second-order quantifiers are restricted to full computation paths. MPL[E] in turn is contained in HyperQCTL*, the extension of HyperCTL* with propositional quantification. HyperQCTL* is as expressive as full monadic second-order logic with the equal-level predicate (MSO[E]) [5].

In this paper, we study this hierarchy of logics from the perspective of the model checking problem. Our starting point is the model checking algorithm for HyperLTL, which reduces the model checking problem to the language empti-ness problem of a Büchi automaton [10]. The construction is similar to the idea of self-composition in that for every trace variable a separate copy of the sys-tem is introduced. Quantifiers are then eliminated by existential and universal projection on the language of the automaton. This basic construction can be extended with propositional quantification, which is also handled by projection. The construction can also be extended to branching time, by tracking the pre-cise state of each computation, rather than just the trace label. However, it is not possible to implement both extensions at the same time: the model checking problem of HyperQCTL* is undecidable [5].

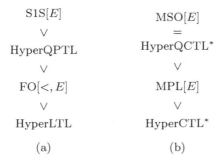

Fig. 1. The hierarchy of hyperlogics [5]: (a) linear time, (b) branching time.

The undecidability of HyperQCTL* is unfortunate, because many interesting properties, such as branching-time knowledge, can be expressed in HyperQCTL*, but not in HyperCTL*. It turns out, however, that MPL[E], whose expres-siveness lies strictly between HyperCTL* and HyperQCTL*, still has a decid-able model checking problem. As the only original contribution of this paper (everything else is based on previously published results), we present the first model checking algorithm for MPL[E]. MPL[E] is a very attractive compro-mise. MPL[E] subsumes both HyperCTL* and HyperKCTL* [5], the extension of HyperCTL* with the knowledge operator.

2 HyperLTL

HyperLTL is a generalization of linear-time temporal logic (LTL). We quickly review the syntax and semantics of LTL and then describe the extension to HyperLTL. Let AP be a finite set of atomic propositions. A trace over AP is a map $t\colon \mathbb{N} \to 2^{\mathrm{AP}}$, denoted by $t(0)t(1)t(2)\cdots$. Let $(2^{\mathrm{AP}})^\omega$ denote the set of all traces over AP.

LTL. The formulas of linear-time temporal logic (LTL) [16] are generated by the following grammar:

$$\varphi ::= a \mid \neg\varphi \mid \varphi \wedge \varphi \mid \mathbf{X}\,\varphi \mid \varphi\,\mathbf{U}\,\varphi$$

where $a \in \mathrm{AP}$ is an *atomic proposition*, the Boolean connectives $\neg$ and $\wedge$ have the usual meaning, $\mathbf{X}$ is the temporal *next* operator, and $\mathbf{U}$ is the temporal *until* operator. We also consider the usual derived Boolean connectives, such as $\vee$, $\to$, and $\leftrightarrow$, and the derived temporal operators *eventually* $\mathbf{F}\,\varphi \equiv \mathbf{tt}\,\mathbf{U}\,\varphi$, *globally* $\mathbf{G}\,\varphi \equiv \neg\mathbf{F}\,\neg\varphi$, and *weak until*: $\varphi\,\mathcal{W}\,\psi \equiv (\varphi\,\mathbf{U}\,\psi) \vee \mathbf{G}\,\varphi$. The satisfaction of an LTL formula φ over a trace t at a position $i \in \mathbb{N}$, denoted by $t, i \models \varphi$, is defined as follows:

$$
\begin{aligned}
t, i &\models a & &\text{iff} & &a \in t(i), \\
t, i &\models \neg\varphi & &\text{iff} & &t, i \not\models \varphi, \\
t, i &\models \varphi_1 \wedge \varphi_2 & &\text{iff} & &t, i \models \varphi_1 \text{ and } t, i \models \varphi_2, \\
t, i &\models \mathbf{X}\,\varphi & &\text{iff} & &t, i+1 \models \varphi, \\
t, i &\models \varphi_1 \mathbf{U}\varphi_2 & &\text{iff} & &\exists k \geq i : t, k \models \varphi_2 \wedge \forall i \leq j < k : t, j \models \varphi_1.
\end{aligned}
$$

We say that a trace t satisfies a sentence φ, denoted by $t \models \varphi$, if $t, 0 \models \varphi$. For example, the LTL formula $\mathbf{G}\,(a \to \mathbf{F}\,b)$ specifies that every position in which a is true must eventually be followed by a position where b is true.

HyperLTL. The formulas of HyperLTL [3] are generated by the grammar

$$
\begin{aligned}
\varphi &::= \exists\pi.\ \varphi \mid \forall\pi.\ \varphi \mid \psi \\
\psi &::= a_\pi \mid \neg\psi \mid \psi \wedge \psi \mid \mathbf{X}\,\psi \mid \psi\,\mathbf{U}\,\psi
\end{aligned}
$$

where a is an atomic proposition from a set AP and π is a trace variable from a set $\mathcal{V}$. Further Boolean connectives and the temporal operators $\mathbf{F}$, $\mathbf{G}$, and $\mathcal{W}$ are derived as for LTL. A sentence is a closed formula, i.e., the formula has no free trace variables.

The semantics of HyperLTL is defined with respect to a trace assignment, a partial mapping $\Pi\colon \mathcal{V} \to (2^{\mathrm{AP}})^\omega$. The assignment with empty domain is denoted by $\Pi_\emptyset$. Given a trace assignment Π, a trace variable π, and a trace t, we denote by $\Pi[\pi \to t]$ the assignment that coincides with Π everywhere but at π, which is mapped to t. The satisfaction of a HyperLTL formula φ over a trace assignment Π and a set of traces T at a position $i \in \mathbb{N}$, denoted by $T, \Pi, i \models \varphi$, is defined as follows:

$$
\begin{aligned}
T, \Pi, i &\models a_\pi & \text{iff} \quad & a \in \Pi(\pi)(i), \\
T, \Pi, i &\models \neg\psi & \text{iff} \quad & T, \Pi, i \not\models \psi, \\
T, \Pi, i &\models \psi_1 \wedge \psi_2 & \text{iff} \quad & T, \Pi, i \models \psi_1 \text{ and } T, \Pi, i \models \psi_2, \\
T, \Pi, i &\models \mathbf{X}\,\psi & \text{iff} \quad & T, \Pi, i+1 \models \psi, \\
T, \Pi, i &\models \psi_1 \, \mathbf{U} \, \psi_2 & \text{iff} \quad & \exists k \geq i : T, \Pi, k \models \psi_2 \\
& & & \wedge \forall i \leq j < k : T, \Pi, j \models \psi_1, \\
T, \Pi, i &\models \exists \pi.\, \varphi & \text{iff} \quad & \exists t \in T : T, \Pi[\pi \to t], i \models \psi, \\
T, \Pi, i &\models \forall \pi.\, \varphi & \text{iff} \quad & \forall t \in T : T, \Pi[\pi \to t], i \models \psi.
\end{aligned}
$$

We say that a set T of traces satisfies a sentence φ, denoted by $T \models \varphi$, if $T, \Pi_\emptyset, 0 \models \varphi$.

System Properties. A *Kripke structure* is a tuple $K = (S, s_0, \delta, \mathrm{AP}, L)$ consisting of a set of states S, an initial state s_0, a transition function $\delta : S \to 2^S$, a set of *atomic propositions* AP, and a *labeling function* $L : S^* \to 2^{\mathrm{AP}}$ that assigns a set of atomic propositions that are true after a given sequence of states has been traversed. We require that each state has a successor, that is $\delta(s) \neq \emptyset$, to ensure that every execution of a Kripke structure can always be continued to infinity. In a *finite* Kripke structure, S is a finite set. We furthermore assume that in a finite Kripke structure, L only depends on the last state, so that L can also be given as a function $S \to 2^{\mathrm{AP}}$.

A *path* of a Kripke structure is an infinite sequence $s_0 s_1 \ldots \in S^\omega$ such that s_0 is the initial state of K and $s_{i+1} \in \delta(s_i)$ for all $i \in \mathbb{N}$. By $Paths(K, s)$, we denote the set of all paths of K starting in state $s \in S$. A *trace* of a path $\sigma = s_0 s_1 \ldots$ is a sequence of labels $l_0 l_1 \ldots$ with $l_i = L(s_0 s_1 \ldots s_i)$ for all $i \in \mathbb{N}$. $Tr(K, s)$ is the set of all traces of paths of a Kripke structure K starting in state s. A Kripke structure K with initial state s_0 satisfies an LTL formula φ, denoted by $K \models \varphi$ iff for all traces $\pi \in Tr(K, s_0)$, it holds that $\pi \models \varphi$. Likewise, the Kripke structure satisfies a HyperLTL formula φ, also denoted by $K \models \varphi$, iff $Tr(K, s_0) \models \varphi$.

Model Checking. The HyperLTL model checking problem is to decide, for a given finite Kripke structure K and a given HyperLTL formula ψ, whether or not $K \models \psi$. The following basic construction (described in more detail in [10]) reduces the model checking problem to the language emptiness problem of a Büchi automaton: the given Kripke structure satisfies the formula if and only if the language of the resulting automaton is empty.

The construction starts by negating ψ, so that it describes the existence of an error. Since we assume that a HyperLTL formula begins with a quantifier prefix, this means that we dualize the quantifiers and then negate the inner LTL formula. Let us assume that the resulting HyperLTL formula has the form $Q_n \pi_{n-1} Q_2 \pi_{n-1} \ldots Q_1 \pi_1.\, \varphi$ where $Q_1, Q_2, \ldots Q_n$ are trace quantifiers in $\{\exists, \forall\}$ and φ is a quantifier-free formula over atomic propositions indexed by trace variables $\{\pi_1, \ldots \pi_n\}$.

Similar to standard LTL model checking, we convert the LTL formula φ into an equivalent Büchi automaton $\mathcal{A}_0$ over the alphabet $(2^{AP})^n$. Each letter is a tuple of n sets of atomic propositions, where the ith element of the tuple represents the atomic propositions of trace π_i.

Next, the algorithm eliminates the quantifiers. For this purpose, it carries out n steps that each eliminate one component from the tuple of the input alphabet. In the ith step, we eliminate the ith component, corresponding to trace variable π_i. Let us consider the ith step. Over the previous steps, the automaton $\mathcal{A}_{i-1}$ over alphabet $(2^{AP})^{(n-i)}$ has been constructed, and now the first component of the tuple corresponds to π_i. If the trace quantifier Q_i is existential, we intersect $\mathcal{A}_{i-1}$ with the Kripke structure K so that, in the sequence of letters, the first component of the tuple is chosen consistently with some path in K. Subsequently, we eliminate the first component of the tuple by existential projection on the automaton. If Q_i is universal, then we combine $\mathcal{A}_{i-1}$ with the Kripke structure K so that only sequences in which the first component is chosen consistently with some path in K need to be accepted by $\mathcal{A}_{i-1}$. Subsequently, we eliminate the first component of the tuple by universal projection on the automaton. This results in the next automaton $\mathcal{A}_i$.

After n such steps, all quantifiers have been eliminated and the language of the resulting automaton is over the one-letter alphabet (consisting of the empty tuple). The HyperLTL formula is satisfied if and only if the language of automaton $\mathcal{A}_n$ is empty.

3   HyperQPTL

HyperQPTL [5,17] extends HyperLTL with quantification over atomic propositions. To easily distinguish quantification over traces $\exists \pi, \forall \pi$ and quantification over propositions $\exists p, \forall p$, we use boldface for the latter. The formulas of Hyper-QPTL are generated by the following grammar:

$$\varphi ::= \exists \pi.\, \varphi \mid \forall \pi.\, \varphi \mid \psi \mid \exists p.\, \varphi \mid \forall p.\, \varphi \mid \psi$$

$$\psi ::= a_\pi \mid p \mid \neg \psi \mid \psi \wedge \psi \mid \mathbf{X}\, \psi \mid \mathbf{F}\, \psi$$

where $a, p \in AP$ and $\pi \in \mathcal{V}$. The semantics of HyperQPTL corresponds to the semantics of HyperLTL with additional rules for propositional quantification:

$$T, \Pi, i \models \exists q.\, \varphi \quad \text{iff} \quad \exists t \in (2^{\{q\}})^\omega.\, T, \Pi[\pi_q \mapsto t], i \models \varphi$$

$$T, \Pi, i \models \forall q.\, \varphi \quad \text{iff} \quad \forall t \in (2^{\{q\}})^\omega.\, T, \Pi[\pi_q \mapsto t], i \models \varphi$$

$$T, \Pi, i \models q \quad \text{iff} \quad q \in \Pi(\pi_q)(i).$$

Expressiveness. As discussed in the introduction, HyperQPTL can express *promptness* [14], which states that there is a bound, common for all traces, until which an eventuality has to be fulfilled. Another common type of property that can be expressed in HyperQPTL is *knowledge*. Epistemic temporal logics extend temporal logics with a so-called *knowledge* operator $\mathcal{K}_A\varphi$, denoting that an agent A knows φ. HyperQPTL can be extended to HyperQPTL$_K$ as follows [17]:

$$T, \Pi, i \models \mathcal{K}_{A,\pi}\varphi \quad \text{iff} \quad \forall t' \in T.\, \Pi(\pi)[0, i] =_A t'[0, i] \rightarrow T, \Pi[\pi \mapsto t'], i \models \varphi$$

In this definition, $t[0, i]$ denotes the prefix of a trace t up to position i. Two sequences t, t' are equivalent with respect to agent A, denoted by $t =_A t'$, if A cannot distinguish t and t'. We assume that A is given as a set of atomic propositions $A \subseteq AP$. Then $t =_A t'$ holds if t and t' agree on all propositions in A.

As shown in [17], the knowledge operator can be eliminated, resulting in an equivalent HyperQPTL formula. The idea is to replace an application of the knowledge operator $\mathcal{K}_{A,\pi}\psi$ with an existentially quantified proposition u and add the following requirement to ensure that u is only true at positions where the knowledge formula is satisfied:

$$\forall r.\,\forall \pi'.\,((r\;\mathcal{U}\;(u \wedge r \wedge \bigcirc \square \neg r)) \wedge \square(r \rightarrow A_\pi = A_{\pi'}) \rightarrow \square(r \wedge \bigcirc \neg r \rightarrow \psi[\pi'/\pi]))$$

In this definition, $A_\pi = A_{\pi'}$ is an abbreviation for the conjunction over all propositions in A that ensures that each proposition has the same value in π and in π'. For each position where the knowledge formula is claimed to be true, the universally quantified proposition r changes from true to false at exactly that position, thus marking the prefix leading to this point. The knowledge formula is then true iff ψ holds on all traces π' that agree with respect to A on the prefix.

HyperQPTL is also strictly more expressive than FO$[<, E]$, the extension of the first-order logic of order with the equal-level predicate E [5]. Given a set V_1 of first-order variables, the formulas φ of FO$[<, E]$ are generated by the following grammar [11]:

$$\varphi ::= \psi \mid \neg\varphi \mid \varphi_1 \vee \varphi_2 \mid \exists x.\varphi$$
$$\psi ::= P_a(x) \mid x < y \mid x = y \mid E(x, y),$$

where $a \in AP$ and $x, y \in V_1$. We interpret FO$[<, E]$ formulas over a set of traces T. We assign first-order variables to elements from the domain $T \times \mathbb{N}$. We define the satisfaction relation $T, V_1 \models \varphi$ with respect to a valuation V_1 assigning all free variables in V_1' as follows:

$T, V_1 \models P_a(x)$ iff $a \in t(n)$ where $(t, n) = V_1(x)$
$T, V_1 \models x < y$ iff $t_1 = t_2 \wedge n_1 < n_2$ where $(t_1, n_1) = V_1(x)$ and $(t_2, n_2) = V_1(y)$
$T, V_1 \models x = y$ iff $V_1(x) = V_1(y)$
$T, V_1 \models E(x, y)$ iff $n_1 = n_2$ where $(t_1, n_1) = V_1(x)$ and $(t_2, n_2) = V_1(y)$
$T, V_1 \models \neg\varphi$ iff $T, V_1 \not\models \varphi$
$T, V_1 \models \varphi_1 \vee \varphi_2$ iff $T, V_1 \models \varphi_1$ or $T, V_1 \models \varphi_2$
$T, V_1 \models \exists x.\varphi$ iff $\exists (t, n) \in T \times \mathbb{N}.$
$\qquad\qquad\qquad T, V_1[x \mapsto (t, n)] \models \varphi,$

where $V_1[x \mapsto v]$ updates a valuation. A trace set T satisfies a closed FO$[<, E]$ formula φ, written $T \models \varphi$, if $T, \emptyset \models \varphi$, where $\emptyset$ denotes the empty valuation.

Model Checking. The only required modification to the model checking algorithm described in Sect. 2 is the treatment of the propositional quantifiers. Since the valuation of the propositions is not restricted by the given Kripke structure, we omit the intersection with the Kripke structure for quantified propositions, and instead eliminate the quantifier by existential or universal projection only.

4   Beyond HyperQPTL

The model checking problems of linear-time hyperlogics beyond HyperQPTL quickly become undecidable. Two examples of such logics are HyperQPTL$^+$ and S1S[E].

HyperQPTL$^+$. HyperQPTL$^+$ [9] differs from HyperQPTL in the role of the propositional quantification. Rather than interpreting the quantified propositions with an additional sequence of values, HyperQPTL$^+$ modifies the interpretation on the existing traces. The syntax of HyperQPTL$^+$ is thus slightly simpler, because also the quantified propositions appear indexed with trace variables:

$$\varphi ::= \forall \pi. \varphi \mid \exists \pi. \varphi \mid \forall a. \varphi \mid \exists a. \varphi \mid \psi$$
$$\psi ::= a_\pi \mid \neg \psi \mid \psi \vee \psi \mid \mathbf{X} \psi \mid \mathbf{F} \psi .$$

In the semantics, the rules for propositional quantification are changed accordingly:

$$T, \Pi, i \models \exists a. \varphi \quad \text{iff} \quad \exists T' \subseteq (2^{\mathrm{AP}})^\omega . T' =_{\mathrm{AP} \setminus \{a\}} T \wedge T', \Pi, i \models \varphi$$
$$T, \Pi, i \models \forall a. \varphi \quad \text{iff} \quad \forall T' \subseteq (2^{\mathrm{AP}})^\omega . T' =_{\mathrm{AP} \setminus \{a\}} T \rightarrow T', \Pi, i \models \varphi .$$

S1S[E]. S1S[E] is monadic second-order logic with one successor (S1S) extended with the equal-level predicate. Let $V_1 = \{x_1, x_2, \ldots\}$ be a set of first-order variables, and $V_2 = \{X_1, X_2, \ldots\}$ a set of second-order variables. The formulas φ of S1S[E] are generated by the following grammar:

$$\tau ::= x \mid min(x) \mid Succ(\tau)$$
$$\varphi ::= \tau \in X \mid \tau = \tau \mid E(\tau, \tau) \mid \neg \varphi \mid \varphi \vee \varphi \mid \exists x. \varphi \mid \exists X. \varphi,$$

where $x \in V_1$ is a first-order variable, *Succ* denotes the successor relation, and $min(x)$ indicates the minimal element of the traces addressed by x. Furthermore, $E(\tau, \tau)$ is the equal-level predicate and $X \in V_2 \cup \{X_a \mid a \in AP\}$. We interpret S1S[$E$] formulas over a set of traces T. As for FO[$<, E$], the domain of the first-order variables is $T \times \mathbb{N}$. Let $\mathcal{V}_1 : V_1 \rightarrow T \times \mathbb{N}$ and $\mathcal{V}_2 : V_2 \rightarrow 2^{(T \times \mathbb{N})}$ be the first-order and second-order valuation, respectively. The value of a term is defined as follows:

$$[x]_{\mathcal{V}_1} = \mathcal{V}_1(x)$$
$$[min(x)]_{\mathcal{V}_1} = (proj_1(\mathcal{V}_1(x)), 0)$$
$$[S(\tau)]_{\mathcal{V}_1} = (proj_1([\tau]_{\mathcal{V}_1}), proj_2([\tau]_{\mathcal{V}_1}) + 1),$$

where $proj_1$ and $proj_2$ denote the projection to the first and second component, respectively. Let φ be an S1S[E] formula with free first-order and second-order variables $V_1' \subseteq V_1$ and $V_2' \subseteq V_2 \cup \{X_a \mid a \in AP\}$, respectively. We define the satisfaction relation $T, \mathcal{V}_1, \mathcal{V}_2 \models \varphi$ with respect to two valuations $\mathcal{V}_1, \mathcal{V}_2$ assigning all free variables in V_1' and V_2' as follows:

$$
\begin{aligned}
T, \mathcal{V}_1, \mathcal{V}_2 &\models \tau \in X && \text{iff } [\tau]_{\mathcal{V}_1} \in \mathcal{V}_2(X) \\
T, \mathcal{V}_1, \mathcal{V}_2 &\models \tau_1 = \tau_2 && \text{iff } [\tau_1]_{\mathcal{V}_1} = [\tau_2]_{\mathcal{V}_1} \\
T, \mathcal{V}_1, \mathcal{V}_2 &\models E(\tau_1, \tau_2) && \text{iff } proj_2([\tau_1]_{\mathcal{V}_1}) = proj_2([\tau_2]_{\mathcal{V}_1}) \\
T, \mathcal{V}_1, \mathcal{V}_2 &\models \neg\varphi && \text{iff } T, \mathcal{V}_1, \mathcal{V}_2 \not\models \varphi \\
T, \mathcal{V}_1, \mathcal{V}_2 &\models \varphi_1 \vee \varphi_2 && \text{iff } T, \mathcal{V}_1, \mathcal{V}_2 \models \varphi_1 \text{ or } T, \mathcal{V}_1, \mathcal{V}_2 \models \varphi_2 \\
T, \mathcal{V}_1, \mathcal{V}_2 &\models \exists x.\varphi && \text{iff } \exists (t, n) \in T \times \mathbb{N}. \\
& && \quad T, \mathcal{V}_1[x \mapsto (t, n)], \mathcal{V}_2 \models \varphi \\
T, \mathcal{V}_1, \mathcal{V}_2 &\models \exists X.\varphi && \text{iff } \exists A \subseteq T \times \mathbb{N}. \\
& && \quad T, \mathcal{V}_1, \mathcal{V}_2[X \mapsto A] \models \varphi,
\end{aligned}
$$

where $\mathcal{V}_i[x \mapsto v]$ updates a valuation. A trace set T satisfies a closed S1S[E] formula φ, written $T \models \varphi$, if $T, \emptyset, \mathcal{V}_2 \models \varphi$, where $\emptyset$ denotes the empty first-order valuation and $\mathcal{V}_2$ assigns each free X_a in φ to the set $\{(t, n) \in T \times \mathbb{N} \mid a \in t[n]\}$.

Model Checking. The model checking problems of HyperQPTL$^+$ and S1S[E] are both undecidable, as shown in [9] and [5], respectively.

5   HyperCTL*

Extending the path quantifiers of CTL* by *path variables* leads to the logic HyperCTL*, which subsumes both HyperLTL and CTL*. The formulas of Hyper-CTL* are generated by the following grammar:

$$
\varphi \quad ::= \quad a_\pi \quad | \quad \neg\varphi \quad | \quad \varphi \vee \varphi \quad | \quad \bigcirc\varphi \quad | \quad \varphi\, \mathbf{U}\, \varphi \quad | \quad \exists\pi.\, \varphi
$$

We require that temporal operators only occur inside the scope of path quantifiers. The semantics of HyperCTL* is given in terms of assignments of variables to *paths*, which are defined analogously to trace assignments. Given a Kripke structure K, the satisfaction of a HyperCTL* formula φ at a position $i \in \mathbb{N}$, denoted by $K, \Pi, i \models \varphi$, is defined as follows:

$$
\begin{aligned}
K, \Pi, i &\models a_\pi && \text{iff} && a \in L\big(\Pi(\pi)[0 \ldots i]\big), \\
K, \Pi, i &\models \neg\varphi && \text{iff} && \Pi, K, i \not\models \varphi, \\
K, \Pi, i &\models \varphi_1 \vee \varphi_2 && \text{iff} && K, \Pi, i \models \varphi_1 \text{ or } K, \Pi, i \models \varphi_2, \\
K, \Pi, i &\models \bigcirc\varphi && \text{iff} && K, \Pi, i+1 \models \varphi, \\
K, \Pi, i &\models \varphi_1\, \mathbf{U}\, \varphi_2 && \text{iff} && \exists k \geq i : K, \Pi, k \models \varphi_2 \text{ and} \\
& && && \forall i \leq j < k : K, \Pi, j \models \varphi_1, \\
K, \Pi, i &\models \exists\pi.\, \varphi && \text{iff} && \exists p \in Paths(K, \Pi(\varepsilon)(i)) : \\
& && && K, \Pi[\pi \mapsto p,\ \varepsilon \mapsto p], i \models \varphi,
\end{aligned}
$$

where ε is a special path variable that denotes the path most recently added to Π (i.e., closest in scope to π). For the empty assignment $\Pi_\emptyset$, we define $\Pi_\emptyset(\varepsilon)(i)$ to yield the initial state. A Kripke structure $K = (S, s_0, \delta, \mathrm{AP}, L)$ satisfies a HyperCTL* formula φ, denoted with $K \models \varphi$, iff $K, \Pi_\emptyset \models \varphi$.

Expressiveness. HyperCTL* can express the flow of information that appears in different branches of the computation tree. Consider, for example, the following Kripke structure (taken from [8]):

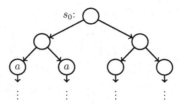

An observer who sees a can infer which branch was taken in the first nondeterministic choice, but not which branch was taken in the second nondeterministic choice. This is expressed by the HyperCTL* formula

$$\forall \pi. \mathbf{X} \forall \pi'. \mathbf{X} (a_\pi \leftrightarrow a_{\pi'}).$$

Model Checking. The modification to the model checking algorithm from Sect. 2 needed to take care of branching time is to change to alphabet of the automata from $(2^{\mathrm{AP}})^n$, i.e., tuples of sets of atomic propositions, to S^n, i.e., tuples of states of the Kripke structure. The model checking algorithm is described in detail in [10]. The algorithm again starts by translating the inner LTL formula φ of the negated specification into an equivalent Büchi automaton $\mathcal{A}_0$ over the alphabet $(2^{\mathrm{AP}})^n$; this automaton is then translated into an automaton over alphabet S^n by applying the labeling function L to the individual positions of the tuple. The algorithm then proceeds as described in Sect. 2, eliminating in each step one path quantifier. In the elimination of the quantifier, the automaton is combined as before with the Kripke structure, ensuring that the state sequence corresponds to a path in the Kripke structure. After n steps, all quantifiers have been eliminated, and the language of the resulting automaton is, as before. over the one-letter alphabet (consisting of the empty tuple). The HyperCTL* formula is satisfied if and only if the language of the resulting automaton is empty.

6   HyperQCTL*

HyperQCTL* [5] extends HyperCTL* with quantification over atomic propositions. The formulas of HyperQCTL* are generated by the following grammar:

$$\varphi \quad ::= \quad a_\pi \quad | \quad \neg\varphi \quad | \quad \varphi \vee \varphi \quad | \quad \bigcirc\varphi \quad | \quad \varphi \, \mathbf{U} \, \varphi \quad | \quad \exists \pi. \, \varphi \quad | \quad \exists p. \, \varphi$$

where $a, p \in \mathrm{AP}$ and $\pi \in \mathcal{V}$. The semantics of HyperQCTL* corresponds to the semantics of HyperCTL* with an additional rule for propositional quantification.

In QPTL, a propositional quantifier over a proposition p determines a sequence in $(2^p)^\omega$; i.e., the value of the proposition depends on the position in the sequence. In HyperQCTL*, the quantification modifies the interpretation on the entire computation tree.

$$K, \Pi, i \models \exists q.\varphi \text{ iff } \exists L' : S^* \rightarrow 2^{AP \cup \{q\}}. \ \forall w \in S^*.$$
$$L'(w) =_{AP \setminus \{q\}} L(w) \wedge K[L'/L], \Pi, i \models \varphi.$$

We say that a Kripke structure K satisfies a HyperQCTL* formula φ, written $K \models \varphi$, if $K, \emptyset, 0 \models \varphi$.

Expressiveness. HyperQCTL* is strictly more expressive than HyperCTL*. In particular, HyperQCTL* subsumes the extension of HyperCTL* with the knowledge operator. The formula $K_{A,\pi}\varphi$ states that the agent who can observe the propositions $A \subseteq$ AP on path π knows that φ holds. The semantics of $K_{A,\pi}$ is defined (analogously to the linear-time version in Sect. 3) as follows:

$$K, \Pi, i \models \mathcal{K}_{A,\pi}\varphi \quad \text{iff} \quad \forall p \in Paths(K, s_0). \ \Pi(\pi)[0, i] =_A p[0, i] \rightarrow$$
$$T, \Pi[\pi \mapsto p], i \models_K \varphi$$

HyperQCTL* also has the same expressiveness as second-order modadic logic equipped with the equal-level predicate (MSO[E]), i.e., the extension of FO[$<, E$] (as defined in Sect. 3) with second-order quantification [5].

Model Checking. The model checking problem of HyperQCTL* is undecidable [5].

7   Monadic Path Logic

Monadic path logic equipped with the equal-level predicate (MPL[E]) is the extension of FO[$<, E$] (as defined in Sect. 3) with second-order quantification, where the second-order quantification is restricted to full paths in the Kripke structure.

Let $V_1 = \{x_1, x_2, \ldots\}$ be a set of first-order variables, and $V_2 = \{X_1, X_2, \ldots\}$ a set of second-order variables. The formulas φ of MPL[E] are generated by the following grammar:

$$\varphi ::= \psi \mid \neg\varphi \mid \varphi_1 \vee \varphi_2 \mid \exists x.\varphi \mid \exists X.\varphi$$
$$\psi ::= P_a(x) \mid x < y \mid x = y \mid x \in X \mid E(x, y),$$

where $a \in$ AP, $x, y \in V_1$, and $X \in V_2$. In the semantics of MPL[E], we assign first-order variables to sequences of states that form a prefix of a path in the Kripke structure, and second-order variables to the infinite prefix-closed sets of prefixes of the paths of the Kripke structure.

We define the satisfaction relation $K, \mathcal{V}_1, \mathcal{V}_2 \models \varphi$ for a Kripke structure K and two valuations $\mathcal{V}_1, \mathcal{V}_2$ as follows:

$$
\begin{aligned}
K, \mathcal{V}_1, \mathcal{V}_2 &\models P_a(x) &&\text{iff} && a \in L(\mathcal{V}_1(x)) \\
K, \mathcal{V}_1, \mathcal{V}_2 &\models x < y &&\text{iff} && \mathcal{V}_1(x) \sqsubseteq \mathcal{V}_1(y) \\
K, \mathcal{V}_1, \mathcal{V}_2 &\models x = y &&\text{iff} && \mathcal{V}_1(x) = \mathcal{V}_1(y) \\
K, \mathcal{V}_1, \mathcal{V}_2 &\models x \in X &&\text{iff} && \mathcal{V}_1(x) \in \mathcal{V}_2(X) \\
K, \mathcal{V}_1, \mathcal{V}_2 &\models E(x, y) &&\text{iff} && |\mathcal{V}_1(x)| = |\mathcal{V}_1(y)| \\
K, \mathcal{V}_1, \mathcal{V}_2 &\models \neg\varphi &&\text{iff} && K, \mathcal{V}_1, \mathcal{V}_2 \not\models \varphi \\
K, \mathcal{V}_1, \mathcal{V}_2 &\models \varphi_1 \vee \varphi_2 &&\text{iff} && K, \mathcal{V}_1, \mathcal{V}_2 \models \varphi_1 \vee K, \mathcal{V}_1, \mathcal{V}_2 \models \varphi_2 \\
K, \mathcal{V}_1, \mathcal{V}_2 &\models \exists x.\varphi &&\text{iff} && \exists p \in S^*, p' \in Paths(K, s_0).\ p \sqsubseteq p' \wedge \\
& && && K, \mathcal{V}_1[x \mapsto p], \mathcal{V}_2 \models \varphi \\
K, \mathcal{V}_1, \mathcal{V}_2 &\models \exists X.\varphi &&\text{iff} && \exists p \in Paths(K, s_0).\ \mathcal{V}_1, \mathcal{V}_2[X \mapsto Prefixes(p)] \models \varphi
\end{aligned}
$$

where $\mathcal{V}_i[x \mapsto v]$ updates a valuation, $p_1 \sqsubseteq p_2$ denotes that p_1 is a prefix of p_2, and $Prefixes(p)$ is the set of prefixes of p. A Kripke structure K satisfies a closed MPL[E] formula φ, written $K \models \varphi$, if $T, \emptyset, \mathcal{V}_2 \models \varphi$, where $\emptyset$ denotes the empty first-order valuation and $\mathcal{V}_2$ assigns each free X_a in φ to the set $\{p \in S^* \mid a \in L(p)\}$.

Expressiveness. The expressiveness of MPL[E] falls strictly between HyperCTL* and HyperQCTL*. Like HyperQCTL*, MPL[E] can, however, express the properties of HyperKCTL*, i.e., the extension of HyperCTL* with the knowledge operator [5].

Model Checking. Similar to the model checking algorithm of Sect. 2, we reduce the model checking problem of MPL[E] to the language emptiness problem of a Büchi automaton. Let φ be the negation of the given formula. We translate φ into an automaton $\mathcal{A}$ over the tuple alphabet $(S \cup \{\bot\})^{\mathcal{V}_1 \cup \mathcal{V}_2}$ such that the language of $\mathcal{A}$ is empty iff the original formula is satisfied by the Kripke structure. The automaton is constructed recursively as follows:

- If $\varphi = P_a(x)$, then $\mathcal{A}$ accepts all infinite sequences where the first time the component of component of x becomes $\bot$ at some point, and stays $\bot$ from thereon after, and a is contained in $L(w)$ where w is the sequence of states in x's component up to that point.
- If $\varphi = x < y$, then $\mathcal{A}$ accepts all infinite sequences where the components of x and y each become and stay $\bot$ at some point, and until x becomes $\bot$ the components are the same.
- If $\varphi = x=y$, then $\mathcal{A}$ accepts all infinite sequences where the components of x and y each become and stay $\bot$ at the same point, and until then the components are the same.
- If $\varphi = x \in X$, then $\mathcal{A}$ accepts all infinite sequences where the component of x becomes and stays $\bot$ at some point, and until then the components of x and X are the same.

- If $\varphi = E(x, y)$, then $\mathcal{A}$ accepts all infinite sequences where the components of x and y become and stay $\perp$ at the same point.
- If $\varphi = \neg\psi$, then we first compute and negate the automaton for ψ. $\mathcal{A}$ is then the intersection of that automaton with an automaton that ensures that, for every $x \in \mathcal{V}_1$, the component of x eventually becomes and stays $\perp$.
- If $\varphi = \exists x.\psi$, then we first compute the automaton for ψ. We then combine the automaton with the Kripke structure to ensure that the component for x forms a prefix of a path in the Kripke structure and ends in $\perp$. $\mathcal{A}$ is then the existential projection of that automaton, where the component for x is eliminated.
- If $\varphi = \exists X.\psi$, then we also first compute the automaton for ψ. We then combine the automaton with the Kripke structure to ensure that the component for X forms a full path in the Kripke structure. $\mathcal{A}$ is then the existential projection of that automaton, where the component for X is eliminated.

8   Conclusions

We have studied the hierarchy of hyperlogics from the perspective of the model checking problem. For the logics considered here, HyperQPTL is clearly the most interesting linear-time logic, because it can still be checked using the basic model checking algorithm, while for more expressive logics like HyperQPTL$^+$ and S1S[E] the model checking problem is already undecidable. Among the branching-time logics, MPL[E] has a similar position, more expressive than HyperCTL*, but, unlike HyperQCTL*, still with a decidable model checking problem.

From a practical point of view, the key challenge that needs to be addressed in all these logics is the treatment of quantifier alternations. In the model checking algorithm quantifier alternations lead to alternations between existential and universal projection on the constructed automaton. Such alternations can in theory be implemented using complementation; in practice, however, the exponential cost of complementation is too expensive. Model checking implementations like MCHyper therefore instead rely on quantifier elimination via strategies [6]. In this approach, the satisfaction of a formula of the form $\varphi = \forall\pi_1.\exists\pi_2.\psi$ is analyzed as a game between a *universal* player, who chooses π_1, and an *existential* player, who chooses π_2. The formula φ is satisfied if the existential player has a strategy that ensures that ψ becomes true.

Acknowledgement. Most of the work reported in this paper has previously appeared in various publications [3,5,6,9–11]. I am indebted to my coauthors Michael R. Clarkson, Norine Coenen, Christopher Hahn, Jana Hofmann, Masoud Koleini, Kristopher K. Micinski, Markus N. Rabe, César Sánchez, Leander Tentrup, and Martin Zimmermann. This work was partially supported by the Collaborative Research Center "Foundations of Perspicuous Software Systems"(TRR: 248, 389792660) and the European Research Council (ERC) Grant OSARES (No. 683300).

References

1. Barthe, G., D'Argenio, P.R., Rezk, T.: Secure information flow by self-composition. Math. Struct. Comput. Sci. **21**(6), 1207–1252 (2011)
2. Bozzelli, L., Maubert, B., Pinchinat, S.: Unifying Hyper and Epistemic Temporal Logics. In: Pitts, A. (ed.) FoSSaCS 2015. LNCS, vol. 9034, pp. 167–182. Springer, Heidelberg (2015). https://doi.org/10.1007/978-3-662-46678-0_11
3. Clarkson, M.R., Finkbeiner, B., Koleini, M., Micinski, K.K., Rabe, M.N., Sánchez, C.: Temporal logics for hyperproperties. In: Abadi, M., Kremer, S. (eds.) POST 2014. LNCS, vol. 8414, pp. 265–284. Springer, Heidelberg (2014). https://doi.org/10.1007/978-3-642-54792-8_15
4. Clarkson, M.R., Schneider, F.B.: Hyperproperties. J. Comput. Secur. **18**(6), 1157–1210 (2010)
5. Coenen, N., Finkbeiner, B., Hahn, C., Hofmann, J.: The hierarchy of hyperlogics. In: 34th Annual ACM/IEEE Symposium on Logic in Computer Science, LICS 2019, Vancouver, BC, Canada, June 24–27, 2019, pp. 1–13. IEEE (2019)
6. Coenen, N., Finkbeiner, B., Sánchez, C., Tentrup, L.: Verifying hyperliveness. In: Dillig, I., Tasiran, S. (eds.) CAV 2019. LNCS, vol. 11561, pp. 121–139. Springer, Cham (2019). https://doi.org/10.1007/978-3-030-25540-4_7
7. Dimitrova, R., Finkbeiner, B., Torfah, H.: Probabilistic hyperproperties of Markov decision processes. In: Hung, D.V., Sokolsky, O. (eds.) ATVA 2020. LNCS, vol. 12302, pp. 484–500. Springer, Cham (2020). https://doi.org/10.1007/978-3-030-59152-6_27
8. Finkbeiner, B.: Temporal hyperproperties. Bulletin of the EATCS, 123 (2017)
9. Finkbeiner, B., Hahn, C., Hofmann, J., Tentrup, L.: Realizing ω-regular hyperproperties. In: Lahiri, S.K., Wang, C. (eds.) CAV 2020. LNCS, vol. 12225, pp. 40–63. Springer, Cham (2020). https://doi.org/10.1007/978-3-030-53291-8_4
10. Finkbeiner, B., Rabe, M.N., Sánchez, C.: Algorithms for model checking HyperLTL and HyperCTL*. In: Kroening, D., Păsăreanu, C.S. (eds.) CAV 2015. LNCS, vol. 9206, pp. 30–48. Springer, Cham (2015). https://doi.org/10.1007/978-3-319-21690-4_3
11. Finkbeiner, B., Zimmermann, M.: The first-order logic of hyperproperties. In: 34th Symposium on Theoretical Aspects of Computer Science, STACS 2017, Hannover, Germany, March 8–11, 2017, pp. 30:1–30:14 (2017)
12. Goguen, J.A., Meseguer, J.: Security policies and security models. In: IEEE Symposium on Security and Privacy, pp. 11–20, April 1982
13. Huisman, M., Worah, P., Sunesen, K.: A temporal logic characterisation of observational determinism. In: Proceedings of the IEEE Computer Security Foundations Workshop, pp. 3–15, July 2006
14. Kupferman, O., Piterman, N., Vardi, M.Y.: From liveness to promptness. Formal Methods Syst. Des. **34**(2), 83–103 (2009)
15. McCullough, D.: Noninterference and the composability of security properties. In: Proceedings of the IEEE Symposium on Security and Privacy, pp. 177–186, April 1988
16. Pnueli, A.: The temporal logic of programs. FOCS **1977**, 46–57 (1977)
17. Rabe, M.N.: A temporal logic approach to information-flow control. Ph.D. thesis, Saarland University (2016)
18. van der Meyden, R., Zhang, C.: Algorithmic verification of noninterference properties. Electr. Notes Theor. Comput. Sci. (ENTCS) **168**, 61–75 (2007)

Algebra-Based Synthesis of Loops and Their Invariants (Invited Paper)

Andreas Humenberger and Laura Kovács$^{(\boxtimes)}$

TU Wien, Wien, Austria
laura.kovacs@tuwien.ac.at

Abstract. Provably correct software is one of the key challenges in our software-driven society. While formal verification establishes the correctness of a given program, the result of program synthesis is a program which is correct by construction. In this paper we overview some of our results for both of these scenarios when analysing programs with loops. The class of loops we consider can be modelled by a system of linear recurrence equations with constant coefficients, called C-finite recurrences. We first describe an algorithmic approach for synthesising all polynomial equality invariants of such non-deterministic numeric single-path loops. By reverse engineering invariant synthesis, we then describe an automated method for synthesising program loops satisfying a given set of polynomial loop invariants. Our results have applications towards proving partial correctness of programs, compiler optimisation and generating number sequences from algebraic relations.

1 Introduction

The two most rigorous approaches for providing correct software are given by formal program verification and program synthesis [43]. The task of formal verification is to prove correctness of a given program with respect to a given logical specification [6,9,17]. On the other hand, program synthesis aims at generating programs which adhere to a given specification [2,34]. The result of a synthesis problem is therefore a program which is correct by construction with respect to the specification. While formal verification has received considerable attention with impressive results, for example, in ensuring safety of device drivers [3] and security of web services [7], program synthesis turns out to be an algorithmically much more difficult challenge [33].

Both in the setting of verification and synthesis, one of the main challenges is to verify or synthesise programs with loops/recursion. In formal verification, solving this challenge requires for example *synthesising loop invariants* [20,30,39]. Intuitively, a loop invariant is a formal description of the behaviour of the loop, expressing loop properties that hold at arbitrary loop iterations. For the purpose of automating formal verification, synthesising loop invariants that are inductive is of critical importance, as inductive invariants describe program properties/safety assertions that hold before and after each loop iteration.

© Springer Nature Switzerland AG 2021
F. Henglein et al. (Eds.): VMCAI 2021, LNCS 12597, pp. 17–28, 2021.
https://doi.org/10.1007/978-3-030-67067-2_2

Invariant Synthesis

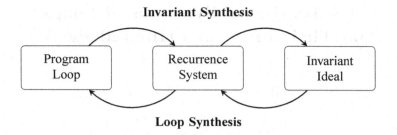

Loop Synthesis

Fig. 1. Algebra-based synthesis of loops and their invariants.

In program synthesis, reasoning with loops requires answering the question whether there exists a loop satisfying a given loop invariant and synthesising a loop with respect to a given invariant. We refer to this task of synthesis as *loop synthesis*. As such, we consider loop synthesis as the reverse problem of loop invariant generation/synthesis: rather than generating invariants summarising a given loop, we synthesise loops whose summaries are captured by a given invariant property.

In this paper, we overview algebra-based algorithms for automating reasoning about loops and their invariants. The key ingredients of our work come with deriving and solving algebraic recurrences capturing the functional behaviour of loops to be verified and/or synthesised. To this end, we consider additional requirements on the loops to be verified/synthesised, in particular by imposing syntactic constraints on the form of loop expressions. The imposed constraints allow us to reduce the verification/synthesis task to the problem of solving algebraic recurrences of special forms. Here, we mainly focus on loops whose functional summaries are precisely captured by so-called C-finite recurrences [27], that is linear recurrences with constant coefficients, for which closed form solutions always exist. We use symbolic summation techniques over C-finite recurrences to compute closed forms and combine these closed forms with additional constraints to ensure that (i) algebraic relations among closed forms yield polynomial loop invariants and (ii) loops synthesised from such polynomial loop invariants implement only affine assignments.

Figure 1 overviews our approach towards synthesising loops and/or their invariants. In order to generate invariants, we extract a system of C-finite recurrence equations describing loop updates. We then compute the polynomial ideal, called the *polynomial invariant ideal*, containing all polynomial equality invariants of the loop, by using recurrences solving and Gröbner basis computation [4]. Any polynomial invariant of the given loop is then a logical consequence of the polynomials from the computed polynomial ideal basis [31]. On the other hand, for loop synthesis, we take a basis of the polynomial invariant ideal generated by given polynomial loop invariants and construct a polynomial constraint problem. This constraint problem precisely characterises the set of all C-finite recurrence systems for which the given polynomial invariants yield algebraic relations among requires $N > 0$ requires $N > 0$

$(x, y, z) \leftarrow (0, 0, 0)$ $(x, y) \leftarrow (0, 0)$

while $y < N$ do   while $y < N$ do

$\quad x \leftarrow x + z + 1$ $\quad x \leftarrow x + 2y + 1$

$\quad z \leftarrow z + 2$ $\quad y \leftarrow y + 1$

$\quad y \leftarrow y + 1$ end

end

ensures $x = N^2$ ensures $x = N^2$

(a) Invariant synthesis for partial correctness.   (b) Loop synthesis to "optimize" Figure 2a.

Fig. 2. Motivating example for invariant and loop synthesis.

the induced C-finite number sequences. Every solution of the constraint problem gives thus rise to a system of C-finite recurrence equations, which is then turned into a loop for which the given polynomial relations are loop invariants [23].

In the rest of this paper, we first motivate our results on examples for invariant and loop synthesis (Sect. 2). We then report on algebra-based approaches for invariant generation (Sect. 3) and loop synthesis (Sect. 4), by summarising our main results published at [23,31].

2   Motivating Examples for Synthesising Invariants and Loops

Loop Invariant Synthesis. Verifying safety conditions and establishing partial correctness of programs is one use case of invariant generation. Consider for example the program in Fig. 2a, annotated with pre- and post-conditions specified respectively by the **requires** and **ensures** constructs. The program of Fig. 2a is clearly safe as the post-condition is satisfied when the loop is exited. However, to prove program safety we need additional loop properties, i.e. inductive loop invariants, that hold at any loop iteration. It is not hard to derive that after any iteration n of the loop (assuming $0 \le n \le N$), the linear invariant relation $y \le N$ holds. It is also not hard to argue that, upon exiting the loop, the value of y is N. However, such properties do not give us much information about the (integer-valued) program variable x. For proving program safety, we need to derive loop invariants relating the values of x, y, z at an arbitrary loop iteration n. Our work in [31] generates such loop invariants by computing the polynomial ideal $I = \langle x - y^2, z - 2y \rangle$ as the so-called *polynomial invariant ideal*. The conjunction $x = y^2 \wedge z = 2y$ of the polynomial relations corresponding to the basis polynomials of I is an inductive loop invariant, which together with the invariant $y \le N$ is sufficient to prove partial correctness of Fig. 2a.

Loop Synthesis. One use case of loop synthesis is program optimisation. To reduce execution time spent within loops, compiler optimisation techniques, such

$(x, y) \leftarrow (0, 2)$
while $y < N$ do
    $x \leftarrow x + y$
    $y \leftarrow y + 1$
end

$(x, y, z) \leftarrow (0, 0, 0)$
while $y < N$ do
    $x \leftarrow x + z + 1$
    $z \leftarrow z + 2$
    $y \leftarrow y + 1$
end

$(x, y) \leftarrow (0, 0)$
while $y < N$ do
    $x \leftarrow x + 2y + 1$
    $y \leftarrow y + 1$
end

(a) Erroneous loop

(b) Synthesised loop

(c) Synthesised loop

Fig. 3. Program repair via loop synthesis. Figures b–c, corresponding also to the programs of Figs. 2a–2b, are revised versions of Fig. a such that $x = y^2$ is an invariant of Figs. b–c.

as strength reduction [8], aim at replacing expensive loop operations with semantically equivalent but less expensive operations and/or reducing the number of loop variables used within loops. The burden of program optimisation in the presence of loops comes however with identifying inductive loop variables and invariants to be used for loop optimisation. Coming back to the loop in Fig. 2a, as argued before, $x = y^2 \wedge z = 2y \wedge y \leq N$ is a loop invariant of Fig. 2a. Moreover, only $x = y^2$ is already a loop invariant of Fig. 2a. Our loop synthesis procedure can be used to synthesise the affine loop of Fig. 2b from the polynomial invariant $x = y^2$, such that the synthesised loop uses less variables and arithmetic operations than Fig. 2a. Note that program repair can also be considered as an instance of program optimisation: while maintaining a given polynomial loop invariant, the task is to revise and repair a given program such that it satisfies the given invariant. Our synthesis approach therefore also provides a solution to program repair, as illustrated in Fig. 3.

3   Algebra-Based Synthesis of Loop Invariants

Overview of State-of-the-Art. One of the most related approaches to our work in automating the synthesis of polynomial loop invariants comes with the seminal work of [14], where a method for refining a user-given partial invariant was introduced to prove partial correctness of a given program. One of the first fully automatic invariant generation procedures was then given by [26] for inferring affine relations within affine programs. Since then, loop invariant generation was intensively studied and the level of automation and expressivity with respect to programs and their invariants steadily increased. Here we overview the most related techniques to our work.

The approach of [35] generalised [26] and provided a method for computing all polynomial equality relations for affine programs up to an a priori fixed degree. Recently, [18] constructively proved that the set of all polynomial equality invariants is computable for affine programs.

The works of [40] and [11] fix a polynomial template invariant and derive a constraint problem that encodes properties of loop invariants, such as inductiveness. These constraint problems are then solved by linear or polynomial algebra. The methods of [36] and [38] use abstract interpretation in combination with Gröbner bases computations for computing polynomial invariants of bounded degree. In [5], the abstract interpretation approach from [36] and the constraint-based approach from [40] is combined, yielding a procedure for computing invariants of bounded degree without resorting to Gröbner bases.

The techniques in [12, 28–30] approximate an arbitrary loop by a single-path loop and then apply recurrence solving to infer nonlinear invariants. They include guards in loops and conditionals in their reasoning, and are also able to infer inequalities as loop invariant. A data-driven approach to invariant generation is given in [41] using the guess-and-check methodology. Linear algebra is used to guess candidate invariants from data generated by concrete program executions where an upper bound on the polynomial degree of the candidate is user-given. An SMT solver is then used to validate the candidates with respect to the properties of loop invariants. If this is not the case, then the candidate is refined based on the output of the SMT solver.

Our work for invariant generation does neither use abstract interpretation nor constraint solving, and does not fix an a priori bound on the degree of the polynomial invariants to be synthesised. Instead, we restrict the class of loops our work can handle to non-deterministic loops whose loop updates yield special classes of algebraic recurrences in the loop counter, and hence we cannot handle loops with arbitrary nestedness as in [30]. We rely on results of [39] proving that the set of all polynomial equality invariants for a given (non-deterministic) loop forms a polynomial ideal. In [31], we use the ideal-theoretic result of [39] and compute all polynomial invariants of the class of non-deterministic loops that can be modelled by C-finite recurrence equations. Our results can further be extended to more complex recurrences equations by allowing restricted multiplications, and hence restricted classes of linear recurrences with polynomial coefficients, among loop variables - as detailed in [20, 22].

Algebra-Based Synthesis of Loop Invariants. We now summarise our algebra-based algorithm for synthesising polynomial loop invariants. To this end, we define our task of loop invariant synthesis as follows:

LOOP INVARIANT SYNTHESIS
- **Given:** A non-deterministic single-path loop $\mathcal{L}$ with program variables $\boldsymbol{x}$ such that each variable from $\boldsymbol{x}$ induces a C-finite number sequence in $\mathcal{L}$;
- **Generate:** A polynomial ideal I of all polynomials $p(\boldsymbol{x})$ such that $p(\boldsymbol{x}) = 0$ is a loop invariant of $\mathcal{L}$.

The main steps of our algorithm for loop invariant synthesis are as follows:

1. The non-deterministic single-path loop $\mathcal{L}$ is transformed into the regular expression π^*, where π is the block of assignments from the loop body of $\mathcal{L}$ and π^* denotes an arbitrary number of executions of π.
2. We extract a system of C-finite recurrence equations for π^*, by describing the C-finite number sequences for each program variable $x_i \in \boldsymbol{x}$ of $\mathcal{L}$ via a C-finite recurrence equation. To this end, we write $x_i(n)$ to denote the value of the program variable $x_i \in \boldsymbol{x}$ at an arbitrary loop iteration $n \geq 0$ as well as to refer to the number sequence $x_i(n)$ induced by the values of x_i at arbitrary loop iterations $n \geq 0$.
3. We solve the resulting C-finite recurrences of π^*, yielding a functional representation of values of $x_i(n)$ depending only on n and some initial values.
4. As a result, we derive closed forms $x_i(n) = f_i(n)$, where f_i are linear combinations of polynomial and exponential expressions in n. We also compute algebraic relations $a_i(n)$ as valid polynomial relations among exponential expressions in n.
5. A polynomial ideal I of all polynomials $p(\boldsymbol{x})$ such that $p(\boldsymbol{x}) = 0$ is a loop invariant of $\mathcal{L}$ is then computed by using Gröbner basis computation to eliminate n from the ideal generated by $\langle x_i - f_i(n), a_i(n) \rangle$. The ideal I is called the *polynomial invariant ideal* of $\mathcal{L}$.

Example 1 (Loop invariant synthesis). We illustrate our algorithm for loop invariant synthesis on the loop of Fig. 2a. The loop guard of Fig. 2a is ignored. Using matrix notation, the block π of loop body assignments induces the following coupled system of C-finite recurrence equations for π^*, with $n \geq 0$:

$$\begin{pmatrix} x(n+1) \\ z(n+1) \\ y(n+1) \end{pmatrix} = \begin{pmatrix} 2 & 0 & 1 \\ 0 & 1 & 0 \\ 0 & 0 & 1 \end{pmatrix} \begin{pmatrix} x(n) \\ z(n) \\ y(n) \end{pmatrix} + \begin{pmatrix} 1 \\ 2 \\ 1 \end{pmatrix}$$

The closed form solutions of the above recurrence system are given by

$$\begin{cases} x(n) = x(0) + n^2 \\ z(n) = z(0) + 2n \\ y(n) = y(0) + n \end{cases}$$

with $x(0) = 0$, $y(0) = 0$ and $z(0) = 0$ from the initial value assignments of Fig. 2a. By eliminating n from $\langle x - n^2, z - 2n, y - n \rangle$, we derive the polynomial invariant ideal $I = \langle x - y^2, z - 2y \rangle$ of π^*, yielding the polynomial loop invariant $x = y^2 \wedge z = 2y$.

Automation and Implementation. Our algorithm for loop invariant synthesis is fully automated within the open-source Julia package **Aligator**, which is available at:

https://github.com/ahumenberger/Aligator.jl.

For experimental summary and comparisons with other tools, in particular with [30], we refer to [19,21].

4   Algebra-Based Synthesis of Loops

Overview of State-of-the-Art. The classical setting of program synthesis has been to synthesise programs from proofs of logical specifications that relate the inputs and the outputs of the program [34]. Thanks to recent successful trends in formal verification based on automated reasoning [10,32], this traditional view of program synthesis has been refined to the setting of syntax-guided synthesis (SyGuS) [2]. In addition to logical specifications, SyGuS approaches consider further constraints on the program template to be synthesised, limiting thus the search space of possible solutions. A wide range of efficient applications of SyGuS have so far emerged, for example programming by examples [16], component-based synthesis [24] with learning [13] and sketc.hing [37].

Most synthesis approaches exploit counterexample-guided synthesis [2,13,37, 42] within the SyGuS framework. These methods take input-output examples satisfying a given property and synthesise a candidate program that is consistent with the given inputs. Correctness of the candidate program with respect to the given property is then checked using formal verification, in particular using SMT-based reasoning. Whenever verification fails, a counterexample violating the given property is generated as an additional input and a new candidate program is generated. Our work does not use an iterative refinement of the input-output values satisfying a given property $p(\boldsymbol{x}) = 0$. Rather, we consider a precise characterisation of the solution space of loops with invariant $p(\boldsymbol{x}) = 0$ to describe all, potentially infinite input-output values of interest. Similarly to sketches [37,42], we consider loop templates restricting the search for solutions to synthesis. Yet, our templates support non-linear arithmetic, which is not yet the case in [13,37].

The programming by example approach of [15] learns programs from input-output examples and relies on lightweight interaction to refine the specification of programs to be synthesised. The approach has further been extended in [25] with machine learning, allowing to learn programs from just one (or even none) input-output example by using a simple supervised learning setup. Program synthesis from input-output examples is shown to be successful for recursive programs [1], yet synthesising loops and handling non-linear arithmetic is not yet supported by this line of research. Our work precisely characterises the solution space of all loops to be synthesised by a system of algebraic recurrences and does not use statistical models supporting machine learning.

To the best of our knowledge, existing synthesis approaches are restricted to linear invariants, see e.g. [43], whereas our work supports loop synthesis from non-linear polynomial properties. We note that many interesting program properties can be best expressed using non-linear arithmetic, for example programs implementing powers (see e.g. Fig. 2), square roots and/or Euclidean divison require non-linear invariants.

Algebra-Based Synthesis of Loops. Our work in [23] addresses the challenging task of loop synthesis, by relying on algebraic recurrence equations and constraint solving over polynomials. Following the SyGuS setting, we consider additional requirements on the loop to be synthesised and define the task of loop synthesis as follows:

LOOP SYNTHESIS
- **Given:** A polynomial ideal I containing polynomials $p(\boldsymbol{x})$ over a set $\boldsymbol{x}$ of variables;
- **Generate:** A loop $\mathcal{L}$ with program variables $\boldsymbol{x}$ such that
  (i) $p(\boldsymbol{x}) = 0$ is an invariant of $\mathcal{L}$ for every $p \in I$, and
  (ii) each variable from $\boldsymbol{x}$ in $\mathcal{L}$ induces a C-finite number sequence.

The main steps of our loop synthesis algorithm are summarised below.

1. We take a basis B of the polynomial invariant ideal I as our input.
2. We fix a non-deterministic loop template $\mathcal{T}$ whose loop updates define a C-finite recurrence system template $\mathcal{S}$, over variables $\boldsymbol{x}$ and of size s. If not specified, the size s of $\mathcal{S}$ is considered to be the number of variables in $\boldsymbol{x}$.
3. We construct a polynomial constraint problem (PCP) which can be divided into two clause sets C_1 and C_2. The first set C_1 describes the closed form solutions of the C-finite recurrence system $\mathcal{S}$. To this end, we exploit properties of C-finite recurrences and define templates for the closed forms of $\boldsymbol{x}$ by ensuring a one-to-one correspondence between the recurrence template $\mathcal{S}$ and the closed form templates of $\boldsymbol{x}$. Intuitively, the clause set C_1 mimics the procedure for computing the closed forms for the recurrence system $\mathcal{S}$. The second clause set C_2 of our PCP makes sure that, for every $p \in B$, $p(\boldsymbol{x})$ is an algebraic relation for the closed form templates of $\boldsymbol{x}$. Since B is a basis of I it follows that $p(\boldsymbol{x}) = 0$ for all $p \in I$. The solution space of our PCP $C_1 \wedge C_2$ captures thus the set of all C-finite recurrence systems of the form $\mathcal{S}$ such that $p(\boldsymbol{x}(n)) = 0$ holds for all $n \geq 0$ and for all $p \in I$, where $\boldsymbol{x}(n)$ denotes the number sequences induced by the loop variables in $\boldsymbol{x}$ (as discussed on page 5).
4. By solving our PCP, we derive C-finite recurrence systems of the form $\mathcal{S}$. These instances of $\mathcal{S}$ can however be considered as non-deterministic programs with simultaneous updates. Thus, any C-finite recurrence system solution of our PCP can directly be translated into a non-deterministic loop $\mathcal{L}$ with sequential updates, by introducing auxiliary variables. Solving our PCP yields therefore a solution to our task of loop synthesis.

In [23], we prove that our approach to loop synthesis is both sound and complete. By completeness we mean, that if there is a loop $\mathcal{L}$ with at most s variables satisfying the invariant $p(\boldsymbol{x}) = 0$ such that the loop body meets the C-finite syntactic requirements of $\mathcal{S}$, then this loop $\mathcal{L}$ is synthesised by our method. As show-cased by Fig. 3, given a loop invariant $p(\boldsymbol{x}) = 0$, one can synthesise a potentially infinite set of loops such that each loop (i) has $p(\boldsymbol{x}) = 0$ as its invariant and (ii) is "better" with respect to a user-defined preference/measure. Our loop synthesis approach can thus be used to synthesise loops with respect to some pre-defined measure.

Example 2 (Loop invariant synthesis). We illustrate our algorithm for loop synthesis on Fig. 2b. To this end, we are interested in synthesising loops from the non-linear polynomial relation $x = y^2$. The invariant we consider is therefore $p(x, y) = x - y^2 = 0$.

We start by (initially) setting $s = 2$ and defining a loop template $\mathcal{T}$ of the form

$$
\begin{aligned}
&(x, y) \leftarrow (a_1, a_2) \\
&\textbf{while } true \textbf{ do} \\
&\quad x \leftarrow b_{11}x + b_{12}y + b_{13} \\
&\quad y \leftarrow b_{21}x + b_{22}y + b_{23} \\
&\textbf{end}
\end{aligned}
\tag{1}
$$

where the a_i and b_{ij} are rational-valued symbolic constants. By denoting with $n \geq 0$ the loop counter, the loop body of (1) can then be modeled by the following C-finite recurrence system:

$$
\begin{pmatrix} x(n+1) \\ y(n+1) \end{pmatrix} = \begin{pmatrix} b'_{11} & b'_{12} \\ b'_{21} & b'_{22} \end{pmatrix} \begin{pmatrix} x(n) \\ y(n) \end{pmatrix} + \begin{pmatrix} b'_{13} \\ b'_{23} \end{pmatrix},
\tag{2}
$$

where $x(n)$ and $y(n)$ represent the values of variables x and y at iteration n (as discussed on page 5), with $x(0) = a_1$ and $y(0) = a_2$. Note that the values of b_{ij} and b'_{ij} might differ as the sequential assignments of (1) correspond to simultaneous assignments in the algebraic representation (2) of the loop.

We next exploit properties of C-finite recurrences. For simplicity and w.l.o.g, we set up the following closed form templates for $x(n)$ and $y(n)$:

$$
\begin{pmatrix} x(n) \\ y(n) \end{pmatrix} = \begin{pmatrix} c_1 \\ c_2 \end{pmatrix} \omega^n + \begin{pmatrix} d_1 \\ d_2 \end{pmatrix} \omega^n n + \begin{pmatrix} e_1 \\ e_2 \end{pmatrix} \omega^n n^2
\tag{3}
$$

where c_i, d_i, e_i are rational-valued symbolic constants and ω are symbolic algebraic numbers. We then generate the clause set C_1 that ensures that we have a one-to-one correspondence between the number sequences described by the recurrence equations and the closed forms. For making sure that the equation $x - y^2 = 0$ is indeed a polynomial invariant, we plug the closed form templates (3) into the equation, and get

$$
c_1\omega^n + d_1\omega^n n + e_1\omega^n n^2 - (c_2\omega^n + d_2\omega^n n + e_2\omega^n n^2)^2 = 0.
\tag{4}
$$

The above Eq. (4) has to hold for all $n \in \mathbb{N}$ as $x - y^2 = 0$ should be a loop invariant. That is, we want to find $c_1, c_2, d_1, d_2, e_1, e_2$ and ω such that (4) holds for all $n \in \mathbb{N}$. The properties of C-finite number sequences allow us to reduce this $\exists\forall$ problem containing exponential expressions into a finite set of polynomials

$$
C_2 = \{c_1\omega - c_2^2\omega^2 = 0, d_1\omega - 2c_2d_2\omega^2 = 0,
$$
$$
e_1\omega - (2c_2e_2 - d_2^2)\omega^2 = 0, 2d_2e_2\omega^2 = 0, e_2^2\omega^2 = 0\}
$$

In summary, we get a PCP consisting of clause sets C_1 and C_2 containing 27 polynomial constraints over the unknowns $a_i, b'_{ij}, c_i, d_i, e_i, \omega$ from (1)–(3). The solution space of our PCP captures the set of all C-finite recurrence systems of the form (2) such that $x(n) - 2y(n)^2 = 0$ holds for all $n \geq 0$. That is, any solution of our PCP yields a loop with an invariant $x = y^2$.

Figures 3(b)–(c) illustrate two solutions of the PCP problem of our example: each program of Fig. 3(b)–(c) is an instance of (1), has $x - 2y^2 = 0$ as its invariant and can be synthesised using our work. The loop of Fig. 3(b), and thus of Fig. 2b, is synthesised by considering the size s of (1) to be 2, whereas Fig. 3(c) is computed by increasing the size s of (1) to 3.

Automation and Implementation. We implemented our approach to loop synthesis in the new open-source Julia package **Absynth**, available at

https://github.com/ahumenberger/Absynth.jl.

Our experiments using academic benchmarks on loop analysis as well as on generating number sequences in algorithmic combinatorics are available in [19,23].

5   Conclusions

We overviewed algebra-based algorithms for loop invariant synthesis and loop synthesis. The key ingredient of our work comes by modeling loops as algebraic recurrences, in particular by C-finite recurrences. To this end, we consider non-deterministic loops whose loop updates induce C-finite number sequences among loop variables. In the case of loop invariant synthesis, our work generates the polynomial ideal of all polynomial invariants of such loops by using symbolic summation in combination with properties of polynomial ideals. Extending this approach to (multi-path) loops inducing more complex recurrence equations supporting for example arbitrary multiplications among (some of the) variables is an interesting line for future work. When synthesising loops from polynomial invariants, we use symbolic summation to generate polynomial constraints whose solutions yield loops that exhibit the given invariant. Solving our constraint system requires satisfiability solving in non-linear arithmetic, opening up new directions for SMT-based reasoning with polynomial constraints. For example, we believe searching for solutions over finite domains would improve the scalability of our loop synthesis method. Extending our loop synthesis task to generate loops that are optimal with respect to a user-specified measure is another challenge to further investigate. To this end, understanding and efficiently encoding the best optimisation measures into our approach is an interesting line for future work.

Acknowledgment. We thank Maximillian Jaroschek (TU Wien) for joint work allowing to extend our invariant generation approaches to more complex loops and number sequences. We also thank Sumit Gulwani (Microsoft) and Manuel Kauers (JKU Linz) for valuable discussions on ideas leading to our loop synthesis framework. Practical aspects of our loop synthesis approach and using loop synthesis for strength reduction involve joint work with Nikolaj Bjørner (Microsoft).

We acknowledge funding from the ERC Starting Grant 2014 SYMCAR 639270, the ERC Proof of Concept Grant SYMELS 842066, the Wallenberg Academy Fellowship TheProSE, and the Austrian FWF research project W1255-N23.

References

1. Albarghouthi, A., Gulwani, S., Kincaid, Z.: Recursive program synthesis. In: CAV, pp. 934–950 (2013)
2. Alur, R., et al.: Syntax-guided synthesis. In: Dependable Software Systems Engineering, vol. 40, pp. 1–25. IOS Press (2015)
3. Ball, T., Levin, V., Rajamani, S.K.: A decade of software model checking with SLAM. Commun. ACM **54**(7), 68–76 (2011)
4. Buchberger, B.: An algorithm for finding the basis elements of the residue class ring of a zero dimensional polynomial ideal. J. Symbolic Comput. **41**(3–4), 475–511 (2006)
5. Cachera, D., Jensen, T.P., Jobin, A., Kirchner, F.: Inference of polynomial invariants for imperative programs: a farewell to Gröbner bases. In: SAS, pp. 58–74 (2012)
6. Clarke, E.M., Allen Emerson, E.: Design and synthesis of synchronization skeletons using branching-time temporal logic. In: Logics of Programs, pp. 52–71 (1981)
7. Cook, B.: Formal reasoning about the security of amazon web services. In: CAV, pp. 38–47 (2018)
8. Cooper, K.D., Taylor Simpson, L., Vick, C.A.: Operator strength reduction. ACM Trans. Program. Lang. Syst. **23**(5), 603–625 (2001)
9. Cousot, P., Cousot, R.: Abstract interpretation: a unified lattice model for static analysis of programs by construction or approximation of fixpoints. In: POPL, pp. 238–252 (1977)
10. De Moura, L., Bjørner, N.: Z3: an efficient SMT solver. In: TACAS, pp. 337–340 (2008)
11. de Oliveira, S., Bensalem, S., Prevosto, V.: Polynomial invariants by linear algebra. In: ATVA, pp. 479–494 (2016)
12. Farzan, A., Kincaid, Z.: Compositional recurrence analysis. In: FMCAD, pp. 57–64 (2015)
13. Feng, Y., Martins, R., Bastani, O., Dillig, I.: Program synthesis using conflict-driven learning. In: PLDI, pp. 420–435 (2018)
14. German, S.M., Wegbreit, B.: A synthesizer of inductive assertions. IEEE Trans. Software Eng. **1**(1), 68–75 (1975)
15. Gulwani, S.: Automating string processing in spreadsheets using input-output examples. In: POPL, pp. 317–330 (2011)
16. Gulwani, S.: Programming by examples: applications, algorithms, and ambiguity resolution. In: IJCAR, pp. 9–14 (2016)
17. Hoare, C.A.R.: An axiomatic basis for computer programming. Commun. ACM **12**(10), 576–580 (1969)
18. Hrushovski, E., Ouaknine, J., Pouly, A., Worrell, J.: On strongest algebraic program invariants. J. ACM., to appear
19. Humenberger, A.: Algebra-based loop reasoning. Ph.D. thesis, TU Wien 2021
20. Humenberger, A., Jaroschek, M., Kovács, L.: Automated generation of non-linear loop invariants utilizing hypergeometric sequences. In: ISSAC, pp. 221–228 (2017)
21. Humenberger, A., Jaroschek, M., Kovács, L.: Aligator.jl - a Julia package for loop invariant generation. In: CICM, pp. 111–117 (2018)

22. Humenberger, A., Jaroschek, M., Kovács, L.:: Invariant generation for multi-path loops with polynomial assignments. In: VMCAI, pp. 226–246 (2018)
23. Humenberger, A., Kovács, L., Bjørner, N.: Algebra-based loop synthesis. In: iFM (2020, to appear)
24. Jha, S., Gulwani, S., Seshia, S.A., Tiwari, A.: Oracle-guided component-based program synthesis. In: ICSE, pp. 215–224 (2010)
25. Kalyan, A., Mohta, A., Polozov, O., Batra, D., Jain, P., Gulwani, S.: Neural-guided deductive search for real-time program synthesis from examples. In: ICLR (2018)
26. Karr, M.: Affine relationships among variables of a program. Acta Informatica **6**, 133–151 (1976)
27. Kauers, M., Paule, P.: The Concrete Tetrahedron - Symbolic Sums, Recurrence Equations, Generating Functions, Asymptotic Estimates. Texts & Monographs in Symbolic Computation. Springer, Vienna (2011). https://doi.org/10.1007/978-3-7091-0445-3
28. Kincaid, Z., Breck, J., Boroujeni, A.F., Reps, T.W.: Compositional recurrence analysis revisited. In: PLDI, pp. 248–262 (2017)
29. Kincaid, Z., Breck, J., Cyphert, J., Reps, T.W.: Closed forms for numerical loops. PACMPL **3**(POPL), 55:1–55:29 (2019)
30. Kincaid, Z., Cyphert, J., Breck, J., Reps, T.W.: Non-linear reasoning for invariant synthesis. PACMPL **2**(POPL), 541–5433 (2018)
31. Kovács, L.: Reasoning algebraically about p-solvable loops. In: TACAS, pp. 249–264 (2008)
32. Kovács, L., Voronkov, A.: First-order theorem proving and vampire. In: CAV, pp. 1–35 (2013)
33. Kuncak, V., Mayer, M., Piskac, R., Suter, P.: Software synthesis procedures. Commun. ACM **55**(2), 103–111 (2012)
34. Manna, Z., Waldinger, R.J.: A deductive approach to program synthesis. ACM Trans. Program. Lang. Syst. **2**(1), 90–121 (1980)
35. Müller-Olm, M., Seidl, H.: A note on Karr's algorithm. In: ICALP, pp. 1016–1028 (2004)
36. Müller-Olm, M., Seidl, H.: Computing polynomial program invariants. Inf. Process. Lett. **91**(5), 233–244 (2004)
37. Nye, M., Hewitt, L., Tenenbaum, J., Solar-Lezama, A.: Learning to infer program sketches. In: ICML, pp. 4861–4870 (2019)
38. Rodríguez-Carbonell, E., Kapur, D.: Automatic generation of polynomial invariants of bounded degree using abstract interpretation. Sci. Comput. Program. **64**(1), 54–75 (2007)
39. Rodríguez-Carbonell, E., Kapur, D.: Generating all polynomial invariants in simple loops. J. Symb. Comput. **42**(4), 443–476 (2007)
40. Sankaranarayanan, S., Sipma, H., Manna, Z.: Non-linear loop invariant generation using Gröbner bases. In: POPL, pp. 318–329 (2004)
41. Sharma, R., Gupta, S., Hariharan, B., Aiken, A., Liang, P., Nori, A.V.: A data driven approach for algebraic loop invariants. In: Felleisen, M., Gardner, P. (eds.) ESOP 2013. LNCS, vol. 7792, pp. 574–592. Springer, Heidelberg (2013). https://doi.org/10.1007/978-3-642-37036-6_31
42. Solar-Lezama, A.: The Sketching approach to program synthesis. In: APLAS, pp. 4–13 (2009)
43. Srivastava, S., Gulwani, S., Foster, J.S.: From program verification to program synthesis. In: POPL, pp. 313–326 (2010)

Generative Program Analysis and Beyond: The Power of Domain-Specific Languages (Invited Paper)

Bernhard Steffen$^{(\boxtimes)}$ and Alnis Murtovi

Chair of Programming Systems, TU Dortmund University, Otto-Hahn-Str. 14,
44227 Dortmund, Germany
{steffen,alnis.murtovi}@cs.tu-dortmund.de

Abstract. In this paper we position Linear Time Temporal Logic (LTL), structural operational semantics (SOS), and a graphical generalization of BNF as central DSLs for program analysis and verification tasks in order to illustrate the impact of language to the mindset: (1) Specifying program analyses in LTL changes the classical algorithmic 'HOW' thinking into a property-oriented 'WHAT' thinking that allows one to logically combine analysis goals and eases proofs. (2) Playing with the original store component in SOS configurations allows one to elegantly realize variants of abstract program interpretations, and to align different aspects, like e.g., the symbolic values of variables and path conditions. (3) Specializing languages by refining their BNF-like meta models has the power to lift certain verification tasks from the program to the programming language level. We will illustrate the advantages of the change of mindset imposed by these three DSLs, as well as the fact that these advantages come at low price due to available adequate generator technology.

Keywords: Generative programming · Domain-specific languages · Meta modelling · Program analysis · (Second-order) model checking · Modal transition systems · Context-free/procedural transition systems · Modal refinement · Predicate/property transformers · Binary decision diagram

1 Introduction

Languages influence and reflect the way of thinking. This is known for natural languages, but it is even more true for artificial languages like programming or modeling languages. E.g., programming in imperative or object-oriented languages requires a completely different mindset from thinking in functional or logical languages. Domain-specific languages (DSLs, [58]) aim at leveraging this effect in order to support specific purposes, e.g., SQL [6] has been designed to query data bases, BNF [26] is the de facto standard for defining syntax, Structural Operational Semantics (SOS, [39]) allows one to conveniently define operational semantics without the burden of dealing with machine architectures, and

© Springer Nature Switzerland AG 2021
F. Henglein et al. (Eds.): VMCAI 2021, LNCS 12597, pp. 29–51, 2021.
https://doi.org/10.1007/978-3-030-67067-2_3

temporal logics [3] are the language of choice for specifying properties of reactive systems.

In this paper we position Linear Time Temporal Logic (LTL, [40]), SOS, and a graphical generalization of BNF as central DSLs for program analysis and verification tasks. We will argue that

- (Bi-directional) LTL [54] is a mindset-changing DSL for specifying program analysis [43,44,47,48]: LTL does not only allow very concise specifications of data flow analyses from which highly efficient implementations can be automatically generated. Rather, it changes the perspective from the HOW, the required fixpoint computation, to the WHAT, the desired property. Thinking in properties, i.e., in logical terms, which allows one to stepwise refine the desired properties using logical connectors. We will illustrate the power of this thinking in Sect. 2 via the development of our lazy code motion algorithm [24]: The corresponding WHAT perspective is so natural that the formal correctness and optimality proofs are quite straightforward.
- SOS is particular powerful in combination with abstract interpretation (cf. also [54]): Abstracting from data naturally provides a correct-by-construction flow graph construction, symbolic execution simply needs a symbolic treatment of data, and varying forms of semantics-based structural refinements can be realized simply by providing adequate domains. An illustrative example is given by using the powerset of program expressions for modeling redundancy information which immediately solved an old problem: how to eliminate all partial redundancies (c.f. Sect. 3).
- Our graphical BNF generalization allows one to lift certain analysis tasks from the program level up to the programming language level [52]: As will be illustrated in Sect. 4, this allows one, e.g., to verify interesting properties for an entire programming language. The impact of this method grows with the specificity of the language making it particularly suitable in the context of domain-specific languages as it allows one to validate certain guarantees already at the corresponding meta level (c.f. Sect. 4). Together with a suitable notion of language refinement this leads to a concept of property preserving language refinement [52] that guarantees that properties that have been verified for some DSL remain valid under further language specialization.

It is the goal of the following three sections to illustrate by example the advantages of the change of mindset imposed by these three DSLs, as well as the fact that these advantages come at low price due to available adequate generator technology. All this can be regarded as a development that started with using temporal logics for program analysis in the early nineties [47,48].[1] We will include some original slides in order to also provide some feeling about the corresponding chronological development. The paper closes in Sect. 5 with a conclusion and some directions to future work.

---

[1] This work was based on bi-directional branching time temporal logics, which has later been replaced by bi-directional LTL.

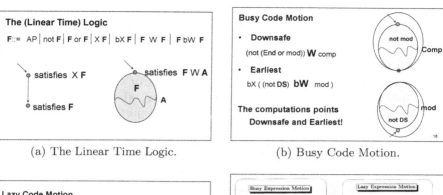

(a) The Linear Time Logic.   (b) Busy Code Motion.

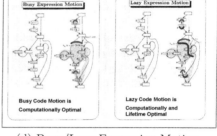

(c) Lazy Code Motion.   (d) Busy/Lazy Expression Motion.

Fig. 1. LTL and Busy&Lazy Code Motion.

2 The LTL Mindset

The syntax of bi-directional LTL is shown in Fig. 1(a) and its semantics is defined as follows:

Definition 1 (Semantics of Linear Time Logic (LTL) [8,40]**).** *Let AP be a set of atomic propositions. A model σ for a formula φ is an infinite sequence of truth assignments to atomic propositions. Given a model* $\sigma = \sigma_0, \sigma_1, \ldots$, *we denote by* σ_i *the set of atomic propositions at position i. For a formula φ and a position* $i \geq 0$, *we say that φ holds at position i of σ, written* $\sigma, i \vDash \phi$, *and define it inductively as follows:*

- *For* $p \in AP, \sigma, i \vDash p$ *iff* $p \in \sigma_i$
- $\sigma, i \vDash \neg\phi$ *iff* $\sigma, i \nvDash \phi$
- $\sigma, i \vDash \phi \vee \psi$ *iff* $\sigma, i \vDash \phi$ *or* $\sigma, i \vDash \psi$
- $\sigma, i \vDash X\phi$ *iff* $\sigma, i + 1 \vDash \phi$
- $\sigma, i \vDash bX\phi$ *iff* $i > 0$ *and* $\sigma, i - 1 \vDash \phi$
- $\sigma, i \vDash \phi\,W\,\psi$ *iff (there exists* $k \geq i$ *such that* $\sigma, k \vDash \psi$ *and* $\sigma, j \vDash \phi$ *for all* $j, i \leq j < k$) *or* $(\sigma, j \vDash \phi$ *for all* $j, 0 < j \leq |\sigma|)$
- $\sigma, i \vDash \phi\,bW\,\psi$ *iff (there exists* k, $0 \leq k \leq i$ *such that* $\sigma, k \vDash \psi$ *and* $\sigma, j \vDash \phi$ *for all* $j, k < j \leq i$) *or* $(\sigma, j \vDash \phi$ *for all* $j, 0 \leq j \leq i)$

If $\sigma, 0 \vDash \phi$, then we say that ϕ holds on σ and denote it by $\sigma \vDash \phi$. A set of models M, often represented by a Kripke structure, satisfies ϕ, denoted $M \vDash \phi$, if every model in M satisfies ϕ.

Remark: This definition coincides with the definition given in [8] except for the use of W for Weak Until (or Unless) in contrast to U (Strong Until).[2] Of course, due to duality, each of these notions of Until allows one to define the other. Focusing here on weak Until in the definition is just a matter of emphasis. In fact, for program analysis based on (non-deterministic) flow graphs (Strong Until does not make much sense, because loops immediately cause violation. In contrast, *relative liveness*, in the sense that some property must hold before some other property may become valid resembles an adequate notion of 'partial correctness' (cf. the definitions of Downsafety and Earliest in Fig. 1b).

We experienced the power of temporal logics for specifying program analyses first in the context of partial redundancy elimination [24, 25]:

An expression t occurring on an edge (u, v) of the control flow graph is called *redundant*, if there is a t-occurrence on every program path reaching u such that no operand of t is modified in between these occurrences. Redundant computations can be eliminated by storing the computed value into a temporary variable which is then accessed instead of recomputing the redundant expression. If in the above definition of redundancy a weaker requirement is considered where t-occurrences have to be present only on *some* paths reaching u, the t-occurrence on the edge (u, v) is called *partially redundant* [33].

Classically, partially redundant computations were eliminated by code motion [21, 22, 24, 25, 33], a technique based on the observation that moving computations against the direction of the control flow may move computations into positions where they are totally redundant and can thus be eliminated.

Figure 2 shows the algorithm for partial redundancy elimination as presented by Morel and Renvoise [33] in 1979. This algorithm is rather involved as it comprises intertwined forward and backward computations as well as minimal and maximal fixpoint computations:

- Σ indicates maximal fixpoints, whereas Π indicates minimal fixpoint.
- The reference 'pred' to predecessors indicates forward computations, where 'succ' indicates backward computation.

It is therefore not surprising that the corresponding correctness proof is rather involved and really takes some effort to be digested.

Things change quite a bit when moving to the LTL formulation shown in Fig. 1(b) which directly specifies the idea behind partial redundancy elimination: Move computations up as far as possible without violating safety, i.e., without introducing computations in paths where they have not been originally:

- Downsafety guarantees the second property: on each path starting at a down-safe point it is guaranteed that the considered computation has to happen

---

[2] $\phi U \psi$, in contrast to $\phi W \psi$, requires ψ to hold eventually.

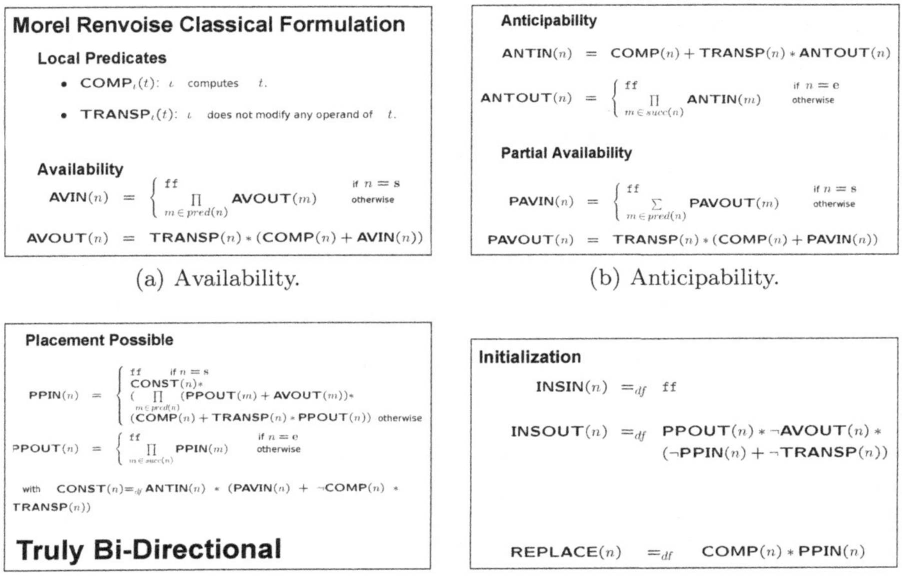

(a) Availability.

(b) Anticipability.

(c) Placement Possible.

(d) Initialization.

Fig. 2. Morel Renvoise classical formulation.

before termination: comp indicates that the considered expression will be evaluated before the arguments change value, indicated by mod, or the program terminates. For the correctness of the specification this strengthening causes no problem, only for the optimality which was not even considered by Morel and Renvoise. Showing that the strengthening to Downsafety has no effect in conjunction with Earliest is in fact the most tricky part of the optimality proof which is otherwise straightforward.

- Earliest guarantees that the computation cannot be moved up further without violating downsafety. This is not quite as general as formulated above, because it uses downsafety instead of safety. However, as mentioned above, this strengthening has no effect.

Remark: [47, 48] are based on a variant of CTL and labelled transitions systems as program models which complicates the formal treatment. The transformation into Kripke structures that introduce a separate node for each statement as done here combined with using LTL allows the elegant formulation shown here. This formulation confirms that both forward and backward computations as well as minimal and maximal fixpoint computations are required, but they need not be intertwined. In fact, the minimal fixpoint only arises as the negation of Downsafety in the definition of Earliest, and there is just one forward computation followed by one backward computation.

Of course, our algorithm can also be 'coded' in Morel/Renvoise style and thereby disentangle the complicated structure as shown in Fig. 3. In retrospect

Busy Code Motion: Morel Renvoise-Style

Local Predicates

- $COMP_\iota(t)$: ι computes t.

- $TRANSP_\iota(t)$: ι does not modify any operand of t.

Up-Safety

$$N\text{-}USAFE_\iota = \begin{cases} ff & \text{if } \iota = s \\ \prod_{\hat{\iota} \in pred(\iota)} X\text{-}USAFE_{\hat{\iota}} & \text{otherwise} \end{cases}$$

$$X\text{-}USAFE_\iota = (N\text{-}USAFE_\iota + COMP_\iota) \cdot TRANSP_\iota$$

Down-Safety

$$N\text{-}DSAFE_\iota = COMP_\iota + X\text{-}DSAFE_\iota \cdot TRANSP_\iota$$

$$X\text{-}DSAFE_\iota = \begin{cases} ff & \text{if } \iota = e \\ \prod_{\hat{\iota} \in succ(\iota)} N\text{-}DSAFE_{\hat{\iota}} & \text{otherwise} \end{cases}$$

Insertion Points (,,Earliestness")

$$N\text{-}INSERT_\iota^{BCM} =_{df} N\text{-}DSAFE_\iota^* \cdot \prod_{\hat{\iota} \in pred(\iota)} (\overline{X\text{-}USAFE_{\hat{\iota}}^*} + \overline{X\text{-}DSAFE_{\hat{\iota}}^*})$$

$$X\text{-}INSERT_\iota^{BCM} =_{df} X\text{-}DSAFE_\iota^* \cdot \overline{TRANSP_\iota}$$

(a) Local Predicates, Up-Safety.   (b) Down-Safety, Inserion Points.

Fig. 3. Busy code motion: Morel Renvoise-style

one might ask why Morel and Renvoise came up with such a complicated algorithm where there is such a simple solution. For us the answer is clear: They had an inadequate mindset. They where thinking in terms of information flow and how it has to be combined rather than in terms properties that can nicely be composed.

The superiority of the LTL mindset can be nicely illustrated along an algorithmic refinement. One major criticism of Morel/Renvoise's algorithm (and similarly of busy code motion) is that it imposes high register pressure. Moving computations up as far as possible means that the corresponding values have to be stored (ideally in registers) for a long time before they are actually used. The attempts to reduce the register pressure led to heuristics that complicated the original algorithmic formulation even more [11,12]. The, indeed optimal solution to this problem in the LTL mindset is, however, quite easy. In a sense similar to Earliest, one has to define a predicate Delayed that intuitively indicates how far the previously hoisted computations can be moved down again without missing any original computation (cf. Fig. 1d). Computation points are then simply the endpoints of such a delay process.

It should be noted, however, that what is considered simple or intuitive is a very personal matter. Indeed we were able to publish our results only in Morel Renvoise style because the program analysis community was not used to temporal logics at that time.

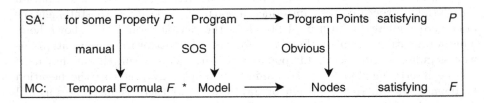

Fig. 4. Static analysis generation.

As a proper DSL for specifying program analyses, LTL also comes with corresponding automatic code generation, in fact in two possible ways:

- Figure 4 sketches a way that exploits a corresponding model checker. This requires a straightforward transformation of the program into a Kripke structure, e.g., via a flow graph construction as indicated in the next section, as well as a global model checker that solves the model checking problem for each state.
- An alternative way is to generate code for program analysis frameworks in the way indicated in Fig. 3.

The presented algorithm is optimal as long as we forbid to change the structure of the original flow graph. The next section will show, in particular, how all partial redundancies can be eliminated when we drop this constraint.

3   The SOS Mindset

Structural operational semantics (SOS) [39] is an intuitive and elegant method for describing the semantics of programming languages. In this section we will see that the underlying 'design pattern' can be exploited much more generally, and that it can be combined nicely with abstract interpretation [10]: already the trivial abstraction to the one point domain resembles classical control flow analysis. We will illustrate the specification power of the SOS language format in various scenarios which, additionally, allows one to automatically generate quite universal interpreters from SOS-based rule systems [2, 9].

3.1   Standard SOS

Let us consider sequential programs from a simple imperative **while** language:

$$S ::= x = a \mid \textbf{skip} \mid S; S \mid \textbf{if } (b) \ \{S\} \textbf{ else } \{S\} \mid \textbf{while } (b) \ \{S\}$$

SOS assigns meaning to programs in terms of partially defined state transformers[3] $\Sigma \xrightarrow{part} \Sigma$. States $\sigma \in \Sigma$ map variables to integer values. We inductively extend the notion of states to arithmetic expressions. For the sake of simplicity we further abuse 1 and 0 as Boolean values true and false.

The core of SOS is given in terms of syntax-oriented rules which define a small-step transition relation among configurations. Configurations are either pairs $\langle S, \sigma \rangle$ capturing a residual statement and a state which occurs during a program's execution or in case of final configurations states alone. For our model language the standard SOS-rules are as follows:

---

[3] Please note that the meaning of 'state' in this section only concerns Σ, in contrast to the other sections, where 'state' denotes nodes of a transitions system.

$$\frac{-}{\langle \mathbf{skip}, \sigma \rangle \Rightarrow \sigma} \qquad\qquad \frac{-}{\langle x = \mathsf{a}, \sigma \rangle \Rightarrow \sigma\{\sigma(a)/x\}}$$

$$\frac{\langle S_1, \sigma \rangle \Rightarrow \langle S_1', \sigma' \rangle}{\langle S_1; S_2, \sigma \rangle \Rightarrow \langle S_1'; S_2, \sigma' \rangle} \qquad\qquad \frac{\langle S_1, \sigma \rangle \Rightarrow \sigma'}{\langle S_1; S_2, \sigma \rangle \Rightarrow \langle S_2, \sigma' \rangle}$$

$$\frac{-}{\langle \mathbf{if}\ (b)\ \{S_0\}\ \mathbf{else}\ \{S_1\}, \sigma \rangle \Rightarrow \langle S_i, \sigma \rangle} \quad i = 1 - \sigma(b)$$

$$\frac{-}{\langle \mathbf{while}\ (b)\ \{S\}, \sigma \rangle \Rightarrow \langle \mathbf{if}\ (b)\ \{S; \mathbf{while}\ (b)\ \{S\}\}\ \mathbf{else}\ \{\mathbf{skip}\}, \sigma \rangle}$$

Based on the above rules the standard SOS-semantics $[\![\, S \,]\!]$ of our model language is given by:

$$[\![\, S \,]\!](\sigma) = \begin{cases} \sigma' & \text{if } \langle S, \sigma \rangle \Rightarrow^* \sigma' \\ \text{undefined} & \text{otherwise} \end{cases}$$

Hence for a given state σ the program either reaches a final configuration σ' or diverges with an infinite sequence of non-final configurations.

Due to infinite data domains, SOS's for realistic programming languages typically define infinite transitions systems, and are therefore more a concept than an actual tool. This may change, however, when considering finite abstract interpretations [10].

3.2   Control Flow Analysis: The One Point Domain

Collapsing Σ to just one point, $\bullet$, and adding the chosen elementary statement as transitions label, we obtain:

$$\frac{-}{\langle \mathbf{skip}, \bullet \rangle \overset{\mathbf{skip}}{\Longrightarrow} \bullet} \qquad\qquad \frac{-}{\langle x = \mathsf{a}, \bullet \rangle \overset{x\,=\,\mathsf{a}}{\Longrightarrow} \bullet}$$

$$\frac{\langle S_1, \bullet \rangle \overset{\alpha}{\Longrightarrow} \langle S_1', \bullet \rangle}{\langle S_1; S_2, \bullet \rangle \overset{\alpha}{\Longrightarrow} \langle S_1'; S_2, \bullet \rangle} \qquad\qquad \frac{\langle S_1, \bullet \rangle \overset{\alpha}{\Longrightarrow} \bullet}{\langle S_1; S_2, \bullet \rangle \overset{\alpha}{\Longrightarrow} \langle S_2, \bullet \rangle}$$

$$\frac{-}{\langle \mathbf{if}\ (b)\ \{S_0\}\ \mathbf{else}\ \{S_1\}, \bullet \rangle \overset{i}{\Longrightarrow} \langle S_i, \bullet \rangle} \quad i \in \{0, 1\}$$

$$\frac{-}{\langle \mathbf{while}\ (b)\ \{S\}, \bullet \rangle \overset{\mathbf{skip}}{\Longrightarrow} \langle \mathbf{if}\ (b)\ \{S; \mathbf{while}\ (b)\ \{S\}\}\ \mathbf{else}\ \{\mathbf{skip}\}, \bullet \rangle}$$

This rule set can be used to automatically generate control flow graphs in transition system format, in our experience a format superior to the classical node-centric formats, where data flow information needs to be qualified as *pre* and *post*. We used this fact for our Fixpoint Analysis Machine [50] for front end generation. The effect can be nicely illustrated using the following simple sample program S_{fac} for computing the factorial of an argument variable n:

```
f = 1;
 while (n != 1){
   f = f * n;
   n = n-1
}
```

Using abbreviations

S_1 = **while** (n != 1) {f = f*n; n=n-1},
S_2 = **if** (n != 1) {f = f*n; n = n-1; S_1} **else skip**,
S_3 = (f = f*n; n = n-1; S_1) and
S_4 = (n = n-1; S_1)

we obtain the control flow graph depicted in Fig. 5.

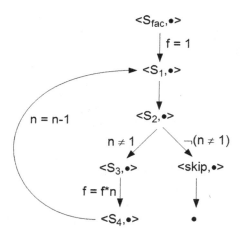

Fig. 5. Stateless SOS unrolls the control flow graph of the factorial program.

Flow graphs obtained in this way can easily be refined by replacing the one point domain to some abstract domain. This has been illustrated in [54] for the odd/even analysis. Flow graph refinements like this were called *property-oriented expansions* in [49], where it was shown how to elegantly obtain powerful join-free (which, in some sense, means loss-free) program analyses, as will be discussed in the next section.

3.3 Property Oriented Expansion via SOS

Classical SOS can be regarded as a typically infinite refinement of the pure control flow graph of Fig. 5. Finite refinements that result from abstract interpretation, like the abovementioned odd/even analysis, are called *Property-Oriented*

Expansions (POE) [49]. POE applies to any (flow) graph structure and any (data flow) property. Indeed, classical SOS can be regarded as such an expansion of the control flow graph with the standard semantics taken as property. Moreover, any set of data flow properties together with its transfer functions defines a POE, which can be regarded as a *meet/join-free* data flow analysis, as no merging of information is required: Properties (e.g. data flow facts) are simply propagated along paths in the control flow graph, and whenever ambivalent information is propagated to a join point separate copies of the node annotated by their properties are created. This simple procedure has nice applications, as for example:

Eliminating All Partial Redundancies: Figure 6(a) shows an example program where all the computations of $a + b$ except the first one are partially redundant. However, the computations cannot be eliminated via code motion as the rightmost $a + b$-free path prohibits any sound code movement.[4]

In contrast to classical partial redundancy elimination (cf. Sect. 2), POE has no problems with this worst-case pattern for partial redundancy elimination. One simply needs to exploit the corresponding redundancy information (typically just bit vectors indicating whether a certain computation is redundant or not) as a driver for the expansion, with the result that at each node of the expanded graph each computation is either totally redundant of fully required. All 'partiality' is automatically eliminated (the *quality* aimed for here)! Subsequently, one simply needs to eliminate the total redundancies as usual in order to arrive at Fig. 6(b). Applying classical automata minimization, as proposed in [49] together with the first solution for eliminating all partial redundancies results in Fig. 6(c).[5]

Perhaps even more illuminating than the worst-case pattern for partial redundancy elimination of Fig. 6 is the treatment of the one state irreducible program graph of Fig. 7(a) which our POE transforms into the optimal three state program graph of Fig. 7(b) without any need of automata minimization.

POE straightforwardly applies to forward oriented program analyses with finite domains. However, in the original paper [49] the extension towards backwards oriented problems, like *partial dead code elimination* [21], is also addressed, and in [23] we extended POE based redundancy elimination towards the much more general notion of *semantic redundancies*, a problem with an infinite data domain [42, 46].

In fact, also symbolic execution is naturally realized via SOS as indicated in Fig. 8, where path conditions and the symbolic values of each variable are explicitly recorded. This is, however, just one possible version of representing the corresponding information. One could, e.g., also provide a single equivalent logic term in order to avoid redundancy and to support minimization via SMT solving. More involved is the symbolic execution underlying our aggres-

---

[4] For the sake of simplicity, we use an uniform assignment pattern $x = a + b$ in the example. This allows us to eliminate complete statements without keeping track on temporaries. A detailed discourse on the issue of assignment vs. expression motion can be found in [22].

[5] In a realistic setting minimization would take conditions of branching into account.

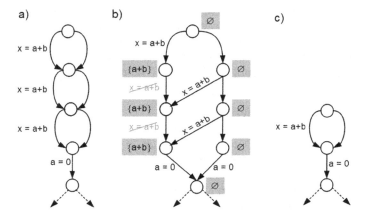

Fig. 6. a) Partially redundant computations that cannot be eliminated by standard techniques. b) Complete redundancy elimination by POE. Nodes are expanded according to the attached redundancy sets. c) Expanded model after minimization.

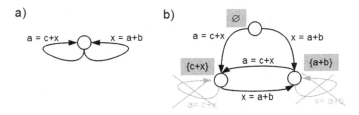

Fig. 7. a) Irreducible program loop with partially redundant computations. b) Optimal program due to POE.

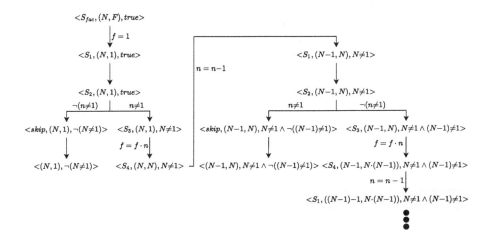

Fig. 8. SOS semantics wrt. symbolic execution.

sive aggregation paradigm [14] which aims at clearly separating the conditional structure underlying the control flow from the computational aspects in order to enable powerful optimizations. The conceptual idea in all these cases is the same: incrementally explore the symbolic execution tree, and, if wished, apply abstraction/aggregation to obtain sound finite representations.

4   The Modal Meta Mindset

In this section, we present *Context-Free Modal Transition Systems* (CFMTSs) which can be regarded as a conceptual generalization of BNF as a graphical DSL for meta-level reasoning and variation control. CFMTSs extend *Modal Transition Systems* (MTSs) [29] to mutually recursive systems of MTSs (see [52] for the corresponding formal definition).[6] We will illustrate our approach by considering a hierarchy of families of sub-languages of PL/0 [59]: The point here is to show the impact of property preserving language refinement in terms of modal refinement [52,55].[7] This is particular interesting in the context of DSL engineering where it guarantees that further specialization preserves established guarantees.

The programming language PL/0 introduced by Niklaus Wirth [59] is a general-purpose language which was intended to be used for educational purpose. Its Extended Backus-Naur form (EBNF) is given below.

```
Program    = Block "."
Block      = ["const" Ident "="Number {"," Ident "="Number} ";"]
             ["var" Ident {","Ident} ";"]
             {"procedure" Ident ";" Block ";"} Statement
Statement  = [Ident ":=" Expression | "call" Ident | "?" Ident
           |  "!" Expression
           |  "begin" Statement {";" Statement } "end"
           |  "if" Condition "then" Statement
           |  "while" Condition "do" Statement]
Condition  = "odd" Expression
           |  Expression ("=" | "#" | "<" | "<=" | ">" | ">=" ) Expression
Expression = ["+" | "-"] Term {("+" | "-") Term}
Term       = Factor {("*"|"/") Factor}
Factor     = Ident | Number | "("Expression")"
```

This specification can straightforwardly be transformed into a CFMTS which comprises one procedural modal transition system (PMTS) for each non-terminal. Figure 9 shows the PMTSs for the non-terminals **Factor** and **Expression**.

---

[6] Alternatively, one can regard CFMTSs also as extensions of Context-Free Process Systems [5] to allow **may** transitions.

[7] Modal refinement preserves properties specified in branching-time temporal logic [30].

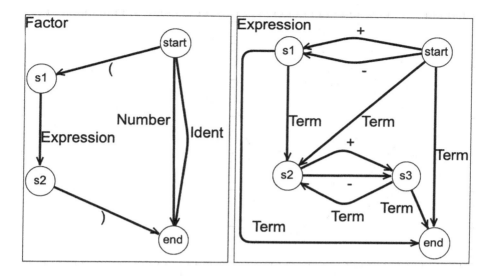

Fig. 9. Factor and Expression as PMTSs.

Figures 9 and 10 should suffice to get an impression of the DSL aspect of the graphical modeling language: We are just dealing with systems of named PMTS, like `Factor`, `Expression` and `Statement` that

- have PMTS names as action labels that, semantically, represent calls to the respective PMTS (cf. the occurrences of `Expression` in the `Factor` and `Statement` PMTS), and
- that possess so-called **may** transitions that are indicated by dotted lines, like the dotted `call` transition in the `Statement` PMTS. This dotted line means that languages conforming to this meta model may provide `call` statements, but they are not required to.

Whereas the first property allows one to specify context-free systems, the second property supports a refinement relation that preserves branching time temporal logics [30]. During refinement, **may** transitions may be eliminated or turned into **must** transitions (just the normal transitions). [52] provides the corresponding formal details also comprising the model checking aspects.

For the remainder of the section the following intuition about modal refinement should suffice:

- CFMTS containing **may** transitions are in fact families of languages. The elements of these families arise from refinement, i.e., either by eliminating the **may** transitions or turning them into **must** transitions. Please note that modal refinement is insensitive to loop unrolling which may result in a CFMTS where an original **may** transitions occurs many times which can all be individually either eliminated or turned into **must** transitions.

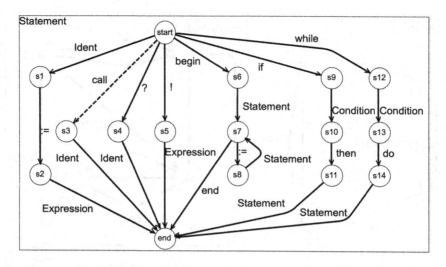

Fig. 10. The Statement PMTS.

- Modal refinement preserves properties specified in branching time temporal logics like CTL [7] or the μ-calculus [27]. Thus all languages, i.e., CFMTS without **may** transitions, that are refinements of some CFMTS share the properties of that CFMTS. This 'meta' property of preservation is very useful for the management of variants.

Playing with Variations of PL/0. This section considers eleven families of variants of Wirth's PL/0 in order to illustrate the impact of **may** transitions and how modal meta model checking (M3C) [52] can provide vital feedback when engineering (specification/programming) languages (cf. Table 13). The theme of our discussion is set by the popular property that *no call to a procedure is possible unless the called procedure is declared.*

For the ease of presentation we will assume for the rest of the section that there is just one procedure which is declared via **procedure** and called by **call**. In this simplified setting, property A of Fig. 15 is a μ-calculus formalization of the considered (intuitive) property.[8]

For our discussion, we introduced a further non-terminal, **Decl**, with corresponding PMTS (cf. Fig. 14) to abbreviate the declaration part for the PMTS in Fig. 11 and the transformed PMTS of Fig. 12. Important is the difference

---

[8] The treatment of multiple procedures can be achieved either via a preprocess that constructs individual 'A'-like properties for each procedure, or by enhancing the modeling language towards an adequate notion of Context-Free Modal Register Automata (cf. [16] for the definition of register automata). Whereas the former approach is rather straightforward the latter approach is part of our envisioned future work which, in particular, concerns the corresponding model checking problems.

between the two block PMTSs: The PMTS of Fig. 12 results from a three step transformation which will be denoted by t in the following:

1. Unroll the `Decl` `may` loop, which does not change the semantics.
2. Disallow `call` statements which are not guaranteed to be preceded by a `may` `Decl` transition. This imposes the required semantical change: `call` statements are now 'guarded' by a `Decl` transition.
3. Minimize the PMTS up to bisimulation equivalence [4].

Transformations like this lie at the core of 'DSL-engineering' which is characterized by enforcing vital properties with syntactical means.

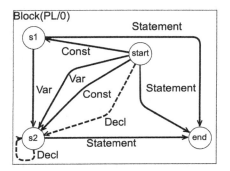

Fig. 11. The `Block` PMTS of variant Nr.8 dC.

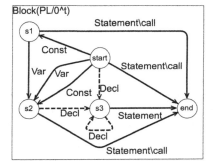

Fig. 12. The `Block` PMTS of variant Nr.9 dC^t.

In the reminder of the section we use the following notation for identifying the different families of PL/0 variants based on the procedure declaration and calling potential. The letter d stands for declaration (`Decl` in the block PMTS), and c for `call` (`call` in the `Statement` PMTS). Are these letters capitalized the corresponding transitions in the respective CFMTSs are **must** transitions, otherwise they are **may** transitions. Figure 13 summarizes the corresponding families we considered in our study: Four families arise simply from the d-c classification described above, and additional four families result from applying the transformation 't' to their CFMTSs. The remaining three families have either only D (denoted WD) or C (denoted WC) as **must** transitions, or neither of them at all (denoted W). Please note, in this notation DC corresponds to the family that just contains full PL/0 and W to the family that only contains its while sub-language.

Not all of these languages make sense. E.g., every program of WC that is not already in W is deemed to violate property A, and any program in WD that is not in W has redundant declarations. The situation is not as bad for dC and Dc, as they allow for language implementations that permit programs with correct `calls`.

Nr.	Variant	Decl	call
1)	WHILE(W)	-	-
2)	WD	Must	-
3)	WC	-	Must
4)	DC	Must	Must
5)	DC^t	Must	Must
6)	dc	May	May
7)	dc^t	May	May
8)	dC	May	Must
9)	dC^t	May	Must
10)	Dc	Must	May
11)	Dc^t	Must	May

Fig. 13. The eleven PL/0 variants.

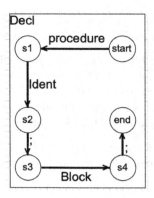

Fig. 14. The Decl PMTS.

Figure 16 provides an overview of the considered landscape partially ordered by modal refinement: dc as the most general family can be refined to all the other families, and, in particular to all the leaves of the refinement DAG.[9] Please note that this refinement hierarchy resembles set inclusion between language families which guarantees that properties proved for some family also holds for each of its refinements.

In order to illustrate this let us consider the following four properties specified in the modal μ-calculus where we use the following conventional notation $[\neg\alpha]\,\phi = \bigwedge_{\beta \in Act, \alpha \neq \beta}[\beta]\,\phi$ where Act is the action alphabet and ϕ is an arbitrary formula of the modal μ-calculus [27]:

$A)$: $\nu X.([call]\text{ff} \wedge [\neg procedure]X)$

$B)$: $\mu X.(\langle call\rangle tt \vee \langle \cdot\rangle X)$ (In CTL:$EF\langle call\rangle tt$)

$C)$: $\mu X.(\langle procedure\rangle tt \vee \langle \cdot\rangle X)$ (In CTL:$EF\langle procedure\rangle tt$)

$D)$: $\nu X.[procedure](\mu Y.\langle call\rangle tt \vee \langle \cdot\rangle Y) \wedge [\cdot]X$

Fig. 15. The properties to be checked on the PL/0 CFMTS.

Property A is the formalization of our central property *no call to a procedure is possible unless the called procedure is declared*. Of course this simple formalization hinges on the restriction to programs with at most one **procedure**, which we made for the ease of presentation. Property B and C simply state that a **call** transition respectively a **procedure** transition is eventually possible. Finally, Property D states the universal extension of Property B that whenever a **procedure** transition is traversed, *at all times a call transition is eventually possible*.

---

[9] Directed Acyclic Graph [56].

We have already briefly discussed that property A of Fig. 15 does not hold for 'standard' PL/0 and how to overcome this problem by an easy transformation here indicated by 't'. In fact this holds even independently from the other choices: the entire sub-DAG of dc^t satisfies A. Moreover, Fig. 16 illustrates that further specialization, i.e., narrowing of the language family, allows one to successively decide more properties, until, at the leaves of the DAG, all properties can be decided.

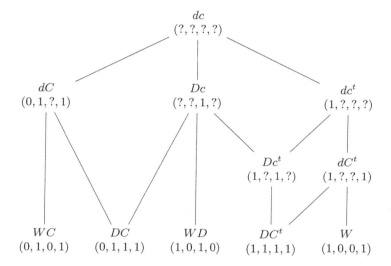

Fig. 16. Hasse-Diagram: Refinement ordering of variations.

Thus, CFMTSs provide DSL engineers with a nice framework to tailor their DSLs according to their needs within a property-preserving, meta-level refinement hierarchy. In particular, it is possible to use M3C [52] to model check properties in branching time temporal logic in order to arrive at overviews as indicated by Fig. 16 where the various languages families are associated with their respective properties. In this figure, going down the DAG structure means refinement and the four tuples associated with each of the DAG nodes record the model checking result for each of the four formulas of Fig. 15. E.g., the 1 in the first component of the dc^t means that property A holds, and the three subsequent question marks that none of the other properties can be decided for this family, as some of its members satisfy these properties, but other do not.

Figure 16 indicates a number of insights:

1. Refinement is property preserving: Going down the DAG, digits are not changed, only question marks may successively turn into digits. Property preservation is a proven fact!
2. The t transformation is effective: All families that result from a t transformation satisfy property A. In the given case, t is effective for the most general

language family dc. Thus the property preservation of refinement guarantees that t is indeed effective also for all the refinements of dc.

3. As refinements can be interpreted as projections to a subset of the considered family of languages, the refinement hierarchy is, indeed, a sub lattice of the powerset lattice.
4. Refinement stops at the one language family for which all the properties can be decided.
5. Model checking of refinement hierarchies should aim at proving properties as far up in the hierarchy as possible in order to exploit property preservation. This means, in particular, that it is economic to search for and refine the lowest adequate spot in the refinement hierarchy when designing a new DSL in order to profit from the already gathered knowledge.

In [53] we call properties that can be enforced directly by an appropriate meta model *rigid archimedean points*. As grammar-based syntax specifications certainly are considered part of a meta model, the four properties discussed here can all be made rigid without imposing unwanted additional constraints. Moreover, using adequate language workbenches like Xtext/EMF [1], MPS [57], Spoofax [19], Marama [15], MetaEdit [20], and Cinco [35], entire IDEs for the resulting DSLs can automatically be generated.

5   Conclusions and Perspectives

We have positioned Linear Time Temporal Logic (LTL), structural operational semantics (SOS), and a graphical generalization of BNF as central DSLs for program analysis and verification tasks in order to illustrate the impact of language to the mindset: (1) Specifying program analyses in LTL changes the classical algorithmic 'HOW' thinking into a property-oriented 'WHAT' thinking that allows one to logically combine analysis goals and eases proofs. (2) Playing with the original store component in SOS configurations allows one to elegantly realize variants of abstract program interpretations, and to align different aspects, like e.g., the symbolic values of variables and path conditions. (3) Specializing languages by refining their BNF-like meta models has the power to lift certain verification tasks from the program up to the programming language level.

Common in all cases is the aim for simplicity for 'the many' (the users of the DSL) on the price of some difficulties for 'the few' [31] that make these DSLs operational, e.g. via some integrated development environment (IDE), a task that is today supported by language workbenches like MPS [57], Spoofax [19], and Cinco [35]. This concerns, e.g., the easy refinement of specifications in LTL using logical operators, the incremental extension of SOS for new language constructs by just adding some additional rules or for new semantical aspects by adding some (abstract) semantic domains, and the modal refinement of language family specifications in CFMTS for a property-preserving variation management.

Interesting is the self-application aspect inherent in DSL development. In fact, all three proposed DSLs are at the heart of language workbench design:

meta modeling and the specification of semantics must be supported by each language workbench which typically also provides numerous static analyses. Thus improvements of one of the considered DSLs may directly enter some language workbench in order to ease further improvements also of this very DSL.

Currently, we are investigating different application scenarios where a change of mindset imposed by one of the described direction may be profitable. One of these scenarios concerns the family of temporal logics comprising, e.g., the μ-calculus [27], CTL [7], LTL [40], and CTL* [13]. There are numerous variants both of linear time and branching time temporal logics, e.g., concerning the underlying model structure (LTS [32], Kripke structures [28], or Kripke transitions systems [34]) or some syntactic restrictions like excluding the nexttime operator. The modal meta mindset might help here both, to systematically organize this landscape and to achieve efficient implementations, e.g., by moving otherwise additional constraints directly into the meta model.

This is not an entirely new idea. The side condition that variables in the μ-calculus have to appear within the range of an even number of negations can, e.g., be enforced via the so-called positive normal form [3], i.e., via syntactic restriction. The same trick also applies to ACTL [36] which is defined by (semantically) forbidding existential path quantification. Moving the side conditions like this (which may impose interesting user-level properties of the logic) into the syntax has various benefits, e.g., concerning corresponding IDEs.

The property that variables in the μ-calculus have to appear within the range of an even number of negations can well be expressed as a temporal formula itself. Thus M3C would allow one to automatically verify whether the considered logical language (family) guarantees this property, with the consequence that the property is guaranteed to be taken care of by the syntax checker for the logic.

The modal meta mindset can also profitably be applied in completely different scenarios, e.g., DTD-based shop configurations[10] [41]: The conceptual idea here is to specify processes via (DTD-based) requirements on their respective documentation which is meant to comprise the actual protocol of its execution. Successful process executions are then characterized by documentations that conform to the underlying DTD.[11] As DTDs can well be translated in CFMTS we can use M3C to automatically check these DTDs for vital properties, like, e.g., that the goods are not send before the payment is confirmed. If this is proved for the DTD, successful process execution is guaranteed whenever the corresponding document is DTD-conform [55].

We are convinced that DSLs will have a major economic impact in the future [51]. They narrow the semantic gap – ideally, the application expert can use it herself in her own mindset – and they typically come with efficient code generators. Thus the move from the WHAT to the HOW is essentially for free. And where it is not, we simply have to develop an appropriate DSL for getting it done

---

[10] DTD stands for Document Type Descriptions.

[11] This leads to very tolerant process specifications, similar to what is aimed at it with CMMN [38] in order to overcome the over specification easily imposed when using e.g. BPMN [37].

(cf. e.g., [17,18,45,51]). This way DSLs become a means to extend the typically very generic language guaranteed correctness-by-construction, e.g. in terms of typing, to also comprise application-specific structural properties.

Acknowledgements. We would like to thank David Schmidt for his constructive comments that helped us to significantly improve the readability of the paper.

References

1. Xtext - Language Engineering Made Easy! http://www.eclipse.org/Xtext/. Accessed 16 Nov 2020
2. Bloom, B.: Structured operational semantics as a specification language. In: Cytron, R.K., Lee, P. (eds.) Conference Record of POPL 1995: 22nd ACM SIGPLAN-SIGACT Symposium on Principles of Programming Languages, San Francisco, California, USA, 23–25 January 1995, pp. 107–117. ACM Press (1995)
3. Bradfield, J.C., Stirling, C.: Modal mu-calculi. In: Blackburn, P., van Benthem, J.F.A.K., Wolter, F. (eds.) Handbook of Modal Logic, Studies in Logic and Practical Reasoning, vol. 3, pp. 721–756. North-Holland (2007)
4. Burkart, O., Caucal, D., Steffen, B.: Bisimulation collapse and the process taxonomy. In: Montanari, U., Sassone, V. (eds.) CONCUR 1996. LNCS, vol. 1119, pp. 247–262. Springer, Heidelberg (1996). https://doi.org/10.1007/3-540-61604-7_59
5. Burkart, O., Steffen, B.: Model checking for context-free processes. In: Cleaveland, W.R. (ed.) CONCUR 1992. LNCS, vol. 630, pp. 123–137. Springer, Heidelberg (1992). https://doi.org/10.1007/BFb0084787
6. Chamberlin, D.D., Boyce, R.F.: SEQUEL: a structured English query language. In: Rustin, R. (ed.), Proceedings of 1974 ACM-SIGMOD Workshop on Data Description, Access and Control, Ann Arbor, Michigan, USA, 1–3 May 1974, vol. 2, pp. 249–264. ACM (1974)
7. Clarke, E.M., Emerson, E.A.: Design and synthesis of synchronization skeletons using branching time temporal logic. In: Kozen, D. (ed.) Logic of Programs 1981. LNCS, vol. 131, pp. 52–71. Springer, Heidelberg (1982). https://doi.org/10.1007/BFb0025774
8. Clarke, E.M., Henzinger, T.A., Veith, H., Bloem, R. (eds.): Handbook of Model Checking. Springer, Cham (2018). https://doi.org/10.1007/978-3-319-10575-8
9. Cleaveland, R., Madelaine, E., Sims, S.: A front-end generator for verification tools. In: Brinksma, E., Cleaveland, W.R., Larsen, K.G., Margaria, T., Steffen, B. (eds.) TACAS 1995. LNCS, vol. 1019, pp. 153–173. Springer, Heidelberg (1995). https://doi.org/10.1007/3-540-60630-0_8
10. Cousot, P., Cousot, R.: Abstract interpretation: a unified lattice model for static analysis of programs by construction or approximation of fixpoints. In: Conference on Record of the 4th, Los Angeles, CA, 1977, pp. 238–252 (1977)
11. Dhamdhere, D.M.: A fast algorithm for code movement optimisation. ACM SIG-PLAN Not. **23**(10), 172–180 (1988)
12. Dhamdhere, D.M., Keith, J.S.: Characterization of program loops in code optimization. Comput. Lang. **8**(2), 69–76 (1983)
13. Emerson, E.A., Halpern, J.Y.: "sometimes" and "not never" revisited: on branching versus linear time. In: Wright, J.R., Landweber, L., Demers, A.J., Teitelbaum, T. (eds.) Conference Record of the Tenth Annual ACM Symposium on Principles of Programming Languages, Austin, Texas, USA, January 1983, pp. 127–140. ACM Press (1983)

14. Gossen, F., Jasper, M., Murtovi, A., Steffen, B.: Aggressive aggregation: a new paradigm for program optimization. CoRR, abs/1912.11281 (2019)
15. Grundy, J., Hosking, J., Li, K.N., Ali, N.M., Huh, J., Li, R.L.: Generating domain-specific visual language tools from abstract visual specifications. IEEE Trans. Software Eng. **39**(4), 487–515 (2013)
16. Howar, F., Steffen, B., Jonsson, B., Cassel, S.: Inferring canonical register automata. In: Kuncak, V., Rybalchenko, A. (eds.) VMCAI 2012. LNCS, vol. 7148, pp. 251–266. Springer, Heidelberg (2012). https://doi.org/10.1007/978-3-642-27940-9_17
17. Jörges, S.: Construction and Evolution of Code Generators - A Model-Driven and Service-Oriented Approach. LNCS, vol. 7747. Springer, Heidelberg (2013). https://doi.org/10.1007/978-3-642-36127-2
18. Jörges, S., Margaria, T., Steffen, B.: Genesys: service-oriented construction of property conform code generators. Innov. Syst. Softw. Eng. **4**(4), 361–384 (2008)
19. Kats, L.C.L., Visser, E.: The spoofax language workbench: rules for declarative specification of languages and ides. In: Cook, W.R., Clarke, S., Rinard, M.C. (eds.) Proceedings of the 25th Annual ACM SIGPLAN Conference on Object-Oriented Programming, Systems, Languages, and Applications, OOPSLA 2010, Reno/Tahoe, Nevada, USA, 17–21 October 2010, pp. 444–463. ACM (2010)
20. Kelly, S., Tolvanen, J.-P.: Domain-Specific Modeling: Enabling Full Code Generation. Wiley-IEEE Computer Society Press, Hoboken (2008)
21. Knoop, J., Rüthing, O., Steffen, B.: Partial dead code elimination. In: Proceedings of the 1994, Orlando, FL, June 1994, vol. 29, no. 6, pp. 147–158 (1994)
22. Knoop, J., Rüthing, O., Steffen, B.: The power of assignment motion. In: Proceedings of the 1995, La Jolla, CA, June 1995, vol. 30, no. 6, pp. 233–245 (1995)
23. Knoop, J., Rüthing, O., Steffen, B.: Expansion-based removal of semantic partial redundancies. In: Jähnichen, S. (ed.) CC 1999. LNCS, vol. 1575, pp. 91–106. Springer, Heidelberg (1999). https://doi.org/10.1007/978-3-540-49051-7_7
24. Knoop, J., Rüthing, O., Steffen, B.: Lazy code motion. In: Feldman, S.I., Wexelblat, R.L. (eds.) Proceedings of the ACM SIGPLAN 1992 Conference on Programming Language Design and Implementation (PLDI), San Francisco, California, USA, 17–19 June 1992, pp. 224–234. ACM (1992)
25. Knoop, J., Rüthing, O., Steffen, B.: Lazy code motion (with retrospective). In: McKinley, K.S. (ed.) 20 Years of the ACM SIGPLAN Conference on Programming Language Design and Implementation 1979–1999, A Selection, pp. 460–472. ACM (1992)
26. Knuth, D.E.: Backus normal form vs. Backus Naur form. Commun. ACM **7**(12), 735–736 (1964)
27. Kozen, D.: Results on the propositional mu-calculus. Theor. Comput. Sci. **27**, 333–354 (1983)
28. Kripke, S.: Semantical considerations on modal logic. Acta Phil. Fennica **16**, 83–94 (1963)
29. Larsen, K.G., Thomsen, B.: A modal process logic. In: [1988] Proceedings. Third Annual Symposium on Logic in Computer Science, pp. 203–210 (1988)
30. Larsen, K.G.: Modal specifications. In: Sifakis, J. (ed.) CAV 1989. LNCS, vol. 407, pp. 232–246. Springer, Heidelberg (1990). https://doi.org/10.1007/3-540-52148-8_19
31. Margaria, T., Steffen, B.: Simplicity as a driver for agile innovation. Computer **43**(6), 90–92 (2010)
32. Milner, R.: Communication and Concurrency. PHI Series in Computer Science. Prentice Hall, Upper Saddle Rive (1989)

33. Morel, E., Renvoise, C.: Global optimization by suppression of partial redundancies. Commun. ACM **22**(2), 96–103 (1979)
34. Müller-Olm, M., Schmidt, D., Steffen, B.: Model-Checking: a tutorial introduction. In: Cortesi, A., Filé, G. (eds.) SAS 1999. LNCS, vol. 1694, pp. 330–354. Springer, Heidelberg (1999). https://doi.org/10.1007/3-540-48294-6_22
35. Naujokat, S., Lybecait, M., Kopetzki, D., Steffen, B.: CINCO: a simplicity-driven approach to full generation of domain-specific graphical modeling tools. STTT **20**(3), 327–354 (2018)
36. De Nicola, R., Vaandrager, F.: Action versus state based logics for transition systems. In: Guessarian, I. (ed.) LITP 1990. LNCS, vol. 469, pp. 407–419. Springer, Heidelberg (1990). https://doi.org/10.1007/3-540-53479-2_17
37. Object Management Group (OMG): Documents Associated with BPMN Version 2.0.1, September 2013. http://www.omg.org/spec/BPMN/2.0.1/. Accessed 16 Nov 2020
38. Object Management Group (OMG): Documents Associated with Case Management Model and Notation (CMMN), Version 1.0, May 2014. http://www.omg.org/spec/CMMN/1.0/. Accessed 16 Nov 2020
39. Plotkin, G.: A structural approach to operational semantics. Technical report, Aarhus Univ., Computer Science Dept., Denmark 1981. DAIMI FN-19
40. Pnueli, A.: The temporal logic of programs. In: 18th Annual Symposium on Foundations of Computer Science, Providence, Rhode Island, USA, 31 October - 1 November 1977, pp. 46–57. IEEE Computer Society (1977)
41. Ray, E.T.: Learning XML - Creating Self-Describing Data: Cover Schemas, 2 edn. O'Reilly, Sebastopol (2003)
42. Rüthing, O., Knoop, J., Steffen, B.: Detecting equalities of variables: combining efficiency with precision. In: Cortesi, A., Filé, G. (eds.) SAS 1999. LNCS, vol. 1694, pp. 232–247. Springer, Heidelberg (1999). https://doi.org/10.1007/3-540-48294-6_15
43. Schmidt, D.A.: Data flow analysis is model checking of abstract interpretations. In: MacQueen, D.B., Cardelli, L. (eds.) Proceedings of the 25th ACM SIGPLAN-SIGACT Symposium on Principles of Programming Languages, POPL 1998, San Diego, CA, USA, 19–21 January 1998, pp. 38–48. ACM (1998)
44. Schmidt, D.A., Steffen, B.: Program analysis as model checking of abstract interpretations. In: Levi, G. (ed.) SAS 1998. LNCS, vol. 1503, pp. 351–380. Springer, Heidelberg (1998). https://doi.org/10.1007/3-540-49727-7_22
45. Smyth, S.: Interactive model-based compilation. Ph.D. thesis, CAU Kiel, to appear
46. Steffen, B., Knoop, J., Rüthing, O.: The value flow graph: a program representation for optimal program transformations. In: Jones, N. (ed.) ESOP 1990. LNCS, vol. 432, pp. 389–405. Springer, Heidelberg (1990). https://doi.org/10.1007/3-540-52592-0_76
47. Steffen, B.: Data flow analysis as model checking. In: Ito, T., Meyer, A.R. (eds.) TACS 1991. LNCS, vol. 526, pp. 346–364. Springer, Heidelberg (1991). https://doi.org/10.1007/3-540-54415-1_54
48. Steffen, B.: Generating data flow analysis algorithms from modal specifications. Sci. Comput. Program. **21**(2), 115–139 (1993)
49. Steffen, B.: Property-oriented expansion. In: Cousot, R., Schmidt, D.A. (eds.) SAS 1996. LNCS, vol. 1145, pp. 22–41. Springer, Heidelberg (1996). https://doi.org/10.1007/3-540-61739-6_31
50. Steffen, B., Claßen, A., Klein, M., Knoop, J., Margaria, T.: The fixpoint-analysis machine. In: Lee, I., Smolka, S.A. (eds.) CONCUR 1995. LNCS, vol. 962, pp. 72–87. Springer, Heidelberg (1995). https://doi.org/10.1007/3-540-60218-6_6

51. Steffen, B., Gossen, F., Naujokat, S., Margaria, T.: Language-driven engineering: from general-purpose to purpose-specific languages. In: Steffen, B., Woeginger, G. (eds.) Computing and Software Science. LNCS, vol. 10000, pp. 311–344. Springer, Cham (2019). https://doi.org/10.1007/978-3-319-91908-9_17

52. Steffen, B., Murtovi, A.: $M3C$: modal meta model checking. In: Howar, F., Barnat, J. (eds.) FMICS 2018. LNCS, vol. 11119, pp. 223–241. Springer, Cham (2018). https://doi.org/10.1007/978-3-030-00244-2_15

53. Steffen, B., Naujokat, S.: Archimedean points: the essence for mastering change. Trans. Found. Mastering Chang. 1, 22–46 (2016)

54. Steffen, B., Rüthing, O.: Quality engineering: leveraging heterogeneous information. In: Jhala, R., Schmidt, D. (eds.) VMCAI 2011. LNCS, vol. 6538, pp. 23–37. Springer, Heidelberg (2011). https://doi.org/10.1007/978-3-642-18275-4_4

55. Tegeler, T., Murtovi, A., Frohme, M., Steffen, B.: Product line verification via modal meta model checking. In: ter Beek, M.H., Fantechi, A., Semini, L. (eds.) From Software Engineering to Formal Methods and Tools, and Back. LNCS, vol. 11865, pp. 313–337. Springer, Cham (2019). https://doi.org/10.1007/978-3-030-30985-5_19

56. Thulasiraman, K., Swamy, M.N.S.: Graphs - Theory and Algorithms. Wiley, New York (1992)

57. Voelter, M., Pech, V.: Language modularity with the MPS language workbench. In: Glinz, M., Murphy, G.C., Pezzè, M. (eds.) 34th International Conference on Software Engineering, ICSE 2012, Zurich, Switzerland, 2–9 June 2012, pp. 1449–1450. IEEE Computer Society (2012)

58. Völter, M., et al.: DSL Engineering - Designing, Implementing and Using Domain-Specific Languages (2013). dslbook.org

59. Wirth, N.: Compilerbau - Eine Einführung. Teubner (1977)

Hyperproperties and Infinite-State Systems

Compositional Model Checking
for Multi-properties

Ohad Goudsmid[1]([✉]), Orna Grumberg[1], and Sarai Sheinvald[2]

[1] Department of Computer Science, The Technion, Haifa, Israel
goudsmidohad@cs.technion.ac.il
[2] Department of Software Engineering, ORT Braude College of Engineering,
Karmiel, Israel

Abstract. *Hyperproperties* lift conventional trace properties in a way
that describes how a system behaves in its entirety, and not just based
on its individual traces. We generalize this notion to *multi-properties*,
which describe the behavior of not just a single system, but of a set of
systems, which we call a *multi-model*. We demonstrate the usefulness
of our setting with practical examples. We show that model-checking
multi-properties is equivalent to model-checking hyperproperties. However, our framework has the immediate advantage of being *compositional*.
We introduce sound and complete compositional proof rules for model-
checking multi-properties, based on over- and under-approximations of
the systems in the multi-model. We then describe methods of computing
such approximations. The first is abstraction-refinement based, in which
a coarse initial abstraction is continuously refined using counterexamples, until a suitable approximation is found. The second, tailored for
models with finite traces, finds suitable approximations via the L^* learning algorithm. Our methods can produce much smaller models than the
original ones, and can therefore be used for accelerating model-checking
for both multi-properties and hyperproperties.

1 Introduction

Temporal logics, such as LTL, are widely used for specifying program behaviors.
An LTL property characterizes a set of traces, each of which satisfies the property.
It has recently been shown that trace properties are insufficient for characterizing
and verifying security vulnerabilities or their absence.

The notion of *hyperproperties* [9], a generalization of trace properties, provides a uniform formalism for specifying properties of *sets of traces*. Hyperproperties are particularly suitable for specifying security properties. For instance,
secure information flow may be characterized by identifying low-security variables that may be observable to the environment, and high-security variables
that should not be observable outside. Secure information flow is maintained in

---

This research was partially supported by the Mel Berlin fellowship and partially by
the Israel Science Foundation.

F. Henglein et al. (Eds.): VMCAI 2021, LNCS 12597, pp. 55–80, 2021.
https://doi.org/10.1007/978-3-030-67067-2_4

a system if for every two traces, if their low-security inputs are identical then so are their low-security outputs, regardless of the values of high-security variables. This property cannot be characterized via single traces.

While hyperproperties are highly useful, they are still limited: they can only refer to the system as a whole. Systems often comprise several components, and it is desired to relate traces from one component to traces of another. A prominent such example is *diversity* [16]. Diversity generalizes the notion of security policies by considering policies of a set of systems. The systems are all required to implement the same functionality but to differ in their implementation details. As noticed in [9], such a set of policies could, in principle, be modeled as a hyperproperty on a single system, which is a product of all the systems in the set. This, however, is both unnatural and highly inefficient.

We remedy this situation by presenting a framework which explicitly describes the system as a set of systems called a *multi-model*, and provides a specification language, MultiLTL, which explicitly relates traces from the different components in the multi-model. Our framework enables to directly and naturally describe properties like diversity, while avoiding the need for a complex translation.

Our framework also has the immediate advantage of being *compositional*. We thus suggest a sound and complete compositional model-checking rule. The rule is based on abstracting each of the components by over- and under-approximations, thus achieving additional gain.

We then suggest methods of computing such approximations. The first is based on *abstraction-refinement*, in which a coarse initial abstraction is continuously refined by using counterexamples, until a suitable approximation is found. The second, tailored for models with finite traces, finds suitable approximations via the L^* learning algorithm. Our methods can produce much smaller models than the original ones, and can therefore be used for accelerating model-checking for both multi-properties and hyperproperties.

We now describe our work in more detail. Our framework consists of multi-models, which are tuples of Kripke structures. The logic we focus on, called MultiLTL, is an extension of HyperLTL [8]. MultiLTL allows indexed quantifications, $\forall^i$ and $\exists^i$, referring to the i'th component-model in the multi-model.

We show that there is a two-way reduction between the model-checking problem for HyperLTL and the model-checking problem for MultiLTL. We emphasize, that even though the two model-checking problems are equivalent, our new framework is clearly more powerful as it enables a direct specification and verification of the whole system by explicitly referring to its parts.

We exploit this power by introducing two compositional proof rules, which are based on over- and under-approximations for each system component separately. These proof rules are capable of proving a MultiLTL property or its negation for a given multi-model.

We suggest two approaches to computing these approximations for the compositional proof rules. The first approach is based on *abstraction-refinement*. The approximations are computed gradually, starting from coarse approximations and refined based on counterexamples. The abstraction-refinement approach is implemented using one of two algorithms. In both algorithms, when model-checking the abstract multi-model is successful, we conclude that model-checking for the original multi-model holds. Otherwise, a counterexample is returned.

The first algorithm is based on counterexamples from the multi-model only. For each component-model, we find a behavior that should be eliminated from an over-approximated component-model or added to an under-approximated component-model, and refine the components accordingly.

The second algorithm is applicable for a restricted type of MultiLTL properties, in which the quantification consists of a sequence of $\forall$ quantifiers followed by a sequence of $\exists$ quantifiers. In hyperproperties, this is a useful fragment which allows specifying noninterference and generalized noninterference, observational determinism, and more. The counterexamples in this case come directly from the unsuccessful model-checking process, and therefore refer both to the model and to the property. Notice that, since the abstract component-models are typically much smaller than the original component-models, their model-checking is much faster.

The logics of MultiLTL and the model of Kripke structure are designed for describing and modeling the behavior of on-going systems. However, to do the same for terminating programs with finite traces, a more suitable description is needed. Therefore, we turn our attention to multi-models and multi-properties with finite traces. In this context, we use nondeterministic finite automata (NFA) to describe a system, and a set of NFAs (*multi-NFA*) to describe a set of such systems. For the specification language, we use nondeterministic finite-word hyper-automata (NFH) suggested in [7]. NFH can be thought of as the regular-language counterpart of HyperLTL, and are able to describe the regular properties of sets of finite-word languages, just as HyperLTL is able to describe the properties of a language of infinite traces. Also like HyperLTL, NFH can be easily adjusted to describe multi-properties, a model that we call *multi-NFH*.

We show that, as in the infinite-trace case, there is a two-way reduction between the model-checking problem for NFH and the model-checking problem for multi-NFH. We then proceed to present a compositional model-checking framework for multi-NFH. As in the case of infinite-traces, this framework is based on finding approximations for the NFAs in the multi-model. The method for finding these approximations for this case, however, is learning-based.

Learning-based model-checking [15] seeks candidate approximations by running an automata learning algorithm such as L^* [2]. In the L^* algorithm, a *learner* constructs a finite-word automaton for an unknown regular language $\mathcal{L}$, through a sequence of *membership queries* ("is the word w in $\mathcal{L}$?") and *equivalence queries* ("is $\mathcal{A}$ an automaton for $\mathcal{L}$?"), to which it receives answers from a *teacher* who knows the language. The learner continually constructs and submits candidate automata, until the teacher confirms an equivalence query.

In our algorithm, the learner constructs a set of candidate automata in every iteration, one for every NFA in the multi-model. The key idea is treating these candidate automata as candidate approximations. When an equivalence query is submitted, we (as the teacher) check whether the NFAs that the learner submitted are suitable approximations. If they are not, we return counterexamples to the learner, based on the given multi-NFA, which it uses to construct the next set of candidates. If they are suitable approximations, we model-check the multi-NFA of the approximations against the multi-NFH. Since the automata that the learner constructs are relatively small, model-checking the candidates multi-model is much faster than model-checking the original multi-model.

In [15], the learning procedure aims at learning the *weakest assumption W*, which is a regular language that contains all the traces that under certain conditions satisfy the specification. The construction of W relies on counterexample words provided by the model checking. We can derive such counterexamples for a certain fragment of multi-NFH. Moreover, we define a suitable weakest assumption for this case, prove that it is regular, and use it as a learning goal in an improved algorithm. Both of these improvements – extracting counterexamples from the model-checker, and learning the weakest assumption rather than the model itself – allow for an even quicker convergence of the model-checking process for this type of multi-properties.

Related Work. *Hyperproperties*, introduced in [9], provide a uniform formalism for specifying properties of sets of traces. Hyperproperties are particularly suitable for specifying security properties, such as secure information flow and non-interference. Two logics for hyperproperties are introduced in [8]: HyperLTL and hyperCTL*, which generalize LTL and CTL*, respectively. Other logics for hyperproperties have been studied in [1,5,6,10,13,14,20].

One of the first sound and complete methods for model-checking hyperproperties is called *self-composition* [4]. Self-composition combines several disjoint copies of the same program, allowing to express relationships among multiple traces. This reduces the k-trace hyperproperty model-checking to trace property model-checking. Unfortunately, the size of the product model increases exponentially with the number of copies. Thus, reasoning directly on the product program is prohibitive.

Many approaches have been suggested for dealing with the high complexity of self-composition. Methods to increase the efficiency of SMT solvers for hyperpropery model-checking have been suggested in [3,19], while a generalization of Hoare triplets for safety-hyperproperties has been presented in [18].

Different approaches to avoid the construction of the full product are presented in [17,21]. The former exploits taint analysis or Bounded Model Checking. The latter infers a self-composition function together with an inductive invariant, suitable for verification.

An automata based algorithm for HyperLTL and HyperCTL* is proposed in [12]. It combines self-composition with ideas from LTL model-checking using alternating automata. A representation of hyperproperties in a form of finite-word automata is developed in [11]. This work introduces a canonical automata representation for regular-k-safety hyperproperties, which are only-universally-quantified safety-hyperproperties.

The first representation of general hyperproperties using finite automata is introduced in [7]. This representation, called *hyperautomata*, allows running multiple quantified words on an automaton. The authors show that hyperautomata can express regular hyperproperties and explore the decidability of nonemptiness (satisfiability) and membership (model-checking) problems. Additionally, they describe an L^*-based learning algorithm for some fragments of hyperautomata.

2   Preliminaries

Kripke Structures are a standard model for ongoing finite-state systems.

Definition 1. *Given a finite set of atomic propositions AP, a* Kripke structure *is a 4-tuple $\mathcal{M} = (S, I, R, L)$, where S is a finite set of states, $I \subseteq S$ is a non-empty set of initial states, $R \subseteq S \times S$ is a total transition relation and $L : S \to 2^{AP}$ is a labeling function.*

A *path* in $\mathcal{M}$ is an infinite sequence of states $p = s_0, s_1, s_2, \ldots$ such that $(s_i, s_{i+1}) \in R$ for every $i \in \mathbb{N}$. A *trace over AP* is an infinite sequence $\tau \in \left(2^{AP}\right)^{\omega}$. We sometimes refer to a trace as a *word* over 2^{AP}. A *trace property over AP* is a set of traces over AP.

The *trace that corresponds to a path p* is the trace $\tau(p) = \tau_0, \tau_1, \tau_2, \ldots$ in which $\tau_i = L(s_i)$ for every $i \in \mathbb{N}$. Notice that since R is total, there exists an infinite path from every state. We denote by τ^i the trace $\tau_i, \tau_{i+1}, \ldots$.

Given a word $w = w_0, w_1, \cdots \in (2^{AP})^{\omega}$, a *run of $\mathcal{M}$ on w* is a path $p = s_0, s_1 \ldots$ in $\mathcal{M}$ such that $L(s_n) = w_n$ for every $n \in \mathbb{N}$. The *language $\mathcal{L}(\mathcal{M})$* of $\mathcal{M}$ is the set of all traces corresponding to paths in $\mathcal{M}$ that start in I. The *prefix language $\mathcal{L}_f(\mathcal{M})$* of $\mathcal{M}$ is the set of all finite prefixes of traces in $\mathcal{L}(\mathcal{M})$. For two Kripke structures $\mathcal{M}, \mathcal{M}'$, we write $\mathcal{M} \models \mathcal{M}'$ to denote that $\mathcal{L}(\mathcal{M}) \subseteq \mathcal{L}(\mathcal{M}')$.

The following is a known result, which can be proven by König's Lemma.

Lemma 1. *For Kripke structures $\mathcal{M}$ and $\mathcal{M}'$, it holds that $\mathcal{L}(\mathcal{M}) = \mathcal{L}(\mathcal{M}')$ iff $\mathcal{L}_f(\mathcal{M}) = \mathcal{L}_f(\mathcal{M}')$.*

2.1   Hyperproperties and HyperLTL

Trace properties and the logics that express them are commonly used to describe desirable system behaviors. However, some behaviors cannot be expressed by referring to each trace individually. In [9], properties describing the behavior of a combination of traces are formalized as *hyperproperties*. Thus, a hyperproperty is a set of sets of traces: all sets that behave according to the hyperproperty. HyperLTL [8] is an extension of *linear temporal logic* (LTL), a widely used temporal logic for trace properties, to hyperproperties. The formulas of HyperLTL are given by the following grammar:

$$\varphi ::= \exists \pi.\, \varphi \mid \forall \pi.\, \varphi \mid \psi$$
$$\psi ::= a_{\pi} \mid \neg \psi \mid \psi \vee \psi \mid \mathsf{X}\psi \mid \psi \mathsf{U}\psi \qquad \text{for every } a \in AP$$

Intuitively, $\exists \pi.\varphi$ means that there exists a trace that satisfies φ and $\forall \pi.\varphi$ means that φ holds for every trace. a_π means that a holds in the first state of π. The semantics of X, U and the Boolean operators are similar to those in LTL: $\mathsf{X}\psi$ means that ψ holds in the next state and $\psi_1 \mathsf{U} \psi_2$ means that ψ_1 holds until ψ_2 holds. Based on these operators we define additional operators commonly defined in LTL: $\mathsf{F}\psi$ means that ψ holds eventually and $\mathsf{G}\psi$ means that ψ holds throughout the entire trace.

The semantics of HyperLTL is defined as follows. Let $T \subseteq (2^{AP})^\omega$ be a set of traces over AP, let $\mathcal{V}$ be a set of *trace variables*, and $\Pi : \mathcal{V} \to T$ be a trace assignment. Let $\Pi[\pi \to t]$ be the function obtained from Π, by mapping π to t. Let Π^i be the function defined by $\Pi^i(\pi) = (\Pi(\pi))^i$.

$$\Pi \models_T \exists \pi.\psi \quad \text{iff there exists } t \in T \text{ such that } \Pi[\pi \to t] \models_T \psi$$
$$\Pi \models_T \forall \pi.\psi \quad \text{iff for every } t \in T, \ \Pi[\pi \to t] \models_T \psi$$
$$\Pi \models_T a_\pi \quad \text{iff } a \in \Pi(\pi)[0]$$
$$\Pi \models_T \neg\varphi \quad \text{iff } \Pi \not\models_T \varphi$$
$$\Pi \models_T \varphi_1 \vee \varphi_2 \quad \text{iff } \Pi \models_T \varphi_1 \text{ or } \Pi \models_T \varphi_2$$
$$\Pi \models_T \mathsf{X}\varphi \quad \text{iff } \Pi^1 \models_T \varphi$$
$$\Pi \models_T \varphi_1 \mathsf{U} \varphi_2 \quad \text{iff there exists } i \geq 0 \text{ such that } \Pi^i \models_T \varphi_2$$
$$\text{and for all } 0 \leq j < i, \ \Pi^j \models_T \varphi_1$$

Notice that when all trace variables of a HyperLTL formula $\mathbb{P}$ are in the scope of a quantifier (i.e, when $\mathbb{P}$ is *closed*), then the satisfaction is independent of the trace assignment, in which case we write $T \models \mathbb{P}$. Given a Kripke structure $\mathcal{M}$ and a HyperLTL formula $\mathbb{P}$, the *model-checking problem* is to decide whether $\mathcal{L}(\mathcal{M}) \models \mathbb{P}$ (which we denote by $\mathcal{M} \models \mathbb{P}$).

By abuse of notation, given traces $w_1, \ldots, w_k$ over AP, we write $\langle w_1, \ldots, w_k \rangle \models \mathbb{Q}_1 \pi_1 \ldots \mathbb{Q}_k \pi_k \psi(\pi_1, \ldots, \pi_k)$ if $\Pi \models \psi(\pi_1, \ldots, \pi_k)$, where $\Pi(\pi_i) = w_i$.

3   Multi-models and Multi-properties

We generalize hyperproperties to *multi-properties*, which reason about the connections between several models, which we call a *multi-model*.

Definition 2. *Given* $k \in \mathbb{N}$, *a* k-multi-model *is a* k-tuple $\mathbb{M} = \langle \mathcal{M}_1, \mathcal{M}_2, \ldots, \mathcal{M}_k \rangle$ *of Kripke structures over a common set of atomic propositions* AP. *A* k-multi-property *is a set of tuples* $\mathbb{P} \subseteq (2^{(2^{AP})^\omega})^k$.

$\mathbb{M}$ *is a* multi-model *if it is a* k-multi-model *for some* k, *and similarly* $\mathbb{P}$ *is a* multi-property.

Intuitively, in a multi-property $\mathbb{P}$, every $T \in \mathbb{P}$ is a tuple of k sets of traces, each interpreted in a model.

We now present MultiLTL, a logic for describing multi-properties. A MultiLTL formula is interpreted over a multi-model $\mathbb{M} = \langle \mathcal{M}_1, \ldots, \mathcal{M}_k \rangle$. We use $[a, b]$, where $a \leq b$ are integers, to denote the set $\{a, a + 1, \ldots, b\}$. MultiLTL formulas are defined inductively as follows.

$$\varphi ::= \exists^j \pi.\, \varphi \mid \forall^j \pi.\, \varphi \mid \psi \qquad \text{where } j \in [1, k]$$
$$\psi ::= a_\pi \mid \neg\psi \mid \psi \vee \psi \mid \mathsf{X}\psi \mid \psi \mathsf{U}\psi$$

The only difference in syntax from HyperLTL is that trace quantifiers are now indexed. This index is taken from the set $[1, k]$ for some $k \in \mathbb{N}$. The formula $\exists^j \pi.\varphi$ means that there exists a trace in $\mathcal{M}_j$ that satisfies φ and $\forall^j \pi.\varphi$ means that φ holds for every trace in $\mathcal{M}_j$.

The semantics of MultiLTL is defined as follows. Let $\mathbb{T} = \langle T_1, \ldots T_k \rangle$ be a multi-model over AP. Let $\mathcal{V}$ be a set of trace quantifiers, and let $\Pi : \mathcal{V} \to \bigcup_{i \in [1,k]} T_i$.

$$\Pi \models_{\mathbb{T}} \exists^i \pi.\psi \quad \text{iff there exists } t \in T_i \text{ such that } \Pi[\pi \to t] \models_{\mathbb{T}} \psi$$
$$\Pi \models_{\mathbb{T}} \forall^i \pi.\psi \quad \text{iff } \Pi[\pi \to t] \models_{\mathbb{T}} \psi \text{ for every } t \in T_i$$

The semantics of the temporal operators is defined as in HyperLTL. Since every MultiLTL formula describes a multi-property, we refer to the formulas themselves as multi-properties.

As with HyperLTL, when a MultiLTL formula $\mathbb{P}$ is closed, satisfaction is independent of Π, and we denote $\mathbb{M} \models \mathbb{P}$ for a multi-model $\mathbb{M}$. The *model-checking problem* for MultiLTL is to decide whether $\mathbb{M} \models \mathbb{P}$.

For a MultiLTL formula $\mathbb{P} = \mathbb{Q}_{i_1}^1 \ldots \mathbb{Q}_{i_n}^n \varphi$, we define $I_\exists(\mathbb{P}) = \{i \mid \mathbb{Q}_{i_j}^i = \exists \text{ and } i_j \in [1, n]\}$, and $I_\forall(\mathbb{P}) = \{i \mid \mathbb{Q}_{i_j}^i = \forall \text{ and } i_j \in [1, n]\}$. We write $I_\exists$ and $I_\forall$ when $\mathbb{P}$ is clear from the context.

3.1   Examples

We demonstrate the usefulness of MultiLTL and multi-models with several examples. The multi-models we consider consist of models that interact with each other via an asynchronous communication channel (which is not modeled). This assumption is not necessary outside the scope of the examples, where other forms of interactions across models can take place (e.g., shared variables).

Example 1. Consider a multi-model consisting of a client model C and a server model S. We would like to check whether $\langle C, S \rangle \models \forall^C \pi_1 \forall^S \pi_2.\mathsf{G}(r\_sent_{\pi_1} \to \mathsf{F}r\_received_{\pi_2})$. In this formula, $r\_sent_{\pi_1}$ means that a request is sent in C and $r\_received_{\pi_2}$ means that a request is received in S. The formula specifies that for every run of the client and for every run of the server, every request sent by the client is eventually received by the server. This is a form of a liveness property that specifies that messages are guaranteed to eventually arrive at their destination. Note that, whether this property holds or not depends in fact on the reliability of the asynchronous communicating channel, connecting the client and the server.

Example 2. Consider again the multi-model of Example 1. Assume that the interaction between the client and the server is as follows. At the beginning of the interaction, the client sends its username and password to the server. Immediately afterwards the server updates its authentication flag and informs the client whether the authentication was successful or not. The client gets this notification one clock cycle after the server authentication flag has been updated. Consider the specification $\mathbb{P}_2$.

$$\mathbb{P}_2 = \forall^S \pi_1 \exists^C \pi_2 \forall^C \pi_3.\ (userDB_{\pi_1} = user_{\pi_2}) \land (passDB_{\pi_1} = pass_{\pi_2}) \land (\mathsf{X}aut_{\pi_1} \land \mathsf{X}\mathsf{X}aut_{\pi_2})$$
$$\land\ ((userDB_{\pi_1} = user_{\pi_3}) \land ((passDB_{\pi_1} \neq pass_{\pi_3})) \to (\mathsf{X}\neg aut_{\pi_1} \land \mathsf{X}\mathsf{X}\neg aut_{\pi_3})$$

The first line of $\mathbb{P}_2$ states that for every trace of the server there is a trace of the client whose username and password match the username and password in the server database. If so, the authentication succeeds. The second line assures that for each username in the server database there is only one valid password with which the authentication succeeds.

Note that in this example, we describe a property which cannot be described using LTL. Further, it cannot be expressed naturally in HyperLTL. MultiLTL, which explicitly refers to traces in different models within a multi-model, naturally expresses it.

Example 3. We demonstrate again the power of MultiLTL to *naturally* express properties that are not naturally expressible in HyperLTL. *Diversity* [16] refers to security policies of a set of systems. The systems constitute different implementations of the same high-level program. They differ in their implementation details[1], but are equivalent with respect to the input-output they produce. In [16], diversity has been advocated as a successful way to resist attacks that exploit memory layout or instruction sequence specifics.

Assume that we are given a high-level program P and two low-level implementations M_1 and M_2. The following MultiLTL properties describe the fact that all implementations are equivalent to P.

$$\mathbb{P}_1 = \forall^P \pi \exists^{M_1} \pi_1 \exists^{M_2} \pi_2.(input_\pi = input_{\pi_1} = input_{\pi_2}) \land$$
$$\mathsf{G}(end_\pi \land end_{\pi_1} \land end_{\pi_2} \to output_\pi = output_{\pi_1} = output_{\pi_2})$$
$$\mathbb{P}_2 = \forall^{M_1} \pi_1 \exists^P \pi.(input_{\pi_1} = input_\pi) \land \mathsf{G}(end_{\pi_1} \land end_\pi \to output_{\pi_1} = output_\pi)$$
$$\mathbb{P}_3 = \forall^{M_2} \pi_2 \exists^P \pi.(input_{\pi_2} = input_\pi) \land \mathsf{G}(end_{\pi_2} \land end_\pi \to output_{\pi_2} = output_\pi)$$

Note that these properties cannot naturally be expressed in HyperLTL since they require an explicit reference to the models from which the related traces are taken.

---

[1] For instance, the call stack of procedures is obfuscated by changing the order of variables, the specific memory location of arguments and local variables, etc. The obfuscations differ in the different implementations.

3.2 Model-Checking MultiLTL

We now show that although MultiLTL is a generalization of HyperLTL, the model-checking problems for these logic types is equivalent.

For the first direction, it is easy to see that the model-checking problem for a model $\mathcal{M}$ and a HyperLTL formula $\mathcal{P}$ is equivalent to the model checking problem for $\langle \mathcal{M} \rangle$ and the MultiLTL formula obtained from $\mathcal{P}$ by indexing all of its quantifiers with the same index 1.

For the other direction, we first introduce some definitions. We use the notation $\uplus$ for disjoint union.

Definition 3. *Given a multi-model* $\mathbb{M} = \langle \mathcal{M}_1, \ldots, \mathcal{M}_k \rangle$ *over* AP, *its* union model *denoted* $\cup\mathbb{M}$ *is* $(\uplus_{i=1}^n S_i, \uplus_{i=1}^n I_i, \uplus_{i=1}^n R_i, L)$, *where* $L(s) = L_i(s) \uplus \{i\}$ *for every* i *and* $s \in S_i$.

The indexing *by* i *of a trace* $\tau = t_0, t_1, \ldots$ *over* AP *is the trace* $\mathsf{ind}_i(\tau) = t_0 \cup \{i\}, t_1 \cup \{i\}, \ldots$

Notice that for a trace τ and a multi-model $\mathbb{M} = \langle \mathcal{M}_1, \ldots, \mathcal{M}_k \rangle$, it holds that $\tau \in \mathcal{L}(\mathcal{M}_i) \iff \mathsf{ind}_i(\tau) \in \mathcal{L}(\cup\mathbb{M})$.

Theorem 1. *The model-checking problem for* MultiLTL *is polynomialy reducable to the model-checking problem for* HyperLTL.

Proof Sketch. Let $\mathbb{M} = \langle \mathcal{M}_1, \ldots, \mathcal{M}_n \rangle$ be a multi-model over AP, and $\mathbb{P} \in$ MultiLTL. We assume that $\mathbb{P}$ is of the form $\mathbb{Q}_1^1 \pi_1 \ldots \mathbb{Q}_n^n \pi_n \varphi$, where φ is in negation normal form. Note that this means that each model is quantified exactly once[2]. Define $\mathcal{M} = \cup\mathbb{M}$. Each (indexed) trace in $\mathcal{M}$ corresponds to one model in $\mathbb{M}$ by its index. Let $\mathcal{P} = \mathbb{Q}_1 \pi_1 \ldots \mathbb{Q}_n \pi_n \varphi'$, where φ' is obtained from φ by applying the following changes: for every $a \in AP$, we replace every occurrence of a literal $l = a_\pi$ or $l = \neg a_\pi$ by $\mathbf{i} \rightarrow l$ if π is quantified by $\forall^i$, and by $\mathbf{i} \wedge l$ if π is quantified by $\exists^i$. Intuitively, for $\forall^i$, for every trace $\tau \in \mathcal{M}$, if τ originates from $\mathcal{M}_i$ then we require that τ fulfill the formula and otherwise we require nothing. For $\exists^i$, we require the existence of a trace in $\mathcal{M}$ that originates from $\mathcal{M}_i$ that fulfills the formula. It can be shown by induction that $\mathbb{M} \models \mathbb{P}$ iff $\mathcal{M} \models \mathcal{P}$.   □

In [12], the authors presented an algorithm for model-checking HyperLTL that can be easily adjusted for MultiLTL. Thus, there is no need to use the reduction in Theorem 1. The algorithm relies roughly on the repeated intersection of the models under $\exists$ with an automaton for φ, the quantifier-free part of the formula, or, in the case of $\forall$ quantifiers, for $\neg\varphi$ (which involves complementation). Accordingly, the complexity is a tower in the number of models, and the size of the models greatly influences the run-time. In case of a model under $\forall$, a word that is accepted by the intersection is a counterexample for the satisfaction of the $\forall$ requirement. Therefore, in case that the formula $\mathbb{P}$ begins with a sequence of $\forall$ quantifiers followed by a sequence of $\exists$ quantifiers (a fragment which we denote by $\forall^*\exists^*$MultiLTL), it is possible to extract a counterexample for every model under $\forall$ in the multi-model. To summarize, we have the following.

---

[2] This can be achieved by duplicating components of the multi-model and reordering them so that they match the order of quantification.

Lemma 2. *1. There is a direct algorithm for model-checking $\mathbb{M} \models \mathbb{P}$.*
2. For $\mathbb{P} \in \forall^* \exists^*$ MultiLTL with n quantifiers such that $|I_\forall(\mathbb{P})| = k$, if $\mathbb{M} \not\models \mathbb{P}$ then the model-checking algorithm can also extract a counterexample $\langle w_1, \ldots, w_k \rangle$ such that $w_i \in \mathcal{L}(\mathcal{M}_i)$ for $i \in [1, k]$. For $\langle w_1, \ldots, w_k \rangle$ it holds that there are no $w_i \in \mathcal{L}(\mathcal{M}_i)$ for $i \in [k+1, n]$ such that $\langle w_1, \ldots, w_n \rangle \models \mathbb{P}$.

Note 1. For $\exists$ quantifiers, there is no natural counterexample in the form of a single word. Indeed, a counterexample in this case would need to convince of the lack of existence of an appropriate word.

4 Compositional Proof Rules for Model-Checking MultiLTL

We present two complementing compositional proof rules for the MultiLTL model-checking problem. Let $\mathbb{M}$ be a k-multi-model, and let $\mathbb{P} = \mathbb{Q}_1^{i_1} \pi_1 \ldots \mathbb{Q}_m^{i_m} \pi_m \varphi$ be a MultiLTL formula. The rule (PR) aims at proving $\mathbb{M} \models \mathbb{P}$, and $(\overline{\text{PR}})$ aims at proving the contrary, that is, $\mathbb{M} \models \neg \mathbb{P}$. Every model $\mathcal{A}_i$ in the rules is an *abstraction*. Since some models may be multiply quantified, a model $\mathcal{M}_i$ may have several different abstractions, according to the quantifiers under which $\mathcal{M}_i$ appears in $\mathbb{P}$.

$$\frac{\forall i \in I_\forall.\ \mathcal{M}_{i_j} \models \mathcal{A}_i \quad \forall i \in I_\exists.\ \mathcal{A}_i \models \mathcal{M}_{i_j} \quad \langle \mathcal{A}_1, \ldots, \mathcal{A}_m \rangle \models \mathbb{Q}_1^{i_1} \pi_1 \ldots \mathbb{Q}_m^{i_m} \pi_m \varphi}{\langle \mathcal{M}_1, \ldots, \mathcal{M}_k \rangle \models \mathbb{Q}_1^{i_1} \pi_1 \ldots \mathbb{Q}_m^{i_m} \pi_m \varphi} \tag{PR}$$

$$\frac{\forall i \in I_\forall.\ \mathcal{A}_i \models \mathcal{M}_{i_j} \quad \forall i \in I_\exists.\ \mathcal{M}_{i_j} \models \mathcal{A}_i \quad \langle \mathcal{A}_1, \ldots, \mathcal{A}_m \rangle \models \neg(\mathbb{Q}_1^{i_1} \pi_1 \ldots \mathbb{Q}_m^{i_m} \pi_m \varphi)}{\langle \mathcal{M}_1, \ldots, \mathcal{M}_k \rangle \models \neg(\mathbb{Q}_1^{i_1} \pi_1 \ldots \mathbb{Q}_m^{i_m} \pi_m \varphi)} \tag{$\overline{\text{PR}}$}$$

Intuitively, in (PR), we use an over-approximation for every model under $\forall$, and an under-approximation for every model under $\exists$. The rule $(\overline{\text{PR}})$ behaves dually to (PR) for the negation of $\mathbb{P}$.

Lemma 3. *The proof rules (PR) and $(\overline{\text{PR}})$ are sound and complete.*

Proof Sketch. For completeness, we can choose $\mathcal{A}_i = \mathcal{M}_{i_j}$ for every $i \in [1, m]$. For soundness of (PR), let $\mathcal{A}_1, \ldots, \mathcal{A}_m$ be models for which the premise of (PR) holds. For every universally quantified model $\mathcal{M}_{i_j}$, its abstraction $\mathcal{A}_i$ includes all of its traces (and maybe more). For every existentially quantified model $\mathcal{M}_{i_j}$, a subset of its traces are included in $\mathcal{A}_i$. Therefore, by the semantics of the quantifiers, it is "harder" for each $\mathcal{A}_i$ to satisfy $\mathbb{P}$ than it is for $\mathcal{M}_{i_j}$. Since $\langle \mathcal{A}_1, \ldots, \mathcal{A}_m \rangle \models \mathbb{P}$, we conclude that $\mathbb{M} \models \mathbb{P}$.

For $(\overline{\text{PR}})$, notice that $\neg \mathbb{P} \equiv \overline{\mathbb{Q}}_1^{i_1} \pi_1 \ldots \overline{\mathbb{Q}}_1^{i_m} \pi_m \neg \varphi$, where $\overline{\forall} = \exists$ and $\overline{\exists} = \forall$, conforming to (PR). □

5 Abstraction-Refinement Based Implementation of (PR) and ($\overline{\text{PR}}$)

In this section, we present methods for constructing over- and under-approximations using an abstraction-refinement based approach. We first define the notion of *simulation*.

Definition 4. *Let $\mathcal{M}_1 = (S_1, I_1, R_1, L_1)$ and $\mathcal{M}_2 = (S_2, I_2, R_2, L_2)$ be Kripke structures over AP. A simulation from $\mathcal{M}_1$ to $\mathcal{M}_2$ is a relation $H \subseteq S_1 \times S_2$ such that for every $(s_1, s_2) \in H$:*

- *$L(s_1) = L(s_2)$*
- *For every $(s_1, s_1') \in R_1$ there exists $s_2' \in S_2$ such that $(s_2, s_2') \in R_2$ and $(s_1', s_2') \in H$.*

If additionally, for every $s_0 \in I_1$ there exists $s_0' \in I_2$ such that $(s_0, s_0') \in H$, we denote $\mathcal{M}_1 \leq_H \mathcal{M}_2$. We denote $\mathcal{M}_1 \leq \mathcal{M}_2$ if $\mathcal{M}_1 \leq_H \mathcal{M}_2$ holds for some simulation H.

Lemma 4. *Let $\mathcal{M}_1, \mathcal{M}_2$ be two Kripke structures such that $\mathcal{M}_1 \leq \mathcal{M}_2$. Then $\mathcal{M}_1 \models \mathcal{M}_2$.*

Lemma 4 is a well-known property of simulation. Next, we describe how to construct sequences of over- and under-approximations for a given model $\mathcal{M}$. Each approximation in these sequences is closer to the original model than its previous. We later incorporate these sequences in a MultiLTL abstraction-refinement based model-checking algorithm using our proof rules.

5.1 Constructing a Sequence of Over-Approximations

Given a Kripke structure $\mathcal{M} = (S, I, R, L)$ over AP, we construct an over-approximations sequence $\mathcal{A}_0 \geq \mathcal{A}_1 \geq \cdots \mathcal{A}_k \geq \mathcal{M}$, where $\mathcal{A}_{i+1}$ is a *refinement* of $\mathcal{A}_i$, which we compute by using counterexamples. A *counterexample* is a word $w \in \mathcal{L}(\mathcal{A}_i)$ yet $w \notin \mathcal{L}(\mathcal{M})$. By Lemma 1, it suffices to consider finite prefixes of w, since there is an index j for which $w_0, w_1, \ldots, w_{j-1} \in \mathcal{L}(\mathcal{A}_i) \setminus \mathcal{L}(\mathcal{M})$.

We use a sequence of *abstraction functions* $h_0, \ldots, h_k$, each defining an abstract model.

Definition 5. *Let $\hat{S}$ be a finite set of abstract states. A function $h : S \to \hat{S}$ is an abstraction function if h is onto, and for every $\hat{s} \in \hat{S}$, it holds that $L(s_1) = L(s_2)$ for every $s_1, s_2 \in h^{-1}(\hat{s})$.*

Definition 6. *For an abstraction function $h : S \to \hat{S}$, the $\exists\exists$ abstract model induced by h is $\mathcal{A}_h = (\hat{S}, \hat{I}, \hat{R}, \hat{L})$, where $\hat{I} = \{\hat{s} \mid \exists s_0 \in I, h(s_0) = \hat{s}\}$, where for every $\hat{s} \in \hat{S}$ we set $\hat{L}(\hat{s}) = L(s)$ for some s such that $h(s) = \hat{s}$, and $(\hat{s}, \hat{s}') \in \hat{R}$ iff there exist $s, s' \in S$ such that $(s, s') \in R$, $h(s) = \hat{s}$ and $h(s') = \hat{s}'$.[3]*

---

[3] $\hat{L}$ is well defined since by Definition 5, only equilabeled states are mapped to the same abstract state.

Lemma 5. *Let $\mathcal{M} = (S, I, R, L)$ be a Kripke structure and $\mathcal{A}_h = (\hat{S}, \hat{I}, \hat{R}, \hat{L})$ be the $\exists\exists$ abstract model induced by an abstraction function $h : S \to \hat{S}$. Then, $\mathcal{M} \leq \mathcal{A}_h$.*

Proof. The relation $H = \{(s, h(s)) | s \in S\}$ is a simulation from $\mathcal{M}$ to $\mathcal{A}_h$. □

Definition 7. *Let $\mathcal{M}$ and $\mathcal{M}'$ be Kripke structures such that $\mathcal{M} \leq \mathcal{M}'$ by a simulation H, and let $r' = s'_0, s'_1, \ldots$ be a run of $\mathcal{M}'$ on w. The run $r = s_0, s_1, \ldots, s_j$ is a maximal induced run of r' in $\mathcal{M}$, if for every $i \in [0, j]$ it holds that $(s_i, s'_i) \in H$, and for every $i \in [0, j-1]$ it holds that $(s_i, s_{i+1}) \in R$. Moreover, there is no state $s^* \in S$ such that $(s^*, s'_{j+1}) \in H$ and $(s_j, s^*) \in R$. If no such j exists then r is infinite, and for every $i \geq 0$ it holds that $(s_i, s'_i) \in H$ and $(s_i, s_{i+1}) \in R$.*

In the sequel, we fix a Kripke structure $\mathcal{M} = (S, I, R, L)$.

Over-Approximation Sequence Construction

Initialization. Define $\hat{S}_0 = \{s_P \mid P \subseteq AP \text{ and } \exists s \in S : L(s) = P\}$. That is, there is a state in $\hat{S}_0$ for every labeling in $\mathcal{M}$. The initial over-approximation $\mathcal{A}_0$ is the $\exists\exists$ model induced by $h_0 : S \to \hat{S}_0$ defined by $h_0(s) = s_{L(s)}$. Since h_0 is an abstraction function, by Lemma 5 we have that $\mathcal{M} \leq \mathcal{A}_0$.

Refinement. Let $h_i : S \to \hat{S}_i$ be an abstraction function. Let $\mathcal{A}_i = (\hat{S}_i, \hat{I}_i, \hat{R}_i, \hat{L}_i)$ be the $\exists\exists$ model induced by h_i. By Lemma 5 we have that $\mathcal{M} \leq \mathcal{A}_i$. Let $w \in \mathcal{L}(\mathcal{A}_i) \backslash \mathcal{L}(\mathcal{M})$ be a counterexample. Let $\hat{r}_i = \hat{s}_0, \hat{s}_1 \ldots$ be a run of $\mathcal{A}_i$ on w, and $r = s_0 \ldots, s_j$ be a maximal induced run of $\mathcal{M}$ on w. Since $w \notin \mathcal{L}(\mathcal{M})$, we have that r is finite. We define $\mathcal{A}_{i+1}$ to be the $\exists\exists$ model induced by h_{i+1}, where $h_{i+1} : S \to \hat{S}_{i+1}$ for $\hat{S}_{i+1} = \hat{S}_i \uplus \{\hat{s}'\}$, defined as follows, for every $s \in S$.

$$h_{i+1}(s) = \begin{cases} h_i(s), & \text{if } h_i(s) \neq \hat{s}_j \\ h_i(s), & \text{if } h_i(s) = \hat{s}_j \text{ and } \exists s' \in S \text{ such that } h_i(s') = \hat{s}_{j+1} \text{ and } (s, s') \in R \\ \hat{s}', & \text{if } h_i(s) = \hat{s}_j \text{ and } \neg\exists s' \in S \text{ such that } h_i(s') = \hat{s}_{j+1} \text{ and } (s, s') \in R \end{cases}$$

The intuition for the refinement is presented in Fig. 1 (a). Concrete states are the full circles and abstract states are the dashed ovals. The purple line is a maximal induced run of $\hat{s}_0, \hat{s}_1 \ldots$ in $\mathcal{M}$, which ends at $\hat{s}_j$. Since there is an infinite run in the abstract model, we can split $\hat{s}_j$ into two abstract states: one that includes all states that can continue to $\hat{s}_{j+1}$, and another that includes all the states with no such transitions. Clearly, the former set includes only states that are not reachable by the maximal induced run of $\hat{s}_0, \hat{s}_1 \ldots$, else the induced run would not have been maximal.

Lemma 6. *For every $i \in \mathbb{N}$, for every state $\hat{s} \in \hat{S}_i$, there exists a state $s \in S$ such that $h_i(s) = \hat{s}$.*

Proof. By induction on i. **Base:** By construction, for every $\hat{s}_P \in \hat{S}_0$ there exists a state $s \in S$ such that $L(s) = P$, and so $h_0(s) = \hat{s}_P$.

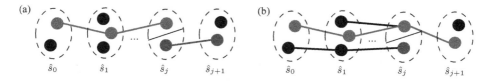

Fig. 1. Refinements (a) ∃∃, and (b) ∀∃.

Step: Assume towards contradiction that there is an abstract state $\hat{s} \in \hat{S}_{i+1}$ such that for every $s \in S$, it holds that $h_{i+1}(s) \neq \hat{s}$. Since $\mathcal{A}_i$ fulfills the required property, $\hat{s} \notin \hat{S}_i$. Then $\hat{s}$ is the new state $\hat{s}'$. Let $s_0, \dots, s_j$ be a maximal induced run of $\mathcal{M}$ on the counterexample w. There is no state $s' \in h_i^{-1}(\hat{s}_{j+1})$ such that $(s_j, s') \in R$. Thus, by construction, $h_{i+1}(s_j) = \hat{s}'$, a contradiction.   □

Lemma 7. *For every $i \geq 0$, it holds that $\mathcal{M} \leq \mathcal{A}_{i+1} \leq \mathcal{A}_i$*

Proof. According to Lemma 5, it is left to show is that $\mathcal{A}_{i+1} \leq \mathcal{A}_i$. The relation $H \subseteq \hat{S}_{i+1} \times \hat{S}_i$, defined by $H = \{(\hat{s}, \hat{s}') \mid h_{i+1}^{-1}(\hat{s}) \subseteq h_i^{-1}(\hat{s}')\}$ is a simulation from $\mathcal{A}_{i+1}$ to $\mathcal{A}_i$.   □

Following Lemma 7, we have that $\mathcal{M} \leq \cdots \leq \mathcal{A}_1 \leq \mathcal{A}_0$. Thus, the refinements get more precise with every refinement step. Moreover, for $i > 0$, the model $\mathcal{A}_i$ is obtained from $\mathcal{A}_{i-1}$ by splitting a state. In a finite-state setting, this guarantees termination at the latest when reaching $\mathcal{A}_i = \mathcal{M}$.

Lemma 8. *Let $\mathcal{M}$ be a Kripke structure and let $\mathcal{A}_0 \geq \mathcal{A}_1 \cdots \geq \mathcal{M}$ be our sequence of over-approximations. Then, there exists $m \in \mathbb{N}$ for which $\mathcal{A}_m = \mathcal{A}_{m+1}$.*

5.2 Constructing a Sequence of Under-Approximations

Given $\mathcal{M} = (S, I, R, L)$ over AP, we construct a sequence of under-approximations $\mathcal{A}_0 \leq \mathcal{A}_1 \leq \cdots \leq \mathcal{A}_k \leq \mathcal{M}$ via a sequence of abstraction functions using counterexamples. In this case, a counterexample is a word $w \notin \mathcal{L}(\mathcal{A})$, yet $w \in \mathcal{L}(\mathcal{M})$. Again, we can consider a prefix of w.

Definition 8. *Given an abstraction function $h : S \to \hat{S}$, the $\forall\exists$ abstract model induced by h is $\mathcal{A}_h = (\hat{S}, \hat{I}, \hat{R}, \hat{L})$, where $\hat{I}$ and L are as in Definition 6, and $(\hat{s}, \hat{s}') \in \hat{R}$ iff for every $s \in S$ such that $h(s) = \hat{s}$ there exists $s' \in S$ such that $(s, s') \in R$ and $h(s') = \hat{s}'$.*

Notice that the transition relation $\hat{R}$ of the $\forall\exists$ abstract model might not be total, i.e., there may exist a state with no outgoing transitions.

Lemma 9. *Let $\mathcal{M} = (S, I, R, L)$ be a Kripke structure and $\mathcal{A}_h = (\hat{S}, \hat{I}, \hat{R}, \hat{L})$ be the $\forall\exists$ abstract model induced by an abstraction function $h : S \to \hat{S}$. Then, $\mathcal{A}_h \leq \mathcal{M}$.*

Proof. $H = \{(h(s), s)|s \in S\}$ is a simulation from $\mathcal{A}_h$ to $\mathcal{M}$.   □

Under-approximation Sequence Construction
Initialization. Let $\hat{S}_0$ and h_0 be as in Sect. 5. We set the initial under-approximation $\mathcal{A}_0$ of $\mathcal{M}$ to be the ∀∃ abstract model induced by h_0. By Lemma 9, we have $\mathcal{A}_0 \le \mathcal{M}$.

Refinement. Let $\mathcal{A}_i = (\hat{S}_i, \hat{I}_i, \hat{R}_i, \hat{L}_i)$ be an ∀∃ abstract model induced by an abstraction function $h_i : S \to \hat{S}_i$. Recall that $\mathcal{A}_i \le \mathcal{M}$. Let $w \in \mathcal{L}(\mathcal{M}) \backslash \mathcal{L}(\mathcal{A}_i)$ be a counterexample. Let $r = s_0, s_1, \ldots$ be a run of $\mathcal{M}$ on w, and let $\hat{r} = \hat{s}_0, \ldots, \hat{s}_j$ be a maximal induced run of $\mathcal{A}_i$ on w. We define $\mathcal{A}_{i+1}$ to be the ∀∃ abstract model induced by $h_{i+1} : S \to \hat{S}_{i+1}$ where $\hat{S}_{i+1} = \hat{S}_i \uplus \{\hat{s}'\}$, and where:

$$h_{i+1}(s) = \begin{cases} h_i(s), & \text{if } h_i(s) \ne \hat{s}_j \\ h_i(s), & \text{if } h_i(s) = \hat{s}_j \text{ and } \exists s' \in S \text{ such that } h_i(s') = h_i(s_{j+1}) \text{ and } (s, s') \in R \\ \hat{s}', & \text{if } h_i(s) = \hat{s}_j \text{ and } \neg \exists s' \in S \text{ such that } h_i(s') = h_i(s_{j+1}) \text{ and } (s, s') \in R \end{cases}$$

The idea behind this refinement is represented in Fig. 1 (b). The purple states and lines represent the run in $\mathcal{M}$. Note that in $\hat{s}_j$ there is a red state with no transition to states in $h_i(s_{j+1})$. Thus there is no ∀∃ abstract transition from $\hat{s}_j$ to $h_i(s_{j+1})$. To add such a transition, we split $\hat{s}_j$ into two states: one with all states that have a transition to a state in $h_i(s_{j+1})$, and another with all states that have no such transition. As a result, $\mathcal{A}_{i+1}$ includes a ∀∃ transition from $\hat{s}_j$ to $h_i(s_{j+1})$.

Similarly to over-approximation, we have the following, which assures correctness and termination.

Lemma 10. *Let $\mathcal{M}$ be a model and let $\mathcal{A}_0, \mathcal{A}_1, \ldots$ be the sequence of under-approximations described above. Then, the following holds.*

- $\mathcal{A}_0 \le \mathcal{A}_1 \le \cdots \le \mathcal{M}$.
- *There exists $m \in \mathbb{N}$ such that $\mathcal{A}_m = \mathcal{A}_{m+1}$.*

5.3 Abstraction-Refinement Guided MultiLTL Model-Checking Using (PR) and $(\overline{\text{PR}})$

Following Sects. 5.1 and 5.2, we present an abstraction-refinement inspired approach for model-checking multi-properties. We are given a MultiLTL formula $\mathbb{P} = \mathbb{Q}_1^1 \pi_1 \ldots \mathbb{Q}_n^n \pi_n \, \varphi$ and a multi-model $\mathbb{M} = \langle \mathcal{M}_1, \ldots, \mathcal{M}_n \rangle$ over AP (see footnote 2). The model-checking procedure for $\mathbb{M} \models \mathbb{P}$ is described in Algorithm 1, which we detail next.

The procedure MMC($\mathbb{M}, \mathbb{P}$) performs model-checking as per Lemma 2 (1) and returns **true** if $\mathbb{M} \models \mathbb{P}$, and **false** otherwise. REFINE refines every approximation $\mathcal{A}_i$ for which there is a counterexample w_i in the vector $\langle w_1, \ldots, w_n \rangle$ of counterexamples.

Algorithm 1: Abstraction-refinement based MultiLTL model-checking

Input: $\mathbb{M} = \langle \mathcal{M}_1, \ldots, \mathcal{M}_n \rangle$, $\mathbb{P} = \mathbb{Q}_1^1 \pi_1 \ldots \mathbb{Q}_n^n \pi_n \ \varphi(\pi_1, \ldots, \pi_n)$.
Output: $\mathbb{M} \models \mathbb{P}$?

1 $\mathbb{A}, \mathbb{B} = \text{INITIALIZE}(\mathbb{M}, \mathbb{P})$
2 **while** *true* **do**
3 $\quad$ $res = \text{MMC}(\mathbb{A}, \mathbb{P})$
4 $\quad$ **if** $res == true$ **then**
5 $\quad\quad$ | $\quad$ **return** $\mathbb{M} \models \mathbb{P}$
6 $\quad$ **else**
7 $\quad\quad$ | $\quad$ $\langle w_1, \ldots, w_n \rangle = \text{GET\_CEX}(\mathbb{A}, \mathbb{M}, \text{PR})$
8 $\quad\quad$ | $\quad$ $\mathbb{A} = \text{REFINE}(\langle w_1, \ldots, w_n \rangle, \mathbb{A})$
9 $\quad$ $res = \text{MMC}(\mathbb{B}, \neg \mathbb{P})$
10 $\quad$ **if** $res == true$ **then**
11 $\quad\quad$ | $\quad$ **return** $\mathbb{M} \not\models \mathbb{P}$
12 $\quad$ **else**
13 $\quad\quad$ | $\quad$ $\langle w_1, \ldots, w_n \rangle = \text{GET\_CEX}(\mathbb{B}, \mathbb{M}, \overline{\text{PR}})$
14 $\quad\quad$ | $\quad$ $\mathbb{B} = \text{REFINE}(\langle w_1, \ldots, w_n \rangle, \mathbb{B})$
15 **endwhile**

Initialization. In INITIALIZE (Line 1), for every model $\mathcal{M}_i$ such that $\mathbb{Q}_i^i = \forall$, we initialize abstract models $\mathcal{A}_i$ and $\mathcal{B}_i$ as described Sects. 5.1 and 5.2, respectively. For every model $\mathcal{M}_i$ such that $\mathbb{Q}_i^i = \exists$, we initialize abstract models $\mathcal{A}_i$ and $\mathcal{B}_i$ as described in Sects. 5.2 and 5.1, respectively. Thus, $\mathcal{B}_i \leq \mathcal{M}_i \leq \mathcal{A}_i$ for every $i \in I_\forall$ and $\mathcal{A}_i \leq \mathcal{M}_i \leq \mathcal{B}_i$ for every $i \in I_\exists$. In Algorithm 1, $\mathbb{A} = \langle \mathcal{A}_1, \ldots, \mathcal{A}_n \rangle$ is used for (PR) and $\mathbb{B} = \langle \mathcal{B}_1, \ldots \mathcal{B}_n \rangle$ for $(\overline{\text{PR}})$.

Abstraction-Refinement. Lines 3–8 apply the rule (PR). When reaching line 3, it is guaranteed that $\mathcal{M}_i \leq \mathcal{A}_i$ for every $i \in I_\forall$ and $\mathcal{A}_i \leq \mathcal{M}_i$ for every $i \in I_\exists$. Thus, we try to apply (PR). We model-check $\mathbb{A} \models \mathbb{P}$ (Line 3). If the result is **true**, then by the correctness of (PR), we have $\mathbb{M} \models \mathbb{P}$ (Line 5). Otherwise, $\mathbb{A} \not\models \mathbb{P}$. As noted in Note 1, for $\mathcal{A}_i$ where $i \in I_\exists$, no single word counterexample can be obtained from the model-checking. Instead, we call GET_CEX (Line 7), which returns a sequence of words that lead to more precise abstractions. For (PR), GET_CEX returns an arbitrary $w_i \in \mathcal{L}(\mathcal{A}_i) \setminus \mathcal{L}(\mathcal{M}_i)$ for every $i \in I_\forall$ and an arbitrary $w_i \in \mathcal{L}(\mathcal{M}_i) \setminus \mathcal{L}(\mathcal{A}_i)$ for every $i \in I_\exists$. For $(\overline{\text{PR}})$, GET_CEX behaves dually on $\mathbb{B}$ for $I_\forall$ and $I_\exists$. If for some i such a word w_i does not exist, GET_CEX returns **null** as w_i. REFINE uses $\langle w_1, \ldots, w_n \rangle$ to refine each abstraction in $\mathbb{A}$ as described in Sects. 5.1, 5.2, obtaining closer abstractions to the original models.

Lines 9–14 apply the rule $(\overline{\text{PR}})$. When we reach line 9, it is guaranteed that $\mathcal{B}_i \leq \mathcal{M}_i$ for every $i \in I_\forall$ and $\mathcal{M}_i \leq \mathcal{B}_i$ for every $i \in I_\exists$. Thus, we try to apply $(\overline{\text{PR}})$ in a similar manner as before. We model-check $\mathbb{B} \models \neg \mathbb{P}$. If the result is **true**, then by the correctness of $(\overline{\text{PR}})$, we have $\mathbb{M} \models \neg \mathbb{P}$ which implies $\mathbb{M} \not\models \mathbb{P}$. Otherwise, we call GET_CEX (Line 13) and refine $\mathbb{B}$ using $\langle w_1, \ldots, w_n \rangle$ (Line 14).

In the worst case, all approximations converge to their respective models (as per Lemmas 8, 10), upon which no further counterexamples are found. Therefore, the run is guaranteed to terminate. Of course, the run terminates much earlier in case that appropriate approximations are found. Correctness follows from the correctness of (PR) and $(\overline{\text{PR}})$. Hence, we have the following.

Lemma 11. *Algorithm 1 terminates with the correct result.*

Example. Consider $\mathcal{M}_1, \mathcal{M}_2$ (Fig. 2) and $\mathbb{P} = \forall^1 \pi \exists^2 \tau. \ \mathsf{G}(p_\pi \oplus \mathsf{X} p_\pi \oplus \mathsf{XX} p_\pi) \wedge$ $\mathsf{G}(p_\pi \to q_\tau)$, where $\oplus$ denotes XOR. For brevity, we ignore $\mathbb{B}$ since $\langle \mathcal{M}_1, \mathcal{M}_2 \rangle \models$ $\mathbb{P}$. When running Algorithm 1 for $\langle \mathcal{M}_1, \mathcal{M}_2 \rangle \models \mathbb{P}$, we first construct $\mathcal{A}_1^0, \mathcal{A}_2^0$ as over- and under-approximations of $\mathcal{M}_1, \mathcal{M}_2$, respectively (Fig. 2). Then, we check whether $\langle \mathcal{A}_1^0, \mathcal{A}_2^0 \rangle \models \mathbb{P}$. This does not hold, and MMC returns counterexamples $\langle \emptyset p \emptyset^\omega, \emptyset q^\omega \rangle$. We refine the abstractions according to these counterexamples.

Next, we find the maximal induced run of $\emptyset p \emptyset^\omega$ in $\mathcal{M}_1$, which is the path $\mathbf{1}, \mathbf{2}, \mathbf{3}, \mathbf{1} \bot$. Since the path for $\emptyset p \emptyset^\omega$ is $\mathbf{4}, \mathbf{5}, \mathbf{4}, \mathbf{4}^\omega$ in $\mathcal{A}_1^0$, we need to refine the state $\mathbf{4}$ in $\mathcal{A}_1^0$. By similar analysis of $\emptyset q^\omega$, state $\mathbf{8}$ is to be split in $\mathcal{A}_2^0$. Thus, we split state $\mathbf{4}$ from $\mathcal{A}_1^0$ to states $\mathbf{6,7}$ in $\mathcal{A}_1^1$. In $\mathcal{A}_2^0$, we split state $\mathbf{8}$ to states $\mathbf{9,10}$ in $\mathcal{A}_2^1$. Then, model-checking $\langle \mathcal{A}_1^1, \mathcal{A}_2^1 \rangle \models \mathbb{P}$ passes, and we return $\langle \mathcal{M}_1, \mathcal{M}_2 \rangle \models \mathbb{P}$.

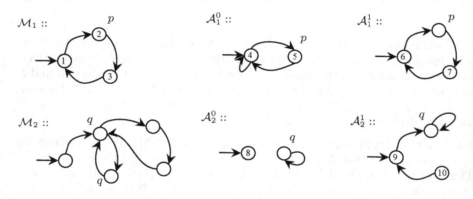

Fig. 2. Model-Checking for $\langle \mathcal{M}_1, \mathcal{M}_2 \rangle \models \mathbb{P}$

5.4   Counterexample Guided MultiLTL Model-Checking Using (PR)

Algorithm 1 is guided by the difference between the abstract models and the original models. We now consider the $\forall^* \exists^*$ fragment of MultiLTL. By Lemma 2, when model-checking $\forall^* \exists^*$ MultiLTL fails, we can get counterexamples for the models under $\forall$. We use these counterexamples to further improve our model-checking scheme for this fragment.

We are given a $\forall^* \exists^*$ MultiLTL formula $\mathbb{P} = \forall_1^1 \pi_1 \ldots \forall_k^k \pi_k \exists_{k+1}^{k+1} \ldots \exists_n^n \pi_n \ \varphi$ and a multi-model $\mathbb{M} = \langle \mathcal{M}_1, \ldots, \mathcal{M}_n \rangle$ over AP as input. Our model-checking procedure is described in Algorithm 2.

Algorithm 2: CEGAR-based $\forall^*\exists^*$ MultiLTL model-checking

---

Input: $\mathbb{M} = \langle \mathcal{M}_1, \ldots, \mathcal{M}_n \rangle$, $\mathbb{P} = \forall_1^1 \pi_1 \ldots \forall_k^k \pi_k \exists_{k+1}^{k+1} \ldots \exists_n^n \pi_n\; \varphi(\pi_1, \ldots, \pi_n)$.

Output: $\mathbb{M} \models \mathbb{P}$?

1 $\mathbb{A} = \text{INITIALIZE}\forall^*\exists^*(\mathbb{M}, \mathbb{P})$
2 **while** *true* **do**
3    $(res, cex) = \text{MMC}(\mathbb{A}, \mathbb{P})$
4   **if** $res == true$ **then**
5 | **return** $\mathbb{M} \models \mathbb{P}$
6    $spuriousList = \text{SPURIOUS}(cex, \mathbb{M})$
7   **if** $\text{ISEMPTY}(spuriousList)$ **then**
8 | **return** $\mathbb{M} \not\models \mathbb{P}$
9    $\mathbb{A} = \text{REFINE}(cex, spuriousList, \mathbb{A}, \mathbb{M})$
10 **endwhile**

The procedure $\text{MMC}(\mathbb{M}, \mathbb{P})$ performs multi-property model-checking, and returns $(true, \emptyset)$ if $\mathbb{M} \models \mathbb{P}$, and otherwise returns $(false, cex)$, where cex is a counterexample vector $\langle w_1, \ldots, w_k \rangle$ such that $w_i \in \mathcal{L}(\mathcal{M}_i)$ for every $i \in [1, k]$ and there are no $w_i \in \mathcal{L}(\mathcal{M}_i)$ for $i \in [k+1, n]$ such that $\langle w_1, \ldots, w_n \rangle \models \mathbb{P}$, as per Lemma 2 (2). We fix every $\mathcal{A}_i$ under $\exists$ to be $\mathcal{M}_i$. Thus, it is guaranteed that the model-checking failure is not caused by words that are missing from the under-approximations, yet do exist in the concrete models. A counterexample w_i from $\langle w_1, \ldots, w_k \rangle$ is *spurious* if $w_i \in \mathcal{L}(\mathcal{A}_i)$ yet $w_i \notin \mathcal{L}(\mathcal{M}_i)$. That is, w_i cannot serve as proof that $\mathbb{M} \not\models \mathbb{P}$. REFINE refines every approximation $\mathcal{A}_i$ for which there is a tuple (i, w_i) in $spuriousList$, the list of spurious counterexamples, by removing w_i from $\mathcal{A}_i$.

Initialization. In INITIALIZE$\forall^*\exists^*$ (Line 1), for every model $\mathcal{M}_i$ such that $\mathbb{Q}_i^i = \forall$, we initialize an abstract model $\mathcal{A}_i$ as described in 5.1. For every model $\mathcal{M}_i$ such that $\mathbb{Q}_i^i = \exists$, we fix $\mathcal{A}_i$ to be $\mathcal{M}_i$. Thus, $\mathcal{M}_i \leq \mathcal{A}_i$ for every $i \in [1, k]$ and $\mathcal{A}_i \leq \mathcal{M}_i$ for every $i \in [k+1, n]$.

Model-Checking. When we reach line 3, it is guaranteed that $\mathcal{M}_i \leq \mathcal{A}_i$ for every $i \in I_\forall$ (and $\mathcal{A}_i \leq \mathcal{M}_i$ for every $i \in I_\exists$, since $\mathcal{A}_i = \mathcal{M}_i$). Thus, we try to apply the proof rule (PR), and model-check $\langle \mathcal{A}_1, \ldots, \mathcal{A}_n \rangle \models \mathbb{P}$ (Line 3) by running MMC. If the result is **true**, then by (PR), we have $\mathbb{M} \models \mathbb{P}$ (Line 5). Otherwise, we get a counterexample vector of the form $\langle w_1, \ldots, w_k \rangle$.

Counterexample Analysis. (Lines 6–9). The procedure SPURIOUS iterates over the words in the counterexample $\langle w_1, \ldots, w_k \rangle$, and returns a list of tuples (i, w_i) such that $w_i \notin \mathcal{L}(\mathcal{M}_i)$. Note that since $\langle w_1, \ldots, w_k \rangle$ is a counterexample, it holds that $w_i \in \mathcal{L}(\mathcal{A}_i)$ for every $i \in [1, k]$. Thus, every w_i in the list of (i, w_i) is spurious. If there are no spurious counterexamples, then we return $\mathbb{M} \not\models \mathbb{P}$ (Line 8). Otherwise, we refine the approximations based on the spurious counterexamples.

In the worst case, the run iterates until $\mathcal{M}_i = \mathcal{A}_i$ for every $i \in [1, n]$, in which case there are no spurious counterexamples. Of course, termination may happen much earlier. Correctness follows from the correctness of (PR). Hence, we have the following.

Lemma 12. *Algorithm 2 terminates with the correct result.*

Algorithm 2 improves Algorithm 1 in several ways. First, in order to compute the counterexamples there is no need to complement the models, which comes with an exponential price. Second, the counterexamples are provided by the model-checking process. As such, they are of "higher quality", in the sense that they take into account the checked property and are guaranteed to remove refuting parts from the abstractions. This, in turn, leads to faster convergence.

6 Multi-properties for Finite Traces

We now consider models whose traces are finite. This setting is natural, for example, when modeling terminating programs. In this case, a model is a finite-word language, and hyperproperties can be expressed by nondeterminisitic finite hyperautomata (NFH) [7]. To explain the idea behind NFH, we first review nondeterministic automata.

Definition 9. *A nondeterministic finite-word automaton (NFA) is a tuple $A = (\Sigma, Q, Q_0, \delta, F)$, where Σ is an alphabet, Q is a nonempty finite set of states, $Q_0 \subseteq Q$ is a set of initial states, $F \subseteq Q$ is a set of accepting states, and $\delta \subseteq Q \times \Sigma \times Q$ is a transition relation.*

Given a word $w = \sigma_1 \sigma_2 \cdots \sigma_n$ over Σ, a *run of A on w* is a sequence of states $(q_0, q_1, \ldots q_n)$, such that $q_0 \in Q_0$, and for every $0 < i \leq n$, it holds that $(q_{i-1}, \sigma_i, q_i) \in \delta$. The run is *accepting* if $q_n \in F$. The *language* of A, denoted $\mathcal{L}(A)$, is the set of all words on which A has an accepting run. A language $\mathcal{L}$ is called *regular* if there exists an NFA such that $\mathcal{L}(A) = \mathcal{L}$.

An NFA A is called *deterministic* (DFA) if $|Q_0| = 1$, and for every $q \in Q$ and $\sigma \in \Sigma$, there exists exactly one q' for which $(q, \sigma, q') \in \delta$. It is well-known that every NFA has an equivalent DFA.

We now turn to explain NFH. An NFH $\mathcal{A}$ consists of a set of *word variables*, an NFA $\mathsf{nfa}(\mathcal{A})$ that runs on words that are assigned to these variables (which is akin to the unquantified LTL formula in a HyperLTL formula), and a *quantification condition* that describes the requirements for these assignments (which is akin to the quantifiers in a HyperLTL formula). Thus, NFH can be thought of as the regular-language counterpart of HyperLTL. We demonstrate NFH with an example.

Example 4. Consider the NFH $\mathcal{A}$ in Fig. 3 (left) over the alphabet $\Sigma = \{a, b\}$ and two word variables x and y. The NFA part $\mathsf{nfa}(\mathcal{A})$ of $\mathcal{A}$ reads two words simultaneously: one is assigned to x and the other to y. Accordingly, the letters that $\mathsf{nfa}(\mathcal{A})$ reads are tuples of the form $\{\sigma_x, \sigma'_y\}$, where σ is the current letter in the word that is assigned to x, and similarly for σ' and y. The symbol $\#$ is used for padding at the end if one of the words is shorter than the other. In the example, for two words w_1, w_2 that are assigned to x and y, respectively, nfa($\mathcal{A}$) requires that (1) w_1, w_2 agree on their a positions, and (2) once one of the words has ended, the other must only contain b letters. Since the quantification condition of $\mathcal{A}$ is $\forall x \forall y$, in a language S that $\mathcal{A}$ accepts, every two words agree on their a positions. As a result, all the words in S must agree on their a positions. The *hyperlanguage* of $\mathcal{A}$ is then the set of all finite-word languages in which all words agree on their a positions.

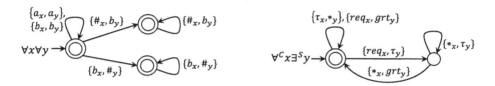

Fig. 3. The NFH $\mathcal{A}$ (left) and the MNFH $\mathcal{B}$ (right).

The *model-checking problem for NFH* is to decide, given a language S and an NFH $\mathcal{A}$, whether $\mathcal{A}$ accepts S, in which case we denote $S \models \mathcal{A}$. When S is given as an NFA, the model-checking problem is decidable (albeit, as for HyperLTL, by a nonelementary algorithm) [7].

6.1 Multi-languages and Multi-NFH

As in the case of models with infinite traces, we generalize languages and NFH to *multi-languages* and *multi-NFH* (MNFH). Thus, a multi-language is a tuple $\langle S_1, S_2, \ldots S_k \rangle$ of finite-word languages, and an MNFH $\mathcal{A}$ is an NFH with indexed quantifiers. The semantics is similar to that of Sect. 3, i.e., a quantifier $\mathbb{Q}^i$ in the quantification condition of $\mathcal{A}$ refers to S_i (rather than all quantifiers referring to the same language in the case of standard NFH).

We consider multi-languages that consist of regular languages. We can express such a multi-language $\langle L_1, L_2, \ldots, L_k \rangle$ by a tuple $\mathbb{M} = \langle \mathcal{M}_1, \mathcal{M}_2, \ldots, \mathcal{M}_k \rangle$ of NFAs, where $\mathcal{L}(\mathcal{M}_i) = L_i$ for every $i \in [1, k]$. We call $\mathbb{M}$ a *multi-NFA* (MNFA). We define the model-checking problem for MNFA accordingly, and denote $\mathbb{M} \models \mathbb{P}$ if an MNFH $\mathbb{P}$ accepts $\mathbb{M}$.

Example 5. Consider an MNFA $\langle S, C \rangle$, where S models a server and C models a client, and the MNFH $\mathcal{B}$ of Fig. 3 (right) over $\Sigma = \{req, grt, \tau\}$, where req is a request sent to the server, grt is a grant given to the client and τ is a non-communicating action.

The multi-model $\langle S, C \rangle$ satisfies $\mathcal{B}$ iff for every run of C there exists a run of S such that every request by C is eventually granted by S. This means that the server does not starve the client.

From now on, we assume without loss of generality that the quantification conditions of the MNFH that we consider are of the form $\mathbb{Q}_1^1 x_1 \mathbb{Q}_2^2 x_2 \ldots \mathbb{Q}_k^k x_k$.

We now show that the model-checking problem for MNFH is equivalent to the model-checking problem for NFH. For the first direction, it is easy to see that a language S is accepted by an NFH $\mathcal{A}$ iff $\langle S \rangle$ is accepted by the MNFH $\mathcal{A}'$ obtained from $\mathcal{A}$ by indexing all quantifiers in the quantification condition of $\mathcal{A}$ by the same index 1. We now show the second direction.

Theorem 2. *Let* $\mathbb{P}$ *be an MNFH, and let* $\mathbb{M} = \langle \mathcal{M}_1, \ldots \mathcal{M}_n \rangle$ *be an MNFA. Then there exist an NFA* $\mathcal{M}$ *and an NFH* $\mathcal{P}$ *such that* $\mathbb{M} \models \mathbb{P}$ *iff* $\mathcal{M} \models \mathcal{P}$.

Proof Sketch. We first mark the individual traces of every NFA in $\mathbb{M}$ by adding its index to all its letters. That is, we replace every letter σ in $\mathcal{M}_i$ with (σ, i). Then, we union all the NFAs in the updated MNFA $\mathbb{M}$ to a single NFA $\mathcal{M}$. Now, every word w in $\mathcal{L}(\mathcal{M})$ is marked with the index of the NFA in $\mathbb{M}$ from which it originated.

We translate the MNFH $\mathbb{P}$ to an NFH $\mathcal{P}$ as follows. First, we remove the indices from the quantifiers in the quantification condition α of $\mathbb{P}$. Next, recall that a letter in $\mathsf{nfa}(\mathbb{P})$ is in fact a letter-set of the form $\{\sigma_{1_{x_1}}, \ldots \sigma_{k_{x_k}}\}$. We update these letters according to $\mathcal{M}$: for every variable x, if x is under the quantifier $\mathbb{Q}^i x$ in α, then we replace every occurrence of σ_x in $\mathsf{nfa}(\mathbb{P})$ with $(\sigma, i)_x$.

Every $\exists^i x$ in α requires the existence of a word $w \in \mathcal{L}(\mathcal{M}_i)$ that is assigned to x and is accepted by $\mathsf{nfa}(\mathbb{P})$ (along with other words assigned to the other variables). Accordingly, $\mathcal{P}$ now requires the existence of a word $w \in \mathcal{L}(\mathcal{M})$ that originates from $\mathcal{L}(\mathcal{M}_i)$ that is assigned to x and is accepted by $\mathsf{nfa}(\mathcal{P})$. That is, the requirement for $\exists$ quantifiers is maintained.

To maintain the requirements for $\forall$ quantifiers, we add a new accepting sink q to $\mathsf{nfa}(\mathcal{P})$, and add transitions to q from every state with every letter-set in which a letter $(\sigma, j)_x$ occurs, where α includes $\forall^i x$ for $i \neq j$. Intuitively, $\forall$ quantifiers in $\mathcal{P}$ require that every word from $\mathcal{L}(\mathcal{M})$ that is assigned to x is accepted by $\mathsf{nfa}(\mathcal{P})$. Since in $\mathbb{P}$ we only required every word from $\mathcal{L}(\mathcal{M}_i)$ to be accepted, we use q to accept words from all the other NFAs in $\mathbb{M}$ that are assigned to x. □

The construction in the proof of Theorem 2 uses an alphabet whose size is polynomial in the original alphabet. The model $\mathcal{M}$ that we construct is linear in the size of $\mathbb{M}$, and the state space of $\mathcal{P}$ is linear in that of $\mathbb{P}$. However, since the size of the alphabet is larger, and the letters of $\mathcal{P}$ are set-letters, there may be exponentially many transitions in $\mathcal{P}$ compared with $\mathbb{P}$.

However, the model-checking algorithm from [7] can be easily altered to handle MNFH, without going through the reduction. Additionally, when $\mathbb{M} \not\models \mathbb{P}$, it is possible to extract a counterexample $\langle w_1, \ldots, w_k \rangle$ when $\mathbb{Q}_i = \forall$ for $i \in [1, k]$.

Lemma 13. *There is a direct algorithm for model-checking MNFH.*

7 Learning-Based Multi-property Model-Checking

We now describe ways of finding approximations according to the proof rules (PR) and $(\overline{\text{PR}})$ described in Sect. 4, for the multi-models of MNFA and multi-properties of MNFH of Sect. 6. The correctness of our rules stems only from the semantics of the quantifiers and so still holds.

The L^* algorithm [2] is a learning algorithm that finds a minimal DFA for an unknown regular language U. We exploit the fact that MNFA consist of regular languages to introduce an L^*-based algorithm for constructing approximations for the languages in the MNFA and for model-checking MNFH. To explain the idea behind our method, we first describe the L^* algorithm.

The L^* Algorithm. L^* consists of two entities: a *learner*, whose goal is to construct a DFA for U, and a *teacher*, who helps the learner by answering *membership queries* – "is $w \in U$?", and *equivalence queries* – "is A a DFA for U?". In case that $\mathcal{L}(A) \neq U$, the teacher also returns a counterexample: a word which is accepted by A and is not in U, or vice versa.

The learner maintains an *observation table* T that contains words for which a membership query was issued, along with the answers the teacher returned for these queries. Once T fulfills certain conditions (in which case we say that T is *steady*), it can be translated to a DFA A_T whose language is consistent with T. If $\mathcal{L}(A_T) = U$ then L^* terminates. Otherwise, the teacher returns a counterexample with which the learner updates T, and the run continues.

In each iteration, the learner is guaranteed to steady T, and L^* is guaranteed to terminate successfully. The sizes of the DFAs that the learner produces grow from one equivalence query to the next (while never passing the minimal DFA for U). The runtime of L^* is polynomial in the size of a minimal DFA for U and in the length of the longest counterexample that is returned by the teacher.

The main idea behind learning-based model-checking algorithms is to use the candidates produced by the learner as potential approximations. Since these candidates may be significantly smaller than the original models, model-checking is accelerated.

We first introduce our algorithm for the general case, in which L^* aims to learn the models themselves. Then, we introduce an improved algorithm in case that the quantification condition is of the type $\forall\exists$, in which case we can both define stronger learning goals, and use the counterexamples provided by the model-checker to reach these goals more efficiently.

7.1   Learning Assumptions for General Multi-properties

Consider an MNFA $\mathbb{M} = \langle \mathcal{M}_1, \mathcal{M}_2, \ldots \mathcal{M}_k \rangle$, and an MNFH $\mathbb{P}$ with a quantification condition $\alpha = \mathbb{Q}_1^1 x_1 \mathbb{Q}_2^2 x_2 \cdots \mathbb{Q}_k^k x_k$. Algorithm L^*_{MNFH}, described in Algorithm 3, computes an over-approximation for every $\mathcal{M}_i$ under $\forall$, and an under-approximation for every $\mathcal{M}_i$ under $\exists$. It does so by running L^* for every $\mathcal{M}_i$ in parallel, aiming to learn $\mathcal{M}_i$. Thus, the learner maintains a set $T_1, \ldots T_k$ of observations tables, one for every $\mathcal{M}_i$. Whenever all tables are steady, the learner submits the DFAs $A_{T_1}, \ldots A_{T_k}$ that it produces as candidates for the approximations via an equivalence query. The result of the equivalence query either resolves $\mathbb{M} \models \mathbb{P}$ according to (PR) and $(\overline{\text{PR}})$, or returns counterexamples with which the learner updates the tables to construct the next round of candidates.

In Algorithm 3, The methods INITIALIZE and STEADY are learner functions used for initializing an observation table, and reaching a steady observation table, respectively. The method ADDCEX updates the table when a counterexample is returned from an equivalence query.

Handling membership queries is rather straightforward: when the learner submits a query w for an NFA $\mathcal{M}_i$, we return **true** iff $w \in \mathcal{L}(\mathcal{M}_i)$. We now describe how to handle equivalence queries.

Equivalence Queries. The learner submits its candidate $\mathbb{A}$, which includes its set of candidates. We first check that they are approximations for (PR), by checking whether $\mathcal{M}_i \models \mathcal{A}_{T_i}$ for every over-approximation and $\mathcal{A}_{T_i} \models \mathcal{M}_i$ for every under-approximation.

If all checks pass, then we model-check $\mathbb{A} \models \mathbb{P}$. If the check passes, we return $\mathbb{M} \models \mathbb{P}$. If the candidates are not approximations for (PR) but are approximations for $(\overline{\text{PR}})$, we model-check $\mathbb{A} \models \neg\mathbb{P}$. If the check passes, we return $\mathbb{M} \not\models \mathbb{P}$.

If none of the above has triggered a return value, then there exists at least one candidate $\mathcal{A}_i$ such that $\mathcal{L}(\mathcal{A}_i) \neq \mathcal{L}(\mathcal{M}_i)$. We can locate these candidates during the over- and under-approximation checks, while computing a word $w \in \mathcal{L}(\mathcal{M}_i) \setminus \mathcal{L}(\mathcal{A}_i)$ (in case that we found $\mathcal{A}_i$ not to be an over-approximation), or a word $w \in \mathcal{L}(\mathcal{A}_i) \setminus \mathcal{L}(\mathcal{M}_i)$ (in the dual case). We then return the list of counterexamples according to the candidates for which we found a counterexample.

Algorithm 3: L^*_{MNFH}

Input: $\mathbb{M} = \langle \mathcal{M}_1, \ldots, \mathcal{M}_k \rangle$, $\mathbb{P}$ with $\alpha = \mathbb{Q}^1_1 \pi_1 \ldots \mathbb{Q}^k_k \pi_k$.
Output: $\mathbb{M} \models \mathbb{P}$?

1 INITIALIZE($T_1, \ldots T_k$)
2 **while** *true* **do**
3 $\quad$ **foreach** $i \in [1, k]$ **do**
4 $\quad\quad$ $T_i = \text{STEADY}(T_i)$
5 $\quad\quad$ Construct $\mathcal{A}_{T_i}$ from T_i
6 $\quad$ $\mathbb{A} = \langle \mathcal{A}_{T_1}, \mathcal{A}_{T_2}, \ldots \mathcal{A}_{T_k} \rangle$
7 $\quad$ $(CexList, pass) = \text{EQUIV}(\mathbb{A}, \mathbb{M}, \mathbb{P})$
8 $\quad$ **if** $CexList == null$ **then**
9 $\quad\quad$ **if** *pass* **then**
10 $\quad\quad\quad$ **return** $\mathbb{M} \models \mathbb{P}$
11 $\quad\quad$ **else**
12 $\quad\quad\quad$ **return** $\mathbb{M} \not\models \mathbb{P}$
13 $\quad$ **foreach** $(w_i, i) \in CexList$ **do**
14 $\quad\quad$ ADDCEX(T_i, w_i)
15 **endwhile**

Since L^* is guaranteed to terminate when learning a regular language, Algorithm 3 is guaranteed to terminate. The correctness of (PR) and $(\overline{\text{PR}})$ guarantee that L^*_{MNFH} terminates correctly at the latest after learning $\mathbb{M}$ (and terminates earlier if it finds smaller appropriate approximations).

7.2   Weakest Assumption for $\forall\exists$

We introduce a *weakest assumption* in the context of multi-properties with a quantification condition $\forall\exists$. Intuitively, a weakest assumption is the most general language that can serve as an over-approximation. We prove that the weakest assumption is regular, and show how to incorporate it in a learning-based multi-property model-checking algorithm based on (PR).

We denote MNFH with a quantification condition of the form $\forall_1^1 x \exists_2^2 y$ by $\text{MNFH}_{\forall\exists}$. The weakest assumption is the goal of the learning Algorithm 4 below.

Definition 10. *Let* $\mathbb{M} = \langle \mathcal{M}_1, \mathcal{M}_2 \rangle$ *be an MNFA and let* $\mathbb{P}$ *be an MNFH$_{\forall\exists}$. The weakest assumption for* $\mathbb{P}$ *w.r.t.* $\mathcal{M}_2$ *is as follows.*

$$W^{\mathcal{M}_2 : \mathbb{P}} = \bigcup_{\mathcal{A} \ s.t. \ \langle \mathcal{A}, \mathcal{M}_2 \rangle \models \mathbb{P}} \mathcal{L}(\mathcal{A})$$

That is, $W^{\mathcal{M}_2 : \mathbb{P}}$ is the union of all languages that along with $\mathcal{M}_2$ satisfy $\mathbb{P}$.

Lemma 14. *Let* $\mathcal{A}$ *and* $\mathcal{M}_2$ *be NFA, and* $\mathbb{P}$ *be an MNFH$_{\forall\exists}$. Then* $\mathcal{L}(\mathcal{A}) \subseteq W^{\mathcal{M}_2 : \mathbb{P}}$ *iff* $\langle \mathcal{A}, \mathcal{M}_2 \rangle \models \mathbb{P}$.

Proof. If $\langle \mathcal{A}, \mathcal{M}_2 \rangle \models \mathbb{P}$ then the claim holds by the definition of $W^{\mathcal{M}_2 : \mathbb{P}}$.
For the other direction, if $\mathcal{L}(\mathcal{A}) \subseteq W^{\mathcal{M}_2 : \mathbb{P}}$, then for every $w \in \mathcal{L}(\mathcal{A})$ there exists an NFA $\mathcal{A}_w$, with $\mathcal{L}(\mathcal{A}_w) = \{w\}$ s.t. $\langle \mathcal{A}_w, \mathcal{M}_2 \rangle \models \mathbb{P}$. Therefore, for every $w \in \mathcal{L}(\mathcal{A})$, there exists a word $w' \in \mathcal{L}(\mathcal{M}_2)$ s.t. $\mathbb{P}$ accepts $\{w_x, w'_y\}$, and so by the semantics of MNFH, we have that $\langle \mathcal{A}, \mathcal{M}_2 \rangle \models \mathbb{P}$. □

We note that a similar approach to Lemma 14 cannot work for general quantification conditions, since their satisfying assignments are generally not closed under union.

To justify using $W^{\mathcal{M}_2 : \mathbb{P}}$ as the objective of a learning algorithm, we show that $W^{\mathcal{M}_2 : \mathbb{P}}$ is regular.

In the following Lemma, $\mathcal{A}_{\Sigma^*}$ is an NFA that accepts all words over Σ, and $\cap$ denotes the intersection construction for NFA. Also, for NFA $\mathcal{A}$ and $\mathcal{B}$, the NFA $\mathcal{A} \times \mathcal{B}$ denotes the NFA over letters of the type $\{\sigma_x, \sigma'_y\}$ where σ_x is from $\mathcal{A}$ and σ'_y is from $\mathcal{B}$ that is formed by running both NFA in parallel, each with its own word (with $\#$ padding the end of the shorter word), and $\downarrow_i$ denotes the projection of the parallel construction to the i'th NFA.

Lemma 15. *Let* $\mathbb{P}$ *be an MNFH$_{\forall\exists}$ and let* $\mathbb{M} = \langle \mathcal{M}_1, \mathcal{M}_2 \rangle$ *be an MNFA. Then* $w \in W^{\mathcal{M}_2 : \mathbb{P}}$ *iff* $w \in \mathcal{L}((\text{nfa}(\mathbb{P}) \cap (\mathcal{A}_{\Sigma^*} \times \mathcal{M}_2)) \downarrow_1)$.

That is, we can derive $W^{\mathcal{M}_2 : \mathbb{P}}$ by taking the lefthand-side projection of the parallel run of $\text{nfa}(\mathbb{P})$ with a multi-language consisting of an NFA that accepts all words in Σ^*, and $\mathcal{M}_2$ (while ignoring the $\#$ symbols). Intuitively, this projection includes all the words which can be matched with a word in $\mathcal{M}_2$ in a way that is accepted by $\text{nfa}(\mathbb{P})$. We can therefore deduce the following.

Corollary 1. $W^{\mathcal{M}_2 : \mathbb{P}}$ *is regular.*

Algorithm 4: $L^*_{\forall\exists}$

Input: An MNFH$_{\forall\exists}$ $\mathbb{P}$, an MNFA $\mathbb{M} = \langle \mathcal{M}_1, \mathcal{M}_2 \rangle$.
Output: $\mathbb{M} \models \mathbb{P}$?

1 INITIALIZE(T)
2 **while** *true* **do**
3     $T = $ STEADY(T)
4   Construct $\mathcal{A}_T$ from T
5     $(cex, pass) = $ EQUIV($\mathcal{A}_T, \mathbb{M}, \mathbb{P}$)
6   **if** *cex* **then**
7 | ADDCEX(T, cex)
8   **else**
9   **if** *pass* **then**
10 | **return** $\langle \mathcal{M}_1, \mathcal{M}_2 \rangle \models \mathbb{P}$
11   **else**
12 | **return** $\langle \mathcal{M}_1, \mathcal{M}_2 \rangle \not\models \mathbb{P}$
13 **endwhile**

7.3 Learning Assumptions for $\forall\exists$

Let $\mathbb{P}$ be an MNFH$_{\forall\exists}$ and let $\mathbb{M} = \langle \mathcal{M}_1, \mathcal{M}_2 \rangle$ be an MNFA. We now introduce our $L^*_{\forall\exists}$ learning-based algorithm for model-checking $\mathbb{M} \models \mathbb{P}$. As we have mentioned in 7.2, the learning goal in our $L^*_{\forall\exists}$ algorithm is $W^{\mathcal{M}_2:\mathbb{P}}$, as it is an over-approximation of $\mathcal{M}_1$ (when $\mathbb{M} \models \mathbb{P}$). However, in this case, notice that every $\mathcal{A}$ such that $\mathcal{L}(\mathcal{M}_1) \subseteq \mathcal{L}(\mathcal{A}) \subseteq W^{\mathcal{M}_2:\mathbb{P}}$ suffices. $L^*_{\forall\exists}$ then runs L^* while using every DFA $\mathcal{A}$ that is produced by the learner during the run as a candidate for an over-approximation of $\mathcal{M}_1$.

We now describe our implementation for answering the membership and equivalence queries.

Membership Queries. When the learner submits a membership query $w \in^?$ $\mathcal{L}(\mathcal{A})$, we model-check $\langle \mathcal{A}_w, \mathcal{M}_2 \rangle \models \mathbb{P}$, where $\mathcal{A}_w$ is a DFA whose language is $\{w\}$. If the check passes, then there exists a word $w' \in \mathcal{L}(\mathcal{M}_2)$ such that $\langle w, w' \rangle \models \mathbb{P}$. Therefore, we return **true**. Otherwise, $\langle w, w' \rangle \not\models \mathbb{P}$ for every $w' \in \mathcal{L}(\mathcal{M}_2)$, and thus we do not include w in $\mathcal{L}(\mathcal{A})$, and return **false**.

Equivalence Queries. We first check that $\mathcal{A}$ is a potential over-approximation, by checking if $\mathcal{M}_1 \models \mathcal{A}$. If not, then we return a counterexample $w \in \mathcal{L}(\mathcal{M}_1) \setminus \mathcal{L}(\mathcal{A})$. Otherwise, we model-check $\langle \mathcal{A}, \mathcal{M}_2 \rangle \models \mathbb{P}$. If the model-checking passed, then we can conclude $\mathbb{M} \models \mathbb{P}$. Otherwise, a counterexample w is returned for a word in $\mathcal{L}(\mathcal{M}_1)$ which has no match in $\mathcal{L}(\mathcal{M}_2)$. We now need to check if w is spurious. If $w \notin \mathcal{L}(\mathcal{M}_1)$, then we return w as a counterexample to the learner. Otherwise, we can conclude that $\mathbb{M} \not\models \mathbb{P}$.

Since L^* is guaranteed to terminate when learning a regular language, $L^*_{\forall\exists}$ is guaranteed to terminate. In both cases, when $\mathbb{M} \models \mathbb{P}$ or $\mathbb{M} \not\models \mathbb{P}$, the correctness of PR and the properties of $W^{\mathcal{M}_2:\mathbb{P}}$ guarantee that the algorithm terminates with a correct answer, at most after learning $W^{\mathcal{M}_2:\mathbb{P}}$ (and may terminate earlier if it finds a smaller appropriate over-approximation).

There are several advantages to using Algorithm 4 over Algorithm 3. First, $W^{\mathcal{M}_2:\mathbb{P}}$ may be smaller than $\mathcal{M}_1$ which leads to quicker convergence. Second, there is no need to complement $\mathcal{M}_1$ for the equivalence query, since we only check if $\mathcal{M}_1$ is contained in the candidate submitted by the learner (which is a DFA and can be easily complemented). Finally, we can now use the more targeted counterexample provided by the model-checking process, again leading to quicker convergence.

While we have defined the weakest assumption and Algorithm 4 for a quantification condition of the type $\forall\exists$, both can be easily extended to handle a sequence of $\exists$ quantifiers rather than a single one.

8   Conclusion

We have introduced multi-models and multi-properties – useful notions that generalize hyperproperties to handle multiple systems. We have formalized these notions for both finite- and infinite-trace systems, and presented compositional proof rules for model-checking multi-properties.

For infinite-trace systems, we have introduced MultiLTL, a generalization of HyperLTL, and have applied our proof rules in abstraction-refinement and CEGAR based algorithms. For finite-trace systems, we have introduced multi-NFH, which offer an automata-based specification formalism for regular multi-properties. Here, we have applied our proof rules in automata-learning algorithms. The algorithms for both approaches accelerate model-checking by computing small abstractions, that allow avoiding model-checking the full multi-model.

References

1. Ábrahám, E., Bonakdarpour, B.: HyperPCTL: a temporal logic for probabilistic hyperproperties. In: McIver, A., Horvath, A. (eds.) QEST 2018. LNCS, vol. 11024, pp. 20–35. Springer, Cham (2018). https://doi.org/10.1007/978-3-319-99154-2_2
2. Angluin, D.: Learning regular sets from queries and counterexamples. Inf. Comput. **75**(2), 87–106 (1987)
3. Barthe, G., Crespo, J.M., Kunz, C.: Relational verification using product programs. In: Butler, M., Schulte, W. (eds.) FM 2011. LNCS, vol. 6664, pp. 200–214. Springer, Heidelberg (2011). https://doi.org/10.1007/978-3-642-21437-0_17
4. Barthe, G., D'Argenio, P.R., Rezk, T.: Secure information flow by self-composition. In: Proceedings. 17th IEEE Computer Security Foundations Workshop, 2004, pp. 100–114. IEEE (2004)
5. Bérard, B., Haar, S., Hélouët, L.: Hyper partial order logic. In: 38th IARCS Annual Conference on Foundations of Software Technology and Theoretical Computer Science, p. 1 (2018)
6. Bohrer, B., Platzer, A.: A hybrid, dynamic logic for hybrid-dynamic information flow. In: Proceedings of the 33rd Annual ACM/IEEE Symposium on Logic in Computer Science, pp. 115–124 (2018)
7. Bonakdarpour, B., Sheinvald, S.: Automata for hyperlanguages. arXiv preprint arXiv:2002.09877 (2020)

8. Clarkson, M.R., Finkbeiner, B., Koleini, M., Micinski, K.K., Rabe, M.N., Sánchez, C.: Temporal logics for hyperproperties. In: Abadi, M., Kremer, S. (eds.) POST 2014. LNCS, vol. 8414, pp. 265–284. Springer, Heidelberg (2014). https://doi.org/10.1007/978-3-642-54792-8_15

9. Clarkson, M.R., Schneider, F.B.: Hyperproperties. J. Comput. Secur. **18**(6), 1157–1210 (2010)

10. Dimitrova, R., Finkbeiner, B., Kovács, M., Rabe, M.N., Seidl, H.: Model checking information flow in reactive systems. In: Kuncak, V., Rybalchenko, A. (eds.) VMCAI 2012. LNCS, vol. 7148, pp. 169–185. Springer, Heidelberg (2012). https://doi.org/10.1007/978-3-642-27940-9_12

11. Finkbeiner, B., Haas, L., Torfah, H.: Canonical representations of k-safety hyperproperties. In: 2019 IEEE 32nd Computer Security Foundations Symposium (CSF), pp. 17–1714. IEEE (2019)

12. Finkbeiner, B., Rabe, M.N., Sánchez, C.: Algorithms for model checking HyperLTL and HyperCTL*. In: Kroening, D., Păsăreanu, C.S. (eds.) CAV 2015. LNCS, vol. 9206, pp. 30–48. Springer, Cham (2015). https://doi.org/10.1007/978-3-319-21690-4_3

13. Finkbeiner, B., Zimmermann, M.: The first-order logic of hyperproperties. In: 34th Symposium on Theoretical Aspects of Computer Science (STACS 2017). Schloss Dagstuhl-Leibniz-Zentrum fuer Informatik (2017)

14. Nguyen, L.V., Kapinski, J., Jin, X., Deshmukh, J.V., Johnson, T.T.: Hyperproperties of real-valued signals. In: Proceedings of the 15th ACM-IEEE International Conference on Formal Methods and Models for System Design, pp. 104–113 (2017)

15. Păsăreanu, C.S., Giannakopoulou, D., Bobaru, M.G., Cobleigh, J.M., Barringer, H.: Learning to divide and conquer: applying the L* algorithm to automate assume-guarantee reasoning. Form. Meth. Syst. Des. **32**(3), 175–205 (2008)

16. Pucella, R., Schneider, F.B.: Independence from obfuscation: a semantic framework for diversity. J. Comput. Secur. **18**(5), 701–749 (2010). https://doi.org/10.3233/JCS-2009-0379

17. Shemer, R., Gurfinkel, A., Shoham, S., Vizel, Y.: Property directed self composition. In: Dillig, I., Tasiran, S. (eds.) CAV 2019. LNCS, vol. 11561, pp. 161–179. Springer, Cham (2019). https://doi.org/10.1007/978-3-030-25540-4_9

18. Sousa, M., Dillig, I.: Cartesian hoare logic for verifying k-safety properties. In: Proceedings of the 37th ACM SIGPLAN Conference on Programming Language Design and Implementation, pp. 57–69 (2016)

19. Terauchi, T., Aiken, A.: Secure information flow as a safety problem. In: Hankin, C., Siveroni, I. (eds.) SAS 2005. LNCS, vol. 3672, pp. 352–367. Springer, Heidelberg (2005). https://doi.org/10.1007/11547662_24

20. Thomas, W.: Path logics with synchronization. In: Perspectives in Concurrency Theory, pp. 469–481 (2009)

21. Yang, W., Vizel, Y., Subramanyan, P., Gupta, A., Malik, S.: Lazy self-composition for security verification. In: Chockler, H., Weissenbacher, G. (eds.) CAV 2018. LNCS, vol. 10982, pp. 136–156. Springer, Cham (2018). https://doi.org/10.1007/978-3-319-96142-2_11

Decomposing Data Structure Commutativity Proofs with mn-Differencing

Eric Koskinen[1($\boxtimes$)] and Kshitij Bansal[2]

[1] Stevens Institute of Technology, Hoboken, USA
eric.koskinen@stevens.edu
[2] Google, Inc., Menlo Park, USA

Abstract. Commutativity of data structure methods is of ongoing interest in contexts such as parallelizing compilers, transactional memory, speculative execution and software scalability. Despite this interest, we lack effective theories and techniques to aid commutativity verification.

In this paper, we introduce a novel decomposition to improve the task of verifying method-pair commutativity conditions from data structure implementations. The key enabling insight—called mn-differencing—defines the precision necessary for an abstraction to be fine-grained enough so that commutativity of method implementations in the abstract domain entails commutativity in the concrete domain, yet can be less precise than what is needed for full-functional correctness. We incorporate this decomposition into a proof rule, as well as an automata-theoretic reduction for commutativity verification. Finally, we discuss our simple proof-of-concept implementation and experimental results showing that mn-differencing leads to more scalable commutativity verification of some simple examples.

1 Introduction

For an object o, with state σ and methods m, n, etc., let $\bar{x}$ and $\bar{y}$ denote argument vectors and $m(\bar{x})/\bar{r}$ denote a method signature, including a vector of corresponding return values $\bar{r}$. *Commutativity* of two methods, denoted $m(\bar{x})/\bar{r} \bowtie n(\bar{y})/\bar{s}$, are circumstances where operations m and n, when applied in either order, lead to the same final state and agree on the intermediate return values $\bar{r}$ and $\bar{s}$. A *commutativity condition* is a logical formula $\varphi_m^n(\sigma, \bar{x}, \bar{r})$ indicating, for a given state σ, whether the methods will always commute, as a function of parameters.

Commutativity conditions are typically much smaller than full specifications, yet they are powerful: it has been shown that they are an enabling ingredient in correct, efficient concurrent execution in the context of parallelizing compilers [39], optimistic parallelism [33], transactional memory [16,24,29,30,36], race detection [17], speculative execution, features [13], layered concurrent programs [31], etc. More broadly, a paper from the systems community [15] found

E. Koskinen—Supported in part by NSF award #1813745 and #2008633.

© Springer Nature Switzerland AG 2021
F. Henglein et al. (Eds.): VMCAI 2021, LNCS 12597, pp. 81–103, 2021.
https://doi.org/10.1007/978-3-030-67067-2_5

that, when software fragments are implemented so that they commute, better scalability is achieved. Commutativity captures independence and when combined with linearizability proofs (*e.g.*, [12,43]) enables concurrent execution. Naturally, it is important that commutativity be correct and, in recent years, growing effort has been made toward reasoning about commutativity conditions automatically. At present, these works are either unsound [4,21] or else they rely on data structure specifications as intermediaries [7,27] which, interestingly, can lead to unsound commutativity conclusions (see Sect. 2).

Our goal in this paper is to improve the task of verifying a commutativity property φ_m^n directly from the data-structure source code of methods m and n. Toward this goal, we first provide a straight-forward way to formulate the problem as a multi-trace (2-safety) question, *i.e.*, relating the behaviors in one circumstance with those in another. This first automata-theoretic reduction (called REDUCE_m^n) is a product program, but with the pre-condition strengthened by only considering reachable data-structure states and the post-condition weakened to observational equivalence. Although REDUCE_m^n is sound, it does not employ any commutativity-specific abstractions and, thus, reachability solvers struggle to verify the resulting encoding, for lack of the ability to decompose the problem in a manner suitable to commutativity.

The key idea of this paper is a decomposition geared toward improving commutativity verification. We introduce the concept of an mn-differencing abstraction (α, R_α) which gives a requirement for how precise an abstraction α must be so that one can reason in that abstract domain and relate abstract post-states with R_α, and yet entail return value agreement in the concrete domain. Intuitively, R_α captures the differences between the behavior of pairs of operations when applied in either order (*e.g.* how push and pop effect the top element of stack), while abstracting away state reads or mutations that would be the same, regardless of the order in which they are applied (*e.g.* those elements deeper in the stack that are untouched). R_α relations capture return value agreement, but they do not quite capture commutativity. We show the pieces fit together by combining R_α with a relation C that tracks the unmodified, cloned portion of the state and an ADT-specific observational equivalence relation I_β. Proving that I_β is an observational equivalence relation is then done using a separate ADT-specific abstraction β.

We then return to algorithms, introducing a second reduction DAREDUCE_m^n that exploits mn-differencing. DAREDUCE_m^n emits two reachability tasks: automata $\mathcal{A}_{\mathbf{A}}(m, n, \varphi_m^n, I)$ and $\mathcal{A}_{\mathbf{B}}(I)$, thus allowing reachability analyses to synthesize separate abstractions (α, R_α) and C for $\mathcal{A}_{\mathbf{A}}(m, n, \varphi_m^n, I)$ and β for $\mathcal{A}_{\mathbf{B}}(I)$. Moreover, $\mathcal{A}_{\mathbf{B}}(I)$ is independent of m, n and φ_m^n, so it can be proved safe once and then reused for every subsequent φ_m^n query.

We implement our reductions in a simple prototype tool called CITYPROVER, on top of Ultimate [22] and CPAchecker [10]. CITYPROVER takes as input simple data structures in C (with integers, structs, arrays) and a candidate formula φ_m^n. It then uses the reductions to discover a proof that φ_m^n is a valid commutativity condition or else produce a counterexample. We report encouraging preliminary results verifying commutativity properties of some simple data structures such as a memory cell, counter, two-place Set, array stack, array queue and rudimentary hash table. In all examples, CITYPROVER was able to discover α, R_α, C and β automatically. In some cases we manually provided simple I relations. Since we reduce to automaton reachability, there was no need for any other user input (such as invariants, preconditions, predicates, lemmas, etc.). We further consider the merits of users providing I relations as opposed to the pre/post-specifications in prior work [7,27], and discuss benefits pertaining to soundness, automation, simplicity and usability. Finally, our experiments show that mn-differencing improves commutativity verification. DAREDUCE_m^n performs better than REDUCE_m^n: it is typically faster and suffers from timeouts less frequently.

Contributions. In summary, our contributions are:

- A reduction REDUCE_m^n that strengthens the pre-condition to reachable ADT states and weakens the post-condition to observational equivalence. (Sect. 4)
- A decomposition of commutativity reasoning that gives a requirement for how precise an abstraction must be to entail concrete commutativity. (Sect. 5)
- An improved reduction DAREDUCE_m^n, which exploits mn-differencing and observational equivalence relations. (Sect. 6)
- A proof-of-concept implementation, that uses these reductions to verify candidate commutativity conditions. (Sect. 7)
- Preliminary experiments showing that DAREDUCE_m^n out-performs REDUCE_m^n on some simple numeric data structures such as a memory cell, counter, two-place Set, array stack, array queue and rudimentary hash table. (Sect. 7)

Some results have been abridged. An extended version is available [28].

Our verified commutativity conditions can be used with existing concurrent implementations (compilers [39], graph algorithms [33,36], STM [16,24], etc.). Moreover, with some further research, they could be combined with linearizability proofs and used inside parallelizing compilers. We believe this to be a promising direction for future work.

Limitations. mn-differencing is defined semantically and could be applied to a wide range of programs, parametric data-structures, etc. Our implementation relies on underlying reachability solvers which are typically limited to programs with simple arrays and simple pointers, with limited support for quantified invariants. Thus, although mn-differencing and DAREDUCE_m^n support ADTs with parameterized sizes (such as ArrayStack), our experiments instead compared REDUCE_m^n-vs-DAREDUCE_m^n for (infinite state) ADTs of a fixed size. We were also limited by these tools' capability of performing permutation reasoning (*e.g.* limited disjunctive power).

2 Overview

Motivating Examples. Consider the SimpleSet data structure shown at the left of Fig. 1. This data structure is a simplification of a Set, capable of storing up to two natural numbers using private integers a and b. Value -1 is reserved to indicate that nothing is stored in the variable. Method add(x) checks to see if

```
class SimpleSet {                              class ArrayStack {
  private int a, b, sz;                          private int A[MAX], top;
  SimpleSet() { a=b=−1; sz=0; }                  ArrayStack() { top = −1; }
  void add(uint x) {                             bool push(int x) {
    if (sz == 0) { a=x; sz++; ret; }               if (top==MAX−1) ret false;
    if (a==x || b==x) { ret; }                     A[top++] = x; ret true;
    if (a==−1) { a=x; sz++; ret; }               }
    if (b==−1) { b=x; sz++; ret; }               int pop() {
    ret;                                           if (top == −1) ret −1;
  }                                                else ret A[top−−]; }
  bool isin (uint y) { ret (a==y||b==y);}        bool isempty() { ret (top==−1); }
  int getsize () { ret sz; }                   }
  void clear () { a=−1; b=−1; sz = 0; }
}
```

Fig. 1. On the left, a SimpleSet data structure, capable of storing up to two natural numbers (using integer fields a and b) and tracking the size sz of the Set. On the right, a simple ArrayStack, that implements a stack using an array A and a top index.

there is space available and that x is not already in the Set, and then stores x in an open slot (either a or b). **ret** means return. Methods isin (y), getsize () and clear () are straightforward.

A commutativity condition, written as a logical formula φ_m^n, describes the conditions under which two methods $m(\bar{x})$ and $n(\bar{y})$ commute, in terms of the argument values and the state of the data structure σ. Two methods isin (x) and isin (y) always commute because neither modifies the ADT, so we say $\varphi_{\text{isin}(x)}^{\text{isin}(y)} \equiv$ true. The commutativity condition of methods add(x) and isin (y) is more involved: $\varphi_{\text{add}(x)}^{\text{isin}(y)} \equiv x \neq y \vee (x = y \wedge \mathsf{a} = x) \vee (x = y \wedge \mathsf{b} = x)$. This condition specifies three situations (disjuncts) in which the two operations commute. In the first case, the methods are operating on different values. Method isin (y) is a read-only operation and since $y \neq x$, it is not affected by an attempt to insert x. Moreover, regardless of the order of these methods, add(x) will either succeed or not (depending on whether space is available) and this operation will not be affected by isin (y). In the other disjuncts, the element being added is already in the Set, so method invocations will observe the same return values regardless of the order and no changes (that could be observed by later methods) will be made by either of these methods. Note that there can be multiple concrete ways of representing the same semantic data structure state: $\mathsf{a} = 5 \wedge \mathsf{b} = 3$ is the same as $\mathsf{a} = 3 \wedge \mathsf{b} = 5$. Other commutativity conditions include: $\varphi_{\text{isin}(y)}^{\text{clear}} \equiv (\mathsf{a} \neq y \wedge \mathsf{b} \neq y)$, $\varphi_{\text{isin}(y)}^{\text{getsize}} \equiv$ true, $\varphi_{\text{add}(x)}^{\text{clear}} \equiv$ false, $\varphi_{\text{clear}}^{\text{getsize}} \equiv \mathsf{sz} = 0$ and $\varphi_{\text{add}(x)}^{\text{getsize}} \equiv \mathsf{a} = x \vee \mathsf{b} = x \vee (\mathsf{a} \neq x \wedge \mathsf{a} \neq -1 \wedge \mathsf{b} \neq x \wedge \mathsf{b} \neq -1)$.

As a second running example, let us consider an array based implementation of Stack, given at the right of Fig. 1. ArrayStack maintains array A for data, a top index to indicate end of the stack, and has operations push and pop.

The capacity of ArrayStack, MAX is parametric. The commutativity condition $\varphi^{\mathsf{pop}}_{\mathsf{push}(x)} \equiv \mathsf{top} > -1 \wedge \mathsf{A[top]} = x \wedge \mathsf{top} < \mathsf{MAX}$ captures that they commute provided that there is at least one element in the stack, the top value is the same as the value being pushed and that there is enough space to push.

The above examples illustrate that commutativity conditions, even for small data-structures, can quickly become tricky to reason about. Nonetheless, correctness of these conditions is important to avoid unsafe concurrency when they are used in parallelization strategies [13,15,16,24,31,33,36]. Some prior works have described unsound methods for verifying commutativity [4,21] and others [7,27] have built upon ADT specifications which, as we discuss below, can lead to unsound commutativity conditions.

What's Hard About This Problem? Toward proving that a candidate φ^n_m is a commutativity condition for $m(\bar{x}) \bowtie n(\bar{y})$, one can begin by posing the problem as 2-safety [14], perhaps using Hoare quadruple notation [44] below on the left:

$$\text{Hoare Quad.}\quad \begin{array}{l} \{\varphi^n_m(\sigma_1) \wedge \sigma_1 = \sigma_2\} \\ r^1_m := m(\bar{a}); \big| r^2_n := n(\bar{b}); \\ r^1_n := n(\bar{b}); \ \big| r^2_m := m(\bar{a}); \\ \{r^1_m = r^2_m \wedge r^1_n = r^2_n \wedge \sigma'_1 = \sigma'_2\} \end{array} \qquad \text{Example}\quad \begin{array}{l} \{\varphi^{\mathsf{pop}()}_{\mathsf{push}(x)} \wedge \sigma_1 = \sigma_2\} \\ r^1_m := \mathsf{push}(x); \big| r^2_n := \mathsf{pop}(); \\ r^1_n := \mathsf{pop}(); \ \big| r^2_m := \mathsf{push}(x); \\ \{r^1_m = r^2_m \wedge r^1_n = r^2_n \wedge \sigma'_1 = \sigma'_2\} \end{array}$$

Intuitively, this Hoare quadruple (similar to a product program [8] or self-composition [9,41]) involves two *copies* of the program, shown on either side of the vertical bar. The pre-condition is a relation on the states of these two programs, as is the post-condition. For commutativity, we start by letting the precondition require that the commutativity condition φ^n_m holds and that the two programs begin in the same ADT states. Meanwhile, the post condition asserts that return values will agree and that the post-states are equivalent. Above on the right is an example: ArrayStack with $\varphi^{\mathsf{pop}()}_{\mathsf{push}(x)} \equiv \mathsf{A[top]} = x \wedge \mathsf{top} > 1 \wedge \mathsf{top} < \mathsf{MAX}$. Running an existing tool (*e.g.* a product program [8] and Ultimate [22]) yields a counterexample, with starting state: $\mathsf{A} = [z, y, x, \alpha] \wedge \mathsf{top} = 2$. The counterexample shows that in this case the post states are different. Depending on the order methods are applied, one reaches either $\mathsf{A} = [z, y, x, \alpha] \wedge \mathsf{top} = 2$ or else $\mathsf{A} = [z, y, x, x] \wedge \mathsf{top} = 2$. Our knowledge of stack semantics tells us that these are the same state (because the value in the 3rd array slot does not matter), but automated tools do not know these states are equivalent: concrete equality is too strict. Similarly, for SimpleSet $\varphi^{\mathsf{add}(y)}_{\mathsf{add}(x)} \equiv x \neq y$ we would obtain a counterexample complaining that $(\mathsf{a} = x \wedge \mathsf{b} = y)$ is different from $(\mathsf{a} = y \wedge \mathsf{b} = x)$.

It appears we need a better notion of equality for the post-states. We might then be tempted to exploit specifications, as is done in prior work [7,27]. Then we can ask whether $Post_m(Post_n(\sigma)) = Post_n(Post_m(\sigma))$[1]. Unfortunately, it is unclear what precision is appropriate for commutativity. Let's take, for example, a coarse specification such as $\{\mathsf{true}\}\mathsf{push}(x)\{\mathsf{true}\}$. Using this in our Hoare

---

[1] Note: as discussed in Sect. 3, we employ the technique discussed in Sect. 4 of Bansal *et al.* [7] to avoid the need for under-approximation or quantifier alternation.

quadruple, we might conclude a post-relation true, seemingly indicating that all post-states are related. We would thus be inclined to incorrectly conclude that any φ_m^n is a valid commutativity condition. When specifications are too coarse like this one, Bansal *et al.* [7] would incorrectly synthesize commutativity condition $\varphi_{\mathsf{push}(x)}^{\mathsf{push}(y)} \equiv$ true. The problem is that abstraction does not capture effects of $\mathsf{push}(x)$ that are relevant to commutativity.

Meanwhile, fine-grained specifications can be close to what is needed for full-functional correctness and it is not clear that we need this level of granularity: much of the post-condition is irrelevant to commutativity. When considering $\mathsf{push}(x)$ and pop, the interaction is limited to the top element of the stack (as well as whether the stack is empty or full), whereas the deeper part of the stack is the same regardless of the order of these methods.

Decomposition and Reductions for Commutativity. We now summarize the challenges and contributions of our work in the context of these examples.

(Section 4). We first observe that we do not strictly need pre/post specifications for commutativity verification and, instead, can work with observational equivalence relations. As a simple start, we describe a straight-forward reduction $\textsc{Reduce}_m^n$ from verifying commutativity conditions of an ADT to an automaton reachability problem. $\textsc{Reduce}_m^n$ emits an automaton $\mathcal{A}(\varphi_m^n)$ whose safety entails that φ_m^n is a valid commutativity condition for methods m and n. To this end, the reduction (i) ensures that we only concern ourselves with commutativity from an over-approximation of the *reachable* states of the object and (ii) weakens the post-condition to a notion of *observational* equivalence. While $\textsc{Reduce}_m^n$ is sound, it does not lead to scalable tools: reachability solvers struggle to decompose the problem.

(Section 5). The main question we ask in this paper is: *What is the right abstraction granularity for commutativity?* Not knowing this has hindered prior works as well as the performance of $\textsc{Reduce}_m^n$. First, the necessary precision depends on methods under consideration. For example, when concerned with return values arising in commutativity of SimpleSet's isin $(y)/$ clear, it is sufficient to use an abstraction that ignores sz. We only need to reason about whether y is stored in a or b. We can use, *e.g.*, an abstraction with predicates $\mathsf{a} = y$ and $\mathsf{b} = y$ (along with their negations). This also ignores all other possible values for a and b: for showing return value agreement, the only relevant aspect of the state is whether or not y is in the set. Similarly, for ArrayStack $\mathsf{push}(x)/\mathsf{pop}()$, we only need to consider the top value and we can abstract away deeper parts of the stack, that are untouched in either method order. While, on the other hand, for $\mathsf{pop}() \bowtie \mathsf{pop}()$, the second-from-top also matters.

Formally, we give a requirement for an abstraction α and a relation R_α in that domain, that it be precise enough so that reasoning about return value agreement in the abstract domain faithfully covers reasoning about agreement in the concrete domain. We call this pair (α, R_α) an mn-differencing abstraction and relation. For the SimpleSet example with $\text{isin}(x)/\text{clear}()$, we can define α to be based on the above mentioned predicates, and then use the relation:

$$R_\alpha(\sigma_1, \sigma_2) \equiv (\mathsf{a} = x)_1 \vee (\mathsf{b} = x)_1 \Leftrightarrow (\mathsf{a} = x)_2 \vee (\mathsf{b} = x)_2, \qquad (1)$$

i.e. the relation that tracks whether σ_1 and σ_2 agree on those predicates. (Subscripts mean that the predicate holds in the correspondingly numbered state.) R_α is a relation on abstract states and summarizes the possible pairs of post-states that will have agreed on return values. For methods $\text{push}(x)/\text{pop}$ on ArrayStack, we can define an abstraction α with predicates $\{\text{top} \geq 0, \mathsf{A}[\text{top}] = x\}$, and use

$$R_\alpha \equiv (\text{top} \geq 0)_1 = (\text{top} \geq 0)_2 \ \wedge \ (\mathsf{A}[\text{top}] = x)_1 = (\mathsf{A}[\text{top}] = x)_2 \qquad (2)$$

This abstraction simply tracks that the ArrayStack is non-empty and whether the top element is x or not. Meanwhile, the remaining portion of the state is *identical* between the two states because it came from cloning the reachable initial state. The equivalence reasoning can easily be tracked with direct, inductive equality: a cloned & unmodified frame relation C. For this example, $C \equiv \forall i < \text{top}_1. \mathsf{A}_1[i] = \mathsf{A}_2[i]$. We will later see that our algorithms and tools will be able to synthesize these (α, R_α) mn-differencing abstractions/relations and cloned frame C.

While so far we have addressed return values, states that are related by $R_\alpha \wedge C$ may not necessarily be observationally equivalent. We show the pieces fit together by working with observational equivalence *relations*. For reasoning about this equivalence, we use a separate abstraction β, more geared toward relational equivalence, and a relation I_β in that abstract domain. For the ArrayStack and SimpleSet examples, we can use the following such relations:

$$I_{AS}(\sigma_1, \sigma_2) \equiv \text{top}_1 = \text{top}_2 \wedge (\forall i.0 \leq i \leq \text{top}_1 \Rightarrow \mathsf{A}_1[i] = \mathsf{A}_2[i]) \qquad (3)$$

$$I_{SS}(\sigma_1, \sigma_2) \equiv ((\mathsf{a}_1 = \mathsf{a}_2 \wedge \mathsf{b}_1 = \mathsf{b}_2) \vee (\mathsf{a}_1 = \mathsf{b}_2 \wedge \mathsf{b}_1 = \mathsf{a}_2)) \ \wedge \ (\text{sz}_1 = \text{sz}_2) \qquad (4)$$

I_{AS} says that the two states agree on the (ordered) values in the Stack. (top_1 means the value of top in σ_1, etc.) For SimpleSet, I_{SS} specifies that two states are equivalent provided that they are storing the same values—perhaps in different ways—and they agree on the size. These observational equivalence relations can sometimes be inferred and, otherwise, are typically compact. Crucially, however, unlike pre/post specifications, if I is an observational equivalence relation, then it is guaranteed to lead to sound commutativity conclusions. Putting it all together, our decomposition can be posed as a proof rule on the right.

The notation $[s_m]^1(\bar{x})$ means the implementation of method m, under a (standard) translation [8,9,41] to act on the σ_1 copy of the state, with arguments $\bar{x}$. Premise (i) incorporates observational equivalence, while (ii) summarizes mn-differencing. Notice

$$(i) \quad : \{I_\beta\}[s_m]^1(\bar{x}) \mid [s_m]^2(\bar{y})\{I_\beta\}$$
$$(ii) \quad : \{Rch \wedge \varphi_m^n\}\,{}^{[s_m]^1(\bar{x});}_{[s_n]^1(\bar{x})} \mid {}^{[s_n]^2(\bar{y});}_{[s_m]^2(\bar{y})}\{R_\alpha \wedge C\}$$
$$(iii) : (R_\alpha \wedge C) \implies I_\beta$$

φ_m^n is a commut. cond. for $m(\bar{x}) \bowtie n(\bar{y})$

that premise (i) does not involve φ_m^n, R_α or C. An outcome of this decomposition is that automated reasoning about I_β (which pertains to all methods of the ADT) can be separated from reasoning about $R_\alpha \wedge C$ (which pertains to a given triple m, n, φ_m^n). Consequently, (i) can be done once globally for the ADT, and then (ii) and (iii) can be done for each new commutativity validity query. Note also that $R_\alpha \wedge C$ is typically *stronger* than I_β (and hence can imply I_β) because it is more specialized to the m/n method-pair under consideration. Meanwhile, I_β is a weaker relation characterizing overall ADT equivalence.

(**Section 6**). We next describe an improved reduction DAREDUCE_m^n, which employs our decomposition. DAREDUCE_m^n emits a pair of automata $\mathcal{A}_\mathbf{A}(m, n, \varphi_m^n, I)$ and $\mathcal{A}_\mathbf{B}(I)$, such that if we prove both are safe then φ_m^n must be a valid commutativity condition. Again, this separation allows tools to synthesize (α, R_α) and C separately from β and I_β.

(**Section 7**). Finally, we describe a proof-of-concept implementation of REDUCE_m^n and DAREDUCE_m^n, and employing Ultimate and CPAchecker as reachability solvers. We report experiments comparing the performance of the two reductions, when applied to some simple ADTs including the above SimpleSet, ArrayStack, Queue and a rudimentary HashTable. While DAREDUCE_m^n has some initial overhead, its use of mn-differencing abstractions appears to enable it to perform better than REDUCE_m^n.

3   Preliminaries

We work with a simple model of a (sequential) object-oriented language. We will denote an object by o. Objects can have member fields $o.a$ and, for the purposes of this paper, we assume them to be integers, structs or integer arrays. Methods are denoted $o.m(\bar{x}), o.n(\bar{y}), \ldots$ where $\bar{x}$ is a vector of the arguments. We often will omit the o. We use the notation $m(\bar{x})/\bar{r}$ to refer to the return variables $\bar{r}$. We use $\bar{a}$ to denote a vector of argument *values*, $\bar{u}$ to denote a vector of return *values* and $m(\bar{a})/\bar{u}$ or $n(\bar{b})/\bar{v}$ to denote a corresponding invocation of a method which we call an *action*. Methods' source code is parsed from C into control-flow automata (CFA) [23] using **assume** to represent branching and loops. (See [28] for details on our CFA-based implementation.) Edges are labeled with straight-line ASTs consisting of **assume**, assignment, and sequential composition. We use s_m to refer to the source code of object method m. For simplicity, we assume that one object method cannot call another, and that all object methods terminate.

Commutativity and Commutativity Conditions. We fix a single object o, denote that object's concrete state space Σ, and assume decidable equality. We denote $\sigma \xrightarrow{m(\bar{a})/\bar{u}} \sigma'$ for the big-step semantics in which the arguments are provided, the entire method is reduced and return values given in $\bar{u}$. For lack of space, we omit the small-step semantics $[\![s]\!]$ of individual statements. For the big-step semantics, we assume that such a successor state σ' is always defined (total) and is unique (determinism). Programs can be transformed so these conditions hold, via wrapping [7] and prophecy variables[2] [3], respectively.

---

[2]   For example, we can use prophecy variables to translate a method such as int m(a) { if (nondet()) x := a; } into one that has does not have nondeterminism in its transition system: int m(a, rho) { if (rho) x := a; }.

Definition 1 (Observational equivalence for commutativity (*e.g.* [29]**).**
We define relation $\simeq\,\subseteq\,\Sigma\times\Sigma$ *as the following greatest fixpoint*

$$\frac{\forall m(\bar{a})\in M.\ \sigma_1\xrightarrow{\ m(\bar{a})/\bar{r}_1\ }\sigma_1'\quad\sigma_2\xrightarrow{\ m(\bar{a})/\bar{r}_2\ }\sigma_2'\quad\bar{r}_1=\bar{r}_2\quad\sigma_1'\simeq\sigma_2'}{\sigma_1\simeq\sigma_2}$$

The above co-inductive definition expresses that two states σ_1 and σ_2 of an object are observationally equivalent $\simeq$ provided that, when any given method invocation $m(\bar{a})$ is applied to both σ_1 and σ_2, then the respective return values agree. Moreover, the resulting post-states maintain the $\simeq$ relation. A (logical) observational equivalence *relation* I is a formula such that $[\![I]\!]\Rightarrow\simeq$. I_{AS} from the previous section is one such relation. A counterexample to observational equivalence is a finite sequence of method operations $m_1(\bar{a}_1),...,m_k(\bar{a}_k)$ applied to both σ_1 and σ_2 such that for $m_k(\bar{a}_k)$, the return values disagree, *i.e.*, $\bar{r}_1^k\neq\bar{r}_2^k$.

We next use observational equivalence to define commutativity. As is typical [7,17] we define commutativity first at the layer of an action, which are particular *values*, and second at the layer of a method, which includes a quantification over all of the possible values for the arguments and return variables.

Definition 2 (Commutativity of m and n). *For values $\bar{a},\bar{b}$, we say* **actions** $m(\bar{a})$ *and* $n(\bar{b})$ *commute, denoted* $m(\bar{a})\bowtie n(\bar{b})$, *if for all* $\sigma,\bar{u}_1,\bar{u}_2,\bar{v}_1,\bar{v}_2,\sigma_m,$ $\sigma_n,\sigma_{mn},\sigma_{nm}$ *such that* $\sigma\xrightarrow{\ m(\bar{a})/\bar{u}_1\ }\sigma_m\xrightarrow{\ n(\bar{b})/\bar{v}_1\ }\sigma_{mn}$ *and* $\sigma\xrightarrow{\ n(\bar{b})/\bar{v}_2\ }\sigma_n\xrightarrow{\ m(\bar{a})/\bar{u}_2\ }$ σ_{nm}, *then* $(\bar{u}_1=\bar{u}_2\wedge\bar{v}_1=\bar{v}_2\wedge\sigma_{mn}\simeq\sigma_{nm})$. **Methods** m *and* n *commute denoted* $m\bowtie n$ *provided that* $\forall\bar{a}\ \bar{b}.\ m(\bar{a})\bowtie n(\bar{b})$.

The quantification $\forall\bar{a}\ \bar{b}$, etc. means vectors of all possible argument values. Our work extends to a more fine-grained notion of commutativity: an asymmetric version called left-movers and right-movers [34], where a method commutes in one direction and not the other.

We will work with commutativity conditions for methods m and n as logical formulae over initial states and the arguments of the methods. We denote a logical commutativity formula as φ_m^n and assume a computable interpretation of formulae: $[\![\varphi_m^n]\!]:(\sigma,\bar{x},\bar{y})\rightarrow\mathbb{B}$. (We tuple the arguments for brevity.) The first argument is the initial state. Commutativity *post-* and *mid-*conditions can also be written over return values [27] but here, for simplicity, we focus on commutativity *pre-*conditions. We may write $[\![\varphi_m^n]\!]$ as φ_m^n when it is clear from context that φ_m^n is meant to be interpreted.

Definition 3 (Commutativity Condition). *Logical formula φ_m^n is a commutativity condition for m and n provided that* $\forall\sigma\ \bar{a}\ \bar{b}.\ [\![\varphi_m^n]\!]\ \sigma\ \bar{a}\ \bar{b}\ \Rightarrow m(\bar{a})\bowtie n(\bar{b})$.

4   One-Shot Reduction to Reachability

We now take a first stab at the goal of reducing commutativity verification to reachability (*i.e.*, verifying non-reachability of an error location). The problems do not exactly align because commutativity verification is instead defined over an object implementation, method pairs, a formula φ_m^n and a notion of equivalence for objects. We thus pose commutativity as reachability intuitively as follows:

Pre-condition :
$$\begin{cases} \sigma_1.\text{init}(); \\ \text{while}(*)\{[s_m]^1(\bar{a}); \text{ where } m(\bar{a}) \text{ chosen nondeterministically }\} \\ \text{assume}(\varphi_m^n(\sigma_1, \bar{a}, \bar{b})); \\ \sigma_2 = \sigma_1.\text{clone}(); \end{cases}$$

Product :
$$\begin{cases} r_m^1 := [s_m]^1(\bar{a}); \big| r_n^2 := [s_n]^2(\bar{b}); \\ r_n^1 := [s_n]^1(\bar{b}); \big| r_m^2 := [s_m]^2(\bar{a}); \end{cases}$$

Post-condition :
$$\begin{cases} \text{assert}(r_m^1 = r_m^2 \wedge r_n^1 = r_n^2); \\ \text{while}(*)\{ \text{ for any } m(\bar{a}) \text{ chosen nondetermistically:} \\ \quad r_1 = [s_m]^1(\bar{a}); r_2 = [s_m]^2(\bar{a}); \\ \quad \text{assert}(r_1 = r_2); \} \end{cases}$$

(A formalization can be found in the extended version [28].) Ignoring the pre-/post conditions, in the above quadruple, we have used a product program [8], which encodes two programs (one for each order of method implementations s_m and s_n), each applied to a replica of the state σ, similar to self-composition and other techniques [6,8,9,18–20,40,41].

Strengthening the Pre-condition for Reachable ADT States σ_1 and σ_2. Above the pre-condition: (i) loops, symbolically applying an arbitrary number of method implementations on σ_1, (ii) assumes φ_m^n of the resulting state and (iii) duplicates that state to σ_2. This has the effect that σ_1 and σ_2 will be identical, restricted to only reachable ADT states, and φ_m^n will hold. That is, the precondition can be thought of as: $\{\textbf{Reachable}(\sigma_1) \wedge \varphi_m^n(\sigma_1, \bar{a}, \bar{b}) \wedge \sigma_1 = \sigma_2\}$. Verification tools will typically over-approximate **Reachable**.

Weakening the Post-condition to Observational Equivalence. Meanwhile, the post-condition asserts return value agreement, and then loops, symbolically executing a nondeterministically chosen method and argument values on both σ_1 and σ_2, and then asserting that return values agree. Thus the post-condition ensures return value agreement and that there is no sequence of methods that could be applied to both of them, witnessing further disagreement. That is, the postcondition can be thought of as: $\{r_m^1 = r_m^2 \wedge r_n^1 = r_n^2 \wedge \textbf{ObsEq}(\sigma_1, \sigma_2)\}$.

Formally, $\textsc{Reduce}_m^n(\varphi_m^n, m, n, M)$ is a transformation over an input object implementation CFA to an output CFA automaton $\mathcal{A}(\varphi_m^n)$ with an error state q_{er}. We prove that if q_{er} is unreachable in the output encoding $\mathcal{A}(\varphi_m^n)$, then φ_m^n is a valid commutativity condition for m and n. That is, if $\mathcal{A}(\varphi_m^n)$ is safe, then φ_m^n is a commutativity condition. (Detail in the extended version [28]).

Example. Figure 2 is a pseudo-code illustration of $\mathcal{A}(\varphi_{\text{add}(x)}^{\text{isin}(y)})$, the output generated when $\textsc{Reduce}_m^n$ is applied to methods $\text{add}(x)$ and $\text{isin}(y)$ of SimpleSet from Sect. 2. When a candidate formula $\varphi_{\text{add}(x)}^{\text{isin}(y)}$ is supplied and a program analysis tool for reachability is applied, the tool performs the reasoning necessary for commutativity. In sum, $\textsc{Reduce}_m^n$ uses the implementation of the ADT itself (including other methods such as clear) in order to symbolically represent reachable states s1 and s2 for the Pre-condition and require that the post-state pairs be observationally equivalent in the Post-condition.

Multiple Commutations. Relational reasoning is needed for post-state equivalence but, when commutativity proofs are used in (most) compilers or runtime systems, only one method ordering will actually be executed. The pair-wise commutativity proofs generalize to multiple commutations due to the fact that each possible post-state in one pair's proof is another possible reachable initial state for another pair.

While $\textsc{Reduce}^n_m$ is sound we show in Sect. 7 that tools don't scale well

```
1 SimpleSet s1 = new SimpleSet();          Pre-cond.
2 while(*) { int t = *; assume (t>0); switch(*) {
3    case 1: [add]¹(t); case 2: [isin]¹(t);
4    case 3: [size]¹(); case 4: [clear]¹(); }}
5 int x = *; int y = *;
6 assume( φ_{add(x)}^{isin (y)}(s1,x,y) );
7 SimpleSet s2 = s1.clone();
```

```
8  r¹_m = [add]¹(x); | r²_n = [isin]²(y);      Quad.
   r¹_n = [isin]¹(y); | r²_m = [add]²(x);
9 assert(r¹_m=r²_m && r¹_n=r²_n);
```

```
                                            Post-cond.
10 while(true){ int t=*; assume(t>0); switch(*) {
11    case 1: assert([add]¹(t) == [add]²(t));
12    case 2: assert([isin]¹(t) == [isin]²(t));
13    case 3: assert([clear]¹() == [clear]²());
14    case 4: assert([size]¹() == [size]²()); } }
```

Fig. 2. $\textsc{Reduce}^n_m$ applied to add(x)/ isin (y).

at proving the safety of $\textsc{Reduce}^n_m$'s output. In the next Sect. 5 we describe an abstraction targeted at proving commutativity to better enable automated reasoning. In the subsequent Sect. 6, we employ that abstraction in an improved reduction $\text{DA}\textsc{Reduce}^n_m$.

5   Decomposing Commutativity with mn-differencing

The problem with reductions like $\textsc{Reduce}^n_m$, is that general-purpose reachability tools do not know how to find the right abstraction for commutativity reasoning and those tools end up veering toward searching for unnecessarily intricate abstractions for full-functional verification. We now present a decomposition to mitigate this problem.

Consider the ArrayStackpush(x)/pop example and a (symbolic) state such as $[a, b, c]$ with top $= 2$ and condition $\varphi_{\text{push}(x)}^{\text{pop}} \equiv x = \text{A[top]}$. When applying a general-purpose reachability solver to $\textsc{Reduce}^n_m$, it will consider deep stack values such as a and b because those values could be reachable in a post-state after a further sequence of pop operations. But the solver is actually doing unnecessary work and is not inherently capable of noticing that those deep stack values will be the same, regardless of the order that push(x) and pop are applied.

Even with the sophisticated and automatic abstraction techniques available in today's tools, we do not currently have a notion of what is the *right* abstraction for commutativity and consequently, today's tools often end up diverging searching for an overly precise abstraction. In this section we address this problem and answer the question: how coarse-grained can an abstraction be, while still being fine-grained enough to reason about commutativity?

The idea of mn-differencing can be visualized via the diagram on the right. We start with two states σ_1 and σ_2 that are exactly equal. The product program leads to post states σ_1' and σ_2'. For these post states, we require return value agreement, denoted $\mathcal{X} \equiv r_m^1 = r_m^2 \wedge r_n^1 = r_n^2$. Next, we have an

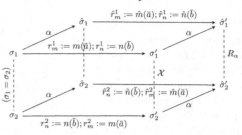

abstraction α, specific to this m/n pair, and a product program in this abstract domain.

The key idea is that (i) relation R_α relates abstract post-states whose return values agree in the abstract domain, and (ii) α is required to be precise enough that return values agree for all state pairs in the concretization of R_α. We can then check whether an initial assumption of φ_m^n on σ_1 implies such an R_α, *i.e.*, checking return value agreement using α which is just precise enough to do so. For $\mathsf{isin}\,(x)/\,\mathsf{clear}$, define an abstraction α with predicates $\{\mathsf{a} = x, \mathsf{a} \neq x, \mathsf{b} = x, \mathsf{b} \neq x\}$ that tracks whether x is in the set. Then

$$R_\alpha^1(\sigma_1, \sigma_2) \equiv (\mathsf{a} = x)_1 \vee (\mathsf{b} = x)_1 \Leftrightarrow (\mathsf{a} = x)_2 \vee (\mathsf{b} = x)_2,$$

i.e. the relation that tracks if σ_1 and σ_2 agree on those predicates. Meanwhile, for $\mathsf{pop}/\mathsf{pop}$ on $\mathsf{ArrayStack}$, we can define a different α with predicates $\{\mathsf{top} > 1, \mathsf{A}[\mathsf{top} - 1] = \mathsf{A}[\mathsf{top}]\}$, and use the relation

$$R_\alpha^2 \equiv (\mathsf{top} > 1)_1 = (\mathsf{top} > 1)_2 \ \wedge \ (\mathsf{A}[\mathsf{top} - 1] = \mathsf{A}[\mathsf{top}])_1 = (\mathsf{A}[\mathsf{top} - 1] = \mathsf{A}[\mathsf{top}])_2$$

This relation characterizes state pairs which agree on the stack having at least two elements, and agree that the top and penultimate elements are the same. As we will see, these abstractions and relations, although they are quite weak, are just strong enough so that they capture whether return values will agree.

5.1   Formal Definition

We now formalize mn-differencing. Where noted below, some definitions are omitted and can be found in the extended version [28]. First, we define a set of state pairs denoted $\mathsf{posts}(\sigma, m, \bar{a}, n, \bar{b})$ to be the set of all pairs of post-states (each denoted $(\sigma_{mn}, \sigma_{nm})$) originating from σ after the methods are applied in the two alternate orders:

$$\mathsf{posts}(\sigma, m, \bar{a}, n, \bar{b}) \equiv \{(\sigma_1, \sigma_2) \mid \sigma \xrightarrow{m(\bar{a})/\bar{r}_m^1} \sigma' \xrightarrow{n(\bar{b})/\bar{r}_n^1} \sigma_1 \wedge \sigma \xrightarrow{n(\bar{b})/\bar{r}_n^2} \sigma'' \xrightarrow{m(\bar{a})/\bar{r}_m^2} \sigma_2\}$$

We also define return value agreement denoted $\mathsf{rvsagree}(\sigma, m, \bar{a}, n, \bar{b})$ as a predicate indicating that all such post-states originated from σ agree on return values:

$$\mathsf{rvsagree}(\sigma, m, \bar{a}, n, \bar{b}) \equiv$$
$$\forall \bar{r}_m^1, \bar{r}_n^1, \bar{r}_n^2, \bar{r}_m^2 \text{ such that } (\sigma \xrightarrow{m(\bar{a})/\bar{r}_m^1} \sigma_1 \xrightarrow{n(\bar{b})/\bar{r}_n^1} \sigma_1' \wedge \sigma \xrightarrow{n(\bar{b})/\bar{r}_n^2} \sigma_2 \xrightarrow{m(\bar{a})/\bar{r}_m^2} \sigma_2').,$$
$$\bar{r}_m^1 = \bar{r}_m^2 \wedge \bar{r}_n^2 = \bar{r}_n^1$$

Definition 4 (mn-differencing Abstraction (α, R_α)). *For an object with state space Σ, and two methods m and n. Let $\alpha : \Sigma \to \Sigma^\alpha$ be an abstraction of the states, and $\gamma : \Sigma^\alpha \to \mathcal{P}(\Sigma)$ the corresponding concretization. A relation $R_\alpha \subseteq \Sigma^\alpha \times \Sigma^\alpha$ with its abstraction (α, R_α) is an mn-differencing abstraction if*

$$\forall \sigma_1^\alpha, \sigma_2^\alpha \in \Sigma^\alpha . R_\alpha(\sigma_1^\alpha, \sigma_2^\alpha) \wedge \forall \sigma\ \bar{a}\ \bar{b}.\ \mathit{posts}(\sigma, m, \bar{a}, n, \bar{b}) \in \gamma(\sigma_1^\alpha) \times \gamma(\sigma_2^\alpha) \Rightarrow$$
$$\mathit{rvsagree}(\sigma, m, \bar{a}, n, \bar{b})$$

The above definition requires that α be a precise enough abstraction so that R_α can discriminate in the abstract domain between pairs of post-states where return values will have agreed versus disagreed in the concrete domain.

A relation R_α may not hold for every initial state σ. For example, the above R_α^2 for pop/pop does not hold when the stack is empty. Hence, we need to ask whether R_α holds, under the assumption that φ_m^n holds in the pre-condition. We say that φ_m^n *implies* (α, R_α) if

$$\forall \sigma\ \bar{a}\ \bar{b}.\ \varphi_m^n(\sigma, \bar{a}, \bar{b}) \Rightarrow \forall (\sigma_1, \sigma_2) \in \mathsf{posts}(\sigma, m, \bar{a}, n, \bar{b}) \Rightarrow R_\alpha(\alpha(\sigma_1), \alpha(\sigma_2))$$

For SimpleSet $\mathsf{isin}\,(x)/\,\mathsf{clear}$, if we let $\varphi_{\mathsf{isin}\,(x)}^{\mathsf{clear}} \equiv \mathsf{a} \neq x \wedge \mathsf{b} \neq x$, this will imply R_α^1 in the posts. Let's see why. If this commutativity condition $\varphi_{\mathsf{isin}\,(x)}^{\mathsf{clear}}$ holds, then x will not be in the set. Neither method adds x to the set and an abstract domain, tracking only whether $\mathsf{a} = x$ and $\mathsf{b} = x$ hold, will lead to post states that agree on whether x is in the set and this carries over to the agreeing on whether x is in the set in the concrete domain.

Cloned and Untouched Frame. The components of the state that are abstracted away by an mn-differencing abstraction include portions of the state that are *unmodified* in either method order (or are both modified in the same way). For example, the deeper elements of ArrayStack remain untouched regardless of the order that methods push and pop are applied. We refer to these state components via a *cloning relation* $C \subseteq \Sigma \times \Sigma$, that we use in conjunction with R_α. Because this relation $C(\sigma_1, \sigma_2)$ always holds when $\sigma_1 = \sigma_2$, and the two method orderings both begin from the same starting point σ, a program analysis can begin with the fact $C(\sigma_0, \sigma_0)$ and then inductively prove that $\mathsf{posts}(\sigma_0, m, \bar{a}, n, \bar{b}) \Rightarrow C$. The cloning relation can instead be thought of as simply a strengthening of R_α, but we present it here separately to emphasize that C captures components of the states that are directly equal, whereas R_α may abstract away unequal components.

Post-state Equivalence. $R_\alpha \wedge C$ is specific to the method pair under consideration and, as such, it can exploit the particular specific effects of the method pair. For example, the R_α for SimpleSet clear/clear can simply say that both sets are empty. On the other hand, these relations alone are not enough to characterize commutativity. States that are R_α-related are not necessarily equivalent. What's needed is to show that method-pair-specific $R_\alpha \wedge C$ relation on the post-states of this method is *strong enough* to imply so that they are observationally equivalent.

We achieve this by using ADT-specific (rather than mn-specific) logical observational equivalence *relations* I_β and separate abstractions I_β there for.

The standard concept of observational equivalence relations [11] is visualized on the right. Importantly, we can use an abstraction β here that is separate from α; this will become useful in the subsequent sections. Formally, I_β is an

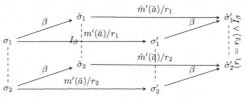

observational equivalence relation iff: $\forall \sigma_1^\beta, \sigma_2^\beta \in \Sigma^\beta.\ I_\beta(\sigma_1^\beta, \sigma_2^\beta) \Rightarrow \forall \sigma_1 \in \delta(\sigma_1^\beta),$ $\sigma_2 \in \delta(\sigma_2^\beta).\ \sigma_1 \simeq \sigma_2$. Relations I_{SS} and I_{AS}, defined earlier, are such relations.

5.2   Connecting the Pieces Together

Finally, we connect R_α and C with I_β and show that they can be used to reason about whether φ_m^n is a valid commutativity condition. The idea is summarized in the proof rule on the right. (Soundness of the rule is given in the extended version [28].) The first judgment (i), presented as a Hoare quadruple, ensures that I_β is an observational equivalence

$$
\begin{array}{l}
(i) \quad : \{I_\beta\}[s_m]^1(\bar{x}) \mid [s_m]^2(\bar{y})\{I_\beta\} \\
(ii) \quad : \{Rch \wedge \varphi_m^n\}\,{}^{[s_m]^1(\bar{x});}_{[s_n]^1(\bar{x})} \mid {}^{[s_n]^2(\bar{y});}_{[s_m]^2(\bar{y})}\{R_\alpha \wedge C\} \\
(iii) : (R_\alpha \wedge C) \implies I_\beta \\
\hline
\varphi_m^n \text{ is a commut. cond. for } m(\bar{x}) \bowtie n(\bar{y})
\end{array}
$$

relation. This judgment can be concluded once per ADT and, subsequently, I_β can be used repeatedly, whenever we wish to verify a new commutativity condition via the other judgments. The second judgment (ii) starts from a reachable ADT state where the commutativity condition φ_m^n holds, and has a post-relation $R_\alpha \wedge C$ consisting of an mn-differencing relation, along with a *cloned, untouched frame* C. Finally judgment (iii) combines the mn-differencing abstraction R_α with the cloned aspects of the state C to imply I_β.

Although an $R_\alpha \wedge C$ may *imply* an I_β, this does not mean that R_α is itself an observational equivalence relation. $R_\alpha \wedge C$ is typically stronger than I_β, but specific to the method-pair. For clear / clear, $R_\alpha \wedge C$ could relate SimpleSet states that are empty. While this implies the SimpleSet observational equivalence relation I_{SS} (Eq. 4 in Sect. 2), this R_α is of course *not* an observational equivalence relation: as soon as add(x) is added to both states, the relation is violated. What's important is simply that R_α implies I_β and, *separately*, that I_β itself is an observational equivalence relation.

Semantically, this decomposition can always be done because we can use $\simeq$ as the notion of observational equivalence and an overly precise R_α. Logically, however, completeness depends on whether a logical observational equivalence relation exists and can be expressed in the assertion language. We leave delving into the details of the assertion language (*e.g.* heap logics) as future work.

6 mn-differencing for Automata-Based Verification

As we show in Sect. 7, REDUCE_m^n given in Sect. 4 yields encodings for which general-purpose reachability solvers quickly diverge: the abstractions they search for become tantamount to what's needed for full-functional verification. In this section, we employ mn-differencing to introduce an improved reduction called DAREDUCE_m^n that decomposes the reasoning into two phases: (**A**) finding a sufficient R_α and frame C that implies I_β and then (**B**) proving that I_β is an observational equivalence relation. The output of DAREDUCE_m^n are a pair of output automata $\mathcal{A}_\mathbf{A}(m, n, \varphi_m^n, I)$ and $\mathcal{A}_\mathbf{B}(I)$, which informally can be thought of as follows:

$\underline{\mathcal{A}_\mathbf{A}(m, n, \varphi_m^n, I)}$

$\sigma_1.\text{init}();$
$\text{while}(*)\{\sigma_1.m(\bar{a}); \text{ where } m(\bar{a}) \text{ chosen nondet.}\}$
$\text{assume}(\varphi_m^n(\sigma_1, \bar{a}, \bar{b})); \quad \sigma_2 = \sigma_1.\text{clone}();$
$r_m^1 := \sigma_1.m(\bar{a}); \Big| r_m^2 := \sigma_2.n(\bar{b});$
$r_n^1 := \sigma_1.n(\bar{b}); \Big| r_m^2 := \sigma_2.m(\bar{a});$
$\text{assert}(r_m^1 = r_m^2 \wedge r_n^1 = r_n^2); // R_\alpha$
$\text{assert}(I(\sigma_1, \sigma_2)); // R_\alpha \wedge C \implies I$

$\underline{\mathcal{A}_\mathbf{B}(I)}$
$\text{assume}(I(\sigma_1, \sigma_2));$
$\text{let } m(\bar{a}) \text{ chosen nondet. in}$
$\quad r_1 = \sigma_1.m(\bar{a}); r_2 = \sigma_2.m(\bar{a});$
$\quad \text{assert}(r_1 = r_2 \wedge I(\sigma_1, \sigma_2));$

DAREDUCE_m^n is formalized as a transformation over CFAs in the extended version [28]. Unlike REDUCE_m^n, $\mathcal{A}_\mathbf{A}(m, n, \varphi_m^n, I)$ ends early with assertions that return values agree and that I must hold. Thus, an analysis on $\mathcal{A}_\mathbf{A}(m, n, \varphi_m^n, I)$ will construct an abstraction α and an mn-differencing relation R_α, as well as a cloned frame C such that $R_\alpha \wedge C \Rightarrow I$. Meanwhile, $\mathcal{A}_\mathbf{B}(I)$ is designed so that a safety proof on $\mathcal{A}_\mathbf{B}(I)$ entails that I is an observational equivalence relation. A pre-condition that assumes I, and then a nondeterministic choice of any ADT method m with nondeterministically selected method arguments $\bar{a}$. To prove that I is an observational equivalence relation, a reachability solver will synthesize an appropriate abstraction β for I in $\mathcal{A}_\mathbf{B}(I)$. If both $\mathcal{A}_\mathbf{A}(m, n, \varphi_m^n, I)$ and $\mathcal{A}_\mathbf{B}(I)$ are safe, then φ_m^n is a valid commutativity condition (as shown in the extended version [28].)

DAREDUCE_m^n improves over REDUCE_m^n by decomposing the verification problem with separate abstraction goals, making it more amenable to automation (see Sect. 7). Moreover, as in the proof rule (Sect. 5), a proof of safety of $\mathcal{A}_\mathbf{B}(I)$ can be done once for the entire ADT. Then, for a given method pair and candidate condition φ_m^n, one only needs to prove the safety of $\mathcal{A}_\mathbf{A}(m, n, \varphi_m^n, I)$.

Automation. Synthesis of α, R_α, C and β is automated. The definition of $\mathcal{A}_\mathbf{B}(I)$ can be amended so that a reachability solver could potentially infer I. The below amended version encodes the search for a (relational) observational equivalence as the search for a (non-relational) loop invariant.

$$\text{amended } \mathcal{A}_{\mathbf{B}}(I) : \begin{cases} \text{while(true)}\{\text{let } m(\bar{a}) \text{ chosen nondetermistically in} \\ r_1 = \sigma_1.m(\bar{a}); r_2 = \sigma_2.m(\bar{a}); \\ \text{assert}(r_1 = r_2); \} \end{cases}$$

7   Evaluation

Our goals were to evaluate (1) whether mn-differencing abstractions ease commutativity verification, *i.e.*, whether $\mathrm{DAREDUCE}^n_m$ outperforms REDUCE^n_m, and (2) how automated our strategy can be.

We implemented a proof-of-concept tool called CITYPROVER[3]. CITYPROVER takes, as input, C-style source code, using structs for object state. Examples are included with the CITYPROVER release. We have written them as C macros so that our experiments focus on commutativity rather than testing existing tools' inter-procedural reasoning power. Also provided as input to CITYPROVER is a commutativity condition φ^n_m and the method names m and n. CITYPROVER then implements REDUCE^n_m and $\mathrm{DAREDUCE}^n_m$ via a program transformation.

Experiments. We created some small examples (with integers, structs and arrays) and ran CITYPROVER on them. Our experiments were run on a Quad-Core Intel(R) Xeon(R) CPU E3-1220 v6 at 3.00 GHz, inside a QEMU VM. We began with single-field objects including: (M) a Memory cell; (A) an Accumulator with increment, decrement, and a check whether the value is 0; and (C) a Counter that also has a clear method. For each object, we considered some example method pairs with both a valid commutativity condition and an incorrect commutativity condition (to check that the tool discovers a counterexample).

ADT	Methods	$\varphi^{n(y_1)}_{m(x_1)}$	Exp.	REDUCE^n_m		DAREDUCE^n_m	
				cpa	ult	cpa	ult
M	rd ⋈ wr	s1.x = y_1	✓	1.4 ✓	0.7 ✓	3.9 ✓	1 ✓
M	rd ⋈ wr	true	✗	1.4 ✗	0.2 ✗	1.3 ✗	0.2 ✗
M	wr ⋈ wr	$y_1 = x_1$	✓	1.4 ✓	0.5 ✓	3.9 ✓	0.8 ✓
M	wr ⋈ wr	true	✗	1.3 ✗	0.3 ✗	2.4 ✗	0.4 ✗
M	rd ⋈ rd	true	✓	1.4 ✓	0.6 ✓	3.9 ✓	1 ✓
A	dec ⋈ isz	s1.x > 1	✓	1.5 ✓	2.2 ✓	4 ✓	2.6 ✓
A	dec ⋈ isz	true	✗	1.5 ✗	0.7 ✗	1.2 ✗	0.6 ✗
A	dec ⋈ inc	s1.x > 1	✓	1.5 ✓	1.3 ✓	4.1 ✓	1.7 ✓
A	dec ⋈ inc	true	✓	1.5 ✓	1.2 ✓	4 ✓	1.5 ✓
A	inc ⋈ isz	s1.x > 1	✓	1.5 ✓	3.3 ✓	4.1 ✓	2.9 ✓
A	inc ⋈ isz	true	✗	1.6 ✗	0.7 ✗	1.2 ✗	0.6 ✗
A	inc ⋈ inc	true	✓	1.4 ✓	1.5 ✓	4.1 ✓	1.6 ✓
A	dec ⋈ dec	true	✓	1.5 ✓	1.5 ✓	3.9 ✓	1.6 ✓
A	dec ⋈ dec	s1.x > 1	✓	1.5 ✓	2.6 ✓	4 ✓	1.9 ✓
A	isz ⋈ isz	true	✓	1.4 ✓	4.3 ✓	4 ✓	3.4 ✓
C	dec ⋈ dec	true	✗	1.9 ✗	1.5 ✗	4.2 ✓✗	1.2 ✗
C	dec ⋈ dec	s1.x ≥ 2	✓	1.5 ✓	13.0 ✓	4.1 ✓	5.9 ✓
C	dec ⋈ inc	true	✗	1.6 ✗	0.3 ✗	1.4 ✗	0.3 ✗
C	dec ⋈ inc	s1.x ≥ 1	✓	1.6 ✓	6.8 ✓	4.2 ✓	3.8 ✓
C	inc ⋈ isz	true	✗	1.5 ✗	0.8 ✗	1.2 ✗	0.7 ✗
C	inc ⋈ isz	s1.x > 0	✓	1.5 ✓	5.3 ✓	4.1 ✓	2.6 ✓
C	inc ⋈ isz	s1.x > 0	✗	1.9 ?	TO ?	4.4 ✗	6.9 ✗
C	inc ⋈ clr	true	✗	1.3 ✗	0.4 ✗	2.5 ✗	0.4 ✗

Fig. 3. Verifying commutativity properties of simple benchmarks. For each, we report time to use REDUCE^n_m vs. $\mathrm{DAREDUCE}^n_m$. A more detailed table is in the extended version [28].

---

[3] https://github.com/erickoskinen/cityprover.

The objects, method pairs and commutativity conditions are shown in the first few columns of Fig. 3, along with the **Exp**ected result. We used both the REDUCE$_m^n$ (Sect. 4) and DAREDUCE$_m^n$ (Sect. 6) algorithms and, in each case, compared using CPAchecker [10] and Ultimate [22] as the solver. For DAREDUCE$_m^n$, we report the total time taken for both Phase **A** and Phase **B**. A more detailed version of this table can be found in the extended version [28]. Benchmarks for which **A** succeed can all share the results of a single run of Phase **B**; meanwhile, when **A** fails, the counterexample can be found without needing **B**. These experiments confirm we can verify commutativity conditions from source. In one case, CPAchecker returned an incorrect result. While DAREDUCE$_m^n$ often takes slightly more time (due to the overhead of starting up a reachability analysis twice), it does not suffer from a timeout (in the case of Counter inc / isz).

We next turned to simple data structures that store and manipulate elements. While mn-differencing and DAREDUCE$_m^n$ support parametric/unbounded ADTs, automated reasoning about the cloned frame C typically requires quantified invariants. Automata reachability tools typically do not currently have robust support quantifiers, so we evaluate these ADTs with a fixed size. We mainly used Ultimate as we had trouble tuning CPAchecker (perhaps owing to our limited experience). In some cases (marked in blue), Ultimate failed to produce a timely response for either reduction, so we tried CPAchecker instead. Figure 4 shows the results of applying REDUCE$_m^n$ and DAREDUCE$_m^n$ on these examples. In each example, we first list the running time for DAREDUCE$_m^n$'s ADT-specific Phase **B**, and then list the times for Phases **A**i and **A**ii, as well as the total time.

For (SS) SimpleSet (Fig. 1), in almost all cases DAREDUCE$_m^n$ outperformed REDUCE$_m^n$, with an average speedup of **3.88×**. For

ADT	$m(x_1), n(y_1)$	$\varphi^{n(y_1)}_{m(x_1)}$	Exp.	REDU$_m^n$ Ult	DARE$_m^n$ Ult
SS	isin ⋈ isin	true	✓	137.8 ✓	36.7 ✓
SS	isin ⋈ add	$x_1 \neq y_1$	✓	84.8 ✓	37.1 ✓
SS	isin ⋈ add	true	✗	2.4 ✗	1.5 ✗
SS	isin ⋈ clear	true	✗	2.6 ✗	1.6 ✗
SS	isin ⋈ clear	$x_1 \neq y_1$	✗	2.4 ✗	1.6 ✗
SS	isin ⋈ clear	$a \neq x_1 \wedge b \neq y_1$	✗	3.1 ✗	1.4 ✗
SS	isin ⋈ clear	$a \neq x_1 \wedge b \neq x_1$	✓	14.0 ✓	19.3 ✓
SS	isin ⋈ getsize	true	✓	41.3 ✓	24.2 ✓
AS	push ⋈ pop	$A[top] = x_1 \wedge top > 1 \wedge top < 4$	✓	MO –	95.5 ✓
AS	push ⋈ pop	true	✗	2.2 ✗	2.0 ✗
AS	push ⋈ push	true	✗	7.6 ✗	17.0 ✗
AS	push ⋈ push	$top < 3$	✗	3.9 ✗	230.7 ✗
AS	push ⋈ push	$x_1 = y_1$	✗	19.8 ✗	17.3 ✗
AS	push ⋈ push	$x_1 = y_1 \wedge top < 3$	✓	MO –	155.1 ✓
AS	pop ⋈ pop	$top = -1$	✓	TO –	38.0 ✓
AS	pop ⋈ pop	true	✗	2.1 ✗	1.4 ✗
Q	enq ⋈ enq	true	✗	39.8 ✗	35.0 ✗
Q	deq ⋈ deq	true	✗	3.5 ✗	3.1 ✗
Q	deq ⋈ deq	$size = 0$	✓	TO –	174.4 ✓
Q	enq ⋈ enq	true	✗	27.8 ✗	23.3 ✗
Q	enq ⋈ enq	$x_1 = y_1$	✗	63.8 ✗	22.6 ✗
Q	emp ⋈ emp	true	✓	TO –	TO –
Q	enq ⋈ deq	$size = 1 \wedge x_1 = A[front]$	✓	TO –	472.0 ✓
Q	enq ⋈ deq	true	✗	MO –	8.4 ✗
Q	enq ⋈ emp	$size > 0$	✓	MO –	TO –
Q	enq ⋈ emp	true	✗	MO –	7.4 ✗
Q	deq ⋈ emp	$size = 0$	✓	MO –	135.8 ✓
Q	deq ⋈ emp	true	✗	MO –	6.5 ✗
HT	put ⋈ put	$_1\varphi^{put}_{put}$	✗	262.5 ✗	97.5 ✗
HT	put ⋈ put	$_2\varphi^{put}_{put}$	✗	202.7 ✗	136.9 ✗
HT	put ⋈ put	$_3\varphi^{put}_{put}$	✓	TO –	TO –
HT	put ⋈ put	$_3\varphi^{put}_{put}$	✓	566.5 ✓	297.5 ✓
HT	put ⋈ put	true	✗	TO –	102.3 ✗
HT	get ⋈ get	$keys = 0$	✓	TO –	TO –
HT	get ⋈ get	true	✓	TO –	TO –
HT	get ⋈ get	true	✓	50.0 ✓	56.8 ✓
HT	get ⋈ put	$x_1 \neq y_1$	✓	TO –	TO –
HT	get ⋈ put	true	✗	1.3 ✗	0.9 ✗

Fig. 4. Results of applying CITYPROVER to ArrayStack, SimpleSet and Queue. A more detailed breakdown of DAREDUCE$_m^n$ can be found in the extended version [28].

(AS) ArrayStack (Fig. 1), REDUCE_m^n found some counterexamples quickly. However, in the other cases REDUCE_m^n ran out of memory, while DAREDUCE_m^n was able to prove all cases. For (Q) Queue, we implemented a simple array-based queue and were able to verify all but two commutativity conditions. Finally, we implemented a rudimentary (HT) HashTable, in which hashing is done only once and insertion gives up if there is a collision. Some commutativity conditions are as follows:

$$^1\varphi_{\text{put}}^{\text{put}} \equiv x_1 \neq y_1, \qquad ^2\varphi_{\text{put}}^{\text{put}} \equiv x_1 \neq y_1 \wedge \text{tb}[x_1\%\text{cap}].k = -1 \wedge \text{tb}[y_1\%\text{cap}].k = -1$$
$$^3\varphi_{\text{put}}^{\text{put}} \equiv x_1 \neq y_1 \wedge x_1\%\text{cap} \neq y_1\%\text{cap} \wedge \text{tb}[x_1\%\text{cap}].k = -1 \wedge \text{tb}[y_1\%\text{cap}].k = -1$$

For HT, Ultimate timed out on Phase **B** and in some cases had some trouble mixing modulus with array reasoning, so we used CPAchecker. We still used Ultimate in some Phase **A** cases, because it can report a counterexample in Phase **A** even if it timed out in **B**. We also could use Ultimate for Phase **A**, given that CPAchecker already proved Phase **B**, with the same I_β. We also had to introduce a prophecy variable to assist the verifiers in knowing that array index equality distributes over modulus of equal keys.

Overall, for REDUCE_m^n there were 15 cases where it reached the 15-minute timeout or out-of-memory. DAREDUCE_m^n performed better: it only reached the timeout in 6 cases. In 24 cases (out of 37), CITYPROVER returned a proof or counterexample in under 2 min. In summary, these experiments confirm that DAREDUCE_m^n improves over REDUCE_m^n: in most cases it is faster, sometimes by as much as 2× or 3×. In **7** cases, DAREDUCE_m^n is able to generate an answer, while REDUCE_m^n suffers from a timeout/memout. (Timeouts typically occurred during refinement loops.)

In all examples, our implementation inferred α, R_α, C and β. For those in Fig. 4, we provided I manually. For the Queue and HashTable, we used (fixed size versions of) the following:

$$I_Q \equiv \text{front}_1 = \text{front}_2 \wedge \text{rear}_1 = \text{rear}_2 \wedge \text{sz}_1 = \text{sz}_2 \wedge \forall i \in [\text{front}_1, \text{rear}_1].\text{q}_1[i] = \text{q}_2[i]$$
$$I_{HT} \equiv \text{keys}_1 = \text{keys}_2 \wedge \forall i \in [0, \text{max}).\text{tb}_1[i].k \geq 0 \Rightarrow \text{tb}_1[i].k = \text{tb}_2[i].k \wedge \text{tb}_1[i].v = \text{tb}_2[i].v$$

I_Q states that the queues have the same size, and that the values agree in the range of the queue. It is possible to weaken this relation but commutativity does not need this weakening. For the HashTable, I_{HT} states that the HashTables have the same number of keys and, in each non-empty slot, they agree on the key and value. Apart from these I relations (which someday could be inferred) our technique is otherwise completely automated: a user only provides guesses for the commutativity conditions and CITYPROVER returns a proof or counterexample.

Working with Observational Equivalence (Obs-Eq) Relations. As compared to pre/post specifications, observational equivalence relations are simpler to work with and do not suffer from the potential to lead to unsound commutativity conclusions. There are several points to consider. *Soundness.* If a relation is an obs-eq relation then it is guaranteed to be precise enough for commutativity proofs (Thm 5.1). By contrast (see Sect. 2) pre/post specifications run the risk of being too coarse grained (and then unsound commutativity conclusions) or too fine grained (accounting for unnecessary detail). *Simplicity.* With an obs-eq relation, we only need to reason about the structure of the abstraction described by that relation. By contrast, pre/post specifications may be superfluous or unnecessarily detailed for commutativity (*e.g.* post-condition of HashTable.clear). Methods with branching or loops quickly veer toward detailed disjunctive post-conditions but, for commutativity, it only matters that an obs-eq relation holds. Even with Queue.enq, there are three cases, but these are unneeded in the obs-eq relation. *Centralized.* Unlike specs, a single obs-eq relation applies to all methods, so they are more centralized and typically less verbose. *Automation.* We feel that inferring an obs-eq relation is a more well-defined and achievable goal, akin to how numerous other verification techniques/tools prefer to synthesize loop invariants rather than synthesizing specifications. Also, many specification inference tools, to be tractable, end up with shallow specifications which, for commutativity, runs the unsoundness risk. *Usability.* We aim to make commutativity verification accessible to non-experts and, given the above mentioned unsoundness risk with imprecise specifications, asking them to write pre/post conditions is perhaps not the best strategy. Even if the non-expert succeeds in writing a correct pre/post condition, they can still lead to unsound conclusions about commutativity.

Experience. In some cases CITYPROVER caught our mistakes/typos. We also tried to use CITYPROVER to help us narrow down on a commutativity condition via repeated guesses. In the HashTable example the successive conditions $^i\varphi_{\mathsf{put}}^{\mathsf{put}}$ (defined in the extended version [28].) represent our repeated attempts to guess commutativity conditions. CITYPROVER's counterexamples pointed out collisions and capacity cases. Commutativity conditions are applied in practice through the use of commutativity-based formats such as abstract locking [24], access point specifications [17] and conflict abstractions [16].

Summary. With REDUCE_m^n, tools often struggle to converge on appropriate abstractions but we show that DAREDUCE_m^n (employing mn-differencing) leads to a more plausible algorithmic strategy: DAREDUCE_m^n can promptly validate commutativity conditions for 31 out of 37 examples. An important direction for future work is to further improve performance and scalability.

8 Related Work

To our knowledge, mn-differencing and reductions based on mn-differencing (*e.g.* DAREDUCE_m^n) have not occurred in the literature. We now survey related works on commutativity reasoning, k-safety, product programs, etc., beyond those that we have already mentioned.

Commutativity Reasoning. Bansal *et al.* [7] synthesize commutativity conditions from provided pre/post specifications, rather than implementations. They assume these specifications are precise enough to faithfully represent all effects relevant to commutativity. As discussed in Sect. 2, if specifications are coarse, Bansal *et al.* would emit unsound commutativity conditions. By contrast, our relations capture just what is needed for commutativity. Gehr *et al.* [21] describe a method based on black-box sampling, but lack a soundness guarantee. Both Aleen and Clark [4] and Tripp *et al.* [42] identify sequences of actions that commute (via random interpretation and dynamic analysis, resp.). Kulkarni et al. [32] point out that degrees of commutativity specification precision are useful. Kim and Rinard [27] verify commutativity conditions from specifications. Commutativity is also used in dynamic analysis [17]. Najafzadeh *et al.* [35] describe a tool for weak consistency, that reports commutativity checking of formulae, but not ADT implementations. Houshmand *et al.* [25] describe commutativity checking for replicated data types (CRDTs). This complementary work is geared toward CRDTs written in a high-level specification language (transitions on tuples of Sets) that can be represented in SMT with user-provided invariants.

k-safety, Product programs, Reductions. Self-composition [9,41] reduces some forms of hyper-properties [14] to properties of a single program. More recent works include product programs [8,18] and techniques for automated verification of *k*-safety properties. Cartesian Hoare Logic [40] is a program logic for reasoning about *k*-safety properties, automated via a tool called DESCARTES. Antonopoulos *et al.* [5] described an alternative automated *k*-safety technique based on partitioning the traces within a program. Farzan and Vandikas [19] discuss a technique and tool WEAVER for verifying hypersafety properties, based on the observation that a proof of some representative runs in a product program can be sufficient to prove that the hypersafety property holds of the original program. Others explore logical relational reasoning across multiple programs [6,20].

9   Discussion and Future Work

We have described a theory (mn-differencing), algorithm (DAREDUCE_m^n) and tool for decomposing commutativity verification of ADT implementations.

mn-differencing can be instantiated to reason about heap ADTs by using, *e.g.*, separation logic [37,38] as an assertion language. Using the separating conjunction, we can frame the mn-differencing relation apart from the cloning relation. For example, we can consider push(x)/pop on a list-based implementation of a stack containing n elements: $stk \mapsto [e_n, s_n] * \cdots * [e_1, \bot]$. We can define mn-differencing R_α to focuses on whether two list-stack states agree on the top element, and frame the rest with a relation C that specifies exact (shape and value) equivalence. It is unclear whether DAREDUCE_m^n is the right strategy for automating mn-differencing heap assertions; integrating mn-differencing into heap-based tools (*e.g.* [1,2,26]) is an interesting direction for future work.

The results of our work can be used to incorporate more commutativity conditions soundly and obtain speed ups in transactional object systems [16,24]. Further research is needed to use our commutativity proofs with parallelizing compilers. Specifically, in the years to come, parallelizing compilers could combine our proofs of commutativity with automated proofs of linearizability [12] to execute more code concurrently and safely.

Acknowledgments. We would like to thank Marco Gaboardi, Maurice Herlihy, Michael Hicks, David Naumann and the anonymous reviewers for their helpful feedback on earlier drafts of this work. This work was supported in part by NSF award #1813745 and #2008633.

References

1. Infer static analyzer. https://fbinfer.com/
2. Verifast. https://github.com/verifast/verifast
3. Abadi, M., Lamport, L.: The existence of refinement mappings. Theor. Comput. Sci. **82**, 253–284 (1991)
4. Aleen, F., Clark, N.: Commutativity analysis for software parallelization: letting program transformations see the big picture. In: Proceedings of the 14th International Conference on Architectural Support for Programming Languages and Operating Systems (ASPLOS-XII) (2009), ACM, pp. 241–252 (2009)
5. Antonopoulos, T., Gazzillo, P., Hicks, M., Koskinen, E., Terauchi, T., Wei, S.: Decomposition instead of self-composition for proving the absence of timing channels. In: Cohen, A., Vechev, M.T. (eds.) Proceedings of the 38th ACM SIGPLAN Conference on Programming Language Design and Implementation, PLDI 2017, Barcelona, Spain, 18–23 June 2017, pp. 362–375. ACM (2017)
6. Banerjee, A., Naumann, D. A., and Nikouei, M. Relational logic with framing and hypotheses. In: 36th IARCS Annual Conference on Foundations of Software Technology and Theoretical Computer Science (FSTTCS 2016). Schloss Dagstuhl-Leibniz-Zentrum fuer Informatik (2016)
7. Bansal, K., Koskinen, E., Tripp, O.: Automatic generation of precise and useful commutativity conditions. In: Beyer, D., Huisman, M. (eds.) TACAS 2018. LNCS, vol. 10805, pp. 115–132. Springer, Cham (2018). https://doi.org/10.1007/978-3-319-89960-2_7
8. Barthe, G., Crespo, J.M., Kunz, C.: Relational verification using product programs. In: Butler, M., Schulte, W. (eds.) FM 2011. LNCS, vol. 6664, pp. 200–214. Springer, Heidelberg (2011). https://doi.org/10.1007/978-3-642-21437-0_17
9. Barthe, G., D'Argenio, P.R., Rezk, T.: Secure information flow by self-composition. In: CSFW (2004)
10. Beyer, D., Keremoglu, M.E.: CPACHECKER: a tool for configurable software verification. In: Gopalakrishnan, G., Qadeer, S. (eds.) CAV 2011. LNCS, vol. 6806, pp. 184–190. Springer, Heidelberg (2011). https://doi.org/10.1007/978-3-642-22110-1_16
11. Bolognesi, T., Smolka, S.A.: Fundamental results for the verification of observational equivalence: a survey. In: PSTV, pp. 165–179 (1987)
12. Bouajjani, A., Emmi, M., Enea, C., Hamza, J. On reducing linearizability to state reachability. In Automata, Languages, and Programming - 42nd International Colloquium, ICALP 2015, Kyoto, Japan, 6–10 July 2015, Proceedings, Part II, pp. 95–107 (2015)
13. Chechik, M., Stavropoulou, I., Disenfeld, C., Rubin, J.: FPH: efficient non-commutativity analysis of feature-based systems. In: Russo, A., Schürr, A. (eds.) FASE 2018. LNCS, vol. 10802, pp. 319–336. Springer, Cham (2018). https://doi.org/10.1007/978-3-319-89363-1_18
14. Clarkson, M.R., Schneider, F.B.: Hyperproperties. J. Comput. Secur. **18**(6), 1157–1210 (2010)

15. Clements, A.T., Kaashoek, M.F., Zeldovich, N., Morris, R.T., Kohler, E.: The scalable commutativity rule: designing scalable software for multicore processors. ACM Trans. Comput. Syst. **32**(4), 10 (2015)
16. Dickerson, T.D., Koskinen, E., Gazzillo, P., Herlihy, M.: Conflict abstractions and shadow speculation for optimistic transactional objects. In: Programming Languages and Systems - 17th Asian Symposium, APLAS 2019, Nusa Dua, Bali, Indonesia, 1–4 December 2019, Proceedings, pp. 313–331 (2019)
17. Dimitrov, D., Raychev, V., Vechev, M., Koskinen, E.: Commutativity race detection. In: Proceedings of the 35th ACM SIGPLAN Conference on Programming Language Design and Implementation (PLDI 2014) (2014)
18. Eilers, M., Müller, P., Hitz, S.: Modular product programs. ACM Trans. Programm. Lang. Syst. (TOPLAS) **42**(1), 1–37 (2019)
19. Farzan, A., Vandikas, A.: Automated hypersafety verification. In: Dillig, I., Tasiran, S. (eds.) CAV 2019. LNCS, vol. 11561, pp. 200–218. Springer, Cham (2019). https://doi.org/10.1007/978-3-030-25540-4_11
20. Frumin, D., Krebbers, R., Birkedal, L.: Reloc: a mechanised relational logic for fine-grained concurrency. In: Proceedings of the 33rd Annual ACM/IEEE Symposium on Logic in Computer Science, pp. 442–451 (2018)
21. Gehr, T., Dimitrov, D., Vechev, M. T. Learning commutativity specifications. In: Computer Aided Verification - 27th International Conference, CAV 2015, San Francisco, CA, USA, 18–24 July 2015, Proceedings, Part I, 307–323 (2015)
22. Heizmann, M., et al.: Ultimate automizer with SMTInterpol. In: Piterman, N., Smolka, S.A. (eds.) TACAS 2013. LNCS, vol. 7795, pp. 641–643. Springer, Heidelberg (2013). https://doi.org/10.1007/978-3-642-36742-7_53
23. Henzinger, T.A., Jhala, R., Majumdar, R., Necula, G.C., Sutre, G., Weimer, W.: Temporal-safety proofs for systems code. In: Computer Aided Verification, 14th International Conference, CAV 2002, Copenhagen, Denmark, 27–31 July 2002, Proceedings, pp. 526–538 (2002)
24. Herlihy, M., Koskinen, E.: Transactional boosting: a methodology for highly concurrent transactional objects. In: Proceedings of the 13th ACM SIGPLAN Symposium on Principles and Practice of Parallel Programming (PPoPP 2008) (2008)
25. Houshmand, F., Lesani, M.H.: replication coordination analysis and synthesis. Proc. ACM Program. Lang. **3**(POPL), 74:1–74:32 (2019)
26. Juhasz, U., Kassios, I.T., Müller, P., Novacek, M., Schwerhoff, M., Summers, A.J.: Viper: a verification infrastructure for permission-based reasoning. Technical report, ETH Zurich (2014)
27. Kim, D., Rinard, M.C. :Verification of semantic commutativity conditions and inverse operations on linked data structures. In: Proceedings of the 32nd ACM SIGPLAN Conference on Programming Language Design and Implementation, PLDI 2011, ACM, pp. 528–541 (2011)
28. Koskinen, E., Bansal, K.: Reducing commutativity verification to reachability with differencing abstractions. CoRR abs/2004.08450 (2020)
29. Koskinen, E., Parkinson, M.J.: The push/pull model of transactions. In: Proceedings of the 36th ACM SIGPLAN Conference on Programming Language Design and Implementation, Portland, OR, USA, June 15–17, 2015, pp. 186–195 (2015)
30. Koskinen, E., Parkinson, M.J., Herlihy, M.: Coarse-grained transactions. In: Proceedings of the 37th ACM SIGPLAN-SIGACT Symposium on Principles of Programming Languages, ACM, pp. 19–30 (2010)
31. Kragl, B., Qadeer, S.: Layered concurrent programs. In: Chockler, H., Weissenbacher, G. (eds.) CAV 2018. LNCS, vol. 10981, pp. 79–102. Springer, Cham (2018). https://doi.org/10.1007/978-3-319-96145-3_5

32. Kulkarni, M., Nguyen, D., Prountzos, D., Sui, X., Pingali, K.: Exploiting the commutativity lattice. In: Proceedings of the 32nd ACM SIGPLAN Conference on Programming Language Design and Implementation, PLDI 2011, pp. 542–555. ACM (2011)

33. Kulkarni, M., Pingali, K., Walter, B., Ramanarayanan, G., Bala, K., Chew, L.P.: Optimistic parallelism requires abstractions. In: Ferrante, J., McKinley, K.S. (eds.) Proceedings of the ACM SIGPLAN 2007 Conference on Programming Language Design and Implementation (PLDI 2007), pp. 211–222. ACM (2007)

34. Lipton, R.J.: Reduction: a method of proving properties of parallel programs. Commun. ACM **18**(12), 717–721 (1975)

35. Najafzadeh, M., Gotsman, A., Yang, H., Ferreira, C., Shapiro, M.: The CISE tool: proving weakly-consistent applications correct. In: Proceedings of the 2nd Workshop on the Principles and Practice of Consistency for Distributed Data, PaPoC@EuroSys 2016, London, United Kingdom, 18 April 2016, pp. 2:1–2:3 (2016)

36. Ni, Y., et al.: Open nesting in software transactional memory. In: Proceedings of the 12th ACM SIGPLAN Symposium on Principles and Practice of Parallel Programming, PPOPP 2007, pp. 68–78. ACM (2007)

37. O'Hearn, P., Reynolds, J., Yang, H.: Local reasoning about programs that alter data structures. In: Fribourg, L. (ed.) CSL 2001. LNCS, vol. 2142, pp. 1–19. Springer, Heidelberg (2001). https://doi.org/10.1007/3-540-44802-0_1

38. Reynolds, J.C.: Separation logic: a logic for shared mutable data structures. In: Proceedings 17th Annual IEEE Symposium on Logic in Computer Science, pp. 55–74. IEEE (2002)

39. Rinard, M.C., Diniz, P.C.: Commutativity analysis: a new analysis technique for parallelizing compilers. ACM Trans. Program. Lang. Syst. (TOPLAS) **19**(6), 942–991 (1997)

40. Sousa, M., Dillig, I.: Cartesian hoare logic for verifying k-safety properties. In: Krintz, C., Berger, E. (eds.) Proceedings of the 37th ACM SIGPLAN Conference on Programming Language Design and Implementation, PLDI 2016, Santa Barbara, CA, USA, 13–17 June 2016, pp. 57–69. ACM (2016)

41. Terauchi, T., Aiken, A.: Secure information flow as a safety problem. In: SAS (2005)

42. Tripp, O., Manevich, R., Field, J., Sagiv, M.: JANUS: exploiting parallelism via hindsight. In: ACM SIGPLAN Conference on Programming Language Design and Implementation, PLDI 2012, pp. 145–156 (2012)

43. Vafeiadis, V.: Automatically proving linearizability. In: Touili, T., Cook, B., Jackson, P. (eds.) CAV 2010. LNCS, vol. 6174, pp. 450–464. Springer, Heidelberg (2010). https://doi.org/10.1007/978-3-642-14295-6_40

44. Yang, H.: Relational separation logic. Theor. Comput. Sci. **375**(1–3), 308–334 (2007)

Proving the Existence of Fair
Paths in Infinite-State Systems

Alessandro Cimatti, Alberto Griggio, and Enrico Magnago[(✉)]

Fondazione Bruno Kessler, Trento, Italy
{cimatti,griggio,magnago}@fbk.eu

Abstract. In finite-state systems, true existential properties admit witnesses in form of lasso-shaped fair paths. When dealing with the infinite-state case (e.g. software non-termination, model checking of hybrid automata) this is no longer the case. In this paper, we propose a compositional approach for proving the existence of fair paths of infinite-state systems. First, we describe a formal approach to prove the existence of a non-empty under-approximation of the original system that only contains fair paths. Second, we define an automated procedure that, given a set of hints (in form of basic components), searches for a suitable composition proving the existence of a fair path. We experimentally evaluate the approach on examples taken from both software and hybrid systems, showing its wide applicability and expressiveness.

1 Introduction

LTL model checking for infinite-state systems is a well-known undecidable problem. Most of the research has concentrated on proving that the properties are universally verified, i.e. all traces satisfy the property. In this work, we focus on its dual problem: the falsification of LTL properties, which amounts to proving that one trace satisfies (the negation of) the property. Notable instances of this problem are proving software non-termination (with the fair path to be found corresponding to a non-terminating execution) and finding counterexamples and scenarios in hybrid systems and in infinite-state fair transition systems. Model checking can be reduced to proving the language emptiness of an infinite-state fair transition system. In order to prove that the LTL property does not hold it is necessary and sufficient to prove the existence of a fair infinite execution.

The problem is conceptually harder than in the finite-state case, since fair paths may have no regular structure. Hence, in general they cannot be presented in lasso-shaped form as $\alpha \cdot \beta^\omega$, where α and β are finite sequences of states and β^ω is the infinite repetition of β.

In this paper, we propose an approach to prove the existence of fair paths in infinite-state fair transition systems. The approach is based on the following insights. We define an underapproximation of the given transition system, extended with formulae describing regions of the state space of the system, which we call $\mathcal{R}$-abstraction. We identify a set of conditions over the underapproximation that are sufficient for the existence of a fair path. Such abstraction enjoys

© Springer Nature Switzerland AG 2021
F. Henglein et al. (Eds.): VMCAI 2021, LNCS 12597, pp. 104–126, 2021.
https://doi.org/10.1007/978-3-030-67067-2_6

the property that each fair loop over its regions entails the existence of a fair path in the original system. In this sense, each lasso-shaped execution over the regions represents a non-empty envelope containing only fair paths of the original system. We formally present the hypotheses necessary for the $\mathcal{R}$-abstraction to represent a suitable non-empty under-approximation of the fair transition system. This argument, based on a monolithic underapproximation, is refined into a compositional approach. Intuitively, the monolithic underapproximation is presented as the composition of smaller transition systems enriched with a set of regions and assumptions. We define a set of conditions that, if satisfied by the components, entail that the composition proves the existence of the fair path.

Based on this framework, we describe a search procedure to identify a compositional presentation of the under-approximation. The procedure takes in input a candidate set of components, and looks for a suitable composition of a subset of them that represents an adequate under-approximation of the original system.

We study a generalization to enforce the divergence of a specific symbol. This is required, for example, to deal with conditions resulting from the conversion of hybrid systems into fair transition systems, and the analysis is to be restricted to non-zeno paths, where time diverges to infinity.

We implemented and evaluated the proposed approach. The procedure works on symbolically represented infinite-state fair transition systems, and is able to produce suitable compositions and to exhibit proofs of existence of fair paths based on manual hints produced with moderate effort. The results, obtained for benchmarks of diverse nature, derived from software termination and hybrid automata, demonstrate the expressiveness of the framework and the effectiveness of the approach.

The paper is organised as follows. In Sect. 2 and 3 we present the background and a running example. In Sect. 4 and 5, we define the monolithic and compositional frameworks. The search procedure is described in Sect. 6. In Sect. 7 we discuss symbol-divergence. In Sect. 8 we contrast our approach with related work. Section 9 reports the experimental evaluation of the approach. Section 10 concludes and outlines future works. The proofs of all the theorems are reported in the extended version of this document[1].

2   Background

We work in the setting of SMT, with the theory of quantified real arithmetic. We assume the standard notions of interpretation, model, satisfiability, validity and logical consequence. We write $\text{NNF}(\phi)$ for the negation normal form of ϕ. A symbolic fair transition system M is a tuple $\langle S, I, T, F \rangle$, where S is the set of state variables; I and F are formulae over S, representing respectively the initial and fair states; T is a formula over S and S' representing the transitions, where $S' \doteq \{s' | s \in S\}$ and the primed version of a variable refers to the next state. We denote with $\boldsymbol{S}$ or $\boldsymbol{s}$ a total assignment over S, i.e. a state. A fair path of M is

---

[1] The extended version is available at https://enricomagnago.com/proving_the_existence_of_fair_paths_in_infinite-state_systems_extended.pdf.

an infinite sequence of states, $s_0, s_1, \ldots$, such that $s_0 \models I$, $s_i s'_{i+1} \models T$ for all i, and for each i there exists $j > i$ such that $s_j \models F$. A deadlock is a reachable state that has no outgoing transitions.

We also assume the standard notions of trace, reachability, and temporal logic model checking, using $\mathbf{E}, \mathbf{A}$ for path quantifiers and $\mathbf{G}, \mathbf{F}$ for "always" and "eventually" (CTL* [17]).

We overload the $\models$ symbol: when ϕ and ψ are SMT formulae, then $\phi \models \psi$ stands for entailment in SMT; when M is a fair transition system and ψ is a temporal property, then $M \models \psi$ is to be interpreted with the LTL semantics.

3 Running Example

For explanatory purposes, we consider a bouncing ball subject to the gravitational acceleration. The ball follows the classical laws of a uniformly accelerated motion, losing a fraction of its velocity at every bounce. The bounce is an instantaneous transition where $v' = -v\frac{c}{c+1}$, with v being the velocity and c the number of bounces. It is also possible for the ball to get stuck to the ground. Let h be the distance of the ball from the ground. The dynamics are partitioned into three phases: in the first phase, the ball is falling down ($v < 0 \wedge h > 0$); in the second, the ball is bouncing $h = 0$; finally, the ball is moving upwards ($v > 0 \wedge h > 0$). Unless stopped, the ball goes infinitely through the phases, but for shorter and shorter periods of time: the interval between two consecutive bounces c and $c+1$ is given by $\frac{1}{c}$.

```
1  MODULE main
2    VAR h : real; v : real; delta : real; c : integer;
3        stop : boolean;
4    DEFINE g := 9.81;
5    INIT c = 1 & h = 0 & v = g / 2;
6    INVAR (h = 0 & v < 0) -> delta = 0;
7    INVAR delta >= 0 & h >= 0;
8    TRANS (h = 0 & v < 0) -> next(c) = c + 1;
9    TRANS !(h = 0 & v < 0) -> next(c) = c;
10   TRANS (stop & h = 0) -> (next(h) = 0 & next(v) = 0);
11   TRANS (!stop & h = 0 & v = 0) -> (next(h) = 0 & next(v) = 0);
12   TRANS (!stop & h = 0 & v < 0) -> (next(h) = 0 &
13                      next(v) = - v*c / (c + 1));
14   TRANS (!stop & !(h = 0 & v <= 0)) -> (next(v) = v - g*delta &
15          next(h) = h + v * delta - 0.5 * g * pow(delta, 2));
16   LTLSPEC ! G F (h = 0 & v > 0);
```

Fig. 1. The SMV encoding of the bouncing ball

Systems like the bouncing ball are usually described as hybrid systems. Here we consider the corresponding infinite state transition system, presented symbolically in Fig. 1 using a variant of the SMV language. The symbol delta represents the amount of time elapsing at each transition. The nondeterministic `stop` variable controls the ball getting stuck to the ground. The (universal) property states that the ball cannot bounce up infinitely often.

4   Fair Paths: Sufficient Conditions

This section presents the main argument used to prove the existence of a fair path for a fair transition system M. First, we identify a transition system, A, organized according to a set of regions $\mathcal{R}$, each corresponding to a location. Then, we show that if A is a non-empty under-approximation of M and satisfies some conditions, then the existence of a fair cycle in M is ensured. When clear from context, with a slight abuse of notation, we write $\mathcal{R}$ for the formula $\bigvee_{i=0}^{m-1} R_i$ denoting the region space.

We call A an $\mathcal{R}$-abstraction with respect to a system M and regions $\mathcal{R}$ if the following conditions hold. The region space $\mathcal{R}$ must be reachable in M - intuitively, this corresponds to finding the "stem" of the fair path. A must be an underapproximation of M, so that the transitions taken in a path in A can be performed also in M. A must never deadlock in $\mathcal{R}$, and there must be no outgoing transitions from $\mathcal{R}$, so that from every state in $\mathcal{R}$ there exists an infinite path starting from it and contained in $\mathcal{R}$. Finally, we require that the set of fair locations F_A is visited infinitely often. These conditions are formalised in the following definition.

Definition 1 ($\mathcal{R}$-abstraction).   *Let* $M \doteq \langle S_M, I_M(S_M), T_M(S_M, S_M'), F_M$ $(S_M) \rangle$ *be a fair transition system. A transition system* $A \doteq \langle S_A, I_A(S_A),$ $T_A(S_A, S_A') \rangle$ *is an* $\mathcal{R}$-*abstraction of* M *with respect to a list of formulae* $\mathcal{R}(S_A) \doteq [R_0(S_A), \dots, R_{m-1}(S_A)]$, *also called regions, iff the following hold:*

H.0 $S_M \subseteq S_A$,

H.1 *There exists some initial state in* M *from which it is possible to reach an initial state of* A, *for some assignment to the* $S_A \backslash S_M$:

$$M \not\models \mathbf{AG} \neg I_A(S_A)$$

H.2 *The set of initial states of* A *is a subset of the union of the regions:*

$$A \models \mathcal{R}(S_A)$$

H.3 *The transition relation of* A *underapproximates the transition relation of* M:

$$\mathcal{R}(S_A) \wedge T_A(S_A, S_A') \models T_M(S_M, S_M')$$

H.4 *Every state in* R_0, *projected over the symbols in* S_M *corresponds to a fair state of* M:

$$A \models \mathbf{AG}(R_0(S_A) \rightarrow F_M(S_M))$$

H.5 *Every reachable state in A has at least one successor via its transition relation T_A:*

$$A \models \mathbf{AGEX} \top$$

H.6 *For each region $R_i \in \mathcal{R}$, with $i > 0$, every state in R_i can remain in such region at most a finite number of steps and must eventually reach a region with a lower index $j < i$:*

$$A \models \bigwedge_{i=1}^{m-1} \mathbf{AG}(R_i \rightarrow \mathbf{A}[R_i \mathbf{U} \bigvee_{j=0}^{i-1} R_j])$$

H.7 *All states reachable in one step from R_0 are in $\mathcal{R}$:*

$$A \models \mathbf{AG}(R_0 \rightarrow \mathbf{AX} \bigvee_{i=0}^{m-1} R_i)$$

In order to prove the existence of a fair path in M, we seek a $\mathcal{R}$-abstraction A. This is sufficient since, as shown by the following theorem, *all* paths of A are fair paths in M.

Theorem 1. *Let $M \doteq \langle S_M, I_M, T_M, F_M \rangle$ be a fair transition system. Let A be an $\mathcal{R}$-abstraction of M with respect to a sequence of regions $\mathcal{R}$ over S. Then M admits a fair path, i.e. $M \not\models \mathbf{FG}\neg F_M(S_M)$, and all infinite paths of A starting from some state reachable in M correspond to a fair path of M.*

Example. Consider the LTL model checking problem defined in Fig. 1 and let $M \doteq \langle S^M, I^M, T^M, F^M \rangle$ be the fair transition system whose fair executions are counterexamples for the LTL property. Then, I^M and T^M are defined as in the system described in Fig. 1 and the fairness condition is $F^M \doteq h = 0 \wedge v > 0$.

Figure 2 shows a possible $\mathcal{R}$-abstraction A for M that proves the existence of at least one counterexample for the LTL property. A has two regions R_0 and R_1. The transition relation T_A is shown with annotations on the edges connecting the two locations. In both regions the ball is on the ground ($h = 0$), but its velocity is negative in R_1 and positive in R_0, hence the latter is fair. More formally, A is defined as $\langle S, R_0 \vee R_1, T_A \rangle$ over two regions $\{R_0, R_1\}$, where:

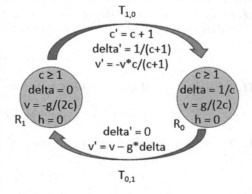

Fig. 2. $\mathcal{R}$-abstraction for the running example.

$$R_0 \doteq c \geq 1 \wedge delta = \frac{1}{c} \wedge v = \frac{g}{2c} \wedge h = 0$$

$$R_1 \doteq c \geq 1 \wedge delta = 0 \wedge v = -\frac{g}{2c} \wedge h = 0$$

$$T_{0,1} \doteq c' = c \wedge delta' = 0 \wedge v' = v - g * delta \wedge h' = h$$

$$T_{1,0} \doteq c' = c + 1 \wedge delta' = \frac{1}{c+1} \wedge v' = -v\frac{c}{c+1} \wedge h' = h$$

$$T_A \doteq \bigvee_{i \in \{0,1\}} (R_i \wedge T_{i,1-i} \wedge R_{1-i}').$$

It is easy to see that A is an $\mathcal{R}$-abstraction and satisfies all required hypotheses of Definition 1.

4.1   Comparison with Recurrent Sets

In the context of software non-termination the notion of recurrent set has been introduced by Gupta et al. in [25]. They show that the existence of an (open) recurrent set is a sufficient and necessary condition for a not well-founded relation. Cook et al. in [9] introduce the notion of closed recurrence sets, which is used also in [14]. Closed recurrence sets, instead of characterising a set of states that contain some infinite sequence, require the existence of at least one sequence in the set and that every sequence remaining in such set is infinite. In the same work they show that every closed recurrence set is also an open recurrent set and that if a open recurrent set exists, then there exists a corresponding closed recurrence set for some underapproximation of the transition relation.

These works are concerned with software non-termination and do not consider fairness conditions. Since, as we show below, an $\mathcal{R}$-abstraction corresponds to a closed recurrent set when the fairness condition is trivial (i.e. $\top$), our notion of $\mathcal{R}$-abstraction is strictly more expressive than what considered in the works above.

A not well-founded relation exists iff there exists an open recurrent set [25]. Cook et al. [14] show that if a system admits some recurrent set then there exist an underapproximation of it that admits a closed recurrence set. Therefore, Theorem 2 below implies that a not well-founded relation exists, for a system with trivial fairness, iff it admits an $\mathcal{R}$-abstraction.

We report the definition of closed recurrence set from [9], where we explicitly state that we are interested in an underapproximation of the transition relation. A set $\mathcal{G}$ is a closed recurrence set for a transition system $M \doteq \langle S, I(S), T(S, S') \rangle$, with respect to some underapproximation $T_{\mathcal{G}}$ of T iff the following hold:

$$\exists S : \mathcal{G}(S) \wedge I(S)$$
$$\forall S \exists S' : \mathcal{G}(S) \to T_{\mathcal{G}}(S, S')$$
$$\forall S, S' : \mathcal{G}(S) \wedge T_{\mathcal{G}}(S, S') \to \mathcal{G}(S')$$
$$\forall S, S' : T_{\mathcal{G}}(S, S') \to T(S, S')$$

Theorem 2. *A system $M \langle S, I(S), T(S, S'), \top \rangle$ admits an $\mathcal{R}$-abstraction $A \doteq \langle S_A, I_A(S_A), T_A(S_A, S_A') \rangle$ if and only if there exists a closed recurrence set $\mathcal{G}$.*

5   Decomposition of the Sufficient Conditions

Finding a monolithic $\mathcal{R}$-abstraction satisfying all the hypotheses for some fair transition system is a challenging problem. Here we refine the framework to present the $\mathcal{R}$-abstraction compositionally, as a network of smaller components, by considering a subset of the symbols at a time. For each subset of the symbols we identify some smaller components that could represent the behaviour of the system projected only on those variables. The monolithic $\mathcal{R}$-abstraction is the composition of these smaller components, one for each subset of variables. We describe the interaction between the components in an assume-guarantee fashion. Each component, that we call $\mathcal{AG}$-skeleton (for Assume-Guarantee skeleton), describes the behaviour of a subset of the symbols while assuming some properties about the others. These properties represent the conditions that are necessary for this behaviour to be enabled and we need to prove that such conditions are ensured by some other $\mathcal{AG}$-skeleton.

The following is the outline of the approach. We first formally define $\mathcal{AG}$-skeletons and a composition operator over such structures. In order to find an $\mathcal{R}$-abstraction, given a set of $\mathcal{AG}$-skeletons we apply such operator until we obtain a composed $\mathcal{AG}$-skeleton with an empty set of assumptions, which, by definition of the composition operator, implies that we considered one $\mathcal{AG}$-skeleton for each subset of the symbols. This $\mathcal{AG}$-skeleton is a transition system associated with a list of regions that either does not allow any loop over the regions or satisfies hypotheses H.5, H.6 and H.7. Among all possible compositions the procedure described in Sect. 6 searches for one that admits at least one such loop that also satisfies H.1, H.2, H.3 and H.4, hence an $\mathcal{R}$-abstraction.

Formally, let M be given. Let $\{S^0, \ldots, S^{n-1}\}$ be pairwise disjoint and a covering[2] of S^M. Let $\{H^j\}_{j=0}^{n-1}$ be a set of transition systems of the form $\langle S^j \cup S^{\neq j}, I^j, T^j \rangle$ and $m^j \in \mathbb{N}$ be the number of regions of H^j. We say that S^j are the symbols controlled by H^j or its local symbols. We also write S for $\bigcup_{j=0}^{n-1} S^j$ and $S^{\neq i}$ for $S \setminus S^i$. Let $\mathcal{R}^j \doteq \{R_i^j(S)|0 \leq i < m^j\}$ be the set of regions of H^j and $\mathcal{A}^j \doteq \{A_i^j(S^{\neq j})|0 \leq i < m^j\}$ the set of assumptions of H^j. Let $A_i^j(S^{\neq j})$ be the assumptions of H^j in its ith region on the other components. We assume such assumptions are in *cartesian* form, by requiring

$$A_i^j(S^{\neq j}) \doteq \bigwedge_{k \neq j} A_i^{j,k}(S^k)$$

where $A_i^{j,k}(S^k)$ are (independent) assumptions on H^k of H^j in the ith region.

Notice that the regions $R_i^j(S)$ of H^j can depend on all the variables S, while the assumptions $A_i^j(S^{\neq j})$ cannot refer to the "local variables" S^j of H^j. The *restricted region i of H^j* is $(R_i^j \wedge A_i^j)$.

Every $\mathcal{AG}$-skeleton H^j must satisfy the following condition.

I. If there is pair of states satisfying the transition relation, such that the first one is in the restricted region i and the latter in the restricted region i', then

---

[2] Hence, $S^M \subseteq \bigcup_j S^j$ and $\forall j \neq k : S^j \cap S^k = \emptyset$

for every state in the restricted region i the transition relation allows for a successor state in the restricted region i':

$$\forall i, i' : 0 \le i < m^j \wedge 0 \le i' < m^j \rightarrow$$

$$\exists S, S' : (R_i^j(S) \wedge A_i^j(S^{\neq j}) \wedge T^j(S, S') \wedge R_{i'}^j(S') \wedge A_{i'}^j(S^{\neq j'})) \models$$

$$\forall S \exists S^{j'} \forall S^{\neq j'} : R_i^j(S) \wedge A_i^j(S^{\neq j}) \wedge A_{i'}^j(S^{\neq j'}) \rightarrow R_{i'}^j(S') \wedge T^j(S, S')$$

This is related to *must*-abstractions, presented for example in [36], in the sense that for every assignment to the current state symbols S there must exist an assignment to the next state symbols. However, in our case we restrict the existential quantification only to the symbols local to the $\mathcal{AG}$-skeleton $S^{j'}$.

Definition 2 (compatible transitions). *Let* $\{H^{j_0}, \ldots, H^{j_k}\} \subseteq \{H^i\}_{i=0}^{n-1}$ *be a subset of the $\mathcal{AG}$-skeletons. A transition from state $\hat{S}$ to $\hat{S}'$ is compatible iff the transitions of the $\mathcal{AG}$-skeletons, from every pair of states in the same regions, meet the respective assumptions of the $\mathcal{AG}$-skeletons.*

$$compatible_{\{j_0,\ldots,j_k\}}(\hat{S}, \hat{S}') \doteq \forall S, S' : \bigwedge_{0 \le i_0 < m^{j_0}, 0 \le i'_0 < m^{j_0}, \ldots, 0 \le i_k < m^{j_k}, 0 \le i'_k < m^{j_k}}$$

$$(R_{i_0}^{j_0}(\hat{S}) \wedge A_{i_0}^{j_0}(\hat{S}) \wedge R_{i'_0}^{j_0}(\hat{S}') \wedge A_{i'_0}^{j_0}(\hat{S}') \wedge \ldots \wedge R_{i_k}^{j_k}(\hat{S}) \wedge A_{i_k}^{j_k}(\hat{S}) \wedge R_{i'_k}^{j_k}(\hat{S}') \wedge A_{i'_k}^{j_k}(\hat{S}') \rightarrow$$

$$\bigwedge_{0 \le t \le k} ((R_{i_t}^t(S) \wedge A_{i_t}^t(S^{\neq j_t}) \wedge A_{i'_t}^t(S^{\neq \{j_s\}_{s=1}^k}') \wedge$$

$$\bigwedge_{0 \le s \le k \wedge s \ne t} T^s(S, S') \wedge R_{i'_s}^s(S') \wedge A_{i'_s}^s(S^{\neq j_s'})) \rightarrow \bigwedge_{0 \le h \le k \wedge h \ne t} A_{i'_t}^{t, j_h}(S^{j_h'})$$

$$)$$

$$)$$

Compatible holds iff the existence of a transition from some state $\hat{S}$ to $\hat{S}'$ in the intersection of some restricted regions, implies that every transition between the same intersection of restricted regions implies that the assumptions made by each $\mathcal{AG}$-skeleton are met.

We now define the composition of $\mathcal{AG}$-skeletons as the standard product of transition systems restricted to the *compatible* transitions and show that this operation is closed: the composition of k $\mathcal{AG}$-skeletons is an $\mathcal{AG}$-skeleton.

Definition 3 (composition of $\mathcal{AG}$-skeletons). *We define the composition of* $\{H^{j_0}, \ldots, H^{j_k}\} \subseteq \{H^j\}_{j=0}^{n-1}$, *such that the sets of local symbols* $\{S^{j_i}\}_{i=0}^k$ *are pairwise disjoint, as* $H^c \doteq \bigotimes_{t=0}^k H^{j_t} = \langle S, I^c, T^c \rangle$ *where:*

- $S^c \doteq \bigcup_{t=0}^k S^{j_t}$;
- $m^c \doteq \prod_{t=0}^k m^{j_t}$;
- $\mathcal{R}^c \doteq \{\bigwedge_{t=0}^k R_{i_t}^{j_t}(S) \wedge \bigwedge_{0 \le s \le k \wedge s \ne t} A_{i_t}^{j_t, j_s}(S^{j_s}) | \forall t \in \{0, \ldots, k\}, i_t \in \{0, \ldots, m^{j_t} - 1\} : R_{i_t}^{j_t}(S) \in \mathcal{R}^{j_t}$ and $\forall s . 0 \le s \le k \wedge s \ne t : A_{i_t}^{j_t, j_s}(S^{j_s}) \in \mathcal{A}^{j_t}\}$;
- $\mathcal{A}^c \doteq \{\bigwedge_{t=0}^k \bigwedge_{j_s \notin \{j_0, \ldots, j_k\}} A_{i_t}^{j_t, j_s}(S^{j_s}) | \forall t \in \{0, \ldots, k\}, j_s \notin \{j_0, \ldots, j_k\}, i_t \in \{0, \ldots, m^{j_t} - 1\} : A_{i_t}^{j_t, j_s}(S^{j_s}) \in \mathcal{A}_{i_t}^{j_t}(S^{\neq j_t})\}$;

- $I^c(S) \doteq \bigwedge_{t=0}^{k} I^{j_t}(S);$
- $T^c(S, S') \doteq compatible_{j_0, \ldots, j_k}(S, S') \wedge \bigwedge_{t=0}^{k} T^{j_t}(S, S').$

For compactness we will use $S^{\neq c}$ for $S \setminus S^c$ which is equal also to $\bigcup_{t=0}^{k} S^{\neq j_t}$ and $A_i^j(S^{\neq c})$ for $\bigwedge_{j_s \notin \{j_0, \ldots, j_k\}} A_i^{j, j_s}(S^{j_s})$.

Theorem 3 ($\mathcal{AG}$-skeletons are closed under $\otimes$). *Given a set of $\mathcal{AG}$-skeletons $\{H^{j_0}, \ldots, H^{j_k}\} \subseteq \{H^j\}_{j=0}^{n-1}$, their composition $H^c \doteq \bigotimes_{t=0}^{k} H^{j_t} = \langle S, I^c, T^c \rangle$ is still an $\mathcal{AG}$-skeleton, i.e. it satisfies hypothesis I.*

By composing a sequence of $\mathcal{AG}$-skeletons such that their local symbols are pairwise disjoint and cover the set of symbols S^M of the fair transition system M, we obtain an $\mathcal{AG}$-skeleton with an empty set of assumptions. By definition, the composition satisfies I: every pair of regions either do not admit any transition between them or from one it is always possible to reach the other in one step and there is no deadlock. Therefore, such $\mathcal{AG}$-skeleton is a transition system associated with a list of regions such that H.5 and H.6 hold, and, in case a region is a subset of the fair states of M, also H.7 holds. In the next section we describe a procedure that (i) computes such a composition of $\mathcal{AG}$-skeletons, and (ii) among all possible compositions it looks for one that admits some loop over the regions satisfying also the remaining hypotheses (H.1, H.2, H.3 and H.4), thus ensuring that it is an $\mathcal{R}$-abstraction.

5.1   Example: Decomposition

In the following, for compactness, we write R^j for $R^j(S)$, A^j for $A^j(S^{\neq j})$, T^j for $T^j(S, S')$ and $R^{j\,'}$, $A^{j\,'}$ for $R^j(S')$ and $A^j(S^{\neq j\,'})$ respectively. We now show how the $\mathcal{R}$-abstraction in Fig. 2 can be represented as composition of smaller $\mathcal{AG}$-skeletons. Consider the partitioning of S given by $S^C \doteq \{c\}$, $S^H \doteq \{h\}$ and $S^{DV} \doteq \{d, v\}$. We define three corresponding $\mathcal{AG}$-skeletons:

$$C \doteq \langle S^C, c \geq 1, c' = c + 1 \vee c' = c \rangle$$

with no assumptions and a single region $c \geq 1$.

$$H \doteq \langle S^H, (R_0^H \wedge A_0^H) \vee (R_1^H \wedge A_1^H),$$
$$(R_0^H \wedge A_0^H \wedge T_{0,0}^H \wedge R_0^{H\,'} \wedge A_0^{H\,'}) \vee$$
$$(R_0^H \wedge A_0^H \wedge T_{0,1}^H \wedge R_1^{H\,'} \wedge A_1^{H\,'}) \vee$$
$$(R_1^H \wedge A_1^H \wedge (T_{1,0,0}^H \vee T_{1,0,1}^H) \wedge R_0^{H\,'} \wedge A_0^{H\,'}) \rangle$$

where $R_0^H \equiv R_1^H \doteq h = 0$, $A_0^H \doteq delta = 0$, $A_1^H \doteq delta = \frac{2v}{g}$, $T_{0,0}^H \equiv T_{0,1}^H \equiv T_{1,0,0}^H \doteq h' = h$ and $T_{1,0,1}^H \doteq h' = h + v * delta - \frac{g}{2} delta^2$. Finally we define

$$DV \doteq \langle S^{DV}, (R_0^{DV} \wedge A_0^{DV}) \vee (R_1^{DV} \wedge A_1^{DV}),$$
$$(R_0^{DV} \wedge A_0^{DV} \wedge T_{0,1}^{DV} \wedge R_1^{DV\,'} \wedge A_1^{DV\,'}) \vee$$
$$(R_1^{DV} \wedge A_1^{DV} \wedge T_{1,0}^{DV} \wedge R_0^{DV\,'} \wedge A_0^{DV\,'})'\rangle$$

where $R_0^{DV} \doteq delta = 0 \land v = -\frac{g}{2c}$ and $R_1^{DV} \doteq delta = \frac{1}{c} \land v = \frac{g}{2c}$, the two assumptions are $A_0^{DV} \equiv A_1^{DV} = c \geq 1 \land h = 0$ and the two components of the transition relation are defined as $T_{0,1}^{DV} \doteq delta' = \frac{1}{c+1} \land v' = -v\frac{c}{c+1}$ and $T_{1,0}^{DV} \doteq delta' = 0 \land v' = v - g * delta$.

The three $\mathcal{AG}$-skeletons satisfy I. Applying the composition operator and removing empty regions and transitions we obtain

$$B \doteq C \otimes DV \otimes H = \langle S^B, R_0^B \lor R_1^B, (R_0^B \land T_{0,1}^B \land R_1^{B'}) \lor (R_1^B \land T_{1,0}^B \land R_0^{B'}) \rangle$$

with two regions $\{R_0^B, R_1^B\}$ and no assumptions, where:

$$R_0^B \doteq c \geq 1 \land delta = \frac{1}{c} \land v = \frac{g}{2c} \land h = 0$$

$$R_1^B \doteq c \geq 1 \land delta = 0 \land v = -\frac{g}{2c} \land h = 0$$

$$T_{0,1}^B \doteq c' = c \land delta' = 0 \land v' = v - g * delta \land h' = h$$

$$T_{1,0}^B \doteq c' = c + 1 \land delta' = \frac{1}{c+1} \land v' = -v\frac{c}{c+1} \land h' = h$$

Region R_0^B implies the fairness condition $h = 0 \land v > 0$ and we obtain the $\mathcal{R}$-abstraction $\langle S, \{R_0^B, R_1^B\}, T^B \rangle$, where $T^B \doteq \bigvee_{i \in \{0,1\}} (R_i^B \land T_{i,1-i}^B \land R_{1-i}^{B'})$ which is exactly the definition of H shown in Fig. 2.

6   Search of the Composition

Let $M \doteq \langle S, I(S), T(S, S'), F(S) \rangle$ be a fair transition system and $\mathcal{H}$ be a set of $\mathcal{AG}$-skeletons. We want to find a subset $\{H^0, \ldots, H^n\} \subseteq \mathcal{H}$, with a composition $C \doteq H^0 \otimes \ldots \otimes H^n$ such that: (i) the symbols associated to the $\mathcal{AG}$-skeletons in the subset are pairwise disjoint and define a covering of S; (ii) C is an underapproximation of M; (iii) C admits a loop over the regions such that there exists a reachable region in the loop and one of the regions underapproximates the fair states $F(S)$ of M.

We propose an incomplete procedure to find such C, that relies on a reduction to a sequence of reachability problems and SMT queries. Algorithm 1 shows the main steps required by our procedure. The function FILTER-INCORRECT-HINTS (line 1) filters the list of hints by keeping only those that satisfy condition I: a satisfiability query checks whether two regions admit some transition between them and if this is the case the unsatisfiability of the $\exists \forall \exists$ formula is decided by employing a variant of the approach presented in [16]. Once the correctness of the $\mathcal{AG}$-skeletons has been established the problem of identifying an $\mathcal{R}$-abstraction is encoded as a reachability problem by calling the function GET-REACHABILITY-PROBLEM (line 6). Then, CHECK-REACHABILTY (line 7) relies on a model checker to identify a witness for the reachability problem. From the witness COMPOSITION-FROM-TRACE (line 11) constructs a candidate composition. At this point CHECK-ASSUMPTIONS (line 12) checks whether the candidate composition satisfies also the compatibility requirement of the composition operator, via a sequence of SMT validity checks. If all those checks succeed then we found a composition that meets all the requirements and the procedure stops; otherwise, at least one validity check failed, and the SMT solver provides an assignment that describes a transition for each $\mathcal{AG}$-skeleton such that those transitions are not *compatible*. In the pseudocode, we refer to this assignment as *bad*. We can refine our reachability encoding by forbidding such composition, by adding $\neg bad$ as an additional invariant constraint to the reachabiliy problem. In this way, we keep refining the encoding and asking the model checker for a candidate composition, until either a valid composition is found or the target state becomes unreachable. In this second case the procedure must stop without providing a definite answer (line 9).

Algorithm 1. FIND-COMPOSITION(M, $\mathcal{H}$)

1: $\mathcal{H} \leftarrow$ FILTER-INCORRECT-HINTS($\mathcal{H}$)
2: $constr \leftarrow \top$
3: $bad \leftarrow \bot$
4: **while** true **do**
5:    $constr \leftarrow constr \wedge \neg bad$
6:    $prob \leftarrow$ GET-REACHABILITY-PROBLEM($\mathcal{H}, M, constr$)
7:    $trace \leftarrow$ CHECK-REACHABILTY($prob$)
8:    **if** $trace = \emptyset$ **then**
9:       **return** $\emptyset$
10:   **end if**
11:   $comp \leftarrow$ COMPOSITION-FROM-TRACE($trace, \mathcal{H}$)
12:   $bad \leftarrow$ CHECK-ASSUMPTIONS($comp$)
13:   **if** $bad = \bot$ **then**
14:      **return** $comp$
15:   **end if**
16: **end while**

We now describe how we build the transition system and the reachability problem returned in line 6. We begin by computing, using a sequence of SMT validity checks, underapproximations of T and F that will allow us to construct a composition satisfying conditions H.3 and H.4, while H.5, H.6 and H.7 are implied by I if the composition allows for at least a loop over the regions.

Condition H.3 [resp. H.4] requires us to decide whether the transition relation [resp. some region] of the composed $\mathcal{AG}$-skeleton implies the transition relation [resp. fairness condition] of M. The transition relation and regions of the composed $\mathcal{AG}$-skeleton, by definition of the composition operator, are given by the conjunction of the transition relations and restricted regions of the $\mathcal{AG}$-skeletons involved in the composition. Therefore, we need to decide the validity of a formula of shape $(\bigwedge_{j=0}^{k} c_j) \rightarrow \phi$, where ϕ is either the transition relation or the fairness condition of M and the c_j are, respectively, the transition relations or the restricted regions of the components. Assume ϕ is in negated normal form. We apply the following rewriting recursively:

$$((\bigwedge_{j=0}^{k} c_j) \to \phi) \mapsto \begin{cases} ((\bigwedge_{j=0}^{k} c_j) \to \phi_0) \wedge ((\bigwedge_{j=0}^{k} c_j) \to \phi_1) & \text{if } \phi \doteq \phi_0 \wedge \phi_1 \\ ((\bigwedge_{j=0}^{k} c_j) \to \phi_0) \vee ((\bigwedge_{j=0}^{k} c_j) \to \phi_1) & \text{if } \phi \doteq \phi_0 \vee \phi_1 \end{cases}$$

Notice that in the second case, if the formulae contain some non-convex theory it might be the case that the original formula holds while our rewritten formula does not. Therefore, we are guaranteed that if the rewritten formula holds, so does the original implication, but the vice-versa might not hold. We apply this rewriting until we obtain a formula that is the conjunction and disjunction of implications with a single positive or negated literal on the right hand side. Finally, we again underapproximate the truth assignment of each implication $(\bigwedge_{j=0}^{k} c_j) \to l$, where l is either a positive or negative literal by checking whether for some c_j the following is valid: $c_j \to l$. We rely on the SMT-solver to decide the validity of such implications, and include such results in our encoding of the problem such that any composition will satisfy conditions H.3 and H.4. In the following we detail how we include these observations in the encoding of our problem. We remark that we need to handle the case in which the SMT-solver is unable to provide a definite answer (e.g. because it runs out of resources and/or the support for the underlying theory is incomplete). Let $\mathcal{P}^T$ and $\mathcal{P}^F$ be the set of atomic formulas occurring in $\text{NNF}(T)$ and $\text{NNF}(F)$ respectively. We introduce, for each $\mathcal{AG}$-skeleton H^j in $\mathcal{H}$, for each predicate $f_k \in \mathcal{P}^F$, a boolean variable $\text{IST}(f_k^H, i)$, and for each predicate $t_k \in \mathcal{P}^T$, a boolean variable $\text{IST}(t_k^H, i, i')$. We define, for each regions $R_i^j, R_{i'}^j \in \mathcal{R}^j$,

$$eval(\text{IST}(f_k^H, i)) := \begin{cases} \top & \text{if } R_i^j \wedge A_i^j \models p_k^F \\ \bot & \text{if } R_i^j \wedge A_i^j \models \neg p_k^F \\ ? & \text{otherwise} \end{cases}$$

$$eval(\text{IST}(t_k^H, i, i')) := \begin{cases} \top & \text{if } R_i^j \wedge A_i^j \wedge T^j \wedge \\ & R_{i'}^j \wedge A_{i'}^j \models p_k^F \\ \bot & \text{if } R_i^j \wedge A_i^j \wedge T^j \wedge \\ & R_{i'}^j \wedge A_{i'}^j \models \neg p_k^F \\ ? & \text{otherwise} \end{cases}$$

We then combine the predicates for all $\mathcal{AG}$-skeletons in $\mathcal{H}$ by defining

$$\text{IST}(f_k, i) \doteq (\bigvee_{H^j \in \mathcal{H}} \text{IST}(f^{H^j}, i) = \top) \wedge \bigwedge_{H^j \in \mathcal{H}} \text{IST}(f^{H^j}, i) \neq \bot$$

and its negated counterpart as

$$\text{ISF}(f_k, i) \doteq (\bigvee_{H^j \in \mathcal{H}} \text{IST}(f^{H^j}, i) = \bot) \wedge \bigwedge_{H^j \in \mathcal{H}} \text{IST}(f^{H^j}, i) \neq \top$$

Similarly we define $\text{IST}(t_k, i, i')$ and $\text{ISF}(t_k, i, i')$ over the $\text{IST}(t^{H^j}, i, i')$. The *universal abstraction* of F, denoted as $\widehat{F}$, at region R_i is obtained by replacing in $\text{NNF}(F)$ every positive literal f_k with $\text{IST}(f_k, i)$ and every negative literal $\neg f_k$ with $\text{ISF}(f_k, i)$. The universal abstraction of T, denoted as $\widehat{T}$, between regions R_i and $R_{i'}$ is obtained similarly by replacing in $\text{NNF}(T)$ every positive [negative, resp.] occurrence $t_k \in T$ with $\text{IST}(t_k, i, i')$ [$\text{ISF}(t_k, i, i')$, resp.].

Since $\widehat{T} \models T$ and $\widehat{F} \models F$, in our encoding we need to ensure that $\widehat{T}$ holds in every transition and that there exists a region in the loop that satisfies $\widehat{F}$.

With the construction above, we can now define the transition system $E \doteq \langle S^E, I^E, T^E, F^E \rangle$ as follows:

- $S^E \doteq S \cup S^H \cup S^{Choice} \cup \{prefix\} \cup S^{l2s} \cup S^P$, where:
  - S are the symbols of the input system M;
  - $S^H \doteq \{l_{H^j} \mid H^j \in \mathcal{H}\}$ are symbols used to keep track of the index of the current region of each $\mathcal{AG}$-skeleton H^j;
  - $S^{Choice} \doteq \{enable_{H^j} \mid H^j \in \mathcal{H}\}$ is a set of booleans;
  - $prefix$ is an integer;
  - $S^{l2s} \doteq \{inLoop, fairLoop\} \cup \{lBack_{H^j} \mid H^j \in \mathcal{H}\}$, where the first two are booleans and the $lBack_{H^j}$ are used to nondeterministically choose the loop-back region for the $\mathcal{AG}$-skeleton H^j;
  - $S^P \doteq \{\text{IST}(f_k^{H^j}) | p_k^F \in F \text{ and } H^j \in \mathcal{H}\} \cup \{\text{IST}(t_k^{H^j}) | p_k^T \in T \text{ and } H^j \in \mathcal{H}\}$ are symbols with domain $\{\top, \bot, ?\}$;
- $I^E \doteq I \wedge prefix > 0 \wedge \neg inLoop \wedge \neg fairLoop \wedge I^{Choice}$ is the initial condition, where I^{Choice} constrains the assignments over S^{Choice} such that the symbols of the enabled components are pairwise disjoint and a covering of S (where the set of enabled components in a state s is $\{H^j \in \mathcal{H} \mid s \models enable_{H^j}\}$).
- $T^E \doteq T^{Enable} \wedge T^{Prefix} \wedge T^{Loop}$, where:
  - $T^{Enable} \doteq \bigwedge_{enable_H \in S^{Choice}} enable'_H = enable_H$ ensures that the choice of enabled components is fixed for each trace;
  - $T^{Prefix} \doteq prefix > 0 \rightarrow T(S, S') \wedge prefix' = prefix - 1 \wedge \neg inLoop' \wedge \neg fairLoop'$ allows E to perform $prefix$ steps following the transition relation of M; this prefix ensures the reachability of the resulting composition (hypothesis H.1);
  - $T^{Loop} \doteq prefix = 0 \rightarrow T^{Aut} \wedge T^{l2s} \wedge \widehat{T} \wedge prefix' = 0$ ensures that, as soon as the prefix finishes, $\widehat{T}$, which implies T, holds at every step (hypothesis H.3) and E must follow the transition relation of the enabled $\mathcal{AG}$-skeletons, where:
    * $T^{l2s} \doteq inLoop' = (inLoop \vee lBack) \wedge fairLoop' = (fairLoop \vee \widehat{F})$ and $lBack \doteq \bigwedge_{H^j \in \mathcal{H}} l_{H^j} = lBack_{H^j}$ holds iff all components are in their loopback location.
    * $T^{Aut} \doteq \bigwedge_{H^j \in \mathcal{H}}(enable_{H^j} \rightarrow T^{H^{j\,enabled}}) \wedge (\neg enable_{H^j} \rightarrow l_{H^j} = l'_{H^j} \wedge \bigwedge_{p^H \in S^P} p^H = ?)$ defines how the $\mathcal{AG}$-skeletons evolve: disabled components never change their location and they cannot contribute in satisfying $\widehat{T}$ and $\widehat{F}$, whereas enabled ones evolve according to their transition relation: $T^{H^{j\,enabled}} \doteq T_{H^j}^{PredAbs} \wedge T^{H^j}(S, S') \bigwedge_{i,i'}(l_{H^j} = i \wedge l'_{H^j} = i') \rightarrow R_i^{H^j}(S) \wedge A_i^{H^j}(S)$, where $T_{H^j}^{PredAbs}$ encodes the truth assignments to the S^P as follows: $T_{H^j}^{PredAbs} \doteq (\bigwedge_{R_i \in \mathcal{R}^{H^j}} l_{H^j} = i \rightarrow$

$$\bigwedge_{p_k \in F} \text{IST}(f_k^{H^j}, i) = eval(\text{IST}(f_k^{H^j}, i)) \wedge (\bigwedge_{R_i, R_{i'} \in \mathcal{R}^{H^j}} (l_{H^j} = i \wedge l'_{H^j} =$$
$$i') \rightarrow \bigwedge_{p_k \in T} \text{IST}(t_k^H, i, i') = eval(\text{IST}(t_k^{H^j}, i, i')),$$

where $eval(\text{IST}(f_k^{H^j}, i))$ and $eval(\text{IST}(t_k^{H^j}, i, i'))$ are the assignments we computed previously for the fairness and transition predicates respectively. This transition relation requires to find an assignment for S and S' such that the conjunction of the enabled transitions is satisfied, ensuring that hypothesis I is not trivially satisfied because of the lack of any transition between the regions.

Using this encoding, the reachability problem asks whether there exists a path in E that reaches a state in which $fairLoop \wedge lBack$ holds. T^{l2s} ensures that the path found by the model checker (line 7) will be a lasso-shape over the regions[3], and there will be at least one region in the loop that satisfies $\widehat{F}$, which implies F.

If the model checker finds a path (line 7), the assignments to $enable_{H^j}$ and l_{H^j} for each $H^j \in \mathcal{H}$ describe the subset of $\mathcal{AG}$-skeletons, the locations and transitions to be considered at every state and transition to obtain the composed $\mathcal{R}$-abstraction. In this way we can construct the candidate composition from the obtained trace (line 11).

In the following we show that the $\mathcal{AG}$-skeleton found by Algorithm 1 meets all the hypothesis required for an $\mathcal{R}$-abstraction.

- Hypothesis H.0 holds since in the initial condition I^E we ensure that the local symbols of the $\mathcal{AG}$-skeletons are pairwise disjoint and cover S^M.
- Hypothesis H.1 holds since in the encoding we allow for $prefix$ steps starting from I^M before reaching some conjunction of the regions of the enabled $\mathcal{AG}$-skeletons.
- Hypothesis H.2 holds since the initial condition of the $\mathcal{R}$-abstraction is exactly the state reached after prefix steps, which by construction is in one of the regions.
- Hypothesis H.3 holds since T holds at every step in which $prefix > 0$, and for $prefix = 0$ $\widehat{T}$ must hold, which implies T.
- The liveness-to-safety construction ensures that there exist a region in the composed $\mathcal{AG}$-skeleton that satisfies $\widehat{F}$, and hence implies F. We call such region R_0 in the $\mathcal{R}$-abstraction, hence H.4 holds.
- Hypotheses H.5, H.6 and H.7 are implied by I. The liveness-to-safety construction allows the procedure to find a sequence of regions $R_0, \ldots, R_k$, such that R_0 is fair and $R_k = R_0$, then the encoding E ensures that for all $0 \leq i < k$, $\exists S, S' : R_i(S) \wedge T(S, S') \wedge R_{i+1}(S')$, hence I is not trivially satisfied due to the lack of transitions.

7   Ensuring Divergence of a Given Symbol

In timed and hybrid systems there is an additional requirement for an infinite counterexample to be valid: there is an explicit notion of "time" whose assignments must diverge to infinity. When encoding a hybrid system as a transition

---

[3] Note that this is the liveness-to-safety construction of [7].

system, time is typically modeled with an additional variable δ representing the duration of each transition (where $\delta = 0$ for discrete transitions and $\delta \geq 0$ for transitions corresponding to time elapses). In order for a transition system trace (of infinite length) to be valid for the original hybrid system, it must not impose any upper bound on the total time elapsed; in other words, the assignments of δ along the trace must describe a series that diverges to infinity. We call such traces *non-zeno*.

This section identifies an approach to restrict the language of an $\mathcal{AG}$-skeleton or a $\mathcal{R}$-abstraction to a non-empty set such that "time" is guaranteed to diverge to infinity in all infinite executions in the language. Theorem 4 shows that the composition operator preserves this property.

Theorem 4. *If all infinite executions of the $\mathcal{AG}$-skeleton A responsible for δ are non-zeno, then also every infinite path of every composition, involving A, is non-zeno.*

Therefore, if it is possible to prove this property locally for the $\mathcal{AG}$-skeleton we are guaranteed that the composition will preserve it. However, if the local information is insufficient to determine whether all its traces are non-zeno, a global analysis of the final composition is required. For this reason, we show how to shrink the language of an $\mathcal{AG}$-skeleton or a $\mathcal{R}$-abstraction so that all its paths are non-zeno, while preserving hypothesis I in the first case, and the hypotheses required by Definition 1 of $\mathcal{R}$-abstraction in the second one.

In the following we will refer generically to regions and transitions meaning the restricted region $R_i \wedge A_i$ in the case of an $\mathcal{AG}$-skeleton and the region R_i in the case of an $\mathcal{R}$-abstraction. We write $a +_n b$, with $n \in \mathbb{N}$ to represent the sum of a and b modulo n. We assume that the domain of δ are the positive reals and that the predicates involving δ in every region i and transition from region i to $i +_n 1$ can be written respectively as $\delta \bowtie f(S \setminus \{\delta\})$ and $\delta' \bowtie g(S \setminus \{\delta\}, S' \setminus \{\delta'\})$, where $\bowtie \in \{<, \leq, =, \geq, >\}$.

Consider one loop over the regions at a time. Let $n \in \mathbb{N}$ be the length of such loop and $R_i(S_i)$ be the ith region in the loop. For each transition $T_{i,i+_n 1}(S, S') \doteq R_i(S) \wedge T(S, S') \wedge R_{i+_n 1}(S')$ from R_i to $R_{i+_n 1}$ in the loop assume we are given a function $low_{i,i+_n 1} : S \to \mathbb{R}$ that maps every assignment in $R_i(S)$ to a real value such that:

$$\sum_{it=0}^{\infty} \sum_{i=0}^{n-1} low_{i,i+_n 1}(S_i^{it}) = +\infty$$

where S_i^{it} is the assignment prescribed by the infinite unrolling of the loop at location i during the it^{th} iteration. We want to restrict the paths corresponding to our loop over the regions to only the paths such that:

$$\bigwedge_{i=0}^{n-1} R_i(S_i^{it}) \wedge T_{i,i+_n 1}(S_i^{it}, S_{i+_n 1}^{it}) \wedge \delta_{i+_n 1}^{it} \geq low_{i,i+_n 1}(S_i^{it})$$

for all iterations it and where $\delta_{i+_n 1}$ is the evaluation of δ at location $i +_n 1$. Since the sum of the $low_{i,i+_n 1}$ diverges to infinity and it is a lower bound for the assignments to δ, every path satisfying the condition above is non-zeno.

We now identify some sufficient conditions for this additional constraint to preserve the required hypotheses.

The sufficient condition requires $low_{i,i+_n1}$ to be a lower bound for the smallest upper bound for $\delta_{i,i+_n1}$ at every transition $T_{i,i+_n1}$ for all paths starting from some S_0. We define such bound for transition $T_{i,i+_n1}$ as $min_\delta(S_i, S_{i+_n1})$. $min_\delta(S_i, S_{i+_n1})$ is the minimum of all $g(S_i, S_{i+_n1})$ and $f(S_{i+_n1})$ such that $\delta' \lesssim g(S_i, S_{i,i+_n1}) \in T_{i,i+_n1}(S_i, S_{i+_n1})$ and $\delta' \lesssim f(S_{i+_n1}) \in R_{i+_n1}(S_{i+_n1})$, for some $\lesssim \in \{<, \leq\}$ and functions f, g that do not contain any of δ and δ'. We define the following condition for $low_{i,i+_n1}$:

$$\models \forall S_0, \ldots, S_{n-1} : (\bigwedge_{i=0}^{n-1} R_i(S_i) \wedge T_{i,i+_n1}(S_i, S_{i+_n1}) \wedge R_{i+_n1}(S_{i+_n1})) \rightarrow$$
$$\sum_{i=0}^{n-1} min_\delta(S_i, S_{i+_n1}) > low_{i,i+_n1}(S_i)$$

Theorem 5. *Given a loop over $n \in \mathbb{N}$ regions $R_0(S), \ldots, R_{n-1}(S)$ and n functions $low_{i,i+_n1} : S \rightarrow \mathbb{R}$ that map every state in $R_i(S)$ to a real value, such that the following holds:*

$$\models \forall S_0, \ldots, S_{n-1} : (\bigwedge_{i=0}^{n-1} R_i(S_i) \wedge T_{i,i+_n1}(S_i, S_{i+_n1}) \wedge R_{i+_n1}(S_{i+_n1})) \rightarrow$$
$$\sum_{i=0}^{n-1} min_\delta(S_i, S_{i+_n1}) > low_{i,i+_n1}(S_i)$$

where $min_\delta(S_i, S_{i+_n1})$ is defined as above. Then replacing every transition $T_{i,i+_n1}(S_i, S_{i+_n1})$ with $T_{i,i+_n1}(S_i, S_{i+_n1}) \wedge \delta_{i+_n1} \geq low_{i,i+_n1}(S_i)$ preserves hypothesis I in the case of an $\mathcal{AG}$-skeleton and all the hypotheses of Definition 1 in the case of a $\mathcal{R}$-abstraction.

7.1   Example: Diverging "Time"

Consider the $\mathcal{AG}$-skeleton DV defined in Subsect. 5.1 for the bouncing ball example. We know that in every loop of DV *delta* is equal to zero in region R_0^{DV} and to $\frac{1}{c}$ in R_1^{DV}. However, we do not have any information about c and we are unable to conclude anything about the summation of the assignments to the symbol δ in its executions. Then, we need to consider the $\mathcal{R}$-abstraction represented in Fig. 2. In this case we also know that $c \geq 1$ and its value increases by 1 in every iteration. We can define $low_{1,0}(c) \doteq \frac{1}{c+1}$ and $low_{0,1}(c) \doteq 0$. Their summation can be written as:

$$\sum_{it=0}^{+\infty} low_{0,1}(c^{it}) + low_{1,0}(c^{it}) = \sum_{it=0}^{+\infty} \frac{1}{c^{it} + 1}$$

This corresponds to the well-known diverging harmonic series. Therefore, we can use $low_{0,1}$ and $low_{1,0}$ as lower bounds for δ. In this case this has no effect on the language of $\mathcal{R}$-abstraction, hence all its executions were already non-zeno paths.

8 Related Work

Most of the literature in verification of temporal properties of infinite-state transition systems, hybrid automata and termination analysis focuses on the universal case, while the existential one has received relatively little attention.

The most closely related works to ours are proving *program non-termination*. [25] and [14] are based on the notion of closed recurrence set, that corresponds to proving the non-termination of a relation. We compare our approach with such techniques in Subsect. 4.1 [9] and [32] search for non-terminating executions via a sequence of safety queries. Other approaches look for specific classes of programs ([21] and [26] prove the decidability of termination for linear loops over the integers), or specific non-termination arguments (in [33] non-termination is seen as the sum of geometric series).

A first obvious difference is that these approaches rely on the existence of a control flow graph, whereas we work at the level of transition system. Moreover, none of these works deals with fairness and our approach can be seen as building a generalization of a closed recurrence set to the fair case. Another key difference with all the above approaches is that they synthesize a monolithic non-termination argument. We propose the composition of a finite number of partial non-termination arguments to prove the non-termination of the whole system. Assume-guarantee style compositional reasoning [23] is a broad topic concerned with the verification of properties. Instead, we employ such kind of reasoning for the falsification of temporal properties.

The only work that explicitly deals with fairness for infinite-state programs is [15], that supports full CTL* and is able to deal with existential properties and to provide fair paths as witnesses. The approach is fully automatic, but it focuses on programs manipulating integer variables, with an explicit control-flow graph, rather than more general symbolic transition systems expressed over different theories (including non-linear real arithmetic). Another approach supporting full CTL* is proposed in [28]. The work presents a model checking algorithm for the verification of CTL* on finite-state systems and a deductive proof system for CTL* on infinite-state systems. In the first case they reduce the verification of CTL* properties to the verification of properties without temporal operators and a single fair path quantifier in front of the formula. To the best of our knowledge there is no generalisation of this algorithm, first reported in [29] and then also in [30], to the infinite-state setting. The rules presented in the second case have been exploited in [6] to implement a procedure for the verification of CTL properties, while our objective is the falsification of LTL properties.

Moreover, in these settings [15,28] there is no notion of non-zenoness.

The analysis of *hybrid systems* deals with more general dynamics than our setting. Most of the works focus on the computation of the set of reachable states, with tools such as FLOW* [10], SpaceEx [20], CORA [1], PHAVer [18] and PHAVerLite [3], that compute an overapproximation of the reachable states using different structures, for example Taylor models, polytopes, polyhedra, support functions. Interestingly, Ariadne [5] computes both an over and under approximation of the reachable set, and can prove and disprove a property, but limited to the case of reachability properties. The few works on *falsification of temporal properties* [35,37,38] have the common trait of being the restriction to logic fragments (*bounded-time* MTL, LTL safety properties) for which finite witnesses are sufficient. Tools in this context, such as TALIRO [2], rely on simulations to find such finite witnesses. Instead, we are interested in identifying infinite witnesses for more general temporal properties. Finally, the HyCOMP model checker [13] supports hybrid systems verification of LTL via a reduction to infinite-state model checking. Its verification procedure k-zeno [12] can only disprove the property when lasso-shaped counterexamples exist.

The works on *timed automata* are less relevant: although the concrete system may exhibit no lasso-shape witnesses, due to the divergence of clocks, the problem is decidable, and lasso-shaped counterexamples exist in finite bi-simulating abstractions. This view is adopted in Uppaal [4], CTAV [34] and LTSmin [27]. Other tools directly search for non lasso-shaped counterexamples, but the proposed techniques are specific for the setting of timed automata [11,31] and lack the generality of the method proposed in this paper.

9 Experimental Evaluation

In order to evaluate the practical feasibility of our approach, we have implemented the procedure described in Sect. 6 by relying on the PYSMT library [22] to interact with SMT solvers, and the NUXMV model checker [8] to perform the reachability checks. Our prototype tool FAIRFIND takes as input a symbolic transition system, a fairness condition and a set of $\mathcal{AG}$-skeletons used as building blocks (or *hints*) for constructing the $\mathcal{R}$-abstraction and implements Algorithm 1. When successful, FAIRFIND returns a suitable set of regions $\mathcal{R}$ and a $\mathcal{R}$-abstraction A of M satisfying all the conditions H.0–H.7 presented in Sect. 4. A is the result of a suitable composition of a subset of the input hints[4]. The prototype does not prove the divergence of symbols and the user can rely of the approach presented in Sect. 7 to achieve this. When successful, FAIRFIND is able to produce a *proof* of the validity of the produced $\mathcal{R}$-abstraction as a

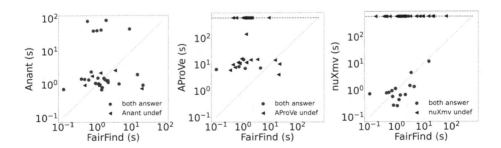

Fig. 3. Execution time of FAIRFIND compared to ANANT, APROVE and NUXMV.

---

[4] Artifact DOI: https://doi.org/10.5281/zenodo.4271411.

sequence of SMT queries, which can be independently checked. This additional check increases the confidence on the correctness of the obtained results. In our evaluation, we have successfully verified the correctness of our results in all cases except 3, for which this additional correctness check fails to provide a definite answer. This fact supports the significance of the approach in the sense that it was able to identify a $\mathcal{R}$-abstraction for which we are unable to directly prove the validity of the required hypotheses.

We have tested FAIRFIND on 43 benchmark instances: 31 are non-linear software non-termination problems, and 12 are LTL verification problems, 9 on hybrid systems and 3 on infinite state transition systems. 29 of the software benchmarks have been taken from [14], while the remaining 2 are new benchmarks we defined. Among the hybrid systems benchmarks, 4 are variations of our running example, whereas the remaining 5 have been taken from the ARCH competition on hybrid systems verification [19]. In our experiment, we have defined the hints manually. In most cases, the $\mathcal{AG}$-skeletons are responsible for the evolution of a single variable of the input system. We defined an average of 5 hints per benchmark (with a minimum of 2 and a maximum of 17). We ran FAIRFIND with a total timeout of 600 s per benchmark, and a timeout of 5 s for each SMT query[5]. FAIRFIND was able to produce a witness $\mathcal{R}$-abstraction for all the benchmarks, suggesting the practical viability of the approach.

We also compared FAIRFIND with two fully automatic procedures for program (non-)termination, ANANT [14] and APROVE [24] (limited to the software non-termination benchmarks), and with the LTL model checker NUXMV [8] (on all the benchmarks). The objective is not to directly contrast the performance of the various tools, as they operate under very different assumptions: FAIRFIND is more general, but it requires human assistance, whereas ANANT and APROVE are specialised tools for software (non-)termination, and NUXMV has very limited support for LTL counterexamples on infinite-state systems [11]. Rather, the goal here is to assess the significance of the benchmarks w.r.t. the state of the art. The results of this experiments are presented in the scatter plots of Fig. 3.

From the plots, we can see that none of the other tools is able to solve all the benchmarks solved by FAIRFIND, and in fact there are 13 instances that are uniquely solved by FAIRFIND (3 of the software benchmarks, 1 of the transition systems and all the hybrid benchmarks).

Figure 4 shows the increase in execution time of FAIRFIND as we increase the number of $\mathcal{AG}$-skeletons provided. The objective of this eval-

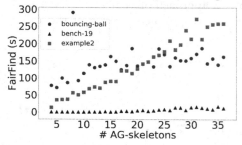

Fig. 4. Execution time of FAIRFIND with increasing number of $\mathcal{AG}$-skeletons.

---

[5] This allows the procedure to make progress even if the solver is unable to provide a definite answer for some query. Many of the benchmarks require reasoning in mixed integer/real non-linear arithmetic (in general undecidable).

uation is to test the robustness of the approach with respect to an increasing number of unnecessary and/or redundant hints. For this reason we increase the number of $\mathcal{AG}$-skeletons such that in all cases the procedure selects the same set of hints. We considered 3 benchmarks: our non-linear, hybrid, running example, one of the software benchmarks taken from [14] (*bench-19*) and one of the non-linear software benchmarks we defined (*example-2*). We let FAIRFIND run with a number of $\mathcal{AG}$-skeletons ranging from 4 to 36. We observe a worst case linear increase in execution time in these experiments. In addition, these benchmarks show two different behaviours. In the bouncing ball and example-2 cases the execution time is dominated by the time required to compute the validity of the implications required for the approximations $\hat{T}$ and $\hat{F}$. In the bench-19 case, the execution time is much lower than in the other two cases, but FAIRFIND performs a higher number of refinements of candidate compositions. In all these cases the procedure has to deal with many non-linear expressions, and this could cause high execution times and instabilities; in fact, sometimes, by increasing the number of $\mathcal{AG}$-skeletons the required time decreases. However, the results we obtained seem promising and we did not observe a blow-up in the time required to identify the $\mathcal{R}$-abstraction.

10 Conclusions

We tackled the problem of proving the existence of fair paths in infinite-state fair transition systems, proposing a deductive framework based on a combination of under-approximations. The framework also encompasses diverging fair paths, required to deal with zenoness. Then, we defined and implemented a procedure to search for a proof based on a suitable composition of $\mathcal{AG}$-skeletons. The experimental evaluation shows that the framework is highly expressive, and the procedure effectively finds fair paths on benchmarks from software non-termination and hybrid systems falsification.

In the future, we will extend the automation of the search procedure and integrate it with a complementary procedure to demonstrate the dual universal property. In order to increase the automation we plan to exploit current techniques in the context of software non-termination and syntax-guided approaches as procedures to synthesise $\mathcal{AG}$-skeletons. Many of the $\mathcal{AG}$-skeletons that have been used in our benchmarks could be synthesised by such techniques. However, some of them, such as the ones in our running example, require the ability to heavily reason about non-linear systems and might be harder to synthesise automatically. For this reason the possibility of taking and verifying hints from the user might be relevant to successfully identify an $\mathcal{R}$-abstraction for complex systems.

We will also experiment the applicability in the finite state case, and integrate the method into satisfiability procedures for temporal logics over hybrid traces.

References

1. Althoff, M.: An introduction to CORA 2015. In: Frehse, G., Althoff, M. (eds.) 1st and 2nd International Workshop on Applied Verification for Continuous and Hybrid Systems, ARCH@CPSWeek 2014, Berlin, Germany, 14 April 2014/ARCH@CPSWeek 2015, Seattle, WA, USA, 13 April 2015. EPiC Series in Computing, vol. 34, pp. 120–151. EasyChair (2015). http://www.easychair.org/publications/paper/248657
2. Annpureddy, Y., Liu, C., Fainekos, G., Sankaranarayanan, S.: S-TaLiRo: a tool for temporal logic falsification for hybrid systems. In: Abdulla, P.A., Leino, K.R.M. (eds.) TACAS 2011. LNCS, vol. 6605, pp. 254–257. Springer, Heidelberg (2011). https://doi.org/10.1007/978-3-642-19835-9_21
3. Becchi, A., Zaffanella, E.: Revisiting polyhedral analysis for hybrid systems. In: Chang, B.-Y.E. (ed.) SAS 2019. LNCS, vol. 11822, pp. 183–202. Springer, Cham (2019). https://doi.org/10.1007/978-3-030-32304-2_10
4. Behrmann, G., David, A., Larsen, K.G.: A tutorial on Uppaal. In: Bernardo, M., Corradini, F. (eds.) SFM-RT 2004. LNCS, vol. 3185, pp. 200–236. Springer, Heidelberg (2004). https://doi.org/10.1007/978-3-540-30080-9_7
5. Benvenuti, L., Bresolin, D., Collins, P., Ferrari, A., Geretti, L., Villa, T.: Assume-guarantee verification of nonlinear hybrid systems with ariadne. Int. J. Robust Nonlinear Control 24(4), 699–724 (2014)
6. Beyene, T.A., Popeea, C., Rybalchenko, A.: Solving existentially quantified horn clauses. In: Sharygina, N., Veith, H. (eds.) CAV 2013. LNCS, vol. 8044, pp. 869–882. Springer, Heidelberg (2013). https://doi.org/10.1007/978-3-642-39799-8_61
7. Biere, A., Artho, C., Schuppan, V.: Liveness checking as safety checking. Electron. Notes Theor. Comput. Sci. 66(2), 160–177 (2002). https://doi.org/10.1016/S1571-0661(04)80410-9
8. Cavada, R., et al.: The nuXmv symbolic model checker. In: Biere, A., Bloem, R. (eds.) CAV 2014. LNCS, vol. 8559, pp. 334–342. Springer, Cham (2014). https://doi.org/10.1007/978-3-319-08867-9_22
9. Chen, H.-Y., Cook, B., Fuhs, C., Nimkar, K., O'Hearn, P.: Proving nontermination via safety. In: Ábrahám, E., Havelund, K. (eds.) TACAS 2014. LNCS, vol. 8413, pp. 156–171. Springer, Heidelberg (2014). https://doi.org/10.1007/978-3-642-54862-8_11
10. Chen, X., Sankaranarayanan, S., Ábrahám, E.: Flow* 1.2: more effective to play with hybrid systems. In: Frehse, G., Althoff, M. (eds.) 1st and 2nd International Workshop on Applied Verification for Continuous and Hybrid Systems, ARCH@CPSWeek 2014, Berlin, Germany, 14 April 2014/ARCH@CPSWeek 2015, Seattle, WA, USA, 13 April 2015. EPiC Series in Computing, vol. 34, pp. 152–159. EasyChair (2015). http://www.easychair.org/publications/paper/248659
11. Cimatti, A., Griggio, A., Magnago, E., Roveri, M., Tonetta, S.: Extending nuXmv with timed transition systems and timed temporal properties. In: Dillig, I., Tasiran, S. (eds.) CAV 2019. LNCS, vol. 11561, pp. 376–386. Springer, Cham (2019). https://doi.org/10.1007/978-3-030-25540-4_21
12. Cimatti, A., Griggio, A., Mover, S., Tonetta, S.: Verifying LTL properties of hybrid systems with K-Liveness. In: Biere, A., Bloem, R. (eds.) CAV 2014. LNCS, vol. 8559, pp. 424–440. Springer, Cham (2014). https://doi.org/10.1007/978-3-319-08867-9_28

13. Cimatti, A., Griggio, A., Mover, S., Tonetta, S.: HyComp: an SMT-based model checker for hybrid systems. In: Baier, C., Tinelli, C. (eds.) TACAS 2015. LNCS, vol. 9035, pp. 52–67. Springer, Heidelberg (2015). https://doi.org/10.1007/978-3-662-46681-0_4

14. Cook, B., Fuhs, C., Nimkar, K., O'Hearn, P.W.: Disproving termination with over-approximation. In: Formal Methods in Computer-Aided Design, FMCAD 2014, Lausanne, Switzerland, 21–24 October 2014, pp. 67–74. IEEE (2014). https://doi.org/10.1109/FMCAD.2014.6987597

15. Cook, B., Khlaaf, H., Piterman, N.: Verifying increasingly expressive temporal logics for infinite-state systems. J. ACM **64**(2), 15:1–15:39 (2017). https://doi.org/10.1145/3060257

16. Dutertre, B.: Solving exists/forall problems with yices. In: Workshop on satisfiability modulo theories (2015)

17. Emerson, E.A., Halpern, J.Y.: "Sometimes" and "not never" revisited: on branching versus linear time temporal logic. J. ACM **33**(1), 151–178 (1986). https://doi.org/10.1145/4904.4999

18. Frehse, G.: PHAVer: algorithmic verification of hybrid systems past HyTech. In: Morari, M., Thiele, L. (eds.) HSCC 2005. LNCS, vol. 3414, pp. 258–273. Springer, Heidelberg (2005). https://doi.org/10.1007/978-3-540-31954-2_17

19. Frehse, G., Althoff, M. (eds.): ARCH19. 6th International Workshop on Applied Verification of Continuous and Hybrid Systemsi, part of CPS-IoT Week 2019, Montreal, QC, Canada, 15 April 2019, EPiC Series in Computing, vol. 61. EasyChair (2019)

20. Frehse, G., et al.: SpaceEx: scalable verification of hybrid systems. In: Gopalakrishnan, G., Qadeer, S. (eds.) CAV 2011. LNCS, vol. 6806, pp. 379–395. Springer, Heidelberg (2011). https://doi.org/10.1007/978-3-642-22110-1_30

21. Frohn, F., Giesl, J.: Termination of triangular integer loops is decidable. In: Dillig, I., Tasiran, S. (eds.) CAV 2019. LNCS, vol. 11562, pp. 426–444. Springer, Cham (2019). https://doi.org/10.1007/978-3-030-25543-5_24

22. Gario, M., Micheli, A.: Pysmt: a solver-agnostic library for fast prototyping of SMT-based algorithms. In: SMT Workshop 2015 (2015)

23. Giannakopoulou, D., Namjoshi, K.S., Păsăreanu, C.S.: Compositional reasoning. Handbook of Model Checking, pp. 345–383. Springer, Cham (2018). https://doi.org/10.1007/978-3-319-10575-8_12

24. Giesl, J., et al.: Proving termination of programs automatically with AProVE. In: Demri, S., Kapur, D., Weidenbach, C. (eds.) IJCAR 2014. LNCS (LNAI), vol. 8562, pp. 184–191. Springer, Cham (2014). https://doi.org/10.1007/978-3-319-08587-6_13

25. Gupta, A., Henzinger, T.A., Majumdar, R., Rybalchenko, A., Xu, R.: Proving non-termination. In: Necula, G.C., Wadler, P. (eds.) Proceedings of the 35th ACM SIGPLAN-SIGACT Symposium on Principles of Programming Languages, POPL 2008, San Francisco, California, USA, 7–12 January 2008, pp. 147–158. ACM (2008). https://doi.org/10.1145/1328438.1328459

26. Hosseini, M., Ouaknine, J., Worrell, J.: Termination of linear loops over the integers. In: Baier, C., Chatzigiannakis, I., Flocchini, P., Leonardi, S. (eds.) 46th International Colloquium on Automata, Languages, and Programming, ICALP 2019, 9–12 July 2019, Patras, Greece. LIPIcs, vol. 132, pp. 118:1–118:13. Schloss Dagstuhl - Leibniz-Zentrum für Informatik (2019). https://doi.org/10.4230/LIPIcs.ICALP.2019.118

27. Kant, G., Laarman, A., Meijer, J., van de Pol, J., Blom, S., van Dijk, T.: LTSmin: high-performance language-independent model checking. In: Baier, C., Tinelli, C. (eds.) TACAS 2015. LNCS, vol. 9035, pp. 692–707. Springer, Heidelberg (2015). https://doi.org/10.1007/978-3-662-46681-0_61
28. Kesten, Y., Pnueli, A.: A compositional approach to CTL* verification. Theor. Comput. Sci. **331**(2–3), 397–428 (2005). https://doi.org/10.1016/j.tcs.2004.09.023
29. Kesten, Y., Pnueli, A., Raviv, L.: Algorithmic verification of linear temporal logic specifications. In: Larsen, K.G., Skyum, S., Winskel, G. (eds.) ICALP 1998. LNCS, vol. 1443, pp. 1–16. Springer, Heidelberg (1998). https://doi.org/10.1007/BFb0055036
30. Kesten, Y., Pnueli, A., Raviv, L., Shahar, E.: Model checking with strong fairness. Formal Methods Syst. Des. **28**(1), 57–84 (2006). https://doi.org/10.1007/s10703-006-4342-y
31. Kindermann, R., Junttila, T., Niemelä, I.: Beyond lassos: complete SMT-based bounded model checking for timed automata. In: Giese, H., Rosu, G. (eds.) FMOODS/FORTE -2012. LNCS, vol. 7273, pp. 84–100. Springer, Heidelberg (2012). https://doi.org/10.1007/978-3-642-30793-5_6
32. Larraz, D., Nimkar, K., Oliveras, A., Rodríguez-Carbonell, E., Rubio, A.: Proving non-termination using max-SMT. In: Biere, A., Bloem, R. (eds.) CAV 2014. LNCS, vol. 8559, pp. 779–796. Springer, Cham (2014). https://doi.org/10.1007/978-3-319-08867-9_52
33. Leike, J., Heizmann, M.: Geometric nontermination arguments. In: Beyer, D., Huisman, M. (eds.) TACAS 2018. LNCS, vol. 10806, pp. 266–283. Springer, Cham (2018). https://doi.org/10.1007/978-3-319-89963-3_16
34. Li, G.: Checking timed Büchi automata emptiness using LU-abstractions. In: Ouaknine, J., Vaandrager, F.W. (eds.) FORMATS 2009. LNCS, vol. 5813, pp. 228–242. Springer, Heidelberg (2009). https://doi.org/10.1007/978-3-642-04368-0_18
35. Nghiem, T., Sankaranarayanan, S., Fainekos, G.E., Ivancic, F., Gupta, A., Pappas, G.J.: Monte-carlo techniques for falsification of temporal properties of non-linear hybrid systems. In: Johansson, K.H., Yi, W. (eds.) Proceedings of the 13th ACM International Conference on Hybrid Systems: Computation and Control, HSCC 2010, Stockholm, Sweden, 12–15 April 2010, pp. 211–220. ACM (2010). https://doi.org/10.1145/1755952.1755983
36. Pasareanu, C.S., Pelánek, R., Visser, W.: Predicate abstraction with under-approximation refinement. Log. Methods Comput. Sci. **3**(1) (2007). https://doi.org/10.2168/LMCS-3(1:5)2007
37. Plaku, E., Kavraki, L.E., Vardi, M.Y.: Falsification of LTL safety properties in hybrid systems. Int. J. Softw. Tools Technol. Transf. **15**(4), 305–320 (2013). https://doi.org/10.1007/s10009-012-0233-2
38. Sankaranarayanan, S., Fainekos, G.E.: Falsification of temporal properties of hybrid systems using the cross-entropy method. In: Dang, T., Mitchell, I.M. (eds.) Hybrid Systems: Computation and Control (part of CPS Week 2012), HSCC 2012, Beijing, China, 17–19 April 2012, pp. 125–134. ACM (2012). https://doi.org/10.1145/2185632.2185653

A Self-certifying Compilation Framework for WebAssembly

Kedar S. Namjoshi[1]([⊠]) and Anton Xue[2]

[1] Nokia Bell Labs, Murray Hill, NJ 07974, USA
kedar.namjoshi@nokia-bell-labs.com
[2] University of Pennsylvania, Philadelphia, PA 19104, USA
antonxue@seas.upenn.edu

Abstract. A *self-certifying* compiler is designed to generate a correctness proof for each optimization performed during compilation. The generated proofs are checked automatically by an independent proof validator. The outcome is formally verified compilation, achieved *without* formally verifying the compiler. This paper describes the design and implementation of a self-certifying compilation framework for WebAssembly, a new intermediate language supported by all major browsers.

1 Introduction

Compiling is everywhere, in astonishing variety. A compiler systematically transforms a source program into an executable program through a series of "optimizations"—program transformations that improve run-time performance by, for instance, rewriting instructions or compacting memory use. It is vital that each transform preserves input-output behavior, so that the behavior of the final executable is identical to that of the original source program. Compiler writers put considerable care into programming these transforms, but when mistakes happen they are often difficult to detect.

The obvious importance of correct compilation has prompted decades of research on compiler verification. The gold standard is a *verified* compiler, where each transform is formally proved correct. Originally proposed in the 1960s [21], verified compilers have been constructed for Lisp (the CLI stack [4]) and for C (CompCert [18,19]). The proofs require considerable mathematical expertise and substantial effort, of the order of multiple person-years. As an illustration, a proof of the key Static Single Assignment (SSA) transform required about a person-year of effort and approximately 10,000 lines of Coq proof script [36].

© Springer Nature Switzerland AG 2021
F. Henglein et al. (Eds.): VMCAI 2021, LNCS 12597, pp. 127–148, 2021.
https://doi.org/10.1007/978-3-030-67067-2_7

Our research goal is to "democratize" this process by making it feasible for compiler developers who are not also theorem-proving experts to build a provably correct compiler. This requires relaxing the notion of correctness. Rather than establish that a transform is correct for *all* programs, we establish that each *specific application* of the transform is correct. We do so by instrumenting every transform to additionally generate a proof object that (if valid) guarantees that the original and transformed programs have the same input-output behavior. Thus, the work of formal verification is divided between a compiler writer, who writes auxiliary code to generate proofs, and an automated validation program, which checks each proof. We call such a compiler *self-certifying*, for it justifies its own correctness.

An invalid proof exposes either an error in the transform code or a gap in the compiler-writer's understanding of its correctness argument, which are both valuable outcomes. It is important to note that a self-certifying compiler may still contain latent errors: its guarantee applies only to an instance of compilation. Yet, in practice, that is what is desired: a programmer cares (selfishly) only about the correct compilation of their own program.

Self-certification may seem unfamiliar, but it is a recurring concept. A model checker is self-certifying, as a counterexample trace certifies a negative result. A SAT solver is also self-certifying, as an assignment certifies a positive result. For the other outcomes, a deductive proof acts as a certificate: cf. [23,29] for model checking and [35] for SAT. Self-certification for parsing is described in [15]. In each case, the certificate is easy to check, while it justifies the outcome of a rather complex calculation.

This paper describes the design and implementation of a self-certifying optimization framework for WebAssembly, a recently-introduced intermediate language that is supported by all major browsers [14]. Programs in C, C++, Rust, and LLVM IR can be compiled to WebAssembly and run within a browser. We choose to focus on WebAssembly for two main reasons: it is an open and widely-adopted standard, and it has a compact, well-designed instruction set with a precisely defined semantics.

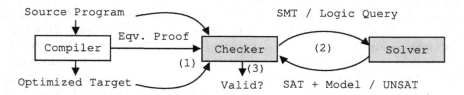

Fig. 1. Self-certification overview. Trusted components are shaded gray.

Figure 1 illustrates the framework. Its core is the proof checker. That takes as input two WebAssembly programs (the source and target of a transform) and a purported equivalence proof, and uses SMT methods to check the validity of this proof. Fortunately, correctness proofs for many standard optimizations can be expressed in logics that are well-supported by SMT solvers.

Armed with a proof validator, one can proceed to augment each optimization with a proof generator. A typical generator records auxiliary information during the transformation and uses it to produce an equivalence proof. In our experience, it is an enjoyable exercise to design proof generators and straightforward to implement them. For instance, proof generation for SSA (described later) requires only about 100 lines of code, and the entire certifying transform was written in three person-weeks.

Self-certification for compilers was originally proposed by Rinard [31] as "credible compilation" and rediscovered in [27] as "witnessing." It is closely related to Translation Validation (TV) [6, 28, 30, 32] but with crucial differences. In TV, a validator has access to only the source and target programs. As program equivalence is undecidable, heuristics are necessary to show equivalence. This has drawbacks: heuristics differ across transforms, and each must be separately verified. In a self-certifying compiler, although the content of a proof depends on the transform, all proofs are checked by the same validator.

Self-certification also has a close relationship to deductive proof. In a deductive proof, the correctness of a transform τ is established by proving that for all programs P, there exists an input-output-preserving simulation relation R such that $\tau(P)$ refines P via R. Through Skolemization, this is equivalent to the existence of a function G such that for all programs P, $\tau(P)$ refines P via $G(P)$. In a self-certifying compiler, the mathematical object G is turned into a computational proof-generator for the transform τ. The generated proof object is the relation $G(P)$, and a validator is thus a generic refinement checker.

While conceptually simple, self-certification is challenging to implement. The first implementations were for a textbook-style language [20]. The most advanced implementation is Crellvm [16], for LLVM. In Crellvm, proofs are syntax-directed, based on relational Hoare logic. While this suffices for many transforms, the authors note in [16] that it cannot support transformations such as loop unrolling that make large alterations to control structure. Our proof format can handle those transforms. An in-depth comparison is given later in the paper.

The central contribution of this work is in defining and implementing a self-certifying compilation framework for a widely-used language.[1] The current system is best thought of as a fledgling compiler for WebAssembly. We have implemented a variety of optimizations, among them SSA, dead store removal, constant propagation and loop unrolling. Experience shows that proof generation imposes only a small programming burden: the typical generator is about a hundred lines of code. Experiments show that the run-time overhead of proof generation is small, under 20%. Proof-checking, on the other hand, may take substantial time (though it is easily parallelized). That is not caused by logical complexity, it is due to the sheer number of lemmas that must be discharged.

---

[1] The implementation is available as open source at https://github.com/nokia/web-assembly-self-certifying-compilation-framework.

The current system has some limitations. Proof-checking is slow, but we believe that can be improved through careful engineering, as each proof is logically simple. A technical limitation is that the proof-checker does not support transforms with unbounded instruction reordering (such as loop tiling), or interprocedural transforms. This is because refinement relations for both require quantification over unbounded auxiliary state. Those transforms *can* be validated with specialized rules that have simpler hypotheses (cf. [1,25,34,37]). Integrating those transforms into the system is a direction for future work.

2   Overview

We illustrate self-certification with the loop unrolling transform. A loop is given as "loop B". For instance, the sum of the first N natural numbers may be expressed as follows. (For readability, this is in pseudo-code, not WebAssembly.)

```
sum := 0; i := 0;
loop {if i >= N then goto Exit; sum := sum + i; i := i+1;}
Exit:
```

The unrolling transformation simply changes the program to "loop (B;B)". This may appear to be of little use. However, unrolling facilitates further analysis and transformation. For the example, assuming N is even, an analysis phase computes invariants such as the assertion below. Then, control-flow simplification applies this invariant to eliminate the second copy of the conditional. The resulting loop executes only half as many conditional tests as the original.

```
assume (N is even); sum := 0; i := 0;
loop {if i >= N then goto Exit; sum := sum + i; i := i+1;
      assert (i < N and i is odd); sum := sum+i; i := i+1;}
Exit:
```

Figure 2 illustrates the template for loop unrolling and its refinement relation. A program is expressed here in the familiar control-flow graph (CFG) form. The refinement relation connects the two state spaces, in this case it is simply the identity relation. It is the responsibility of a compiler writer to think carefully about the correctness argument for a transform and to program a proof generator that produces the right refinement relation and any additional hints.

The proof validator tests the inductiveness of the refinement relation over loop-free path segments by generating lemmas in SMT form. In this example, assuming that states are identical at edges e_0 and f_0, they must be identical after the path segments $f_0; B; f_1$ and $e_0; B; e_1$. Continuing from that point, the segment $f_1; B; f_2$ is matched by $e_1; B; e_1$; segment $f_1; B; f_4$ is matched by $e_1; B; e_2$; and so forth. The proof-generator suggests the segment matches as hints, while the validator ensures that all path segments in the target CFG are covered.

The inductiveness checks combined with segment coverage ensure that validation is sound; i.e., it never accepts an incorrect proof. The use of SMT-supported logics to define the refinement relation ensures that a wide range of proofs can

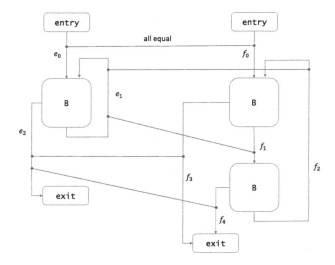

Fig. 2. Loop Unrolling, with refinement relation shown by horizontal lines.

be checked automatically. Fortunately, logical theories that SMT solvers handle well—equality, uninterpreted functions, arrays and integer arithmetic—suffice for many intra-procedural optimizations.

3   WebAssembly: Syntax and Semantics

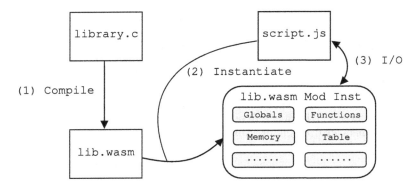

Fig. 3. WebAssembly usage

We summarize the structure and notable features of WebAssembly[2]. A typical setup is shown in Fig. 3. A C program `library.c` is (1) compiled using

---

[2] The full specification is at https://webassembly.github.io/spec/.

tools such as LLVM to produce a WebAssembly module, `lib.wasm`. This module is (2) loaded by a browser via JavaScript to create a sandboxed instance. Communication is bidirectional (3): the JavaScript code may invoke functions of `library.wasm`, and the WebAssembly code invokes JavaScript functions through a foreign-function interface for input and output actions.

$$
\begin{aligned}
\tau \quad &::= \text{i32} \mid \text{i64} \mid \text{f32} \mid \text{f64} \\
\tau^\rightarrow &::= \tau^* \rightarrow \tau^* \quad \text{(Function Type)} \\
\tau_p \quad &::= \text{i8} \mid \text{i16} \mid \text{i32} \quad \text{(Pack Size)} \\
x \quad &::= i_{32} \quad \text{(Variable)} \\
c \quad &::= i_{32} \mid i_{64} \mid f_{32} \mid f_{64} \text{ (Constant)} \\
a \quad &::= i \quad \text{(Address)} \\
o \quad &::= i \quad \text{(Offset)} \\
sx \quad &::= \text{U} \mid \text{S} \quad \text{(Signage)}
\end{aligned}
$$

$unop_i$ ::= Clz | Ctz | Popcnt
$unop_f$ ::= Neg | Abs | Ceil | Floor
        Trunc | Nearest | Sqrt

$binop_i$ ::= Add | Sub | Mul | Div_sx |
       Rem_sx | And | Or | Xor |
       Shl | Shr_sx | Rotl | Rotr
$binop_f$ ::= Add | Sub | Mul | Div |
       Min | Max | CopySign

$testop$ ::= Eqz

$relop_i$ ::= Eq | Ne | Lt_sx |
       Gt_sx | Le_sx | Ge_sx
$relop_f$ ::= Eq | Ne | Lt | Gt | Le | Ge

$cvtop$ ::= ReinterpretFloat |
       ReinterpretInt |
       ExtendSI32 | ...

e ::= (Numeric Instructions)
Const c | Unary $unop$ | Binary $binop$ |
Test $testop$ | Compare $relop$ | Convert $cvtop$ |

(Type-Parametric Instructions)
Nop | Drop | Select |

(Variable Instructions)
LocalGet x | LocalSet x | LocalTee x |
GlobalGet x | GlobalSet x |

(Memory Instructions)
Load τ a o $\tau_p^?$ | Store τ a o $(\tau_p\, sx)^?$ |
MemorySize | MemoryGrow |

(Control Flow Instructions)
Block $\tau^\rightarrow$ e^* | Loop $\tau^\rightarrow$ e^* | If $\tau^\rightarrow$ e^* |
Br x | BrIf x | BrTable x^* x |
Return | Call x | CallIndirect x |
Unreachable

$$
\begin{aligned}
tys \quad &::= \text{types } \{x \rightarrow \tau^\rightarrow\} \\
f \quad &::= \text{function } x\,\tau^*\, e^* \\
funcs &::= \text{functions } \{x \rightarrow f\} \\
glob \quad &::= \text{global } x\, c \\
mem \quad &::= \text{memory } \{a \rightarrow i\} \\
tab \quad &::= \text{table } \{x \rightarrow a\} \\
mod \quad &::= \text{module } tys\, funcs\, glob\, tab\, mem
\end{aligned}
$$

Fig. 4. The WebAssembly instruction set of the reference interpreter: ($\star$) denotes zero or more occurrences, (?) denotes zero or one occurrence. The SSA transform introduces a "phi" assignment instruction, described in Sect. 5.

3.1 The WebAssembly Instruction Set

The core WebAssembly instruction set is shown in Fig. 4. Our presentation is closely based on that in the reference interpreter[3]. The instruction set is a rather standard set of instructions designed for a stack machine with auxiliary local

---
[3] https://github.com/WebAssembly/spec.

and global memory. A module instance contains a stack of values, local variable stores, a global variable store, a linear memory array, and a function table. These spaces are disjoint from each other, a security feature.

WebAssembly programs operate on a small set of basic data types: integer data (i32, i64) and floating point data (f32, f64). Booleans are i32 values. The sign interpretation for integer values is determined by each operator in its own way (e.g., LeU and LeS). The memory model is simple. Each module has a global memory store. Each function has its own local memory store. The global *linear memory* map is a contiguous, byte-addressable memory from index 0 to an (adjustable) MemorySize. A function table stores references to functions, which are invoked via the CallIndirect instruction. All input or output is carried out through indirect calls to JavaScript functions.

Evaluation is stack based. *Numeric instructions* operate over values obtained from the top of the evaluation stack and return the result to the top of the evaluation stack. Many instructions (e.g., add) are polymorphic and could be partially defined (e.g., no divide by 0). Execution halts (*"traps"*) if the next instruction is undefined at the current state. *Type-parametric instructions* are used to modify the evaluation stack. For instance, drop pops the topmost value on the stack, while select pops the three topmost values and pushes back one chosen value. *Variable instructions* are used to access the local variables of a function (which include its parameters), and the global store. *Memory instructions* are used to access the linear memory, and are parametrized with the index, offset, size, and type of the data to be stored or retrieved.

Unusually for a low-level language, control flow in WebAssembly is structured. Break (jump) instructions like Br transfer control only to labels defined in the surrounding scope. A branch instruction is parametrized by an i32 value that determines the number of nested levels to break out of. The Block, Loop, and If instructions generate new, well-nested labels. A function invocation via Call pops the appropriate number of arguments from the top of the stack and pushes back the return values when completed via Return. A trapping state is entered with the Unreachable instruction, which aborts execution.

3.2   WebAssembly Semantics

The standard semantics of WebAssembly [14] is syntax-directed, combining control and execution state in a single stack. While this is mathematically convenient, compiler optimizations are typically framed in a control-flow graph representation that separates control from execution: control is represented by the edges and execution by operations labeling vertices. The translation of a WebAssembly program to a control-flow graph is illustrated in Fig. 5.

A *control-flow graph* (CFG) is a labeled directed graph $G = (V, E, \mathsf{label})$, where V is the set of vertices, $E \subseteq V \times V$ is the set of edges, and label is a labeling function. It has a single *entry* vertex with indegree 0 and outdegree 1 (the entry edge), and a single *exit* vertex with indegree 1 (the exit edge) and outdegree 0. A *path* is a sequence of vertices where each adjacent pair is an edge. Vertex m is reachable from vertex n if there is a path where the initial vertex is

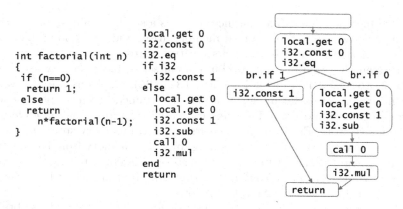

Fig. 5. Conversion from C to WebAssembly to a CFG. The `factorial` function is invoked recursively as (`call 0`) in WebAssembly.

n and the final vertex is m. Every vertex is reachable from the entry vertex and reaches the exit vertex.

The labeling function associates each vertex with a list of basic instructions, called a *basic block*; the entry vertex is mapped to the empty list and the exit vertex to a single return instruction (the only block with this instruction). Each function call is its own block, labeling a node with indegree and outdegree 1. Every edge is labeled by a Boolean-valued function; the entry edge is labeled *true*. These structural conditions simplify the validation of witnesses.

A *labeled transition system* (LTS for short) is defined by a tuple of the form (S, I, T, Σ) where S is a set of states, $I \subseteq S$ is a non-empty set of initial states, Σ is an alphabet, and $T \subseteq S \times (\Sigma \cup \{\tau\}) \times S$ is a (labeled) transition relation, where τ is a symbol not in Σ. An (infinite) *execution* from a state s is an infinite sequence of alternating states and labels $s_0 = s, a_0, s_1, a_1, s_2, \ldots$ such that for each i, the triple (s_i, a_i, s_{i+1}) is in T. The *observation* sequence of this execution is the projection of the sequence $a_0, a_1, \ldots$ on Σ. A *computation* is an execution from an initial state. The *language* of an LTS is the set of observation sequences produced by its computations.

An *evaluation context* for a function, denoted cxt, is a tuple (K, L, G, M) where K is an evaluation stack for that function, L maps local variables (including parameters) to values, G maps global variables to values, and M maps natural numbers to values, representing the linear memory.

WebAssembly Semantics. The semantics of a program P is given as an LTS lts(P), defined as follows. The set of states S consists of tuples of the form (C, G, M) where C is a *call stack* (defined next) and G and M represent the global and linear memory maps, respectively. There is a special trap state, with a self-loop. A call stack is a sequence of *frames* (also called "activation records"). A frame is a tuple $(f, K, L, (e, k))$ where f is a function name; K is an evaluation stack (a list of values); L is a local variable map whose domain includes the function parameters; and (e, k) is a *location* within the CFG for f, where e is a CFG edge and k is an index into the basic block associated with the vertex that the target of e.

The initial state is $(\hat{C}, \hat{G}, \hat{M})$. The initial call stack $\hat{C}$ contains a single activation record for the start function of a WebAssembly module. The local, global and memory maps are initialized as defined by the WebAssembly specification, edge e is the entry edge of the start function CFG, and $k = 0$.

A transition is either a local transition modifying only the top frame on the call stack; a function call, adding a frame; or a function return, removing the top frame. Undefined behavior (e.g., a division by 0) results in a transition to the trap state. The precise definition of transitions is in the full paper.

Input and output in WebAssembly is via the foreign-function interface; the browser also has access to the global and linear memories. The only observable transitions are therefore foreign function invocations and the final transition returning from the start function with its associated global and linear memories.

Definition 1 (Transformation Correctness). *A program transformation modifying program P to program Q is correct if the language of the transition system for Q is a subset of the language of the transition system for P.*

Transformation correctness therefore requires that calls to foreign functions are carried out in the same order and with the same actual arguments and memory maps in both source and target programs, and that the memory values upon termination of the WebAssembly program are identical. In our proof validator, we strengthen the foreign call requirement to apply to all function calls.

4   Witness Structure and Validation

We consider a program transformation that changes the structure and labeling of a CFG for a single function, keeping parameters and entry and exit nodes unchanged. Let $\mathcal{G}$ denote the source CFG and $\mathcal{H}$ the modified CFG for that function. A *proof witness* is defined by a correspondence between the execution contexts of $\mathcal{H}$ and $\mathcal{G}$ that meets certain inductiveness conditions. We prove that these conditions suffice to establish transformation correctness. The structure of a witness is defined by the following components:

A witness identifies a subset of the edges of each graph, referred to as the *checkpoint* edges and denoted $\mathsf{ckpt}(X)$ for graph X. This set must include the entry and exit edge of the graph and form a feedback-edge set (i.e., every cycle in the graph contains a checkpoint edge). For each node labeled with a function call, its adjacent edges must be checkpoint edges.

From these structural conditions, it follows that every path from a checkpoint edge must eventually cross another checkpoint edge. Let $\mathsf{frontier}(X, e)$ be the set of finite paths in graph X that start at edge e and end at a checkpoint edge with no checkpoint edges in between.

A witness specifies a partial function $W : \mathsf{ckpt}(\mathcal{H}) \times \mathsf{ckpt}(\mathcal{G}) \to (\mathsf{cxt}(\mathcal{H}) \to$ $\mathsf{cxt}(\mathcal{G}) \to \mathsf{Bool})$. This defines the relationship between source and target states that holds on the given pair of edges: concretely, the value of $W(f, e)$ for an edge pair (f, e) is a predicate defined on target and source contexts. The entry edges of $\mathcal{H}, \mathcal{G}$ must be in the domain of W.

The final component of a witness is a function choice that maps a pair of edges (f, e) in the domain of W and a path q in $\mathsf{frontier}(\mathcal{H}, f)$ to a path p in $\mathsf{frontier}(\mathcal{G}, e)$. This relates paths in the target to paths in the source.

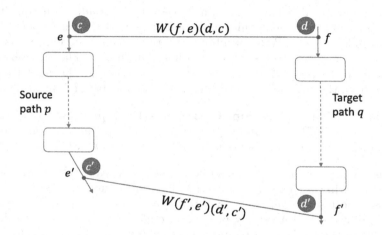

Fig. 6. Path matching and inductiveness. Note the mnemonic patterns: edges (e/f), paths (p/q), and contexts (c/d) for the source/target programs.

Valid Witnesses As illustrated in Fig. 6, let (f, e) be an edge pair such that $W(f, e)$ is defined. Let q be a path in $\mathsf{frontier}(\mathcal{H}, f)$ and let $p = \mathsf{choice}((f, e), q)$ be its matching path in $\mathsf{frontier}(\mathcal{G}, e)$. Let f', e' be the final edges on the paths q, p respectively.

A *basic* path is one where no vertex is labeled with a function call or return. Every basic path q induces a sequence denoted $\mathsf{actions}(q)$ that contains only non-call-or-return instructions labeling the vertices and Boolean guards labeling the edges on the path. The semantics of each action a in context d is specified by (1) predicate $\mathsf{def}(a, d)$ which is true if a is well-defined at d; (2) predicate $\mathsf{en}(a, d)$ which is true (assuming a is well-defined) if a is enabled at d; and (3) a partial function $\mathsf{eval}(a, d)$ (defined if a is well-defined and enabled) which produces a new context. For WebAssembly instructions, eval is defined in Fig. 8; def and en are defined in the full version of this paper.

For an action sequence σ, the predicate $\mathsf{enabled}(\sigma, d)$ is recursively defined as follows, where $d' = \mathsf{eval}(a, d)$:

$$\mathsf{enabled}(\epsilon, d) = true$$
$$\mathsf{enabled}(a : x, d) = \mathsf{def}(a, d) \wedge \mathsf{en}(a, d) \wedge \mathsf{enabled}(x, d').$$

Similarly, if σ is enabled at d, then $\mathsf{exec}(\sigma, d)$ and $\mathsf{trapped}(\sigma, d)$ are defined by

$$\mathsf{exec}(\epsilon, d) = d$$
$$\mathsf{exec}(a : x, d) = \mathsf{exec}(x, d')$$
$$\mathsf{trapped}(\epsilon, d) = false$$
$$\mathsf{trapped}(a : x, d) = \neg\mathsf{def}(a, d) \vee (\mathsf{en}(a, d) \wedge \mathsf{trapped}(x, d')).$$

We define $\mathsf{enabled}(q, d)$ for a path q as $\mathsf{enabled}(\mathsf{actions}(q), d)$, and similarly define $\mathsf{eval}(q, d)$ and $\mathsf{trapped}(q, d)$. The witness validity conditions are defined as follows:

Initiality. For the entry edges $\hat{f}, \hat{e}$ of $\mathcal{H}$ and $\mathcal{G}$, respectively, $W(\hat{f}, \hat{e})$ must be the identity relation.

Path Matching. q and p are either basic paths; or both have only a single vertex that is labeled either with return, or with identical function calls.

Enabledness. Path p is enabled if q is enabled. That is[4],

$$[W(f, e)(d, c) \wedge \mathsf{enabled}(q, d) \;\Rightarrow\; \mathsf{enabled}(p, c)]$$

Trapping. If path q leads to a trap, so does path p.

$$[W(f, e)(d, c) \wedge \mathsf{trapped}(q, d) \;\Rightarrow\; \mathsf{trapped}(p, c)]$$

Non-blocking: Basic Path. Execution of q cannot be blocked. Precisely, for a basic path q, the Boolean guard on edges on q other than the initial and final edge must be true for every initial context d such that $W(f, e)(c, d)$ holds.

Inductiveness: Basic Path. The context obtained by executing the instructions on path q is related by W to the context obtained by executing instructions on path p.

$$[W(f, e)(d, c) \wedge \mathsf{enabled}(q, d) \wedge d' = \mathsf{exec}(q, d)$$
$$\wedge \; c' = \mathsf{exec}(p, c) \;\Rightarrow\; W(f', e')(d', c')].$$

Inductiveness: Function Call. The paths have identical call instructions. The call state (global, linear memory, and parameter values) should be identical prior to the call. Assuming the call requires k parameters, the length k stack prefixes $d(K)[0..k)$ and $c(K)[0..k)$, which represent the top k values on the respective stacks, must be identical.

$$[W(f, e)(d, c) \;\Rightarrow\; d(G, M, K[0..k)) = c(G, M, K[0..k))]$$

---

[4] The formal statements follow Dijkstra-Scholten convention [9], where $[\varphi]$ indicates that the expression φ is valid. We use $d(X, Y, \ldots)$ to abbreviate $(d(X), d(Y), \ldots)$.

W must also hold of the stacks obtained after removing the call arguments:

$$[W(f,e)(d,c) \wedge d'(L,G,M) = d(L,G,M) \wedge d'(K) = d(K[k..])$$
$$\wedge \ c'(L,G,M) = c(L,G,M) \wedge c'(K) = c(K[k..]) \ \Rightarrow \ W(f,e)(d',c')]$$

These conditions ensure that corresponding calls behave identically. After the calls, $W(f',e')$ must hold with the (unspecified but same) result v:

$$[W(f,e)(d,c) \wedge d'(G,M) = c'(G,M)$$
$$\wedge \ d'(K) = v : d(K[k..]) \wedge c'(K) = v : c(K[k..])$$
$$\wedge \ c'(L) = c(L) \wedge d'(L) = d(L) \ \Rightarrow \ W(f',e')(d',c')]$$

Inductiveness: Function Return. The values at the top of the stack must be identical, as must the global and linear memories. I.e.,

$$[W(f,e)(d,c) \ \Rightarrow \ d(G,M) = c(G,M) \wedge d(K)[0] = c(K)[0]]$$

Theorem 1. *(Soundness) If there is a valid proof witness for a transformation from program P (CFG $\mathcal{G}$) to program Q (CFG $\mathcal{H}$), the transformation from P to Q is correct.*

Proof. (Sketch) We have to show that the language of $\mathsf{lts}(Q)$ is a subset of the language of $\mathsf{lts}(P)$. This is done by setting up a simulation relation between the (unbounded) state spaces of these transition systems. Roughly speaking, this relation matches the sequence of frames on the source call stack with those on the target call stack, relating frames for unmodified functions with the identity relation, and relating frames for the modified function by W. The complete proof (in the full paper) establishes that under the witness validity conditions, this relation is a stuttering simulation that preserves observations.   □

5   Proof Generation

We illustrate, using the example of the SSA transform, how a compiler writer programs a proof generator by weaving it into the optimization algorithm. Besides SSA, the system includes proof generating versions of several common optimizations, such as dead store elimination, loop unrolling, constant propagation and folding, a "compress-locals" transform peculiar to WebAssembly which compacts the local memory array, removing unused entries and renaming the others, and finally the unSSA transformation that takes a program out of SSA form. In each case, the proof generator is approximately 100 lines of code; the actual transform is between 500–700 lines of code.

The safety net provided by the validator is analogous to the safety guarantee provided by a strong type system. Programming can proceed as usual, with the reassurance that validation will not allow incorrect compilation. Indeed, we have occasionally made mistakes in programming optimizations (common mistakes such as cut-and-paste errors and missing cases), which have been caught by the proof validator.

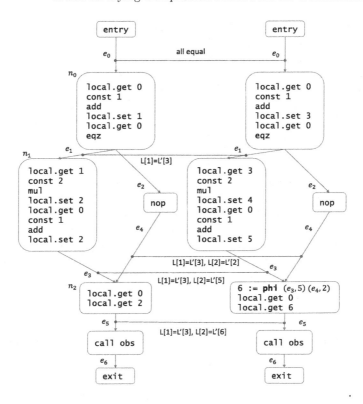

Fig. 7. Example SSA transform. Source on the left, result on the right.

SSA is a key transformation in modern compilers. It ensures that in the target program, every variable appears on the left hand side of at most one assignment statement (hence the name). The transformation does not improve performance; instead, it essentially builds definition-use chains into the program text. This structural property considerably simplifies follow-on transformations that do optimize performance, such as dead store elimination (DSE).

For WebAssembly, we apply the SSA transformation to local memory, accessed via `LocalGet`, `LocalSet` and `LocalTee` operations. An example of the SSA transform is shown in Fig. 7. The source program is on the left, the target on the right. Notice that the two assignments to index 2 at node n_1 have been replaced with assignments to fresh indexes 4 and 5 in the target program.

SSA introduces the new, so-called "phi" assignment statement. There are two distinct paths in the source program that reach the node n_2. The value of $L[2]$ differs along those paths: in the SSA version it is represented as $L'[5]$ for the left-hand path and as $L'[2]$ for the right-hand path. Those values must necessarily be merged to correctly represent the value of $L[2]$ at source node n_2. This is the role of the phi assignment. The syntax $6 := \mathsf{phi}\,(e_3, 5)(e_4, 2)$ represents that

$L'[6]$ should get the value of $L'[5]$ on an execution that follows edge e_3 and the value of $L'[2]$ on an execution that follows edge e_4.

The witness validation conditions are easily adapted to take phi-instructions into account: phi-instructions on a node of a source or target path are resolved to a simple assignment based on the path edge that enters the node.

As should be clear from this example, the SSA transformation is in essence a renaming of variables—but with a twist, in that the renaming is not uniform over the program. For example, $L[2]$ is represented at various points in the target program by $L'[2]$, $L'[4]$, $L'[5]$, and $L'[6]$. The correspondence between source and target program must reflect this fact. To avoid clutter, the figure only shows the important portions of the correspondence[5]. It should be easy to check that the full correspondence is inductive and that (as the stack and global memories are identical) the call to the obs function (short for "observable") must obtain identical actual parameters and thus produce identical results.

A proof generator must generate such a correspondence for the SSA transformation on *any* program. We explain next how this is done. Proof generation is necessarily dependent on the algorithm used for SSA conversion. We base the explanation on the well known algorithm of Cytron et al [7], which is implemented in our framework.

SSA Algorithm. The SSA conversion algorithm operates in two stages. Our description must necessarily be brief; for more detail, please refer to the original article [7]. In Stage 1, the location and form of the necessary phi-assignments is determined, while Stage 2 fills in the details of those assignments.

The first stage is technically complex. First, for each local index k, the set of nodes asgn(k) is determined, this is the set of nodes that contain an assignment to k (through LocalSet or LocalTee). Then the *iterated dominance frontier* of asgn(k) is determined; those are precisely the nodes that must have a phi-assignment for k. Dominance is a standard notion in program analysis. In short, node n *dominates* node m if every path in the CFG from the entry node to m must pass through node n. A node m is in the *dominance frontier* of node n if m is *not* strictly dominated by n but some predecessor of m is dominated by n. The dominance frontier of a set X of nodes (denoted $\mathsf{DF}(X)$) is the union of the individual dominance frontiers. The *iterated* dominance frontier (IDF) of a set X is defined as the least fixed point of the function $(\lambda Z : \mathsf{DF}(X \cup Z))$.

For our source program, asgn$(2) = \{\text{entry}, n_1\}$; it includes the entry node as all variables are initialized. The IDF of this set is just the singleton $\{n_2\}$. Thus there must be a phi-assignment for $L[2]$ at node n_2. However, the details of this assignment; in particular, which renamed versions of $L[2]$ reach this node, is not yet known. That information is filled in by Stage 2.

The second stage does a depth-first traversal of the CFG. For each original index, the traversal carries a stack of fresh index values that are used to rename it. For instance the stack for $L[2]$ on entering edge e_3 is $[5; 4; 2]$ with index 5

---

[5] The full correspondence for edge e_3 is that $K, G, M = K', G', M'$ (stack, global, and main memories are identical) and that $L[0] = L'[0]$, $L[1] = L'[3]$, and $L[2] = L'[5]$.

being the top entry, while the stack for $L[2]$ on entering edge e_4 is just $[2]$. In processing the instructions at a node, a (LocalGet k) instruction is replaced with (LocalGet k') where k' is the index at the *top* of the stack for k. A (LocalSet k) instruction is replaced with (LocalSet k') where k' is a *fresh* index, which is pushed on to the stack for $L[k]$. (A similar replacement occurs for instances of LocalTee.) For the example program, the phi-assignment $6 := \mathsf{phi}\,(e_3, 5)(e_4, 2)$ at node n_2 is filled in by taking the indexes $5, 2$ at the top of the stacks for $L[2]$ for edges e_3 and e_4, respectively, and generating a fresh index 6.

Proof Generation. We now turn to proof generation. First, note that the SSA transformation does not alter CFG structure. Thus, the correspondence relates identical edges in source and target. Moreover, the contents of the value stack K and the memories G and M are uninfluenced by this transformation. Thus, the focus is entirely on the local variables. The key to defining the relation on each edge is knowing which fresh local index represents an original local index k on that edge. Fortunately, this information is easy to obtain. In the second stage above, the fresh index corresponding to original index k at edge e is precisely the index at the top of the stack for $L[k]$ when edge e is traversed (each edge is traversed exactly once). Thus, the template for the full correspondence at edge e is that $K, G, M = K', G', M'$ and for each original index k, $L[k] = L'[k']$ where k' is the fresh index at the top of the stack for $L[k]$ at edge e.

We have implemented the SSA transformation in about 700 lines of OCaml code (including comments). That includes the iterated dominance frontier calculation but not the calculation of the base dominance relationship, which is done separately in about 300 lines of OCaml. Proof generation is implemented in an additional 130 lines of OCaml (including comments). The implementation of the SSA algorithm and the proof generator took (we estimate) about 3 person-weeks.

6   Validator Implementation

We have so far laid out the design of the self-certifying framework and shown how to write proof generators. In this section, we describe the implementation of the validator, which builds on the reference WebAssembly implementation. It is about 6300 source lines of OCaml source code[6], which includes the proof checking algorithm, an interface to the Z3 SMT solver [22], code for manipulating control flow graphs, and utility functions. The code has substantial explanatory comments. It was developed in roughly 7 person-months of effort.

The method is defined as Algorithm 1. It receives as input two CFGs for the same WebAssembly function (the source CFG $\mathcal{G}$ and the target CFG $\mathcal{H}$), and a candidate witness object (ckpt, W, frontier, choice). The algorithm then checks the witness for validity against $\mathcal{G}$ and $\mathcal{H}$, through a simple workset algorithm that repeatedly invokes the back-end SMT solver to check the validity of the given formula; the witness check fails if the formula is invalid.

---

[6] Excluding comments. Measured with `cloc`: https://github.com/AlDanial/cloc.

Context c	Label a	eval(a,c)	Condition
(K,L,G,M)	Const c	$\hookrightarrow$ $(c:K,L,G,M)$	
$(v_1:K,L,G,M))$	Unary op	$\hookrightarrow$ $(v:K,L,G,M)$	if $v = op(v_1)$
$(v_1:v_2:K,L,G,M)$	Binary bop	$\hookrightarrow$ $(v:K,L,G,M)$	if $v = op(v_1,v_2)$
$(v_1:K,L,G,M)$	Test op	$\hookrightarrow$ $(v:K,L,G,M)$	if $v = op(v_1)$
$(v_1:v_2:K,L,G,M)$	Compare op	$\hookrightarrow$ $(v:K,L,G,M)$	if $v = op(v_1,v_2)$
$(v_1:v_2:K,L,G,M)$	Convert op	$\hookrightarrow$ $(v:K,L,G,M)$	if $v = op(v_1,v_2)$
(K,L,G,M)	Nop	$\hookrightarrow$ (K,L,G,M)	
$(v:K,L,G,M)$	Drop	$\hookrightarrow$ (K,L,G,M)	
$(i:v_1:v_2:K,L,G,M)$	Select	$\hookrightarrow$ $(v_1:K,L,G,M)$	if $i = 0_{i32}$
$(i:v_1:v_2:K,L,G,M)$	Select	$\hookrightarrow$ $(v_2:K,L,G,M)$	if $i \neq 0_{i32}$
(K,L,G,M)	LocalGet x	$\hookrightarrow$ $(v:K,L,G,M)$	if $v = L(x)$
$(v:K,L,G,M)$	LocalSet x	$\hookrightarrow$ (K,L',G,M)	$L' = L[x \mapsto v]$
$(v:K,L,G,M)$	LocalTee x	$\hookrightarrow$ $(v:K,L',G,M)$	$L' = L[x \mapsto v]$
(K,L,G,M)	GlobalGet x	$\hookrightarrow$ $(v:K,L,G,M)$	if $v = G(x)$
$(v:K,L,G,M)$	GlobalSet x	$\hookrightarrow$ (K,L,G',M)	$G' = G[x \mapsto v]$
$(x:K,L,G,M)$	Load o	$\hookrightarrow$ $(v:K,L,G,M)$	if $v = M(x+o)$
$(v:x:K,L,G,M)$	Store o	$\hookrightarrow$ (K,L,G,M')	$M' = M[x+o \mapsto v]$
(K,L,G,M)	MemorySize	$\hookrightarrow$ $(v:K,L,G,M)$	$v =$ MEMORY_SIZE
$(d:K,L,G,M)$	MemoryGrow	$\hookrightarrow$ $(v:K,L,G,M)$	$v =$ MEMORY_SIZE
(K,L,G,M)	Br	$\hookrightarrow$ (K,L,G,M)	
$(v:K,L,G,M)$	If $true$	$\hookrightarrow$ (K,L,G,M)	$v \neq 0_{i32}$
$(v:K,L,G,M)$	If $false$	$\hookrightarrow$ (K,L,G,M)	$v = 0_{i32}$
$(v:K,L,G,M)$	BrIf $true$	$\hookrightarrow$ (K,L,G,M)	$v \neq 0_{i32}$
$(v:K,L,G,M)$	BrIf $false$	$\hookrightarrow$ (K,L,G,M)	$v = 0_{i32}$
$(v:K,L,G,M)$	BrIndex d	$\hookrightarrow$ (K,L,G,M)	$v = d$
$(v:K,L,G,M)$	BrDefault l	$\hookrightarrow$ (K,L,G,M)	$l \leq v$

Fig. 8. The definition of $c' = $ eval(a,c), where c is the current evaluation context, a is a local transition action label, and c' is the following context. Basic instructions are in the top group; branch conditions are in the bottom group; transitions not defined are assumed to trap by default. The notation $L[x \mapsto v]$ denotes a map identical to L except at element x where its value is v.

The witness conditions defined in Sect. 4 and checked by Algorithm 1 ultimately depend on the semantics of individual actions. We supply this semantics in Fig. 8 for the context $c = (K,L,G,M)$; this defines the resulting context $c' = $ eval(a,c). Instruction semantics is defined in the top group, branch conditions at the bottom. MemoryGrow has no effect; the memory is assumed to be of a large fixed size. Label-context pairs not listed here are undefined. The bulk of the implementation effort is in the encoding this semantics in SMT terms.

Algorithm 1. Witness Checking Algorithm

1: **procedure** REFINEMENTCHECK($\mathcal{G}$, $\mathcal{H}$, witness = (ckpt, W, frontier, choice))
2:     Initialize workset to $\{(\hat{f}, \hat{e})\}$, the entry edges
3:     **while** workset is not empty **do**
4:         remove checkpoint edge pair (f, e) from workset, mark it as visited
5:         if (f, e) is not in domain(W), **abort** (bad witness structure)
6:         **for all** paths q in frontier($\mathcal{H}, f$) **do**
7:             let f' be the final edge of q
8:             let $p = \text{choice}((f, e), q)$ be the corresponding source path, final edge e'
9:             invoke an SMT solver to check witness conditions from Section 4 on q, p
10:            add (f', e') to the workset if not visited
11:        **end for**
12:    **end while**
13: **end procedure**

6.1 Encoding into SMT

We now describe how the action semantics can be encoded into appropriate first-order logical theories. Conceptually, the process is straightforward; nevertheless, an actual implementation must resolve or work around several complexities.

The *fully interpreted* encoding must represent the i32, i64, f32 and f64 datatypes precisely. Integer types are represented with bitvectors to properly account for low-level bit manipulation with Xor and Rotr instructions. However, encoding floating point types is a challenge. The current fully interpreted encoding applies only to programs over i32 values, that do not use MemoryGrow, correctly specify MEMORY_SIZE, and where load and store memory operations are i32-aligned. This encoding is used to check proofs for constant propagation and folding on i32 values.

On the other hand, proofs of several transformations (including all other implemented transformations and others such as loop peeling and common subexpression elimination) amount to reasoning about substitution under equality. For such proofs, a *fully uninterpreted* encoding suffices to check refinement. A significant advantage of the uninterpreted encoding is that the validator can handle *all* WebAssembly programs, without restrictions. Proof witnesses also specify the encoding that is to be used to check their validity.

These two options naturally suggest a third, a *partially interpreted* SMT encoding where, say, all int32 and int64 operations are fully interpreted in the theory of bitvectors, while floating point operations are uninterpreted. We are in the process of developing such an interpretation; it would remove many of the restrictions currently placed by the fully interpreted encoding.

6.2 Evaluation

The goal of our evaluation was to test how well our prototype implementation scales on real programs. To do this, we ran our checker against the proofs generated by proof-generating optimizations on two benchmarks: the WebAssembly reference interpreter's test suite (https://github.com/WebAssembly/spec/) and the WebP image library (https://github.com/webmproject/libwebp). We found that nearly all proofs are easily verified, although a small percentage of checks fail because the SMT solver is a bottleneck.

Procedure. We first gathered WebAssembly S-expression (WAST) files from each benchmark. This was either already provided in the case of the reference interpreter (73 files, 3036 functions, 49113 LoC, total 2.6 MB), or in the case of WebP's C implementation, can be compiled to WebAssembly using Emscripten[7] (1 file, 953 functions, 328780 LoC, total 6.8 MB).

Next, for each function of each module of each file we ran the following:

(1) Convert the function into a source CFG.
(2) Run an optimization (either SSA, SSA + unSSA, SSA + DSE, or Loop unroll), which generates a target CFG and a proof witness to be checked.
(3) For each witness, generate SMT lemmas as in Algorithm 1 and pass those to the Z3 SMT solver if they meet a heuristic size restriction. If the lemma is too large or if the solver times out, the check is considered unsuccessful.

All experiments were run with Z3 4.8.7 on a machine with 30 GB RAM and an AMD Ryzen 7 PRO 3700U CPU. The proof validation process is parallelizable: each function of each module can be checked separately. All proof lemmas associated with a source-target pair of CFGs can also be checked separately. We do not, however, use parallelization in this evaluation, and this is reflected in the relatively low CPU (typically < 30%) and RAM (typically < 25%) usage throughout the experiments.

Results and Discussion. Our results are summarized in Fig. 9. First, $101/237460$ ($\approx 0.04\%$) of SSA + unSSA's lemmas are *potentially* faulty, as the solver returns Unknown on these instances rather than Unsat (correct) or Sat (faulty). However, upon isolating several of these cases and re-running the solver with longer timeouts, the sampled Unknowns were in fact Unsat, and therefore correct. In a similar vein, some lemmas are unchecked because of heuristic size restrictions. Thus, although we have not completely verified the optimizations on the reference interpreter and WebP, we have, however, succeeded in verifying a significant portion. Furthermore, every skipped lemma that we have manually extracted and checked has also been valid.

Second, the solver calls dominate runtime in all experiments, which is expected in part due to the sheer amount of queries. Fortunately the check of each lemma is usually fast, on average we check about 11 lemmas per second, but without timeout settings we have observed exceptional outliers. For simplicity, SMT lemmas are written out as SMT-LIB2 strings that are piped into Z3 rather than via Z3's direct OCaml bindings; this reduces performance somewhat.

Finally, an obvious point is that additional machine resources would improve the evaluation results. For one, increasing the size restriction allows more lemmas

---

[7] https://developer.mozilla.org/en-US/docs/WebAssembly/C_to_wasm.

Reference Interpreter (49113 LoC)			
	SMT/Total Time (s)	Checked/Total SMT	Faulty
SSA	1412.4/1415.5 $\approx 99.8\%$	45376/45380 $\approx 99.9\%$	0
SSA + unSSA	2374.2/2377.7 $\approx 99.8\%$	77584/77592 $\approx 99.9\%$	0
SSA + DSE	1547.9/1551.3 $\approx 99.8\%$	49596/49604 $\approx 99.9\%$	0
Loop Unroll	12.6/14.6 $\approx 86.3\%$	488/488 $= 100\%$	0
WebP Image Library (328780 LoC)			
	SMT/Total Time (s)	Checked/Total SMT	Faulty
SSA	13593.4/13617.5 $\approx 99.8\%$	135088/135156 $\approx 99.9\%$	0
SSA + unSSA	27339.3/27364.4 $\approx 99.9\%$	237460/266492 $\approx 89.1\%$	101?
SSA + DSE	21068.5/21095.8 $\approx 99.9\%$	231068/266116 $\approx 86.8\%$	0
Loop Unroll	3589.4/3606.0 $\approx 99.5\%$	38036/38036 $= 100\%$	0

Fig. 9. We examine four optimizations on two different benchmarks. The total number of SMT lemmas is a multiple of four because we check that the source-target paths are (1) inductive, (2) enabled, (3) non-trapping, and (4) non-blocking. A checked lemma is correct if the solver (Z3 with timeout = 2 sec) returns Unsat; it is considered faulty if the solver returns Sat and potentially faulty if the solver returns Unknown. We do not check lemmas that are too large with respect to a size heuristic.

to be checked. Additionally, Z3 and the overall pipeline would also be faster — all this without parallelizing proof checking. In summary, the evaluation results here give us confidence that self-certification can be feasibly adopted in practice.

7   Related Work and Conclusions

This work is inspired by and builds upon a large body of prior work on compiler verification. We highlight the most closely related work below.

Mechanized Proof. The seminal work on mechanized proof of compiler optimizations is by McCarthy and Painter from 1960s [21]. Mechanized proofs have been carried out in several settings, notable ones are for the Lisp compiler in the CLI stack [4] and for the C compiler CompCert [18, 19]. Such proofs require enormous effort and considerable mathematical expertise—the CompCert and CLI proofs each required several person-years. A proof of a roughly 800-line SSA transformation needed nearly a person-year and over 10,000 lines of Coq proof script [36], illustrating the difficulty of the problem. As explained in the Introduction, there are close connections between deductive proof methods and self-certification.

Translation Validation. Translation Validation (TV) [1, 6, 8, 28, 30, 32, 37] is a form of result checking [5]. Compilation is treated as a black-box process; the validator has access only to the input and output programs. As explained in the Introduction, specialized heuristics must be crafted for each optimization. Incompleteness of these heuristics shows up in missed equivalences, for instance [8] report that about 25% of equivalences were not detected on a particular test suite. The complexity of some TV validators raises the question of whether the validators are themselves correct. Unfortunately, verifying a TV validator is difficult. For instance, the verification of a 1000-line TV validator for SSA [2] needed over a person-year of effort and 15,000 lines of Coq proof script.

Self-certification avoids the introduction of transformation-specific heuristics. In principle, self-certification is complete. In practice, it is possible for SMT solvers to run out of time or memory and thus produce an "unknown" result.

Self Certification. We discuss prior work on compiler self-certification in the Introduction; we do so now in more detail. Credible compilation was first implemented in [20] for a basic textbook-style intermediate language. It has proved to be challenging to implement self-certification for languages used in practice. The implementation of witnessing for LLVM in [11,26] handles only a small subset of LLVM IR and simple optimizations. Validation of the LLVM SSA transform is shown in [24], but that validator uses a simplified LLVM semantics and proof generation is somewhat incomplete.

The most thorough implementation of certification to date is in the Crellvm system for LLVM [16]. A Crellvm proof consists of Extended Relational Hoare Logic (ERHL) assertions (cf. [3]) that connect corresponding source and target program points, together with hints for instantiating inference rules. The validator applies the given hints to check the inductiveness of the supplied ERHL assertions. The limitations arise from (1) the ERHL logic, which is syntax-driven, and thus cannot be used to witness the correctness of transformations which modify control structure, such as loop unrolling; and from (2) the large collection of custom-built inference rules (221 in the current system), each of which must be formally verified. In contrast, our WebAssembly validator is based on a small set of refinement proof rules, with all of the detailed logical and arithmetic reasoning left to a generic SMT solver. This modular design simplifies the validator implementation, while the proof format is sufficiently expressive to support all of the Crellvm optimizations and more, including loop unrolling.

Regression Verification. A related line of work is that of regression verification [12,13,17], which establishes the equivalence of structurally similar recursive programs. Each procedure body is loop-free (loops are converted to recursion), simplifying equivalence checking through SMT encoding. The original work bases equivalence on a fixed relation with identical parameter values. Some of these limitations have been overcome in later work [6,10,33] through stronger program equivalence heuristics. The key difference is that self-certification, by design, involves the compiler writer in the process and thus does not require heuristics.

Several enhancements are of interest. One is the extension of self-certification to complex transformations that require specialized proof methods. Rules for validating loop transformations were developed and implemented in the TVOC project [1,37] and re-implemented for LLVM [25]. Rules for validating interprocedural transformations such as tail-recursion elimination and inlining are developed in [34]. A second interesting project is to produce a formally verified validator, mechanizing the soundness proof of Theorem 1.

Acknowledgments. This material is based upon work supported by the National Science Foundation under Grant CCF-1563393. Any opinions, findings, and conclusions or recommendations expressed in this material are those of the author(s) and do not necessarily reflect the views of the National Science Foundation.

References

1. Barrett, C.W., Fang, Y., Goldberg, B., Hu, Y., Pnueli, A., Zuck, L.D.: TVOC: a translation validator for optimizing compilers. In: CAV, pp. 291–295 (2005)
2. Barthe, G., Demange, D., Pichardie, D.: Formal verification of an SSA-based middle-end for CompCert. ACM Trans. Program. Lang. Syst. **36**(1), 4 (2014)
3. Benton, N.: Simple relational correctness proofs for static analyses and program transformations. In: POPL, pp. 14–25 (2004)
4. Bevier, W.R., Hunt, W.A., Moore, J.S., Young, W.D.: An approach to systems verification. J. Autom. Reasoning **5**(4), 411–428 (1989)
5. Blum, M., Kannan, S.: Designing programs that check their work. J. ACM **42**(1), 269–291 (1995)
6. Churchill, B.R., Padon, O., Sharma, R., Aiken, A.: Semantic program alignment for equivalence checking. In: PLDI, pp. 1027–1040 (2019)
7. Cytron, R., Ferrante, J., Rosen, B.K., Wegman, M.N., Zadeck, F.K.: Efficiently computing static single assignment form and the control dependence graph. ACM Trans. Program. Lang. Syst. **13**(4), 451–490 (1991)
8. Dahiya, M., Bansal, S.: Modeling undefined behaviour semantics for checking equivalence across compiler optimizations. In: HVC, pp. 19–34 (2017)
9. Dijkstra, E.W., Scholten, C.S.: Predicate calculus and program semantics. In: Texts and Monographs in Computer Science, Springer, New York (1990). https://doi.org/10.1007/978-1-4612-3228-5
10. Fedyukovich, G., Gurfinkel, A., Sharygina, N.: Automated discovery of simulation between programs. In: Davis, M., Fehnker, A., McIver, A., Voronkov, A. (eds.) LPAR 2015. LNCS, vol. 9450, pp. 606–621. Springer, Heidelberg (2015). https://doi.org/10.1007/978-3-662-48899-7_42
11. Gjomemo, R., Namjoshi, K.S., Phung, P.H., Venkatakrishnan, V.N., Zuck, L.D.: From verification to optimizations. In: D'Souza, D., Lal, A., Larsen, K.G. (eds.) VMCAI 2015. LNCS, vol. 8931, pp. 300–317. Springer, Heidelberg (2015). https://doi.org/10.1007/978-3-662-46081-8_17
12. Godlin, B., Strichman, O.: Regression verification. In: Proceedings of the 46th Design Automation Conference, DAC 2009, San Francisco, CA, USA, July 26–31, 2009, pp. 466–471 (2009)
13. Godlin, B., Strichman, O.: Regression verification: proving the equivalence of similar programs. Softw. Test., Verif. Reliab. **23**(3), 241–258 (2013)
14. Haas, A., et al.: Bringing the web up to speed with WebAssembly. In: PLDI, pp. 185–200 (2017)
15. Jourdan, J., Pottier, F., Leroy, X.: Validating LR(1) parsers. In: ESOP, pp. 397–416 (2012)
16. Kang, J., Kim, Y., et al.: Crellvm: verified credible compilation for LLVM. In: PLDI, pp. 631–645 (2018)
17. Lahiri, S.K., Hawblitzel, C., Kawaguchi, M., Rebêlo, H.: SYMDIFF: a language-agnostic semantic diff tool for imperative programs. In: CAV, pp. 712–717 (2012)
18. Leroy, X.: Formal certification of a compiler back-end or: programming a compiler with a proof assistant. In: POPL, pp. 42–54. ACM (2006)

19. Leroy, X.: Formal verification of a realistic compiler. Commun. ACM **52**(7), 107–115 (2009)
20. Marinov, D.: Credible Compilation. Master's thesis, Massachusetts Institute of Technology (2000)
21. McCarthy, J., Painter, J.: Correctness of a compiler for arithmetic expressions, pp. 33–41. American Mathematical Society (1967)
22. de Moura, L., Bjørner, N.: Z3: an efficient SMT solver. In: Ramakrishnan, C.R., Rehof, J. (eds.) TACAS 2008. LNCS, vol. 4963, pp. 337–340. Springer, Heidelberg (2008). https://doi.org/10.1007/978-3-540-78800-3_24
23. Namjoshi, K.S.: Certifying model checkers. In: CAV, pp. 2–13 (2001)
24. Namjoshi, K.S.: Witnessing an SSA transformation. In: VeriSure Workshop, CAV (2014). https://kedar-namjoshi.github.io/papers/Namjoshi-VeriSure-CAV-2014.pdf
25. Namjoshi, K.S., Singhania, N.: Loopy: Programmable and formally verified loop transformations. In: SAS, pp. 383–402 (2016)
26. Namjoshi, K.S., Tagliabue, G., Zuck, L.D.: A witnessing compiler: a proof of concept. In: RV, pp. 340–345 (2013)
27. Namjoshi, K.S., Zuck, L.D.: Witnessing program transformations. In: Logozzo, F., Fähndrich, M. (eds.) SAS 2013. LNCS, vol. 7935, pp. 304–323. Springer, Heidelberg (2013). https://doi.org/10.1007/978-3-642-38856-9_17
28. Necula, G.: Translation validation of an optimizing compiler. In: (PLDI) 2000, pp. 83–95 (2000)
29. Peled, D.A., Pnueli, A., Zuck, L.D.: From falsification to verification. In: FSTTCS, pp. 292–304 (2001)
30. Pnueli, A., Shtrichman, O., Siegel, M.: The code validation tool (CVT)- automatic verification of a compilation process. Software Tools Technol. Transfer **2**(2), 192–201 (1998)
31. Rinard, M.: Credible Compilation. Tech. Rep. MIT-LCS-TR-776, MIT (1999)
32. Samet, H.: Automatically proving the correctness of translations involving optimized code - research sponsored by Advanced Research Projects Agency, ARPA order no. 2494. Ph.D. thesis, Stanford University (1975)
33. Strichman, O., Veitsman, M.: Regression verification for unbalanced recursive functions. In: Fitzgerald, J., Heitmeyer, C., Gnesi, S., Philippou, A. (eds.) FM 2016. LNCS, vol. 9995, pp. 645–658. Springer, Cham (2016). https://doi.org/10.1007/978-3-319-48989-6_39
34. Zaks, A., Pnueli, A.: Program analysis for compiler validation. In: PASTE, pp. 1–7 (2008)
35. Zhang, L., Malik, S.: Validating SAT solvers using an independent resolution-based checker: practical implementations and other applications. In: DATE, pp. 10880–10885 (2003)
36. Zhao, J., Nagarakatte, S., Martin, M.M.K., Zdancewic, S.: Formal verification of SSA-based optimizations for LLVM. In: PLDI 2013, pp. 175–186 (2013)
37. Zuck, L.D., Pnueli, A., Goldberg, B., Barrett, C.W., Fang, Y., Hu, Y.: Translation and run-time validation of loop transformations. Formal Methods Syst. Des. **27**(3), 335–360 (2005)

Concurrent and Distributed Systems

Concurrent Correctness in Vector Space

Christina Peterson[✉][ID], Victor Cook[ID], and Damian Dechev[ID]

University of Central Florida, Orlando, FL 32816, USA
{clp8199,victor.cook}@knights.ucf.edu,
dechev.dechev@ucf.edu

Abstract. Correctness verification of a concurrent history is challenging and has been proven to be an NP-complete problem. The reason that verifying correctness cannot be solved in polynomial time is a consequence of the way correctness is defined. Traditional correctness conditions require a concurrent history to be equivalent to a legal sequential history. The worst case number of legal sequential histories for a concurrent history is $O(n!)$ with respect to n methods invoked. Existing correctness verification tools improve the time complexity by either reducing the size of the possible legal sequential histories or improving the efficiency of generating the possible legal sequential histories. Further improvements to the time complexity of correctness verification can be achieved by changing the way correctness of concurrent programs is defined. In this paper, we present the first methodology to recast the correctness conditions in literature to be defined in vector space. The concurrent histories are represented as a set of method call vectors, and correctness is defined as properties over the set of vectors. The challenge with defining correctness in vector space is accounting for method call ordering and data structure semantics. We solve this challenge by incorporating a priority assignment scheme to the values of the method call vectors. Using our new definitions of concurrent correctness, we design a dynamic analysis tool that checks the vector space correctness of concurrent data structures in $O(n^2)$ with respect to n method calls, a significant improvement over $O(n!)$ time required to analyze legal sequential histories. We showcase our dynamic analysis tool by using it to check the vector space correctness of a variety of queues, stacks, and hashmaps.

Keywords: Concurrent programs · Correctness condition · Dynamic analysis

1 Introduction

Concurrent programming is difficult due to non-determinism associated with unpredictable thread scheduling, hardware interrupts, and software interrupts.

This work was funded by NSF grants 1740095 and 1717515.

© Springer Nature Switzerland AG 2021
F. Henglein et al. (Eds.): VMCAI 2021, LNCS 12597, pp. 151–173, 2021.
https://doi.org/10.1007/978-3-030-67067-2_8

This challenge has motivated considerable research on tools and techniques for verifying that a concurrent program is correct. Correctness conditions in literature [1,4,21,25,34] define correctness of a concurrent history in terms of possible sequential histories based on allowable method call ordering. The subproblem of verifying correctness for a single concurrent history is also challenging. Papadimitriou [34] proves that testing a concurrent history for serializability is NP-complete. Gibbons et al. [19] prove that verifying sequential consistency of a concurrent history and verifying linearizability of a concurrent history are both NP-complete problems. Proving that a concurrent system is sequentially consistent or linearizable is undecidable [2,6].

The reason that verifying correctness for a single concurrent history cannot be solved in polynomial time resides in the way correctness is defined. The property shared by the correctness conditions in literature is that a concurrent history must be equivalent to a sequential history. Consider a concurrent program with n processes, where each process executes one method on a concurrent data structure. If all method calls overlap, then the concurrent history could observe the method calls in any order. This yields $n!$ possible legal sequential histories that this concurrent history could be equivalent to and be considered correct. The worst case growth rate of legal sequential histories is $O(n!)$ with respect to n method calls invoked on the concurrent data structure. Many verification tools address this problem by reducing the size of the sequential histories [14,27,33,39] or generating the sequential histories more efficiently [22,28,36,37]. Of the tools that place no constraints on the data structure type and do not require knowledge of linearization points, the best upper bound time complexity achieved is $O(p \cdot n^{d-1})$, where p is the number of threads, n is the number of methods, and d is a linearizability depth [33].

We use the vector space representation of concurrent systems introduced by Cook et al. [10] to recast the correctness conditions in literature. Instead of referencing sequential histories, the concurrent histories are represented as a set of method call vectors and the correctness condition is defined as properties over the set of vectors. We do not claim that the revised definition solves the NP-complete problem of generating all possible legal sequential histories for correctness verification. However, we do claim that the revised definition reframes correctness so that correctness verification is a polynomial time problem. The main challenge with defining concurrent correctness in vector space is handling method call ordering and data structure semantics. We address this challenge by incorporating a priority assignment scheme to the values of the method call vectors. Method calls either promote or demote another method call's priority based on the method call ordering required by the correctness condition and the data structure semantics. We capitalize on our proposed definitions of concurrent correctness to design an efficient dynamic analysis tool that checks the vector space correctness of concurrent data structures. The worst case time complexity of our dynamic analysis tool is $O(n^2)$, where n is the number of method calls. Our dynamic analysis tool does not require model checkers, annotations, or source code modifications, making it applicable to real programs with large workloads.

The contributions of this paper include:

1. We propose definitions of well-known correctness conditions [1, 4, 21, 25, 34] in vector space.
2. We present a priority assignment scheme for the method call vectors that captures the method call ordering required by the correctness condition and the data structure semantics.
3. We develop an efficient dynamic analysis tool that checks the correctness of concurrent data structures in $O(n^2)$ time. The correctness conditions incorporated in our tool include the vector space versions of linearizability, sequential consistency, quiescent consistency, and quasi-linearizability.
4. We evaluate our tool by using it to check the correctness of queues, stacks, and hashmaps. Additionally, we enhance our tool by enabling the vector computations to be performed on the Graphics Processing Unit (GPU).

2   System Model

A concurrent system comprises sequential threads, referred to as *processes*, that communicate through shared data structures called *concurrent objects* (or simply *objects*) [21]. An *item* is data to be stored in a concurrent object. An *abstract data type* defines a set of possible values for a concurrent object and defines the behavior (*semantics*) of a set of methods that enable the processes to manipulate the concurrent object. An *event* is an *invocation* or *response* of a method. An execution of a concurrent system is modeled by a *concurrent history* (or simply *history*), which is a finite series of events. A *method call* in history H is a pair consisting of an invocation and next matching response in H [20]. A method call m_0 *precedes* method call m_1 if the response event of m_0 occurs before the invocation event of m_1. A method call m_0 *happens-before* method call m_1 if m_0 takes effect before m_1. An invocation is *pending* in history H if no matching response follows the invocation. For a history H, *complete(H)* is the maximal subsequence of H consisting only of invocations and matching responses. For a history H, an *extension* of H is a history constructed by appending responses to zero or more pending invocations of H. An *object subhistory*, denoted $H|x$, is a subsequence of the events of H for object x. A *thread subhistory*, denoted $H|t$, is a subsequence of the events of H for thread t. A history H is sequential if the first event of H is an invocation and each invocation, except possibly the last, is immediately followed by a matching response. A *sequential specification* for an object is a set of sequential histories for that object. A sequential history is *legal* if each object subhistory is legal for that object.

A *vector* is an ordered n-tuple of numbers, where n is an arbitrary positive integer. A *column vector* is a vector with a n by 1 (row-by-column) dimension. Each method call in a concurrent history is represented as a column vector, where each position of the vector represents a unique combination of objects/items, referred to as a *configuration*, encountered by the concurrent system, where this representation is uniform among the set of vectors.

A *producer* is a method that generates an item to be placed in a concurrent object. A *consumer* is a method that removes an item from a concurrent object.

A *reader* is a method that reads an item from a concurrent object. A *writer* is a method that writes to an existing item in a concurrent object. A *method call set* is an unordered set of method calls in a history.

3   Methodology

Our reframed correctness conditions represent method calls in a concurrent history as a set of vectors in vector space, and define correctness according to properties over the set of vectors. We leverage the correctness conditions defined in vector space to design an efficient dynamic analysis tool for checking the vector space correctness of concurrent data structures.

3.1   Correctness Defined in Vector Space

The general idea of our approach is to represent the method calls in a concurrent history as a set of vectors and determine correctness according to properties over the set of vectors. To achieve this we must recast the standard definitions of concurrent correctness to be in vector space. The vector space definition for correctness condition c is denoted by the term "vector space c." The correctness conditions in literature establish two properties regarding a concurrent history. First, the history of method calls must be equivalent to a legal sequential history, i.e. the method calls appear atomic. Second, the order that the method calls take effect is in compliance with the corresponding definition of correctness. To define concurrent correctness in vector space, we want the vectors representing the method calls to be able to express 1) that the method calls appear atomic, and 2) the order that the method calls should take effect.

To illustrate our reasoning, consider a simple producer-consumer data structure where the only correctness requirement is that the method calls appear atomic. The following value assignment scheme captures atomicity of method calls. Let method call m be represented by vector V whose elements are initialized to zero. Let o, i be an index in V associated with the configuration for object O and item I. If m is a producer method that produces item I in object O, then $V[o, i] = 1$. If m is a consumer method that produces item I in object O, then $V[o, i] = -1$. Let V_{sum} be the sum of all vectors obtained by converting the method calls in a concurrent history to their vector representation using the previously described value assignment scheme. The concurrent history is atomic if for all indices o, i, $V_{sum}[o, i] \geq 0$ because if $V_{sum}[o, i] < 0$ for some index o, i, this indicates that I is consumed from O that no longer exists in O.

Consider a producer/consumer data structure where the method calls must appear atomic and take effect according to real-time order. The behavior of the method calls when they take effect is dependent on the semantics of the data structure. For example, a First-In-First-Out (FIFO) queue requires that the items are dequeued in the same order that they are enqueued. A Last-In-First-Out (LIFO) stack requires that the items are popped in the reverse order that they are pushed. This expected ordering of method calls in conjunction with the expected behavior of the method calls can be captured using a priority system for the value assignments of the method call vectors. We can use a similar strategy as the value assignment for atomicity such that $V[o, i] = 1$ if item I has the highest priority to be removed from object O. $V[o, i] = 0$ if item I has the lowest priority to be removed from object O. An item I that is removed from object O that does not have the highest priority will cause $V_{sum}[o, i] < 0$.

The priority assignments are not static and must be updated based on data structure semantics and the ordering of the method calls defined by the correctness condition. We assign priorities using a promotion/demotion scheme based on the geometric series $\frac{1}{2} + \frac{1}{4} + \frac{1}{8} + ... + \frac{1}{2^n}$. When an item is produced in an object, it is initially assigned a value of 1. If an item is determined to have a lesser priority than another item based on method call ordering and data structure semantics, it is demoted. For every jth demotion applied to item I in object O, $V[o, i] = V[o, i] - \frac{1}{2^j}$, where the domain of j is the set of positive integers, $\mathcal{Z}^+$. Since $\sum_{n=1}^{\infty} \left(\frac{1}{2} \right)^n = 1$, the range of the sum of the demotions for index o, i is $\left(-1, -\frac{1}{2} \right]$, guaranteeing that $V[o, i] > 0$. Once I is removed from O, it must promote all items that were previously demoted due to this item. For every jth promotion applied to I in O which has been previously demoted k times, $V[o, i] = V[o, i] + \frac{1}{2^j}$, where the domain of j is $[1, k]$. After an item has been promoted k times, it will be assigned the highest priority value 1.

Consider the concurrent history in Fig. 1. The correctness condition for this history is linearizability, a correctness property such that each method takes effect at some moment between its invocation and response and the history is equivalent to a legal sequential history. This history comprises three processes that each enqueue an item into object x. The vector representation of the method calls up to time $t1$ is shown in Eq. 1. Since $x.enq(7)$ and $x.enq(8)$ overlap, their value assignment is 1 because it is unknown which of these method calls linearizes first. The invocation of $x.enq(9)$ occurs after the response of $x.enq(7)$, so $x.enq(9)$ must demote itself resulting in a value assignment of $\frac{1}{2}$. Each element of the sum of the method call vectors is greater than zero, indicating that the history is vector space linearizable up to time $t1$.

The vector representation of the method calls up to time $t2$ is shown in Eq. 2. The value assignment for $x.deq(8)$ is -1. Since each element of the sum of the method call vectors is greater than zero, the history is vector space linearizable up to time $t2$. If item 9 had been dequeued instead of item 8, the sum of the method call vectors for index $x, 9$ would have been $-\frac{1}{2}$, indicating that the history is not vector space linearizable at time $t2$. The vector representation of the method calls up to time $t3$ is shown in Eq. 3. Since $x.enq(9)$ was previously demoted due to method call $x.enq(7)$, $x.enq(9)$ must be promoted by adding $\frac{1}{2^1} = \frac{1}{2}$ to the method call vector for $x.enq(9)$. Item 9 now has a value assignment of 1 and has the highest priority to be dequeued next. The history is vector space linearizable up to time $t3$ since each element of the sum of the method call vectors is greater than zero. A similar evaluation can be applied when reasoning about other correctness conditions in vector space.

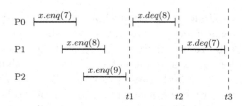

Fig. 1. FIFO queue concurrent history

$$
t1 : conf. : \begin{bmatrix} x,7 \\ x,8 \\ x,9 \end{bmatrix} \quad \overset{method}{\underset{calls}{}} : \overset{x.enq(7)}{\begin{bmatrix} 1 \\ 0 \\ 0 \end{bmatrix}} + \overset{x.enq(8)}{\begin{bmatrix} 0 \\ 1 \\ 0 \end{bmatrix}} + \overset{x.enq(9)}{\begin{bmatrix} 0 \\ 0 \\ \frac{1}{2} \end{bmatrix}} = \begin{bmatrix} 1 \\ 1 \\ \frac{1}{2} \end{bmatrix} \tag{1}
$$

$$
\overset{t2 : conf.}{\begin{bmatrix} x,7 \\ x,8 \\ x,9 \end{bmatrix}} \quad \overset{x.enq(7)}{\begin{bmatrix} 1 \\ 0 \\ 0 \end{bmatrix}} + \overset{x.enq(8)}{\begin{bmatrix} 0 \\ 1 \\ 0 \end{bmatrix}} + \overset{x.enq(9)}{\begin{bmatrix} 0 \\ 0 \\ \frac{1}{2} \end{bmatrix}} + \overset{x.deq(8)}{\begin{bmatrix} 0 \\ -1 \\ 0 \end{bmatrix}} = \begin{bmatrix} 1 \\ 0 \\ \frac{1}{2} \end{bmatrix} \tag{2}
$$

$$
\overset{t3 : conf.}{\begin{bmatrix} x,7 \\ x,8 \\ x,9 \end{bmatrix}} \quad \overset{x.enq(7)}{\begin{bmatrix} 1 \\ 0 \\ 0 \end{bmatrix}} + \overset{x.enq(8)}{\begin{bmatrix} 0 \\ 1 \\ 0 \end{bmatrix}} + \overset{x.enq(9)}{\begin{bmatrix} 0 \\ 0 \\ 1 \end{bmatrix}} + \overset{x.deq(8)}{\begin{bmatrix} 0 \\ -1 \\ 0 \end{bmatrix}} + \overset{x.deq(7)}{\begin{bmatrix} -1 \\ 0 \\ 0 \end{bmatrix}} = \begin{bmatrix} 0 \\ 0 \\ 1 \end{bmatrix} \tag{3}
$$

Algorithm 1. Type Definitions

```
1: #define MAX constant      ▷ Total number of       16:    Semantics semantics      ▷ Data structure
    object/item configurations                              semantics, e.g. FIFO, LIFO
2: enum OpType                                        17:    void* obj
3:    Producer                                        18:    Item* item
4:    Consumer                                        19:    Item* previtem
5:    Reader                                          20:    int V[MAX]
6:    Writer                                          21:    int exp      ▷ Number of times a method is
7: enum OpResult                                             demoted
8:    Success                                         22:    OpResult outcome
9:    Fail                                            23:    list <Method >promote_items
10: struct Item                                       24:    long int invocation
11:    void* value                                    25:    long int response
12:    int readcount      ▷ Number of times an        26: function INDEX(void* object, void* item)
    item is read
13:    int failcount      ▷ Number of times a         27: function PRODUCERMETHOD(int index)
    method fails                                      28: function    ISBALANCED(set    <Method
14: struct Method                                         >methods)
15:    OpType type
```

The type definitions for the promotion/demotion scheme are presented in Algorithm 1. INDEX on line 1.26 returns the index in the method call vector associated with a specified object and item. PRODUCERMETHOD on line 1.27 returns the producer method that produced the item associated with a configuration index. Algorithm 2 presents the promotion/demotion scheme. The logic

Algorithm 2. Promotion/Demotion Scheme

```
1: function PROMOTEDEMOTE(set < Method > methods, Method start, long int min)
2:     stack < Method > stack_consumer
3:     Method prev, curr
4:     for curr = start; curr != methods.end(); ++curr do
5:         if curr.invocation > min then min = curr.response; start = curr; break        ▷ Discard
       non-overlapping methods
6:         if curr.type == Producer then curr.V[INDEX(curr.obj, curr.item)] = 1        ▷ Initial assignment
7:             for prev = methods.begin(); prev != curr; ++prev do
8:                 if prev happens-before curr then
9:                     if prev.type == Producer and curr.semantics == FIFO then
10:                         prev.promote_items.push(curr)
11:                         curr.V[INDEX(curr.obj, curr.item)]        =        curr.V[INDEX(curr.obj, curr.item)]        −
       ( 1/2 )^{++(curr.exp)}                                                            ▷ Demote
12:                     else if prev.type == Producer and curr.semantics == LIFO then
13:                         curr.promote_items.push(prev)
14:                         prev.V[INDEX(prev.obj, prev.item)]        =        prev.V[INDEX(prev.obj, prev.item)]        −
       ( 1/2 )^{++(prev.exp)}                                                            ▷ Demote
15:                 else if curr.type == Consumer and curr.outcome == Success then
16:                     curr.V[INDEX(curr.obj, curr.item)] = −1
17:                     methods.remove(PRODUCERMETHOD(INDEX(curr.obj, curr.item)))
18:                     stack_consumer.push(curr)
19:                 else if curr.type == Consumer and curr.outcome == Fail then
20:                     curr.V[INDEX(curr.obj, curr.item)] = − ( 1/2 )^{++(curr.item.failcount)}        ▷ Demote all items in
       object for deq/pop
21:                 else if curr.type == Writer then
22:                     Method prev_method = PRODUCERMETHOD(INDEX(curr.obj, curr.previtem))
23:                     curr.V[INDEX(curr.obj, curr.item)] = prev_method.V[INDEX(curr.obj, curr.previtem)]        ▷ Adopt
       priority
24:                     curr.V[INDEX(curr.obj, curr.previtem)] = −prev_method.V[INDEX(curr.obj, curr.previtem)]
25:                 else if curr.type == Reader then
26:                     curr.V[INDEX(curr.obj, curr.item)] = − ( 1/2 )^{++(curr.item.readcount)}        ▷ Demote read
27:     while !stack_consumer.empty() do
28:         Method top = stack_consumer.top()
29:         for int i = 0; i < top.promote_items.size(); ++i do
30:             int index = INDEX(top.promote_items[i].obj, top.promote_items[i].item)
31:             top.promote_items[i].V[index]        =        top.promote_items[i].V[index]        +
       ( 1/2 )^{(top.promote_items[i].exp)--}                                            ▷ Promote
32:         methods.remove(top)
33:         stack_consumer.pop()
```

for the happens-before relation on line 2.8 varies based on the correctness condition. The initial value assignment is performed on line 2.6 and the demotion is performed on line 2.11 or line 2.14. The items to be promoted are maintained in the *promote_items* list, shown on lines 2.10 and 2.13. The promotion is performed on line 2.31.

Reads also utilize the promotion/demotion scheme. Let method call m be represented by vector V whose elements are initialized to zero. Let RC be a vector such that $RC[o,i]$ is a read count for item I in object O. When m performs a read on I in O, it is demoted such that $RC[o,i] = RC[o,i] + 1$, $V[o,i] = -\frac{1}{2^{RC[o,i]}}$ shown on line 2.26. The sum of the reader methods will always be between $\left(-1, -\frac{1}{2}\right]$ due to $\sum_{n=1}^{\infty} \left(\frac{1}{2}\right)^n = 1$. Let V_{sum} be the summation of the producer, consumer, and writer methods. Let R_{sum} be the summation of the reader methods. Applying the ceiling function to V_{sum} will cause $\lceil V_{sum}[o,i] \rceil = 1$ for each index o, i if I exists in O and $\lceil V_{sum}[o,i] \rceil = 0$ if I does not exist in O. If a read is performed on I that does not exist in O, then $\lceil V_{sum}[o,i] \rceil + R_{sum}[o,i] < 0$ for index o, i, indicating an incorrect history in vector space.

A write simultaneously does two actions: 1) it consumes the previous value held by an item, and 2) it produces a new value to be held by an item. We assume that the write does not affect its priority in the object. Let m be a writer method that overwrites item I_{prev} in object O with item I in object O. Let m be represented by vector V whose elements are initialized to zero. Let V_{prev} be the vector associated with the method call that produced item I_{prev} for object O. Let the index corresponding to the configuration for object O and item I_{prev} be position o, i_{prev} in V. Then $V[o,i] = V_{prev}[o,i_{prev}]$ shown on line 2.23, and $V[o,i_{prev}] = -V_{prev}[o,i_{prev}]$ shown on line 2.24. Defining the method call vector for a writer method in this way transfers the priority of the previous item to the new item. If a write is performed on an item that hasn't been produced, then the value assignment depends on program semantics. If the program allows the write to succeed by producing the corresponding item, then the value assignment is treated as a producer. If the program requires the write to fail, then this is an instance of *conditional semantics*, where the method call will take no action and return false when reaching an undefined state of the data structure (i.e. a dequeue applied to an empty queue).

Conditional semantics require special handling, which we now discuss. Let method call m be represented by vector V whose elements are initialized to zero. Let J be a count of false return values. When m attempts to perform an operation on an item I in object O that takes no action and returns false, it is demoted such that $J[o,i] = J[o,i] + 1$, $V[o,i] = -\frac{1}{2^{J[o,i]}}$ shown on line 2.20. If the consume action is not for a specific item (i.e. dequeue or pop), then all elements of V are demoted. The sum of the failed consumer methods will always be between $\left(-1, -\frac{1}{2}\right]$ due to $\sum_{n=1}^{\infty} \left(\frac{1}{2}\right)^n = 1$. Let V_{sum} be the summation of the producer, consumer (successful), and writer methods. Let F_{sum} be the summation of the failed consumer methods. Applying the ceiling function to V_{sum} will cause $\lceil V_{sum}[o,i] \rceil = 1$ for each index o, i if I exists in O and $\lceil V_{sum}[o,i] \rceil = 0$ if I does not exist in O. If a consume is performed on I and fails because I does not exist in O, then $\lceil V_{sum}[o,i] \rceil + F_{sum}[o,i] < 0$. Otherwise, if a consume is performed on I and fails even though I does exist in O, then $\lceil V_{sum}[o,i] \rceil + F_{sum}[o,i] > 0$. Multiplying $\lceil V_{sum}[o,i] \rceil + F_{sum}[o,i]$ by -1 for each index o, i if $F_{sum}[o,i] \neq 0$ will result in a value that is less than zero if a consumer method fails and I exists in O, or greater than zero if a consumer method fails and I does not exist in O.

The time intervals in which method call vectors need to be checked is dependent on the correctness condition. Definition 1 establishes conditions that must be satisfied for a history to be correct in vector space at an arbitrary time t.

Definition 1. *Let vectors P_{sum}, C_{sum}, W_{sum}, R_{sum}, and F_{sum} be the sum of producer method vectors, successful consumer method vectors, writer method vectors, reader method vectors, and failed consumer method vectors, respectively,* *up to time t. Let N be a vector such that $N[i] = 0$ if $F_{sum}[i] = 0$ and $N[i] = -1$ if $F_{sum}[i] \neq 0$. A concurrent history up to time t is balanced if:*

for each *index i,*
$(P_{sum}[i] + C_{sum}[i] + W_{sum}[i]) \geq 0,$ *and*
$\lceil (P_{sum}[i] + C_{sum}[i] + W_{sum}[i]) \rceil + R_{sum}[i] \geq 0,$ *and*
$(\lceil (P_{sum}[i] + C_{sum}[i] + W_{sum}[i]) \rceil + F_{sum}[i]) \cdot N[i] \geq 0$

Since applying the ceiling function to the sum of the producer, successful consumer, and writer methods loses information regarding item priorities, Definition 1 must check the sum of the producer, successful consumer, and writer methods prior to checking the reader methods or failed consumer methods. To revise the existing definitions of correctness to be in vector space, we define when a method call happens-before another method call for the application of PROMOTEDEMOTE to a history, and the intervals in which a history must be balanced. We are now ready to reframe concurrent correctness in vector space.

Linearizability. Linearizability is the correctness property such that the concurrent history is equivalent to a legal sequential history and all method calls take effect in real-time order.

The definition of vector space linearizability is provided in Definition 2. The PROMOTEDEMOTE function is applied to method calls according to real-time order. The history must be balanced at the end of every method response. Two method calls are *overlapping* if one of the method call's invocation event occurs before the other method call's response event. Overlapping methods must be included when determining if a history is balanced since a method that overlaps with another method could affect its outcome.

Definition 2 *(Vector Space). Let H be a history. Let h be the subhistory of H up to method response t and extension h′ includes all method calls overlapping with t. History H is vector space linearizable if for every method response t, 1) PROMOTEDEMOTE is applied to the method calls in complete(h′) such that method call m_0 happens-before method call m_1 if m_0 and m_1 are invoked on the same object and m_0 precedes m_1 in complete(h′), and 2) h is balanced up to method response t.*

Sequential Consistency. Sequential Consistency is the correctness property such that the concurrent history is equivalent to a legal sequential history and all method calls take effect in program order.

The definition of vector space sequential consistency is provided in Definition 3. The PROMOTEDEMOTE function is applied to method calls according to program order or dependencies between methods called by different threads. A dependency exists between method call m_0 and method call m_1 if m_0 and m_1 are invoked on the same object and called by different threads and m_0 is consumed before m_1. In this case, all methods that precede m_0 and are called by the same process as m_0 must happen before all methods that occur after m_0. Enforcing the happens-before relationship between methods with dependencies enables the detection of non-sequentially consistent behavior due to cyclic dependencies. Since sequential consistency does not enforce real-time order of method calls, checking that the history is balanced must occur at the end of the history.

Definition 3 *(Vector Space). Let H be a history. Let h be the subhistory of H up to method response t and extension h' includes all method calls overlapping with t. History H is vector space sequentially consistent if for the last method response t, 1) PROMOTEDEMOTE is applied to the method calls in complete(h') such that method call m_0 happens-before method call m_1 if m_0 and m_1 are invoked on the same object and m_0 and m_1 are called by the same process and m_0 precedes m_1 in complete(h'), or m_0 and m_1 are invoked on the same object and m_0 is called by process p_0 and m_1 is called by process p_1 ($p_0 \neq p_1$) and there exist method calls m_0' called by p_0 and m_1' called by p_1 and m_0' and m_1' are invoked on the same object and m_0' is consumed before m_1' and m_0 precedes m_0' in complete(h'), and 2) h is balanced up to method response t.*

Quiescent Consistency. Quiescent Consistency is the correctness property such that the concurrent history is equivalent to a legal sequential history and all method calls take effect in real-time order when separated by a period of quiescence (no active method calls).

The definition of vector space quiescent consistency is provided in Definition 4. The PROMOTEDEMOTE function is applied to method calls according to real-time order when separated by a period of quiescence. The history must be balanced at the end of every quiescent period.

Definition 4 *(Vector Space). Let H be a history. Let h be the subhistory of H up to method response t and extension h' includes all method calls overlapping with t. History H is vector space quiescently consistent if for every method response t preceding a period of quiescence, 1) PROMOTEDEMOTE is applied to the method calls in complete(h') such that method call m_0 happens-before method call m_1 if m_0 and m_1 are invoked on the same object and m_0 and m_1 are separated by a period of quiescence and m_0 precedes m_1 in complete(h'), and 2) h is balanced up to method response t.*

Quasi-Linearizability. Quasi-linearizability is the correctness property such that the concurrent history is equivalent to a legal sequential history and all method calls separated by a distance of length k take effect in real-time order.

The definition of vector space quasi-linearizability is provided in Definition 5. The PROMOTEDEMOTE function is applied to method calls according to real-time order when separated by a distance of length k. The history must be balanced at the end of every method response t at distance k.

Definition 5 *(Vector Space) . Let H be a history. Let h be the subhistory of H up to method response t and extension h' includes all method calls overlapping with t. History H is vector space quasi-linearizable if for every method response t at distance k, 1) PROMOTEDEMOTE is applied to the method calls in complete(h') such*

Algorithm 3. Dynamic Analysis Algorithm

```
1: #define NUM_THRDS constant                                    ▷ Total number of threads
2: function               VERIFY(list < Method >                     thrd_list[NUM_THRDS],
   int thrd_list_count[NUM_THRDS])
3:     int count[NUM_THRDS]
4:     list < Method >::iterator position[NUM_THRDS]
5:     set < Method > methods                                    ▷ Sorted by response time
6:     list < Method >::iterator start, temp, start_prev
7:     start = temp = start_prev = methods.begin()
8:     long int min = LONG_MAX
9:     while true do
10:        for int i = 0; i <NUM_THRDS; ++i do
11:            if count[i] < thrd_list_count[i].load() then
12:                if count[i] == 0 then position[i] = thrd_list[i].begin() else ++position[i]
13:                Method m = *position[i]
14:                temp = methods.insert(m)
15:                count[i] = count[i] + 1
16:                if m.response < min then min = m.response; start = start_prev = temp
17:        PROMOTEDEMOTE(methods, start, min)
18:        if ! ISBALANCED(methods) then History not balanced at time min
19:        if start == start_prev then min = LONG_MAX
20:        if All threads finished then break
21:    PROMOTEDEMOTE(methods, start, LONG_MAX )
22:    if ! ISBALANCED(methods) then History not balanced at final time
```

that method call m_0 happens-before method call m_1 if m_0 and m_1 are invoked on the same object and m_0 and m_1 are separated by a distance k and m_0 precedes m_1 in complete(h'), and 2) h is balanced up to method response t.

4   Dynamic Correctness Tool Implementation

We use the correctness conditions defined in vector space to build an efficient dynamic tool to verify program correctness. The algorithm for the dynamic correctness tool is presented in Algorithm 3. The tool runs a verification thread simultaneously with a user program that checks the specified correctness condition (vector space linearizability, vector space sequential consistency, vector space quiescent consistency, or vector space quasi-linearizability). When a user program thread executes a method, it writes a method object to its thread-local list of methods. It then atomically updates a thread-local counter to indicate the tail position of the thread-local method list. The verification thread will continuously loop through the thread-local method lists on line 3.10 and will insert methods in the method call set one at a time per thread as they become available on line 3.14.

The verification step applies PROMOTEDEMOTE to the current method call set on line 3.17 and then checks that the method call set is balanced on line 3.18. At every loop iteration, the verification thread tracks the most recent response time that is the minimum among the threads on line 3.16, and only performs the verification step up to this response time to prevent skipping over methods that respond after the verification step is performed. The verification thread maintains a method iterator on line 3.16 for the starting point of the verification step that is updated as the method list is traversed to prevent re-checking methods that have already been checked. Methods that overlap with the minimum response time are also included in the verification step because they could affect the method with the minimum response time. Overlapping methods are included in the verification step by the if-statement on line 2.5 because only methods with an invocation greater than the minimum response time are discarded. In this case, the start iterator and minimum response time are set to the method with the earliest response time that does not overlap with the previously recorded minimum time. If the start iterator is never updated by PROMOTEDE-MOTE called on line 3.17, then *min* is reset to LONG_MAX on line 3.19.

Since the method call vectors are sparse, we maintain a sum with each Item/Object and update the sums when performing PROMOTEDEMOTE to the method call set. Using this strategy, we reduce the required space and avoid the overhead costs of applying addition to the method call vectors at frequent time intervals. The most expensive aspect of the tool with respect to time is determining the happens-before relationship between methods during PROMOT-EDEMOTE. We reduce this time cost by removing consumer methods and the corresponding producer methods that produced the consumed item since these methods will no longer impact other methods regarding the happens-before relationship. To avoid losing precision due to floating-point numbers, we maintain the numerator and denominator of the fraction that represents the method call vector sum for a particular element.

4.1 Time Complexity

The while-loop on line 3.9 will continue until all n methods have been encountered. At each iteration of the while-loop, the verification thread will read one method from each of the thread-local method lists and assign the method with the minimum response as the start method for PROMOTEDEMOTE on line 3.17. Within the PROMOTEDEMOTE function, the for-loop on line 2.4 will advance through the method call set until it reaches the first method that does not overlap with the starting method on line 2.5. In this case, the starting method is set to the current method. Since the starting method is advanced by the while-loop on line 3.9 and the for-loop on line 2.4, both of these loops will take at most $O(n)$ time. The for loop on line 2.7 always starts at the beginning of the method call set to handle the happens-before relationship between methods, which takes at most $O(n)$ time. Since the for-loop on line 2.7 is nested within the for-loop on line 2.4, the total time complexity of Algorithm 3 is $O(n^2)$.

4.2 Correctness

We now demonstrate that the dynamic analysis tool is 1) *sound* - it reports an error if the observed trace is non-linearizable, i.e. no false negatives, and 2) *complete* - it reports an error only for non-linearizable traces, i.e. no false positives. We use the term *vector space linearizability* to refer to our proposed definition of linearizability and the term *linearizability* to refer to the standard definition of linearizability [21]. The soundness and completeness proofs are limited to producer, consumer, reader, and writer methods.

Theorem 1 *(Soundness). Let H be a concurrent history. If H is not linearizable, then H is not vector space linearizable.*

Proof A history H is not linearizable if any of the following scenarios occur: 1) the method calls do not take effect in real-time order, or 2) the history is not equivalent to a legal sequential history. For the first scenario, if the method calls do not take effect in real-time order, then the following cases may occur: 1) an item is consumed from object O that does not have the highest priority in O, 2) an item is read before it is produced or written in object O, or 3) a consumer method fails when the item to be consumed exists in object O. A proof by cases is provided to show that if the method calls do not take effect in real-time order, then H is not vector space linearizable.

Case 1. There must exist some method response t' where an item I is consumed that does not have the highest priority in object O. The method call vector for the consume is set to -1 at index o, i. Since this item does not have the highest priority in O, the value assignment at index o, i of the method call vector that produced the item is less than one. The sum of the method call vectors at index o, i is less than zero, which is not vector space linearizable.

Case 2. There must exist some method response t' where an item I is read that does not exist in object O. The method call vector for the jth read for an item is set to $-\frac{1}{2^j}$ at index o, i. Since I does not exist in O, the sum of the method call vectors at index o, i is less than zero, which is not vector space linearizable.

Case 3. There must exist some method response t' where a consumer method fails when the item I to be consumed exists in object O. The method call vector $\boldsymbol{F}$ is set to $-\frac{1}{2^j}$ at index o, i for the jth failed consume applied to I in O. If $\boldsymbol{F}_{sum}[i] \neq 0$, then $\boldsymbol{N}[i] =$-1 by Definition 1. Since the item corresponding to index o, i exists, $\lceil(\boldsymbol{P}_{sum}[o, i] + \boldsymbol{C}_{sum}[o, i] + \boldsymbol{W}_{sum}[o, i])\rceil = 1$. Since $\lceil(\boldsymbol{P}_{sum}[o, i] + \boldsymbol{C}_{sum}[o, i] + \boldsymbol{W}_{sum}[o, i])\rceil + \boldsymbol{F}_{sum}[o, i] > 0$, $(\lceil(\boldsymbol{P}_{sum}[o, i] + \boldsymbol{C}_{sum}[o, i] + \boldsymbol{W}_{sum}[o, i])\rceil + \boldsymbol{F}_{sum}[o, i]) \cdot \boldsymbol{N}[o, i] < 0$, which is not vector space linearizable.

For the second scenario, if the history is not equivalent to a legal sequential history, then the following cases may occur for producer, consumer, reader, or writer methods: 1) item I is consumed from object O that never existed in O, 2) item I is read that never existed in object O, or 3) a consumer method fails and item I to be consumed always existed in object O. A proof by cases is provided to show that if the history is not equivalent to a legal sequential history, then H is not vector space linearizable.

Case 1. If item I to be consumed never existed in O, then the method call vector for the consume is set to -1 at index o, i and all other method call vectors at index o, i are zero. The sum of the method call vectors over the entire history is -1 at index o, i, which is not vector space linearizable.

Case 2. The same reasoning for Case 2 of the first scenario, where method response t' is the end of the concurrent history, applies to this case.

Case 3. The same reasoning for Case 3 of the first scenario, where method response t' is the end of the concurrent history, applies to this case.

In all cases, if H is not linearizable, then H is not vector space linearizable.

Theorem 2 *(Completeness). Let H be a concurrent history. If H is not vector space linearizable, then H is not linearizable.*

Proof A history H is not vector space linearizable if for some method response t', the subhistory h' of H up to method response t', including method calls that overlap with t', is not balanced. History h' is not balanced if any of the following cases occur for some index o, i: 1) $\boldsymbol{P}_{sum}[o, i] + \boldsymbol{C}_{sum}[o, i] + \boldsymbol{W}_{sum}[o, i] < 0$, or 2) $\lceil (\boldsymbol{P}_{sum}[o, i] + \boldsymbol{C}_{sum}[o, i] + \boldsymbol{W}_{sum}[o, i]) \rceil + \boldsymbol{R}_{sum}[o, i] < 0$, or 3) $(\lceil (\boldsymbol{P}_{sum}[o, i] + \boldsymbol{C}_{sum}[o, i] + \boldsymbol{W}_{sum}[o, i]) \rceil + \boldsymbol{F}_{sum}[o, i]) \cdot \boldsymbol{N}[o, i] < 0$. A proof by cases is provided to show that if H is not vector space linearizable, then H is not linearizable. For all cases, the priority assignments are applied to the method call vectors according to data structure semantics and the happens-before relation, where method call m_0 happens-before method call m_1 if m_0 and m_1 are invoked on the same object and m_0 precedes m_1 in complete(h').

Case 1. The case for $\boldsymbol{P}_{sum}[o, i] + \boldsymbol{C}_{sum}[o, i] + \boldsymbol{W}_{sum}[o, i] < 0$ occurs when item I is consumed from object O that does not have the highest priority to be removed from O. The value assignment for a consumer method call is -1 at index o, i. The value assignment for a producer method call is 1 for the highest priority and less than one for all other priorities at index o, i. The sum $\boldsymbol{P}_{sum}[o, i] + \boldsymbol{C}_{sum}[o, i] + \boldsymbol{W}_{sum}[o, i]$ is less than zero if the value assignment of -1 for a consumer method call is added to a priority that is less than one. Since the item being consumed does not have the highest priority to be consumed, the method call ordering based on the data structure semantics and the happens-before relation is violated, which implies a non-linearizable history.

Case 2. The case for $\lceil (\boldsymbol{P}_{sum}[o, i] + \boldsymbol{C}_{sum}[o, i] + \boldsymbol{W}_{sum}[o, i]) \rceil + \boldsymbol{R}_{sum}[o, i] < 0$ occurs when I is read before it has been produced or written in O. The sum $\boldsymbol{P}_{sum}[o, i] + \boldsymbol{C}_{sum}[o, i] + \boldsymbol{W}_{sum}[o, i]$ is greater than zero if I exists in O. When the ceiling function is applied to $\boldsymbol{P}_{sum}[o, i] + \boldsymbol{C}_{sum}[o, i] + \boldsymbol{W}_{sum}[o, i]$, the resulting value is one if I exists in O; the resulting value is zero if I does not exist in O. The value assignment for method call vector $\boldsymbol{R}$ performing the jth read of an item is set to $-\frac{1}{2^j}$ at index o, i. Since $\lceil (\boldsymbol{P}_{sum}[o, i] + \boldsymbol{C}_{sum}[o, i] + \boldsymbol{W}_{sum}[o, i]) \rceil + \boldsymbol{R}_{sum}[o, i] < 0$, I does not exist in O which implies a non-linearizable history.

Case 3. The case for $(\lceil (\boldsymbol{P}_{sum}[o, i] + \boldsymbol{C}_{sum}[o, i] + \boldsymbol{W}_{sum}[o, i]) \rceil + \boldsymbol{F}_{sum}[o, i]) \cdot \boldsymbol{N}[o, i] < 0$ occurs when a consumer method fails and item I to be consumed exists in object O. The method call vector $\boldsymbol{F}$ at index o, i is set to $-\frac{1}{2^j}$ for the jth failed consume applied to I in O. The sum $(\lceil (\boldsymbol{P}_{sum}[o, i] + \boldsymbol{C}_{sum}[o, i] + \boldsymbol{W}_{sum}[o, i]) \rceil + \boldsymbol{F}_{sum}[o, i]) > 0$ if a consumer method fails and I to be consumed exists in O; otherwise, $(\lceil (\boldsymbol{P}_{sum}[o, i] + \boldsymbol{C}_{sum}[o, i] + \boldsymbol{W}_{sum}[o, i]) \rceil + \boldsymbol{F}_{sum}[o, i]) < 0$ if a consumer method fails and I does not exist in O. The vector element $\boldsymbol{N}[o, i] = 0$ if $\boldsymbol{F}_{sum}[o, i] = 0$ by Definition 1; otherwise, $\boldsymbol{N}[o, i] = -1$ if $\boldsymbol{F}_{sum}[o, i] \neq 0$. Since the sum $(\lceil (\boldsymbol{P}_{sum}[o, i] + \boldsymbol{C}_{sum}[o, i] + \boldsymbol{W}_{sum}[o, i]) \rceil + \boldsymbol{F}_{sum}[o, i]) \cdot \boldsymbol{N}[o, i] < 0$, a consumer method fails when I exists in O, which implies a non-linearizable history.

In all cases, if H is not vector space linearizable, then H is not linearizable. A similar logic can be applied for reasoning about soundness and completeness of the other vector space correctness conditions.

5   Discussion

Correctness defined in vector space is not limited to only producer, consumer, reader, and writer methods. It is possible to apply the vector space verification technique to polling methods such as size or contains. For example, a size method can be handled by applying the ceiling function to the method call vector sums and computing the *taxicab norm*, $||x|| = \sum_{i=1}^{n} |x_i|$, of the resulting method call vector sums. The taxicab norm represents the total number of items in the data structure, which can be used to verify correctness of a size polling method. A contains method can be handled by checking the method call vector sum at the index corresponding to the item of interest. If contains returns false, the sum should be zero; if contains returns true, the sum should be greater than zero.

The main limitation of verifying correctness in vector space is that it assumes a single total order in which all threads observe operations in the same order. This presents a challenge for weak memory concurrency models such as Total Store Order (TSO) [32] where threads may observe updates in their local write buffers but not observe updates in remote write buffers. To extend our approach to support correctness conditions where threads observe a different order of operations, the vector space analysis must be maintained on a per-thread basis.

6   Experimental Evaluation

We evaluate our dynamic analysis tool by checking the vector space correctness of an Intel TBB Queue [23], a k-FIFO queue [24], a Boost Library [5] lock-free stack, a Tervel Library [16] lock-free stack, an Intel TBB hashmap [23], and a Tervel Library [16] wait-free hashmap. The data structures are checked for vector space linearizability, vector space sequential consistency, vector space quiescent consistency, and vector space quasi-linearizability. The tests are conducted on a 32-core AMD EPYC 7551 @ 2 GHz with Ubuntu 18.04.1 LTS operating system. The thread count for each test is fixed at 32. We hold the thread count fixed because our approach is unaffected by the total number of threads. We vary the number of methods called by each thread from 10 to 10000. The number of keys is set to the number of method calls. The method call distribution for the queue data type is 50% enqueue and 50% dequeue. The method call distribution for the stack data type is 50% push and 50% pop. The method call distribution for the hashmap data type is 33% insert, 33% delete, and 34% find. We set k (quasi-linearization factor) to 2 for the k-FIFO queue.

All data structures satisfied the evaluated correctness conditions except for the k-FIFO queue. The k-FIFO queue satisfied vector space quasi-linearizabiltiy when k is set to 2, but does not satisfy the other correctness conditions. The verification time of our dynamic analysis tool is presented in Fig. 2. The n^2 trend

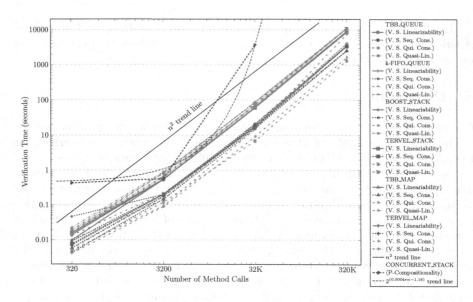

Fig. 2. Vector space (V. S.) verification times of concurrent data structures

line is plotted to demonstrate that all vector space correctness conditions scale at the rate of $O(n^2)$. The n^2 line is plotted as $6.25 \times 10^{-7} n^2$, where n is the number of method calls.

Table 1. Vector space (V. S.) verification time (in seconds) for 320,000 method calls (32 threads, 10,000 method calls each)

Data Structure	V.S. Linearizability		V. S. Sequential Consistency		V. S. Quiescent Consistency		V. S. Quasi-Linearizability	
	Program	Verify	Program	Verify	Program	Verify	Program	Verify
TBB Queue	0.11	8938	0.09	3473	0.10	4033	0.11	10949
k-FIFO Queue	0.21	9110	0.21	3495	0.21	2530	0.21	11294
Boost Stack	0.21	8613	0.21	3425	0.19	4109	0.19	10876
Tervel Stack	0.46	4483	0.46	3403	0.43	1312	0.47	10830
TBB Map	0.02	7831	0.01	2559	0.01	7333	0.02	9005
Tervel Map	0.72	7181	0.73	2555	0.70	1625	0.69	8381

The main factor that affects the verification time is the application of the priority scheme to the method calls due to the overhead associated with promoting and demoting methods. The fastest correctness condition to check is vector space quiescent consistency. Vector space quiescent consistency encounters less overhead due to the priority scheme in comparison to the other correctness conditions since the priority scheme is only enforced at the quiescent periods. Vector space sequential consistency takes more time to check than vector space quiescent consistency because the priority scheme is enforced when methods are called by the same thread. Vector space linearizability takes more time to check than vector space sequential consistency because the priority scheme is enforced for every method call. Vector space quasi-linearizability takes more time to check than vector space linearizability because an additional for-loop of length k is required to determine if methods are separated by a distance k when establishing if a method call happens-before another method call.

We compare our dynamic analysis tool with the P-Compositionality [22] verification technique applied to a concurrent stack. P-Compositionality is an efficient solution to the NP-complete problem of comparing to legal sequential histories. We compare to P-Compositionality to provide motivation for the revised definitions of correctness in vector space by showcasing the potential performance improvements achievable when correctness verification is a polynomial time problem. The thread count for each test is fixed at 32 and the number of methods called by each thread varies from 10 to 10000. The verification time follows an exponential trend, where $2^{0.0004*n-1.16}$ was computed using interpolation. The approach timed out at the 10000 method calls per thread (320K total) configuration. A stack is a particularly challenging abstract data type because a stack history can only be partitioned at instants in which the stack is empty. With this limitation, P-Compositionality cannot overcome the exponential growth with respect to the number of methods called.

A snapshot of the verification time at 320,000 method calls is shown in Table 1. The program time (in seconds) is the measured time of the slowest thread to execute their assigned method calls. The verification time (in seconds) is the measured time of the verification thread to check the correctness of the tested data structure. Although the program execution time is short compared to the verification time, the problem size with respect to the number of threads is much larger than state-of-the-art dynamic analysis correctness tools [22,28]. There is a large amount of variance in the quiescent periods for each execution, leading to a lower consistency in the time to check vector space quiescent consistency for each of the tested data structures. The verification time for the other correctness conditions is generally consistent among each of the tested data structures because the priority scheme is applied at intervals that do not deviate between different executions. In general, the map data type takes less time to verify than the other data types because inserting or removing items in the map does not affect the priority of the other items in the map.

A notable observation regarding the verification time for the different correctness conditions is that some of the relaxed correctness conditions (vector space sequential consistency and vector space quiescent consistency) are faster to verify than vector space linearizability. This result is quite different from the theoretical time to check correctness for standard relaxed correctness conditions by searching for an equivalent legal sequential history since the relaxed correctness conditions have more possible legal sequential histories than linearizability.

6.1   Enhancements Using the GPU

Verifying correctness in vector space is further enhanced by utilizing the Graphics Processing Unit (GPU) to check that the concurrent history is balanced (i.e.

the method call vector sums are ≥ 0) in parallel. The tests are conducted on an AMD - Ryzen 5 2400G 3.6 GHz Quad-Core Processor with the OpenCL [30] standard programming environment. The results for the Intel TBB queue are shown in Fig. 3. The verification times with the label 'OpenCL' indicate that the computation to determine if the concurrent history is balanced is performed on the GPU. The verification times without the label 'OpenCL' indicate that the computation to determine if the concurrent history is balanced is performed using a for-loop. At 320, 3200, and 32K method calls, the overhead of OpenCL outweighs the benefits of using the GPU to check if the concurrent history is balanced. At the 320K method call configuration, the verification time is reduced by 27% for vector space linearizability, 27% for vector space sequential consistency, and 20% for vector space quasi-linearizability when performing the balance computation on the GPU. No time reduction is observed for vector space quiescent consistency because the time required to verify vector space quiescent consistency increases as the number of quiescent periods increases, leading to inconsistent verification times. In general, the verification time reduction motivates utilizing the GPU for large method call counts. The $O(n^2)$ time complexity required for determining the happens-before relationship between method calls limits the potential performance benefits of GPU computation, which provides further motivation for the development of correctness conditions that are not constrained by a happens-before relationship.

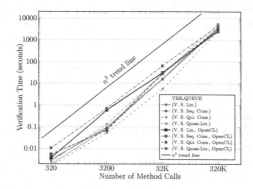

Fig. 3. Vector space (V. S.) verification times of Intel TBB Queue on AMD - Ryzen

7   Related Work

There is a large amount of previous research focused on checking correctness properties of concurrent objects. The literature comprises two fundamentally different approaches for checking correctness: static checking [3,8,11,14,15,15, 26,27,29,31,33,35,38,40,42,45] and dynamic checking [7,9,12,13,17,18,22,28, 36,37,41,43,44]. Due to space constraints, we dedicate the remainder of this section for a direct comparison with existing correctness tools.

7.1   Comparison of the Proposed Dynamic Analysis Tool to Existing Tools

The main advantage of our dynamic analysis tool over other tools for correctness checking is that we avoid the time costs of generating all possible legal sequential histories of a concurrent history. There is a special case of linearizability where correctness checking of a single history can be performed in $O(n)$ time if a single atomic instruction can be identified as the linearization point of a method. In this case, a concurrent history only has one possible legal sequential history which can be checked in $O(n)$ time. Vechev et al. [40] and Ou et al. [31] present tools that accept user annotated linearization points, while Vafeiadis [39] and Long et al. [27] present tools to automatically identify potential linearization points. However, these approaches are not applicable to the common case where method calls have non-fixed linearization points.

Table 2. Time complexity analysis of correctness verification techniques

Verification Technique	Time Complexity	Description
Vector Space Analysis	$O(n^2)$	n is the number of method calls
Strong Hitting Schedules [33]	$O(p \cdot n^{d-1})$	p is the number of threads, n is the number of operations, d is the linearizability depth, empirically holds for small d, where upper bound of d is 5
Reduction to Satisfiability [14]	$O(n^k)$	n is the number of clauses, k is the rank of input-operation order signature
P-Compositionality [22]	$O((n/k+1) \cdot 2^p \cdot B)$	p is the number of threads, n is the number of method calls, B is a bound on the states of the sequential specification, and k is the number of partitions applied to a history
Just-In-Time [28]	$O((n+1) \cdot 2^p \cdot B)$	p is the number of threads, n is the number of method calls, and B is a bound on the states of the sequential specification
Round-Up [44]	$O((1+k)!^{n/(1+k)})$	k is the quasi factor, n is the number of method calls

Recent dynamic analysis tools have significantly pruned the search space of possible legal sequential histories to consider when checking correctness [22,28]. The time complexity of the dynamic analysis tool by Lowe [28] is $O((n+1) \cdot 2^p \cdot B)$, where p is the number of threads, n is the number of method calls, and B is a bound on the states of the sequential specification. Horn et al. [22] optimize Lowe's dynamic analysis tool by a partitioning scheme that reduces n by a constant factor, but the time complexity of solving the smaller partitions is still $O((n+1) \cdot 2^p \cdot B)$, which is exponential with respect to the number of threads. The partitioning scheme is highly effective for the set and map abstract data type because a history can be partitioned according to operations on individual keys since these operations are commutative. However, the partitioning scheme has limited applicability for sets and maps if a size polling method is invoked, or for other abstract data types such as stacks and queues where commutativity of operations is dependent on the state of the data structure. Since our dynamic analysis tool has a time complexity of $O(n^2)$, it is capable of checking the correctness of large method call workloads for an arbitrary number of threads more efficiently than the tools by Horn et al. [22] and Lowe [28].

A summary of the time complexity analysis of concurrent correctness verification techniques is presented in Table 2. Ozkan et al. [33] empirically demonstrate that most linearizable histories have a witness schedule in a strong d-hitting family for $d \leq 5$, yielding a worst-case time complexity of $O(p \cdot n^4)$, where p is the number of processes. Horn et al. [22] and Lowe et al. [28] present verification techniques that are exponential with respect to the number of threads. Roundup [44] enumerates all possible quasi-linearizations, yielding a worst-case time complexity that is exponential with respect to the number of method calls.

Emmi et al. [14]'s reduction of correctness verification to a logical satisfiability problem guarantees a worst-case time complexity of $O(n^k)$ for a fixed rank k of input-operation order signature. This approach is limited to collection abstract data types whose methods are value-invariant, local, parametric, and reducible. Our proposed vector space analysis does not have these limitations. The proposed vector space analysis of writer methods enables a priority adoption for values that may be changed by method calls and can therefore handle value-variant methods. Although the presented theory for vector space analysis is only provided for local methods (methods that touch exactly the values appearing in its label), it is possible to handle non-local methods such as size and contains in vector space using mathematical strategies in Sect. 5. Our proposed vector space analysis is not limited to parametric methods because the logic for handling writer method calls in vector space can be applied to handle method calls where value renaming does not yield admitted behavior. Additionally, our proposed vector space analysis is not limited to reducible methods because the worst-case time complexity is $O(n^2)$, where n is the number of method calls. Therefore, our approach does not need to be characterized by small representative behaviors.

8   Conclusion

We revised the traditional correctness conditions in literature to be defined in vector space. We use the proposed theory to design an efficient dynamic analysis tool that checks the vector space correctness of concurrent data structures in $O(n^2)$ time, where n is the number of method calls. The key benefit of our dynamic analysis tools is that it shines in areas where other correctness tools fall short. For example, the dynamic analysis tools by Horn et al. [22] and Lowe [28] have a time complexity that scales exponentially with respect to the number of threads, while our approach is not impacted by number of threads. Additionally, our dynamic analysis tool can check relaxed vector space correctness conditions as efficiently as vector space linearizability which is much different than the observed verification time for tools that take more time to check standard relaxed correctness condition due to the search space for possible legal sequential histories [44]. The experimental evaluation demonstrates that our dynamic analysis tool can check the vector space correctness of practical concurrent data structures for an arbitrary number of threads with large workloads.

References

1. Afek, Y., Korland, G., Yanovsky, E.: Quasi-linearizability: relaxed consistency for improved concurrency. In: Lu, C., Masuzawa, T., Mosbah, M. (eds.) OPODIS 2010. LNCS, vol. 6490, pp. 395–410. Springer, Heidelberg (2010). https://doi.org/10.1007/978-3-642-17653-1_29
2. Alur, R., McMillan, K., Peled, D.: Model-checking of correctness conditions for concurrent objects. In: Proceedings 11th Annual IEEE Symposium on Logic in Computer Science, pp. 219–228. IEEE (1996)
3. Amit, D., Rinetzky, N., Reps, T., Sagiv, M., Yahav, E.: Comparison under abstraction for verifying linearizability. In: Damm, W., Hermanns, H. (eds.) CAV 2007. LNCS, vol. 4590, pp. 477–490. Springer, Heidelberg (2007). https://doi.org/10.1007/978-3-540-73368-3_49
4. Aspnes, J., Herlihy, M., Shavit, N.: Counting networks. J. ACM (JACM) **41**(5), 1020–1048 (1994)
5. Boost: Boost c++ library (2019). https://www.boost.org/
6. Bouajjani, A., Emmi, M., Enea, C., Hamza, J.: Verifying concurrent programs against sequential specifications. In: Felleisen, M., Gardner, P. (eds.) ESOP 2013. LNCS, vol. 7792, pp. 290–309. Springer, Heidelberg (2013). https://doi.org/10.1007/978-3-642-37036-6_17
7. Bouajjani, A., Emmi, M., Enea, C., Hamza, J.: Tractable refinement checking for concurrent objects. In: Proceedings of the 42nd Annual ACM SIGPLAN-SIGACT Symposium on Principles of Programming Languages (POPL 2015), vol. 50, no. 1, pp. 651–662 (2015)
8. Burckhardt, S., Dern, C., Musuvathi, M., Tan, R.: Line-up: a complete and automatic linearizability checker. In: Proceedings of the 31st ACM SIGPLAN Conference on Programming Language Design and Implementation (PLDI 2010) vol. 45, no.6, pp. 330–340 (2010)
9. Burnim, J., Elmas, T., Necula, G., Sen, K.: Ndseq: Runtime checking for nondeterministic sequential specifications of parallel correctness. In: Proceedings of the 32nd ACM SIGPLAN Conference on Programming Language Design and Implementation (PLDI '11), vol. 46, pp. 401–414. ACM (2011)
10. Cook, V., Peterson, C., Painter, Z., Dechev, D.: Quantifiability: Concurrent correctness from first principles. arXiv preprint arXiv:1905.06421 (2019)
11. Doolan, P., Smith, G., Zhang, C., Krishnan, P.: Improving the scalability of automatic linearizability checking in SPIN. In: Duan, Z., Ong, L. (eds.) ICFEM 2017. LNCS, vol. 10610, pp. 105–121. Springer, Cham (2017). https://doi.org/10.1007/978-3-319-68690-5_7
12. Elmas, T., Tasiran, S.: Vyrdmc: driving runtime refinement checking with model checkers. Electron. Notes Theor. Comput. Sci. **144**(4), 41–56 (2006)
13. Elmas, T., Tasiran, S., Qadeer, S.: Vyrd: verifying concurrent programs by runtime refinement-violation detection. In: Proceedings of the 2005 ACM SIGPLAN conference on Programming language design and implementation (PLDI 2005), vol. 40, pp. 27–37. ACM (2005)

14. Emmi, M., Enea, C.: Sound, complete, and tractable linearizability monitoring for concurrent collections. In: Proceedings of the ACM on Programming Languages, vol. 2(POPL), p. 25 (2017)
15. Emmi, M., Enea, C., Hamza, J.: Monitoring refinement via symbolic reasoning. In: Proceedings of the 36th ACM SIGPLAN Conference on Programming Language Design and Implementation (PLDI 2015), vol. 50, pp. 260–269. ACM (2015)
16. Feldman, S., LaBorde, P., Dechev, D.: Tervel: A unification of descriptor-based techniques for non-blocking programming. In: 2015 International Conference on Embedded Computer Systems: Architectures, Modeling, and Simulation (SAMOS), pp. 131–140. IEEE (2015)
17. Flanagan, C., Flanagan, C., Freund, S.N.: Atomizer: a dynamic atomicity checker for multithreaded programs. In: Proceedings of the 31st ACM SIGPLAN-SIGACT Symposium on Principles of Programming Languages (POPL 2004), vol. 39, pp. 256–267. ACM (2004)
18. Flanagan, C., Freund, S.N., Yi, J.: Velodrome: a sound and complete dynamic atomicity checker for multithreaded programs. Proceedings of the 29th ACM SIGPLAN Conference on Programming Language Design and Implementation (PLDI 2008) 43(6), 293–303 (2008)
19. Gibbons, P.B., Korach, E.: Testing shared memories. SIAM J. Comput. **26**(4), 1208–1244 (1997)
20. Herlihy, M., Shavit, N.: The Art of Multiprocessor Programming. Morgan Kaufmann. Revised Reprint. ISBN: 0123973375, August 2012
21. Herlihy, M.P., Wing, J.M.: Linearizability: a correctness condition for concurrent objects. ACM Trans. Program. Lang. Syst. (TOPLAS) **12**(3), 463–492 (1990)
22. Horn, A., Kroening, D.: Faster linearizability checking via P-compositionality. In: Graf, S., Viswanathan, M. (eds.) FORTE 2015. LNCS, vol. 9039, pp. 50–65. Springer, Cham (2015). https://doi.org/10.1007/978-3-319-19195-9_4
23. Intel: Intel thread building blocks (2019). https://www.threadingbuildingblocks.org/
24. Kirsch, C.M., Lippautz, M., Payer, H.: Fast and scalable, lock-free k-FIFO queues. In: Malyshkin, V. (ed.) PaCT 2013. LNCS, vol. 7979, pp. 208–223. Springer, Heidelberg (2013). https://doi.org/10.1007/978-3-642-39958-9_18
25. Lamport, L.: How to make a multiprocessor computer that correctly executes multiprocess programs. IEEE Trans. Comput. **100**(9), 690–691 (1979)
26. Liu, Y., Chen, W., Liu, Y.A., Sun, J.: Model checking linearizability via refinement. In: Cavalcanti, A., Dams, D.R. (eds.) FM 2009. LNCS, vol. 5850, pp. 321–337. Springer, Heidelberg (2009). https://doi.org/10.1007/978-3-642-05089-3_21
27. Long, Z., Zhang, Y.: Checking linearizability with fine-grained traces. In: Proceedings of the 31st Annual ACM Symposium on Applied Computing, pp. 1394–1400. ACM (2016)
28. Lowe, G.: Testing for linearizability. Concurrency and Computation: Practice and Experience **29**(4), e3928 (2017)
29. Nanevski, A., Banerjee, A., Delbianco, G.A., Fábregas, I.: Specifying concurrent programs in separation logic: Morphisms and simulations. arXiv preprint arXiv:1904.07136 (2019)
30. OpenCL: The opencl specification (2010). https://www.khronos.org/opencl/
31. Ou, P., Demsky, B.: Checking concurrent data structures under the c/c++ 11 memory model. In: Proceedings of the 22nd ACM SIGPLAN Symposium on Principles and Practice of Parallel Programming (PPoPP 2017), vol. 52, pp. 45–59. ACM (2017)

32. Owens, S., Sarkar, S., Sewell, P.: A better x86 memory model: x86-TSO. In: Berghofer, S., Nipkow, T., Urban, C., Wenzel, M. (eds.) TPHOLs 2009. LNCS, vol. 5674, pp. 391–407. Springer, Heidelberg (2009). https://doi.org/10.1007/978-3-642-03359-9_27

33. Ozkan, B.K., Majumdar, R., Niksic, F.: Checking linearizability using hitting families. In: Proceedings of the 24th Symposium on Principles and Practice of Parallel Programming (PPoPP 2019), pp. 366–377. ACM (2019)

34. Papadimitriou, C.H.: Serializability of concurrent database updates. J. Assoc. Comput. Machinery **26**(4), 631–653 (1979)

35. Sergey, I., Nanevski, A., Banerjee, A., Delbianco, G.A.: Hoare-style specifications as correctness conditions for non-linearizable concurrent objects. In: Proceedings of the 2016 ACM SIGPLAN International Conference on Object-Oriented Programming, Systems, Languages, and Applications (OOPSLA 2016), vol. 51(10), pp. 92–110 (2016)

36. Shacham, O., Bronson, N., Aiken, A., Sagiv, M., Vechev, M., Yahav, E.: Testing atomicity of composed concurrent operations. In: Proceedings of the 2011 ACM International Conference on Object Oriented Programming Systems Languages and Applications (OOPSLA 2011), vol. 46, pp. 51–64. ACM (2011)

37. Shacham, O., et al.: Verifying atomicity via data independence. In: Proceedings of the 2014 International Symposium on Software Testing and Analysis, pp. 26–36. ACM (2014)

38. Siegel, S.F., et al.: Civl: the concurrency intermediate verification language. In: SC 2015: Proceedings of the International Conference for High Performance Computing, Networking, Storage and Analysis, pp. 1–12. IEEE (2015)

39. Vafeiadis, V.: Automatically proving linearizability. In: Touili, T., Cook, B., Jackson, P. (eds.) CAV 2010. LNCS, vol. 6174, pp. 450–464. Springer, Heidelberg (2010). https://doi.org/10.1007/978-3-642-14295-6_40

40. Vechev, M., Yahav, E., Yorsh, G.: Experience with model checking linearizability. In: Păsăreanu, C.S. (ed.) SPIN 2009. LNCS, vol. 5578, pp. 261–278. Springer, Heidelberg (2009). https://doi.org/10.1007/978-3-642-02652-2_21

41. Wang, L., Stoller, S.D.: Runtime analysis of atomicity for multithreaded programs. IEEE Trans. Software Eng. **32**(2), 93–110 (2006)

42. Wing, J.M., Gong, C.: Testing and verifying concurrent objects. J. Parallel Distributed Comput. **17**(1–2), 164–182 (1993)

43. Wu, S., Yang, C., Chan, W.: ASR: abstraction subspace reduction for exposing atomicity violation bugs in multithreaded programs. In: 2015 IEEE International Conference on Software Quality, Reliability and Security, pp. 272–281. IEEE (2015)

44. Zhang, L., Chattopadhyay, A., Wang, C.: Round-up: runtime verification of quasi linearizability for concurrent data structures. IEEE Trans. Softw. Eng. **41**(12), 1202–1216 (2015)

45. Zomer, O., Golan-Gueta, G., Ramalingam, G., Sagiv, M.: Checking linearizability of encapsulated extended operations. In: Shao, Z. (ed.) ESOP 2014. LNCS, vol. 8410, pp. 311–330. Springer, Heidelberg (2014). https://doi.org/10.1007/978-3-642-54833-8_17

Verification of Concurrent Programs
Using Petri Net Unfoldings

Daniel Dietsch, Matthias Heizmann, Dominik Klumpp[(✉)], Mehdi Naouar,
Andreas Podelski, and Claus Schätzle

University of Freiburg, Freiburg im Breisgau, Germany
`klumpp@informatik.uni-freiburg.de`

Abstract. Given a verification problem for a concurrent program (with
a fixed number of threads) over infinite data domains, we can construct
a model checking problem for an abstraction of the concurrent program
through a Petri net (a problem which can be solved using McMillan's
unfoldings technique). We present a method of abstraction refinement
which translates Floyd/Hoare-style proofs for sample traces into additional synchronization constraints for the Petri net.

Keywords: Petri nets · Unfoldings · Concurrency · Verification

1   Introduction

The verification of concurrent programs is an active topic of research, and since
it is also an old topic of research, there is a large body of literature covering
a wide area of aspects of the problem; see, e.g., [2,3,7,8,10,11,15,17,19,21]. In
this paper, we address the verification problem for programs composed of a fixed
number of threads over an infinite data domain.

This verification problem poses two major challenges. First, the challenge of
interleavings. In contrast to sequential programs, the control-flow of concurrent
programs is much more permissive: an execution trace is not a cohesive sequence
of statements from one process but an interleaved sequence of execution traces
of all processes. Hence we have to account for a gigantic number of possible
orderings of statements of the system's independent processes. For finite state
systems the problem has been successfully approached by *Petri net unfoldings*.
If the finite state system is represented by a bounded Petri net (i.e., a Petri
net where each place can only take a pre-defined fixed amount of tokens), an
unfolding is a mathematical structure that allows us to see all reachable states
without exploring all interleavings explicitly. Unfoldings explicitly preserve the
concurrent nature of Petri nets and can be exponentially more concise than a
naive reachability graph.

The second challenge that we are facing is that our variables take their
value from an infinite data domain and hence we cannot directly apply algorithms for finite state systems. For sequential programs this second challenge is
often approached by abstracting the program by a finite state system. If such

F. Henglein et al. (Eds.): VMCAI 2021, LNCS 12597, pp. 174–195, 2021.
https://doi.org/10.1007/978-3-030-67067-2_9

an abstraction represents all executions of the program but does not have any erroneous execution, we know that the program is correct. Finding a suitable abstraction is difficult. Algorithms for finding abstractions usually follow the counterexample-guided abstraction refinement scheme (CEGAR). There, the algorithm constructs abstractions iteratively. In each iteration the algorithm uses Floyd/Hoare-style annotations obtained from counterexamples to refine the abstraction.

In this paper, we present a method of abstraction refinement which, given a verification problem for a program composed of a fixed number of threads over an infinite data domain, constructs a model checking problem for a Petri net. The idea is to translate Floyd/Hoare-style annotations into synchronization constraints; by adding synchronization constraints to the Petri net, we refine the abstraction of the concurrent program through the Petri net. In summary, the method of abstraction refinement constructs a bounded Petri net and thus gives us the possibility to use Petri net unfoldings for the verification of programs composed of a fixed number of threads over an infinite data domain.

Let us motivate our approach by illustrating shortcomings of naive sequentialization, a straightforward approach to the verification of concurrent programs. Sequentialization means that we translate the concurrent program into a sequential program which allows us to apply all verification techniques for sequential programs. In its most basic form, the sequentialization produces a control flow graph (CFG) that is the product of the CFGs of the concurrent program's threads. However, this basic approach does not scale well: The product CFG must explicitly represent the many different interleavings. Hence the number of locations in the CFG grows exponentially with the number of threads. As an example, consider the schema for a concurrent program shown in Fig. 1. Given a number N, this yields a concurrent program with N threads. After the variable x is initially set to 0, the different threads all repeatedly modify x for a nondeterministically chosen number of times. The control flow graph for each thread is simple, it only requires 3 locations (loop head, location between both assignments, and loop exit). But the resulting product CFG has 3^N locations, it grows exponentially in the number of threads. For large N, even the construction of the product CFG may thus run out of time and memory. In our approach we do not construct this product but a Petri net that has for each thread one token and whose places are the locations of all CFGs. Hence our Petri net grows only linearly in the number of threads.

This paper is organized as follows. In Sect. 2 we demonstrate our approach on the example above and another example. Section 3 introduces our notation and terminology for finite automata and Petri nets. We use Petri nets to introduce the considered verification problem formally in Sect. 4. In Sect. 5 we present our algorithm for this verification problem, and in Sect. 6 we present an automata-theoretic difference operation required by our verification algorithm. In Sect. 7 we discuss how the difference operation introduces synchronization constraints. Finally, we discuss related work in Sect. 8 and conclude with Sect. 9.

```
1  x := 0 // initialization
```

```
1  thread1() {          1  thread2() {                    1  threadN() {
2    while (*) {         2    while (*) {                   2    while (*) {
3      x := x + 1        3      x := x + 2                   3      x := x + N
4      x := x * 1        4      x := x * 2       • • •       4      x := x * N
5    }                   5    }                              5    }
6  }                     6  }                              6  }
```

Specification: After all threads have terminated, the value of x is non-negative.

Fig. 1. A concurrent program schema with a scalable (but fixed) number of threads N

2 Examples

In this section we illustrate two aspects of our method of abstraction refinement. Our method takes as input a verification problem for a concurrent program (i.e., a program composed of a fixed number of threads over an infinite data domain). The program's control flow is represented by a bounded Petri net. The property to be verified is encoded as unreachability of a special *error place* ℓ_{err} in this Petri net. Our method proceeds by iteratively adding synchronization to the input Petri net, in order to represent *data constraints* over the infinite program state space, i.e., the constraints on the control flow that are due to updates and tests of data values.

We begin by examining the example in Fig. 1 a bit closer, and we will demonstrate on this example the strength of our approach: Through its lazy synchronization and the use of unfoldings, we verify the program efficiently, regardless of the number of threads. The second example will illustrate how our approach adds synchronization where necessary.

2.1 Retaining Concurrency of Different Threads

Consider again the concurrent program schema in Fig. 1. This program schema can be instantiated for any number of threads N. In Fig. 2a we see the instantiation of the schema in Fig. 1 for $N = 2$ threads. In our approach, we represent such a concurrent program in the form of a Petri net, in this case shown in Fig. 2b. Each transition of the Petri net is labeled with a statement of the concurrent program. Here, the first transition is labeled with the initialization statement for the global variable x. This transition starts the two threads. After some number of iterations, the threads can decide nondeterministically to exit their respective loops. Then, the last transition is enabled, which is labeled with the negated postcondition and leads to the *error place* ℓ_{err}. This Petri net is our initial abstraction of the concurrent program. The term *abstraction* refers to the fact that the actions labeling the transitions of the Petri net serve as reference; they are not interpreted for the operational semantics of the Petri net. The state of the Petri is purely defined by the number of tokens on each of its places. Hence, in Fig. 2b, the error place ℓ_{err} is reachable.

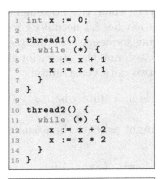

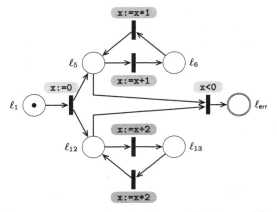

Specification: When all threads have terminated, x is non-negative.

(a) Instance of the schema in Fig. 1 for $N = 2$ threads,

(b) A Petri net representing the verification problem posed by Fig. 2a. In this Petri net, an error state (a marking with a token on the place ℓ_{err}) is reachable.

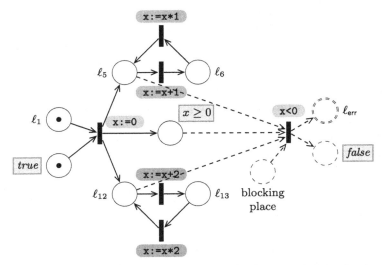

(c) A refined version of the Petri net in Fig. 2b where synchronization has been added parsimoniously. The dashed arcs and places are unreachable.

Fig. 2. Example. Parsimoniously added synchronization (reflecting data constraints) reveals the unreachability of an error place in the program. Synchronization is avoided when the interleavings between actions of different threads are irrelevant in the abstract – even though they may be relevant in the concrete.

The verification task now consists of showing that, when the statement semantics *are* taken into account, no firing sequence that reaches ℓ_{err} actually corresponds to a program execution. We pick one such firing sequence and analyse the corresponding sequence of statements, taking into account the operational semantics of the statements. This yields the following two data constraints:

1. After executing the statement `x:=0`, the program is in a state where $x \geq 0$ holds.
2. If the program is in a state where $x \geq 0$ holds, it cannot execute the assume statement `x<0`.

Next, our algorithm constructs the Petri net depicted in Fig. 2c by adding synchronization that reflects the two data constraints above to the initial Petri net of Fig. 2b. The synchronization constraints are implemented by adding three additional places (labeled by *true*, $x \geq 0$ and *false*) that represent the knowlege about the program's data that we want to replicate. Intuitively, the places are used to abstract the program's data values. The transitions labeled `x:=0` and `x<0` are connected to the new places. The order in which the statements `x:=x+1`, `x:=x*1`, `x:=x+2` and `x:=x*2` are executed is relevant for the concurrent program (i.e., for the final value of x). It is, however, irrelevant for the correctness proof that uses the state assertion $x \geq 0$. Since these four statements are not relevant for establishing the state assertion $x \geq 0$, and this state assertion is preserved by these statements, our algorithm does not connect the transitions labeled with these statements with one of the new places.

In the resulting *refined* Petri net Fig. 2c, the transition labeled `x:=0` can fire if there is a token in the *true* place, and moves this token to the place labeled $x \geq 0$. Now the transitions in the two threads can fire repeatedly, without moving the token in $x \geq 0$. When at some point both the places ℓ_5 and ℓ_{12} have a token, the transition labeled $x < 0$ could fire. However, this would put a token in the place labeled *false*, representing a violation of the data constraints. Hence we prevent this transition from ever firing by adding a *blocking place* as predecessor, which will never have a token. As a result, the place ℓ_{err} is unreachable, and we conclude that the concurrent program satisfies its specification.

Our approach proceeds in the same way for all instantiations of the concurrent program of Fig. 1, for every number of threads N: The state assertions *true*, $x \geq 0$ and *false* are added to the Petri net, and synchronized only with the statements `x:=0` and `x<0`. However, synchronization with each thread is not necessary. As a result, the size of the final refined Petri net grows only linearly in the number of threads N. Through the use of unfoldings, we can check the reachability of the error place efficiently, without explicitly considering all interleavings of transitions in the Petri net.

```
1  int x;
2
3  thread1() {
4    x := 42
5    assert x == 42
6  }
7
8  thread2() {
9    x := x + 1
10  }
```

Specification: The statement `assert x == 42` never fails.

(a) Concurrent program whose threads operate on a shared variable x.

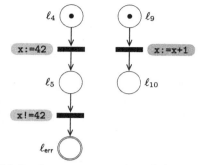

(b) Petri net representation of the program in Fig. 3a. In this Petri net, an error state (a marking with a token on the place ℓ_{err}) is reachable.

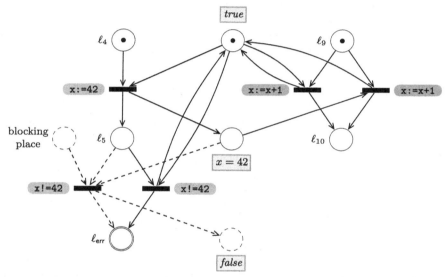

(c) Petri net constructed by adding synchronization constraints to the Petri net in Fig. 3b. Dashed lines indicate parts that are unreachable. The error place ℓ_{err} remains reachable.

Fig. 3. Example. Our approach represents the concurrent program in Fig. 3a as the Petri net in Fig. 3b. To this initial abstraction, we add synchronization reflecting *data constraints* on the control flow of the concurrent program. The resulting Petri net is shown in Fig. 3c.

2.2   Adding Synchronization Lazily

Consider now the concurrent program depicted in Fig. 3a. Here, the first thread sets a global variable x to the value 42, and then asserts that it holds said value. The second thread on the other hand increments x. We represent this program through the Petri net depicted in Fig. 3b. Once again, transitions are labeled by statements of the concurrent program, which only serve as reference; they are not interpreted for the operational semantics of the Petri net. The transition labeled with the negation of the assertion condition leads to the error place ℓ_{err}. The place ℓ_{err} is reachable by a firing sequence of the Petri net.

As before, our algorithm analyses the sequence of statements along a firing sequence that reaches ℓ_{err}, for instance the sequence `x:=42` `x!=42`. The analysis of this sequence of statements, taking into account the operational semantics of the statements, yields the following two data constraints:

1. After executing the assignment `x:=42`, the program is in a state where $x = 42$ holds.
2. If the program is in a state where $x = 42$ holds, the assertion condition is not violated, i.e., the assume statement `x!=42` cannot be executed.

Next, the algorithm constructs the Petri net depicted in Fig. 3c, by adding synchronization to the initial Petri net. As before, we add three additional places (labeled by *true*, $x = 42$ and *false*) to reflect our data constraints. However, in this example, the order and number of firings of the transitions in the two threads is not irrelevant to our data constraints: In particular, if the program is in a state where $x = 42$ holds and the second thread now executes `x:=x+1`, then it is no longer guaranteed that $x = 42$ holds. Hence, we must connect the transitions to the new places. We have two copies of the transition labeled `x:=x+1`: One copy can fire if there is a token in the *true* place, and puts the token back into the *true* place. The second copy can fire if there is a token in the place labeled $x = 42$, and moves that token into the *true* place. Similarly for the two copies of the transition labeled `x!=42`: One copy takes a token from the *true* place and puts it back, the other takes a token from the $x = 42$ place and moves it to the *false* place. This however would represent a violation of the data constraints, and thus we again add a *blocking place* to prevent this transition from firing. The transition labeled `x:=42` moves a token from the *true* place to the $x = 42$ place. We omit the second copy of this transition (with predecessor $x = 42$), as it would be unreachable.

In the resulting Petri net Fig. 3c, an execution of the Petri net labeled with the sequence `x:=42` `x!=42` is no longer possible. However, the ℓ_{err} place is still reachable through a firing sequence labeled with the statements `x:=42` `x:=x+1` `x!=42`. Hence our algorithm now analyses this sequence, taking into account the semantics, and determines that there are no data constraints preventing the execution of this sequence of statements. We conclude that the concurrent program is incorrect: The assertion may indeed be violated. Because of the introduced synchronization, the reachability check in this example has to explicitly consider the different orderings between transitions from the two threads. This explains our focus on avoiding synchronization wherever possible, in order to maintain the efficiency of our approach. However, in this case a separate consideration of the different orderings is inevitable, as exactly one of them can be executed and leads to an error.

3   Petri Net and Finite Automata

In this section we introduce our notation and terminology for Petri nets and finite automata. Analogously to finite automata we will introduce Petri nets as acceptors of languages. Throughout this paper we will only work with *bounded* Petri nets, but we will define a bounded Petri net as a special case of a (general) Petri net.

3.1   Finite Automata

A *finite automaton* $\mathcal{A} = (\Sigma, Q, \delta, q_{\mathsf{init}}, Q_{\mathsf{acc}})$ consists of an alphabet Σ, a finite set of states Q, a transition relation $\delta \subseteq Q \times \Sigma \times Q$, an initial state $q_0 \in Q$ and a set of accepting states $Q_{\mathsf{acc}} \subseteq Q$. The elements of Σ are called *letters*, and sequences $w \in \Sigma^*$ are *words*. We say that a word $w = a_1 \ldots a_n \in \Sigma^*$ is accepted by $\mathcal{A}$ iff there exists a corresponding run of states $q_0 \ldots q_n$ such that

- $q_0 = q_{\mathsf{init}}$ is the initial state,
- for all $i \in \{1, \ldots, n\}$, it holds that $(q_{i-1}, a_i, q_i) \in \delta$,
- and $q_n \in Q_{\mathsf{acc}}$ is accepting.

The set of all words accepted by $\mathcal{A}$ is the language $L(\mathcal{A})$ recognized by the automaton.

We say that $\mathcal{A}$ is *deterministic* iff for all $q \in Q$ and $a \in \Sigma$, there exists at most one q' such that $(q, a, q') \in \delta$. Dually, we say that $\mathcal{A}$ is *total* iff there always exists at least one such q'. Hence, the transition relation of a deterministic total automaton is a function, and we write $\delta(q, a) = q'$ in place of $(q, a, q') \in \delta$. It is well-known that for every finite automaton $\mathcal{A}$, one can compute a deterministic total automaton $\mathcal{A}'$ that recognizes the same language, $L(\mathcal{A}) = L(\mathcal{A}')$. We abbreviate *deterministic total automaton* as *DFA*.

We call a transition $(q, a, q') \in \delta$ a *self-loop* iff $q = q'$.

3.2   Petri Nets as Language Acceptors

We define a Petri net as a 7-tuple $\mathcal{N} = (\Sigma, P, T, F, m_{\mathsf{init}}, \lambda, P_{\mathsf{fin}})$ where Σ is an alphabet, P are *places*, T are *transitions* with $P \cap T = \emptyset$, $F \subseteq (P \times T) \cup (T \times P)$ is a *flow relation*, $m_{\mathsf{init}} : P \to \mathbb{N}$ is an *initial marking*, $\lambda : T \to \Sigma$ is a *labeling* of transitions, and $P_{\mathsf{fin}} \subseteq P$ is a set of *accepting places*. We will sometimes use an infix notation for the flow relation and write e.g. $p \mathrel{F} t$ instead of $(p, t) \in F$.

We define a *marking* as a map $m : P \to \mathbb{N}$ that assigns a token count to each place. We write M to denote that set of all markings over P. A marking $m \in M$ *covers* a place $p \in P$ iff m assigns at least one token to p.

$$m \text{ covers } p \Leftrightarrow m(p) > 0$$

We call a marking $m \in M$ *accepting* iff it covers at least one accepting place.

With $m \rhd_t m'$ we denote that transition $t \in T$ can be *fired* from marking m, i.e., all predecessor places have a token, and the firing of t results in the marking m'. Formally, we define the *firing relation* $\rhd \subseteq M \times T \times M$ as

$$m \rhd_t m' \Leftrightarrow \begin{array}{ll} \forall p \in P : p \: F \: t \to m(p) > 0 & \text{and} \\ \forall p \in P : m'(p) = m(p) - |\{t \in T \mid p \: F \: t\}| + |\{t \in T \mid t \: F \: p\}| \end{array}$$

A *firing sequence* in $\mathcal{N}$ is then an alternating sequence $m_0 \rhd_{t_1} m_1 \rhd_{t_2} \dots \rhd_{t_n} m_n$ of markings $m_i \in M$ and transitions $t_i \in T$, such that (a) $m_0 = m_{\text{init}}$ is the initial marking and (b) the sequence adheres to the firing relation, i.e. $m_{i-1} \rhd_{t_i} m_i$ for all $i \in \{1, \dots, n\}$. A firing sequence ending in an accepting marking is called *accepting*. We say that a marking m is reachable iff there exists a firing sequence $m_0 \rhd_{t_1} m_1 \rhd_{t_2} \dots \rhd_{t_n} m_n$ with $m_n = m$.

We define the language that is recognized by a Petri net as follows:

$$L(\mathcal{N}) := \left\{ a_1 a_2 \dots a_n \in \Sigma^* \: \middle| \: \begin{array}{l} \exists \text{ accepting firing sequence} \\ \quad m_0 \rhd_{t_1} m_1 \rhd_{t_2} \dots \rhd_{t_n} m_n \\ \text{such that } \forall \: i \in \{1, \dots n\} : \lambda(t_i) = a_i \end{array} \right\}$$

A net is *bounded* (also known as *1-safe* or just *safe*) iff all reachable markings have at most one token per place. In this paper we consider only bounded Petri nets and we will often use *Petri net* as a synonym for *bounded Petri net*. We identify markings $m : P \to \mathbb{N}$ with sets $m' \subseteq P$.

$$m \equiv m' \quad \Leftrightarrow \quad \forall p \in P : m(p) = 1 \leftrightarrow p \in m'$$

4   Petri Programs

In this section we describe our formal setting, based on the notion of Petri nets as language acceptors as presented in Sect. 3.2. We then make precise the verification problem solved by our algorithm.

4.1   Program Semantics

We assume a fixed set of program variables **Var** and a language of statements **Stmt**. A *program state* $s \in$ **State** maps program variables to their values, which may lie in an infinite data domain (such as $\mathbb{Z}$). Each statement $st \in$ **Stmt** is assigned a semantics $[\![st]\!] \subseteq$ **State** $\times$ **State**, which relates input states to possible output states. We call a sequence of statements $\tau \in$ **Stmt*** a *trace*, and extend the semantics in a straightforward way:

Definition 1 (Trace Semantics, Infeasibility). *The* semantics *of a trace* $\tau \in \mathbf{Stmt}^*$ *is recursively defined as*

$$[\![\varepsilon]\!] = id \qquad\qquad [\![st.\tau]\!] = [\![st]\!] \circ [\![\tau]\!]$$

We call τ infeasible *iff* $[\![\tau]\!] = \emptyset$.

The semantics of a trace is hence exactly the set of all pairs of program states (s, s') such that, starting from s, τ can be executed in its entirety, and can (depending on nondeterministic choices) reach the state s'. If no such pair exists, it follows that data constraints prevent the execution of the trace: It is infeasible.

A *state assertion* is a logical formula φ over variables in **Var**. We write $s \models \varphi$ to signify that program state s satisfies the state assertion φ. A valid Hoare triple $\{\varphi\}\, st\, \{\psi\}$ consists of state assertions φ, ψ and a statement st, such that for each pair $(s, s') \in [\![st]\!]$ it holds that $s \models \varphi$ implies $s' \models \psi$. An *infeasibility proof* for a trace $\tau = st_1 \ldots st_n$ is a sequence of state assertions $\varphi_0 \ldots \varphi_n$ such that $\varphi_0 = \textit{true}$, $\varphi_n = \textit{false}$ and $\{\varphi_i\}\, st_{i+1}\, \{\varphi_{i+1}\}$ is a valid Hoare triple for $i \in \{0, \ldots, n-1\}$. As the name implies, if there exists an infeasibility proof for a trace τ, then τ is infeasible. In a sense, an infeasibility proof consists of data constraints blocking the execution of the trace τ.

Our algorithm considers bounded Petri nets $\mathcal{N}$ over a finite alphabet $\Sigma \subseteq \mathbf{Stmt}$. We use the term *Petri net* when we want to stress that it is only viewed as a language acceptor, ignoring the semantics of statements. By contrast, the term *Petri program* refers to the infinite-state program, which is derived by assigning semantics to the alphabet statements. The Petri net represents the control flow of this program. In fact, it could be called the program's *control flow Petri net*, in analogy to *control flow graphs* for sequential programs.

4.2 Verification Problem

In addition to the control flow, a Petri net $\mathcal{N}$ also encodes its correctness specification. This is achieved by the accepting places of the Petri net, which represent *error locations*, i.e., locations that should not be reached by any execution of the corresponding Petri program. In the program text from which the net is derived, these error locations are typically expressed as assert statements.

Example 2 (Specifications). For instance, the net in Fig. 3b encodes the program with the assert statement `assert x==42`. If this assert condition is *violated*, i.e., $x \neq 42$, the error location ℓ_{err} is reached.

An accepted trace $\tau \in L(\mathcal{N})$ is thus a trace for which at least one thread would reach an error location, provided the trace actually has a corresponding execution in the Petri program. We thus call these traces *error traces*. It now becomes clear that the verification task must consist of showing that no error trace has a corresponding execution in the Petri program, i.e., all error traces are *infeasible*.

Example 3 (Infeasible and Error Traces). Consider again the example shown in Fig. 2b. Here, the trace `x:=0` `x:=x+2` `x:=x*2` `x<0` is an error trace. It is however infeasible, as there is no output state s of `x:=0` `x:=x+2` `x:=x*2` which can execute `x<0`.

Conversely, the trace `x:=0` `x:=x+1` `x:=x+2` of Fig. 2b is feasible, its semantics contains for instance the pair of states $(\{x \mapsto 17\}, \{x \mapsto 3\})$. It is however not an error trace.

While the *language* $L(\mathcal{N})$ accepted by the Petri net represents the Petri program's control flow aspects, the *semantic relation* additionally takes into account the program's data and summarizes the program's semantics:

Definition 4 (Semantic Relation). *Let $\mathcal{N}$ be a Petri program. The* semantic relation $[\![\mathcal{N}]\!]$ *of $\mathcal{N}$ is defined as*

$$[\![\mathcal{N}]\!] := \bigcup_{\tau \in L(\mathcal{N})} [\![\tau]\!]$$

We conclude the section by formally stating the verification task:

Definition 5 (Petri Program Correctness). *A Petri program $\mathcal{N}$ is correct if and only if its semantic relation is empty:*

$$[\![\mathcal{N}]\!] = \emptyset$$

i.e., if and only if all error traces are infeasible.

5 Verification Algorithm

We now describe our verification algorithm. It is an adaptation of the *Trace Abstraction* approach [16] to Petri programs.

As defined above, the verification algorithm must determine if the semantic relation of a given Petri program $\mathcal{N}$ is empty, i.e., $[\![\mathcal{N}]\!] = \emptyset$. The simplest case where this holds is the case where the Petri net recognizes the empty language, i.e., $L(\mathcal{N}) = \emptyset$. This holds if and only if no accepting marking is reachable in $\mathcal{N}$. This reachability problem can be solved efficiently using the algorithm for the construction of *complete finite prefixes of the unfolding of a Petri net* proposed by McMillan [9,20]. This prefix is a finite initial part of the unfolding which contains full information about the reachable markings of the Petri net.

Our algorithm aims to reduce every verification problem to the simple case $L(\mathcal{N}) = \emptyset$, and thus to purely automata-theoretic reasoning. It does so by iteratively transforming the Petri program $\mathcal{N}$ to a Petri program $\mathcal{N}'$ that is equivalent, i.e., it has the same semantic relation: $[\![\mathcal{N}]\!] = [\![\mathcal{N}']\!]$. The transformed Petri net $\mathcal{N}'$ accepts only a subset of the traces accepted by $\mathcal{N}$, i.e., $L(\mathcal{N}') \subseteq L(\mathcal{N})$. If the algorithm eventually reaches a Petri net $\mathcal{N}'$ with $L(\mathcal{N}') = \emptyset$, as determined by the unfolding algorithm, then it holds that $[\![\mathcal{N}]\!] = [\![\mathcal{N}']\!] = \emptyset$, and the original Petri program $\mathcal{N}$ is correct.

Petri program $\mathcal{N}$

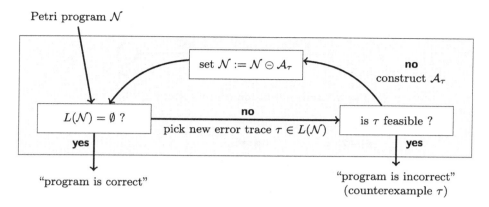

Fig. 4. Trace Abstraction CEGAR loop.

In order to achieve this iterative refinement, the algorithm employs a counter-example guided abstraction refinement (CEGAR) loop, illustrated in Fig. 4. In each iteration, the complete finite prefix of the unfolding of $\mathcal{N}$ is constructed in order to search for an error trace τ accepted by the current Petri net $\mathcal{N}$, the (possibly spurious) counterexample. Our algorithm then checks this counterexample for feasibility using an SMT solver. If the counterexample is feasible, i.e., non-spurious, then the program is incorrect and the verification is stopped. If τ is infeasible on the other hand, the algorithm constructs a finite automaton $\mathcal{A}_\tau$ that accepts at least τ and possibly infinitely many other infeasible traces. The refined Petri net is then constructed as the difference $\mathcal{N} \ominus \mathcal{A}_\tau$ of the current $\mathcal{N}$ and $\mathcal{A}_\tau$. We will describe the automata-theoretic difference operation $\ominus$ in Sect. 6. For the moment, suffice it to say that this difference operation takes as input a Petri net $\mathcal{N}$ and a finite automaton $\mathcal{A}$. It then constructs a version of the Petri net with additional synchronization, as seen in Sect. 2. The resulting Petri net satisfies $L(\mathcal{N} \ominus \mathcal{A}) = L(\mathcal{N}) \setminus L(\mathcal{A})$.

We now discuss how to construct the automaton $\mathcal{A}_\tau$. This automaton extracts the data constraints from an infeasibility proof of the trace τ and generalizes them to other traces. To this end, we introduce the following class of automata:

Definition 6 (Floyd/Hoare-Automata). *A* Floyd/Hoare-automaton *is a finite automaton* $\mathcal{A} = (\Sigma, Q, \delta, q_{\text{init}}, Q_{\text{acc}})$ *over the alphabet of program statements* Σ, *such that there exists a mapping* β *that assigns each automaton state* $q \in Q$ *a state assertion* $\beta(q)$ *with*

- $\beta(q_{\text{init}}) = true$,
- *if* $(q, st, q') \in \delta$, *then* $\{\beta(q)\}$ st $\{\beta(q')\}$ *is a valid Hoare triple,*
- *and for all* $q \in Q_{\text{acc}}$, $\beta(q) = false$.

For each trace τ accepted by a Floyd/Hoare-automaton $\mathcal{A}$, there exists an infeasibility proof, given by application of β to the accepting run of states. Hence $\mathcal{A}$

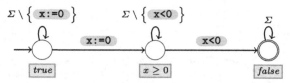

(a) Floyd/Hoare-automaton for a trace of Fig. 2b.

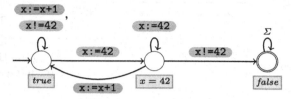

(b) Floyd/Hoare-automaton for a trace of Fig. 3b.

Fig. 5. Examples of deterministic total Floyd/Hoare-automata for the examples from Sect. 2.

can only accept infeasible traces. For details on how to construct a Floyd/Hoare-automaton $\mathcal{A}_\tau$ from an infeasible trace τ, we refer the reader to Heizmann et al. [16]. Note that in particular, one can always construct a deterministic total Floyd/Hoare-automaton, assuming the set of state assertions used to label states is closed under conjunctions.

Example 7 (Floyd/Hoare-Automata). Consider again an error trace from Fig. 2b, for instance `x:=0` `x:=x+1` `x:=x+2` `x:=x*2` `x:=x*1` `x<0`. A possible infeasibility proof is $true, x \geq 0, x \geq 0, x \geq 0, x \geq 0, x \geq 0, false$. A Floyd/Hoare-automaton corresponding to this infeasibility proof is shown in Fig. 5a. Subtraction of this Floyd/Hoare-automaton from the Petri net yields the Petri net shown in Fig. 2c.

Similarly, the error trace `x:=42` `x!=42` from Fig. 3b is proven infeasible by the sequence $true, x = 42, false$. A corresponding Floyd/Hoare-automaton is given in Fig. 5b. The Petri net shown in Fig. 3c represents the difference of the original net and this Floyd/Hoare-automaton.

After presenting the difference operation in Sect. 6, we will discuss in Sect. 7 how its usage combined with Floyd/Hoare-automata achieves the additional synchronization using data constraints. We conclude this section with a discussion of soundness of our approach. We begin by showing that the subtraction of a Floyd-Hoare automaton does not modify the Petri program's semantics.

Lemma 8 (Semantics-Preserving Refinement). *Let $\mathcal{A}_\tau$ be an automaton accepting only infeasible traces, and let $\mathcal{N}' = \mathcal{N} \ominus \mathcal{A}_\tau$. Then $\mathcal{N}$ is equivalent to $\mathcal{N}'$, i.e., $\llbracket \mathcal{N} \rrbracket = \llbracket \mathcal{N}' \rrbracket$.*

Proof. Since $L(\mathcal{N}') \subseteq L(\mathcal{N})$, it follows that $[\![\mathcal{N}']\!] \subseteq [\![\mathcal{N}]\!]$. On the other hand, $L(\mathcal{N}) \subseteq L(\mathcal{N}') \cup L(\mathcal{A}_\tau)$. It follows that

$$[\![\mathcal{N}]\!] \subseteq [\![\mathcal{N}']\!] \cup \bigcup_{\tau \in L(\mathcal{A}_\tau)} [\![\tau]\!] = [\![\mathcal{N}']\!] \cup \bigcup_{\tau \in L(\mathcal{A}_\tau)} \emptyset = [\![\mathcal{N}']\!]$$

Thus it holds that $[\![\mathcal{N}]\!] = [\![\mathcal{N}']\!]$.

Intuitively, the argument for the equivalence of $\mathcal{N}$ and $\mathcal{N}'$ is this: We only remove traces $\tau \in L(\mathcal{A}_\tau)$ which are accepted by the Floyd/Hoare-automaton $\mathcal{A}_\tau$. But then such traces τ must be infeasible, i.e., there do not exist corresponding executions of the Petri program. Hence we only remove traces that are artefacts of the finite-state abstraction given by the Petri net, we never remove actual feasible program traces. In other words, we *refine* the abstraction $\mathcal{N}$ to the equivalent, but strictly less coarse abstraction $\mathcal{N}'$. We arrive at the soundness result for our algorithm:

Theorem 9 (Soundness). *Our verification algorithm is sound, i.e., whenever it concludes that a given input Petri program $\mathcal{N}$ is correct, then $[\![\mathcal{N}]\!] = \emptyset$.*

Proof. The algorithm iteratively transforms $\mathcal{N}$ to some Petri program $\mathcal{N}'$. By repeated application of Lemma 8, we have that $[\![\mathcal{N}]\!] = [\![\mathcal{N}']\!]$. The algorithm concludes correctness only if $L(\mathcal{N}') = \emptyset$ (by soundness of McMillan's unfolding algorithm [9,20]), and hence $[\![\mathcal{N}]\!] = [\![\mathcal{N}']\!] = \emptyset$.

6 Difference Operation

In this section we present a difference operation $\mathcal{N} \ominus \mathcal{A}$ for a Petri net $\mathcal{N}$ and a finite automaton $\mathcal{A}$. This difference operation implements the addition of synchronization discussed in Sect. 2, and is used by our verification algorithm as presented in Sect. 5. We give a purely automata theoretic presentation of this operation here, and we discuss in Sect. 7 how this operation implements the addition of synchronization constraints.

The inputs of our operation are a bounded Petri net $\mathcal{N} = (\Sigma, P, T, F, m_0, \lambda, P_{\mathsf{fin}})$ and a *deterministic total* finite automaton $\mathcal{A} = (\Sigma, Q, \delta, q_0, Q_{\mathsf{acc}})$ over the same alphabet which satisfies the property

$$L(\mathcal{A}) = L(\mathcal{A}) \circ \Sigma^*$$

i.e., the language of $\mathcal{A}$ is closed under concatenation with Σ^*. We call the Petri net $\mathcal{N}$ the *minuend* of the operation and we call the finite automaton $\mathcal{A}$ the *subtrahend* of the operation.

The basic idea of the construction is to run the Petri net and the DFA in parallel and to let the result block as soon as the DFA is going to enter an accepting state. The basic construction rule is illustrated in Fig. 6: For each Petri net transition t with predecessor places $p_1, \ldots p_n$ and successor places $p'_1, \ldots p'_m$, and for each edge in the finite automaton that has predecessor q, successor q'

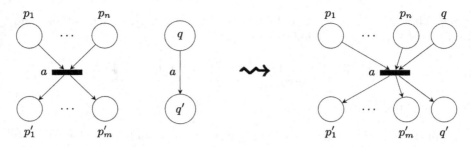

Fig. 6. Basic construction rule for the difference operation whose minuend is a Petri net, whose subtrahend is a deterministic total finite automaton and whose result is a Petri net.

and is labeled by $\lambda(t)$, we add a transition that is labeled by labeled by $\lambda(t)$ and has predecessor places are $p_1, \ldots p_n, q$ and successor places $p'_1, \ldots p'_m, q'$. There are however two exceptions to this basic construction rule.

E1: If the successor state q' is an accepting state, the transition must never fire. Hence we add a special *blocking place* as predecessor, which can never have a token.

E2: If a letter $a \in \Sigma$ occurs only in self-loops of the DFA, then we just copy the Petri net transitions that are labeled by a without adding an additional predecessor or successor.

The exception E1 ensures that words of $L(\mathcal{A})$ are not accepted by the result. The exception E2 is an optimization that reduces the number of transitions and the elements of the flow relation. While this optimization is not directly necessary for the correctness of the operation, we will discuss in Sect. 7 why it is crucial to our approach. In order to implement exception E2, we define the subset $\Sigma_{\mathsf{looper}} \subseteq \Sigma$ that consists of all letters $a \in \Sigma$ that occur only in self-loops of the subtrahend $\mathcal{A}$.

$$\Sigma_{\mathsf{looper}} := \{a \in \Sigma \mid \delta(q, a) = q \text{ for all } q \in Q\}$$

We define the result of the synchronization operation $\mathcal{N}' := \mathcal{N} \ominus \mathcal{A}$ formally as

$$\mathcal{N}' := (\Sigma, P', T', F', m'_0, \lambda', P'_{\mathsf{fin}})$$

The set of places is the disjoint union of the minuend's places, the subtrahend's states and one auxiliary place.

$$P' := P \,\dot{\cup}\, Q \,\dot{\cup}\, \{p_{\mathsf{block}}\}$$

The set of transitions and the flow relation is defined according to the construction rule of Fig. 6 and the exceptions E1 and E2.

$$
\begin{aligned}
T' := \ & \{t \mid t \in T, \lambda(t) \in \Sigma_{\text{looper}}\} \\
& \cup \{(q, t, q') \mid t \in T, \lambda(t) \notin \Sigma_{\text{looper}}, q \in Q, \delta(q, \lambda(t)) = q'\} \\
F' := \ & \{(p, t'), (t', p') \mid t' \in T, (p, t) \in F, (t, p') \in F\} \\
& \cup \{(q, t'), (t', q') \mid t' = (q, t, q'), q \in Q, t \in T, q' \in Q\} \\
& \cup \{(p, t'), (t', p') \mid t' = (q, t, q'), (p, t) \in F, (t, p') \in F\} \\
& \cup \{(p_{\text{block}}, t') \mid t' = (q, t, q'), q' \in Q_{\text{acc}}\}
\end{aligned}
$$

Transition labels are copied from the minuend.

$$
\lambda(t') := \begin{cases} \lambda(t') & \text{if } t' \in T \\ \lambda(t) & \text{if } t' = (q, t, q') \text{ for some } q \in Q, t \in T, q' \in Q \end{cases}
$$

The initial marking is the disjoint union of the minuend's initial marking and the initial state of the subtrahend.

$$
m_0' := m_0 \,\dot\cup\, \{q_0\}
$$

The set of accepting places is the minuend's set of accepting places.

$$
P'_{\text{fin}} := P_{\text{fin}}
$$

We show that this operation does indeed implement the language-theoretic difference between the given Petri net and the automaton:

Theorem 10. *Given a Petri net $\mathcal{N}$ and a DFA $\mathcal{A}$. If $\mathcal{A}$ is total and closed under concatenation with Σ^*, then the Petri net $\mathcal{N} \ominus \mathcal{A}$ recognizes the set theoretic difference of $L(\mathcal{N})$ and $L(\mathcal{A})$, i.e.,*

$$
L(\mathcal{N} \ominus \mathcal{A}) = L(\mathcal{N}) \backslash L(\mathcal{A}).
$$

Proof. Let $\mathcal{N} = (\Sigma, P, T, F, m_0, \lambda, P_{\text{acc}})$, $\mathcal{A} = (\Sigma, Q, \delta, q_0, Q_{\text{acc}})$, and $\mathcal{N}' = \mathcal{N} \ominus \mathcal{A} = (\Sigma, P', T', F', m_0', \lambda', P'_{\text{acc}})$. Let $a_1 \ldots a_n \in \Sigma^*$ be a word. We prove by induction over the length n the following: The sequence $m_0 \cup \{q_0\} \,\triangleright_{t_1'}\, m_1 \cup \{q_1\} \,\triangleright_{t_2'}\, \ldots \,\triangleright_{t_n'}\, m_n \cup \{q_n\}$ is a firing sequence of $\mathcal{N}'$ iff $m_0 \,\triangleright_{t_1}\, m_1 \,\triangleright_{t_2}\, \ldots \,\triangleright_{t_n}\, m_n$ is a firing sequence of $\mathcal{N}$ and $q_0, q_1, \ldots, q_n$ is a run of $\mathcal{A}$ such that no q_i is an accepting state, where $t_i' = t_i$ if $a_i \in \Sigma_{\text{looper}}$ and $t_i' = (q_{i-1}, t_i, q_i)$ if $a_i \notin \Sigma_{\text{looper}}$. In the induction step, we use that the DFA $\mathcal{A}$ is total and that our auxiliary place p_{block} ensures that the firing sequence of $\mathcal{N}'$ cannot contain an accepting state of $\mathcal{A}$. Since $\mathcal{A}$ is total it cannot block and since it is deterministic and closed under concatenation with Σ^* is can never leave the set of accepting states once it entered an accepting state. Together with the fact that the accepting places of $\mathcal{N}'$ are the accepting places of $\mathcal{N}$ we conclude that $a_1 \ldots a_n \in L(\mathcal{N}')$ iff $a_1 \ldots a_n \in L(\mathcal{N})$ and $a_1 \ldots a_n \notin L(\mathcal{A})$.

7   Discussion

The approach we have presented avoids eager synchronization: It does not initially represent the many different interleavings of a concurrent program explicitly, and hence avoids the associated state explosion. Instead, synchronization is added lazily, only where it is needed: We derive data constraints from the analysis of infeasible interleavings, represented as a finite automaton. Our difference operation then uses this automaton to add synchronization to the Petri net. Here too we carefully avoid unnecessary synchronization.

Example 11 (Synchronization based on data constraints). Let us discuss the synchronization based on data constraints on our example programs. Consider the Petri net in Fig. 2c, the result of our difference construction applied to the Petri net in Fig. 2b and the Floyd/Hoare-automaton in Fig. 5a. Observe that there is no synchronization between the transitions labeled `x:=x+1` , `x:=x*1` , `x:=x+2` and `x:=x*2` . While the ordering between these statements does have an impact on the behaviour of the program (in particular, on the final value of x), it is irrelevant to the data constraint $x \geq 0$, which prevents the program from reaching the error place. Correspondingly, these statements only occur as self-loops in the Floyd/Hoare-automaton, and are thus not synchronized by our difference operation (exception E2). By contrast, the statement `x:=0` establishes the data constraint $x \geq 0$, and `x<0` contradicts it. Hence, the transitions labeled with these statements are modified to have additional predecessor and successor places corresponding to the automaton states. If the transition labeled `x<0` was to fire, the token would move to the place labeled *false*. This place corresponds to an accepting state of the Floyd/Hoare-automaton, or in other words, a violation of the data constraints. Hence the transition must not fire: It requires a token from the blocking place, which never has a token. In summary, we only synchronize the initialization statement and the check of the postcondition. The two threads however remain completely unsynchronized.

Compare this to our second example program, and to the difference of Fig. 3b and Fig. 5b, as shown in Fig. 3c. Here, synchronization between all three statements has been introduced: Each transition has as predecessor and as successor a place corresponding to an automaton state, resp. a data constraint. The reason for this lies in the fact that none of the statements is irrelevant to the data constraints. Hence synchronization is necessary to keep track of these constraints. The statement `x:=42` establishes the data constraint $x = 42$, and hence moves a token from the *true* place to the place labeled $x = 42$. The statement `x!=42` contradicts the data constraint $x = 42$, and hence we have a transition labeled with this statement, which takes a token out of the $x = 42$ place and puts it in the *false* place. However, we again prevent this transition from firing through the addition of a blocking place. Note that we have a second transition with the same statement: If the constraint $x = 42$ has not been established, the statement may execute without contradicting the trivial constraint *true*. No such second transition is necessary for the statement `x:=42` , as it is not possible to reach the data constraint $x = 42$ and then execute the statement (again). Finally, the statement `x:=x+1` is also synchronized: While it neither establishes nor contradicts the data constraint, this synchronization is necessary as it can invalidate the constraint. Here too we have two copies of the transition: If no constraint on the data has been established (a token is in the *true* place), the statement can execute and establishes no new data constraint (the token is put back into the *true* place). On the other hand, if the data constraint $x = 42$ holds (i.e., there is a token in the place labeled with this constraint), then `x:=x+1` invalidates the constraint (and moves the token into the *true* place). As a result of the added synchronization, only one (out of three) interleavings of the statements remains possible in the Petri net.

Optimization E2. Through the use of McMillan's unfolding technique, we are able to check emptiness of the refined Petri net resulting from our difference operation. The efficiency of this check and our whole approach relies crucially on the optimization E2 in the definition of the difference operation. Unfoldings do not explicitly consider the many different orderings between concurrent transitions, i.e., transitions t_1, t_2 that are both enabled in a reachable marking m and have disjoint sets of predecessors. The ability to preserve the concurrency of such transitions is the source of the efficiency of the unfolding technique. Without exception E2, the difference Petri net would not have any concurrent transitions: If the marking m can be reached from the initial marking through a firing sequence labeled with a word w, then by Theorem 10, m contains exactly one place corresponding to a state q of the finite automaton, namely the state that the automaton reaches after reading w. Without exception E2, q would be a predecessor place for both transitions t_1 and t_2, and hence the transitions would not be concurrent. Since unfoldings explicitly consider the ordering between non-concurrent transitions, they would suffer the same exponential explosion as naive sequentialization. Thus, our difference operation is specifically designed to optimize for the application of the unfolding technique.

Scalability. The result is a verification algorithm that, for many concurrent programs, is significantly more efficient than classical Trace Abstraction based on sequentialization. We demonstrate this efficiency improvement using our example concurrent program schema from Fig. 1. To this effect, we analyzed instances of this program schema for up to 60 threads, both with classical Trace Abstraction and with the method presented here. We ran both analyses on a machine with an AMD EPYC 7351P 16-Core CPU 2.4 GHz and 128 GB RAM running Linux 5.8.12 und Java 1.8.0_202 64bit, and monitored them using the benchmarking tool benchexec [4]. The results can be seen in Fig. 7. The classical, automata-based Trace Abstraction (shown in red) falls victim to the state explosion problem, and reaches the timeout (15 min) for 12 threads or more. On the other hand, our approach (shown in blue) scales much better, and can analyse even the 60-thread instance in approximately 15 s. Similarly, the memory consumption of classical Trace Abstraction explodes quickly, while the memory consumption of our approach scales well. The erratic memory consumption of the classical approach for more than 12 threads is due to the timeouts.

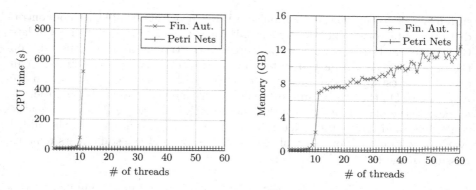

Fig. 7. Resources used in the analysis of instantiations of the program schema from Fig. 1 for up to 60 threads, with classical (automata-based) Trace Abstraction and with our Petri net-based approach.

8   Related Work

Partial Order Reduction (POR) is another technique used to deal with the complex control flow of concurrent systems, and has recently been applied for infinite-state program verification [5,6,12,13,22]. Closest to our approach are the works that combine POR with Trace Abstraction, such as the work by Cassez and Ziegler [5] as well as the works of Farzan and Vandikas [12,13]. Cassez and Ziegler apply a variant of POR, where two statements that do not write to common variables are independent. They apply this POR to the sequentialization of the concurrent program once, and then verify the resulting program using classical Trace Abstraction. Farzan and Vandikas on the other hand use a form of Büchi tree automata to represent an infinite range of reductions of the program and use an adaptation of Trace Abstraction to find a proof for one of these infinitely many reductions. We share the general idea of POR, namely to avoid explicitly representing many different interleavings. However, POR selects representative interleavings, while we consider all interleavings but represent them concisely. Furthermore, the works of Farzan and Vandikas in particular focus on proof simplicity . By contrast, our focus is on the combinatorial explosion of interleavings.

Bounded model checking (BMC) is among the most popular techniques for concurrent program verification. The basic idea in BMC is to search for a counterexample in executions whose length is bounded by some integer k. This problem can be efficiently reduced to a satisfiability problem, and can therefore be solved by SAT or SMT methods. BMC has the disadvantage of not being able to prove the absence of errors in general. There are many program verification tools based on bounded model checking, e.g., CBMC [1], DARTAGNAN [14], LAZY-CSEQ [18], and YOGAR-CBMC [23]. CBMC implements a bit-precise bounded model checking for C programs and uses POR to deal with the problem of interleavings. YOGAR-CBMC uses a scheduling constraint based abstraction refinement method for bounded model checking of concurrent programs. In order to obtain effective refinement constraints, two graph-based algorithms have been devised over the so-called Event Order Graph for counterexample validation and refinement generation. LAZY-CSEQ translates a multi-threaded C program into a nondeterministic sequential C program that preserves reachability for all round-robin schedules with a given bound on the number of rounds and re-uses existing BMC tools as backends for the sequential verification problem.

Thread-Modular Abstraction Refinement [17] performs thread-modular assume-guarantee reasoning to overcome the challenge of the large number of interleavings of multithreaded programs. Thread modularity means that one explores the state space of one thread at a time, making assumptions about how the environment can interfere. This approach uses counterexample-guided predicate-abstraction refinement to overcome the challenge of the infinite state space.

Inductive data flow graphs [11] consist of data flow graphs with incorporated inductive assertions. They consider a set of dependencies between data operations in interleaved thread executions and generate the set of concurrent program traces which give rise to these dependencies. The approach first constructs an inductive data flow graph and then checks whether all program traces are represented.

SLAB [8] is a certifying model checker for infinite-state concurrent systems. For a given transition system and a safety property it either delivers a counterexample or generates a certificate of system correctness in the form of an inductive verification diagram. SLAB considers the control-flow constraints of a program as data constraints over program counter variables. Hence SLAB can also abstract the control-flow of a program and does not have to build a product of CFGs initially. The abstraction is iteratively refined by predicates that are obtained from Craig interpolation.

9   Conclusion

We presented a verification approach for concurrent programs composed of a fixed number of threads over an infinite data domain. The contribution of the paper is to propose a solution to the two challenges raised by this verification problem: find a finite state abstraction for the concurrent program and deal with the problem of interleavings. Our solution is to use bounded Petri nets as finite state abstractions of the concurrent program. This enables us to apply algorithms based on unfoldings [9,20], i.e., algorithms that are used to analyze concurrent systems without falling victim to the problem of interleavings. Our algorithm for finding abstractions is based on the scheme of counterexample-guided abstraction refinement, specifically in the automata-based setting of Trace Abstraction [16]. We have shown that the automata-theoretic difference operation used in this setting can be implemented through the addition of (automatically generated) synchronization constraints to a Petri net.

References

1. Alglave, J., Kroening, D., Tautschnig, M.: Partial orders for efficient bounded model checking of concurrent software. In: Sharygina, N., Veith, H. (eds.) CAV 2013. LNCS, vol. 8044, pp. 141–157. Springer, Heidelberg (2013). https://doi.org/10.1007/978-3-642-39799-8_9
2. Apt, K.R., de Boer, F.S., Olderog, E.R.: Verification of Sequential and Concurrent Programs. Springer Science & Business Media, Verlag (2009). https://doi.org/10.1007/978-1-84882-745-5
3. Berdine, J., Lev-Ami, T., Manevich, R., Ramalingam, G., Sagiv, M.: Thread quantification for concurrent shape analysis. In: Gupta, A., Malik, S. (eds.) CAV 2008. LNCS, vol. 5123, pp. 399–413. Springer, Heidelberg (2008). https://doi.org/10.1007/978-3-540-70545-1_37
4. Beyer, D., Löwe, S., Wendler, P.: Reliable benchmarking: requirements and solutions. Int. J. Softw. Tools Technol. Transf. 21(1), 1–29 (2017). https://doi.org/10.1007/s10009-017-0469-y
5. Cassez, F., Ziegler, F.: Verification of concurrent programs using trace abstraction refinement. In: Davis, M., Fehnker, A., McIver, A., Voronkov, A. (eds.) LPAR 2015. LNCS, vol. 9450, pp. 233–248. Springer, Heidelberg (2015). https://doi.org/10.1007/978-3-662-48899-7_17
6. Chu, D.-H., Jaffar, J.: A framework to synergize partial order reduction with state interpolation. In: Yahav, E. (ed.) HVC 2014. LNCS, vol. 8855, pp. 171–187. Springer, Cham (2014). https://doi.org/10.1007/978-3-319-13338-6_14
7. Donaldson, A., Kaiser, A., Kroening, D., Wahl, T.: Symmetry-aware predicate abstraction for shared-variable concurrent programs. In: Gopalakrishnan, G., Qadeer, S. (eds.) CAV 2011. LNCS, vol. 6806, pp. 356–371. Springer, Heidelberg (2011). https://doi.org/10.1007/978-3-642-22110-1_28
8. Dräger, K., Kupriyanov, A., Finkbeiner, B., Wehrheim, H.: SLAB: a certifying model checker for infinite-state concurrent systems. In: Esparza, J., Majumdar, R. (eds.) TACAS 2010. LNCS, vol. 6015, pp. 271–274. Springer, Heidelberg (2010). https://doi.org/10.1007/978-3-642-12002-2_22
9. Esparza, J., Römer, S., Vogler, W.: An improvement of McMillan's unfolding algorithm. Formal Methods Syst. Des. 20(3), 285–310 (2002). https://doi.org/10.1023/A:1014746130920
10. Farzan, A., Kincaid, Z.: Verification of parameterized concurrent programs by modular reasoning about data and control. ACM SIGPLAN Not. 47(1), 297–308 (2012)
11. Farzan, A., Kincaid, Z., Podelski, A.: Inductive data flow graphs. ACM SIGPLAN Not. 48(1), 129–142 (2013)
12. Farzan, A., Vandikas, A.: Automated hypersafety verification. In: Dillig, I., Tasiran, S. (eds.) CAV 2019. LNCS, vol. 11561, pp. 200–218. Springer, Cham (2019). https://doi.org/10.1007/978-3-030-25540-4_11
13. Farzan, A., Vandikas, A.: Reductions for safety proofs. Proc. ACM Program. Lang. 4(POPL), 13:1–13:28 (2020)
14. Gavrilenko, N., Ponce-de-León, H., Furbach, F., Heljanko, K., Meyer, R.: BMC for weak memory models: relation analysis for compact SMT encodings. In: Dillig, I., Tasiran, S. (eds.) CAV 2019. LNCS, vol. 11561, pp. 355–365. Springer, Cham (2019). https://doi.org/10.1007/978-3-030-25540-4_19
15. Gupta, A., Popeea, C., Rybalchenko, A.: Predicate abstraction and refinement for verifying multi-threaded programs. In: Proceedings of the 38th Annual ACM SIGPLAN-SIGACT Symposium on Principles of Programming Languages, pp. 331–344. ACM (2011)

16. Heizmann, M., Hoenicke, J., Podelski, A.: Software model checking for people who love automata. In: Sharygina, N., Veith, H. (eds.) CAV 2013. LNCS, vol. 8044, pp. 36–52. Springer, Heidelberg (2013). https://doi.org/10.1007/978-3-642-39799-8_2

17. Henzinger, T.A., Jhala, R., Majumdar, R., Qadeer, S.: Thread-modular abstraction refinement. In: Hunt, W.A., Somenzi, F. (eds.) CAV 2003. LNCS, vol. 2725, pp. 262–274. Springer, Heidelberg (2003). https://doi.org/10.1007/978-3-540-45069-6_27

18. Inverso, O., Trubiani, C.: Parallel and distributed bounded model checking of multi-threaded programs. In: Proceedings of the 25th ACM SIGPLAN Symposium on Principles and Practice of Parallel Programming, pp. 202–216. ACM (2020)

19. Kahlon, V., Sankaranarayanan, S., Gupta, A.: Semantic reduction of thread interleavings in concurrent programs. In: Kowalewski, S., Philippou, A. (eds.) TACAS 2009. LNCS, vol. 5505, pp. 124–138. Springer, Heidelberg (2009). https://doi.org/10.1007/978-3-642-00768-2_12

20. McMillan, K.L.: Using unfoldings to avoid the state explosion problem in the verification of asynchronous circuits. In: von Bochmann, G., Probst, D.K. (eds.) CAV 1992. LNCS, vol. 663, pp. 164–177. Springer, Heidelberg (1993). https://doi.org/10.1007/3-540-56496-9_14

21. Miné, A.: Static analysis of run-time errors in embedded critical parallel C programs. In: Barthe, G. (ed.) ESOP 2011. LNCS, vol. 6602, pp. 398–418. Springer, Heidelberg (2011). https://doi.org/10.1007/978-3-642-19718-5_21

22. Wachter, B., Kroening, D., Ouaknine, J.: Verifying multi-threaded software with Impact. In: Formal Methods in Computer-Aided Design, pp. 210–217. IEEE (2013)

23. Yin, L., Dong, W., Liu, W., Wang, J.: On scheduling constraint abstraction for multi-threaded program verification. IEEE Trans. Softw. Eng. **46**(5), 549–565 (2020)

Eliminating Message Counters in
Synchronous Threshold Automata

Ilina Stoilkovska[1,2(✉)], Igor Konnov[2], Josef Widder[2], and Florian Zuleger[1]

[1] TU Wien, Vienna, Austria
{stoilkov,zuleger}@forsyte.at
[2] Informal Systems, Vienna, Austria
{igor,josef}@informal.systems

Abstract. In previous work, we introduced synchronous threshold automata for the verification of synchronous fault-tolerant distributed algorithms, and presented a verification method based on bounded model checking. Modeling a distributed algorithm by a threshold automaton requires to correctly deal with the semantics for sending and receiving messages based on the fault assumption. This step was done manually so far, and required human ingenuity. Motivated by similar results for asynchronous threshold automata, in this paper we show that one can start from a faithful model of the distributed algorithm that includes the sending and receiving of messages, and then automatically obtain a threshold automaton by applying quantifier elimination on the receive message counters. In this way, we obtain a fully automated verification pipeline. We present an experimental evaluation, discovering a bug in our previous manual encoding. Interestingly, while quantifier elimination in general produces larger threshold automata than the manual encoding, the verification times are comparable and even faster in several cases, allowing us to verify benchmarks that could not be handled before.

1 Introduction

Formal modeling and automated verification of fault-tolerant distributed algorithms [2,28] received considerable attention recently, e.g., [8,20,29,32,38]. In the more classic approach towards distributed algorithms' correctness, algorithms are described in pseudo code, using send and receive operations whose semantics are typically not formalized, but given in English. As a result, this may lead to ambiguities that are an obstacle both for implementing distributed algorithms faithfully, as well as for computer-aided verification. Threshold automata were introduced as a formalization of fault-tolerant distributed algorithms with precise semantics [5,23,26], and effective automated verification methods have been introduced both for the asynchronous [22] and for the synchronous [36] case. While they are a concise model that allows to capture precisely the non-determinism distributed systems exhibit due to the communication model and

Partially supported by: Interchain Foundation, Switzerland; Austrian Science Fund (FWF) via doctoral college LogiCS W1255.

© Springer Nature Switzerland AG 2021
F. Henglein et al. (Eds.): VMCAI 2021, LNCS 12597, pp. 196–218, 2021.
https://doi.org/10.1007/978-3-030-67067-2_10

partial faults, threshold automata in fact constitute a manual abstraction: a threshold automaton has to capture two major ingredients of a distributed system: (i) the local program control flow that is based on received messages and (ii) the semantics of send and receive operations in a fault-prone environment. For many classical distributed algorithms, this manual abstraction is quite immediate, but as has been observed in [37], more involved distributed algorithms are harder to abstract manually. This manual process consists in understanding how a fault assumption—that typically is well-understood but not formalized—changes the semantics of sending and receiving messages, which is a formalization step that typically requires human ingenuity. The more desirable approach is to have a precise and formal description of (i) and (ii), and to construct the abstraction automatically. This also allows to reuse (ii), that is, the formalization of given distributed computing model for new benchmarks. Indeed, in [37], for asynchronous algorithms, we introduced a method that takes as input formalizations of (i) and (ii) and automatically constructs threshold automata. By this, we have reduced the required expertise of the user, increased the degree of automation on the verification process, and indeed found some bugs in manual abstractions of asynchronous algorithms. However, the approach in [37] focuses on (asynchronous) interleaving semantics, and asynchronous message passing, which pose different challenges than the synchronous setting.

While distributed algorithms are mostly designed for asynchronous systems, there exists a considerable amount of literature that focuses on *synchronous* distributed algorithms. The synchronous computation model is relevant, both theoretically and practically: (a) a well-known impossibility result [18] reveals a class of problems for which a solution in the asynchronous model does not exist, but which can be solved in the synchronous model, (b) some real-time systems are actually built on top of synchronous distributed algorithms [24], and (c) several verification approaches reduce the asynchronous to the synchronous setting [4,12,13,15,19,25], enabling the transfer of verification techniques. For these reasons, verification in the synchronous setting received significant interest recently [1,17,29]. Applying verification techniques discovered a bug in an already published synchronous consensus algorithm, as reported in [27].

In [36], we proposed a synchronous variant of threshold automata along with an automated verification method based on bounded model checking. We experimentally evaluated our approach on a large number of benchmarks coming from the distributed systems literature. However, the framework in [36] is based on the manual abstraction described above.

Our Contributions. In this paper, we bring the automatic generation of threshold automata to the synchronous setting. We propose a *synchronous* threshold automata (STA) framework that allows us to:

1. model a given algorithm with an STA, whose guards are linear integer arithmetic expressions over the number of *received* messages, such that the obtained STA is in one-to-one correspondence with the pseudo code,

2. model the implicit assumptions imposed by the computation and fault models explicitly, using a so-called *environment assumption*, which is specific to the respective fault model and can be reused for different algorithms,
3. automatically translate the guards over the *local receive* variables into guards over the number of *globally sent* messages, using quantifier elimination,
4. pass the output of the translation as input to the verification tool proposed in [36], which implements a semi-decision procedure for computing the diameter, and performs bounded model checking.

In [36], the STA given as input to the verification tool was produced manually, that is, the steps 1–3 above were done by the user. By automating these steps, we reduce the ingenuity required by the user. We encoded the control flow and the environment assumptions of several synchronous algorithms in our framework and compared the resulting STA with the existing manual encodings from [34]. We confirm that manual abstraction is error-prone, as we discovered glitches in previous manually encoded STA. For all benchmarks, the automatically generated STA are comparable with the manual encodings. For some, the automatically generated STA could be verified faster. Thus in addition to increasing the degree of automation, we also gained in performance.

2 Our Approach at a Glance

Synchronous Distributed Algorithms. A distributed algorithm is a collection of n processes that perform a common task and exchange messages. At most t of the n processes can be faulty, and f processes are actually faulty. The numbers n, t, f are parameters, where n and t are "known", that is, they appear in the code (see Fig. 1), while f may differ according to the individual executions. In the synchronous computation model, the actions that a process takes locally depend on the messages that the process has received in the current round by other processes. Often, a process checks whether a quorum has been obtained (e.g., majority, two-thirds, etc.) by counting the number of messages it has received. Obtaining a quorum means that the number of *received* messages has to pass a given threshold, which should guarantee that it is safe for a correct process to take an action, and move to a new local state.

The threshold automata framework [23] is based on the observation that from the viewpoint of enabled transitions in a transition system, we may substitute the check whether a quorum of messages has been *received* with a check whether enough messages have been *sent*. For some algorithms, this substitution is straightforward, but others have more complicated guard expressions over the number of received messages. Consider, for example, the pseudo code of the algorithm PhaseQueen [6,9], presented in Fig. 1. The algorithm operates in phases, with two rounds per phase (lines 3–8 and 9–11). In round 1, all processes broadcast their value stored in the variable v (line 3), receive messages from other processes (line 4), and count the number of messages with value 0 (line 5) and value 1 (line 6). If a process received more than $2t$ messages with value 1, then it sets its value to 1 (line 7), otherwise it sets its value to 0 (line 8). In round 2,

```
1   v := input({0, 1})
2   for each phase 1 through t + 1 do
3       broadcast v  /* round 1: full message exchange */
4       receive messages from other processes
5       C[0] := number of received 0's
6       C[1] := number of received 1's
7       if C[1] > 2t then v := 1
8       else v := 0
9       if phase = i then broadcast v  /* round 2: queen's broadcast */
10      receive queen's message v_q
11      if C[v] < n - t then v := v_q
```

Fig. 1. The pseudo code of the Byzantine consensus algorithm PhaseQueen

a process i acts as a queen, if the number of the current phase is equal to i (line 9), and it is the only process that broadcasts (line 9). Each process receives the queen's value v_q (line 10), and checks if in round 1, it received less than $n - t$ messages with value equal to its own value v. If this is the case, the process sets its value to the value v_q received from the queen (line 11). This algorithm satisfies the property *agreement*: it ensures that after phase $t + 1$, i.e., after the loop on line 2 terminates, all correct processes have the same value v.

Receive Synchronous Threshold Automata. In Sect. 3, we propose a *new variant* of synchronous threshold automata, rSTA, with guards expressed over receive variables. Figure 2 shows the rSTA of the algorithm PhaseQueen. It corresponds to the control flow of the pseudo code in Fig. 1 as follows. The following locations capture local states of correct processes that are currently not a queen:

- Vi encodes that a process has the value $i \in \{0, 1\}$,
- R1Vi encodes that after the first round a process sets its value to $i \in \{0, 1\}$, and that it has received at least $n - t$ messages that have its value (i.e., the condition from line 11 evaluates to false),
- R1ViQ encodes that after the first round a process sets its value to $i \in \{0, 1\}$, and that it has received less than $n - t$ messages that have its value. Such a process will use the queen's message to update its value at the end of the second round (that is, the condition in line 11 evaluates to true),
- R2Vi encodes that after the second round a process sets its value to $i \in \{0, 1\}$.

From the location R2Vi, we have outgoing rules that bring the process back to the beginning of the next phase, i.e., to Vi, for $i \in \{0, 1\}$. Additionally, a process might move from the location R2Vi to QVi, for $i \in \{0, 1\}$, and thus become a queen in the next phase. The locations QVi, R1QVi, R2QVi, for $i \in \{0, 1\}$, capture the behavior of a correct process acting as a queen in the current phase. The Byzantine processes can act arbitrary, and their behavior is not explicitly modeled in the automaton. However, in some phase, the queen may be Byzantine. To capture this, we introduce locations, populated by a single Byzantine process, namely the locations $F = \{\text{F}, \ldots, \text{R2QF}\}$. The queen is Byzantine in some phase, if the single Byzantine process moves from the location R2F to the location QF.

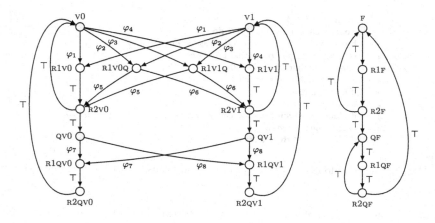

$$\mathsf{sent}(m_0) = \{\mathrm{v0, Qv0}\} \qquad \varphi_1 \equiv \mathsf{nr}(m_1) \le 2t \wedge \mathsf{nr}(m_0) \ge n - t \qquad \varphi_5 \equiv \mathsf{nr}(m_{q0}) \ge 1$$

$$\mathsf{sent}(m_1) = \{\mathrm{v1, Qv1}\} \qquad \varphi_2 \equiv \mathsf{nr}(m_1) \le 2t \wedge \mathsf{nr}(m_0) < n - t \qquad \varphi_6 \equiv \mathsf{nr}(m_{q1}) \ge 1$$

$$\mathsf{sent}(m_{q0}) = \{\mathrm{R1Qv0}\} \qquad \varphi_3 \equiv \mathsf{nr}(m_1) > 2t \wedge \mathsf{nr}(m_1) \ge n - t \qquad \varphi_7 \equiv \mathsf{nr}(m_1) \le 2t$$

$$\mathsf{sent}(m_{q1}) = \{\mathrm{R1Qv1}\} \qquad \varphi_4 \equiv \mathsf{nr}(m_1) > 2t \wedge \mathsf{nr}(m_1) < n - t \qquad \varphi_8 \equiv \mathsf{nr}(m_1) > 2t$$

Fig. 2. The rSTA for the algorithm PhaseQueen [6], where $n > 4t \wedge t \ge f$.

Processes in locations $\mathrm{v}i, \mathrm{Qv}i$ send messages of type m_i, that is, messages containing the value $i \in \{0, 1\}$. The message types m_{qi} are used to encode that the queen in the current phase sent a message with value $i \in \{0, 1\}$. When the queen process is Byzantine, it can send messages of type m_{q0} or m_{q1}. We write $\mathsf{sent}(m)$ to denote the set of locations where processes send a message of type m, and $\#\mathsf{sent}(m)$ for the number of sent messages of type m.

The receive guards $\varphi_1, \dots, \varphi_8$ express conditions over the number of received messages of some message type, and capture expressions which appear in the pseudo code. We denote by $\mathsf{nr}(m_i)$ and $\mathsf{nr}(m_{qi})$ the number of messages containing the value $i \in \{0, 1\}$ that a process received from all processes in the first round of the phase (i.e., the value $\mathsf{C}[i]$ in the pseudo code, lines 5, 6) and by the queen in the second round of the phase, respectively. For example, the receive guard φ_1, occurring on rules that move processes to the location R1v0, checks if a process received at most $2t$ messages of type m_1 (the **else** branch is taken in line 8), and at least $n - t$ messages of type m_0 (the condition in line 11 is false).

We explicitly encode the relationship between the number of received and sent messages using an *environment assumption* Env, which bounds the number of received messages: (i) from below by the number of messages sent by the correct processes, and (ii) from above by the number of messages sent by both the correct and faulty processes. The bound (i) captures the assumptions of the synchronous communication, which requires that all messages sent by correct processes in a round are received in the same round, and the bound (ii) captures the non-determinism introduced by the faulty processes. E.g., in the algorithm PhaseQueen, we have f Byzantine processes, which may send messages of arbitrary types. For the receive variable $\mathsf{nr}(m_i)$, we have the constraint $\#\mathsf{sent}(m_i) \leq \mathsf{nr}(m_i) \leq \#\mathsf{sent}(m_i) + f$ in the environment assumption Env.

The agreement property stated above is a safety property. To check if it holds, it suffices to check that after $t + 1$ phases, either all processes are in locations v0, QV0, or in locations v1, QV1. The precise formalization of the properties we are interested in verifying can be found in [36].

Our Approach. In Sect. 6, we eliminate the receive variables in an rSTA using quantifier elimination for Presburger arithmetic [14,30,31]. We strengthen the receive guards by the environment assumption Env that imposes bounds on the values of the receive variables, which are existentially quantified. As a result, a quantifier-free guard expression over the number of sent messages is obtained. For example, the result of applying quantifier elimination to the guard φ_1 over the receive variables from Fig. 2, strengthened by the upper and lower bounds in the environment assumption Env, is the guard $\widehat{\varphi}_1$ with no receive variables:

$$\widehat{\varphi}_1 \equiv \#\mathsf{sent}(m_1) \leq 2t \land \#\mathsf{sent}(m_0) + f \geq n - t \land \widehat{\mathsf{Env}}$$

where $\widehat{\mathsf{Env}}$ are the residual constraints from eliminating the receive variables from the environment assumption Env. The condition $\mathsf{nr}(m_1) \leq 2t$ in the guard φ_1 is translated to $\#\mathsf{sent}(m_1) \leq 2t$, and the condition $\mathsf{nr}(m_0) \geq n - t$ to $\#\mathsf{sent}(m_0) + f \geq n - t$. That is, when translating the guards, the number of the faulty processes f is used in guards that check if the number of sent messages passes a threshold, whereas f is not used in guards that check if the number of sent messages is below a threshold. (Byzantine processes send messages arbitrarily.)

The STA where all guards over the receive variables are replaced by the automatically generated guards over the number of sent messages constitutes a valid input to the bounded model checking technique for STA from [36], which we use to verify their safety properties. We show that this method is sound and complete by showing the existence of a bisimulation between the composition of n copies of rSTA and the composition of n copies of the produced STA. Thus, eliminating the receive message counters preserves temporal properties. We implemented this technique and used it to automatically generate STA for a set of benchmarks, and compared them to the existing manually encoded STA for the same benchmarks. We discuss our the experimental results in Sect. 7.

3   Synchronous Threshold Automata

We recall synchronous threshold automata from [36] and extend them with receive variables below. A *synchronous threshold automaton (STA)* is the tuple $\mathsf{STA} = (\mathcal{L}, \mathcal{I}, \mathcal{R}, \Pi, RC, \mathsf{Env})$, whose locations $\mathcal{L}$, initial locations $\mathcal{I}$, rules $\mathcal{R}$, parameters Π, and resilience condition RC are defined below. We define the environment assumption Env in Sect. 3.2.

Parameters Π, Resilience Condition RC. We assume that the set Π of *parameters* contains at least the parameter n, denoting the total number of processes.

The *resilience condition RC* is a linear arithmetic expression over the parameters from Π. We call the vector $\boldsymbol{\pi} = \langle \pi_1, \ldots, \pi_{|\Pi|} \rangle$ the *parameter vector*, and the vector $\mathbf{p} = \langle \mathsf{p}_1, \ldots, \mathsf{p}_{|\Pi|} \rangle \in \mathbb{N}^{|\Pi|}$ a *valuation* of $\boldsymbol{\pi}$. The set $\mathbf{P}_{RC} = \{ \mathbf{p} \in \mathbb{N}^{|\Pi|} \mid \mathbf{p}$ is a valuation of $\boldsymbol{\pi}$ and $\mathbf{p}$ satisfies $RC \}$ contains the *admissible valuations* of $\boldsymbol{\pi}$. The mapping $N : \mathbf{P}_{RC} \to \mathbb{N}$ maps an admissible valuation $\mathbf{p} \in \mathbf{P}_{RC}$ to the number $N(\mathbf{p}) \in \mathbb{N}$ of *participating processes*, i.e., the number of processes whose behavior is modeled using the STA. We denote by $N(\boldsymbol{\pi})$ the linear combination of parameters that defines the number of participating processes.

Locations $\mathcal{L}, \mathcal{I}$. The *locations* $\ell \in \mathcal{L}$ encode the current value of the local variables of a process, together with information about the program counter. We assume that each local variable and the program counter ranges over a finite set of values, that is, we assume that the set $\mathcal{L}$ of locations is a finite set. The *initial locations* in $\mathcal{I} \subseteq \mathcal{L}$ encode the initial values of the local variables.

Message Types $\mathcal{M}$. Let $\mathcal{M}$ denote the set of *message types*. To encode sending messages in the STA, we define a mapping $\mathsf{sent} : \mathcal{M} \to 2^{\mathcal{L}}$, that maps a message type $m \in \mathcal{M}$ to a set $\mathsf{sent}(m) \subseteq \mathcal{L}$ of locations, such that $\mathsf{sent}(m) = \{ \ell \in \mathcal{L} \mid$ a process in ℓ sends message of type $m \}$.

Let $L \subseteq \mathcal{L}$ denote a set of locations, and let $\#L$ denote the number of processes in locations from the set L. To define guards over the sent messages and express temporal properties, we define *c-propositions*:

$$\#L \geq \boldsymbol{a} \cdot \boldsymbol{\pi} + b \text{ for } L \subseteq \mathcal{L}, \, \boldsymbol{a} \in \mathbb{Z}^{|\Pi|}, \text{ and } b \in \mathbb{Z}$$

We denote by CP the set of *c*-propositions. If the set L of locations in the *c*-proposition is equal to the set $\mathsf{sent}(m)$, for some $m \in \mathcal{M}$, the *c*-proposition is used to check whether the number of messages of type $m \in \mathcal{M}$ is greater than or equal to a linear combination of the parameters, also called a *threshold*. Formally, the *c*-propositions are evaluated in tuples $(\boldsymbol{\kappa}, \mathbf{p})$, where $\boldsymbol{\kappa} \in \mathbb{N}^{|\mathcal{L}|}$ is an $|\mathcal{L}|$-dimensional vector of *counters*, and $\mathbf{p} \in \mathbf{P}_{RC}$ is an admissible valuation:

$$(\boldsymbol{\kappa}, \mathbf{p}) \models \#L \geq \boldsymbol{a} \cdot \boldsymbol{\pi} + b \quad \text{iff} \quad \sum_{\ell \in L} \kappa[\ell] \geq \boldsymbol{a} \cdot \mathbf{p} + b \tag{1}$$

Rules $\mathcal{R}$. A *rule* $r \in \mathcal{R}$ is a tuple $(\textit{from}, \textit{to}, \varphi)$, where: $\textit{from}, \textit{to} \in \mathcal{L}$ are locations, and φ is a *guard*, i.e., a Boolean combination of *c*-propositions. The guards $r.\varphi$, for $r \in \mathcal{R}$, analogously to (1), are evaluated in tuples $(\boldsymbol{\kappa}, \mathbf{p})$, and the semantics of the Boolean connectives is standard.

3.1   Receive Synchronous Threshold Automata

A *receive STA* is the tuple $\mathsf{rSTA} = (\mathcal{L}, \mathcal{I}, \mathcal{R}^{\Delta}, \Delta, \Pi, RC, \mathsf{Env}^{\Delta})$, whose locations $\mathcal{L}$, initial locations $\mathcal{I}$, parameters Π, and resilience condition RC are defined as for STA. We define the receive variables Δ and rules $\mathcal{R}^{\Delta}$ below, and the environment assumption Env^{Δ} in Sect. 3.2.

Receive Variables Δ. The set Δ contains *receive variables* $\mathsf{nr}(m)$ that store the number of messages of type $m \in \mathcal{M}$ that were received by a process. Thus, $|\Delta| = |\mathcal{M}|$, as in Δ there is exactly one receive variable $\mathsf{nr}(m)$ per message type $m \in \mathcal{M}$. The values of the receive variables depend on the number of messages sent in a given round (discussed in more detail in Sect. 3.2).

Let $M \subseteq \mathcal{M}$ denote a set of message types, and let $\#M$ denote the total number of messages of types $m \in M$, received by some process. Observe that the notation $\#M$ is a shorthand for $\sum_{m \in M} \mathsf{nr}(m)$. We will use these two notations interchangeably. Further, when M is a singleton set, that is, when $M = \{m\}$, we will simply use the notation $\mathsf{nr}(m)$ to denote $\#\{m\}$. For the purpose of expressing guards over the receive variables $\mathsf{nr}(m)$, for $m \in \mathcal{M}$, we define *r-propositions*:

$$\#M \geq \boldsymbol{a} \cdot \boldsymbol{\pi} + b, \text{ such that } M \subseteq \mathcal{M}, \boldsymbol{a} \in \mathbb{Z}^{|\Pi|}, b \in \mathbb{Z}$$

We denote by RP the set of *r*-propositions. The intended meaning of the *r*-propositions is to check whether the total number of messages of types $m \in M$ received by some process i passes some threshold. Formally, they are evaluated in tuples $(\mathbf{d}, \mathbf{p})$, where $\mathbf{d} \in \mathbb{N}^{|\mathcal{M}|}$ is a vector of values assigned to each receive variable $\mathsf{nr}(m)$, for $m \in \mathcal{M}$, and $\mathbf{p} \in \mathbf{P}_{RC}$. We define:

$$(\mathbf{d}, \mathbf{p}) \models \#M \geq \boldsymbol{a} \cdot \boldsymbol{\pi} + b \quad \text{iff} \quad \sum_{m \in M} \mathbf{d}[m] \geq \boldsymbol{a} \cdot \mathbf{p} + b \quad (2)$$

Rules $\mathcal{R}^{\Delta}$. Similarly to the way we defined rules of STA above, the rules $r^{\Delta} \in \mathcal{R}^{\Delta}$ in rSTA are tuples $r^{\Delta} = (from, to, \varphi)$, where $r^{\Delta}.from, r^{\Delta}.to \in \mathcal{L}$ are locations, and $r^{\Delta}.\varphi$ is a *receive guard*, which is a Boolean combination of *c*-propositions and *r*-propositions. The receive guards $r^{\Delta}.\varphi$, for $r^{\Delta} \in \mathcal{R}^{\Delta}$, are evaluated in tuples $(\mathbf{d}, \boldsymbol{\kappa}, \mathbf{p})$. Given a tuple $(\mathbf{d}, \boldsymbol{\kappa}, \mathbf{p})$, where $\mathbf{d} \in \mathbb{N}^{|\mathcal{M}|}$ is a vector of valuations of the receive variables $\mathsf{nr}(m)$, for $m \in \mathcal{M}$, $\boldsymbol{\kappa} \in \mathbb{N}^{|\mathcal{L}|}$ is an $|\mathcal{L}|$-dimensional vector of counters, and $\mathbf{p} \in \mathbf{P}_{RC}$ is an admissible valuation, we evaluate *c*-propositions and *r*-propositions (the semantics of the Boolean connectives is standard):

$$(\mathbf{d}, \boldsymbol{\kappa}, \mathbf{p}) \models \#L \geq \boldsymbol{a} \cdot \boldsymbol{\pi} + b \quad \text{iff} \quad (\boldsymbol{\kappa}, \mathbf{p}) \models \#L \geq \boldsymbol{a} \cdot \boldsymbol{\pi} + b \quad \text{(cf. (1))}$$
$$(\mathbf{d}, \boldsymbol{\kappa}, \mathbf{p}) \models \#M \geq \boldsymbol{a} \cdot \boldsymbol{\pi} + b \quad \text{iff} \quad (\mathbf{d}, \mathbf{p}) \models \#M \geq \boldsymbol{a} \cdot \boldsymbol{\pi} + b \quad \text{(cf. (2))}$$

3.2 Environment Assumption and Modeling Faults

Depending on the fault model, when constructing a (receive) STA that models the behavior of a process running a given algorithm, we typically need to introduce additional locations or rules that are used to capture the behavior of the faulty processes. Additionally, to faithfully model the faulty environment, we will introduce constraints on the number of processes in given locations in both STA and rSTA, expressed using *c*-propositions, as well as constraints on the values of the receive variables of the rSTA, expressed using *e-propositions*:

$$\#M \geq \#L + \boldsymbol{a} \cdot \boldsymbol{\pi} + b, \text{ such that } M \subseteq \mathcal{M}, L \subseteq \mathcal{L}, \boldsymbol{a} \in \mathbb{Z}^{|\Pi|}, b \in \mathbb{Z}$$

We denote by EP the set of e-propositions. The e-propositions are evaluated in tuples $(\mathbf{d}, \boldsymbol{\kappa}, \mathbf{p})$ where $\mathbf{d} \in \mathbb{N}^{|\mathcal{M}|}$ is a vector of valuations of the receive variables, $\boldsymbol{\kappa} \in \mathbb{N}^{|\mathcal{L}|}$ is an $|\mathcal{L}|$-dimensional vector of counters, and $\mathbf{p} \in \mathbf{P}_{RC}$. We say that:

$$(\mathbf{d}, \boldsymbol{\kappa}, \mathbf{p}) \models \#M \geq \#L + \boldsymbol{a} \cdot \boldsymbol{\pi} + b \quad \text{iff} \quad \sum_{m \in M} \mathbf{d}[m] \geq \sum_{\ell \in L} \boldsymbol{\kappa}[\ell] + \boldsymbol{a} \cdot \mathbf{p} + b$$

The e-propositions will be used to express that the number of received messages is in the range from the number of messages sent by *correct* processes to the total number of sent messages (sent by both correct and faulty processes).

For STA, the environment assumption Env is a conjunction of c-propositions and their negations. For rSTA, the environment assumption Env^{Δ} is a conjunction of c-propositions, e-propositions and their negations. The c-propositions restrict the number of processes in certain locations, while the e-propositions restrict the values of the receive variables by relating them to the number of sent messages of the same type. We define the environment assumptions Env and Env^{Δ} of the STA and rSTA, respectively, as $\mathsf{Env} \equiv \mathsf{Env}_{\mathrm{CP}}$ and $\mathsf{Env}^{\Delta} \equiv \mathsf{Env}_{\mathrm{CP}} \wedge \mathsf{Env}_{\mathrm{EP}}$, where $\mathsf{Env}_{\mathrm{CP}}$ and $\mathsf{Env}_{\mathrm{EP}}$ are conjunctions of c-propositions and e-propositions and their negations, respectively, such that:

$$\mathsf{Env}_{\mathrm{CP}} \equiv \mathsf{C1} \wedge \mathsf{C2} \wedge \mathsf{Env}_{\mathrm{CP},*} \quad \text{and} \quad \mathsf{Env}_{\mathrm{EP}} \equiv \mathsf{E1} \wedge \mathsf{Env}_{\mathrm{EP},*}$$

where, irrespective of the fault model, we have the following constraints:

(C1) $\bigwedge_{\ell \in \mathcal{L}} \#\{\ell\} \geq 0$, i.e., the number of processes in a location ℓ is non-negative,

(C2) $\#\mathcal{L} = N(\boldsymbol{\pi})$, i.e., the number of processes in all locations $\mathcal{L}$ is equal to the number of participating processes,

(E1) $\bigwedge_{m \in \mathcal{M}} \#\mathsf{sent}(m) \leq \mathsf{nr}(m)$, i.e., the number $\mathsf{nr}(m)$ of received messages of each message type $m \in \mathcal{M}$ is bounded from below by the number $\#\mathsf{sent}(m)$ of messages of type m, sent by correct processes.

The formulas $\mathsf{Env}_{\mathrm{CP},*}$ and $\mathsf{Env}_{\mathrm{EP},*}$ for $* \in \{\mathsf{cr}, \mathsf{so}, \mathsf{byz}\}$, depend on the fault model, i.e., on whether we model crash, send omission, or Byzantine faults.

Crash Faults. Crash-faulty processes stop executing the algorithm prematurely and cannot restart. To model the behavior of the crash-faulty processes, the set $\mathcal{L}$ of locations of the (receive) STA is the set: $\mathcal{L} = \mathcal{L}_{\mathsf{corr}} \cup \mathcal{L}_{\mathsf{cr}} \cup \{\ell_{\mathsf{fld}}\}$, where $\mathcal{L}_{\mathsf{corr}}$ is a set of *correct* locations, $\mathcal{L}_{\mathsf{cr}} = \{\ell_{\mathsf{cr}} \mid \ell_{\mathsf{cr}} \text{ is a fresh copy of } \ell \in \mathcal{L}_{\mathsf{corr}}\}$ is a set of *crash* locations, and ℓ_{fld} is a *failed* location. The crash locations $\ell_{\mathsf{cr}} \in \mathcal{L}_{\mathsf{cr}}$ model the same values of the local variables and program counter as their correct counterpart $\ell \in \mathcal{L}_{\mathsf{corr}}$. The difference is that processes in the crash locations $\ell_{\mathsf{cr}} \in \mathcal{L}_{\mathsf{cr}}$ are flagged by the environment to crash in the current round. After crashing, they move to the failed location ℓ_{fld}, where they remain forever. This models that the crashed processes cannot restart.

A crash-faulty process may send a message to a subset of the other processes in the round in which it crashes. To model this, we introduce the mapping $\mathsf{sent}_{\mathsf{cr}} : \mathcal{M} \to 2^{\mathcal{L}_{\mathsf{cr}}}$, which defines, for each $m \in \mathcal{M}$, the set of crash locations $\mathsf{sent}_{\mathsf{cr}}(m) \subseteq$

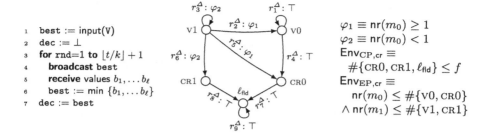

1 **best** := input(V)
2 **dec** := ⊥
3 **for** rnd=1 **to** ⌊t/k⌋ + 1
4   **broadcast best**
5   **receive** values $b_1, \ldots b_\ell$
6   **best** := min $\{b_1, \ldots b_\ell\}$
7   **dec** := **best**

$\varphi_1 \equiv \mathsf{nr}(m_0) \geq 1$
$\varphi_2 \equiv \mathsf{nr}(m_0) < 1$
$\mathsf{Env}_{\mathrm{CP,cr}} \equiv$
  $\#\{\mathrm{CR0, CR1}, \ell_{\mathsf{fld}}\} \leq f$
$\mathsf{Env}_{\mathrm{EP,cr}} \equiv$
  $\mathsf{nr}(m_0) \leq \#\{\mathrm{v0, CR0}\}$
  $\wedge\, \mathsf{nr}(m_1) \leq \#\{\mathrm{v1, CR1}\}$

Fig. 3. The pseudo code of the algorithm FloodMin for $k = 1$ [28], which tolerates crash faults, and the receive STA encoding its loop body.

$\mathcal{L}_{\mathrm{cr}}$ where processes send a message of type m. Then, $\#(\mathsf{sent}(m) \cup \mathsf{sent}_{\mathrm{cr}}(m))$ denotes the number of messages sent by correct and crash-faulty processes. In addition to the new locations, we add the following new rules:

(cr1) for every rule $r \in \mathcal{R}$, if $r.\mathit{from} \in \mathcal{L}_{\mathrm{corr}}$ and $r.\mathit{to} \in \mathcal{L}_{\mathrm{corr}}$, then we add the rule $(r.\mathit{from}, \ell_{\mathrm{cr}}, r.\varphi)$, where $\ell_{\mathrm{cr}} \in \mathcal{L}_{\mathrm{cr}}$ is the crash location corresponding to $r.\mathit{to}$,
(cr2) for every crash location $\ell_{\mathrm{cr}} \in \mathcal{L}_{\mathrm{cr}}$, we add the rule $(\ell_{\mathrm{cr}}, \ell_{\mathsf{fld}}, \top)$,
(cr3) for the failed location ℓ_{fld}, we add the rule $(\ell_{\mathsf{fld}}, \ell_{\mathsf{fld}}, \top)$.

The rules (cr1) move processes from the correct to the crash locations, in rounds where the environment flags them as crashed. The rules (cr2) move processes from the crashed locations to the failed location, where they can only apply the self-loop rule (cr3), which keeps them in the failed location.

We model the behavior of crash-faulty processes explicitly, that is, we have $N(\pi) = n$. The constraints $\mathsf{Env}_{\mathrm{CP,cr}}$ and $\mathsf{Env}_{\mathrm{EP,cr}}$ for the crash fault model are:

$$\mathsf{Env}_{\mathrm{CP,cr}} = \#(\mathcal{L}_{\mathrm{cr}} \cup \{\ell_{\mathsf{fld}}\}) \leq f$$

$$\mathsf{Env}_{\mathrm{EP,cr}} \equiv \bigwedge_{m \in \mathcal{M}} \mathsf{nr}(m) \leq \#(\mathsf{sent}(m) \cup \mathsf{sent}_{\mathrm{cr}}(m))$$

The formula $\mathsf{Env}_{\mathrm{CP,cr}}$ ensures that there are no more than f faults. The formula $\mathsf{Env}_{\mathrm{EP,cr}}$ restricts the values of the receive variables by ensuring that the number of received messages of type $m \in \mathcal{M}$ for each process is a value, bounded from above by the number $\#(\mathsf{sent}(m) \cup \mathsf{sent}_{\mathrm{cr}}(m))$ of messages of type m, sent by the correct processes and the processes flagged as crashed in the current round.

Figure 3 depicts the pseudo code and the rSTA of the crash-tolerant k-set agreement algorithm FloodMin, for $k = 1$ [28]. We identify the sets $\mathcal{L}_{\mathrm{corr}} = \{\mathrm{v0, v1}\}$ of correct locations, $\mathcal{L}_{\mathrm{cr}} = \{\mathrm{CR0, CR1}\}$ of crash locations, $\mathcal{M} = \{m_0, m_1\}$ of message types. The location $\mathrm{v}i$ encodes that a correct process has its variable **best** set to $i \in \{0, 1\}$, the location $\mathrm{CR}i$ encodes that the value of **best** of a crashed process is $i \in \{0, 1\}$, and the message type m_i encodes a message containing the value $i \in \{0, 1\}$. The failed location is ℓ_{fld}. We define $\mathsf{sent}(m_i) = \{\mathrm{v}i\}$ and $\mathsf{sent}_{\mathrm{cr}}(m_i) = \{\mathrm{CR}i\}$, for $i \in \{0, 1\}$. The two receive guards

$$r_3^{\Delta}: \varphi_2 \qquad\qquad r_1^{\Delta}: \top$$

v1 $\overset{r_2^{\Delta}: \varphi_1}{\longrightarrow}$ v0

$$r_6^{\Delta}: \varphi_2 \qquad\qquad r_4^{\Delta}: \top$$

so1 $\overset{r_5^{\Delta}: \varphi_1}{\longrightarrow}$ so0

$$\mathsf{Env}_{\mathsf{CP,so}} \equiv \#\{\mathsf{v0}, \mathsf{v1}\} = n - f$$
$$\wedge \#\{\mathsf{so0}, \mathsf{so1}\} = f$$
$$\mathsf{Env}_{\mathsf{EP,so}} \equiv \mathsf{nr}(m_0) \leq \#\{\mathsf{v0}, \mathsf{so0}\}$$
$$\wedge \mathsf{nr}(m_1) \leq \#\{\mathsf{v1}, \mathsf{so1}\}$$

Fig. 4. The receive STA encoding the loop body of the algorithm FMinOmit for $k = 1$, which tolerates send omission faults and whose pseudo code is given in Fig. 3.

$\varphi_1 \equiv \mathsf{nr}(m_0) \geq 1$ and $\varphi_2 \equiv \mathsf{nr}(m_0) < 1$ check if a process received at least one message of type m_0 (i.e., if the minimal value 0 has been received in line 5 of the pseudo code) and no message of type m_0, respectively. The constraint $\mathsf{Env}_{\mathsf{CP,cr}}$ ensures that there are not more than f processes in the locations $\mathrm{CR0}, \mathrm{CR1}$, and ℓ_{fld} together. The constraint $\mathsf{Env}_{\mathsf{EP,cr}}$ bounds the values of the receive variables $\mathsf{nr}(m_i)$ from above by the number of processes in locations $\mathrm{v}i, \mathrm{CR}i$, for $i \in \{0, 1\}$.

Send Omission Faults. A send-omission-faulty process may omit to send a message, but acts as a correct process on the receiving side. We model algorithms tolerating send omission faults similarly to crash faults: the set $\mathcal{L}$ of locations is $\mathcal{L} = \mathcal{L}_{\mathsf{corr}} \cup \mathcal{L}_{\mathsf{so}}$, where $\mathcal{L}_{\mathsf{corr}}$ is a set of *correct* locations and $\mathcal{L}_{\mathsf{so}} = \{\ell_{\mathsf{so}} \mid \ell_{\mathsf{so}} \text{ is a fresh copy of } \ell \in \mathcal{L}_{\mathsf{corr}}\}$ is a set of *send-omission* locations. For every rule $r \in \mathcal{R}$ connecting two locations $\ell, \ell' \in \mathcal{L}_{\mathsf{corr}}$, there exists a rule $(\ell_{\mathsf{so}}, \ell'_{\mathsf{so}}, r.\varphi) \in \mathcal{R}$, connecting their two corresponding send-omission locations $\ell_{\mathsf{so}}, \ell'_{\mathsf{so}} \in \mathcal{L}_{\mathsf{so}}$. We introduce the mapping $\mathsf{sent}_{\mathsf{so}} : \mathcal{M} \to 2^{\mathcal{L}_{\mathsf{so}}}$, which defines the set of send-omission locations where processes send a message of type $m \in \mathcal{M}$.

As there are no rules that connect the locations from $\mathcal{L}_{\mathsf{corr}}$ to the locations from $\mathcal{L}_{\mathsf{so}}$, the automaton consists of two parts: one used by the correct processes, and one used by the send-omission-faulty processes. The behavior of the send-omission-faulty processes is encoded explicitly, using locations and rules in the automaton, hence, we define $N(\boldsymbol{\pi}) = n$. The constraint $\mathsf{Env}_{\mathsf{CP,so}}$ ensures that the number of processes populating the correct locations is $n - f$, and the number of processes populating the send-omission locations is f. The constraint $\mathsf{Env}_{\mathsf{EP,so}}$ ensures that the number of received messages of type $m \in \mathcal{M}$ for each process is bounded from above by the number $\#(\mathsf{sent}(m) \cup \mathsf{sent}_{\mathsf{so}}(m))$ of messages of type m, sent by the correct and the send-omission-faulty processes. Formally:

$$\mathsf{Env}_{\mathsf{CP,so}} = \#\mathcal{L}_{\mathsf{corr}} = n - f \wedge \#\mathcal{L}_{\mathsf{so}} = f$$

$$\mathsf{Env}_{\mathsf{EP,so}} \equiv \bigwedge_{m \in \mathcal{M}} \mathsf{nr}(m) \leq \#(\mathsf{sent}(m) \cup \mathsf{sent}_{\mathsf{so}}(m))$$

Figure 4 depicts the rSTA for the k-set agreement algorithm FMinOmit, for $k = 1$, which is a variant of the algorithm FloodMin (Fig. 3) that tolerates send omission faults. We identify the sets $\mathcal{L}_{\mathsf{corr}} = \{\mathrm{v0}, \mathrm{v1}\}$ of correct locations, $\mathcal{L}_{\mathsf{so}} = \{\mathrm{so0}, \mathrm{so1}\}$ of send-omission locations, and $\mathcal{M} = \{m_0, m_1\}$ of message types. We define $\mathsf{sent}(m_i) = \{\mathrm{v}i\}$ and $\mathsf{sent}_{\mathsf{so}}(m_i) = \{\mathrm{so}i\}$, for $i \in \{0, 1\}$. The

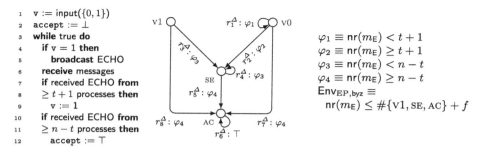

Fig. 5. The pseudo code of the algorithm RB [21], which tolerates Byzantine faults, and the receive STA encoding its loop body.

constraint $\mathsf{Env}_{\mathrm{CP,so}}$ ensures that there are exactly $n - f$ processes in the correct locations $\mathrm{v0}, \mathrm{v1}$, and exactly f processes in the send-omission locations $\mathrm{so0}, \mathrm{so1}$. The receive guards φ_1 and φ_2 are the syntactically same as in the rSTA for the crash-tolerant version of the algorithm FloodMin, for $k = 1$. However, the environment constraint $\mathsf{Env}_{\mathrm{EP,so}}$ differs from $\mathsf{Env}_{\mathrm{EP,cr}}$: it restricts the number $\mathsf{nr}(m_i)$ of received messages of type m_i to a value which is less than or equal to the number of processes in locations $\mathrm{v}i, \mathrm{so}i$, for $i \in \{0, 1\}$.

Byzantine Faults. To model the behavior of the Byzantine-faulty processes, which can act arbitrary, no new locations and rules are introduced in the (receive) STA. Instead, the (receive) STA is used to model the behavior of the correct processes, and the effect that the Byzantine-faulty processes have on the correct ones is captured in the guards (and environment assumption). The number of messages sent by Byzantine-faulty processes is overapproximated by the parameter f, which denotes the number of faults. That is, for a message type $m \in \mathcal{M}$, the number $\#\mathsf{sent}(m) + f$ is the upper bound on the number of messages sent by correct and Byzantine-faulty processes.

The (receive) STA for Byzantine faults is used to model the behavior of the correct processes, hence $N(\pi) = n - f$. As we do not introduce new locations or rules, we have $\mathsf{Env}_{\mathrm{CP,byz}} \equiv \top$. The constraint $\mathsf{Env}_{\mathrm{EP,byz}}$ encodes the effect that the Byzantine-faulty processes have on the correct processes, by bounding the receive variables $\mathsf{nr}(m)$ by $\mathsf{sent}(m) + f$ from above, for $m \in \mathcal{M}$:

$$\mathsf{Env}_{\mathrm{EP,byz}} \equiv \bigwedge_{m \in \mathcal{M}} \mathsf{nr}(m) \leq \mathsf{sent}(m) + f$$

Figure 5 shows the pseudo code of the Byzantine reliable broadcast algorithm RB [21]. The locations $\mathcal{L} = \{\mathrm{v0}, \mathrm{v1}, \mathrm{SE}, \mathrm{AC}\}$ model the behavior of the correct processes. The location $\mathrm{v}i$ encodes that a process has value $i \in \{0, 1\}$, the location SE that a process has sent an ECHO message, and the location AC that a process sets its value to 1 in line 12. There is a single message type, m_{E}, which encodes a message containing the value ECHO. There are four receive guards, $\varphi_1, \ldots, \varphi_4$. The guard φ_2, for example, checks that at least $t + 1$ ECHO messages are received, capturing line 8 of the pseudo code. The set of processes that send an ECHO message is $\mathsf{sent}(m_\mathsf{E}) = \{\mathrm{V1}, \mathrm{SE}, \mathrm{AC}\}$. The constraint $\mathsf{Env}_{\mathrm{EP,byz}}$ ensures that there are not more than $\#\{\mathrm{V1}, \mathrm{SE}, \mathrm{AC}\} + f$ received messages of type m_E.

Remark on Algorithms with a Coordinator. When modeling Byzantine-tolerant algorithms where a process acts as a coordinator (such as, e.g., the algorithm PhaseQueen in Fig. 1), we need to take into account that at some point, the coordinator will be Byzantine. Thus, we add locations $\mathcal{L}_\mathsf{byz} \subseteq \mathcal{L}$ for a single Byzantine process, disjoint from the locations that are used by the correct processes. The new locations do not encode any values of the local variables; they ensure that the Byzantine process (which may become a coordinator) moves synchronously with the other processes. In the rSTA for the algorithm PhaseQueen (Fig. 2), we defined $\mathcal{L}_\mathsf{byz} = F = \{\mathrm{F}, \ldots, \mathrm{R2QF}\}$. As we model the behavior of a single Byzantine process explicitly, we have $N(\boldsymbol{\pi}) = n - f + 1$.

In this case, we define the constraints $\mathsf{Env}_{\mathrm{CP,co}}$, which restrict the number of processes in given locations. We also identify locations $\mathcal{L}_\mathsf{co} \subseteq \mathcal{L}$, which only a (correct or Byzantine) coordinator is allowed to populate. The environment constraint $\mathsf{Env}_{\mathrm{CP,co}}$ for Byzantine-tolerant algorithms with a coordinator is:

$$\mathsf{Env}_{\mathrm{CP,co}} \equiv \#\mathcal{L}_\mathsf{co} = 1 \wedge \#\mathcal{L}_\mathsf{byz} = 1$$

where $\#\mathcal{L}_\mathsf{co} = 1$ (resp. $\#\mathcal{L}_\mathsf{byz} = 1$) ensures that there is exactly one process in the coordinator locations $\mathcal{L}_\mathsf{co}$ (resp. in the Byzantine locations $\mathcal{L}_\mathsf{byz}$).

Additionally, we have message types $m_\mathsf{co} \in \mathcal{M}$ that model the coordinator messages, and denote by ℓ_F the location where the Byzantine process performs the coordinator broadcast. The constraint $\mathsf{Env}_{\mathrm{EP,co}}$ states that the number of received coordinator messages of type m_co does not exceed the total number of coordinator messages of type m_co sent by the correct and Byzantine coordinators:

$$\mathsf{Env}_{\mathrm{EP,co}} \equiv \mathsf{Env}_{\mathrm{EP,byz}} \wedge \bigwedge_{m_\mathsf{co} \in \mathcal{M}} \mathsf{nr}(m_\mathsf{co}) \leq \#(\mathsf{sent}(m_\mathsf{co}) \cup \{\ell_F\})$$

Thus, for the algorithm PhaseQueen, whose rSTA we depicted in Fig. 2:

$$\mathsf{Env}_{\mathrm{CP,co}} \equiv \#\{\mathrm{QV0}, \ldots, \mathrm{R2QV1}, \mathrm{QF}, \ldots, \mathrm{R2QF}\} = 1 \wedge \#\{\mathrm{F}, \ldots, \mathrm{R2QF}\} = 1$$

$$\mathsf{Env}_{\mathrm{EP,co}} \equiv \bigwedge_{i \in \{0,1\}} (\mathsf{nr}(m_i) \leq \#\mathsf{sent}(m_i) + f \wedge \mathsf{nr}(m_{qi}) \leq \#(\mathsf{sent}(m_{qi}) \cup \{\mathrm{R1QF}\}))$$

4 Counter Systems

For an $\mathsf{STA} = (\mathcal{L}, \mathcal{I}, \mathcal{R}, \Pi, RC, \mathsf{Env})$ and an admissible valuation $\mathbf{p} \in \mathbf{P}_{RC}$, we recall the definition of a counter system from [36]. A *counter system* w.r.t. an admissible valuation $\mathbf{p} \in \mathbf{P}_{RC}$ and an $\mathsf{STA} = (\mathcal{L}, \mathcal{I}, \mathcal{R}, \Pi, RC, \mathsf{Env})$ is the tuple $\mathsf{CS}(\mathsf{STA}, \mathbf{p}) = (\Sigma(\mathbf{p}), I(\mathbf{p}), R(\mathbf{p}))$, representing a system of $N(\mathbf{p})$ processes whose behavior is modeled using the STA, where $\Sigma(\mathbf{p})$ is the set of *configurations*, $I(\mathbf{p})$ is the set of *initial configurations*, and $R(\mathbf{p})$ is the *transition relation*.

A *configuration* $\sigma \in \Sigma(\mathbf{p})$ is a tuple $(\boldsymbol{\kappa}, \mathbf{p})$, where $\mathbf{p} \in \mathbf{P}_{RC}$ is an admissible valuation, and $\boldsymbol{\kappa} \in \mathbb{N}^{|\mathcal{L}|}$ is an $|\mathcal{L}|$-dimensional vector of *counters*, such that $\sigma \models$ Env. For every $\sigma \in \Sigma(\mathbf{p})$, we have $\sum_{\ell \in \mathcal{L}} \sigma.\boldsymbol{\kappa}[\ell] = N(\mathbf{p})$. This follows from $\sigma \models$ Env, in particular from $\sigma \models \#\mathcal{L} = N(\boldsymbol{\pi})$, the definition of $N(\mathbf{p})$, and the semantics of the c-propositions. A configuration $\sigma \in \Sigma(\mathbf{p})$ is *initial*, i.e., $\sigma \in I(\mathbf{p}) \subseteq \Sigma(\mathbf{p})$, iff $\sigma.\boldsymbol{\kappa}[\ell] = 0$, for every $\ell \in \mathcal{L} \setminus \mathcal{I}$. That is, the value $\sigma.\boldsymbol{\kappa}[\ell]$ of the counter for each non-initial location $\ell \in \mathcal{L} \setminus \mathcal{I}$ is set to 0 in $\sigma \in \mathcal{I}$.

To define the transition relation $R(\mathbf{p})$, we first define the notion of a transition. A *transition* is a function $tr : \mathcal{R} \to \mathbb{N}$ that maps each rule $r \in \mathcal{R}$ to a *factor* $tr(r) \in \mathbb{N}$. Given a valuation $\mathbf{p}$ of $\boldsymbol{\pi}$, the set $Tr(\mathbf{p}) = \{tr \mid \sum_{r \in \mathcal{R}} tr(r) = N(\mathbf{p})\}$ contains transitions whose factors sum up to $N(\mathbf{p})$. For a transition tr and a rule $r \in \mathcal{R}$, the factor $tr(r)$ denotes the number of processes that act upon this rule. By restricting the set $Tr(\mathbf{p})$ to contain transitions whose factors sum up to $N(\mathbf{p})$, we ensure that in a transition, every process takes a step. This captures the semantics of synchronous computation. A transition $tr \in Tr(\mathbf{p})$ is *enabled* in a tuple $(\boldsymbol{\kappa}, \mathbf{p})$, where $\boldsymbol{\kappa}$ is an $|\mathcal{L}|$- dimensional vector of counters and $\mathbf{p} \in \mathbf{P}_{RC}$ an admissible valuation, iff for every $r \in \mathcal{R}$, such that $tr(r) > 0$, it holds that $(\boldsymbol{\kappa}, \mathbf{p}) \models r.\varphi$, and for every $\ell \in \mathcal{L}$, we have $\boldsymbol{\kappa}[\ell] = \sum_{r \in \mathcal{R} \wedge r.from=\ell} tr(r)$. The former condition ensures that processes only use rules whose guards are satisfied, and the latter that every process moves in an enabled transition.

Given a transition $tr \in Tr(\mathbf{p})$, we define the *origin* $o(tr) = (\boldsymbol{\kappa}, \mathbf{p})$ of tr, where for every location $\ell \in \mathcal{L}$, we have $\boldsymbol{\kappa}[\ell] = \sum_{r \in \mathcal{R} \wedge r.from=\ell} tr(r)$, and the *goal* $g(tr) = (\boldsymbol{\kappa}', \mathbf{p})$ of tr, where for every location $\ell \in \mathcal{L}$, we have $\boldsymbol{\kappa}'[\ell] = \sum_{r \in \mathcal{R} \wedge r.to=\ell} tr(r)$. The origin $o(tr)$ is the unique tuple $(\boldsymbol{\kappa}, \mathbf{p})$ where the transition tr is enabled, while its goal $g(tr)$ is the unique tuple $(\boldsymbol{\kappa}', \mathbf{p})$ that is obtained by applying the transition tr to its origin $o(tr)$. The *transition relation* $R(\mathbf{p})$ is the relation $R(\mathbf{p}) \subseteq \Sigma(\mathbf{p}) \times Tr(\mathbf{p}) \times \Sigma(\mathbf{p})$, such that $\langle \sigma, tr, \sigma' \rangle \in R(\mathbf{p})$ iff $\sigma = o(tr)$ is the origin and $\sigma' = g(tr)$ is the goal of the transition tr.

5   Synchronous Transition Systems

Let $\mathsf{rSTA} = (\mathcal{L}, \mathcal{I}, \mathcal{R}^{\Delta}, \Delta, \Pi, RC, \mathsf{Env}^{\Delta})$ be a receive STA, and $\mathbf{p} \in \mathbf{P}_{RC}$ an admissible valuation of the parameter vector $\boldsymbol{\pi}$. A *synchronous transition system* (or *system*), w.r.t. an admissible valuation $\mathbf{p} \in \mathbf{P}_{RC}$ and an rSTA is the triple $\mathsf{STS}(\mathsf{rSTA}, \mathbf{p}) = \langle S(\mathbf{p}), S_0(\mathbf{p}), T(\mathbf{p}) \rangle$, representing a system of $N(\mathbf{p})$ processes whose behavior is modeled using the rSTA, where $S(\mathbf{p})$ is the set of *states*, $S_0(\mathbf{p})$ is the set of *initial states*, and $T(\mathbf{p})$ is the *transition relation*.

Recall that the environment assumption Env^{Δ} of the rSTA is the conjunction $\mathsf{Env}^{\Delta} \equiv \mathsf{Env}_{\mathrm{CP}} \wedge \mathsf{Env}_{\mathrm{EP}}$. A *state* $s \in S(\mathbf{p})$ is a tuple $s = \langle \boldsymbol{\ell}, \mathbf{nr}_1, \ldots, \mathbf{nr}_{N(\mathbf{p})}, \mathbf{p} \rangle$, where $\boldsymbol{\ell} \in \mathcal{L}^{N(\mathbf{p})}$ is an $N(\mathbf{p})$-dimensional vector of locations, and $\mathbf{nr}_i \in \mathbb{N}^{|\mathcal{M}|}$, for $1 \leq i \leq N(\mathbf{p})$, is a vector of valuations of the receive variables $nr(m)$, with $m \in \mathcal{M}$, for each process i, such that $s \models \mathsf{Env}_{\mathrm{CP}}$. In a state $s \in S(\mathbf{p})$, the vector $\boldsymbol{\ell}$ of locations is used to store the current location $s.\boldsymbol{\ell}[i] \in \mathcal{L}$ for each process i, while the vector $\mathbf{nr}_i \in \mathbb{N}^{|\mathcal{M}|}$ stores the values of the receive variables for each process i, with $1 \leq i \leq N(\mathbf{p})$. Further, each state $s \in S(\mathbf{p})$ satisfies $\mathsf{Env}_{\mathrm{CP}}$.

To formally define that a state $s \in S(\mathbf{p})$ satisfies the environment constraint $\mathsf{Env}_{\mathrm{CP}}$, we define the semantics of c-propositions w.r.t. states $s \in S(\mathbf{p})$. Let $\mathsf{counters}_\mathbf{p} : S(\mathbf{p}) \times \mathcal{L} \to \mathbb{N}$ denote a mapping that maps a state $s \in S(\mathbf{p})$ and a location $\ell \in \mathcal{L}$ to the number of processes that are in location ℓ in the state s, that is, $\mathsf{counters}_\mathbf{p}(s, \ell) = |\{i \mid 1 \leq i \leq N(\mathbf{p}) \wedge s.\boldsymbol{\ell}[i] = \ell\}|$. Further, let $\boldsymbol{\kappa}(s) \in \mathbb{N}^{|\mathcal{L}|}$ denote the $|\mathcal{L}|$-dimensional vector of counters w.r.t. the state $s \in S(\mathbf{p})$, where for every location $\ell \in \mathcal{L}$, we have that $\boldsymbol{\kappa}(s)[\ell]$ stores the number of processes that are in location ℓ in the state s, that is, $\boldsymbol{\kappa}(s)[\ell] = \mathsf{counters}_\mathbf{p}(s, \ell)$. We say that $s \models \#L \geq \boldsymbol{a} \cdot \boldsymbol{\pi} + b$ iff $(\boldsymbol{\kappa}(s), s.\mathbf{p}) \models \#L \geq \boldsymbol{a} \cdot \boldsymbol{\pi} + b$. A state $s \in S(\mathbf{p})$ satisfies the environment constraints $\mathsf{Env}_{\mathrm{CP}}$, that is, $s \models \mathsf{Env}_{\mathrm{CP}}$ iff $(\boldsymbol{\kappa}(s), s.\mathbf{p}) \models \mathsf{Env}_{\mathrm{CP}}$.

In an *initial state* $s_0 \in S_0(\mathbf{p})$, the vector $\boldsymbol{\ell}$ of locations stores only initial locations, i.e., $\boldsymbol{\ell}[i] \in \mathcal{I}$, for $1 \leq i \leq N(\mathbf{p})$, and all receive variables of all processes are initialized to 0. Formally, a state $s_0 = \langle \boldsymbol{\ell}, \mathbf{nr}_1, \ldots, \mathbf{nr}_{N(\mathbf{p})}, \mathbf{p} \rangle$ is *initial*, i.e., $s_0 \in S_0(\mathbf{p})$, if $s_0.\boldsymbol{\ell} \in \mathcal{I}^{N(\mathbf{p})}$ and $s_0.\mathbf{nr}_i[m] = 0$, for $1 \leq i \leq N(\mathbf{p})$ and $m \in \mathcal{M}$.

We now define the transition relation $T(\mathbf{p}) \subseteq S(\mathbf{p}) \times S(\mathbf{p})$, where we will use the environment constraint $\mathsf{Env}_{\mathrm{EP}}$ to restrict the values of the receive variables. A transition $(s, s') \in T(\mathbf{p})$ encodes one round in the execution of the distributed algorithm. In a round, the processes send and receive messages, and update their variables based on the received messages. Further, all the messages sent in the current round are received in the same round. The process variable updates are captured by moving processes from one location to another, based on the values of the receive variables. The *transition relation* $T(\mathbf{p})$ is a binary relation $T(\mathbf{p}) \subseteq S(\mathbf{p}) \times S(\mathbf{p})$, where $(s, s') \in T(\mathbf{p})$ iff for every process i, with $1 \leq i \leq N(\mathbf{p})$:

1. $0 \leq s'.\mathbf{nr}_i[m] \leq N(\mathbf{p})$, such that $(s'.\mathbf{nr}_i, \boldsymbol{\kappa}(s), s.\mathbf{p}) \models \mathsf{Env}_{\mathrm{EP}}$, for $m \in \mathcal{M}$,
2. there exists $r^\Delta \in \mathcal{R}^\Delta$ such that:
   - $s.\boldsymbol{\ell}[i] = r^\Delta.from$,
   - $(s'.\mathbf{nr}_i, \boldsymbol{\kappa}(s), s.\mathbf{p}) \models r^\Delta.\varphi$,
   - $s'.\boldsymbol{\ell}[i] = r^\Delta.to$.
3. $s'.\mathbf{p} = s.\mathbf{p}$ and $s' \models \mathsf{Env}_{\mathrm{CP}}$.

In a transition $(s, s') \in T(\mathbf{p})$, the receive variables and locations of each process are updated. That is, the value $s'.\mathbf{nr}_i[m]$ of the receive variable $\mathsf{nr}(m)$ of process i is assigned a value in the range from 0 to $N(\mathbf{p})$ non-deterministically, such that the environment constraint $\mathsf{Env}_{\mathrm{EP}}$ is satisfied. This ensures that the number of received messages of type m is non-negative, that it does not exceed the number of participating processes, and that the receive variables of each process are assigned values that satisfy the constraints of the environment assumption. In the case of the synchronous computation model, this captures that all messages sent by correct processes in a round are received in the same round, and that the number of messages of type m, received by process i, is bounded by above by the total number of messages of type m, sent by both correct and faulty processes. To update the locations, each process i picks a rule $r^\Delta \in \mathcal{R}^\Delta$ that it applies to update its location, if the process i is in location $r^\Delta.from$ in the state s, and if the newly assigned values of the receive variables of process i in the state s' satisfy the receive guard $r^\Delta.\varphi$. If this is the case, the process i updates its location to $r^{\Delta}.to$ in the state s'. The parameter values remain unchanged, and we require that the state s' satisfies $\mathsf{Env}_{\mathrm{CP}}$, i.e., it is a valid state.

6 Abstracting rSTA to STA

Given an rSTA, our goal is to construct an STA, which differs from the rSTA only in the guards on its rules and the environment assumption. For each rule $r^{\Delta} \in \mathcal{R}^{\Delta}$ in the rSTA, whose guard $r^{\Delta}.\varphi$ is a receive guard, we will construct a rule $r \in \mathcal{R}$ in the STA, such that the guard $r.\varphi$ is a Boolean combination of c-propositions. We will perform the abstraction in two steps: (i) we will strengthen each receive guard $r^{\Delta}.\varphi$, occurring on the rules $r^{\Delta} \in \mathcal{R}^{\Delta}$ of the rSTA, with the constraints imposed by the faulty environment and the synchronous computation model, encoded in the environment assumption Env^{Δ}, and (ii) we will eliminate the receive variables from the receive guards and environment assumptions of rSTA to obtain the guards and environment assumption of STA.

6.1 Guard Strengthening

Let $\mathsf{rSTA} = (\mathcal{L}, \mathcal{I}, \mathcal{R}^{\Delta}, \Delta, \Pi, RC, \mathsf{Env}^{\Delta})$ be a receive STA, where the rules $r^{\Delta} \in \mathcal{R}^{\Delta}$ have guards containing expressions over the receive variables $\mathsf{nr}(m) \in \Delta$, and where the environment assumption $\mathsf{Env}^{\Delta} \equiv \mathsf{Env}_{\mathrm{CP}} \wedge \mathsf{Env}_{\mathrm{EP}}$ is a conjunction of two environment constraints, $\mathsf{Env}_{\mathrm{CP}}$ and $\mathsf{Env}_{\mathrm{EP}}$, where the latter restricts the values of the receive variables. Recall that in Sect. 3.2, we defined different environment constraints $\mathsf{Env}_{\mathrm{EP}}$ for the different fault models. In general, these constraints express that for each message type $m \in \mathcal{M}$, the receive variable $\mathsf{nr}(m)$ is assigned a value which is greater or equal to the number of messages of type m sent by correct processes, and which is smaller or equal to the total number of messages of type m, sent by both correct and faulty processes (e.g., $\#\mathsf{sent}(m) \leq \mathsf{nr}(m) \leq \#\mathsf{sent}(m) + \#\mathsf{sent}_{\mathrm{cr}}(m)$ for crash faults). As a first step towards eliminating the receive variables from the receive guards, we strengthen the rules from the set $\mathcal{R}^{\Delta}$, such that we add the environment constraints $\mathsf{Env}_{\mathrm{EP}}$ to their guards in order to bound the values of the receive variables.

Definition 1. *Given* $r^{\Delta} \in \mathcal{R}^{\Delta}$, *its* strengthened rule *is* $\widehat{r}^{\Delta} = \mathsf{strengthen}(r^{\Delta})$, *such that:* $\widehat{r}^{\Delta}.from = r^{\Delta}.from$, $\widehat{r}^{\Delta}.to = r^{\Delta}.to$, $\widehat{r}^{\Delta}.\varphi = r^{\Delta}.\varphi \wedge \mathsf{Env}_{\mathrm{EP}}$.
  We denote by $\widehat{\mathcal{R}}^{\Delta} = \{\mathsf{strengthen}(r^{\Delta}) \mid r^{\Delta} \in \mathcal{R}^{\Delta}\}$ *the set of strengthened rules in* $\mathsf{rSTA} = (\mathcal{L}, \mathcal{I}, \mathcal{R}^{\Delta}, \Delta, \Pi, RC, \mathsf{Env}^{\Delta})$, *where* $\mathsf{Env}^{\Delta} \equiv \mathsf{Env}_{\mathrm{CP}} \wedge \mathsf{Env}_{\mathrm{EP}}$.

6.2 Eliminating the Receive Variables

Let $\mathsf{rSTA} = (\mathcal{L}, \mathcal{I}, \mathcal{R}^{\Delta}, \Delta, \Pi, RC, \mathsf{Env}^{\Delta})$ be a receive STA, and let $\widehat{\mathcal{R}}^{\Delta}$ be the set of strengthened rules (Definition 1). We define an $\mathsf{STA} = (\mathcal{L}, \mathcal{I}, \mathcal{R}, \Pi, RC, \mathsf{Env})$ whose locations, initial locations, and parameters are the same as in rSTA, while we construct the rules $\mathcal{R}$ and the environment assumption Env of the STA below.

  Recall that $\mathsf{Env}^{\Delta} \equiv \mathsf{Env}_{\mathrm{CP}} \wedge \mathsf{Env}_{\mathrm{EP}}$. To define the environment assumption Env of the constructed STA, we set $\mathsf{Env} \equiv \mathsf{Env}_{\mathrm{CP}}$. Before we define the rules of the constructed STA, we define the mapping eliminate.

Definition 2. *Let* ϕ *be a propositional formula over r-, c-, and e-propositions. Let* $\boldsymbol{\delta} = \langle \mathsf{nr}(m_1), \ldots, \mathsf{nr}(m_{|\mathcal{M}|}) \rangle$ *denote the* $|\mathcal{M}|$-*dimensional receive variables vector, and* QE *denote the quantifier elimination procedure for Presburger arithmetic. The formula* $\mathsf{eliminate}(\phi) = \mathsf{QE}(\exists \boldsymbol{\delta}\ \phi)$ *is a quantifier-free formula, with no occurrence of receive variables* $\mathsf{nr}(m) \in \Delta$, *which is logically equivalent to* $\exists \boldsymbol{\delta}\ \phi$.

To construct a rule $r \in \mathcal{R}$ of an STA, given a rule $r^\Delta \in \mathcal{R}^\Delta$ of an rSTA, we will apply the mapping eliminate to each guard of the strengthened rule $\widehat{r}^\Delta \in \widehat{\mathcal{R}}^\Delta$, where $\widehat{r}^\Delta = \mathsf{strengthen}(r^\Delta)$. The result of quantifier elimination is a quantifier-free formula over c-propositions, which is logically equivalent to $\exists \boldsymbol{\delta}\ \widehat{r}^\Delta.\varphi$.

Definition 3. *Given* $r^\Delta \in \mathcal{R}^\Delta$, *its constructed rule is* $r = \mathsf{construct}(r^\Delta) \in \mathcal{R}$, *such that:* $r.from = r^\Delta.from$, $r.to = r^\Delta.to$, $r.\varphi = \mathsf{eliminate}(\widehat{r}^\Delta.\varphi)$, *where* $\widehat{r}^\Delta = \mathsf{strengthen}(r^\Delta)$.

Proposition 1. *For every strengthened rule* $\widehat{r}^\Delta \in \widehat{\mathcal{R}}^\Delta$ *and every tuple* $(\mathbf{d}, \boldsymbol{\kappa}, \mathbf{p})$, *where* $\mathbf{d} \in \mathbb{N}^{|\mathcal{M}|}$, $\boldsymbol{\kappa} \in \mathbb{N}^{|\mathcal{L}|}$, *and* $\mathbf{p} \in \mathbf{P}_{RC}$, *we have:*

$$(\mathbf{d}, \boldsymbol{\kappa}, \mathbf{p}) \models \widehat{r}^\Delta.\varphi \quad implies \quad (\boldsymbol{\kappa}, \mathbf{p}) \models \mathsf{eliminate}(\widehat{r}^\Delta.\varphi)$$

Proposition 1 is a consequence of quantifier elimination. Note that the converse of this proposition does not hold in general. That is, $(\boldsymbol{\kappa}, \mathbf{p}) \models \mathsf{eliminate}(\widehat{r}^\Delta.\varphi)$ does not imply that $(\mathbf{d}, \boldsymbol{\kappa}, \mathbf{p}) \models \widehat{r}^\Delta.\varphi$, for every $\mathbf{d} \in \mathbb{N}^{|\mathcal{M}|}$. However, by quantifier elimination, we have that $(\boldsymbol{\kappa}, \mathbf{p}) \models \mathsf{eliminate}(\widehat{r}^\Delta.\varphi)$ implies $(\boldsymbol{\kappa}, \mathbf{p}) \models \exists \boldsymbol{\delta}\ \widehat{r}^\Delta.\varphi$.

6.3   Soundness and Completeness

This construction of an STA is sound and complete. That is, given a rSTA and an admissible valuation $\mathbf{p} \in \mathbf{P}_{RC}$, we show that there exists a bisimulation relation between the system $\mathsf{STS}(\mathsf{rSTA}, \mathbf{p})$, induced by rSTA and $\mathbf{p}$, and a counter system $\mathsf{CS}(\mathsf{STA}, \mathbf{p})$, induced by the constructed STA and $\mathbf{p}$. The existence of a bisimulation implies that $\mathsf{STS}(\mathsf{rSTA}, \mathbf{p})$ and $\mathsf{CS}(\mathsf{STA}, \mathbf{p})$ satisfy the same CTL* formulas [3]. To express temporal formulas, as atomic propositions we use the c-propositions from the set CP. We define two labeling functions, $\lambda_{S(\mathbf{p})}$ and $\lambda_{\Sigma(\mathbf{p})}$, where $\lambda_{S(\mathbf{p})} : S(\mathbf{p}) \to 2^{\mathrm{CP}}$ assigns to a state $s \in S(\mathbf{p})$ the set of c-propositions that hold in it (the function $\lambda_{\Sigma(\mathbf{p})} : \Sigma(\mathbf{p}) \to 2^{\mathrm{CP}}$ is defined analogously).

We introduce an *abstraction mapping* $\alpha_\mathbf{p} : S(\mathbf{p}) \to \Sigma(\mathbf{p})$ that maps states $s \in S(\mathbf{p})$ of $\mathsf{STS}(\mathsf{rSTA}, \mathbf{p})$ to configurations $\sigma \in \Sigma(\mathbf{p})$ of $\mathsf{CS}(\mathsf{STA}, \mathbf{p})$, such that $\sigma = \alpha_\mathbf{p}(s)$ iff $\sigma = (\boldsymbol{\kappa}(s), s.\mathbf{p})$. By the definition of the abstraction mapping $\alpha_\mathbf{p}$ and the semantics of c-propositions, we have that a state and its abstraction satisfy the same c-propositions. Further, given a configuration $\sigma \in \Sigma(\mathbf{p})$, we can construct a state $s \in S(\mathbf{p})$, such that $\sigma = \alpha_\mathbf{p}(s)$. While this is always possible, the constructed state s might not be reachable in any execution of the system $\mathsf{STS}(\mathsf{rSTA}, \mathbf{p})$. However, we can use the constraint $\mathsf{Env}_{\mathrm{EP}}$ to restrict the value of the receive variables in the constructed state s, such that it is a valid state in the system $\mathsf{STS}(\mathsf{rSTA}, \mathbf{p})$. The main result of this section is stated below. The detailed proof of this result can be found in the first author's PhD thesis.

Theorem 1. *The binary relation* $B(\mathbf{p}) = \{(s, \sigma) \mid s \in S(\mathbf{p}), \sigma \in \Sigma(\mathbf{p}), \sigma = \alpha_{\mathbf{p}}(s)\}$ *is a bisimulation relation.*

7   Experimental Evaluation

To show the usefulness of translating rSTA to STA, we: (i) encoded synchronous fault-tolerant distributed algorithms using rSTA, (ii) implemented the method from Sect. 6 in a prototype, (iii) compared the output to the existing manual encodings from [34], some of which are artifacts of the experimental evaluation from [36] and were given as examples throughout this paper, and (iv) verified the properties of the generated STA using the technique from [36].

Encoding Algorithms as rSTA. We extended the STA encoding from [36], to support (i) declarations of receive variables and (ii) constraints given by the environment assumption. The algorithms we encoded are listed in Table 1, and their rSTA can be found in [35]. For each of them, there already existed a manually produced STA [34]. The manually produced rSTA and STA have the same structure w.r.t. locations and rules, and differ only in the guards that occur on the rules: in the rSTA, we have receive guards, which are Boolean combinations of r-propositions and c-propositions, while in the manually encoded STA, the guards are Boolean combinations of c-propositions.

Applying Quantifier Elimination. We implemented a script that parses the input rSTA and creates an STA whose rules have guards that are Boolean combinations of c-propositions, according to the abstraction from Sect. 6. To automate the quantifier elimination step, we applied Z3 [16] tactics for quantifier elimination [10,11], to formulas of the form $\exists \delta \ \widehat{r^{\Delta}}.\varphi$, where $\widehat{r^{\Delta}}.\varphi \equiv r^{\Delta}.\varphi \wedge \mathsf{Env}_{\mathrm{EP}}$ is the strengthened guard of the receive guard $r^{\Delta}.\varphi$, for $r^{\Delta} \in \mathcal{R}^{\Delta}$. For all our benchmarks, the STA is generated within seconds, as reported in Table 1.

Analyzing the Automatically Generated STA. We compared the guards of the automatically generated STA (autoSTA) to the manually encoded STA (manSTA). Syntactically, the guards of autoSTA are larger in general, as they contain additional constraints that result from quantifier elimination. Semantically, we check whether the guards for the autoSTA imply the guards of the manSTA. For each automatically generated guard φ_{auto}, we check whether its corresponding guard φ_{man} from the manual encoding is implied by φ_{auto}, for all values of the parameters and number of sent messages by checking the validity of the formula:

$$\forall \mathbf{p} \in \mathbf{P}_{RC} \ \forall L_1 \dots \forall L_{|\mathcal{M}|} \ \varphi_{\mathsf{auto}}(L_1, \dots, L_{|\mathcal{M}|}) \to \varphi_{\mathsf{man}}(L_1, \dots, L_{|\mathcal{M}|}) \quad (3)$$

where $L_j = \mathsf{sent}(m_j)$, for $m_j \in \mathcal{M}$ and $1 \le j \le |\mathcal{M}|$, denotes the set of locations where processes send messages of type m_j. We automate the validity check of (3) using an SMT solver, such as Z3, to check the unsatisfiability of its negation. With this check we are able to either verify that the earlier manSTA faithfully model the benchmark algorithms, or detect discrepancies, which we investigated

Table 1. The algorithms we encoded as rSTA and the results of applying the verification technique from [36]. The column QE states the time needed to produce an autoSTA from an rSTA. The column ⇒ states if (3) is valid all, some, or none of guards. We report on the time it took the solvers Z3 and CVC4 to (i) check the guard implications (only Z3), (ii) compute the diameter for the autoSTA, and (iii) check the safety properties of the autoSTA, (iv) compute the diameter for the manSTA, (v) check the safety properties of the manSTA, using the SMT-based procedure from [36].

algorithm	QE Z3	⇒	(i) ⇒ time Z3	d	(ii) autoSTA d time Z3	CVC4	(iii) autoSTA BMC time Z3	CVC4	(iv) manSTA d time Z3	CVC4	(v) manSTA BMC time Z3	CVC4
RB	0.16s	all	0.18s	2	0.09s	0.26s	0.03s	0.03s	0.07s	0.27s	0.02s	0.03s
HybridRB	0.39s	all	0.41s	2	0.14s	0.75s	0.03s	0.06s	0.09s	0.67s	0.03s	0.05s
OmitRB	0.34s	all	0.36s	2	0.11s	0.69s	0.03s	0.05s	0.09s	0.67s	0.02s	0.04s
FairCons	0.25s	all	0.44s	2	0.17s	2.82s	0.07s	0.16s	0.14s	2.68s	0.06s	0.14s
FloodMin, $k = 1$	0.10s	all	0.19s	2	0.07s	0.25s	0.06s	0.11s	0.06s	0.25s	0.06s	0.09s
FloodMin, $k = 2$	0.26s	all	0.35s	2	0.13s	1.72s	0.07s	0.19s	0.15s	2.22s	0.06s	0.17s
FMinOmit, $k = 1$	0.10s	all	0.13s	1	0.03s	0.03s	0.01s	0.01s	0.06s	0.04s	0.01s	0.01s
FMinOmit, $k = 2$	0.27s	all	0.26s	1	0.05s	0.08s	0.01s	0.03s	0.05s	0.08s	0.01s	0.03s
FloodSet	0.20s	all	0.31s	2	0.11s	0.71s	0.07s	0.17s	0.10s	0.90s	0.06s	0.15s
kSetOmit, $k = 1$	0.59s	all	0.52s	3	2.71s	53.36s	0.22s	0.85s	1.09s	1m8s	0.23s	0.81s
kSetOmit, $k = 2$	1.43s	all	1.18s	–	t.o.	t.o.	–	–	t.o.	t.o.	–	–
PhaseKing	1.19s	all	1.57s	4	3.53s	16.51s	0.24s	1.57s	3.67s	15.80s	0.25s	1.47s
ByzKing	1.16s	all	1.58s	4	1.92s	1m19s	0.27s	1.97s	3.73s	38.50s	0.24s	2.26s
HybridKing	3.59s	some	3.03s	4	0.33s	6.34s	0.18s	1.11s	t.o.	t.o.	–	–
OmitKing	3.09s	all	2.79s	4	0.26s	6.12s	0.15s	0.91s	1h15m	t.o.	9.08s	1m27s
PhaseQueen	0.42s	all	0.90s	3	0.37s	4.46s	0.04s	0.61s	0.40s	4.72s	0.06s	0.50s
ByzQueen	0.42s	all	0.91s	3	0.39s	17.15s	0.09s	0.58s	0.53s	10.6s	0.08s	0.61s
HybridQueen	1.34s	some	1.77s	3	0.13s	2.04s	0.05s	0.37s	t.o.	t.o.	–	–
OmitQueen	1.13s	all	1.56s	3	0.13s	2.18s	0.20s	0.46s	0.57s	8.87s	0.27s	1.21s

further. Our translation technique produces the strongest possible guards, due to the soundness and completeness result. Hence, we expected that the implication holds for all the guards of all the benchmarks we considered. This is however not the case for the algorithms HybridKing and HybridQueen which are designed to tolerate hybrid faults, in particular, send omissions and Byzantine faults. There, we found that one automatically generated guard does not imply its corresponding manual guard, and concluded that this is due to a flaw in the manual encoding by manual inspection. We found a similar problem with a missing rule in the (purely) Byzantine versions of these algorithms, namely ByzKing and ByzQueen. By adding these rules and correcting the appropriate manual guards, we were able to establish the validity of (3) for all guards.

Model Checking of Safety Properties. We gave the STA we obtained as output of our translation procedure as input to the bounded model checking tool from [36], which computes a diameter of a counter system and performs bounded model checking for safety properties. The experiments were run on a machine with 2.8 GHz Quad-Core Intel(R) Core(TM) i7 CPU and 16GB. The results of applying the SMT-based procedure from [36] to the autoSTA, as well as to the extended set [34] of manSTA from [36], are presented in Table 1. The timeout, denoted by t.o. in the table, was set to 24 h. For all algorithms, we note that bounded model checking with both Z3 and CVC4 performs similarly for both autoSTA and manSTA. For computing the diameter, we observe that for the algorithms: RB [21] (Fig. 5), HybridRB, OmitRB [9], FairCons [33], FloodMin, for $k = 1$ (Fig. 3) and $k = 2$ [28], FMinOmit, for $k = 1$ (Fig. 4) and $k = 2$ [28], kSetOmit, for $k = 2$ [33], FloodSet [28], PhaseKing [7], and PhaseQueen [6] (Fig. 1), we obtain comparable results on both the autoSTA and manSTA. For the other algorithms, we found:

- computing the diameter for the autoSTA of kSetOmit, with $k = 1$ [33], is slightly slower with Z3 and slightly faster with CVC4 than for the manSTA;
- Z3 performs better when computing the diameter for the autoSTA than for the manSTA of both ByzKing and ByzQueen [9], while CVC4 performs worse. Note that in Table 1 we report the times for the manSTA of ByzKing and ByzQueen that have missing rules. After adding the rules to the manSTA, computing the diameter on the autoSTA is still faster with both solvers;
- Z3 and CVC4 compute the diameter for the autoSTA of HybridKing and HybridQueen [9] within seconds, in contrast to both timing out for the manSTA;
- computing the diameter with Z3 is significantly faster for the autoSTA than for the manSTA of OmitKing [9]. CVC4 computes the diameter for autoSTA of OmitKing, while for manSTA it times out. The computed diameter d = 4 for autoSTA is smaller than the diameter 8, computed for manSTA;
- Z3 and CVC4 compute the diameter for the autoSTA of OmitQueen [9] faster than for manSTA.

8 Conclusions

We established a fully automated pipeline that for a synchronous distributed algorithm: (1) starts from a formal model that captures its pseudo code, (2) produces a formal model suitable for verification, and (3) automatically verifies its safety properties. Our technique thus closes the gap between the original description of an algorithm (using received messages) and the synchronous threshold automaton of the algorithm given as an input to a verification tool.

There are two major differences to the asynchronous case considered in [37]. First, the asynchronous model uses interleaving semantics, while in the synchronous model all processes take a step in a transition. Second, in the asynchronous model, there are no limitations when a message will be delivered. The lower bound on the number of received messages, given in the synchronous model by the number of sent messages by correct processes, is only *eventually* satisfied in the asynchronous model, and thus is not used in the process of eliminating the receive variables from the receive guards.

We did extensive experimental evaluation of our method. We attribute the better performance of the bounded model checking technique from [36] on the automatically generated STA to the fact that the automatically generated guards contain more additional constraints, coming from the environment assumption, which help guide the SMT solvers. Moreover, not only do we obtain the diameter bounds faster, we also obtain better bounds for the automatically generated STA of some benchmarks. These findings confirm the conjecture that manual encoding of distributed algorithms is a tedious and error-prone task and suggest that there is a real benefit of producing guards automatically.

References

1. Aminof, B., Rubin, S., Stoilkovska, I., Widder, J., Zuleger, F.: Parameterized model checking of synchronous distributed algorithms by abstraction. VMCAI 2018. LNCS, vol. 10747, pp. 1–24. Springer, Cham (2018). https://doi.org/10.1007/978-3-319-73721-8_1
2. Attiya, H., Welch, J.: Distributed Computing, 2nd edn. Wiley, Hoboken (2004)
3. Baier, C., Katoen, J.P.: Principles of Model Checking. MITP, United States (2008)
4. Bakst, A., von Gleissenthall, K., Kici, R.G., Jhala, R.: Verifying distributed programs via canonical sequentialization. PACMPL 1(OOPSLA), 1–27 (2017)
5. Balasubramanian, A.R., Esparza, J., Lazić, M.: Complexity of verification and synthesis of threshold automata. In: ATVA (2020)
6. Berman, P., Garay, J.A., Perry, K.J.: Asymptotically Optimal Distributed Consensus. Technical report, Bell Labs (1989). http://plan9.bell-labs.co/who/garay/asopt.ps
7. Berman, P., Garay, J.A., Perry, K.J.: Towards optimal distributed consensus (Extended Abstract). In: FOCS, pp. 410–415 (1989)
8. Bertrand, N., Konnov, I., Lazić, M., Widder, J.: Verification of randomized consensus algorithms under round-rigid adversaries. In: CONCUR, pp. 1–15 (2019)
9. Biely, M., Schmid, U., Weiss, B.: Synchronous consensus under hybrid process and link failures. Theor. Comput. Sci. 412(40), 5602–5630 (2011)
10. Bjørner, N.: Linear quantifier elimination as an abstract decision procedure. In: Giesl, J., Hähnle, R. (eds.) IJCAR 2010. LNCS (LNAI), vol. 6173, pp. 316–330. Springer, Heidelberg (2010). https://doi.org/10.1007/978-3-642-14203-1_27
11. Bjørner, N., Janota, M.: Playing with quantified satisfaction. LPAR 35, 15–27 (2015)
12. Bouajjani, A., Enea, C., Ji, K., Qadeer, S.: On the completeness of verifying message passing programs under bounded asynchrony. In: Chockler, H., Weissenbacher, G. (eds.) CAV 2018. LNCS, vol. 10982, pp. 372–391. Springer, Cham (2018). https://doi.org/10.1007/978-3-319-96142-2_23
13. Chaouch-Saad, M., Charron-Bost, B., Merz, S.: A reduction theorem for the verification of round-based distributed algorithms. In: Bournez, O., Potapov, I. (eds.) RP 2009. LNCS, vol. 5797, pp. 93–106. Springer, Heidelberg (2009). https://doi.org/10.1007/978-3-642-04420-5_10
14. Cooper, D.C.: Theorem proving in arithmetic without multiplication. Mach. Intell. 7(91–99), 300 (1972)
15. Damian, A., Drăgoi, C., Militaru, A., Widder, J.: Communication-closed asynchronous protocols. In: Dillig, I., Tasiran, S. (eds.) CAV 2019. LNCS, vol. 11562, pp. 344–363. Springer, Cham (2019). https://doi.org/10.1007/978-3-030-25543-5_20

16. de Moura, L., Bjørner, N.: Z3: an efficient SMT solver. In: Ramakrishnan, C.R., Rehof, J. (eds.) TACAS 2008. LNCS, vol. 4963, pp. 337–340. Springer, Heidelberg (2008). https://doi.org/10.1007/978-3-540-78800-3_24

17. Drăgoi, C., Henzinger, T.A., Veith, H., Widder, J., Zufferey, D.: A logic-based framework for verifying consensus algorithms. In: McMillan, K.L., Rival, X. (eds.) VMCAI 2014. LNCS, vol. 8318, pp. 161–181. Springer, Heidelberg (2014). https://doi.org/10.1007/978-3-642-54013-4_10

18. Fischer, M.J., Lynch, N.A., Paterson, M.S.: Impossibility of distributed consensus with one faulty process. J. ACM **32**(2), 374–382 (1985)

19. Gleissenthall, K.V., Gökhan Kici, R., Bakst, A., Stefan, D., Jhala, R.: Pretend synchrony. In: POPL (2019)

20. Hawblitzel, C., et al.: Ironfleet: proving safety and liveness of practical distributed systemsp. Commun. ACM **60**(7), 83–92 (2017)

21. Srikanth, T.K., Toueg, S.: Optimal clock synchronization. J. ACM **34**(3), 626–645 (1987)

22. Konnov, I., Lazić, M., Veith, H., Widder, J.: A short counterexample property for safety and liveness verification of fault-tolerant distributed algorithms. In: POPL, pp. 719–734 (2017)

23. Konnov, I., Veith, H., Widder, J.: On the completeness of bounded model checking for threshold-based distributed algorithms: reachability. Inf. Comput. **252**, 95–109 (2017). https://doi.org/10.1016/j.ic.2016.03.006

24. Kopetz, H., Grünsteidl, G.: TTP - a protocol for fault-tolerant real-time systems. IEEE Comput. **27**(1), 14–23 (1994). https://doi.org/10.1109/2.248873

25. Kragl, B., Qadeer, S., Henzinger, T.A.: Synchronizing the asynchronous. In: CONCUR, pp. 1–17 (2018)

26. Kukovec, J., Konnov, I., Widder, J.: Reachability in parameterized systems: all flavors of threshold automata. In: CONCUR. LIPIcs, vol. 118, pp. 1–17 (2018)

27. Lincoln, P., Rushby, J.: A formally verified algorithm for interactive consistency under a hybrid fault model. In: FTCS, pp. 402–411 (1993)

28. Lynch, N.: Distributed Algorithms. Morgan Kaufman (1996)

29. Marić, O., Sprenger, C., Basin, D.: Cutoff bounds for consensus algorithms. In: Majumdar, R., Kunčak, V. (eds.) CAV 2017. LNCS, vol. 10427, pp. 217–237. Springer, Cham (2017). https://doi.org/10.1007/978-3-319-63390-9_12

30. Presburger, M.: Über die vollständigkeit eines gewissen systems der arithmetik ganzer zahlen, in welchem die addition als einzige operation hervortritt. Comptes Rendus du I congres de Mathématiciens des Pays Slaves, pp. 92–101 (1929)

31. Pugh, W.: A practical algorithm for exact array dependence analysis. Commun. ACM **35**(8), 102–114 (1992)

32. Rahli, V., Guaspari, D., Bickford, M., Constable, R.L.: Formal specification, verification, and implementation of fault-tolerant systems using EventML. ECEASST **72** (2015)

33. Raynal, M.: Fault-tolerant agreement in synchronous message-passing systems. Synth. Lect. Distrib. Comput. Theory **1**(1), 1–189 (2010)

34. Stoilkovska, I.: Manually Encoded Synchronous Threshold Automata. https://github.com/istoilkovska/syncTA/algorithms. Accessed Oct 2020

35. Stoilkovska, I.: Receive Synchronous Threshold Automata. https://github.com/istoilkovska/syncTA/receiveSTA. Accessed Oct 2020

36. Stoilkovska, I., Konnov, I., Widder, J., Zuleger, F.: Verifying safety of synchronous fault-tolerant algorithms by bounded model checking. In: Vojnar, T., Zhang, L. (eds.) TACAS 2019. LNCS, vol. 11428, pp. 357–374. Springer, Cham (2019). https://doi.org/10.1007/978-3-030-17465-1_20

37. Stoilkovska, I., Konnov, I., Widder, J., Zuleger, F.: Eliminating message counters in threshold automata. In: Hung, D.V., Sokolsky, O. (eds.) ATVA 2020. LNCS, vol. 12302, pp. 196–212. Springer, Cham (2020). https://doi.org/10.1007/978-3-030-59152-6_11
38. Wilcox, J.R., et al.: Verdi: a framework for implementing and formally verifying distributed systems. In: PLDI, pp. 357–368 (2015)

A Reduction Theorem for Randomized Distributed Algorithms Under Weak Adversaries

Nathalie Bertrand[1] , Marijana Lazić[2(✉)] , and Josef Widder[3]

[1] Univ Rennes, Inria, CNRS, IRISA, Rennes, France
nathalie.bertrand@inria.fr
[2] Technical University of Munich, Munich, Germany
lazic@in.tum.de
[3] Informal Systems, Vienna, Austria
josef@informal.systems

Abstract. Weak adversaries are a way to model the uncertainty due to asynchrony in randomized distributed algorithms. They are a standard notion in correctness proofs for distributed algorithms, and express the property that the adversary (scheduler), which has to decide which messages to deliver to which process, has no means of inferring the outcome of random choices, and the content of the messages.

In this paper, we introduce a model for randomized distributed algorithms that allows us to formalize the notion of weak adversaries. It applies to randomized distributed algorithms that proceed in rounds and are tolerant to process failures. For this wide class of algorithms, we prove that for verification purposes, the class of weak adversaries can be restricted to simple ones, so-called round-rigid adversaries, that keep the processes tightly synchronized. As recently a verification method for round-rigid adversaries has been introduced, our new reduction theorem paves the way to the parameterized verification of randomized distributed algorithms under the more realistic weak adversaries.

Keywords: Communication closure · Reduction · Distributed algorithms · Randomized consensus · Weak adversaries · Parameterized verification

1 Introduction

Automated verification of fault-tolerant distributed algorithms faces the combinatorial explosion problem. The asynchronous parallel composition of many processes leads to a huge number of executions. Recently, several verification methods [5,6,9,11,15] are based on the idea that for many distributed algorithms, instead of considering all these asynchronous executions, it is sufficient

This project has received funding from Interchain Foundation (Switzerland), and the European Research Council (ERC) under the European Union's Horizon 2020 research and innovation programme under grant agreement No 787367 (PaVeS).

© Springer Nature Switzerland AG 2021
F. Henglein et al. (Eds.): VMCAI 2021, LNCS 12597, pp. 219–239, 2021.
https://doi.org/10.1007/978-3-030-67067-2_11

to consider only fewer (representative) synchronous executions. The central argument is similar to the reductions (also know as, mover analysis) by Lipton [16] and Elrad and Francez [10]: given an arbitrary execution, by repeatedly swapping neighboring transitions, one arrives at one of the representative (synchronous) executions. As this argument works on executions (traces), it works for reachability properties, and for specific stuttering-insensitive linear temporal properties.

In this paper, we extend this idea to randomized distributed algorithms and probabilistic properties [2,4,17]. Rather than arguing on traces, probabilistic guarantees require us to reason on Markov decision processes (MDPs). In MDPs the non-determinism is resolved by using adversaries, that is, by functions that map an execution prefix to the next action taken. In case the next action is a coin toss, we obtain a branching, where each branch is associated with a probability. As a result, an MDP together with an adversary induce a computation tree with probabilistic branching. As the adversary is a function on the prefix, it is not clear whether in the presence of this branching, it is possible to conduct a swapping argument on the computation tree that maintains probabilistic properties. The technical challenge we face is to characterize a family of adversaries that permits a swapping argument in order to arrive at a computation tree that corresponds to a synchronous execution. Restricting to synchronous executions considerably decreases the verification effort, by reducing the number of executions to check. For the analysis of distributed consensus algorithms, there are two well-researched classes of adversaries, namely strong and weak adversaries. Strong adversaries have full knowledge of the execution prefix, while weak adversaries are based on a projection (abstraction) of the execution prefix, in particular, they do not have access to the content of the exchanged messages and the outcomes of coin tosses. In this paper, we formalize weak adversaries, and make explicit that they inherently impose restrictions on the local code of a distributed algorithm, that is, they can only be defined for a class of distributed algorithms (which was not apparent from their mathematical definition in the literature).

Intuitively, these algorithms expose some form of symmetry regarding the local control flow. Consider a formalization of Ben-Or's consensus algorithm [4] in Fig. 1. The subscript in the locations (nodes) encode the local estimate of the consensus value, for instance D_0 and D_1 are locations where processes decide 0 and 1, respectively. We observe that the control flows on the 0 side and the 1 side are symmetric: if we ignore the subscripts the paths through the graph are identical. In contrast, consider the (made-up) example in Fig. 2. If at location J there would be a branching due to receiving messages with different consensus estimates, the two paths that lead to F differ in length. An adversary may observe whether a process has taken the left path or the right path which allows the adversary to infer knowledge on the consensus value that led to branching at location J. However, typical randomized consensus algorithms from the literature [4,7,17,18] have a structure similar to Fig. 1. Almost sure termination of these algorithms have been automatically verified in [5] under synchronous executions formalized via round-rigid adversaries. In this paper we show that for these distributed algorithms the computation trees that are defined by weak adversaries can be reduced to round-rigid computation trees by a swapping argument. As a result we show that *the verification results from* [5] *apply to a wider class of adversaries than originally claimed*.

More formally, our new reduction theorem says that for each weak adversary there exists a round-rigid adversary that maintains the original probabilities of properties. For strong adversaries, we were not able to derive such a reduction argument, which indicates that the verification problem for strong adversaries is harder. This would also explain why the mathematical proofs in the literature for strong adversaries are considerably more involved [1].

Contributions. We present in Sect. 2 a new formalization of randomized distributed algorithms that allows us to define the weak adversary model from the literature [2]. Our model is based on threshold automata [13] and their probabilistic extension [5]. To faithfully express the weak adversaries, we introduce a process-based semantics, i.e., rather than the counter system semantics from [5,13], we propose semantics based on processes that exchange messages. We then prove our reduction in two steps. First, in Sect. 3, we reduce adversaries to communication-closed [10] adversaries, that is, adversaries that to a process in round r only deliver messages of round $r' \leq r$. Then, in Sect. 4, we reduce weak communication-closed adversaries to round-rigid adversaries.

2   Modeling Randomized Threshold-Based Algorithms

Probabilistic threshold automata with semantics based on counter systems were introduced in [5]. For a discussion on the operation of threshold-based distributed algorithms, and how they are captured by threshold automata we refer to [5]. Here we provide more concrete semantics based on processes and message buffers (modeled as sets). A *probabilistic threshold automaton with processes*, PTA$_\mathbb{P}$, is a tuple $(\mathcal{L}, \mathcal{Z}, \mathcal{R}, RC)$, where

- $\mathcal{L}$ is a non-empty finite set of locations that contains the disjoint subsets: *initial locations* $\mathcal{I}$, *final locations* $\mathcal{F}$, and *border locations* $\mathcal{B}$, with $|\mathcal{B}| = |\mathcal{I}|$.
- $\mathcal{Z}$ is a disjoint union of the following five sets:
  - Π is a set of *parameter variables*;
  - $\mathbb{P} = \{p_1, \ldots, p_n\}$, for some $n \geq 1$, is a finite set of *processes*; It is the disjoint union of $\mathbb{C}$ and $\mathbb{F}$, representing sets of correct and faulty processes, respectively;
  - $\mathcal{T}$ is a finite set of *types* of messages
  - $\mathcal{V}$ is a finite set of *values* of messages, typically $\mathcal{V} = \{0, 1\}$;
  - $\Lambda \subseteq \{x_{t,v} \mid t \in \mathcal{T}, \ v \in \mathcal{V}\}$ is a set of *local receive variables*;
- $\mathcal{R}$ is a finite set of *rules*; and
- RC, the *resilience condition*, is a constraint over parameter variables.

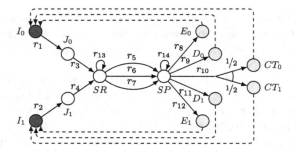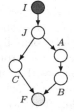

Fig. 1. Ben-Or's randomized consensus algorithm as a probabilistic threshold automaton with processes.

Fig. 2. Asymmetric threshold automaton used in Example 5.

Table 1. The rules of the probabilistic threshold automaton for Ben-Or's algorithm from Fig. 1, where $z_i \in \{x_0, x_1, y_0, y_1, y_?\}$ refers to messages of type z and value i.

Rule	Guard	Update	Rule	Guard	Update
r_1	true	$\emptyset$	r_8	$y_0 + y_1 + y_? \geq n-t \ \wedge \ y_0 \geq t+1$	$\emptyset$
r_2	true	$\emptyset$	r_9	$y_0 + y_1 + y_? \geq n-t \ \wedge \ y_0 > (n+t)/2$	$\emptyset$
r_3	true	$\{x_0\}$	r_{10}	$y_0 + y_1 + y_? \geq n-t \ \wedge$	
r_4	true	$\{x_1\}$		$y_0 < t+1 \ \wedge \ y_1 < t+1$	$\emptyset$
r_5	$x_0 + x_1 \geq n-t \ \wedge \ x_0 \geq (n+t)/2$	$\{y_0\}$	r_{11}	$y_0 + y_1 + y_? \geq n-t \ \wedge \ y_1 > (n+t)/2$	$\emptyset$
r_6	$x_0 + x_1 \geq n-t \ \wedge \ x_1 \geq (n+t)/2$	$\{y_1\}$	r_{12}	$y_0 + y_1 + y_? \geq n-t \ \wedge \ y_1 \geq t+1$	$\emptyset$
r_7	$x_0 + x_1 \geq n-t \ \wedge$		r_{13}	true	$\emptyset$
	$x_0 < (n+t)/2 \ \wedge \ x_1 < (n+t)/2$	$\{y_?\}$	r_{14}	true	$\emptyset$

Example 1. Figure 1 depicts a $\mathsf{PTA}_\mathbb{P}$ that formalizes the seminal consensus algorithm by Ben-Or [4]. It has locations $\mathcal{L} = \mathcal{B} \cup \mathcal{I} \cup \mathcal{F} \cup \{SR, SP\}$, where $\mathcal{B} = \{I_0, I_1\}$ are border locations, $\mathcal{I} = \{J_0, J_1\}$ are initial locations, and $\mathcal{F} = \{E_0, E_1, D_0, D_1, CT_0, CT_1\}$ are final locations. The set of parameters is $\Pi = \{n, t, f\}$, where n is the total set of processes, f is the number of faulty processes, and t is an upper bound on the number of faults. The 14 rules of the $\mathsf{PTA}_\mathbb{P}$ from Fig. 1 are given in Table 1 (and detailed later). There are two message types, $\mathcal{T} = \{x, y\}$, and three values $\mathcal{V} = \{0, 1, ?\}$, where x-messages can only have values 0 and 1, and y-messages all three values. The local receive variables from Λ are thus written $x_0, x_1, y_0, y_1, y_?$ where we write shortly, e.g., type-value pair $(x, 0)$.

See [5] for an in-detail exposition of Ben-Or's algorithm and its formalization as threshold automaton. There, one can observe that the pseudo-code of this algorithm consists of a while loop, and one loop iteration is refered to as a *round*. In the threshold automaton in Fig. 1, the solid arrows represent local transitions within a round, while dashed arrows represent local transitions to the next round. In each round, each process starts in I_0 or I_1. The subscript of the locations show what is the process' current estimate of the consensus value.

A process informs its peers about its consensus estimate by firing rule r_3 or r_4 and sending a message of type x_0 or x_1, respectively. Then it waits in SR until sufficiently many—given by the guards—messages are received to fire r_5, r_6, and r_7, etc. If the thresholds are chosen properly, this shall ensure that if a process enters D_0 in some round, and thus decides 0, no process ever enters D_1 in some round and decided 1 (agreement of consensus). The randomization is introduced in rule r_{10}: this is a coin toss where a process chooses its estimate for the next round if there was no clear majority around a value. The dashed arrows then show how a process transitions from a final location of round r to the beginning of round $r + 1$. Performing an infinite number of rounds, and (if necessary) coin tosses, shall ensure that eventually every process decides.

Resilience Condition. Let $\mathbb{N}_0$ denote the set of natural numbers including zero. A resilience condition RC defines the set of *admissible parameter values* $\mathbf{P}_{RC} = \{\mathbf{p} \in \mathbb{N}_0^{|\Pi|} : \mathbf{p} \models RC\}$, for which the algorithm is designed to be correct. For example, Ben-Or's consensus algorithm is correct when $n/5 > t \geq f \geq 0$. We introduce a function $N : \mathbf{P}_{RC} \to \mathbb{N}_0$ that maps a vector of admissible parameters to a number of modeled processes in the system. For instance, for the automaton in Fig. 1, N is the function $(n, t, f) \mapsto n-f$, as we model only the $n-f$ correct processes explicitly, while the effect of Byzantine faulty processes is captured in non-deterministic choices between different guards. For crash-resilient algorithms, where all processes are initially correct (until they crash), we model them all explicitly, that is, $N(n, t, f) = n$. The set of modeled processes is then $\mathbb{C} = \{p_1, \ldots, p_N\}$.

Messages. The set of all messages is $\mathcal{M} = (\mathbb{P} \times \mathcal{T} \times \mathcal{V} \times \mathbb{N}_0)$. A message m is a tuple $(sen, type, val, rnd)$ where the process $sen \in \mathbb{P}$ is the sender, the message type is $type \in \mathcal{T}$, the value is $val \in \mathcal{V}$, and the message is sent in the round $rnd \in \mathbb{N}_0$. Note that we do not make explicit the process receiving the message, because we focus on broadcast communications, and thus messages are sent to every process.

Let $\mathcal{M}_{\mathbb{F}} = \mathbb{F} \times \mathcal{T} \times \mathcal{V} \times \mathbb{N}_0$ be the subset of all messages where the sender is a faulty process, and $\mathcal{M}_{\mathbb{C}} = \mathbb{C} \times \mathcal{T} \times \mathcal{V} \times \mathbb{N}_0$ the subset of messages sent by correct processes. In our example from Fig. 1 we have $|\mathbb{F}| = f$ and $|\mathbb{C}| = n - f$.

In the sequel, we assume $\mathcal{M}$ is equipped with a total order $<_{\mathcal{M}}$. This total order can be naturally derived from the order on $\mathbb{N}_0$, and fixed orders on the processes, on the types, and on the values.

Rules. We introduce rules in detail, and give syntactic restrictions that model the local transitions of a distributed algorithm from/to particular locations. A rule r is a tuple $(from, \delta_{to}, \varphi, \boldsymbol{u})$ where $from \in \mathcal{L}$ is the *source* location, $\delta_{to} \in$ Dist($\mathcal{L}$) is a probability distribution over the *destination* locations, $\boldsymbol{u} \subseteq \mathcal{T} \times \mathcal{V}$ is the *update set*, and φ is a guard, *i.e.*, a conjunction of expressions of the form $\sum_{v \in \mathcal{V}} (b_v \cdot x_{t,v}) \square \bar{a} \cdot \mathbf{p}^{\mathsf{T}} + a_0$ where $t \in \mathcal{T}$ is a fixed message type; for a message value $v \in \mathcal{V}$, $b_v \in \mathbb{N}_0$ is a non-negative integer and $x_{t,v} \in \Lambda$ is a local receive variable; $\square \in \{\geq, <\}$, $\bar{a} \in \mathbb{Z}^{|\Pi|}$ is a vector of integers, $a_0 \in \mathbb{Z}$, and $\mathbf{p}$ is the vector of all parameters. If a guard contains only one conjunct, we sometimes call it *a simple threshold guard* (or just *a simple guard*). The set of all simple guards that appear in a probabilistic threshold automaton PTA$_\mathbb{P}$ is denoted by $\mathcal{G}(\mathsf{PTA}_\mathbb{P})$.

If $r.\delta_{to}$ is a Dirac distribution, *i.e.*, if there exists $\ell \in \mathcal{L}$ such that $r.\delta_{to}(\ell) = 1$, we call r a *Dirac rule*, and simply denote it $(from, \ell, \varphi, \boldsymbol{u})$.

Probabilistic threshold automata model algorithms with multiple rounds that follow the same code. They represent the behaviour each correct process follows within a round. Informally, a round happens between border locations and final locations. The round switch rules let processes move from final locations of a given round to border locations of the next round. From each border location there is exactly one Dirac rule to an initial location, and it has a form $(\ell, \ell', \texttt{true}, \emptyset)$ where $\ell \in \mathcal{B}$ and $\ell' \in \mathcal{I}$. As $|\mathcal{B}| = |\mathcal{I}|$, one can think of border locations as copies of initial locations. It remains to model from which final locations to which border location (that is, initial for the next round) processes move. This is done by *round switch rules*. They can be described as Dirac rules $(\ell, \ell', \texttt{true}, \emptyset)$ with $\ell \in \mathcal{F}$ and $\ell' \in \mathcal{B}$. The set of round switch rules is denoted by $\mathcal{S} \subseteq \mathcal{R}$. A location belongs to $\mathcal{B}$ iff all the incoming edges are in $\mathcal{S}$. Similarly, a location is in $\mathcal{F}$ iff there is only one outgoing edge and it is in $\mathcal{S}$.

Example 2. Back to our running example, the only rule that is not a Dirac rule is r_{10}, and round switch rules are represented by dashed arrows. Also the update sets are either empty sets or singletons, where we again write shortly, *e.g.*, x_0 instead of the type-value pair $(x, 0)$.

2.1 Symmetry in PTA$_\mathbb{P}$

In the distributed algorithm community, weak adversaries are typically defined by not being able to observe message content and the outcome of coin tosses. In the PTA$_\mathbb{P}$ model, one can often retrieve information about the outcome of a coin toss by the location a process ends up in, or about the message contents by the rule that is taken. For instance, in our example, depending on the outcome of a coin toss, a process goes either to location CT_0 or CT_1. Also, firing r_5 or r_6 reveals which messages of type x—with value 0 or 1—are in the majority. This motivates the introduction of two equivalence relations, one on locations and one on guards (and thus rules). In our example on the one hand, the locations CT_0 and CT_1 should be equivalent, and on the other hand the rules r_5 and r_6 should be equivalent. In the following, we formalize weak adversaries using such symmetries in threshold automata.

Equivalence Relations on Guards and Rules. Let us first define a correspondence between threshold guards. Fix two simple threshold guards

$$\varphi_1 \colon \sum_{v \in \mathcal{V}} (b_{t_1,v} \cdot x_{t_1,v}) \,\square_1\, \bar{a} \cdot \mathbf{p}^{\mathsf{T}} + a_0 \quad \text{and} \quad \varphi_2 \colon \sum_{v \in \mathcal{V}} (d_{t_2,v} \cdot x_{t_2,v}) \,\square_2\, \bar{c} \cdot \mathbf{p}^{\mathsf{T}} + c_0.$$

We say that φ_1 and φ_2 *correspond to each other*, denoted by $\varphi_1 \equiv_\varphi \varphi_2$, if:

- $\square_1$ and $\square_2$ are the same relation, either $\geq$ or $<$,
- coefficients are the same, that is, $\bar{a} = \bar{c}$ and $a_0 = c_0$,
- message types are the same, that is, $t_1 = t_2$,
- there exists a permutation π on the set of values $\mathcal{V}$, such that $b_{t_1,v} = d_{t_2,\pi(v)}$.

We extend this definition to threshold guards. Let $\varphi_A = \varphi_1^A \wedge \ldots \wedge \varphi_k^A$ and $\varphi_B = \varphi_1^B \wedge \ldots \wedge \varphi_m^B$ be threshold guards, and each φ_i^A and φ_j^B be a simple guard. We say φ_A and φ_B correspond to each other, and write $\varphi_A \equiv_\varphi \varphi_B$, if $k = m$ and there is a permutation ρ on the set $\{1, \ldots, k\}$ such that $\varphi_i^A \equiv_\varphi \varphi_{\rho(i)}^B$ for every $1 \leq i \leq k$.

Example 3. In case $x, y \in \mathcal{T}$ and $0, 1, 2 \in \mathcal{V}$, we have $y_0 \geq n - 2t \equiv_\varphi y_1 \geq n - 2t$ and $y_0 + 3y_1 < t + 1 \equiv_\varphi y_1 + 3y_2 < t + 1$. In the example from Table 1 we have $r_5 \equiv_\varphi r_6$, $r_8 \equiv_\varphi r_{12}$, and $r_9 \equiv_\varphi r_{11}$.

The equivalence relation over guards, allows us to define an equivalence relation $\equiv_\mathcal{R} \subseteq \mathcal{R} \times \mathcal{R}$ on rules. Let r_1 and r_2 be two rules from $\mathcal{R}$. We have $r_1 \equiv_\mathcal{R} r_2$ if and only if it holds that: $r_1.\varphi \equiv_\varphi r_2.\varphi$, and there exists a permutation π on the set of values $\mathcal{V}$, such that $(t, v) \in r_1.\boldsymbol{u}$ if and only if $(t, \pi(v)) \in r_2.\boldsymbol{u}$.

Example 4. Consider again our example from Table 1. The rules r_1, r_2, r_3, r_4 have trivial guards, which are therefore all in the same equivalence class of $\equiv_\varphi$. In contrast, not all the rules are equivalent w.r.t. relation $\equiv_\mathcal{R}$, as their update sets are different. Thus, we have $r_1 \equiv_\mathcal{R} r_2$ and $r_3 \equiv_\mathcal{R} r_4$.

Equivalence Relation on Locations. We define equivalence relation $\equiv_\mathcal{L} \subseteq \mathcal{L} \times \mathcal{L}$ on locations inductively as follows:

- The set of border locations $\mathcal{B}$ is one equivalence class of $\equiv_\mathcal{L}$, that is, for every $\ell_1, \ell_2 \in \mathcal{B}$ and every $\ell_3 \notin \mathcal{B}$ it holds that $\ell_1 \equiv_\mathcal{L} \ell_2$, and $\ell_1 \not\equiv_\mathcal{L} \ell_3$.
- Let ℓ_1 and ℓ_2 be two locations from $\mathcal{L} \setminus \mathcal{B}$. We have $\ell_1 \equiv_\mathcal{L} \ell_2$ if and only if there exist rules r_1 and r_2 and locations ℓ_1^s and ℓ_2^s such that
  - ℓ_i^s is a source location of r_i, for $i = 1, 2$, that is, $r_i.from = \ell_i^s$,
  - ℓ_i is a destination location for r_i, formally, $r_i.\delta_{to}(\ell_i) > 0$, for $i = 1, 2$,
  - $\ell_1^s \equiv_\mathcal{L} \ell_2^s$, and $r_1 \equiv_\mathcal{R} r_2$.
- The set of final locations $\mathcal{F}$ is either one equivalence class of $\equiv_\mathcal{L}$ or a union of finitely many equivalence classes of $\equiv_\mathcal{L}$. As a consequence, there are no two locations $\ell_1 \in \mathcal{F}$ and $\ell_2 \notin \mathcal{F}$ such that $\ell_1 \equiv_\mathcal{L} \ell_2$.

Let $\mathsf{PTA}_\mathbb{P}$ be a probabilistic threshold automaton with processes, equipped with equivalence relations $\equiv_\mathcal{L}$ and $\equiv_\mathcal{R}$. Assume $\ell, \ell_0, \ell_1 \in \mathcal{L}$ are locations, and $r = (from, \delta_{to}, \varphi, \boldsymbol{u}) \in \mathcal{R}$ is a non-Dirac rule such that its source location is ℓ ($r.from = \ell$), and ℓ_0 and ℓ_1 are its destination locations. Then $\ell_0 \equiv_\mathcal{L} \ell_1$. In words, all destinations of a non-Dirac rule are equivalent locations.

Example 5. In Fig. 1 we have 7 equivalence classes w.r.t. $\equiv_\mathcal{L}$, namely $\{I_0, I_1\}$, $\{J_0, J_1\}$, $\{SR\}$, $\{SP\}$, $\{E_0, E_1\}$, $\{D_0, D_1\}$, and $\{CT_0, CT_1\}$.

Such an equivalence relation does not always exist, due to the last requirement on final locations. For instance, on the automaton from Fig. 2, where $I \in \mathcal{B}$, $J \in \mathcal{I}$, $F \in \mathcal{F}$, where all rules have guard *true* and empty update set, it is not possible to define $\equiv_\mathcal{L}$. Intuitively, an adversary is able to infer whether the left or the right branch is taken, and consequently in similar asymmetric automata it may infer information about message content or coin tosses. However, typical randomized consensus algorithms from the literature [4,7,17,18] have a structure similar to the one in Fig. 1, and are thus symmetric.

2.2 Semantics of a PTA$_\mathbb{P}$

The semantics of a probabilistic threshold automaton with processes is an infinite-state Markov decision process (MDP), which we formally define below.

Given a PTA$_\mathbb{P}$ and a function N (defined earlier), we define the semantics, called *probabilistic system with processes* Sys(PTA$_\mathbb{P}$), to be infinite-state MDP $(\Sigma, I, \text{Act}, \Delta)$, where Σ is the set of configurations for PTA$_\mathbb{P}$ among which $I \subseteq \Sigma$ are initial, the set of actions is $\text{Act} = \mathcal{P}(\mathcal{M}) \times \mathbb{C}$, and $\Delta \colon \Sigma \times \text{Act} \to \text{Dist}(\Sigma)$ is the probabilistic transition function.

Configurations. A configuration σ is a tuple $(\mathbf{s}, Sent, Rcvd, \mathbf{p})$, where the components are defined as follows:

- $\sigma.\mathbf{s} \colon \mathbb{C} \to \mathcal{L} \times \mathbb{N}_0$ is a function that describes the control states of processes, that is, the location and the round of each correct process,
- $\sigma.Sent \subseteq \mathcal{M}_\mathbb{C}$ is a set of messages sent by correct processes,
- $\sigma.Rcvd \colon \mathbb{C} \to \mathcal{P}(\mathcal{M})$ is a function that keeps track of the received messages for every correct process.
- $\sigma.\mathbf{p} \in \mathbb{N}_0^{|\Pi|}$ is a vector of parameter values.

We write $\sigma.Rcvd[p]_{|t,v,k}$ for the set of messages from $\sigma.Rcvd[p]$ of type t and value v that are sent in round k. Formally,

$$\sigma.Rcvd[p]_{|t,v,k} = \{m \in \sigma.Rcvd[p] \mid m.type = t \wedge m.val = v \wedge m.rnd = k\}.$$

We write $\sigma.\mathbf{s}_{\text{loc}} \colon \mathbb{C} \to \mathcal{L}$ and $\sigma.\mathbf{s}_{\text{rnd}} \colon \mathbb{C} \to \mathbb{N}_0$ for the projections to the first and the second component of $\sigma.\mathbf{s}$, respectively.

A configuration $\sigma = (\mathbf{s}, Sent, Rcvd, \mathbf{p})$ is *initial* if all processes are in border locations of round 0, and there are no sent nor received messages in any round:

- $\sigma.Sent = \emptyset$,
- for every $p \in \mathbb{C}$ we have $\sigma.Rcvd[p] = \emptyset$,
- for every $p \in \mathbb{C}$ there is a location $\ell \in \mathcal{B}$ such that $\sigma.\mathbf{s}[p] = (\ell, 0)$.

A threshold guard evaluates to true in a configuration σ for a process p and a round k, written $\sigma, p, k \models \varphi$, if for all its conjuncts $\sum_{v \in \mathcal{V}}(b_v \cdot x_{t,v}) \geq \bar{a} \cdot \mathbf{p}^\mathsf{T} + a_0$ we have $\sum_{v \in \mathcal{V}}(b_v \cdot |\sigma.Rcvd[p]_{|t,v,k}|) \geq \bar{a} \cdot (\sigma.\mathbf{p}^\mathsf{T}) + a_0$, and similarly for conjuncts of the other form, *i.e.*, $\sum_{v \in \mathcal{V}}(b_v \cdot x_{t,v}) < \bar{a} \cdot \mathbf{p}^\mathsf{T} + a_0$.

Actions. An action $\alpha = (M, p) \in \text{Act}$ stands for the atomic execution of the following two steps: (i) process p receives the set of messages $M \subseteq \mathcal{M}$, and after that (ii) process p makes progress by executing a rule, if possible.

An action $\alpha = (M, p)$ is *applicable* to a configuration σ if each message from M has either been sent by a correct process or it comes from a faulty process, i.e., for every $m \in M$ we have: $m \in \sigma.Sent$ or $m \in \mathcal{M}_\mathbb{F}$.

A rule $r = (from, \delta_{to}, \varphi, \mathbf{u})$ is *executable* by a process p in a configuration σ with $\sigma.\mathbf{s}[p] = (\ell, k)$ if: (i) p is in the source location of the rule, that is, $from = \ell$, and (ii) the guard evaluates to true in σ for p and k, that is, $\sigma, p, k \models \varphi$. In every configuration for every process there is at most one executable rule.

It is also important to note the role of the round number k in the definition of an executable rule. Whether a rule r is executable by p in σ depends only on the messages from the round in which this process is in σ. Thus, threshold automata are communication-closed [9,10] by construction and thus provide an effective model for many communication-closed fault-tolerant distributed algorithms in the literature. We consider this notion in more detail in Sect. 3.

Let σ be a configuration and let action $\alpha = (M, p)$ be applicable to σ. When α is applied to σ, process p receives messages from M, which results in configuration σ_{aux}, and then executes a rule r that is executable by p in σ_{aux} (if there is an executable rule), which finally results in σ'. Note that $M = \emptyset$ implies that $\sigma = \sigma_{aux}$, and if there is no executable rule in σ_{aux} then we have $\sigma_{aux} = \sigma'$.

Let us define a function $exec : \Sigma \times \mathsf{Act} \to \mathcal{R} \cup \{\bot\}$ that given a configuration σ and an action $\alpha = (M, p)$ applicable to σ, outputs (i) the unique rule r that is executable by p in configuration σ_{aux} obtained from σ by changing only $\sigma_{aux}.Rcvd[p] = \sigma.Rcvd[p] \cup M$, if such a rule exists, and (ii) it outputs $\bot$ if no such rule exists. We define $exec(\sigma, \alpha) = \bot$ if α is not applicable to σ.

Let $\alpha = (M, p)$ be an action applicable to σ, and let ℓ be either a potential destination location of $exec(\sigma, \alpha) \neq \bot$, or ℓ is the location of p in σ if $exec(\sigma, \alpha) = \bot$. We write $apply(\sigma, \alpha, \ell)$ for the resulting configuration: parameters are unchanged, all messages from M are added to $\sigma.Rcvd[p]$, and if $exec(\sigma, \alpha) = r \neq \bot$, then new messages from $\mathcal{M}$ are added to $\sigma.Sent$ according to the update set $r.\boldsymbol{u}$, and finally while the location and the round of all processes except p are unchanged, we have that location of p becomes ℓ and its round is unchanged (or increased by 1 if r is a round switch rule).

Formally, if $\alpha = (M, p)$, we have that $apply(\sigma, \alpha, \ell) = \sigma'$ if and only if $apply(\sigma, \alpha, \ell)$ is defined and the following holds:

- The parameter values do not change: $\sigma'.\mathbf{p} = \sigma.\mathbf{p}$.
- Process p receives all messages from M, formally, $\sigma'.Rcvd[p] = \sigma.Rcvd[p] \cup M$.
- The control states of processes, that is, their locations and rounds given by the function $\sigma'.\mathbf{s}$, are updated as follows:
  - After updating $\sigma.Rcvd[p]$, if there is no executable r for p, that is, if $exec(\sigma, \alpha) = \bot$, then the control states of all processes remain the same: $\sigma'.\mathbf{s} = \sigma.\mathbf{s}$.
  - Otherwise, if $exec(\sigma, \alpha) = r \neq \bot$, then the control states for all the processes except for p remain the same. Formally, $\sigma'.\mathbf{s}[q] = \sigma.\mathbf{s}[q]$ for every $q \neq p$.

  Process p moves to location ℓ and either (i) it stays in the same round if $r \notin \mathcal{S}$ is not a round switch rule, or (ii) it moves to the following round if $r \in \mathcal{S}$. Formally, if we denote the round of p in σ by $\sigma.\mathbf{s}_{\mathrm{rnd}}[p] = k$, then we have that $\sigma'.\mathbf{s}[p] = (\ell, k)$ if r is not a round switch, and $\sigma'.\mathbf{s}[p] = (\ell, k+1)$ if r is a round switch rule.
- The set of sent messages is updated as follows:
  - If $exec(\sigma, \alpha) = \bot$, then no rule is fired and thus no message is sent, that is, $\sigma'.Sent = \sigma.Sent$.

- If $exec(\sigma, \alpha) = r \neq \bot$ then the rule r is fired, and the update set $r.\boldsymbol{u}$ dictates the set of messages (their types and values) that process p sends to all in round $k = \sigma.\mathbf{s}_{\mathrm{rnd}}[p]$, that is, $\sigma'.Sent = \sigma.Sent \cup \{(p, t, v, k) \mid (t, v) \in r.\boldsymbol{u}\}$.

Let $\alpha = (M, p)$ be applicable to σ, and let process p be in round k in configuration σ, that is, $\sigma.\mathbf{s}(p) = (\ell, k)$ for some location ℓ and round k. Then we define the *round of action* α *in configuration* σ to be k, and denote this by $rnd_\sigma(\alpha) = k$. When it is clear from the context which configuration we refer to, we only write $rnd(\alpha)$ instead of $rnd_\sigma(\alpha)$.

Probabilistic Transition Function. The probabilistic transition function Δ is defined such that for every two configurations σ and σ' and for every action α applicable to σ, with $exec(\sigma, \alpha) = r \in \mathcal{R} \cup \{\bot\}$, we have

$$\Delta(\sigma, \alpha)(\sigma') = \begin{cases} r.\delta_{to}(\ell) & \text{if } apply(\sigma, \alpha, \ell) = \sigma' \text{ for some } \ell \in \mathcal{L} \\ 0 & \text{otherwise.} \end{cases}$$

Note that if $r = \bot$ we define $r.\delta_{to}(\ell) = 1$, and if there exists a location ℓ with $apply(\sigma, \alpha, \ell) = \sigma'$, this location is uniquely defined.

Paths. A (finite or infinite) *path* in $\mathsf{Sys}(\mathsf{PTA})$ is an alternating sequence of configurations and actions $\sigma_0, \alpha_0, \sigma_1, \alpha_1 \ldots$, such that for $i > 0$, there exists a location ℓ_i such that $apply(\sigma_{i-1}, \alpha_{i-1}, \ell_i) = \sigma_i$. We denote the set of all paths by Paths and the set of all finite paths (ending with a configuration) by Paths_{fin}. The length of a finite path $\rho = \sigma_0, \alpha_0, \sigma_1, \alpha_1 \ldots, \sigma_k$ is the number of actions taken, that is, $|\rho| = k$. Wlog if ρ is an infinite path, we let $|\rho| = \infty$. We sometimes consider prefixes of a (finite or infinite) path ρ, and for $s < |\rho|$ write ρ_s for $\sigma_0, \alpha_0, \ldots, \sigma_s$. Also the last configuration σ_k of a finite path $\rho = \sigma_0, \alpha_0 \ldots, \alpha_{k-1}, \sigma_k$ is written $last(\rho)$. As sent messages cannot be unsent, the set of sent messages can only grow along a path. Thus, the set $last(\rho).Sent$ contains the set $\sigma_i.Sent$ for every $0 \leq i \leq k$. That is why we often write $\rho.Sent$ instead of $last(\rho).Sent$.

2.3 Message Identities

An adversary formalizes which messages will be received next. When formalizing weak adversaries, we have to capture that the adversary can pick a message without being aware of the content of the message. For this we introduce message identities in the model. Note that every action may include sending a finite number of messages. Therefore, in a finite path there are finitely many sent messages, and we can assign them their identities (IDs for short). For a path $\rho \in \mathsf{Paths}_{fin}$, we define IDs of messages sent by correct processes along ρ by a function $ID[\rho] : \rho.Sent \to \mathbb{N}$ defined recursively on the length ρ:

Base Case. If ρ is a degenerative path $\rho = \sigma_0$, then σ_0 is an initial configuration, and therefore, there are no sent messages in it. Formally, $\sigma_0.Sent = \emptyset$ and there is nothing to assign.

Recursion. Let $\rho = \tau \alpha \sigma \in \mathsf{Paths}_{fin}$ be a non-degenerative finite path. We distinguish two cases depending if new messages were sent while executing α.

- If no message is sent when applying α to $last(\tau)$, *i.e.*, if either no rule is executed $exec(last(\tau), \alpha) = \bot$, or if there is an executed rule $exec(last(\tau), \alpha) = r \neq \bot$ but $r.\boldsymbol{u} = \emptyset$, then the function ID is unchanged: we set $ID[\rho] = ID[\tau]$.
- Otherwise, let $r = exec(last(\tau), \alpha)$ and let the set of messages sent when executing rule r from $last(\tau)$ be $r.\boldsymbol{u} = \{m_1, \ldots, m_k\}$ for some $k \geq 1$, with $m_1 <_{\mathcal{M}} m_2 \cdots <_{\mathcal{M}} m_k$. Then the function $ID[\rho]$ is defined as follows:

$$ID[\rho](m) = \begin{cases} ID[\tau](m) & \text{if } m \in \tau.Sent, \\ |\tau.Sent| + i & \text{if } m = m_i \in r.\boldsymbol{u} \text{ for } 1 \leq i \leq k \end{cases}$$

Revealing Messages from their IDs. It is important to notice that for every natural number $n \leq |\tau.Sent|$ there is a unique message $m \in \tau.Sent$ with that identity, that is, with $ID(m) = n$. We define an inverse of msg when defined. Given a path $\rho \in \mathsf{Paths}_{fin}$ we define a function $rev\text{-}msg[\rho] : \{1, 2, \ldots, |\rho.Sent|\} \to \rho.Sent$, such that for every n with $1 \leq n \leq |\rho.Sent|$ we have $rev\text{-}msg[\rho](n) = m$ if and only if $ID[\rho](m) = n$.

We extend this definition to a set of IDs, and define $rev\text{-}msg[\rho]$ of a set of natural numbers $N \subset \mathbb{N}$ to be $rev\text{-}msg[\rho](N) = \{rev\text{-}msg[\rho](n) \mid n \in N\}$.

Faulty Messages. Recall that $\mathcal{M}_{\mathbb{F}} = \mathbb{F} \times \mathcal{T} \times \mathcal{V} \times \mathbb{N}_0$ is the set of messages $m = (p, t, v, k) \in \mathcal{M}$ with the sender being a faulty process, that is, $p \in \mathbb{F}$. Note that this set has countably infinitely many elements, and therefore there exists a bijection between the set of natural numbers and $\mathcal{M}_{\mathbb{F}}$. We choose one such bijection $ID_f : \mathcal{M}_{\mathbb{F}} \to \mathbb{N}$ to be an enumerating function for the set of the faulty messages.

Similarly, we define a reveal function $rev\text{-}msg_f : \mathbb{N} \to \mathcal{M}_{\mathbb{F}}$ as the inverse of the identity function, that is, $rev\text{-}msg_f = ID_f^{-1}$. Moreover, for a set of natural numbers $N \subset \mathbb{N}$ we define $rev\text{-}msg_f(N) = \{rev\text{-}msg_f(n) \mid n \in N\}$.

2.4 Adversaries

The non-determinism in Markov decision processes is traditionally resolved by a so-called adversary, see *e.g.* [3, Chap. 10]. An *adversary* is a function $\mathsf{a} : \mathsf{Paths}_{fin} \to 2^{\mathbb{N} \times \{c,f\}} \times \mathbb{C}$ that given a finite path $\rho = \sigma_0, \alpha_0, \sigma_1, \ldots, \sigma_k$ of $\mathsf{Sys}(\mathsf{PTA}_{\mathbb{P}})$ selects a set of message IDs with the nature of their senders (a set of elements from $\mathbb{N} \times \{c\}$ or $\mathbb{N} \times \{f\}$) together with a correct process (thus from $\mathbb{C}$) to whom these messages are delivered.

As an adversary only gives message IDs, we need to understand which messages correspond to them. This is why we introduce the function $reveal[\mathsf{a}] : \mathsf{Paths}_{fin} \to \mathsf{Act}$ that reveals the next action in a path according to the choice of the adversary a. Let $\mathsf{a}(\rho) = (N_1 \times \{c\} \times \{p\}) \cup (N_2 \times \{f\} \times \{p\})$, where N_1 and N_2 are finite sets of natural numbers, and $p \in \mathbb{C}$ is a correct process. Then we define $reveal[\mathsf{a}](\rho)$ to be the action $(M_1 \cup M_2, p)$, where $M_1 = rev\text{-}msg[\rho](N_1)$ and $M_2 = rev\text{-}msg_f(N_2)$.

Given a path ρ, we also define a function $choice[\rho] : 2^{\rho.Sent} \times \mathbb{C} \to 2^{\mathbb{N} \times \{c,f\}} \times \mathbb{C}$ that tells us which choice $\mathsf{a}(\rho)$ should the adversary take in order to obtain the expected action. Let $(M, p) \in 2^{\rho.Sent} \times \mathbb{C}$, with $M = M_1 \cup M_2$ where M_1 are messages sent by correct processes and M_2 are messages sent by faulty processes. Let $N_1 = \{ID[\rho](m) \mid m \in M_1\}$ and let $N_2 = \{ID_f(m) \mid m \in M_2\}$. Then we have $choice[\rho](M, p) = (N, p)$, where $N = (N_1 \times \{c\}) \cup (N_2 \times \{f\})$.

Given an initial configuration σ_0, an adversary a generates a set $\mathsf{paths}(\sigma_0, \mathsf{a})$ of infinite paths $\sigma_0, \alpha_0, \sigma_1, \ldots$ with the following property: for every $i > 0$, $\alpha_i = reveal[\mathsf{a}](\sigma_0, \sigma_1, \ldots, \sigma_{i-1})$ and there exists a location ℓ_i such that $\sigma_i = apply(\sigma_{i-1}, \alpha_i, \ell_i)$. Every infinite path $\pi \in \mathsf{paths}(\sigma_0, \mathsf{a})$, and every finite path ρ which is a prefix of an infinite path $\pi \in \mathsf{paths}(\sigma_0, \mathsf{a})$, are said to be *induced by* a.

The MDP $\mathsf{Sys}(\mathsf{PTA}_{\mathbb{P}})$ together with an initial configuration σ_0 and an adversary a induce a Markov chain, denoted by $\mathcal{M}_{\mathsf{a}}^{\sigma_0}$. Precisely, the state space of $\mathcal{M}_{\mathsf{a}}^{\sigma_0}$ is Paths_{fin}, its initial state is the initial configuration σ_0—which is also a path of length 0—and the probabilistic transition function $\delta_{\mathsf{a},\sigma_0} : \mathsf{Paths}_{fin} \to \mathsf{Dist}(\mathsf{Paths}_{fin})$ is defined for every $\tau \in \mathsf{Paths}_{fin}$ starting in σ_0 and ending in some configuration σ, for every action α, and every $\sigma' \in \Sigma$ by:

$$(\delta_{\mathsf{a}}(\tau))(\tau\alpha\sigma') = \Delta(\sigma, reveal[\mathsf{a}](\tau))(\sigma').$$

In words, the probability in $\mathcal{M}_{\mathsf{a}}^{\sigma_0}$ to move from state τ to state $\tau\alpha\sigma'$ is non-zero as soon as there exists an action α' such that $\sigma' = apply(\sigma, \alpha', \ell)$ and a picks α'. This equals the probability that the corresponding process moves to ℓ if the adversary a picks action α'. Note that the Markov chain $\mathcal{M}_{\mathsf{a}}^{\sigma_0}$ is acyclic, and even has the shape of a tree, since its states are the finite paths in Paths_{fin}. We write $\mathbf{P}_{\mathsf{a}}^{\sigma_0}$ for the probability measure over infinite paths starting at σ_0 in $\mathcal{M}_{\mathsf{a}}^{\sigma_0}$.

Given σ_0, a and a finite path $\rho = \sigma_0, \alpha_0, \ldots, \sigma_k \in \mathsf{Paths}_{fin}$, we write $\mathcal{M}_{\mathsf{a}}^{\rho}$ for the Markov chain which corresponds to the part of $\mathcal{M}_{\mathsf{a}}^{\sigma_0}$ with initial state ρ. The probability measure $\mathbf{P}_{\mathsf{a}}^{\rho}$ in $\mathcal{M}_{\mathsf{a}}^{\rho}$ is inherited from the one in $\mathcal{M}_{\mathsf{a}}^{\sigma_0}$.

Weak Adversaries. In order to define weak adversaries, we introduce an equivalence relation on paths.

For two sets of messages M_1 and M_2 we say they are *equivalent up to message values* if there is a bijection $f : M_1 \to M_2$ such that for every $m \in M_1$ we have that m and $f(m)$ have the same sender, type and round. Formally, we have $m.sen = f(m).sen$, $m.type = f(m).type$, $m.rnd = f(m).rnd$.

The weak observation relation relates two configurations that differ only in message content and symmetric locations of processes. Formally:

Definition 1. *The* weak observation relation *is the equivalence relation* $\equiv_w \subseteq \Sigma^2$ *such that* $\sigma \equiv_w \sigma'$ *if and only if*

- *for every correct process* $p \in \mathbb{C}$, *if* $\sigma.\mathsf{s}(p) = (\ell_1, k_1)$ *and* $\sigma'.\mathsf{s}(p) = (\ell_2, k_2)$, *then* $k_1 = k_2$ *and* $\ell_1 \equiv_{\mathcal{L}} \ell_2$.
- $\sigma.Sent$ *and* $\sigma'.Sent$ *are equivalent up to message values*
- *for all* $p \in \mathbb{C}$, $\sigma.Rcvd(p)$ *and* $\sigma'.Rcvd(p)$ *are equivalent up to message values*
- $\sigma.\mathbf{p} = \sigma'.\mathbf{p}$

We extend the relation to finite paths of the same length: if $\pi = \sigma_1, \sigma_2, \ldots, \sigma_k$ and $\pi' = \sigma'_1, \sigma'_2, \ldots, \sigma'_k$, then we write $\pi \equiv_w \pi'$ if $\sigma_i \equiv_w \sigma'_i$ for every $1 \leq i \leq k$.

An adversary a is *weak* if for every two finite paths π and π' with $\pi \equiv_w \pi'$ we have that $\mathsf{a}(\pi) = \mathsf{a}(\pi')$. In words, a weak adversary does not distinguish two paths if they are equivalent, and thus makes the same choice for equivalent paths.

Note that for threshold automata on which $\equiv_\mathcal{L}$ cannot be defined, we can also not define $\equiv_w$. Therefore, weak adversaries are a property of only those distributed algorithms that can be modeled by symmetric automata.

Lemma 1. *Let $\pi = \sigma_0, \ldots, \sigma_k, \alpha_k, \sigma_{k+1}$ and $\bar{\pi} = \sigma_0, \ldots, \sigma_k, \alpha_k, \bar{\sigma}_{k+1}$ be two paths such that $exec(\sigma_k, \alpha_k) = r$ is a non-Dirac rule with two destination locations $\ell \neq \bar{\ell}$, with $apply(\sigma_k, \alpha_k, \ell) = \sigma_{k+1}$ and with $apply(\sigma_k, \alpha_k, \bar{\ell}) = \bar{\sigma}_{k+1}$. Then for every weak adversary a we have $\mathsf{a}(\pi) = \mathsf{a}(\bar{\pi})$.*

Proof. Fix an arbitrary weak adversary a. By definition of weak adversaries, it is enough to show that $\pi \equiv_w \bar{\pi}$, and thus to prove that $\sigma_{k+1} \equiv_w \bar{\sigma}_{k+1}$.

We check all conditions for two configurations to be weakly-equivalent. Of course, $\sigma_{k+1}.\mathbf{p} = \bar{\sigma}_{k+1}.\mathbf{p}$. Let $\alpha_k = (M, p)$.

For every correct process $q \neq p$, $\sigma_{k+1}.\mathbf{s}(q) = \bar{\sigma}_{k+1}.\mathbf{s}(q)$. Writing $\sigma_{k+1}.\mathbf{s}(p) = (\ell, k)$ and $\bar{\sigma}_{k+1}.\mathbf{s}(p) = (\bar{\ell}, \bar{k})$, then the rounds k and $\bar{k}$ are trivially equal, and $\ell \equiv_\mathcal{L} \bar{\ell}$ holds by definition of the equivalence relation on locations.

Moreover, the update is defined by the rule r, and is independent of the destination location, so that the sent messages coincide: $\sigma_{k+1}.Sent = \sigma_k.Sent \cup r.\boldsymbol{u} = \bar{\sigma}_{k+1}.Sent$.

We now compare receive sets, and again they do not depend on the destination location, but only on r. For each correct process $q \neq p$ it trivially holds that $\sigma_{k+1}.Rcvd(q) = \bar{\sigma}_{k+1}.Rcvd(q)$. Also $\sigma_{k+1}.Rcvd(p) = \sigma_k.Rcvd(p) \cup M = \bar{\sigma}_{k+1}.Rcvd(p)$. □

We define two more notions for adversaries: An adversary a is *communication-closed* if for every finite path ρ the action $reveal[\mathsf{a}](\rho) = \alpha = (M, p)$ is such that each message $m \in M$ is sent before or in the same round in which process p is in $last(\rho)$. Formally, $m.rnd \leq rnd(\alpha)$. An adversary a is *round-rigid* if for every finite path ρ the action $reveal[\mathsf{a}](\rho) = \alpha = (M, p)$ has the smallest possible round, that is, there is no applicable action α' such that $rnd(\alpha') < rnd(\alpha)$. In the sequel, we show that weak round-rigid adversaries are as expressive as weak adversaries (see Theorem 1 and Theorem 2).

2.5 Atomic Propositions and Stutter Equivalence

Properties of threshold-based distributed algorithms are expressed in temporal logic. More precisely, we consider a stutter-insensitive fragment of LTL, namely, LTL$_{\mathsf{-X}}$ [3, Chapter 7]. The atomic propositions describe the non-emptiness of a location in a given round, *i.e.*, whether there is at least one correct process in location $\ell \in \mathcal{L} \setminus \mathcal{B}$ in round k [5]. The set of all such propositions for a round $k \in$

$\mathbb{N}_0$ is denoted by $\mathrm{AP}_k = \{\mathrm{ap}(\ell, k) \colon \ell \in \mathcal{L} \setminus \mathcal{B}\}$. For every k we define a labeling function $\lambda_k \colon \Sigma \to 2^{\mathrm{AP}_k}$ such that $\mathrm{ap}(\ell, k) \in \lambda_k(\sigma)$ iff $\exists p \in \mathbb{C}$. $\sigma.\mathbf{s}(p) = (\ell, k)$.

For a path $\pi = \sigma_0, \alpha_1, \sigma_1, \ldots, \alpha_n, \sigma_n$, $n \in \mathbb{N}$, and a round k, a trace $\mathrm{trace}_k(\pi)$ w.r.t. the labeling function λ_k is the sequence $\lambda_k(\sigma_0)\lambda_k(\sigma_1)\ldots\lambda_k(\sigma_n)$. Similarly, if a path is infinite $\pi = \sigma_0, \alpha_1, \sigma_1, \alpha_2, \sigma_2, \ldots$, then $\mathrm{trace}_k(\pi) = \lambda_k(\sigma_0)\lambda_k(\sigma_1)\ldots$.

We say that two finite traces are stutter equivalent w.r.t. AP_k, denoted $\mathrm{trace}_k(\pi_1) \triangleq \mathrm{trace}_k(\pi_2)$, if there is a finite sequence $A_0 A_1 \ldots A_n \in (2^{\mathrm{AP}_k})^+$, $n \in \mathbb{N}_0$, such that both $\mathrm{trace}_k(\pi_1)$ and $\mathrm{trace}_k(\pi_2)$ are contained in the language given by the regular expression $A_0^+ A_1^+ \ldots A_n^+$. If traces of π_1 and π_2 are infinite, then stutter equivalence $\mathrm{trace}_k(\pi_1) \triangleq \mathrm{trace}_k(\pi_2)$ is defined in the standard way [3]. To simplify notation, we say that paths π_1 and π_2 are stutter equivalent w.r.t. AP_k, and write $\pi_1 \triangleq_k \pi_2$, instead of referring to specific path traces. Two stutter equivalent paths satisfy the same $\mathsf{LTL}_{\text{-X}}$ formulas [3, Theorem 7.92].

Remark. We emphasize that atomic propositions cannot check emptiness of border locations from the set $\mathcal{B}$. The specifications cannot observe the moment of transition from one round to another. This allows us to swap transitions of adjacent rounds below.

The following lemma expresses that an action may only change atomic propositions of its own round, as it only affects a process in that round.

Lemma 2. *Let $\pi = \sigma_0, \alpha_1, \sigma_1, \ldots, \sigma_{s-1}, \alpha_s, \sigma_s$ be a finite path. Then, for every round $k \neq \mathrm{rnd}(\alpha_s)$, it holds that $\lambda_k(\sigma_{s-1}) = \lambda_k(\sigma_s)$.*

Proof. Let $\mathrm{ap}(\ell, k) \in \lambda_k(\sigma_{s-1})$, meaning that for some correct process $p \in \mathbb{C}$, $\sigma_{s-1}.\mathbf{s}(p) = (\ell, k)$. Since $\mathrm{rnd}(\alpha_s) \neq k$, we have $\alpha_s = (M, q)$ for a set of messages M and some correct process $q \neq p$. Thus, application of α_s does not affect p, and $\sigma_s.\mathbf{s}(p) = (\ell, k)$. In other words, $\mathrm{ap}(\ell, k) \in \lambda_k(\sigma_s)$. This holds for every $\mathrm{ap}(\ell, k) \in \lambda_k(\sigma_{s-1})$, concluding the proof. $\qquad\square$

Using Lemma 2, it is easy to prove that swapping two actions of different rounds in a path yield a stutter equivalent path w.r.t. AP_k for every $\in \mathbb{N}_0$:

Lemma 3. *Let $\pi = \sigma_0, \ldots, \sigma_s, \sigma_{s+1}, \sigma_{s+2}$ and $\pi' = \sigma_0, \ldots, \sigma_s, \sigma'_{s+1}, \sigma'_{s+2}$ be two paths with $\pi_s = \pi'_s = \sigma_0, \ldots, \sigma_s$, and such that there are two actions α and α' with $\mathrm{rnd}(\alpha) \neq \mathrm{rnd}(\alpha')$, and there are locations ℓ and ℓ' with*

$$\sigma_{s+1} = \mathrm{apply}(\sigma_s, \alpha, \ell) \qquad\qquad \sigma_{s+2} = \mathrm{apply}(\sigma_{s+1}, \alpha', \ell')$$
$$\sigma'_{s+1} = \mathrm{apply}(\sigma_s, \alpha', \ell') \qquad\qquad \sigma'_{s+2} = \mathrm{apply}(\sigma'_{s+1}, \alpha, \ell)$$

Then $\sigma_{s+2} = \sigma'_{s+2}$ and for every $k \in \mathbb{N}_0$, $\pi \triangleq_k \pi'$.

Proof. Let us first prove that $\sigma_{s+2} = \sigma'_{s+2}$. Both σ_{s+2} and σ'_{s+2} are obtained from σ_s by applying α with ℓ and α' with ℓ', just in different orders. By standard communication-closure arguments [8–10], if an action from a smaller round happens in an execution after an action of larger round, it is easy to prove that these two actions do not affect each other. Thus, in any order they will lead to the same configuration.

Let us now fix an arbitrary $k \in \mathbb{N}_0$ and prove that $\pi \triangleq_k \pi'$. As these two paths have the same prefix of length s, it suffices to prove that $\sigma_s, \sigma_{s+1}, \sigma_{s+2} \triangleq_k \sigma_s, \sigma'_{s+1}, \sigma_{s+2}$. We distinguish three cases: (i) $k \neq rnd(\alpha)$ and $k \neq rnd(\alpha')$, (ii) $k = rnd(\alpha)$, and (iii) $k = rnd(\alpha')$. Cases (ii) and (iii) are symmetrical, so that we only prove (ii).

(i) By Lemma 2 we have $\lambda_k(\sigma_s) = \lambda_k(\sigma_{s+1}) = \lambda_k(\sigma'_{s+1}) = \lambda_k(\sigma_{s+2})$, which trivially yields the required statement.

(ii) As in this case $k \neq rnd(\alpha')$, we can apply Lemma 2 and obtain that $\lambda_k(\sigma_{s+1}) = \lambda_k(\sigma_{s+2})$ and $\lambda_k(\sigma_s) = \lambda_k(\sigma'_{s+1})$. Therefore, $\mathrm{trace}_k(\sigma_s, \sigma_{s+1}, \sigma_{s+2}) = \lambda_k(\sigma_s)\lambda_k(\sigma_{s+2})\lambda_k(\sigma_{s+2})$, and $\mathrm{trace}_k(\sigma_s, \sigma'_{s+1}, \sigma_{s+2}) = \lambda_k(\sigma_s)\lambda_k(\sigma_s)\lambda_k(\sigma_{s+2})$, and they are clearly stutter equivalent w.r.t. k. □

3   Reduction to Communication-Closed Adversaries

In this section we show that in the threshold automata framework (which models communication-closed algorithms by construction, cf. Sect. 2.2), for every adversary, there exists an "equivalent" communication-closed adversary. This step is quite intuitive: if the adversary delivers a message m of round r to a process in round $r' \neq r$, this is "similar" to an adversary that instead does not deliver m now, but delivers m later when the process enters r. However, we need to formalize this, in order to set the stage of our central reduction in Sect. 4.

For a set of messages M and a round k we denote by $M|_k$ the set of messages from M sent in round k, that is, $M|_k = \{m \in M \mid m.rnd = k\}$. Similarly, we define $M|_{\leq k} = \cup_{i \leq k} M|_i$ the set of messages from M sent in any round $i \leq k$.

Communication-Closed Configurations and Markov Chains. The definition of rules *executable* in σ in Sect. 2.2 yields that messages received from the "future", *i.e.*, from a round $k > \sigma.\mathbf{s}_{\mathrm{rnd}}(p)$, do not play a role for process p in σ. Namely, if two configurations σ and σ' differ only in the messages that processes have received from future rounds, then the same rules are executable in σ and σ'. That is why for every σ we define $\tilde{\sigma}$ to be a configuration in which each process only has received messages from "past" and "present", i.e., from a round $k \leq \sigma.\mathbf{s}_{\mathrm{rnd}}(p)$. As border locations can be seen as borders between consecutive rounds, we decide to let processes from border locations in $\tilde{\sigma}$ receive messages only from the "past", as if they were not yet in the next round. Formally, $\tilde{\sigma}.\mathbf{s} = \sigma.\mathbf{s}$ and $\tilde{\sigma}.Sent = \sigma.Sent$ and $\tilde{\sigma}.\mathbf{p} = \sigma.\mathbf{p}$ and for all $p \in \mathbb{C}$, if $\mathbf{s}_{\mathrm{loc}}(p) \in \mathcal{B}$ then $\tilde{\sigma}.Rcvd(p) = \sigma.Rcvd(p)|_{\leq \mathbf{s}_{\mathrm{rnd}}(p)-1}$ otherwise $\tilde{\sigma}.Rcvd(p) = \sigma.Rcvd(p)|_{\leq \mathbf{s}_{\mathrm{rnd}}(p)}$. A configuration σ is communication-closed if $\sigma = \tilde{\sigma}$.

Recall that a path has the form $\sigma_0, \alpha_0, \ldots, \alpha_{s-1}, \sigma_s$, but given a sequence of configurations $\sigma_0, \ldots, \sigma_s$ of a path generated by an adversary $\mathbf{a}$, we can easily recover the missing actions. This allows us to consider the states of Markov chains to be finite sequences of configurations rather than finite paths. Both representations are equivalent, and thus in this section we consider paths as sequences of configurations. We can lift the notion of communication-closed configurations to communication-closed paths, such that given a path $\rho = \sigma_0, \ldots, \sigma_k$ we define $\mu(\rho) = \tilde{\sigma}_0, \ldots, \tilde{\sigma}_k$. Finally, we obtain a communication-closed Markov chain $\widetilde{\mathcal{M}}_{\mathbf{a}}^{\sigma_0}$ by replacing each state ρ in $\mathcal{M}_{\mathbf{a}}^{\sigma_0}$ by $\mu(\rho)$.

Communication-Closed Adversaries. Given an arbitrary adversary a, we define its corresponding communication-closed adversary $cc(a)$ as follows. If a process p is scheduled by a it is also scheduled by $cc(a)$, but it receives different messages: if p is not at the beginning of a round, $cc(a)$ should check which messages a would give to p, and among them $cc(a)$ should choose only those messages that do not come from future rounds. Once a process reaches a round (when it is at a border location in $\mathcal{B}$), it receives all the messages from that round and all those that were previously sent to it, but the process could not receive it earlier (because at that time these were messages from the future.)

As $cc(a)$ has to know the behavior of a, we show how to recover a path generated by a (if it exists) if we are given a communication-closed path. Formally, given an adversary a and a communication-closed path ρ, we define $\nu_a(\rho)$ to be a path τ generated by a, such that $\mu(\tau) = \rho$, if such a path exists; otherwise, $\nu_a(\rho)$ is undefined. Observe that if ρ is a path generated by a, then $\rho = \nu_a(\mu(\rho))$.

Finally, we define a communication-closed version of an adversary formally. Recall that τ_i denotes the prefix of τ of length i.

Definition 2. *Let* a *be an adversary. For a given finite path ρ, if $\nu_a(\mu(\rho))$ is undefined then $cc(a)(\rho)$ is an arbitrary action. Otherwise, if $\nu_a(\mu(\rho)) = \tau = \sigma_0, \ldots, \sigma_s$, let reveal[a]$(\tau_i) = \alpha_i = (M_i, p_{j_i})$, for each $0 \leq i \leq s$ and some $p_{j_i} \in \mathbb{C}$. If $\alpha_s = (M_s, p)$, in order to define $cc(a)(\rho)$ we distinguish two cases:*

– *If $\sigma_s.s[p] = (\ell, k)$ with $\ell \notin \mathcal{B}$, then*

$$cc(a)(\rho) = choice[\tau](M_s|_{\leq k}, p).$$

– *If $\sigma_s.s[p] = (\ell, k)$ with $\ell \in \mathcal{B}$, then for $S_p = \{i \mid 1 \leq i < s \wedge \alpha_i = (M_i, p)\}$ being the set of indices of the actions involving process p:*

$$cc(a)(\rho) = choice[\tau](M, p), \text{ for } M = M_s|_{\leq k} \cup \bigcup_{i \in S_p} M_i|_k.$$

Theorem 1. *For every adversary* a, $\widetilde{\mathcal{M}}_a^{\sigma_0} = \widetilde{\mathcal{M}}_{cc(a)}^{\sigma_0}$.
Moreover, for every LTL$_{\text{-X}}$ *formula ψ,* $\mathbf{P}_a^{\sigma_0}(\psi) = \mathbf{P}_{cc(a)}^{\sigma_0}(\psi)$.

4   From Weak to Round-Rigid Adversaries

In this section we reduce a communication-closed weak adversary to a round-rigid adversary. More precisely, we show that we can transform the Markov chain defined by the weak adversary to a round-rigid Markov chain that satisfies specific temporal logic formulas with the same probabilities.

Swapping Function for Paths and Swapped Adversaries. We first define a swapping function for a path $\rho = \sigma_0, \alpha_0, \sigma_1, \ldots, \sigma_s, \alpha_s, \sigma_{s+1}, \alpha_{s+1}, \sigma_{s+2} \ldots$ and $s \in \mathbb{N}$ a *swapping index* for ρ, such that $rnd(\alpha_s) > rnd(\alpha_{s+1})$. It applies to a path $\bar{\rho} = \bar{\sigma}_0, \ldots, \bar{\sigma}_s, \bar{\alpha}_s, \bar{\sigma}_{s+1}, \bar{\alpha}_{s+1}, \bar{\sigma}_{s+2}, \ldots$ such that $\bar{\rho}_s \equiv_w \rho_s$, and swaps its actions (and target locations) at steps s and $s+1$. Formally, if $\bar{\ell}_s$, $\bar{\ell}_{s+1}$ are the destination locations at step s and $s+1$, *i.e.* $apply(\bar{\sigma}_s, \bar{\alpha}_s, \bar{\ell}_s) = \bar{\sigma}_{s+1}$ and $apply(\bar{\sigma}_{s+1}, \bar{\alpha}_{s+1}, \bar{\ell}_{s+1}) = \bar{\sigma}_{s+2}$, then for $\sigma'_{s+1} = apply(\bar{\sigma}_s, \bar{\alpha}_{s+1}, \bar{\ell}_{s+1})$ we define

$$
\mathsf{sw}[\rho, s](\bar{\rho}) = \begin{cases} \bar{\sigma}_0, \ldots, \bar{\sigma}_s, \bar{\alpha}_{s+1}, \sigma'_{s+1}, \bar{\alpha}_s, \bar{\sigma}_{s+2}, \ldots & \text{if } \bar{\rho}_s \equiv_w \rho_s \\ \bar{\rho} & \text{otherwise.} \end{cases}
$$

Note that the configurations in $\bar{\rho}$ and $\mathsf{sw}[\rho, s](\bar{\rho})$ may only differ at position $s+1$, and that $\bar{\rho}$ and $\mathsf{sw}[\rho, s](\bar{\rho})$ are stutter-equivalent. Hence, for every $\mathsf{LTL_{\text{-}X}}$ formula ψ, $\bar{\rho} \models \psi$ iff $\mathsf{sw}[\rho, s](\bar{\rho}) \models \psi$. If $\rho' = \mathsf{sw}[\rho, s](\bar{\rho})$, we also write $\mathsf{sw}[\rho, s]^{-1}(\rho') = \bar{\rho}$.

Now, given a weak communication-closed adversary a, a path ρ, and a swapping index s for ρ, we define the *swapped adversary* $\mathsf{a}' = \mathsf{swap}[\rho, s](\mathsf{a})$ that, intuitively, will implement the swapping function $\mathsf{sw}[\rho, s]$ over a-induced paths. Formally, for any finite path ρ', the definition distinguishes whether $\rho'_s \equiv \rho_s$, and depends on the length of ρ':

(i) if $|\rho'| < s$, then $\mathsf{a}'(\rho') = \mathsf{a}(\rho')$;
(ii) if $\rho'_s \not\equiv_w \rho_s$ and $|\rho'| \geq s$, then $\mathsf{a}'(\rho') = \mathsf{a}(\rho')$;
(iii) if $\rho'_s \equiv_w \rho_s$ and $|\rho'| = s$, then

$$
\mathsf{a}'(\rho') = choice[\rho'](reveal[\mathsf{a}](\rho_{s+1}));
$$

(iv) if $\rho'_s \equiv_w \rho_s$ and $|\rho'| = s+1$, then

$$
\mathsf{a}'(\rho') = choice[\rho'](reveal[\mathsf{a}](\rho_s));
$$

(v) if $\rho'_s \equiv_w \rho_s$ and $|\rho'| \geq s+2$, then

$$
\mathsf{a}'(\rho') = choice[\rho'](reveal[\mathsf{a}](\mathsf{sw}[\rho, s]^{-1}(\rho'))).
$$

Let us give some intuition on the definition of the swapped adversary $\mathsf{swap}[\rho, s](\mathsf{a})$. Cases (i) and (ii) concern paths that are not involved in the swapping: either they are shorter than the position s at which the swap occurs, or their prefix of length s is not weakly-equivalent to the one of ρ. In these easy cases, $\mathsf{a}' = \mathsf{swap}[\rho, s](\mathsf{a})$ is defined as a. Case (iii) applies to all paths of length s that are weakly-equivalent to ρ_s, and the goal is to define $\mathsf{swap}[\rho, s](\mathsf{a})$ so that it selects action α_{s+1}. However, under a and $\mathsf{swap}[\rho, s](\mathsf{a})$, the identities of messages may be different along paths (and their extensions) that are equivalent to ρ_s. We thus need to use the $reveal[\mathsf{a}]$ and $choice[\_]$ functions to define that the action prescribed by $\mathsf{swap}[\rho, s](\mathsf{a})$ is α_{s+1}. Case (iv) applies to paths of length $s+1$, whose prefix of length s is weakly-equivalent to ρ_s. For them, the decision $\mathsf{swap}[\rho, s](\mathsf{a})$ should results in action α_s. Finally, (v) deals with longer paths, for which a and $\mathsf{swap}[\rho, s](\mathsf{a})$ take the same decisions, up to the renaming of message identities, and the earlier swapping of α_s and α_{s+1}.

Excerpts of the Markov chains $\mathcal{M}_{\mathsf{a}}^{\sigma_0}$ and $\mathcal{M}_{\mathsf{a}'}^{\sigma_0}$ in Fig. 3 illustrate the transformation to the swapped adversary. Observe that swapping α_s and α_{s+1} relies on the fact that a is weak. Indeed, the same action α_{s+1} applies after α_s even if α_s induces a non-Dirac distribution. Observe that $\mathsf{swap}[\rho, s](\mathsf{a})$ is still a weak adversary, since it is defined uniformly over weakly-equivalent paths.

Adversaries a and $\mathsf{swap}[\rho, s](\mathsf{a})$ are tightly related. First, the successor configurations in two steps after a path $\rho' \equiv_w \rho_s$ are the same, and they have the same probabilities to happen. Second, the Markov chains from these points are identical. Finally the probabilities of $\mathsf{LTL\_X}$ formulas are preserved.

Proposition 1. *Let* a *be a weak communication-closed adversary,* ρ *an* a-*induced path and* s *a swapping index. Then, the swapped adversary* $\mathsf{a}' = \mathsf{swap}[\rho, s](\mathsf{a})$ *is again a weak communication-closed adversary, and it satisfies:*

1. *for every* $\rho' \equiv_w \rho_s$ *and every* $\sigma \in \Sigma$, *we have*

$$\mathbf{P}_{\mathsf{a}}^{\rho'}(\mathbf{F}^{=2}\sigma) = \mathbf{P}_{\mathsf{a}'}^{\rho'}(\mathbf{F}^{=2}\sigma)$$

2. *for every path* $\bar{\rho}$ *with* $|\bar{\rho}| = s+2$, *we have*

$$\mathcal{M}_{\mathsf{a}}^{\bar{\rho}} = \mathcal{M}_{\mathsf{a}'}^{\mathsf{sw}[\rho, s](\bar{\rho})}$$

3. *for every* $\mathsf{LTL\_X}$ *formula* ψ, *we have*

$$\mathbf{P}_{\mathsf{a}}^{\sigma_0}(\psi) = \mathbf{P}_{\mathsf{a}'}^{\sigma_0}(\psi)$$

Proof. Remark that indeed $\mathsf{swap}[\rho, s](\mathsf{a})$ is weak, because it is defined uniformely for weakly-equivalent paths. It is also communication-closed, as a is.

Let us now prove the three statements.

1. Let $\rho' \equiv_w \rho_s$, and let σ be a configuration with $\mathbf{P}_{\mathsf{a}}^{\rho'}(\mathbf{F}^{=2}\sigma) > 0$. Then there exists an a-induced path $\rho' \alpha_s \sigma_{s+1} \alpha_{s+1} \sigma$ and locations ℓ_s, ℓ_{s+1} such that

$$\sigma_{s+1} = apply(\sigma_s, \alpha_s, \ell_s)$$
$$\sigma = apply(\sigma_{s+1}, \alpha_{s+1}, \ell_{s+1})$$

Let $\bar{\rho} = \mathsf{sw}[\rho, s](\rho' \alpha_s \sigma_{s+1} \alpha_{s+1} \sigma)$. By definition of $\mathsf{swap}[\rho, s](\mathsf{a})$, $\bar{\rho}$ is a path induced by $\mathsf{swap}[\rho, s](\mathsf{a})$, and it ends in σ. More precisely, letting

$$\alpha'_{s+1} = choice[\rho'](reveal[\mathsf{a}](\rho'))$$
$$\sigma'_{s+1} = apply(\sigma_s, \alpha'_{s+1}, \ell_{s+1})$$
$$\alpha'_s = choice[\rho' \alpha'_{s+1} \sigma'_{s+1}](reveal[\mathsf{a}'](\rho' \alpha_s \sigma_{s+1}))$$
$$\sigma'_{s+2} = apply(\sigma'_{s+1}, \alpha'_s, \ell_s)$$

then $\sigma'_{s+2} = \sigma$ and $\bar{\rho} = \rho' \alpha'_{s+1} \sigma'_{s+1} \alpha'_s \sigma$. Thus $\mathbf{P}_{\mathsf{swap}[\rho, s](\mathsf{a})}^{\rho'}(\mathbf{F}^{=2}\sigma) > 0$. Moreover, by commutativity of multiplication, the probabilities of reaching σ in two steps in $\mathcal{M}_{\mathsf{a}}^{\rho'}$ and $\mathcal{M}_{\mathsf{swap}[\rho, s](\mathsf{a})}^{\rho'}$ coincide: they are equal to $\alpha_s.\delta_{to}(\ell_s) \times \alpha_{s+1}.\delta_{to}(\ell_{s+1})$.

2. To prove that the Markov chains after $\bar{\rho}$ of length $s+2$ under a, and the one after $\mathsf{sw}[\rho, s](\bar{\rho})$ under $\mathsf{swap}[\rho, s](\mathsf{a})$ are equal, we observe that, for paths longer than $s+2$,

$$\mathsf{a}'(\rho') = choice[\rho'](reveal[\mathsf{a}](\mathsf{sw}[\rho, s]^{-1}(\rho'))).$$

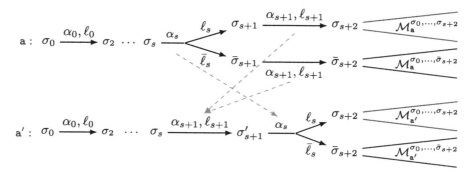

Fig. 3. Parts of Markov chains $\mathcal{M}_{\mathsf{a}}^{\sigma_0}$ (above) and $\mathcal{M}_{\mathsf{a}'}^{\sigma_0}$ (below) following Proposition 1. We assume here α_s is a non-Dirac action with two destination locations ℓ_s and $\bar{\ell}_s$, and α_{s+1} is a Dirac action with destination location ℓ_{s+1}. If some of actions $\alpha_0, \ldots, \alpha_{s-1}$ are non-Dirac, we omit drawing branches that are irrelevant for Proposition 1. Note that $reveal[\mathsf{a}](\sigma_0, \ldots, \sigma_{s+1})$ and $reveal[\mathsf{a}](\sigma_0, \ldots, \bar{\sigma}_{s+1})$ must be the same action α_{s+1}, as a is a weak adversary. This is the key insight that allows swapping, which would not be possible for a strong adversary with $reveal[\mathsf{a}](\sigma_0, \ldots, \sigma_{s+1}) \neq reveal[\mathsf{a}](\sigma_0, \ldots, \bar{\sigma}_{s+1})$.

This is (v) in the definition of $\mathsf{swap}[\rho, s](\mathsf{a})$, and also applies if $\rho' \not\equiv_w \rho_s$, in which case $\mathsf{sw}[\rho, s]^{-1}(\rho') = \rho'$. In words, $\mathsf{swap}[\rho, s](\mathsf{a})$ consists in applying a on the reverse swapped path. Therefore, the subsequent Markov chains are equal, as illustrated on Fig. 3.

3. Finally, to prove that the probabilities of $\mathsf{LTL_{-X}}$ formulas are preserved, we argue that $\mathcal{M}_{\mathsf{a}}^{\sigma_0}$ and $\mathcal{M}_{\mathsf{swap}[\rho, s](\mathsf{a})}^{\sigma_0}$ are essentially the same, up to the swapping of some paths at positions s and $s+1$. Remember that they both are tree-shaped. First, they are equal up to depth s. Then item (i) shows that the successors from depth s in two steps are the same, and they happen with same probabilities. Last, item (ii) shows that the subsequent Markov chains are identical. To conclude, we use Lemma 3 to justify that even if actions are swapped at positions s and $s+1$, they satisfy the same $\mathsf{LTL_{-X}}$ formulas.

$\square$

Theorem 2. *For every weak communication-closed adversary* a *under which every round terminates, there exists a weak round-rigid adversary* a' *such that for every $\mathsf{LTL_{-X}}$ formula ψ we have* $\mathbf{P}_{\mathsf{a}}^{\sigma_0}(\psi) = \mathbf{P}_{\mathsf{a}'}^{\sigma_0}(\psi)$.

Proof (sketch). Theorem 2 is obtained by applying iteratively Proposition 1 to consecutive actions that are in reverse order. Since every round is assumed to terminate under a, one can start by moving towards the beginning all actions of round 1 that happen after actions of later rounds; then one swaps all actions of round 2, and so on, to obtain in the limit a weak adversary which is round-rigid.

5   Conclusions

Parameterized verification of safety and almost sure termination of a class of distributed consensus algorithms [4,7,17,18] has been recently considered in [5]. For almost sure termination, the authors limited themselves to so-called "round-rigid" adversaries, which were introduced by the authors for that purpose. Verification under these adversaries was reduced to verification of specifications in a linear temporal logic that can be checked (within a few minutes) with the ByMC model checker [14].

In this paper, we have shown that automated verification under weak adversaries can be reduced to verification of round-rigid adversaries. More precisely, in order to verify randomized distributed algorithms under weak adversaries, one only needs to verify their behavior under round-rigid adversaries, which has been done in [5] for various randomized consensus algorithms. In order to define weak adversaries, we were forced to reason within a system model with semantics that explicitly talks about processes with IDs and messages. In contrast, the standard semantics of threshold automata, namely, counter systems is used in [5] and in ByMC. For a complete chain of proof we would need to connect process-based semantics to counter systems. This is a rather standard technical argument so that we do not give it here. From a theoretical viewpoint we find our reduction from weak adversaries to round-rigid adversaries more interesting: reductions for concurrent distributed systems is typically done for reachability properties [10,12,16] or linear temporal properties [8,9,13]. As a result, the reduction argument is conducted on traces generated by the system: one shows that by swapping transitions in a trace we arrive at another, yet "simpler" trace of the system. In this paper, we lifted this reasoning from traces to computation trees and MDPs which shows that reductions are not only efficient in non-deterministic systems but also in probabilistic systems defined by distributed algorithms. This mirrors the recent "synchronizing" trend in the verification of non-deterministic fault-tolerant distributed algorithms [5,6,9,11,15], and opens this domain to automated parameterized verification of *randomized* distributed algorithms.

References

1. Aguilera, M., Toueg, S.: The correctness proof of Ben-Or's randomized consensus algorithm. Distrib. Comput. **25**(5), 371–381 (2012)
2. Aspnes, J.: Randomized protocols for asynchronous consensus. Distrib. Comput. **16**(2–3), 165–175 (2003)
3. Baier, C., Katoen, J.P.: Principles of Model Checking. MIT Press, Cambridge (2008)
4. Ben-Or, M.: Another advantage of free choice: completely asynchronous agreement protocols (extended abstract). In: PODC, pp. 27–30 (1983)
5. Bertrand, N., Konnov, I., Lazic, M., Widder, J.: Verification of randomized consensus algorithms under round-rigid adversaries. In: CONCUR. LIPIcs, vol. 140, pp. 33:1–33:15 (2019)

6. Bouajjani, A., Enea, C., Ji, K., Qadeer, S.: On the completeness of verifying message passing programs under bounded asynchrony. In: CAV, pp. 372–391 (2018)
7. Bracha, G.: Asynchronous Byzantine agreement protocols. Inf. Comput. **75**(2), 130–143 (1987)
8. Chaouch-Saad, M., Charron-Bost, B., Merz, S.: A reduction theorem for the verification of round-based distributed algorithms. In: Bournez, O., Potapov, I. (eds.) RP 2009. LNCS, vol. 5797, pp. 93–106. Springer, Heidelberg (2009). https://doi.org/10.1007/978-3-642-04420-5_10
9. Damian, A., Drăgoi, C., Militaru, A., Widder, J.: Communication-closed asynchronous protocols. In: Dillig, I., Tasiran, S. (eds.) CAV 2019. LNCS, vol. 11562, pp. 344–363. Springer, Cham (2019). https://doi.org/10.1007/978-3-030-25543-5_20
10. Elrad, T., Francez, N.: Decomposition of distributed programs into communication-closed layers. Sci. Comput. Program. **2**(3), 155–173 (1982)
11. Gleissenthall, K., Gökhan Kici, R., Bakst, A., Stefan, D., Jhala, R.: Pretend synchrony. In: POPL, pp. 59:1–59:30 (2019)
12. Konnov, I., Lazic, M., Veith, H., Widder, J.: Para^2: Parameterized path reduction, acceleration, and SMT for reachability in threshold-guarded distributed algorithms. Formal Methods Syst. Des. **51**(2), 270–307 (2017)
13. Konnov, I., Lazić, M., Veith, H., Widder, J.: A short counterexample property for safety and liveness verification of fault-tolerant distributed algorithms. In: POPL, pp. 719–734 (2017)
14. Konnov, I., Widder, J.: ByMC: Byzantine model checker. In: Margaria, T., Steffen, B. (eds.) ISoLA 2018. LNCS, vol. 11246, pp. 327–342. Springer, Cham (2018). https://doi.org/10.1007/978-3-030-03424-5_22
15. Kragl, B., Qadeer, S., Henzinger, T.A.: Synchronizing the asynchronous. In: CONCUR. LIPIcs, vol. 118, pp. 21:1–21:17 (2018)
16. Lipton, R.J.: Reduction: a method of proving properties of parallel programs. Commun. ACM **18**(12), 717–721 (1975)
17. Mostéfaoui, A., Moumen, H., Raynal, M.: Randomized k-set agreement in crash-prone and Byzantine asynchronous systems. Theoretical Comput. Sci. **709**, 80–97 (2018)
18. Song, Y.J., van Renesse, R.: Bosco: one-step Byzantine asynchronous consensus. In: Taubenfeld, G. (ed.) DISC 2008. LNCS, vol. 5218, pp. 438–450. Springer, Heidelberg (2008). https://doi.org/10.1007/978-3-540-87779-0_30

Abstract Interpretation and Model Checking

Runtime Abstract Interpretation for Numerical Accuracy and Robustness

Franck Védrine[1], Maxime Jacquemin[1],
Nikolai Kosmatov[1,2(✉)] ,
and Julien Signoles[1]

[1] Université Paris-Saclay, CEA, List,
Palaiseau, France
{franck.vedrine,maxime.jacquemin,
julien.signoles}@cea.fr
[2] Thales Research and Technology, Palaiseau, France
nikolaikosmatov@gmail.com

Abstract. Verification of numerical accuracy properties in modern software remains an important and challenging task. One of its difficulties is related to unstable tests, where the execution can take different branches for real and floating-point numbers. This paper presents a new verification technique for numerical properties, named Runtime Abstract Interpretation (RAI), that, given an annotated source code, embeds into it an abstract analyzer in order to analyze the program behavior at runtime. RAI is a hybrid technique combining abstract interpretation and runtime verification that aims at being sound as the former while taking benefit from the concrete run to gain greater precision from the latter when necessary. It solves the problem of unstable tests by surrounding an unstable test by two carefully defined program points, forming a so-called split-merge section, for which it separately analyzes different executions and merges the computed domains at the end of the section. Our implementation of this technique in a toolchain called FLDBox relies on two basic tools, FLDCompiler, that performs a source-to-source transformation of the given program and defines the split-merge sections, and an instrumentation library FLDLib that provides necessary primitives to explore relevant (partial) executions of each section and propagate accuracy properties. Initial experiments show that the proposed technique can efficiently and soundly analyze numerical accuracy for industrial programs on thin numerical scenarios.

1 Introduction

Verification of numerical accuracy properties of critical software is an important and complex task. In programs with floating-point operations, the results of computations are approximated with respect to ideal computations on real numbers [30]. An accumulation of rounding errors can result in costly or even

F. Henglein et al. (Eds.): VMCAI 2021, LNCS 12597, pp. 243–266, 2021.
https://doi.org/10.1007/978-3-030-67067-2_12

disastrous bugs[1,2,3]. Therefore, verifying that such behaviors do not happen, and so that *accuracy properties* do hold, is of the utmost importance. It remains a challenging research problem [28] for both dynamic and static analysis.

Abstract interpretation [8] and runtime verification [18] are two well-established program analysis techniques for verifying program properties. The former is a static technique that soundly over-approximates the program behaviors in order to verify at compile time that all of them satisfy some property of interest $\mathcal{P}$, while the latter is a dynamic technique that monitors a concrete execution in order to check that this execution satisfies $\mathcal{P}$ at runtime. Both techniques have many successful applications [5,33], but suffer from intrinsic limitations: abstract interpretation may be too slow and imprecise to be tractable, while runtime verification cannot soundly reason about all possible executions and may have a hard time dealing with properties that rely on non-executable models (e.g. real numbers) or several execution traces.

This paper presents a new verification technique for verifying numerical accuracy properties, named *Runtime Abstract Interpretation (RAI)*, as a hybrid verification technique combining abstract interpretation and runtime verification. Similar to [12] and modern symbolic execution tools [6], the main idea of RAI is to turn a given program into an abstract interpreter for that program, following—in the simplest case—the same control-flow structure. It replaces (i) concrete values by abstract values in an abstract domain and (ii) concrete floating-point operations and comparisons by abstract transformers and predicates. By embedding an abstract interpretation engine into a runtime program execution, it aims at being sound as the former while taking benefit from the concrete run to retrieve the precision of the latter (even if the execution context is unknown at compile time, e.g. in the presence of numerical inputs from an external database). It can also take into account uncertainty of program inputs (e.g. coming from sensors), providing guarantees on their *robustness* [22].

The main difficulty of numerical property verification consists in handling unstable tests in a sound way. Indeed, an *unstable test* happens for instance when the guard of a conditional statement depends on a floating-point expression and can be evaluated to a boolean value different from the one relying on the real values. For example, if we have x∈ [0.9, 1.1] (e.g. due to input uncertainty or rounding errors) before the statement if(x<1.0)...else..., the theoretical execution for the exact (real) value can follow the then branch, while the machine (floating-point) values can lead to the else branch. In such a case, the program execution flow diverges from the theoretical one in real numbers. For a sound analysis of the program, both branches should be considered and a possible imprecision of variables in the rest of the program should be computed comparing different control flows. Some tools [14,21,39] can soundly support unstable tests, but do not scale to large industrial code with >10,000 LOC.

---

[1] http://www-users.math.umn.edu/arnold/disasters/patriot.html.

[2] https://en.wikipedia.org/wiki/Vancouver_Stock_Exchange.

[3] http://www-users.math.umn.edu/arnold/disasters/sleipner.html.

RAI solves this issue by surrounding an unstable test by two carefully defined program points, *split* and *merge*, delimiting a so-called *split-merge section*, for which it separately analyzes different executions and soundly merges the computed abstract values at the end of the section. To make the technique efficient, the (partial) executions of the section are enumerated and separately analyzed only within the section itself, without repeating each time a common execution prefix and suffix before and after the section, thanks to storing and retrieving the context at the split point. A split-merge section is defined as the smallest part of the program that suits the analysis goals, while the lists of variables to save and to merge are carefully minimized. To further reduce repeated execution segments, split-merge sections can be nested: the section defined for some unstable test can be a strict subset of that for another test.

We have implemented FLDBox, a prototype RAI toolchain for verifying numerical accuracy and robustness properties on C code. Numerical properties can be specified using a set of dedicated primitives, or more generally, as annotations in the ACSL specification language [2], which are then translated into instrumented C code using these primitives by the (existing) runtime assertion checker E-ACSL [37] recently extended for their support [25]. The main steps of FLDBox rely on two new tools, FLDCompiler, that defines the split-merge sections, and an instrumentation library FLDLib[4], that provides necessary primitives to explore partial executions of a section and propagate accuracy properties. Each component can be used separately, or can be easily replaced. For instance, it is possible to replace FLDLib by Cadna [23] to obtain accuracy verification by stochastic propagation instead of conservative propagation. We have evaluated FLDBox on several small-size numerical C programs, and on two industrial case studies of synchronous reactive systems of several dozens of thousands of lines of code. The results show that the proposed technique can efficiently and soundly analyze numerical accuracy for industrial programs on *thin numerical scenarios* (where each input is replaced by a small interval of values around it).

Summary of Contributions:

- a *new hybrid verification technique*, named Runtime Abstract Interpretation, for *verifying numerical accuracy and robustness properties*, that embeds an abstract interpreter into the code and relies on split-merge sections;
- a *modular prototype implementation* of RAI, called FLDBox, based on two main components: FLDCompiler and FLDLib;
- an *empirical evaluation* of the whole FLDBox toolchain on representative programs, including industrial case studies (artifact available at [42]).

2   Motivating Numerical Example

Floating-point operations approximate ideal computations on real numbers [30] and, therefore, can introduce rounding errors. Accuracy properties express that

---

[4]   The source code of FLDLib is available at https://github.com/fvedrine/fldlib.

these errors stay in acceptable bounds. Robustness of the system means that a small perturbation of the inputs (e.g. due to possible sensor imprecision [22]) will cause only small perturbations on its outputs.

Consider for instance the C function of Fig. 1. It implements an interpolation table tbl composed of n measures for linear approximation of a continuous function on a point in $\in [0, n-1]$. Such tables are quite common in numerical analysis. We are interested in two properties:

accuracy: the round-off error of the result (out) increases the imprecision of the input (in) by at most twice the biggest difference between two consecutive measures of the table;

robustness: the previous property is satisfied not only for every concrete input value in, but also near it, in $[\text{in} - \varepsilon, \text{in} + \varepsilon]$, for a given small $\varepsilon > 0$.

```
1   double interpolate(double *tbl, int n, double in) {
2      double out;
3      int idx = (int) in; // truncation to an integer
4      if (idx < 0 || idx >= n-1) // out-of-bound values
5         out = (idx < 0) ? tbl[0] : tbl[n-1];
6      else // computation from the two closest integer values
7         out = tbl[idx] + (in - idx) * (tbl[idx+1] - tbl[idx]);
8      return out;
9   }
```

Fig. 1. Motivating example: an interpolation table.

The first property will be (more precisely) expressed by the assertion of Fig. 4, as we will explain in Sec. 3. Both properties are verified for in $\in [0, n-1]$, but fail for values around -1. Indeed, for two close values -1 and $-1 + \varepsilon$ of in (with a small $\varepsilon > 0$), idx is equal to -1 and 0 respectively. Therefore the result out is equal to tbl[0] and tbl[0]$+(-1+\varepsilon)\times$(tbl[1]$-$tbl[0]) $\approx 2\times$tbl[0]$-$tbl[1] respectively: that is an obvious discontinuity. Any tool checking this property should raise an alarm if (and, optimally, only if) such an input is encountered.

Numerical analysis of a complex computation-intensive industrial application (typically, >10,000 lines of code) for the whole set of possible inputs is not feasible in the majority of cases. A suitable numerical property can be complex to define (and even in this example, the property above should be slightly corrected to become true, as we explain in Sect. 3). Expressing such properties for a large interval of values (like the interval in $\in [0, n-1]$ in our example) is not always possible (e.g. for more complex properties or functions) or not sufficient to ensure the desired precision (e.g. on irregularly-spaced interpolation data when the table entries become greater on some sub-intervals while a more precise estimate is required for other sub-intervals, or in the presence of singularities). A more precise estimate can often be found on smaller intervals (as we will illustrate on Fig. 6 in Sect. 4.2).

In practice, industrial engineers often seek to ensure accuracy and robustness properties by considering a rich test suite and by replacing in each test case the concrete value of each input variable by an interval around this concrete value, thus creating a *thin numerical scenario* from the test case. This approach allows engineers to check accuracy and robustness on such thin scenarios, better understand the numerical properties of the program, and possibly prepare their later proof if it is required. The purpose of the present work is to provide a practical and sound technique for this goal.

Dynamic analysis tools cannot soundly assess robustness and accuracy for an interval of values because they do not reason on intervals and can only check properties for a specific execution with given concrete inputs *(Issue 1)*, and because of unstable tests, like at lines 3–4: the branch taken at runtime for machine values may be different from the theoretical execution with real numbers. The imprecision of computation of `in` (prior to the call to this function) could lead to executing, say, the positive branch at runtime while the negative branch should be executed in real numbers *(Issue 2a)*.

Abstract interpreters may have a hard time dealing with (possibly, nested) unstable tests [22,39] *(Issue 2b)*. They also hardly keep precise relationships between variables, e.g. between `idx` and `in` after the truncation from `double` to `int` at line 3. That usually leads to imprecise analysis results *(Issue 3)*. In addition, a practical abstract interpreter usually requires to stub input-output (I/O) functions such as communications with the environment in order to model possible behaviors outside the analysis scope *(Issue 4)*. In our example, the interpolation table values can be read during system initialization from a file by another function, like we often observed in industrial code.

Last but not least, the user needs to express the accuracy properties in a formal way and the analysis tools need to understand them. For that purpose, a formal specification language for numerical properties is required *(Issue 5)*.

In this paper, we propose a new hybrid verification technique for verifying accuracy and robustness properties, named Runtime Abstract Interpretation (RAI), embedding an abstract interpretation engine into the code, where:

- a dedicated extension of a formal specification language solves Issue 5 (Sect.4.1);
- relying on concrete runs solves Issue 4, with two possibilities: either by taking the concrete values from the environment (when these values are known to be fixed) or by defining value and error intervals for them (when not fixed);
- Issue 3 is solved since the relations between variables are implicitly kept by the execution flow, while the RAI toolchain automatically replaces the concrete floating-point values and operations by their abstract counterparts that soundly take into account round-off errors (Sect. 4.2);
- representing concrete values by abstract ones solves Issue 1;
- analyzing possible executions solves Issues 2a and 2b (Sect. 4.3).

3 Overview of Runtime Abstract Interpretation

Figure 2 describes the whole process of RAI. **Bold** font shows the main steps and elements (detailed in Sect. 4) that we have designed from scratch or extended from earlier work. We illustrate these steps for the function `abs` of Fig. 5a.

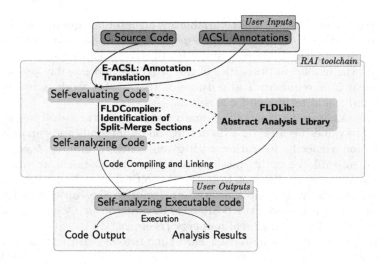

Fig. 2. Principle of Runtime Abstract Interpretation.

A key element of our RAI toolchain FLDBox is FLDLib, the Abstract Analysis Library (presented in Sect. 4.2). It implements (in C++) the required primitives of the analyzer (e.g. abstract domain types, transfer functions, join operators of abstract domains, split and merge instructions). Its implementation is eventually linked to the user code to produce a Self-Analyzing Executable Code, but only its API is required at compile time to allow calls to its primitives.

Our RAI toolchain takes as inputs a C source code with formal annotations in the ACSL specification language [2] that express numerical properties to be verified in the code. The first step consists in encoding the annotations as additional source code in order to evaluate them at runtime. It produces an instrumented code, that we call here Self-evaluating Code. This step is performed by the pre-existing runtime assertion checker of the Frama-C verification platform [24], namely the E-ACSL tool [16,37], that we have extended to support the target numerical properties (cf. Sect. 4.1). Alternatively, the user can manually instrument the code with property checking instructions using primitives provided by FLDLib.

For example, the assertion on lines 27–29 of Fig. 5a (stating that the absolute error x_e of x at that point is between the given bounds) will be translated by E-ACSL into C code using the corresponding primitive (`accuracy_assert_ferr`) of FLDLib. For short, we will give a pseudo-code translation on line 29 of Fig. 5b.

The second step of RAI is performed by FLDCompiler that embeds an abstract analyzer into the code by extending the behavior of all numerical operations. It leads to Self-analyzing code (in C++) able to analyze the target annotations in addition to the normal code behavior. For that purpose, the **double** and **float** types are overloaded and become abstract domains represented by struct types. So, a variable **float** x becomes a tuple of abstract values $x = (x_\mathrm{r}, x_\mathrm{f}, x_\mathrm{e}, x_\mathrm{rel})$

whose elements represent the ideal (real) domain x_r, the machine (floating-point) domain x_f, the absolute error domain x_e, and the relative error domain x_rel. Numerical comparisons and operations are overloaded to soundly propagate these domains (cf. Sect. 4.2). To handle unstable tests, FLDCompiler defines split-merge sections allowing the analyzer to run some execution segments several times when it is necessary to relate machine and real values of diverging executions (cf. Sect. 4.3).

For the example of Fig. 5a, FLDCompiler inserts split and merge instructions on lines 8 and 23 in order to surround the unstable test on line 14 and allow the analyzer to re-execute the code between them when necessary. Let $b^\mathrm{r}, b^\mathrm{f}$ denote the branches (i.e. the truth values of b) executed, resp., for a real and a machine value of x. Basically, RAI *partitions* the domain of values of x into four subsets such that $(b^\mathrm{r}, b^\mathrm{f}) = (0,0)$, $(0,1)$, $(1,0)$ or $(1,1)$. The corresponding execution paths within the limits of the section are analyzed separately for each subset, and the results are soundly merged at the end of the section. For example, the subset $(b^\mathrm{r}, b^\mathrm{f}) = (1,0)$ is here defined by $x_\mathrm{r} < 0, x_\mathrm{f} \geq 0$. For this subset the section will be executed twice: once forcing the true branch $b = 1$ to compute the expected real domain, and once forcing the false branch $b = 0$ to compute the resulting machine domain, both being needed to soundly merge the results and compute errors. If another unstable test is met inside the section, the tool (dynamically) partitions the current subset into smaller subsets to explore relevant execution flows for the domains of values that do lead to these flows. Broadly inspired by dynamic symbolic execution [6,7] (but more complex in our case due to the need of soundly merging/re-slitting subexecutions to make the approach efficient), this exploration is the most technical part of the contribution. Its main ideas will be presented below in Sect. 4.3 using Fig. 5b, the source code being available online.

The third step of RAI is "compile & link" using a standard C++ compiler. It embeds the abstract analysis primitives' code into the final executable. Its execution performs the analysis, evaluates the annotations and produces the code output as if executed in a normal way, without RAI. If an annotation fails, the failure can be reported and, if desired, the execution can be aborted.

4 The RAI Technique in More Detail

4.1 Primitives to Express Numerical Properties

We rely on (a rich, executable subset of) the ACSL specification language [2,35] to express accuracy properties on C programs. It is a powerful language, well supported by the Frama-C [24] platform. Among others, it comes with a runtime assertion checker, named E-ACSL [37], that converts the formal annotations into C code to check them at runtime.

Specification. ACSL annotations are logical properties enclosed in special comments /*@...*/. They include pre-/postconditions and assertions that may be written before any C instruction. They can contain logical functions, predicates and comparison operators over terms. All constants and numerical operators

Built-in name	: type
accuracy_get_[f,d][rel]err	$: \mathbb{F} \to \mathbb{Q}^2$
accuracy_get_[f,d]real	$: \mathbb{F} \to \mathbb{Q}^2$
accuracy_get_[f,d]impl	$: \mathbb{F} \to \mathbb{Q}^2$
accuracy_enlarge_[f,d]val_err:	$\mathbb{F} \times \mathbb{Q}^4 \to$ bool
accuracy_assert_[f,d][rel]err	$: \mathbb{F} \times \mathbb{Q}^2 \to$ bool
[f,d]print	$: \mathbb{F} \to$ bool

Fig. 3. Numerical built-ins extending ACSL. The first three lines are logic functions, while the others are predicates. Their counterparts exist in FLDLib.

```
1   /*@ assert
2       \let (err_min, err_max) = accuracy_get_derr(in);   // primitive
3       \let cst = max_distance(tbl, n);                   // logic function
4       \let (val_min, val_max) = accuracy_get_dimpl(out); // primitive
5       \let bound = max(-val_min, val_max);               // logic function
6       accuracy_assert_derr(out,
7           -2.0 * cst * max(-err_min, err_max) - 1e-16 * bound,
8           +2.0 * cst * max(-err_min, err_max) + 1e-16 * bound); */
```

Fig. 4. ACSL assertion expressing—more precisely—the accuracy property of Sec. 2 for the function of Fig. 1.

are over mathematical numbers (integers in $\mathbb{Z}$, or rationals in $\mathbb{Q}$, depending on the context). C integers and floating-point values are implicitly coerced to their mathematical counterparts.

To express numerical properties, we have extended ACSL with a rich set of numerical built-ins presented in Fig. 3, in which $\mathbb{F}$ denotes either type float (if f) or double (if d). These primitives have their C counterparts supported by the FLDLib library. The two built-ins starting with accuracy_enlarge enlarge the intervals of values and the absolute errors to the two pairs of bounds provided as arguments. The accuracy_assert built-ins check whether the absolute or (if rel is indicated) the relative error is included within the given bounds. The accuracy_get_[rel]err built-ins return the lower and upper bounds of the absolute or relative error, while the accuracy_get_real/impl built-ins return the bounds of the real-number or implementation domain. The last built-ins print the FLDLib representation (x_r, x_f, x_e, x_{rel}) of a floating-point variable x. Thanks to these built-ins, numerical properties can be easily expressed in ACSL.

A simple ACSL assertion, stating that the absolute error is in the provided bounds, is given on lines 27–29 of Fig. 5a. As another example, the accuracy property stated in Sect. 2 for the program of Fig. 1 can be expressed—more precisely—by the assertion of Fig. 4. Here, the logic function max_distance computes the maximal distance between two successive elements of y, that is, $\max_{i=0,\dots,n-2} |y[i+1] - y[i]|$. Lines 4–5 compute the upper bound for $|\text{out}|$, which is used in the last terms on lines 7–8, added to take into account a small round-off error from the addition operation on line 7 in Fig. 1. This correction illustrates the difficulty to define correct error bounds for machine computation.

Robustness follows from this assertion: a small input error leads to a small output error.

Encoding for Runtime Checking. We have extended the E-ACSL tool in two ways to support numerical properties. First, the numerical built-ins of Fig. 3 are directly compiled into their FLDLib counterparts. Second, since the ACSL specification language relies on mathematical integers and rational numbers, the generated code cannot soundly use standard C operators over integral or floating-point types. Instead, E-ACSL generates special code relying on GMP library[5] to soundly represent mathematical integers and rationals. This translation has been optimized to rely on the machine representation as much as possible, when the values fit it, and generate GMP code only when necessary. This second extension was presented in [25] and is outside of the main scope of this paper.

4.2 Propagating Abstract Values at Runtime

As the design of RAI is very technical, the following presentation focuses on the key design ideas illustrated by Fig. 5 that provides a (simplified pseudo-code) version of the resulting Self-analyzing Code for function **abs**. The reader can refer to the open-source code of FLDLib for more detail.

FLDLib is an open-source instrumentation library that infers accuracy properties over C or C++ code. It implements numerical abstract domains inspired by those implemented in the close-source tool Fluctuat [21]. Since these domains themselves are not a key contribution of this paper, we present them briefly.

FLDLib only deals with detecting numerical errors and computing domains of numerical variables. Discrete values (pointers included) are only enumerated. In particular, it has no pointer analysis. Therefore, it is better used on *thin scenarios* that encompass concrete test cases in small intervals. In such scenarios, pointers have only one or two possible value(s). This way, RAI scales to large numerical codes or pieces of code inside bigger developments ($>10,000$ lines of code).

Domains. FLDLib domains combine intervals and *zonotopes* [20]. Zonotopes allow to maintain linear relationships between program variables V that share the same perturbations (noise symbols) by mapping V to affine forms. Sharing noise symbols between variables helps at keeping precise information since it means that the source of uncertainty is the same. We do not detail the zonotope domain here for lack of space, but Fig. 6 illustrates the benefits of combining zonotopes and intervals, in particular with a domain subdivision. For instance, if $x \in [0,1]$, an interval is more precise than a zonotope for representing x^2 (providing an interval $x^2 \in [0,1]$ instead of $[-0.25,1]$, cf. the projection of abstractions onto the $x \times x$ axis in Fig. 6a), but less precise for representing $x - x^2$ ($[-1,1]$ instead of $[0,0.25]$, cf. the distance from the diagonal in Fig. 6a). The intersection of both abstractions provides more precise results (Fig. 6b). A subdivision of the input interval into two sub-intervals significantly improves the results

---

[5] https://gmplib.org/.

(a)

```
1 float abs(float x) {
2
3
4
5
6 // Here FLDCompiler
7 // will insert:
8 // split(x);
9
10
11
12
13
14   int b = (x < 0);
15   if (b) {
16     x = -x;
17   }
18
19
20
21 // Here FLDCompiler
22 // will insert:
23 // merge(x);
24
25
26 // Will be translated to C by E-ACSL:
27 /*@ assert
28     accuracy_assert_ferr(x,
29     -1e-5, 1e-5);*/
30   return x;
31 }
```

(b)

```
1 float abs(float_fld x){//x = (xr,xf,xe) =(real,float,error)
2   int bʳ, bᶠ, bᵉˣᵉᶜ;
3   float_fld xˢᵃᵛᵉ, xᵐᵉʳᵍᵉᵈ, xᵗᵐᵖ;
4   xˢᵃᵛᵉ = x;  // store init. domains at split-merge section entry
5   xᵐᵉʳᵍᵉᵈ = (⊥,⊥,⊥);  // set merged domains to empty
6   // fix branches taken for real and machine values:
7   for (bʳ,bᶠ ∈ {0,1}){
8     xᵗᵐᵖ = (⊥,⊥,⊥);  // store empty domains in xᵗᵐᵖ
9     for (bᵉˣᵉᶜ ∈ {bʳ,bᶠ}){  // fix the branch bᵉˣᵉᶜ to follow now
10       x = xˢᵃᵛᵉ;  // start each execution from initial domains
11       // reduce domains to execute the chosen branches bʳ,bᶠ:
12       if (bʳ)  Assume(xᵣ < 0)  else  Assume(xᵣ ≥ 0);
13       if (bᶠ)  Assume(xf < 0)  else  Assume(xf ≥ 0);
14       int b = bᵉˣᵉᶜ;  // ensure we follow the chosen branch
15       if (b) {  // deduce new domains after num. operations:
16         x = ComputeUnitOp(-,x);  // propagates x = -x;
17       }
18       // if real/machine executions diverge, i.e. bʳ ≠ bᶠ:
19       if (bʳ != bᶠ){  // then merge them separately
20         if (bᵉˣᵉᶜ == bʳ)  xᵣᵗᵐᵖ = Joinᵣ(xᵣᵗᵐᵖ,xᵣ);
21         if (bᵉˣᵉᶜ == bᶠ)  xfᵗᵐᵖ = Joinf(xfᵗᵐᵖ,xf);
22         xₑᵗᵐᵖ = ComputeErr(xᵣᵗᵐᵖ,xfᵗᵐᵖ);
23         x = xᵗᵐᵖ;
24       }
25     }  // end of enumeration of subcases for bᵉˣᵉᶜ ∈ {bʳ,bᶠ}
26     xᵐᵉʳᵍᵉᵈ = Join(xᵐᵉʳᵍᵉᵈ,x);  // merge output variables
27   }  // end of enumeration of possibles cases for bʳ,bᶠ ∈ {0,1}
28   x = xᵐᵉʳᵍᵉᵈ;  // set resulting merged domains
29   assert (-10⁻⁵ ≤ xₑ ≤ 10⁻⁵);  // translated ACSL assert
30   return x;
31 }
```

Fig. 5. (a) Function **abs** with an assertion and a split-merge section to be inserted by FLDCompiler, and (b) the resulting (simplified) Self-analyzing Code for RAI. For simplicity, we omit here the relative error x_{rel} in $x = (x_r, x_f, x_e, x_{\mathrm{rel}})$.

(Fig. 6c,d)—the orange area of Fig. 6d is much less than in Fig. 6b. As mentioned in Sec. 2, using thin scenarios helps to keep precise relationships between variables.

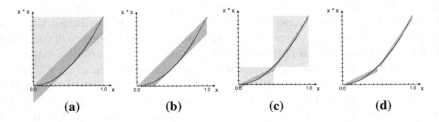

(a)   (b)   (c)   (d)

Fig. 6. Function x^2 abstracted (a) with intervals (yellow) and affine forms (orange) shown separately, and (b) the resulting intersection. The same abstractions with a subdivision, (c) shown separately, and (d) the resulting intersection. (Color figure online)

Type Redefinition and Operation Overloading. A key principle of FLDLib consists in redefining `double` and `float` types and overloading all related operations. The `float` type becomes a structure that is called in this paper `float_fld` (cf. line 1 in Fig. 5a,b). A variable `float x;` becomes a variable `float_fld` x; that, mathematically speaking, contains a tuple of abstract values (x_r, x_f, x_e, x_{rel}) whose elements represent the real domain x_r as a zonotope, the floating-point domain x_f as an interval, the absolute error domain x_e as a zonotope, and the relative error domain x_{rel} as an interval. For simplicity, we omit the relative error computation in our examples.

Like Cadna [23] (for an execution with concrete values), FLDLib uses C++ operator overloading to propagate these domains over the program execution (with abstract values). All arithmetic operations and comparisons, as well as casts from floating-point to integral types are redefined as abstract transformers.

For instance, the unary operation assignment `x = -x;` can be replaced in the resulting Self-analyzing Code as a primitive $x = ComputeUnitOp(-, x)$; (cf. line 16 in Fig. 5a,b) that computes the resulting abstract values of the components of x after the operation. Similarly, a binary operation `x = x + y;` is replaced by a primitive $x = ComputeBinOp(+, x, y)$;. Such abstract operations (transfer functions) are well-known and we do not detail them here.

In addition to abstract versions of all numerical operations, FLDLib provides other useful primitives for constraint propagation. In the (simplified) examples of this paper, we also use a primitive $Assume(\texttt{<cond>})$ to assume a condition (and propagate it to all relevant domains), a primitive $Join(x', x'')$ to merge (join) the domains coming from different execution paths, its variants $Join_r(x'_r, x''_r)$ and $Join_f(x'_f, x''_f)$ to merge the domains for real or machine numbers only, and $ComputeErr(x_r, x_f)$ to compute a new error (e.g. after such a separate merge).

Operator overloading is particularly convenient in our context since it limits necessary source-to-source transformations. We also have promising initial experiments on Ada programs that support operator overloading through the libadalang library[6]. A similar approach could be applied to C programs with no operator overloading capabilities, where such a transformation can be automatically done e.g. by the Clang compiler.

4.3   Covering All Executions for Unstable Tests

Unstable Tests by Example. The key difficulty of our method is related to unstable tests. For instance, for the conditional at line 15 in Fig. 5a, if the domains and precision of x ensure that both the real number and the machine number satisfy `x<0` and thus execute the same branch (b = 1), the Self-analyzing Code needs to execute only this branch and perform the analysis (thanks to the overloaded operations) along this path to obtain a sound result. In general, the evaluation of the condition for real numbers (denoted b^r) can lead to the true or false branch (we write $b^r = 1$ or 0, resp.), while the condition for machine numbers (denoted b^f) does not necessarily lead to the same branch. Therefore, the Self-analyzing

---

[6] https://github.com/AdaCore/libadalang.

Code has to consider four cases: $(b^r, b^f) \in \{0,1\}^2$ (cf. line 7 in Fig. 5b) which create a partition of the set of possible values. It analyzes each case separately (saving and restoring initial values, cf. lines 4, 10 in Fig. 5b) and finally merges the results of all cases (cf. lines 5, 26 in Fig. 5b). For each case, the domains are reduced to fit the assumption of the case (cf. lines 12–13 in Fig. 5b) before a new execution starts. The domains of the four cases are indeed different: even if, say, b^f is the same, different assumptions on b^r lead to different domains.

We denote by b^{exec} the branch(es) to be executed in each case. For each of the two cases with $b^r = b^f$ (where real and machine numbers activate the same branch), it is sufficient to execute only that branch, that is, $b^{exec} = b^r = b^f$, since its execution by assumption (and thanks to the overloaded operations) computes both the new real values and the new machine values. However, in each of the two diverging cases (with $b^r \neq b^f$), we need to execute the real value flow (taking $b^{exec} = b^r$) to evaluate the new real values, and the machine value flow (taking $b^{exec} = b^f$) to evaluate the new machine values (cf. lines 9, 14–15 in Fig. 5b). Both subcases are then merged accordingly: real values from the real value branch, machine values from the machine value branch (cf. line 8, 19–24 in Fig. 5b) before being merged as a complete case (cf. line 28 in Fig. 5b). Incomplete data written on lines 22–23 after the first subcase are ignored and overwritten by the second subcase. So, the machine domains coming from the execution for real values ($b^{exec} = b^r$) and the real domains coming from the execution for machine values ($b^{exec} = b^f$) are indeed ignored. Overall, line 15 is executed 6 times.

Assume we have $|x_e| = |x_f - x_r| \leq 10^{-5}$ for the input value. Then the assertion on line 29 will be satisfied. For instance, for the unstable case $b_r = 1$, $b_f = 0$, the *Assume*'s on lines 12–13 reduce domains to $-x_r$, $x_f \in [0, 10^{-5}]$. After executing both subcases, i.e. after lines 20–22 in the second iteration of the internal loop, the RAI computes $x_r^{tmp}, x_f^{tmp} \in [0, 10^{-5}]$, hence $x_e^{tmp} \in [-10^{-5}, 10^{-5}]$. The constraint $x_e \in [-10^{-5}, 10^{-5}]$ being respected in all cases, it remains respected after the merge on line 26. Notice that the execution of the Self-analyzing Code after the merge point continues as a unique execution (unless a subsequent split-merge section splits it again). In this way, RAI reruns the execution segments only when it is necessary for a sound analysis of the program.

Split-Merge Sections. As illustrated by Fig. 5, in order to be sound, RAI encloses each unstable test b within a loop that executes its body several times to analyze all possible cases of evaluation of b for real and machine numbers. FLDBox provides two directives to delimit those loops: split marks the start of a block of code B that must be run multiple times to analyze all possible executions, while merge marks the point of convergence where all memory states after the executions of B must be joined into a unique state. Such a block B enclosed between these directives is called a *split-merge section*. Such sections can include several branches and be nested (for instance, for nested conditional statements). The split-merge directives are provided by FLDLib and inserted into the generated code by FLDCompiler.

In the general case, split is parameterized by the variables that must be restored before a new execution in order to ensure that the initial memory state

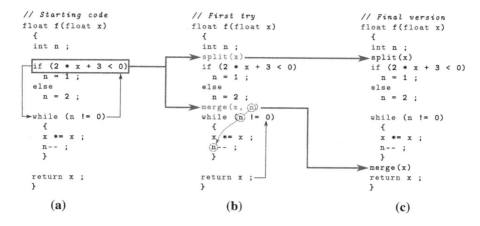

Fig. 7. (a) A code and (b),(c) transformation steps performed by FLDCompiler.

$$save\text{-}list(p) = \{x \mid \exists (s_1, s_2), (x, s_1) \in maydef(p) \land (x, s_2) \in mayref(p)\},$$
$$merge\text{-}list(p) = \{x \mid \exists (s_1, s_2), (x, s_1) \in maydef(p) \land (s_1, s_2, x) \in datadep(\mathcal{F}(p)) \land s_2 \notin p\},$$
where $\mathcal{F}(p)$ is the body of the function containing p.

Fig. 8. Computation of *save-list* and *merge-list*.

is the same at each loop iteration (i.e. each execution of the section runs from the same state), while merge is parameterized by the variables to be joined after different executions. A simple example of a split-merge section is shown in Fig. 5a, where the split and merge directives become, resp., lines 2–13 and 18–28 in Fig. 5b. They are parameterized by x since x must be restored before a new execution (it may have been overwritten by a previous one at line 16) and x is the only section's output to be merged (cf. lines 4, 10, 26 in Fig. 5b).

For the example of Fig. 1, FLDCompiler inserts a split directive with no argument (since in is never overwritten) before the cast at line 3, while a merge directive parameterized by out is inserted before line 8. Indeed, a cast from a floating-point value to an integer is a form of unstable test since the real value can be casted to a different integer than the floating-point one. The merge directive cannot be placed earlier because out would not be computed yet.

Annotation Criteria. FLDCompiler is a source-to-source program transformation that automatically annotates a program with the needed split and merge directives together with their parameters. For the sake of performance and precision, a generated split-merge section should be minimal (as small as possible), split should only restore what is needed, and merge should only join variables that are modified by the section and used afterward. Positioning the split-merge sections is done by a greedy algorithm that expands them through the code until three criteria, presented below, are satisfied. These criteria are illustrated on the example of Fig. 7 that contains the unstable test if(2 * x + 3 < 0).

Criterion 1. *A split must strictly dominate its associated merge. Conversely, a merge must strictly post-dominate its associated split.*

Dominance and post-dominance relations [32] used in this criterion state that all paths that go through split must go through its associated merge and, conversely, all paths that go through merge must have gone through its associated split. This criterion ensures that the memory allocations performed by split are eventually freed by merge. The other way round, the memory freed by merge must have been initially allocated by split. In our example, the if statement is *post-dominated* by the while, which is *dominated* by the if. Therefore, a split (resp. merge) directive is added before the if (resp. while).

Criterion 2. *A split-merge section must start and end in the same block.*

A split-merge section is enclosed in a loop that starts in the part generated by split and ends in the part generated by merge. The criterion must be satisfied to produce a syntactically valid C code, as in Fig. 5a and Fig. 7b,c.

Criterion 3. *Non floating-point variables must be kept unchanged in every memory state generated by a split and joined by its associated merge.*

This criterion is mandatory because the FLDLib library has no abstraction for non floating-point variables: merging them would lead to an error. For example, Fig. 7b presents a first positioning attempt for the split-merge section that actually violates Criterion 3. Indeed, because the value of the integer variable n is modified in the if and is needed after the merge, its values must be joined. To fix this, merge is delayed as shown in Fig. 7c. This criterion enables to prove the robustness propety in our motivating example in Fig. 1 whereas linear domains usually fail at keeping enough relationships between the idx variable and the input in.

In some cases, e.g. when an integer variable depending on the result of an unstable test is part of the outputs of the function, the split-merge section cannot be closed inside the function. In such cases (met only in one industrial example for <10% of unstable tests), the user may need to move the section to the caller(s) to respect this criterion. The user can indeed adjust the split-merge directives manually, e.g. making one section instead of two consecutive sections. This can sometimes increase precision, since domain merging is done later on the path and fewer times, at the cost of increasing the number of paths to analyze and analysis time. A similar observation is true for nested sections: without a nested section inside another one, the analysis can be more precise (with less merges) but can take longer (since more and longer path segments are replayed).

Arguments of split and merge. As said previously, split and merge take parameters that specify, resp., the variables to restore before a new execution of the section, and the ones to be eventually merged after it. To minimize the analysis cost, only necessary parameters should be generated. For example, if a variable is never modified, restoring its value is useless. These parameters for split and merge are respectively computed by a *save-list* and a *merge-list* whose computation is explained below. They are based on a dedicated data dependency analysis inspired from [26]. More precisely, for each statement p, this analysis gathers four sets, informally defined as follows:

***mustdef** (p)*: a set of variables necessarily modified in p (that is, all executions modify them). For instance, variable n of Fig. 7 is in the *mustdef* set of if.

***maydef** (p)*: a set of pairs (x, s) where s is a sub-statement of p that may modify the variable x. In Fig. 7, the *maydef* set of the while loop contains (x, x+=x). However, x does not belong to the *mustdef* set of while because, if n = 0, then x is left unchanged. An important difference in our approach w.r.t. [26] is that the floating-point variables read *in the branching conditions* in p are also considered in *maydef(p)* since the analysis of a branch b adds the constraints $Assume(b_r)$ and $Assume(b_f)$ (cf. lines 12–13 in Fig. 5b) that are propagated to these variables and may thus modify their domains.

***mayref** (p)*: a set of pairs (x, s) where s is a statement of p that may read the variable x. In Fig. 7, x belongs to the *mayref* set of if because it is read by its condition. For sequence of statements S, this set does not contain variables that are read after being assigned in S. For instance, x (paired to any statement) does not belong to *mayref* of sequence $S \equiv$ (x = 2; y = x + 3;).

***datadep** (p)*: a set of tuples (s_1, s_2, x) in which s_1 writes a variable x that is later read by s_2 (without intermediate writings). Its computation uses the three previous sets. For the example of sequence S above, variable x is modified by x = 2; and then read by y = x + 3, so $(x = 2, y = x + 3, x) \in datadep(S)$.

The *save-list* and *merge-list* of a split-merge section are computed as shown in Fig. 8. A variable x is added to the *save-list* of a section p if there is a statement inside p that may modify x and another statement that may read x. Said another way, if a new execution may depend on the value of a variable that could have been modified in another execution, then we need to restore it before a new execution. Dually, a variable x is added to the *merge-list* of a section p if there is a statement in p that may modify x and there is another statement outside the section that may read that modified value afterwards.

FLDCompiler is implemented as a Frama-C plug-in [36] and relies on its kernel to pretty-print the generated code. It visits the whole source code and generates the split-merge sections based on the declared type of variables. The basic version has no notion of alias, so if a pointer iterates on the cells of a floating-point array, it does not add them to the *save-list* and the *merge-list*, which may produce unsound results. To soundly solve this problem, FLDCompiler relies on Eva [4], the value analysis plugin of Frama-C, in order to know all possible targets of pointers to be added to the *save-list* and the *merge-list*. It may add unnecessary variables since Eva's analysis by abstract interpretation is conservative. Finally, FLDCompiler issues a warning if it tries to add to the lists something that is dynamically allocated and thus that does not exist at compile-time.

Path Exploration within Split-Merge Sections. The example of Fig. 5 illustrated the key ideas of the exploration This simplified approach would not be directly suitable though for nested conditions, loops or nested split-merge sections.

The actual implementation is much more technical (and cannot be presented here for lack of space): it performs a depth-first exploration of path segments inside each section, dynamically discovers new branches and records (dynamically allocated) execution contexts in a worklist of executions to be explored. Nested split-merge sections are treated by storing a section context in a stack. Since the abstract values of outcoming variables are merged at the end of the path segment of the inner section, they can be used to continue the considered execution for the outer section in a transparent way. Thanks to this approach, the directives split(*id*, *save-list*) and merge(*id*, *merge-list*), (which, in practice, have a unique identifier *id* for each section) are defined as macros. The interested reader may find all implementation details in the open-source code of FLDLib.

5   Experimental Results

Our RAI toolchain FLDBox has been evaluated [42] on (i) variations of the motivating example with different sizes of the table, (ii) a benchmark of small-size C examples, and (iii) on two large industrial case studies. They were run on an Intel Core i7 CPU, 2.60 GHz with 32 Gb RAM (on an artifact virtual machine, execution time can depend on the provided resources and be longer).

Motivating Example with Different Table Sizes. We first consider a version of the motivating example of Fig. 1 that loads the measures of the interpolation table from a file and calls interpolate with a large scenario in $\in [0, n-1]$. This is a very frequent code pattern in industrial code. It uses an external I/O library that is compiled with standard options and is not instrumented with our custom floating-point domains. We compare time (see Fig. 9) and precision of the tools supporting unstable tests (Fluctuat, Rosa and Precisa) and FLDBox for different sizes of the table. Rosa and Precisa do not manage such examples that generate a combinatorial explosion: with 2 elements Rosa takes 9 s, with 3 elements it takes 111 s and more than 20 min for 4 elements; Precisa takes 9.1 s for 8 elements, 37 s for 9 elements, 131 s for 10 elements. Since FLDBox accepts dynamic values, the Self-analyzing Executable is compiled only once and can be used with different files, unlike Fluctuat that parses the interpolation table in the source code.

FLDBox reports an accuracy error on the result of 8×10^{-6}, while Fluctuat reports a maximal accurracy error of 0.89. Hence RAI shows that the interpolate function is robust, whereas Fluctuat cannot show it, at least, without additional subdivision annotations from the user that can be tricky to find.

Benchmarks. We use benchmarks from [13,22] with unstable tests and present in [10]. They contain several small-size C examples in several categories (cf. Fig. 10). *Simple examples* show basic computations that focus on accuracy properties. *Unstable branches* are robustness tests for unstable branch handling.

Table size	10	20	100	200	400	1000	2000
FLDBox	0.01s	0.02s	0.14s	0.47s	1.85s	11.6s	69s
Fluctuat	0.05s	0.09s	0.16s	0.28s	7.00s	92.0s	838s
Precisa	131s	TO	TO	TO	TO	TO	TO
Rosa	TO	TO	TO	TO	TO	TO	TO

Fig. 9. Analysis time for the motivating example. Timeout (TO) is set to 20 min.

Interpolation tables contain various ways to compute an interpolation table . They also focus on testing robustness of unstable branches. *Maths* models functions of `math.h` for error estimation. *Miscellaneous* contain other examples. File `filter.c` is a second order linear filter that focuses on accuracy. File `patriot.c` is a historical example that contains a sum of 0.1 whose error shifts over time. File `complex_LU.c` finds a vector X such that $M(X) = (Y)$ for a square matrix M with a Lower/Upper decomposition. File `complex_intersect.c` shows iterative computations. File `scanf.c` shows how to manage external library functions not related to floating-point operations. The variable whose precision is analyzed is given after the file name.

Results. Each example has been annotated with ACSL assertions modeling the expected properties to use our toolchain. All of them have also been run with a timeout of 20 min in Fluctuat [21], Precisa [39] and Rosa [13]. Figure 10 presents the accuracy and time (either on top of the whole category for very small values, or per example otherwise). ko identifies a case where the tool failed to treat the example. n/t means "not translated" into PVS for Precisa or into Scala for Rosa due to the difficulty or impossibility to give an equivalent encoding of the C version. The best accuracy for a particular example is written in bold. Therefore, the table clearly shows that **FLDBox has almost always the best accuracy.**

The results of FpDebug were also recorded to show an under-approximation of the precision, where "unstable" means that FpDebug detects an unstable test and exits. They show that the results of our RAI toolchain, while being obtained using over-approximations, are not very far from the results returned by FpDebug and providing an under-approximation. Hence, **on the considered examples, FLDBox remains reasonably precise.**

Since FLDLib uses the same reasoning as Fluctuat except for constraint management, many results are merely the same. However, Fluctuat has only a limited support for unstable branches. Rosa manages them well but chains of `if`'s lead to a combinatorial explosion. Rosa approximates the errors on constant values but it is the most precise tool on non-linear computations. Precisa was used without the SMT optimization with FPRock. It is left as future work to evaluate if it can scale better with it. Nevertheless FLDBox aims at providing **guaranteed accuracy analysis with unstable branches on real-life C code** containing loops and thousands of lines of code, while Precisa (as Rosa) is more concerned with robustness proofs of smaller algorithms. Finally, unlike the other two sound tools (Fluctuat, Precisa), **Rosa and FLDBox did not report any false alarms on these examples,** whereas Rosa has timed out on some.

Target file/variable	FLDBox	Fluctuat	Rosa	Precisa	FpDebug
Simple examples:	< 0.01s	< 0.01s	< 0.6s	< 0.2s	
absorption.c/z	**1e-8**	**1e-8**	5.96e-8	5.96e-8	1e-8
associativity.c/u	**6.67e-16**	1.55e-15	1.55e-15	4.21e-15	-2.22e-16
division.c/z2	**1.805e-16**	5.55e-16	5.55e-16	5.55e-16	-1.57e-17
exp.c/y	**4.47e-13**	5.61e-13	n/t	4.45e-12	ko
polynome.c/t	1.066e-14	9.21e-15	**7.33e-15**	1.80e-14	-2.41e-16
relative.c/z	**2.33e-12**	**2.33e-12**	**2.33e-12**	6.59e-12	1.82e-13
triangle.c/A	**2.59e-13**	**2.59e-13**	1.58e-12	2.58e-8	-5.6e-21
Unstable branches:	< 0.01s	< 0.01s	see below	< 0.2s	
comp_abs.c/z	**4.44e-16**	2 (false al.)	3.73e-9/0.3s	4 (false al.)	-2.85e-8
comp_cont.c/y	**5.03e-5**	9.03e-5	7.0e-5/0.2s	3 (false al.)	-2.25e-8
comp_cont_nested.c/w	**1.67e-18**	**1.67e-18**	4.52e-16/3e4s	n/t	-1.0e-18
comp_cont_mult.c/res	**3.30e-5**	105 (false al.)	3.41e-5/0.4s	192 (false al.)	unstable
comp_disc_nested.c/z	**0.1** (true al.)	**0.1**	0.3/1.6s	n/t	ko
comp_disc.c/z	1.0	1.0	**0.5** (true al.)/0.2s	ko	ko
comp_model_err.c/S	**0.023** (true al.)	3.82e-1	**0.024**/2.2s	ko	ko
smartRoot.c/VAR	**1.52e-15**	0.27	1.61e-15/25s	ko	1.38e-17
cav10.c/VAR	102	101	**2.9**/1.4s	101	-3.3e-17
squareRoot3.c/VAR	**1.25e-11**	0.43	2.75e-9/4.5s	2.71 (false al.)	7.27e-17
squareRoot3Inv.c/VAR	**1.25e-9**	0.43	3.93e-9/4.5s	2.71	7.27e-17
Interpolation tables:	< 0.1s	< 0.1s	see below	see below	
inter_cond.c/res	**1.33e-5**	105 (false al.)	192/0.5s	191/0.02s	4.77e-7
inter_loop.c/result	**1.45e-6**	4.17e-6	ko	33/0.05s	-4.60e-7
inter_tbl_cast.c/out	**4e-6**	77.1 (false al.)	time out	time out	-1.04e-15
inter_tbl_loop.c/res	**4e-8**	time out	n/t	n/t	-1.04e-15
motiv_example.c/out1	**1.19e-7**	77.1 (false al.)	time out	time out	-1.04e-8
motiv_example.c/out2	**4** (true al.)	95.1	time out	time out	ko
Maths:	< 0.2s	< 0.1s	see below	see below	
sin_model_error.c/res	**2.57e-16**	**2.57e-16**	n/t	n/t	8.79e-18
sqrt_unroll.c/t.v	**7.11e-15**	7.82e-14	n/t	n/t	-4.81e-15
sqrt_fixpoint.c/Output	**3.15e-15**	1.39e-14	n/t	n/t	3.51e-16
Miscellaneous:	see below	see below	see below	see below	
filter.c/S	**1.65e-14**/0.13s	**1.65e-14**/1s	time out	time out	1.44e-16
NBody.c/VAR	**1.13e-6**/4.4s	time out	time out	n/t	1.91e-6
patriot.c/t	**1.91e-4**/0.05s	**1.91e-4**/0.8s	time out	time out	7.14e-15
complex_LU.c/det	**7.15e-15**/0.01s	n/t	n/t	n/t	n/t
complex_intersect.c/x	0.53/0.27s	**0.2**/0.6s	n/t	n/t	n/t
scanf.c/res	**4.57e-7**/0.04s	n/t	n/t	n/t	n/t

Fig. 10. Tool comparison over small-size C examples.

Industrial Case Studies. We also experimented FLDBox on two (non public) industrial case studies (synchronous reactive systems of several dozens of thousands of lines of code) on thin scenarios coming from existing tests with relative error, resp, 10^{-6} and 10^{-16}. The first one was automatically generated in C, whereas the second one was manually written in C++. Thus only Fluctuat and our tool were used on the first, and only our tool on the second. The first one contains computations that represent physical models, with many components like interpolation tables, but also linear filters, threshold functions. The second one contains solving algorithms coming from the C++ template library for linear algebra eigen[7], which is very convenient for our instrumentation mechanism as all the floating-point code is inlined.

---

[7] https://gitlab.com/libeigen/eigen.

Results. On the first case study, FLDCompiler added about 50 `split-merge` sections whose nested depth was up to 5. Even if we only used its syntactic version (that is not based on the Eva plug-in of Frama-C, resulting in a loss of precision), the results were very useful. Our tool exercised all interesting split-merge sections by performing the simulation of 80,000 loop cycles in <24h! It took only 2s to analyze one loop cycle with FLDLib (while Fluctuat took 1h, so did not scale). All these sections have been proved to be continuous. More precisely, when the output absolute value was >0.1, the relative error was $<10^{-2}$, otherwise the absolute error was $<10^{-3}$, that was acceptable for that case study.

The second case study with eigen demonstrated the need to extend FLD-Compiler to provide better results on some linear algebra algorithms and some discontinuous unstable branches. For example, the determinant computation is a continuous formula but often internally uses a LU (Lower/Upper) matrix decomposition that contains many unstable branches due to the choice of the best pivoting number. In this case, we have manually defined 25 split-merge sections (it took only about 3 h) whose depth was up to 4. FLDBox was able to successfully analyze between 10 and 20 cycles and validate the robustness of the unstable tests. The relative error was proved to be $< 10^{-10}$ for the first 7 cycles, and then progressively increased, e.g., to $< 10^{-4}$ for the 15th cycle.

FLDBox scales better than Fluctuat on these case studies for the reasons mentioned in Sec. 2 and since it does not care about pointers. Nevertheless, its scalability is directly related to the trade-off between precision and analysis time: if the number of noise symbols in zonotopes is not bounded, the analysis may be quadratic. To address this issue, FLDLib offers an option to set a bound (typically, $\sim$15) for the number of noise symbols introduced in an affine form.

On the first industrial C code, FLDBox succeeds in keeping a reasonable error for a thin scenario and thus avoiding excessive over-approximations. On the second industrial C++ code, the guaranteed numerical error delivered by FLDLib increases at every loop cycle, so that, for 20 cycles, false alarms appear from the accumulation of overapproximations because more and more unstable branches are detected. In this case, FLDLib helped to identify and better understand the tricky numerical parts of a big code.

All in all, these industrial use cases demonstrate that **FLDBox scales on thin scenarios** up to several dozens of thousands of lines of code. At worst, a few `split-merge` directives have to be manually adjusted and FLDLib provides a helpful support for this task. It is also worth noting that FLDLib can be replaced by Cadna to obtain a stochastic analysis that scales better, even if the results are non-necessarily sound but close to the expected ones. We also experimented the exact part of FLDLib (without domains) that works like FpDebug, but at source code level, and obtained the same under-approximated results as FpDebug.

6   Related Work

Many techniques and tools [1,3,9,11,13–15,17,19–21,23,27,34,38–41] have been developed for analysis of numerical properties in the last fifteen years. They can be roughly classified in two categories: *testing* and *static analysis* tools.

Among testing tools, FpDebug [3] and Herbgrind [34] are based on Valgrind [31] and detect accuracy property failures with few false alarms. FpDebug relies on MPFR[8] to associate a highly-precise value to each floating-point value of the tested program; its results are under-approximations. Herbgrind uses symbolic execution to detect sudden important accuracy loss. Both tools scale up on bigger programs. However, unlike FLDBox, they cannot guarantee the absence of failures even on thin scenarios. Verrou [19], Cadna [23], and Verificarlo [17] aim at reporting possible instances of errors with stochastic arithmetic. The core idea consists in randomly (with a selected probability) changing the rounding mode used for each floating-point operation during the program execution. For each execution, the obtained floating-point values differ, and with enough executions, an accuracy estimation can be made with a good confidence. Like FLDBox, those tools do not avoid false alarms because of the stochastic process, but their results are rather realistic and robust. However, unlike RAI, they cannot guarantee the absence of errors.

Among static analysis tools, Fluctuat [21], Gappa [15], Rosa [13,14] and Daisy [11] use a data-flow approach with interval or zonotope abstract domains. Precisa [39], FPTaylor [38] and real2Float [27] use optimization-based approaches. Gappa, Daisy, FPTaylor, real2Float, and Precisa allow formal verification in a theorem prover by generating proof scripts or certificates. Among all these tools, only Fluctuat, Rosa and Precisa have support for unstable tests.

These last tools have different design choices and trade-offs between scalability and tightness of over-approximations. Fluctuat [21] favor some scalability with forward propagation of domains. Fluctuat scales reasonably well for programs of a few thousand lines of code. Precisa uses interval arithmetic combined with branch-and-bound optimization and symbolic error computations; Rosa uses external SMT solver like Z3 [29], while Fluctuat relies on the zonotope abstract domain [20] to represent values and errors. Compared to Rosa, Precisa and Fluctuat, FLDBox scales better and can handle I/O and memory manipulations without stubs.

FPTaylor [38] favors tightness: it handles bounding errors as an optimization problem that is soundly solved by first-order Taylor approximations of arithmetic expressions. FPTaylor generally provides tighter approximations than our toolchain. However, unlike FLDBox, it cannot analyze large programs and handles neither loops, nor I/O operations, nor unstable tests. Finally, Gappa [15] presents a third possible trade-off. Indeed, Gappa is intended to help verifying and formally proving properties on numerical programs. It is based on interval arithmetic and rewriting rules for floating-point rounding errors expressions.

Rosa [13,14] and PVS-based tools [40,41] generate suitable optimized types for given accuracy and manage unstable tests using constraint solvers. Rosa optimizes the format of the floating-point variables given a required accuracy whereas [41] generates programs with contracts to check the stability of tests. Salsa [9] improves the accuracy of programs but it does not treat unstable tests.

---

[8] https://www.mpfr.org.

RAI combines abstract interpretation [8] and runtime verification [18]. The idea of computing abstract domains at runtime (but without handling unstable tests) was proposed e.g. in [12]. Modern symbolic execution tools [6,7] also combine static and dynamic analyses by replacing concrete values by symbolic ones and exploring execution paths. But they do not need to merge/re-split/re-merge several executions to treat unstable tests, and soundly define relevant points, which constitutes the key difficulty of RAI.

Relying on various ideas of previous work (type overloading, abstract domains and transformers, enriching concrete execution with additional symbolic features, program dependency analysis), RAI combines and enriches them in order to support unstable tests, bringing specific technical contributions on how to efficiently and soundly analyze relevant executions segments several times, how to define split-merge sections and find minimal lists of variables to save/merge. To the best of our knowledge, such a combined technique for numerical analysis has never been proposed before. The main benefits of FLDBox lie in its ability to scale up well for thin scenarios while preserving soundness, and in its management of I/O and memory manipulations without the need of stubs.

7   Conclusion and Perspectives

Assessment of numerical accuracy in critical programs is crucial to prevent accumulation of rounding errors that can provoke dangerous bugs. This work has presented an original hybrid verification technique for verification of numerical accuracy and robustness, Runtime Abstract Interpretation (RAI), that combines abstract interpretation and runtime verification and is able to soundly and efficiently handle unstable tests. We implemented FLDBox, a prototype RAI toolchain, and evaluated it on a representative set of numerical C programs and on two industrial case studies. The results show that RAI can efficiently and soundly analyze numerical accuracy for industrial programs on thin numerical scenarios.

An interesting work perspective is to integrate our toolchain into a continuous integration process. For that purpose, it only requires to instrument the unit test files. Any other file (including library files) can remain unchanged. Future work also includes a larger evaluation on real-life programs and an extension of FLDBox to support all features of the C programming language. It is planned to continue the research on these topics in the ANR project Interflop.

Acknowledgement. The authors thank Romain Soulat and Thales Research and Technology for providing case studies and participation in the evaluation. We are also grateful to Jean Gassino, Gregory de la Grange and IRSN for their support and evaluation on additional case studies, as well as to the anonymous reviewers for their valuable comments.

References

1. Bard, J., Becker, H., Darulova, E.: Formally verified roundoff errors using SMT-based certificates and subdivisions. In: ter Beek, M.H., McIver, A., Oliveira, J.N. (eds.) FM 2019. LNCS, vol. 11800, pp. 38–44. Springer, Cham (2019). https://doi.org/10.1007/978-3-030-30942-8_4
2. Baudin, P., Filliâtre, J.C., Marché, C., Monate, B., Moy, Y., Prevosto, V.: ACSL: ANSI/ISO C Specification Language. http://frama-c.com/acsl.html
3. Benz, F., Hildebrandt, A., Hack, S.: A dynamic program analysis to find floating-point accuracy problems. In: Conference on Programming Language Design and Implementation (PLDI 2012) (2012)
4. Blazy, S., Bühler, D., Yakobowski, B.: Structuring abstract interpreters through state and value abstractions. In: Bouajjani, A., Monniaux, D. (eds.) VMCAI 2017. LNCS, vol. 10145, pp. 112–130. Springer, Cham (2017). https://doi.org/10.1007/978-3-319-52234-0_7
5. Boulanger, J.: Static Analysis of Software: The Abstract Interpretation (2011)
6. Cadar, C., et al.: Symbolic execution for software testing in practice: preliminary assessment. In: The 33rd International Conference on Software Engineering (ICSE 2011), pp. 1066–1071. ACM (2011). https://doi.org/10.1145/1985793.1985995
7. Cadar, C., Sen, K.: Symbolic execution for software testing: three decades later. Commun. ACM (2013)
8. Cousot, P., Cousot, R.: Abstract interpretation: a unified lattice model for static analysis of programs by construction or approximation of fixpoints. In: Symposium on Principles of Programming Languages (POPL 1977) (1977)
9. Damouche, N., Martel, M.: Salsa: An automatic tool to improve the numerical accuracy of programs. In: Automated Formal Methods, AFM@NFM (2017)
10. Damouche, N., Martel, M., Panchekha, P., Qiu, J., Sanchez-Stern, A., Tatlock, Z.: Toward a standard benchmark format and suite for floating-point analysis. In: NSV 2016 (2016)
11. Darulova, E., Izycheva, A., Nasir, F., Ritter, F., Becker, H., Bastian, R.: Daisy - framework for analysis and optimization of numerical programs (Tool paper). In: Beyer, D., Huisman, M. (eds.) TACAS 2018. LNCS, vol. 10805, pp. 270–287. Springer, Cham (2018). https://doi.org/10.1007/978-3-319-89960-2_15
12. Darulova, E., Kuncak, V.: Trustworthy numerical computation in scala. In: The 26th Annual ACM SIGPLAN Conference on Object-Oriented Programming, Systems, Languages, and Applications (OOPSLA 2011), part of SPLASH 2011, pp. 325–344. ACM (2011). https://doi.org/10.1145/2048066.2048094
13. Darulova, E., Kuncak, V.: Sound compilation of reals. In: Symposium on Principles of Programming Languages (POPL) (2014)
14. Darulova, E., Kuncak, V.: Towards a compiler for reals. ACM Trans. Program. Lang. Syst (2017)
15. Daumas, M., Melquiond, G.: Certification of bounds on expressions involving rounded operators. Trans. Math. Softw. (2010). https://doi.org/10.1145/1644001.1644003
16. Delahaye, M., Kosmatov, N., Signoles, J.: Common specification language for static and dynamic analysis of C programs. In: The 28th Annual ACM Symposium on Applied Computing, Software Verification and Testing Track (SAC-SVT 2013), pp. 1230–1235. ACM (2013). https://doi.org/10.1145/2480362.2480593
17. Denis, C., de Oliveira Castro, P., Petit, E.: Verificarlo: Checking floating point accuracy through monte carlo arithmetic. In: Symposium on Computer Arithmetic (ARITH) (2016). https://doi.org/10.1109/ARITH.2016.31

18. Falcone, Y., Havelund, K., Reger, G.: A tutorial on runtime verification. In: Engineering Dependable Software Systems. IOS Press (2013)
19. Févotte, F., Lathuilière, B.: Studying the numerical quality of an industrial computing code: a case study on code_aster. In: Numerical Software Verification (NSV) (2017). https://doi.org/10.1007/978-3-319-63501-9_5
20. Ghorbal, K., Goubault, E., Putot, S.: The zonotope abstract domain Taylor1+. In: Bouajjani, A., Maler, O. (eds.) CAV 2009. LNCS, vol. 5643, pp. 627–633. Springer, Heidelberg (2009). https://doi.org/10.1007/978-3-642-02658-4_47
21. Goubault, E., Putot, S.: Static analysis of finite precision computations. In: International Conference on Verification, Model Checking, and Abstract Interpretation (VMCAI) (2011)
22. Goubault, E., Putot, S.: Robustness analysis of finite precision implementations. In: Asian Symposium on Programming Languages and Systems (APLAS) (2013)
23. Jézéquel, F., Chesneaux, J.M.: CADNA: a library for estimating round-off error propagation. Comput. Phys. Commun. (2008)
24. Kirchner, F., Kosmatov, N., Prevosto, V., Signoles, J., Yakobowski, B.: Frama-C: a software analysis perspective. Formal Aspects Comput. (2015)
25. Kosmatov, N., Maurica, F., Signoles, J.: Efficient runtime assertion checking for properties over mathematical numbers. In: Deshmukh, J., Ničković, D. (eds.) RV 2020. LNCS, vol. 12399, pp. 310–322. Springer, Cham (2020). https://doi.org/10.1007/978-3-030-60508-7_17
26. Léchenet, J.-C., Kosmatov, N., Le Gall, P.: Cut branches before looking for bugs: certifiably sound verification on relaxed slices. Formal Aspects Comput. **30**(1), 107–131 (2017). https://doi.org/10.1007/s00165-017-0439-x
27. Magron, V., Constantinides, G.A., Donaldson, A.F.: Certified roundoff error bounds using semidefinite programming. ACM Trans. Math. Softw. **43**(4), 34:1–34:31 (2017). https://doi.org/10.1145/3015465
28. Monniaux, D.: The pitfalls of verifying floating-point computations. Trans. Program. Lang. Syst. (TOPLAS) (2008)
29. de Moura, L., Bjørner, N.: Z3: an efficient SMT solver. In: Ramakrishnan, C.R., Rehof, J. (eds.) TACAS 2008. LNCS, vol. 4963, pp. 337–340. Springer, Heidelberg (2008). https://doi.org/10.1007/978-3-540-78800-3_24
30. Muller, J., et al.: Handbook of Floating-Point Arithmetic. Birkhäuser (2010). https://doi.org/10.1007/978-0-8176-4705-6
31. Nethercote, N., Seward, J.: Valgrind: A framework for heavyweight dynamic binary instrumentation. In: Conference on Programming Language Design and Implementation (PLDI) (2007)
32. Prosser, R.T.: Applications of Boolean Matrices to the Analysis of Flow Diagrams. In: Eastern Joint IRE-AIEE-ACM Computer Conference (1959). https://doi.org/10.1145/1460299.1460314
33. Sánchez, C., et al.: A survey of challenges for runtime verification from advanced application domains (Beyond software). Formal Methods Syst. Des. (2019)
34. Sanchez-Stern, A., Panchekha, P., Lerner, S., Tatlock, Z.: Finding root causes of floating point error. ACM Sigplan Notice (2018). http://arxiv.org/abs/1705.10416
35. Signoles, J.: E-ACSL: Executable ANSI/ISO C Specification Language. http://frama-c.com/download/e-acsl/e-acsl.pdf
36. Signoles, J., Antignac, T., Correnson, L., Lemerre, M., Prevosto, V.: Frama-C Plug-in Development Guide. http://frama-c.com/download/plugin-developer.pdf

37. Signoles, J., Kosmatov, N., Vorobyov, K.: E-ACSL, a runtime verification tool for safety and security of C programs. Tool Paper. In: International Workshop on Competitions, Usability, Benchmarks, Evaluation, and Standardisation for Runtime Verification Tools (RV-CuBES) (2017)

38. Solovyev, A., Baranowski, M.S., Briggs, I., Jacobsen, C., Rakamaric, Z., Gopalakrishnan, G.: Rigorous estimation of floating-point round-off errors with symbolic taylor expansions. Trans. Program. Lang. Syst. (2018). https://doi.org/10.1145/3230733

39. Titolo, L., Feliú, M.A., Moscato, M.M., Muñoz, C.A.: An abstract interpretation framework for the round-off error analysis of floating-point programs. In: Verification, Model Checking, and Abstract Interpretation - 19th International Conference, VMCAI 2018, Los Angeles, CA, USA, January 7–9, Proceedings (2018). https://doi.org/10.1007/978-3-319-73721-8_24

40. Titolo, L., Moscato, M., Muñoz, C.A.: Automatic generation and verification of test-stable floating-point code. arXiv e-prints (2020)

41. Titolo, L., Muñoz, C.A., Feliú, M.A., Moscato, M.M.: Eliminating unstable tests in floating-point programs. In: Logic-Based Program Synthesis and Transformation (LOPTSR) (2018). https://doi.org/10.1007/978-3-030-13838-7_10

42. Védrine, F., Jacquemin, M., Kosmatov, N., Signoles, J.: Companion artifact evaluated by the VMCAI 2021 artifact evaluation committee. Zenodoo (2020). https://doi.org/10.5281/zenodo.4275521

Twinning Automata and Regular Expressions for String Static Analysis

Luca Negrini[1,2], Vincenzo Arceri[1(✉)], Pietro Ferrara[1], and Agostino Cortesi[1]

[1] Ca' Foscari University of Venice, Venice, Italy
{vincenzo.arceri,pietro.ferrara,cortesi}@unive.it
[2] JuliaSoft S.r.l., Verona, Italy
luca.negrini@unive.it

Abstract. In this paper we formalize TARSIS, a new abstract domain based on the abstract interpretation theory that approximates string values through finite state automata. The main novelty of TARSIS is that it works over an alphabet of strings instead of single characters. On the one hand, such an approach requires a more complex and refined definition of the widening operator, and the abstract semantics of string operators. On the other hand, it is in position to obtain strictly more precise results than state-of-the-art approaches. We implemented a prototype of TARSIS, and we applied it to some case studies taken from some of the most popular Java libraries manipulating string values. The experimental results confirm that TARSIS is in position to obtain strictly more precise results than existing analyses.

Keywords: String analysis · Static analysis · Abstract interpretation

1 Introduction

Strings play a key role in any programming language due to the many and different ways in which they are used, for instance to dynamically access object properties, to hide the program code by using string-to-code statements and reflection, or to manipulate data-interchange formats, such as JSON, just to name a few. Despite the great effort spent in reasoning about strings, static analysis often failed to manage programs that heavily manipulate strings, mainly due to the inaccuracy of the results and the prohibitive amount of resources (time, space) required to retrieve useful information on strings. On the one hand, finite height string abstractions [16] are computable in a reasonable time, but precision is suddenly lost when using advanced string manipulations. On the other hand, more sophisticated abstractions (e.g., the ones reported in [8,14]) compute precise results but they require a huge, and sometimes unrealistic, computational cost, making such code intractable for these abstractions. A good representation of such abstractions is the finite state automata domain [8]. Over-approximating strings into finite state automata has shown to increase string analysis accuracy in many scenarios, but it does not scale up to real world programs dealing with statically unknown inputs and long text manipulations.

© Springer Nature Switzerland AG 2021
F. Henglein et al. (Eds.): VMCAI 2021, LNCS 12597, pp. 267–290, 2021.
https://doi.org/10.1007/978-3-030-67067-2_13

In this paper we introduce TARSIS, a new abstract domain for string values based on finite state automata (FSA). Standard FSA has been shown to provide precise abstractions of string values when all the components of such strings are known, but with high computational cost. Instead of considering standard finite automata built over an alphabet of single characters, TARSIS considers automata that are built over an alphabet of strings. The alphabet comprises a special value to represent statically unknown strings. This avoids the creation of self-loops with any possible character as input, which otherwise would significantly degrade performance. We define the abstract semantics of mainstream string operations, namely substring, length, indexOf, replace, concat and contains, either defined directly on the automaton or on its equivalent regular expression.

TARSIS has been implemented into a prototypical static analyzer supporting a subset of Java. By comparing TARSIS with other cutting-edge domains for string analysis, results show that (i) when applied to simple code that causes a precision loss in simpler domains, TARSIS correctly approximates string values within a comparable execution time, (ii) on code that makes the standard automata domain unusable due to the complexity of the analysis, TARSIS is in position to perform in a limited amount of time, making it a viable domain for complex and real codebases, and (iii) TARSIS is able to precisely abstract complex string operations that have not been addressed by state-of-the-art domains.

The rest of the paper is structured as follows. Section 2 introduces a motivating example. Section 3 defines the mathematical notation used throughout the paper. Section 4 formalizes TARSIS and its abstract semantics. Section 5 reports experimental results and comparison with other domains, while Sect. 6 concludes.

1.1 Related Work

The problem of statically analyzing strings has been already tackled in different contexts in the literature [2,8,13,14,16,25,29]. The original finite state automata abstract domain was defined in [8] in the context of dynamic languages, providing an automata-based abstract semantics for common ECMAScript string operations. The same abstract domain has been integrated also for defining a sound-by-construction analysis for string-to-code statements [7]. The authors of [4] provided an automata abstraction merged with interval abstractions for analyzing JavaScript arrays and objects. In [13], the authors proposed a static analysis of Java strings based on the abstraction of the control-flow graph as a context-free grammar. Regular strings [12] is an abstraction of the finite state automata domain and approximates strings as a strict subset of regular expressions. Even if it is does not tackle the problem of analyzing strings, in [28] a lattice-based generalization of regular expressions was proposed, showing a regular expressions-based domain parametric from a lattice of reference. An interesting automata-based model is symbolic automata [21], that differs from the standard one having an alphabet of predicates (that can potentially be infinite) instead of single characters. Examples of applications of symbolic automata in the context of static analysis are regex processing, sanitizer analysis [32] and their usage as program model for mixing syntactic and semantic abstractions over the program [30]. Finally, orthogonally to static analysis of strings by abstract interpretation, a big effort was spent in

```
1   int countMatches(String str, String sub) {
2       int count = 0;
3       int len = sub.length();
4       while (str.contains(sub)) {
5           int idx = str.indexOf(sub);
6           count = count + 1;
7           int start = idx + len;
8           int end = str.length();
9           str = str.substring(start, end);
10      }
11      return count;
12  }
```

Fig. 1. A program that counts the occurrences of a string into another one

the context of string constraints verification, focusing on the study of decidable fragments of the string constraint formulas [3] or proposing new efficient decidable procedures or string constraints representations [3,5,11] also based on automata, such as [33,34], or involving type conversion string constraints [1].

2   Motivating Example

Consider the code of Fig. 1 that counts the occurrences of string sub into string str. This code is (a simplification of) the *Apache commons-lang* library method StringUtils.countMatches[1], one of the most popular Java libraries providing extra functionalities over the core classes of the Java *lang* package (that contains class String as well). Proving properties about the value of count after the loop is particularly challenging, since it requires to correctly model a set of string operations (namely length, contains, indexOf, and substring) and their interaction. State-of-the-art string analyses fail to precisely model most of such operations, since their abstraction of string values is not rigorous enough to deal with such situations. This loss of precision usually leads to failure in proving string-based properties (also on non-string values) in real-world software, such as the numerical bounds of the value returned by countMatches when applied to a string.

The goal of this paper is to provide an abstract interpretation-based static analysis, in order to deal with complex and nested string manipulations similar to the one reported in Fig. 1. As we will discuss in Sect. 5, TARSIS models (among the others) all string operations used in countMatches, and it is precise enough to infer, given the abstractions of str and sub, the precise range of values that count might have at the end of the method.

3   Preliminaries

Mathematical Notation. Given a set S, S^* is the set of all finite sequences of elements of S. If $s = s_0 \ldots s_n \in S^*$, s_i is the i-th element of s, $|s| = n + 1$ is its length, and $s[x/y]$ is the sequence obtained replacing all occurrences of x in s with y. When s' is a subsequence of s, we write $s' \curvearrowright_s s$. We denote by

---

[1] https://commons.apache.org/proper/commons-lang/.

$s^n, n \geq 0$ the n-times repetition of the string s. Given two sets S and T, $\wp(S)$ is the powerset of S, $S \setminus T$ is the set difference, $S \subset T$ is the strict inclusion relation between S and T, $S \subseteq T$ is the inclusion relation between S and T, and $S \times T$ is the Cartesian product between S and T.

Ordered Structures. A set L with a partial ordering relation $\leq \subseteq L \times L$ is a poset, denoted by $\langle L, \leq \rangle$. A poset $\langle L, \leq, \vee, \wedge \rangle$, where $\vee$ and $\wedge$ are respectively the least upper bound (lub) and greatest lower bound (glb) operators of L, is a lattice if $\forall x, y \in L \,.\, x \vee y$ and $x \wedge y$ belong to L. It is also complete if $\forall X \subseteq L$ we have that $\bigvee X, \bigwedge X \in L$. A complete lattice L, with ordering $\leq$, lub $\vee$, glb $\wedge$, top element $\top$, and bottom element $\bot$ is denoted by $\langle L, \leq, \vee, \wedge, \top, \bot \rangle$.

Abstract Interpretation. Abstract interpretation [17,18] is a theoretical framework for sound reasoning about semantic properties of a program, establishing a correspondence between the concrete semantics of a program and an approximation of it, called abstract semantics. Let C and A be complete lattices, a pair of monotone functions $\alpha : C \to A$ and $\gamma : A \to C$ forms a *Galois Connection* (GC) between C and A if $\forall x \in C, \forall y \in A : \alpha(x) \leq_A y \Leftrightarrow x \leq_C \gamma(y)$. We denote a GC as $C \xleftrightarrow[\alpha]{\gamma} A$. Given $C \xleftrightarrow[\alpha]{\gamma} A$, a concrete function $f : C \to C$ is, in general, not computable. Hence, a function $f^\sharp : A \to A$ that must *correctly* approximate the function f is needed. If so, we say that the function $f^\sharp$ is *sound*. Given $C \xleftrightarrow[\alpha]{\gamma} A$ and a concrete function $f : C \to C$, an abstract function $f^\sharp : A \to A$ is sound w.r.t. f if $\forall c \in C. \, \alpha(f(c)) \leq_A f^\sharp(\alpha(c))$. Completeness [24] can be obtained by enforcing the equality of the soundness condition and it is called *backward completeness*. Given $C \xleftrightarrow[\alpha]{\gamma} A$, a concrete function $f : C \to C$ and an abstract function $f^\sharp : A \to A$, $f^\sharp$ is backward complete w.r.t. f if $\forall c \in C. \, \alpha(f(c)) = f^\sharp(\alpha(c))$.

Finite State Automata and Regular Expression Notation. We follow the notation reported in [8] for introducing finite state automata. A finite state automaton (FA) is a tuple $\mathtt{A} = \langle Q, \Sigma, \delta, q_0, F \rangle$, where Q is a finite set of states, $q_0 \in Q$ is the initial state, Σ is a finite alphabet of symbols, $\delta \subseteq Q \times \Sigma \times Q$ is the transition relation and $F \subseteq Q$ is the set of final states. If $\delta : Q \times \Sigma \to Q$ is a function then $\mathtt{A}$ is called deterministic finite state automaton. The set of all the FAs is $\mathrm{F_A}$. If $\mathscr{L} \subseteq \Sigma^*$ is recognized by a FA, we say that $\mathscr{L}$ is a regular language. Given $\mathtt{A} \in \mathrm{F_A}$, $\mathscr{L}(\mathtt{A})$ is the language accepted by $\mathtt{A}$. From the Myhill-Nerode theorem, for each regular language uniquely exists a minimum FA (w.r.t. the number of states) recognizing the language. Given a regular language $\mathscr{L}$, $\mathsf{Min}(\mathtt{A})$ is the minimum FA $\mathtt{A}$ s.t. $\mathscr{L} = \mathscr{L}(\mathtt{A})$. Abusing notation, given a regular language $\mathscr{L}$, $\mathsf{Min}(\mathscr{L})$ is the minimal FA recognizing $\mathscr{L}$. We denote as $\mathsf{paths}(\mathtt{A}) \in \wp(\delta^*)$ the set of sequences of transitions corresponding to all the possible paths from the initial state q_0 to a final state $q_n \in F$. When $\mathtt{A}$ is cycle-free, the set $\mathsf{paths}(\mathtt{A})$ is finite and computable. Given $\pi \in \mathsf{paths}(\mathtt{A})$, $|\pi|$ is its length, meaning the sum of the lengths of the symbols that appear on the transitions composing the path. Furthermore, $|\mathsf{minPath}(\mathtt{A})| \in \mathbb{N}$ denotes the (unique) length of a minimum path. If $\mathtt{A}$ is a cycle-free automaton, $|\mathsf{maxPath}(\mathtt{A})| \in \mathbb{N}$ denotes the (unique) length of a maximum path. Given $\pi = t_0 \dots t_n \in \mathsf{paths}(\mathtt{A})$, σ_{π_i} is the symbol read by the transition t_i, $i \in [0, n]$, and $\sigma_\pi = \sigma_{\pi_0} \dots \sigma_{\pi_n}$ is the string recognized by such

```
a ∈ AE ::= x ∈ ID  |  n ∈ ℤ  |  a + a  |  a - a  |  a * a  |  a / a
       |  length(s)  |  indexOf(s,s)
b ∈ BE ::= x ∈ ID  |  true  |  false  |  b && b  |  b || b  |  ! b
       |  e < e  |  e == e  |  contains(s₁,s₂)
s ∈ SE ::= x ∈ ID  |  "σ"  |  substr(s,a,a)
       |  concat(s,s)  |  replace(s,s,s)    (σ ∈ Σ*)
e ∈ E ::= a  |  b  |  s
st ∈ STMT ::= st ; st  |  skip  |  x = e  |  if (b) {st} else {st}
       |  while (b) {st}
P ∈ IMP ::= st ;
```

Fig. 2. IMP syntax

path. Predicate cyclic(A) holds if and only if the given automaton contains a cycle. Throughout the paper, it could be more convenient to refer to a finite state automaton by its regular expression (regex for short), being equivalent. Given two regexes r_1 and r_2, $r_1 \| r_2$ is the disjunction between r_1 and r_2, $r_1 r_2$ is the concatenation of r_1 with r_2, $(r_1)^*$ is the Kleene-closure of r_1.

The Finite State Automata Abstract Domain. Here, we report the necessary notions about the finite state automata abstract domain presented in [8], over-approximating string properties as the minimum deterministic finite state automaton recognizing them. Given an alphabet Σ, the finite state automata domain is defined as $\langle \mathrm{FA}_{/\equiv}, \sqsubseteq_{\mathrm{FA}}, \sqcup_{\mathrm{FA}}, \sqcap_{\mathrm{FA}}, \mathrm{Min}(\varnothing), \mathrm{Min}(\Sigma^*) \rangle$, where $\mathrm{FA}_{/\equiv}$ is the quotient set of FA w.r.t. the equivalence relation induced by language equality, $\sqsubseteq_{\mathrm{FA}}$ is the partial order induced by language inclusion, $\sqcup_{\mathrm{FA}}$ and $\sqcap_{\mathrm{FA}}$ are the lub and the glb, respectively. The minimum is $\mathrm{Min}(\varnothing)$, that is, the automaton recognizing the empty language, and the maximum is $\mathrm{Min}(\Sigma^*)$, that is, the automaton recognizing any possible string over Σ. We abuse notation by representing equivalence classes in $\mathrm{FA}_{/\equiv}$ by one of its automaton (usually the minimum), i.e., when we write $A \in \mathrm{FA}_{/\equiv}$ we mean $[A]_{\equiv}$. Since $\mathrm{FA}_{/\equiv}$ does not satisfy the Ascending Chain Condition (ACC), i.e., it contains infinite ascending chains, it is equipped with the parametric widening ∇_{FA}^n. The latter is defined in terms of a state equivalence relation merging states that recognize the same language, up to a fixed length $n \in \mathbb{N}$, a parameter used for tuning the widening precision [10,23]. For instance, let us consider the automata $A, A' \in \mathrm{FA}_{/\equiv}$ recognizing the languages $\mathscr{L} = \{\epsilon, a\}$ and $\mathscr{L}' = \{\epsilon, a, aa\}$, respectively. The result of the application of the widening ∇_{FA}^n, with $n = 1$, is $A \nabla_{\mathrm{FA}}^n A' = A''$ s.t. $\mathscr{L}(A'') = \{ a^n \mid n \in \mathbb{N} \}$.

Core Language and Semantics. We introduce a minimal core language IMP, whose syntax is reported in Fig. 2. Such language supports the main operators over strings. In particular, IMP supports arithmetic expressions (AE), Boolean expressions (BE) and string expressions (SE). Primitives values are $\mathrm{VAL} = \mathbb{Z} \cup \Sigma^* \cup \{\mathrm{true}, \mathrm{false}\}$, namely integers, strings and booleans. Programs states $\mathbb{M} : \mathrm{ID} \to \mathrm{VAL}$ map identifiers to primitives values, ranged over the meta-variable $\mathfrak{m}$. The concrete semantics of IMP statements is captured by the function $[\![\mathrm{st}]\!]$:

$$[\![\, \texttt{substr}(\texttt{s},\texttt{a},\texttt{a}') \,]\!]m = \sigma_i \ldots \sigma_j \qquad \text{if } i \leq j < |\sigma|, i = [\![\, \texttt{s} \,]\!]m, j = [\![\, \texttt{s}' \,]\!]m$$

$$[\![\, \texttt{length}(\texttt{s}) \,]\!]m = |\sigma|$$

$$[\![\, \texttt{indexOf}(\texttt{s},\texttt{s}') \,]\!]m = \begin{cases} \min\{\, i \mid \sigma_i \ldots \sigma_j = \sigma' \,\} & \text{if } \exists i, j \in \mathbb{N}.\, \sigma_i \ldots \sigma_j = \sigma' \\ -1 & \text{otherwise} \end{cases}$$

$$[\![\, \texttt{replace}(\texttt{s},\texttt{s}',\texttt{s}'') \,]\!]m = \begin{cases} \sigma[\sigma'/\sigma''] & \text{if } \sigma' \curvearrowright_{\mathsf{s}} \sigma \\ \sigma & \text{otherwise} \end{cases}$$

$$[\![\, \texttt{concat}(\texttt{s},\texttt{s}') \,]\!]m = \sigma \cdot \sigma'$$

$$[\![\, \texttt{contains}(\texttt{s},\texttt{s}') \,]\!]m = \begin{cases} \texttt{true} & \text{if } \exists i, j \in \mathbb{N}.\, \sigma_i \ldots \sigma_j = \sigma' \\ \texttt{false} & \text{otherwise} \end{cases}$$

$$\text{where } \sigma = [\![\, \texttt{s} \,]\!]m, \sigma' = [\![\, \texttt{s}' \,]\!]m, \sigma'' = [\![\, \texttt{s}'' \,]\!]m$$

Fig. 3. Concrete semantics of IMP string expressions

$M \to M$. The semantics is defined in a standard way and for this reason has been omitted. Such semantics relies on the one of expressions, that we capture, abusing notation, as $[\![\, e \,]\!] : M \to \text{VAL}$. While the semantics concerning arithmetic and Boolean expressions is straightforward (and not of interest of this paper), we define the part concerning strings in Fig. 3.

4   The TARSIS abstract domain

In this section, we recast the original finite state abstract domain working over an alphabet of characters Σ, reported in Sect. 3, to an augmented abstract domain based on finite state automata over an alphabet of strings.

4.1   Abstract Domain and Widening

The key idea of TARSIS is to adopt the same abstract domain, changing the alphabet on which finite state automata are defined to a set of strings, namely Σ^*. Clearly, the main concern here is that Σ^* is infinite and this would not permit us to adopt the finite state automata model, that requires the alphabet to be finite. Thus, in order to solve this problem, we make this abstract domain *parametric* to the program we aim to analyze and in particular to its strings. Given an IMP program P, we denote by Σ_{P}^* any substring of strings appearing in P,[2] *delimiting* the space of string properties we aim to check only on P.

At this point, we can instantiate the automata-based framework proposed in [8] with the new alphabet as

$$\langle \mathcal{T}\text{FA}_{/\equiv}, \sqsubseteq_{\mathcal{T}}, \sqcup_{\mathcal{T}}, \sqcap_{\mathcal{T}}, \text{Min}(\varnothing), \text{Min}(\mathbb{A}_{\mathsf{P}}^*) \rangle$$

---

[2] The set Σ_{P}^* can be easily computed collecting the constant strings in P by visiting its abstract syntax tree and then computing their substrings.

The alphabet on which finite state automata are defined is $\mathbb{A}_P \triangleq \Sigma_P^* \cup \{T\}$, where T is a special symbol that we intend as *"any possible string"*. Let $\mathcal{T}$FA be the set of any deterministic finite state automaton over the alphabet $\mathbb{A}_P$. Since we can have more automata recognizing a language, $\mathcal{T}$FA$_{/\equiv}$ is the quotient set of $\mathcal{T}$FA w.r.t. the equivalence relation induced by language equality, that is, the elements of domain are equivalence classes. For simplicity, when we write $A \in \mathcal{T}$FA$_{/\equiv}$, we intend the equivalence class of A. $\sqsubseteq_{\mathcal{T}}$ is the partial order induced by language inclusion, $\sqcup_{\mathcal{T}}$ and $\sqcap_{\mathcal{T}}$ are the lub and the glb over elements of $\mathcal{T}$FA$_{/\equiv}$, computing the equivalence class of the union and the intersection of the two automata representing the corresponding classes, respectively. The bottom element is $\mathsf{Min}(\varnothing)$, corresponding to the automaton recognizing the empty language, and the maximum is $\mathsf{Min}(\mathbb{A}_P^*)$, namely the automaton recognizing any string over $\mathbb{A}_P$.

Like in the standard finite state automata domain FA$_{/\equiv}$, also $\mathcal{T}$FA$_{/\equiv}$ is not a complete lattice and, consequently, it does not form a Galois Connection with the string concrete domain $\wp(\Sigma^*)$. This comes from the non-existence, in general, of the best abstraction of a string set in $\mathcal{T}$FA$_{/\equiv}$ (e.g., a context-free language has no best abstract element in $\mathcal{T}$FA$_{/\equiv}$ approximating it). Nevertheless, this is not a concern since weaker forms of abstract interpretation are still possible [19] still guaranteeing soundness relations between concrete and abstract elements (e.g., polyhedra [20]). In particular, we can still ensure soundness comparing the concretizations of our abstract elements (cf. Section 8 of [19]). Hence, we define the concretization function $\gamma_{\mathcal{T}} : \mathcal{T}FA_{/\equiv} \rightarrow \wp(\Sigma^*)$ as $\gamma_{\mathcal{T}}(A) \triangleq \bigcup_{\sigma \in \mathscr{L}(A)} \mathsf{Flat}(\sigma)$, where Flat converts a string over $\mathbb{A}_P$ into a set of strings over Σ^*. For instance, $\mathsf{Flat}(a\, T T\, bb\, c) = \{\ a\sigma bbc \mid \sigma \in \Sigma^*\ \}$. Note that, the language of strings (over the alphabet Σ) recognized by A corresponds to the concretization function reported above, namely $\mathscr{L}(A) = \gamma_{\mathcal{T}}(A)$.

Widening. Similarly to the standard automata domain FA$_{/\equiv}$, also $\mathcal{T}$FA$_{/\equiv}$ does not satisfy ACC, meaning that fix-point computations over $\mathcal{T}$FA$_{/\equiv}$ may not converge in a finite time. Hence, we need to equip $\mathcal{T}$FA$_{/\equiv}$ with a widening operator to ensure the convergence of the analysis. We define the widening operator $\nabla_{\mathcal{T}}^n : \mathcal{T}FA_{/\equiv} \times \mathcal{T}FA_{/\equiv} \rightarrow \mathcal{T}FA_{/\equiv}$, parametric in $n \in \mathbb{N}$, taking two automata as input and returning an over-approximation of the least upper bounds between them, as required by widening definition. We rely on the standard automata widening reported in Sect. 3, that, informally speaking, can be seen as a *subset construction* algorithm [22] up to languages of strings of length n. In order to explain the widening $\nabla_{\mathcal{T}}^n$, consider the following function manipulating strings.[3]

```
1  function f(v) {
2      res = "";
3      while (?)
4          res = res + "id = " + v;
5      return res;
6  }
```

---

[3] For the sake of readability, in the program examples presented in this paper the plus operation between strings corresponds to the string concatenation.

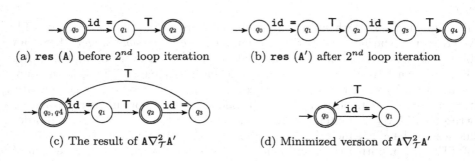

(a) res (A) before 2nd loop iteration   (b) res (A') after 2nd loop iteration

(c) The result of $A \nabla_T^2 A'$ (d) Minimized version of $A \nabla_T^2 A'$

Fig. 4. Example of widening application

The function f takes as input parameter v and returns variable res. Let us suppose that v is a statically unknown string, corresponding to the automaton recognizing T (i.e., $\mathsf{Min}(\{T\})$). The result of the function f is a string of the form id =T, repeated zero or more times. Since the while guard is unknown, the number of iterations is statically unknown, and in turn, also the number of performed concatenations inside the loop body. The goal here is to over-approximate the value returned by the function f, i.e., the value of res at the end of the function.

Let A, reported in Fig. 4a, be the automaton abstracting the value of res before starting the second iteration of the loop, and let A', reported in Fig. 4b be the automaton abstracting the value of res at the end of the second iteration. At this point, we want to apply the widening operator ∇_T^n, between A and A', working as follows. We first compute $A \sqcup_T A'$ (corresponding to the automaton reported in Fig. 4b except that also q_0 and q_2 are final states). On this automaton, we merge any state that recognizes the same $\mathbb{A}_P$-strings of length n, with $n \in \mathbb{N}$. In our example, let n be 2. The resulting automaton is reported in Fig. 4c, where q_0 and q_4 are put together, the other states are left as singletons since they cannot be merged with no other state. Figure 4d depicts the minimized version of Fig. 4c.

The widening ∇_T^n has been proved to meet the widening requirements (i.e., over-approximation of the least upper bounds and convergence on infinite ascending chains) in [23]. The parameter n, tuning the widening precision, is arbitrary and can be chosen by the user. As highlighted in [8], the higher n is, the more the corresponding widening operator is precise in over-approximating lubs of infinite ascending chains (i.e., in fix-point computations).

A classical improvement on widening-based fix-point computations is to integrate a threshold [15], namely widening is applied to over-approximate lubs when a certain threshold (usually over some property of abstract values) is overcome. In fix-point computations, we decide to apply the previously defined widening ∇_T^n only when the number of the states of the lubbed automata overcomes the threshold $\tau \in \mathbb{N}$. This permits us to postpone the widening application, getting more precise abstractions when the automata sizes do not overcome the threshold. At the moment, the threshold τ is not automatically inferred, since it surely requires further investigations.

4.2   String Abstract Semantics of IMP

In this section, we define the abstract semantics of the string operators defined in Sect. 3 over the new string domain $\mathcal{T}\mathsf{FA}_{/\equiv}$. Since IMP supports strings, integers and Booleans values, we need a way to merge the corresponding abstract domains. In particular, we abstract integers with the well-known interval abstract domain [17] defined as $\mathsf{Intv} \triangleq \{ \, [a, b] \mid a \in \mathbb{Z} \cup \{-\infty\}, b \in \mathbb{Z} \cup \{+\infty\}, a \leq b \, \} \cup \{\perp_{\mathsf{Intv}}\}$ and Booleans with $\mathsf{Bool} \triangleq \wp(\{\mathtt{true}, \mathtt{false}\})$. As usual, we denote by $\sqcup_{\mathsf{Intv}}$ and $\sqcup_{\mathsf{Bool}}$ the lubs between intervals and Booleans, respectively. In particular, we merge such abstract domains in $\mathrm{VAL}^{\sharp}$ by the coalesced sum abstract domain [6] as

$$\mathrm{VAL}^{\sharp} \triangleq \mathcal{T}\mathsf{FA}_{/\equiv} \oplus \mathsf{Intv} \oplus \mathsf{Bool}$$

Informally, the coalesced sum abstract domain introduces a new bottom and top element, and it *coalesces* the bottom elements of the involved domains.

The program state is represented through abstract program memories $\mathbb{M}^{\sharp}$: $\mathrm{ID} \rightarrow \mathrm{VAL}^{\sharp}$ from identifiers to abstract values. The abstract semantics is captured by the function $\langle\!\langle \mathtt{st}\rangle\!\rangle : \mathbb{M}^{\sharp} \rightarrow \mathbb{M}^{\sharp}$, relying on the abstract semantics of expressions defined by, abusing notation, $\langle\!\langle \mathtt{e}\rangle\!\rangle : \mathbb{M}^{\sharp} \rightarrow \mathrm{VAL}^{\sharp}$. We focus on the abstract semantics of string operations[4], while the semantics of the other expressions is standard and does not involve strings.

In order to define the abstract semantics of IMP over TARSIS, it is worth to highlight that one can think to reuse the one adopted in the standard finite state automata abstract domain [8]: unfortunately, this is not possible since the one reported in [8] only deals with automata over alphabet of single characters (not strings), and does not handle the character $\top$ used in TARSIS alphabet, that must be treated, as we will see soon, as a special symbol.

Length. Given $\mathsf{A} \in \mathcal{T}\mathsf{FA}_{/\equiv}$, the abstract semantics of `length` returns an interval $[c_1, c_2]$ such that $\forall \sigma \in \mathscr{L}(\mathsf{A}) \, . \, c_1 \leq |\sigma| \leq c_2$. We recast the original idea of the abstract semantics of `length` over standard finite state automata. Let $\mathsf{s} \in \mathrm{SE}$, supposing that $\langle\!\langle \mathsf{s}\rangle\!\rangle\mathsf{m}^{\sharp} = \mathsf{A} \in \mathcal{T}\mathsf{FA}_{/\equiv}$. The `length` abstract semantics is:

$$\langle\!\langle \mathtt{length(s)}\rangle\!\rangle\mathsf{m}^{\sharp} \triangleq \begin{cases} [|\mathsf{minPath}(\mathsf{A})|, +\infty] & \text{if } \mathsf{cyclic}(\mathsf{A}) \vee \mathsf{readsTop}(\mathsf{A}) \\ [|\mathsf{minPath}(\mathsf{A})|, |\mathsf{maxPath}(\mathsf{A})|] & \text{otherwise} \end{cases}$$

where $\mathsf{readsTop}(\mathsf{A}) \Leftrightarrow \exists q, q' \in Q \, . \, (q, \top, q') \in \delta$. Note that, when evaluating the length of the minimum path, $\top$ is considered to have a length of 0. For instance, consider the automaton A reported in Fig. 5a. The minimum path of A is $(q_0, aa, q_1), (q_1, \top, q_2), (q_2, bb, q_4)$ and its length is 4. Since a transition labeled with $\top$ is in A (and its length cannot be statically determined), the abstract `length` of A is $[4, +\infty]$. Consider the automaton A' reported in Fig. 5b. In this case, A' has no cycles and has no transitions labeled with $\top$ and the length of any string recognized by A' can be determined. The length of the minimum path of A' is 3 (below path of A'), the length of the maximum path of A' is 7 (above path of A') and consequently the abstract `length` of A' is $[3, 7]$.

---

[4] The abstract semantics of `concat` does not add any further important technical detail to the paper hence it is not reported.

Fig. 5. (a) A s.t. $\mathscr{L}(\text{A}) = \{bbb\ bbb, aa\ \text{T}\ bb\}$, (b) A′ s.t. $\mathscr{L}(\text{A}') = \{a\ b\ c, aa\ bbb\ cc\}$

Contains. Given $\text{A}, \text{A}' \in \mathcal{T}\text{FA}_{/\equiv}$, the abstract semantics of `contains` should return `true` if any string of A′ is surely contained into some string of A, `false` if no string of A′ is contained in some string of A and $\{\texttt{true}, \texttt{false}\}$ in the other cases. For instance, consider the automaton A depicted in Fig. 6a and suppose we check if it contains the automaton A′ recognizing the language $\{aa, a\}$. The automaton A′ is a *single-path automaton* [9], meaning that any string of A′ is a prefix of its longest string. In this case, the containment of the longest string (on each automaton path) implies the containment of the others, such as in our example, namely it is enough to check that the longest string of A′ is contained into A. Note that, a single-path automaton cannot read the symbol T. We rely on the predicate $\textsf{singlePath}(\text{A})$ when A is a non-cyclic single-path automaton and we denote by $\sigma_{\textsf{sp}}$ its longest string. Let $\text{s}, \text{s}' \in \text{SE}$, supposing that $\langle\!\langle \text{s} \rangle\!\rangle \text{m}^{\sharp} = \text{A} \in \mathcal{T}\text{FA}_{/\equiv}$, $\langle\!\langle \text{s}' \rangle\!\rangle \text{m}^{\sharp} = \text{A}' \in \mathcal{T}\text{FA}_{/\equiv}$. The `contains` abstract semantics is:

$$\langle\!\langle \texttt{contains}(\text{s}, \text{s}') \rangle\!\rangle \text{m}^{\sharp} \triangleq \begin{cases} \texttt{false} & \text{if } \text{A}' \sqcap_{\mathcal{T}} \textsf{FA}(\text{A}) = \text{Min}(\varnothing) \\ \texttt{true} & \text{if } \textsf{singlePath}(\text{A}') \\ & \wedge \forall \pi \in \textsf{paths}(\text{A}^{ac}) . \sigma_{\textsf{sp}} \curvearrowright_{\textsf{s}} \sigma_{\pi} \\ \{\texttt{true}, \texttt{false}\} & \text{otherwise} \end{cases}$$

In the first case, we denote by $\textsf{FA}(\text{A})$ the factor automaton of A, i.e., the automaton recognizing any substring of A. In particular, if A does not share any substring of A′, the abstract semantics safely returns `false` (checking the emptiness of the greatest lower bound between $\textsf{FA}(\text{A})$ and A′). Then, if A′ is a single path automaton, the abstract semantics returns `true` if any path of A^{ac} reads the longest string of A′, with A^{ac} being a copy of A where all the cycles have been removed. Here, we abuse notation denoting with $\sigma_{\textsf{sp}} \curvearrowright_{\textsf{s}} \sigma_{\pi}$ the fact that $\sigma_{\textsf{sp}}$ is a substring of each string in $\textsf{Flat}(\sigma_{\pi})$. Otherwise, $\{\texttt{true}, \texttt{false}\}$ is returned.

IndexOf. Given $\text{A}, \text{A}' \in \mathcal{T}\text{FA}_{/\equiv}$, the `indexOf` abstract semantics returns an interval of the first indexes of the strings of $\mathscr{L}(\text{A}')$ inside strings of $\mathscr{L}(\text{A})$, recalling that when there exists a string of $\mathscr{L}(\text{A}')$ that is not a substring of at least one string of $\mathscr{L}(\text{A}')$, the resulting interval must take into account -1 as well. Let $\text{s}, \text{s}' \in \text{SE}$ and suppose $\langle\!\langle \text{s} \rangle\!\rangle \text{m}^{\sharp} = \text{A}$ and $\langle\!\langle \text{s}' \rangle\!\rangle \text{m}^{\sharp} = \text{A}'$. The abstract semantics of `indexOf` is defined as:

$$\langle\!\langle\texttt{indexOf(s,s')}\rangle\!\rangle\textsf{m}^{\sharp} \triangleq \begin{cases} [-1,+\infty] & \text{if } \mathsf{cyclic}(\texttt{A}) \vee \mathsf{cyclic}(\texttt{A}') \vee \mathsf{readsTop}(\texttt{A}') \\ [-1,-1] & \text{if } \forall\sigma' \in \mathscr{L}(\texttt{A}') \, \nexists\sigma \in \mathscr{L}(\texttt{A}).\, \sigma' \curvearrowright_{\mathsf{s}} \sigma \\ \bigsqcup_{\sigma \in \mathscr{L}(\texttt{A}')}^{\mathsf{Intv}} \mathsf{IO}(\texttt{A},\sigma) & \text{otherwise} \end{cases}$$

If one of the automata has cycles or the automaton abstracting strings we aim to search for ($\texttt{A}'$) has a T-transition, we return $[-1,+\infty]$. Moreover, if none of the strings recognized by $\texttt{A}'$ is contained in a string recognized by $\texttt{A}$, we can safely return the precise interval $[-1,-1]$ since any string recognized by $\texttt{A}'$ is never a substring of a string recognized by $\texttt{A}$.[5] If none of the aforementioned conditions is met, we rely on the auxiliary function $\mathsf{IO} : \mathcal{TFA}_{/\equiv} \times \Sigma^* \to \mathsf{Intv}$, that, given an automaton $\texttt{A}$ and a string $\sigma \in \Sigma^*$, returns an interval corresponding to the possible first positions of σ in strings recognized by $\texttt{A}$. Since $\texttt{A}'$ surely recognizes a finite language (i.e., has no cycles), the idea is to apply $\mathsf{IO}(\texttt{A},\sigma)$ to each $\sigma \in \mathscr{L}(\texttt{A}')$ and to return the upper bound of the resulting intervals. In particular, the function $\mathsf{IO}(\texttt{A},\sigma)$ returns an interval $[i,j] \in \mathsf{Intv}$ where, i and j are computed as follows.

$$i = \begin{cases} -1 & \text{if } \exists\pi \in \mathsf{paths}(\texttt{A}).\, \sigma \not\curvearrowright_{\mathsf{s}} \sigma_{\pi} \\ \displaystyle\min_{\pi \in \mathsf{paths}(\texttt{A})} \left\{ i \, \middle| \, \begin{matrix} \sigma_f \in \mathsf{Flat}(\sigma_{\pi}) \\ \wedge \sigma_{f_i} \ldots \sigma_{f_{i+n}} = \sigma \end{matrix} \right\} & \text{otherwise} \end{cases}$$

$$j = \begin{cases} -1 & \text{if } \forall\pi \in \mathsf{paths}(\texttt{A}).\, \sigma \not\curvearrowright_{\mathsf{s}} \sigma_{\pi} \\ +\infty & \text{if } \exists\pi \in \mathsf{paths}(\texttt{A}).\, \sigma \curvearrowright_{\mathsf{s}} \sigma_{\pi} \\ & \wedge \pi \text{ reads } \mathsf{T} \text{ before } \sigma \\ \displaystyle\max_{\pi \in \mathsf{paths}(\texttt{A})} \left\{ i \, \middle| \, \begin{matrix} \sigma_f \in \mathsf{Flat}(\sigma_{\pi}) \\ \wedge \sigma_{f_i} \ldots \sigma_{f_{i+n}} = \sigma \\ \wedge \sigma \not\curvearrowright_{\mathsf{s}} \sigma_{f_0} \ldots \sigma_{f_{i+n-1}} \end{matrix} \right\} & \text{otherwise} \end{cases}$$

As for the abstract semantics of **contains**, we abuse notation denoting with $\sigma \curvearrowright_{\mathsf{s}} \sigma_{\pi}$ the fact that σ is a substring of each string in $\mathsf{Flat}(\sigma_{\pi})$. Given $\mathsf{IO}(\texttt{A},\sigma) = [i,j] \in \mathsf{Intv}$, i corresponds to the minimal position where the first occurrence of σ can be found in $\texttt{A}$, while j to the maximal one. Let us first focus on the computation of the minimal position. If there exists a path π of $\texttt{A}$ s.t. σ is not recognized by σ_{π}, then the minimal position where σ can be found in $\texttt{A}$ does not exist and -1 is returned. Otherwise, the minimal position where σ begins across π is returned. Let us consider now the computation of the maximal position. If all paths of the automaton do not recognize σ, then -1 is returned. If there exists a path where σ is recognized but the character T appears earlier in the path, then $+\infty$ is returned. Otherwise, the maximal index of the first occurrences of σ across the paths of $\texttt{A}$ is returned.

---

[5] Note that this is a decidable check since $\texttt{A}$ and $\texttt{A}'$ are cycle-free, otherwise the interval $[-1,+\infty]$ would be returned in the first case.

Fig. 6. Example of may-replacement

Replace. In order to give the intuition about how the abstract semantics of replace will work, consider the three automata $A, A_s, A_r \in \mathcal{T}FA_{/\equiv}$. Roughly speaking, the abstract semantics of replace substitutes strings of A_s with strings of A_r inside strings of A. Let us refer to A_s as the *search automaton* and to A_r as the *replace automaton*. We need to specify two types of possible replacements, by means of the following example. Consider $A \in \mathcal{T}FA_{/\equiv}$ that is depicted in Fig. 6a and suppose that the search automaton A_s is the one recognizing the string *bbb* and the replace automaton A_r is a random automaton. In this case, the replace abstract semantics performs a *must-replace* over A, namely substituting the sub-automaton composed by q_1 and q_2 with the replace automaton A_r. Instead, let us suppose that the search automaton A_s is the one recognizing *bbb* or *cc*. Since it is unknown which string *must* be replaced (between *bbb* and *cc*), the replace abstract semantics needs to perform a *may-replace*: when a string recognized by the search automaton is met inside a path of A it is left unaltered in the automaton and, in the same position where the string is met, the abstract replace only extends A with the replace automaton. An example of may replacement is reported in Fig. 6, where A is the one reported in Fig. 6a, the search automaton A_s is the one recognizing the language $\{bbb, cc\}$ and the replace automaton A_r is the one recognizing the string *rr*.

Before introducing the abstract semantics of replace, we define how to replace a string into an automaton. In particular, we define algorithm RP in Algorithm 1, that given $A \in \mathcal{T}FA_{/\equiv}$, a replace automaton A^r and $\sigma \in \Sigma^* \cup \{T\}$, it returns a new automaton that is identical to A except that σ is replaced with A^r.

Algorithm 1 searches the given string σ across all paths of A, collecting the sequences of transitions that recognize the search string σ and extracting them from the paths of A (lines 2–3): an ϵ-transition is introduced going from the first state of the sequence to the initial state of A', and one such transition is also introduced for each final state of A', connecting that state with the ending state of the sequence (lines 4–5). Then, the list of states composing the sequence of transitions is iterated backwards (lines 6–7), stopping at the first state that has a transition going outside of such list. All the states traversed in this way (excluding the one where the iteration stopped) are removed from the resulting automaton, with the transitions connecting them (lines 8–9), since they were needed only to recognize the string that has been replaced. Note that RP corresponds to a must-replace. At this point, we are ready to define the

---

Algorithm 1: RP algorithm

Data: $A^o = \langle Q^o, \mathbb{A}, \delta^o, q_0^o, F^o \rangle, A^r = \langle Q^r, \mathbb{A}, \delta^r, q_0^r, F^r \rangle \in \mathcal{T}FA_{/\equiv}, \sigma \in \Sigma^* \cup \{T\}$
Result: $A \in \mathcal{T}FA_{/\equiv}$

1   $Q^{result} \leftarrow Q^o \cup Q^r$; $\delta^{result} \leftarrow \delta^o \cup \delta^r$;
2   **foreach** $\pi \in$ paths(A^o) **do**
3   **foreach** $(q_i, \sigma_0, q_{i+1}), \ldots, (q_{i+n-1}, \sigma_n, q_{i+n}) \in \pi$ **do**
4       $\delta^{result} \leftarrow \delta^{result} \cup (q_i, \epsilon, q_0^r)$;
5       $\delta^{result} \leftarrow \delta^{result} \cup \{ (q_f, \epsilon, q_{i+n}) \mid q_f \in F^r \}$;
6   **foreach** $k \in [i+n-1, i+1]$ **do**
7   **if** $\nexists(q_k, \sigma', q) \in \delta^o : q \neq q_{k+1}$ **then**
8         $Q^{result} \leftarrow Q^{result} \setminus \{q_k\}$;
9         $\delta^{result} \leftarrow \delta^{result} \setminus \{(q_k, \sigma', q_{k+1})\}$;
10   **else break**;
11 **return** $\langle Q^{result}, \mathbb{A}, \delta^{result}, q_0^o, F^o \rangle$;

---

replace abstract semantics. In particular, if either A or A_s have cycles or A_s has a T-transition, we return Min($\{T\}$), namely the automaton recognizing T. Otherwise, the **replace** abstract semantics is:

$$\langle \mathtt{replace}(s, s_s, s_r) \rangle m^{\sharp} \triangleq \begin{cases} A & \text{if } \forall \sigma_s \in \mathscr{L}(A_s) \\ & \nexists \sigma \in \mathscr{L}(A). \\ & \sigma_s \curvearrowright_s \sigma \\ RP(A, \sigma_s, A_r) & \text{if } \mathscr{L}(A_s) = \{\sigma_s\} \\ \bigsqcup_{\sigma \in \mathscr{L}(A_s)} RP(A, \sigma, A_r \sqcup_{\mathcal{T}} \text{Min}(\{\sigma\})) & \text{otherwise} \end{cases}$$

In the first case, if none of the strings recognized by the search automaton A_s is contained into strings recognized by A, we can safely return the original automaton A without any replacement. In the special case where $\mathscr{L}(A_s) = \{\sigma_s\}$, we return the automaton obtained by performing a replacement calling the function $RP(A, \sigma_s, A_r)$. In the last case, for each each string $\sigma \in \mathscr{L}(A_s)$, we perform a may replace of σ with A_r: note that, this exactly corresponds to a call RP where the replace automaton is $A_r \sqcup_{\mathcal{T}} \text{Min}(\{\sigma\})$, namely σ is not removed. The so far obtained automata are finally lubbed together.

Substring. Given $A \in \mathcal{T}FA_{/\equiv}$ and two intervals i, j $\in$ Intv, the abstract semantics of **substring** returns a new automaton A' soundly approximating any substring from i to j of strings recognized by A, for any $i \in$ i, $j \in$ j s.t. $i \leq j$.

Given $A \in \mathcal{T}FA_{/\equiv}$, in the definition of the **substring** semantics, we rely on the corresponding regex r since the two representations are equivalent and regexes allow us to define a more intuitive formalization of the semantics of **substring**. Let us suppose that $\langle s \rangle m^{\sharp} = A \in \mathcal{T}FA_{/\equiv}$ and let us denote by r the regex corresponding to the language recognized by A. At the moment, let us consider exact intervals representing one integer value, namely $\langle a_1 \rangle m^{\sharp} = [i, i]$ and $\langle a_2 \rangle m^{\sharp} = [j, j]$, with $i, j \in \mathbb{Z}$. In this case, the abstract semantics is defined as:

$$\langle \mathtt{substr}(s, a_1, a_2) \rangle m^{\sharp} \triangleq \bigsqcup \text{Min}(\{ \sigma \mid (\sigma, 0, 0) \in Sb(r, i, j - i) \})$$

where Sb takes as input a regex r, two indexes $i, j \in \mathbb{N}$, and computes the set of substrings from i to j of all the strings recognized by r. In particular, Sb is

---

Algorithm 2: Sb algorithm

Data: r regex over $\mathbb{A}$, $i, j \in \mathbb{N}$
Result: $\{ (\sigma, n_1, n_2) \mid \sigma \in \Sigma^*, n_1, n_2 \in \mathbb{N} \}$

1 **if** $j = 0 \vee r = \varnothing$ **then**
2 | **return** $\varnothing$;
3 **else if** $r = \sigma \in \Sigma^*$ **then**
4 | **if** $i > |\sigma|$ **then return** $\{(\epsilon, i - |\sigma|, j)\}$;
5 | **else if** $i + j > |\sigma|$ **then return** $\{(\sigma_i \ldots \sigma_{|\sigma|-1}, 0, j - |\sigma| + i)\}$;
6 | **else return** $\{(\sigma_i \ldots \sigma_{i+j}, 0, 0)\}$;
7 **else if** $r = \mathsf{T}$ **then**
8 | result $\leftarrow \{(\epsilon, i - k, j) : 0 \le k \le i, k \in \mathbb{N}\}$;
9 | result $\leftarrow$ result $\cup \{ (\bullet^k, 0, j - k) \mid 0 \le k \le j, k \in \mathbb{N} \}$;
10 | **return** result;
11 **else if** $r = r_1 r_2$ **then**
12 | result $\leftarrow \varnothing$;
13 | subs$_1 \leftarrow$ Sb(r_1, i, j);
14 | **foreach** $(\sigma_1, i_1, j_1) \in$ subs$_1$ **do**
15 | | **if** $j_1 = 0$ **then**
16 | | | result $\leftarrow$ result $\cup \{(\sigma_1, i_1, j_1)\}$;
17 | | **else**
18 | | | result $\leftarrow$ result $\cup \{ (\sigma_1 \cdot \sigma_2, i_2, j_2) \mid (\sigma_2, i_2, j_2) \in$ Sb$(r_2, i_1, j_1) \}$;
19 | **return** result;
20 **else if** $r = r_1 \| r_2$ **then**
21 | **return** Sb$(r_1, i, j) \cup$ Sb(r_2, i, j);
22 **else if** $r = (r_1)^*$ **then**
23 | result $\leftarrow \{(\epsilon, i, j)\}$; partial $\leftarrow \varnothing$;
24 | **repeat**
25 | | result $\leftarrow$ result $\cup$ partial; partial $\leftarrow \varnothing$;
26 | | **foreach** $(\sigma_n, i_n, j_n) \in$ result **do**
27 | | | **foreach** (suff, $i_s, j_s) \in$ Sb$(r_1, i_n, i_n + j_n)$ **do**
28 | | | | **if** $\nexists(\sigma', k, w) \in$ result . $\sigma' = \sigma_n \cdot$ suff $\wedge k = i_s \wedge w = j_s$ **then**
29 | | | | partial $\leftarrow$ partial $\cup \{(\sigma_n \cdot$ suff, $i_s, j_s)\}$;
30 | **until** partial $\neq \varnothing$;
31 | **return** result;

---

defined by Algorithm 2 and, given a regex r and $i, j \in \mathbb{N}$, it returns a set of triples of the form (σ, n_1, n_2), such that σ is the *partial substring* that Algorithm 2 has computed up to now, $n_1 \in \mathbb{N}$ tracks how many characters have still to be skipped before the substring can be computed and $n_2 \in \mathbb{N}$ is the number of characters Algorithm 2 needs still to look for to successfully compute a substring. Hence, given Sb(r, i, j), the result is a set of such triples; note that given an element of the resulting set (σ, n_1, n_2), $n_2 = 0$ means that no more characters are needed and σ corresponds to a proper substring of r from i to j. Thus, from the resulting set, we can filter out the partial substrings, and retrieve only proper substrings of r from i to j, by only considering the value of n_2. Algorithm 2 is defined by case on the structure of the input regex r:

1. $j = 0$ or $r = \varnothing$ (lines 1–2): $\varnothing$ is returned since we either completed the substring or we have no more characters to add;
2. $r = \sigma \in \Sigma^*$ (lines 3–6): if $i > |\sigma|$, the requested substring happens after this atom, and we return a singleton set $\{\epsilon, i - |\sigma|, j\}$, thus tracking the consumed characters before the start of the requested substring; if $i + j > |\sigma|$, the substring begins in σ but ends in subsequent regexes, and we return a

singleton set containing the substring of σ from i to its end, with $n_1 = 0$ since we begun collecting characters, and $n_2 = j - |\sigma| + i$ since we collected $|\sigma| - i$ characters; otherwise, the substring is fully inside σ, and we return the substring of σ from i to $i + j$, setting both n_1 and n_2 to 0;

3. $\mathbf{r} = \mathsf{T}$ (lines 7–10): since $\mathbf{r}$ might have any length, we generate substrings that (a) gradually consume all the missing characters before the substring can begin (line 8) and (b) gradually consume all the characters that make up the substring, adding the unknown character $\bullet$ (line 9);

4. $\mathbf{r} = \mathbf{r}_1\mathbf{r}_2$ (lines 11–20): the desired substring can either be fully found in $\mathbf{r}_1$ or $\mathbf{r}_2$, or could overlap them; thus we compute all the partial substrings of $\mathbf{r}_1$, recursively calling Sb (line 13); for all $\{\sigma_1, i_1, j_1\}$ returned, substrings that are fully contained in $\mathbf{r}_1$ (i.e., when $j_1 = 0$) are added to the result (line 16) while the remaining ones are joined with ones computed by recursively calling Sb on $\mathbf{r}_2$ with $n_1 = j_1$ and $n_2 = j_2$;

5. $\mathbf{r} = \mathbf{r}_1 || \mathbf{r}_2$ (lines 20–21): we return the partial substring of $\mathbf{r}_1$ and the ones of $\mathbf{r}_2$, recursively calling Sb on both of them;

6. $\mathbf{r} = (\mathbf{r}_1)^*$ (lines 22–31): we construct the set of substrings through fixpoint iteration, starting by generating $\{\epsilon, i, j\}$ (corresponding to $\mathbf{r}_1$ repeated 0 times - line 23) and then, at each iteration, by joining all the partial results obtained until now with the ones generated by a further recursive call to Sb, keeping only the joined results that are new (lines 24–30).

Above, we have defined the abstract semantics of **substring** when intervals are constant. When $\langle a_1 \rangle m^{\sharp} = [i, j]$ and $\langle a_2 \rangle m^{\sharp} = [l, k]$, with $i, j, l, k \in \mathbb{Z}$, the abstract semantics of **substring** is

$$\langle \mathtt{substr}(\mathsf{s}, \mathsf{a}_1, \mathsf{a}_2) \rangle m^{\sharp} \triangleq \bigsqcup_{a \in [i,j], b \in [l,k], a \leq b} \bigsqcup \mathsf{Min}(\{\ \sigma \mid (\sigma, 0, 0) \in \mathsf{Sb}(\mathbf{r}, a, b - a)\ \})$$

We do not precisely handle the cases when the intervals are unbounded (e.g., $[1, +\infty]$). These cases have been already considered in [8] and treated in an ad-hoc manner and one may recast the same proposed idea in our context. Nevertheless, when these cases are met, our analysis returns the automaton recognizing any possible substring of the input automaton, still guaranteeing soundness.

5   Experimental Results

TARSIS has been compared with five other domains, namely the prefix (PR), suffix (SU), char inclusion (CI), bricks (BR) domains (all defined in [16]), and $\mathrm{FA}_{/\equiv}$ (defined in [8], adapting their abstract semantics definition for Java, without altering their precision).

All domains have been implemented in a prototype of a static analyzer for a subset of the Java language, similar to IMP (Sect. 3), plus the assert statement. In particular, our analyzer raises a *definite* alarm (DA for short) when a failing assert (i.e., whose condition is definitely false) is met, while it raises a *possible* alarm (PA for short) when the assertion *might* fail (i.e., the assertion's condition

```
1   void substring () {
2     String res = "substring test";
3     if (nondet)
4       res = res + " passed";
5     else
6       res = res + " failed";
7     result = res.substring (5, 18);
8     assert (res.contains("g"));
9     assert (res.contains("p"));
10    assert (res.contains("f"));
11    assert (res.contains("d"));
12  }
```

```
1   void loop () {
2     String value = read ();
3     String res = "Repeat: ";
4     while (nondet)
5       res = res + value + "!";
6     assert (res.contains("t"));
7     assert (res.contains("!"));
8     assert (res.contains("f"));
9   }
```

(a) Program SUBS   (b) Program LOOP

Fig. 7. Program samples used for domain comparison

evaluates to $\top_{\mathsf{Bool}}$). Comparisons have been performed by analyzing the code through the coalesced sum domain specified in Sect. 4.2 with trace partitioning [31] (note that all traces are merged when evaluating an assertion), plugging in the various string domains. All experiments have been performed on a HP EliteBook G6 machine, with an Intel Core i7-8565U @ 1.8 GHz processor and 16 GB of RAM memory.

To achieve a fair comparison with the other string domains, the subjects of our evaluation are small hand-crafted code fragments that represent standard string manipulations that occur regularly in software. PR, SU, CI and BR have been built to model simple properties and to work with integers instead of intervals, and have been evaluated on small programs: Sect. 5.1 compares them to TARSIS and $FA_{/\equiv}$ without expanding the scope of such evaluations. Section 5.2 instead focuses on slightly more advanced and complex string manipulations that are not modeled by the aforementioned domains, but that $FA_{/\equiv}$ and TARSIS can indeed tackle, highlighting differences between them.

It is important to notice that performances of programs relying on automata (highlighted in Sect. 5.3) are heavily dependent on their implementation. Both $FA_{/\equiv}$ and TARSIS (whose sources are available on GitHub[6,7]) come as non-optimized proof-of-concept libraries (specifically, TARSIS has been built following the structure of $FA_{/\equiv}$ to ensure a fair performance comparison) whose performances can be greatly improved.

5.1 Precision of the Various Domains on Test Cases

We start by considering programs SUBS (Fig. 7a) and LOOP (Fig. 7b). SUBS calls substring on the concatenation between two strings, where the first is constant and the second one is chosen in a non-deterministic way (i.e., nondet condition is statically unknown, lines 3–6). LOOP builds a string by repeatedly appending a suffix, which contains a user input (i.e., an unknown string), to a constant

---

[6] $FA_{/\equiv}$ source code: https://github.com/SPY-Lab/fsa.
[7] TARSIS source code: https://github.com/UniVE-SSV/tarsis.

value. Table 1 reports the value approximation for res for each abstract domain and analyzed program when the first assertion of each program is met, as well as if the abstract domain precisely dealt with the program assertions. For the sake of readability, TARSIS and $FA_{/\cong}$ approximations are expressed as regexes.

When analyzing SUBS, both PR and SU lose precision since the string to append to res is statically unknown. This leads, at line 7, to a partial substring of the concrete one with PR, and to an empty string with SU. Instead, the substring semantics of CI moves every character of the receiver in the set of possibly contained ones, thus the abstract value at line 7 is composed by an empty set of included characters, and a set of possibly included characters containing the ones of both strings. Finally, BR, $FA_{/\cong}$ and TARSIS are expressive enough to track any string produced by any concrete execution of SUBS.

When evaluating the assertions of SUBS, a PA should be raised on lines 9 and 10, since "p" or "f" might be in res, together with a DA alarm on line 11, since "d" is surely not contained in res. No alarm should be raised on line 8 instead, since "g" is part of the common prefix of both branches and thus will be included in the substring. Such behavior is achieved when using BR, $FA_{/\cong}$, or TARSIS. Since the substring semantics of CI moves all characters to the set of possibly contained ones, PAs are raised on all four assertions. Since SU loses all information about res, PAs are raised on lines 7–10 when using such domain. PR instead tracks the definite prefix of res, thus the PA at line 7 is avoided.

When analyzing LOOP, we expect to obtain no alarm at line 6 (since character "t" is always contained in the resulting string value), and PA at lines 7 and 8. PR infers as prefix of res the string "Repeat: ", keeping such value for the whole analysis of the program. This allows the analyzer to prove the assertion at line 6, but it raises PAs when it checks the ones at lines 7 and 8. Again, SU loses any information about res since the lub operation occurring at line 3 cannot find a common suffix between "Repeat: " and "!", hence PAs are raised on lines 6–8. Since the set of possible characters contains T, CI can correctly state that any character might appear in the string. For this reason, two PAs are reported on lines 7 and 8, while no alarm is raised on line 6 (again, this is possible since the string used in the contains call has length 1). The alternation of T and "!" prevents BR normalization algorithm from merging similar bricks. This will eventually lead to overcoming the length threshold k_L, hence resulting in the

Table 1. Values of res at the first assert of each program

Domain	Program SUBS		Program LOOP	
PR	ring test	✗	Repeat:	✗
SU	ϵ	✗	ϵ	✗
CI	[] [abdefgilnprstu]	✗	[:aepRt] [!:aepRt T]	✓
BR	[{ring test fai, ring test pas}] $(1, 1)$	✓	[{T}] $(0, +\infty)$	✗
$FA_{/\cong}$	ring test (pas||fai)	✓	Repeat: $(T)^*$	✓
TARSIS	(ring test pas||ring test fai)	✓	Repeat: $(T!)^*$	✓

```
1   void toString(String[] names) {
2     String res="People: {";
3     int i=0;
4     while(i<names.length){
5       res=res+names[i];
6       if(i!=names.length −1)
7         res=res+",";
8       i=i+1;
9     }
10    res=res+"}";
11    assert(res.contains("People"));
12    assert(res.contains(","));
13    assert(res.contains("not"));
14  }
```

```
1   void count(boolean nondet) {
2     String str;
3     if(nondet) str="this is the thing";
4     else str="the throat";
5     int count=countMatches(str, "th")
6     assert(count>0);
7     assert(count==0);
8     assert(count==3);
9   }
```

(a) Program TOSTRING   (b) Program COUNT

Fig. 8. Programs used for assessing domain precision

$[\{T\}]\,(0,+\infty)$ abstract value. In such a situation, BR returns T_{Bool} on all contains calls, resulting in PAs on lines 6–8. The parametric widening of $FA_{/\equiv}$ collapses the colon into T. In TARSIS, since the automaton representing res grows by two states each iteration, the parametric widening defined in Sect. 4.1 can collapse the whole content of the loop into a 2-states loop recognizing T!. The precise approximation of res of both domains enable the analyzer to detect that the assertion at line 6 always holds, while PAs are raised on lines 7 and 8.

In summary, PR and SU failed to produce the expected results on both SUBS and LOOP, while CI and BR produced exact results in one case (LOOP and SUBS, respectively), but not in the other. Hence, $FA_{/\equiv}$ and TARSIS were the two only domains that produced the desired behavior in these rather simple test cases.

5.2   Evaluation on Realistic Code Samples

In this section, we explore two real world code samples. Method TOSTRING (Fig. 8a) transforms an array of names that come as string values into a single string. While it resembles the code of LOOP in Fig. 7b (thus, results of all the analyses show the same strengths and weaknesses), now assertions check contains predicates with a multi-character string. Method COUNT (Fig. 8b) makes use of

Table 2. Values of res and count at the first assert of the respective program

Domain	Program TOSTRING		Program COUNT	
PR	People: {	✗	$[0,+\infty]$	✗
SU	ϵ	✗	$[0,+\infty]$	✗
CI	$[\{\}{:}\mathsf{Peopl}\,]\,[\{\}{:}{,}\mathsf{Peopl}\,\mathsf{T}]$	✗	$[0,+\infty]$	✗
BR	$[\{T\}]\,(0,+\infty)$	✗	$[0,+\infty]$	✗
$FA_{/\equiv}$	People: $\{(T)^*T\}$	✓	$[2,3]$	✓
TARSIS	People: $\{\}\|\|$People: $\{(T,)^*T\}$	✓	$[2,3]$	✓

Table 3. Execution times of the domains on each program

Domain	SUBS	LOOP	TOSTRING	COUNT
PR	11 ms	3 ms	78 ms	29 ms
SU	10 ms	2 ms	92 ms	29 ms
CI	10 ms	3 ms	90 ms	29 ms
BR	13 ms	3 ms	190 ms	28 ms
FA$_{/\equiv}$	10 ms	52013 ms	226769 ms	4235 ms
TARSIS	34 ms	38 ms	299 ms	39 ms

COUNTMATCHES (reported in Sect. 2) to prove properties about its return value. Since the analyzer is not inter-procedural, we inlined COUNTMATCHES inside COUNT. Table 2 reports the results of both methods (stored in res and count, respectively) evaluated by each analysis at the first assertion, as well as if the abstract domain precisely dealt with the program assertions.

As expected, when analyzing TOSTRING, each domain showed results similar to those of LOOP. In particular, we expect to obtain no alarm at line 11 (since "People" is surely contained in the resulting string), and two PAs at line 12 and 13. PR, SU, CI and BR raise PAs on all the three assert statements. FA$_{/\equiv}$ and TARSIS detect that the assertion at line 11 always holds. Thus, when using them, the analyzer raises PAs on lines 12 and 13 since: comma character is part of res if the loop is iterated at least once, and T might match "not".

If COUNT (with the inlined code from COUNTMATCHES) was to be executed, count would be either 2 or 3 when the first assertion is reached, depending on the choice of str. Thus, no alarm should be raised at line 6, while a DA should be raised on line 7, and a PA on line 8. Since PR, SU, CI and BR do not define most of the operations used in the code, the analyzer does not have information about the string on which COUNTMATCHES is executed, and thus abstract count with the interval $[0, +\infty]$. Thus, PAs are raised on lines 6–8. Instead, FA$_{/\equiv}$ and TARSIS are instead able to detect that sub is present in all the possible strings represented by str. Thus, thanks to trace partitioning, the trace where the loop is skipped and count remains 0 gets discarded. Then, when the first indexOf call happens, $[0, 0]$ is stored into idx, since all possible values of str start with sub. Since the call to length yields $[10, 17]$, all possible substrings from $[2, 2]$ (idx plus the length of sub) to $[10, 17]$ are computed (namely, "e throat", "is the", "is the", ..., "is the thing"), and the resulting automaton is the one that recognizes all of them. Since the value of sub is still contained in every path of such automaton, the loop guard still holds and the second iteration is analyzed, repeating the same operations. When the loop guard is reached for the third time, the remaining substring of the shorter starting string (namely "roat") recognized by the automaton representing str will no longer contain sub: a trace where count equals $[2, 2]$ will leave the loop. A further iteration is then analyzed, after which sub is no longer contained in any of the strings that str might hold. Thus, a second and final trace where count equals $[3, 3]$ will reach the assertions, and will be merged by interval lub, obtaining $[2, 3]$ as final value for count. This allows TARSIS and $\text{FA}_{/\cong}$ to identify that the assertion at line 7 never holds, raising a DA, while the one at line 8 might not hold, raising a PA.

5.3 Efficiency

The detailed analysis of two test cases, and two examples taken from real-world code underlined that TARSIS and $\text{FA}_{/\cong}$ are the only ones able to obtain precise results on them. We now discuss the efficiency of the analyses. Table 3 reports the execution times for all the domains on the case studies analyzed in this section. Overall, PR, SU, CI, and BR are the fastest domains with execution times usually below 100 msecs. Thus, if on the one hand these domains failed to prove some of the properties of interest, they are quite efficient and they might be helpful to prove simple properties. TARSIS execution times are higher but still comparable with them (about 50% overhead on average). Instead, $\text{FA}_{/\cong}$ blows up on three out of the four test cases (and in particular on TOSTRING). Hence, TARSIS is the only domain that executes the analysis in a limited time while being able to prove all the properties of interest on these four case studies.

The reason behind the performance gap between TARSIS and $\text{FA}_{/\cong}$ can be accounted on the alphabets underlying the automata. In $\text{FA}_{/\cong}$, automata are built over an alphabet of single characters. While this simplifies the semantic operations, it also causes state and transition blow up w.r.t. the size of the string that needs to be represented. This does not happen in TARSIS, since atomic strings (not built through concatenation or other string manipulations) are part of the alphabet and can be used as transition symbol. Having less states and transitions to operate upon drastically lowers the time and memory requirements of automata operations, making TARSIS faster than $\text{FA}_{/\cong}$.

TARSIS's alphabet has another peculiarity w.r.t. $\text{FA}_{/\cong}$'s: it has a special symbol for representing the unknown string. Having such a symbol requires some fine-tuning of the algorithms to have them behave differently when the symbol is encountered, but without additional tolls on their performances. $\text{FA}_{/\cong}$'s alphabet does not have such a symbol, thus representing the unknown string is achieved through a state having one self-loop for each character in the alphabet (including the empty string). This requires significantly more resources for automata algorithms, leading to higher execution times.

6   Conclusion

In this paper we introduced TARSIS, an abstract domain for sound abstraction of string values. TARSIS is based on finite state automata paired with their equivalent regular expression: a representation that allows precise modeling of complex string values. Experiments show that TARSIS achieves great precision also on code that heavily manipulate string values, while the time needed for the analysis is comparable with the one of other simpler domains.

The analysis proposed in this paper is intra-procedural and we are currently working on extending it to an inter-procedural analysis. Moreover, in order to further improve the performance of our analysis, sophisticated techniques such as abstract slicing [26,27] can be integrated to keep the size of automata arising during abstract computations as low as possible, by focusing the analysis only on the string variables of interest. Finally, in this paper, we did not investigate completeness property of TARSIS w.r.t. the considered operations of interest. This would ensure that no loss of information is related to $\mathcal{T}\mathrm{FA}_{/\equiv}$ due to the input abstraction process [9]. Our future directions will include a deeper study about $\mathcal{T}\mathrm{FA}_{/\equiv}$ completeness, and possibly the application of completion processes when incompleteness arises for a string operation [24].

References

1. Abdulla, P.A., et al.: Efficient handling of string-number conversion. In: Donaldson, A.F., Torlak, E. (eds.) Proceedings of the 41st ACM SIGPLAN International Conference on Programming Language Design and Implementation, PLDI 2020, London, UK, 15–20 June 2020, pp. 943–957. ACM (2020). https://doi.org/10.1145/3385412.3386034
2. Abdulla, et al.: String constraints for verification. In: Biere, A., Bloem, R. (eds.) Computer Aided Verification - 26th International Conference, CAV 2014, Held as Part of the Vienna Summer of Logic, VSL 2014, Vienna, Austria, 18–22 July 2014. Proceedings. Lecture Notes in Computer Science, vol. 8559, pp. 150–166. Springer (2014). https://doi.org/10.1007/978-3-319-08867-9_10
3. Abdulla, P.A., Atig, M.F., Diep, B.P., Holík, L., Janku, P.: Chain-free string constraints. In: Chen, Y., Cheng, C., Esparza, J. (eds.) Automated Technology for Verification and Analysis - 17th International Symposium, ATVA 2019, Taipei, Taiwan, 28–31 October 2019, Proceedings. Lecture Notes in Computer Science, vol. 11781, pp. 277–293. Springer (2019). https://doi.org/10.1007/978-3-030-31784-3_16
4. Almashfi, N., Lu, L.: Precise string domain for analyzing javascript arrays and objects. In: 2020 3rd International Conference on Information and Computer Technologies (ICICT), pp. 17–23 (2020)
5. Amadini, R., Gange, G., Stuckey, P.J.: Dashed strings for string constraint solving. Artif. Intell. **289**, 103368 (2020). https://doi.org/10.1016/j.artint.2020.103368
6. Arceri, V., Maffeis, S.: Abstract domains for type juggling. Electron. Notes Theor. Comput. Sci. **331**, 41–55 (2017). https://doi.org/10.1016/j.entcs.2017.02.003
7. Arceri, V., Mastroeni, I.: A sound abstract interpreter for dynamic code. In: Hung, C., Cerný, T., Shin, D., Bechini, A. (eds.) SAC 2020: The 35th ACM/SIGAPP Symposium on Applied Computing, online event, [Brno, Czech Republic], 30 March–3 April 2020. pp. 1979–1988. ACM (2020). https://doi.org/10.1145/3341105.3373964
8. Arceri, V., Mastroeni, I., Xu, S.: Static analysis for Ecmascript string manipulation programs. Appl. Sci. **10**, 3525 (2020). https://doi.org/10.3390/app10103525

9. Arceri, V., Olliaro, M., Cortesi, A., Mastroeni, I.: Completeness of abstract domains for string analysis of javascript programs. In: Hierons, R.M., Mosbah, M. (eds.) Theoretical Aspects of Computing - ICTAC 2019–16th International Colloquium, Hammamet, Tunisia, 31 October–4 November 2019, Proceedings. Lecture Notes in Computer Science, vol. 11884, pp. 255–272. Springer (2019). https://doi.org/10. 1007/978-3-030-32505-3_15

10. Bartzis, C., Bultan, T.: Widening arithmetic automata. In: Alur, R., Peled, D.A. (eds.) Computer Aided Verification, 16th International Conference, CAV 2004, Boston, MA, USA, 13–17 July 2004, Proceedings. Lecture Notes in Computer Science, vol. 3114, pp. 321–333. Springer (2004). https://doi.org/10.1007/978-3-540-27813-9_25

11. Chen, T., Hague, M., Lin, A.W., Rümmer, P., Wu, Z.: Decision procedures for path feasibility of string-manipulating programs with complex operations. Proc. ACM Program. Lang. 3(POPL), 49:1–49:30 (2019). https://doi.org/10.1145/3290362

12. Choi, T., Lee, O., Kim, H., Doh, K.: A practical string analyzer by the widening approach. In: Kobayashi, N. (ed.) Programming Languages and Systems, 4th Asian Symposium, APLAS 2006, Sydney, Australia, 8–10 November 2006, Proceedings. Lecture Notes in Computer Science, vol. 4279, pp. 374–388. Springer (2006). https://doi.org/10.1007/11924661_23

13. Christensen, A.S., Møller, A., Schwartzbach, M.I.: Precise analysis of string expressions. In: Cousot, R. (ed.) Static Analysis, 10th International Symposium, SAS 2003, San Diego, CA, USA, 11–13 June 2003, Proceedings. Lecture Notes in Computer Science, vol. 2694, pp. 1–18. Springer (2003). https://doi.org/10.1007/3-540-44898-5_1

14. Cortesi, A., Olliaro, M.: M-string segmentation: A refined abstract domain for string analysis in C programs. In: Pang, J., Zhang, C., He, J., Weng, J. (eds.) 2018 International Symposium on Theoretical Aspects of Software Engineering, TASE 2018, Guangzhou, China, 29–31 August 2018, pp. 1–8. IEEE Computer Society (2018). https://doi.org/10.1109/TASE.2018.00009

15. Cortesi, A., Zanioli, M.: Widening and narrowing operators for abstract interpretation. Comput. Lang. Syst. Struct. 37(1), 24–42 (2011). https://doi.org/10.1016/j.cl.2010.09.001

16. Costantini, G., Ferrara, P., Cortesi, A.: A suite of abstract domains for static analysis of string values. Softw. Pract. Exp. 45(2), 245–287 (2015). https://doi.org/10.1002/spe.2218

17. Cousot, P., Cousot, R.: Abstract interpretation: a unified lattice model for static analysis of programs by construction or approximation of fixpoints. In: Graham, R.M., Harrison, M.A., Sethi, R. (eds.) Conference Record of the Fourth ACM Symposium on Principles of Programming Languages, Los Angeles, California, USA, January 1977, pp. 238–252. ACM (1977). https://doi.org/10.1145/512950. 512973

18. Cousot, P., Cousot, R.: Systematic design of program analysis frameworks. In: Aho, A.V., Zilles, S.N., Rosen, B.K. (eds.) Conference Record of the Sixth Annual ACM Symposium on Principles of Programming Languages, San Antonio, Texas, USA, January 1979, pp. 269–282. ACM Press (1979). https://doi.org/10.1145/567752. 567778

19. Cousot, P., Cousot, R.: Abstract interpretation frameworks. J. Log. Comput. 2(4), 511–547 (1992). https://doi.org/10.1093/logcom/2.4.511

20. Cousot, P., Halbwachs, N.: Automatic discovery of linear restraints among variables of a program. In: Aho, A.V., Zilles, S.N., Szymanski, T.G. (eds.) Conference Record of the Fifth Annual ACM Symposium on Principles of Programming Languages, Tucson, Arizona, USA, January 1978, pp. 84–96. ACM Press (1978). https://doi.org/10.1145/512760.512770
21. D'Antoni, L., Veanes, M.: Minimization of symbolic automata. In: Jagannathan, S., Sewell, P. (eds.) The 41st Annual ACM SIGPLAN-SIGACT Symposium on Principles of Programming Languages, POPL 2014, San Diego, CA, USA, 20–21 January 2014, pp. 541–554. ACM (2014). https://doi.org/10.1145/2535838.2535849
22. Davis, M.D., Sigal, R., Weyuker, E.J.: Computability, Complexity, and Languages: Fund. of Theor. CS. Academic Press Professional, Inc. (1994)
23. D'Silva, V.: Widening for Automata. MsC Thesis, Inst. Fur Inform. - UZH (2006)
24. Giacobazzi, R., Ranzato, F., Scozzari, F.: Making abstract interpretations complete. J. ACM **47**(2), 361–416 (2000). https://doi.org/10.1145/333979.333989
25. Madsen, M., Andreasen, E.: String analysis for dynamic field access. In: Cohen, A. (ed.) Compiler Construction - 23rd International Conference, CC 2014, Held as Part of the European Joint Conferences on Theory and Practice of Software, ETAPS 2014, Grenoble, France, 5–13 April, 2014. Proceedings. Lecture Notes in Computer Science, vol. 8409, pp. 197–217. Springer (2014). https://doi.org/10.1007/978-3-642-54807-9_12
26. Mastroeni, I., Nikolic, D.: Abstract program slicing: From theory towards an implementation. In: Dong, J.S., Zhu, H. (eds.) Formal Methods and Software Engineering - 12th International Conference on Formal Engineering Methods, ICFEM 2010, Shanghai, China, 17–19 November 2010. Proceedings. Lecture Notes in Computer Science, vol. 6447, pp. 452–467. Springer (2010). https://doi.org/10.1007/978-3-642-16901-4_30
27. Mastroeni, I., Zanardini, D.: Abstract program slicing: an abstract interpretation-based approach to program slicing. ACM Trans. Comput. Log. **18**(1), 7:1–7:58 (2017). https://doi.org/10.1145/3029052
28. Midtgaard, J., Nielson, F., Nielson, H.R.: A parametric abstract domain for lattice-valued regular expressions. In: Rival, X. (ed.) Static Analysis - 23rd International Symposium, SAS 2016, Edinburgh, UK, 8–10 September 2016, Proceedings. Lecture Notes in Computer Science, vol. 9837, pp. 338–360. Springer (2016). https://doi.org/10.1007/978-3-662-53413-7_17
29. Park, C., Im, H., Ryu, S.: Precise and scalable static analysis of jquery using a regular expression domain. In: Ierusalimschy, R. (ed.) Proceedings of the 12th Symposium on Dynamic Languages, DLS 2016, Amsterdam, The Netherlands, 1 November 2016, pp. 25–36. ACM (2016). https://doi.org/10.1145/2989225.2989228
30. Preda, M.D., Giacobazzi, R., Lakhotia, A., Mastroeni, I.: Abstract symbolic automata: mixed syntactic/semantic similarity analysis of executables. In: Rajamani, S.K., Walker, D. (eds.) Proceedings of the 42nd Annual ACM SIGPLAN-SIGACT Symposium on Principles of Programming Languages, POPL 2015, Mumbai, India, 15–17 January 2015, pp. 329–341. ACM (2015). https://doi.org/10.1145/2676726.2676986
31. Rival, X., Mauborgne, L.: The trace partitioning abstract domain. ACM Trans. Program. Lang. Syst. 29(5), 26-es, August 2007. https://doi.org/10.1145/1275497.1275501

32. Veanes, M.: Applications of symbolic finite automata. In: Konstantinidis, S. (ed.) Implementation and Application of Automata - 18th International Conference, CIAA 2013, Halifax, NS, Canada, July 16–19, 2013. Proceedings. Lecture Notes in Computer Science, vol. 7982, pp. 16–23. Springer (2013). https://doi.org/10.1007/978-3-642-39274-0_3
33. Wang, H., Chen, S., Yu, F., Jiang, J.R.: A symbolic model checking approach to the analysis of string and length constraints. In: Huchard, M., Kästner, C., Fraser, G. (eds.) Proceedings of the 33rd ACM/IEEE International Conference on Automated Software Engineering, ASE 2018, Montpellier, France, 3–7 September 2018, pp. 623–633. ACM (2018). https://doi.org/10.1145/3238147.3238189
34. Yu, F., Alkhalaf, M., Bultan, T., Ibarra, O.H.: Automata-based symbolic string analysis for vulnerability detection. Formal Meth. Syst. Des. **44**(1), 44–70 (2013). https://doi.org/10.1007/s10703-013-0189-1

Unbounded Procedure Summaries from Bounded Environments

Lauren Pick[1]($\boxtimes$), Grigory Fedyukovich[2], and Aarti Gupta[1]

[1] Princeton University, Princeton, NJ, USA
lpick@cs.princeton.edu
[2] Florida State University, Tallahassee, FL, USA

Abstract. Modular approaches to verifying interprocedural programs involve learning summaries for individual procedures rather than verifying a monolithic program. Modern approaches based on use of Satisfiability Modulo Theory (SMT) solvers have made much progress in this direction. However, it is still challenging to handle mutual recursion and to derive adequate procedure summaries using scalable methods. We propose a novel modular verification algorithm that addresses these challenges by learning lemmas about the relationships among procedure summaries and by using *bounded environments* in SMT queries. We have implemented our algorithm in a tool called CLOVER and report on a detailed evaluation that shows that it outperforms existing automated tools on benchmark programs with mutual recursion while being competitive on standard benchmarks.

Keywords: Program verification · Modular verification · Procedure summaries · Bounded environments · CHC solvers

1 Introduction

Automated techniques for modular reasoning about interprocedural recursive programs have a rich history with various techniques spanning interprocedural dataflow analysis [55,57], abstract interpretation [18], and software model checking [6]. These techniques exploit the inherent modularity in a program by deriving a *summary* for each procedure. Procedure summaries can be viewed as specifications or interface contracts, where internal implementation details have been abstracted away. In addition to aiding code understanding and maintenance, they can be combined to verify the full program. A modular verification approach that infers and composes procedure summaries may scale better than a monolithic one that considers all procedure implementations at once.

A popular modern approach is to encode interprocedural program verification problems as Constrained Horn Clauses (CHCs) [32], in which uninterpreted predicates represent placeholders for procedure summaries. A CHC solver then finds interpretations for these predicates such that these interpretations correspond to summaries, enabling generation of procedure summaries.

© Springer Nature Switzerland AG 2021
F. Henglein et al. (Eds.): VMCAI 2021, LNCS 12597, pp. 291–324, 2021.
https://doi.org/10.1007/978-3-030-67067-2_14

CHC solvers [13, 27, 32, 39, 42, 49, 60] query to backend SMT (Satisfiability Modulo Theory) solvers [8] to find interpretations that make all CHC rules valid. In addition to classic fixpoint computations,

CHC solvers use model checking techniques, e.g., counterexample guided abstraction refinement (CEGAR) [17], interpolation [46], property-directed reachability (PDR) [12, 23], and guess-and-check procedures [25]. They can thus find procedure summaries adequate for verification but not necessarily least or greatest fixpoints. CHC-based verifiers have been successfully applied to a range benchmark programs, but there remain significant challenges in handling mutual recursion and in scalability.

We aim to address these challenges by leveraging program structure during solving and learning relevant facts. Typical CHC-based verifiers may not maintain a program's structure when encoding it into CHCs. In contrast, our method uses the program call graph, which can be preserved easily in a CHC encoding, to guide proof search.

For improving scalability, we ensure that the *SMT queries in our method are always bounded in size* even when more of the program is explored. We wish both to maintain scalability *and* to avoid learning over-specialized facts. We do this by leveraging the call graph of the program, i.e., analyzing a procedure in the context of a bounded number of levels in the call graph. Furthermore, such a notion of a *bounded environment* enables us to refer to bounded call paths in the program and learn special lemmas, called *EC (Environment-Call) Lemmas*, to capture relationships among summaries of different procedures on such paths. These lemmas are beneficial in *handling mutual recursion*.

Other techniques also trade off scalability and relevance by considering a bounded number of levels in a call graph, e.g., in bounded context-sensitivity or k-sensitive pointer/alias analysis [51], stratified inlining [44], and depth cutoff [40] in program verification. However, other than SPACER [42], which is restricted to $k = 1$ bounded environments, existing CHC solvers do not use bounded environments to limit size of the SMT queries.

Summary of Contributions. This paper's contributions are as follows:

- We propose a new CHC-solving method for generating procedure summaries for recursive interprocedural programs (Sect. 6).
- We propose to handle mutual recursion by explicitly learning EC Lemmas to capture relationships among different procedures on a call path (Sect. 5).
- We propose to use bounded environments (with bound $k \geq 1$) (Sect. 4) to compute individual procedure summaries. The SMT queries formulated in our method are always bounded in size, thereby improving scalability.
- We have implemented our method in a tool called CLOVER and report on its evaluation on several benchmark programs, along with a detailed comparison against existing tools (Sect. 7).

To the best of our knowledge, EC Lemmas and bounded environments, the main features of our algorithm, are novel for summary generation in modular verifiers.

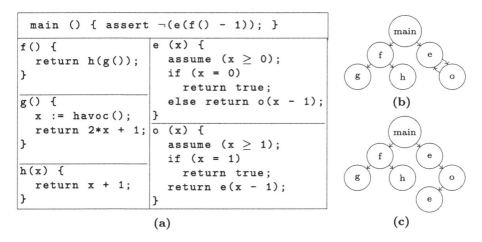

```
main () { assert ¬(e(f() - 1)); }
```

```
f () {                    e (x) {
  return h(g());            assume (x ≥ 0);
}                           if (x = 0)
─────────────────             return true;
g() {                       else return o(x - 1);
  x := havoc();           }
  return 2*x + 1;         ─────────────────────
}                         o (x) {
─────────────────           assume (x ≥ 1);
h(x) {                      if (x = 1)
  return x + 1;               return true;
}                           return e(x - 1);
                          }
```

(a)   (c)

Fig. 1. Example: (a) source code, (b) call graph, and (c) final derivation tree.

2 Motivating Example

We illustrate the main steps of our modular algorithm on the example program shown in Fig. 1a. To keep our focus on intuition, we describe our algorithm in terms of the program (CHC encodings are described later).

In Fig. 1a, e and o are defined mutually recursively and return *true* iff their argument is respectively even or odd. Procedure f returns the (always-even) result of calling h on g's result, where g returns an arbitrary odd number and h adds one to its input. The safety specification is that $e(f() - 1)$ never holds. We aim to infer over-approximate procedure summaries so that the assertion's truth follows from replacing procedure calls in main with these summaries.

We maintain context-insensitive *over-* and *under-approximate* summaries for all procedures , each of which captures both pre- *and* post-conditions of its procedure. All over- (resp. under-) approximate summaries are initially ⊤ (resp. ⊥). At each step, we choose a target procedure p and its bounded environment, then update p's summaries based on the results of SMT queries on its over- or under-approximate body. We also allow the bounded environment to be over- or under-approximated, leading to four kinds of SMT queries. These queries let us over- and under-approximate any procedure that is called before or after the target, unlike SPACER [42] or SMASH [31], which use two kinds of SMT queries.

Table 1 lists non-trivial verification steps that update various procedure summaries. (Steps that do not update any summary are not listed.) The first column lists the call path that is visited in each step, in which the last call is the current *target* procedure whose summary is updated, and the call path is used to generate its bounded environment. The "Environment" (resp. "Target") column shows whether the bounded environment (resp. target) is over- or under-approximated.

Table 1. Relevant steps to verify program in Fig. 1a.

Call graph path	Environment	Target	Deductions (universally quantified)
main → e	Over	Under	$x = 0 \land y = true \Rightarrow e(x, y)$
main → f → h	Over	Under	$y = x + 1 \Rightarrow h(x, y)$
main → e → o	Over	Under	$x = 1 \land y = true \Rightarrow o(x, y)$
main → f → g	Over	Under	$y \bmod 2 \neq 0 \Rightarrow g(y)$
main → f → g	Under	Over	$g(y) \Rightarrow y \bmod 2 \neq 0$
main → f → h	Under	Over	$h(x, y) \Rightarrow y = x + 1$
main → f	Over	Under	$y \bmod 2 = 0 \Rightarrow f(y)$
main → f	Under	Over	$f(y) \Rightarrow y \bmod 2 = 0$
main → e → o → e	Over	Over	$(o(x, y) \Rightarrow y \Leftrightarrow ((1 + x) \bmod 2 = 0)) \Rightarrow$ $(e(m, n) \Rightarrow n \Leftrightarrow (m \bmod 2 = 0))$
main → e → o	Over	Over	$o(x, y) \Rightarrow y \Leftrightarrow ((1 + x) \bmod 2 = 0))$ $e(x, y) \Rightarrow x > 1 \land y \Leftrightarrow ((1 + x) \bmod 2 = 0)$

The "Deductions" column lists deductions resulting from SMT queries in that step. Note that formulas in this column (and in the remainder of this section) are implicitly universally quantified over all variables and involve uninterpreted predicates (e.g., $h(x, y)$ in row 2). Except in row 9, all these formulas are implications that represent procedure summaries. Row 9 shows an implication between two such formulas – this is an instance of an EC lemma (described later).

2.1 Using the Program Call Graph

Our algorithm chooses environment-target pairs based on the call graph of the program, shown in Fig. 1b. It maintains explored paths through the call graph in a data structure called a *derivation tree*, initially consisting of only one node that represents entry procedure main. Figure 1c shows the tree just before the algorithm converges. The subset A of nodes *available* to be explored is also maintained, and it is this subset that guides exploration in our algorithm.

To improve scalability, we use *bounded* environments from call paths to use in SMT queries at each step. These bounded environments include bodies of the ancestors of the target procedure, but only up to level k above the target in the call graph. Ancestors at $l > k$ above the target are soundly abstracted away so that these environments capture at least the behaviors of the program before and after the target procedure that may lead to a counterexample. Approximations of these environments and of the bodies of target procedures help us learn new facts about the targets. In this example, we use $k = 2$. When we target the last call to e along path main → e → o → e, main's body will be abstracted.

2.2 Summary Updates Using SMT Queries

We now consider the four SMT queries on a chosen environment-target pair at each step. Suppose our algorithm has already considered the path to o on row 3 (Table 1) and now chooses node $g \in A$ in path main → f → g. Here, the bounded environment includes calls to h (called by f) and e (called by main), so we use their over-approximate summaries (both currently ⊤). We under-approximate the environment using summaries for h and e learned in rows 2 and 1, respectively. Over- and under-approximations of g are just its body with local variables rewritten away (i.e., 2 * havoc() + 1), since it has no callees.

In checks that over-approximate the procedure body, we try to learn an interpolant that proves the absence of a subset of counterexamples along this path in the program. Since target procedure body is over-approximated, any interpolant found that separates its encoding from the counterexample captured by the environment will be an over-approximate summary for the target procedure, expressing a fact about all behaviors of the procedure. Such over-approximate summaries allow us to prove safety in a modular way. In checks that under-approximate the procedure body, we try to find (part of) a bug. Since the target procedure body is under-approximated, the interpolant is instead an under-approximate summary, describing behaviors the procedure *may* exhibit. Under-approximate summaries allow us to construct counterexamples in the case where the program is unsafe. Approximating the environment and target procedure body allows us to keep queries small.

Both the *over-over* and *under-under* checks fail here, so no updates are made. A weaker version of the *under-under* check is the *over-under* check, in which the environment is now *over-approximated*. Because it is weaker, it may result in learning under-approximate summaries that may not be necessary, since the over-approximated environment may contain spurious counterexamples. When our algorithm performs this check, it finds a path that goes through the over-approximated environment and the under-approximation of g's body and thus augments g's under-approximation (row 4).

A corresponding weaker version of the *over-over* check is the *under-over* check, in which the environment is *under-approximated*. Because the under-approximated environment may not capture all counterexamples, the learned interpolant by itself could be too weak to prove safety. Our algorithm refines g's over-approximation with the interpolant learned in this query (row 5).

Note that these two weaker checks are crucial in our algorithm. Consider a different main function that contains only assert(f() mod 2 = 0). To prove safety, we would need to consider paths main → f → h and main → f → g, but for these paths, both "stronger" checks fail. Paths through the derivation tree must be paths through the call graph, so we would not consider the bodies of h and g simultaneously; the "weaker" checks allow us to learn summary updates.

2.3   Explicit Induction and EC lemmas

To demonstrate the need for and use of induction and EC lemmas for handling mutual recursion, we now consider row 9 in Table 1, where we perform an *over-over* check for the final call to e in the call path. The current derivation tree has the same structure as the final derivation tree, shown in Fig. 1c.

No Induction. At this stage, our over-approximation for f precisely describes all possible behaviors of f (rows 7, 8), but no interpolant can be learned because the over-approximation ⊤ of o in the body of procedure e is too coarse. Without using induction, we cannot make any assumptions about this call to o, and are stuck with this coarse over-approximation. Even if we inlined the body of o, we would similarly still have an overly-coarse over-approximation for e.

Induction with EC Lemmas. We can instead try to use induction on the body of e. Its over-approximated environment includes counterexample paths that we would like to prove spurious. Let formula $\phi(x, y)$ denote property $e(x, y) \Rightarrow (y \Leftrightarrow x \bmod 2 = 0)$. The consequent in this implication is generated by examining the environment for e, i.e., the environment implies the negation of the consequent [1]. Problems arise when trying to prove this property by induction because there is no opportunity to apply the inductive hypothesis about e. When the else branch is taken, facts about o are needed to finish the proof for $\phi(x, y)$ and $x > 0$.

If we were to inline o and assume inductive hypothesis that $\phi(x, y)$ holds for the inner call to e, an inductive proof would succeed without using EC lemmas. However, such an inlining approach can lead to poor scalability and precludes inference of summaries (e.g., for o) that could be useful in other call paths.

EC Lemmas. Our algorithm discovers additional lemmas in the form of implications over certain procedure summaries (Sect. 5). Let formula $\theta(m, n) \stackrel{\text{def}}{=} o(m, n) \Rightarrow (n \Leftrightarrow (1 + m) \bmod 2 = 0)$. (Again, the consequent in this implication is generated by examining the environment for o.) Let $\psi(x, y, m, n) \stackrel{\text{def}}{=} \theta(m, n) \Rightarrow \phi(x, y)$, i.e., ψ is similar to ϕ property, but with an additional assumption θ about o.

Validity of ψ is proved by case analysis: $\psi(1, true, m, n)$ is trivially true, and the proof of $\psi(x, y, m, n)$ for $x > 0$ works because of the assumption θ. Thus, the formula $\psi(x, y, m, n)$ is learned as an *EC lemma* (see row 9).

Now, we reconsider the call to o along call path main $\rightarrow$ e $\rightarrow$ o. The discovered EC lemma allows us to prove formula θ valid by induction. This new over-approximate fact for o is combined with the EC lemma allowing the algorithm to learn $e(x, y) \Rightarrow (y \Leftrightarrow x \bmod 2 = 0)$. This step corresponds to row 10.

3   Preliminaries

In this section, we define our notion of a program, introduce CHC notions and encodings, and define contexts and derivation trees.

Programs. A program P is a set of procedures with entry point *main*. Each procedure p has vectors of input and output variables in_p and out_p and a body $body_p$, which may contain calls to other procedures or recursive calls to p. When p is clear from context, we omit it in the variables' subscripts, e.g., $p(in, out)$. We encode a program as a system of CHCs $\mathcal{C}$.

---

[1] Expressions such as $x \bmod 2 = 0$ can be generated by existentially quantifying local variables and then performing quantifier elimination.

Body of `main`:

```
assert (¬(e(f() - 1)));
```

CHC for `main`:

$$f(x) \wedge e(x - 1, y) \wedge y \Rightarrow \perp$$

Body of `e`:

```
assume (x ≥ 0);
if (x = 0) return true;
else return o(x - 1);
```

CHC for `even`:

$$x = 0 \Rightarrow e(x, \top)$$
$$x \neq 0 \wedge o(x - 1, y) \Rightarrow e(x, y)$$

Unfolding `e` in `main`:

```
assume(f() - 1 ≥ 0);
if (f() - 1 = 0) return true;
else return o(f() - 2);
```

Unfolding `e` in `main` (CHCs):

$$f(x) \wedge x - 1 = 0 \Rightarrow \perp$$
$$f(x) \wedge x - 1 \geq 0 \wedge x - 1 \neq 0 \wedge o(x - 2, y) \Rightarrow \perp$$

Fig. 2. Unfoldings (and intermediate steps) of `e` in the body of `main` from Fig. 1a. Program snippets are shown on the left and CHC encodings on the right.

Definition 1. *A CHC C is an implicitly universally-quantified implication formula in first-order logic with theories of the form body $\Rightarrow$ head. Let $\mathcal{R}$ be a set of uninterpreted predicates. The formula head may take either the form $R(\vec{y})$ for $R \in \mathcal{R}$ or $\perp$. Implications in which head $= \perp$ are called* queries. *The formula body may take the form $\phi(\vec{x})$ or $\phi(\vec{x}) \wedge R_0(\vec{x}_0) \wedge \ldots \wedge R_n(\vec{x}_n)$, where each R_i is an uninterpreted predicate, and $\phi(\vec{x})$ is a fully interpreted formula over $\vec{x}$ (i.e., it contains only theory predicates), which may contain all variables in each $\vec{x}_i$ and (if the head is of the form $R(\vec{y})$) all variables in $\vec{y}$.*

A system of CHCs for a program can be generated by introducing an uninterpreted predicate per procedure and encoding the semantics of each procedure using these and theory predicates. Each application $R(\vec{x})$ in the body of a CHC corresponds to a procedure call to a procedure p, where $\vec{y} = (in_p, out_p)$. By analogy, we refer each such R as a *callee* of the predicate in the head of the CHC. For each $C \in \mathcal{C}$ with uninterpreted predicate applications $\{R_0(\vec{x}_0), \ldots, R_n(\vec{x}_n)\}$ in its body, we let *callee*$_C$ be a one-to-one mapping from $0, \ldots, n$ to these applications.

This mapping allows us to distinguish between different applications of the same predicate within the same CHC body, which we can understand as distinguishing between different callsites of the same callee within a procedure. We abuse notation and denote the corresponding predicate for a procedure $p \in P$ in encoding $\mathcal{C}$ as p. We assume that in any application $p(\vec{y})$ in the head of a CHC in $\mathcal{C}$, $\vec{y}$ is the same vector of variables in_p, out_p. We let $C.body$ and $C.head$ denote the body and head of CHC C respectively. We let loc_C denote $fv(C.body) \setminus fv(C.head)$, where for a formula F, $fv(F)$ denotes the free variables in F. We assume that all $C, C' \in \mathcal{C}$ are such that $loc_C \cap loc_{C'} = \emptyset$ and let $loc_p = \bigcup \{loc_C \mid C.head = p(\vec{y})\}$. Note that disjunction $\bigvee_i \{body_i \mid body_i \Rightarrow p(\vec{y}) \in \mathcal{C}\}$ gives the semantics of $body_p$. We abuse notation to use $body_p$ to refer to this disjunction.

Corresponding CHC encodings are shown in Fig. 2 for demonstration. We assume the use of an encoding that preserves the call graph structure of the program in CHCs; i.e., there will be a CHC with head containing p with an application of q in its body iff p calls q.

Definition 2 (Solution). *A solution for a system of CHCs C is an interpretation M for uninterpreted predicates $\mathcal{R}$ that makes all CHCs in C valid.*

A CHC encoding is such that if it has a solution, the original program is safe. To remember facts learned during our algorithm, we maintain two sets of first-order interpretations of $\mathcal{R}$ called O and U, functioning as mappings from procedures to their over- and under-approximate summaries, respectively.

Definition 3 (Procedure Summaries). *The over- (O) and under-approximate (U) summaries are such that all non-query CHCs body $\Rightarrow$ head $\in C$ are valid under O and that implication head $\Rightarrow$ body is valid under U.*

From Definition 3, it is clear that for all p, $O[p] = \top$ and $U[p] = \bot$ are valid summaries. We use these as *initial* summaries in the algorithm presented in Sect. 6. Note that when O is a solution for the system of CHCs C (i.e., O makes the query CHCs valid). When U is such that a query CHC is *not* valid, then verification fails and a counterexample exists.

Definition 4 (Approximation). *Given a formula Π and an interpretation $M \in \{O, U\}$, an approximation $\widehat{\Pi}_M$ is defined as follows:*

$$\widehat{\Pi}_M \stackrel{\text{def}}{=} \Pi \wedge \bigwedge_{p(in, out) \text{ in } \Pi} M[p](in, out)$$

In addition to approximations, we can manipulate CHCs using *renaming* and *unfolding*.

Definition 5 (Renaming). *For a formula F containing variables $\vec{x}$, $F[\vec{x} \mapsto \vec{y}]$ denotes the simultaneous renaming of variables $\vec{x}$ to $\vec{y}$ in F.*

Definition 6 (Unfolding). *Let C be a system of CHCs. Let $C \in C$ be a CHC $R_0(\vec{x}_0) \wedge \ldots \wedge R_n(\vec{x}_n) \wedge \phi(\vec{x}) \Rightarrow R(\vec{y})$ where $callee_C(i) = R_i(\vec{x}_i)$ for each $i \in \{0, \ldots, n\}$. There is an unfolding of $callee_C(k)$ per CHC in C whose head is an application of predicate R_k. For such a CHC body $\Rightarrow R_k(\vec{y}_k) \in C$, the unfolding of $R_k(\vec{x}_k)$ in C is given by the following:*

$$\bigwedge_{i \in \{0, \ldots, n\}, i \neq k} R_i(\vec{x}_i) \wedge body[\vec{y}_k \mapsto \vec{x}_k] \wedge \phi(\vec{x}) \Rightarrow (\vec{y})$$

An unfolding is essentially a one-level inlining of one CHC in another. Figure 2 illustrates what an unfolding of CHCs correponds to on our motivating example, where e is unfolded in `main`.

Definition 7 (Environment). *For a CHC C of the form $\bigwedge_{i \in \{1..n\}} R_i(\vec{x}_i) \wedge \phi(\vec{x_1}, \ldots, \vec{x_n}) \Rightarrow \bot$, the environment for $R_k(\vec{x_k})$ is given by the following:*

$$\bigwedge_{i \in \{1..n\}, i \neq k} R_i(\vec{x}_i) \wedge \phi(\vec{x_1}, \ldots, \vec{x_n})$$

By analogy with programs, the environment for $R_k(\vec{x_k})$ intuitively captures the procedure calls in C before and after the procedure call for $R_k(\vec{x_k})$. Note that if C is simply an encoding of a single procedure body, then the environment will only capture the immediate callees of that procedure. On the other hand, if C is, for example, an unfolding of the CHC representing main, then the environment may contain any calls before and after the call corresponding to $R_k(\vec{x_k})$ in a full but potentially spurious counterexample run of the program so long as they have corresponding predicate applications in the unfolding C.

Definition 8 (Derivation Tree). *A derivation tree $D = \langle N, E \rangle$ for system of CHCs P is a tree with nodes N and edges E, where each $n \in N$ is labeled with uninterpreted predicate $p = proc(n)$, a context query CHC $ctx(n)$, and an index $i = idx(n)$ such that $callee_{ctx(n)}(i)$ is an application of p.*

Our algorithm uses the derivation tree is capture the already-explored unfoldings starting from the encoding of *main* and to further guide exploration. Each node $n \in N$ represents a *verification subtask*, where the body of $ctx(n)$ represents a set of (potentially spurious) counterexamples. The goal of each subtask is to find a solution for the system of CHCs consisting of all non-query CHCs in $\mathcal{C}$ with the query CHC $ctx(n)$ and refine the over-approximation $O[proc(n)]$ to reflect the learned facts, or, if this cannot be done, to expand $proc(n)$'s under-approximation $U[proc(n)]$ to demonstrate (part of) a real counterexample.

A program's initial derivation tree consists of only one node labeled with procedure *main* and a query CHC from the system $\mathcal{C}$. We maintain the invariant that if s is the parent of t, then the $ctx(t)$ must be able to be constructed by unfolding a predicate in $ctx(s)$. Furthermore, we require that the unfolded predicate is one of the predicates that was added in the previous unfolding step to get $ctx(s)$. This notion of a derivation tree is similar to other CHC-based work [49,60], but our invariant restricts the way in which we can expand the tree (i.e., the way in which we can unfold from *main*) – *every derivation tree path corresponds to a call graph path*. We let $e(n)$ refer to the environment for $callee_{ctx(n)}(idx(n))$ in $ctx(n)$.

For a derivation tree path d (of length $|d|$) whose final node is n, the *full* context $ctx(n)$ can be derived by unfolding all of $proc(n)$'s ancestors in the root node's context CHC along the corresponding call graph path for the original program[2]. We also denote this full context as $unfold(d, |d|)$. For $k < |d|$, $unfold(d, k)$ corresponds to unfolding the bodies of the last $k - 1$ procedure calls in d into the body of $proc(n)$'s k^{th} ancestor. Note that $unfold(d, k)$ only unfolds ancestors on the call path; any other of the ancestors remain represented as uninterpreted predicates. For $k \geq |d|$, $unfold(d, k) = unfold(d, |d|)$. (See also Definition 9.)

4   Bounded Contexts and Environments

Here we define *bounded* contexts and environments. Our algorithm uses these bounded versions in all SMT queries described later.

---

[2] We lift the ancestor relationship from nodes to their procedures.

Definition 9 (Bounded context). *For a given bound k, and a path $d = n_0 \to \ldots \to n_{m-1} \to n_m$ in a derivation tree, a k-bounded context for n_m is a formula $bctx(n_m)$ over variables $bvs \stackrel{\text{def}}{=} fv(unfold(d,k))$, defined as follows:*

$$bctx(n_m) \stackrel{\text{def}}{=} unfold(d,k).body \wedge interface(d,k) \wedge summ(d,k) \Rightarrow \bot$$

Here, we also have the following:

- *$interface(d,k)$ is a formula over the inputs and outputs of the procedure for node n_{m-k}, $k < m$ (or $\top$, if $k \geq m$)*
- *$summ(d,k)$ is a formula over the inputs and outputs of the other callees of the k-bounded ancestors of $proc(n_m)$.*

Note $unfold(d,k)$ ignores any restrictions due to ancestors that are more than k-levels above $proc(n_m)$. Such restrictions are expressed in $interface(d,k)$, which represents the interface between the k-bounded context and the rest of the context above it. In practice, we compute $interface(d,k)$ as $\mathrm{QE}(\exists fv(e(n_m)) \setminus bvs.\widehat{e(n_m)}_{O,\ell})$, where QE denotes quantifier elimination. We approximate quantifier elimination using the standard model-based projection technique [10]. We can always use $interface(d,k) = \top$, which treats ancestor procedures above bound k as havocs; we found this choice ineffective in practice.

In what follows, we refer to $unfold(d,k).body \wedge interface(d,k)$ as $B(d,k)$ or simply as B when d and k are clear. Again, we require that each $bctx(n_m)$ (and thus each $B(d,k)$) can be computed from its parent n_{m-1}'s bounded context via a single unfolding. Given our choice of $interface(d,k)$, using such a method to compute a child node's bounded context lets us avoid (approximate) quantifier elimination on large formulas since only one procedure body's variables need to be eliminated when starting from the parent's bounded context.

The $summ(d,k)$ formula can be either $\top$ or a conjunction that adds approximation constraints based on summaries for the other callee procedures. We use $bctx.body = B$ when $summ(d,k) = \top$, or $bctx.body = \widehat{B}_M$ or $bctx.body = \widehat{b}_M$ for $M \in \{O,U\}$, where b is the environment for $callee_{ctx(n_m)}(idx(n_m))$ (when $summ(d,k)$ is the conjunction from approximating with M).

Example 1. The figure shows a bounded context for predicate p with bound 2 for the derivation tree path shown with solid edges. Ancestor predicates q_1, q_2 are unfolded in $unfold(d,2)$, and $summ(d,2)$ approximates callees r_0, r_1, r_2:

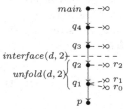

For scalability, our algorithm (Sect. 6) considers verification subtasks with the *bounded* context of a given procedure. Our algorithm' queries use *bounded environments*, which can be computed from bounded contexts.

Definition 10 (Bounded environment). *For a node n, its bounded environment $benv(n)$ is the environment for the predicate $callee_{ctx(n)}(idx(n))$ in $ctx(n)$.*

We define a bounded parent relationship between nodes $s, t \in N$, where $s \to t$ is not necessarily in E, but where $ctx(s)$ has $proc(t)$ as a callee.

Definition 11 (Bounded parent). *A node s is a bounded parent of node t in derivation tree D, denoted $s \in Bparent(t, D)$, iff there is some index i such that $callee_{ctx(s)}(i)$ is an application of $proc(t)$ and $b_t \Leftrightarrow next(b_s, proc(t), i)$, where b_t and b_s are bodies of the bounded contexts of s and t.*

Note that the parent of a node n is always a bounded parent for n, and that n may have several bounded parents because the approximation of different full environments may lead to the same bounded environment. We use bounded parents in our algorithm (Sect. 6) to avoid considering redundant verification subtasks.

5 EC Lemmas

We also learn a set L of *EC lemmas*, which are implications capturing assumptions under which a procedure has a particular over-approximation.

Definition 12 (Environment-Call (EC) Lemmas). *Let $proc(n) = p$ for some node n in a derivation tree. An EC lemma for p, where n has ancestors with procedures $\{q_i\}$ along a derivation tree path, is of the following form:*

$$\forall fv(S_i) \ \cup \ in \ \cup \ out. \bigwedge_i S_i \Rightarrow (p(in, out) \Rightarrow prop)$$

Here, prop is a formula with $fv(prop) \subseteq in \ \cup \ out$, each S_i is of the form $q_i(in_i, out_i) \Rightarrow prop_i$, where q_i is some ancestor's uninterpreted predicate, and $prop_i$ is a formula with $fv(prop_i) \subseteq in_i \cup out_i$.

Intuitively, an EC lemma allows us to learn that *prop* is an over-approximation of procedure p under the assumptions $\{S_i\}$ about its ancestors with procedures $\{q_i\}$. Each S_i itself is an assumption that $prop_i$ over-approximates q_i. These ancestors are in target p's environment, so we call these formulas Environment-Call (EC) Lemmas. In practice, we learn EC lemmas involving ancestors whose procedures are callees of p to help set up induction for mutual recursion.

6 Modular Verification Algorithm

We now describe our modular verification algorithm. We first outline the top-level procedure (Sect. 6.1) based on iteratively processing nodes in the derivation tree. Then we describe how each node is processed using SMT queries (Sect. 6.2), the order in which SMT queries are performed (Sect. 6.3), and how induction is performed and how EC lemmas are learned and used (Sect. 6.4). We present the correctness and the progress property of our algorithm and discuss limitations (Sect. 6.5). (Additional heuristics are described in Appendix C [52].)

Algorithm 1. Modular Verification Procedure

1: **procedure** VERIFY( )
2:     $N \leftarrow \{n\}$ with $proc(n) = main$
3:     $Goal \leftarrow \langle N, \emptyset \rangle, N, O, U, \emptyset, \mathcal{C} \vdash Res$
4:     **while** $Goal.A \neq \emptyset$ or summaries are insufficient **do**
5:         $Goal \leftarrow$ PROCESSNODE(n, $Goal$) for $n \in Goal.A$
6:     **return** RESULT($Goal$)

6.1   Algorithm Outline

Our algorithm constructs a derivation tree based on the call graph of the program, which is used to guide the selection of CHCs to explore. We *achieve scalability* by considering only bounded environments in all our SMT queries. We present these queries as part of proof rules that capture the major steps of our algorithm. The use of induction and EC lemmas enables handling of *mutually recursive programs*. The state during verification is captured by *proof (sub)goals*.

Definition 13 (Proof (sub)Goal). *For system of CHCs $\mathcal{C}$, derivation tree $D = \langle N, E \rangle$, a subset $A \subseteq N$ of* available *nodes, over- and under-approximate summary maps O and U, a set of EC lemmas L, and $Res \in \{\top, \bot\}$, a proof (sub)subgoal is denoted $D, A, O, U, L, \mathcal{C} \vdash Res$.*

Main Loop. Algorithm 1 shows the top-level procedure for our method. The VERIFY procedure constructs an initial proof goal containing an initial derivation tree, initial summary maps, and empty sets of lemmas. Initially all nodes in the derivation tree are available, i.e., they are in A. It then iteratively chooses an available node and tries to update its summaries (using routine PROCESSNODE), thereby updating the current goal. The loop terminates when no more nodes are available or when the current summaries are sufficient to prove/disprove safety. RESULT returns *safe* if the summaries are sufficient for proving safety, *unsafe* if they are sufficient for disproving safety, or *unknown* otherwise.

Choice of Procedures and Environments. PROCESSNODE can be viewed as making queries on an environment-procedure pair. If the algorithm chooses node n, then the pair consists of $benv(n)$ and the procedure corresponding to $proc(n)$. Note that the call graph guides the choice of the target since all paths in D correspond to call graph paths, and the bounded environment, which is computed by unfolding the k-bounded ancestors of the target. Importantly, the chosen node must be in A; this choice can be heuristic as long as no node in A is starved.

Summary Inference. Our algorithm learns new summaries for target predicates by applying four proof rules. For ease of exposition, we first describe these proof rules without induction (next subsection), followed by rules for induction and EC lemma. While these proof rules resemble those in SMASH [31], our queries involve k-bounded environments with $k \geq 1$ and our summaries are first-order theory formulas; in SMASH, queries use bounded environments with $k = 1$ and summaries are pre-/post-condition pairs over predicate abstractions. Additional proof rules specify the removal and addition of nodes in D and A. Appendix B [52] provides the complete set of rules, omitted here due to space constraints.

6.2   Proof Rules Without Induction

The algorithm updates the current *Goal* whenever a proof rule can be applied. Note that we are building a proof tree from the bottom-up, so an application of a rule here involves matching the conclusion to the current *Goal*. We abbreviate some common premises with names as shown in Fig. 3. For a node $n \in A$, let p be its procedure and b be its bounded environment. Also let *body* be the renaming of the body of p. The distinct feature of our algorithm is that the proof rules use only bounded environments.

$$
\begin{array}{ll}
\text{AVAIL} \;\; n \in A \;\; \text{PROC} \;\; p = proc(n) \;\; \text{BENV} \;\; b = benv(n) \;\; \text{IDX} \;\; i = idx(n) \\
\quad \text{BODY} \;\; body = body_p[in, out \mapsto fv(callee_{bctx(n)}(i)), loc_p \mapsto fresh(loc_p)] \\
\quad \text{PROP} \;\; hyp = \forall in, out \in fv(body).p(in, out) \Rightarrow indProp \\
\quad \text{IND} \;\;\;\; indProp = \forall vars(\psi) \setminus (in_p \cup out_p).\mathbb{I}
\end{array}
$$

Fig. 3. Abbreviated premises, where $fresh(\vec{x})$ returns a vector $\vec{x'}$ of fresh variables.

SAFE
O is a solution for $\mathcal{C}$
$$\overline{D, A, O, U, L, \mathcal{C} \vdash \bot}$$

UNSAFE
$\exists body \Rightarrow \bot \in \mathcal{C}.\widehat{body}_U \not\Rightarrow \bot$
$$\overline{D, A, O, U, L, \mathcal{C} \vdash \top}$$

OVER-OVER (OO)
$$
\frac{\widehat{body}_O \Rightarrow \mathbb{I} \quad\; \begin{array}{cccc} \text{AVAIL} & \text{PROC} & \text{BENV} & \text{BODY} \\ \mathbb{I} \Rightarrow \neg\widehat{b}_O & O' = O[p \mapsto O[p] \wedge \mathbb{I}] & D, A, O', U, L, \mathcal{C} \vdash Res \end{array}}{D, A, O, U, L, \mathcal{C} \vdash Res}
$$

UNDER-UNDER (UU)
$$
\frac{\begin{array}{ccccc} \text{AVAIL} & \text{PROC} & \text{BENV} & \text{IDX} & body \Rightarrow p(in, out) \in \mathcal{C} \\ \multicolumn{5}{c}{\pi = body[in, out \mapsto fv(callee_{bctx(n)}(i)), loc_C \mapsto fresh(loc_C)]} \\ \widehat{\pi}_U \wedge \widehat{b}_U \not\Rightarrow \bot & U' = U[p \mapsto U[p] \vee \exists loc_C.\pi] & D, A, O, U', L, \mathcal{C} \vdash Res \end{array}}{D, A, O, U, L, \mathcal{C} \vdash Res}
$$

Fig. 4. Proof rules without induction.

The SAFE and UNSAFE rules (Fig. 4) allow us to conclude the safety or find a counterexample of the original program P using over- or under-approximate summaries, respectively. In the latter case, the underapproximate summaries

Algorithm 2. Procedure to learn from a node.
```
1: procedure PROCESSNODE(n, Goal)
2:     for C ∈ C with C.head = proc(n)(in, out) do
3:         if OU(n, C, Goal) then UU(n, C, Goal)
4:     if no UU call above returned true then
5:         if ¬OO(n, Goal) then UO(n, Goal)
6:     if no UU nor OO call above returned true then ADDNODES(n, Goal)
7:     updated ← any summaries were updated above
8:     PROCESSED(n, updated, Goal)
9:     return Goal
```

demonstrate that there is no solution for set of CHCs C. If either rule is applicable to the proof goal, we have found sufficient summaries.

The OVER-OVER (OO) rule (Fig. 4) can be used to update a predicate p's over-approximate summary. If the conjunction of over-approximation of $body_p$ and the bounded environment is unsatisfiable, then we can find an interpolant $\mathbb{I}$ and use it to refine the map O for p.

The UNDER-OVER (UO) rule (Appendix B [52]) is similar, except it uses an under-approximation of the environment.

Example 2. Recall the example in Fig. 1a. Row 5 in Table 1 shows the over-approximate summary $y \bmod 2 \neq 0$ for procedure g obtained as a result of UO.

The UNDER-UNDER (UU) rule (Fig. 4) can be used to update predicate p's under-approximation.

Let π be the body of a CHC whose head is $p(\vec{y})$, where variables $\vec{y}$ have been renamed to the variables that p is applied to in $callee_{bctx(n)}(i)$ and the rest of the variables have been renamed to fresh ones. If the conjunction of the under-approximations of π and b is satisfiable, then we can update p's under-approximate summary U with $\exists loc_C.\pi$.

If the environment were unbounded, then this check being satisfiable would actually indicate a *concrete* counterexample, since the context would be an unfolding of a query CHC and UNSAFE would hold, but since our environment is *bounded*, the context may not be an unfolding of the query CHC, since it may be missing some constraints. We can only conclude that there might be a counterexample that involves unfolding this application of p. We want to remember the part that goes through p so that we do not need to unfold it in the full context and thus add $\exists loc_p.\pi$ to $U[p]$. The OVER-UNDER (OU) rule (Appendix B [52]) is the same as UU but over-approximates the bounded environment.

Example 3. Recall the example in Fig. 1a. Row 7 in Table 1 shows the under-approximate summary $y \bmod 2 = 0$ for procedure f obtained as a result of OU.

6.3 Ordering and Conditions for SMT Queries

The way in which proof rules are applied to process a node is shown in Algorithm 2. In the pseudocode, OO, UO, OU, and UU refer to attempts to apply the corresponding rules (e.g., $OO(n, Goal)$ tries to apply the OO rule with $n \in A$ as the AVAIL premise). Rules that update under-approximations (UU, OU) are applied per CHC with head $proc(n)^3$, whereas rules that update over-approximations (OO, UO) are applied to the disjunction of all such CHCs' bodies. They return *true* upon successful application (and update *Goal*), or *false* otherwise.

If we have neither found any counterexamples through the bounded environment (i.e., all UU attempts failed), nor eliminated the bounded verification subtask (i.e., the OO attempt failed), then we try to derive new facts by adding new available nodes for the callees of $proc(n)$. Procedure ADDNODES adds these nodes while avoiding adding redundant nodes to D (more details in Appendix D [52]). If any summary updates were made for $proc(n)$, then the procedure PROCESSED (line 8) will add the bounded parents of n to A, so that new information can be propagated to the parents' summaries. It then removes n from A.

6.4 Proof Rules for Induction

For programs with unbounded recursion, the OO and UO rules (Fig. 4) are insufficient for proving safety; we therefore extend the rules with induction where the goal is to show that the paths in the approximated bounded environment are spurious. For ease of exposition, we first discuss an extension of OO that does not use EC lemmas and then discuss one that does. (Corresponding extensions for rule UO are similar and can be found in Appendix B [52].)

Without EC lemmas. The rule OVER-OVER-IND (OOI) in Fig. 5 is a replacement for OO that uses induction to find new over-approximate facts. The first five premises are the same as in rule OO. As before, we aim to learn a refinement $\mathbb{I}$ for the over-approximate summary of p, where $\mathbb{I} \Rightarrow \neg \widehat{b}_O$.

The base case is that $\mathbb{I}$ over-approximates p for all CHCs that do not have any applications of p in their body, i.e. for all $body \Rightarrow p(\vec{y}) \in \mathcal{C}$ where p does not occur in $body$, $body \Rightarrow \mathbb{I}$. For the inductive step, we consider such CHCs where $body$ contains calls to P. The inductive hypothesis, which is captured by formula hyp, is that $\mathbb{I}$ over-approximates all recursive calls to p inside these bodies. We check both the base case and the inductive step at once with the implication $\widehat{body}_O \wedge hyp \Rightarrow \mathbb{I}$. If the induction succeeds, then we strengthen $O[p]$ with $\mathbb{I}$.

With EC lemmas. The OVER-OVER-IND-LEMMAS (OOIL) proves weaker properties than OOIL by doing induction under certain *assumptions*. These properties are *EC lemmas*.

OOIL makes assumptions for current node n and performs induction using these assumptions and known EC lemmas. In particular, $assumps(n, D)$ is a

---

^{3} In the implementation, multiple checks can be done together.

OVER-OVER-IND (OOI)

AVAIL	PROC	BENV	BODY	IND	PROP

$$\frac{\widehat{body}_O \wedge hyp \Rightarrow \mathbb{I} \quad\quad \mathbb{I} \Rightarrow \neg \widehat{b}_O \quad\quad O' = O[p \mapsto O[p] \wedge \mathbb{I}] \quad\quad D, A, O', U, L, \mathcal{C} \vdash Res}{D, A, O, U, L, \mathcal{C} \vdash Res}$$

OVER-OVER-IND-LEMMAS (OOIL)

AVAIL	PROC	BENV	BODY	IND	PROP

$$\frac{\begin{array}{c} S = assumps(n, D) \quad\quad \widehat{body}_O \wedge Inst(L) \wedge Inst(S) \wedge hyp \Rightarrow \mathbb{I} \quad\quad \mathbb{I} \Rightarrow \neg \widehat{b}_O \\ L' = L \cup \{\forall vars(S), in, out. \bigwedge S \Rightarrow (p(in, out) \Rightarrow \mathbb{I})\} \quad\quad D, A, O, U, L', \mathcal{C} \vdash Res \end{array}}{D, A, O, U, L, \mathcal{C} \vdash Res}$$

Fig. 5. Proof rules for induction.

set of assumptions $\{a_i \mid 1 \leq i \leq j\}$ for some $j \geq 0$. When $j = 0$, the set of assumptions is empty, and OOIL has the same effect as applying OOI. Each assumption a_i is of the following form:

$$q_i(in_{q_i}, out_{q_i}) \Rightarrow \forall vars(b_i) \setminus in_{q_i} \cup out_{q_i} . \neg b_i,$$

where q_i is the predicate for an ancestor of n and q_i is called by target p in some CHC. The ancestor node's bounded environment is b_i. Intuitively, each assumption is that the ancestor's bounded verification subtask has been discharged.

The *Inst* function takes a set of formulas, conjoins them, and replaces each application of an uninterpreted predicate with its interpretation in O. When applied to a set of assumptions S, it has an additional step that precedes the others: it first adds a conjunct $a_i[in_{q_i} \mapsto x, out_{q_i} \mapsto y]$ for each predicate application $q_i(x, y)$ in *body* to each element $a_i \in S$. This corresponds to applying the assumption in the induction hypothesis. If induction succeeds, we learn the EC lemma that $\mathbb{I}$ over-approximates $p(in, out)$ under the assumptions S.

Example 4. In §2, when we chose procedure e and proved an EC lemma, we used $j = 1$ to make an assumption about its caller o.

Appendix B [52] contains additional rules that allow lemmas to be simplified. There may be multiple attempts at applying the OOIL proof rule with different j values. For scalability, we require that j not exceed the bound k used for bounded contexts, limiting the number of these attempts.

6.5 Correctness and Progress

The correctness and progress claims for Algorithm 1 are stated below.

Theorem 1 (Correctness). *Algorithm 1 returns safe (resp. unsafe) only if the program with entry point* main *never violates the assertion (resp. a path in* main *violates the assertion).*

Proof. (Sketc.h) The CHC encoding is such that there is solution to the system of CHCs $\mathcal{C}$ iff the program does not violate the assertion. As a result, if the over-approximate summaries O constitute a solution and proof rule SAFE can be applied, the program does not violate the assertion. The under-approximate summaries U in every proof subgoal are guaranteed to be such that for any $p \in \mathcal{C}$, $U[p]$ implies any over-approximation $O[p]$. If UNSAFE can be applied, then the under-approximate summaries U imply that there is no possible solution O. The summaries in U can be used to reconstruct a counterexample path through the original program in this case.

Theorem 2 (Progress). *Processing a node in the derivation tree leads to at least one new (non-redundant) query.*

Proof. (Sketch) Initially, no nodes in A have been processed, and after a node is processed, it is removed from the derivation tree. The only way that a node can be processed and not have a new query made about it is if an already-processed node is re-added to A and this node does not have a new query that can be made about it. The ADDNODES and MAKEUNAVAILABLE procedures are the only ones that add nodes to A. The ADDNODES procedure, by definition, will only add a node to A if there is a new query that can be made about it. MAKEUNAVAILABLE only adds bounded parents of nodes whose summaries were updated. For any such bounded parent, at least one approximation of its procedure's body must be different than it was the last time the bounded parent was processed, since one of its callee's summaries was updated.

Limitations. If the underlying solver is unable to find appropriate interpolants, the algorithm may generate new queries indefinitely. (The underlying problem is undecidable, so this is not unusual for modular verifiers.) Note, however, that because environments are bounded, each query's size is restricted.

7   Evaluation and Results

We implemented our algorithm in a tool called CLOVER on top of CHC solver FREQHORN [25] and SMT solver Z3 [50]. We evaluated CLOVER and compared it with existing CHC-based tools on three sets of benchmarks (described later) that comprise standard collections and some new examples that include mutual recursion.

We aimed to answer the following questions in our evaluation:

– Is CLOVER able to solve standard benchmarks?
– Is CLOVER more effective than other tools at handling mutual recursion?
– To what extent do EC lemmas help CLOVER solve benchmarks?
– How does the bound k for environments affect CLOVER's performance?

We compared CLOVER against tools entered in the annual CHC-solver competition (CHC-Comp) in 2019: SPACER [42], based on PDR [12]; ELDARICA [39],

based on CEGAR [17]; HoIce [13], based on ICE [29]; PCSat [56]; and Ultimate Unihorn [22], based on trace abstraction [35].

For all experiments, we used a timeout of 10 min (as used in CHC-Comp).
We ran Clover on a MacBook Pro, with a 2.7 GHz Intel Core i5 processor and
8 GB RAM, but the other tools were run using StarExec [59]. Clover was not
run on StarExec due to difficulties with setting up the tool with StarExec[4].

7.1   Description of Benchmarks

To evaluate Clover, we gathered three sets of varied benchmarks. The first
set's benchmarks range from 10–7200 lines, and the latter two sets have smaller
but nontrivial code (100 lines). The latter two sets were manually encoded into
CHCs, and we plan to contribute them to CHC-Comp. Additional details follow.

CHC-Comp. We selected 101 benchmarks from CHC-Comp [14] that were contributed by HoIce and PCSat, since their encodings preserve procedure calls
and feature nonlinear CHCs (which can represent procedures with multiple
callees per control-flow path)[5].

Real-World. Two families of benchmarks are based on real-world code whose correctness has security implications. The *Montgomery* benchmarks involve properties about the sum of Montgomery representations [41] of concrete numbers.
The *s2n* benchmarks are based on Amazon Web Services' s2n library [3] and
involve arrays of unbounded length (not handled by the tool PCSat).

Mutual Recursion. This set of benchmarks containing mutual recursion was
created because few CHC-Comp benchmarks exhibit mutual recursion, likely due
to lack of tool support. *Even-Odd* benchmarks involve various properties of e
and o (defined as in Sect. 2) and extensions that handle negative inputs. Another
benchmark family is based on the *Hofstadter* Figure-Figure sequence [38]. *Mod*
n benchmarks consider mutually-recursive encodings of $\lambda x.x \bmod n = 0$ for $n =$
$3, 4, 5$. These serve as proxies for recursive descent parsers, which may have deep
instances of mutual recursion. We could not directly conduct experiments on
such parsers, since existing front-ends [21,33] cannot handle them. *Combination*
benchmarks result from combining Montgomery and Even-Odd benchmarks.

7.2   Results and Discussion

Table 2 gives a summary of results. It reports the number of benchmarks solved
for each benchmark set by Clover with bound parameter k being 2, 9, and
10 (the best-performing bounds for the three benchmark sets) and by the other
tools. It also reports results for Clover with $k = 10$ but without EC lemmas.
Figure 6 show the timing results for other tools against Clover for Real-World
and Mutual Recursion benchmarks.

---

[4] We expect that our platform is less performant than the StarExec platform.

[5] We did not compare against FreqHorn since it cannot handle nonlinear CHCs.

Table 2. Number of benchmarks solved by CLOVER and competing tools.

	CLOVER				SPACER	ELDA-RICA	HOICE	PCSAT	ULTI-MATE AUTO-MIZER
	k = 2	k = 9	k = 10	k = 10, no EC lemmas					
CHC-comp (101)	80	77	77	72	93	94	92	81	76
Montgomery (12)	0	11	12	12	5	12	12	3	11
s2n (4)	3	4	4	4	3	0	2	N/A	4
Even-odd (24)	24	24	24	0	12	0	9	0	0
Hofstadter (5)	4	5	4	5	1	4	5	5	0
Mod n (15)	0	15	15	0	0	0	0	0	0
Combination (2)	0	2	2	0	0	0	0	0	0
Total solved (163)	145	171	171	127	133	110	120	89	91

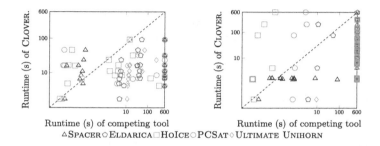

Runtime (s) of competing tool   Runtime (s) of competing tool

△ SPACER ○ ELDARICA □ HOICE ○ PCSAT ◇ ULTIMATE UNIHORN

Fig. 6. Timing results for the Real World (left) and Mutual Recursion (right) benchmarks. Points below the diagonal line are those for which CLOVER outperforms the corresponding tool. Points on the right edge indicate timeouts of the other tool.

Efficacy on Standard Benchmarks. As can be seen in Table 2, CLOVER performs comparably with other tools on the CHC-Comp benchmarks, and significantly outperforms them on the other two sets of benchmarks. We expect that we can further improve the performance of CLOVER with additional optimizations and heuristics, such as those that improve the quality of interpolants.

Efficacy on Mutual Recursion Benchmarks. Table 2 and Fig. 6 demonstrate that CLOVER is more effective and often more efficient at solving Mutual Recursion benchmarks than the other tools. Few tools are able to handle the Even-Odd benchmarks, which CLOVER (with EC lemmas) can solve at any bound value greater than 2. Other tools are unable to solve even half of the Mutual Recursion benchmarks, reinforcing that CLOVER is a useful addition to existing tools that enables handling of mutual recursion as a first class concern.

Usefulness of EC lemmas. Running CLOVER with and without EC lemmas using bound $k = 10$ revealed their usefulness for many of the benchmarks. In particular, the columns for bound 10 with and without EC lemmas in Table 2 show that EC lemmas are needed to allow CLOVER to solve several CHC-Comp benchmarks and all the Mutual Recursion benchmarks except the Hofstadter ones. These results indicate that CLOVER's ability to outperform other tools on the these benchmarks relies on EC lemmas.

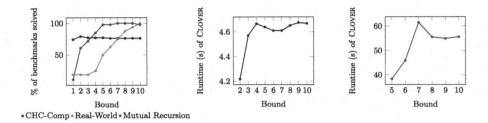

Fig. 7. Left: Percentage of benchmarks CLOVER solves with different bounds on different benchmark categories; **Center, Right**: Timing results on a representative benchmark from CHC-Comp and Mutual Recursion, respectively.

Comparison of Different Bounds. Figure 7 (left) shows the number of benchmarks successfully solved by CLOVER in each set as the bound value is varied. Running CLOVER with *too small* a bound impedes its ability to prove the property or find a counterexample, since the environment is unable to capture sufficient information. On the other hand, running CLOVER with *too large* a bound affects the runtime negatively. This effect can be observed in Fig. 7 center and right, which show how the runtime varies with the bound for a representative benchmark from the CHC-Comp and Mutual Recursion sets, respectively. Note that at a bound $k < 2$, CLOVER does not solve the given CHC-Comp benchmark, and at $k < 5$, CLOVER does not solve the given Mutual Recursion benchmark. These results confirm the expected trade-off between scalability and environment relevance. The appropriate trade-off – i.e., the best bound parameter to use – depends on the type of program and property. As seen in Fig. 7 (left), the bound values that lead to the most benchmarks being solved differ per benchmark set. Rather than having a fixed bound, or no bound at all, the ability to choose the bound parameter in CLOVER allows the best trade-off for a particular set of programs. If the best bound is not known a priori, bound parameters of increasing size can be determined empirically on representative programs.

We also report data on how the number and solving time for each type of SMT query varies with the bound k, averaged over benchmarks in each set. Figure 8 shows the statistics on the average number of queries of each type (top), on the average time taken to solve the query (bottom). These data are from all runs for which CLOVER is successful and gives an answer of *safe* or *unsafe*.

We can use these data along with the data in Fig. 7 to (roughly) compare an approach restricted to $k = 1$ with an approach that allows $k > 1$ in bounded environments. Note that CLOVER differs significantly in other respects from tools

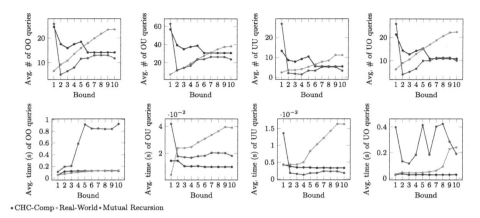

Fig. 8. Average statistics (**top four** plots: number, **bottom four**: solve times) of SMT queries made by CLOVER as the bound changes (for successful runs).

like SPACER and SMASH that enforce $k = 1$ in environments[6], making it difficult to perform controlled experiments to compare this aspect alone.

Note from Fig. 8 that for the CHC-Comp and Mutual Recursion sets of benchmarks, the number of SMT queries of all types is lower at $k > 1$ in comparison to $k = 1$. This result indicates that benchmarks that can be solved with $k > 1$ require on average fewer updates to procedure summaries than are needed on average for benchmarks that can be solved with $k = 1$, confirming the benefit of improved relevance when going beyond a restricted environment with $k = 1$. The data for the Real-World does not follow this trend because a higher bound ($k = 10$) is needed to solve the examples (as can be seen in Fig. 7).

From Fig. 8, it is clear that the OU and UU queries are cheaper than OO and UO queries, which is expected since the latter require over-approximating the target's body. Unsurprisingly, OO queries are the most expensive. Average times of non-OO queries for $k > 1$ are lower than (or about the same as) average times for $k = 1$ for the CHC-Comp and Mutual Recursion sets but continue to increase with k in the Real-World set because solving the Montgomery benchmarks relies on propagating under-approximations from increasingly large call graph depths.

8 Related Work

There is a large body of existing work that is related in terms of CHC solving, program analysis, and specification inference.

---

[6] Unlike SPACER it does not use PDR to derive invariants, and unlike SMASH it is not limited to predicate abstractions.

8.1 CHC-solving for Program Verification

Program verification problems, including modular verification, can be encoded into systems of CHCs [21,32,33,49]. There are many existing CHC-solver based tools [13,15,26,32,39,42,48,60,62] that can solve such systems. CLOVER has many algorithmic differences from these efforts.

Most existing tools do not place any bounds on the environments (if they are used at all). This includes approaches that unfold a relation at each step [48,60] and CEGAR-based approaches [32,39] where counterexamples can be viewed as environments. These tools face scalability issues as environments grow; DUALITY makes larger interpolation queries as more relations are unfolded [49], and ELDARICA makes larger tree/disjunctive interpolation queries for counterexamples that involve more procedures [39].

SPACER [42], which is based on PDR [12,23], considers bounded environments but only allows a bound of one ($k = 1$). The difference between DUALITY and a PDR-like approach has been referred to as the *variable elimination trade-off* [48], where eliminating too many variables can lead to over-specialization of learned facts (PDR) and eliminating no variables can lead to larger subgoals (DUALITY). Our parameterizable bounded environments enable a trade-off between the two. Another significant difference between SPACER and CLOVER is that the former uses PDR-style bounded assertion maps to perform induction, whereas we use induction explicitly and derive EC lemmas. DUALITY may also implicitly use assumptions, and some other tools [13,60] learn lemmas with implications, but none of them learn lemmas in the form of EC lemmas.

HOICE [13], FREQHORN [26], and LINEARARBITRARY [62] are based on guessing summaries and do not have any notion of environments similar to ours. All of these approaches have trade-offs between scalability of the search space and expressivity of guessed summaries.

8.2 Program Analysis and Verification

Techniques such as abstract interpretation [18,19,24] and interprocedural dataflow analysis [55,57] can infer procedure summaries and perform modular verification.

These approaches often use fixed abstractions and path-insensitive reasoning, which may result in over-approximations that are too coarse for verification.

The software model checker BEBOP [6] in SLAM [7] extended interprocedural dataflow analysis with path sensitivity. Related model checkers include a direct precursor to DUALITY [47] and other adaptations of PDR to software [16,37]. Of these, GPDR [37] is similar to SPACER, but lacks modular reasoning and under-approximations. Specification inference (including HOUDINI-style learning [28]) has also been used to enable modular verification of relational programs [43,53].

Another tool SMASH [31] is closely related to our work. It uses over- and under-approximate procedure summaries, and alternation between them. However, it does not have any notion of a parameterizable bounded environment. The environment for a procedure call is expressed as a pair of a precondition and a postcondition, where the former is an under-approximation of the program execution preceding the call, and the latter is an over-approximation of the program execution following the call. These environments are thus bounded environments with a fixed bound of 1. More importantly, procedure summaries in SMASH are comprised of predicate abstractions. In contrast, our summaries are richer formulas in first-order logic theories. We do not rely on predicate abstraction unlike SMASH and other related tools [30, 31, 34].

8.3 Specification Inference

Existing work on specification inference is also relevant. Many past efforts [2, 4, 9, 54, 58, 61] focused on learning coarse interface specifications or rules specifying the correct usage of library API calls, rather than learning logical approximations of procedures. Other specification inference techniques learn procedure summaries for library API procedures by using abstract interpretation [19, 36] or learn information-flow properties about the procedures [45, 53]. Other related work [1] infers maximal specifications for procedures with unavailable bodies, and other techniques assume an angelic environment setting [11, 20] – specifications inferred by these techniques may not be valid over-approximations. Another technique [5] also uses interpolation to infer over-approximate summaries but is not applicable to recursive programs.

9 Conclusions

We have presented a modular algorithm for generating procedure summaries and safety verification of interprocedural programs that addresses the challenges of handling mutual recursion and scalability of SMT queries. The novel features of our algorithm are use of bounded environments to limit the size of SMT queries, and a mechanism for performing induction under assumptions that uses these bounded environments to learn EC lemmas that capture relationships between summaries of procedures on call paths in the program.

We have implemented our algorithm in a CHC-based tool called CLOVER. An evaluation demonstrates that CLOVER is competitive with state-of-the-art tools on benchmarks from CHC-Comp and based on real-world examples, and is especially effective at solving benchmarks containing mutual recursion. Our algorithm can also be combined with existing invariant-generation techniques to successfully solve benchmarks with unbounded arrays.

Acknowledgements. This material is based upon work supported by the National Science Foundation Graduate Research Fellowship Program under Grant No. DGE-1656466. Any opinions, findings, and conclusions or recommendations expressed in this material are those of the author(s) and do not necessarily reflect the views of the National Science Foundation. This work was supported in part by the National Science Foundation award FMitF 1837030.

A   Renaming and Unfolding

Here, a formula f ranging over variables v is denoted $f(v)$. For example, a procedure body is encoded by some formula $body_p(in_p, out_p, local_p)$ and a path within it is encoded by some formula $\pi_p(in_p, out_p, local_p)$.

Definition 14 (Renaming). *Given a set of program paths $\Pi(v, y, x)$ that contain the statement $\ell : y := p(x)$, the renaming of a formula $\Pi_p(in, out, locs)$ that represents a subset of all paths in procedure p is defined as follows:*

$$rename\big(\Pi_p(in, out, locs), \Pi(v, x, y), \ell\big) \stackrel{\text{def}}{=}$$

$$\begin{cases} \Pi_p\big(x, y, fresh(v, x, y)\big), & \text{if } \ell:\ y := p(x) \text{ in } \Pi(v, x, y) \\ \Pi_p(x, y, locs), & \text{otherwise} \end{cases}$$

where $fresh(v, x, y)$ is a vector of fresh variables not present already in v, x, or y.

Definition 15 (Unfolding). *Let ℓ be a location at which procedure p is called. Given set of program paths Π that all go through location ℓ, an unfolding of p is a one-level inlining at location ℓ of one of the control-flow paths π_p in the body of p:*

$$\pi(v, x, y)[p(x, y) \mapsto rename(\{\pi_p\}, \Pi(v, x, y), \ell)]$$

B   Full Set of Derivation Rules

$$
\begin{array}{ll}
\text{AVAIL } n \in A & \text{PROC } p = proc(n) \in P \\
\text{BENV } b = bctx(n).env & \text{LOC } \quad \ell = bctx(n).loc \\
\text{NODE } n \in D.N & \text{PATH path } \pi \text{ in } body \\
\text{BODY } body = rename(body_p, bctx(n)) \\
\text{CALL } \text{ procedure call to } proc(n') \in P \text{ at location } \ell' \text{ in } \pi \\
\text{NCTX } ctx(n') = (b[p(in, out) \mapsto rename(\{\pi\}, body_n, \ell)], \ell') \\
\text{PROP } hyp = \forall in, out \in vars(body).p(in, out) \Rightarrow indProp \\
\text{IND } \quad indProp = \forall vars(\psi) \setminus (in_p \cup out_p).\mathbb{I}
\end{array}
$$

SAFE

$$\dfrac{m = body_{main} \qquad \widehat{m}_O \Rightarrow \bot}{D, A, O, U, L, P \vdash \bot}$$

UNSAFE

$$\dfrac{m = body_{main} \qquad \widehat{m}_U \not\Rightarrow \bot}{D, A, O, U, L, P \vdash \top}$$

OVER-OVER (OO)

$$\dfrac{AVAIL \quad PROC \quad BENV \quad BODY \quad \widehat{body}_O \Rightarrow \mathbb{I} \quad \mathbb{I} \Rightarrow \neg\widehat{b}_O \quad O' = O[p \mapsto O[p] \wedge \mathbb{I}] \quad D, A, O', U, L, P \vdash Res}{D, A, O, U, L, P \vdash Res}$$

UNDER-OVER (UO)

$$\frac{AVAIL \quad PROC \quad BENV \quad LOC \quad BODY}{\dfrac{\widehat{body_O} \Rightarrow \mathbb{I} \qquad \mathbb{I} \Rightarrow \neg \widehat{b}_{U,\ell}}{O' = O[p \mapsto O[p] \wedge \mathbb{I}] \qquad D, A, O', U, L, P \vdash Res}}{D, A, O, U, L, P \vdash Res}$$

UNDER-UNDER (UU)

$$\frac{AVAIL \quad PROC \quad BENV \quad LOC \quad BODY \quad PATH}{\dfrac{\widehat{\pi}_U \wedge \widehat{b}_{U,\ell} \not\Rightarrow \bot \qquad U' = U[p \mapsto U[p] \vee \exists locals_p.\pi]}{D, A, O, U', L, P \vdash Res}}{D, A, O, U, L, P \vdash Res}$$

OVER-UNDER (OU)

$$\frac{AVAIL \quad PROC \quad BENV \quad BODY \quad PATH}{\dfrac{\widehat{\pi}_U \wedge \widehat{b}_O \not\Rightarrow \bot \qquad U' = U[p \mapsto U[p] \vee \exists locals_p.\pi]}{D, A, O, U', L, P \vdash Res}}{D, A, O, U, L, P \vdash Res}$$

ADD-NODE (AN)

$$\frac{AVAIL \quad PROC \quad PATH \quad CALL \quad NCTX}{\dfrac{D'.E = D.E \cup \{n \to n'\} \qquad \forall n'' \in D.N.bctx(n') \neq bctx(n'')}{A' = A \cup \{n'\} \qquad D', A', O, U, L, P \vdash Res}}{D, A, O, U, L, P \vdash Res}$$

MAKE-AVAILABLE (MA)

$$\frac{NODE \quad PROC \quad PATH \quad CALL \quad NCTX}{\dfrac{n'' \in D.N \qquad bctx = bctx(n'')}{A' = A \cup \{n''\} \qquad D, A', O, U, L, P \vdash Res}}{D, A, O, U, L, P \vdash Res}$$

MAKE-UNAVAILABLE (MU)

$$\frac{AVAIL \qquad D, (A \setminus \{n\}), O, U, L, P \vdash Res}{D, A, O, U, L, P \vdash Res}$$

OVER-OVER-IND-LEMMAS (OOIL)

$$\frac{AVAIL \quad PROC \quad BENV \quad BODY \quad IND \quad PROP}{\dfrac{S = assumps(n, D) \qquad \widehat{body_O} \wedge Inst(L) \wedge Inst(S) \wedge hyp \Rightarrow \mathbb{I}}{\dfrac{\mathbb{I} \Rightarrow \neg \widehat{b}_O \qquad L' = L \cup \{\forall vars(S), in, out. \bigwedge S \Rightarrow (p(in, out) \Rightarrow \mathbb{I})\}}{D, A, O, U, L', P \vdash Res}}}{D, A, O, U, L, P \vdash Res}$$

UNDER-OVER-IND-LEMMAS (UOIL)

$$AVAIL \quad PROC \quad BENV \quad BODY \quad IND \quad PROP$$

$$S = underAssumps(n, D) \quad \widehat{body}_O \wedge Inst(L) \wedge Inst(S) \wedge hyp \Rightarrow \mathbb{I}$$

$$\mathbb{I} \Rightarrow \neg\widehat{b}_{U,\ell} \quad L' = L \cup \{\forall vars(S), in, out. \bigwedge S \Rightarrow (p(in, out) \Rightarrow \mathbb{I})\}$$

$$D, A, O, U, L', P \vdash Res$$

$$\overline{D, A, O, U, L, P \vdash Res}$$

REDUCE-LEMMAS (RL)

$$ec = \forall vars(S), in, out. \bigwedge S \Rightarrow (p(in, out) \Rightarrow \psi) \in L$$

$$a \in S \quad p' \in P \quad (p'(in, out) \Rightarrow O[p']) \Rightarrow a \quad S' = S \setminus \{a\}$$

$$L' = (L \setminus \{ec\}) \cup \{\forall vars(S'), in, out. \bigwedge S' \Rightarrow (p(in, out) \Rightarrow \psi)\}$$

$$D, A, O, U, L', P \vdash Res$$

$$\overline{D, A, O, U, L, P \vdash Res}$$

ELIM-LEMMAS (EL)

$$ec = \forall in, out. \top \Rightarrow (p(in, out) \Rightarrow prop) \in L$$

$$O' = O[p \mapsto O[p] \wedge prop]$$

$$D, A, O', U, L \setminus \{ec\}, P \vdash Res$$

$$\overline{D, A, O, U, L, P \vdash Res}$$

C   Heuristics

C.1   Prioritizing Choice of Node

The VERIFY procedure from Fig. 1 employs a heuristic to choose which node in the set A to call PROCESSNODE on next. The factors that contribute toward an node's priority are as follows, with ties in one factor being broken by the next factor, where $depth(n)$ denotes the depth of node n in D and $previous(n)$ denotes the number of times that the node n has been chosen previously:

- A lower $\alpha * depth(n) + \beta * previous(n)$ score gives higher priority, where α and β are weights
- A lower call graph depth of $proc(n)$ gives higher priority
- A later call location $ctx(n).loc$ gives higher priority

We prioritize nodes n with lower $depth(n)$ values because they are more likely to help propagate learned summaries up to the *main* procedure's callees. This priority is moderated by the $previous(n)$ score which should prevent the starvation of nodes with larger $depth(n)$ values. Our current heuristic search is more BFS-like, but for some examples, a DFS-like search is better. We plan to improve our heuristics in future work.

C.2   Avoiding Redundant Queries

If we have previously considered a node n that we are now processing, we can avoid making the same queries that we have previously made. E.g., if none of the over-approximate summaries for any of the procedures in $bctx(n).env$ nor any of over-approximate summaries for any of the procedures called by $proc(n)$ have been updated since the last time n was processed, we do not need to redo the over-over check.

C.3   Learning Over-approximate Bodies

Although there are many existing methods to interpolate, in many cases they are useless (recall our motivating example where an interpolant is just $\top$). To improve our chances of learning a refinement for an over-approximate summary, whenever we apply one of the proof rules that involves over-approximating the procedure body (e.g., OO, UO, OOIL, UOIL), we ensure that we at least learn the result of over-approximating the procedure body as an over-approximate fact about that procedure. For example, if we consider doing this for OO, we would simply replace premise $O' = O[p \mapsto O[p] \wedge \mathbb{I}]$ with $O' = O[p \mapsto O[p] \wedge \mathbb{I} \wedge \exists locals_p.\widehat{body}_O]$. Note that the result of applying quantifier elimination to $\mathbb{I} \wedge \exists locals_p.\widehat{body}_O$ is also an interpolant. Similarly, if we consider doing this for OOIL, we replace the goal $D, O, U, L', P \vdash Res$ with $D, O[p \mapsto \exists locals_p.\widehat{body}_O], U, L', P \vdash Res$.

C.4   Preventing Summaries from Growing too Large

Although we want to increase our chances of learning useful refinements of over-approximations as we have just discussed, we still wish to prevent summaries from becoming too complicated. We can achieve this in a few ways.

Quantifier Elimination. One way that we can achieve this is to use quantifier elimination or an approximation thereof on each conjunct (resp. disjunct) that we add to an over- (resp. under-) approximate summary. For example, we can replace $U' = U[p \mapsto U[p] \vee \exists locals_p.\pi]$ with $U' = U[p \mapsto U[p] \vee \mathrm{QE}(\exists locals_p.\pi)]$ in the UU rule. We illustrate how to do this using two examples:

- Instead of using premise $O' = O[p \mapsto O[p] \wedge \mathbb{I} \wedge \exists locals_p.\widehat{body}_O]$ for the OO rule as just discussed, we use the following premise: $O' = O[p \mapsto O[p] \wedge \mathbb{I} \wedge \mathrm{QE}(\exists locals_p.\widehat{body}_O)]$
- We can also apply this to properties we learn by induction. Instead of using the premise $L' = L \cup \{\forall vars(A). \bigwedge A \Rightarrow (p(in, out) \Rightarrow indProp)$ for rule OOIL, use the following premise: $L' = L \cup \{\forall vars(A). \bigwedge A \Rightarrow (p(in, out) \Rightarrow \mathrm{QE}(indProp))$
- Replace premise $U' = U[p \mapsto U[p] \vee \exists locals_p.\pi]$ with $U' = U[p \mapsto U[p] \vee \mathrm{QE}(\exists locals_p.\pi)]$ in the UU rule.

Algorithm 3. Procedure for adding nodes in derivation tree

---

procedure ADDNODES(n, *Goal*)
    for control-flow path π through $body_{proc(n)}$ **do**
        for procedure call to p at location ℓ in π **do**
            if $\neg$TRYADDNODE(n, π, p, ℓ, *Goal*) **then**
                MAKEAVAILABLEIFNEW(n, π, p, ℓ, *Goal*)

This use of QE leads to quantifier-free summaries.

When we update over- (resp. under-) approximate summaries, we can use over- (resp. under-) approximate QE. By comparison, under- (resp. over-) approximate QE would lead to unsoundness. Approximating QE is not only cheaper but can also further simplify the resulting summary.

Selective Updates. We can also prevent summaries from growing too quickly syntactically by only performing semantic updates. For example, consider O from the goal of the OO rule and O' from its subgoal. If $O[p] \Rightarrow O'[p]$, then although $O'[p]$ contains more conjuncts than $O[p]$, it does not provide any new information. In this case, we avoid the update and simply use O in the subgoal instead of O'. Similarly, if we consider U from the goal of UU and U' from its subgoal, then we only want to update the under-approximation if we have that $U'[p] \not\Rightarrow U[p]$. Over-approximate summaries become monotonically more constrained, so if $O[p] \Rightarrow O'[p]$, then $O[p] \Leftrightarrow O'[p]$ must hold. Under-approximations become monotonically less constrained.

D   Addition of Nodes in Derivation Tree

The ADDNODES procedure is shown in Algorithm 3. For every path π through $body_{proc(n)}$, it calls procedure
TRYADDNODE(n, π, p, ℓ, *Goal*), which tries to apply AN to *Goal* with premises $n \in A$ (AVAIL), path π in *body* (PATH), and procedure call to $p = proc(n') \in P$ at location ℓ in π (CALL). If TRYADDNODE succeeds in applying AN, then it updates *Goal* to be the subgoal of the application and returns *true*. If it fails, then it performs no updates and returns *false*. If TRYADDNODE fails, then there is already a node n'' in D with the same bounded environment that the new node n' would have. In this case, ADDNODES calls MAKEAVAILABLEIFNEW, which applies MA if either of the following hold:

- n'' has never been processed before
- n'' has previously been processed with summaries O_{prev} and U_{prev} and the body *body* of $proc(n)$ or the bounded environment *benv* for n'' has a different over- or under-approximation than before, i.e., $\widehat{body}_{M_{prev}} \neq \widehat{body}_M$ or else $\widehat{benv}_{M_{prev}} \neq \widehat{benv}_M$ for $M \in \{O, U\}$

Similarly to TRYADDNODE, the procedure
MAKEAVAILABLEIFNEW(n, π, p, ℓ, *Goal*) applies MA with premises $n \in D.N$

(NODE), path π in *body* (PATH), and procedure call to $proc(n') \in P$ at location ℓ in π (CALL). Both TRYADDNODE and MAKEAVAILABLEIFNEW have the side-effect of updating *Goal* to be the subgoal of the applied rule (if any).

E   Correctness and Progress Proof Sketches

Theorem 3 (Correctness). *Algorithm 1 returns safe (resp. unsafe) only if* **main**'s *semantics are such that it never violates the assertion (resp. a path in* **main** *violates the assertion).*

Proof. The over-approximate summaries O in every proof subgoal are guaranteed to be such that for any procedure $p \in P$, the semantics of p, given by interpreted predicate $R_p(in, out)$, imply $O[p]$ (see Definition 3), so approximation $\widehat{m}_O$ contains at least all of the behaviors of the **main** procedure. The proof rule SAFE can only be applied when $\widehat{m}_O \Rightarrow \bot$, i.e., when the over-approximate summary of **main**'s body does not violate the assertion along any path, indicating that the actual semantics of **main** also cannot violate the assertion. Similarly, the under-approximate summaries U in every proof subgoal are guaranteed to be such that for any $p \in P$, $U[p]$ imply $R_p(in, out)$, so the approximation $\widehat{m}_U$ only contains behaviors that are behaviors of the **main** procedure. The proof rule UNSAFE can only be applied when $\widehat{m}_U \Rightarrow \top$, i.e., when the under-approximation of **main** violates the assertion along some path, which thus indicates that the actual semantics of **main** also includes assertion-violating behaviors.

Theorem 4 (Progress). *Processing a node in the derivation tree leads to at least one new (non-redundant) query.*

Proof. Initially, no nodes in A have been processed, and after a node is processed, it is removed from the derivation tree. The only way that a node can be processed and not have a new query made about it is if an already-processed node is re-added A and this node does not have a new query that can be made about it. The ADDNODES and MAKEUNAVAILABLE procedures are the only ones that add nodes to A. The ADDNODES procedure, by definition, will only add a node to A if there is a new query that can be made about it. MAKEUNAVAILABLE only adds bounded parents of nodes whose summaries were updated. For any such bounded parent, at least one approximation of its procedure's body must be different than it was the last time the bounded parent was processed, since one of its callee's summaries was updated.

F   Additional Experimental Results

Figures 9 and 10 compare timing results for other tools against CLOVER for Real-World and Mutual Recursion benchmarks.

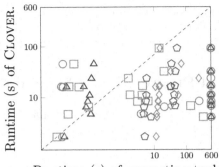

Runtime (s) of competing tool:

△Spacer ⚲Eldarica □HoIce ○PCSat ◇Ultimate Unihorn

Fig. 9. Timing results for the Real-World benchmarks. Points below the diagonal line are those for which CLOVER outperforms the corresponding tool. Points on the right edge indicate timeouts of the corresponding tool.

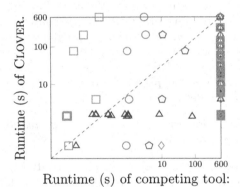

Runtime (s) of competing tool:

△Spacer ⚲Eldarica □HoIce ○PCSat ◇Ultimate Unihorn

Fig. 10. Timing results for the Mutual Recursion benchmarks. Points below the diagonal line are those for which CLOVER outperforms the corresponding tool. Points on the right edge indicate timeouts of the corresponding tool. Points on the top edge indicate a timeout for CLOVER.

References

1. Albarghouthi, A., Dillig, I., Gurfinkel, A.: Maximal specification synthesis. ACM SIGPLAN Notices **51**(1), 789–801 (2016)
2. Alur, R., Cerný, P., Madhusudan, P., Nam, W.: Synthesis of interface specifications for java classes. In: Proceedings of the 32nd ACM SIGPLAN-SIGACT symposium on Principles of programming languages, pp. 98–109. ACM (2005)
3. Amazon Web Services: https://github.com/awslabs/s2n (2019)
4. Ammons, G., Bodík, R., Larus, J.R.: Mining specifications. ACM Sigplan Notices **37**(1), 4–16 (2002)

5. Asadi, S., et al.: Function summarization modulo theories. In: LPAR. EPiC Series in Computing, vol. 57, pp. 56–75 (2018)
6. Ball, T., Rajamani, S.K.: Bebop: a path-sensitive interprocedural dataflow engine. In: Proceedings of the 2001 ACM SIGPLAN-SIGSOFT Workshop on Program Analysis for Software Tools and Engineering, pp. 97–103. ACM (2001)
7. Ball, T., Rajamani, S.K.: The SLAM toolkit. In: Berry, G., Comon, H., Finkel, A. (eds.) CAV 2001. LNCS, vol. 2102, pp. 260–264. Springer, Heidelberg (2001). https://doi.org/10.1007/3-540-44585-4_25
8. Barrett, C., Tinelli, C.: Satisfiability modulo theories. Handbook of Model Checking, pp. 305–343. Springer, Cham (2018). https://doi.org/10.1007/978-3-319-10575-8_11
9. Beckman, N.E., Nori, A.V.: Probabilistic, modular and scalable inference of type-state specifications. In: Proceedings of the 32nd ACM SIGPLAN Conference on Programming Language Design and Implementation, pp. 211–221. ACM (2011)
10. Bjørner, N., Janota, M.: Playing with quantified satisfaction. LPAR (short papers) **35**, 15–27 (2015)
11. Blackshear, S., Lahiri, S.K.: Almost-correct specifications: a modular semantic framework for assigning confidence to warnings. In: Proceedings of the 34th ACM SIGPLAN Conference on Programming Language Design and Implementation, pp. 209–218. ACM (2013)
12. Bradley, A.R.: SAT-based model checking without unrolling. In: Jhala, R., Schmidt, D. (eds.) VMCAI 2011. LNCS, vol. 6538, pp. 70–87. Springer, Heidelberg (2011). https://doi.org/10.1007/978-3-642-18275-4_7
13. Champion, A., Kobayashi, N., Sato, R.: HoIce: an ICE-based non-linear horn clause solver. In: Ryu, S. (ed.) APLAS 2018. LNCS, vol. 11275, pp. 146–156. Springer, Cham (2018). https://doi.org/10.1007/978-3-030-02768-1_8
14. CHC-Comp: https://chc-comp.github.io (2019)
15. Chen, Y.-F., Hsieh, C., Tsai, M.-H., Wang, B.-Y., Wang, F.: Verifying recursive programs using intraprocedural analyzers. In: Müller-Olm, M., Seidl, H. (eds.) SAS 2014. LNCS, vol. 8723, pp. 118–133. Springer, Cham (2014). https://doi.org/10.1007/978-3-319-10936-7_8
16. Cimatti, A., Griggio, A.: Software model checking via IC3. In: Madhusudan, P., Seshia, S.A. (eds.) CAV 2012. LNCS, vol. 7358, pp. 277–293. Springer, Heidelberg (2012). https://doi.org/10.1007/978-3-642-31424-7_23
17. Clarke, E., Grumberg, O., Jha, S., Lu, Y., Veith, H.: Counterexample-guided abstraction refinement. In: Emerson, E.A., Sistla, A.P. (eds.) CAV 2000. LNCS, vol. 1855, pp. 154–169. Springer, Heidelberg (2000). https://doi.org/10.1007/10722167_15
18. Cousot, P., Cousot, R.: Static determination of dynamic properties of recursive procedures. In: IFIP Conference on Formal Description of Programming Concepts, St. Andrews, NB, Canada, pp. 237–278 (1977)
19. Cousot, P., Cousot, R., Fähndrich, M., Logozzo, F.: Automatic inference of necessary preconditions. In: Proceedings of International Conference on Verification, Model Checking, and Abstract Interpretation, VMCAI, pp. 128–148 (2013)
20. Das, A., Lahiri, S.K., Lal, A., Li, Y.: Angelic verification: precise verification modulo unknowns. In: Kroening, D., Păsăreanu, C.S. (eds.) CAV 2015. LNCS, vol. 9206, pp. 324–342. Springer, Cham (2015). https://doi.org/10.1007/978-3-319-21690-4_19

21. De Angelis, E., Fioravanti, F., Pettorossi, A., Proietti, M.: VeriMAP: a tool for verifying programs through transformations. In: Ábrahám, E., Havelund, K. (eds.) TACAS 2014. LNCS, vol. 8413, pp. 568–574. Springer, Heidelberg (2014). https://doi.org/10.1007/978-3-642-54862-8_47

22. Dietsch, D., Heizmann, M., Hoenicke, J., Nutz, A., Podelski, A.: Ultimate TreeAutomize. HCVS/PERR. EPTCS **296**, 42–47 (2019)

23. Eén, N., Mishchenko, A., Brayton, R.K.: Efficient implementation of property directed reachability. In: Formal Methods in Computer-Aided Design (FMCAD), pp. 125–134. IEEE (2011)

24. Fähndrich, M., Logozzo, F.: Static contract checking with abstract interpretation. In: Beckert, B., Marché, C. (eds.) FoVeOOS 2010. LNCS, vol. 6528, pp. 10–30. Springer, Heidelberg (2011). https://doi.org/10.1007/978-3-642-18070-5_2

25. Fedyukovich, G., Kaufman, S.J., Bodík, R.: Sampling invariants from frequency distributions. In: Formal Methods in Computer Aided Design (FMCAD), pp. 100–107. IEEE (2017)

26. Fedyukovich, G., Prabhu, S., Madhukar, K., Gupta, A.: Solving constrained horn clauses using syntax and data. In: Formal Methods in Computer Aided Design (FMCAD), pp. 170–178. ACM (2018)

27. Fedyukovich, G., Prabhu, S., Madhukar, K., Gupta, A.: Quantified invariants via syntax-guided synthesis. In: Dillig, I., Tasiran, S. (eds.) CAV 2019. LNCS, vol. 11561, pp. 259–277. Springer, Cham (2019). https://doi.org/10.1007/978-3-030-25540-4_14

28. Flanagan, C., Leino, K.R.M.: Houdini, an annotation assistant for ESC/Java. In: Oliveira, J.N., Zave, P. (eds.) FME 2001. LNCS, vol. 2021, pp. 500–517. Springer, Heidelberg (2001). https://doi.org/10.1007/3-540-45251-6_29

29. Garg, P., Löding, C., Madhusudan, P., Neider, D.: ICE: a robust framework for learning invariants. In: Proceedings of the International Conference on Computer Aided Verification (CAV), pp. 69–87 (2014)

30. Godefroid, P., Huth, M., Jagadeesan, R.: Abstraction-based model checking using modal transition systems. In: Larsen, K.G., Nielsen, M. (eds.) CONCUR 2001. LNCS, vol. 2154, pp. 426–440. Springer, Heidelberg (2001). https://doi.org/10.1007/3-540-44685-0_29

31. Godefroid, P., Nori, A.V., Rajamani, S.K., Tetali, S.: Compositional may-must program analysis: unleashing the power of alternation. In: Proceedings of the 37th Annual ACM SIGPLAN-SIGACT Symposium on Principles of Programming Languages, pp. 43–56. ACM (2010)

32. Grebenshchikov, S., Lopes, N.P., Popeea, C., Rybalchenko, A.: Synthesizing software verifiers from proof rules. ACM SIGPLAN Notices **47**(6), 405–416 (2012)

33. Gurfinkel, A., Kahsai, T., Komuravelli, A., Navas, J.A.: The seaHorn verification framework. In: Kroening, D., Păsăreanu, C.S. (eds.) CAV 2015. LNCS, vol. 9206, pp. 343–361. Springer, Cham (2015). https://doi.org/10.1007/978-3-319-21690-4_20

34. Gurfinkel, A., Wei, O., Chechik, M.: YASM: a software model-checker for verification and refutation. In: Ball, T., Jones, R.B. (eds.) CAV 2006. LNCS, vol. 4144, pp. 170–174. Springer, Heidelberg (2006). https://doi.org/10.1007/11817963_18

35. Heizmann, M., Hoenicke, J., Podelski, A.: Refinement of trace abstraction. In: Palsberg, J., Su, Z. (eds.) SAS 2009. LNCS, vol. 5673, pp. 69–85. Springer, Heidelberg (2009). https://doi.org/10.1007/978-3-642-03237-0_7

36. Henzinger, T.A., Jhala, R., Majumdar, R.: Permissive interfaces. In: Proceedings of the 10th European Software Engineering Conference Held Jointly with 13th ACM SIGSOFT International Symposium on Foundations of Software Engineering, pp. 31–40. ACM (2005)

37. Hoder, K., Bjørner, N.: Generalized property directed reachability. In: Cimatti, A., Sebastiani, R. (eds.) SAT 2012. LNCS, vol. 7317, pp. 157–171. Springer, Heidelberg (2012). https://doi.org/10.1007/978-3-642-31612-8_13

38. Hofstadter, D.R., et al.: Gödel, Escher, Bach. An eternal golden braid, vol. 20. Basic books New York (1979)

39. Hojjat, H., Rümmer, P.: The ELDARICA horn solver. In: Formal Methods in Computer Aided Design (FMCAD), pp. 1–7. IEEE (2018)

40. Ivancic, F., et al.: DC2: a framework for scalable, scope-bounded software verification. In: IEEE/ACM International Conference on Automated Software Engineering (ASE), pp. 133–142 (2011)

41. Koc, C.K., Acar, T., Kaliski, B.S.: Analyzing and comparing montgomery multiplication algorithms. IEEE micro **16**(3), 26–33 (1996)

42. Komuravelli, A., Gurfinkel, A., Chaki, S.: Smt-based model checking for recursive programs. Formal Methods Syst. Des. **48**(3), 175–205 (2016)

43. Lahiri, S.K., McMillan, K.L., Sharma, R., Hawblitzel, C.: Differential assertion checking. In: Proceedings of the 2013 9th Joint Meeting on Foundations of Software Engineering, pp. 345–355. ACM (2013)

44. Lal, A., Qadeer, S., Lahiri, S.K.: A solver for reachability modulo theories. In: Proceedings of the International Conference on Computer Aided Verification (CAV), pp. 427–443 (2012)

45. Livshits, V.B., Nori, A.V., Rajamani, S.K., Banerjee, A.: Merlin: specification inference for explicit information flow problems. ACM Sigplan Not. **44**(6), 75–86 (2009)

46. McMillan, K.L.: Interpolation and SAT-based model checking. In: Hunt, W.A., Somenzi, F. (eds.) CAV 2003. LNCS, vol. 2725, pp. 1–13. Springer, Heidelberg (2003). https://doi.org/10.1007/978-3-540-45069-6_1

47. McMillan, K.L.: Lazy annotation for program testing and verification. In: Touili, T., Cook, B., Jackson, P. (eds.) CAV 2010. LNCS, vol. 6174, pp. 104–118. Springer, Heidelberg (2010). https://doi.org/10.1007/978-3-642-14295-6_10

48. McMillan, K.L.: Lazy annotation revisited. In: Biere, A., Bloem, R. (eds.) CAV 2014. LNCS, vol. 8559, pp. 243–259. Springer, Cham (2014). https://doi.org/10.1007/978-3-319-08867-9_16

49. McMillan, K.L., Rybalchenko, A.: Solving constrained horn clauses using interpolation. Tech. Rep. MSR-TR-2013-6 (2013)

50. de Moura, L., Bjørner, N.: Z3: an efficient SMT solver. In: Ramakrishnan, C.R., Rehof, J. (eds.) TACAS 2008. LNCS, vol. 4963, pp. 337–340. Springer, Heidelberg (2008). https://doi.org/10.1007/978-3-540-78800-3_24

51. Nielson, F., Nielson, H.R., Hankin, C.: Principles of Program Analysis. Springer-Verlag (1999)

52. Pick, L., Fedyukovich, G., Gupta, A.: Unbounded Procedure Summaries from Bounded Environments (2020). https://cs.princeton.edu/%7Eaartig/papers/clover-vmcai21-extended.pdf

53. Pick, L., Fedyukovich, G., Gupta, A.: Automating modular verification of secure information flow. In: FMCAD. TU Wien Academic Press, pp. 158–168. IEEE (2020)

54. Ramanathan, M.K., Grama, A., Jagannathan, S.: Static specification inference using predicate mining. ACM SIGPLAN Not. **42**(6), 123–134 (2007)

55. Reps, T.W., Horwitz, S., Sagiv, S.: Precise interprocedural dataflow analysis via graph reachability. In: Proceedings of the 22nd ACM SIGPLAN-SIGACT Symposium on Principles of Programming Languages, pp. 49–61. ACM (1995)
56. Satake, Y., Kashifuku, T., Unno, H.: PCSat: Predicate constraint satisfaction (2019). https://chc-comp.github.io/2019/chc-comp19.pdf
57. Sharir, M., Pnueli, A.: Two Approaches to Interprocedural Data Flow Analysis. In: Program Flow Analysis: Theory and Applications, pp. 189–233 (1981)
58. Shoham, S., Yahav, E., Fink, S., Pistoia, M.: Static specification mining using automata-based abstractions. In: ISSTA, pp. 174–184. ACM (2007)
59. Stump, A., Sutcliffe, G., Tinelli, C.: StarExec: a cross-community infrastructure for logic solving. In: Demri, S., Kapur, D., Weidenbach, C. (eds.) IJCAR 2014. LNCS (LNAI), vol. 8562, pp. 367–373. Springer, Cham (2014). https://doi.org/10.1007/978-3-319-08587-6_28
60. Unno, H., Torii, S., Sakamoto, H.: Automating induction for solving horn clauses. In: Majumdar, R., Kunčak, V. (eds.) CAV 2017. LNCS, vol. 10427, pp. 571–591. Springer, Cham (2017). https://doi.org/10.1007/978-3-319-63390-9_30
61. Yang, J., Evans, D., Bhardwaj, D., Bhat, T., Das, M.: Perracotta: mining temporal API rules from imperfect traces. In: Proceedings of the 28th International Conference on Software Engineering, pp. 282–291. ACM (2006)
62. Zhu, H., Magill, S., Jagannathan, S.: A data-driven CHC solver. ACM SIGPLAN Not. **53**(4), 707–721 (2018)

Syntax-Guided Synthesis for Lemma Generation in Hardware Model Checking

Hongce Zhang$^{(\boxtimes)}$, Aarti Gupta, and Sharad Malik

Princeton University, Princeton, NJ 08544, USA
{hongcez,aartig,sharad}@princeton.edu

Abstract. In this work we propose to use Syntax-Guided Synthesis (SyGuS) for lemma generation in a word-level IC3/PDR framework for bit-vector problems. Hardware model checking is moving from bit-level to word-level problems, and it is expected that model checkers can benefit when such high-level information is available. However, for bit-vectors, it is challenging to find a good word-level interpolation strategy for lemma generation, which hinders the use of word-level IC3/PDR algorithms.

Our SyGuS-based procedure, SyGuS-$\mathcal{A}$PDR, is tightly integrated with an existing word-level IC3/PDR framework $\mathcal{A}$PDR. It includes a predefined grammar template and term production rules for generating candidate lemmas, and does not rely on any extra human inputs. Our experiments on benchmarks from the hardware model checking competition show that SyGuS-$\mathcal{A}$PDR can outperform state-of-the-art Constrained Horn Clause (CHC) solvers, including those that implement bit-level IC3/PDR. We also show that SyGuS-$\mathcal{A}$PDR and these CHC solvers can solve many instances faster than other leading word-level hardware model checkers that are not CHC-based. As a by-product of our work, we provide a translator Btor2CHC that enables the use of CHC solvers for general hardware model checking problems, and contribute representative bit-vector benchmarks to the CHC-solver community.

Keywords: Hardware model checking · Syntax-guided synthesis (SyGuS) · Bit-vector theory · Lemma generation · CHC solver

1 Introduction

Hardware bugs are circuit design errors that can cause malfunction or security breaches, which could further lead to system failures or economic losses. Compared to software bugs, hardware bugs tend to be more costly to fix due to the need for a physical replacement and high non-recurring expenses for respins. Therefore, it is very important to ensure the correctness of hardware designs before manufacturing. Model checking [18], which formally checks whether certain correctness properties hold in a state transition system, has been successfully applied in finding hardware bugs or proving there are no property violations.

In hardware model checking, descriptions of the circuit and properties to be checked are given as inputs to an automated tool. The design description,

© Springer Nature Switzerland AG 2021
F. Henglein et al. (Eds.): VMCAI 2021, LNCS 12597, pp. 325–349, 2021.
https://doi.org/10.1007/978-3-030-67067-2_15

until recently, was typically provided using a bit-level format called AIGER [7], which uses the and-inverter graph (AIG) representation. The AIGER format is compact and close to a post-logic-synthesis hardware implementation. However, it lacks word-level information which could be helpful in improving scalability of hardware model checking. Recently, in 2019, the hardware model checking competition (HWMCC) started to advocate use of a word-level description called Btor2 [49]. It follows similar principles as the bit-level AIGER format, but instead uses SMT-LIB2 [6] logics for bit-vectors and arrays. This format preserves the word-level information in the circuit description. For example, a 32-bit adder in Btor2 can be represented succinctly using a single "add" operator (namely the modular addition function bvadd in SMT-LIB2), whereas in AIGER format, it is bit-blasted into single-bit half and full adders represented using 378 AIG nodes. The Btor2 format allows model checkers to potentially take advantage of the high-level circuit structure.

Along with the Btor2 word-level format, there has been interest in using Constrained Horn Clauses (CHCs) to describe digital circuits and properties at the word-level, and CHC solvers have been used or developed to synthesize environment invariants [59]. Although CHC solvers have largely been used in software verification [13, 24, 30, 35, 39, 48], the associated techniques to find invariants may also be helpful in hardware verification. Many CHC solvers can successfully find invariants in linear integer/real arithmetic (LIA/LRA) and array theories. For example, SPACER [39] extends the IC3/PDR algorithm [11, 21] to $\mathcal{A}$PDR [8, 32] (and also other variants) for LIA/LRA, where Craig interpolants are used to generate *lemmas* that are conjoined to construct an invariant.

However, when it comes to supporting bit-vectors, the lack of a native word-level interpolation strategy hinders the use of $\mathcal{A}$PDR and similar techniques. Indeed, our experiments on bit-vector problems show that directly using word-level interpolants from an SMT solver for lemma generation in $\mathcal{A}$PDR can actually incur a performance loss.

In this paper, we propose our solution to address this problem. We propose to use Syntax-Guided Synthesis (SyGuS) [2] for generating lemmas for invariants, in a new method called SyGuS-$\mathcal{A}$PDR. It is tightly integrated with an IC3/PDR framework, where models from deductive reasoning in IC3/PDR are used to guide the generation of lemmas. In particular, it uses a general grammar template with predicate and term production rules without any need of extra human input, and where the search space of predicates and terms is pruned based on the deduced models. It also tightens previous frames in IC3/PDR to allow a larger set of lemma candidates to be considered. In addition to this tight integration, our method includes other known techniques [21, 37] specialized here to support word-level reasoning for bit-vectors—generalization of lemma candidates by extracting minimal UNSAT subset (MUS), and partial model generation in predecessor generalization. These features are summarized in Fig. 1.

We have implemented our proposed SyGuS-$\mathcal{A}$PDR algorithm using SMT-Switch [44], which provides an interface to various SMT (Satisfiability Modulo Theory) solvers in the backend. We describe an extensive evaluation of SyGuS-

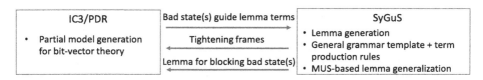

Fig. 1. Integration of IC3/PDR with SyGuS-based lemma generation

$\mathcal{A}$PDR against state-of-the-art CHC solvers and hardware model checkers on benchmarks from the bit-vector track of HWMCC'19. Our experiments show that SyGuS-$\mathcal{A}$PDR outperforms state-of-the-art CHC solvers with more solved instances. Furthermore, we show that CHC solvers can deliver better performance on a notable portion of the benchmarks, in comparison to other hardware model checkers that are not CHC-based. Finally, as part of this evaluation, we have developed a translator that can convert Btor2 to the standard CHC format. This enables other CHC solvers to be used on word-level hardware model checking problems.

Summary of Contributions:

- We present a novel algorithm SyGuS-$\mathcal{A}$PDR that uses SyGuS-based lemma generation for word-level bit-vector reasoning in an IC3/PDR framework. It is distinctive in using a tight integration between the two, where: (1) the space of lemma candidates is guided both by a general grammar template and models provided by IC3/PDR, (2) existing functionality in IC3/PDR is used to tighten previous frames, which allows a larger set of lemma candidates to be considered.
- We have implemented SyGuS-$\mathcal{A}$PDR and provide an extensive empirical evaluation against other tools on the HWMCC'19 benchmarks.
- We enable application of CHC solvers on hardware model checking problems via a translation tool `Btor2CHC` developed as part of this work. We have made the translated HWMCC'19 benchmarks publicly available [58].

The paper is organized as follows. We start with some background in the next section, and describe a motivating example (Sect. 3). In Sect. 4, we present the SyGuS-$\mathcal{A}$PDR algorithm. Section 5 describes the experimental evaluation and results, followed by related work and conclusions.

2   Background and Notation

2.1   Constrained Horn Clauses (CHCs)

A Constrained Horn Clause is a first order logic (FOL) formula over some background theory $\mathcal{A}$ in the following form:

$$\forall v_1, v_2, ..., v_n, \phi\left(V\right) \wedge \left(\bigwedge_k p_k\left(V_k\right)\right) \rightarrow h\left(V_h\right) \tag{1}$$

Here $v_1, v_2, v_3, ..., v_n$ form the set of variables V from theory $\mathcal{A}$. ϕ is an interpreted constraint over the functions and variables in $\mathcal{A}$, and p_k and h are uninterpreted predicate symbols over sets of variables V_k and V_h, respectively. V_k and V_h are subsets of V, and can be empty. A CHC is satisfiable if there exists an interpretation $\mathcal{I}$ for the predicate symbols p_k and h that makes the formula valid. A set of CHCs is satisfiable if there exists an interpretation $\mathcal{I}$ for all the predicate symbols that make all CHC formulas valid.

2.2   Hardware Model Checking Using CHCs

Here we focus on safety properties in hardware model checking. A digital circuit can be viewed as a state transition system: $\langle V, Init, T \rangle$, where V is a set of state variables (along with the primed version of variables V' that denote next states), $Init$ is a predicate representing initial states, and T is a transition relation. Note that for hardware model checking, the transition relation T is functional, i.e., $T(V, V') := V' = Next(V)$. For a given safety property P, we would like to check if the transition system will ever reach a state (the bad state) where P does not hold. If all bad states are unreachable, we would like to get a proof showing P is valid. One such proof is an inductive invariant (Inv):

$$Init(V) \rightarrow Inv(V) \tag{2}$$
$$Inv(V) \wedge T(V, V') \rightarrow Inv(V') \tag{3}$$
$$Inv(V) \rightarrow P(V) \tag{4}$$

In other words, Inv should hold in the initial states (2), it should be inductive (3), and it should imply safety (4). These three constraints are in the form of CHCs (with an implicit universal quantification over all variables), where Inv is an uninterpreted predicate. If these CHCs are satisfiable, then the interpretation of Inv is the inductive invariant that forms the proof of safety.

2.3   IC3/PDR and $\mathcal{A}$PDR

The IC3/PDR algorithm [11,21] constructs inductive invariants to check safety. It maintains a sequence of forward reachable sets of states (FRS): F_i, which are over-approximations of all reachable states in i steps. They satisfy the following properties.

$$F_0(V) = Init(V) \tag{5}$$
$$F_i(V) \wedge T(V, V') \rightarrow F_{i+1}(V') \tag{6}$$
$$F_i(V) \rightarrow F_{i+1}(V) \tag{7}$$
$$F_i(V) \rightarrow P(V) \tag{8}$$

The algorithm converges if at any point $F_{i+1}(V) \rightarrow F_i(V)$. As F_i is in the form of a conjunction of clauses (for bit-level PDR) or lemmas (for word-level PDR), when it is clear from the context, we interchangeably use F_i to refer to either the conjunction or the set of clauses/lemmas.

The procedure for constructing FRS can be viewed as iteratively blocking bad states or their predecessors (states that can reach bad states following the transitions) by applying the following rules in an indefinite order. (We refer the readers to [32] for details.)

- **Unreachable.** If $\exists i, F_{i+1} \rightarrow F_i$, the system is safe ($P$ holds) and the algorithm converges.
- **Unfold.** For the last FRS: F_N in the series, if $F_N \wedge T \rightarrow P'$, then extend the series with $F_{N+1} \leftarrow P$ and $N \leftarrow N + 1$.
- **Candidate.** For the last FRS: F_N in the series, if $\exists m, m \models F_N \wedge T \wedge \neg P'$, then we need to add $\langle m, N \rangle$ as a proof obligation (meaning that we would like to try blocking m at step N as it can lead to the failure of P).
- **Predecessor.** For a proof obligation $\langle m, i + 1 \rangle$, according to the transition relation T, if there is a predecessor m_i of it at step i, then we will also add $\langle m_i, i \rangle$ to the proof obligation.
- **NewLemma.** For a proof obligation $\langle m, i+1 \rangle$, if we found no predecessor of it at step i, then try to find a lemma l showing m is infeasible at $i + 1$, and update all $F_j, j \leq i + 1$ with l to remember this (explained in details in Sect. 4.1).
- **Push.** For a lemma l in F_i, see if it also holds at step $i + 1$.
- **ReQueue.** For a proof obligation $\langle m, i \rangle$, if we found it has no predecessor at $i - 1$, then also add m to the proof obligation at step $i + 1$.
- **Reachable.** If we get a proof obligation at step 0, then the system is unsafe. The algorithm stops.

For CHCs in different theories, the theory-dependent techniques used in the above procedures may vary. In particular, $\mathcal{A}$PDR [8] (in SPACER [39]) implements the two procedures—**Predecessor** and **NewLemma**—using model-based projection [39] and Craig interpolation [46], respectively, to adapt IC3/PDR for LIA/LRA theories.

2.4   CHC Solving Techniques for Bit-Vectors

As the hardware model checking problems require bit-vectors, here we focus our discussion on solving CHCs in bit-vector theory.

Bit-Blasting. The original IC3/PDR algorithm [11,21] is applicable if the BV problems are *bit-blasted*, i.e., transformed into propositional logic with one Boolean variable for each bit in each bit-vector variable. This is the general approach implemented in SPACER [39] for bit-vectors. For the special case where a problem contains only arithmetic operators in the BV theory, SPACER can attempt the translation method described below.

Translation and Abstraction. Another approach for solving bit-vector problems is to translate them into another theory (e.g., LIA or LRA), derive a safe inductive invariant, and then port it back soundly to the bit-vector theory. This approach is discussed in related work [33] and implemented in the PDR engine in SPACER.

Table 1. A simple transition system: $\langle V, Init, T \rangle$

V	$\{a,b,c,e,i\}$, a,b,c,i: (_BitVec 16), e : Bool
$Init$	$a = 0 \wedge b = 0 \wedge c = 0$
T	$a' = \text{ite}\,(e, i, a + 1) \wedge b' = \text{ite}\,(e, i, b) \wedge c' = \text{ite}\,(e, 0, c + 1)$

Another CHC solver, ELDARICA [35], handles bit-vector theory through abstraction, as well as translation. It applies lazy Cartesian predicate abstraction [5,29], in combination with a variant of counterexample-guided abstraction refinement (CEGAR) [4,17]. Bit-vectors are lazily mapped to quantifier-free Presburger constraints, and then solved and interpolated by an SMT solver. Using the abstractions, it constructs an abstract reachability graph (ARG). To eliminate spurious counterexamples in the abstract reachability relation, it obtains additional predicates from Craig interpolation.

Learning-Based Methods. There have also been other efforts that use learning-based or guess-and-check approaches for CHC solving, e.g., Synth-Horn [61], FreqHorn [23–25], HoICE [13], Code2Inv [54]. However, to the best of our knowledge, these tools currently do not offer support for bit-vector theory.

3   A Motivating Example

We use an example to illustrate why word-level reasoning is beneficial and also how word-level interpolants for bit-vectors can fail to converge. Table 1 shows a simple transition system. This is a case simplified from a verification problem of a domain-specific accelerator design we encountered in our previous hardware verification work [59].

For simplicity of presentation, we use "+" to represent bit-vector addition: bvadd, which will wrap-around in the case of overflow and we use ite as the short form for "if-then-else". Variables a, b, and c correspond to three registers in the circuit, and e and i are primary inputs. All variables except e are 16-bit wide. a and c will count up if $e = \bot$ (false), while a and b will be loaded with input i and c will be cleared if $e = \top$ (true). A simple property to check can be, for example, if state $(a, b, c) = (6, 4, 1)$ is reachable. For a human looking at this transition system, it is not hard to find that $a = b + c$ is an inductive invariant. Initially a, b, c are all 0. Subsequently, if $e = \top$, then $a = b$ and $c = 0$, and the relation holds; if $e = \bot$, then a and c both increase by 1 (and may cause both sides of the equality to wrap-around) so the equality relation still holds. This relation is easy to find for a human analyzer, however, it turns out to be hard for a bit-level model checker because the bit-blasting breaks the word addition into bit-level operations and the invariant becomes much more complex.

On the other hand, when we directly use a word-level bit-vector interpolator [31] out-of-the-box, to generate lemmas for blocking $(a, b, c) = (6, 4, 1)$ or other models that lead to it, we actually get these lemmas: $l_1 : a = b \vee b \neq 4$,

$l_2 : a = b + 2 \lor a = b + 1 \lor a = b \lor b = 4$, $l_3 : (b, c) \neq (4, 65535)$. There are several issues with these lemmas: (1) They only hold for the frames explored so far. This is true for all three lemmas shown here. (2) Although some may look similar to an inductive invariant, they are not general enough (e.g., l_2). (3) Some are overly generalized, like l_3, which drops a and will become invalid after 65536 steps. In general, interpolation in BV theory is hard, because unlike LIA/LRA, there is no counterpart to the Farkas's lemma [22] in BV theory that can directly provide a word-level interpolant.

In this work, we address these issues by using SyGuS in a tight integration with an IC3/PDR framework, as described in detail in the next section.

4   Integrating SyGuS with IC3/PDR

A SyGuS-based guess-and-check approach is flexible, but it can be quite expensive when the search space of candidate lemmas is large, and enumerating through the candidates is expensive. We address these issues by using SyGuS in a tight integration with an IC3/PDR framework where the distinctive features are: (1) We use the models from IC3/PDR to guide and prune the search space of predicates in lemma candidates. (2) We provide a general grammar template and production rules to generate new terms in lemma candidates. These rules use hardware-specific insights as heuristics to prioritize the search and term generation. (3) We use procedures in IC3/PDR to tighten previous frames to allow using lemmas that are otherwise not considered. In addition, we use UNSAT core minimization to create a more general lemma from a set of predicates, and use partial model generation for predecessor generalization to support bit-vector theory in IC3/PDR on the word-level.

4.1   Lemma Formulation

In IC3/PDR, a lemma is needed when some previously generated bad state(s) m in F_{i+1} should be blocked because it has no predecessor in F_i, i.e., when the following implication is valid:

$$(F_i(V) \land T(V, V')) \lor Init(V') \rightarrow Q(V') \tag{9}$$

Here, F_i is a set of lemmas learned at step i, and $Q(V') := \neg \bigwedge_k (V'_k = c_k)$, where c_k is the assignment to variable V_k in the bad state m. This is illustrated in Fig. 2(a). To learn this fact for future use, we would like to add it (i.e., conjoin it) with F_{i+1}. Although formula Q can itself be conjoined with F_{i+1} (as well as all $F_j, j \leq i$, thanks to the monotonicity of the series of F), typical IC3/PDR procedures will try to find a stronger lemma l such that $l \rightarrow Q$, and conjoin l with F_{i+1} instead. It is hoped that l can potentially block more unreachable states.

For LIA/LRA, the $\mathcal{A}$PDR algorithm uses Craig interpolants to derive lemma l. For bit-vectors, although there are existing word-level interpolation methods [3,31] using techniques like equality and uninterpreted function (EUF) layering, equality substitution, linear integer encoding and lazy bit-blasting etc.,

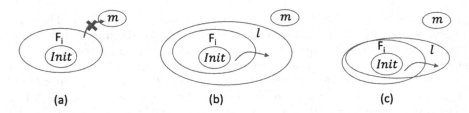

Fig. 2. (a) A bad state(s) m can be blocked when it has no predecessor in F_i. (b) Using constraint (10) for lemma generation and (c) using constraint (12) for lemma generation

our experiments in Sect. 5 show that using these interpolants actually incurs a performance loss and makes the word-level IC3/PDR slower than bit-blasting.

When viewing interpolation as constraint-based synthesis, the interpolator can be seen as trying to find a candidate l that satisfies the following two constraints (there is an implicit universal quantification over all variables):

$$(F_i(V) \wedge T(V, V')) \vee Init(V') \rightarrow l(V') \tag{10}$$
$$l(V') \rightarrow Q(V') \tag{11}$$

These requirements are sufficient but not necessary conditions for a lemma l. In fact, (10) can be relaxed to the following form (similar to what is used for inductive generalization in IC3 [11]):

$$(l(V) \wedge F_i(V) \wedge T(V, V')) \vee Init(V') \rightarrow l(V') \tag{12}$$

The difference between (10) and (12) is that the latter applies l on the previous frame also. Any candidate l that satisfies (10) will also satisfy (12), but the reverse is not true. In fact, using constraint (12) allows finding a lemma l that can also tighten F_i at the same time, whereas (10) finds lemmas that contain all states in F_i and also all states that are one-step reachable from F_i. Therefore, using (12) is helpful if the previously generated lemmas in F_i are too weak. The difference between using (10) or (12) for lemma generation is illustrated in Fig. 2(b) and (c).

As an example, if the over-approximation introduced by F_i is already too coarse, even if we can somehow "magically" guess a safe inductive invariant Inv correctly, Inv may not even hold for (10). On the other hand, choosing (12) instead of (10) will shift the cost to lemma generation. Note that while (12) is similar to prior work [11,12], we target lemmas with bit-vectors rather than Boolean clauses. Our solution to this problem is to have a tightening procedure that will also generate lemmas in F_i while still using (10) as the constraint. This will be explained in Sect. 4.5. As we choose (10), our method can be viewed as SyGuS-based interpolation, combined with an additional tightening procedure (usually available) in the IC3/PDR framework.

$$\langle \texttt{Cand} \rangle ::= \neg \langle \texttt{Conj} \rangle$$
$$\langle \texttt{Conj} \rangle ::= \langle \texttt{Pred} \rangle \mid \langle \texttt{Pred} \rangle \wedge \langle \texttt{Conj} \rangle$$
$$\langle \texttt{Pred} \rangle ::= \langle \texttt{Term} \rangle \; Comparator_{BV} \; \langle \texttt{Term} \rangle$$
$$\langle \texttt{Term} \rangle ::= \langle \texttt{Constant} \rangle \mid \langle \texttt{Variable} \rangle \mid \langle \texttt{Term} \rangle \; Operator_{BV} \; \langle \texttt{Term} \rangle$$

Fig. 3. The grammar template for lemmas, where operators and terms are dynamically generated.

4.2 SyGuS-Based Interpolation

The grammar template that we use for learning an interpolant, i.e., the lemma l, is shown in Fig. 3. The top-level lemma candidate ($\langle \texttt{Cand} \rangle$) is a negated conjunction of predicates over BV theory. The predicates and terms used in the predicates are dynamically generated and pruned due to a tight integration of SyGuS with IC3/PDR. We would like to first give an overview of our SyGuS-based approach, and leave the discussion of operators and terms to Sect. 4.4.

At a high-level, our SyGus-based lemma generation procedure is shown in Algorithm 1). For given bad state(s) m, our method first checks if we have encountered m before (due to the ReQueue rule in $\mathcal{A}$PDR, it may have been blocked at some previous frame j, $j \leq i$). If so, the previously generated predicate set is reused (Line 2) to save the work of predicate generation. Otherwise, it will invoke the predicate generation procedure to get an initial set of predicates based on m (Line 4). For a set of predicates L, it will check if L is sufficient to generate a lemma (Line 5). If the current set is insufficient, it will try to tighten the previous frame first (Line 7). If after tightening, the current predicate set is still insufficient, it will then incrementally construct more predicates, while factoring

---

Algorithm 1: NEWLEMMA($Init, F_i, T, m$): Generating lemma when m has no predecessor in F_i

Input: $Init$: initial states, F_i: set of lemmas at step i, T: transition relation, m: the bad state to block at step $i + 1$

Output: the lemma that blocks m

1 **if** m has been blockable on/before step i **then**
2       $L \leftarrow$ GETPREVIOUSLYGENERATEDPREDSET (m) ;
3 **else**
4       $L \leftarrow$ GENINITIALPREDSET (m) ;
5 **while** $\neg$ PREDSUFFICIENT (F_i, T, L) **do**
6       $(n, n') \leftarrow$ MODEL $(\;((F_i \wedge T) \vee Init') \wedge \neg l_L\;)$;
7   **if** $\neg$ RECBLOCK (n, i, MAY) **then**
8           $L \leftarrow L \cup$ MOREPRED (m, n, n') ;
9 $base \leftarrow (F_i \wedge T) \vee Init'$;
10 $L \leftarrow$ MUS $(L \cup \{base\})$;
11 **return** $\neg \bigwedge_{p \in L} p$;

in both m and the model (n, n') demonstrating L is insufficient (Line 8). After L finally becomes sufficient, it will invoke the MUS procedure (Line 10) to get a minimal set of predicates using UNSAT cores.

In Algorithm 1, GETPREVIOUSLYGENERATEDPREDSET is simply to retrieve the cached predicates for the same model. GENINITIALPREDSET and PREDSUF-FICIENT will be described in Sect. 4.3. Our approach to generate new terms to make new predicates in MOREPRED is presented in Sect. 4.4. MUS is briefly discussed in Sect. 4.6, and RECBLOCK is the recursive blocking function provided by an IC3/PDR framework.

Note that our SyGuS-based method is tightly integrated with the IC3/PDR framework and uses the results from deductive solving to guide the generation of predicates (Line 4 and 8), and uses procedures in IC3/PDR to tighten previous frames to allow using lemmas that are otherwise not considered (Line 7). It checks the sufficiency of a set of predicates using a single SMT query to expedite candidate validation (Line 5) and uses UNSAT core minimization (Line 10) to construct a more general lemma.

Theorem 1. *For bit-vector problems, IC3/PDR converges when using Algorithm 1 for lemma generation.*

This is because the lemmas generated by Algorithm 1 will block the given bad states, and the rest follows from correctness of the original IC3/PDR algorithm.

4.3 Lemma Generation and Validation

Pruning Based on Bad State. The lemma generation procedure is invoked if formula (9) is found to be valid, and we need to find a candidate l that satisfies (10) and (11). Our SyGuS method starts with handling constraint (11) first. Note that l is in the form of $\neg (p_1 \wedge p_2 \wedge ... \wedge p_n)$ according to the grammar in Fig. 3 and the equivalent contrapositive of (11) is $\neg Q \rightarrow \neg l$. Therefore, $\neg Q$ should imply every predicate $p_1, p_2, ... p_n$ in l. For a given Q, our SyGuS approach will only construct predicates from the grammar that can be implied from $\neg Q$, i.e., model m. This is shown as pruning on the initial predicate set based on model m (Line 4, GETINITIALPREDSET in Algorithm 1).

Candidate Validation. After generating predicates that satisfy (11), we consider the constraint (10). Our method starts with a candidate set of simple syntactic structures and incrementally adds more complex predicates if the current set is not sufficient. To test if a set of predicates L is sufficient, we conjoin all predicates in L to form $l_L = \neg(\bigwedge_{p \in L} p)$, and check if l_L makes (10) valid. This is the PREDSUFFICIENT procedure in Algorithm 1. In other words, if the following is UNSAT, it is adequate to construct a lemma:

$$((F_i(V) \wedge T(V, V')) \vee Init(V')) \wedge \neg l_L(V') \tag{13}$$

Pruning Due to Inadequate Batch. If the batch is inadequate (i.e., formula (13) is satisfiable), we construct a formula $c := \bigwedge_i V_i' = a_i$, where a_i is the assignment to V_i' in the model of (13). Since c is constructed from the model, $\forall p \in L, c \to p$. If there is a good set of predicates $L' \supset L$, then within L', there must be a predicate p_c such that $c \to \neg p_c$. Therefore, we can use the extracted formula c to guide the generation of new predicates. This constitutes additional pruning of the search space (Line 8 in Algorithm 1).

4.4 Generating Terms in the Grammar

As shown in Algorithm 1, our SyGuS method starts from an initial set of predicates (constructed from the initial set of terms) and incrementally generates new terms to create more predicates.

The Initial Set of Terms and Comparators. We extract the terms and predicates in the original problem from the syntax tree of the initial state predicate *Init*, the transition relation T, and the given property P), and select a subset to form the set of initial predicates. For a given Q (recall that Q encodes the model to block), all predicates containing only the variables in Q are added to the initial predicate set. While for the terms, only those that (a) contain only the variables in Q and (b) whose bit-width is less than a threshold H_p are added to the initial term set. We also expand the term set with additional constants when bit-widths are less than a threshold H_c. The rationale behind this strategy is that we want to find lemmas in the "control space" first, which is often beneficial as shown in previous work [42,59]. Instead of relying on user input (as in [59]), we differentiate between the terms that are *likely* control- or data-related. *Specifically, we use a heuristic that terms with a larger bit-width are more likely to be data-related, and a specific constant for data-related terms would not be useful in the inductive invariants.* In our experiments, we empirically set thresholds $H_c = 4$ and $H_p = 8$, to balance between the expressiveness and the cost of extra predicates. For the bit-vector comparators in the predicates, initially we begin with only `Equal` and `NotEqual`.

Adding More Existing Terms and Comparators. If the predicates constructed from the initial terms and operators are not able to generate a lemma, in the next call to MOREPRED, we will add back all the existing terms that contain no variables outside Q. Comparators like `bvult` ("unsigned less than") and `bvule` ("unsigned less than or equal") will be added also if they exist in the original problem.

Generating New Terms. The above procedure adds terms and comparators that are already present in the original problem formulation. However, this set of terms is often insufficient. Therefore, we use a procedure for generating new terms based on the following three rules – Construct, Replace, and Bit-Blast.

Construct Rule. Assume that we already have a set of terms $\{t\}$ and operators $\{op\}$. For each operator op and vector of terms $\langle t_0, t_1, ... \rangle$, we will construct a new term (op t_0 t_1 ...) if it is well-formed. In the examples we have seen in the HWMCC benchmarks, the set of operators is usually not very large, which are mainly logic operators like **and**, arithmetic operators like **add**, some bit-field manipulations, and **ite**. *As a heuristic, we prioritize using bit-field extraction and arithmetic operators for wide terms, and will use only logical operators on the narrow ones (separated also by the bit-width threshold H_p).* Furthermore, we avoid having multiple terms that can be simplified to the same form, by using the rewriting capability of the underlying SMT solver implicitly. Some solvers, e.g., Boolector [49], simplify and rewrite the terms upon their creation. We create the terms in the solver, then retrieve the simplified form and compute a syntactic hash to detect duplicate terms. The construction process of this rule can be applied iteratively, where we use the newly generated terms to create more new terms. However, in our implementation, we restrict it to a single iteration per invocation, to avoid overwhelming the algorithm with too many predicates.

Replace Rule. This rule replaces a sub-term with another. Suppose there is an existing term t with the following form: (op t_0 t_1 ...). For each of the sub-terms (e.g., t_0), we will try to see if there is another term with the same sort that can replace it in t and result in a new term. Instead of trying all potential replacements, we look for replacement pairs using information from the transition relation as follows.

As stated in Algorithm 1, we invoke the MOREPRED procedure for new term production at times when the check (13) had returned SAT and we need more terms to form more predicates. At this point, we can evaluate the existing terms using the model of (13) and check which pairs of them have the same value. This is similar to running simulation to identify potential correlations of signals in a circuit. Terms are evaluated twice, once on the assignment to current state variables and once on the primed ones. In addition to finding correlation in the primed evaluation (where predicates become insufficient), we also detect correlation between the current state and the next state. For example, suppose that a term $t_1(V)$ evaluates to c_1 under M and another term $t_2(V')$ evaluates to c_2 under M. If $c_1 = c_2$, we will also identify t_1 and t_2 as a replacement pair. Here, the term t_1 being replaced is evaluated based on current state variables V and the term t_2 is evaluated as if it is on the next state variables V'. This difference on the current and next state variable set *allows us to find temporal correlations that are potential causes and effects.*

Bit-Blast Rule. For hardware model checking problems, it is also possible that no good word-level invariant exists or the desired word-level invariant cannot be generated from existing terms and operators. Therefore we keep this rule as a fallback option. When applied, it creates terms using the **extract** operator to extract every single bit of a state variable. We prioritize using it first on the state variables which have been used in other terms with an **extract** operator. The rationale for this heuristic is that if the original problem contains bit-fields that are extracted from signals derived from such a state variable, the state variable is likely to be more "bit-level" rather than "word-level." If we continuously apply this rule, eventually all bits from all state variables will be added to the term set.

At this point, the set is guaranteed to be sufficient, and the algorithm degenerates to finding bit-level invariants in the worst case.

In our implementation, we apply these rules in the following order. First, we continuously apply **Replace** until it generates no more new terms or the predicate set becomes sufficient. Then we try **Construct**, where we prioritize different operators for wide and narrow terms and terminate if the prioritized terms are already sufficient. This is followed by another round of **Replace**, and finally **Bit-Blast** with the prioritization on variables that are more "bit-level." For any rule, if the prioritized terms are already sufficient, the procedure returns. Similar to the sharing of predicates among lemmas blocking the same model, the term set is also shared when two models in the proof-obligation have the same set of variables.

Example. Consider an illustration for creation of new terms according to these three rules. For the example transition system in Sect. 3, suppose at some point, there is a proof obligation: block model $(a, b, c) = (6, 4, 1)$ at F_2. The initial term set is listed in Fig. 4. For F_1 there are already lemmas added using the these terms on variables a, b, c, however, they cannot generate sufficient predicates to block the model (predicates after initial pruning are shown in the figure). A model for (13) can be extracted: $(a, b, c, e, a', b', c') = (3, 3, 0, \perp, 4, 3, 1)$. Readers can check the assignments to the primed variables in the model make all initial predicates evaluate to true. When applying the **Replace** rule, existing terms will be evaluated on variable sets $(a, b, c) = (3, 3, 0)$ and $(a', b', c') = (4, 3, 1)$ to identify potential correlations between pairs. In this example, we find 7 possible replacement pairs, which result in 4 new terms, shown in the bottom-left table in Fig. 4, where replacement is based on the correlated value in the first column and the replacement pair $\langle t_1, t_2 \rangle$ means t_1 is replaced by t_2. If these were not sufficient, we could further apply the **Construct** rule, and more new terms would be generated using operator bvadd on the existing terms. Finally if these were still not sufficient, we would fall back to **Bit-Blast**.

For the specific proof obligation here, the above term generation process will actually stop after the **Replace** rule, where the predicates with term $b + c$ will be sufficient, and the invariant $a = b + c$ will be discovered. (For this proof obligation, the term $b + 1$ also works, which can produce predicate $a = b + 1$, but it is not as general, and will be dropped by the MUS procedure.) Note that the discovery of $a = b + c$ in this example is not simply by chance. The two replacements needed – a to b, and 1 to c – are found by our method that looks for correlation between terms, which leads to finding this invariant. Interestingly, these correspond to the two cases in the induction step in our human reasoning process in Sect. 3.

4.5   Tightening Previous Frames in IC3/PDR

As we discussed in Sect. 4.1, using constraint (12) instead of (10) allows a larger space of lemmas. But on the other hand, having l on both sides of the implication breaks the monotonicity of predicate minimization. For (10), after a predicate

F_1	$\neg(c \neq 0 \land c \neq 1) \land \neg(a \neq b \land c = 0) \land \neg(b \neq 0 \land c \neq 0) \land \neg(a \neq 1 \land c \neq 0)$

Terms on $\{a, b, c\}$: $\{0, 1, a, b, c, a+1, c+1\}$

Initial predicates on $(a, b, c) = (6, 4, 1)$:
$$a \neq 0, a \neq 1, b \neq 0, b \neq 1, c \neq 0, c = 1,$$
$$a \neq b, b \neq c, a \neq c, b \neq a+1, c \neq a+1, b \neq c+1$$

Replace: Term Substitution

	0	1	a	b	c	$a+1$	$c+1$
V	0	1	3	3	0	4	1
V'	0	1	4	3	1	5	2

	Replacement Pairs	New Terms
0	$\langle c, 0 \rangle$	
1	$\langle c+1, 1 \rangle, \langle 1, c \rangle,$ $\langle c+1, c \rangle, \langle c, 1 \rangle$	$a + c, c + c$
3	$\langle a, b \rangle$	$b + 1, b + c$
4	$\langle a+1, a \rangle$	

Construct: Making New Terms

Existing terms
$$0, 1, a, b, c, a+1, c+1, a+c, \ldots$$

Existing operators: $+$

New terms:
$$a+2, c+2, a+c+1, a+b, \ldots$$

Bit-Blast: Extract Bit-fields

V	New Terms
a	$a[0], a[1], \ldots, a[15]$
b	$b[0], b[1], \ldots, b[15]$
c	$c[0], c[1], \ldots, c[15]$

Fig. 4. An illustration of the three term generation rules.

is removed, (10) could stay UNSAT or become SAT. But once it becomes SAT, removing more predicates will not make (10) UNSAT. The same does not hold for (12), as removing predicates also shrinks the pre-image. This makes minimizing the set of predicates in (12) much harder. As a trade-off between allowing a larger space of lemmas and ease of minimizing the set of sufficient predicates, we choose the latter and decide to stick with constraint (10). To mitigate the associated problem—potentially missing a good lemma due to coarse frames, we add a procedure to tighten the previous frames, as described below.

We design a lazy approach to tighten previous frames (Line 7 in Algorithm 1). When the check (13) indicates that L is insufficient (i.e., we get a SAT result for (13)), instead of immediately generating more terms to construct more candidate predicates, we first check whether the current state variable assignment from the satisfiable model in (13) is blockable. This blocking operation will introduce new lemmas in the previous frame F_i and could potentially turn (10) into (12) by introducing the same lemma. This may then allow the predicates in L to be used. On the other hand, if the model cannot be blocked, it means no lemmas can be generated from the current predicate set, even using (12) instead of (10). So we will indeed need to construct more terms to enrich the set of predicates.

Instead of requiring any big change, the blocking operation suggested above can use an existing recursive blocking function utility available in an IC3/PDR framework (denoted as RECBLOCK in Algorithm 1). However, this blocking is different from blocking of models generated from (9), which *must* be blocked, otherwise P will fail. Thus, we need to distinguish between a "may-proof-obligation"

Algorithm 2: MUS(U): Minimizing the set U of UNSAT constraints

---

Input: U: $\{base\} \cup L$, a set of constraints
Output: U': a minimal UNSAT subset of U

1 **while** *true* **do**
2      $U' \leftarrow$ UNSATCORE(U) ;
3   **if** $|U'| = |U|$ **then**
4   **break**;
5      $U \leftarrow U'$;
6 SORT($U' - \{base\}$) , by syntax complexity ;
7 **for** $u \in (U' - \{base\})$ **do**
8   **if** $U' - \{u\}$ *is UNSAT* **then**
9          $U' \leftarrow$ UNSATCORE($U' - \{u\}$) ;
10 **return** U';

---

and a "must-proof-obligation" for blocking a model. Note also that this distinction is not a special requirement of SyGuS-$\mathcal{A}$PDR. For example, in the existing IC3/PDR framework QUIP [36], a "may-proof-obligation" arises due to failures of lemma pushing. Here, we simply reuse this facility to design our lazy frame tightening procedure.

4.6   Generalizing the Lemma by Using UNSAT Cores

When constructing lemmas from a set of predicates, we would like to get a more general lemma using fewer predicates. This is done through minimal unsatisfiable subset (MUS) extraction from the unsatisfiable formula (13), where we treat each predicate $p_i \in L$ as an individual constraint, and the rest of the formula (*base*) as one constraint.

Our MUS procedure (shown in Algorithm 2) follows standard approaches, as it first computes a small UNSAT core by iteratively using UNSAT core extraction of the SMT solver until reaching a fixed-point of the core size [60] (Line 1–5). Then it further reduces the core size by trying to drop constraints. Here, we use a new heuristic based on the *syntax-complexity*, defined as the number of nodes in the syntax tree plus the occurrence of constants as an extra penalty. Our contraint-dropping is done iteratively in descending order of the syntax-complexity of constraints (Line 6–9). This allows us to get an MUS where the predicates have simpler syntactic structure and also fewer constants, which may generalize better in the overall algorithm.

4.7   Partial Model Generation for Word-Level Reasoning in Bit-Vectors

We also propose to use partial model generation in the **Predecessor** procedure for *word-level* bit-vector reasoning in IC3/PDR. Our method can handle hardware model checking problems where the transition relation is functional. (We leave the general case of adapting it in model-based projection for bit-vectors to future work).

Our implementation of partial model generation mimics the ternary simulation method used in the original PDR implementation [21], but at the word-level. For some bit-vector operators like bvand and ite, there is a masking effect. For example, consider a satisfiable SMT formula that contains a fragment (bvand a b), if we know that variable a is assigned to all 0s in the model extracted from the query, then the assignment to b does not affect the evaluation of the fragment. If b does not appear elsewhere in the formula, we can remove the assignment to b and get a partial model while the formula still evaluates to true under the reduced set of assignments. Using partial model generation, we can derive a reduced set of variable assignments representing multiple bad states. This benefits the SyGuS-based interpolation because when we later generate lemma candidates to block it, we can limit the search space to candidates containing only those variables in the partial model.

5   Experimental Evaluations

We implemented the SyGuS-$\mathcal{A}$PDR methods on top of an $\mathcal{A}$PDR framework that we developed according to the algorithm presented in previous work [32]. We used the solver-agnostic interfacing library SMT-Switch [44], and used Boolector [49] for SMT queries and UNSAT core extraction.

5.1   Experiment Setup

Environment of the Experiments. The experiments were conducted on a cluster of machines with Xeon Gold 6142 CPUs running Springdale Linux 7.8, and each tool is allocated 8 cores and 64 GB of memory. Similar to the HWMCC setting, we set the time-out limit to be one hour wall-clock time.

Benchmark Examples. We use the benchmarks from the bit-vector track of 2019's HWMCC. It has 317 test cases in the Btor2 format. We use our conversion tool Btor2CHC to convert them into CHCs.

Tools for Comparison. We test our SyGuS-$\mathcal{A}$PDR tool against state-of-the-art CHC solvers on the HWMCC'19 benchmarks. For comparison, we also report the performance of word-level hardware model checkers that participated in HWMCC'19 (and were run with the same configuration). The tools we compared with are listed as follows.

- SyGuS-$\mathcal{A}$PDR is our tool that uses the syntax-guided lemma generation procedure described in Sect. 4.
- BvITP is a tool we constructed that uses the word-level interpolants [31] from MathSAT [16] out-of-the-box to generate lemmas in $\mathcal{A}$PDR.
- SPACER [32,40] is a state-of-the-art CHC solver and part of Z3 [19]. We test the newest release version 4.8.9, but it actually solves fewer instances (83 vs. 90) compared to an older version 4.8.7.
  We did not further investigate the reason of the performance degradation, but will report the results from 4.8.7.

Table 2. Number of solved instances

Solver		# Solved	Safe	Unsafe
Our work	SyGuS-$\mathcal{A}$PDR	126	**112**	14
CHC solvers	BvItp	22	22	0
	Z3/Spacer	90	87	3
	Eldarica	4	4	0
HW model checkers	AVR	**157**	111	**46**
	CoSA2 (Pono)	137	96	41
	BtorMC	108	67	41
	CoNPS-btormc-THP	40	0	40

- ELDARICA is a CHC solver that makes use of counter-example-guided abstraction refinement (CEGAR) method. As ELDARICA can use different interpolation abstraction templates, we start 4 parallel running engines each with a different template configuration and report the best result, using the latest release version 2.0.4.
- AVR (abstractly verifying reachability) is a collection of 11 parallel running engines including 3 variants of BMC and 8 variants of IC3 integrated with multiple abstraction techniques [27]. We use the binary release available from the Github tagged with `hwmcc19` for the experiment.
- CoSA2 (successor of CoSA [45], now named Pono) is a model checker based on the solver-agnostic framework SMT-Switch [44]. It runs four parallel engines: BMC, BMC simple-path, k-induction and the interpolation-based method [47]. We were unable to compile using the source code tagged with `hwmcc19`. Instead we use a development version with a commit hash `6d72613`. Our experiment results show it actually solves more instances than reported in HWMCC'19.
- BtorMC (version 3.2.0) is a tool based on the SMT solver Boolector [49], equipped with two engines: BMC and k-induction. In our experiment, we run two instances in parallel and record the shorter time.
- CoNPS-btormc-THP is from Norbert Manthey. It is a specially configured BtorMC using huge pages for mapping memory and is linked against a modified GlibC library. We obtained the tool from the author.

5.2 The Overall Result

We plot the wall-clock time vs. the number of solved instances in Fig. 5. A table summarizing the number of solved instances is shown in Table 2. Our results on the hardware model checkers are mostly consistent with the results from the HWMCC'19 report [52], with minor difference which is probably due to difference in the machine configurations or the version of tools that we use.

Among the tools, AVR solves the most instances. Our SyGuS-$\mathcal{A}$PDR solves about the same number of safe instances as AVR, but fewer unsafe instances.

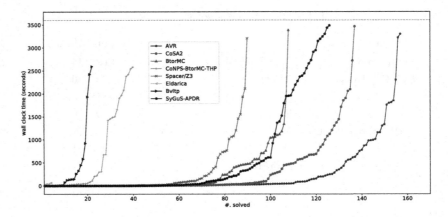

Fig. 5. Wall clock time vs. number of solved instances.

This is because in the unsafe case, even though a bad model leading to the violation of the property will become reachable at some point, in the first several frames, it is still blockable, and SyGuS-$\mathcal{A}$PDR will still try to construct lemmas to block it. We can make up for this disadvantage by having a BMC engine run in parallel with it, similar to what typical model checkers do. However, our focus is on lemma generation for proofs, so we leave this for future work.

5.3   Effectiveness of SyGuS-$\mathcal{A}$PDR in Improving Lemmas

We plot the comparison between SyGuS-$\mathcal{A}$PDR and BVITP in Fig. 6(a)—SyGuS-$\mathcal{A}$PDR shows a clear improvement over BVITP. In our experiments, we found that the word-level bit-vector interpolants from MathSAT often contain conjunctions

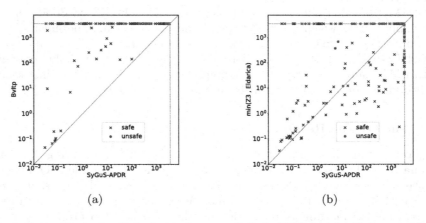

Fig. 6. Comparison of wall-clock time between SyGuS-$\mathcal{A}$PDR and (a) BVITP or (b) the faster time from Z3/SPACER or ELDARICA.

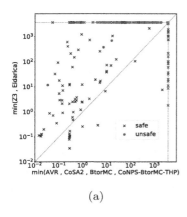
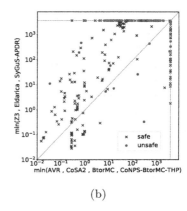

(a)   (b)

Fig. 7. Comparison of wall-clock time between word-level hardware model checkers and CHC solvers (a) without, or (b) with SyGuS-𝒜PDR.

of a large number of equality relations in the form of $v = c$, where v is a state variable and c is a constant. This makes the interpolants very specific to the models, and they often trap the algorithm in the first few frames with hundreds or even thousands of lemmas. This explains why BVITP performs badly. And on the unsafe systems, it must reach a minimum bound to discover the shortest counterexample, therefore it is not able to find any unsafe instances. Removing some equalities in such an interpolant in BVITP, as we have attempted, often makes it no longer an interpolant. SyGuS-𝒜PDR, on the other hand, uses syntax-based guidance to steer the interpolants and can select simpler, and hopefully more general, predicates to mitigate such issues.

Figure 6(b) shows the comparison of SyGuS-𝒜PDR and the faster of either Z3/SPACER or ELDARICA. ELDARICA solves only 4 instances, two of which contain complex arithmetic operations in the transition relation and are solved by neither Z3/SPACER nor SyGuS-𝒜PDR. SyGuS-𝒜PDR solves 56 instances that are not solved by Z3/SPACER or ELDARICA, and within the 70 instances that both categories solve, SyGuS-𝒜PDR runs faster on 36.

5.4   CHC Solvers Vs. Hardware Model Checkers

We also compare the results from the two existing CHC solvers (referred to as the CHC group in the following text) with the collection of word-level model checkers that participated in HWMCC'19 (referred to as the HMC group). A comparison of solving time is shown in Fig. 7. Although the CHC group solves fewer instances (92 vs. 196), there are 22 instances solved exclusively by CHC group. Among the 70 instances solved by both groups, the CHC group is faster on 16. This indicates that the CHC group has some complementary strengths that are worth further investigation.

For example, there is one test case `analog_estimation_convergence` where SPACER derives a safe inductive invariant in less than one second, whereas AVR does not converge within one hour. We took a closer look at the invariant produced by Z3/SPACER. It contains fragments with similar structure as a linear relation in LIA theory. This is likely an outcome of the translation technique, and it makes Z3/SPACER the fastest solver on this instance. When we also include SyGuS-𝒜PDR in the CHC group, the group now solves 148 (significant improvement from 92), where 27 are not solved by the HMC group. Among the 121 instances solved by both groups, CHC group is faster in 33 test cases.

Around the time of preparing the final version of the paper, two new tools become available: GSPACERBV [28] and a new version of AVR for HWMCC'20 competition (referred to as AVR-20). We conducted further experiments after paper submission, and for completeness, include a summary here. Detailed results can be found in [57]. GSPACERBV shows an improvement from SPACER thanks to its global guidance rules in lemma generation [41] and the model-based projection procedure for bit-vectors, yet it solves fewer instances than SyGuS-𝒜PDR (101 vs. 126). AVR-20 shows a great performance gain compared to its previous generation (249 vs. 157) as it doubles the portfolio size with more techniques integrated. Though, AVR-20 solves more safe instances than SyGuS-𝒜PDR (205 vs. 112), SyGuS-𝒜PDR runs faster on almost half of the instances it solves (50) and is there supplementary to the portfolio used in AVR-20.

6 Related Work

Enhancing the Interpolants. There are many existing works that aim to enhance the interpolants used in model checking. For example, Albarghouthi and McMillan [1] propose to reduce the number of disjuncts of linear inequality constraints to get simpler interpolants. Blicha *et al.* [10] propose to decompose the interpolants to mitigate the divergence problem. GSPACER [41] incorporates global guidance in the lemma. These works are mostly for interpolation in the infinite domain (e.g., LIA/LRA) theories.

In the bit-vector theory, there is no native word-level bit-vector interpolation strategy in the first place. Existing methods rely on EUF layering, translation to (non)-linear integer arithmetic, application of certain forms of quantifier elimination etc. [3,31]. Additionally, compared to LIA/LRA, the bit-vector theory has a more diverse set of operators allowing bit-field manipulation as well as logical and arithmetic operations. This often introduces non-linear relations that are hard to translate to other theories.

In the LIA/LRA domain, the closest approach to ours is [43], which also uses templates to guide the generation of interpolants. It introduces interpolation abstractions in the SMT query but leaves the construction of interpolants completely to the solver, whereas SyGuS-𝒜PDR constructs the interpolants *outside* the solver, and therefore has more direct control on the generated lemma. Previous works [9,14,20] also construct interpolant outside the SAT/SMT solver, while SyGuS-𝒜PDR incorporates syntax guidance and further integrates it with IC3/PDR framework to make use of models and procedures from deductive reasoning in IC3/PDR.

Word-Level IC3/PDR Algorithms for Bit-Vectors. Previous efforts on the word-level BV can be mainly categorized as: (1) adding an abstraction layer so that the core algorithm remains at the bit-level, (e.g., word-level abstraction [34], word-level predicate abstraction [38], IC3ia [15], data-path abstraction [42] and syntax-guided abstraction [26]) (2) using specific types of atomic reasoning units (ARUs) [55,56], or (3) translating the BV problem to another theory [33]. SyGuS-$\mathcal{A}$PDR differs from the existing works in that: (1) it does not need an explicit abstraction-refinement loop—the models in the proof obligations and the transition relation are all kept concrete and the interpretation of the predicates are always revealed to the solver; (2) the grammar allows lemmas that are in general more flexible compared to the ARUs; and (3) while translation is feasible for arithmetic and some related operations, it does not work for all the operators available in BV theory, especially bit manipulation operators. In comparison, SyGuS-$\mathcal{A}$PDR is native on the BV theory and supports all BV operators.

Syntax-Guided Inductive Invariant Synthesis. Syntax-guided synthesis has been applied on the inductive invariant synthesis problem before, e.g., LOOP-INVGEN [50,51], CVC4SY [53], FREQHORN [23–25] and GRAIN [59]. A key feature of SyGuS-$\mathcal{A}$PDR is its tight integration with IC3/PDR framework, which allows use of *both deductive reasoning as well as grammars* to guide candidate lemma generation and prune the search space.

7   Conclusions and Future Work

In this work, we present our technique of using syntax-guided synthesis for lemma generation for unbounded hardware model checking. This is also an attempt to attack the challenges of BV interpolation with the help of a tighter integration with the IC3/PDR framework. Although our motivation for reasoning about problems in BV theory comes from hardware verification applications, the techniques we present may also benefit software verification, especially low-level software (e.g., device driver or firmware) where bit manipulation is essential.

To achieve better performance, our SyGuS-based lemma generation algorithm can be further integrated with other techniques, e.g., an abstraction refinement framework, or with other parallel running engines.

Acknowledgements. This work was supported in part by the Applications Driving Architectures (ADA) Research Center, a JUMP Center co-sponsored by SRC and DARPA; by the DARPA POSH and DARPA SSITH programs; and by NSF Grant No. 1628926.

References

1. Albarghouthi, A., McMillan, K.L.: Beautiful interpolants. In: Sharygina, N., Veith, H. (eds.) CAV 2013. LNCS, vol. 8044, pp. 313–329. Springer, Heidelberg (2013). https://doi.org/10.1007/978-3-642-39799-8_22

2. Alur, R., et al.: Syntax-guided synthesis. In: FMCAD, pp. 1–8 (2013)
3. Backeman, P., Rummer, P., Zeljic, A.: Bit-vector interpolation and quantifier elimination by lazy reduction. In: 2018 Formal Methods in Computer Aided Design (FMCAD), pp. 1–10 (2018)
4. Ball, T., Majumdar, R., Millstein, T., Rajamani, S.K.: Automatic predicate abstraction of C programs. In: Proceedings of the ACM SIGPLAN 2001 Conference on Programming Language Design and Implementation, pp. 203–213 (2001)
5. Ball, T., Podelski, A., Rajamani, S.K.: Boolean and cartesian abstraction for model checking C programs. In: Margaria, T., Yi, W. (eds.) TACAS 2001. LNCS, vol. 2031, pp. 268–283. Springer, Heidelberg (2001). https://doi.org/10.1007/3-540-45319-9_19
6. Barrett, C.W., Sebastiani, R., Seshia, S.A., Tinelli, C.: Satisfiability modulo theories. Handb. Satisfiability 185, 825–885 (2009)
7. Biere, A., Heljanko, K., Wieringa, S.: AIGER 1.9 and beyond. Technical Report 11/2, Institute for Formal Models and Verification, Johannes Kepler University, Altenbergerstr. 69, 4040 Linz, Austria (2011)
8. Bjørner, N., Gurfinkel, A.: Property directed polyhedral abstraction. In: VMCAI, pp. 263–281 (2015)
9. Bjørner, N., Gurfinkel, A., Korovin, K., Lahav, O.: Instantiations, zippers and EPR interpolation. In: LPAR, pp. 35–41 (2013)
10. Blicha, M., Hyvärinen, A.E.J., Kofroň, J., Sharygina, N.: Decomposing Farkas interpolants. In: Vojnar, T., Zhang, L. (eds.) TACAS 2019. LNCS, vol. 11427, pp. 3–20. Springer, Cham (2019). https://doi.org/10.1007/978-3-030-17462-0_1
11. Bradley, A.R.: SAT-based model checking without unrolling. In: VMCAI, pp. 70–87 (2011)
12. Bradley, A.R., Manna, Z.: Checking safety by inductive generalization of counterexamples to induction. In: Formal Methods in Computer Aided Design (FMCAD 2007), pp. 173–180. IEEE (2007)
13. Champion, A., Kobayashi, N., Sato, R.: HoIce: an ICE-based non-linear horn clause solver. In: APLAS (2018)
14. Chockler, H., Ivrii, A., Matsliah, A.: Computing interpolants without proofs. In: Biere, A., Nahir, A., Vos, T. (eds.) HVC 2012. LNCS, vol. 7857, pp. 72–85. Springer, Heidelberg (2013). https://doi.org/10.1007/978-3-642-39611-3_12
15. Cimatti, A., Griggio, A., Mover, S., Tonetta, S.: IC3 modulo theories via implicit predicate abstraction. In: Ábrahám, E., Havelund, K. (eds.) TACAS 2014. LNCS, vol. 8413, pp. 46–61. Springer, Heidelberg (2014). https://doi.org/10.1007/978-3-642-54862-8_4
16. Cimatti, A., Griggio, A., Schaafsma, B.J., Sebastiani, R.: The MathSAT5 SMT solver. In: Piterman, N., Smolka, S.A. (eds.) TACAS 2013. LNCS, vol. 7795, pp. 93–107. Springer, Heidelberg (2013). https://doi.org/10.1007/978-3-642-36742-7_7
17. Clarke, E., Grumberg, O., Jha, S., Lu, Y., Veith, H.: Counterexample-guided abstraction refinement for symbolic model checking. J. ACM (JACM) 50(5), 752–794 (2003)
18. Clarke, E.M., Grumberg, O., Peled, D.: Model Checking. MIT Press, Cambridge (1999)
19. De Moura, L., Bjørner, N.: Z3: An efficient SMT solver. In: TACAS, pp. 337–340 (2008)
20. Drews, S., Albarghouthi, A.: Effectively propositional interpolants. In: Chaudhuri, S., Farzan, A. (eds.) CAV 2016. LNCS, vol. 9780, pp. 210–229. Springer, Cham (2016). https://doi.org/10.1007/978-3-319-41540-6_12

21. Een, N., Mishchenko, A., Brayton, R.: Efficient implementation of property directed reachability. In: FMCAD, pp. 125–134 (2011)
22. Farkas, J.: Theorie der einfachen ungleichungen. J. für die reine und angewandte Mathematik **1902**(124), 1–27 (1902)
23. Fedyukovich, G., Bodík, R.: Accelerating syntax-guided invariant synthesis. In: TACAS, pp. 251–269 (2018)
24. Fedyukovich, G., Kaufman, S., Bodík, R.: Sampling invariants from frequency distributions. In: FMCAD, pp. 100–107 (2017)
25. Fedyukovich, G., Prabhu, S., Madhukar, K., Gupta, A.: Solving constrained horn clauses using syntax and data. In: FMCAD, pp. 170–178 (2018)
26. Goel, A., Sakallah, K.: Model checking of Verilog RTL using IC3 with syntax-guided abstraction. In: Badger, J.M., Rozier, K.Y. (eds.) NFM 2019. LNCS, vol. 11460, pp. 166–185. Springer, Cham (2019). https://doi.org/10.1007/978-3-030-20652-9_11
27. Goel, A., Sakallah, K.: AVR: abstractly verifying reachability. TACAS 2020. LNCS, vol. 12078, pp. 413–422. Springer, Cham (2020). https://doi.org/10.1007/978-3-030-45190-5_23
28. Govind, H., Fedyukovich, G., Gurfinkel, A.: Word level property directed reachability. In: International Conference on Computer Aided Design (2020)
29. Graf, S., Saidi, H.: Construction of abstract state graphs with PVS. In: Grumberg, O. (ed.) CAV 1997. LNCS, vol. 1254, pp. 72–83. Springer, Heidelberg (1997). https://doi.org/10.1007/3-540-63166-6_10
30. Grebenshchikov, S., Lopes, N.P., Popeea, C., Rybalchenko, A.: Synthesizing software verifiers from proof rules. In: PLDI, pp. 405–416. ACM (2012)
31. Griggio, A.: Effective word-level interpolation for software verification. In: Proceedings of the International Conference on Formal Methods in Computer-Aided Design, pp. 28–36, FMCAD 2011, FMCAD Inc, Austin, Texas (2011)
32. Gurfinkel, A.: IC3, PDR, and friends. Summer School on Formal Techniques (2015)
33. Gurfinkel, A., Belov, A., Marques-Silva, J.: Synthesizing safe bit-precise invariants. In: Ábrahám, E., Havelund, K. (eds.) TACAS 2014. LNCS, vol. 8413, pp. 93–108. Springer, Heidelberg (2014). https://doi.org/10.1007/978-3-642-54862-8_7
34. Ho, Y.S., Mishchenko, A., Brayton, R.: Property directed reachability with word-level abstraction. In: FMCAD, pp. 132–139 (2017)
35. Hojjat, H., Rümmer, P.: The ELDARICA Horn Solver. In: FMCAD, pp. 158–164. IEEE (2018)
36. Ivrii, A., Gurfinkel, A.: Pushing to the top. In: 2015 Formal Methods in Computer-Aided Design (FMCAD), pp. 65–72 (2015)
37. Ivrii, A., Gurfinkel, A., Belov, A.: Small inductive safe invariants. In: 2014 Formal Methods in Computer-Aided Design (FMCAD), pp. 115–122. IEEE (2014)
38. Jain, H., Kroening, D., Sharygina, N., Clarke, E.: Word level predicate abstraction and refinement for verifying RTL Verilog. In: Proceedings of the 42nd annual Design Automation Conference, pp. 445–450 (2005)
39. Komuravelli, A., Gurfinkel, A., Chaki, S.: SMT-based model checking for recursive programs. FMSD **48**(3), 175–205 (2016)
40. Komuravelli, A., Gurfinkel, A., Chaki, S., Clarke, E.M.: Automatic abstraction in SMT-based unbounded software model checking. In: CAV, pp. 846–862 (2013)
41. Vediramana Krishnan, H.G., Chen, Y.T., Shoham, S., Gurfinkel, A.: Global guidance for local generalization in model checking. In: Lahiri, S.K., Wang, C. (eds.) CAV 2020. LNCS, vol. 12225, pp. 101–125. Springer, Cham (2020). https://doi.org/10.1007/978-3-030-53291-8_7

42. Lee, S., Sakallah, K.A.: Unbounded scalable verification based on approximate property-directed reachability and datapath abstraction. In: Biere, A., Bloem, R. (eds.) CAV 2014. LNCS, vol. 8559, pp. 849–865. Springer, Cham (2014). https://doi.org/10.1007/978-3-319-08867-9_56

43. Leroux, J., Rümmer, P., Subotić, P.: Guiding Craig interpolation with domain-specific abstractions. Acta Informatica 53(4), 387–424 (2016)

44. Mann, M., Wilson, A., Tinelli, C., Barrett, C.: SMT-switch: a solver-agnostic C++ api for smt solving. arXiv preprint arXiv:2007.01374 (2020)

45. Mattarei, C., Mann, M., Barrett, C., Daly, R.G., Huff, D., Hanrahan, P.: CoSA: Integrated verification for agile hardware design. In: 2018 Formal Methods in Computer Aided Design (FMCAD), pp. 1–5. IEEE (2018)

46. McMillan, K.: Applications of Craig interpolation to model checking. In: Marcinkowski, J., Tarlecki, A. (eds.) CSL 2004. LNCS, vol. 3210, pp. 22–23. Springer, Heidelberg (2004). https://doi.org/10.1007/978-3-540-30124-0_3

47. McMillan, K.L.: Interpolation and SAT-based model checking. In: Hunt, W.A., Somenzi, F. (eds.) CAV 2003. LNCS, vol. 2725, pp. 1–13. Springer, Heidelberg (2003). https://doi.org/10.1007/978-3-540-45069-6_1

48. McMillan, K.L., Rybalchenko, A.: Solving constrained horn clauses using interpolation (2013)

49. Niemetz, A., Preiner, M., Wolf, C., Biere, A.: BTOR2, BtorMC and Boolector 3.0. In: Chockler, H., Weissenbacher, G. (eds.) CAV 2018. LNCS, vol. 10981, pp. 587–595. Springer, Cham (2018). https://doi.org/10.1007/978-3-319-96145-3_32

50. Padhi, S., Millstein, T., Nori, A., Sharma, R.: Overfitting in synthesis: theory and practice. In: Dillig, I., Tasiran, S. (eds.) CAV 2019. LNCS, vol. 11561, pp. 315–334. Springer, Cham (2019). https://doi.org/10.1007/978-3-030-25540-4_17

51. Padhi, S., Sharma, R., Millstein, T.D.: Data-driven precondition inference with learned features. In: PLDI, pp. 42–56. ACM (2016)

52. Preiner, M., Biere, A.: Hardware model checking competition 2019. http://fmv.jku.at/hwmcc19/. Accessed 10 Sep 2020

53. Reynolds, A., Barbosa, H., Nötzli, A., Barrett, C., Tinelli, C.: cvc4sy: smart and fast term enumeration for syntax-guided synthesis. In: CAV, pp. 74–83 (2019)

54. Si, X., Naik, A., Dai, H., Naik, M., Song, L.: Code2Inv: a deep learning framework for program verification. In: Lahiri, S.K., Wang, C. (eds.) CAV 2020. LNCS, vol. 12225, pp. 151–164. Springer, Cham (2020). https://doi.org/10.1007/978-3-030-53291-8_9

55. Welp, T., Kuehlmann, A.: QF_BV model checking with property directed reachability. In: 2013 Design, Automation & Test in Europe Conference & Exhibition (DATE), pp. 791–796. IEEE (2013)

56. Welp, T., Kuehlmann, A.: Property directed reachability for QF_BV with mixed type atomic reasoning units. In: Asia and South Pacific Design Automation Conference, pp. 738–743. IEEE (2014)

57. Zhang, H.: Figures for additional experiment results. https://github.com/zhanghongce/HWMCC19-in-CHC/blob/logs/figs/compare.md. Accessed 14 Nov 2020

58. Zhang, H.: HWMCC19 benchmark in constrained horn clauses. https://github.com/zhanghongce/HWMCC19-in-CHC. Accessed 08 Oct 2020

59. Zhang, H., Yang, W., Fedyukovich, G., Gupta, A., Malik, S.: Synthesizing environment invariants for modular hardware verification. In: Beyer, D., Zufferey, D. (eds.) VMCAI 2020. LNCS, vol. 11990, pp. 202–225. Springer, Cham (2020). https://doi.org/10.1007/978-3-030-39322-9_10

60. Zhang, L., Malik, S.: Extracting small unsatisfiable cores from unsatisfiable boolean formulas. In: International Conference on Theory and Applications of Satisfiability Testing (SAT) (2003)
61. Zhu, H., Magill, S., Jagannathan, S.: A data-driven CHC solver. In: Proceedings of the 39th ACM SIGPLAN Conference on Programming Language Design and Implementation, PLDI 2018, pp. 707–721. Association for Computing Machinery, New York (2018). https://doi.org/10.1145/3192366.3192416

Synthesis and Repair

Approximate Bit Dependency Analysis to Identify Program Synthesis Problems as Infeasible

Marius Kamp[✉] and Michael Philippsen

Programming Systems Group,
Friedrich-Alexander University Erlangen-Nürnberg (FAU),
Erlangen, Germany
{marius.kamp,michael.philippsen}@fau.de

Abstract. Bit-vector-based program synthesis is an important building block of state-of-the-art techniques in computer programming. Some of these techniques do not only rely on a synthesizer's ability to return an appropriate program if it exists but also require a synthesizer to detect if there is no such program at all in the entire search space (i.e., the problem is infeasible), which is a computationally demanding task.

In this paper, we propose an approach to quickly identify some synthesis problems as infeasible. We observe that a specification function encodes dependencies between input and output bits that a correct program must satisfy. To exploit this fact, we present approximate analyses of essential bits and use them in two novel algorithms to check if a synthesis problem is infeasible. Our experiments show that adding our technique to applications of bit vector synthesis can save up to 33% of their time.

1 Introduction

Program synthesis is the construction of a program that satisfies a declarative specification. Its ability to create a program that implements a specification function and consists of some given bit vector operations has recently propelled research in computer programming. For example, program synthesizers craft instruction selection rules in compilers [4], superoptimize code [18], generate code for unusual architectures [17], optimize machine learning kernels [5], or enumerate rewrite rules for SMT solvers [16]. As it is often not a priori known which and how many operations to use for a synthesized program, some applications formulate multiple synthesis problems that differ in the used operations [4] or in the length of the program [18]. Other works search over a collection of synthesis tasks [2] or generate synthesis problems based on a symbolic execution of a program [14]. All these approaches have a common trait: for some of the synthesis problems, there may not be a program that implements the specification *and* consists of the available operations. These problems are called *infeasible*. Infeasible problems tend to be harder than feasible ones of comparable size because

© Springer Nature Switzerland AG 2021
F. Henglein et al. (Eds.): VMCAI 2021, LNCS 12597, pp. 353–375, 2021.
https://doi.org/10.1007/978-3-030-67067-2_16

synthesizers have to show that there is no such program in the entire solution space. If infeasible problems occur frequently, the performance of an application "critically depends on the performance of unsatisfiable queries" [14] (i.e., infeasible problems). Thus, applications get faster by quickly identifying infeasible problems as such without invoking the costly synthesizer.

We present such an infeasibility checker for bit vector synthesis problems (f, Ops) with a specification function f plus a collection of available operations Ops that bounds the number of times an operation may occur in the constructed program. To illustrate our approach, our running example is the problem of computing the average of two integers x and y by rounding up fractional solutions. The program $(x \vee y) - ((x \oplus y) \gg 1)$ satisfies this specification [21]. When human programmers want to find such a program, they intuitively know that they need to divide by 2 or right shift by 1 to compute the average (suppose for now that the constant belongs to the operation). Alas, program synthesizers lack this intuition. We can, however, find out that the synthesized program indeed needs such an operation by inspecting the dependencies between input and output bits of the specification: The $i+1$-th input bits of both x and y influence the i-th output bit. To see this, consider $x = 2$, $y = 0$, and the result 1. If we turn off the second bit of x, the result is 0. Hence, the second bit of x influences the first output bit. Since this bit dependency must also exist in the synthesized program, we need an operation that can provide it. Thus, we analyze the dependencies between input and output bits of both the specification function and each of the available operations. Since this analysis is NP-complete, Sect. 3 proposes approximations. Once we know the bit dependencies of both the specification and the operations, we can check if the operations cannot be combined to satisfy the bit dependencies of the specification. In this case, the synthesis problem is infeasible and we do not need to invoke the synthesizer. We derive a checking algorithm in Sect. 4 that uses an abstraction of the concrete bit dependencies called *shapes*.

The collective bit dependencies of an output bit come in two flavors. These correspond to the value the output bit takes if all of the input bits it depends on are set to 0. All output bits of our running example come in the same flavor, but if we modify the specification to compute the average of $\neg x$ and y instead, the highest (most significant) output bit will take the value 1 for $x = 0$ and $y = 0$. Hence, the highest output bit comes in a different flavor than the other output bits. We give a second algorithm in Sect. 4 that detects if some output bit cannot get the right flavor using the given operations. Although both algorithms may miss infeasible problems, they never flag a feasible problem as infeasible. We evaluate our contributions in Sect. 5 and discuss related work in Sect. 6.

2   Fundamentals

A (fixed-width) *bit vector* is a vector of Boolean variables (the *bits*) of constant length (the *width*). Let B_k be the set of all bit vectors of width k. A *bit vector function* is then a function $B_{k_1} \times \cdots \times B_{k_n} \to B_{k_o}$. If all $k_1, \ldots, k_n, k_o = 1$, the function is a *Boolean function*.

Well-known bit vector functions include bitwise operations like conjunction ($\wedge$), inclusive ($\vee$) and exclusive ($\oplus$) disjunction, arithmetic operations ($+$, $-$, $\times$, $\div$, rem), and bit shifts ($\ll$, $\gg$). The specification function, the operations, and the resulting program are also bit vector functions. Without loss of generality, we assume the same bit width for all of them.

A bit vector function with arguments of width $k_1, \dots, k_n$ may be transformed into a bit vector function with $\sum_{i=1}^{n} k_i$ arguments of width 1; and also into k_o functions of output width 1. Then, every function represents the calculation of one output bit. Thus, every bit vector function f corresponds to a collection of Boolean functions $f_1, \dots, f_{k_o}$.

$f_{|x_i=c}(x_1, \dots, x_n) = f(x_1, \dots, x_{i-1}, c, x_{i+1}, \dots, x_n)$ is the *restriction* of f to $x_i = c$. An input variable x_i is *essential in* f if there exist constants $c_1, \dots, c_n$ such that $f_{|x_i=0}(c_1, \dots, c_n) \neq f_{|x_i=1}(c_1, \dots, c_n)$. Intuitively, the essential variables are exactly those variables that influence the result of f.

A Boolean function f can be uniquely represented by the *Zhegalkin polynomial* [6] with coefficients $a_K \in \{0, 1\}$:

$$f(x_1, \dots, x_n) = \bigoplus_{K \subseteq \{1, \dots, n\}} a_K \wedge \bigwedge_{i \in K} x_i.$$

For example, $\neg(x_1 \wedge x_2) = 1 \oplus (x_1 \wedge x_2)$ with $a_{\{1\}} = a_{\{2\}} = 0$ and $a_{\emptyset} = a_{\{1,2\}} = 1$. The *Reed–Muller decomposition* $f(X) = f_{|x_i=0}(X) \oplus (x_i \wedge (f_{|x_i=0}(X) \oplus f_{|x_i=1}(X)))$ for $X = x_1, \dots, x_n$ factors out x_i from this polynomial [21].

In this work, (undirected) graphs must not have multiple edges between the same vertices (*parallel edges*), whereas this is permitted for directed graphs. $N(X)$ denotes the *neighbors* of all vertices in X. A bipartite graph G (with partition $\{A, B\}$) contains a matching of all vertices of A if and only if $|N(X)| \geq |X|$ for all $X \subseteq A$ (Hall's Marriage Theorem [8]).

3   Approximation of Essential Bits

We use the dependencies between input and output bits to identify synthesis problems as infeasible. If every program using the given operations violates the bit dependencies of the specification function, the synthesis problem is infeasible. We view the operations and the specification function as collections of Boolean functions f. The essential bits of f provide its bit dependencies. As computing all essential bits of an arbitrary f is NP-complete [6], we approximate them. To do this, we present two underapproximations and one overapproximation.

In this section, we view f as a circuit of $\oplus$ and $\wedge$ gates and the constant 1. Since the well-known bit vector functions have circuits of polynomial size [22], their analysis is still tractable. As both the specification function and custom operations are usually defined with these functions, we can obtain their circuits by combining the circuits of the well-known bit vector functions. A circuit that computes the 2nd bit of our running example is $x_3 \oplus y_3 \oplus (x_1 \wedge (x_2 \oplus y_2) \wedge (y_1 \oplus 1)) \oplus (x_2 \wedge (y_1 \oplus y_2))$ provided that x and y have at least 3 bits. To define our approximations, it hence suffices to supply rules for the constant 1, a bit x_i as well as the operations $\oplus$ and $\wedge$. The cornerstone of our approximations is:

Lemma 1. *The bit x_i is essential in a Boolean function f if and only if the Zhegalkin polynomial of f has at least one coefficient $a_K = 1$ with $i \in K$.*

Proof. If x_i is essential, the Zhegalkin polynomial must contain x_i. Conversely, if x_i is not essential, then $f_{|x_i=0} \oplus f_{|x_i=1} = 0$. By the Reed–Muller decomposition, $f = f_{|x_i=0} \oplus \left(x_i \wedge (f_{|x_i=0} \oplus f_{|x_i=1})\right) = f_{|x_i=0}$. Since the Zhegalkin polynomial of $f_{|x_i=0}$ does not contain x_i, the same holds for f. □

As the number of a_K is exponential in the number of input bits, we do not enumerate all non-zero a_K but only check if some a_K are non-zero. Our underapproximation UA_1 of the essential bits of f only considers the coefficients a_K with $|K| \leq 1$. UA_1 is a set over the x_i and 1. If $x_i \in UA_1$, $a_{\{i\}} = 1$ and x_i is essential according to Lemma 1. The rules to compute UA_1 for 1 and a bit x_i are $UA_1(1) = \{1\}$ and $UA_1(x_i) = \{x_i\}$.

The rule for $f = g \oplus h$ is $UA_1(g \oplus h) = UA_1(g) \triangle UA_1(h)$ with the symmetric set difference $X \triangle Y = (X \setminus Y) \cup (Y \setminus X)$ because the Zhegalkin polynomial of $g \oplus h$ has a non-zero coefficient for $\{i\}$ if either g or h has such a coefficient (since $x_i \oplus x_i = 0$). Thus, $x_i \in UA_1(f)$ iff $x_i \in UA_1(g)$ "xor" $x_i \in UA_1(h)$.

To derive a rule for $f = g \wedge h$, we look at the single monomials g_i of $g = g_1 \oplus \cdots \oplus g_m$ and h_j of $h = h_1 \oplus \cdots \oplus h_n$. Then $f = g \wedge h = (g_1 \oplus \cdots \oplus g_m) \wedge (h_1 \oplus \cdots \oplus h_n) = (g_1 \wedge h_1) \oplus \cdots \oplus (g_1 \wedge h_n) \oplus \cdots \oplus (g_m \wedge h_1) \oplus \cdots \oplus (g_m \wedge h_n)$. For two monomials g_i and h_j, $g_i \wedge h_j$ forms again a monomial and hence has a single non-zero coefficient. Let a_G and a_H be the non-zero coefficients of g_i and h_j respectively. Since the conjunction is idempotent (i.e., $x_i \wedge x_i = x_i$), the non-zero coefficient of $g_i \wedge h_j$ is $a_{G \cup H}$.

Using the known rules, we obtain $UA_1(g \wedge h) = UA_1(g_1 \wedge h_1) \triangle \cdots \triangle UA_1(g_1 \wedge h_n) \triangle \cdots \triangle UA_1(g_m \wedge h_1) \triangle \cdots \triangle UA_1(g_m \wedge h_n)$. Since UA_1 only considers coefficients a_K with $|K| \leq 1$, we can ignore all those $g_i \wedge h_j$ that do not have such a coefficient. For $|G \cup H| \leq 1$, either $G = H$ and $|G| = |H| \leq 1$ or $|G| = 1$ and $H = \emptyset$ (or vice versa). We thus group the $UA_1(g_i \wedge h_j)$ into three sets.

By definition of UA_1, all those monomials that fulfill the first condition are included in $UA_1(g) \cap UA_1(h)$. The set of monomials satisfying the second condition depends on the presence of the NeuTral element 1:

$$\mathrm{NT}(k_1, k_2) = \begin{cases} UA_1(k_1) \setminus \{1\} & \text{if } 1 \in UA_1(k_2) \\ \emptyset & \text{otherwise.} \end{cases}$$

As either G or H may be empty according to the second condition, $UA_1(f)$ depends on $\mathrm{NT}(g, h)$ and $\mathrm{NT}(h, g)$. Since these sets and $UA_1(g) \cap UA_1(g)$ are not necessarily disjoint, the above expansion of $g \wedge h$ requires that we take their symmetric difference: $UA_1(g \wedge h) = (UA_1(g) \cap UA_1(h)) \triangle \mathrm{NT}(g, h) \triangle \mathrm{NT}(h, g)$. For the 2nd bit of our running example, UA_1 holds $\{x_3, y_3\}$.

In general, a combination of $UA_1(g)$ and $UA_1(h)$ does not yield an underapproximation of $f = g \circ h$. For example, let $g(x_1, x_2) = x_2 \oplus (x_1 \wedge x_2)$ and

$h(x_1, x_2) = x_1 \oplus x_2 \oplus (x_1 \wedge x_2)$. Then, $x_2 \in UA_1(g)$ but $x_2 \notin UA_1(g \circ h)$ since $g(h(x_1, x_2), x_2) = x_2 \oplus (x_1 \wedge x_2) \oplus x_2 \oplus (x_1 \wedge x_2) = 0$. Thus, to compute $UA_1(g \circ h)$, the circuit for $g \circ h$ must be constructed explicitly.

Next, we show how to use UA_1 to compute the set UA_2 of the coefficients a_K with $|K| \leq 2$. For some bit x_i, the Reed–Muller decomposition splits a function f into a part $f_{|x_i=0}$ that does not depend on x_i and a part $x_i \wedge (f_{|x_i=0} \oplus f_{|x_i=1})$ in which every monomial contains x_i. Hence, $UA_1(f_{|x_i=0} \oplus f_{|x_i=1})$ contains all those x_j such that $a_{\{i,j\}} = 1$ in the Zhegalkin polynomial of f. If this set is non-empty, x_i and all $x_j \in UA_1(f_{|x_i=0} \oplus f_{|x_i=1})$ are essential bits of f. By taking the union of these essential bits for all bits x_i of f (and additionally $UA_1(f)$), we obtain $UA_2(f)$. For the 2nd bit of our running example, UA_2 is $\{x_1, x_2, x_3, y_1, y_2, y_3\}$ and thus contains all essential bits.

In contrast, our overapproximation OA holds those x_i that possibly occur in some set K with $a_K = 1$ as well as 1 if $a_\emptyset = 1$. As these x_i may occur in arbitrary monomials, we have to adjust our rules. (The rule whether $1 \in OA(f)$ is a special case. It is the same as for UA_1 since this rule is exact in this case.) Again, the first two are $OA(1) = \{1\}$ and $OA(x_i) = \{x_i\}$.

$f = g \oplus h$ has exactly those non-zero coefficients that occur in either g or h. The number of non-zero a_K may be exponential. But since every non-zero coefficient of f is included in the set union of the non-zero coefficients of g and h, the set union overapproximates them: $OA(g \oplus h) = OA(g) \cup OA(h)$.

If x_i is neither essential in g nor h, it is also not essential in $f = g \wedge h$. We can thus also resort to a set union but with one caveat. If g or h is the constant 0 function, the result should also be the constant 0 function, which has no essential bits. Note that $OA(g) = \emptyset$ implies $g = 0$ (similar for h):

$$OA(g \wedge h) = \begin{cases} \emptyset & \text{if } OA(g) = \emptyset \text{ or } OA(h) = \emptyset \\ OA(g) \cup OA(h) & \text{otherwise.} \end{cases}$$

For the 2nd bit of the running example, OA is the same as UA_2 and hence also yields an exact result. In contrast to UA (both UA_1 and UA_2), replacing a bit in $OA(g)$ by $OA(h)$ (i.e., removing x_i and adding $OA(h)$ instead) overapproximates the essential bits of $g \circ h$. As the UA and OA of bit vector functions is the collection of the UAs and OAs of their corresponding Boolean functions, we can derive the OA of a program from the OA of its operations.

4   Flagging Synthesis Problems as Infeasible

The specification function f and its implementing program P represent equivalent bit vector functions and have the same essential bits for each output bit. In terms of approximations, the following two tests $UA(f) \subseteq OA(P)$ and $UA(P) \subseteq OA(f)$ must hold. Hence, to check whether a synthesis problem is infeasible, it suffices to either show that the allowed operations do not admit a program P_U (the *upper bound*) with $UA(f) \subseteq OA(P_U)$ or a program P_L (the *lower bound*) with $UA(P_L) \subseteq OA(f)$. Our definition does not require that upper and lower bounds perform the same computation as P. Proving that these do not exist for a function f is as costly as identifying infeasibility with a standard synthesizer. As our approximations require to build the full circuit for P_L before evaluating $UA(P_L)$, we do not attempt to prove the non-existence of lower bounds. Instead, we show that there is no upper bound by tackling the complementary problem: If we cannot find an upper bound for f using the approximations of essential bits, the synthesis problem must be infeasible. But it is not necessary to examine all possible programs during this search: With relaxed upper bounds (Sect. 4.1) we only need to consider programs that are trees (Sect. 4.2) and are constructed by expanding a program consisting of at most two operations (Sect. 4.4); and we can use bipartite matchings (Sect. 4.3) to speed up the search. We give an algorithm relying on essential bits (Sect. 4.4) and another one that determines the "flavor" of the bit dependencies by tracking the 1 in the Zhegalkin polynomial (Sect. 4.5).

Note that loop-free programs correspond to *directed acyclic graphs* (DAG) with a single source node (the result). Its nodes are input variables and operations, its edges point to the operands of operation nodes. We call an outgoing edge of an operation o an *argument edge* (short: arg-edge) of o.

4.1 Bit Dependency Shapes

We discovered that the essential bits of an input variable often follow one of four regular patterns that we call *bit shapes*. When the essential bits follow a *simple* shape (symbol: $\diagup$), the i-th output bit is solely based on the i-th input bit, e.g., in operations like $\wedge$. In an *ascending* shape ($\blacktriangle$), input bits $j \leq i$ influence the i-th output bit, e.g., in $+$. In a *descending* shape ($\blacktriangledown$), the i-th output bit depends on input bits $j \geq i$, e.g., the bits of x in $x \gg y$. In a *block* shape ($\blacksquare$), arbitrary input bits influence an output bit, e.g., the bits of y in $x \div y$.

These shapes are partially ordered and form a lattice [7]: a larger shape subsumes all input-output dependencies of a smaller shape. Figure 1 shows this ordering. $\blacktriangle$ and $\blacktriangledown$ are incomparable, denoted by $\blacktriangle \parallel \blacktriangledown$. The smallest/largest element is $\diagup / \blacksquare$.

Fig. 1. Lattice.

The shape of an input variable of a specification function resp. the shape of an operand of an operation is the smallest shape that fits to the approximated essential bits of the input variable or operand. We discard both the operands with no influence on the output (no shape) and the operations without operands (e.g., constants). For example, the program that computes the average from Sect. 1 uses the operations $\wedge$, $\oplus$, $\gg 1$, and $-$. For two input variables x and y, the i-th output bit of $x \wedge y$ depends only on the i-th input bit of both x and y. Since this pattern corresponds to a $\diagup$ shape, we say that $\wedge$ is an operation with two inputs in shape $\diagup$. Hence, the list $[\diagup, \diagup]$ is an abstraction of $\wedge$. Similarly, $[\diagup, \diagup]$, $[\blacktriangle, \blacktriangle]$, and $[\blacktriangledown]$ are the shape abstractions of $\oplus$, $-$, and $\gg 1$ respectively.

We derive the shapes of the input variables of a program P via its DAG representation and the computed shape abstractions of its operations. Since a shape abstraction contains one shape per operand, each arg-edge of the DAG is associated with a shape. According to Sect. 3, for an operation o_1 that uses the result of its operand o_2 we can obtain an overapproximation of $o_1 \circ o_2$ by replacing an essential bit x_i in $OA(o_1)$ by all elements of OA of the i-th Boolean function of o_2. To transfer this property to shapes, consider for example $x - (y \gg 1)$ with the operations $-$ and $\gg 1$. The 2nd bit of y influences the 1st output bit of $\gg 1$, which in turn influences the 1st and 3rd output bits of $-$, among others. Hence, the shape abstraction for $x - (y \gg 1)$ is [▲,■]. This suggests that the composition of shape abstractions is related to the join $\sqcup$ of the shape lattice since [▲,▲] is the shape abstraction of $-$, [▶] is the shape abstraction of $\gg 1$, and ▲ $\sqcup$ ▶ $=$ ■ is the smallest element greater than or equal to both ▲ and ▶.

To show this, assume that o_2 is connected to an arg-edge a_1 of shape s_1 of o_1. Now examine an arg-edge a_2 of o_2 that is in shape s_2. If $s_1 = \diagup$, then the i-th input bit of a_1 affects at most the i-th output bit of o_1. Thus, if we replace these bits by those from the corresponding entry of $OA(o_2)$, a_2 is at most in the shape s_2 in $OA(o_1 \circ o_2)$. Similarly, if $s_1 = ▲$ and $s_2 = \diagup$, then a_2 is at most in the shape ▲ in $OA(o_1 \circ o_2)$ because the i-th input bit of o_2 influences only the i-th output bit and o_1 spreads the i-th input bit only to the output bits $j \geq i$. An exhaustive analysis of all cases reveals that the shape of a_2 in $o_1 \circ o_2$ is at most $s_1 \sqcup s_2$. Thus, for a path $a_1, \ldots, a_n$ in P from the source to an input variable over arg-edges a_i of shape s_i, the total Path Shape $\mathrm{PS}_P(a_1, \ldots, a_n) = \bigsqcup_{1 \leq i \leq n} s_i$. The shape of an input variable v of P is the join of the path shapes of all paths that reach v. For example, the two paths that reach x in Fig. 2 have shapes ▲ $\sqcup$ $\diagup$ $=$ ▲ and ▲ $\sqcup$ ▶ $\sqcup$ $\diagup$ $=$ ■, hence the shape of variable x is ▲ $\sqcup$ ■ $=$ ■. If there is only one unique path, we use a simplified notation $\mathrm{PS}_P(a_n) = \mathrm{PS}_P(a_1, \ldots, a_n)$.

Fig. 2. Shapes of the running example.

If P has an input variable v with a shape in P (computed via OA) that is not greater or equal to the shape in f (computed via UA), there must be an output bit that is essential in some input bit in f but not in P. Hence, $UA(f) \nsubseteq OA(P)$. If there is no P such that all input variables have greater or equal shape in P than in f, there is no upper bound and thus the synthesis problem is infeasible.

4.2   Tree Upper Bounds

The program $(x \vee y) - ((x \oplus y) \gg 1)$ is not the only upper bound for our example synthesis task. Figure 3 shows another upper bound with some special properties. First, some operations do not refer to an operand (denoted by "?"). Arbitrary values may be inserted here. As our infeasibility checker only uses the leaf shapes of a program and does not run it, we may keep these "loose ends" in our programs.

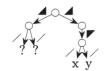

Fig. 3. Tree program.

Second, the result of every operation and every input variable is only used once. Hence, this program is formed like a tree. Does existence of an upper bound imply existence of such a tree upper bound? Luckily, we show below that whenever there is an upper bound program for a specification function f, there is also an upper bound whose underlying undirected graph (that results from replacing all directed edges $a \to b$ by a single undirected edge) is a tree. Hence, parallel arg-edges collapse to a single edge in the underlying undirected graph. Instead of a (hopefully failing) exhaustive search for an upper bound among arbitrary programs, it hence suffices to check the much smaller search space of tree programs that use each input variable only once. Such tree programs are not "real" programs in the sense that they can be executed since some operands are unconnected (as in Fig. 3). Their only purpose is to provide a simple skeleton that abstracts several real programs. In the following proof, we transform an arbitrary upper bound into a tree program. If the underlying undirected graph of a program is not a tree, it must contain a cycle. We reduce these cycles until they can be eliminated from the program. These transformations ensure that the shape of the input variables of the resulting program are at least as large as in the original program.

Lemma 2. *Suppose P is an upper bound of f. Then there is an upper bound P′ that uses the same operations but whose underlying undirected graph is a tree.*

Proof. We construct a sequence of upper bounds $P_0, \dots, P_n$ such that $P_0 = P$ and $P_n =: P'$.

If for an arbitrary $i \geq 0$ the underlying undirected graph G_i of P_i is a tree, then $n := i$. Otherwise, $\overline{G_i}$ has a cycle C of minimal length with an operation o that has a minimal distance from the source among the operations in C. Then C contains exactly two non-parallel arg-edges a_1, a_2 of o with shapes s_1, s_2. Let p_1, p_2 be the (unique and distinct) paths in P_i from o to a common end o' that include a_1 resp. a_2 such that their union forms an orientation of C.

Cycle reduction: Assume that $|p_1| > 1$ and $|p_2| > 1$. Let q_1 (resp. q_2) be the operation that directly precedes o' on p_1 (resp. p_2). Since P_i is a DAG, P_i cannot contain both a path from q_1 to q_2 and from q_2 to q_1. Assume that P_i does not contain a path from q_2 to q_1 (the other case is similar). Then P_{i+1} results from the transformation shown in Fig. 4a. To show that P_{i+1} is also an upper bound, let p be an arbitrary path from the source to an arbitrary variable x in P_i. If p does not contain the edge (q_1, o'), p is also a path in P_{i+1}. Otherwise, we can obtain a corresponding path p' in P_{i+1} by replacing (q_1, o') by the two edges (q_1, q_2)

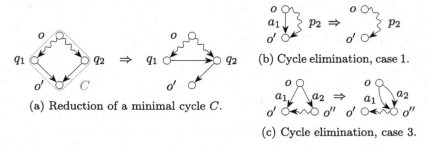

(a) Reduction of a minimal cycle C.

(b) Cycle elimination, case 1.

(c) Cycle elimination, case 3.

Fig. 4. Tree construction. ⤳➤: paths that may include arg-edges a_1 or a_2.

and (q_2, o'). The edge (q_1, o') in P_i and (q_1, q_2) in P_{i+1} correspond to the same operand of q_1 and hence have the same shape. Let s be the shape of the operand corresponding to the edge (q_2, o'). Then $\mathrm{PS}_{P_{i+1}}(p') = \mathrm{PS}_{P_i}(p) \sqcup s \geq \mathrm{PS}_{P_i}(p)$. As this holds for all paths p and variables x, P_{i+1} is also an upper bound. G_{i+1} has a smaller cycle than the minimal C of G_i.

Cycle elimination, $|p_1| = 1$ ($|p_2| = 1$ is similar): Case 1, $s_1 \leq \mathrm{PS}_{P_i}(p_2)$: Define P_{i+1} by removing the arg-edge a_1 in P_i (Fig. 4b). Then P_{i+1} is also an upper bound: For each path p over a_1 in P_i we get a path p' in both P_i and P_{i+1} by replacing a_1 with p_2 such that $\mathrm{PS}_{P_i}(p) \leq \mathrm{PS}_{P_i}(p')$. Hence, $\mathrm{PS}_{P_i}(p) \sqcup \mathrm{PS}_{P_i}(p') = \mathrm{PS}_{P_{i+1}}(p')$. P_{i+1} is an upper bound as the join of the shapes of all paths reaching a variable x is the same in P_i and P_{i+1}. G_{i+1} has fewer cycles than G_i. Case 2, $s_1 > \mathrm{PS}_{P_i}(p_2)$: Similar to case 1 but remove the last arg-edge of p_2 instead of a_1. Case 3, $s_1 \parallel \mathrm{PS}_{P_i}(p_2)$: Define P_{i+1} by reconnecting a_1 to the operation o'' that a_2 refers to (Fig. 4c). To show that P_{i+1} is an upper bound, let p be an arbitrary path from the source to an arbitrary variable x in P_i. If p does not contain a_1, p is also a path in P_{i+1}. Otherwise, there is a path p' to x in P_{i+1} that contains the reconnected a_1 and all edges except a_2 from p_2 since a_1 and p_2 have a common end in P_i. Similar to above, $\mathrm{PS}_{P_{i+1}}(p') \geq \mathrm{PS}_{P_i}(p)$ and hence the join of the shapes of all paths from the source to x is at least as large in P_{i+1} as in P_i. Since p and x are arbitrary, all variables are in at least the same shape in P_{i+1} as in P_i and P_{i+1} is also an upper bound. G_{i+1} has fewer cycles than G_i.

As these transformations keep the upper bound property and eventually remove all cycles, G_n is a tree.   □

Note that our infeasibility checker never constructs a tree program from a general program. It only explores the search space of tree programs. It even suffices to explore tree programs without parallel edges as such edges can be transformed away without affecting the upper bound property: For parallel edges with shapes $s_1 \leq s_2$ it suffices to keep the edge for s_2. We omit the case of incomparable shapes as there are no such arg-edges in the synthesis problems of our evaluation in Sect. 5 and hence it is unlikely that they occur in practice.

4.3   Bipartite Matching of Variables to Usage Locations

A (hopefully failing) exhaustive search for upper bounds among the tree programs examines many tree programs that differ only in the usages of the input variables. In the tree program in Fig. 3, we can, for example, swap x with y or one of the "?". In total, there are $\binom{4}{2} = 12$ ways to connect the given variables to this arrangement of operations. An exhaustive search would examine these 12 possibilities for each possible arrangement of the operations. To tune the search and avoid many redundant configurations, we simply omit the variables during the search. Hence, the search space shrinks to the space of *leaves programs* that use placeholder nodes (*leaves*) instead of variables (see Fig. 5). Then we view the problem of replacing the leaves by variables as a bipartite matching problem. Recall that in an upper bound each input variable must have a shape that is greater or equal to its respective shape in the specification function. To tailor our search towards upper bounds, a variable can only be matched to a leaf if this puts the variable in a shape required by an upper bound. In Fig. 5, for example, x may only be matched to one of the two rightmost leaves.

Consequently, we search for an upper bound using the operations alone and then obtain a bipartite matching from the variables to leaves that gives them at least the *variable shapes* of the input ↑variables of the specification function f. The multiset V holds all variable shapes of f. The path shape of the unique path from the root to a placeholder is its *leaf shape*. The multiset $L(P)$ contains

Fig. 5. Leaves program.

all leaf shapes of a leaves programs P. A leaves program is an upper bound if there is a matching of each variable v to a leaf ℓ whose shape is at least as large as the shape of v. If no leaves program admits such a matching, the synthesis problem is infeasible. It thus suffices to compute the size ν of a maximum matching, which can be done efficiently with the formula we give in Lemma 3.

As we did in the proof of Lemma 2, we shall later transform upper bounds, making use of the condition in Lemma 4 that guarantees that a second leaves program T can match at least as many variables as P. Hence, if P is an upper bound, so is T (needed in the search space reduction in Sect. 4.4). Finding a program with a maximum number of matched variables is an optimization problem yielding an optimum program. If this optimum program does not admit a matching of all variables, the synthesis problem is infeasible.

In the course of the search, we expand leaves programs by adding an operation. If an incomplete leaves program cannot be expanded to an optimum program, it may be ignored during the search. Lemma 5 extends Lemma 4 to also consider further expansions.

Some more notations: Restrictions of variable/leaf shapes to some set of shapes X: $V(X) = \{x \in V \mid x \in X\}$ and $L(P,X) = \{x \in L(P) \mid x \in X\}$; universe of shapes U; *downward closure* $\downarrow X = \{y \in U \mid \exists x \in X. x \geq y\}$ of a set of shapes X. Analogously, $\uparrow X = \{y \in U \mid \exists x \in X. x \leq y\}$. Leaf shape difference w.r.t. a set of shapes X: $\delta(P,T,X) = \{y \in L(P) \setminus L(T) \mid y \in X\}$. Missing proofs for the lemmas can be found in the artifact for the paper [13].

Lemma 3. *The maximum number of matched variables of a leaves program P is $\nu(P) = |L(P)| - \max_X(|L(P,\downarrow X)| - |V(\downarrow X)|)$.*

To compute ν, we only need to consider those sets X with distinct $\downarrow X$, which are $\{\diagup\}, \{\blacktriangleleft\}, \{\blacktriangleright\}, \{\blacktriangleleft,\blacktriangleright\}, \{\blacksquare\}$. A single iteration that counts the leaf shapes for each of these sets then yields all $|L(P,\downarrow X)|$. This is a lot easier than trying each possibility of assigning the variables to the leaves. Besides, the check whether a leaves program P is an upper bound reduces to $\nu(P) = |V|$.

Next, we relate the size of maximum matchings for two leaves programs. Intuitively, if a leaves program T has larger leaf shapes than P, it should match at least as many variables as P. The next lemma formalizes this insight.

Lemma 4. *Suppose P and T are leaves programs with $|\mathrm{L}(P)| = |\mathrm{L}(T)|$. If for all sets of shapes X, $|\delta(P, T, \uparrow X)| \leq |\delta(T, P, \uparrow X)|$, then $\nu(T) \geq \nu(P)$.*

If as many leaves of P as possible match to leaves of T with the same shape and if the remaining leaves of P match to larger leaves of T, Hall's Marriage Theorem provides the necessary condition for Lemma 4. This is handy if T is the result of some transformation on P because we can prove that the transformation preserves optimality if we can obtain such a matching by examining its steps.

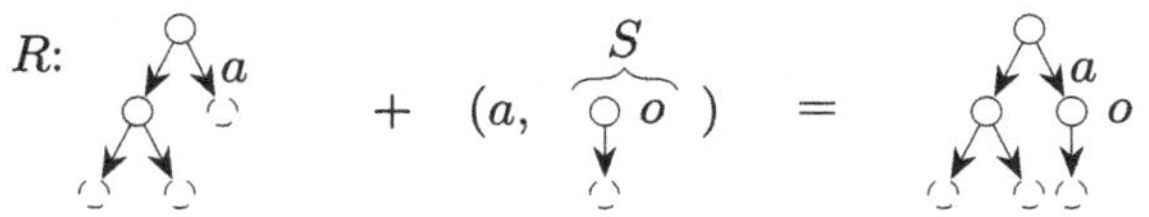

Fig. 6. Expansion of a leaves program (placeholder: $\circlearrowleft$).

A leaves program R is a *root* of a leaves program P if R and P have the same root operation and R is an induced subtree of P. (R and P have the same structure except that the successor of an operation may be another operation in P but a leaf in R.) An exhaustive search can then expand R to get closer to P by replacing a leaf arg-edge a with a subtree S formed of several operations, see Fig. 6, notation: $R + (a, S)$. Suppose we can expand a leaves program R by either γ_1 or γ_2. If we choose the better expansion according to Lemma 4, is it possible that this choice must lead to a worse program after subsequent expansions? Lemma 5 shows that this is impossible:

Lemma 5. *If a leaves program P is rooted in $R + \gamma_1$ and there is another expansion γ_2 of R such that γ_2 comprises the same operations as γ_1 and for all sets of shapes X, $|\delta(R + \gamma_1, R + \gamma_2, \uparrow X)| \leq |\delta(R + \gamma_2, R + \gamma_1, \uparrow X)|$, then there is a P' rooted in $R + \gamma_2$ with $\nu(P') \geq \nu(P)$.*

4.4   Infeasibility Checks with Upper Bounds

Although a (hopefully failing) exhaustive search constructs leaves programs only to get their leaf shapes, the order in which the search considers operations matters. For example, Fig. 7 shows an optimal leaves program if we pick the operations with $\diagup$ operand shapes first and the operation with $\blacktriangleright$ operand shape last. This leaves program is, however, not an optimum program and hence no upper bound because it admits a matching of only one variable in contrast to Fig. 5. The reason is the position of the operations that provide $\blacktriangle$ and $\blacktriangleright$ shapes. As these two operations together supply a $\blacktriangle \sqcup \blacktriangleright = \blacksquare$ shape, it intuitively makes sense to pick these operations first and the other operations that cannot further enlarge this shape later. We show below that there are always at most two operations that should be picked first (although we do not always know which). The remaining operations can then be considered in an arbitrary order.

But let us first introduce three transformations T1 to T3 for leaves programs and conditions under which they do not reduce ν. We shall use T1 to T3 in the proofs below. Readers may wish to skip these on a cursory read.

As Fig. 8 shows, $\mathrm{T1}(P, a)$ removes a subtree S_1 connected to a and connects the remaining tree to an arbitrary leaf ℓ of S_1.

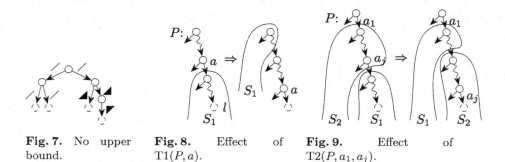

Fig. 7. No upper bound.

Fig. 8. Effect of $\mathrm{T1}(P, a)$.

Fig. 9. Effect of $\mathrm{T2}(P, a_1, a_j)$.

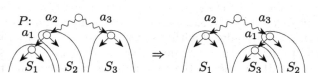

Fig. 10. Effect of $\mathrm{T3}(P, a_1, a_2, a_3)$.

Lemma 6. *Suppose $a_1, \dots, a_n$ is a path in a leaves program P. If for $1 \leq i < j \leq n$, $\mathrm{PS}_P(a_{j-1}) = \diagup < \mathrm{PS}_P(a_j)$, then $\nu(\mathrm{T1}(P, a_i)) \geq \nu(P)$.*

$\mathrm{T2}(P, a_1, a_j)$ swaps the subtree S_1 connected to the arg-edge a_j with the subtree S_2 connected to a_1, see Fig. 9.

Lemma 7. *Suppose $a_1, \dots, a_n$ is a path in a leaves program P. If for $1 \leq j \leq n$, $\mathrm{PS}_P(a_1) = \mathrm{PS}_P(a_j)$, then $\nu(\mathrm{T2}(P, a_1, a_j)) \geq \nu(P)$.*

$\mathrm{T3}(P, a_1, a_2, a_3)$ removes the subtrees S_1, S_2, S_3 connected to arg-edges a_1, a_2, a_3 respectively. Then it connects S_2 to a_3, S_3 to a_1, and S_1 to a_2, see Fig. 10.

Lemma 8. *Suppose P is a program with arg-edges a_1, a_2, a_3 such that (a) $\mathrm{PS}_P(a_2) \leq \mathrm{PS}_P(a_3)$, (b) there is no path that contains both a_2 and a_3, (c) an operation o is connected to a_2, a_1 is an arg-edge of o, and $\mathrm{PS}_P(a_2) = \mathrm{PS}_P(a_1)$. Then $\nu(\mathrm{T3}(P, a_1, a_2, a_3)) \geq \nu(P)$.*

Lemma 5 already revealed that expanding only one leaf arg-edge for every leaf shape suffices because expanding a second arg-edge of the same shape with the same operations cannot yield a better program. Now we show that it even suffices to consider (almost) only a single arbitrary permutation of operations during the search for upper bounds: We first show that there is a leaves program consisting of at most two operations (a so-called *seed*) that can be expanded to an optimum solution. Second, we show that there is a seed that can be expanded to an optimum program with the remaining operations in an arbitrary order.

Lemma 9. *There is an optimum program O rooted in a seed D of at most two operations with $\max(\mathrm{L}(D)) = \max(\mathrm{L}(O))$.*

Proof. Let Q be an arbitrary optimum leaves program with root operation r. If $\max(\mathrm{L}(Q))$ is a subset of the set of arg-edge shapes of r, r alone satisfies the Lemma. Otherwise, there is a shape in $\max(\mathrm{L}(Q))$ that is not provided by r. If r has only arg-edges of shape $\diagup$, there is a path $a_1, \ldots, a_i$ in Q with $\mathrm{PS}_Q(a_{i-1}) = \diagup < \mathrm{PS}_Q(a_i)$. By Lemma 6, $\mathrm{T1}(Q, a_{i-1})$ is also optimum and is rooted in an operation with an arg-edge of non-$\diagup$ shape. Hence, assume that r has a non-$\diagup$ arg-edge a_r of shape s_r. This implies that there is exactly one shape s_m in $\max(\mathrm{L}(Q))$ that is not an arg-edge shape of r. There are three cases. (a) If Q has a path $a'_1, \ldots, a'_n$ with $\mathrm{PS}_Q(a'_1) = \mathrm{PS}_Q(a'_{n-1})$ and $\mathrm{PS}_Q(a'_n) = s_m$, then $\mathrm{T2}(Q, a'_1, a'_{n-1})$ is also optimum by Lemma 7 and r plus the operand of a'_1 form its seed. For the remaining cases, the missing shape s_m is ■ and Q has a path $a'_1, \ldots, a'_n$ and a $1 < i < n$ with $\mathrm{PS}_Q(a'_1) = \diagup$, $\mathrm{PS}_Q(a'_n) = ■$. (b) If $\mathrm{PS}_Q(a'_i) = s_r$, then the disjoint subtrees connected to a'_i and a'_r may be swapped without altering any leaf shape. For the resulting program, case (a) applies. (c) If $\mathrm{PS}_Q(a'_i) \parallel s_r$, then $\mathrm{T1}(P, a'_{i-1})$ is also optimum by Lemma 6. Moreover, the prefix of $\diagup$ arg-edges is removed from the path so that case (a) applies.   □

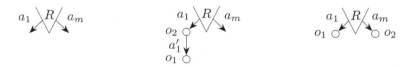

Fig. 11. Constellations in the proof of Lemma 10.

If a seed D cannot be expanded to an optimum program by picking the operations in an arbitrary order, the next Lemma shows that there is a "stronger" seed (that we can systematically search for). In its proof, we try to swap the order of two operations in an optimum program. In almost all cases, we can connect the swapped operations so that the resulting leaves program is still optimum. Otherwise, the two swapped operations provide the "stronger" seed.

Lemma 10. *Suppose that O is an optimum program rooted in a seed D with $\max(\mathrm{L}(D)) = \max(\mathrm{L}(O))$ and that no optimum program O' has a leaf shape $s \in \max(\mathrm{L}(O'))$ that is larger than some shape in $\max(\mathrm{L}(O))$.*

Let R be a program, a_1 an arg-edge of R, and a_2 an arg-edge of $R + (a_1, o_1)$ such that R is rooted in D and O is rooted in $R + (a_1, o_1) + (a_2, o_2)$. If no arg-edges a_2' of R and a_1' of $R + (a_2', o_2)$ exist such that $R + (a_2', o_2) + (a_1', o_1)$ is a root of an optimum program, then there is a seed D' that is the root of an optimum program with $\max(L(D')) = \max(L(O))$ and there is an $s_D \in L(D)$ such that, for all leaf shapes $s_{D'} \in L(D')$, $s_D < s_{D'}$.

Proof. Since $\max(L(O)) = \max(L(D))$, $\max(L(R)) = \max(L(O))$. Let $s_1 = PS_O(a_1)$ and $s_2 = PS_O(a_2)$. If there are arg-edges a_2' of R and a_1' of $R + (a_2', o_2)$ such that $PS_R(a_2') = s_2$ and $PS_{R+(a_2', o_2)}(a_1') = s_1$, then $L(R + (a_2', o_2) + (a_1', o_1)) = L(R + (a_1, o_1) + (a_2, o_2))$. Hence, $R + (a_2', o_2) + (a_1', o_1)$ can also be expanded to an optimum program by Lemma 5. Otherwise, there are two cases:

(1) $s_2 \notin L(R)$. Since $\max(L(R)) = \max(L(O))$, R must have some arg-edge a_m of shape $s_m > s_2 > s_1$ (see Fig. 11, left). There are three sub-cases:

(1a) All arg-edges of o_2 have a larger shape than s_2. Then o_2 may also be connected to arg-edges of smaller shape than s_2. If o_2 is connected to a_1 of R and o_1 is connected to an arg-edge a_1' of o_2 (see Fig. 11, center), the leaves provided by o_2 in $R + (a_1, o_1) + (a_2, o_2)$ are still present in the resulting program (since a_2 is an arg-edge of o_1, the shape of a_1' is still present). For every leaf shape contributed by o_1 in $R + (a_1, o_1) + (a_2, o_2)$, o_1 contributes a leaf that is at least as large in $R + (a_1, o_2) + (a_1', o_1)$ because the shape of a_1' is larger than s_1. By Lemma 5, this is also a root of an optimum program.

(1b) There is some arg-edge of o_2 with shape $t \le s_2$. If o_2 is connected to a_m and o_1 is connected to a_1 (see Fig. 11, right; since $s_m > s_2 > s_1$, these are distinct arg-edges), the leaves provided by o_1 in $R + (a_1, o_1) + (a_2, o_2)$ (plus $s_2 \ge t$) are still present in the resulting program. For every leaf shape contributed by o_2 in $R + (a_1, o_1) + (a_2, o_2)$, o_2 contributes a leaf that is at least as large in $R + (a_m, o_2) + (a_1, o_1)$. Viewed as a matching, the leaf of a_m in $R + (a_1, o_1) + (a_2, o_2)$ and the leaf of a_2 in $R + (a_m, o_2) + (a_1, o_1)$ are unmatched. But for the arg-edge a_t of shape t, we have $PS_{R+(a_1,o_1)+(a_2,o_2)}(a_t) = s_2$ and $PS_{R+(a_m,o_2)+(a_1,o_1)}(a_t) = s_m$. Thus, the premise of Lemma 5 holds and $R + (a_m, o_2) + (a_1, o_1)$ is also the root of an optimum program.

(1c) The smallest arg-edge shape of o_2 is incomparable to s_2. Then $s_m = \blacksquare$ and $\max(L(O)) = \{\blacksquare\}$. Also, since $s_m > s_2 > s_1$, $s_1 = \diagup$. If o_1 has an arg-edge $a_\diagup$ of shape $\diagup$, $T3(O, a_\diagup, a_1, a_m)$ is also optimum by Lemma 8. Since o_1 and o_2 occur in shape s_m in $T3(O, a_\diagup, a_1, a_m)$, there exists an expansion by o_2 followed by o_1 (as seen before).

Now, assume that no expansion by o_2 and then o_1 is a root of an optimum program. Hence, o_1 cannot have an arg-edge of shape $\diagup$. Since the program $o_1 + (a_2, o_2)$ can provide the shape $\blacksquare = s_m$, the program has no leaf of shape $\diagup$, and $s_1 = \diagup$, we know by Lemma 6 that this program is the root of the optimum program $T1(O, a_1)$. Hence, $o_1 + (a_2, o_2)$ is the required seed as it has no leaf of shape $\diagup = s_1$ and consists of two operations.

(2) There is an arg-edge a_2' of R with $PS_R(a_2') = s_2$ but $s_1 \notin L(R + (a_2', o_2))$. As $s_1 \in L(R)$ by assumption, o_2 must be connected to the only arg-edge a_2' with

$\text{PS}_R(a_2') = s_2 = s_1$. If we connect o_1 to any arg-edge of o_2, each leaf of o_1 in this program is larger than or equal to its counterpart in $R + (a_1, o_1) + (a_2, o_2)$. Thus, by Lemma 5, this can also be expanded to an optimum program. □

We can simply try to expand all possible seeds and pick the best program because Lemmas 9 and 10 guarantee that this will be an optimum program. In our running example, we then eventually pick a seed consisting of the operations with shape abstractions $[\blacktriangle, \blacktriangle]$ and $[\blacktriangleright]$ and grow the optimum program shown in Fig. 5 from this seed. This is the idea behind Algorithm 1.

Now we show that Algorithm 1 only flags synthesis problems as infeasible that are truly infeasible. Since we deal with leaves programs, we need to show that the algorithm only returns "infeasible" if there is no leaves program with a matching of all variables to some leaf. To compute the size of a maximum matching, Algorithm 1 uses the matching function ν that is defined in Lemma 3.

Theorem 1. *Algorithm 1 returns "infeasible" if and only if there is no leaves program P with $\nu(P) = |V|$.*

Proof. By Lemmas 9 and 10, there is a seed D of at most two operations that can be expanded to an optimum program by all permutations of operations. The main loop (lines 2–10) considers all these seeds and hence considers D.

```
   input  : Operations Ops, Variable shapes V
   output : Feasibility flag
 1 B ← ∅;
 2 foreach seed D of at most two operations do
 3 │   S₀ ← {D}; ROps ← Ops \ {o | D contains operation o};
 4 │   for i ← 1 to |ROps| do                                    // ops-loop
 5 │   │   Sᵢ ← ∅;
 6 │   │   foreach T ∈ Sᵢ₋₁ do
 7 │   │   │   foreach s ∈ L(T) do
 8 │   │   │   │   a ←Leaf arg-edge with PS_T(a) = s;
 9 │   │   │   └   Sᵢ ← Sᵢ ∪ (T + (a, ROps[i]));
10 │   B ← B ∪ {arg max_{T∈S_{|ROps|}}(ν(T))};
11 if ν(arg max_{T∈B}(ν(T))) = |V| then
12 │   return unknown
13 return infeasible
```

Algorithm 1. Checking the existence of an upper bound.

Suppose that a permutation π of operations can expand D and that in iteration i of the ops-loop (lines 4–9) some program T in S_{i-1} can be expanded to an optimum program. Then there is some arg-edge a of T such that $T + (a, o_{\pi_i})$ can be expanded to an optimum program. For all a' with $\text{PS}_T(a') = \text{PS}_T(a)$, $T + (a', o_{\pi_i})$ can also be expanded to an optimum program by Lemma 5. As the inner loop considers $\text{PS}_T(a)$, it also expands an arg-edge of shape $\text{PS}_T(a)$ and includes the expansion in S_i. As every iteration of the ops-loop produces a program that can be expanded to an optimum program, $S_{|ROps|}$ contains an optimum program O that line 10 adds to $\mathcal{B}$. Hence, Algorithm 1 returns "infeasible" if and only if $\nu(O) < |V|$. □

4.5   Infeasibility Check with the 1 in the Zhegalkin Polynomial

As Sect. 1 shows, bit dependencies come in two flavors. For example, the highest output bit of an average of $\neg x$ and y behaves differently than the other bits. The reason is that only the Zhegalkin polynomial of the highest bit contains a non-zero coefficient $a_\emptyset$ (i.e., the Zhegalkin polynomial contains a 1). Hence, the presence of a 1 determines the flavor of an output bit.

Recall that our definition of an upper bound implies that its Zhegalkin polynomial for an output bit must contain a 1 if the same holds for the specification. If such a program does not exist, the synthesis problem is infeasible. If it exists, such a program may use two ways to realize a 1 in some output bit: First, certain operations (e.g., constants) provide some 1s. Second, some operations can *propagate* a 1 from an input bit to another output bit. Consider, for example, the program $2 + 2$. As the Zhegalkin polynomial of the 2nd bit of 2 but only the 3rd bit of the result is 1, the operation $+$ can at least propagate the 2nd to the 3rd bit. An infeasibility checker may thus compute all possible propagations and then check if these suffice to let the sources of 1 reach the required output bits.

Although OA contains all possible propagations, it is too imprecise for this infeasibility checker. Consider an operation $o(x, y)$ with the Zhegalkin polynomial $x_1 \wedge y_2$ for the 1st output bit. Then $OA(o_1) = \{x_1, y_2\}$ but a 1 in y_2 can never reach the 1st output bit if x_1 does not also contain 1. Thus, o does not help to propagate 1 from the 2nd to the 1st bit. Luckily, we may use the following trick to overapproximate the propagations from other input bits: For each output bit i we compute $OA(o_i)$ with the i-th input bits of all its operands forced to 0. Then this $OA(o_i)$ contains the overapproximated input bits that can reach the i-th output bit independently of the i-th input bit of each operand.

Next, we combine the propagations of all operations. Let the goal set G be the set of i such that $1 \in UA(f_i)$ for a specification function f. To check if 1 can never reach all output bits in G, Algorithm 2 computes a set J of propagations. It then flags a synthesis problem as infeasible if it is impossible to propagate a 1 from its possible sources to the output bits in G.

Theorem 2. *If Algorithm 2 returns "infeasible", there is an $i \in G$ such that no program comprising the operations Ops has a 1 in the Zhegalkin polynomial of its i-th output bit.*

Proof. Suppose that Algorithm 2 returns "infeasible". Then there is an output bit $i \in G$ but J does not contain a propagation from a bit in *Srcs* to i (lines 8–9). We show by induction on $|Ops|$ that J holds at least all propagations of all programs using a subset of the operations *Ops*. Initially, J holds the propagations of the empty program. Suppose an operation $o \notin Ops$ propagates bit j to i. Let P be an arbitrary program using operations $Ops \cup \{o\}$. Then there are disjoint sets

input : Bit width w, Operations Ops, Goal G
output: Feasibility flag

```
1  Srcs ← ∅; J ← {(i, i) | 1 ≤ i ≤ w};
2  foreach Operation o ∈ Ops do
3  |  NJ ← J;
4  |  foreach Propagation of o from bit j to i do
5  |  |  NJ ← NJ ∪ {(k, ℓ) | (k, j) ∈ J, (i, ℓ) ∈ J};
6  |  Srcs ← Srcs ∪ {i | 1 ≤ i ≤ w, i-th output bit of o contains 1};
7  |  J ← NJ;
8  if ∃i ∈ G. ∀j ∈ Srcs. (j, i) ∉ J then
9  |  return infeasible
10 return unknown
```

Algorithm 2. Checking the propagations of 1.

$A, B \subseteq Ops$ such that o depends on the operations in A and the operations in B depend on o in P. By the induction hypothesis, J holds all possible propagations for A and B. Thus, if A propagates bit k to j and B propagates bit i to ℓ, then line 5 adds (k, ℓ) to J. Hence, J holds at least all possible propagations.

Also, $Srcs$ contains the bit positions of all sources of 1. Thus, if J lacks a propagation from a bit in $Srcs$ to i, then no program comprising the operations Ops has a 1 in the Zhegalkin polynomial of its i-th output bit.   □

5 Evaluation

This section addresses three questions: (RQ1) How fast and accurate are our approximations compared with an exact computation? (RQ2) How much do Algorithms 1 and 2 impact the solution time for synthesis problems? (RQ3) Do Algorithms 1 and 2 detect hard infeasible problems?

As we are not aware of a benchmark of infeasible synthesis problems, we use specifications from four sources: The bit vector rewrite rules of Nötzli et al. [16], the code optimizations of Buchwald [3], the test cases in the public repository of Sasnauskas et al. [18] without undefined behavior, and the Syntax Guided Synthesis competition benchmark [1]. As we are restricted to bit vector specifications with a single equality constraint and without precondition, this yields $26 + 56 + 23 + 19 = 124$ specifications. To turn them into synthesis problems that may be infeasible, we use them as input to an existing application in Sects. 5.2 and 5.3 that adds collections of available operations.

For comparative purposes, we implemented the synthesis method of Gulwani et al. [10] on top of the mature state-of-the-art SMT solver Yices 2.6.2 [9]. We implemented this synthesis method, our approximations, plus Algorithms 1 and 2 straightforwardly in Java, without a lot of manual fine-tuning. All measurements ran on a computer equipped with an Intel i7-6920HQ processor and 32 GB of RAM running a Linux 5.7.11 kernel and Java 11.0.8 + 10.

5.1   Quality of the Approximations (RQ1)

The approximations UA_1, UA_2, and OA are one of the contributions of this paper. We examine how well they are suited for an analysis of the 124 specifications and how large the advantage of UA_2 is over UA_1.

To obtain the exact set of essential bits for each output bit, according to Sect. 2 we formulate for each synthesis problem multiple Yices queries "Does output bit i depend on input bit j?", one for each i and j.

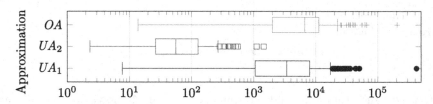

Fig. 12. Speedup of approximations over exact computation.

Figure 12 shows that computing UA_1 and OA is almost always at least three orders of magnitude faster than the exact computation. UA_2 is still 50 times faster in about half the cases. Figure 13 shows that UA_1 and OA deliver perfect results for more than 50% of the specifications. UA_2 almost reaches 75% and can avoid the low agreement of UA_1 in some cases. UA_2 takes at most 120 ms for analyzing a single specification, whereas Yices requires up to 3 min, a disproportionate amount of time.

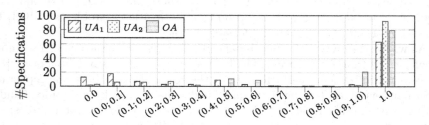

Fig. 13. Agreement with exact computation.

5.2   Impact of Algorithms 1 and 2 (RQ2)

Synthesizers for bit vector programs of bounded length usually detect infeasible synthesis problems. They benefit from our work if the runtime saving from avoiding the costly infeasibility proof exceeds the added runtime of our infeasibility check for all considered synthesis problems. This is what we evaluate here.

As a generator for synthesis problems and an example synthesizer we use Synapse [2], a technique that synthesizes optimal programs w.r.t. a user-specified cost model that assigns a cost to each operation. Such a problem lies at the heart of many applications [5, 17–19]. Later, we supply the generated synthesis problems to a second synthesizer. We feed Synapse the 124 specifications. Synapse uses a specification-specific set of operations (see below) and enumerates synthesis problems in order of increasing total cost of its collection of available operations. If a synthesis problem is infeasible or cannot be solved within the time limit, Synapse continues searching. If Synapse finds a program for a (feasible) synthesis problem, it stops and returns this program. Hence, all but the last synthesis problem are infeasible or time out. To reduce the risk that Synapse hits its time limit (which we set to 10 min), we use the enumeration scheme by Buchwald, Fried, and Hack [4]. We stop the enumeration for a single specification if Synapse cannot find a solution within 4 h. For simplicity, our cost model assigns a cost of 1 to all operations.

We set the specification-specific set of operations according to its benchmark source. For each source, this set comprises the union of operations used by programs implementing the specification functions from that source.[1] Since one of these sets of operations contains 9 custom operations, we also evaluate how well our checkers can handle operations beyond the well-known bit vector operations.

Table 1. Performance without and with Algorithms 1 and 2 (runtimes are total times).

| Synthesizer | Default | | With pre-checking for infeasibility | | | | | |
	Total	Timeouts	UA_2, OA	Alg. 1	Alg. 2	Total	Timeouts	Speedup
Synapse	13.1 h	5	11.1 min	3.9 s	207.3 s	8.8 h	5	32.93%
GJTV	490.1 h	1,818				455.6 h	1,730	7.04%

Table 2. Number of synthesis problems flagged as infeasible by Algorithms 1 and 2 versus number of all synthesis problems for varying level of hardness.

Synthesizer	[0 ms; 100 ms]	(100 ms; 1 s]	(1 s; 10 s]	(10 s; 60 s]	(60 s; ∞)
Synapse	1,606/2,582	4,198/16,417	774/3,767	446/987	16/34
GJTV	2,884/5,900	1,663/6,328	1,646/4,227	497/2,875	350/4,457

In total, Synapse generates 23,787 synthesis problems. For 2 specifications, Synapse hits the enumeration time limit of 4 h. Thus, 122 of the 23,787 synthesis problems are known to be feasible whereas 23,660 are infeasible and 5 are too difficult for Synapse to solve within the 10 min time limit. To avoid that our

---

[1] The benchmark sources provide a means to obtain the correct program. For example, some sources specify rewrite rules. Here, the left hand side corresponds to the specification function and the right hand side is an implementing program.

results are specific to Synapse, we also feed the 23, 787 synthesis problems to our implementation of the synthesis algorithm by Gulwani et al. [10] (GJTV).[2]

To evaluate the impact of our work, we apply Algorithms 1 and 2 on *all* of these problems (including the feasible ones) and omit the costly synthesizer on the ones that our algorithms flag as infeasible, see Table 1. Algorithms 1 and 2 flag 5, 261 resp. 3, 013 (total: 7, 040) synthesis problems as infeasible.

With our checkers, Synapse and GJTV take 33% resp. 7% less time. Although the improvement for GJTV is less strong (since the number of long-running problems is higher, see next section), our checkers can clearly speed up applications of bit vector synthesis. The total runtime of our checkers is 14.6 min, which is negligible compared with the runtimes of the synthesizers. Computing the approximations takes up to 170 times longer than running the algorithms. This shows the effectiveness of our search space reduction.

5.3   Hardness of Flagged Synthesis Problems (RQ3)

To the best of our knowledge, there is no objective measure of the hardness of a synthesis problem. But we may define the hardness of a problem for a specific synthesizer as its runtime on that problem. To do this, we use the runtimes of Synapse and GJTV for the 23, 787 synthesis problems from Sect. 5.2. For easier presentation, we put the runtimes into five distinct bins, easy to hard, with boundaries at 100 ms, 1 s, 10 s, and 60 s. Then we investigate the proportion of synthesis problems that are flagged infeasible to all synthesis problems in a bin.

As Table 2 shows, the problems that our infeasibility checker flags as infeasible are spread over all bins. For Synapse, our checker flags almost half of the problems in the two hardest bins as infeasible. The percentage of flagged problems in these bins is lower for GJTV, but our checker can flag problems as infeasible on which GJTV hits the timeout. Thus, our work can also deal with hard synthesis problems.

5.4   Threats to Validity

Our results might be affected by implementation errors. We wrote more than 5, 500 test cases and performed billions of random tests to minimize this threat. Also, the selected specifications might not be representative. To mitigate this threat, we used four different sources for specifications. Last, the results might be specific to a synthesis algorithm or underlying solver. To make our results representative, we used two different synthesis algorithms that each uses a different solver (Z3 [15] and Yices). We make our implementation publicly available [13].

---

[2] We observed that synthesizers for the class of Syntax Guided Synthesis problems perform poorly due to the necessary restrictions, as others noted before us [4].

6   Related Work

Usually, infeasible problems are only addressed using domain-specific knowledge [4,19] or by restricting the space of considered programs (e.g., to trees instead of DAGs [14]), so that infeasibility is detected faster at the cost of missing some feasible solutions.

To the best of our knowledge, Warren's right-to-left computability test [20,21] is the only application of bit dependencies to the program feasibility problem. In our terminology, it states that, given a specification function, there is an implementing program composed of an arbitrary number of $+$, $-$, $\wedge$, $\vee$, and $\neg$ operations if and only if all variables are at most in shape ◢. Our work generalizes his test by supporting different kinds of shapes and arbitrary operations. Also, we present an algorithm to obtain the variable shapes.

Hu et al. [11] present an infeasibility check for unbounded synthesis problems that are constrained by a grammar. They reduce the infeasibility check to a program reachability problem that they tackle with a verification tool. For bounded bit vector synthesis problems as considered in this work, such a tool would be an SMT solver that the synthesis algorithms that we considered in Sect. 5 already rely on. Thus, the work of Hu et al. [11] and ours tackle disjoint problems.

Another infeasibility checker by Hu et al. [12] relies on a set of example input-output pairs to compute an abstraction of the set of terms that the grammar can generate via an extension of a dataflow analysis to grammars. Its performance depends on a good selection of examples. The checker only deals with unbounded synthesis problems in the theory of linear integer arithmetic. The choice of a good abstraction for bit vector synthesis tasks is an open problem.

7   Conclusion

The presented algorithms use bit dependencies to quickly flag some bit vector synthesis problems as infeasible. We also proposed approximations to compute the essential bits. As our techniques speed up synthesizers on infeasible problems by up to 33%, it is an interesting open problem to find further properties of bit vector functions to improve program synthesis.

References

1. Alur, R., et al.: Syntax-guided synthesis. In: FMCAD 2013: Formal Methods in Computer-Aided Design, Portland, OR, pp. 1–8 (2013). https://sygus.org
2. Bornholt, J., Torlak, E., Grossman, D., Ceze, L.: Optimizing synthesis with metasketches. In: POPL 2016: Principles of Programming Languages, St. Petersburg, FL, pp. 775–788 (2016). https://doi.org/10.1145/2837614.2837666
3. Buchwald, S.: OPTGEN: a generator for local optimizations. In: Franke, B. (ed.) CC 2015. LNCS, vol. 9031, pp. 171–189. Springer, Heidelberg (2015). https://doi.org/10.1007/978-3-662-46663-6_9

4. Buchwald, S., Fried, A., Hack, S.: Synthesizing an instruction selection rule library from semantic specifications. In: CGO 2018: Code Generation and Optimization, Vienna, Austria, pp. 300–313 (2018). https://doi.org/10.1145/3168821

5. Cowan, M., Moreau, T., Chen, T., Bornholt, J., Ceze, L.: Automatic generation of high-performance quantized machine learning kernels. In: CGO 2020: Code Generation and Optimization, San Diego, CA, pp. 305–316 (2020). https://doi.org/10.1145/3368826.3377912

6. Crama, Y., Hammer, P.L.: Fundamental concepts and applications. In: Boolean Functions: Theory, Algorithms, and Applications, pp. 3–66. Cambridge University Press, Cambridge (2011). ISBN: 978-0-521-84751-3. https://doi.org/10.1017/CBO9780511852008.002

7. Davey, B.A., Priestley, H.A.: Introduction to Lattices and Order. Cambridge University Press, Cambridge (2002)

8. Diestel, R.: Graph Theory. Springer, Berlin (2017). https://doi.org/10.1007/978-3-662-53622-3

9. Dutertre, B.: Yices 2.2. In: Biere, A., Bloem, R. (eds.) CAV 2014. LNCS, vol. 8559, pp. 737–744. Springer, Cham (2014). https://doi.org/10.1007/978-3-319-08867-9_49

10. Gulwani, S., Jha, S., Tiwari, A., Venkatesan, R.: Synthesis of loop-free programs. In: PLDI 2011: Programming Language Design and Implementation, San Jose, CA, pp. 62–73 (2011). https://doi.org/10.1145/1993498.1993506

11. Hu, Q., Breck, J., Cyphert, J., D'Antoni, L., Reps, T.: Proving unrealizability for syntax-guided synthesis. In: Dillig, I., Tasiran, S. (eds.) CAV 2019. LNCS, vol. 11561, pp. 335–352. Springer, Cham (2019). https://doi.org/10.1007/978-3-030-25540-4_18

12. Hu, Q., Cyphert, J., D'Antoni, L., Reps, T.W.: Exact and approximate methods for proving unrealizability of syntax-guided synthesis problems. In: PLDI 2020: Programming Language Design and Implementation, London, UK, pp. 1128–1142 (2020). https://doi.org/10.1145/3385412.3385979

13. Kamp, M., Philippsen, M.: Artifact for "approximate bit dependency analysis to identify program synthesis problems as infeasible", October 2020. https://doi.org/10.5281/zenodo.4275482

14. Mechtaev, S., Griggio, A., Cimatti, A., Roychoudhury, A.: Symbolic execution with existential second-order constraints. In: ESEC/FSE 2018: European Software Engineering Conference and Symposium on the Foundations of Software Engineering, Lake Buena Vista, FL, pp. 389–399 (2018). https://doi.org/10.1145/3236024.3236049

15. de Moura, L., Bjørner, N.: Z3: an efficient SMT solver. In: Ramakrishnan, C.R., Rehof, J. (eds.) TACAS 2008. LNCS, vol. 4963, pp. 337–340. Springer, Heidelberg (2008). https://doi.org/10.1007/978-3-540-78800-3_24

16. Nötzli, A., et al.: Syntax-guided rewrite rule enumeration for SMT solvers. In: Janota, M., Lynce, I. (eds.) SAT 2019. LNCS, vol. 11628, pp. 279–297. Springer, Cham (2019). https://doi.org/10.1007/978-3-030-24258-9_20

17. Phothilimthana, P.M., Jelvis, T., Shah, R., Totla, N., Chasins, S., Bodik, R.: Chlorophyll: synthesis-aided compiler for low-power spatial architectures. ACM SIGPLAN Not. 49(6), 396–407 (2014). https://doi.org/10.1145/2666356.2594339

18. Sasnauskas, R., et al.: Souper: a synthesizing superoptimizer (2018). arXiv:1711.04422, April 2018. https://github.com/google/souper

19. Van Geffen, J., Nelson, L., Dillig, I., Wang, X., Torlak, E.: Synthesizing JIT compilers for in-kernel DSLs. In: Lahiri, S.K., Wang, C. (eds.) CAV 2020. LNCS, vol. 12225, pp. 564–586. Springer, Cham (2020). https://doi.org/10.1007/978-3-030-53291-8_29
20. Warren Jr., H.S.: Functions realizable with word-parallel logical and two's-complement addition instructions. Commun. ACM **20**(6), 439–441 (1977). https://doi.org/10.1145/359605.359632
21. Warren Jr., H.S.: Hacker's Delight. Addison-Wesley, Upper Saddle River (2012)
22. Wegener, I.: The Complexity of Boolean Functions. B. G. Teubner, Stuttgart (1987)

Automated Repair of Heap-Manipulating Programs Using Deductive Synthesis

Thanh-Toan Nguyen[1(✉)], Quang-Trung Ta[1], Ilya Sergey[1,2], and Wei-Ngan Chin[1]

[1] School of Computing, National University of Singapore, Singapore, Singapore
{toannt,taqt,ilya,chinwn}@comp.nus.edu.sg
[2] Yale-NUS College, Singapore, Singapore

Abstract. We propose a novel method to automatically repairing buggy heap-manipulating programs using constraint solving and deductive synthesis. Given an input program C and its formal specification in the form of a Hoare triple: $\{\mathcal{P}\}$ C $\{\mathcal{Q}\}$, we use a separation-logic-based verifier to verify if program C is correct w.r.t. its specifications. If program C is found buggy, we then repair it in the following steps. First, we rely on the verification results to collect a list of suspicious statements of the buggy program. For each suspicious statement, we temporarily replace it with a template patch representing the desired statements. The template patch is also formally specified using a pair of unknown pre- and postcondition. Next, we use the verifier to analyze the temporarily patched program to collect constraints related to the pre- and postcondition of the template patch. Then, these constraints are solved by our constraint solving technique to discover the suitable specifications of the template patch. Subsequently, these specifications can be used to synthesize program statements of the template patch, consequently creating a candidate program. Finally, if the candidate program is validated, it is returned as the repaired program. We demonstrate the effectiveness of our approach by evaluating our implementation and a state-of-the-art approach on a benchmark of 231 buggy programs. The experimental results show that our tool successfully repairs 223 buggy programs and considerably outperforms the compared tool.

1 Introduction

The goal of automated program repair (APR) is to identify fragments of a program that contains bugs and then to discover a patch that can be applied to fix the issue. This intuitive definition of APR and its evident practical utilities have aroused a lot of interest and researchers have proposed various approaches to automatically fixing buggy programs, using ideas from mutation testing [21,29,41,52,53], mining of semantic constraints [35–37], symbolic analysis of the reference implementations [34,46], and deep learning [15,33].

However, one of the current limitations in APR is that few studies focus on repairing heap-manipulating programs. One of them is a mutation-based approach [28] that combines formal verification and genetic programming to repair

© Springer Nature Switzerland AG 2021
F. Henglein et al. (Eds.): VMCAI 2021, LNCS 12597, pp. 376–400, 2021.
https://doi.org/10.1007/978-3-030-67067-2_17

buggy programs. Concretely, this approach uses genetic programming operators, such as *mutate, insert, delete*, to generate mutated programs, and then use a verifier to validate these programs. However, these tactics are insufficient to repair non-trivial bugs in heap-manipulating programs. In another study, Verma and Roy [50] enable users to express their expected program's graphical states at different program points in a debug-and-repair process. Their synergistic method is effective in fixing various bug patterns of heap-manipulating programs, but not fully automated. In contrast, we aim to build a fully automated method that requires only program specifications in the form of pre- and postconditions. Similar to our approach in using formal specifications, the previous approaches [17,49] leverage the static verifier Infer [2,3] to repair buggy programs. Although they target large-scale projects, these tools can fix only memory-related bugs, such as *null dereferences, memory leaks*, and *resource leaks*. In contrast, our work aims to repair more complicated bugs related to the functional correctness of heap-manipulating programs.

In this work, we introduce a fully automated approach to repairing heap-manipulating programs using constraint solving and deductive synthesis. It is inspired by recent advances in program synthesis using formal specification [40, 42]. However, our usage of program synthesis only applies to buggy statements to leave the repaired program with the least changes. The inputs of our approach are a program C, its precondition $\mathcal{P}$, its postcondition $\mathcal{Q}$. The input program C is first verified w.r.t. its specifications $\mathcal{P}$ and $\mathcal{Q}$, using a separation-logic-based verifier. If the input program does not satisfy its specifications, it is considered buggy, and we start the repair process as follows.

Firstly, our approach localizes a list of suspicious statements using invalid verification conditions in the verification step. Each suspicious statement is subsequently replaced by a template patch TP, consequently making a *template program*. The key idea is to find program statements of TP to make the template program satisfy w.r.t. the specifications $\mathcal{P}$ and $\mathcal{Q}$. Next, the verifier is used to analyze the template program w.r.t. the specifications $\mathcal{P}$ and $\mathcal{Q}$ to generate constraints related to the specifications of the template patch TP. These constraints are then solved using our constraint solving technique to discover the definition of the pre- and postcondition of the template patch. In the next step, these specifications are used to synthesize program statements of the template patch TP. Then, synthesized program statements replace TP in the template program to produce a candidate program. The candidate program is validated using the verifier to finally return a repaired program.

Contributions. This paper makes the following contributions.

- We propose a novel approach to repairing buggy heap-manipulating programs. To fix a buggy program, we first use constraint solving to infer the specifications of a patch. Then, from these inferred specifications, we use deductive synthesis to synthesize program statements of the patch.
- We introduce a list of inference rules and an algorithm to formally infer the specifications of a patch. We also present synthesis rules and an algorithm to synthesize program statements of the patch using the inferred specifications.

– We implement the proposed approach in a prototype and evaluate it in a benchmark of buggy heap-manipulating programs. Our tool can repair 223 out of 231 buggy programs and outperforms a state-of-the-art repair tool.

2   Motivation

We illustrate our repair approach using the program dll-append in Fig. 1 which implements a buggy version of a function that should append two disjoint doubly-linked lists (DLLs). The function append takes as parameters two pointers of the structure node. Each node is an element of a doubly-linked list and stores pointers to the previous and next elements of the list. Following the definition of the structure node (lines 1–3) is a separation logic (SL) *inductive predicate* dll, which recursively describes the shape of a symbolic-heap fragment that stores a DLL of length n. That is, a DLL is either a NULL-pointer with the empty heap predicate emp and zero-length (line 5), or a non-NULL pointer p to the head of the structure node (denoted via $p \mapsto \{q, r\}$) such that the pointer q points to the

```
1: typedef struct node {
2:     struct node* prev;
3:     struct node* next;} node;
4:
5: // dll(p, q, n) ≜ (p=null ∧ n=0 ∧ emp)
6: //        ∨ (∃r. p↦{q,r} * dll(r, p, n−1))
7:
8: void append(node* x, node* y)
9: // requires dll(x, a, n) * dll(y, b, m) ∧ n>0
10: // ensures dll(x, a, n+m);
11: {
12:     if (x->next == NULL) {
13:         x->next = y;
14:         if (y != NULL)
15:             y->next = x;
16:     } else append(x->next, y);
17: }
```

Fig. 1. A buggy dll-append program.

"tail" of the DLL, with the recursively repeating dll-structure, and a length decremented by one (line 6).

The SL specifications for the function append are given by a precondition and a postcondition that follow the syntax of **requires** and **ensures**, respectively. The precondition specifies that x and y both are the heads of two disjoint DLLs (the disjointness is enforced by the *separating conjunction* $*$), and the first DLL's length is positive (line 9). The postcondition expects that the result of append is a DLL, starting at x, with a length equal to the sum of the lengths of the initial lists (line 10). Here, the predicate definitions and program specifications are written after the notation //.

An astute reader could have noticed the bug we have planted on line 15 of Fig. 1: upon reaching the end of the x-headed DLL, the implementation does incorrectly set the pointer y->next to point to x. Let us now present how this mistake can be automatically discovered and fixed using our approach.

Firstly, the starting program state is the precondition $\mathsf{dll}(a, x, n) * \mathsf{dll}(y, b, m) \wedge n > 0$. Then, we use separation logic rules to update a program state. When the condition x->next == NULL at line 12 is true, the predicate $\mathsf{dll}(x, a, n)$ is unfolded as $\exists u.\ x \mapsto \{a,u\} \wedge n{=}1 \wedge u{=}\mathsf{null}$. Consequently, the program state is $\exists u.\ x \mapsto \{a,u\} * \mathsf{dll}(y,b,m) \wedge n{=}1 \wedge u{=}\mathsf{null}$. Next, at line 13, we have the following Hoare triple $\{\exists u.\ x \mapsto \{a,u\}\}$ `x->next = y;` $\{\exists u.\ x \mapsto \{a,y\}\}$, leading to the program state of $\exists u.\ x \mapsto \{a,y\} * \mathsf{dll}(y,b,m) \wedge n{=}1 \wedge u{=}\mathsf{null}$. This program state could be simplified as $x \mapsto \{a,y\} * \mathsf{dll}(y,b,m) \wedge n{=}1$. Then, when the condition `y != NULL` at line 14 is true, the predicate $\mathsf{dll}(y,b,m)$ is unfolded as $\exists v.\ y \mapsto \{b,v\} * \mathsf{dll}(v,y,m{-}1)$. As a result, the program state upon reaching line 15 is $\exists v.\ x \mapsto \{a,y\} * y \mapsto \{b,v\} * \mathsf{dll}(v,y,m{-}1) \wedge n{=}1$. After executing the statement at line 15, the state is $\exists v.\ x \mapsto \{a,y\} * y \mapsto \{b,x\} * \mathsf{dll}(v,y,m{-}1) \wedge n{=}1$. Then, this state has to entail the postcondition, but the following entailment is invalid: $\exists v.\ x \mapsto \{a,y\} * y \mapsto \{b,x\} * \mathsf{dll}(v,y,m{-}1) \wedge n{=}1 \nvdash \mathsf{dll}(x,a,n{+}m)$. Hence, the function `append` is buggy.

Our approach repairs this buggy function by replacing a buggy statement with a template patch. The idea is to infer the specifications of the template patch. Then, these specifications are used to synthesize program statements of the template patch. We will elaborate on the details of our approach in the next sections, and use the motivating example to illustrate each step of our approach.

Note that the mutation-based approach [28] is not able to repair this motivating example. That approach relies on mutation operators, such as *mutate*, *delete*, *insert*. However, there is no expression `y->prev` or statement `y->prev = x` available in the program `dll-append` to replace the buggy expression or statement at line 15. Besides, as discussed in the Introduction (Sect. 1), the semi-automated approach [50] requires a user to specify program states at various points to repair this motivating example while our automated approach only requires a pair of pre- and postcondition of the input program.

3   Overview of Program Repair Using Deductive Synthesis

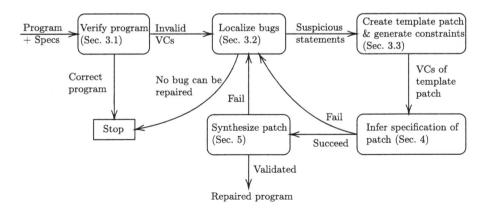

Fig. 2. Our automated program repair workflow.

Figure 2 presents an overview of our program repair approach. An input program is first verified w.r.t. its specifications using a separation-logic-based verifier (Sect. 3.1). Concretely, the HIP/SLEEK verifier [7] is used. If the input program does not satisfy its specifications, it is considered buggy, and we start our repair process. Firstly, our approach collects a list of suspicious statements and rank them by their likelihood to trigger the bug (Sect. 3.2), based on the invalid verification conditions (VCs) and program traces generated during the verification step. Secondly, each suspicious statement stmt, starting from the highest-ranked one, is replaced by a template patch TP_{stmt}, consequently creating a *template program* (Sect. 3.3). This template patch TP_{stmt} is accompanied by an initially unknown precondition $\mathcal{P}_{tp}$ and a postcondition $\mathcal{Q}_{tp}$. Thirdly, the approach invokes the verifier to analyze the template program to generate VCs related to unknown predicates $\mathcal{P}_{tp}$ and $\mathcal{Q}_{tp}$. These VCs are subsequently solved by our constraint solving technique to discover the definition of $\mathcal{P}_{tp}$ and $\mathcal{Q}_{tp}$ (Sect. 4). Then, these specifications $\mathcal{P}_{tp}$ and $\mathcal{Q}_{tp}$ is used to synthesize program statements of the template patch TP_{stmt} (Sect. 5). If the synthesis step succeeds, a candidate program is created by replacing the template TP_{stmt} with the synthesized statements. Finally, the candidate program is validated using the verifier to return a repaired program. Note that HIP/SLEEK is able to prove program termination [25,26]. Hence, the repaired program always terminates.

We will elaborate on the details of our framework in the rest of Sect. 3 and Sects. 4 and 5. We also formalize our repair algorithm in Sect. 6.

3.1 Program Verification Using Separation Logic

Figure 3 presents the syntax of the formula of our specification language. They are formulae that follow the pre- and postcondition syntax (**requires** and **ensures**) as introduced in the motivating example (Fig. 1). Our separation logic fragment is called SL_R and contains inductive heap predicates and linear arithmetic. In this fragment, x, k, null denote a variable, an integer constant, and a null pointer, respectively. A term t can be an arithmetic expression e or a memory address expression a. Moreover, emp is the predicate describing the empty memory, and $x \overset{\iota}{\mapsto} \{t_1, ..., t_n\}$ is a singleton predicate representing a single data structure of the type ι [1], pointed to by x, having n fields $t_1, ..., t_n$. Besides, $P(t_1, ..., t_n)$ is an inductive predicate modeling a recursive data structure (Definition 1). These predicates compose a *spatial formula* Σ via the separating conjunction operator $*$. Moreover, Π denotes a *pure formula* in the first-order theory of equality and linear arithmetic. Finally, F is a *symbolic-heap formula*.

---

[1] For brevity, we omit ι when presenting examples.

$$t \ ::= e \mid a \qquad e \ ::= k \mid x \mid -e \mid e_1 + e_2 \mid e_1 - e_2 \mid k \cdot e \qquad a \ ::= \mathsf{null} \mid x$$

$$\Pi \ ::= \mathsf{true} \mid \mathsf{false} \mid a_1 = a_2 \mid a_1 \neq a_2 \mid e_1 = e_2 \mid e_1 \neq e_2 \mid e_1 > e_2 \mid e_1 \geq e_2 \mid e_1 < e_2 \mid e_1 \leq e_2 \mid$$
$$\neg \Pi \mid \Pi_1 \wedge \Pi_2 \mid \Pi_1 \vee \Pi_2 \mid \Pi_1 \to \Pi_2 \mid \forall x . \Pi \mid \exists x . \Pi$$

$$\Sigma \ ::= \mathsf{emp} \mid x \overset{\iota}{\mapsto} \{t_1, ..., t_n\} \mid \mathsf{P}(t_1, ..., t_n) \mid \Sigma_1 * \Sigma_2 \qquad F \ ::= \Sigma \mid \Pi \mid \Sigma \wedge \Pi \mid \exists x . F$$

Fig. 3. syntax of formulae in $\mathrm{SL_R}$.

Definition 1 (Inductive heap predicate). *A system of k inductive heap predicates P_i, with $i = 1, ..., k$, is defined as follows, where each F_j^i is called a definition case of P_i, and is denoted as $F_j^i \overset{\mathrm{def}}{\Rightarrow} \mathsf{P}_i$:*

$$\left\{ \mathsf{P}_i(x_1^i, ..., x_{n_i}^i) \overset{\mathrm{def}}{=} F_1^i(x_1^i, ..., x_{n_i}^i) \vee ... \vee F_{m_i}^i(x_1^i, ..., x_{n_i}^i) \right\}_{i=1}^k$$

Example 1 (Doubly linked-list). The doubly-linked list in Sect. 2 is an example of an inductive heap predicate, which has one base case and one inductive case.
$$\mathsf{dll}(p, q, n) \overset{\mathrm{def}}{=} (\mathsf{emp} \wedge p = \mathsf{null} \wedge n = 0) \ \vee \ \exists r . (p \mapsto \{q, r\} * \mathsf{dll}(r, p, n - 1))$$

Figure 4 presents the semantics of formulae in our separation logic $\mathrm{SL_R}$. Given a set Var of variables, Sort of sorts, Val of values, Loc of memory addresses ($\mathsf{Loc} \subset \mathsf{Val}$), a model of a formula consists of: a *stack* model s, which is a function $s \colon \mathsf{Var} \to \mathsf{Val}$, and a *heap* model h, which is a partial function $h \colon (\mathsf{Loc} \times \mathsf{Sort}) \rightharpoonup \mathsf{Val}^+$. In this model, $[\![\Pi]\!]_s$ denotes the value of a pure formula Π under the stack model s. Likewise, $\mathrm{dom}(h)$ is the domain of h; $h \# h'$ shows that h and h' have disjoint domains, i.e., $\mathrm{dom}(h) \cap \mathrm{dom}(h') = \varnothing$; and $h \circ h'$ is the union of two disjoint heap models h and h'. In addition, $[f \mid x{:}y]$ is a function like f except that it returns y for the input x. Regarding the semantics of an inductive heap predicate, we follow the standard *least fixed point semantics* [1] by interpreting an inductive predicate symbol P as the least fixed point $[\![\mathsf{P}]\!]$ of a monotone operator constructed from its inductive definition.

$$
\begin{array}{lll}
s, h \models \Pi & \text{iff} & [\![\Pi]\!]_s = \mathsf{true} \text{ and } \mathrm{dom}(h) = \varnothing \\
s, h \models \mathsf{emp} & \text{iff} & \mathrm{dom}(h) = \varnothing \\
s, h \models x \overset{\iota}{\mapsto} \{x_1, ..., x_n\} & \text{iff} & \mathrm{dom}(h) = \{s(x)\} \text{ and } h(s(x), \iota) = (s(x_1), ..., s(x_n)) \\
s, h \models \mathsf{P}(x_1, ..., x_n) & \text{iff} & (h, [\![x_1]\!]_s, ..., [\![x_n]\!]_s) \in [\![\mathsf{P}]\!] \\
s, h \models \Sigma_1 * \Sigma_2 & \text{iff} & \exists h_1, h_2 : h_1 \# h_2; \ h_1 \circ h_2 = h; \ s, h_1 \models \Sigma_1; \ s, h_2 \models \Sigma_2 \\
s, h \models \Sigma \wedge \Pi & \text{iff} & [\![\Pi]\!]_s = \mathsf{true} \text{ and } s, h \models \Sigma \\
s, h \models \exists x . F & \text{iff} & \exists v \in \mathsf{Val} : [s \mid x{:}v], h \models F
\end{array}
$$

Fig. 4. Semantics of formulae in $\mathrm{SL_R}$.

We follow the literature to use separation logic [5,19,44] to verify the functional correctness of a program w.r.t. its specification. Separation logic follows Hoare logic in using a triple $\{\mathcal{P}\}$ C $\{\mathcal{Q}\}$ to describe how the program state is updated during the execution of the program C. Here, $\mathcal{P}$ and $\mathcal{Q}$ represents the precondition and postcondition of the program C, respectively. The triple $\{\mathcal{P}\}$ C $\{\mathcal{Q}\}$ expresses that given a starting program state of a program C satisfying $\mathcal{P}$, if the program C executes and terminates, then the resulting program state would satisfy $\mathcal{Q}$. Hence, a program C is verified w.r.t. its specifications $\mathcal{P}$ and $\mathcal{Q}$ if the triple $\{\mathcal{P}\}$ C $\{\mathcal{Q}\}$ holds. For instance, in Sect. 2, we have used separation logic rules to update program states and found that the motivating example in Fig. 1 is buggy because there exists an invalid entailment that consequently makes the Hoare triple of the function **append** not valid. Technically, we use the HIP/SLEEK verifier [7] to update program states. In this section, we do not present separation logic rules due to the page limit. Interested readers could refer to [5,19,44].

3.2 Bug Localization

We localize suspicious statements and rank them according to their likelihood to cause a bug by utilizing invalid VCs and program traces collected during the verification step (Sect. 3.1). Firstly, we collect a list of statements belonging to buggy traces. Then, we rank these statements by (i) how many times they appear in the buggy and correct traces and (ii) the distance from it to invalid VCs using program positions. Concretely, a statement is ranked higher if it appears more times in buggy traces and fewer times in the correct traces. Then, if two statements are the same in the first measure, the second measure is used.

For example, the only buggy trace in the motivating example (Fig. 1) is from taking the *if* branches of the two conditional statements. Hence, we collect two statements x->next = y at line 13 and y->next = x at line 15. Moreover, the statement x->next = y also appears in the correct trace when the conditional expression y != NULL at line 14 is **false**. Therefore, the second statement is more likely to cause the bug than the first one, consequently being ranked higher. In summary, we localize two suspicious statements with their corresponding ranking that are subsequently used as inputs of the next phase.

3.3 Template Patch Creation and Constraint Generation

In this phase, each suspicious statement is substituted by a template patch. This replacement will generate a program that our approach regards as a *template program*. Intuitively, the specifications, the pre- and postcondition, of the template patch will be inferred and later used to synthesize program statements of the template patch.

For example, Fig. 5 shows a *template program* created by replacing the highest-ranked suspicious statement y->next = x with the template patch $TP(x, y)$ at line 11. The special statement $TP(x, y)$ is currently encoded as a function call with parameters of all program variables available at that program location. We also encode the pre- and postcondition of this function call using unknown predicates $P(x, y, a, b, n, m)$ and $Q(x, y, a, b, n, m)$, respectively (lines 2, 3). The parameters of these predicates are parameters x, y of the

```
1: void TP(node* x, node* y);
2: // requires P(x, y, a, b, n, m)
3: // ensures Q(x, y, a, b, n, m);
4: void append(node* x, node* y)
5: // requires dll(x, a, n) * dll(y, b, m) ∧ n>0
6: // ensures dll(x, a, n+m);
7: {
8:     if (x->next == NULL) {
9:         x->next = y;
10:        if (y != NULL)
11:            TP(x,y);
12:    } else append(x->next, y);
13: }
```

Fig. 5. A template program.

template patch $TP(x, y)$ and other variables a, b, n, m in the precondition of append.

To generate constraints related to the specifications of a template patch, the separation-logic-based verifier is called to verify the template program. All the entailments related to the specifications (unknown predicates) of the template patch are collected. The aim is to infer the definition of unknown predicates to make all VCs correct, and then use inferred specifications to synthesize statements of the template patch $TP(x, y)$. For example, we collect all VCs containing predicates $P(x, y, a, b, n, m)$ and $Q(x, y, a, b, n, m)$ in Fig. 5. These VCs are later used in Sect. 4 to infer the definition of predicates $P(x, y, a, b, n, m)$ and $Q(x, y, a, b, n, m)$. Finally, these specifications are subsequently used in Sect. 5 to synthesize program statements of the template patch $TP(x, y)$.

Example 2 (VCs of the template patch). The entailments related to unknown predicates $P(x, y, a, b, n, m)$ and $Q(x, y, a, b, n, m)$ of the template patch in Fig. 5 are as follows.

$$x \mapsto \{a, y\} * dll(y, b, m) \wedge n{=}1 \wedge y{\neq}null \vdash P(x, y, a, b, n, m) * K(x, y, a, b, n, m)$$
$$Q(x, y, a, b, n, m) * K(x, y, a, b, n, m) \quad \vdash dll(x, a, m{+}n)$$

where the predicate $K(x, y, a, b, n, m)$ is the frame formula [4] which is obtained after analyzing the function call $TP(x, y)$ with the precondition $P(x, y, a, b, n, m)$.

4   Specification Inference

In Sect. 3.3, we explain how to create a template program and collect entailments related to the specifications of the template patch. In this section, we will describe how our approach solves these entailments to discover the definition of the specifications of the template patch.

4.1 Inference Rules

Figure 6 presents our inference rules to discover the definition of unknown predicates. Each inference rule has zero or more premises, a conclusion, and possibly a side condition. A premise or a conclusion is of the form $\mathsf{S};\ \Delta$, where Δ is a set of entailments, and S is the current discovered solution (a set of definitions of unknown predicates). Furthermore, we write $\Delta, \{F_1 \vdash F_2\}$ to denote a new entailment set obtained by extending Δ with the entailment $F_1 \vdash F_2$. When F is a symbolic-heap formula of the form $\exists \vec{x}.(\Sigma \wedge \Pi)$, we define $F * \Sigma' \triangleq \exists \vec{x}.(\Sigma * \Sigma' \wedge \Pi)$ and $F \wedge \Pi' \triangleq \exists \vec{x}.(\Sigma \wedge \Pi \wedge \Pi')$, given that $\mathsf{fv}(\Sigma') \cap \vec{x} = \varnothing$ and $\mathsf{fv}(\Pi') \cap \vec{x} = \varnothing$. Here, $\mathsf{fv}(F)$ denotes the set of free variables in the formula F. We also write $\vec{u} = \vec{v}$ to denote $(u_1 = v_1) \wedge \ldots \wedge (u_n = v_n)$, given that $\vec{u} \triangleq u_1, \ldots, u_n$ and $\vec{v} \triangleq v_1, \ldots, v_n$ are two variable lists of the same size. Finally, $\vec{u} \mathrel{\#} \vec{v}$ indicates that the two lists $\vec{u}$ and $\vec{v}$ are disjoint, i.e., $\nexists w.(w \in \vec{u} \wedge w \in \vec{v})$.

$$\top \frac{}{\mathsf{S};\ \Delta}\ \Delta = \varnothing \qquad\qquad \vdash_\pi \frac{\mathsf{S};\ \Delta}{\mathsf{S};\ \Delta, \{\Pi_1 \vdash \Pi_2\}}\ \Pi_1 \rightarrow \Pi_2$$

$$\bot_\pi \frac{\mathsf{S};\ \Delta}{\mathsf{S};\ \Delta, \{\Sigma_1 \wedge \Pi_1 \vdash F_2\}}\ \Pi_1 \rightarrow \mathsf{false} \qquad \bot_\sigma \frac{\mathsf{S};\ \Delta}{\mathsf{S};\ \Delta, \{\Sigma_1 * u \overset{\iota_1}{\mapsto} \{\vec{t}\} * u \overset{\iota_2}{\mapsto} \{\vec{r}\} \wedge \Pi_1 \vdash F_2\}}$$

$$\mathsf{P_L} \frac{\mathsf{S};\ \Delta, \{F_1 * F_1^\mathsf{P}(\vec{t}) \vdash F_2\}, \ldots, \{F_1 * F_n^\mathsf{P}(\vec{t}) \vdash F_2\}}{\mathsf{S};\ \Delta, \{F_1 * \mathsf{P}(\vec{t}) \vdash F_2\}}\ \mathsf{P}(\vec{t}) \overset{\text{def}}{=} F_1^\mathsf{P}(\vec{t}) \vee \ldots \vee F_n^\mathsf{P}(\vec{t})$$

$$\mathsf{P_R} \frac{\mathsf{S};\ \Delta, \{F_1 \vdash \exists \vec{x}(F_2 * F_i^\mathsf{P}(\vec{t}))\}}{\mathsf{S};\ \Delta, \{F_1 \vdash \exists \vec{x}.(F_2 * \mathsf{P}(\vec{t}))\}}\ F_i^\mathsf{P}(\vec{t}) \overset{\text{def}}{\Rightarrow} \mathsf{P}(\vec{t}) \qquad =_\mathsf{L} \frac{\mathsf{S};\ \Delta, \{F_1[t/u] \vdash F_2[t/u]\}}{\mathsf{S};\ \Delta, \{F_1 \wedge u = t \vdash F_2\}}$$

$$*{\mapsto} \frac{\mathsf{S};\ \Delta, \{F_1 \vdash \exists \vec{x}.(F_2 \wedge u = v \wedge \vec{t} = \vec{r})\}}{\mathsf{S};\ \Delta, \{F_1 * u \overset{\iota}{\mapsto} \{\vec{t}\} \vdash \exists \vec{x}.(F_2 * v \overset{\iota}{\mapsto} \{\vec{r}\})\}}\ \mathsf{fv}(v, \vec{r}) \mathrel{\#} \vec{x} \qquad \exists_\mathsf{L} \frac{\mathsf{S};\ \Delta, \{F_1[u/v] \vdash F_2\}}{\mathsf{S};\ \Delta, \{\exists v. F_1 \vdash F_2\}}\ u \notin \mathsf{fv}(F_1, F_2)$$

$$*\mathsf{P} \frac{\mathsf{S};\ \Delta, \{F_1 \vdash \exists \vec{x}.(F_2 \wedge \vec{t} = \vec{r})\}}{\mathsf{S};\ \Delta, \{F_1 * \mathsf{P}(\vec{t}) \vdash \exists \vec{x}.(F_2 * \mathsf{P}(\vec{r}))\}}\ \mathsf{fv}(\vec{r}) \mathrel{\#} \vec{x} \qquad \exists_\mathsf{R} \frac{\mathsf{S};\ \Delta, \{F_1 \vdash \exists \vec{x}.F_2[t/u]\}}{\mathsf{S};\ \Delta, \{F_1 \vdash \exists \vec{x}, u.(F_2 \wedge u = t)\}}$$

$$\mathsf{U_L} \frac{\mathsf{S} \cup \{\mathsf{U}(\vec{t}) \overset{\text{def}}{=} F\};\ \Delta[F/\mathsf{U}(\vec{t})], \{F_1 \vdash F_2\}}{\mathsf{S};\ \Delta, \{F_1 * \mathsf{U}(\vec{t}) \vdash F_2 * F\}}\ \mathsf{U} \notin F_1, F_2 \qquad \mathsf{E_L} \frac{\mathsf{S};\ \Delta, \{F_1 \vdash F_2\}}{\mathsf{S};\ \Delta, \{F_1 * \mathsf{emp} \vdash F_2\}}$$

$$\mathsf{U_R} \frac{\mathsf{S} \cup \{\mathsf{U}(\vec{t}) \overset{\text{def}}{=} F\};\ \Delta[F/\mathsf{U}(\vec{t})], \{F_1 \vdash F_2\}}{\mathsf{S};\ \Delta, \{F_1 * F \vdash F_2 * \mathsf{U}(\vec{t})\}}\ \mathsf{U} \notin F_1, F_2 \qquad \mathsf{E_R} \frac{\mathsf{S};\ \Delta, \{F_1 \vdash \exists \vec{x}.F_2\}}{\mathsf{S};\ \Delta, \{F_1 \vdash \exists \vec{x}.(F_2 * \mathsf{emp})\}}$$

Fig. 6. Specification inference rules.

Most of our proposed rules are inspired by the standard entailment checking rules in separation logic literature [47,48]. However, there are two main differences. Firstly, they need to handle multiple entailments generated from the verification of a temporarily patched program. Secondly, they also have to deal with unknown heap predicates. We will explain the details of our rules as follows.

- *Axiom rule* $\top$. This rule will return the current set of discovered specification S if no entailment needs to be handled ($\Delta = \varnothing$).

- *Elimination rules* $\perp_\pi$, $\perp_\sigma$, $\vdash_\pi$. These rules eliminate a valid entailment from the entailment set Δ in their conclusions. Here, we utilize three simple checks for the validity of the candidate entailment when (i) it has a contradiction in the antecedent ($\perp_\pi$), (ii) or it contains overlaid singleton heaps ($\perp_\sigma$), (iii) or it is a pure entailment ($\vdash_\pi$). In the last case, an off-the-shelf prover like Z3 [10] will be invoked to prove the pure entailment.
- *Normalization rules* $\exists_\mathsf{L}$, $\exists_\mathsf{R}$, $=_\mathsf{L}$, E_L, E_R. These rules simplify an entailment in Δ by either eliminating existentially quantified variables ($\exists_\mathsf{L}$, $\exists_\mathsf{R}$), or removing equalities ($=_\mathsf{L}$) or empty heap predicates (E_L, E_R) from the entailment.
- *Unfolding rules* P_L, P_R. These rules derive new entailments from a goal entailment in Δ by unfolding a heap predicate in its antecedent or its consequent. Note that there is a slight difference between these two rules. When a heap predicate in the antecedent is unfolded (P_L), all derived entailments will be added to the set Δ. In contrast, only one derived entailment will be added to the set Δ when a heap predicate in the consequent is unfolded (P_R).
- *Matching rules* $*\mapsto$, $*\mathsf{P}$. These rules remove identical instances of singleton heap predicates ($*\mapsto$) or inductive heap predicates ($*\mathsf{P}$) from two sides of a goal entailment in Δ. Here, we ensure that these instances of predicates are identical by adding equality constraints about their parameters into the consequent of the derived entailment.
- *Solving rules* U_L, U_R. These rules discover the definition of an unknown heap predicate $\mathsf{U}(\vec{t})$ in a goal entailment of Δ and update it to the solution set S. More specifically, if $\mathsf{U}(\vec{t})$ appears in the entailment's antecedent, then the rule U_L chooses the sub-formula of the consequent as the definition of $\mathsf{U}(\vec{t})$. Similarly, when $\mathsf{U}(\vec{t})$ appears in the consequent, then the rule U_R assigns $\mathsf{U}(\vec{t})$ to a sub-formula of the antecedent. In practice, these rules are often used when the entailment contains $\mathsf{U}(\vec{t})$ as its only heap predicate the antecedent (or the consequent). Then, the rule U_L (or U_R) can simply choose the entire consequent (or the entire antecedent) as the definition of $\mathsf{U}(\vec{t})$.

4.2   Inference Algorithm

Figure 7 presents our proof search procedure InferUnknPreds, which is implemented recursively to infer specifications from the unknown entailment set. Its inputs include a set Δ of unknown entailments and a set S of the currently discovered unknown heap predicates. This input pair correlates to a conclusion or a premise of an inference rule. Its output is a set that contains the definitions of the unknown heap predicates. When InferUnknPreds is invoked for the first time the input S is set to an empty list ($\varnothing$).

Given the predicate set S and the unknown entailment set Δ, the algorithm InferUnknPreds considers two cases. The first case is when there exists an entailment $F \vdash G$ that has more than one unknown predicate in G and no unknown predicate in F. Then, the definitions of unknown predicates in G are discovered by defining their spatial and pure formulae (line 2). Firstly, their spatial formulae of unknown predicates are defined by dividing the spatial formula of the antecedent F using the procedure DivideHeapFormula. For instance,

Procedure: InferUnknPreds(S, Δ)

Input: Δ, S are sets of unknown entailments and discovered heap predicates.
Output: The solution set of unknown predicates.

```
 1: if F ⊢ G ∈ Δ ∧ NumOfUnknPred(F) = 0 ∧ NumOfUnknPred(G) > 1 then
 2:    Ω ← DivideHeapFormula(F)              ▷ devide the spatial formula of F
 3:    for each (S_sub, Δ_sub) in Ω do              ▷ One way of dividing
 4:       res ← InferUnknPreds(S_sub, Δ_sub)
 5:       if res ≠ ∅ then return res                  ▷ Discover a solution
 6: else
 7:    R ← FindInferRules(S, Δ)                        ▷ find inference rules
 8:    for each R in R do
 9:       if R = ⊤ then return S                            ▷ axiom rule
10:       else                                     ▷ other inference rules
11:          (S', Δ') ← GetPremise(R)                 ▷ apply the chosen rule
12:          res ← InferUnknPreds(S', Δ')
13:          if res ≠ ∅ then return res               ▷ discover a solution
14:    return ∅                                         ▷ fail to solve Δ
```

Fig. 7. Proof search algorithm for unknown entailments.

the first entailment in Example 2 has two unknown predicate $P(x, y, a, b, n, m)$ and $K(x, y, a, b, n, m)$ in its consequent, and has no unknown predicate in its antecedent. Hence, the pair (P_S, K_S) that contains the corresponding spatial formulae of $P(x, y, a, b, n, m)$ and $K(x, y, a, b, n, m)$ could be either $(\text{emp}, x \mapsto \{a, y\} *$ $\text{dll}(y, b, m))$, or $(x \mapsto \{a, y\}, \text{dll}(y, b, m))$, or pairs in the reverse order. Then, the pure part of an unknown predicate is defined by using constraints in the antecedent F such that the constraints are related to variables in the spatial formula and the parameters of the predicate. For example, if we have $P_S \overset{\text{def}}{=} x \mapsto \{a, y\}$, then we have the following definition: $P(x, y, a, b, n, m) \overset{\text{def}}{=} x \mapsto \{a, y\} \wedge n = 1 \wedge y \neq \text{null}$. Each way of dividing the spatial formula of the antecedent F results in a pair (S_{sub}, Δ_{sub}) where the definitions of unknown predicates are added to the set S to generate S_{sub}. Next, Δ_{sub} is obtained by substituting unknown predicates by their corresponding definitions in Δ. Then, the algorithm with new arguments (S_{sub}, Δ_{sub}) continues recursively (lines 4,5).

In the second case, when there is no such entailment $F \vdash G$, the algorithm first finds from all inference rules presented in Fig. 6 a set of rules $\mathcal{R}$ whose conclusion can be unified with the entailment set Δ (line 7). Then InferUnknPreds subsequently applies each of the selected rules in $\mathcal{R}$ to solve the unknown entailment set Δ. In particular, if the selected rule R is an axiom rule $\top$, the procedure InferUnknPreds immediately returns the current solution set S, which does not derive any new entailment set (line 9). Otherwise, it continues to solve the new set of unknown entailments obtained from the premise of the rule R (lines 11,12) to discover the definitions of the unknown predicates (line 13). Finally,

InferUnknPreds returns an empty set ($\varnothing$) if all selected rules fail to solve the unknown entailment set Δ (line 14).

In practice, to make the proof search more efficient, we also rank the discovered inference rules in $\mathcal{R}$ by their likelihood to solve the unknown entailments. These heuristics are as follows:

- The axiom rule ($\top$) is the most important since it immediately returns the solution set.
- The elimination rules ($\bot_\sigma, \bot_\pi, \vdash_\pi$) are the second most important since they can remove valid entailments from the entailment set Δ.
- The normalization rules ($\exists_L, \exists_R, E_L, E_R, =_L$) are the third most important since they can simplify and make all the entailments more concise.
- Other rules ($P_L, P_R, *\mapsto, *P, P_L, P_R$) generally have the same priority. However, in several special cases, the priority of these rules change as follows:

- The rules $*\mapsto$, $*P$, P_L, P_R have high priority if the following conditions are satisfied. (i) The rule $*\mapsto$ matches and removes singleton heap predicates of the same root. (ii) The rule $*P$ matches and removes identical instances of inductive heap predicates. (iii) In the rule P_L, F_1 is a pure formula and F_2 is emp. (iv) In the rule P_R, F_1 is emp and F_2 is a pure formula.
- The rules $*\mapsto$, $*P$ have high priority when they match and remove heap predicates that have some identical arguments.
- Finally, the rules P_L, P_R are more important if after unfolding, they can introduce heap predicates that have some identical arguments, which can be removed later by the two rules $*\mapsto$, $*P$.

$$\cfrac{\cfrac{\cfrac{}{\mathsf{S} \cup \{\mathsf{Q}(x,y,a,b,n,m) \stackrel{\text{def}}{=} \mathsf{dll}(x,a,m{+}1)\};\ \varnothing} \top}{\mathsf{S};\ \mathsf{Q}(x,y,a,b,n,m) \wedge y{\neq}\mathsf{null} \vdash \mathsf{dll}(x,a,m{+}1)} \mathsf{U_L}}{\mathsf{S};\ \mathsf{Q}(x,y,a,b,n,m) \wedge n{=}1 \wedge y{\neq}\mathsf{null} \vdash \mathsf{dll}(x,a,m{+}n)} =_\mathsf{L}$$

Fig. 8. A proof tree of applying specification inference rules.

Example 3 (Specification inference). We illustrate how to apply specification inference rules to solve the below unknown entailments, given in Example 2.

$$x{\mapsto}\{a,y\} * \mathsf{dll}(y,b,m) \wedge n{=}1 \wedge y{\neq}\mathsf{null} \vdash \mathsf{P}(x,y,a,b,n,m) * \mathsf{K}(x,y,a,b,n,m)$$
$$\mathsf{Q}(x,y,a,b,n,m) * \mathsf{K}(x,y,a,b,n,m) \quad \vdash \mathsf{dll}(x,a,m{+}n)$$

The first entailment has two unknown predicates, namely $\mathsf{P}(x,y,a,b,n,m)$ and $\mathsf{K}(x,y,a,b,n,m)$, in its consequent, and no unknown predicate in its antecedent. Hence, the definitions of $\mathsf{P}(x,y,a,b,n,m)$ and $\mathsf{K}(x,y,a,b,n,m)$ are discovered using DivideHeapFormula to partition the spatial part of the antecedent. One possible solution is that the spatial part of $\mathsf{P}(x,y,a,b,n,m)$ is $x{\mapsto}\{a,y\} * \mathsf{dll}(y,b,m)$ while the spatial part of $\mathsf{K}(x,y,a,b,n,m)$ is emp, as follows:

$$P(x, y, a, b, n, m) \stackrel{\text{def}}{=} x \mapsto \{a, y\} * \mathsf{dll}(y, b, m) \wedge y \neq \mathsf{null}$$
$$K(x, y, a, b, n, m) \stackrel{\text{def}}{=} \mathsf{emp} \wedge n{=}1 \wedge y \neq \mathsf{null}$$

Now, we can replace $K(x, y, a, b, n, m)$ in the second entailment with its actual definition to obtain the following entailment.

$$Q(x, y, a, b, n, m) \wedge n{=}1 \wedge y \neq \mathsf{null} \vdash \mathsf{dll}(x, a, m{+}n)$$

The above entailment can be solved by our inference rules, as presented in the proof tree in Fig. 8 where S contains the definition of predicates $P(x, y, a, b, n, m)$ and $K(x, y, a, b, n, m)$.

5   Deductive Program Synthesis

In this section, we show how program statements of a template patch are synthesized from the specifications inferred in Sect. 4. We first define the notion of synthesis goal, then explain all synthesis rules, and finally introduce an algorithm that synthesizes program statements using synthesis rules.

$$\text{Exists}_{\text{L}} \frac{\Gamma; V; \{F_1[t/u]\} \rightsquigarrow \{F_2\} \mid \mathsf{C}}{\Gamma; V; \{\exists u.F_1\} \rightsquigarrow \{F_2\} \mid \mathsf{C}} \; t \notin \mathsf{fv}(V, F_1, F_2) \qquad \text{Exists}_{\text{R}} \frac{\Gamma; V; \{F_1\} \rightsquigarrow \{\exists \vec{z}.F_2[t/u]\} \mid \mathsf{C}}{\Gamma; V; \{F_1\} \rightsquigarrow \{\exists \vec{z}, u.(F_2 \wedge u{=}t)\} \mid \mathsf{C}}$$

$$\text{Frame}_{\mapsto} \frac{\Gamma; V; \{\Sigma_1 \wedge \Pi_1\} \rightsquigarrow \{\exists \vec{z}.(\Sigma_2 \wedge \Pi_2)\} \mid \mathsf{C}}{\Gamma; V; \{\Sigma_1 * u \xrightarrow{\iota} \{\vec{t}\} \wedge \Pi_1\} \rightsquigarrow \{\exists \vec{z}.(\Sigma_2 * u \xrightarrow{\iota} \{\vec{t}\} \wedge \Pi_2)\} \mid \mathsf{C}} \; \mathsf{fv}(u, \vec{t}) \# \vec{z}$$

$$\text{Frame}_{\text{P}} \frac{\Gamma; V; \{\Sigma_1 \wedge \Pi_1\} \rightsquigarrow \{\exists \vec{z}.(\Sigma_2 \wedge \Pi_2)\} \mid \mathsf{C}}{\Gamma; V; \{\Sigma_1 * P(\vec{t}) \wedge \Pi_1\} \rightsquigarrow \{\exists \vec{z}.(\Sigma_2 * P(\vec{t}) \wedge \Pi_2)\} \mid \mathsf{C}} \; \mathsf{fv}(\vec{t}) \# \vec{z}$$

$$\text{Unfold}_{\text{L}} \frac{\Gamma; V; \{F_1 * F_P^i(\vec{t})\} \rightsquigarrow \{F_2\} \mid \mathsf{C} \quad P(\vec{t}) \stackrel{\text{def}}{=} F_P^1(\vec{t}) \vee \dots \vee F_P^n(\vec{t})}{\Gamma; V; \{F_1 * P(\vec{t})\} \rightsquigarrow \{F_2\} \mid \mathsf{C} \quad 1 \leq i \leq n, \forall j \neq i, F_1 * F_P^j(\vec{t}) \equiv \mathsf{false}}$$

$$\text{Unfold}_{\text{R}} \frac{\Gamma; V; \{F_1\} \rightsquigarrow \{\exists \vec{z}.(F_2 * F_P(\vec{t}))\} \mid \mathsf{C}}{\Gamma; V; \{F_1\} \rightsquigarrow \{\exists \vec{z}.(F_2 * P(\vec{t}))\} \mid \mathsf{C}} \; F_P(\vec{t}) \stackrel{\text{def}}{\Rightarrow} P(\vec{t})$$

$$\text{Call} \frac{\Gamma \cup \{\{G_1\}\mathtt{fname}(\vec{u})\{G_2\}\}; V \cup \{v\}; \{F_1 * G_2\theta[v/res]\} \rightsquigarrow \{F_2\} \mid \mathsf{C}}{\Gamma \cup \{\{G_1\}\mathtt{fname}(\vec{u})\{G_2\}\}; V; \{F_1 * F\} \rightsquigarrow \{F_2\} \mid \mathtt{typ \; v \; = \; fname}(\vec{u}\theta); \; \mathsf{C}} \; \begin{array}{l} G_1\theta = F, \\ \mathsf{fv}(\vec{u}\theta) \in V \end{array}$$

$$\text{Assign} \frac{\Gamma; V \cup \{u\}; \{F_1 \wedge u{=}e\} \rightsquigarrow \{\exists \vec{z}.(F_2 \wedge u{=}e)\} \mid \mathsf{C}}{\Gamma; V \cup \{u\}; \{F_1\} \rightsquigarrow \{\exists \vec{z}.(F_2 \wedge u{=}e)\} \mid \mathtt{u \; = \; e}; \; \mathsf{C}} \; \begin{array}{l} u \notin \vec{z}, u \notin \mathsf{fv}(F_1), \\ \mathsf{fv}(e) \subseteq V \end{array}$$

$$\text{Skip} \frac{}{\Gamma; V; \{F_1\} \rightsquigarrow \{F_2\} \mid \mathtt{skip}} \; F_1 \vdash F_2 \qquad \text{Ret} \frac{}{\Gamma; V; \{F_1\} \rightsquigarrow \{\exists \vec{z}.(F_2 \wedge res{=}e)\} \mid \mathtt{return \; e}; } \; \begin{array}{l} F_1 \vdash \exists \vec{z}.F_2, \\ \mathsf{fv}(e) \subseteq V \end{array}$$

$$\text{Read} \frac{\Gamma; V \cup \{v\}; \{\Sigma_1 * u \xrightarrow{\iota} (\mathtt{fld} : t) \wedge \Pi_1 \wedge v{=}t\} \rightsquigarrow \{F_2\} \mid \mathsf{C}}{\Gamma; V; \{\Sigma_1 * u \xrightarrow{\iota} (\mathtt{fld} : t) \wedge \Pi_1\} \rightsquigarrow \{F_2\} \mid \mathtt{typ \; v \; = \; u\text{-}>fld}; \; \mathsf{C}} \; \begin{array}{l} u \in V, \\ v \notin V \end{array}$$

$$\text{Write} \frac{\Gamma; V; \{F_1 * u \xrightarrow{\iota} (\mathtt{fld} : t)\} \rightsquigarrow \{F_2 * u \xrightarrow{\iota} (\mathtt{fld} : t)\} \mid \mathsf{C}}{\Gamma; V; \{F_1 * u \xrightarrow{\iota} (\mathtt{fld} : r)\} \rightsquigarrow \{F_2 * u \xrightarrow{\iota} (\mathtt{fld} : t)\} \mid \mathtt{u\text{-}>fld \; = \; t}; \; \mathsf{C}} \; \begin{array}{l} \mathsf{fv}(u, t) \subseteq V, \\ r \neq t \end{array}$$

$$\text{Alloc} \frac{\Gamma; V \cup \{u\}; \{\Sigma_1 * u \xrightarrow{\iota} \{\vec{v}\} \wedge \Pi_1\} \rightsquigarrow \{\Sigma_2 * u \xrightarrow{\iota} \{\vec{t}\} \wedge \Pi_2\} \mid \mathsf{C}}{\Gamma; V; \{\Sigma_1 \wedge \Pi_1\} \rightsquigarrow \{\Sigma_2 * u \xrightarrow{\iota} \{\vec{t}\} \wedge \Pi_2\} \mid \mathtt{struct \; \iota \; u \; = \; malloc(sizeof(struct \; \iota))}; \; \mathsf{C}} \; \begin{array}{l} u \notin \mathsf{fv}(V, \Sigma_1) \\ \vec{v} \text{ are fresh} \\ \vec{t} \subseteq V \end{array}$$

$$\text{Free} \frac{\Gamma; V; \{F_1 \wedge \Pi_1\} \rightsquigarrow \{\exists \vec{z}.(\Sigma_2 \wedge \Pi_2)\} \mid \mathsf{C}}{\Gamma; V; \{F_1 * u \mapsto \{\vec{t}\} \wedge \Pi_1\} \rightsquigarrow \{\exists \vec{z}.(\Sigma_2 \wedge \Pi_2)\} \mid \mathtt{free(u)}; \; \mathsf{C}} \; \begin{array}{l} u \notin \mathsf{fv}(\Sigma_2) \\ u, \vec{t} \subseteq V \end{array}$$

Fig. 9. Deductive synthesis rules.

A *synthesis goal* is written as $\Gamma; V; \{F_1\} \rightsquigarrow \{F_2\} \mid$ C, where Γ is a list of declared functions that supports to synthesize function call statements, V consists of all available variables that could be used during the synthesis algorithm, F_1 is a precondition, F_2 is a postcondition, and C is a list of program statements that will be synthesized. Hence, solving a synthesis goal is equivalent to finding program statements C such that the Hoare triple $\{F_1\}$ C $\{F_2\}$ holds.

5.1   Synthesis Rules

Figure 9 presents our synthesis rules to synthesize program statements. A synthesis rule contains zero or more premises, a conclusion, and possible side conditions. A premise or a conclusion of a synthesis rule is a synthesis goal. Here, typ, fld, and fname indicate a variable type, a field of a data structure, and a function name, respectively. Besides, res is a keyword in our specification language to indicate the returned result of a function. Other notations are introduced previously in Sect. 4.1 and Sect. 3.1. All synthesis rules are described as follows.

- *Simplification rules* Exists$_L$ and Exists$_R$. These rules simplify a synthesis goal by removing an existential variable in its precondition (Exists$_L$) or its postcondition (Exists$_R$).
- *Frame rules* Frame$_{\mapsto}$ and Frame$_P$. These rules remove an identical singleton heap predicate (Frame$_{\mapsto}$) or inductive heap predicate (Frame$_P$) from the pre- and postcondition of a synthesis goal.
- *Unfolding rules* Unfold$_L$ and Unfold$_R$. These rules produce a new synthesis goal by unfolding an inductive heap predicate in the precondition (Unfold$_L$) or postcondition (Unfold$_R$) of a synthesis goal. When an inductive heap predicate is unfolded in the precondition (Unfold$_L$), the side conditions ensure that only one definition case $F_P^i(\vec{t})$ of $P(\vec{t})$ is satisfiable. In contrast, unfolding an inductive heap predicate $P(\vec{t})$ in the postcondition (Unfold$_R$) creates multiple subgoals, but solving the current synthesis goal requires only one subgoal to succeed.
- *Rule* Call. This rule invokes a function call fname($\vec{u}$) which has the specification of $\{G_1\}$fname($\vec{u}$)$\{G_2\}$ when all chosen input arguments $\vec{u}\theta$ satisfy the specification of its corresponding parameters. Here, θ is a substitution of arguments to the parameters $\vec{u}$ of the function, i.e., replacing the function's formal parameters with the corresponding actual arguments. Then, updating the precondition of the synthesis goal is similar to update a program state in formal verification when a function call fname($\vec{u}\theta$) is encountered.
- *Rule* Assign. The rule Assign assigns a value e to a variable u that is in the list V ($u \in V$) when a constraint $u=e$ appears in the postcondition but the variable u is not assigned any value in the precondition ($u \notin \mathsf{fv}(F_1)$). Consequently, an assignment statement u = e; is generated.
- *Rules* Skip and Ret. The rule Skip is applicable when there exists a valid entailment $F_1 \vdash F_2$. It also marks that a synthesis goal is solved by producing a skip statement. Meanwhile, the rule Ret generates a statement return e;. It is similar to combining the rule Assign (with u is res) and the rule Skip. These rules have no premises, meaning that they are terminating rules.

- *Rules* Read and Write. The rule Read assigns the value of a field of a heap variable to a new variable. For instance, if a statement `append(x->next, y)` needs to be synthesized when repairing a buggy `dll-append` program, Read is executed to create the statement `node* z = x->next;`. Then, Call is used to synthesize the statement `append(z, y);`. Meanwhile, the rule Write assigns a new value to a field of a heap variable is if the values of the field of the variable in the pre- and postcondition differ (see Example 4).
- *Rules* Alloc and Free. The rule Alloc allocates a new variable u of the data structure ι if all arguments $\vec{t}$ are in the list V. This rule is called when a new heap variable u appears in the spatial formula of the postcondition but not the precondition ($u \notin \mathsf{fv}(\Sigma_1)$). On the other hand, the rule Free deallocates a heap variable u if it is in the spatial formula of the precondition but not in the spatial formula of the postcondition.

5.2 Synthesis Algorithm

Figure 10 shows our synthesis algorithm SynthesizeStmts. Given a list of declared functions Γ, a list of available variables V, a precondition F_1, and a postcondition F_2, the algorithm SynthesizeStmts aims to produce program statements C that solve the synthesis goal $\Gamma; V; \{F_1\} \rightsquigarrow \{F_2\} \mid$ C.

Algorithm: SynthesizeStmts(Γ, V, F_1, F_2)

Input: A list of function declarations Γ, a list of available variables V, a precondition F_1, and a postcondition F_2.

Output: A list of synthesized statements, or Fail if no statement is synthesized.

1:   $\mathcal{R} \leftarrow$ FindSynRules(Γ, V, F_1, F_2) $\triangleright$ find applicable rules
2:   **for each rule R in $\mathcal{R}$ do**
3:      **if** R $\in \{$Skip, Ret$\}$ **then return** DeriveStmt(R) $\triangleright$ a terminating rule
4:      **else if** R $\in \{$Exists$_\mathsf{L}$, Exists$_\mathsf{R}$, Frame$_{\mapsto}$, Frame$_\mathsf{P}$, Unfold$_\mathsf{L}$, Unfold$_\mathsf{R}\}$ **then**
5:        $(\Gamma', V', F_1', F_2') \leftarrow$ DeriveNewGoal(R) $\triangleright$ a normalization rule
6:        **return** SynthesizeStmts(Γ, V', F_1', F_2')
7:      **else** $\triangleright$ other rules
8:        $(\Gamma', V', F_1', F_2'),$ stmt $\leftarrow$ DeriveNewGoalAndStmt(R)
9:        res $\leftarrow$ SynthesizeStmts(Γ', V', F_1', F_2')
10:     **if** res $\neq$ Fail **then return** AppendStmts(stmt, res) $\triangleright$ found a solution
11: **return Fail** $\triangleright$ fail to synthesize

Fig. 10. The SynthesizeStmts algorithm.

The algorithm SynthesizeStmts first finds from all synthesis rules presented in Sect. 5.1 a list of rules $\mathcal{R}$ that is applicable to the current tuple (Γ, V, F_1, F_2) (line 1). If there exists a terminating rule (Skip or Ret), then SynthesizeStmts returns a `skip` statement (Skip) or a return statement (Ret) (line 3). If a normalization rule is selected, then SynthesizeStmts will immediately apply it to derive a new goal and continue the synthesis process (lines 4–6). For other synthesis rules, SynthesizeStmts subsequently executes each of them to derive both a new goal $(\Gamma', V', F_1', F_2')$ and a program statement stmt (line 8). Our algorithm also checks if the rule Call is executed on a smaller sub-heap of the precondition F_1 that consequently ensures termination of a patched program. The algorithm will continue the synthesis process on the new goal (line 9) and will append the previously synthesized statement stmt on the new result res to return all synthesized statements (line 10). Besides, it also returns Fail if all selected rules fail to synthesize program statements from the current inputs (line 11).

In practice, the algorithm SynthesizeStmts also ranks synthesis rules collected by FindSynRules to make it more effective. Firstly, two terminating rules Skip and Ret are the most important since they immediately return a list of synthesized statements. Then, the rules $\mathsf{Exists_L}$, $\mathsf{Exists_R}$, $\mathsf{Unfold_L}$ are the second most important rules because they simplify the current synthesis goal and generate a more concise synthesis goal. Finally, other synthesis rules are ranked equally.

$$\cfrac{\cfrac{\cfrac{\cfrac{\cfrac{\cfrac{\cfrac{\Gamma; V; \{x\mapsto\{a,y\} * y\mapsto\{x,t\}\} \rightsquigarrow \{x\mapsto\{a,y\} * y\mapsto\{x,t\}\} \mid C' \quad C' = \texttt{skip}}{\Gamma; V; \{x\mapsto\{a,y\} * y\mapsto\{x,t\}\} \rightsquigarrow \{x\mapsto\{a,y\} * y\mapsto\{x,t\}\} \mid C} \ \text{Skip}}{\begin{array}{c} C = \texttt{y-> prev = x; } C' \end{array}}}{\Gamma; V; \{x\mapsto\{a,y\} * y\mapsto\{b,t\}\} \rightsquigarrow \{x\mapsto\{a,y\} * y\mapsto\{x,t\}\} \mid C} \ \text{Write}}{\Gamma; V; \{x\mapsto\{a,y\} * y\mapsto\{b,t\} * \mathsf{dll}(t,y,m-1)\} \rightsquigarrow \{\exists k,h.\ x\mapsto\{a,k\} * k\mapsto\{x,h\} * \mathsf{dll}(h,k,m-1)\} \mid C} \ \mathsf{Frame_P}}{\Gamma; V; \{x\mapsto\{a,y\} * y\mapsto\{b,t\} * \mathsf{dll}(t,y,m-1)\} \rightsquigarrow \{\exists k.\ x\mapsto\{a,k\} * \mathsf{dll}(k,x,m)\} \mid C} \ \mathsf{Unfold_R}}{\Gamma; V; \{ x\mapsto\{a,y\} * y\mapsto\{b,t\} * \mathsf{dll}(t,y,m-1)\} \rightsquigarrow \{\mathsf{dll}(x,a,m+1)\} \mid C} \ \mathsf{Unfold_R}}{\Gamma; V; \{\exists t.\ x\mapsto\{a,y\} * y\mapsto\{b,t\} * \mathsf{dll}(t,y,m-1)\} \rightsquigarrow \{\mathsf{dll}(x,a,m+1)\} \mid C} \ \mathsf{Exists_L}}{\Gamma; V; \{x\mapsto\{a,y\} * \mathsf{dll}(y,b,m) \wedge y{\neq}\mathsf{null}\} \rightsquigarrow \{\mathsf{dll}(x,a,m+1)\} \mid C} \ \mathsf{Unfold_L}$$

Fig. 11. Synthesis rules are applied to specifications inferred in Example 3.

Example 4 (The patch to repair the motivating example). Figure 11 explains how our synthesis algorithm applies synthesis rules to synthesize a program statement from the specifications inferred in Example 3. Here, Γ contains a declaration of function append while the list V is $\{x,y\}$. The algorithm SynthesizeStmts first uses the rule $\mathsf{Unfold_L}$ to remove the constraint $y{\neq}\mathsf{null}$ from the precondition. Next, the rule $\mathsf{Exists_L}$ is used to remove the existential variable t from the precondition. Then, the postcondition is unfolded twice using the rule $\mathsf{Unfold_R}$ to have a predicate dll of length $m-1$ like in the precondition. Next, the predicate dll of length $m-1$ is removed from both the pre- and postcondition using the rule $\mathsf{Frame_P}$. Finally, the field prev of the variable y is updated according to the rule Write to terminate the synthesis algorithm with the rule Skip. Therefore, a program statement y->prev = x is synthesized. This statement will replace the template patch TP(x,y) at line 11 in Fig. 5 to produce a candidate program. Finally, the candidate program is validated w.r.t. the specifications of the function append and then returned as the repaired program of the motivating example.

6   Repair Algorithm

We formally introduce the algorithm Repair in Fig. 12. The inputs of the algorithm include a program C, its precondition $\mathcal{P}$, its postcondition $\mathcal{Q}$, and an environment variable Γ containing all declared functions.

The algorithm first verifies if program C is correct against its specifications (line 1). If the verification fails, then C is considered buggy. In this case, all the invalid VCs generated during the verification step are collected (line 2). Next, the algorithm Repair utilizes these VCs to localize a list of suspicious statements S (line 3). It also ranks these suspicious statements according to their likelihood to cause the bug. Then, it attempts to repair each suspicious statement in S, starting from the highest-ranked one (lines 4–14).

Algorithm: Repair($\Gamma, \mathcal{P}, \mathsf{C}, \mathcal{Q}$)

Input: Γ is a list of declared functions that can be used, and C, $\mathcal{P}$, $\mathcal{Q}$ are the program to be repaired, and its corresponding pre- and postcondition.
Output: None if the Hoare triple $\{\mathcal{P}\}$ C $\{\mathcal{Q}\}$ holds, $\bar{\mathsf{C}}$ if C is buggy and $\bar{\mathsf{C}}$ is the repaired solution, or Fail if C is buggy but cannot be repaired.

```
 1:  if Verify(P, C, Q) = Fail then                                    ▷ C is buggy
 2:     VCs ← GetInvalidVCs(P, C, Q)
 3:     S ← LocalizeBuggyStmts(C, VCs)                      ▷ suspicious statements
 4:     for each stmt in S do
 5:        (C_stmt, TP_stmt, P_tp, Q_tp) ← CreateTemplatePatchedProg(C, stmt)
 6:        VCs' ← GetVCs(C_stmt, P, Q)                        ▷ collect entailments
 7:        D ← InferUnknPreds(∅, VCs')                    ▷ specification inference
 8:        if D ≠ ∅ then
 9:           (P̄_tp, Q̄_tp) ← GetPredDefn(D)
10:           V ← GetAvailableVars(C_stmt)
11:           TP̄_stmt ← SynthesizeStmts(Γ, V, P̄_tp, Q̄_tp)       ▷ deductive synthesis
12:           if TP̄_stmt ≠ Fail then
13:              C̄ ← GetCandidateProg(C_stmt, TP̄_stmt)
14:              if Verify(P, C̄, Q) = Valid then return C̄      ▷ discover a patch
15:     return Fail                                              ▷ fail to repair
16:  else return None                                             ▷ C is correct
```

Fig. 12. The algorithm Repair.

Specifically, the algorithm creates a template program $\mathsf{C_{stmt}}$ for each suspicious statement stmt (line 5): it replaces that statement with a template patch $\mathsf{TP_{stmt}}$, which is specified by a pair of unknown pre- and postcondition $\mathcal{P}_{tp}$, $\mathcal{Q}_{tp}$. Then, Repair verifies the template patched program to collect all VCs related to $\mathcal{P}_{tp}$, $\mathcal{Q}_{tp}$ (line 6). These VCs will be solved by the algorithm InferUnknPreds (described in Sect. 4.2) to infer the actual definition of $\mathcal{P}_{tp}$, $\mathcal{Q}_{tp}$ (line 7). If this specification inference succeeds (lines 8, 9), the inferred pre- and postcondition

$\overline{\mathcal{P}}_{\mathtt{tp}}$, $\overline{\mathcal{Q}}_{\mathtt{tp}}$ will be used to synthesize program statements of the template patch (line 13), using the algorithm SynthesizeStmts as explained in Sect. 5.2. When SynthesizeStmts can synthesize a list of program statements, our algorithm Repair will replace the template patch $\mathtt{TP}_{\mathtt{stmt}}$ with synthesized statements to create a candidate program $\overline{\mathtt{C}}$ (line 13). If $\overline{\mathtt{C}}$ can be validated by the procedure Verify, it will be returned as the repaired program (line 14). Otherwise, the algorithm Repair returns Fail if it is unable to fix the input buggy program (line 15). It also returns None if the input program C is correct w.r.t. its specifications (line 16).

We claim that our program repair algorithm in Fig. 12 is sound. We formally state that soundness in the following Theorem 1.

Theorem 1 (Soundness). *Given a program* C, *a precondition* $\mathcal{P}$, *and a postcondition* $\mathcal{Q}$, *if the Hoare triple* $\{\mathcal{P}\}$ C $\{\mathcal{Q}\}$ *does not hold, and the algorithm* Repair *returns a program* $\overline{\mathtt{C}}$, *then the Hoare triple* $\{\mathcal{P}\}$ $\overline{\mathtt{C}}$ $\{\mathcal{Q}\}$ *holds.*

Proof. In our repair algorithm Repair (Fig. 12), an input program C is buggy when $\mathsf{Verify}(\mathcal{P}, \mathtt{C}, \mathcal{Q}) = \mathsf{Fail}$ or the Hoare triple $\{\mathcal{P}\}$ C $\{\mathcal{Q}\}$ does not hold. Then, if a candidate program $\overline{\mathtt{C}}$ is produced (line 13), the algorithm Repair always verifies program $\overline{\mathtt{C}}$ w.r.t. the precondition $\mathcal{P}$ and the postcondition $\mathcal{Q}$ before returning $\overline{\mathtt{C}}$ (line 14). Hence, if $\{\mathcal{P}\}$ C $\{\mathcal{Q}\}$ does not hold and the algorithm Repair returns a program $\overline{\mathtt{C}}$, the Hoare triple $\{\mathcal{P}\}$ $\overline{\mathtt{C}}$ $\{\mathcal{Q}\}$ holds. $\qquad\square$

7   Evaluation

We implemented our prototype tool, called NEM, on top of the HIP/SLEEK verification framework [6,7,38]. The specification inference in Sect. 4 was implemented on top of the Songbird prover [47,48]. Because our approach currently does not synthesize conditional statements, we apply mutation operators, e.g., changing from `x->next != NULL` to `x->prev != NULL`, to repair buggy conditional expressions of the conditional statements. We conducted experiments on a computer with CPU Intel® Core™ i7-6700 (3.4 GHz), 8 GB RAM, and Ubuntu 16.04 LTS. The details of our tool NEM and experiments are available online at https://nem-repair-tool.github.io/.

To evaluate our repair approach, we first selected a list of heap-manipulating programs written in a C-like language that was formally defined in [7]. These programs include algorithms of various data structures, such as singly-linked list (sll), doubly-linked list (dll), sorted linked list (srtll), binary tree (tree), binary search tree (bst), and AVL tree (avl). They include popular algorithms like *insert*, *append*, *delete*, *copy* for linked-lists. Some of these programs are taken from the benchmark used in [50] that are annotated accordingly. Note that our programs are tail-recursive while these in [50] use *while* loops.

Table 1. Evaluation of NEM and a mutation-based tool [28] on repairing buggy heap-manipulating programs. Programs denoted with * are from [50].

Program	#LoC	#Buggy	NEM		Mutation-based tool [28]	
			#Repaired	Avg.time (s)	#Repaired	Avg.time (s)
sll-length	12	11	**11**	3.31	0	–
sll-copy	13	9	**9**	5.4	0	–
sll-append	11	18	**18**	5.84	1	2.13
sll-insert*	11	11	**11**	4.86	1	2.1
sll-delete*	13	17	**17**	5.32	0	–
dll-length	12	12	**12**	3.7	0	–
dll-append	16	20	**16**	10.12	1	5.36
dll-insert	12	11	**11**	4.58	1	2.11
dll-delete	20	20	**20**	15.72	0	–
srtll-insert*	19	20	**20**	18.35	2	6.13
tree-size	13	16	**16**	9.46	0	–
tree-height	16	20	**20**	13.67	0	–
avl-size	17	16	**16**	32.63	0	–
bst-size	13	16	**16**	11.46	0	–
bst-height	16	14	**10**	40.54	0	–
Summary		231	**223**	12.59	6	3.99

To demonstrate the effectiveness of our method, we compared our tool with a state-of-the-art repair tool [28]. This tool uses genetic programming operators, e.g., *mutate, delete, insert*, to generate candidate programs, and then verifies these programs using a verifier. Both program repair tools verify and repair programs according to their provided specifications. Moreover, these two tools also use the HIP/SLEEK verifier to verify input programs and validate candidate programs. Each tool is configured to repair a buggy program within a timeout of 300 s. Regarding our tool NEM, we set both the timeouts of specification inference (Sect. 4) and deductive synthesis (Sect. 5) to 20 s. Besides, we did not include the semi-automated program repair tool Wolverine [50] since we could not obtain the implementation.

We followed a previous approach [50] in building a bug injection tool. This tool modifies program statements of a verified program to introduce errors at various program locations. Our tool modifies directly on the input program and generates readable buggy versions that are close to the input program. In contrast, the bug injection tool in Wolverine creates bugs in the intermediate representation code, consequently not enabling users to compare the buggy versions with the original correct program. Our bug injection tool currently modifies *one* statement or *two* statements in different branches of conditional statements. We also limit the maximum buggy versions of each program to 20.

Table 1 shows the results of running our prototype NEM and the mutation-based tool on the chosen benchmark. For each program, # LoC is the number of lines of code while # Buggy is the number of buggy versions created by the bug injection tool. Regarding the last 4 columns, we compared two evaluated tools in the number of buggy versions repaired, and the average time one tool needs to fix a buggy version. The results show that our tool outperforms the mutation-based one in the number of buggy programs repaired. Concretely, NEM was able to repair 223 buggy versions out of a total of 231 cases while the mutation-based tool only generated 6 correct patches. It is also noteworthy that NEM could handle buggy cases in all 15 programs. On the other hand, the mutation-based tool only gave correct patches for 5/15 programs. This is because our approach synthesizes patch candidates based on constraints collected from program semantics. Meanwhile, the mutation-based approach only uses a list of genetic programming operators, such as *mutate, delete, insert*, which limits the pattern of candidate patches.

Regarding the running time, our tool NEM needed 12.59 s on average to generate one correct patch while the mutation-based approach requires 3.99 s on average. This is because our approach of using specification inference and deductive synthesis is more expensive than mutation operators. However, it is much more effective when it can repair substantially more buggy programs.

There are 8 buggy versions of the 2 programs dll-append and bst-height that NEM could not repair. This is because the constraints collected when repairing these programs are highly complicated that they could not be solved by the current proof search heuristics of our constraint solver. This is a limitation of our work and we aim to resolve it in the future.

8   Related Work

Similar to our approach, a mutation-based approach [28] also aims to enhance APR with deductive verification. Technically, this method requires an iteration of (*i*) generating a patch by employing code mutation operators via GenProg [53] and (*ii*) verifying the patched program via HIP/SLEEK [7]. In contrast, we use specification inference and deductive synthesis to generate program statements of a patch. Hence, our approach is more effective than the mutation-based approach [28] in repairing buggy heap-manipulating programs as shown in Sect. 7.

The initial approaches that repair buggy heap-manipulating programs [11,12] rely on first-order logic formulae for specifications. However, these approaches are limited to detecting and fixing violations of user-provided data structure invariants. Meanwhile, our approach handles a broader class of errors, manifested as violations of specifications for arbitrary programs. The work [13] uses an input program and its specifications to generate constraints, which are then solved using the Alloy solver [20]. The obtained solutions are then translated into a repaired program. However, the repair procedure in [13] is restricted to a specific number of templates. In contrast, our approach uses a fully-fledged deductive synthesis framework, thus, allowing for fixing a larger class of bugs.

Recently, the tool FootPatch [49] relies on the Infer analysis tool [2,3] to detect errors and emit fixes for them. While also grounded in separation logic, this approach is less general than ours, as it only considers a fixed number of classes of bugs. However, it is more scalable thanks to the ability of Infer to detect unsafe memory accesses in large codebases without any user input. Likewise, Logozzo and Ball [31] use abstract interpretation [9] as a way to detect and fix mistakes in programs, but only for a limited number of issues that are captured by the employed analyzer. Similar to our approach, Maple [39] uses program specifications to detect bugs and validate candidate patches in numerical programs.

Our idea of generating correct-by-construction patches is similar to synthesizing programs from Hoare-style specifications [8,40,42]. However, it is applied in the context of program repair where the minimum number of statements is synthesized, leading to patches that are close to the original programs. Similar to our approach, deductive program repair [22] fixes buggy *functional* programs using the specifications from both symbolically executed tests and pre/postconditions and verifying the resulting program using the Leon tool [23].

Traditional APR approaches rely on *test suites* in checking the correctness of programs. Two main approaches of test-based APR are heuristic repair and constraint-based repair [30]. The *heuristic repair* identifies the bugs and the patches in the programs employing the insights that similar code patterns might be observed in sufficiently large codebases [16,43] while the *constraint-based* repair uses the provided test suite to infer symbolic constraints, and then solves those constraints to generate a patch [32,35–37,54]. Test-based APR approaches have been previously applied for fixing bugs in programs with pointers. For instance, a recent approach [50] involves a programmer in the debug-repair process to define correct program states at run-time. In contrast, our approach repairs buggy programs without the involvement of programmers.

9   Limitation and Future Work

We now discuss the limitations of our current approach and our plans to address them. Firstly, our approach mainly focuses on fixing program statements. Consequently, it may remove correct expressions, e.g., the left-hand side of an assignment or a parameter of a function call. This is because it aims to ease the bug localization step in limiting the number of suspicious statements as the number of suspicious expressions would be considerably larger than that of suspicious statements. In the future, we plan to add expression-level program repair by expressing correct expressions as *holes* in program sketc.hes as in ImpSynt [42]. This method could also enhance our approach in repairing multiple locations as our approach currently only repairs *one* buggy statement or *two* buggy statements in different branches of a conditional statement.

Secondly, our approach does not handle omission errors. The debug-and-repair approach [50] can repair these cases by adding program states at various program points. Likewise, we can improve the capabilities of our repair method by inserting template patches at various program locations, and then synthesizing program statements of these patches. Thirdly, our approach could not repair buggy programs using the structure *list segment* in their specifications, e.g., the program schedule3 in the benchmark of [28]. Our early inspections indicate that these cases need *lemmas* in synthesizing program statements. Therefore, we aim to incorporate *lemma synthesis*, e.g., [48], to our repair framework. Fourthly, the buggy programs in our benchmark (Sect. 7) are produced using a bug injection tool. Therefore, we plan to evaluate our approach on student submissions in programming courses, similar to previous approaches [14,18,45,51].

Furthermore, we aim to ease the requirement of providing program specifications from users. To do that, we could either leverage static analyzers that do not require program specifications, e.g., Infer [2,3], or incorporate specification inference techniques, such as [24,27], to automatically infer program specifications. Finally, as discussed in Sect. 7, we plan to improve our constraint-solving technique to handle buggy programs that our approach currently fails to repair.

10 Conclusion

We have proposed a novel approach to fix buggy heap-manipulating programs. If a program is found buggy, we first encode program statements to fix this program in a template patch. Then, the specifications of the template patch are inferred using a constraint solving technique. Finally, from the inferred specifications, we use deductive synthesis to synthesize program statements of the template patch. The experimental results showed that our approach substantially outperformed a mutation-based approach in repairing buggy heap-manipulating programs.

Acknowledgments. This research is supported by the Singapore NRF grant R-252-007-A50-281, the National Research Foundation, Singapore under its Emerging Areas Research Projects (EARP) Funding Initiative, the Singapore NRF National Satellite of Excellence in Trustworthy Software Systems (NSoE-TSS) and Crystal Centre at NUS School of Computing. Any opinions, findings and conclusions or recommendations expressed in this material are those of the author(s) and do not reflect the views of National Research Foundation, Singapore. We are grateful to the anonymous reviewers for their valuable and detailed comments. The first author would like to thank Cristina David for encouraging discussions, and Xuan-Bach D. Le for sharing the implementation of their tool.

References

1. Brotherston, J., Simpson, A.: Sequent calculi for induction and infinite descent. J. Logic Comput. **21**(6), 1177–1216 (2011)
2. Calcagno, C., Distefano, D.: Infer: an automatic program verifier for memory safety of C programs. In: NASA International Symposium on Formal Methods (NFM), pp. 459–465 (2011)

3. Calcagno, C.: Moving fast with software verification. In: NASA International Symposium on Formal Methods (NFM), pp. 3–11 (2015)
4. Calcagno, C., Distefano, D., O'Hearn, P.W., Yang, H.: Compositional shape analysis by means of bi-abduction. J. ACM **58**(6), 26:1–26:66 (2011)
5. Charguéraud, A.: Separation logic for sequential programs (functional pearl). In: International Conference on Functional Programming (ICFP), pp. 116:1–116:34 (2020)
6. Chin, W.N., David, C., Nguyen, H.H., Qin, S.: Enhancing modular OO verification with separation logic. In: Symposium on Principles of Programming Languages (POPL), pp. 87–99 (2008)
7. Chin, W.N., David, C., Nguyen, H.H., Qin, S.: Automated verification of shape, size and bag properties via user-defined predicates in Separation Logic. Sci. Comput. Program. (SCP) **77**(9), 1006–1036 (2012)
8. Costea, A., Zhu, A., Polikarpova, N., Sergey, I.: Concise read-only specifications for better synthesis of programs with pointers. In: European Symposium on Programming (ESOP), pp. 141–168 (2020)
9. Cousot, P., Cousot, R.: Abstract interpretation: a unified lattice model for static analysis of programs by construction or approximation of fixpoints. In: Symposium on Principles of Programming Languages (POPL), pp. 238–252 (1977)
10. de Moura, L.M., Bjørner, N.: Z3: an efficient SMT solver. In: International Conference on Tools and Algorithms for Construction and Analysis of Systems (TACAS), pp. 337–340 (2008)
11. Demsky, B., Rinard, M.C.: Automatic detection and repair of errors in data structures. In: International Conference on Object Oriented Programming Systems Languages & Applications (OOPSLA), pp. 78–95 (2003)
12. Demsky, B., Rinard, M.C.: Data structure repair using goal-directed reasoning. In: International Conference on Software Engineering (ICSE), pp. 176–185 (2005)
13. Gopinath, D., Malik, M.Z., Khurshid, S.: Specification-based program repair using SAT. In: International Conference on Tools and Algorithms for Construction and Analysis of Systems (TACAS), pp. 173–188 (2011)
14. Gulwani, S., Radiček, I., Zuleger, F.: Automated clustering and program repair for introductory programming assignments. In Conference on Programming Language Design and Implementation (PLDI), pp. 465–480 (2018)
15. Gupta, R., Pal, S., Kanade, A., Shevade, S.: Deepfix: fixing common C language errors by deep learning. In: AAAI Conference on Artificial Intelligence (AAAI), pp. 1345–1351 (2017)
16. Harman, M.: Automated patching techniques: the fix is in: technical perspective. Tech. Perspect. Commun. ACM **53**(5), 108 (2010)
17. Hong, S., Lee, J., Lee, J., Oh, H.: Saver: scalable, precise, and safe memory-error repair. In: International Conference on Software Engineering (ICSE) (2020)
18. Hu, Y., Ahmed, U.Z., Mechtaev, S., Leong, B., Roychoudhury, A.: Re-factoring based program repair applied to programming assignments. In: International Conference on Automated Software Engineering (ASE), pp. 388–398 (2019)
19. Ishtiaq, S.S., O'Hearn, P.W.: BI as an assertion language for mutable data structures. In: Symposium on Principles of Programming Languages (POPL), pp. 14–26 (2001)
20. Jackson, D., Vaziri, M.: Finding bugs with a constraint solver. In: International Symposium on Software Testing and Analysis (ISSTA), pp. 14–25 (2000)
21. Kim, D., Nam, J., Song, J., Kim, S.: Automatic patch generation learned from human-written patches. In: International Conference on Software Engineering (ICSE), pp. 802–811 (2013)

22. Kneuss, E., Koukoutos, M., Kuncak, V.: Deductive program repair. In: Kroening, D., Păsăreanu, C.S. (eds.) CAV 2015. LNCS, vol. 9207, pp. 217–233. Springer, Cham (2015). https://doi.org/10.1007/978-3-319-21668-3_13

23. Kneuss, E., Kuraj, I., Kuncak, V., Suter, P.: Synthesis modulo recursive functions. In: International Conference on Object Oriented Programming Systems Languages & Applications (OOPSLA), pp. 407–426 (2013)

24. Le, Q.L., Gherghina, C., Qin, S., Chin, W.-N.: Shape analysis via second-order bi-abduction. In: Biere, A., Bloem, R. (eds.) CAV 2014. LNCS, vol. 8559, pp. 52–68. Springer, Cham (2014). https://doi.org/10.1007/978-3-319-08867-9_4

25. Le, T.C., Gherghina, C., Hobor, A., Chin, W.N.: A resource-based logic for termination and non-termination proofs. In: International Conference on Formal Engineering Methods (ICFEM), pp. 267–283 (2014)

26. Le, T.C., Qin, S., Chin, W.N.: Termination and non-termination specification inference. In: Conference on Programming Language Design and Implementation (PLDI), pp. 489–498 (2015)

27. Le, T.C., Zheng, G., Nguyen, T.: SLING: using dynamic analysis to infer program invariants in separation logic. In: Conference on Programming Language Design and Implementation (PLDI), pp. 788–801 (2019)

28. Le, X.B.D., Le, Q.L., Lo, D., Le Goues, C.: Enhancing automated program repair with deductive verification. In: IEEE International Conference on Software Maintenance and Evolution (ICSME) (2016)

29. Le Goues, C., Nguyen, T.V., Forrest, S., Weimer, W.: Genprog: a generic method for automatic software repair. IEEE Trans. Softw. Eng. (TSE) **38**(1), 54–72 (2012)

30. Goues, C.L., Pradel, M., Roychoudhury, A.: Automated program repair. Commun. ACM **62**(12), 56–65 (2019)

31. Logozzo, F., Ball, T.: Modular and verified automatic program repair. In: International Conference on Object Oriented Programming Systems Languages & Applications (OOPSLA), pp. 133–146 (2012)

32. Long, F., Rinard, M.: Staged program repair with condition synthesis. In: Joint European Software Engineering Conference and Symposium on the Foundations of Software Engineering (ESEC/FSE), pp. 166–178 (2015)

33. Long, F., Rinard, M.: Automatic patch generation by learning correct code. In: Symposium on Principles of Programming Languages (POPL), pp. 298–312 (2016)

34. Mechtaev, S., Nguyen, M.D., Noller, Y., Grunske, L., Roychoudhury, A.: Semantic program repair using a reference implementation. In: International Conference on Software Engineering (ICSE), pp. 129–139 (2018)

35. Mechtaev, S., Yi, J., Roychoudhury, A.: Directfix: looking for simple program repairs. In: International Conference on Software Engineering (ICSE), pp. 448–458 (2015)

36. Mechtaev, S., Yi, J., Roychoudhury, A.: Angelix: scalable multiline program patch synthesis via symbolic analysis. In: International Conference on Software Engineering (ICSE), pp. 691–701 (2016)

37. Nguyen, H.D.T., Qi, D., Roychoudhury, A., Chandra, S.: Semfix: program repair via semantic analysis. In: International Conference on Software Engineering (ICSE), pp. 772–781 (2013)

38. Nguyen, H.H., Chin, W.-N.: Enhancing program verification with lemmas. In: International Conference on Computer Aided Verification (CAV), pp. 355–369 (2008)

39. Nguyen, T.-T., Ta, Q.-T., Chin, W.-N.: Automatic program repair using formal verification and expression templates. In: Enea, C., Piskac, R. (eds.) VMCAI 2019. LNCS, vol. 11388, pp. 70–91. Springer, Cham (2019). https://doi.org/10.1007/978-3-030-11245-5_4

40. Polikarpova, N., Sergey, I.: Structuring the synthesis of heap-manipulating programs. In: Symposium on Principles of Programming Languages (POPL), pp. 72:1–72:30 (2019)

41. Qi, Y., Mao, X., Lei, Y., Dai, Z., Wang, C.: The strength of random search on automated program repair. In: International Conference on Software Engineering (ICSE), pp. 254–265 (2014)

42. Qiu, X., Solar-Lezama, A.: Natural synthesis of provably-correct data-structure manipulations. In: International Conference on Object Oriented Programming Systems Languages & Applications (OOPSLA), pp. 65:1–65:28 (2017)

43. Ray, B., Hellendoorn, V., Godhane, S., Tu, Z., Bacchelli, A., Devanbu, P.: On the "naturalness" of buggy code. In: International Conference on Software Engineering (ICSE), pp. 428–439 (2016)

44. Reynolds, J.C.: Separation logic: a logic for shared mutable data structures. In: Symposium on Logic in Computer Science (LICS), pp. 55–74 (2002)

45. Sakkas, G., Endres, M., Cosman, B., Weimer, W., Jhala, R.: Type error feedback via analytic program repair. In: Conference on Programming Language Design and Implementation (PLDI), pp. 16–30 (2020)

46. Sidiroglou-Douskos, S., Lahtinen, E., Long, F., Rinard, M.: Automatic error elimination by horizontal code transfer across multiple applications. In: Conference on Programming Language Design and Implementation (PLDI), pp. 43–54 (2015)

47. Ta, Q.-T., Le, T.C., Khoo, S.-C., Chin, W.-N.: Automated mutual explicit induction proof in separation logic. In: International Symposium on Formal Methods (FM), pp. 659–676 (2016)

48. Ta, Q.-T., Le, T.C., Khoo, S.-C., Chin, W.-N.: Automated lemma synthesis in symbolic-heap separation logic. In: Symposium on Principles of Programming Languages (POPL), pp. 9:1–9:29 (2018)

49. van Tonder, R., Le Goues, C.: Static automated program repair for heap properties. In: International Conference on Software Engineering (ICSE), pp. 151–162 (2018)

50. Verma, S., Roy, S.: Synergistic debug-repair of heap manipulations. In: Joint European Software Engineering Conference and Symposium on the Foundations of Software Engineering (ESEC/FSE), pp. 163–173 (2017)

51. Wang, K., Singh, R., Su, Z.: Search, align, and repair: data-driven feedback generation for introductory programming exercises. In: Conference on Programming Language Design and Implementation (PLDI), pp. 481–495 (2018)

52. Weimer, W., Fry, Z.P., Forrest, S.: Leveraging program equivalence for adaptive program repair: Models and first results. In: International Conference on Automated Software Engineering (ASE), pp. 356–366 (2013)

53. Weimer, W., Nguyen, T., Le Goues, C., Forrest, S.: Automatically finding patches using genetic programming. In: International Conference on Software Engineering (ICSE), pp. 364–374 (2009)

54. Xuan, J., et al.: Nopol: atomic repair of conditional statement bugs in Java programs. IEEE Trans. Softw. Eng. (TSE) 43(1), 34–55 (2017)

GPURepair: Automated Repair of GPU Kernels

Saurabh Joshi and Gautam Muduganti$^{(\boxtimes)}$

Indian Institute of Technology Hyderabad,
Hyderabad, India
{sbjoshi,cs17resch01003}@iith.ac.in

Abstract. This paper presents a tool for repairing errors in GPU kernels written in CUDA or OpenCL due to data races and barrier divergence. Our novel extension to prior work can also remove barriers that are deemed unnecessary for correctness. We implement these ideas in our tool called GPURepair, which uses GPUVerify as the verification oracle for GPU kernels. We also extend GPUVerify to support CUDA Cooperative Groups, allowing GPURepair to perform inter-block synchronization for CUDA kernels. To the best of our knowledge, GPURepair is the only tool that can propose a fix for intra-block data races and barrier divergence errors for both CUDA and OpenCL kernels and the only tool that fixes inter-block data races for CUDA kernels. We perform extensive experiments on about 750 kernels and provide a comparison with prior work. We demonstrate the superiority of GPURepair through its capability to fix more kernels and its unique ability to remove redundant barriers and handle inter-block data races.

Keywords: GPU · Verification · Automated repair · CUDA · OpenCL

1 Introduction

The part of the program that runs on the GPU (Graphics Processing Unit) is referred to as a *kernel*. Given that multiple cores of the GPU may execute the kernel in parallel, data races and barrier divergence are frequently the cause of several errors that occur in practice. Identifying and repairing these errors early in the development cycle can have a tremendous positive financial impact [14].

In CUDA, a grid consists of blocks, and a block consists of threads. Consider the CUDA kernel in Listing 1.1 without the highlighted line. There is a data race on accesses of the shared array A. The race can be avoided by introducing

---

The author names are in alphabetical order.

© Springer Nature Switzerland AG 2021
F. Henglein et al. (Eds.): VMCAI 2021, LNCS 12597, pp. 401–414, 2021.
https://doi.org/10.1007/978-3-030-67067-2_18

a barrier (__syncthreads()) in the kernel at line 3 in Listing 1.1. This block-level barrier enforces that all threads in a block reach it before any of them can proceed further. A grid-level barrier behaves similarly for the entire grid.

In Listing 1.2, only the threads with an even thread id will reach the barrier. As the threads within a block execute in a *lock-step* manner, this will result in a deadlock as threads with odd ids will never be able to reach the barrier at Line 4. This problem is known as *barrier divergence*.

```
1  __global__ void race (int* A) {
2    int temp = A[threadIdx.x+1];
3    __syncthreads();
4    A[threadIdx.x] = temp;
5  }
```

Listing 1.1. Kernel with Data Race

```
1  __global__ void race (int* A) {
2    if (threadIdx.x % 2 == 0) {
3      int temp = A[threadIdx.x+1];
4      __syncthreads();
5      A[threadIdx.x] = temp;
6    }
7  }
```

Listing 1.2. Kernel with Barrier Divergence

This tool paper makes the following contributions:

- We extend the underlying technique behind AutoSync [9] to provide barrier placements that avoid barrier divergence in addition to data races. Our novel extension may also suggest removing barriers inserted by the programmer if deemed unnecessary, which might help enhance the performance of the input GPU kernel.
- We implement our technique in our tool GPURepair, which is built on top of the GPUVerify [11] framework and uses GPUVerify as an oracle. To the best of our knowledge, ours is the only technique and tool that can propose a fix for both CUDA and OpenCL GPU kernels. Another unique feature of GPURepair is its ability to fix kernels that have inter-block data races.
- Bugle is the component of the GPUVerify toolchain that translates LLVM bitcode to Boogie. We have enhanced it with the ability to translate barrier synchronization statements from the CUDA Cooperative Groups API to Boogie. We have also extended GPUVerify with the semantics to support grid-level barriers. Using these enhancements, GPURepair proposes fixes for inter-block data races.
- We perform an extensive experimental evaluation on 748 GPU kernels written in CUDA and OpenCL. We compare GPURepair against AutoSync, which is the only other tool known that attempts to repair CUDA kernels containing data races.

2   GPURepair

2.1   GPURepair Architecture and Workflow

The implementation of GPURepair builds on top of GPUVerify, as depicted in Fig. 1. In addition to the instrumentation done by GPUVerify to enable verification of GPU kernels, GPURepair adds the instrumentation necessary to impose constraints on the program behavior. On each iteration, GPURepair calls GPUVerify with a proposed solution to check if the program is repaired. If the program

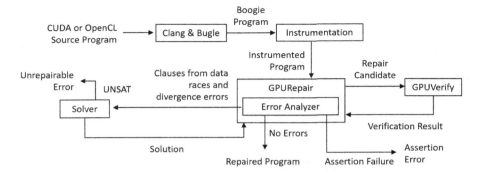

Fig. 1. GPURepair workflow

is not repaired, it calls the *Solver* with the constraints generated from the errors seen so far to obtain a candidate solution suggesting which barriers need to be enabled/disabled in the program. If the program can be repaired, GPURepair generates the Boogie representation of the fixed program and a summary file. The summary file contains the changes that have to be made to fix the program along with the source location details of the original CUDA/OpenCL input kernel. The technique behind GPURepair can, in principle, use any verifier for GPU programs as an oracle.

2.2 Instrumentation

GPUVerify uses a pair of distinct non-deterministically chosen threads for analysis instead of modeling all the threads in the kernel. This two-thread abstraction is used to prove that a kernel is race-free and divergence-free. Details of this abstraction are available in [11] and beyond the scope of this paper. GPUVerify models barriers by resetting read/write flags of shared arrays for the two threads used by the two-thread abstraction if they belong to the same block. We extend this to support grid-level barriers for the repair of inter-block data races. A grid-level barrier is modeled by performing a reset even when the two threads do not belong to the same block.

Since GPURepair attempts to fix errors caused only due to data races or barrier divergence, it proposes a solution that only involves removing existing barriers or adding new ones. Therefore, the instrumentation stage of GPURepair introduces barriers guarded with Boolean variables, referred to as *barrier variables*. The value of a barrier variable acts as a switch to enable or disable the barrier. A barrier guarded by a barrier variable is referred to as an *instrumented barrier*. Consider the kernel in Listing 1.3 without the highlighted lines. This kernel has a data race. The instrumentation process adds an instrumented barrier before a shared variable is either read or written. Function calls involving a shared variable are also taken into consideration, and an instrumented barrier is added before the invocation. Pre-existing barriers in the programs are also guarded with barrier variables to explore if they can be removed without introducing data races.

In addition, the control flow graph (CFG) is analyzed for branch statements and loops to handle scenarios where barriers, if inserted right before the read/write to a shared variable, may introduce barrier divergence. For example, in Listing 1.3, the instrumentation process mentioned above would insert the instrumented barriers right before Line 11 and Line 18. However, the solution to this program would be a barrier before the `if` block at Line 15. The instrumentation process takes these scenarios under consideration by inserting instrumented barriers at the scope boundaries such as entry points of branch statements, loop-heads, and function calls. After instrumentation, the highlighted lines at Lines 9, 13, and 16 in Listing 1.3 are added. For CUDA kernels, if instrumentation of grid-level barriers is enabled, the highlighted lines at Lines 10, 14, and 17 are also added.

Algorithm 1. The Repair Algorithm

1: Input: Instrumented Program P
2: Output: Repaired Program P_φ
3: $\varphi := true$
4: **loop**
5:     $\langle res, sol \rangle := Solve(\varphi)$
6:     **if** $res = UNSAT$ **then**
7:         print Error: Program cannot be repaired
8:         **return** errorcode
9:     **end if**
10:     $\langle result, \pi \rangle := Verify(P_{sol})$
11:     **if** $result = SAFE$ **then**
12:         break
13:     **end if**
14:     **if** $result \neq RACE$ && $result \neq DIVERGENCE$ **then**
15:         print Error: Program cannot be repaired
16:         **return** errorcode
17:     **end if**
18:     $c := GenerateClause(\pi)$
19:     $\varphi := \varphi \cup \{c\}$
20: **end loop**
21: **return** P_{sol}

```
1   bool b1, b2, b3, b4, b5, b6;
2   __device__ void write(int* A, int
        idx) {
3       A[idx] = 50;
4   }
5
6   __global__ void race(int* A) {
7       auto g = this_grid();
8
9       if(b1) { __syncthreads(); }
10      if(b4) { g.sync(); }
11      int temp = A[threadIdx.x+1];
12
13      if(b2) { __syncthreads(); }
14      if(b5) { g.sync(); }
15      if (temp < 50) {
16          if(b3) { __syncthreads(); }
17          if(b6) { g.sync(); }
18          write(A, threadIdx.x);
19      }
20  }
```

Listing 1.3. Example CUDA Kernel

In this example, variables `b1`, . . . , `b6` are initially unconstrained. Their values are constrained by GPURepair iteratively to avoid data races or barrier divergence during the repair process. The repair process also assigns weights to these barrier variables such that introducing barriers at the block-level is preferred over the grid-level. This is done because grid-level barriers have a higher performance penalty [32]. For the same reason, barriers nested within loops are less preferred. Although the examples in this section are in CUDA, it should be noted that the actual working of this stage happens on the Boogie program generated by Bugle to make GPURepair agnostic to the front-end language (i.e., CUDA or OpenCL).

2.3   Preliminaries

Let P be the given input GPU kernel after instrumentation, as described in Sect. 2.2. Let $\{b_1, \ldots, b_m\}$ be the barrier variables introduced as a part of the instrumentation process. Given a formula φ over b_i's, let P_φ denote the instrumented kernel P with values of b_i's constrained to obey φ.

A clause c is called a *positive* (resp. *negative*) *monotone clause* if it has literals with only positive (resp. negative) polarity (e.g., $b_1 \vee b_5 \vee b_{11}$). From now on, we may also denote a clause as a set of literals with disjunctions among the set elements being implicit. A formula or a constraint φ is a set of clauses with conjunction being implicit among the set elements. Note that a formula φ consisting of only positive monotone clauses or only negative monotone clauses is always satisfiable. Let φ^+ (resp. φ^-) denote the set of positive (resp. negative) monotone clauses belonging to φ.

Let C be a set consisting of non-empty sets $S_1, \ldots, S_n$. The set $\mathcal{H}$ is called a *hitting-set* (HS) of C if:

$$\forall_{S_i \in C} \mathcal{H} \cap S_i \neq \emptyset$$

$\mathcal{H}$ is called a *minimal-hitting-set* (*mhs*) if any proper subset of $\mathcal{H}$ is not a hitting-set. $\mathcal{H}$ is called a *Minimum-Hitting-Set* (*MHS*) of C if no smaller hitting set exists for C. Note that a collection C may have multiple *mhs* and multiple *MHS*.

Since we also consider a formula φ as a set of clauses, we shall abuse the notation and use $mhs(\varphi^+)$ to denote the set of literals that constitutes the minimal-hitting-set of φ^+.

Maximum satisfiability (*MaxSAT*) is an optimization version of the *SAT* problem where the goal is to find an assignment that maximizes the number of clauses that are satisfied in a formula. In partial *MaxSAT* (PMS), given a set of hard clauses (φ_h) and a set of soft clauses (φ_s), the goal is to find an assignment that satisfies all the clauses of φ_h while maximizing the number of soft clauses being satisfied. The weighted partial *MaxSAT* (WPMS) problem asks to satisfy all the hard clauses while maximizing the sum of the weights of the satisfied soft clauses. In WPMS, positive weights are associated with each soft clause.

2.4   The Repair Algorithm

Algorithm 1 depicts the repair technique behind GPURepair at a high level. It is very similar to the algorithm presented in AutoSync [9].

Initially, all the barrier variables are unconstrained (Line 3), giving the verifier the freedom to set them to any value that leads to an error. Then, Algorithm 1 iteratively calls the verifier (Line 4–20) until it either finds a solution or determines that it cannot repair the program. A call to the verifier (Line 10) returns an error trace π along with the type of the error being captured in *result*. If the verifier could not find an error (Line 11) with the proposed solution *sol*, then the algorithm exits the loop, and the instrumented Boogie program constrained with *sol* is returned (Line 21). If the verifier returned with an error that is neither a data race nor a barrier divergence (Line 14), then Algorithm 1 terminates with an error stating that it cannot repair the program. Here, we are operating under the assumption that inserting an extraneous barrier may only introduce a barrier divergence error, and removing a programmer-inserted barrier may only cause a data race error.

If the verifier returns with a data race error, then the error trace π would tell us which set of barriers were disabled (i.e., the corresponding barrier variables were set to *false* by the verifier). Let the set of barrier variables that were set to *false* in π be $b_{i_1}, \ldots, b_{i_d}$. To avoid the same error trace π we need to add a constraint represented as a clause c, $(b_{i_1} \vee, \ldots, \vee b_{i_d})$, which is generated by $GenerateClause(\pi)$ (Line 18). Note that such a clause generated from a data race (respectively barrier divergence) error always has only positive (resp. negative) literals. This newly generated clause is added to the constraint φ (Line 19), which consists of one clause per error trace. We need to check if φ is satisfiable (Line 5). If it is not satisfiable (Line 6), it indicates that there is no assignment to barrier variables that avoids all previously seen traces. Algorithm 1 quits with an error (Line 7) in this case. If φ is satisfiable, then the *Solve* method proposes a solution *sol* (Line 5), which is essentially an assignment to some of the barrier variables. We use two different ways to compute *sol* from φ. The first method (the *MaxSAT* strategy) uses a *MaxSAT* solver to minimize the number of barrier variables being set to *true* in *sol* at each iteration. This is done by solving a partial *MaxSAT* problem with φ as hard clauses and $\{\neg b_1, \ldots, \neg b_m\}$ as soft clauses. The second method (the *mhs* strategy) is to compute a minimal-hitting-set (mhs) over φ^+ using a polynomial-time greedy algorithm [21] at each iteration to attempt to minimize the number of b_i's being set to *true*. In this strategy, a single query to a *MaxSAT* solver is needed to ensure that the number of b_i's being set to *true* is the minimum.

A similar approach has been used previously in other works [7,22,23]. It should be noted that the clauses generated in these works are all positive monotone clauses (clauses with only positive literals). In contrast, the clauses generated by Algorithm 1 could be a mix of positive monotone clauses and negative monotone clauses. Because of this added complication, the approach of using the *mhs* is not complete. There could be a scenario where the *mhs* could come up with a solution that causes the negative monotone clauses to be unsatisfiable. Consider an example with the following clauses: { $b1 \vee b3$, $b1 \vee b4$, $b2 \vee b5$, $b2 \vee b6$, $\neg b1 \vee \neg b2$ }. The $mhs(\varphi^+)$ would give us $b1$ and $b2$, which would cause the clause $\neg b1 \vee \neg b2$ to be unsatisfiable. To overcome this, GPURepair falls back to the *MaxSAT* solver whenever the *mhs* approach results in unsatisfiability.

A barrier inside a loop can pose a heavier performance penalty as opposed to a barrier that is not nested inside a loop. Similarly, inter-block synchronization is more expensive compared to intra-block synchronization [32]. In principle, different barrier variables can be given different weights based on loop nesting or profiling information. Then, instead of minimizing the number of barriers, one may want to have barrier placements that minimize the sum of the weights of the enabled barriers. This can easily be achieved by posing this as a weighted

mhs or a weighted partial $MaxSAT$ (WPMS) problem. The weight of a barrier is computed as $((gw * gb) + lw^{ld})$ where gw is the penalty for a grid-level barrier, gb is 0 for block-level barriers and 1 for grid-level barriers, lw is the penalty for a barrier that is inside a loop, and ld is the loop-nesting depth of the barrier.

3   Related Work

The verification of GPU programs has been an active area of research for quite a while. GPUVerify [10,11] defines an operational semantics for GPU kernels called synchronous, delayed visibility (SDV) semantics, which mimics the execution of a kernel by multiple groups of threads and uses this to identify data races and barrier divergence. ESBMC-GPU [28] extends the ESBMC model checker by generating an abstract representation of the CUDA libraries and verifies kernels by checking specific desired properties. VerCors [8,13] builds on permission-based separation logic and extends it to verify GPU programs. PUG [25] is a symbolic verifier that uses SMT solvers to identify bugs in CUDA kernels. Contrary to most of the other verifiers which use static analysis for verification, GKLEE [26] uses concolic verification to identify concrete witnesses for reported bugs.

Automatic program repair is another active area of research that ties-in quite closely with our work. There have been several research efforts in the past for repairing sequential programs [16,18,20,27] as well as concurrent programs [15,17,19,22,23,30,31]. The work done in [17,22,23,31] is very similar to the approach that we take in this paper, where the source code is instrumented, and the repair technique uses the error traces obtained from a verifier to fix the program.

To the best of our knowledge, apart from GPURepair, AutoSync [9] is the only tool that tries to repair a GPU program. AutoSync takes a CUDA program *without any barriers* and introduces barriers at appropriate locations to remove data race errors.

3.1   Comparison with AutoSync

Repair on Source Code vs. Repair on Boogie Code: AutoSync and GPURepair use different types of inputs. AutoSync uses a CUDA program as its input for the repair process, whereas GPURepair uses the Boogie program generated from Bugle. GPURepair is agnostic to the front-end language, allowing it to handle both CUDA and OpenCL. AutoSync, on the other hand, directly takes and manipulates the source code, which makes it fragile to syntactic changes and limits its capabilities to CUDA only.

Consider the kernel in Listing 1.3. When function inlining is enabled, GPU-Verify can accurately identify that Line 3 and Line 11 cause a read-write race through the function call at Line 18. It reports the line information by specifying that the lines inside the functions cause the read-write race and also explicitly specifies the lines from where these functions are invoked. AutoSync, however, does not process this information correctly and ends up with a code error. GPURepair takes these cases into account and has the ability to place the barrier precisely between the function invocations.

Barrier Placement vs. Instrumentation: AutoSync uses GPUVerify to identify the lines of code that cause the data race and tries to insert a barrier between these lines of code. In contrast, GPURepair inserts instrumented barriers at various locations in the intermediate Boogie code based on the usage of global variables and uses the trace information provided in errors to enable/disable barriers. This instrumentation gives GPURepair the ability to remove programmer-inserted barriers that are deemed unnecessary as well as repair errors caused by barrier divergence or data races that require a grid-level barrier. This feature is exclusive to GPURepair.

Consider the statement `A[idx] = A[idx + 1]`, that has a read-write race occurring in a single line of code. Because AutoSync uses the line information of the statements to identify a read/write on shared variables to insert barriers in the middle, it is unable to do so here since the line numbers will be the same. AutoSync ends up in an infinite loop in these scenarios. In contrast, GPURepair can identify such scenarios since this statement from the source file will be split into two statements, a read followed by a write, in the Boogie representation of the kernel.

Error Parsing vs. SMT Variable Analysis: AutoSync uses regular expressions for parsing the error messages generated by GPUVerify to identify the locations responsible for causing the data race. This technique makes AutoSync extremely fragile to any changes in the output of GPUVerify. For example, AutoSync reports that the program has no errors if, in the output, it does not find texts related to data race or barrier divergence errors. This causes it to misclassify programs with assertion violation errors as error-free programs. GPURepair relies on the SMT model provided by GPUVerify to determine which barriers contributed to the error. This approach makes GPURepair robust and indifferent to the textual output format of GPUVerify.

Inter-block Races: GPURepair can propose a fix for inter-block races using CUDA Cooperative Groups for CUDA kernels. No other tool is known to repair inter-block races.

4   Experiments

In this section, we present our comparison of GPURepair and AutoSync on several CUDA benchmarks. In addition, we present our findings for runs of GPURepair on OpenCL benchmarks as AutoSync cannot tackle OpenCL kernels. The source code of GPURepair is available at [2]. The artifacts and the virtual machine used to reproduce the results of this paper are available at [3] and [6], respectively.

4.1   Experimental Setup

Since GPURepair depends on GPUVerify as an oracle, the implementation of GPURepair uses the same technology stack as GPUVerify. The instrumentation and repair stages are built using the .NET Framework with C# as the programming language. As mentioned in Sect. 2.1, there are several tools involved in the pipeline of GPURepair. Specified below are the version numbers of the tools used in the experimentation. We use the Z3 solver [12,29] for determining the barrier assignments. The tools used in GPURepair with their versions are: LLVM 6.0.1, Clang 6.0.1, libclc (Revision 353912), Bugle (Revision 15df0ed), GPUVerify (Revision d5a90ec), and Z3 4.6.0.

The experiments were performed on Standard_F2s_v2 Azure® virtual machine, which has 2 vCPUs and 4 GiB of memory. More details on the virtual machine can be found at [5]. For the experiments, a total of 748 kernels (266 CUDA and 482 OpenCL) were considered. This benchmark set is a union of four independent test suites and publicly available [1] sample programs. Table 1 summarizes the various sources of the kernels. The average number of lines of code for this benchmark set is 17.51, and the median is 11. 14 kernels have more than 100 lines of code, and 47 have more than 50 lines of code.

Table 1. Benchmark Summary

Source	Kernels
GPUVerify Test Suite (Inc. 482 OpenCL Kernels) [4]	658
NVIDIA GPU Computing SDK v5.0 [1]	56
AutoSync Micro Benchmarks [9]	8
GPURepair Test Suite (Inc. 16 examples for CUDA Cooperative Groups)	26

All the experiments were performed with a timeout of 300 seconds for each benchmark for each tool. By default, the weight of a grid-level barrier (gw) is taken as 12, and the weight of a barrier inside a loop (lw) is 10. For nested loops, the loop-depth is computed, and the loop weight (lw) is raised to the power of the loop-depth.

4.2 Results

Table 2 summarizes the results obtained from running the benchmark suite with GPURepair and AutoSync. AutoSync does not support OpenCL; therefore, results for OpenCL are only applicable for GPURepair. Numbers in bold indicate better results.

The table categorizes the results into three categories based on the output of GPUVerify. The first category includes all the kernels for which GPUVerify concluded that there were no errors. For all 152 CUDA kernels that fall in this category, AutoSync crashed in 6 of these benchmarks, and even though GPUVerify did not give any errors, GPURepair suggested removal of unnecessary barriers for 13 CUDA kernels and 25 OpenCL kernels. Removal of unnecessary barriers is a feature exclusive to GPURepair. AutoSync attempts only to insert barriers so as to avoid data race errors.

Table 2. Count of kernels grouped by category

Category	AutoSync	GPURepair	
Total Benchmarks	CUDA 266	CUDA 266	OpenCL 482
Verified by GPUVerify	152	152	331
No changes made by the tool	146	138	293
Changes recommended by the tool	0	**13**	25
Errors	6	**0**	10
Timeouts (300 seconds)	0	1	3
Data Race/Barrier Divergence Errors identified by GPUVerify	89	89	69
Repaired by the tool	31	**43**	33
Repaired using grid-level barriers	0	**15**	0
Could not be repaired by the tool	10	20	34
Errors	14	**0**	0
Timeouts (300 seconds)	34	**11**	2
Unrepairable errors identified by GPUVerify	25	25	82
Handled gracefully by the tool	0	**25**	82
False Positives	24	**0**	0
Errors	1	**0**	0

The second category includes the kernels for which GPUVerify had identified data races or barrier divergence errors. For 10 benchmarks, AutoSync stated that the error could not be repaired. Out of these 10, GPURepair was able to repair 6, it timed out for 2, and it could not repair 2 of these. The final category involves the kernels that had either assertion errors or errors thrown by Clang or Bugle or had invalid invariants. Repairing these kernels is beyond the scope of either AutoSync or GPURepair. AutoSync claimed that a solution was found for 24 out of the 25 CUDA kernels in this category, but those were found to be false positives. AutoSync checks the textual error messages for any information related to data races and barrier divergence, and if it does not find anything, AutoSync treats it as a success. In contrast, GPURepair returned the same error code as GPUVerify for all the benchmarks in this category. This category highlights the fragile nature of AutoSync, as it syntactically depends on the output of GPUVerify.

It is evident that GPURepair provides much more coverage as it can handle OpenCL kernels. Even for CUDA kernels, GPURepair provides better coverage as it can repair more programs, support inter-block synchronization using CUDA Cooperative Groups, and exits gracefully for a larger number of kernels.

As described in Table 2, there were 25 benchmarks in the third category where GPUVerify itself throws an irreparable error (e.g., either an assertion violation or errors thrown by other stages). We provide a time comparison in the form of a

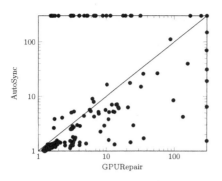

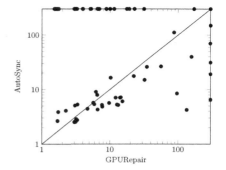

Fig. 2. Runtime in seconds (Log Scale)

Fig. 3. Runtime in seconds - repair candidates (Log Scale)

scatter plot shown in Fig. 2 for the remaining 241 CUDA benchmarks, which are either certified as error-free by GPUVerify or contain data race and/or barrier divergence errors. Each benchmark has been executed 3 times for each of the tools, and the average time for these 3 runs is taken into consideration. We used the average since there was a negligible difference between the median and the average.

Out of the 241 benchmarks, AutoSync was faster in 178 cases, whereas GPURepair was faster for 63 benchmarks. GPUVerify did not show any error for 152 out of these 241 benchmarks. For these benchmarks, AutoSync did not have to put any further efforts. In contrast, GPURepair attempts to determine if there are any programmer-inserted barriers that are unnecessary and could be removed. This explains GPURepair being slower for some of the benchmarks. Figure 3 shows a run time comparison for 89 benchmarks for which GPUVerify found data race/barrier divergence errors. GPURepair performs significantly better than AutoSync when a kernel requires repair. This is evident from Fig. 3 as AutoSync was faster on 32 benchmarks, whereas GPURepair was faster on 57 benchmarks out of these 89 benchmarks. Note that if any of the tools crash on a benchmark, we consider that run to have timed out; that is, as a benchmark run that took 300 seconds.

The default configuration of GPURepair uses the *mhs* strategy to solve the clauses, enables exploring grid-level barriers to find a solution, and inspects pre-existing barriers for removal if deemed unnecessary. The solver type can be changed to *MaxSAT*, and the usage of grid-level barriers and inspection of pre-existing barriers can be disabled through command-line options. In addition, the weight of grid-level barriers and the weight of barriers nested within loops can also be overridden using command-line options. Detailed documentation on how to run GPURepair can be found at [2]. Table 3 compares the time taken by AutoSync and GPURepair on different configurations. The total time taken by AutoSync is higher, primarily because 300 seconds were counted every time any of the tools crashed. This analysis demonstrates that GPURepair is more robust than AutoSync while performing quite close to AutoSync with respect to runtime.

Table 3. Comparison of AutoSync and the various configurations of GPURepair

Tool (Configuration)	All Kernels (241)		Repaired + Unchanged (28 + 133 = 161)		
	Total Time	Median Time	Total Time	Median Time	Verifier Calls
	(in seconds)				
AutoSync	17076	1.43	384	1.24	216
GPURepair	5810	1.76	823	1.57	271
GPURepair --maxsat	5940	1.75	887	1.54	306
GPURepair --disable-grid	4450	1.72	660	1.56	254
GPURepair --disable-inspect	5430	1.81	754	1.56	250
GPURepair --disable-grid --disable-inspect	4225	1.79	621	1.51	235

Additional experiments and analysis are provided in the extended manuscript [24].

5 Conclusion

This tool paper introduces GPURepair, which can fix barrier divergence errors and remove unnecessary barriers in addition to AutoSync's ability to fix data races. GPURepair has the additional capability to handle both CUDA and OpenCL kernels. Most importantly, GPURepair has a unique feature for suggesting a fix for inter-block races using Cooperative Groups in CUDA.

With extensive experimental evaluation on the benchmark suites (consisting of 700+ CUDA/OpenCL kernels), we have affirmed the superiority of our work. Our experimental results clearly show that GPURepair provides far more coverage than AutoSync. For 65% of the total benchmarks, AutoSync was not applicable as 482 out of the 748 benchmarks were OpenCL kernels. Even for CUDA kernels, GPURepair is able to provide more coverage and is able to repair more kernels. GPURepair is also faster than AutoSync when a kernel indeed requires repair.

Acknowledgements. We thank the anonymous reviewers for their helpful comments and the authors of AutoSync for providing the source-code under a public license. We also thank the Ministry of Education, India, for financial support.

References

1. CUDA Toolkit 5.0. https://developer.nvidia.com/cuda-toolkit-50-archive. Accessed 18 Nov 2020
2. GPURepair GitHub Repository. https://github.com/cs17resch01003/gpurepair. Accessed 18 Nov 2020

3. GPURepair VMCAI 2021 Artifacts. https://doi.org/10.5281/zenodo.4276525. Accessed 18 Nov 2020

4. GPUVerify Test Suite. https://github.com/mc-imperial/gpuverify/tree/master/testsuite. Accessed 18 Nov 2020

5. Microsoft Azure Fsv2-Series Virtual Machine Sizes. https://docs.microsoft.com/en-us/azure/virtual-machines/fsv2-series. Accessed 18 Nov 2020

6. VMCAI 2021 Virtual Machine. https://doi.org/10.5281/zenodo.4017292. Accessed 18 Nov 2020

7. Abdulla, P.A., Atig, M.F., Chen, Y.-F., Leonardsson, C., Rezine, A.: Counterexample guided fence insertion under TSO. In: Flanagan, C., König, B. (eds.) TACAS 2012. LNCS, vol. 7214, pp. 204–219. Springer, Heidelberg (2012). https://doi.org/10.1007/978-3-642-28756-5_15

8. Amighi, A., Darabi, S., Blom, S., Huisman, M.: Specification and verification of atomic operations in GPGPU programs. In: Calinescu, R., Rumpe, B. (eds.) SEFM 2015. LNCS, vol. 9276, pp. 69–83. Springer, Cham (2015). https://doi.org/10.1007/978-3-319-22969-0_5

9. Anand, S., Polikarpova, N.: Automatic synchronization for GPU kernels. In: FMCAD 2018, pp. 1–9. IEEE (2018)

10. Betts, A., et al.: The design and implementation of a verification technique for GPU kernels. TOPLAS **37**(3), 10:1–10:49 (2015)

11. Betts, A., Chong, N., Donaldson, A.F., Qadeer, S., Thomson, P.: GPUVerify: a verifier for GPU kernels. In: OOPSLA 2012, pp. 113–132. ACM (2012)

12. Bjørner, N., Phan, A.-D., Fleckenstein, L.: vZ - an optimizing SMT solver. In: Baier, C., Tinelli, C. (eds.) TACAS 2015. LNCS, vol. 9035, pp. 194–199. Springer, Heidelberg (2015). https://doi.org/10.1007/978-3-662-46681-0_14

13. Blom, S., Huisman, M., Mihelcic, M.: Specification and verification of GPGPU programs. Sci. Comput. Program. **95**, 376–388 (2014)

14. Boehm, B.W., Papaccio, P.N.: Understanding and Controlling Software Costs. IEEE Trans. Software Eng. **14**(10), 1462–1477 (1988)

15. Černý, P., Chatterjee, K., Henzinger, T.A., Radhakrishna, A., Singh, R.: Quantitative synthesis for concurrent programs. In: Gopalakrishnan, G., Qadeer, S. (eds.) CAV 2011. LNCS, vol. 6806, pp. 243–259. Springer, Heidelberg (2011). https://doi.org/10.1007/978-3-642-22110-1_20

16. Chandra, S., Torlak, E., Barman, S., Bodík, R.: Angelic debugging. In: ICSE 2011, pp. 121–130. ACM (2011)

17. Deshmukh, J., Ramalingam, G., Ranganath, V.-P., Vaswani, K.: Logical concurrency control from sequential proofs. In: Gordon, A.D. (ed.) ESOP 2010. LNCS, vol. 6012, pp. 226–245. Springer, Heidelberg (2010). https://doi.org/10.1007/978-3-642-11957-6_13

18. Griesmayer, A., Bloem, R., Cook, B.: Repair of boolean programs with an application to C. In: Ball, T., Jones, R.B. (eds.) CAV 2006. LNCS, vol. 4144, pp. 358–371. Springer, Heidelberg (2006). https://doi.org/10.1007/11817963_33

19. Jin, G., Song, L., Zhang, W., Lu, S., Liblit, B.: Automated atomicity-violation fixing. In: PLDI 2011, pp. 389–400. ACM (2011)

20. Jobstmann, B., Griesmayer, A., Bloem, R.: Program repair as a game. In: Etessami, K., Rajamani, S.K. (eds.) CAV 2005. LNCS, vol. 3576, pp. 226–238. Springer, Heidelberg (2005). https://doi.org/10.1007/11513988_23

21. Johnson, D.S.: Approximation algorithms for combinatorial problems. J. Comput. Syst Sci. **9**(3), 256–278 (1974)

22. Joshi, S., Kroening, D.: Property-driven fence insertion using reorder bounded model checking. In: Bjørner, N., de Boer, F. (eds.) FM 2015. LNCS, vol. 9109, pp. 291–307. Springer, Cham (2015). https://doi.org/10.1007/978-3-319-19249-9_19

23. Joshi, S., Lal, A.: Automatically finding atomic regions for fixing bugs in Concurrent programs. CoRR abs/1403.1749 (2014)

24. Joshi, S., Muduganti, G.: GPURepair: Automated Repair of GPU Kernels. https://arxiv.org/abs/2011.08373 (2020)

25. Li, G., Gopalakrishnan, G.: Scalable SMT-based verification of GPU kernel functions. In: FSE 2010, pp. 187–196. ACM (2010)

26. Li, G., Li, P., Sawaya, G., Gopalakrishnan, G., Ghosh, I., Rajan, S.P.: GKLEE: concolic verification and test generation for GPUs. In: PPOPP 2012, pp. 215–224. ACM (2012)

27. Malik, M.Z., Siddiqui, J.H., Khurshid, S.: Constraint-based program debugging using data structure repair. In: ICST 2011, pp. 190–199. IEEE Computer Society (2011)

28. Monteiro, F.R., et al.: ESBMC-GPU a context-bounded model checking tool to verify CUDA programs. Sci. Comput. Program. **152**, 63–69 (2018)

29. de Moura, L., Bjørner, N.: Z3: an efficient SMT solver. In: Ramakrishnan, C.R., Rehof, J. (eds.) TACAS 2008. LNCS, vol. 4963, pp. 337–340. Springer, Heidelberg (2008). https://doi.org/10.1007/978-3-540-78800-3_24

30. Muzahid, A., Otsuki, N., Torrellas, J.: AtomTracker: A Comprehensive approach to atomic region inference and violation detection. In: MICRO 2010, pp. 287–297. IEEE Computer Society (2010)

31. Vechev, M.T., Yahav, E., Yorsh, G.: Abstraction-guided synthesis of synchronization. In: POPL 2010, pp. 327–338. ACM (2010)

32. Zhang, L., Wahib, M., Zhang, H., Matsuoka, S.: A study of single and multi-device synchronization methods in Nvidia GPUs. In: 2020 IEEE International Parallel and Distributed Processing Symposium (IPDPS), New Orleans, 18–22 May 2020, pp. 483–493. IEEE (2020)

Applications

A Synchronous Effects Logic
for Temporal Verification of Pure Esterel

Yahui Song[(✉)] and Wei-Ngan Chin[(✉)]

School of Computing, National University of Singapore,
Singapore, Singapore
{yahuis,chinwn}comp.nus.edu.sg

Abstract. Esterel is an imperative synchronous language that has found
success in many safety-critical applications. Its precise semantics makes
it natural for programming and reasoning. Existing techniques tackle
either one of its main challenges: correctness checking or temporal verification. To resolve the issues simultaneously, we propose a new solution
via a Hoare-style forward verifier and a term rewriting system (TRS)
on *Synced Effects*. The first contribution is, by deploying a novel effects
logic, the verifier computes the deterministic program behaviour via construction rules at the source level, defining program evaluation syntactically. As a second contribution, by avoiding the complex translation from
LTL formulas to Esterel programs, our purely algebraic TRS efficiently
checks temporal properties described by expressive Synced Effects. To
demonstrate our method's feasibility, we prototype this logic; prove its
correctness; provide experimental results, and a number of case studies.

1 Introduction

Esterel [6] is a synchronous programming language for the development of complex reactive systems. Its high-level imperative style allows the simple expression
of parallelism and preemption, making it natural for programmers to specify
and reason about control-dominated model designs. Esterel has found success in
many safety-critical applications such as nuclear power plant control software.

The success with real-time and embedded systems in domains that need
strong guarantees can be partially attributed to its precise semantics and computational model. There exist two main semantics for Esterel [4]: (i) the *operational semantics*: is a small-step semantics, a procedure for running a whole program defined by an interpretation scheme. It analyses control flow and signals
propagation in the reaction; and (ii) the *circuit semantics*: translates Esterel
programs into constructive boolean digital circuits, i.e., systems of equations
among boolean variables. *Existing semantics are particularly useful for code com-
pilation/optimization or tracking the execution, but not ideal for compositional
reasoning in terms of the source program.*

© Springer Nature Switzerland AG 2021
F. Henglein et al. (Eds.): VMCAI 2021, LNCS 12597, pp. 417–440, 2021.
https://doi.org/10.1007/978-3-030-67067-2_19

Esterel treats computation as a series of deterministic reactions to external signals. All parts of a reaction complete in a single, discrete-time step called an *instant*. Besides, instants exhibit deterministic concurrency; each reaction may contain concurrent threads without execution order affecting the result of the computation. Primitives constructs execute in zero time except for the **pause** statement. Hence, time flows as a sequence of logical instants separated by explicit pauses. In each instant, several elementary instantaneous computations take place simultaneously.

To maintain determinism and synchrony, evaluation in one thread of execution may affect code arbitrarily far away in the program. In another words, there is a strong relationship between signal status and control propagation: a signal status determines which branch of a **present** test is executed, which in turn determines which **emit** statements are executed (See Sect. 3.1 for the language syntax). In this paper, we tackle Esterel's *Logical Correctness* issue, caused by these non-local executions, which is simply the requirement that there exists precisely **one** status for each signal that respects the coherence law. For example:

```
1 signal S1 in
2 present S1 then nothing else emit S1 end present end signal
```

Consider the program above. If the local signal S1 were *present*, the program would take the first branch of the condition, and the program would terminate without having emitted S1 (**nothing** leaves S1 with its default value, *absent*). If S1 were absent, the program would choose the second branch and emit the signal. Both executions lead to a contradiction. Therefore there are no valid assignments of signals in this program. This program is logically incorrect.

```
1 signal S1 in
2 present S1 then emit S1 else nothing end present end signal
```

Consider the revised program above. If the local signal S1 were present, the conditional would take the first branch, and S1 would be emitted, justifying the choice of signal value. If the S1 were absent, the signal would not be emitted, and the choice of absence is also justified. Thus there are two possible assignments to the signals in this program, which is also logically incorrect.

```
1 present S1 then emit S1 else nothing end present
```

However, if S1 is an unbounded external input signal, then this program becomes logically correct, as given a certain status of the input signal, there is precisely one reaction, which satisfies the coherence law. *Although logical correctness is decidable, there is a deep lack in the state-of-the-art semantics for Esterel* [12], *which is the ability to reason about unbounded input signals.* We show that our Effects logic resolves the above issues more systematically, by taking the signal statuses (both present and absent) explicitly as arithmetic path constraints and looking ahead of analyzing the whole program.

In this paper, we represent the program behaviours using Synced Effects. By deploying a novel fixpoint logic, the Hoare-style forward verifier computes all the possible execution traces. Logically incorrect programs, having none/multiple assignments for local/output signals w.r.t the same input set, will be rejected. Meantime, we present a term rewriting system (TRS) upon synced effects to support temporal verification, which is another research challenge of Esterel.

Safety properties are typically used to describe the desired properties of reactive systems. One of the widely used languages for specifying temporal behaviour and safety properties is linear-time temporal logic (LTL). Existing approaches to Esterel's temporal verification have neither achieved compositionality nor automation. One prior work [15], recursively translates LTL formula into an Esterel program whose traces correspond to the computations that violate the safety property. The program derived from the formula is then parallel composed with the given Esterel program to be verified. The composed program is compiled using Esterel tools. Lastly, an analysis of the compiler's output then indicates whether or not the property is satisfied by the original program.

In this work, we propose an alternative approach based on our effects logic, which enables a modular *local* temporal verification without any complex translation. More specifically, given a logical correct program $\mathcal{P}$, we compute its synced effects Φ, and express the temporal properties in Φ'; Our TRS efficiently checks the language inclusions $\Phi \sqsubseteq \Phi'$. To the best of the authors' knowledge, this work proposes the first algebraic TRS for Esterel and resolves the correctness checking and temporal verification at the same time. In addition, while existing works for Esterel's temporal verification have designed for a fixed set of temporal primitives such as *finally*, *next*, *until*, we show that our expressive synced effects provide us with more flexibility than existing temporal logics (Sect. 5.2).

We summarize our main contributions as follows:

1. **The Synced Effects:** We define the syntax and semantics of the Synced Effects, to be the specification language, which are sufficient to capture the Esterel program behaviours and non-trivial temporal properties (Sect. 3.2).
2. **Automated Verification System:** Targeting a pure Esterel language (Sect. 3.1), we develop a Hoare-style forward verifier (Sect. 4), to compositionally compute the program effects, and check the logical correctness with the presence of input signals. We present an effects inclusion checker (the TRS), to soundly prove temporal properties represented by synced effects (Sect. 5).
3. **Implementation and Evaluation:** We prototype the novel effects logic, prove the correctness, provide experimental results and case studies to show the feasibility of our method (Sect. 6).

Organization. Section 2 gives motivation examples to highlight the key methodologies and contributions. Section 3 formally presents a pure Esterel language, the syntax and semantics of our synced effects. Section 4 presents the forward verification rules and the logical correctness checking process. Section 5 explains the TRS for effects inclusion checking, and displays the essential auxiliary functions. Section 6 demonstrates the implementation and evaluation.

We discuss related works in Sect. 7 and conclude in Sect. 8. Proofs can be found in the technical report [21].

2   Overview

We now give a summary of our techniques, using Esterel programs shown in Fig. 1 and Fig. 2 Our synced effects can be illustrated with the modules `close` and `manager`, which simulate the operations to constantly open and close a file.

Here, `CLOSE` and `BTN` are declared to be input/output signals. The module `manager` enters into a `loop` after declaring a local signal `OPEN`. Inside of the loop, it emits the signal `OPEN`, indicating the file is now opened; then tests on the status of signal `BTN`. Signals are absent by default, until they are explicitly emitted. If `BTN` is present, a function call to module `close` will be triggered, otherwise, it does `nothing`[1].

The input signal `BTN` denotes a button which can be pressed by the users, and its presence indicates the intention to close the file. Then before exiting from the loop, the `manager` pauses for one time instant.

The module `close` is obligated to simply emit the signal `CLOSE` after a pause, indicating the file is now closed.

```
1 module close:
2 output CLOSE;
3 /*@ requires {OPEN}
4     ensures {}.{CLOSE} @*/
5  pause; emit CLOSE
6 end module
```

Fig. 1. The close module

```
1 module manager:
2 input BTN;
3 output CLOSE;
4 /*@
5 requires {}
6 ensures ({BTN}.{CLOSE}\/{})*
7 @*/
8   signal OPEN in
9    loop
10      emit OPEN;
11      present BTN
12        then run close
13        else nothing
14      end present;
15      pause
16    end loop
17   end signal
18 end module
```

Fig. 2. The manager module

2.1   Synced Effects

We define Hoare-triple style specifications (marked in green) for each program, which leads to a compositional verification strategy, where temporal reasoning can be done locally.

---

[1] `nothing` is the Esterel equivalent of unit, void or skip in other languages.

Synced Effects is a Novel Abstract Semantics Model for Esterel. The process control in such synchronous languages are event driven. Events, represented by signals, are emitted within the environment for instance by sensors or the users. The system generates signals in response which are either internal or external. Following this model, synced effects describe the program behaviours using *sequences of sets of signals* occurring in the macro level.

More specifically, the set of signals to be present in one logical time instance are represented within one {}. For example, the postcondition of module `close`, {} · {CLOSE}, says that the execution leads to two time instances, and only in the second time instance, the signal CLOSE is guaranteed to be present.

Putting the temporal effects in the precondition is new, to represent the required temporal execution history. For example, the precondition of module `close`, {OPEN} requires that before entering into this module, the signal OPEN should be emitted in the current time instance. Besides, to enhance the expressiveness, synced effects allow trace disjunctions via ∨ and trace repetitions via ⋆ and ω. For example, the postcondition in module `manager` ensures a repeating pattern, in which it can be either {BTN} · {CLOSE} or just {}. See Sect. 3.2 for the syntax and semantics of synced effects[2].

1) `loop`
   $\langle \{\} \rangle$

2)   `emit OPEN;`
   $\langle \{\text{OPEN}\} \rangle$ **[FV-Emit]**

3)   `present BTN then`
   $\langle \{\text{OPEN}, \text{BTN}\} \rangle$ **[FV-Present]**

4)   `run close`
   $\{\text{OPEN}, \text{BTN}\} \sqsubseteq \{\text{OPEN}\}$ *(-TRS: check precondition, succeed-)*
   $\langle \{\text{OPEN}, \text{BTN}\} \cdot \{\text{CLOSE}\} \rangle$ **[FV-Call]**

5)   `else nothing`
   $\langle \{\text{OPEN}\} \rangle$ **[FV-Present]**

6)   `end present;`
   $\langle \{\text{OPEN}, \text{BTN}\} \cdot \{\text{CLOSE}\} \vee \{\text{OPEN}\} \rangle$ **[FV-Present]**

7)   `pause`
   $\langle (\{\text{OPEN}, \text{BTN}\} \cdot \{\text{CLOSE}\} \vee \{\text{OPEN}\}) \cdot \{\} \rangle$ **[FV-Pause]**

8) `end loop`
   $\langle (\{\text{OPEN}, \text{BTN}\} \cdot \{\text{CLOSE}\} \vee \{\text{OPEN}\})^{\star} \rangle$ **[FV-Loop]**

9) $(\{\text{OPEN}, \text{BTN}\} \cdot \{\text{CLOSE}\} \vee \{\text{OPEN}\})^{\star} \sqsubseteq (\{\text{BTN}\} \cdot \{\text{CLOSE}\} \vee \{\})^{\star}$ *(-TRS: check postcondition, succeed-)*

Fig. 3. The forward verification example for the loop in module `manager`.

---

[2] The signals shown in one time instance represent the *minimal* set of signals which are required/guaranteed to be there. An empty set {} refers to any set of signals.

2.2   Forward Verification

As shown in Fig. 3, we demonstrate the forward verification process of the loop in module **manager**. The current *effects state* of a program is captured in the form of $\langle \Phi \rangle$. To facilitate the illustration, we label the verification steps by 1), ..., 9). We mark the deployed verification rules in gray. The verifier invokes the TRS to check language inclusions along the way.

The effects state 1) is the initial effects when entering into the loop. The effects state 2) is obtained by [FV-Emit], which simply adds the emitted signal to the current time instance. The effects states 3), 5) and 6) are obtained by [FV-Present], which adds the constraints upon the tested signal into the current state, and unions the effects accumulated from two branches at the end. The effects state 4) is obtained by [FV-Call]. Before each method call, it checks whether the current effects state satisfies the precondition of the callee method. If the precondition is not satisfied, then the verification fails, otherwise it concatenates the postcondition of the callee to the current effects. The effects state 7) is obtained by [FV-Pause]. It concatenates an empty time instance to the current effects, to be the new *current state*. The effects state 8) is obtained by [FV-Loop], which computes a deterministic fixpoint of effects, to be the invariant of executing the loop. After these states transformations, step 9) checks the satisfiability of the declared postcondition by invoking the TRS.

Table 1. The inclusion proving example from the postcondition checking in Fig. 3.

$$\frac{\dfrac{\dfrac{\dfrac{\Phi \sqsubseteq \Phi_{post}(\dagger) \quad \text{[REOCCUR]}}{\mathcal{E} \cdot \Phi \sqsubseteq (\mathcal{E} \vee \bot) \cdot \Phi_{post}}}{\{\text{CLOSE}\} \cdot \Phi \sqsubseteq (\{\text{CLOSE}\} \vee \mathcal{E}) \cdot \Phi_{post}} \text{[UNFOLD]}}{\{\text{OPEN, BTN}\} \cdot \{\text{CLOSE}\} \cdot \Phi \sqsubseteq \Phi_{post}} \text{[UNFOLD]} \qquad \frac{\dfrac{\dfrac{\Phi \sqsubseteq \Phi_{post}(\dagger) \quad \text{[REOCCUR]}}{\mathcal{E} \cdot \Phi \sqsubseteq (\bot \vee \mathcal{E}) \cdot \Phi_{post}}}{\{\text{OPEN}\} \cdot \Phi \sqsubseteq \Phi_{post}} \text{[UNFOLD]}}{\Phi \sqsubseteq \Phi_{post}(\dagger)} \text{[UNFOLD]}$$

where $\Phi = (\{\text{OPEN, BTN}\} \cdot \{\text{CLOSE}\} \vee \{\text{OPEN}\})^\star$; and $\Phi_{post} = (\{\text{BTN}\} \cdot \{\text{CLOSE}\} \vee \{\})^\star$

2.3   The TRS

Our TRS is obligated to check the inclusion among synced effects, an extension of Antimirov and Mosses's algorithm. Antimirov and Mosses [3] present a term rewriting system for deciding the inequalities of regular expressions, based on a complete axiomatic algorithm of the algebra of regular sets. Basically, the rewriting system decides inequalities through an iterated process of checking the inequalities of their *partial derivatives* [2]. There are two important rules: [DISPROVE], which infers false from trivially inconsistent inequalities; and [UNFOLD], which applies Theorem 1 to generate new inequalities. $D_a(r)$ is the partial derivative of r w.r.t the instance a. (Σ is the whole set of the alphabet.)

Theorem 1 (Regular Expressions Inequality (Antimirov)). *For regular expressions* r *and* s, $r \preceq s \Leftrightarrow (\forall a \in \Sigma).\ D_a(r) \preceq D_a(s)$.

Extending to the inclusions among synced effects, we present the rewriting process by our TRS in Table 1, for the postcondition checking shown in Fig. 3 We mark the rules of the inference steps in gray. Note that time instance {OPEN, BTN} entails {BTN} because the former contains more constraints. We formally define the subsumption for time instances in Definition 3. Intuitively, we use [DISPROVE] wherever the left-hand side (LHS) is *nullable*[3] while the right-hand side (RHS) is not. [DISPROVE] is the heuristic refutation step to disprove the inclusion early, which leads to a great efficiency improvement.

Termination is guaranteed because the set of derivatives to be considered is finite, and possible cycles are detected using *memorization*. The rule [REOCCUR] finds the syntactic identity, as a companion, of the current open goal, as a bud, from the internal proof tree [9]. (We use (†) in Fig. 3 to indicate such pairings.)

3   Language and Specifications

In this section, we first introduce a pure Esterel language and then depict our Synced Effects as the specification language.

3.1   The Target Language: Pure Esterel

In this work, we consider the Esterel v5 dialect [4,5] endorsed by current academic compilers, shown in Fig. 4 Pure Esterel is the subset of the full Esterel language where data variables and data-handling primitives are abstracted away. We shall concentrate on the pure Esterel language, as in this work, we are mainly interested in signal status and control propagation, which are not related to data.

(*Program*)	$\mathcal{P} ::=$ meth*	(*Basic Types*)	$\tau ::=$ IN | OUT | INOUT
(*Module Def.*)	module $::=$ x $(\tau\ S)^*$ $\langle$**requires** Φ_{pre} **ensures** $\Phi_{post}\rangle$ p		
(*Statement*)	p q $::=$ nothing | pause | emit S | present S p q		
	$\qquad$ | p ; q | loop p | p || q | trap T p | exit T_d		
	$\qquad$ | signal S p | run x $(S)^*$ | assert Φ		

$S \in$ signal variables	x, $T \in$ **var**	(*Finite List*) *	(Depth)$d \in \mathbb{Z}$

Fig. 4. Pure esterel syntax.

Here, we regard S, x and T as meta-variables. Basic signal types include IN (input signals), OUT (output signals), INOUT (the signals used to be both

---

[3] If the event sequence is possibly empty, i.e. contains $\mathcal{E}$, we call it nullable, formally defined in Definition 1.

input and output). **var** represents the countably infinite set of arbitrary distinct identifiers. We assume that programs we use are well-typed conforming to basic types τ. A program $\mathcal{P}$ comprises a list of method declarations **meth***.

Each module **meth** has a name **x**, a list of well-typed arguments $(\tau\ \mathbf{S})^*$, a statement-oriented body **p**, also is associated with a precondition Φ_{pre} and a postcondition Φ_{post}. (The syntax of effects specification Φ is given in Fig. 6)

Following the language constructs formally defined in Fig. 4, we describe how signals are emitted and how control is transmitted between statements [4]:

- The statement **nothing** terminates instantaneously.
- The statement **pause** pauses exactly one logical instant and terminates in the next instant.
- The statement **emit S** broadcasts the signal **S** to be set to present and terminates instantaneously. The emission of **S** is valid for the current instant only.
- The statement **present S p q** immediately starts **p** **if S** is present in the current instant; otherwise it starts **q** when **S** is absent.
- The sequence statement **p** ; **q** immediately starts **p** and behaves as **p** as long as **p** remains active. When **p** terminates, control is passed instantaneously to **q**, which determines the behaviour of the sequence from then on. If **p** exits a **trap**, so does the whole sequence, **q** being discarded in this case. **q** is never started if **p** always pauses. *(Notice that '*emit **S1** ; emit **S2**' *emits* **S1** *and* **S2** *simultaneously and terminates instantaneously.)*
- The statement **loop p** immediately starts its body **p**. When **p** terminates, it is immediately restarted. If **p** exits a trap, so does the whole loop. The body of a loop is not allowed to terminate instantaneously when started, i.e., it must execute either a pause or an exit statement. For example, '**loop emit** S' is not a correct program. A loop statement never terminates, but it is possible to escape from the loop by enclosing it within a trap and executing an exit statement.
- The parallel statement **p** || **q** starts **p** and **q** in parallel. The parallel statement remains active as long as one of its branches remains active unless some branch exits a trap. The parallel statement terminates when both **p** and **q** are terminated. The branches can terminate in different instants, the parallel waiting for the last one to terminate. Parallel branches may simultaneously exit traps. If, in some instant, one branch exits a trap **T** or both branches exit the same trap **T**, then the parallel exits **T**. If both statements exit distinct traps **T** and **U** in the same instant, then the parallel only exits the higher prioritized one.
- The statement **trap T p** defines a lexically scoped exit point **T** for **p**. When the trap statement meth starts, it immediately starts its body **p** and behaves as **p** until termination or exit. If **p** terminates, so does the trap statement. If **p** exits **T**, then the trap statement terminates instantaneously. If **p** exits an inner trap **U**, this exit is propagated by the trap statement.

– The statement `exit` $\mathbf{T_d}$ instantaneously exits the trap $\mathbf{T}$ with a depth $\mathbf{d}$. The corresponding trap statement is terminated unless an outermost trap is concurrently exited, as an outer trap has a higher priority when being exited concurrently. For example, as shown in Fig. 5, such an encoding of exceptions for Esterel was first advocated for by Gonthier [13]. As usual, we make depths value $\mathbf{d}$ explicit. Here, $\mathbf{T1}$ has depth 1 because of the declaration of trap $\mathbf{U}$ in the middle; $\mathbf{U0}$ and $\mathbf{T0}$ have

```
1  trap T in
2    trap U in
3      [   exit  T1
4      || exit  U0
5      || exit  V3]
6    end trap;
7    exit T0
8  end trap
```

Fig. 5. Nested traps

depth 0 because they are directly enclosed by the trap $\mathbf{U}$ and $\mathbf{T}$ respectively; $\mathbf{V3}$ has depth 3 corresponding to an outer trap, defined outside of this code segment. Therefore Fig. 5 ends up with exiting outermost trap $\mathbf{V3}$.

– The statement `signal` $\mathbf{S}$ $\mathbf{p}$ starts its body $\mathbf{p}$ with a fresh signal $\mathbf{S}$, overriding any that might already exist.
– The statement `run` $\mathrm{x}(\mathbf{S}^*)$ is a call to module x providing the list of IO signals.
– The statement `assert` Φ is used to guarantee the temporal property Φ asserted at a certain point of the programs.

3.2 The Specification Language: Synced Effects

We present the syntax of our Synced Effects in Fig. 6 Effects Φ can be recursively constructed by nil ($\bot$); an empty trace $\mathcal{E}$; one time instant represented by I; effects concatenation $\Phi \cdot \Phi$; effects disjunction $\Phi \vee \Phi$; Kleene star $\star$, a multiple times repetition of the effects Φ (possibly $\mathcal{E}$); Omega ω, an infinite repetition of the effects Φ. One time instant is constructed by a list of mappings from signals to status, recording the current status of all the signals, and will be overwritten if there is a new status of a signal had been determined. The status of a signal can be either **present** or **absent**.

Semantic Model of Effects. To define the model, we use φ (*a trace of sets of signals*) to represent the computation execution, indicating the sequential constraint of the temporal behaviour. Let $\varphi \models \Phi$ denote the model relation, i.e., the linear temporal sequence φ satisfies the synced effects Φ.

$$
\begin{array}{rll}
(Synced\ Effects) & \Phi & ::= \bot \mid \mathcal{E} \mid \mathrm{I} \mid \Phi \cdot \Phi \mid \Phi \vee \Phi \mid \Phi^\star \mid \Phi^\omega \\
(Time\ Instant) & \mathrm{I} & ::= (\mathbf{S} \mapsto \theta)^* \\
(Status) & \theta & ::= \textbf{present} \mid \textbf{absent}
\end{array}
$$

$$
(Omega)\ \omega \qquad (Kleene\ Star)\ \star \qquad (Finite\ List)\ *
$$

Fig. 6. Synced effects.

As shown in Fig. 7, we define the semantics of our synced effects. We use [] to represent the empty sequence; ++ to represent the append operation of two traces; [I] to represent the sequence only contains one time instant.

I is a list of mappings from signals to status. For example, the time instance {**S**} indicates the fact that signal **S** is present regardless of the status of other non-mentioned signals, i.e., the set of time instances which at least contain **S** to be present. Any time instance contains contradictions, such as {**S**, **S̄**}, will lead to false, as a signal **S** can not be both present and absent. We use the overline on top of the signal to denote the constraint of being absent.

$$
\begin{array}{llll}
\varphi \models \mathcal{E} & \textit{iff} & \varphi = [] \\
\varphi \models \mathtt{I} & \textit{iff} & \varphi = [\mathtt{I}] \\
\varphi \models \Phi_1 \cdot \Phi_2 & \textit{iff} & \textit{there exist } \varphi_1, \varphi_2,\ \varphi = \varphi_1 {+}{+} \varphi_2 \textit{ and } \varphi_1 \models \Phi_1 \textit{ and } \varphi_2 \models \Phi_2 \\
\varphi \models \Phi_1 \vee \Phi_2 & \textit{iff} & \varphi \models \Phi_1 \textit{ or } \varphi \models \Phi_2 \\
\varphi \models \Phi^{\star} & \textit{iff} & \varphi \models \mathcal{E} \textit{ or} \\
& & \textit{there exist } \varphi_1, \varphi_2,\ \varphi = \varphi_1 {+}{+} \varphi_2 \textit{ and } \varphi_1 \models \Phi \textit{ and } \varphi_2 \models \Phi^{\star} \\
\varphi \models \Phi^{\omega} & \textit{iff} & \textit{there exist } \varphi_1, \varphi_2,\ \varphi = \varphi_1 {+}{+} \varphi_2 \textit{ and } \varphi_1 \models \Phi \textit{ and } \varphi_2 \models \Phi^{\omega} \\
\varphi \models \bot & \textit{iff} & \textit{false}
\end{array}
$$

Fig. 7. Semantics of effects.

4   Automated Forward Verification

An overview of our automated verification system is given in Fig. 8. It consists of a Hoare-style forward verifier and a TRS. The inputs of the forward verifier are Esterel programs annotated with temporal specifications written in Synced Effects (cf. Fig. 2). The input of the TRS is a pair of effects LHS and RHS, referring to the inclusion LHS ⊑ RHS to be checked *(LHS refers to left-hand side effects, and RHS refers to right-hand side effects.)*. Besides, the verifier calls the TRS to prove produced inclusions, i.e., between the current effects states and pre/post conditions or assertions (cf. Fig. 3).

The TRS will be explained in Sect. 5. In this section, we mainly present the forward verifier by introducing the forward verification rules. These rules transfer program states and systematically accumulate the effects based on the syntax of each statement. We present the intermediate representation of program states in Fig. 9.

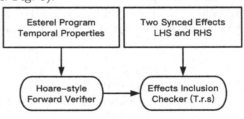

Fig. 8. System overview.

$$
\begin{aligned}
(\textit{Program States}) \quad & \Delta ::= \langle \underline{\Phi}, \ \pi \wedge \phi, \ \mathbf{k} \rangle \\
(\textit{Intermediate Synced Effects}) \quad & \underline{\Phi} ::= \perp \mid \mathcal{E} \mid \pi \wedge \phi \mid \underline{\Phi} \cdot \underline{\Phi} \mid \underline{\Phi} \vee \underline{\Phi} \mid \underline{\Phi}^{\star} \mid \underline{\Phi}^{\omega} \\
(\textit{Current Time Instant}) \ \pi \wedge \phi \quad & ::= (\mathbf{S} = \theta)^{\star} \wedge (\mathbf{S} \mapsto \theta)^{\star}
\end{aligned}
$$

Fig. 9. Intermediate representation for then program states.

Program states Δ are represented by a tuple, where the first element ($\underline{\Phi}$) represents the trace of *history*; the second element represents the *current* time instant containing the path constraints (π) and signal assignments (ϕ)[4]; the third element ($\mathbf{k}$) represents the completion code, keeping track of the exits from nested traps [23]. Let ϱ be the environment containing all the local and output signals.

4.1 Forward Rules

As nothing is the Esterel equivalent of unit, void or skip in other languages, the rule [FV-Nothing] simply obtains the next program state by inheriting the current program state.

$$
\frac{}{\varrho \vdash \langle \underline{\Phi}, \pi \wedge \phi, \mathbf{k} \rangle \ \text{nothing} \ \langle \underline{\Phi}, \pi \wedge \phi, \mathbf{k} \rangle} \ [\text{FV-Nothing}]
$$

The rule [FV-Emit] updates the current assignment of signal $\mathbf{S}$ to present; keeps the history trace and completion code unchanged.

$$
\frac{\phi' = \phi[\mathbf{S} \mapsto \text{present}]}{\varrho \vdash \langle \underline{\Phi}, \pi \wedge \phi, \mathbf{k} \rangle \ \text{emit} \ \mathbf{S} \ \langle \underline{\Phi}, \pi \wedge \phi', \mathbf{k} \rangle} \ [\text{FV-Emit}]
$$

The rule [FV-Pause] archives the current time instance to the history trace; then initializes a new time instant where π' is an empty set, and all the signals from ϱ are set to default absent. The completion code $\mathbf{k}$ remains unchanged.

$$
\frac{\pi' = \{\} \qquad \phi' = \{\mathbf{S} \mapsto \text{absent} \mid \forall \mathbf{S} \in \varrho\}}{\varrho \vdash \langle \underline{\Phi}, \pi \wedge \phi, \mathbf{k} \rangle \ \text{pause} \ \langle (\underline{\Phi} \cdot (\pi \wedge \phi)), \pi' \wedge \phi', \mathbf{k} \rangle} \ [\text{FV-Pause}]
$$

The rule [FV-Decl] obtains a new environment ϱ' by adding the local signal $\mathbf{S}$ into ϱ; sets the status of $\mathbf{S}$ to absent in the current time instance, then behaves as its body $\mathbf{p}$ w.r.t ϱ' and ϕ' accordingly [6].

$$
\frac{\varrho' = \varrho, \mathbf{S} \qquad \phi' = \phi[\mathbf{S} \mapsto \text{absent}] \qquad \varrho' \vdash \langle \underline{\Phi}, \pi \wedge \phi', \mathbf{k} \rangle \ \mathbf{p} \ \langle \underline{\Phi}_1, \pi_1 \wedge \phi_1, \mathbf{k}_1 \rangle}{\varrho \vdash \langle \underline{\Phi}, \pi \wedge \phi, \mathbf{k} \rangle \ \text{signal} \ \mathbf{S} \ \mathbf{p} \ \langle \underline{\Phi}_1, \pi_1 \wedge \phi_1, \mathbf{k}_1 \rangle} \ [\text{FV-Decl}]
$$

---

[4] The difference between $\mathbf{S} = \theta$ and $\mathbf{S} \mapsto \theta$ is: the former one denotes the constraints along the execution path, which creates *false* if there are two different status assignments to the same signal; while the latter one records the current status of one signal, and will be overwritten when the presence of a signal had been determined.

The rule [FV-Present] firstly gets π' and π'' by adding the path constraints (**S**=present) and (**S**=absent) to the current time instance; then derives $\langle \underline{\Phi}_1, \pi_1 \wedge \phi_1, k_1 \rangle$ and $\langle \underline{\Phi}_2, \pi_2 \wedge \phi_2, k_2 \rangle$ from the *then* and *else* branches. We introduce can [12] function which intuitively determines whether the tested signal **S** can be emitted or not. If **S** *cannot* be emitted (can(**S**)=false), the final

```
1   signal SL in
2       present SL
3           then emit S1
4           else emit S2
5       end present
6   end signal
```

Fig. 10. Cannot

states will only come from the else branch **q**; otherwise we say **S** *can* be emitted (can(**S**)=true), the final states will be the union of both branches' execution. For example, as it shown in Fig. 10, to unblock a present expression, one must determine if the tested signal can be emitted or not. One way for that is to detect the none-occurrences of emit **SL**. Here, since can(**SL**)=false, the program will leave **SL** absent and emit **S2**.

$$\frac{\begin{array}{ll} \pi' = \pi \wedge (\mathbf{S}=\text{present}) & \varrho \vdash \langle \underline{\Phi}, \pi' \wedge \phi, k \rangle \; \mathbf{p} \; \langle \underline{\Phi}_1, \pi_1 \wedge \phi_1, k_1 \rangle \\ \pi'' = \pi \wedge (\mathbf{S}=\text{absent}) & \varrho \vdash \langle \underline{\Phi}, \pi'' \wedge \phi, k \rangle \; \mathbf{q} \; \langle \underline{\Phi}_2, \pi_2 \wedge \phi_2, k_2 \rangle \\ \langle \Delta \rangle = \langle \underline{\Phi}_2, \pi_2 \wedge \phi_2, k_2 \rangle & \text{when} \quad \text{can}(\mathbf{S})=\text{false} \\ \langle \Delta \rangle = \langle \underline{\Phi}_1, \pi_1 \wedge \phi_1, k_1 \rangle \vee \langle \underline{\Phi}_2, \pi_2 \wedge \phi_2, k_2 \rangle & \text{when} \quad \text{can}(\mathbf{S})=\text{true} \end{array}}{\varrho \vdash \langle \underline{\Phi}, \pi \wedge \phi, k \rangle \; \text{present } \mathbf{S} \; \mathbf{p} \; \mathbf{q} \; \langle \Delta \rangle} \text{[FV-Present]}$$

The rule [FV-Par] gets $\langle \underline{\Phi}_1, \pi_1 \wedge \phi_1, k_1 \rangle$ and $\langle \underline{\Phi}_2, \pi_2 \wedge \phi_2, k_2 \rangle$ by executing **p** and **q**. The zip function synchronises the effects from these two

```
1   emit A; pause; emit B; emit C
2   ||
3   emit E; pause; emit F; pause; emit G
```

Fig. 11. Parallel composition

branches. For example, as it shown in Fig. 11, the first branch generates effects $\{\mathbf{A}\} \cdot \{\mathbf{B}, \mathbf{C}\}$ while the second branch generates effect $\{\mathbf{E}\} \cdot \{\mathbf{F}\} \cdot \{\mathbf{G}\}$; then the final states should be $\{\mathbf{A}, \mathbf{E}\} \cdot \{\mathbf{B}, \mathbf{C}, \mathbf{F}\} \cdot \{\mathbf{G}\}$. The max function returns the larger value of k_1 and k_2. When both of the branches have exits, the final k_f follows the larger one, as the larger completion code indicates a higher exiting priority.

$$\frac{\varrho \vdash \langle \underline{\Phi}, \pi \wedge \phi, k \rangle \; \mathbf{p} \; \langle \underline{\Phi}_1, \pi_1 \wedge \phi_1, k_1 \rangle \quad \varrho \vdash \langle \underline{\Phi}, \pi \wedge \phi, k \rangle \; \mathbf{q} \; \langle \underline{\Phi}_2, \pi_2 \wedge \phi_2, k_2 \rangle}{\langle \underline{\Phi}_f, \pi_f \wedge \phi_f \rangle = \text{zip} \; (\underline{\Phi}_1, \pi_1 \wedge \phi_1) \; (\underline{\Phi}_2, \pi_2 \wedge \phi_2) \qquad k_f = \max(k_1, k_2)}{\varrho \vdash \langle \underline{\Phi}, \pi \wedge \phi, k \rangle \; \mathbf{p} \parallel \mathbf{q} \; \langle \underline{\Phi}_f, \pi_f \wedge \phi_f, k_f \rangle} \text{[FV-Par]}$$

The rule [FV-Seq] firstly gets $\langle \underline{\Phi}_1, \pi_1 \wedge \phi_1, k_1 \rangle$ by executing **p**. If there is an exceptional exit in **p**, $(k_1 \neq 0)$, it abandons the execution of **q** completely. Otherwise, there is no exits in **p**, $(k_1=0)$, it further gets $\langle \underline{\Phi}_2, \pi_2 \wedge \phi_2, k_2 \rangle$ by continuously executing **q**, to be the final program state.

$$\frac{\begin{array}{c} \varrho \vdash \langle \underline{\Phi}, \pi \wedge \phi, k \rangle \; \mathbf{p} \; \langle \underline{\Phi}_1, \pi_1 \wedge \phi_1, k_1 \rangle \quad \varrho \vdash \langle \underline{\Phi}_1, \pi_1 \wedge \phi_1, k_1 \rangle \; \mathbf{q} \; \langle \underline{\Phi}_2, \pi_2 \wedge \phi_2, k_2 \rangle \\ \langle \Delta \rangle = \langle \underline{\Phi}_1, \pi_1 \wedge \phi_1, k_1 \rangle \qquad \text{when } k_1 \neq 0 \\ \langle \Delta \rangle = \langle \underline{\Phi}_2, \pi_2 \wedge \phi_2, k_2 \rangle \qquad \text{when } k_1 = 0 \end{array}}{\varrho \vdash \langle \underline{\Phi}, \pi \wedge \phi, k \rangle \; \mathbf{p} \; ; \; \mathbf{q} \; \langle \Delta \rangle} \; [\text{FV-Seq}]$$

The rule [FV-Loop] firstly computes a fixpoint $\langle \underline{\Phi}_1, \pi_1 \wedge \phi_1, k_1 \rangle$ by initializing a temporary program state $\langle \mathcal{E}, \pi \wedge \phi, k \rangle$ before executing $\mathbf{p}$. If there is an exit in $\mathbf{p}$, $(k_1 \neq 0)$, the final state will contain a finite trace of history effects, $\underline{\Phi}$ followed by $\underline{\Phi}_1$, and a new current time instance $(\pi_1 \wedge \phi_1)$. Otherwise, there is no exits in $\mathbf{p}$, the final states will contain a infinite trace of effects, constructed by ω. Then anything following an infinite trace will be abandoned. (cf. Table 2)

$$\frac{\begin{array}{c} \varrho \vdash \langle \mathcal{E}, \pi \wedge \phi, k \rangle \; \mathbf{p} \; \langle \underline{\Phi}_1, \pi_1 \wedge \phi_1, k_1 \rangle \\ \langle \Delta \rangle = \langle \underline{\Phi} \cdot \underline{\Phi}_1, \pi_1 \wedge \phi_1, k_1 \rangle \rangle \qquad \text{when } k_1 \neq 0 \\ \langle \Delta \rangle = \langle \underline{\Phi} \cdot (\underline{\Phi}_1 \cdot (\pi_1 \wedge \phi_1))^\omega, \text{none}, k_1 \rangle \quad \text{when } k_1 = 0 \end{array}}{\varrho \vdash \langle \underline{\Phi}, \pi \wedge \phi, k \rangle \; \text{loop } \mathbf{p} \; \langle \Delta \rangle} \; [\text{FV-Loop}]$$

The rule [FV-Trap] gets $\langle \underline{\Phi}_1, \pi_1 \wedge \phi_1, k_1 \rangle$ by executing the trap body $\mathbf{p}$. When there is no exit from the trap body (k=0), or there is an exit which can be exactly caught by the current trap (k=1), we leave the final completion code to be 0. When there is an exit with a higher priority, (k>1), indicating to exit from a outer trap, we get the final k_f by decreasing the completion code by one.

$$\frac{\begin{array}{c} \varrho \vdash \langle \underline{\Phi}, \pi \wedge \phi, k \rangle \; \mathbf{p} \; \langle \underline{\Phi}_1, \pi_1 \wedge \phi_1, k_1 \rangle \\ k_f = 0 \qquad \text{when} \quad k_1 \leq 1 \\ k_f = k_1 \text{-} 1 \qquad \text{when} \quad k_1 > 1 \end{array}}{\varrho \vdash \langle \underline{\Phi}, \pi \wedge \phi, k \rangle \; \text{trap } \mathbf{T} \; \mathbf{p} \; \langle \underline{\Phi}_1, \pi_1 \wedge \phi_1, k_f \rangle} \; [\text{FV-Trap}]$$

As $\texttt{exit } \mathbf{T}_d$ will abort execution up to the (d+1) th enclosing of the trap $\mathbf{T}$. The rule [FV-Exit] sets the value of k using d+1.

$$\frac{}{\varrho \vdash \langle \underline{\Phi}, \pi \wedge \phi, k \rangle \; \text{exit } \mathbf{T}_d \; \langle \underline{\Phi}, \pi \wedge \phi, d+1 \rangle} \; [\text{FV-Exit}]$$

The rule [FV-Call] checks if the precondition of callee, Φ_{pre}, is satisfied by the current effects state; then it obtains the next program state by concatenating the postcondition to the current effects state. (cf. Table 2)

$$\frac{\begin{array}{c} \mathbf{x} \; (\tau \; \mathbf{S})^* \; \langle \textbf{requires} \; \Phi_{\text{pre}} \; \textbf{ensures} \; \Phi_{\text{post}} \rangle \; \mathbf{p} \in \mathcal{P} \\ TRS \vdash \underline{\Phi} \cdot (\pi \wedge \phi) \sqsubseteq \Phi_{\text{pre}} \qquad \langle \Delta \rangle = \underline{\Phi} \cdot (\pi \wedge \phi) \cdot \Phi_{\text{post}} \end{array}}{\varrho \vdash \langle \underline{\Phi}, \pi \wedge \phi, k \rangle \; \text{run x } (\mathbf{S})^* \; \mathbf{p} \; \langle \Delta \rangle} \; [\text{FV-Call}]$$

The rule [FV-Assert] simply checks if the asserted property Φ' is satisfied by the current effects state. If not, a compilation error will be raised.

$$\frac{TRS \vdash \underline{\Phi} \cdot (\pi \wedge \phi) \sqsubseteq \Phi'}{\varrho \vdash \langle \underline{\Phi}, \pi \wedge \phi, k \rangle \; \text{assert } \Phi' \; \langle \underline{\Phi}, \pi \wedge \phi, k \rangle} \; [\text{FV-Assert}]$$

4.2 Correctness Checking

Esterel assumes that the systems are deterministic. Informally, a non-deterministic system does not have a unique response to a given input event; instead, it chooses its response to the input event from a set of possible responses, and an external observer has no way to consistently predict the response that will be chosen by the system. Non-determinism corresponds to unlimited parallelism and not to any stochastic behaviour [17]. All Esterel statements and constructs are guaranteed to be deterministic, in other words, there is no way to introduce non-deterministic behaviour in an Esterel program.

To effectively check logical correctness, in this work, given an Esterel program, after been applied to the forward rules, we compute the possible execution traces in a disjunctive form; then prune the traces contain contradictions, following these principles: (cf. Fig. 12) (i) explicit present and absent; (ii) each local signal should have only one status; (iii) lookahead should work for both present

```
1) present S1 ⟨{}⟩

2)    then nothing ⟨{S1 ∧ S̄1}⟩

3)    else emit S1 ⟨{S̄1 ∧ S1}⟩

4) end present ⟨{false} ∨ {false}⟩
   false → logical incorrect
```

Fig. 12. Logical incorrect.

and absent; (iv) signal emissions are idempotent; (v) signal status should not be contradictory.

Finally, upon each assignment of inputs, programs have none or multiple output traces that will be rejected, corresponding to no-valid or multiple-valid assignments. We regard these programs, which have precisely one *safe* trace reacting to each input assignments, as logical correct.

Lemma 1 (Safe Time Instants). *Given a time instant $\pi \wedge \phi$, we define it is safe if and only if, for any signal S, the binding from the path constraints $[\![\pi]\!]_S$ justifies the status from the time instant mappings $[\![\phi]\!]_S$; otherwise, we say it is a contradicted instant. Formally,*

$$\pi \wedge \phi \text{ is safe iff } \not\exists S.\ [\![\pi]\!]_S \neq [\![\phi]\!]_S$$

Note that, the proof obligations are discharged by the Z3 solver while deciding whether a time instant I is safe or not, represented by $\mathrm{SAT}(\pi \wedge \phi)$.

Corollary 1 (Safe Traces). *A temporal trace Φ is safe iff all the time instants contained in the trace are safe.*

5 Temporal Verification via a TRS

The TRS is a decision procedure (proven to be terminating and sound) to check language inclusions among Synced Effects (cf. Table 1). It is triggered i) prior to temporal property assertions; ii) prior to module calls for the precondition checking; and iii) at the end of verifying a module for the post condition checking. Given two effects Φ_1, Φ_2, the TRS is to decide if the inclusion $\Phi_1 \sqsubseteq \Phi_2$ is valid.

During the effects rewriting process, the inclusions are in the form of $\Gamma \vdash \Phi_1 \sqsubseteq^{\Phi} \Phi_2$, a shorthand for: $\Gamma \vdash \Phi \cdot \Phi_1 \sqsubseteq \Phi \cdot \Phi_2$. To prove such inclusions is to check whether all the possible event traces in the antecedent Φ_1 are legitimately allowed in the possible event traces from the consequent Φ_2. Γ is the proof context, i.e., a set of effects inclusion hypothesis, Φ is the history of effects from the antecedent that have been used to match the effects from the consequent. Note that Γ, Φ are derived during the inclusion proof. The inclusion checking procedure is initially invoked with $\Gamma=\{\}$ and $\Phi=\mathcal{E}$. Formally,

Theorem 2 (Synced Effects Inclusion).
For synced effects Φ_1 and Φ_2, $\Phi_1 \sqsubseteq \Phi_2 \Leftrightarrow (\forall I). \, D_I(\Phi_1) \sqsubseteq D_I(\Phi_2)$.

Next we provide the definitions and implementations of auxiliary functions *Nullable* (δ), *First* (fst) and *Derivative* (D) respectively. Intuitively, the Nullable function $\delta(\Phi)$ returns a boolean value indicating whether Φ contains the empty trace $\mathcal{E}$; the First function fst(Φ) computes a set of possible initial time instants of Φ; and the Derivative function $D_I(\Phi)$ computes a next-state effects after eliminating one time instant I from the current effects Φ.

Definition 1 (Nullable). *Given any effects Φ, we recursively define $\delta(\Phi)$ as:*

$$\delta(\Phi) : \text{bool} = \begin{cases} \text{true} & \text{if } \mathcal{E} \in \Phi \\ \text{false} & \text{if } \mathcal{E} \notin \Phi \end{cases}, \text{ where}$$

$$\delta(\bot)=\text{false} \qquad \delta(\mathcal{E})=\text{true} \qquad \delta(I)=\text{false} \qquad \delta(\Phi_1 \cdot \Phi_2)=\delta(\Phi_1) \wedge \delta(\Phi_2)$$
$$\delta(\Phi_1 \vee \Phi_2)=\delta(\Phi_1) \vee \delta(\Phi_2) \qquad\qquad \delta(\Phi^*)=\text{true} \qquad\qquad \delta(\Phi^\omega)=\text{false}$$

Definition 2 (First). *Let* fst$(\Phi):=\{I \mid (I \cdot \Phi') \in \llbracket \Phi \rrbracket\}$ *be the set of initial time instants derivable from effects Φ. ($\llbracket \Phi \rrbracket$ represents all the traces contained in Φ.)*

$$\text{fst}(\bot)=\{\} \qquad \text{fst}(\mathcal{E})=\{\} \qquad \text{fst}(I)=\{I\} \qquad \text{fst}(\Phi^*)=\text{fst}(\Phi)$$
$$\text{fst}(\Phi^\omega)=\text{fst}(\Phi) \qquad\qquad \text{fst}(\Phi_1 \vee \Phi_2)=\text{fst}(\Phi_1) \cup \text{fst}(\Phi_2)$$
$$\text{fst}(\Phi_1 \cdot \Phi_2)= \begin{cases} \text{fst}(\Phi_1) \cup \text{fst}(\Phi_2) & \text{if } \delta(\Phi_1)=\text{true} \\ \text{fst}(\Phi_1) & \text{if } \delta(\Phi_1)=\text{false} \end{cases}$$

Definition 3 (Instants Subsumption). *Given two time instants* I *and* J, *we define the subset relation* $I \subseteq J$ *as: the set of present signals in* J *is a subset of the set of present signals in* I, *and the set of absent signals in* J *is a subset of the set of absent signals in* I.[5] *Formally,*

$$I \subseteq J \Leftrightarrow \{S \mid (S \mapsto \text{present}) \in J\} \subseteq \{S \mid (S \mapsto \text{present}) \in I\} \text{ and}$$
$$\{S \mid (S \mapsto \text{absent}) \in J\} \subseteq \{S \mid (S \mapsto \text{absent}) \in I\}$$

Definition 4 (Partial Derivative). *The partial derivative* $D_I(\Phi)$ *of effects* Φ *w.r.t. a time instant* I *computes the effects for the left quotient* $I^{-1}[\![\Phi]\!]$.

$$D_I(\bot) = \bot \qquad D_I(\mathcal{E}) = \bot \qquad D_I(J) = \mathcal{E} \ (\textit{if } I \subseteq J) \qquad D_I(J) = \bot \ (\textit{if } I \not\subseteq J)$$
$$D_I(\Phi^\star) = D_I(\Phi) \cdot (\Phi^\star) \qquad D_I(\Phi^\omega) = D_I(\Phi) \cdot (\Phi^\omega) \qquad D_I(\Phi_1 \vee \Phi_2) = D_I(\Phi_1) \vee D_I(\Phi_2)$$

$$D_I(\Phi_1 \cdot \Phi_2) = \begin{cases} D_I(\Phi_1) \cdot \Phi_2 \vee D_I(\Phi_2) & \text{if } \delta(\Phi_1) = \texttt{true} \\ D_I(\Phi_1) \cdot \Phi_2 & \text{if } \delta(\Phi_1) = \texttt{false} \end{cases}$$

5.1 Inference Rules

We now discuss the key steps and related inference rules that we may use in such an effects inclusion proof.

I. **Axiom Rules.** Analogous to the standard propositional logic, $\bot$ (referring to *false*) entails any effects, while no *non-false* effects entails $\bot$.

$$\frac{}{\Gamma \vdash \bot \sqsubseteq \Phi} \ [\text{Bot-LHS}] \qquad\qquad \frac{\Phi \neq \bot}{\Gamma \vdash \Phi \not\sqsubseteq \bot} \ [\text{Bot-RHS}]$$

II. **Disprove (Heuristic Refutation).** This rule is used to disprove the inclusions when the antecedent is nullable, while the consequent is not nullable. Intuitively, the antecedent contains at least one more trace (the empty trace) than the consequent. Therefore, the inclusion is invalid.

$$\frac{\delta(\Phi_1) \wedge \neg\delta(\Phi_2)}{\Gamma \vdash \Phi_1 \not\sqsubseteq \Phi_2} \ [\text{DISPROVE}]$$

III. **Prove.** We use the rule [REOCCUR] to prove an inclusion when there exist inclusion hypotheses in the proof context Γ, which are able to soundly prove the current goal. One of the special cases of this rule is when the identical inclusion is shown in the proof context, we then terminate the procedure and prove it as a valid inclusion.

$$\frac{(\Phi_1 \sqsubseteq \Phi_3) \in \Gamma \qquad (\Phi_3 \sqsubseteq \Phi_4) \in \Gamma \qquad (\Phi_4 \sqsubseteq \Phi_2) \in \Gamma}{\Gamma \vdash \Phi_1 \sqsubseteq \Phi_2} \ [\text{REOCCUR}]$$

---

[5] As in having more constraints refers to a smaller set of satisfying instances.

IV. **Unfolding (Induction).** Here comes the inductive step of unfolding the inclusions. Firstly, we make use of the auxiliary function `fst` to get a set of instants F, which are all the possible initial time instants from the antecedent. Secondly, we obtain a new proof context Γ' by adding the current inclusion, as an inductive hypothesis, into the current proof context Γ. Thirdly, we iterate each element $I \in F$, and compute the partial derivatives (the *next-state* effects) of both the antecedent and consequent w.r.t I. The proof of the original inclusion $\Phi_1 \sqsubseteq \Phi_2$ succeeds if all the derivative inclusions succeeds.

$$\frac{F = \mathtt{fst}(\Phi_1) \quad \Gamma' = \Gamma, (\Phi_1 \sqsubseteq \Phi_2) \quad \forall I \in F. \ (\Gamma' \vdash D_I(\Phi_1) \sqsubseteq D_I(\Phi_2))}{\Gamma \vdash \Phi_1 \sqsubseteq \Phi_2} \ [\text{UNFOLD}]$$

V. **Normalization.** We present a set of normalization rules to soundly transfer the synced effects into a normal form, particular after getting their derivatives. Before getting into the above inference rules, we assume that the effects formulae are tailored accordingly using the lemmas shown in Table 2 We built the lemmas on top of a complete axiom system suggested by Antimirov and Mosses [3], which was designed for finite regular languages and did not include the corresponding lemmas for effects constructed by ω.

Table 2. Some Normalization Lemmas for synced effects.

$\Phi \vee \Phi \rightarrow \Phi$	$\perp \cdot \Phi \rightarrow \perp$	$(\mathcal{E} \vee \Phi)^* \rightarrow \Phi^*$
$\perp \vee \Phi \rightarrow \Phi$	$\Phi \cdot \perp \rightarrow \perp$	$(\Phi_1 \vee \Phi_2) \vee \Phi_3 \rightarrow \Phi_1 \vee (\Phi_2 \vee \Phi_3)$
$\Phi \vee \perp \rightarrow \Phi$	$\perp^\omega \rightarrow \perp$	$(\Phi_1 \cdot \Phi_2) \cdot \Phi_3 \rightarrow \Phi_1 \cdot (\Phi_2 \cdot \Phi_3)$
$\mathcal{E} \cdot \Phi \rightarrow \Phi$	$\perp^* \rightarrow \mathcal{E}$	$\Phi \cdot (\Phi_1 \vee \Phi_2) \rightarrow \Phi \cdot \Phi_1 \vee \Phi \cdot \Phi_2$
$\Phi \cdot \mathcal{E} \rightarrow \Phi$	$\Phi^\omega \cdot \Phi_1 \rightarrow \Phi^\omega$	$(\Phi_1 \vee \Phi_2) \cdot \Phi \rightarrow \Phi_1 \cdot \Phi \vee \Phi_2 \cdot \Phi$

Theorem 3 (Termination). *The rewriting system TRS is terminating.*

Theorem 4 (Soundness). *Given an inclusion $\mathcal{I}$, if the TRS returns* TRUE *when proving $\mathcal{I}$, then $\mathcal{I}$ is valid.*

Proof. Both see in the technical report [21].

5.2 Expressiveness of Synced Effects

Classical LTL extended propositional logic with the temporal operators $\mathcal{G}$ ("globally") and $\mathcal{F}$ ("in the future"), which we also write $\Box$ and $\Diamond$, respectively; and introduced the concept of fairness, which ensures an infinite-paths semantics.

Table 3. Examples for converting LTL formulae into Effects. ($\{\mathbf{A}\}, \{\mathbf{B}\}$ represent different time instants which contain signal $\mathbf{A}$ and $\mathbf{B}$ to be present.)

$\Box\mathbf{A} \equiv \{\mathbf{A}\}^\omega$	$\Diamond\mathbf{A} \equiv \{\}^\star \cdot \{\mathbf{A}\}$	$\mathbf{A}\ \mathcal{U}\ \mathbf{B} \equiv \{\mathbf{A}\}^\star \cdot \{\mathbf{B}\}$
$\mathcal{X}\mathbf{A} \equiv \{\} \cdot \{\mathbf{A}\}$	$\Box\Diamond\mathbf{A} \equiv (\{\}^\star \cdot \{\mathbf{A}\})^\omega$	$\Diamond\Box\mathbf{A} \equiv \{\}^\star \cdot \{\mathbf{A}\}^\omega$

LTL was subsequently extended to include the $\mathcal{U}$ ("until") operator and the $\mathcal{X}$ ("next time") operator. As shown in Table 3, we are able to recursively encode these basic operators into our synced effects, making it possibly more intuitive and readable, mainly when nested operators occur[6].

Besides the high compatibility with standard first-order logic, synced effects makes the temporal verification for Esterel more scalable. It avoids the *must-provided* translation schemas for each LTL temporal operator, as to how it has been done in the prior work [15].

6   Implementation and Evaluation

To show the feasibility of our approach, we have prototyped our automated verification system using OCaml *(Source code and test suite are available from* [19]*)*. The proof obligations generated by the verifier are discharged using constraint solver Z3. We prove termination and soundness of the TRS, our beck-end solver. We validate the front-end forward verifier for conformance, against two Esterel implementations: the Columbia Esterel Compiler (CEC) [11] and Hiphop.js [7,24]:

- **CEC:** It is an open-source compiler designed for research in both hardware and software generation from the Esterel synchronous language to C, Verilog or BLIF circuit description. It currently supports a subset of Esterel V5 [5], and provides pure Esterel programs for testing.
- **Hiphop.js:** It is a DSL for JavaScript, to facilitate the design of complex web applications by smoothly integrating Esterel and JavaScript. To enrich our test suite, we take a subset of Hiphop.js programs (as our verifier does not accept JavaScript code), and translate them into our target language.

Based on these two benchmarks, we validate the verifier using 96 pure Esterel programs, varying from 10 lines to 300 lines. We manually annotate temporal specifications in synced effects for each of them, including both succeeded and failed instances. The remainder of this section presents some case studies.

---

[6] Our implementation provides a LTL-to-Effects translator.

6.1 Loops

As shown in Fig. 13, the program firstly emits signal **A**, then enters into a loop which emits signal **B** followed by a pause followed by emitting signal **C** at the end. The synced effects of it is $\Phi=\{A,B\}\cdot(\{B,C\})^{\omega}$, which says that in the first time instant, signals **A** and **B** will be present, because there is no explicit pause between the `emit A` and the `emit B`; then for the following instants (in an infinite trace), signals **B** and **C** will be present all the time, because after executing `emit C`, it immediately executes from the beginning of the loop, which is `emit B`. As we can see, Esterel's instantaneous nature requires a special distinction when it comes to loop statements, which increases the difficulty of the invariants inference, enabled by our forward verifier.

To further demonstrate the execution of loop statements, we revise the example in Fig. 13 by adding a pause at the beginning of the loop, as shown in Fig. 14 We get an different final effects $\Phi' = \{A\}\cdot(\{B\}\cdot\{C\})^{\omega}$, where only signal **A** is present in the first time instant; Then for the following instances (in an infinite trace), **B** and **C** are not necessarily to be present in the same instances, instead, they will take turns to be present.

6.2 Exception Priority

As shown in Fig. 15, the final effects for this nested trap test contains one time instance with only signal **A** is present. In the nested exception declaration, the outer traps have higher priorities over the inner traps, in other words, the exception of greater depth has always priority. In this example, when `exit T1` and `exit T2` are executed concurrently, as `exit T1` has a higher priority, the control will be transferred directly to the end of `trap T1`, ignoring the `emit B` in line 12. Therefore signal **A** is emitted while signal **B** is not emitted.

```
1  module loopTest1:
2  output A,B,C;
3  /*@
4  require {}
5  ensure {A,B}.({B,C})w
6  @*/
7  emit A;
8  loop
9    emit B; pause; emit C
10 end loop   end module
```

Fig. 13. Loop (1)

```
1  module loopTest2:
2  output A,B,C;
3  /*@
4  require {}
5  ensure {A}.({B}.{C})w
6  @*/
7  emit A;
8  loop
9    pause; emit B;
10   pause; emit C
11 end loop   end module
```

Fig. 14. Loop (2)

```
1  module trapTest:
2  output A,B;
3  /*@
4  require {}
5  ensure {A}
6  @*/
7  trap T1 in
8    trap T2 in
9      emit A;
10     (exit T1)||(exit T2)
11   end trap;
12   emit B
13 end trap
14 end module
```

Fig. 15. Exception priority

6.3   A Gain on Constructiveness

We discovered a bug from the Esterel v5 *Constructive* semantics [4]. As shown in Fig. 16, this program is detected as "non-constructive" and rejected by CEC. Because the status of **S** must be *guessed* prior to its emission; however, in present statements, it is required that the status of the tested signal must be *determined* before executing the sub-expressions.

```
1  module a_bug:
2  output S;
3  /*@
4  require {}
5  ensure {S}
6  @*/
7  signal S in
8    present S then emit S
9    else emit S
10   end present end signal
11 end module
```

Fig. 16. A bug found

Well, this program actually can be constructed, as the only possible assignment to signal **S** is to be present. Our verification system accepts this program, and compute the effects effectively. We take this as an advantage of using our approach to compute the fixpoint of the program effects, which essentially explores all the possible assignments to signals in a more efficient manner.

7   Related Work

7.1   Semantics of Esterel

For the Pure Esterel, an early work [6] (1992) gave two operational semantics, a macrostep logical semantics called the behavioural semantics, and a small-step logical semantics called the execution semantics. A subsequent work [4] (1999) gave an update to the logical behavioural macrostep semantics to make it more *constructive*. The logical behavioural semantics requires existence and uniqueness of a behaviour, while the constructive behavioural semantics introduces *Can* function to determine execution paths in an effective but restricted way.

Our synced effects of Esterel closely follows the work of states-based semantics [4]. In particular, we borrow the idea of internalizing state into effects using *history* and *current* that bind a partial store embedded at any level in a program. However, as the existing semantics are not ideal for compositional reasoning in terms of the source program, our forward verifier can help meet this requirement for better modularity.

A more recent work [12] (2019) proposes a calculus for Esterel, which is different from a reduction system - although there is an equational theory. The deep lack in the calculus is the ability to reason about input signals. However, as explained in Sect. 4.2, our effects logic is able to reason about the correctness with unbounded input signals. Beyond the correctness checking, the computed temporal effects are particularly convenient for the safety checking at the source code level before the runtime. With that, next, we introduce some related works of temporal verification on Esterel programs.

7.2   Temporal Verification of Esterel

In prior work [15], given a LTL formula, they first recursively translate it into an Esterel program whose traces correspond to the computations that violate the safety formula. The program derived from the formula is then composed in parallel with the given Esterel program to be verified. The program resulting from this composition is compiled using available Esterel tools; a trivial analysis of the compiler's output then indicates whether or not the property is satisfied by the original program. By exhaustively generating all the composed program's reachable states, the Esterel compiler, in fact, performs model checking.

However, the overhead introduced by the complex translation makes it particularly inefficient when *disproving* some of the properties. Besides, it is limited by the expressive power of LTL, as whenever a new temporal logic has to be introduced, we need to design a new translation schema for it accordingly.

Informally, we are concerned with the problem: *Given a temporal property* Φ', *how to check that a given behaviour* Φ *satisfies it*. The standard approaches to this *language inclusion* problem are based on the translation of Φ and Φ' into equivalent finite state automata: $\mathcal{M}_{\mathcal{A}}$ and $\mathcal{M}_{\mathcal{B}}$; and then check emptiness of $\mathcal{M}_{\mathcal{A}} \cap \neg \mathcal{M}_{\mathcal{B}}$. However, the worst-case complexity of any efficient algorithm [10] based on such translation also goes exponential in the number of states.

In this work, we provide an alternative approach, inspired by Antimirov and Mosses' work, which presented a TRS [3] for deciding the inequalities of basic regular expressions. A TRS is a refutation method that normalizes regular expressions in such a way that checking their inequality corresponds to an iterated process of checking the inequalities of their *partial derivatives* [2]. Works based on such a TRS [3,14,16] suggest that this method is a better average-case algorithm than those based on the translation into automata. Invigorated by that, in this paper, we present a new solution of extensive temporal verification, which deploys a TRS but solves the language inclusions between Synced Effects.

Similarly, extending from Antimirov's notions of partial derivatives, prior work [8] (Broda et al., 2015) presented a decision procedure for equivalence checking between Synchronous Kleene Algebra (SKA) terms. Next, we discuss the similarities and differences between our work and [8].

7.3   Synchronous Kleene Algebra (SKA)

Kleene algebra (KA) is a decades-old sound and complete equational theory of regular expressions. Our Synced Effects theory draws similarities to SKA [18], which is KA extended with a synchrony combinator for actions. Formally, given a KA is $(A, +, \cdot, \star, 0, 1)$, a SKA over a finite set A_B is $(A, +, \cdot, \times, \star, 0, 1, A_B)$, $A_B \subseteq A$. Our $\bot$ (*false*) corresponds to the 0; our $\mathcal{E}$ (empty trace) corresponds to the 1; our *time instance* containing simultaneous signals can be expressed via $\times$; and the *instants subsumption* (Definition 3) is reflected by SKA's *demanding relation*.

Presently, SKA allows the synchrony combinator $\times$ to be expressed over any two SKA terms to support concurrency. We achieve a similar outcome in Synced Effects by supporting normalization operations during trace synchronization, via a `zip` function in the forward rule of [FV-Par]. This leads to one major difference in the inclusion/equivalence checking procedure, whereby a TRS for SKA would have to rely on *nullable*, *first*, and *partial derivatives* for terms constructed by the added combinator ×, but carefully avoided by our TRS construction. While the original equivalence checking algorithm for SKA terms in [18] has relied on well-studied decision procedures based on classical Thompson ϵ-NFA construction, [8] shows that the use of Antimirov's partial derivatives could result in better average-case algorithms for automata construction. Our present work avoided the consideration for the more general × operation from SKA and customized the TRS for inclusion (instead of equivalence) checking. These decisions led to some opportunities for improvements. Moreover, between TRS and the construction of efficient automata, we have recently shown in [20] that the former has a minor performance advantage (over a benchmark suite) when it is compared with state-of-the-art PAT [22] model checker. Improvement came from the avoidance of the more expensive automata construction process.

Apart from the synchrony combinator, we also introduced the ω constructor to explicitly distinguish infinite traces from the coarse-grained repetitive operator kleene star $\star$. The inclusion of ω constructor allows us to support non-terminating reactive systems, that are often supported by temporal specification and verification to ensure systems dependability. As a consequence, our backend TRS solver is designed to be able to soundly reason about both finite traces (inductive definition) and infinite traces (conductive definition), using cyclic proof techniques of [9].

Another extension from the ready-made KA theory is Kleene algebra with tests (KAT), which provides solid mathematical semantic foundations for many domain-specific languages (DSL), such as NetKAT [1], designed for network programming. In KAT, actions are extended with boolean predicates and the negation operator is added accordingly. Our Synced Effects also support the boolean algebra in a similar way, since each of our signals can be explicitly specified to be either present or absent. Contradictions of such signals are also explicitly captured by $\perp$ (*false*), whenever signal unification fails.

8   Conclusion

We define the syntax and semantics of the novel Synced Effects, capable of capturing Esterel program behaviours and temporal properties. We develop a Hoare-style forward verifier to compute the program effects constructively. The verifier further enables a more systematic logical correctness checking, with the presence of unbounded input signals, which was a profound lack in prior works. We present an effects inclusion checker (the TRS) to verify the annotated temporal properties efficiently. We implement the effects logic and show its feasibility. To the best of our knowledge, our work is the first solution that automates modular verification for Esterel using an expressive effects logic.

Acknowlegement. We would like to thank the referees of VMCAI 2021 for most helpful advices. This work is supported by NRF grant R-252-007-A50-281 and MoE Tier-1 R-252-000-A63-114.

References

1. Anderson, C.J., et al.: NetKAT: semantic foundations for networks. ACM SIG-PLAN Notices **49**(1), 113–126 (2014)
2. Antimirov, V.: Partial derivatives of regular expressions and finite automata constructions. In: Mayr, E.W., Puech, C. (eds.) STACS 1995. LNCS, vol. 900, pp. 455–466. Springer, Heidelberg (1995). https://doi.org/10.1007/3-540-59042-0_96
3. Antimirov, V., Mosses, P.: Rewriting extended regular expressions. Theoret. Comput. Sci. **143**(1), 51–72 (1995)
4. Berry, G.: The constructive semantics of pure Esterel-draft version 3. Draft Version, 3 (1999)
5. Berry, G.: The Esterel v5 language primer: version v5_91. Centre de mathématiques appliquées, Ecole des mines and INRIA (2000)
6. Berry, G., Gonthier, G.: The Esterel synchronous programming language: design, semantics, implementation. Sci. Comput. Program. **19**(2), 87–152 (1992)
7. Berry, G., Nicolas, C., Serrano, M.: Hiphop: a synchronous reactive extension for Hop. In: Proceedings of the 1st ACM SIGPLAN International Workshop on Programming Language and Systems Technologies for Internet Clients, pp. 49–56 (2011)
8. Broda, S., Cavadas, S., Ferreira, M., Moreira, N.: Deciding synchronous Kleene algebra with derivatives. In: Drewes, F. (ed.) CIAA 2015. LNCS, vol. 9223, pp. 49–62. Springer, Cham (2015). https://doi.org/10.1007/978-3-319-22360-5_5
9. Brotherston J.: Cyclic proofs for first-order logic with inductive definitions. In: Beckert B. (eds) Automated Reasoning with Analytic Tableaux and Related Methods. TABLEAUX 2005. LNCS, vol 3702. Springer, Heidelberg (2005). https://doi.org/10.1007/11554554_8
10. De Wulf, M., Doyen, L., Henzinger, T.A., Raskin, J.-F.: Antichains: a new algorithm for checking universality of finite automata. In: Ball, T., Jones, R.B. (eds.) CAV 2006. LNCS, vol. 4144, pp. 17–30. Springer, Heidelberg (2006). https://doi.org/10.1007/11817963_5
11. Edwards, S.A.: The Columbia Esterel Compiler (2006). http://www.cs.columbia.edu/~sedwards/cec/
12. Florence, S.P., You, S.H., Tov, J.A., Findler, R.B.: A calculus for Esterel: if can, can. if no can, no can. Proc. ACM Program. Lang. **3**(POPL), 1–29 (2019)
13. Gonthier, G.: Sémantiques et modèles d'exécution des langages réactifs synchrones: application à ESTEREL. Ph.D. thesis, Paris 11, (1988)
14. Hovland, D.: The inclusion problem for regular expressions. J. Comput. Syst. Sci. **78**(6), 1795–1813 (2012)
15. Jagadeesan, L.J., Puchol, C., Von Olnhausen, J.E.: Safety property verification of Esterel programs and applications to telecommunications software. In: Wolper, P. (ed.) CAV 1995. LNCS, vol. 939, pp. 127–140. Springer, Heidelberg (1995). https://doi.org/10.1007/3-540-60045-0_45
16. Keil, M., Thiemann, P.: Symbolic solving of extended regular expression inequalities. arXiv preprint arXiv:1410.3227 (2014)
17. Palshikar, G.K.: An introduction to Esterel. Embed. Syst. Program. **14**(11), 1–12 (2001)

18. Prisacariu, C.: Synchronous Kleene algebra. J. Logic Algebraic Program. **79**(7), 608–635 (2010)
19. Song, Y.: Synced effects source code (2020). https://github.com/songyahui/SyncedEffects.git
20. Song, Y., Chin, W.-N.: Automated temporal verification of integrated dependent effects. In: International Conference on Formal Engineering Methods (2020)
21. Song, Y., Chin, W.-N.:Technical report (2020). https://www.comp.nus.edu.sg/~yahuis/VMCAI2021.pdf
22. Sun, J., Liu, Y., Dong, J.S., Pang, J.: PAT: towards flexible verification under fairness. In: Bouajjani, A., Maler, O. (eds.) CAV 2009. LNCS, vol. 5643, pp. 709–714. Springer, Heidelberg (2009). https://doi.org/10.1007/978-3-642-02658-4_59
23. Tardieu, O.: A deterministic logical semantics for Esterel. Electron. Notes Theoret. Comput. Sci. **128**(1), 103–122 (2005)
24. Vidal, C., Berry, G., Serrano, M.: Hiphop. js: a language to orchestrate web applications. In: Proceedings of the 33rd Annual ACM Symposium on Applied Computing, pp. 2193–2195 (2018)

A Design of GPU-Based Quantitative Model Checking

YoungMin Kwon[1(✉)] and Eunhee Kim[2]

[1] Department of Computer Science, The State University of New York, Incheon, Korea
youngmin.kwon@sunykorea.ac.kr
[2] 2e Consulting Corporation, Seoul, South Korea
keh@2e.co.kr

Abstract. In this paper, we implement a GPU-based quantitative model checker and compare its performance with a CPU-based one. Linear Temporal Logic for Control (LTLC) is a quantitative variation of LTL to describe properties of a linear system and LTLC-Checker [1] is an implementation of its model checking algorithm. In practice, its long and unpredictable execution time has been a concern in applying the technique to real-time applications such as automatic control systems. In this paper, we design an LTLC model checker using a GPGPU programming technique. The resulting model checker is not only faster than the CPU-based one especially when the problem is not simple, but it has less variation in the execution time as well. Furthermore, multiple counterexamples can be found together when the CPU-based checker can find only one.

Keywords: Quantitative model checking · GPU programming · LTLC

1 Introduction

Temporal logics are a branch of logic that can specify behaviors of a system evolving over time [12]. *Linear Temporal Logic* (LTL) is a temporal logic that describes linear behaviors of a system without considering branching [18,27]. *Linear Temporal Logic for Control* (LTLC) is a quantitative variation of LTL that can describe properties about state trajectories of a linear system or a hybrid system [23,24]. Using the LTLC model checking technique, (i) one can validate whether all state trajectories of a system satisfy an LTLC specification and (ii) one can compute an input to a physical system such that a goal described in LTLC can be achieved. Particularly, we are interested in the second usage in this paper. To compute a control input, a control objective is described in LTLC and then its negation is model checked. A control input can be obtained from a counterexample such that the input obtained this way can drive the system to satisfy the original goal.

Automatic controllers are systems that interface a computer system and a physical system. Typically, an automatic controller takes a reference input from a computer system and makes the output of a physical system conform to the reference value

Y. Kwon—This work was supported by NRF of MSIT, Korea (2019R1F1A1058770).

© Springer Nature Switzerland AG 2021
F. Henglein et al. (Eds.): VMCAI 2021, LNCS 12597, pp. 441–463, 2021.
https://doi.org/10.1007/978-3-030-67067-2_20

while satisfying certain constraints on the state trajectories. In this paper, we adopt the approaches of a *Model Predictive Control* (MPC), where a sequence of control inputs up to an input horizon is computed to make the system reach a steady state by an output horizon [10, 11]. However, unlike MPC, where a single conjunctive set of constraints is considered, LTLC can consider numerous sets of conjunctive constraints together. That is, a wide range of control objectives can be easily expressed in LTLC. There are quantitative model checking or reachability checking techniques that have been applied to control systems [14, 15, 22, 28]. The state space of a physical system is continuous. There are model checking techniques that can handle such infinite state systems [4, 8, 16, 17, 25].

The trend of boosting the performance of a processor by increasing the clock speed has been obstructed by hardware limitations such as the transistor leakage current. As an alternative strategy, a multi-core architecture, with many cores running at reduced clock speed, is introduced and has been successfully adopted [32, 33]. Graphics card industries adopted the trend and they put thousands of cores in a GPU. To utilize this parallel architecture for general programming practices such as scientific computing, a technique called *General-Purpose computing on Graphics Processing Units* (GPGPU) has been invented. To further enhance the flexibility of GPU programming, Nvidia introduced the *Compute Unified Device Architecture* (CUDA) API along with a set of tools including C/C++ compiler extensions [3, 30]. Using the GPGPU technique many successful performance improvement cases have been reported [2, 3, 21].

When control objectives are simple, the CPU-based LTLC checker can find a counterexample relatively quickly. However, as the complexity of the goal and the control horizon increases, the execution time grows exponentially. This is an inherent characteristic of LTL model checking [12, 27]. Not only is the duration of the execution time increased, but its variation is increased as well because of the search space growth. The long duration and its unpredictability have been a major obstacle in adopting the techniques to real-time applications. In this paper, we design a GPU-based LTLC model checker that runs faster and has a more predictable execution time [1] than those of a CPU-based checker. Although these improvements cannot tackle the inherent exponential complexity issue of LTLC model checking, many goals with a practical complexity can be handled within a reasonable amount of time.

In this paper, the LTLC model checker is redesigned to utilize the parallel architecture of GPU devices. Because the LTLC model checking algorithm is converted to a sequence of feasibility checking problems, we modified the algorithm to solve many linear programming problems on thousands of cores on a GPU in parallel. For complex model checking problems, the execution of the new GPU-based checker is significantly faster than the CPU-based checker on average. Furthermore, the variance of the execution time of the GPU-based checker is much smaller than that of the CPU-based one. This predictable execution time makes the model checker a more suitable candidate for a real-time application such as a feedback controller.

The time complexity of LTL model checking is PSPACE-complete. To speed up the model checking process, a parallel BFS algorithm that runs on many cores of a CPU has been developed [19]. This BFS algorithm has been re-engineered to take advantage of the massive parallel architecture of GPU devices [6, 7]. In [34], a piggyback algorithm is used on Rabin automata to check the liveness property on a GPU device. In this paper, we developed a mixed DFS-BFS algorithm. In LTLC model checking, instead of building an intersection automaton, the feasibility of the constraints on state trajectories along each accepting run of a Büchi automaton is checked by Linear Programming. Pruning infeasible search paths as early as an infeasibility is found in their prefixes can expedite the LTLC model checking process. The mixed DFS-BFS algorithm finds these infeasible prefixes and prevents examinations on unnecessary search paths.

In [5], the massive parallel processing capability of a GPU device has been exploited to approximate invariants of a program using *Octagon Abstract Domains* (OADs). OADs are conjunctions of constrains of the form $\pm x \pm y \leq c$, which can be represented by a *Difference Bound Matrix* (DBM) [31]. OADs can efficiently approximate program invariants by several operations: testing the emptiness using Bellman-Ford algorithm, finding the strong closure to reveal the tightest implicit constraints using Floyd-Warshall shortest-path algorithm, widening the domain to approximate fixpoints, handling of guard and assignment operations, etc. In [5], a GPU device is utilized to speed up the OAD operations. In particular, a GPU performs the OAD operations on DBMs, mapped to a 2D texture, whenever a CPU reaches certain program points. While this approach handles many operations efficiently on relatively simple octagon constraints, the proposed technique mainly checks the emptiness of polyhedrons, a more general constraint. The DBM corresponds to the Tableau in LTLC: the former represents the constraints among program variables and the latter represents an LP problem. While a single DBM is handled on a GPU device at a time in [5], in LTLC model checking, multiple Tableaus are processed simultaneously each by a warp of threads. This approach can further increase the degree of parallelism.

2 Linear Temporal Logic for Control

Linear Temporal Logic for Control (LTLC) is a quantitative temporal logic to describe properties of a linear system [23] or a hybrid system [24]. In this paper, we focus on linear systems, the simpler of the two, so that the performance comparisons are more straightforward. In this section, we summarize the syntax, semantics and a model checking algorithm of LTLC before explaining its extension to a GPU-based parallel design.

2.1 Discrete Linear Time Invariant System Model

LTLC describes properties of *discrete-time Linear Time Invariant* (LTI) systems. LTI systems can be represented by a seven-tuple $M = \langle U, Y, X, A, B, C, D \rangle$, where $U = \{u_1, ..., u_{nu}\}$ is a set of inputs, $Y = \{y_1, ..., y_{ny}\}$ is a set of outputs, $X = \{x_1, ..., x_{nx}\}$ is a set of states, and $A \in \mathbb{R}^{nx \times nx}$, $B \in \mathbb{R}^{nx \times nu}$, $C \in \mathbb{R}^{ny \times nx}$, and $D \in \mathbb{R}^{ny \times nu}$ are system matrices, describing the dynamics of the system in the state space form [13].

The relation among the state trajectory $\mathbf{x} : \mathbb{N} \to \mathbb{R}^{nx}$, the output trajectory $\mathbf{y} : \mathbb{N} \to \mathbb{R}^{ny}$, and the input $\mathbf{u} : \mathbb{N} \to \mathbb{R}^{nu}$ can be expressed in the following recurrence equations.

$$\mathbf{x}(t+1) = A \cdot \mathbf{x}(t) + B \cdot \mathbf{u}(t), \quad \mathbf{y}(t) = C \cdot \mathbf{x}(t) + D \cdot \mathbf{u}(t), \tag{1}$$

where $\mathbf{x}(t)_i = x_i$ at time t, $\mathbf{y}(t)_i = y_i$ at time t, and $\mathbf{u}(t)_i = u_i$ at time t.

Solving the recurrence equation, the state trajectory $\mathbf{x}$ and the output trajectory $\mathbf{y}$ can be expressed in terms of the input $\mathbf{u}$ and the initial state $\mathbf{x}(0)$ as follows:

$$\mathbf{x}(t) = A^t \cdot \mathbf{x}(0) + \sum_{i=0}^{t-1} A^{t-i-1} \cdot B \cdot \mathbf{u}(i), \quad \mathbf{y}(t) = C \cdot \mathbf{x}(t) + D \cdot \mathbf{u}(t). \tag{2}$$

A *computational path* π is a function $\pi : \mathbb{N} \to \mathbb{R}^{nu} \times \mathbb{R}^{ny} \times \mathbb{R}^{nx}$ that comprises the input, output, and state trajectories such that $\pi(t) = (\mathbf{u}(t), \mathbf{y}(t), \mathbf{x}(t))$.

2.2 Syntax and Semantics of LTLC

The syntax of an LTLC formula ϕ is as follows:

$$\phi ::= \mathrm{T} \mid \mathrm{F} \mid ap \mid \neg\phi \mid \phi \wedge \varphi \mid \phi \vee \varphi \mid \phi \to \varphi \mid \phi \leftrightarrow \varphi \mid$$
$$\mathrm{X}\,\phi \mid \phi\,\mathrm{U}\,\varphi \mid \phi\,\mathrm{R}\,\varphi \mid \square\,\phi \mid \lozenge\,\phi,$$
$$ap(t) ::= c_1 \cdot v_1(texp_1) + \ldots + c_n \cdot v_n(texp_n) \bowtie d,$$

where ap is an atomic proposition, $texp_i$ is a polynomial of variable t such that $texp_i \geq t$, $c_1, \ldots, c_n$, and d are real numbers, $v_1, \ldots, v_n \in U \cup Y \cup X$ are input, output, or state variables and $\bowtie$ is one of $<, \leq, >, \geq, =$, and $\neq$.

An implicit meaning of LTLC is as follows. The logical connectives, $\neg, \wedge, \vee, \to$, and $\leftrightarrow$ have their usual meanings, i.e., not, and, or, imply and equivalent respectively. The temporal connectives $\mathrm{X}, \mathrm{U}, \mathrm{R}, \square$, and $\lozenge$ mean: $\mathrm{X}\,\phi$ is true at time t iff ϕ is true at time $t + 1$, $\phi\,\mathrm{U}\,\varphi$ is true at time t iff φ eventually becomes true at some time $t' \geq t$ and ϕ is true during $t \leq \tau < t'$, and $\phi\,\mathrm{R}\,\varphi$ is true at time t iff φ holds up to the first time (inclusively) ϕ becomes true, but if ϕ does not become true, φ is true forever. $\square\,\phi$ is true at time t iff ϕ is always true for $\tau \geq t$, and $\lozenge\,\phi$ is true at time t iff ϕ eventually becomes true at some time $\tau \geq t$.

Formally, the meaning of LTLC formulas can be expressed in the ternary satisfaction relation $\models \subseteq \Pi \times \mathbb{N} \times \Phi$ and the binary satisfaction relation $\models \subseteq \mathcal{M} \times \Phi$, where Π is the set of all computational paths, Φ is the set of all LTLC formulas, and $\mathcal{M}$ is the set of all LTI system models. For simplicity we write $\pi, t \models \phi$ for $(\pi, t, \phi) \in\, \models$ and $M \models \phi$ for $(M, \phi) \in\, \models$. The ternary satisfaction relation $\models$ is as follows

$$\pi, t \models \mathrm{T},$$
$$\pi, t \not\models \mathrm{F},$$
$$\pi, t \models c_1 \cdot v_1(texp_1) + \cdots + c_n \cdot v_n(texp_n) \bowtie d \Leftrightarrow \sum_{i=1}^{n} c_i \cdot \theta(v_i(texp_i)) \bowtie d,$$
$$\pi, t \models \neg\phi \quad \Leftrightarrow \pi, t \not\models \phi,$$
$$\pi, t \models \phi \wedge \varphi \Leftrightarrow \pi, t \models \phi \text{ and } \pi, t \models \varphi,$$
$$\pi, t \models \phi \vee \varphi \Leftrightarrow \pi, t \models \phi \text{ or } \pi, t \models \varphi,$$
$$\pi, t \models \mathrm{X}\,\phi \quad \Leftrightarrow \pi, t+1 \models \phi,$$
$$\pi, t \models \phi\,\mathrm{U}\,\varphi \Leftrightarrow \pi, i \models \varphi \text{ for some } i \geq t \text{ and } \pi, j \models \phi \text{ for all } t \leq j < i,$$
$$\pi, t \models \phi\,\mathrm{R}\,\varphi \Leftrightarrow \pi, t \models \varphi \text{ and for } i > t, \pi, i \models \varphi \text{ if } \pi, j \not\models \phi \text{ for all } t \leq j < i,$$

where $\theta(v_i(texp_i))$ is the value of v_i at time $texp_i$.

Using the ternary satisfaction relation, the binary satisfaction relation can be defined as follows.

$$M \models \phi \Leftrightarrow \pi, 0 \models \phi \text{ for all computational paths } \pi \text{ of } M.$$

While the ternary satisfaction relation is about a single computational path, i.e., whether a given path π satisfies a formula ϕ at time t, the binary satisfaction relation is about all paths, i.e., whether all the computational paths of an LTI system M satisfy a formula ϕ at time 0.

2.3 Horizon Constraints

One of the utilities of LTLC model checking technique is to control an LTI system. Specifically, we are interested in finding a sequence of control input that can drive the system to satisfy a goal described in LTLC. As a part of the goal, LTLC adopted the horizon constraints of *Model Predictive Control* (MPC) [10]. The constraints are: the input and the output of the system do not change after the input horizon Hu and after the output horizon Hy respectively.

With the horizon constraints, we do not need to check the computational paths to their infinite length, but up to the output horizon Hy. As a result, the LTLC model checking process is reduced to a finite one. Although, the LTLC model checking may look similar to the bounded model checking technique, the horizon constraints are weaker than those enforced by bounded model checking. For example, $\Box \phi$ is not satisfiable in bounded model checking, but it is satisfiable in LTLC if the system can reach a steady state where ϕ is true by Hy.

The horizon constraints are as follows

$$H : \bigwedge_{i=1}^{nx}(\mathbf{x}_i(Hy + 1) = \mathbf{x}_i(Hy)) \ \wedge \ \bigwedge_{i=1}^{nu} \Box \, (\mathbf{u}_i(Hu + t) = \mathbf{u}_i(Hu)). \tag{3}$$

From Eq. (1), if two consecutive states are the same and the input does not change henceforth, then the state will not change. If the horizon constraints are satisfied, then for $t \geq Hy$,

$$\pi, t \models \mathsf{X}\,\phi \ \Leftrightarrow \ \pi, t \models \phi, \quad \pi, t \models \phi\,\mathsf{U}\,\varphi \ \Leftrightarrow \ \pi, t \models \varphi, \quad \pi, t \models \phi\,\mathsf{R}\,\varphi \ \Leftrightarrow \ \pi, t \models \varphi.$$

Because $\Box \phi \equiv \mathsf{F}\,\mathsf{R}\,\phi$ and $\Diamond \phi \equiv \mathsf{T}\,\mathsf{U}\,\phi$, the equivalences above effectively remove all temporal operators for $t \geq Hy$ and the satisfiability of a computational path π can be decided instantly at time Hy.

2.4 LTLC Model Checking as Feasibility Checking

The Horizon constraints make the LTLC model checking process a finite one, but the infinite number of computational paths needs to be addressed. To satisfy the binary satisfaction relation $M \models \phi$, every computational path π of M should satisfy ϕ at time 0, but there are infinitely many of them: from Eq. (2), any changes in the input $\mathbf{u}(t)$ at a time t or in the initial state $\mathbf{x}(0)$ can make a different computational path π'. Because $\mathbf{u}(t) \in \mathbb{R}^{nu}$ for $0 \leq t \leq Hu$ and $\mathbf{x}(0) \in \mathbb{R}^{nx}$, there are uncountably many computational paths and enumerating them one by one is not possible.

As a first step to tackle this problem, we convert the formula ϕ to a *Disjunctive Normal Form* (DNF) and check the feasibility of each conjunctive term. Observe that without any temporal operators, an LTLC formula ϕ can be converted to a predicate formula and it can further be transformed to a DNF. If there exists a computational path π that can satisfy all the constraints in any of the conjunctive terms of the DNF, ϕ can be satisfied by the computational path π. Particularly, we check the negation of the original formula, $\neg\phi$. Any feasible path π serves as a counterexample witnessing the violation of the original formula ϕ. On the other hand, the non-existence of a feasible path π attests that all computational paths π of M satisfy the original formula ϕ.

Checking the feasibility of conjunctive terms can be done by solving a *Linear Programming* (LP) problem [29]. To speed up the feasibility checking process, we rewrite the atomic propositions at future time steps in terms of an initial state $\mathbf{x}(0)$ and a sequence of input $\mathbf{u}(t)$ for $0 \leq t \leq Hu$ using Eq. (2). Let a vector of variables $\mathbf{v}$ be defined as

$$\mathbf{v} = [\mathbf{x}_1(0), \ldots, \mathbf{x}_{nx}(0), \mathbf{u}_1(0), \ldots, \mathbf{u}_{nu}(0), \ldots, \mathbf{u}_1(Hu), \ldots, \mathbf{u}_{nu}(Hu)]^T .$$

With $\mathbf{v}$, an atomic proposition $c_1 \cdot v_1(texp_1) + \cdots + c_n \cdot v_n(texp_n) \bowtie d$ can be rewritten as $a_1 \cdot \mathbf{v} + \cdots + a_n \cdot \mathbf{v} \bowtie d$. Furthermore, the problem of finding a computational path π that satisfies all atomic propositions in a conjunctive term is converted to finding a feasible vector $\mathbf{v}$ from the conjunctions of the transformed atomic propositions. LP can be employed to find a feasible vector $\mathbf{v}$.

To bring insights into the LTLC model checking algorithm, let us consider a simple LTLC model checking example.

Example 1 (LTLC Model Checking). A linear system M is $M = \langle U, Y, X, A, B, C, D \rangle$, where $U = \{u\}$, $Y = \{y\}$, $X = \{x_1, x_2\}$, $A = \begin{bmatrix} 1 & 1 \\ 2 & 0 \end{bmatrix}$, $B = [2\ 1]^T$, $C = [1\ 1]$, and $D = \mathbf{0}$. An LTLC specification ϕ is $\phi = H \rightarrow \neg(\mathbf{X}\ a \wedge \mathbf{X}\ \mathbf{X}\ a)$, where the atomic proposition $a(t)$ is $y(t) < 3$, and the input and the output horizons for H are $Hu = 2$ and $Hy = 2$ respectively. In the model checking process, we look for a counterexample, a computational path π that satisfies the negation of the specification. That is, find a π such that $\pi, 0 \models \neg\phi$. In particular, we look for the five variables $\mathbf{x}_1(0), \mathbf{x}_2(0), \mathbf{u}(0), \mathbf{u}(1)$, and $\mathbf{u}(2)$ that can satisfy $\neg\phi \equiv H \wedge \mathbf{X}\ a \wedge \mathbf{X}\ \mathbf{X}\ a$ at time 0. Applying Eq. (2), $\mathbf{x}(1), \mathbf{x}(2)$, and $\mathbf{x}(3)$ are

$$\mathbf{x}(1) = \begin{bmatrix} 1 & 1 \\ 2 & 0 \end{bmatrix} \cdot \mathbf{x}(0) + \begin{bmatrix} 2 \\ 1 \end{bmatrix} \cdot \mathbf{u}(0),$$

$$\mathbf{x}(2) = \begin{bmatrix} 1 & 1 \\ 2 & 0 \end{bmatrix}^2 \cdot \mathbf{x}(0) + \begin{bmatrix} 1 & 1 \\ 2 & 0 \end{bmatrix} \cdot \begin{bmatrix} 2 \\ 1 \end{bmatrix} \cdot \mathbf{u}(0) + \begin{bmatrix} 2 \\ 1 \end{bmatrix} \cdot \mathbf{u}(1),$$

$$\mathbf{x}(3) = \begin{bmatrix} 1 & 1 \\ 2 & 0 \end{bmatrix}^3 \cdot \mathbf{x}(0) + \begin{bmatrix} 1 & 1 \\ 2 & 0 \end{bmatrix}^2 \cdot \begin{bmatrix} 2 \\ 1 \end{bmatrix} \cdot \mathbf{u}(0) + \begin{bmatrix} 1 & 1 \\ 2 & 0 \end{bmatrix} \cdot \begin{bmatrix} 2 \\ 1 \end{bmatrix} \cdot \mathbf{u}(1) + \begin{bmatrix} 2 \\ 1 \end{bmatrix} \cdot \mathbf{u}(2),$$

and $\mathbf{y}(t) = [1, 1] \cdot \mathbf{x}(t)$ for $t = 1$ and $t = 2$.

$$\pi, 0 \models H \wedge \mathbf{X} a \wedge \mathbf{X} \mathbf{X} a$$

$$\Leftrightarrow \begin{cases} \mathbf{u}(t + 2) = \mathbf{u}(2) \text{ for } t \geq 0 \wedge & \text{(input horizon constraint)} \\ \mathbf{x}_1(2) = \mathbf{x}_1(3) \wedge \mathbf{x}_2(2) = \mathbf{x}_2(3) \wedge & \text{(output horizon constraint)} \\ \mathbf{y}(1) < 3 \wedge \mathbf{y}(2) < 3 & (\mathbf{X} a \wedge \mathbf{X} \mathbf{X} a) \end{cases}$$

$$\Leftrightarrow \begin{array}{l} [2, 2, 4, 1, 2] \cdot \mathbf{v} = 0 \wedge [4, 0, 2, 3, 1] \cdot \mathbf{v} = 0 \wedge \\ [3, 1, 3, 0, 0] \cdot \mathbf{v} < 3 \wedge [5, 3, 7, 3, 0] \cdot \mathbf{v} < 3, \end{array}$$

where a vector variable $\mathbf{v} \in \mathbb{R}^5$ is $[\mathbf{x}_1(0), \mathbf{x}_2(0), \mathbf{u}(0), \mathbf{u}(1), \mathbf{u}(2)]^T$.

The input horizon constraint can be satisfied because the input to the system can be freely decided. Thus,

$$M \not\models \phi \Leftrightarrow \left\{ \mathbf{v} : \begin{array}{l} [2, 2, 4, 1, 2] \cdot \mathbf{v} = 0 \wedge [4, 0, 2, 3, 1] \cdot \mathbf{v} = 0 \wedge \\ [3, 1, 3, 0, 0] \cdot \mathbf{v} < 3 \wedge [5, 3, 7, 3, 0] \cdot \mathbf{v} < 3, \end{array} \right\} \neq \emptyset.$$

The existence of $\mathbf{v}$ can be checked by Linear Programming. Any feasible solution $\mathbf{v}$ is a counterexample that we are looking for.   □

A practical concern is that depending on the formula and the horizons, there can be numerous conjunctive terms in a transformed DNF. To make the model checking process practical, we build a Büchi automaton [9] $\mathcal{B}_\phi$ for an LTLC formula ϕ using the Expand algorithm [18] and generate the conjunctive terms from $\mathcal{B}_\phi$. In fact, each accepting run of $\mathcal{B}_\phi$ can be regarded as a conjunctive term of a DNF: if all constraints along the run are feasible then the formula ϕ is satisfiable by the feasible solution. If we search $\mathcal{B}_\phi$ for such accepting runs in the *Depth First Search* (DFS) manner, then the runs in a subtree rooted at a node share the common prefix from the root to the node. If an infeasibility is found in the common prefix, all conjunctive terms sharing the prefix are infeasible and they can be skipped. This pruning technique is very effective and makes the LTLC model checking practical.

3   Parallel Model Checker Design

To exploit the parallel architecture of GPUs, we restructured the LTLC model checking algorithm. In this section we briefly explain preliminaries of CUDA programming and then the design overview of our GPU-based LTLC model checking algorithm.

3.1   Preliminary: CUDA

An Nvidia GPU has tens of *Streaming Multiprocessors* (SM) and each SM is equipped with hundreds of cores. A *kernel* code runs on a core, abstracted in a thread. A group of threads, called a thread *block*, runs concurrently in an SM while sharing memory and synchronization barriers. In addition, the hardware employs an architecture called *Single Instruction Multiple Threads* (SIMT), where a unit of 32 threads, called a *warp*, executes a common instruction at a time until they diverge by branches.

A typical CUDA program runs in the following four steps: (1) allocate memory in the *host* (the CPU and its main memory) and in the *device* (the GPU and its memory); (2) copy data from the host to the device; (3) execute kernel codes on the device; (4) copy the result back from the device to the host. In addition, to reduce the overhead of the memory copy, a pipelining scheme, called *streaming*, is supported. That is, while a kernel code is being executed, data transfer between the host and the device can be performed simultaneously.

3.2   GPU-Based LTLC Model Checking Algorithm

In the CPU-based LTLC model checking algorithm, a counterexample is sought using a Büchi automaton. Specifically, given an LTLC formula ϕ, a Büchi automaton $\mathcal{B}_{\neg\phi}$ for the negated formula $\neg\phi$ is constructed and a counterexample is searched on $\mathcal{B}_{\neg\phi}$ in the *Depth First Search* (DFS) manner. The time complexity of the DFS is exponential *with respect to* (w.r.t.) the output horizon Hy. To accelerate the LTLC model checking process, a feasibility check is performed on each step of the DFS against the constraints collected along the path up to the current node: if the constraints are infeasible, all search paths in the subtree rooted at the current node can be pruned as they share the infeasible constraints. In practice, this strategy is very effective as can be observed in Fig. 6. For an output horizon Hy as large as 40, the GPU-based LTLC model checking for the formula, artificially made to be complex, can be finished in less than one *min* in most of the cases.

In this paper, we further improve performance of the LTLC model checking process by increasing the degree of parallelism. One obvious way to achieve a high degree of parallelism is to check a batch of DFS search paths together on a GPU device in parallel. That is, for each search path of depth Hy obtained by unrolling the graph structure of $\mathcal{B}_{\neg\phi}$, check its feasibility in one of the parallel threads running on a GPU core. However, simply increasing the degree of parallelism by checking multiple DFS paths together does not accelerate the model checking process much: a few thousand parallel threads of a GPU are no match for the exponential growth in the number of search paths as Hy extends. To be effective, we need to utilize the pruning strategy.

As a solution, we designed a mixed DFS and *Breadth First Search* (BFS) strategy. In this scheme, we replaced the single steps of the BFS with path fragments in a DFS subtree of height ℓ. Specifically, (1) after removing a path ρ from the BFS queue;[1] (2) check the feasibility of the paths obtained by suffixing ρ with the path fragments in the DFS subtree rooted at the last node of ρ; and (3) enqueue only the feasible ones to the BFS queue. Because the number of path fragments is exponentially proportional to the height ℓ of the DFS subtree, there are sufficiently many feasibility checking problems that can exploit the parallel architecture of a GPU. Furthermore, because only the feasible paths are enqueued, the model checking process can take advantage of the path pruning strategy.

Figure 1 illustrates this mixed search scheme. Overall, the mixed search is a BFS except that each step of the BFS is not a single node, but a DFS path fragment of length ℓ. In the first diagram of the figure, the DFS prefixes *iPPR*, *iPQP*, *iPQQ*, etc. are

---

[1] To distinguish with other queues, we call the queue for the BFS a *BFS queue* or a *BFS-Q*.

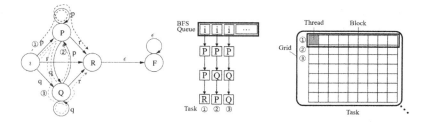

Fig. 1. Task generation and processing steps are illustrated for a Büchi automaton $\mathcal{B}_\phi$ for $\phi = (p \vee q) \cup r$. Prefixes of the runs of $\mathcal{B}_\phi$ up to a predefined length, ℓ, are added to a task queue and then converted to devTasks which are the basic unit of computation in CUDA

queued and checked in the BFS manner when $\ell = 3$. The feasibility of these prefixes is checked on a GPU device in parallel and only the feasible ones participate in the next round of search. Suppose that $iPQP$ is the only feasible prefix, then $iPQPPP$, $iPQPPPQ$, $iPQPPQP$, etc. are queued for the next round. This mixed search ensures that many prefixes of the runs of a Büchi automaton can be checked together. Increasing the degree of parallelism by extending ℓ to its maximum alone does not accelerate the model checking process. By choosing a proper ℓ, we can eliminate subtrees sharing infeasible prefixes while taking advantage of the parallel architecture of GPU devices.

For the mixed search, composite data types of *Task* and *DevTask* are introduced.[2] Among the fields of *Task* are a node of a Büchi automaton called the *current node*, a reference to the *parent task*, and the time step t. The current node and the parent task reference form a subtree representing the active portions of the search tree at the moment. The time step t is equal to the depth of the node in the tree.

While *tasks* are added to the BFS queue during the mixed search, *devTasks* are added to a host-side buffer and transferred between the host-side buffer and a device-side buffer. Each *devTask* has references to the corresponding *task* and to a *tableau*. The *task* reference is to continue the mixed search when the feasibility check is done. That is, depending on the feasibility checking result, either the exploration on that search path is aborted or more DFS paths suffixed with the path fragments rooted at the current node of the task are added to the BFS queue. Whenever a task becomes infeasible, its parent task is informed. If all of the parent's children become infeasible, the parent itself becomes infeasible and is removed after notifying its parent recursively. A *tableau* represents a set of constraints that need to be satisfied together. In addition, the state of the optimization process is recorded in the tableau while solving an LP problem [29]. Particularly, if the Simplex method for LP is paused by a loop-limit, the current state of the process is preserved in the tableau and when the Simplex method is resumed in the next round, it continues from where it was stopped.

Algorithm 1 describes how the tasks are added to the BFS queue. After the feasibility of devTasks is checked on a GPU device (1) the function DFS is called only for feasible tasks; (2) unfinished devTasks are added back to the host-side buffer so that

---

[2] The terms beginning with capital letters like Task and DevTask represent types and those beginning with small letters like task and devTask represent their instances.

Algorithm 1. DFS for task generation

---

function DFS(task, depth)
  if depth = 0 **then**
    add task to BFS-Q
  else
    n = task.node, t = task.t + 1   *{task forms a search path from the node to the root}*
    if $t < Hy$ **then**
      for all m ∈ n.outgoing-nodes **do**
        DFS(new Task(task, m, t), depth-1)   *{Task(parent, current node, step)}*
      end for
    else
      for all ineq ∈ n.final-(in)equalities **do**
        task' = new Task(task, ∅, t)
        add ineq to task'   *{ineq: constraints to reach and cycle an accepting loop}*
        add task' to BFS-Q
      end for
    end if
  end if
end function

---

they can continue from where they were stopped; and (3) the tasks for infeasible dev-Tasks are removed immediately so that the search trees rooted at their current nodes are pruned. Function DFS adds tasks to the BFS queue while traversing the search tree in the DFS manner up to the depth ℓ. On reaching Hy, the function DFS creates a new task for each of the constraint set in final-(in)equalities and adds them to the BFS queue. The final-(in)equalities are the conditions, in DNF, for a run to reach and cycle an accepting loop of a Büchi automaton from the node. The horizon constraint H of Eq. (3) is to bring the system to a steady state and it will be further added to each conjunction in Algorithm 2.

Algorithm 2 describes how the tasks in the BFS queue are added to a page-locked host-side buffer *hostBuf*. A tableau is generated from a task in *BFS-Q* and is added to a devTask along with a reference to the task. The tableau for a task is built to include all constraints from the task's current node to the root by following the *parent task* links. When the task's time step reaches Hy, the horizon constraint of Eq. (3) is added to the tableau in addition to the constraints in a search path. If the hostBuf is full or the BFS queue is empty, the devTasks in the buffer are scheduled to run on a GPU device.

When creating a devTask, its tableau is placed within the host-side buffer together. Once the host-side buffer is ready, it is asynchronously copied to its device-side counter-part, *devBuf*. Therefore, a kernel code can execute its task using the tableau in the device memory. However, after the copy, all the memory references need to be remapped because the host-side buffer address and the device-side buffer address are different. The reference remapping can be done straightforwardly using an offset from an anchor point. In particular, we update all memory references such that their offsets from the beginning of both buffers are the same. Once the kernel tasks are finished, the device-side buffer is copied back to the host-side buffer asynchronously and the memory references are remapped once again.

Algorithm 2. BFS for devTask generation

{*Code fragment for adding devTasks to hostBuf from tasks in BFS-Q*}
while (BFS-Q $\neq \emptyset$ **or** hostBuf $\neq \emptyset$) **and** counterexample is not found **do**
  if BFS-Q $\neq \emptyset$ **then**
    remove a task τ from BFS-Q
    if $\tau.t < Hy$ **then**
      Build a tableau T for τ {*add normalized constraints along τ to T*}
      devTask = new DevTask(T, task)
      add devTask to hostBuf
    else
      Build a tableau T for τ and horizon constraints {*normalized constraints $\cup$ H*}
      devTask = new DevTask(T, task)
      add devTask to hostBuf
    end if
  end if
  if hostBuf is full **or** BFS-Q $= \emptyset$ **then**
    schedule devTasks in hostBuf to run on GPU
  end if
end while

In CUDA, data transfer between the host and the device is a potential performance bottleneck. To mitigate the latency, CUDA supports a pipeline scheme called streaming. In particular, the device has three queues, one is for the kernel computation and the other two are for the data transfer from host to device and from device to host respectively. The operations in different queues can be performed simultaneously. To utilize the streaming capability, we added multiple streams each equipped with its own host-side and device-side buffers. The buffers for each stream are allocated once when the model checker is initialized because memory allocation in the device or page-locked memory allocation in the host will synchronize all other asynchronous operations.

The number of required Simplex iterations would be different from a devTask to a devTask. This is also true for the devTasks in the same stream. As a result, all threads in a stream are synchronized to the slowest one. As a remedy to this issue, we increased the number of streams and reduced the number of devTasks within a stream. That way, the expected execution time of all threads within a stream is reduced. Furthermore, we enforce a loop-limit on the Simplex iterations such that any devTasks that are not finished within the loop-limit are moved to the next round. Hence, quickly finished devTasks do not need to wait long for the slowest one to finish.

Algorithm 3 describes the devTask scheduling procedure. CUDA streams are employed to relieve the latency due to the memory copy. We added a composite data type *Stream* to facilitate the stream processing. Stream has fields *hostBuf* for its page-locked host-side buffer, *devBuf* for its device-side buffer, and *s* for its CUDA stream id. Each devTask is processed by a block of 32 threads. The number of threads in a block is equal to the warp size. In addition, the number of thread blocks is equal to the number of devTasks to process, $devTask_i.size$, in $stream_i$. The argument to the kernel function is $devBuf_i$, containing an array of devTasks and their tableaus. After all of the kernel functions are executed, those devTasks paused by the loop-limit are added back

---

Algorithm 3. GPU task scheduling

{Code fragment for scheduling devTasks to run on a GPU device}
for all stream$_i$ ∈ streams **do**
  if stream$_i$ is ready to run on a GPU **then**
    cudaMemcpyAsync()   *{copy hostBuf$_i$ to devBuf$_i$}*
    lpSolve ≪ devTask$_i$.size, 32, 0, stream$_i$.s ≫ (devBuf$_i$)
    cudaMemcpyAsync()   *{copy devBuf$_i$ to hostBuf$_i$}*
  end if
end for
wait until any stream$_j$ is finished
for all devTasks τ in hostBuf$_j$ **do**
  if the feasibility of τ is not decided **then**
    add τ back to hostBuf$_j$
  else if τ is feasible **then**
    call DFS to add the next round of tasks to BFS-Q
  end if   *{ignore τ if it is infeasible}*
end for

Algorithm 4. GPU kernel - LP problem solver

__global__ **function** lpSolve (parameters)   *{kernel function}*
remap the pointers in the devTask at devBuf$_{blockIdx.x}$
update the cost row in Tableau
for loop = 0 **to** maxLoop-1 **do**
  break if cost cannot be reduced further
  __syncwarp__()   *{memory barrier}*
  find a pivot
  __syncwarp__()   *{memory barrier}*
  update the pivot's row and other rows
end for
set time-out flag of devTask **if** loop = maxLoop
__syncthreads__()
end function

---

to *hostBuf$_i$*; infeasible ones are discarded; and only for the feasible devTasks, DFS is called to generate the next round of tasks.

Algorithm 4 describes the kernel code to solve an LP problem. The first step is the remapping of the references from the host memory address space to the device memory address space. Once the kernel computation is done, the reverse mapping is performed on the host. There is a limit, called *maxLoop*, on the number of row operations for each round. It prevents all devTasks from waiting for the slowest one to finish. The interrupted devTasks by the loop-limit are added back to hostBuf$_i$ so that they can continue solving their LP problems in the next round.

To utilize the SIMT architecture, a block of 32 threads is assigned for each devTask. The 32 threads run in the same warp. However, because the number of tableau columns may not be a multiple of 32, some threads may cover more columns than other threads. Furthermore, if the number of columns is less than 32, some threads do not even participate in the Simplex method. Hence, we added the barriers, __syncwarp, to make the participating threads start certain phases of the Simplex method in synchrony.

For example, the row operations of each thread should be started only after a pivot is selected and the pivot selection can be started only after all row operations are finished.

4   Experiments

In this section, we compare the performances of the CPU-based LTLC-Checker and those of the GPU-based one. For this comparison, we modified the helicopter velocity control example of [23]. Specifically, we adopted the same helicopter dynamics model, but used a more complicated specification to compare their performances.

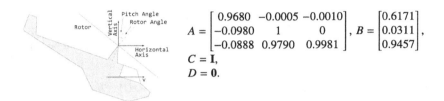

$$A = \begin{bmatrix} 0.9680 & -0.0005 & -0.0010 \\ -0.0980 & 1 & 0 \\ -0.0888 & 0.9790 & 0.9981 \end{bmatrix}, B = \begin{bmatrix} 0.6171 \\ 0.0311 \\ 0.9457 \end{bmatrix},$$
$$C = \mathbf{I},$$
$$D = \mathbf{0}.$$

Fig. 2. A helicopter diagram and its system matrices.

Figure 2 describes the parameters of the helicopter model and its system matrices. The helicopter is controlled by changing the rotor angle, denoted by r. The model has three state variables represented by a column vector $\mathbf{x} \in \mathbb{R}^3$: *pitch rate* $q' = \frac{d}{dt}p = \mathbf{x}_1$, *pitch angle* $p' = \mathbf{x}_2$, and *velocity* $v' = \mathbf{x}_3$. The state variables are regarded as output variables without any transformations. The formal model of the helicopter dynamics is

$$M = \langle U, Y, X, A, B, C, D \rangle, \text{ where } U = \{r\}, \ Y = \{q, p, v\}, \ X = \{q', p', v'\},$$

and the system matrices are on the right side of Fig. 2.

To compare the performances of the two model checkers, we made a rather artificial goal and measured their execution times while changing some of its parameters. With the helicopter model M, let us describe the LTLC specification for this experiment in terms of the initial condition, the constraints, and the goal.

- Initially, the pitch rate, the pitch angle, and the velocity are 0 °/sec, 0 °, and 1 *m/sec* respectively, i.e., $q(0) = 0$, $p(0) = 0$, and $v(0) = 1$.
- We enforced the constraints that the rotor angle is always within ± 20° ($\pm\theta_{r20}$ *radian*) and its rate of change is always within ±10 °/sec($\pm\theta_{r10}$ *radian/sec*).
- The goal is to accelerate the helicopter to reach a velocity *vf m/sec* at some time and then decelerate it to the permanent stop within the output horizon *Hy*. To make the problem more complex, we allow a range of pitch angle of ±15° ($\pm\theta_{p15}$ *radian*) until the stop condition can be achieved by restricting the pitch rate to a range of ±2 °/sec ($\pm\theta_{q2}$ *radian/sec*).

To obtain a control input from a counterexample, we check $M \models \neg\phi$. Particularly, if the result is false, the checker reports a counterexample including $r(t)$ for $t = 0, \ldots, Hu$ such that the original goal ϕ can be achieved. On the other hand, if the result is true, no control input can satisfy the original goal ϕ. We measured the execution times with two different pairs of horizons: $Hy = 40, Hu = 39$ and $Hy = 30, Hu = 29$.

The initial condition can be expressed without any temporal operators as

$$\phi_i = (\mathbf{x}_1(t) = 0 \wedge \mathbf{x}_2(t) = 0 \wedge v(t) = 1).$$

The first part of the goal that *the helicopter should reach the speed of vf m/sec at some time* can be described using the eventually operator $\Diamond$ as

$$\phi_{g1} = \Diamond \, v(t) \geq vf.$$

The second part of the goal that restricts the rotor angle and its rate can be expressed using the always operator $\Box$ as

$$\phi_{g2} = \Box (-\theta_{r10} \leq r(t+1) - r(t) \wedge r(t+1) - r(t) \leq \theta_{r10}).$$

The last part of the goal is to stop the helicopter while allowing the wide pitch angle range until the goal can be achieved only by the small pitch rate range. We will use a nested until formula to describe this goal. As a first step, let us describe the condition that limits the pitch to the smaller range and brings the helicopter to stop. $\Box \, v(t) = 0$ means that the helicopter is permanently stopped. Hence, this step can be described as

$$\phi'_{g3} = (-\theta_{q2} \leq q(t) \wedge q(t) \leq \theta_{q2}) \, U \, (\Box \, v(t) = 0).$$

ϕ'_{g3} can be read as *until the helicopter is permanently stopped q is maintained within* $\pm$ 2°/sec *range*. Finally, the condition that *a wide pitch angle range is allowed until* ϕ'_{g3} *is possible* can be expressed using another until formula as

$$\phi_{g3} = (-\theta_{p15} \leq p(t) \wedge p(t) \leq \theta_{p15}) \, U \, \phi'_{g3}.$$

Combining them together, the whole condition can be expressed as

$$\phi = \phi_i \rightarrow (\phi_{g1} \wedge \phi_{g2} \wedge \phi_{g3}).$$

Figure 3 shows an LTLC-Checker description of the model checking problem. The description has two main sections: model description and goal description. These sections begin with tags `system:` and `specification:` respectively. Scalar or matrix constants are defined in the left side of the figure. The system dynamics equations are described in terms of the input, output, and state variables. The specification block begins with the input and output horizon constraints. Optional definitions of atomic propositions follow the horizon constraints. In the example, the physical limits of the rotor angle and the rotor rate limits are described in *ru, rl, rru* and *rrl*. Following these atomic propositions, constraints about the initial state, the velocity *vf* to reach, the stop condition, and the pitch constraints are described. LTLC-checker checks the last LTLC formula that is the negation of the entire goal described above.

```
############################
# Model description

system:
    ############################
    # constants

    #rotor angle/rate, pitch angle/rate
    const pi = 3.141592, deg = pi/180;
    const rmax = 20*deg, rrmax = 10*deg,
          pmax = 15*deg, qmax = 2*deg,
          vf   = 3.0;

    ############################
    # system dynamics

    #near hover dynamics
    const A = [ 0.9608, -0.0005, -0.0010;
                0.0980,  1,       0;
               -0.0888,  0.9790,  0.9981 ],
          B = [ 0.6171;  0.0311;  0.9457 ];

    #x = [pitch rate, pitch angle, velocity]'
    var x[3]: state,
        r: input,   #rotor angle
        p: output, #pitch angle
        q: output, #pitch rate
        v: output; #velocity

    x = A * x + B * r;
    q = [1, 0, 0] * x;
    p = [0, 1, 0] * x;
    v = [0, 0, 1] * x;
```

```
############################
# Goal description

specification:
    ############################
    # horizon constraints
    output horizon: 40;
    input horizon:  39;

    ############################
    # helper formulas
    ru(t):  r(t) <= rmax;
    rl(t):  r(t) >= -rmax;
    rru(t): r(t+1) - r(t) <= rrmax;
    rrl(t): r(t+1) - r(t) >= -rrmax;

    x0(t): x[0](t) = 0;
    x1(t): x[1](t) = 0;

    vi(t): v(t) = 1;
    vh(t): v(t) >= vf;
    vs(t): v(t) = 0;
    pu(t): p(t) <=  pmax;
    pl(t): p(t) >= -pmax;
    qu(t): q(t) <=  qmax;
    ql(t): q(t) >= -qmax;

    ############################
    # the goal
    !( x0 /\ x1 /\
       [] ( ru /\ rl /\ rru /\ rrl ) /\
       vi /\
       ((pu /\ pl) U ((qu /\ ql) U [] vs)) /\
       <> vh);
```

Fig. 3. LTLC-Checker description of the discrete dynamics of the model (left) and the specification of the goal (right).

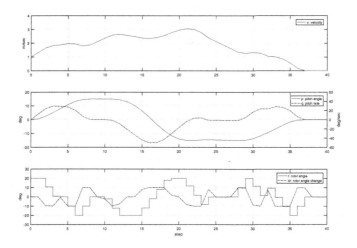

Fig. 4. (Top) velocity, (middle) pitch angle and pitch rate, (bottom) rotor angle and rotor angle change of the helicopter model when the control input found in a counterexample is applied.

As a first step, we checked whether a counterexample satisfies the original goal. Figure 4 shows the input, output, and state trajectories of the helicopter when the control input found in a counterexample is applied. The first graph of Fig. 4 shows how the velocity of the helicopter is changed: the speed of the vehicle reached the speed vf (3.0 m/sec) at step 21 then the vehicle stopped before the output horizon 40. The second graph depicts the pitch angle (solid line) and the pitch rate (dot-dashed line) trajectories over time. The pitch angle line is swinging within the wide range limit of $\pm 15\,^\circ$ and as the vehicle nears the stop condition, the range of the pitch rate is reduced to the narrower limit of $\pm 2\,^\circ/sec$. In the third graph, the rotor angle (solid line) is maintained within the constraint range of $\pm 20\,^\circ$ and the rotor angle change (dot-dashed line) remains with the allowed range of $\pm 10\,^\circ$. Hence, the counterexample satisfies the original goal.

To compare the performances of the two checkers, we measured their execution times while varying the target velocity vf. Because we want to accelerate the helicopter to vf and then decelerate it to stop within a finite horizon, the larger the vf the smaller the solution space will be. In other words, as we increase vf the problem becomes more difficult and the checkers will run longer to find a counterexample. The system used for this experiment is: the host computer is equipped with Intel® Xeon® CPU ES-2360 with hyper-threaded 6 cores running at 2.30 GHz and 32 GB of memory; the graphics card is Nvidia® Titan RTX® with 72 SMs, 4608 CUDA cores and 24 GB of memory.

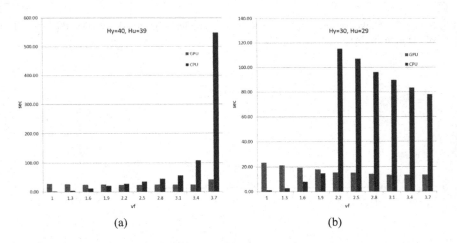

(a)   (b)

Fig. 5. Run times of the GPU-based LTLC model checker (red) and the CPU-based model checker (blue). (a) Comparison result when the output horizon and input horizon are $Hy = 40$ and $Hu = 39$ respectively. Model checking result is false when $vf = 1, \ldots, 3.4$ and true when $vf = 3.7$. (b) Comparison result when the output horizon and input horizon are $Hy = 30$ and $Hu = 29$ respectively. Model checking result is false when $vf = 1, \ldots, 1.9$ and true in other cases. (Color figure online)

Figure 5 shows the results of our performance comparison. While changing vf from 1.0 to 3.7 m/sec in ten equally distributed steps, we measured the execution time of the GPU-based model checker (left-red) and the CPU-based checker (right-blue).

Figure 5(a) and Fig. 5(b) are the results when $Hy = 40$ and when $Hy = 30$ respectively. In both graphs, when vf is small, the CPU-based checker runs faster, but as vf increases the GPU-based checker outperforms the CPU-based one significantly. Furthermore, the execution time of the GPU-based checker does not change much with the changes of vf. On the other hand, the execution time of the CPU-based checker fluctuates widely as vf changes. The jumps when the results become true are because the checker has to search the entire search space. In Fig. 5(b), the time decreases after the jump because infeasible search paths are pruned early.

Figure 6 shows a more detailed performance comparison result. When $Hy = 40$ the GPU-based checker ran 3.27 times faster than the CPU-based checker (26.27 sec vs 85.92 sec) on average, and the former ran 3.57 times faster than the latter (16.65 sec vs 59.58 sec) when $Hy = 30$. However, when the problem is easy (small vf), the CPU-based checker finished earlier than the GPU-based one. The main reason the GPU-based checker under-performed the CPU-based one is the overhead of finding multiple counterexamples together. For example, when $vf = 1$ and $Hy = 40$, although the CPU-based checker ran 15.61 times faster than the GPU-based checker, the GPU-based checker found 1,293 counterexamples simultaneously, while the CPU-based checker found only one.

vf	$Hy = 40, Hu = 39$			$Hy = 30, Hu = 29$		
	GPU (sec)	CPU (sec)	Res.	GPU (sec)	CPU (sec)	Res.
3.7	41.51	547.67	T	13.36	77.91	T
3.4	24.31	108.23	F	13.41	83.34	T
3.1	24.18	56.54	F	13.37	89.61	T
2.8	23.83	44.74	F	14.26	96.14	T
2.5	23.43	35.37	F	15.12	107.00	T
2.2	23.51	27.66	F	15.28	115.04	T
1.9	24.59	20.82	F	17.83	14.80	F
1.6	23.97	12.12	F	19.24	8.04	F
1.3	25.89	4.29	F	21.24	2.80	F
1.0	27.52	1.76	F	23.40	1.12	F
mean	26.27	85.92	·	16.65	59.58	·
std. dev.	5.22	156.73	·	3.42	44.46	·

Fig. 6. Detailed execution times of the GPU-based checker and the CPU-based checker.

This parallel search capability substantially reduces the variance in the execution time of the model checking process. In Fig. 6, the standard deviation of the CPU-based checker is 30.05 times larger than that of the GPU-based one when $Hy = 40$ (156.73 sec vs 5.22 sec) and 13.01 times larger when $Hy = 30$ (44.46 sec vs 3.42 sec). It is because the variations in solving LP problems will be wider when checking a path by solving them sequentially along the path. The overall variation can be reduced by the parallel search: while the GPU cores serving slow tasks will keep working on them, the GPU cores allocated for quickly finished tasks will take new tasks. Moreover, the loop-limit prevents quickly finished tasks from waiting for slower ones to finish. More detailed analyses are in the next section. This reduced variance makes the performance of the model checker more predictable and makes it more attractive for real-time applications.

5   Analysis

In this section, we performed an analysis on the performances of the LTLC model checking algorithm. To simplify the analysis, we assumed that the search depth ℓ of DFS is Hy. We compared the three cases: (1) an algorithm running sequentially on a CPU; (2) an algorithm that picks N DFS paths, checks them in parallel on N GPU cores, and waits for the last to finish before starting the next round; (3) identical to the second case, except that a loop-limit is enforced and paused tasks are moved to the next round.

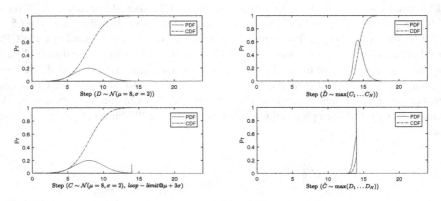

Fig. 7. The CDF and PDF of D: execution time of solving an LP problem; $\hat{D}$: execution time of solving N LP problems in parallel without a loop-limit; C: execution time of solving an LP problem with loop-limit; and $\hat{C}$: execution time of solving N LP problems in parallel with a loop-limit.

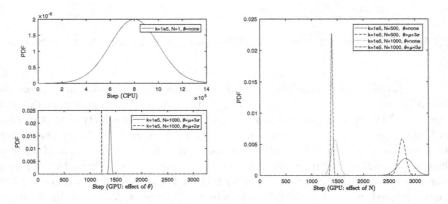

Fig. 8. (top-left) PDF of $A = \sum D_i$; (right) comparing the effect of N: PDFs of $\sum \hat{D}_i$ and $\sum \hat{C}_i$; and (bottom-left) comparing the effect of loop-limit.

First, let us consider the execution time to check a single DFS path. This operation involves checking the feasibility of a set of linear constraints by an LP. An LP problem can be efficiently solved by the Simplex method in polynomial time on average, although the worst case complexity is exponential. To account for this variation, we assumed that the execution time to solve an LP problem follows the Gaussian distribution with the mean μ and the variance σ^2. Let D be a *Random Variable* (RV) representing the execution time to solve an LP problem. Then, $D \sim N(\mu, \sigma^2)$. The top-left side graph in Fig. 7 shows the *Probability Distribution Function* (PDF) and the *Cumulative Distribution Function* (CDF) of D when $\mu = 8$ and $\sigma = 2$.

Suppose that a feasible solution is found at the kth DFS search path. Then, the execution time for the first case is the sum of k *Independent and Identically Distributed* (IID) RVs of D. Let A be a RV representing the execution time of the model checking process. Then, $A = D_1 + D_2 + \cdots + D_k$ and

$$P[A \le x] = G\left(\frac{x-k\cdot\mu}{k\cdot\sigma}\right),$$

where $G(x)$ is the CDF of the Normal distribution: $G = \frac{1}{\sqrt{2\pi}} \int_{-\infty}^{x} e^{-x^2/2}$. The top-left side graph in Fig. 8 shows the PDF of A.

For the second case, let $\hat{D}$ be a RV representing the execution time of the batch of N parallel computations without a loop-limit. That is, $\hat{D}$ is the max of the N IID RVs of D, i.e., $\hat{D} = \max(D_1, \ldots, D_N)$. Then, because $P\left[\hat{D} \le x\right] = P[D_1 \le x \wedge \cdots \wedge D_N \le x]$,

$$P\left[\hat{D} \le x\right] = P[D \le x]^N.$$

The top-right side graph in Fig. 7 shows the PDF and CDF of $\hat{D}$ when $N = 1000$. Because N tasks are waiting for the last one to finish, each round of $\hat{D}$ takes more time than each step of D and the variation is reduced ($\mu_{\hat{D}} = 14.49, \sigma_{\hat{D}} = 0.70$). However, during each round of $\hat{D}$, 1000 times more tasks are executed. Assuming that a GPU core is 100 times slower than a CPU, then the GPU based algorithm will execute 5.52 times more tasks than a CPU based one during the same time period.

Assuming that $k \gg N$, the sum of random variables still follows the Gaussian distribution by the *Central Limit Theorem* (CLT), i.e. $\hat{D}_1 + \hat{D}_2 + \cdots + \hat{D}_{k'} \sim N(k' \cdot \mu_{\hat{D}}, \ k' \cdot \sigma_{\hat{D}})$, where $k' = k/N$, $\mu_{\hat{D}}$ and $\sigma_{\hat{D}}$ are the mean and the standard deviation of the random variable $\hat{D}$ respectively. In the right side graph of Fig. 8, the solid line and the dotted line are the PDFs of the sum of $\hat{D}$ when $N = 500$ and when $N = 1000$ respectively. As the graph shows, increasing the degree of parallelism, N, speeds up the model checking process and reduces the variance as well.

Now, let us consider the third case, where long lasting threads beyond the loop-limit are moved to the next round. Let C be a RV representing the execution time of each thread. The PDF of C is a Gaussian distribution clipped on the right at the time-limit. Let $\hat{C}$ be the RV representing the execution time of the N parallel threads. Then,

$$P[C \le x] = \begin{cases} G\left(\frac{x-\mu}{\sigma}\right) & \text{if } x < \theta \\ 1 & \text{otherwise} \end{cases}, \qquad P\left[\hat{C} \le x\right] = P[C \le x]^N$$

where θ is the cut off time enforced by the loop-limit. The bottom-left side graph of Fig. 7 shows the PDF and CDF of C when $\theta = \mu + 3 \cdot \sigma$. The small jump in the PDF is where the loop-limit is applied. Because of the clipping operation, the mean μ_C and the variance σ_C^2 of C are both reduced from those of D. The bottom-right side graph of Fig. 7 shows the PDF and CDF of $\hat{C}$ when $N = 1000$. Observe that as the number of threads in a batch grows, the likelihood of any of the threads hitting the loop-limit increases exponentially. Hence, there are sharp edges in the PDF and CDF at θ. The mean and the standard deviation of $\hat{C}$ are $\mu_{\hat{C}} = 13.92$ and $\sigma_{\hat{C}} = 0.18$. Compared to $\hat{D}$, the standard deviation is reduced by 4 times by the clipping operation.

Let $a(t)$ be the accumulated number of *devTasks* finished by time t when a new *devTask* is scheduled right after a *devTask* is done. Then, the average number of rounds before checking the kth search path, k'', is the minimum t such that $N \cdot a(t) \geq k$. Let $y(t)$ be the expected number of *devTasks* finished during the interval $(\delta \cdot (t - 1), \delta \cdot t]$, then $a(t) = \sum_{i=1}^{t} y(i)$, where δ is the time duration corresponding to the loop-limit ($2 \cdot \sigma$ or $3 \cdot \sigma$ in this paper). $y(t)$ satisfies the following recurrence equations

$$y(t + 1) = y(t) \cdot P\left[\frac{D-\mu}{\delta} \leq 1\right] + \sum_{i=1}^{t} y(t - i) \cdot P\left[i < \frac{D-\mu}{\delta} \leq i + 1\right],$$

where $y(0) = 1$ to ensure that a *devTask* is started at time 0. This equation is similar to the convolution sum: when $i = t$, the corresponding term $y(0) \cdot P\left[t < \frac{D-\mu}{\delta} \leq t + 1\right]$ is the expectation that a *devTask* started at step 0 is finished in the interval $(\mu + \delta \cdot t, \mu + \delta \cdot (t + 1)]$; when $i = t - 1$, the term $y(1) \cdot P\left[t - 1 < \frac{D-\mu}{\delta} \leq t\right]$ is the expectation that a *devTask* is started at step 1 and is finished in the interval $(\mu + \delta \cdot (t - 1), \mu + \delta \cdot t]$ ($y(1)$ is the expected number of new *devTasks* started at step 1 substituting the finished initial *devTasks*); when $i = t - 2$, the term $y(2) \cdot P\left[t - 2 < \frac{D-\mu}{\delta} \leq t - 1\right]$ is the expectation that a *devTask* is started at step 2 and is finished in the interval $(\mu + \delta \cdot (t - 2), \mu + \delta \cdot (t - 1)]$ ($y(2)$ is the expected number of new *devTasks* started at step 2 substituting the initial *devTasks* finished during their second round and those started at step 1 and are done during their first round); and so on. The first term $y(t) \cdot P\left[\frac{D-\mu}{\delta} \leq 1\right]$ is the expectation that a *devTask* is started at step t and is finished after δ.

Applying the CLT again, the execution time for the model checking algorithm is $\hat{C}_1 + \hat{C}_2 + \cdots + \hat{C}_{k''} \sim N(k'' \cdot \mu_{\hat{C}}, k'' \cdot \sigma_{\hat{C}})$. In the right side graph of Fig. 8, the dashed line and the dot-dashed line are the PDFs of $\hat{C}$ when $N = 500$ and when $N = 1000$ respectively. Like $\hat{D}$, increasing the degree of parallelism speeds up the model checking process and reduces the variance. In addition, compared to $\hat{C}$, enforcing the loop-limit makes the model checking process faster and more predictable. The bottom-left side graph of Fig. 8 compares $\hat{D}$ when the loop-limits are $\theta = \mu + 2 \cdot \sigma$ and $\theta = \mu + 3 \cdot \sigma$. As expected, reducing the loop-limit decreases the waiting time for the last *devTasks* to finish and improves the performance. However, this simplified analysis does not include the overhead of preparing and running tasks on GPUs. As shown in Sect. 4, reducing the loop-limit too much actually harms the performance.

Comparing the performances of the GPU-based checker and those of the CPU-based checker is analogous to comparing the queuing systems with multiple servers and with a performant single server. For example, comparing an M/M/1 queue with a twice more performant server and an M/M/2 queue, there will be more waits in the queue in the M/M/1 system, but the wait time in the whole system in the queue will be smaller [26]. GPU-based checker can be regarded as an M/M/N queuing system where N is the number of parallel threads, whereas-CPU based checker is an M/M/1 system with a performant server. The result in Fig. 6 is because the GPU cores are more performant than $1/N$ of the CPU. Moreover the loop-limit reduces the variance in the service time and the reduced variance decreases the wait time as well.

6 Conclusions

In this paper we designed an LTLC model checking technique to utilize the parallel architecture of GPU devices. We showed that the design speeds up the model checking process and reduces the variation as well. These characteristics make the GPU-based model checker suitable for real-time applications.

As a future research direction, we will further improve the performance of the GPU-based checker. We observed that a few LP tasks took significantly more time to finish than others. To use the GPU cores more efficiently, we can reduce their priority and let faster tasks run more. Another direction we are considering is to improve the LP kernel task itself by adopting faster algorithms like the interior point methods [20].

With the GPGPU techniques and the evolving computational power of GPUs, model checking techniques can be employed as an on-line computation module for an application rather than an off-line validation tool. We wish the proposed research can be a stepping stone towards that direction.

References

1. LTLC-GPU. http://www3.cs.stonybrook.edu/~youngkwon/sw/LTLCCuda.v0.8.190224.zip
2. Ahamed, A.K.C., Magoulès, F.: Parallel sub-structuring methods for solving sparse linear systems on a cluster of GPUs. In: 2014 IEEE International Conference on High Performance Computing and Communications, 2014 IEEE 6th International Symposium on Cyberspace Safety and Security, 2014 IEEE 11th International Conference on Embedded Software and System (HPCC, CSS, ICESS), pp. 121–128. IEEE (2014)
3. Ahamed, A.K.C., Magoulès, F.: GPU accelerated substructuring methods for sparse linear systems. In: 2016 IEEE International Conference on Computational Science and Engineering (CSE) and IEEE International Conference on Embedded and Ubiquitous Computing (EUC) and 15th International Symposium on Distributed Computing and Applications for Business Engineering (DCABES), pp. 614–625. IEEE (2016)
4. Alur, R., Dill, D.L.: A theory of timed automata. Theor. Comput. Sci. **126**, 183–235 (1994)
5. Banterle, F., Giacobazzi, R.: A fast implementation of the octagon abstract domain on graphics hardware. In: Nielson, H.R., Filé, G. (eds.) SAS 2007. LNCS, vol. 4634, pp. 315–332. Springer, Heidelberg (2007). https://doi.org/10.1007/978-3-540-74061-2_20
6. Barnat, J., Bauch, P., Brim, L., Ceska, M.: Employing multiple CUDA devices to accelerate LTL model checking. In: 2010 IEEE 16th International Conference on Parallel and Distributed Systems, pp. 259–266. IEEE (2010)
7. Bartocci, E., DeFrancisco, R., Smolka, S.A.: Towards a GPGPU-parallel SPIN model checker. In: International SPIN Symposium on Model Checking of Software, pp. 87–96. ACM (2014)

8. Bu, L., Li, Y., Wang, L., Li, X.: BACH: bounded reachability checker for linear hybrid automata. In: Formal Methods in Computer Aided Design, pp. 65–68. IEEE Computer Society (2008)

9. Büchi, J.: On a decision method in restricted second order arithmetic. In: Proceedings of the International Conference on Logic, Methodology and Philosophy of Science, pp. 1–11. Stanford University Press (1960)

10. Clarke, D., Mohtai, C., Tuffs, P.: Generalized predictive control. Automatica 23, 137–160 (1987)

11. Clarke, D., Scattolini, R.: Constrained receding-horizon predictive control. In: IEE Proceedings Part D, vol. 138, pp. 347–354 (1991)

12. Clarke, E., Grumberg, O., Peled, D.: Model Checking. MIT Press, Cambridge (2000)

13. Franklin, G.F., Powell, J.D., Emami-Naeini, A.: Feedback control of dynamic systems, vol. 3 (2002)

14. Fränzle, M., Herde, C.: HySAT: an efficient proof engine for bounded model checking of hybrid systems. Formal Methods Syst. Des. 30, 179–198 (2007)

15. Girard, A., Pola, G., Tabuada, P.: Approximately bisimilar symbolic models for incrementally stable switched systems. Trans. Autom. Control 55, 116–126 (2010)

16. Henzinger, T.A.: The theory of hybrid automata. In: Annual Symposium on Logic in Computer Science, pp. 278–292. IEEE Computer Society (1996)

17. Henzinger, T.A., Ho, P.-H., Wong-Toi, H.: HyTech: a model checker for hybrid systems. In: Grumberg, O. (ed.) CAV 1997. LNCS, vol. 1254, pp. 460–463. Springer, Heidelberg (1997). https://doi.org/10.1007/3-540-63166-6_48

18. Holzmann, G.J.: The model checker SPIN. IEEE Trans. Softw. Eng. 23, 279–295 (1997)

19. Holzmann, G.J.: Parallelizing the spin model checker. In: Donaldson, A., Parker, D. (eds.) SPIN 2012. LNCS, vol. 7385, pp. 155–171. Springer, Heidelberg (2012). https://doi.org/10.1007/978-3-642-31759-0_12

20. Karmarkar, N.: A new polynomial-time algorithm for linear programming. In: Combinatorica, vol. 4, pp. 373–395 (1984)

21. Khun, J., Šimeček, I., Lórencz, R.: GPU solver for systems of linear equations with infinite precision. In: 2015 17th International Symposium on Symbolic and Numeric Algorithms for Scientific Computing (SYNASC), pp. 121–124. IEEE (2015)

22. Kloetzer, M., Belta, C.: A fully automated framework for control of linear systems from temporal logic specifications. Trans. Autom. Control 53, 287–297 (2008)

23. Kwon, Y.M., Agha, G.: LTLC: linear temporal logic for control. In: Egerstedt, M., Mishra, B. (eds.) HSCC 2008. LNCS, vol. 4981, pp. 316–329. Springer, Heidelberg (2008). https://doi.org/10.1007/978-3-540-78929-1_23

24. Kwon, Y., Kim, E.: Bounded model checking of hybrid systems for control. IEEE Trans. Autom. Control 60, 2961–2976 (2015)

25. Larsen, K.G., Pettersson, P., Yi, W.: UPPAAL in a nutshell. Int. J. Softw. Tools Technol. Transf. 1, 134–152 (1997)

26. Law, A.M., Kelton, W.D.: Simulation Modeling & Analysis. McGraw-Hill, New York (1991)

27. Lichtenstein, O., Pnueli, A.: Checking that finite state concurrent programs satisfy their linear specification. In: POPL, pp. 97–107 (1985)

28. Liu, J., Ozay, N., Topcu, U., Murray, R.M.: Synthesis of reactive switching protocols from temporal logic specifications. Trans. Autom. Control 58(7), 1771–1785 (2013)

29. Luenberger, D.G.: Linear and Nonlinear Programming, 2nd edn. Addison Wesley, Boston (1989)

30. McClanahan, C.: History and evolution of GPU architecture. A Survey Paper, p. 9 (2010)

31. Miné, A.: The octagon abstract domain. In: Proceedings Eighth Working Conference on Reverse Engineering, pp. 310–319. IEEE (2001)

32. Ramanathan, R.: Intel multi-core processors: making the move to quad-core and beyond. Technology@ Intel Mag. **4**(9), 2–4 (2006)
33. Venu, B.: Multi-core processors-an overview. arXiv preprint arXiv:1110.3535 (2011)
34. Wijs, A.: BFS-based model checking of linear-time properties with an application on GPUs. In: Chaudhuri, S., Farzan, A. (eds.) CAV 2016. LNCS, vol. 9780, pp. 472–493. Springer, Cham (2016). https://doi.org/10.1007/978-3-319-41540-6_26

Formal Semantics and Verification of Network-Based Biocomputation Circuits

Michelle Aluf-Medina[1], Till Korten[2], Avraham Raviv[1], Dan V. Nicolau Jr.[3], and Hillel Kugler[1(✉)]

[1] Bar-Ilan University, Ramat Gan, Israel
hillelk@biu.ac.il
[2] B CUBE - Center for Molecular Bioengineering, TU Dresden, Dresden, Germany
[3] QUT, Brisbane, Australia

Abstract. Network-Based Biocomputation Circuits (NBCs) offer a new paradigm for solving complex computational problems by utilizing biological agents that operate in parallel to explore manufactured planar devices. The approach can also have future applications in diagnostics and medicine by combining NBCs computational power with the ability to interface with biological material. To realize this potential, devices should be designed in a way that ensures their correctness and robust operation. For this purpose, formal methods and tools can offer significant advantages by allowing investigation of design limitations and detection of errors before manufacturing and experimentation. Here we define a computational model for NBCs by providing formal semantics to NBC circuits. We present a formal verification-based approach and prototype tool that can assist in the design of NBCs by enabling verification of a given design's correctness. Our tool allows verification of the correctness of NBC designs for several NP-Complete problems, including the Subset Sum, Exact Cover and Satisfiability problems and can be extended to other NBC implementations. Our approach is based on defining transition systems for NBCs and using temporal logic for specifying and proving properties of the design using model checking. Our formal model can also serve as a starting point for computational complexity studies of the power and limitations of NBC systems.

Keywords: Biological computation · Network-based biocomputation · Model checking · Subset sum problem · Exact cover · Satisfiability

1 Introduction

Engineering biological devices to perform computation is of major interest due to the potential of utilizing inherent parallelism in biological components to

This project has received funding from the European Union's Horizon 2020 research and Innovation programme under grant agreement number 732482 (Bio4Comp) and by the ISRAEL SCIENCE FOUNDATION (Grant No. 190/19).

F. Henglein et al. (Eds.): VMCAI 2021, LNCS 12597, pp. 464–485, 2021.
https://doi.org/10.1007/978-3-030-67067-2_21

speed up computation, construct low energy consuming devices and interface with biological material, opening up potential diagnostic and medical applications. Network-Based Biocomputation Circuits (NBCs) [4,20] offer a new paradigm for solving complex computational problems by utilizing biological agents that operate in parallel to explore manufactured planar devices. Devices should be designed to ensure correctness and robust operation, for which formal reasoning tools can offer significant advantages by assisting in identification of limitations and errors in the design before device manufacturing. Here we define a computational model for NBCs [20] by providing formal semantics, and present a formal verification-based approach and tool that can prove correctness of the design. The tool can be used to verify that a given design contains no logical errors, and allows evaluation of different designs prior to manufacturing. Similar verification tools are now commonplace in the hardware industry, where early identification of design flaws can lead to significant savings in cost (money, development time and reputation).

NBC is an alternative parallel-computation method that was proposed in [20] and solves a given combinatorial problem by encoding it into a graphical, molecular network that is embedded in a nanofabricated planar device. The approach can be applied for solving NP-Complete problems [14] and other types of combinatorial problems. In addition, since biological agents are utilized in NBC, the technology can be used in the future to carry cells through the devices and perform complex computational processing with medical and diagnostic applications. In the NBC approach a device runs biological agents through the network in order to explore it in parallel and thus solve a given combinatorial problem. The combinatorial problem considered in [20] is the Subset Sum Problem (SSP), which is a known NP-complete problem. The SSP problem is given a target goal k, and asks if it can be reached as a sum of some combination of elements in a given set $S = \{s_1 \ s_2 \ \dots \ s_N\}$.

An example NBC circuit for the SSP of $S = \{2 \ 5 \ 9\}$ is shown in Fig. 1a. Molecular agents (actin filaments or microtubules, which are propelled by molecular motors) enter from the top-left corner of the network. At split junctions, the agents have an approximately equal chance of moving down or moving diagonally, while agents continue in the current direction of movement at pass junctions, as seen in Fig. 1b. When a computational agent takes the diagonal path at a split junction, the element for that junction is "added". Agents exiting the network in the bottom row thus have an x coordinate (denoted exit# in Fig. 1a) that represents a possible subset sum, and by utilizing many agents to explore the network in parallel all the possible subset sums can be determined.

More recently, the NBC approach has been extended to encode and solve additional NP-Complete problems [16,32] and work has been done towards improving the scalability of the approach and the design process of the circuits. New encodings include the Exact Cover (ExCov) and the Satisfiability (SAT) problems. An additional feature that could extend the capabilities of NBC is tagging—the ability to mark a protein or filament with a distinguishing attribute. Fluorescence tagging, for example, is common in biological research

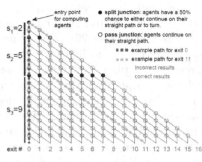

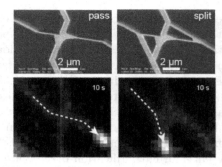

(a) SSP network for set $S = \{2\ 5\ 9\}$.

(b) Pass (left) and split (right) junction structures.

Fig. 1. Network design for SSP (reproduced from [20]). (a) Overall network structure of the SSP for the set $S = \{2\ 5\ 9\}$. Split junctions are denoted as filled black circles and pass junctions as unfilled circles. Agents enter from the top left point of the network. The yellow path corresponds to the sum 11 being computed utilizing 2 and 9. (b) Physical design of pass and split junctions. Pass junctions are designed to maintain the agent's direction of movement, while split junctions are designed to allow agents an approximately equal chance to maintain or change their direction of movement.

and is used to track biomolecules and cells. As an additional component of computation, tagging can be used to track the paths used by computational agents [20,27]. Once the agents reach the end of the network, their tags could be examined and then used to validate the path taken and determine the output result.

Here we provide formal semantics to NBC by defining transition relations that capture the dynamics of an agent in the network. This forms the basis of a translation into the SMV format supported by the NuSMV [9] and nuXMV [7] model checkers and its application to verify design correctness or identify logical errors. We also extend the NBC semantics to a real time stochastic model by mapping NBCs to chemical reaction networks (CRNs) opening up possibilities to utilize stochastic simulation and probabilistic model checking. Finally our formal model can serve as a starting point for computational complexity studies of the power and limitations of NBC systems.

2   Related Work

Engineering biological devices to perform specified computation has the potential of utilizing the inherent parallelism in biological components to speed computation, construct low energy consuming devices and interface with biological material. Seminal work by Adelman [3] has demonstrated a method to use DNA for solving the Hamiltonian path problem, which is known to be NP-Complete. The instance of the Hamiltonian path considered in [3] is a small graph (7 nodes and 14 edges), thus a major challenge since then in the field is overcoming physical and experimental constraints towards scaling up the computation to tackle large systems.

There have been several different paradigms suggested to realize the vision proposed in [3], including DNA Strand Displacement Systems (DSD) [23,25] that utilize the complementarity of DNA base sequences to bind together and perform designed reactions, and DNA self assembly applying a reprogrammable set of DNA tiles, capable of implementing a wide variety of self assembly algorithms [24,28]. DNA walkers are molecular machines that can move along tracks [26,30] and can be used for performing computation or moving cargo for nanotechnology applications. Computational methods and tools have proven to be useful in improving and validating the designs of engineered biological systems [5,15,22] and have served as motivating applications for defining semantics and computational methods for NBC. Formal verification methods assuming discrete semantics have been used to verify the correctness of DNA Strand Displacement Systems and DNA walkers [17,31], and probabilistic model checking has also been applied to these systems [6,11,17]. More broadly, viewing biological systems as reactive systems leads naturally to specifying their behavior using temporal logic and applying model checking (see e.g. [8,13] and references within).

Network-Based Biocomputation (NBC) [20] uses biological agents that operate in parallel to explore manufactured planar devices. To enable the exploration of the solution space effectively, NBC encodes the operations of solving NP-complete problems into graphs, which are then used as templates for the design and fabrication of networks, for instance microfluidic networks. To process the computation in a massively parallel fashion, NBC uses a large number of motile agents to explore the many possible paths towards actual solutions. The actual circuits we have verified here are physically manufactured to be populated with actin filaments or microtubules [4], although similar devices have been experimentally implemented for bacteria [27]. In [29], the SSP problem has been solved by the NBC approach using a laser photonic system rather than molecular motors as in [20]. Our computational methods and tools are applicable to all the variety of experimental implementation strategies currently developed for NBC and can also be extended to support future NBC technology.

3   Formal Semantics

We first describe our general approach for providing semantics to NBC circuits, the definitions are then used and refined to encode specific designs to solve the subset sum (SSP), exact cover (ExCov) and satisfiability (SAT) problems. A network is composed of a set of junctions that are positioned on a 2-dimensional plane, allowing agents to move along the network to nearby junctions according to the type of junction visited. The encoding assumes a single agent traversing the network, and can naturally be used to construct a system consisting of several agents traversing the network in parallel. We define a discrete state semantics that includes nondeterministic choice, and then suggest a translation to chemical reaction networks (CRNs) [10] that provides a stochastic continuous time semantics.

3.1   Discrete Nondeterministic Semantics

Our transition system is defined as:

$$T = \langle V, \theta, \rho, C \rangle$$

Where V are the system variables, θ is the initial condition, ρ is the transition relation and C is a set of compassion requirements. The variables encode the position of the agent in the network and its direction of movement:

$$V = \{x, y, dir\}$$

The variables x and y encode the position of the agent in the network, where $x \in \{0 \cdots max\}$ and $y \in \{0 \cdots max\}$ and max is the sum of all elements in the set in the case of the subset sum problem, determining the size of the device in the general case. The variable dir is a Boolean variable encoding the direction of movement of the agent. In most circuits we assume the initial condition θ is $x = 0 \wedge y = 0$ capturing an agent entering the circuit from the upper left corner, see Fig. 1a. We assume here the initial position is a split junction and do not constrain the value of the dir variable, thus it can be chosen nondeterministically to be either 0 or 1. The variable dir maintains the current movement direction of the filament, where $dir = 0$ means travelling down while $dir = 1$ means travelling diagonally.

The transition relation specifies how the variables get updated depending on the current state:

$$y' = y + 1$$

$$(x' = x \wedge dir = 0) \vee (x' = x + 1 \wedge dir = 1)$$

Agents move from the top row to the bottom row, thus the y variable always gets incremented by 1 specifying this movement. The movement can either be directly down, in which case x is not changed, this happens when the variable dir is 0, or diagonally, in which case x is incremented by 1, when the variable dir is 1. In addition we update the transition relation such that after reaching the bottom row the agent returns back to the top left corner of the network, to the state $x = 0 \wedge y = 0$.

The variable dir determines the direction of movement as explained above. It remains unchanged if the agent is in a pass junction, or makes a nondeterministic choice between 0 (down) or 1 (diagonal) if the agent is in a split junction:

$$dir' = (dir \wedge (x', y') \in pass) \vee (\{0, 1\} \wedge (x', y') \in split)$$

We define the compassion requirement:

$$C = \{\langle (x = m \wedge y = n \wedge (m, n) \in split, x = m \wedge y = n + 1) \rangle,$$

$$\langle (x = m \wedge y = n \wedge (m, n) \in split, x = m + 1 \wedge y = n + 1) \rangle\}$$

A compassion requirement is composed of a set of pairs, each pair is of the form $\langle p, q \rangle$ and requires that if p appears infinitely often then q appears infinitely often. In this case for every split junction if it is visited infinitely often it will take the direction down infinitely often and the direction diagonal infinitely often. This ensures that for every split junction both directions, down and diagonal will eventually be explored. Formally, if the state $x = m \land y = n$ that is a split junction is visited infinitely often, then both of the states $x = m \land y = n + 1$ and $x = m + 1 \land y = n + 1$ will be visited infinitely often.

3.2 Stochastic Semantics

Following from the semantics described above we propose a stochastic semantics extension by providing a mapping to chemical reaction networks (CRNs). CRNs consist of a set of species C and a set of reactions R that allow the species to interact. We introduce species for each of the locations in the network, with a separate species for down or diagonal movement if the position is a pass junction. For split and pass junctions the species are, respectively:

$$C_s = \{x_i y_j | i, j \in \{0 \cdots max\} \land (i, j) \in split\}$$

$$C_p = \{x_i y_j d_k | k \in \{0, 1\}, i, j \in \{0 \cdots max\} \land (i, j) \in pass\}$$

The species will count how many agents are positioned at each location described by state $x = i \land y = j$, allowing to represent multiple agents simultaneously exploring the network. The reactions will correspond to an agent moving to the next location. For each split junction, assuming the next junction is a pass junction, we will define the following two reactions:

$$x_i y_j \rightarrow x_i y_{j+1} d_0$$

$$x_i y_j \rightarrow x_{i+1} y_{j+1} d_1$$

If an agent is in a split junction at position (i, j) there are two reactions as shown above that can be taken, the first will move the agent to position $(i, j+1)$ representing a down movement, whereas the second will move the agent to position $(i + 1, j + 1)$ representing a diagonal movement. If the first equation is fired then the number of copies of species $x_i y_j$ will be decremented by 1 and the number of copies of species $x_i y_{j+1} d_0$ will be incremented by 1, whereas if the second equation is fired, the number of copies of species $x_i y_j$ will be decremented by 1, and the number of copies of species $x_{i+1} y_{j+1} d_1$ will be incremented by 1.

For pass junctions, assuming the next junction is also a pass junction, we define the following reactions, in which according to the first reaction the movement is down and according to the second reaction the movement is diagonally:

$$x_i y_j d_0 \rightarrow x_i y_{j+1} d_0$$

$$x_i y_j d_1 \rightarrow x_{i+1} y_{j+1} d_1$$

If the next position is a split junction we define the following reactions:

$$x_i y_j d_0 \rightarrow x_i y_{j+1}$$
$$x_i y_j d_1 \rightarrow x_{i+1} y_{j+1}$$

The CRN defined above can also have a rate associated with each reaction which is a number that determines the probability of firing the reaction effecting how fast these reactions will fire. These definitions provide a stochastic continuous time semantics for NBCs using the underlying CRN model [10]. An example of a stochastic simulation using these semantics for the SSP network from Fig. 1a is shown in Fig. 2.

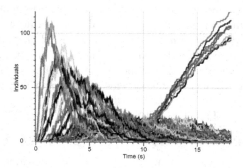

Fig. 2. Stochastic simulation of an SSP network for $S = \{2\ 5\ 9\}$ with 1000 agents. Time is shown in the X axis while the number of individual agents of each species is shown in the Y axis. Each color plot represents a different species at a specific network position. This simulation starts with 1000 individuals at position $(x, y) = (0, 0)$ (plot not shown) that traverse the network assuming no interaction between the agents. The graph is a result of running a CRN model using Gillespie stochastic simulation implemented in the DSD tool [18]. The plots that rise beyond the background values at around 10 time units are the number of agents at each of the 8 possible subset sum exits.

We next explain our encodings of the SSP, ExCov and SAT problems and the temporal logic properties used to specify the correctness of the circuits. Our motivation here is to capture the networks used in the experimental work with the actual biological agents and not to find efficient ways to solve these NP-Complete problems on standard computers. The verification approach can then be generalized and utilized to NBC applications in which the main aim is to interact with living cells for diagnostic and medical applications rather than solve combinatorial problems.

4   Subset Sum Problem (SSP)

The Subset Sum Problem (SSP) is an established NP-Complete problem that returns *true* if a subset exists in a given set S, that sums to some given value k, and returns *false* otherwise.

The SSP network is constructed using variables for rows, columns, junction types, movement direction of computational agents, and a flag. The flag is used to indicate that the computational agent has reached the network output (the last row).

An additional tag variable was added to the network description in order to track at which split junctions the computational agents took a diagonal path, thus "adding" the element for that row. The tag is built by indexing split junctions starting from the top left corner of the network (index 0) and then running through each row and assigning indices to the junctions sequentially. This indexing includes junctions that are considered unreachable in a properly functioning network. Networks using tagging are able to identify the exact path taken to reach a given sum. This allows further investigation into the number of different paths to a given output. In experimentally manufactured NBC devices these tags may also allow for identification of agents that followed erroneous paths.

Agent positioning in the network is indicated by row and column variables that run from zero to the maximum sum of elements in the given set. Only half of these $(row, column)$ points are used due to the network's triangular structure. In order to define the transition relations for the general SSP problem, $S = \{s_1\ s_2\ \dots\ s_N\}$, we first define the maximum sum of set S (Eq. 1), array of split junction rows (Eq. 2) and, if tagging is used, an array of tags (Eq. 3).

$$max = \sum_{i=1}^{N} s_i \tag{1}$$

$$srow = \left[0\ \sum_{i=1}^{index} s_i \right] \text{ where } index = 1, \dots, N-1 \tag{2}$$

$$tag = \left[t_{0,0}\ t_{\sum_{i=1}^{index} s_i, 0} \dots t_{\sum_{i=1}^{index} s_i, \sum_{i=1}^{index} s_i} \right] \text{ where } index = 1, \dots, N-1 \tag{3}$$

The row increases with each transition until reaching the end of the network. This captures the assumption that agents cannot move backwards in the network. Junction type, which depends on the row, is decided according to a sequential sum of elements in the set. The direction of movement is either nondeterministic (when "choosing" at a split junction) or keeps the last selection (when at a pass junction). The full transition relation, without the additional tag variable, can be seen in Eq. 4. The tag's transitions are separately defined in Eq. 5.

$$
\begin{array}{ll}
[r, c, d, j, f] | 0 \leq r, c \leq max, d \in \{down, diag\}, j \in \{split, pass\}, f \in \text{boolean} \\
[r, c, d, split, f] & \rhd\ [r+1, c, down, pass, f] & \text{if } r+1 \notin srow \\
& \rhd\ [r+1, c+1, diag, pass, f] & \text{if } r+1 \notin srow \\
& \rhd\ [r+1, c, down, split, f] & \text{if } r+1 \in srow \\
& \rhd\ [r+1, c+1, diag, split, f] & \text{if } r+1 \in srow \\
[r, c, d, pass, f] & \rhd\ [r+1, c, d, pass, f] & \text{if } d = down \wedge r+1 \notin srow \\
& \rhd\ [r+1, c+1, d, pass, f] & \text{if } d = diag \wedge r+1 \notin srow \\
& \rhd\ [r+1, c, d, split, f] & \text{if } d = down \wedge r+1 \in srow \\
& \rhd\ [r+1, c+1, d, split, f] & \text{if } d = diag \wedge r+1 \in srow \\
[max-1, c, d, j, f] & \rhd\ [max, c, d, j, true] & \text{if } d = down \\
& \rhd\ [max, c+1, d, j, true] & \text{if } d = diag
\end{array}
\tag{4}
$$

$$
\begin{array}{l}
t_{row,col} \in \text{boolean initially } false \text{ for every } t_{row,col} \in tag \\
t_{row,col} \rhd true \quad \text{if } row = r-1 \wedge col = c-1 \wedge d = diag \\
\quad\quad \rhd t_{row,col} \text{ otherwise}
\end{array}
\tag{5}
$$

A duplicate network was built with the addition of two variables, sum and $xsum$, for verification of overall output correctness, rather than specific output correctness. These variables select a value from the set of valid sums and the set of invalid sums respectively, and are used for comparison with the column value when reaching the network output.

Table 1. Network specifications for individual outputs. LTL specification (ltl_k) checks that the output of interest is never reachable. CTL specification (ctl_k) checks if there is any path to the output of interest.

LTLSPEC NAME ltl_k := $G!((flag = TRUE)\&(column = k))$;
CTLSPEC NAME ctl_k := $EF((flag = TRUE)\&(column = k))$;
$column$ is the current sum, k is the output of interest and $flag$ is the output row indicator

Two specification types were used to verify network correctness. The first type (Table 1) uses both Linear Temporal Logic (LTL) and Computational Tree Logic (CTL) to check the validity of a specific sum k by comparing it with the column value at the output. The LTL formula checks the lack of a run where $column = k$, while the CTL formula checks for the existence of at least one run where $column = k$. For the SSP, the value k can range anywhere from zero to the maximum sum value of set S. We use both CTL and LTL although the outcomes of NBC verification will be equivalent, for evaluating and optimizing the performance of model-checking, as discussed in Sect. 7.

The second type of specification (Table 2) uses CTL to check that all valid sums are reachable and all invalid sums are unreachable. When used on networks containing identifiable errors (errors that can be detected by measuring agents at the exit of the network in the bottom row), a counter-example is provided indicating an unreachable valid sum and/or a reachable invalid sum. This specification does not need to get a target sum k but rather checks correctness for any target sum.

Table 2. Network specifications for overall output in CTL. csum checks that the network can exit on all valid sums. nsum checks that the network cannot exit on any invalid sum.

CTLSPEC NAME csum
$:=!(EX(AG((flag = FALSE)|(!(column = sum))))));$
CTLSPEC NAME nsum
$:=!(EF((flag = TRUE)\&(column = xsum)));$

column is the current sum (column in the network), *sum* is one of the set of valid outputs, *xsum* is one of the set of invalid outputs and *flag* is the output row indicator

5   Exact Cover (ExCov)

The Exact Cover problem (ExCov) is another important problem, which is known to be NP-Complete. This problem returns *true* if there exists an exact cover (a union of disjoint sets) of the defined universe U when given a collection of sets SS that contain elements from the universe, and returns *false* otherwise.

We use a reduction to SSP to construct NBCs that solve the ExCov problem [16]. In the reduction, the ExCov is encoded into binary format. This encoding is then used to create the elements of an SSP network. The elements of the universe are treated as an array, where each position can be either 0 or 1, and where each element is given a specific index in the array. The sets to be examined are then each assigned an array of the same length as the universe, where only elements contained in the set are assigned a "one" value. All other elements are assigned a "zero" value. These arrays are then treated as binary numbers and are converted to their respective decimal values, as shown in Table 3.

As the ExCov does not allow the union of non-disjoint sets (the exact cover cannot contain sets that share an element), a "force-down" junction is included in the network to replace such split junctions. This prevents the agents from taking a diagonal path where an element in the current set is already contained in a previously included set on the path.

This construction can be seen in Fig. 3, which depicts the network for the sets given in Table 3. There exist multiple exact covers for this set of subsets, so there are multiple paths in this network that lead to output 15, the binary encoding of the universe. The pink path exhibits the function of the force-down

Table 3. Conversion from set to decimal using binary representation.

Set	Binary representation
$U = \{1\ 2\ 3\ 4\}$	$U = \begin{bmatrix}1\ 1\ 1\ 1\end{bmatrix} = 15$
$S_1 = \{2\}$	$S_1 = \begin{bmatrix}0\ 0\ 1\ 0\end{bmatrix} = 2$
$S_2 = \{3\}$	$S_2 = \begin{bmatrix}0\ 1\ 0\ 0\end{bmatrix} = 4$
$S_3 = \{1\ 4\}$	$S_3 = \begin{bmatrix}1\ 0\ 0\ 1\end{bmatrix} = 9$
$S_4 = \{2\ 3\}$	$S_4 = \begin{bmatrix}0\ 1\ 1\ 0\end{bmatrix} = 6$

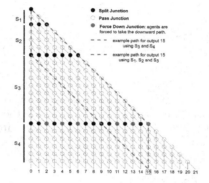

Fig. 3. ExCov network for $U = \{1\ 2\ 3\ 4\}$ and $SS = \{\{2\}, \{3\}, \{1\ 4\}, \{2\ 3\}\}$. Split and pass junctions are as defined in Fig. 1a. Force-down junctions are denoted as filled orange circles. The blue path combines sets S_3 and S_4, constituting an exact cover. (Color figure online)

junctions, where the computational agent is forced into the downward direction instead of having the chance to move diagonally, as in a split junction. In this case, this is due to set S_4 sharing elements with sets S_1 and S_2, which have already been included. In terms of the decision problem encoded in the network, the existence of one path leading to the required output implies that the result should be computed as *true*.

This network is, in essence, an implementation of the SSP network with the addition of a new junction type. Thus, the state of the model is defined by the same combination of variables as that of the SSP. The junction type now depends on both row and column values as the previously defined split junction rows may now contain force-down junctions. The tag variable was added here as well, to track the path taken by the biocomputation agents. The maximum sum of the network, split junction rows, and tags are defined as they were in SSP, where the set elements are now the decimal values of the subsets' binary representation. The transition relation, without the additional tag variable, can be seen in Eq. 6, while the tag's transitions are defined in the same manner as the tags for the SSP (Eq. 5).

$$
\begin{array}{ll}
[r, c, d, j, f] | 0 \leq r, c \leq max, d \in \{down, diag\}, j \in \{split, pass, fdown\}, \\
\quad f \in \text{boolean} \\
[r, c, d, split, f] \quad \triangleright \; [r+1, c(c+1), down(diag), pass, f] \\
\qquad \text{if } r+1 \notin srow \\
\qquad \triangleright \; [r+1, c, down, split, f] \\
\qquad \text{if } r+1 \in srow \\
\qquad \triangleright \; [r+1, c+1, diag, split, f] \\
\qquad \text{if } r+1 \in srow \wedge (r+1, c+1) \notin fdown \\
\qquad \triangleright \; [r+1, c+1, diag, fdown, f] \\
\qquad \text{if } (r+1, c+1) \in fdown \wedge d = diag \\
[r, c, d, pass, f] \quad \triangleright \; [r+1, c, d, pass, f] \\
\qquad \text{if } d = down \wedge r+1 \notin srow \\
\qquad \triangleright \; [r+1, c+1, d, pass, f] \\
\qquad \text{if } d = diag \wedge r+1 \notin srow \\
\qquad \triangleright \; [r+1, c, d, split, f] \\
\qquad \text{if } d = down \wedge r+1 \in srow \\
\qquad \triangleright \; [r+1, c+1, d, split, f] \\
\qquad \text{if } d = diag \wedge r+1 \in srow \\
\qquad \triangleright \; [r+1, c, d, fdown, f] \\
\qquad \text{if } (r+1, c) \in fdown \wedge d = down \\
\qquad \triangleright \; [r+1, c+1, d, fdown, f] \\
\qquad \text{if } (r+1, c+1) \in fdown \wedge d = diag \\
[r, c, d, fdown, f] \quad \triangleright \; [r+1, c, down, pass, f] \\
[max-1, c, d, j, f] \triangleright [max, c, d, j, true] \\
\qquad \text{if } d = down \\
\qquad \triangleright \; [max, c+1, d, j, true] \\
\qquad \text{if } d = diag
\end{array}
\tag{6}
$$

Both LTL and CTL specifications were used to verify the output of interest k, similar to the specifications in Table 1. The difference here is that k is assigned the decimal value of the binary representation of the universe.

6   Satisfiability (SAT)

The Boolean Satisfiability problem (SAT) is considered the classic NP-complete problem. SAT is the problem of determining if there exists an assignment of *true* and *false* values to the variables of a Boolean formula, such that the formula evaluates to *true*. The formula is considered satisfiable if any such assignment exists, and is considered unsatisfiable when no such assignment exists (the formula always evaluates to false). One standard format for SAT problems is Conjunctive Normal Form (CNF), where the Boolean formula φ, consists of a conjunction of a set of clauses $\{C_i\}_{i=1}^{n}$, and each clause consists of a disjunction of a set of literals $\{x_j\}_{j=1}^{m}$.

The initial model designed for SAT used a similar structure to that of the SSP network, as seen in Fig. 4a. Each row represents a literal x_j, and each junction is a split junction. As computational agents progress through this network, they are tagged after each split junction for the clauses their truth assignment satisfies. The two example paths demonstrate cases where all tags are marked (the Boolean formula was satisfied), as well as where there was a tag missing (the Boolean formula was not satisfied). As there exists an output where all tags are marked, the problem is satisfiable.

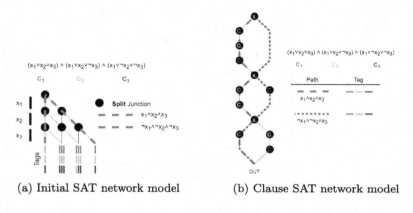

(a) Initial SAT network model   (b) Clause SAT network model

Fig. 4. SAT network models for three literals and three clauses.

The next network model used, seen in Fig. 4b, is structured with individual junctions for literals and clauses, rather than having multiple junctions for each literal as in Fig. 4a. Each literal junction has paths both to the left (*true*) and right (*false*), reflecting their relevant truth assignment. These paths connect to a sequence of clause junctions. Computational agents are tagged at clause junctions with an identifier for the relevant clause satisfied by the truth assignment of the path.

Unlike the SSP and ExCov networks where the output location indicates the result, in the SAT network, the use of tagging is critical as it indicates the clauses satisfied. The final computation result depends on the total collection of tags on the computational agents at output. The problem is considered satisfiable if there exists an agent that collected tags for each clause as measured at output.

Using the clause model, two network descriptions were constructed. One network description has separate variables for clause junctions and tags, while the other unifies them into a single tag variable that merges their behavior in order to minimize the number of variables and possible states created by the NuSMV model checker. The tag variables for these networks are treated as counters that indicate the number of times each clause has been satisfied. As all problems investigated are of the 3-SAT format, the tag for each clause can only be an integer from zero to three, where zero indicates the clause was never satisfied.

The state of the model is defined by a combination of variables for junction type, direction of movement, current literal and it's assigned value, exit flag, and a tag array for the clauses satisfied. The junction type is now divided into clause and literal junctions.

Table 4. SAT clause network LTL and CTL specifications. For satisfiable networks LTL returns *false* and CTL returns *true*. For unsatisfiable networks LTL returns *true* and CTL returns *false*.

LTL	LTLSPEC NAME ltl_sat := $G!((flag = TRUE)\&(\bigwedge\limits_{i \geq 0} tag[i] > 0))$
	There is no path that satisfies all clauses
CTL	CTLSPEC NAME ctl_sat := $EF((flag = TRUE)\&(\bigwedge\limits_{i \geq 0} tag[i] > 0))$
	There exists a path that satisfies all clauses
	Each $tag[i]$ corresponds to a specific clause

Both models use the same LTL and CTL specifications to check if all tags have a positive, non-zero value when reaching the output state. That is, $tag[i] > 0$ for every clause i when $flag = TRUE$. The number of tags directly corresponds with the number of clauses.

7   Experimental Results

We developed a prototype tool [1,2] that automates both the generation of the SMV encodings for each problem (SSP, ExCov and SAT), and the verification of these encodings using the NuSMV model checker [9]. The user selects which problem they would like to solve and then the tool runs as described in the following sections. For the SSP and ExCov problems our tool also automates the translation to chemical reaction networks allowing to run a Gillespie stochastic simulation using the GEC and DSD tools [18,21]. We systematically evaluate the verification capabilities of our tool, by proving correctness of the designs and by identifying errors in designs that were explicitly modified to represent faulty junctions or errors in the NBC encoding. Overall the verification results demonstrate that the approach can handle large NBC circuits and is applicable to the real-world systems currently designed in [4,20,27].

7.1   SSP

Using input sets from the user, the tool builds SMV network descriptions both with and without tags. Once the models have been generated, the tool runs NuSMV on each of the defined specifications. Verifications are first run on the specifications defined in Table 1 using two methods. The first runs all outputs in bulk, and the second runs output by output. This is done for both LTL and CTL specifications separately. Then, verifications are run on the specifications defined in Table 2 for both valid and invalid sums. Each specification's verification result and runtime is parsed and saved for further analysis.

Table 5. SSP all output verification runtimes in minutes

SSP						
ID	Set size	Set	Tag runtimes		No tag runtimes	
			LTL	CTL	LTL	CTL
0	3	[2, 3, 5]	0.0041	0.0016	0.0035	0.0014
1	4	[2, 3, 5, 7]	0.0114	0.0027	0.0073	0.0022
2	5	[2, 3, 5, 7, 11]	0.0478	0.0065	0.0198	0.0038
3	6	[2, 3, 5, 7, 11, 13]	0.2256	0.0218	0.0466	0.0070
4	7	[2, 3, 5, 7, 11, 13, 17]	1.3204	0.0956	0.1028	0.0138
5	8	[2, 3, 5, 7, 11, 13, 17, 19]	18.0535	0.4476	0.2144	0.0278
6	9	[2, 3, 5, 7, 11, 13, 17, 19, 23]	106.7040	2.0753	0.4226	0.0553

While the difference between LTL and CTL verification runtimes in small networks is negligible, the difference in large networks is considerable. As seen in Table 5, LTL runtimes grow at a much faster rate than those of CTL. There is also a drastic increase in runtime when verifying networks utilizing tagging, as additional variables are necessary to define tags for all split junctions. For the first specification type, it is not usually necessary to look at all outputs or both logics. Thus, runtime can be decreased by examining specific outputs of interest using a single specification instead. The increase in verification runtime as a result of larger network size is not as drastic for running individual outputs (Table 6) due to the compounded nature of the runtime when running in bulk.

Verification runtime for the second specification type grows at about the same rate as that of the bulk run on the first specification's CTL format (Table 7 and Table 8). The two are comparable as they both check validity of all network outputs. By using these different specification types, we are able to efficiently verify NBC designs for increasingly large networks.

The second specification type can further be used to identify unreachable valid sums and reachable invalid sums in networks with observable errors. We model here errors that my occur as part of the manufacturing of the NBC devices, and consider a scenario where a certain junction appears to contain an error and we want to check its effect on the correctness of the overall circuit. There are three general types of errors that may be found in SSP networks:

1. Pass junction behaves as a split junction
2. Pass junction forces one direction
   (a) when both paths are valid (block one valid path)
   (b) when one path is valid, and the invalid path is forced
3. Split junction forces one direction

Table 6. SSP output 9 and 10 verification runtimes in minutes.

SSP

ID	Set size	Set	Output	Path exists	Tag runtimes		No tag runtimes	
					LTL	CTL	LTL	CTL
0	3	[2, 3, 5]	9	NO	0.0012	0.0010	0.0011	0.0010
0	3	[2, 3, 5]	10	YES	0.0015	0.0010	0.0013	0.0009
1	4	[2, 3, 5, 7]	9	YES	0.0020	0.0010	0.0015	0.0009
1	4	[2, 3, 5, 7]	10	YES	0.0020	0.0010	0.0015	0.0009
2	5	[2, 3, 5, 7, 11]	9	YES	0.0033	0.0012	0.0019	0.0010
2	5	[2, 3, 5, 7, 11]	10	YES	0.0033	0.0012	0.0019	0.0010
3	6	[2, 3, 5, 7, 11, 13]	9	YES	0.0082	0.0019	0.0023	0.0011
3	6	[2, 3, 5, 7, 11, 13]	10	YES	0.0083	0.0018	0.0023	0.0011
4	7	[2, 3, 5, 7, 11, 13, 17]	9	YES	0.0278	0.0032	0.0030	0.0012
4	7	[2, 3, 5, 7, 11, 13, 17]	10	YES	0.0281	0.0033	0.0030	0.0012
5	8	[2, 3, 5, 7, 11, 13, 17, 19]	9	YES	0.2507	0.0079	0.0041	0.0013
5	8	[2, 3, 5, 7, 11, 13, 17, 19]	10	YES	0.2510	0.0079	0.0041	0.0014
6	9	[2, 3, 5, 7, 11, 13, 17, 19, 23]	9	YES	1.1600	0.0306	0.0057	0.0015
6	9	[2, 3, 5, 7, 11, 13, 17, 19, 23]	10	YES	1.1433	0.0245	0.0057	0.0015

Table 7. SSP general sum verification runtimes in minutes.

SSP

Set size	Set	Runtime			
		csum		nsum	
		Tag	No Tag	Tag	No Tag
3	[2, 3, 5]	0.0011	0.0011	0.0009	0.0009
4	[2, 3, 5, 7]	0.0013	0.0012	0.0009	0.0009
5	[2, 3, 5, 7, 11]	0.0018	0.0013	0.0009	0.0009
6	[2, 3, 5, 7, 11, 13]	0.0037	0.0018	0.0009	0.0009
7	[2, 3, 5, 7, 11, 13, 17]	0.0092	0.0025	0.0009	0.0009
8	[2, 3, 5, 7, 11, 13, 17, 19]	0.0260	0.0042	0.0009	0.0009
9	[2, 3, 5, 7, 11, 13, 17, 19, 23]	0.0821	0.0074	0.0010	0.0009

Examples of these errors are shown in Fig. 5. These errors are not always identifiable by observing the possible exits from the network, as affected junctions may not be reachable, forced paths may converge with valid paths, or blocked paths may not be the only path leading to the affected output. In order to simulate manufacturing errors that would cause unexpected outputs, deliberate errors were added to the network descriptions. A comparison between the

Table 8. SSP general sum verification runtimes in minutes on network with no tag variable. Sets include the first k prime numbers.

SSP		Runtime		
Set size	Set	csum	nsum	Total
5	[2, 3, 5, 7, 11]	0.0055	0.0013	0.0068
10	[2, 3, 5, ... 19, 23, 29]	0.1140	0.0025	0.1165
15	[2, 3, 5, ... 41, 43, 47]	1.5203	0.0024	1.5227
20	[2, 3, 5, ... 61, 67, 71]	7.8919	0.0036	7.8955
25	[2, 3, 5, ... 83, 89, 97]	32.3312	0.0059	32.3371
30	[2, 3, 5, ... 107, 109, 113]	122.3742	0.0112	122.3854

expected verification result of the network and that of the network with added errors is shown in Table 9. The correctness of NBC network design can be checked by examining these errors and their verification results.

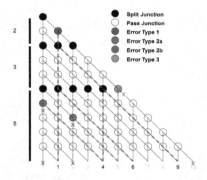

Fig. 5. SSP network for $S = \{2\ 3\ 5\}$ with example errors and their resulting outputs. Each error type is assigned a color. Resulting reachable paths are marked with dashed lines. Blocked paths are marked with an X at the initial and end points.

7.2   ExCov

Using an input file containing a collection of universes and sets of subsets, the tool encodes the given problems into binary format. Then, tagged and not tagged networks are generated using specifications for the output of interest as defined in Table 1. In this case, the output of interest (decimal value of universe's binary encoding) is assigned to variable k. Then, NuSMV is run on both specifications (LTL and CTL) to check for the existence of an exact cover. The tool then parses and saves verification results and runtimes for further analysis.

Table 9. SSP general sum verification results for valid networks and observably invalid networks. Error is denoted as the $(row, column)$ junction location along with the error type as in the error type definitions.

SSP						
Set size	Set	Original network		Faulty network		
		csum	nsum	Error	csum	nsum
3	[2, 3, 5]	VALID	VALID	(3,1) - 2b	INVALID	INVALID
4	[2, 3, 5, 7]	VALID	VALID	(12,2) - 2a	INVALID	VALID
5	[2, 3, 5, 7, 11]	VALID	VALID	(14,4) - 1	VALID	INVALID
6	[2, 3, 5, 7, 11, 13]	VALID	VALID	(17,17) - 3	INVALID	VALID
7	[2, 3, 5, 7, 11, 13, 17]	VALID	VALID	(29,15) - 2a	VALID	VALID

Verification runtimes show similar behavior to those seen with SSP networks. The same difference in growth in runtime of LTL and CTL, as well as the same drastic difference in runtime of tagged as compared to not tagged networks is observed (Table 10).

Table 10. ExCov verification runtimes in minutes.

ExCov								
ID	Universe	# of Subsets	Set of subsets	ExCov exists	Tag runtimes		No tag runtimes	
					LTL	CTL	LTL	CTL
0	[1, 2, 3, 4]	4	[[1, 2], [1], [1, 3], [4]]	NO	0.0015	0.0013	0.0012	0.0011
1	[1, 2, 3, 4]	4	[[1, 2], [1, 3], [1, 3, 4], [1, 2, 3]]	NO	0.0016	0.0015	0.0014	0.0011
2	[1, 2, 3, 4]	4	[[2], [3], [1, 4], [2, 3]]	YES	0.0020	0.0009	0.0017	0.0010
3	[1, 2, 3, 4, 5, 6, 7, 8]	8	[[1, 4, 7], [1, 4], [4, 5, 7], [3, 5, 6], [2, 3, 6, 7], [2, 7], [8], [3, 4, 5]]	YES	666.1414	3.7020	0.0586	0.0079
4	[1, 2, 3, 4, 5, 6, 7, 8]	8	[[1, 4, 7], [1, 4], [4, 5, 7], [3, 5, 6], [2, 3, 6, 7], [2, 7], [4, 8], [3, 4, 5]]	NO	5.1313	6.1802	0.0113	0.0056

As the ExCov NBC design is based off of that of the SSP, the types of errors observed in the SSP may occur here as well. As the translation is more complex due to the addition of "force-down" junctions, it is critical to make sure these junctions are added at all relevant locations. By not including these junctions in the network description properly, incorrect results may be observed when verifying the existence of an exact cover. As the network grows larger, it becomes more difficult to identify such errors. In order to capture such mistakes in network translation, an additional variable was used to switch junction behavior to that of split junctions, in essence switching the network with the SSP equivalent. This type of error does not affect networks where an exact cover exists as the original path to the universe output is not blocked. A comparison of network behavior in both cases is seen in Table 11. This illustrates the utility of the verification method to verify new NBC designs that are complex or include various network optimizations, and may have subtle design errors.

Table 11. ExCov existence verification on networks with properly functioning force-down junctions (Valid) and networks with force-down junctions that behave as split junctions (Invalid).

ExCov				
Universe	Set of subsets	ExCov exists	ExCov found	
			Valid	Invalid
[1, 2, 3, 4]	[[1, 2], [1], [1, 3], [4]]	NO	NO	NO
[1, 2, 3, 4]	[[1, 2], [1, 3], [1, 3, 4], [1, 2, 3]]	NO	NO	YES
[1, 2, 3, 4]	[[2], [3], [1, 4], [2, 3]]	YES	YES	YES
[1, 2, 3, 4, 5, 6, 7, 8]	[[1, 4, 7], [1, 4], [4, 5, 7], [3, 5, 6], [2, 3, 6, 7], [2, 7], [4, 8], [3, 4, 5]]	NO	NO	YES

7.3   SAT

Our tool generates 3-CNF SAT problems of random sizes in DIMACS format using CNFGen [19]. These are then run through the MiniSat SAT Solver to get their satisfiability results [12] for later comparison with NuSMV verification results. The tool then generates two network descriptions for each problem, one with separate clause and tag variables (Clause) and one with merged clause and tag variables (No-Clause). NuSMV is then run on each network description, once with and once without variable re-ordering (VRO). The re-ordering organizes the tag variables by first appearance of the relevant clause in the network. For example, all clauses containing the first literal come before clauses containing the second literal. Verification results and runtimes, for each of the specifications defined in Table 4, are parsed and saved for further analysis. NBC verification results were compared with the MiniSat results, which directly check satisfiability or unsatisfiability of the formula, and were all consistent.

Runtimes are examined using three comparisons; LTL vs. CTL, No VRO vs. VRO and No-Clause vs. Clause (Table 12). The same differences in verification runtime of LTL as compared with CTL specifications seen in SSP and ExCov were observed. While variable re-ordering may improve verification runtime, the re-ordering used here did not generally show improvement for all networks, and no tendency towards either improvement or deterioration was observed. Overall, the No-Clause network description tends to have faster runtimes than the Clause network description, as unification of the tag and clause variable decreases the size of the network description.

Table 12. SAT verification runtimes in minutes.

3-SAT								
# Clauses	# Variables	No-clause runtimes				Clause runtimes			
		No VRO		VRO		No VRO		VRO	
		LTL	CTL	LTL	CTL	LTL	CTL	LTL	CTL
18	31	6.8871	0.1432	100.0822	0.8676	59.2266	0.2711	86.9653	0.5320
19	38	25.7469	0.4413	103.6992	0.3943	369.7850	1.1077	76.2565	0.2613
14	26	5.8769	0.1064	56.8184	0.3577	20.1059	0.1606	13.9620	0.0781
9	23	0.0201	0.0017	0.0959	0.0039	0.0299	0.0022	0.0670	0.0032
15	37	0.4292	0.0138	12.7095	0.0370	11.8577	0.0233	10.9242	0.0284
13	32	0.0334	0.0033	1.7767	0.0104	0.5014	0.0051	1.8381	0.0094
19	27	37.3025	1.0872	194.4493	2.7105	348.9075	3.5467	123.0635	1.2737
10	27	0.0320	0.0025	0.0820	0.0045	0.0548	0.0029	0.0624	0.0032
19	19	1.6001	0.0982	0.1200	0.0106	12.7730	0.2503	1.8869	0.0288
3	9	0.0085	0.0013	0.0090	0.0014	0.0048	0.0012	0.0054	0.0012

8   Summary

We presented a prototype verification tool that takes as input an NBC design and performs formal verification to check the logical correctness of the circuit. The tool verifies the correctness of NBC designs for SSP, ExCov and SAT. For handling SAT problems, we have also implemented tagging in the verification tool, where the agent sets all the labels it gathers while traversing the network to true, and temporal logic queries can also relate to the tagging of the filament when exiting the network. We have used our tool to analyze the efficiency of different methods of verifying encodings and to generate random examples of varying sizes and difficulties using an automatic SAT formula generator. The verification results demonstrate that the approach can handle large NBC circuits and is applicable to the real-world systems currently designed in [4, 20, 27]. Our work is currently used as an integral part of the design phases of new circuits in the Bio4Comp project.

Future work includes further scaling of the methods by evaluating and optimizing additional model checking algorithms and tools. Our translation to chemical reactions can form a basis for applying probabilistic model checking, which can remove some of the restricting assumptions made here. For example, we assume that pass junctions that do not have a manufacturing fault, never allow computational agents to change direction, while it was observed [4, 20] that most but not all of the of the agents traverse through pass junctions correctly. The effects of these errors could be quantified and analyzed using simulation and probabilistic model checking of CRNs to quantitatively estimate the effects of these errors in NBCs.

References

1. Bionetverification. https://github.com/msamedina/bionetverification
2. Zenodo. https://zenodo.org/record/4017293#.X7FIzWgzY2w
3. Adleman, L.M.: Molecular computation of solutions to combinatorial problems. Science **266**(5187), 1021–1024 (1994)
4. Bio4Comp: Bio4Comp project website (2020). www.bio4comp.org
5. Boemo, M.A., Lucas, A.E., Turberfield, A.J., Cardelli, L.: The formal language and design principles of autonomous DNA walker circuits. ACS Synth. Biol. **5**(8), 878–884 (2016)
6. Boemo, M.A., Turberfield, A.J., Cardelli, L.: Automated design and verification of localized DNA computation circuits. In: Phillips, A., Yin, P. (eds.) DNA 2015. LNCS, vol. 9211, pp. 168–180. Springer, Cham (2015). https://doi.org/10.1007/978-3-319-21999-8_11
7. Cavada, R., et al.: The NUXMV symbolic model checker. In: Biere, A., Bloem, R. (eds.) CAV 2014. LNCS, vol. 8559, pp. 334–342. Springer, Cham (2014). https://doi.org/10.1007/978-3-319-08867-9_22
8. Chabrier, N., Fages, F.: Symbolic model checking of biochemical networks. In: Priami, C. (ed.) CMSB 2003. LNCS, vol. 2602, pp. 149–162. Springer, Heidelberg (2003). https://doi.org/10.1007/3-540-36481-1_13
9. Cimatti, A., Clarke, E., Giunchiglia, F., Roveri, M.: Nusmv: a new symbolic model checker. Int. J. Softw. Tools Technol. Transfer **2**(4), 410–425 (2000)
10. Cook, M., Soloveichik, D., Winfree, E., Bruck, J.: Programmability of chemical reaction networks. In: Condon, A., Harel, D., Kok, J., Salomaa, A., Winfree, E. (eds.) Algorithmic Bioprocesses, pp. 543–584. Springer, Heidelberg (2009). https://doi.org/10.1007/978-3-540-88869-7_27
11. Dannenberg, F., Kwiatkowska, M., Thachuk, C., Turberfield, A.J.: DNA walker circuits: computational potential, design, and verification. In: Soloveichik, D., Yurke, B. (eds.) DNA 2013. LNCS, vol. 8141, pp. 31–45. Springer, Cham (2013). https://doi.org/10.1007/978-3-319-01928-4_3
12. Eén, N., Sörensson, N.: An extensible SAT-solver. In: Giunchiglia, E., Tacchella, A. (eds.) SAT 2003. LNCS, vol. 2919, pp. 502–518. Springer, Heidelberg (2004). https://doi.org/10.1007/978-3-540-24605-3_37
13. Fisman, D., Kugler, H.: Temporal reasoning on incomplete paths. In: Margaria, T., Steffen, B. (eds.) ISoLA 2018. LNCS, vol. 11245, pp. 28–52. Springer, Cham (2018). https://doi.org/10.1007/978-3-030-03421-4_3
14. Garey, M.R., Johnson, D.S.: Computers and Intractability, a Guide to the Theory of NP-Completeness. W. H. Freeman and Company, New York (1979)
15. Gautam, V., Long, S., Orponen, P., et al.: Ruledsd: a rule-based modelling and simulation tool for DNA strand displacement systems. In: BIOINFORMATICS, pp. 158–167 (2020)
16. Korten, T., Jr, D.V.N., Diez, S., Kugler, H., Linke, H.: Designing network based bio-computation circuits for the exact cover problem (2020, in preparation)
17. Lakin, M., Parker, D., Cardelli, L., Kwiatkowska, M., Phillips, A.: Design and analysis of DNA strand displacement devices using probabilistic model checking. J. Roy. Soc. Interface **9**(72), 1470–1485 (2012)
18. Lakin, M.R., Phillips, A.: Modelling, simulating and verifying turing-powerful strand displacement systems. In: Cardelli, L., Shih, W. (eds.) DNA 2011. LNCS, vol. 6937, pp. 130–144. Springer, Heidelberg (2011). https://doi.org/10.1007/978-3-642-23638-9_12

19. Lauria, M., Elffers, J., Nordström, J., Vinyals, M.: CNFgen: a generator of crafted benchmarks. In: Gaspers, S., Walsh, T. (eds.) SAT 2017. LNCS, vol. 10491, pp. 464–473. Springer, Cham (2017). https://doi.org/10.1007/978-3-319-66263-3_30
20. Nicolau, D.V., et al.: Parallel computation with molecular-motor-propelled agents in nanofabricated networks. Proc. Natl. Acad. Sci. **113**(10), 2591–2596 (2016)
21. Pedersen, M., Phillips, A.: Towards programming languages for genetic engineering of living cells. J. Roy. Soc. Interface **6**(4), 437–450 (2009)
22. Phillips, A., Cardelli, L.: A programming language for composable DNA circuits. J. Roy. Soc. Interface **6**(4), 1470–1485 (2009)
23. Qian, L., Winfree, E.: Scaling up digital circuit computation with DNA strand displacement cascades. Science **332**(6034), 1196–1201 (2011)
24. Rothemund, P.W., Papadakis, N., Winfree, E.: Algorithmic self-assembly of DNA Sierpinski triangles. PLoS Biol. **2**(12), e424 (2004)
25. Seelig, G., Soloveichik, D., Zhang, D., Winfree, E.: Enzyme-free nucleic acid logic circuits. Science **314**(5805), 1585–1588 (2006)
26. Shin, J.S., Pierce, N.A.: A synthetic DNA walker for molecular transport. J. Am. Chem. Soc. **126**(35), 10834–10835 (2004)
27. Van Delft, F.C., et al.: Something has to give: scaling combinatorial computing by biological agents exploring physical networks encoding NP-complete problems. Interface Focus **8**(6), 20180034 (2018)
28. Woods, D., Doty, D., Myhrvold, C., Hui, J., Zhou, F., Yin, P., Winfree, E.: Diverse and robust molecular algorithms using reprogrammable DNA self-assembly. Nature **567**(7748), 366–372 (2019)
29. Xu, X.Y., et al.: A scalable photonic computer solving the subset sum problem. Sci. Adv. **6**(5) (2020). https://doi.org/10.1126/sciadv.aay5853
30. Yin, P., Yan, H., Daniell, X.G., Turberfield, A.J., Reif, J.H.: A unidirectional DNA walker that moves autonomously along a track. Angew. Chem. **116**(37), 5014–5019 (2004)
31. Yordanov, B., Wintersteiger, C.M., Hamadi, Y., Phillips, A., Kugler, H.: Functional analysis of large-scale DNA strand displacement circuits. In: Soloveichik, D., Yurke, B. (eds.) DNA 2013. LNCS, vol. 8141, pp. 189–203. Springer, Cham (2013). https://doi.org/10.1007/978-3-319-01928-4_14
32. Zhu, J., et al.: Solution of a 3-sat problem based on network-based biocomputation via molecular motors (2020, in preparation)

Netter: Probabilistic, Stateful Network Models

Han Zhang[✉] , Chi Zhang, Arthur Azevedo de Amorim , Yuvraj Agarwal,
Matt Fredrikson, and Limin Jia

Carnegie Mellon University, Pittsburgh, PA, USA
{hzhang3,yuvraj,mfredrik}@cs.cmu.edu
{chiz5,liminjia}@andrew.cmu.edu,
arthur.aa@gmail.com

Abstract. We study the problem of using probabilistic network models
to formally analyze their quantitative properties, such as the effect of
different load-balancing strategies on the long-term traffic on a server
farm. Compared to prior work, we explore a different design space in
terms of tradeoffs between model expressiveness and analysis scalability,
which we realize in a language we call *Netter*. Netter code is compiled
to probabilistic automata, undergoing optimization passes to reduce the
state space of the generated models, thus helping verification scale. We
evaluate Netter on several case studies, including a probabilistic load
balancer, a routing scheme reminiscent of MPLS, and a network defense
mechanism against link-flooding attacks. Our results show that Netter
can analyze quantitative properties of interesting routing schemes that
prior work hadn't addressed, for networks of small size (4–9 nodes and
a few different types of flows). Moreover, when specialized to simpler,
stateless networks, Netter can parallel the performance of previous state-
of-the-art tools, scaling up to millions of nodes.

Keywords: Stateful networks · Probabilistic model checking ·
Discrete-time Markov chains

1 Introduction

Recent years have seen a surge of interest in automated tools for verifying networks [6,27,36], in particular for analyzing their *quantitative* properties—"What
is average latency for this type of traffic?"; "What percentage of packets are
dropped on this link?". Such formal verification tools complement other analysis
approaches, such as simulations, which are often guaranteed to yield accurate
results, but might require a large number of samples to do so.

In contrast to qualitative properties, such as reachability or the absence of
routing loops, quantitative properties are often probabilistic, and thus more
challenging, due to the complexity of computing over probabilistic models in
the presence of the explosion in the number of possible executions. Consider

© Springer Nature Switzerland AG 2021
F. Henglein et al. (Eds.): VMCAI 2021, LNCS 12597, pp. 486–508, 2021.
https://doi.org/10.1007/978-3-030-67067-2_22

Bayonet [6] for instance, a state-of-the-art language in this domain. Bayonet can express complex models that account for router state, queue lengths, randomness, and even different packet orderings. Though useful, this expressiveness limits the scalability of the analysis: currently, Bayonet can handle networks of about 30 nodes and small traffic volumes, on the order of 20 packets [6]. Other proposals achieve better scalability by sacrificing expressiveness to varying degrees. McNetKAT [5, 27], for instance, does not model network state or packet interaction, but in return scales to networks with thousands of nodes [27].

The goal of this paper is to seek a different middle ground between expressiveness and scalability. In particular, we aim to analyze the performance of stateful networks *in the long run*, without a priori bounds on the volume of traffic that traverses them. Moreover, we would like to do so while modeling some interaction between different sources of traffic. Potential applications include the analysis of load balancers, traffic engineering schemes, and other components that use states to improve performance. Given the challenges faced by prior work, it is natural to expect that some compromises will have to be made to handle interesting applications. Our hypothesis is that the behavior of many networks should not be too sensitive to the exact ordering of packet arrivals, but rather to how the traffic is distributed among different classes of flows over sizable time intervals—or, put differently, the main interactions between different types of traffic in these networks happen at a large scale. For example, certain traffic engineering schemes (cf. Sect. 4.2) avoid congestion by periodically reallocating flows on alternative paths based on the volume of data transmitted since the last checkpoint, with typical sampling intervals staying on the order of a few minutes. Based on this insight, we have designed *Netter*, a probabilistic language for modeling and verifying stateful networks. Unlike previous proposals [6, 27], Netter can express interactions between different kinds of traffic while avoiding the combinatorial explosion of having to reason explicitly about all possible packet orderings. Netter programs are compiled to finite-state Markov chains, which can be analyzed by various model checkers, such as PRISM [16] or Storm [8].

We evaluate Netter on a series of case studies: (1) computing failure probabilities on a simple stateless network; (2) a traffic engineering scheme reminiscent of MPLS-TE; (3) a stateful, probabilistic load balancer; and (4) a mitigation strategy for link-flooding attacks from prior work [18]. Our experiments show that Netter can scale to networks of 4–9 nodes, while providing insight into challenging routing questions that prior work had left unaddressed, such as examining the cost of deploying a cheap balancing strategy compared to the optimal one. While these sizes are modest compared to practical networks, we note that Netter can scale to similar orders of magnitude as state-of-the-art tools [27] on the more constrained stateless setting.[1] We expect that Netter's flexibility will allow users to tune between complexity and performance as suits their application.

---

[1] Due to dependency issues, we only managed to run part of the experiment of Smolka et al. [27], so our comparison is mostly based on the numbers reported by the authors. While this prevents us from making a precise comparison, their setup was similar to ours, and we do not expect the performance of their code to change substantially.

To summarize, our paper makes the following technical *contributions*:

- *Netter*, a domain-specific probabilistic language for modeling and verifying network programs (Sects. 2 and 3). By focusing on flow-level modeling and abstracting away from event orderings, Netter can verify asymptotic properties of stateful networks that were previously out of reach [6,27].
- Optimizations for reducing the size of the automata generated by Netter (Sect. 3). To be confident in their correctness, these optimizations were verified in the Coq proof assistant [30].
- A series of case studies evaluating the expressiveness and scalability of Netter (Sect. 4), including a comparative benchmark, a traffic engineering scheme, a stateful load balancer, and a defense against link-flooding attacks. Our results show that Netter scales similarly to state-of-the-art tools on stateless networks, while enabling the automated quantitative analysis of some stateful routing schemes that prior work could not handle.
- Netter is open-source, and available at https://github.com/arthuraa/netter. Our artifacts including case study code and Coq formalization are public available [39] and can be used with the VMCAI virtual machine [7].

The rest of the paper is organized as follows. In Sect. 2, we give a brief overview of the Netter workflow with a simple, but detailed, model of a stateful network, showing how we can reason about its performance characteristics automatically. In Sect. 3, we delve into the Netter language, covering its main functionality and how it departs from prior work. We describe its Haskell implementation and the optimization passes used to improve model checking time. In Sect. 4, we present our case studies. Finally, we discuss related work in Sect. 5 and conclude in Sect. 6.

2 Overview

The workflow of using Netter for analyzing probabilistic quantitative network properties is depicted in Fig. 1. Users provide a Haskell file with a model written in an embedded probabilistic imperative language. The model contains the code of the network, as well as declarations of key performance metrics that the users want to analyze, such as the drop rate of the network. The Netter compiler transforms this model into a probabilistic automaton that encodes a finite-state, discrete-time Markov chain. This automaton is encoded in the language of the PRISM model checker [16], but back-ends to similar tools could be added easily. This Markov chain is then fed to Storm [8], a high-performance probabilistic model checker, along with a set of properties to analyze, such as the expected value of a performance metric in the stationary distribution of the chain.

To illustrate this workflow, consider the network depicted in Fig. 2. Two servers, S1 and S2, sit behind a load balancer LB. When a new flow of traffic arrives, the load balancer simply picks one of the servers at random and routes the traffic through the corresponding link. Any traffic that exceeds the link's

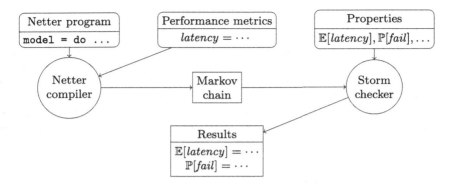

Fig. 1. Netter workflow. Rounded corners denote user-provided inputs, rectangles denote outputs, and circles denote components.

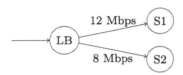

Fig. 2. Example network with two servers, S1 and S2, and a load balancer LB. LB has randomly forward incoming flows to either server. If the new flow traffic size is 10 Mbps, it will experience losses if forwarded to S2.

capacity is dropped, and we are interested in computing the long-term average drop rate of this load-balancing scheme under certain traffic assumptions.

Figure 3 shows a model of this network in Netter. Unlike other network modeling languages [6], Netter does not represent different network nodes as separate entities. Rather, the model presents a global view of the network, where all the state is manipulated by a single program. In our example, this state comprises just the two allocated variables `dest` and `newFlow` (lines 10–11), which represent the state of the load balancer and the state of the current flow. Later examples will show models where other nodes also use state (Sect. 4).

Since Netter programs are compiled to finite-state automata, variables must be bounded, and their bounds are specified in the parameters of the `var` function. The `dest` variable represents the router chosen by the load balancer, while `newFlow` tracks whether a new flow of traffic has just arrived. For now, we assume that there can be only one flow at a time in this network, which transmits data at a rate of 10 Mbps. The `rewards` call (lines 13–15) specifies that we are interested in analyzing the average drop rate of the network. Note that to avoid confusion with standard Haskell functions, many Netter operators are primed (e.g. `when'`) or prefixed with a dot (e.g. `./`). The `.? ... .:` form is the Netter equivalent of the ternary operator in C-like languages.

Figure 3 shows the code representing the execution of one step of the Markov chain. On the first time step, the state variables are set to their lower bound.

Then, the program enters a loop, executing its code once per step. More precisely, the behavior of the network is defined in lines 17–19. Line 17 says that on every step there is a 10% probability that a flow ends and a new one starts. The .<-$ operator samples from a probability distribution specified as a list of probability/value pairs. By changing this distribution, or by adding more state variables, we can model richer traffic patterns (Sect. 4.3). Lines 18–19 say that, whenever a new flow appears, the load balancer chooses its server uniformly at random. The selected server remains stored in dest for the next few time steps, until newFlow becomes 1 again.

```
1   trafficSize = 10
2   bandwidth1 = 12
3   bandwidth2 = 8
4
5   dropRate bw = int dropped ./ int trafficSize
6     where dropped = max 0 (trafficSize - bw)
7
8   model :: Prog ()
9   model = do
10    dest <- var 1 2
11    newFlow <- var 0 1
12
13    rewards "dropRate"
14      (dest .== 1 .? dropRate bandwidth1
15       .: dropRate bandwidth2)
16
17    newFlow .<-$ [(0.1, 1), (0.9, 0)]
18    when' (newFlow .== 1) $ do
19      dest .<-$ [(0.5, 1), (0.5, 2)]
```

Fig. 3. Netter implementation of model in Fig. 2.

Figure 4 shows the probabilistic automaton produced by Netter for this network. Though the execution of the original program happens conceptually in one step, representing this directly as a probabilistic automaton is challenging. It is easier to decompose the code into a series of more elementary steps, where we use the auxiliary *program counter* variable pc_0 to choose which command of the program needs to be executed next. The point pc_0 = 0 marks the beginning of the execution at the source level. (Using a small number of PC values is crucial for keeping the generated model small, an issue that prior work on Probabilistic NetKAT also faced [27]; cf. Sect. 3.) We set the dropRate reward to zero at other PCs to ensure that it is counted only once per source-level step.

To calculate the long-term average drop rate for the incoming flow, we feed Storm the PCTL query R{"dropRate"}=? [LRA] / LRA=? [pc_0=0], to which it replies 0.1. (The adjusting factor LRA=? [pc_0=0] is included to compensate for intermediate steps in the automaton that have no source-level counterpart.)

```
 1  module m0   // load-balance new flow to server
 2  dest_0 : [1..2];
 3  [step] (pc_0!=1) -> true;
 4  [step] ((pc_0=1)&(newFlow_0=1)) -> 0.5:(dest_0'=1) \
 5                                   + 0.5:(dest_0'=2);
 6  [step] ((pc_0=1)&(newFlow_0!=1)) -> (dest_0'=dest_0);
 7  endmodule
 8
 9  module m1   // randomly decide if flow becomes active
10  newFlow_0 : [0..1];
11  [step] (pc_0!=2) -> true;
12  [step] (pc_0=2) -> 0.1:(newFlow_0'=1) \
13                   + 0.9:(newFlow_0'=0);
14  endmodule
15
16  module m2   // manage pc counter
17  pc_0 : [0..2];
18  [step] (pc_0=0) -> (pc_0'=2);
19  [step] (pc_0=1) -> (pc_0'=0);
20  [step] (pc_0=2) -> (pc_0'=1);
21  endmodule
22
23  rewards "dropRate"
24  (pc_0=0) : ((dest_0=1)?0.0:0.2);
25  (pc_0!=0) : 0;
26  endrewards
```

Fig. 4. Compiled DTMC model from Netter implementation in Fig. 3.

3   The Netter Language

Operations. Figure 5 enumerates some of the main operations in Netter. The Expr type represents integer and boolean values in the network program. The type Prog is used for commands and program declarations. It carries the structure of a monad [22], allowing us to easily compose subprograms. Commands have a return type of (), the unit type, which means that they yield no values,

Function	Type	Description
var	Int -> Int -> Prog Expr	Declare a state variable
.+, .-, .&&	Expr -> Expr -> Expr	Arithmetic and logic
.<-	Expr -> Expr -> Prog ()	Deterministic assignment
.<-$	Expr -> [(Double, Expr)] -> Prog ()	Probabilistic assignment
if'	Expr -> Prog () -> Prog () -> Prog ()	Conditional
block	Prog () -> Prog ()	Block for local variables
.!!	[Expr] -> Expr -> Expr	List indexing

Fig. 5. Select Netter primitives.

```
data RouterState = RouterState { reservedBandwidth :: Expr
                               , sampledBandwidth :: Expr }

makeRouter :: Prog RouterState
makeRouter = do
  rb <- var 0 maxBandwidth
  sb <- var 0 maxBandwidth
  return (RouterState { reservedBandwidth = rb, sampledBandwidth = sb })
```

Fig. 6. Netter programs can use Haskell abstractions such as functions and data types.

and are run solely for building the program. Other declarations, however, may produce useful results, such as the variable declaration command `var`, which returns an `Expr` (cf. Fig. 3).

The API highlights important distinctions with respect to prior work. First, unlike Probabilistic NetKAT [5] or Bayonet [6], there are no specialized commands for manipulating packets (though this functionality can be encoded with regular state variables, as we do in Sect. 4.1). Indeed, since Netter is tailored to analyze flow-level behavior, we focus on commands that manipulate the high-level routing decisions (e.g. the `dest` variable in Fig. 3), and assume that these can be implemented in terms of lower-level packet-manipulating primitives. Second, unlike Probabilistic NetKAT, Netter programs can use *arbitrary* expressions in assignments and in the guards of if statements, making it easy to encode typical imperative programs—indeed, most of the case studies in Sect. 4 use this functionality.[2] On the other hand, Probabilistic NetKAT allows programs to perform unbounded iteration, while Netter does not have an analogous construct. This simplifies the semantics of Netter programs, which can be easily described as a stochastic matrix on the finite space of all program states. An entry M_{ij} of this matrix describes the probability of transitioning from state i to state j after running the code. The semantics is similar to that of McNetKAT [27], but includes a semantics for arithmetic expressions, and omits a clause for iteration. (In practice, we have not found the absence of loops to be a limitation, since we could partly emulate iteration by wrapping Netter commands in Haskell loops).

Netter has a phase distinction between *model code*, which is analyzed by the model checker, and *compiler code*, which is responsible for generating the former. The `Expr` type produces expressions that are consumed by the model checker, and thus does not have a well-defined "value" when the model is being generated. This prevents us from operating on expressions as if they were regular values in Haskell; for instance, we cannot test if two model variables hold the same value by writing `x == y`, since the equality operator returns a fixed boolean rather than a symbolic expression. This is why many basic Haskell operators

---

[2] In principle, since variables are bounded, it would be possible to do away with expressions by evaluating them at every possible state. However, this would result in much larger compiled models, making the analysis more costly.

have counterparts for Netter expressions, as we have seen with the ./ and .==
operators of Fig. 3. Despite this phase distinction, the compiler code is free to
use other Haskell types and operations to generate a model, which makes up
for the minimalist set of basic constructs available in Netter. For instance, we
can represent a stateful router with a record that contains Netter variables (cf.
Fig. 6), a functionality that is useful when defining complex network models, as
we will see in Sect. 4.

Implementation. The compilation process that takes a network algorithm
implemented in Netter and generates an *optimized* PRISM model was implemented in about 2k lines of Haskell. First, user-level commands are processed
to build an internal representation of a model in a simple imperative language
called Imp. As depicted in Fig. 7, the program then undergoes a series of compilation passes to produce a Markov-chain model. An important part of this
process is the translation of the program to a control-flow graph (CFG), which
can be more directly represented as an automaton. The size of the resulting
automaton is linear in the size of the CFG, which must be kept to a minimum
to avoid blowing up the state space. This is the job of two optimization passes
of the pipeline: one that inlines as many assignments as possible, and one that
removes stores and variables that are not used to compute the rewards declared
by the user. The inlining pass is particularly challenging. Indeed, in an earlier
version of the compiler, we tried to symbolically execute the Netter program to
remove the need for any intermediate assignments, probabilistic and deterministic alike. However, composing multiple symbolic probabilistic assignments can
quickly lead to bloated models: if an assignment with n probabilistic branches
is expanded in another probabilistic assignment with m branches the result is
generally a probabilistic assignment with $n \cdot m$ branches.

To avoid this issue, we adopted a more conservative strategy where we only
inline deterministic assignments. This requires some care: if a variable x receives
the result of a random sample, we need to stop propagating any inlined expressions that mention x, since they refer to its old value. To increase our confidence
in this step, we have formalized our main optimization passes using the Coq proof
assistant [30], and manually translated the algorithms to Haskell. To define the
semantics of the language, we formalized a core of finite probability theory in
Coq, including infrastructure for reasoning about coupling arguments [10]. Probabilistic NetKAT relies on a similar optimization to compile to PRISM [27],
though its logic is considerably simpler, since only constants can be assigned in
the language (and thus almost no dependencies need to be considered).

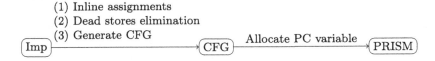

Fig. 7. Netter compilation pipeline.

4   Applications

Now that we have acquainted ourselves with the Netter basics, we discuss four case studies that used the language to model and analyze stateful networks. For all of the following cases, we evaluate Netter on a 12-core VM with 64 GB memory. Unless specified otherwise, we use the Storm [8] model checker with their Sparse backend engine. We set the max memory limit to be 40 GB for Storm, reserving headroom for graceful shutdown in case of memory exhaustion.

4.1   Warming up

As a first case study, we evaluate the performance of Netter on a simple stateless benchmark. This benchmark exercises features that could already be handled in prior work [6, 27], and is a sanity check to ensure that Netter's expressiveness does not incur large performance penalties when it is not needed. Figure 8 presents a network that connects two hosts, H_1 and H_2, via a chain of $4k$ intermediate switches. Each switch $S_{i,1}$ forwards traffic to either $S_{i,2}$ or $S_{i,3}$ with equal probability. Both $S_{i,2}$ and $S_{i,3}$ forward to $S_{i,4}$, but the link $S_{i,3} \to S_{i,4}$ can fail with probability $p = 10^{-3}$. Finally, $S_{i,4}$ forwards to $S_{i+1,1}$. We are interested in the probability that a packet is successfully delivered from H_1 to H_2.

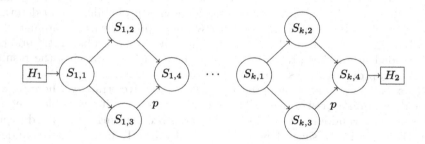

Fig. 8. Chain topology with failures.

We compare the time taken to check the Netter model in Storm against the time taken by PRISM and Storm to check a handwritten model of this network. The handwritten model was taken from an analogous experiment in the McNetKAT paper [27]. We set a timeout of 5 min. Figure 9 presents the results. We observe that Storm takes about the same time to check the Netter and the handwritten models, with the latter being slightly cheaper to process. We checked networks of at most 4M switches. PRISM timed out at 32k switches. For comparison, the authors of McNetKAT [27] reported that their custom solver could analyze 65k switches in 2.5 min running on a cluster with 24 machines, while Bayonet could analyze 32 switches in 25 min. Moreover, their performance figures for checking the handwritten model with PRISM are similar to ours. We did not manage to run the McNetKAT code in our setting, due to dependency issues.

The gap between Bayonet and the other tools is to be expected, as it is based on a much more general solver and accounts for traffic details that the others don't, such as asynchronous event scheduling. (Note that these features should not fundamentally change the analysis, since this experiment considers only one packet.) As for McNetKAT, we believe that the difference in performance can be mostly explained by the use of the Storm back-end; nevertheless, since Storm is compatible with the PRISM language, which can also be targeted by McNetKAT, McNetKAT could readily benefit from advances in other model checkers as well.

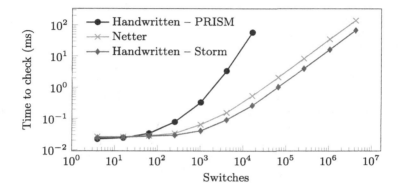

Fig. 9. Checking performance of chain example.

The case for using Netter on an example like this is not so strong, as the handwritten automaton for PRISM is about the same size as our model, and can be checked slightly faster. With the next case studies, we will see examples with non-trivial control flow that would be difficult to encode directly in PRISM.

4.2 Traffic Engineering with MPLS

Traditional IP routing can be too inflexible for traffic-engineering purposes, as every packet is sent through the shortest path between its source and destination. If a link on this path becomes congested, the performance of the network degrades. In modern networks, a popular solution is to manage sections of a path using Multiprotocol Label Switching (MPLS) instead of pure IP.

Originally, MPLS was introduced to speed up the handling of addresses in switches. When packets from other protocols enter an MPLS network, they are encapsulated with a *label* determined by their header and routed through a path in the network until they reach an exit node, when the labels are removed. (In reality, the labels change as packets traverse the network, but this detail is not relevant for our purposes.) Labels are processed in a way that resembles IP addresses, in that the next hop of a packet along a path is determined by its labels. However, labels are much shorter than IP addresses, and thus faster to process in hardware.

As MPLS was extended over the years, it gained the ability to manage labels with more flexibility than IP, making it attractive for traffic engineering. To avoid congestion, for example, MPLS can reserve some bandwidth for each label, and assign them to paths so that the total reserved bandwidth on each link does not exceed its capacity. Moreover, this reserved bandwidth can change dynamically based on traffic demands, causing labels to be reallocated on different paths.

Prior work [24] observed that bad MPLS configurations can allocate labels on sub-optimal paths, leading to *latency inflation*. In the network analyzed by the authors, the weighted latency was 10%–22% higher than the optimal, and some labels could remain on sub-optimal paths for as long as 10 days!

To investigate the causes of latency inflation, we devised an experiment that models the bandwidth adjustment logic used by the main network vendors—the so-called "auto-bandwidth" feature. In this experiment, each flow corresponds to the traffic assigned to one MPLS label; thus, each flow is routed through a particular path in the network, and has a certain bandwidth reserved for it along this path. Our adjustment logic is governed by two parameters: the *sample interval* and the *adjustment interval*. Every sample interval, the network samples the volume of traffic on each flow. When the adjustment interval is completed, the largest sample since the beginning of the interval is compared against the current reserved bandwidth for each flow. If the sample is larger than the reserved bandwidth, the network reallocates the flow on a new path with enough bandwidth, potentially evicting lower-priority flows allocated there. We set the sample interval to 3 time steps, and the adjustment interval to 9 time steps. (Real MPLS deployments expose other configuration options as well, such as the adjustment threshold. For simplicity, we omit those.)

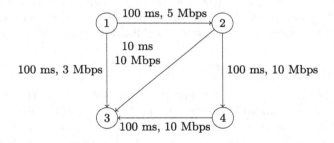

Fig. 10. MPLS network topology.

Figure 10 shows the topology used in our experiment. The link between 2 and 3 is a local link with high bandwidth, whereas the other four are long links with higher latency. There are two flows in this network: $f_{2,3}$, a high-volume flow of 9 Mbps between 2 and 3, and $f_{1,3}$ between 1 and 3. The volume of traffic in $f_{1,3}$ varies between 2 and 4 Mbps according to a random walk, moving up or down if possible with a probability of 25%.

We use Storm to compare the long-term weighted latency of two configurations for this network: one where $f_{2,3}$ has a higher priority than $f_{1,3}$, and the other one where the priorities are reversed. We switch to the Hybrid engine to avoid memory exhaustion for this model. Storm reports that the weighted latency is 101 ms for the first configuration 81 ms for the second one, which corresponds to an increase of about 24%. Intuitively, in the first configuration, when $f_{1,3}$ triggers an adjustment, it ends up evicting $f_{2,3}$ to a much longer path, because it has higher priority. Since $f_{2,3}$ carries more traffic, the weighted latency goes up. In the second configuration, instead, $f_{1,3}$ is reassigned to the path $1 \rightarrow 2 \rightarrow 4 \rightarrow 3$, and the problem does not arise. These observations corroborate the aforementioned empirical results.

As a side note, this case study was one of the original motivations for implementing Netter. We attempted to encode an earlier version of this model directly in the PRISM language, but felt that correctly expressing the control-flow of the autobandwidth logic as an automaton was error prone, especially when trying to express more complex topologies and flow configurations, since there is no convenient way of abstracting the network topology in PRISM. By contrast, our Netter model takes in a high-level description of the network topology as an adjacency matrix, and automatically computes the lists of possible routes for a flow ranked by latency, while ensuring that the available bandwidth on each route is correctly updated.

4.3   Stateful Load Balancers

Load balancers are commonly used to improve web application performance by sharing and distributing a pool of resources. They act as virtual servers to receive incoming client requests and forward requests across different backend servers to manage desirable loads between servers. Many load balancing algorithms require storing internal state information. For example, a Round Robin algorithm needs to remember which server it assigns the previous flows before allocating the next one. Many other algorithms need to compare the current server loads before finding a suitable candidate to allocate the new flow. Although previous works have modeled randomized load balancers [5,6], they do not support the case for stateful load balancers or other complex algorithms. In our experiment, we implement and analyze three different load balancing algorithms.

Max Free Capacity. The Max Free Capacity algorithm requires the load balancer to forward new flows to the server with the largest available capacity, measured as the difference between the server's maximum capacity and the its current load. Intuitively, this strategy should have a very low probability of flow loss because it can find the best server to process all incoming flows. However, the disadvantage is that the load balancer needs to collect information from all servers before making any decisions. This method can be costly, generating too much internal traffic and incurring high latency.

Round Robin. The Round Robin algorithm uses an internal counter to assign new flows to servers. When a new flow arrives, the load balancer forwards it to the server given by the current counter and updates the counter to the next server in line. The advantage of this strategy is that the load balancer doesn't need to check the server load at all. The disadvantage is that it may cause significant server imbalances and packet drops when a server receives too much load while another one is mostly free.

Best of Random 2. In the Best of Random 2 algorithm, the load balancer randomly picks two servers, compares their current load, and sends the new flow to server with the largest available capacity. This simple but powerful algorithm is proven to have a small maximum server load with high probability [21], making it a popular option for many applications [29]. Compared to the previous two algorithms, the Best of Random 2 algorithm is a compromise for avoiding flow losses while reducing internal traffic queries, since it only needs to query two servers instead of all of them.

We implement these three algorithms in Netter in a simple load balancing use case—we put one load balancer in front of a group of servers, and the load balancer forwards incoming flows to any one of the servers. We explore various settings in terms of the number of servers, number of flows, and server capacity, and compare these algorithms' performance. We pick two metrics—average flow loss rate and server load imbalance—to measure these algorithms' performance. Finally, we show the complexity of running Netter in these cases.

During our evaluation, we represent flow traffic with a Markov model. At every timestamp, each inactive flow can be independently activated with a probability of 0.6. Upon activation, the flow randomly selects a volume between 1 and 3 Mbps. Active flows also have a 0.6 probability of deactivating and return to the inactive state at every timestamp. In the following graph, the flow number represents the maximum possible number of flows that could arrive at the load balancer at the same timestamp.

Flow Loss Rates. Figure 11a shows the long-run flow loss percentage for different algorithms in a group of 3 servers with *different capacity*. The percentage of flow loss is calculated by the number of packet drops over total incoming loads. From the figure, we can see that the Max Free Capacity algorithm always has a strictly lower flow loss compared to the other two algorithms. The Round Robin algorithm causes more flow losses than the Best of Random 2 algorithm. This is because the Best of Random 2 will overload a server beyond its capacity only if neither of the two randomly chosen servers has enough free capacity. In comparison, the Round Robin algorithm is agnostic to the server's current load, and it assigns flows periodically in the long run. We can also see that the difference in flow loss for these three strategies is getting smaller when the flow load increases. This is because none of the strategies deal with the case where the incoming flow load is larger than the total server capacity.

This result confirms our intuition that the Max Free Capacity is the best solution among the three algorithms in reliable flow allocation if we ignore its

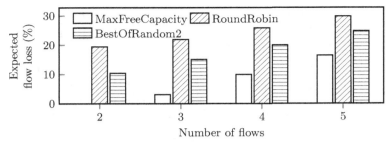

(a) Different capacity, number of servers=3.

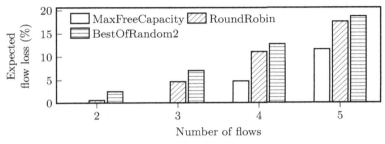

(b) Equal capacity, number of servers=3.

Fig. 11. Model checking results on flow loss rates for the load balancer using different algorithms to allocate flows to 3 servers.

costly nature of querying every server for their load during runtime. Moreover, we can see that the Round Robin algorithm has a larger flow loss rate than the other two algorithms when the servers have different capacity.

Figure 11b shows the long-run flow loss percentage for every algorithm with servers of the *same capacity*. Comparing to the previous figure, we can see the difference in the flow loss rate across all three algorithms. Each algorithm observes less flow loss comparing to the previous case. Similarly, the Max Free Capacity algorithm has the lowest flow loss rate. An interesting observation for this case is that the Round Robin algorithm causes less flow loss than the Best of Random 2 algorithm. This is because, given the parameters set for the Markov flow model, the server is less likely to have an active flow when selected by the Round Robin algorithm (i.e., previous flows must remain active for many rounds) than with the Best of Random 2 algorithm (i.e., server can be picked at any time).

Server Load Imbalances. Figure 12a shows an imbalance among servers by plotting the absolute value of servers' capacity and load. In this case, all servers with the same 3 Mbps capacity are represented as white bars, and the grey bars show the long-run load on the servers. We can see that the Round Robin algorithm and the Best of Random algorithm have the same load allocation among the servers. Yet, the Max Free Capacity algorithm's imbalance is caused by a priority

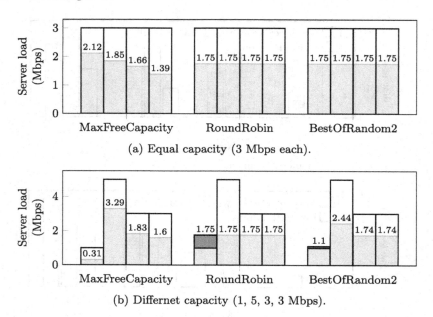

(a) Equal capacity (3 Mbps each).

(b) Differnet capacity (1, 5, 3, 3 Mbps).

Fig. 12. Model checking results on server load imbalance from the three load balancing algorithms to allocate 5 flows to 4 servers. For each algorithm, the four bars represents the four individual servers. White bar indicates server capacity, light grey for average loads, and dark grey for overloads.

among servers when breaking a tie. By default, this algorithm allocates the flow to the server with a smaller index when servers have the same free capacity.

Figure 12b shows the imbalances between servers with unequal capacity. We assign each server with 1 Mbps, 5 Mbps, 3 Mbps, and 3 Mbps maximum capacity, respectively. The dark grey bars in the figure represent overloading servers beyond their maximum capacity. For example, the Round Robin algorithm allocates 1.78 Mbps traffic to server 1, where over 40% will be dropped due to server overload. The root cause of the massive server overload is that the Round Robin algorithm is agnostic to individual server loads when allocating new flows. For simplicity, the load balancer only keeps one next counter to decide where to send the next flow. As a result, the load balancer forwards the incoming flow to the chosen destination, even if the server is busy while others have ample free capacity. In comparison, the Best of Random 2 significantly reduces server utilization imbalance. Instead of deterministically assigning one server for new flows, the load balancer randomly picks two candidates and checks their utilization. Server overload can still happen—when the load balancer picks two busy servers by chance, and neither one can fulfill the new flow without loss. However, the probability of server overload (and imbalance flow allocation) is much smaller than the Round Robin algorithm. On the other hand, the Max Free Capacity algorithm is the optimal strategy in avoiding server overload. This is because the load balancer has a global view of server loads before allocating new flows. It can always pick the capable server to process the new flow if such one exists. Therefore, we observe that no server experiences high or near-max loads.

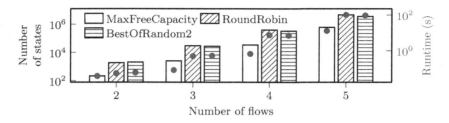

Fig. 13. Model checking complexity in Markov chain state number and runtime for load balancer using each of the three algorithm to allocate flows among 4 servers with same capacity. The runtime is marked as red point scaled on the right side. (Color figure online)

Analysis Runtime. Figure 13 shows the complexity and runtime of using Netter to analyze different algorithms. In the figure, we show that the runtime of model checking is proportional to the number of states the Markov chain needs to calculate. Since different algorithms have different numbers of variables in the model, they vary significantly in model complexity. The Best of Random 2 algorithm uses random choice in picking the servers, which leads to more states for the model checker to explore, especially when comparing against the Max Free Capacity algorithm. The Round Robin algorithm requires a global variable in the model to keep track of the next server to allocate new flow. In addition to the complexity in the algorithm, we must keep auxiliary variables such as flow assignment and flow volume to calculate flow loss rate and server loads at every timestamp. These variables increase the state space exponentially, and thus pose a scalability challenge for exhaustive model checking.

We empirically evaluate different model-checking engines of Storm. We compared their Sparse and Hybrid engines and found out the Sparse engine is universally faster in solving the load balancer models. The Hybrid engine, on the other hand, sacrifices runtime speed for smaller memory usages. Therefore, for problems with larger state space that Sparse engine runs out of memory, we use the hybrid engine. One example is the case study of MPLS in Sect. 4.2.

4.4 Defending Against Link-Flooding Attacks

Link-flooding attacks have become a serious threat to Internet security [34]. As a distributed denial-of-service attack, link-flooding aims to disrupt the availability of specific links between routers (e.g., data centers, Internet exchange points, Autonomous Systems). All services and connections sharing the same victim links in their paths will be affected, regardless of their sources and destinations.

To defend against link-flooding attacks, several prior methods propose routing-based mechanisms to divert the victim's network traffic during attacks [18, 25]. They propose different rate-limiting and routing algorithms to be applied at intermediate routers to coordinate defenses. When hosts detect links in their routing path are under attack, they proactively switch to other alternative routing paths to avoid such links. Although such approaches are intuitive, many practical challenges affect the feasibility of re-routing to alternative paths [31]. For example, before switching, the victim host needs to analyze what latency and bandwidth availability the secondary path can provide. Therefore, it is important to verify the effectiveness and applicability of re-routing techniques based on the specific routing algorithms and global topology.

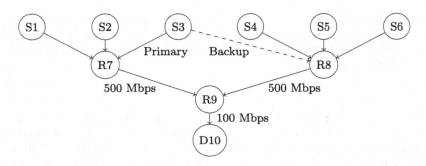

Fig. 14. Topology for DDoS case study in Sect. 4.4. S3 uses R7 as its primary link, but maintains an alternative path through R8 as a backup.

To illustrate, we present a network topology vulnerable to such attacks (cf. Fig. 14). This topology is adapted from the evaluation in the CoDef paper [18], where they implement a simulation network to measure the effectiveness of CoDef rate-limiting and routing algorithm. Node S1–S6 are clients sending traffic to D10 as the final destination, R7–R9 are intermediate routers. S1 and S2 are malicious attackers sending a massive amount of traffic. Both of them send a median of 300 Mbps of traffic following a Pareto distribution. S3 is the victim of the example. It shares the same link as attackers S1 and S2. However, it can switch to its backup link to avoid attackers. S3 and S4 are file transfer applications, greedily expecting to utilize as much bandwidth as possible. S5 and S6 consume 10 Mbps consistently, representing fixed bandwidth flows such as streaming. Meanwhile, S3 maintains a secondary backup link with router R8, but it does not utilize that link under normal circumstances. Using multiple routers from different providers, as S3 does, is commonly known as *multihoming* [1].

We implement three routing algorithms in Netter using the same topology and check the average bandwidth allocated for each flow as properties. To switch between different algorithms, we only need to change the code in the routing module, keeping the rest of the model the same.

CoDef Collaborative Routing. CoDef proposes a collaborative routing algorithm for routers R7–R9 to coordinate and defend against link-flooding attackers S1 and S2. All routers collaboratively label each destination-source pair as a unique path and ensure fair bandwidth utilization on a per-path basis. The algorithm allocates the bandwidth in two passes: first, the router assigns a fair share to each flow, and then allocate additional free bandwidth in a second pass.

Uniformly Random. This algorithm allocates egress bandwidth uniform-randomly based on the proportion of incoming bandwidth. It is a statistically simple allocation algorithm and requires minimal metadata communication between routers. For example, suppose S1 and S2 send a large amount of traffic to router R7 and S3 uses its primary link. The router will allocate a higher share of the available 500 Mbps outgoing bandwidth to these two flows, reducing flow 3's portion.

Type-Aware Priority. The type-aware routing algorithm considers the type of flows. Motivated by the real-world example of classifying traffic into several classes and provide different quality-of-service guarantees [3, 24], routers can assign priorities and available bandwidth accordingly to a different type of traffic. In our example, we enable the routers to prioritize consistent flow transmission; specifically, the fixed bitrate flows 5 and 6. As for the remaining flows, the router follows the same uniform strategy to allocate the available bandwidth.

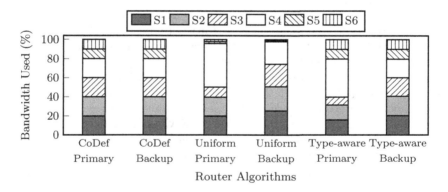

Fig. 15. Model checking results for each flow's portion at the destination (Node 10). S1 and S2 are attacker flows. Each bar indicates a corresponding router algorithm and which router link flow 3 connects to.

Figure 15 compares the model checking results for different algorithms. CoDef algorithm enforces fair allocations regardless of S3's egress link. However, other algorithms present pathological cases when S3 is under direct link-flooding attacks from attackers S1 and S2. The Uniform algorithm equally splits bandwidth between two incoming routers ($7 \rightarrow 9$, $8 \rightarrow 9$). In the Primary case, flows

1–3 and 4–6 use an equal amount, while in Secondary flows 1–2 and 3–6 are the same. The Type-aware algorithm reserves a high priority to flow 5 and 6, and uniformly shares the rest bandwidth among flows 1–4.

We successfully used Netter to analyze a large topology of 10 nodes without the need to scale all numbers by a common factor manually. Switching between the router's rate-limiting algorithms is also relatively easy. We can implement a new rate-limiting algorithm and specify which router to use it. One limitation of Netter model checking is that we cannot use continuous distributions for traffic volumes. Because Netter compiles programs to finite-state models, we use a discrete approximation of the Pareto distribution to represent attacker S1 and S2's traffic model. We calculate the numerical value for every 5th percentile along with their cumulative density function and use these numbers and their percentiles to approximate the probabilistic distribution of flows 1 and 2.

5 Related Work

There is a rich body of work for testing and verifying forwarding behaviors such as reachability and loop freedom, in stateless networks [9,13–15,19,20,32,33,35, 37,38] and stateful networks [4,23,28,36]. The aforementioned projects do not concern quantitative properties of the network such as latency and throughput, which our work focuses on. Moreover, we support probabilistic network models, which differentiates our work from quantitative network analysis based on fixed quantity and SAT solvers [11,12,17].

Next, we discuss related work that is closer to ours, on probabilistic languages to model and analyze quantitative properties of networks [6,27]. NetKAT [2,5,26,27] is a family of network-modeling languages based on Kleene algebra with tests. In the original NetKAT [2], a program denotes a set of packet histories, which are traces of the states of a packet while it traverses the network. Probabilistic NetKAT [5,26,27] adds in probabilistic choice, and has been used to analyze interesting case studies, such as fault tolerance of a data center design [27]. The semantics of Probabilistic NetKAT is similar to Netter's, though the more sophisticated features of the language go beyond finite-state Markov chains, and require continuous distributions. Language-wise, Netter and Probabilistic NetKAT are built on similar primitives, with two main differences: (1) NetKAT programs can only assign constants to variables, whereas Netter programs can assign arbitrary arithmetic and logical expressions, and (2) NetKAT has unbounded iteration, which Netter does not (though Netter programs can simulate iteration by metaprogramming; that is, by writing a Haskell loop that repeatedly calls a code snippet). The restricted assignments are not too limiting for NetKAT, since it is used to model stateless networks, and the assignments encode a network node's actions after matching on the headers of a packet ("if the destination IP is 10.0.0.1, forward the packet to port 10"). Netter, on the other hand, was primarily designed to model stateful networks, which perform more assignments and would be awkward to encode without expressions. Because of its richer assignments, Netter's optimizations are more challenging than NetKAT's [27], since they involve inlining expressions, tracking state dependencies and eliminating dead stores. The McNetKAT dialect of Probabilistic NetKAT can also be compiled to PRISM [27], though it also features a custom solver that outperforms PRISM on large networks.

Bayonet [6] is another recent language for analyzing stateful networks. It is more general than Netter, as even the ordering of network events is taken into account. Moreover, Bayonet programs can condition distribution parameters based on the observations they make, and then run Bayesian inference to determine those parameters. Unfortunately, the complexity of features modeled by the language poses great challenges for scalability. Bayonet requires users to bound the number of packets transmitted in the network and the number of network events that can occur. In the case studies analyzed by the authors, these numbers go to at most 20 packets and to a thousand network events (though in most case studies only a few tens of events are allowed). By contrast, by aggregating traffic at the level of flows, Netter analysis can scale to much larger time frames, since we can compute performance metrics for a network's long-term distribution. On the simple network of Sect. 4.1, we have seen that Netter can scale up to thousands of nodes, while prior work [6, 27] showed that Bayonet's analysis scales up to about 30 nodes (though, admittedly, on a somewhat different setup). On the other hand, Netter scalability degrades substantially when handling more complex networks, such as those of Sect. 4.3, which where limited to four servers. This issue seems challenging to address with Netter's current back-end: if each node in the network comprises 10 possible states, a modest size, the number of states of the system will be proportional to $10^{\#\mathrm{nodes}}$ in the worst case.

6   Conclusion and Future Work

We have presented a framework for formally analyzing the probabilistic quantitative properties of networks. We showed the design and implementation of Netter, a language for verifying quantitative properties of stateful networks. Netter compiles its programs down to PRISM automata, and applies several optimizations to simplify their control flow, thus speeding up the analysis of the generated models. We evaluated Netter on a series of case studies. We observed that the tool scales up to sizable networks when reasoning about simple properties and routing schemes. We demonstrated how to use Netter to model more complex networks as well. Though the scalability of the analysis quickly degrades in these cases, we could still reason about important performance characteristics and use them to compare different routing strategies. In future work, we would like to address these scalability issues, potentially integrating symbolic analysis techniques that do not require explicitly enumerating the network state space.

Acknowledgments. The authors would like to thank Steffen Smolka, Justin Hsu and Timon Gehr for useful discussions and clarifications. This work was partially funded by ONR award N000141812618, NSF award 1513961 and NSF award 1564009.

506   H. Zhang et al.

References

1. Abley, J., Lindqvist, K., Davies, E., Black, B., Gill, V.: IPv4 multihoming practices and limitations. RFC 4116, RFC Editor, July 2005. http://www.rfc-editor.org/rfc/rfc4116.txt
2. Anderson, C.J., et al.: NetKAT: semantic foundations for networks. In: Jagannathan, S., Sewell, P. (eds.) The 41st Annual ACM SIGPLAN-SIGACT Symposium on Principles of Programming Languages, POPL 2014, San Diego, CA, USA, 20–21 January 2014, pp. 113–126. ACM (2014). https://doi.org/10.1145/2535838.2535862
3. Braden, B., Zhang, L., Berson, S., Herzog, S., Jamin, S.: Resource reservation protocol (RSVP) - version 1 functional specification. RFC 2205, RFC Editor, September 1997. http://www.rfc-editor.org/rfc/rfc2205.txt
4. Fayaz, S.K., Yu, T., Tobioka, Y., Chaki, S., Sekar, V.: BUZZ: testing context-dependent policies in stateful networks. In: 13th USENIX Symposium on Networked Systems Design and Implementation (NSDI 2016), pp. 275–289. USENIX Association, Santa Clara (2016). https://www.usenix.org/conference/nsdi16/technical-sessions/presentation/fayaz
5. Foster, N., Kozen, D., Mamouras, K., Reitblatt, M., Silva, A.: Probabilistic NetKAT. In: Thiemann, P. (ed.) ESOP 2016. LNCS, vol. 9632, pp. 282–309. Springer, Heidelberg (2016). https://doi.org/10.1007/978-3-662-49498-1_12
6. Gehr, T., Misailovic, S., Tsankov, P., Vanbever, L., Wiesmann, P., Vechev, M.T.: Bayonet: probabilistic inference for networks. In: Foster, J.S., Grossman, D. (eds.) Proceedings of the 39th ACM SIGPLAN Conference on Programming Language Design and Implementation, PLDI 2018, Philadelphia, PA, USA, 18–22 June 2018, pp. 586–602. ACM (2018). https://doi.org/10.1145/3192366.3192400
7. Henriksen, T.: VMCAI 2021 virtual machine, September 2020. https://doi.org/10.5281/zenodo.4017293
8. Hensel, C., Junges, S., Katoen, J.P., Quatmann, T., Volk, M.: The probabilistic model checker storm. CoRR abs/2002.07080 (2020). https://arxiv.org/abs/2002.07080
9. Horn, A., Kheradmand, A., Prasad, M.: Delta-net: real-time network verification using atoms. In: 14th USENIX Symposium on Networked Systems Design and Implementation (NSDI 2017), pp. 735–749. USENIX Association, Boston (2017). https://www.usenix.org/conference/nsdi17/technical-sessions/presentation/horn-alex
10. Hsu, J.: Probabilistic couplings for probabilistic reasoning. CoRR abs/1710.09951 (2017). http://arxiv.org/abs/1710.09951
11. Jensen, J.S., Krogh, T.B., Madsen, J.S., Schmid, S., Srba, J., Thorgersen, M.T.: P-Rex: fast verification of MPLS networks with multiple link failures. In: Proceedings of the 14th International Conference on Emerging Networking EXperiments and Technologies, CoNEXT 2018 (2018)
12. Juniwal, G., Bjorner, N., Mahajan, R., Seshia, S.A., Varghese, G.: Quantitative network analysis. Technical report (2016). http://cseweb.ucsd.edu/~varghese/qna.pdf
13. Kazemian, P., Chang, M., Zeng, H., Varghese, G., McKeown, N., Whyte, S.: Real time network policy checking using header space analysis. In: Presented as Part of the 10th USENIX Symposium on Networked Systems Design and Implementation (NSDI 2013), pp. 99–111. USENIX, Lombard (2013). https://www.usenix.org/conference/nsdi13/technical-sessions/presentation/kazemian

14. Kazemian, P., Varghese, G., McKeown, N.: Header space analysis: static checking for networks. In: Presented as Part of the 9th USENIX Symposium on Networked Systems Design and Implementation (NSDI 2012), pp. 113–126. USENIX, San Jose (2012). https://www.usenix.org/conference/nsdi12/technical-sessions/presentation/kazemian

15. Khurshid, A., Zou, X., Zhou, W., Caesar, M., Godfrey, P.B.: VeriFlow: verifying network-wide invariants in real time. In: Presented as Part of the 10th USENIX Symposium on Networked Systems Design and Implementation (NSDI 2013), pp. 15–27. USENIX, Lombard (2013). https://www.usenix.org/conference/nsdi13/technical-sessions/presentation/khurshid

16. Kwiatkowska, M., Norman, G., Parker, D.: PRISM 4.0: verification of probabilistic real-time systems. In: Gopalakrishnan, G., Qadeer, S. (eds.) CAV 2011. LNCS, vol. 6806, pp. 585–591. Springer, Heidelberg (2011). https://doi.org/10.1007/978-3-642-22110-1_47

17. Larsen, K.G., Schmid, S., Xue, B.: WNetKAT: a weighted SDN programming and verification language. In: 20th International Conference on Principles of Distributed Systems (OPODIS 2016) (2016)

18. Lee, S.B., Kang, M.S., Gligor, V.D.: CoDef: collaborative defense against large-scale link-flooding attacks. In: Proceedings of the Ninth ACM Conference on Emerging Networking Experiments and Technologies, CoNEXT 2013, p. 417–428. Association for Computing Machinery, New York (2013). https://doi.org/10.1145/2535372.2535398

19. Lopes, N.P., Bjorner, N., Godefroid, P., Jayaraman, K., Varghese, G.: Checking beliefs in dynamic networks. In: 12th USENIX Symposium on Networked Systems Design and Implementation (NSDI 2015), pp. 499–512. USENIX Association, Oakland (2015). https://www.usenix.org/conference/nsdi15/technical-sessions/presentation/lopes

20. Mai, H., Khurshid, A., Agarwal, R., Caesar, M., Godfrey, P.B., King, S.T.: Debugging the data plane with anteater. In: Proceedings of the ACM SIGCOMM 2011 Conference, SIGCOMM 2011, pp. 290–301. ACM, New York (2011). https://doi.org/10.1145/2018436.2018470

21. Mitzenmacher, M., Upfal, E.: Probability and Computing: Randomized Algorithms and Probabilistic Analysis. Cambridge University Press, New York (2005)

22. Moggi, E.: Computational lambda-calculus and monads. In: Proceedings of the Fourth Annual Symposium on Logic in Computer Science (LICS 1989), Pacific Grove, California, USA, 5–8 June 1989, pp. 14–23. IEEE Computer Society (1989). https://doi.org/10.1109/LICS.1989.39155

23. Panda, A., Lahav, O., Argyraki, K., Sagiv, M., Shenker, S.: Verifying reachability in networks with mutable datapaths. In: 14th USENIX Symposium on Networked Systems Design and Implementation (NSDI 2017), pp. 699–718. USENIX Association, Boston, March 2017. https://www.usenix.org/conference/nsdi17/technical-sessions/presentation/panda-mutable-datapaths

24. Pathak, A., Zhang, M., Hu, Y.C., Mahajan, R., Maltz, D.A.: Latency inflation with MPLS-based traffic engineering. In: Thiran, P., Willinger, W. (eds.) Proceedings of the 11th ACM SIGCOMM Internet Measurement Conference, IMC 2011, Berlin, Germany, 2 November 2011, pp. 463–472. ACM (2011). https://doi.org/10.1145/2068816.2068859

25. Smith, J.M., Schuchard, M.: Routing around congestion: defeating DDoS attacks and adverse network conditions via reactive BGP routing. In: 2018 IEEE Symposium on Security and Privacy (SP), pp. 599–617. IEEE (2018)

26. Smolka, S., Kumar, P., Foster, N., Kozen, D., Silva, A.: Cantor meets scott: semantic foundations for probabilistic networks. In: Proceedings of the 44th ACM SIGPLAN Symposium on Principles of Programming Languages, POPL 2017, pp. 557–571. Association for Computing Machinery, New York (2017). https://doi.org/10.1145/3009837.3009843

27. Smolka, S., et al.: Scalable verification of probabilistic networks. In: McKinley, K.S., Fisher, K. (eds.) Proceedings of the 40th ACM SIGPLAN Conference on Programming Language Design and Implementation, PLDI 2019, Phoenix, AZ, USA, 22–26 June 2019, pp. 190–203. ACM (2019). https://doi.org/10.1145/3314221.3314639

28. Stoenescu, R., Popovici, M., Negreanu, L., Raiciu, C.: SymNet: scalable symbolic execution for modern networks. In: Proceedings of the 2016 Conference on ACM SIGCOMM 2016 Conference, SIGCOMM 2016, pp. 314–327. ACM, New York (2016). https://doi.org/10.1145/2934872.2934881

29. Tarreau, W.: Test driving "power of two random choices" load balancing, April 2019. https://www.haproxy.com/blog/power-of-two-load-balancing/

30. The Coq Development Team: The Coq proof assistant, version 8.12.0, July 2020. https://doi.org/10.5281/zenodo.4021912

31. Tran, M., Kang, M.S., Hsiao, H.C., Chiang, W.H., Tung, S.P., Wang, Y.S.: On the feasibility of rerouting-based DDoS defenses. In: 2019 IEEE Symposium on Security and Privacy (SP), pp. 1169–1184. IEEE (2019)

32. Tschaen, B., Zhang, Y., Benson, T., Benerjee, S., Lee, J., Kang, J.M.: SFC-checker: checking the correct forwarding behavior of service function chaining. In: IEEE SDN-NFV Conference (2016)

33. Xie, G.G., et al.: On static reachability analysis of IP networks. In: IEEE Proceedings of the 24th Annual Joint Conference of the IEEE Computer and Communications Societies, INFOCOM 2005, vol. 3, pp. 2170–2183. IEEE (2005)

34. Xue, L., Luo, X., Chan, E.W., Zhan, X.: Towards detecting target link flooding attack. In: 28th Large Installation System Administration Conference (LISA 2014), pp. 90–105 (2014)

35. Yang, H., Lam, S.S.: Real-time verification of network properties using atomic predicates. IEEE/ACM Trans. Netw. 24(2), 887–900 (2016). https://doi.org/10.1109/TNET.2015.2398197

36. Yuan, Y., Moon, S.J., Uppal, S., Jia, L., Sekar, V.: NetSMC: a custom symbolic model checker for stateful network verification. In: Bhagwan, R., Porter, G. (eds.) 17th USENIX Symposium on Networked Systems Design and Implementation, NSDI 2020, Santa Clara, CA, USA, 25–27 February 2020, pp. 181–200. USENIX Association (2020). https://www.usenix.org/conference/nsdi20/presentation/yuan

37. Zeng, H., Kazemian, P., Varghese, G., McKeown, N.: Automatic test packet generation. IEEE/ACM Trans. Netw. 22(2), 554–566 (2014). https://doi.org/10.1109/TNET.2013.2253121

38. Zeng, H., et al.: Libra: divide and conquer to verify forwarding tables in huge networks. In: NSDI 2014, pp. 87–99 (2014)

39. Zhang, H., Zhang, C., Azevedo de Amorim, A., Agarwal, Y., Fredrikson, M., Jia, L.: Netter: probabilistic, stateful network models, October 2020. https://doi.org/10.5281/zenodo.4089060

Decision Procedures

Deciding the Bernays-Schoenfinkel Fragment over Bounded Difference Constraints by Simple Clause Learning over Theories

Martin Bromberger[1(✉)], Alberto Fiori[1,2], and Christoph Weidenbach[1]

[1] Max Planck Institute for Informatics, Saarland Informatics Campus,
Saarbrücken, Germany
{mbromber,afiori,weidenb}@mpi-inf.mpg.de
[2] Graduate School of Computer Science, Saarland Informatics Campus,
Saarbrücken, Germany

Abstract. Simple clause learning over theories SCL(T) is a decision procedure for the Bernays-Schoenfinkel fragment over bounded difference constraints BS(BD). The BS(BD) fragment consists of clauses built from first-order literals without function symbols together with simple bounds or difference constraints, where for the latter it is required that the variables of the difference constraint are bounded from below and above. The SCL(T) calculus builds model assumptions over a fixed finite set of fresh constants. The model assumptions consist of ground foreground first-order and ground background theory literals. The model assumptions guide inferences on the original clauses with variables. We prove that all clauses generated this way are non-redundant. As a consequence, expensive testing for tautologies and forward subsumption is completely obsolete and termination with respect to a fixed finite set of constants is a consequence. We prove SCL(T) to be sound and refutationally complete for the combination of the Bernays Schoenfinkel fragment with any compact theory. Refutational completeness is obtained by enlarging the set of considered constants. For the case of BS(BD) we prove an abstract finite model property such that the size of a sufficiently large set of constants can be fixed a priori.

1 Introduction

Our work is motivated by the modeling, execution and verification of a "supervisor" [10], a component in a technical system that controls system functionality. Examples for a supervisor are the electronic control unit of a combustion engine or a control unit for the lane change assistant in a car. In this context we have been looking for a decsision procedure of a logical fragment that has sufficient expressivity to model supervisor functionality and properties; at the same time the fragment should run efficiently, i.e., generating consequences out of ground facts (inputs), and, finally, it should be push button verifiable

© Springer Nature Switzerland AG 2021
F. Henglein et al. (Eds.): VMCAI 2021, LNCS 12597, pp. 511–533, 2021.
https://doi.org/10.1007/978-3-030-67067-2_23

(decidable). The Bernays Schoenfinkel fragment of first-order logic over linear arithmetic BS(LRA) is a candidate for such a fragment. The first-order part can be used to specify the rules and properties of a supervisor and the linear arithmetic part to deal with technicalities of the application. For example, computing the (real world) injection time of a charged combustion engine contains rules like the one below:

$$P(x) \wedge 150 \leq x \leq 200 \wedge R(y) \wedge 6500 \leq y \leq 7000 \wedge T(x, y, z) \rightarrow I(z + 10)$$

where x is the air pressure in the inlet manifold, y the speed of the engine, T a table lookup for the injection time z and finally 10 is added for engine heat protection. In the real world, the added heat protection part 10 is the result of an additional computation taking temperature of the engine, exhaust gas, inlet air and lambda value into account. In the supervisor context, a decision procedure should also deliver explanations, i.e., explicit (counter) models and proofs. In addition to efficiency, this is another reason why we designed SCL(T) to compute explicit models and proofs.

The combination of linear rational arithmetic (LRA) with the Bernays Schoenfinkel fragment of first-order logic (BS(LRA)) is already undecidable for a single monadic predicate [9,13]. This can be shown by encoding the halting problem of a 2-counter machine [17]. For a number of universally quantified fragments there exist complete methods and some fragments are even decidable [12,16,24]. If the first-order part of BS(LRA) consists only of variables and predicates, then there exist refutationally complete calculi [1].

In this paper we introduce a new calculus SCL(T) (Simple Clause Learning over Theories) for the combination of a background theory with a foreground first-order logic without equality. As usual in a hierarchic setting, we assume the background theory to be term-generated and compact. In this paper we only consider *pure* clause sets where the only symbols occurring in the clause set from the foreground logic are predicates and variables. Reasoning in the SCL(T) calculus is driven by a partial, finite model assumption similar to conflict driven clause learning (CDCL) [14,18,23] and our previous work [11]. In contrast to SMT, the model assumption is not build on an a priori abstraction of ground literals to propositional logic, but from ground background and ground foreground theory literals generated by SCL(T) through instantiation and respecting their semantics. So any SCL(T) trail is always satisfiable in the combined theory. Inferences are performed on the original clauses with variables, similar to hierarchic superposition, where the ordering restrictions of hierarchic superposition are replaced by guidance through the partial ground model assumption. The main advantage of this approach is that learned clauses are never redundant, Lemma 22, and that the partial model assumption can be explored to derive an overall explicit model. SCL(T) is sound, Lemma 9 and Lemma 12, and refutationally complete, Theorem 25. As a running example, we present the combination of linear rational arithmetic (LRA) with the Bernays Schoenfinkel fragment of first-order logic (BS(LRA)).

In order to demonstrate the potential of SCL(T) we prove it can decide the class BS(BD), the Bernays-Schoenfinkel fragment over simple bounds and bounded difference constraints, Sect. 3. This class was known to be decidable before [24], but not on the basis of a sound and complete calculus such as SCL(T).

Related Work: In contrast to variants of hierarchic superposition [1, 4, 16] SCL(T) selects clauses via a partial model assumption and not via an ordering. This has the advantage that SCL(T) does not generate redundant clauses. Where hierarchic superposition builds implicit models via saturated clause sets, SCL(T) builds explicit, finite model candidates that need to be extended to overall models of a clause set, see Example 13 and Sect. 4. One way to deal with universally quantified variables in an SMT setting is via instantiation [12, 21]. This has shown to be practically useful in many applications. It typically comes without completeness guarantees and it does not learn any new clauses with variables. While mcSAT [8] extends the SMT framework with the possibility to create new literals, its learning capabilities are also limited to the ground case. An alternative is to combine SMT techniques with superposition [7] where the ground literals from an SMT model assumption are resolved by superposition with first-order clauses. SCL(T) does not resolve with respect to its ground model assumption but on the original clauses with variables. Program verification through Horn clause reasoning [5] is another research direction related to SMT and SCL(T). Here constrained Horn clauses are considered and various reasoning methods have been developped. Our logic is not restricted to Horn clauses and our reasoning methods are different. In the same way SMT solving can be used to keep track of consistent SCL(T) trails, Horn clause reasoning could be used to explore the propagation space of an SCL(T) run. Background theories can also be built into first-order superposition in a kind of lazy way. This direction has been followed by SPASS+T [19] and Vampire [15]. The idea is to axiomatize part of the background theory in first-order logic and to direct ground literals of the background theory to SMT solver. Also this approach has shown to be practically useful but comes without any completeness guarantees and generated clauses may be redundant. Model evolution [2] has also been extended with linear integer arithmetic [3] where universally quantified integer variables are finitely bound from the beginning. A combination of first-order logic with linear integer arithmetic has also been built into a sequent calculus [22] that operates in the style of a free-variable tableau calculus with incremental closure. No new clauses are learned.

Organization of the Paper: After a section fixing notation, notions and some preliminary work, Sect. 2, the following Sect. 3 introduces the SCL(T) calculus and proves its properties. Missing proofs can be found in an arXiv publication [6]. Section 4 presents decidability of BS(BD) by SCL(T). The final Sect. 5 discusses extensions to model building, further improvements and summarizes the obtained results.

2   Preliminaries

Many-Sorted First-Order Logic Without Equality: A *many-sorted signature* $\Sigma = (\mathcal{S}, \Omega, \Pi)$ is a triple consisting of a finite, non-empty set $\mathcal{S}$ of *sort symbols*, a non-empty set Ω of *operator symbols* (also called *function symbols*) over $\mathcal{S}$ and a finite set Π of *predicate symbols* over $\mathcal{S}$. For every sort from $\mathcal{S}$ there is at least one constant symbol in Ω of this sort. First-order terms, atoms, literals, clauses, formulas and substitutions are defined in the usual many-sorted way where an additional infinite set $\mathcal{X}$ of variables is assumed, such that for each sort from $\mathcal{S}$ there are infinitely many variables of this sort in $\mathcal{X}$. For each sort $S \in \mathcal{S}$, $T_S(\Sigma, \mathcal{X})$ denotes the set of all terms of sort S and $T_S(\Sigma)$ the set of all ground terms of sort S.

For notation, a, b, c are constants from Ω, w, x, y, z variables from $\mathcal{X}$, and if we want to emphasize the sort of a variable, we write x_S for a variable of sort S; t, s denote terms, P, Q, R predicates from Π, A, B atoms, L, K, H denote literals, C, D denote clauses, and N denotes a clause set. For substitutions we write σ, δ, ρ. Substitutions are well-sorted: if $x_s\sigma = t$ then $t \in T_S(\Sigma, \mathcal{X})$, they have a finite domain $\mathrm{dom}(\sigma) = \{x \mid x\sigma \neq x\}$ and their codomain is denoted by $\mathrm{codom}(\sigma) = \{x\sigma \mid x \in \mathrm{dom}(\sigma)\}$. The application of substitutions is homomorphically extended to non-variable terms, atoms, literals, clauses, and formulas. The complement of a literal is denoted by the function comp. For a literal L, $|L|$ denotes its respective atom. The function atoms computes the set of atoms from a clause or clause set. The function vars maps terms, literals, clauses to their respective set of contained variables. The function con maps terms, literals, clauses to their respective set of constants. A term, atom, clause, or a set of these objects is *ground* if it does not contain any variable, i.e., the function vars returns the empty set. A substitution σ is *ground* if $\mathrm{codom}(\sigma)$ is ground. A substitution σ is *grounding* for a term t, literal L, clause C if $t\sigma$, $L\sigma$, $C\sigma$ is ground, respectively. The function gnd computes the set of all ground instances of a literal, clause, or clause set. Given a set of constants B, the function gnd_B computes the set of all ground instances of a literal, clause, or clause set where the grounding is restricted to use constants from B. The function mgu denotes the *most general unifier* of two terms, atoms, literals. As usual, we assume that any mgu of two terms or literals does not introduce any fresh variables and is idempotent.

The semantics of many-sorted first-order logic is given by the notion of an algebra: let $\Sigma = (\mathcal{S}, \Omega, \Pi)$ be a many-sorted signature. A Σ-*algebra* $\mathcal{A}$, also called Σ-*interpretation*, is a mapping that assigns (i) a non-empty carrier set $S^{\mathcal{A}}$ to every sort $S \in \mathcal{S}$, so that $(S_1)^{\mathcal{A}} \cap (S_2)^{\mathcal{A}} = \emptyset$ for any distinct sorts $S_1, S_2 \in \mathcal{S}$, (ii) a total function $f^{\mathcal{A}} : (S_1)^{\mathcal{A}} \times \ldots \times (S_n)^{\mathcal{A}} \rightarrow (S)^{\mathcal{A}}$ to every operator $f \in \Omega$, $\mathrm{arity}(f) = n$ where $f : S_1 \times \ldots \times S_n \rightarrow S$, (iii) a relation $P^{\mathcal{A}} \subseteq ((S_1)^{\mathcal{A}} \times \ldots \times (S_m)^{\mathcal{A}})$ to every predicate symbol $P \in \Pi$ with $\mathrm{arity}(P) = m$. The semantic entailment relation $\models$ is defined in the usual way. We call a Σ-algebra $\mathcal{A}$ *term-generated* if $\mathcal{A}$ fulfills the following condition: whenever $\mathcal{A}$ entails all groundings $C\sigma$ of a clause C (i.e., $\mathcal{A} \models C\sigma$ for all grounding substitutions σ of a clause C), then $\mathcal{A}$ must also entail C itself (i.e., $\mathcal{A} \models C$).

Hierarchic Reasoning: The starting point of a hierarchic reasoning [1,4] is a background theory $\mathcal{T}^{\mathcal{B}}$ over a many-sorted signature $\Sigma^{\mathcal{B}} = (\mathcal{S}^{\mathcal{B}}, \Omega^{\mathcal{B}}, \Pi^{\mathcal{B}})$ and a non-empty set of term-generated $\Sigma^{\mathcal{B}}$-algebras $\mathcal{C}^{\mathcal{B}}$: $\mathcal{T}^{\mathcal{B}} = (\Sigma^{\mathcal{B}}, \mathcal{C}^{\mathcal{B}})$. A constant $c \in \Omega^{\mathcal{B}}$ is called a *domain constant* if $c^{\mathcal{A}} \neq d^{\mathcal{A}}$ for all $\mathcal{A} \in \mathcal{C}^{\mathcal{B}}$ and for all $d \in \Omega^{\mathcal{B}}$ with $d \neq c$. The background theory is then extended via a foreground signature $\Sigma^{\mathcal{F}} = (\mathcal{S}^{\mathcal{F}}, \Omega^{\mathcal{F}}, \Pi^{\mathcal{F}})$ where $\mathcal{S}^{\mathcal{B}} \subseteq \mathcal{S}^{\mathcal{F}}$, $\Omega^{\mathcal{B}} \cap \Omega^{\mathcal{F}} = \emptyset$, and $\Pi^{\mathcal{B}} \cap \Pi^{\mathcal{F}} = \emptyset$. Hierarchic reasoning is based on a background theory $\mathcal{T}^{\mathcal{B}}$ and a respective foreground signature $\Sigma^{\mathcal{F}}$: $\mathcal{H} = (\mathcal{T}^{\mathcal{B}}, \Sigma^{\mathcal{F}})$. It has its associated signature $\Sigma^{\mathcal{H}} = (\mathcal{S}^{\mathcal{F}}, \Omega^{\mathcal{B}} \cup \Omega^{\mathcal{F}}, \Pi^{\mathcal{B}} \cup \Pi^{\mathcal{F}})$ generating *hierarchic* $\Sigma^{\mathcal{H}}$-algebras. A $\Sigma^{\mathcal{H}}$-algebra $\mathcal{A}$ is called *hierarchic* with respect to its background theory $\mathcal{T}^{\mathcal{B}}$, if $\mathcal{A}^{\mathcal{H}}|_{\Sigma^{\mathcal{B}}} \in \mathcal{C}^{\mathcal{B}}$. As usual, $\mathcal{A}^{\mathcal{H}}|_{\Sigma^{\mathcal{B}}}$ is obtained from a $\mathcal{A}^{\mathcal{H}}$-algebra by removing all carrier sets $S^{\mathcal{A}}$ for all $S \in (\mathcal{S}^{\mathcal{F}} \backslash \mathcal{S}^{\mathcal{B}})$, all functions from $\Omega^{\mathcal{F}}$ and all predicates from $\Pi^{\mathcal{F}}$. We write $\models_{\mathcal{H}}$ for the entailment relation with respect to hierarchic algebras and formulas from $\Sigma^{\mathcal{H}}$ and $\models_{\mathcal{B}}$ for the entailment relation with respect to the $\mathcal{C}^{\mathcal{B}}$ algebras and formulas from $\Sigma^{\mathcal{B}}$.

Terms, atoms, literals build over $\Sigma^{\mathcal{B}}$ are called *pure background terms*, *pure background atoms*, and *pure background literals*, respectively. All terms, atoms, with a top-symbol from $\Omega^{\mathcal{B}}$ or $\Pi^{\mathcal{B}}$, respectively, are called *background terms*, *background atoms*, respectively. A background atom or its negation is a *background literal*. All terms, atoms, with a top-symbol from $\Omega^{\mathcal{F}}$ or $\Pi^{\mathcal{F}}$, respectively, are called *foreground terms*, *foreground atoms*, respectively. A foreground atom or its negation is a *foreground literal*. Given a set (sequence) of $\mathcal{H}$ literals, the function bgd returns the set (sequence) of background literals and the function fgd the respective set (sequence) of foreground literals. A substitution σ is called *simple* if $x_S \sigma \in T_S(\Sigma^{\mathcal{B}}, \mathcal{X})$ for all $x_S \in \text{dom}(\sigma)$ and $S \in \mathcal{S}^{\mathcal{B}}$.

As usual, clauses are disjunctions of literals with implicitly universally quantified variables. We often write a $\Sigma^{\mathcal{H}}$ clause as a *constrained clause*, denoted $\Lambda \parallel C$ where Λ is a conjunction of background literals and C is a disjunction of foreground literals semantically denoting the clause $\neg \Lambda \vee C$. A *constrained closure* is denoted as $\Lambda \parallel C \cdot \sigma$ where σ is grounding for Λ and C. A constrained closure $\Lambda \parallel C \cdot \sigma$ denotes the ground constrained clause $\Lambda\sigma \parallel C\sigma$.

In addition, we assume a well-founded, total, strict ordering $\prec$ on ground literals, called an $\mathcal{H}$-order, such that background literals are smaller than foreground literals. This ordering is then lifted to constrained clauses and sets thereof by its respective multiset extension. We overload $\prec$ for literals, constrained clauses, and sets of constrained clause if the meaning is clear from the context. We define $\preceq$ as the reflexive closure of $\prec$ and $N^{\preceq \Lambda \parallel C} := \{D \mid D \in N \text{ and } D \preceq \Lambda \parallel C\}$. An instance of an LPO with according precedence can serve as $\prec$.

Definition 1 (Clause Redundancy). *A ground constrained clause $\Lambda \parallel C$ is redundant* with respect to a set N of ground constrained clauses and an order $\prec$ *if $N^{\preceq \Lambda \parallel C} \models_{\mathcal{H}} \Lambda \parallel C$. A clause $\Lambda \parallel C$ is redundant* with respect to a clause set N, an $\mathcal{H}$-order $\prec$, and a set of constants B *if for all $\Lambda' \parallel C' \in \text{gnd}_B(\Lambda \parallel C)$ the clause $\Lambda' \parallel C'$ is redundant with respect to $\cup_{D \in N} \text{gnd}_B(D)$.*

*Example 2 (*BS(LRA)*).* The running example in this paper is the Bernays-Schoenfinkel clause fragment over linear arithmetic: BS(LRA). The background theory is linear rational arithmetic over the many-sorted signature $\Sigma^{\mathrm{LRA}} = (\mathcal{S}^{\mathrm{LRA}}, \Omega^{\mathrm{LRA}}, \Pi^{\mathrm{LRA}})$ with $\mathcal{S}^{\mathrm{LRA}} = \{\mathrm{LRA}\}$, $\Omega^{\mathrm{LRA}} = \{0, 1, +, -\} \cup \mathbb{Q}$, $\Pi^{\mathrm{LRA}} = \{\leq, <, \neq, =, >, \geq\}$) where LRA is the linear arithmetic sort, the function symbols consist of $0, 1, +, -$ plus the rational numbers and predicate symbols $\leq, <, =, \neq, >, \geq$. The linear arithmetic theory $\mathcal{T}^{\mathrm{LRA}} = (\Sigma^{\mathrm{LRA}}, \{\mathcal{A}^{\mathrm{LRA}}\})$ consists of the linear arithmetic signature together with the standard model $\mathcal{A}^{\mathrm{LRA}}$ of linear arithmetic. This theory is then extended by the free (foreground) first-order signature $\Sigma^{\mathrm{BS}} = (\{\mathrm{LRA}\}, \Omega^{\mathrm{BS}}, \Pi^{\mathrm{BS}})$ where Ω^{BS} is a set of constants of sort LRA different from Ω^{LRA} constants, and Π^{BS} is a set of first-order predicates over the sort LRA. We are interested in hierarchic algebras $\mathcal{A}^{\mathrm{BS(LRA)}}$ over the signature $\Sigma^{\mathrm{BS(LRA)}} = (\{\mathrm{LRA}\}, \Omega^{\mathrm{BS}} \cup \Omega^{\mathrm{LRA}}, \Pi^{\mathrm{BS}} \cup \Pi^{\mathrm{LRA}})$ that are $\Sigma^{\mathrm{BS(LRA)}}$ algebras such that $\mathcal{A}^{\mathrm{BS(LRA)}}|_{\Sigma^{\mathrm{LRA}}} = \mathcal{A}^{\mathrm{LRA}}$.

Note that our definition of the BS(LRA) fragment restricted to the linear arithmetic sort does not restrict expressiveness compared to a definition adding further free sorts to Σ^{BS}. Free sorts containing only constants can be simulated by the linear arithmetic sort in a many-sorted setting.

We call a clause set N *abstracted* if the arguments of any predicate from $\Pi^{\mathcal{F}}$ are only variables. Abstraction can always be obtained by adding background constraints, e.g., the BS(LRA) clause $x > 1 \parallel R(x, 5)$ can be abstracted to $x > 1, y = 5 \parallel R(x, y)$, preserving satisfiability. Recall that even in the foreground signature we only consider background sorts and that the only operators in the foreground signature are constants.

A set N of $\mathcal{H}$ clauses is called *pure* if it does not contain symbols from $\Omega^{\mathcal{F}}$ ranging into a sort of $\mathcal{S}^{\mathcal{B}}$. In this case N is *sufficiently complete* according to [1], hence hierarchic superposition is complete for N [1,4]. As a consequence, a pure clause set N is unsatisfiable iff $\mathrm{gnd}_B(N)$ can be refuted by hierarchic superposition for a sufficiently large set B of constants. We will make use of this result in the completeness proof for our calculus, Theorem 24.

Satisfiability of pure clause sets is undecidable. We already mentioned in the introduction that this can be shown through a reduction to the halting problem for two-counter machines [13,17]. Clause redundancy for pure clause sets cannot be decided as well, still SCL(T) learns only non-redundant clauses.

Lemma 3 (Non-Redundancy for Pure Clause Sets is Undecidable). *For a pure clause set N it is undecidable whether some clause C is non-redundant with respect to N.*

3   SCL(T)

Assumptions: For this section we consider only pure, abstracted clause sets N. We assume that the background theory $\mathcal{T}^{\mathcal{B}}$ is term-generated, compact, contains an equality $=$, and that all constants of the background signature are domain constants. We further assume that the set $\Omega^{\mathcal{F}}$ contains infinitely many constants for each background sort.

Example 4 (Pure Clauses). With respect to BS(LRA) the unit clause $x \geq 5, 3x + 4y = z \parallel Q(x, y, z)$ is abstracted and pure while the clause $x \geq 5, 3x + 4y = a, z = a \parallel Q(x, y, z)$ is abstracted but not pure because of the foreground constant a of the LRA sort, and the clause $x \geq 5, 3x + 4y = 7 \parallel Q(x, y, 7)$ is not abstracted.

Note that for pure, abstracted clause sets, any unifier between two foreground literals is simple and its codomain consists of variables only.

In order for the SCL(T) calculus to be effective, decidability in $\mathcal{T}^{\mathcal{B}}$ is needed as well. For the calculus we implicitly use the following equivalence: A $\Sigma^{\mathcal{B}}$ sentence $\exists x_1, \ldots, x_n \phi$ where ϕ is quantifier free is true, i.e., $\models_{\mathcal{B}} \exists x_1, \ldots, x_n \phi$ iff the ground formula $\phi\{x_1 \mapsto a_1, \ldots, x_n \mapsto a_n\}$ where the a_i are $\Omega^{\mathcal{F}}$ constants of the respective background sorts is $\mathcal{H}$ satisfiable. Together with decidability in $\mathcal{T}^{\mathcal{B}}$ this guarantees decidability of the satisfiability of ground constraints from constrained clauses.

If not stated otherwise, satisfiability means satisfiability with respect to $\mathcal{H}$. The function $\text{adiff}(B)$ for some finite sequence of background sort constants denotes a constraint that implies different interpretations for the constants in B. In case the background theory enables a strict ordering $<$ as LRA does, then the ordering can be used for this purpose. For example, $\text{adiff}([a, b, c])$ is then the constraint $a < b < c$. In case the background theory does not enable a strict ordering, then inequations can express disjointness of the constants. For example, $\text{adiff}([a, b, c])$ is then the constraint $a \neq b \wedge a \neq c \wedge b \neq c$. An ordering constraint has the advantage over an inequality constraint that it also breaks symmetries. Assuming all constants to be different will eventually enable a satisfiability test for foreground literals based on purely syntactic complementarity.

The inference rules of SCL(T) are represented by an abstract rewrite system. They operate on a problem state, a six-tuple $\Gamma = (M; N; U; B; k; D)$ where M is a sequence of annotated ground literals, the *trail*; N and U are the sets of *initial* and *learned* constrained clauses; B is a finite sequence of constants of background sorts for instantiation; k counts the number of decisions in M; and D is a constrained closure that is either $\top$, $\Lambda \parallel \perp \cdot \sigma$, or $\Lambda \parallel C \cdot \sigma$. Foreground literals in M are either annotated with a number, a level; i.e., they have the form L^k meaning that L is the k-th guessed decision literal, or they are annotated with a constrained closure that propagated the literal to become true, i.e., they have the form $(L\sigma)^{(\Lambda \parallel C \vee L) \cdot \sigma}$. An annotated literal is called a decision literal if it is of the form L^k and a propagation literal or a propagated literal if it of in the form $L \cdot \sigma^{(\Lambda \parallel C \vee L) \cdot \sigma}$. A ground foreground literal L is of *level* i with respect to a problem state $(M; N; U; B; k; D)$ if L or $\text{comp}(L)$ occurs in M and the first decision literal left from L ($\text{comp}(L)$) in M, including L, is annotated with i. If there is no such decision literal then its level is zero. A ground constrained clause $(\Lambda \parallel C)\sigma$ is of *level* i with respect to a problem state $(M; N; U; B; k; D)$ if i is the maximal level of a foreground literal in $C\sigma$; the level of an empty clause $\Lambda \parallel \perp \cdot \sigma$ is 0. A ground literal L is *undefined* in M if neither L nor $\text{comp}(L)$ occur in M. The initial state for a first-order, pure, abstracted $\mathcal{H}$ clause set N is $(\epsilon; N; \emptyset; B; 0; \top)$, where B is a finite sequence of foreground constants of background sorts. These constants cannot occur in N, because N is pure. The final state $(\epsilon; N; U; B; 0; \Lambda \parallel \bot)$ denotes unsatisfiability of N. Given a trail M and its foreground literals $\mathrm{fgd}(M) = \{L_1, \dots, L_n\}$ an $\mathcal{H}$ ordering $\prec$ *induced* by M is any $\mathcal{H}$ ordering where $L_i \prec L_j$ if L_i occurs left from L_j in M, or, L_i is defined in M and L_j is not.

The transition rules for SCL(T) are

Propagate. $(M; N; U; B; k; \top) \Rightarrow_{\mathrm{SCL(T)}} (M, L\sigma^{(\Lambda \parallel C_0 \vee L)\delta \cdot \sigma}, \Lambda'\sigma; N; U; B; k; \top)$

provided $\Lambda \parallel C \in (N \cup U)$, σ is grounding for $\Lambda \parallel C$, $\mathrm{adiff}(B) \wedge \mathrm{bgd}(M) \wedge \Lambda\sigma$ is satisfiable, $C = C_0 \vee C_1 \vee L$, $C_1\sigma = L\sigma \vee \dots \vee L\sigma$, $C_0\sigma$ does not contain $L\sigma$, δ is the mgu of the literals in C_1 and L, $\Lambda'\sigma$ are the background literals from $\Lambda\sigma$ that are not yet on the trail, $\mathrm{fgd}(M) \models \neg(C_0\sigma)$, $\mathrm{codom}(\sigma) \subseteq B$, and $L\sigma$ is undefined in M

The rule Propagate applies exhaustive factoring to the propagated literal with respect to the grounding substitution σ and annotates the factored clause to the propagation. By writing $M, L\sigma^{(\Lambda \parallel C_0 \vee L)\delta \cdot \sigma}, \Lambda'\sigma$ we denote that all background literals from $\Lambda'\sigma$ are added to the trail.

Decide. $(M; N; U; B; k; \top) \Rightarrow_{\mathrm{SCL(T)}} (M, L\sigma^{k+1}, \Lambda\sigma; N; U; B; k+1; \top)$

provided $L\sigma$ is undefined in M, $|K\sigma| \in \mathrm{atoms}(\mathrm{gnd}_B(N \cup U))$ for all $K\sigma \in \Lambda\sigma$, $|L\sigma| \in \mathrm{atoms}(\mathrm{gnd}_B(N \cup U))$, σ is grounding for Λ, all background literals in $\Lambda\sigma$ are undefined in M, $\mathrm{adiff}(B) \wedge \mathrm{bgd}(M) \wedge \Lambda\sigma$ is satisfiable, and $\mathrm{codom}(\sigma) \subseteq B$

The number of potential trails of a run is finite because the rules Propagate and Decide make sure that no duplicates of background literals occur on the trail and that only undefined literals over a fixed finite sequence B of constants are added to the trail. Requiring the constants from B to be different by the $\mathrm{adiff}(B)$ constraint enables a purely syntactic consistency check for foreground literals.

Conflict. $(M; N; U; B; k; \top) \Rightarrow_{\mathrm{SCL(T)}} (M; N; U; B; k; \Lambda \parallel D \cdot \sigma)$

provided $\Lambda \parallel D \in (N \cup U)$, σ is grounding for $\Lambda \parallel D$, $\mathrm{adiff}(B) \wedge \mathrm{bgd}(M) \wedge \Lambda\sigma$ is satisfiable, $\mathrm{fgd}(M) \models \neg(D\sigma)$, and $\mathrm{codom}(\sigma) \subseteq B$

Resolve. $(M, L\rho^{\Lambda \parallel C \vee L \cdot \rho}; N; U; B; k; (\Lambda' \parallel D \vee L') \cdot \sigma) \Rightarrow_{\mathrm{SCL(T)}}$
$\qquad (M, L\rho^{\Lambda \parallel C \vee L \cdot \rho}; N; U; B; k; (\Lambda \wedge \Lambda' \parallel D \vee C)\eta \cdot \sigma\rho)$

provided $L\rho = \mathrm{comp}(L'\sigma)$, and $\eta = \mathrm{mgu}(L, \mathrm{comp}(L'))$

Note that Resolve does not remove the literal $L\rho$ from the trail. This is needed if the clause $D\sigma$ contains further literals complementary of $L\rho$ that have not been factorized.

Factorize. $(M; N; U; B; k; (\Lambda \parallel D \vee L \vee L') \cdot \sigma) \Rightarrow_{\mathrm{SCL(T)}}$
$\qquad (M; N; U; B; k; (\Lambda \parallel D \vee L)\eta \cdot \sigma)$

provided $L\sigma = L'\sigma$, and $\eta = \mathrm{mgu}(L, L')$

Note that Factorize is not limited with respect to the trail. It may apply to any two literals that become identical by application of the grounding substitution σ.

Skip. $(M, L; N; U; B; k; \Lambda' \parallel D \cdot \sigma) \Rightarrow_{\text{SCL(T)}} (M; N; U; B; l; \Lambda' \parallel D \cdot \sigma)$

provided L is a foreground literal and $\text{comp}(L)$ does not occur in $D\sigma$, or L is a background literal; if L is a foreground decision literal then $l = k - 1$, otherwise $l = k$

Note that Skip can also skip decision literals. This is needed because we won't eventually require exhaustive propagation. While exhaustive propagation in CDCL is limited to the number of propositional variables, in the context of our logic, for example BS(LRA), it is exponential in the arity of foreground predicate symbols and can lead to an unfair exploration of the space of possible inferences, harming completeness, see Example 7.

Backtrack. $(M, K^{i+1}, M'; N; U; B; k; (\Lambda \parallel D \vee L) \cdot \sigma) \Rightarrow_{\text{SCL(T)}}$
$\qquad\qquad (M, L\sigma^{(\Lambda \parallel D \vee L) \cdot \sigma}, \Lambda'\sigma; N; U \cup \{\Lambda \parallel D \vee L\}; B; i; \top)$

provided $L\sigma$ is of level k, and $D\sigma$ is of level i, $\Lambda'\sigma$ are the background literals from $\Lambda\sigma$ that are not yet on the trail

The definition of Backtrack requires that $L\sigma$ is the only literal of level k in $(D \vee L)\sigma$. Additional occurrences of $L\sigma$ in D have to be factorized first before Backtrack can be applied.

Grow. $(M; N; U; B; k; \top) \Rightarrow_{\text{SCL(T)}} (\epsilon; N; U; B \cup B'; 0; \top)$

provided B' is a non-empty sequence of foreground constants of background sorts distinct from the constants in B

In case the adiff constraint is implemented by a strict ordering predicate on the basis of the sequence B, it can be useful to inject the new constants B' into $B \cup B'$ such that the ordering of the constants from B is not changed. This can help caching background theory results for testing trail satisfiability.

Definition 5. *The rules Propagate, Decide, Grow, and Conflict are called con-flict search rules and the rules Resolve, Skip, Factorize, and Backtrack are called* conflict resolution *rules.*

Recall that the goal of our calculus is to replace the ordering restrictions of the hierarchic superposition calculus with a guiding model assumption. All our inferences are hierarchic superposition inferences where the ordering restrictions are neglected.

The next two examples show that the adiff constraint is needed to produce satisfiable trails and that exhaustive propagation cannot be afforded, respectively.

Example 6 (Inconsistent Trail). Consider a clause set $N = \{R(x, y), x \leq y \parallel \neg R(x, y) \vee P(x), x \geq y \parallel \neg R(x, y) \vee \neg P(y)\}$; if we were to remove the $\text{adiff}(B)$ constraint from the side conditions of rule Propagate we would be able to obtain inconsistent trails. Starting with just $B = \{a, b\}$ as constants it is possible to propagate three times and obtain the trail $M = [R(a, b), P(a), a \leq b, \neg P(b), a \geq b]$, M is clearly inconsistent as $M \models P(a)$, $M \models \neg P(b)$ yet $a = b$.

Example 7 (Exhaustive Propagation). Consider a BS(LRA) clause set $N = \{x = 0 \parallel \text{Nat}(x), \ y = x + 1 \parallel \neg\text{Nat}(x) \vee \text{Nat}(y)\} \cup N'$ where N' is unsatisfiable and nothing can be propagated from N'. Let us further assume that N' is satisfiable with respect to any instantiation of variables with natural numbers. If propagation is not restricted, then the first two clauses will consume all constants in B. For example, if $B = [a, b, c]$ then the trail $[\text{Nat}(a), a = 0, \text{Nat}(b), b = a + 1, \text{Nat}(c), c = b + 1]$ will be derived. Now all constants are fixed to natural numbers. So there cannot be a refutation of N' anymore. An application of Grow will not solve the issue, because again the first two rules will fix all constants to natural numbers via exhaustive propagation.

Definition 8 (Well-formed States). *A state $(M; N; U; B; k; D)$ is well-formed if the following conditions hold:*

1. *all constants appearing in $(M; N; U; B; k; D)$ are from B or occur in N.*
2. *$M \wedge \text{adiff}(B)$ is satisfiable*
3. *$N \models_{\mathcal{H}} U$,*
4. *Propagating clauses remain propagating and conflict clauses remain false:*
   (a) *if $D = \Lambda \parallel C \cdot \sigma$ then $C\sigma$ is false in $\text{fgd}(M)$ and $\text{bgd}(M) \wedge \text{adiff}(B) \wedge \Lambda\sigma$ is satisfiable,*
   (b) *if $M = M_1, L\sigma^{(\Lambda \parallel C \vee L) \cdot \sigma}, M_2$ then $C\sigma$ is false in $\text{fgd}(M_1)$, $L\sigma$ is undefined in M_1, and $\text{bgd}(M_1) \wedge \text{adiff}(B) \wedge \Lambda\sigma$ is satisfiable.*
5. *All clauses in $N \cup U$ are pure. In particular, they don't contain any constants from B.*

Lemma 9 (Rules preserve Well-Formed States). *The rules of SCL(T) preserve well-formed states.*

Definition 10 (Stuck State). *A state $(M; N; U; B; k; D)$ is called stuck if $D \neq \Lambda \parallel \perp \cdot \sigma$ and none of the rules Propagate, Decide, Conflict, Resolve, Factorize, Skip, or Backtrack is applicable.*

Proposition 11 (Form of Stuck States). *If a run (without rule Grow) where Conflict was applied eagerly ends in a stuck state $(M; N; U; B; k; D)$, then $D = \top$ and all ground foreground literals that can be build from the foreground literals in N by instantiation with constants from B are defined in M.*

Lemma 12 (Stuck States Produce Ground Models). *Every stuck state $(M; N; U; B; k; \top)$ produces a ground model, i.e., $M \wedge \text{adiff}(B) \models \text{gnd}_B(N \cup U)$.*

The next example shows that in some cases the finite partial model of a stuck state can be turned into an overall model. For some fragments of BS(LRA) this can be done systematically, see Section 4.

Example 13 (SCL(T) Model Extraction). In some cases it is possible to extract an overall model from the ground trail of a stuck state of an SCL(T) derivation. Consider $B = [a, b, c]$ and a satisfiable BS(LRA) constrained clause set $N = \{x \geq 1 \parallel P(x), x < 0 \parallel P(x), 0 \leq x \wedge x < 1 \parallel \neg P(x), 2x \geq 1 \parallel P(x) \vee Q(x)\}$. Starting from state $(\epsilon; N; \emptyset; B; 0; \top)$ and applying Propagate fairly a regular run can derive the following trail

$$M = P(a)^{x \geq 1 \parallel P(x) \cdot \{x \mapsto a\}}, a \geq 1, P(b)^{x < 0 \parallel P(x) \cdot \{x \mapsto b\}}, b < 0,$$
$$\neg P(c)^{0 \leq x \wedge x < 1 \parallel \neg P(x) \cdot \{x \mapsto c\}}, 0 \leq c, c < 1, Q(c)^{2x \geq 1 \parallel P \vee Q(x) \cdot \{x \mapsto c\}}, 2c \geq 1$$

The state $(M; N; \emptyset; B; 0; \top)$ is stuck and $M \models_{\mathcal{H}} \text{gnd}_B(N)$. Moreover from M we can generate an interpretation $\mathcal{A}^{\text{BS(LRA)}}$ of N by generalizing the foreground constants used for instantiation and interpreting the predicates P and Q as formulas over $\Sigma^{\mathcal{B}}$, $P^{\mathcal{A}} = \{q \in \mathbb{Q} \mid q < 0 \vee q \geq 1\}$ and $Q^{\mathcal{A}} = \{q \in \mathbb{Q} \mid 2q \geq 1 \wedge q < 1\}$.

Lemma 14 (Soundness). *If a derivation reaches the state $(M; N; U; B; k; \Lambda \parallel \bot \cdot \sigma)$, then N is unsatisfiable.*

Definition 15 (Reasonable Run). *A sequence of SCL(T) rule applications is called a* reasonable run *if an application of rule Decide does not enable an application of rule Conflict.*

Proposition 16 (Avoiding Conflicts after Decide). *Let N be a set of constrained clauses and $(M; N; U; B; k; \top)$ be a state derived from $(\epsilon; N; \emptyset; B; 0; \top)$. If an application of rule Decide to $(M; N; U; B; k; \top)$ enables an application of rule Conflict, then Propagate would have been applicable to $(M; N; U; B; k; \top)$.*

Definition 17 (Regular Run). *A sequence of SCL(T) rule applications is called a* regular run *if it is a reasonable run, the rule Conflict has precedence over all other rules, and Resolve resolves away at least the rightmost foreground literal from the trail.*

Proposition 18 (Stuck States at Regular Runs). *Lemma 12 also holds for regular runs.*

Example 19 (SCL(T) Refutation). Given a set of foreground constants $B = [a, b, c]$ and a BS(LRA) constrained clause set $N = \{C_1: x = 0 \parallel P(x), C_2: y = x + 1 \parallel \neg P(x) \vee P(y), C_3: z = 2 \parallel \neg P(z)\}$ the following is a regular derivation

$$(\epsilon; N; \emptyset; B; 0; \top)$$
$$\Rightarrow^{\text{Propagate}}_{\text{SCL(T)}} (P(a)^{C_1 \cdot \{x \mapsto a\}}, a = 0; N; \emptyset; B; 0; \top)$$
$$\Rightarrow^{\text{Propagate}}_{\text{SCL(T)}} (\ldots, P(b)^{C_2 \cdot \{x \mapsto a, y \mapsto b\}}, b = a + 1; N; \emptyset; B; 0; \top)$$
$$\Rightarrow^{\text{Propagate}}_{\text{SCL(T)}} (\ldots, P(c)^{C_2 \cdot \{x \mapsto b, y \mapsto c\}}, c = b + 1; N; \emptyset; B; 0; \top)$$
$$\Rightarrow^{\text{Conflict}}_{\text{SCL(T)}} (\ldots, P(c)^{C_2 \cdot \{x \mapsto b, y \mapsto c\}}, c = b + 1; N; \emptyset; B; 0; z = 2 \parallel \neg P(z) \cdot \{z \mapsto c\})$$
$$\Rightarrow^{\text{Resolve}}_{\text{SCL(T)}} (\ldots, P(c)^{C_2 \cdot \{x \mapsto b, y \mapsto c\}}, c = b + 1; N; \emptyset; B; 0;$$
$$\qquad z = x + 1 \wedge z = 2 \parallel \neg P(x) \cdot \{z \mapsto c, x \mapsto b\})$$
$$\Rightarrow^{\text{Skip}}_{\text{SCL(T)}} (\ldots, P(b)^{C_2 \cdot \{x \mapsto a, y \mapsto b\}}, b = a + 1; N; \emptyset; B; 0;$$
$$\qquad z = x + 1 \wedge z = 2 \parallel \neg P(x) \cdot \{z \mapsto c, x \mapsto b\})$$
$$\Rightarrow^{\text{Resolve}}_{\text{SCL(T)}} (\ldots, P(b)^{C_2 \cdot \{x \mapsto a, y \mapsto b\}}, b = a + 1; N; \emptyset; B; 0;$$
$$\qquad z = x + 1 \wedge z = 2 \wedge x = y + 1 \parallel \neg P(y) \cdot \{z \mapsto c, x \mapsto b, y \mapsto a\})$$
$$\Rightarrow^{\text{Skip}}_{\text{SCL(T)}} (P(a)^{C_1 \cdot \{x \mapsto a\}}, a = 0; N; \emptyset; B; 0;$$
$$\qquad z = x + 1 \wedge z = 2 \wedge x = y + 1 \parallel \neg P(y) \cdot \{z \mapsto c, x \mapsto b, y \mapsto a\})$$
$$\Rightarrow^{\text{Resolve}}_{\text{SCL(T)}} (P(a)^{C_1 \cdot \{x \mapsto a\}}, a = 0; N; \emptyset; B; 0;$$
$$\qquad z = x + 1 \wedge z = 2 \wedge x = y + 1 \wedge y = 0 \parallel \bot \cdot \{z \mapsto c, x \mapsto b, y \mapsto a\})$$

N is proven unsatisfiable as we reach a state in the form $(M; N; U; B; k; \Lambda \parallel \bot \cdot \sigma)$.

Example 20 (SCL(T) Clause learning). Given an initial constant set $B = [a]$ and a BS(LRA) constrained clause set $N = \{C_1 : x \geq y \parallel \neg P(x, y) \vee Q(z), C_2 : z = u + v \parallel \neg P(u, v) \vee \neg Q(z)\}$ the following is an example of a regular run

$$(\epsilon; N; \emptyset; B; 0; \top)$$
$$\Rightarrow^{\text{Decide}}_{\text{SCL(T)}} (P(a, b)^1; N; \emptyset; B; 1; \top)$$
$$\Rightarrow^{\text{Propagate}}_{\text{SCL(T)}} (P(a, a)^1, Q(a)^{C_1 \cdot \{x \mapsto a, y \mapsto a, z \mapsto a\}}, a \geq a; N; \emptyset; B; 1; \top)$$
$$\Rightarrow^{\text{Conflict}}_{\text{SCL(T)}} (P(a, a)^1, Q(a)^{C_1 \cdot \{u \mapsto a, v \mapsto a, z \mapsto a\}}, a \geq a; N; \emptyset; B; 1;$$
$$\qquad C_2 \cdot \{x \mapsto a, y \mapsto a, z \mapsto a\})$$
$$\Rightarrow^{\text{Resolve}}_{\text{SCL(T)}} (P(a, a)^1, Q(a)^{C_1 \cdot \{x \mapsto a, y \mapsto a, z \mapsto a\}}, a \geq a; N; \emptyset; B; 1;$$
$$\qquad x \geq y \wedge z = u + v \parallel$$
$$\qquad \neg P(x, y) \vee \neg P(u, v) \cdot \{x \mapsto a, y \mapsto a, z \mapsto a, u \mapsto a, v \mapsto a\})$$
$$\Rightarrow^{\text{Skip*}}_{\text{SCL(T)}} (P(a, a)^1; N; \emptyset; B; 1; x \geq y \wedge z = u + v \parallel$$
$$\qquad \neg P(x, y) \vee \neg P(u, v) \cdot \{x \mapsto a, y \mapsto a, z \mapsto a, u \mapsto a, v \mapsto a\})$$
$$\Rightarrow^{\text{Factorize}}_{\text{SCL(T)}} (P(a, a)^1; N; \emptyset; B; 1; x \geq y \wedge z = x + y \parallel$$
$$\qquad \neg P(x, y) \cdot \{x \mapsto a, y \mapsto a, z \mapsto a\})$$
$$\Rightarrow^{\text{Backtrack}}_{\text{SCL(T)}} (\neg P(a, a)^{(x \geq y \wedge z = x + y \parallel \neg P(x,y)) \cdot \{x \mapsto a, y \mapsto a\}}, a \geq a, a = a + a; N;$$
$$\qquad \{x \geq y \wedge z = x + y \parallel \neg P(x, y)\}; B; 1; \top)$$

The learned clause $x \geq y \wedge z = x + y \parallel \neg P(x, y)$ contains two distinct variables even if we had to use a single constant for instantiations in conflict search.

Corollary 21 (Regular Conflict Resolution). *Let N be a set of constrained clauses. Then any conflict in an SCL(T) regular run admits a regular conflict resolution if the run starts from state $(\epsilon; N; \emptyset; B; 0; \top)$.*

Lemma 22 (Non-Redundant Clause Learning). *Let N be a set of constrained clauses, and let $\Lambda_n \parallel D \vee L$ be a clause learned in an SCL(T) regular run such that $(\epsilon; N; \emptyset; B; 0; \top) \Rightarrow^{*}_{SCL(T)} \Rightarrow^{Backtrack}_{SCL(T)} (M, L\sigma^{(\Lambda_n \parallel D \vee L) \cdot \sigma}, \Lambda'_n \sigma; N; U \cup \{\Lambda_n \parallel D \vee L\}; B; i; \top)$. Then $\Lambda_n \parallel D \vee L$ is not redundant with respect to any $\mathcal{H}$ ordering $\prec$ induced by the trail M.*

Of course, in a regular run the ordering of foreground literals on the trail will change, i.e., the ordering underlying Lemma 22 will change as well. Thus the non-redundancy property of Lemma 22 reflects the situation at the time of creation of the learned clause. A non-redundancy property holding for an overall run must be invariant against changes on the ordering. However, the ordering underlying Lemma 22 also entails a fixed subset ordering that is invariant against changes on the overall ordering. This means that our dynamic ordering entails non-redundancy criteria based on subset relations including forward redundancy. From an implementation perspective, this means that learned clauses need not to be tested for forward redundancy. Current resolution, or superposition based provers spent a reasonable portion of their time in testing forward redundancy of newly generated clauses. In addition, also tests for backward reduction can be restricted knowing that learned clauses are not redundant.

Lemma 23 (Termination of SCL(T)). *Let N be a set of constrained clauses and B be a finite set of background constants. Then any regular run with start state $(\epsilon; N; \emptyset; B; 0; \top)$ that uses Grow only finitely often terminates.*

Theorem 24 (Hierarchic Herbrand Theorem). *Let N be a finite set of clauses. N is unsatisfiable iff there exists a finite set $N' = \{\Lambda_1 \parallel C_1, \ldots, \Lambda_n \parallel C_n\}$ of variable renamed copies of clauses from N and a finite set B of fresh constants and a substitution σ, grounding for N' where $\mathrm{codom}(\sigma) = B$ such that $\bigwedge_i \Lambda_i \sigma$ is $\mathcal{T}^B$ satisfiable and $\bigwedge_i C_i \sigma$ is first-order unsatisfiable over $\Sigma^{\mathcal{F}}$.*

Finally, we show that an unsatisfiable clause set can be refuted by SCL(T) with any regular run if we start with a sufficiently large sequence of constants B and apply Decide in a fair way. In addition, we need a Restart rule to recover from a stuck state. Of course, an unrestricted use of rule Restart immediately leads to non-termination.

Restart. $(M; N; U; B; k; \top) \Rightarrow_{SCL(T)} (\epsilon; N; U; B; 0; \top)$

Theorem 25 (Refutational Completeness of SCL(T)). *Let N be an unsatisfiable clause set. Then any regular SCL(T) run will derive the empty clause provided (i) Rule Grow and Decide are operated in a fair way, such that all possible trail prefixes of all considered sets B during the run are eventually explored, and (ii) Restart is only applied to stuck states.*

Condition (i) of the above theorem is quite abstract. It can, e.g., be made effective by applying rule Grow only after all possible trail prefixes with respect to the current set B have been explored and to make sure that Decide does not produce the same stuck state twice.

4   SCL(T) Decides BS(BD)

As mentioned in Lemma 12, all stuck states produce ground models for $\mathrm{gnd}_B(N)$. This does not mean that all stuck states produce a full hierarchic algebra $\mathcal{A}$ that satisfies N, i.e., a model over the full and potentially infinite carrier sets of our theory (e.g., $\mathbb{R}$) instead of a model over a finite set of sample elements (i.e., our constants B). In this section, we explain on the example of the Bernays-Schoenfinkel clause fragment with bounded difference constraints (BS(BD)) how to formalize an extraction criterion, i.e., a condition that guarantees that a satisfying algebra $\mathcal{A}$ can be extracted from a stuck state that fulfills the condition. We also explain how $\mathcal{A}$ can be constructed explicitly from such a stuck state and which conditions on N guarantee that SCL(T) finds a stuck state that fulfills the extraction criterion.

Definition 26 (BS(BD)). *The Bernays-Schoenfinkel fragment with bounded difference constraints is a subset of* BS(LRA) *that only allows theory atoms of the form* $x \triangleleft c$, $x \triangleleft y$, *or* $x - y \triangleleft c$ *where c may be any integer number, $x, y \in \mathcal{X}$, and $\triangleleft \in \{\leq, <, \neq, =, >, \geq\}$. Moreover, we require for all considered clauses $\Lambda \| C$ that the theory part Λ may only contain an atom of the form $x - y \triangleleft c$ if Λ also bounds x and y, i.e., Λ also contains atoms $c_x \leq x$, $x \leq d_x$, $c_y \leq y$, and $y \leq d_y$, where c_x, d_x, c_y, d_y are integers.*

For the rest of this section we fix a finite set of BS(BD) clauses N, where κ is the maximal absolute value of any integer occurring in N and η is the maximal number of distinct variables in any single clause in N. Moreover, we define the function $\mathrm{fr}(b) = b - \lfloor b \rfloor$ that returns the *fractional/decimal part* of a real number.

The first step of defining an extraction criterion is the definition of an equivalence relation that ranges over all possible argument tuples/grounding substitutions for literals and clauses in N. This equivalence relation must fulfill two conditions: (i) it has only finitely many equivalence classes and (ii) for every theory atom A in N it holds that A is satisfied by all elements in an equivalence class or by none. Unbounded region equivalence $\cong_\kappa^\eta$ is such an equivalence class for BS(BD):

Definition 27 (**Unbounded Region Equivalence** $\cong_\kappa^\eta$ [24,25]). *We define the equivalence relation* $\cong_\kappa^\eta$ *on* $\mathcal{R} = \bigcup_{k=0}^\eta \mathbb{Q}^k$ *in such a way that* $\bar{r} \cong_\kappa^\eta \bar{s}$ *for $\bar{r}, \bar{s} \in \mathcal{R}$ if and only if*

1. *$\bar{r}$ and $\bar{s}$ have the same dimension, i.e., $\bar{r} = \langle r_1, \dots, r_m \rangle$ and $\bar{s} = \langle s_1, \dots, s_m \rangle$;*
2. *for every i*
   (a) $r_i > \kappa$ if and only if $s_i > \kappa$,

(b) $r_i < -\kappa$ if and only if $s_i < -\kappa$,
(c) if $-\kappa < r_i, s_i < \kappa$, then $\lfloor r_i \rfloor = \lfloor s_i \rfloor$, and
(d) if $-\kappa < r_i, s_i < \kappa$, then $\mathrm{fr}(r_i) = 0$ if and only if $\mathrm{fr}(s_i) = 0$;
3. for all i, j
(a) if $r_i, r_j > \kappa$ or $r_i, r_j < -\kappa$, then $r_i \leq r_j$ if and only if $s_i \leq s_j$,
(b) if $-\kappa < r_i, r_j < \kappa$, then $\mathrm{fr}(r_i) \leq \mathrm{fr}(r_j)$ if and only if $\mathrm{fr}(s_i) \leq \mathrm{fr}(s_j)$.

Corollary 28. *Let A be a BD atom and let $\sigma_r = \{x_1 \mapsto r_1, \ldots, x_m \mapsto r_m\}$ and $\sigma_s = \{x_1 \mapsto s_1, \ldots, x_m \mapsto s_m\}$ be two grounding assignments for A such that $\bar{r} \cong_\kappa^\eta \bar{s}$. Then $A \cdot \sigma_r$ is satisfied if and only if $A \cdot \sigma_s$ is satisfied.*

The first condition for our equivalence class is necessary so we can express all argument tuples over our theories potentially infinite carrier sets with argument tuples over just a finite set of sample elements (i.e., our constants B). The second condition is necessary because the algebras we are looking for are supposed to be uniform in a given equivalence class, i.e., for every atom A in N it holds that A is satisfied by all elements in an equivalence class or by none.

Definition 29 ($\cong_\kappa^\eta$-Uniform Algebras [24,25]). *Consider an algebra $\mathcal{A}$ for N. We call $\mathcal{A}$ $\cong_\kappa^\eta$-uniform over N if it interprets all $\cong_\kappa^\eta$-equivalence classes uniformly, i.e., for all predicates P in N and all $\bar{r} \cong_\kappa^\eta \bar{s}$ with $m = \mathrm{arity}(P)$ and $\bar{r}, \bar{s} \in \mathbb{Q}^m$ it holds that $\bar{r} \in P^{\mathcal{A}}$ if and only if $\bar{s} \in P^{\mathcal{A}}$.*

Based on these definitions, an extraction criterion guarantees the following properties for a stuck state $(M'; N; U; B; k; \top)$: (i) our trail can be extended to $M = M', M^p$ in such a way that there exists an argument tuple in B^m for every equivalence class and (ii) the literals in $\mathrm{fgd}(M')$ describe a uniform model, i.e., for every literal $|L| \in \mathrm{atoms}(N)$ it holds that $L \cdot \sigma \in M'$ if and only if $L \cdot \tau \in M'$, where σ and τ are two grounding substitutions over B that belong to the same equivalence class.

Definition 30 ($\cong_\kappa^\eta$-Extraction-Criterion). *A stuck state $(M'; N; U; B; k; \top)$ fulfills the $\cong_\kappa^\eta$-extraction-criterion if:*

1. $B = \{b_1, ..., b_{|B|}\}$ is large enough, i.e., $|B| \geq 2\kappa \cdot (\eta + 1) + 2\eta + 1$
2. M' has a $\cong_\kappa^\eta$-uniform trail extension M, M^p such that $M' \wedge M^p \wedge \mathrm{adiff}(B)$ is satisfiable and M^p is a sequence of theory atoms constructed as follows:[1]
   (a) Let $\pi : \mathbb{N} \to \{-\kappa - 1, -\kappa, \ldots, \kappa - 1, \kappa\}$ be the function with $\pi(i) = -\kappa - 1 + \lfloor i/(\eta + 1) \rfloor$ for $1 \leq i \leq 2\kappa \cdot (\eta + 1) + \eta$, and $\pi(i) = \kappa$ for $2\kappa \cdot (\eta + 1) + \eta < i \leq |B|$.
   (b) Let $\rho : \mathbb{N} \to \mathbb{N}$ be the function with $\rho(i) = i\%(\eta + 1)$ for $1 \leq i \leq 2\kappa \cdot (\eta + 1) + \eta$, and $\rho(i) = i - 2\kappa \cdot (\eta + 1) + \eta + 1$ for $2\kappa \cdot (\eta + 1) + \eta < i \leq |B|$.
   (c) Intuitively, we use $\pi(i)$ and $\rho(i)$ to partition the constants in B over the intervals $(-\infty, -\kappa), [-\kappa, -\kappa + 1), \ldots, [\kappa - 1, -\kappa)[\kappa, \infty)$ such that the interval $(-\infty, -\kappa)$ contains η constants, each interval $[i, i+1)$ with $-\kappa \leq i < \kappa$ contains $\eta + 1$ constants, and the interval $[\kappa, \infty)$ contains at least $\eta + 1$ constants.

---

[1] The added theory atoms correspond exactly to the different cases in the unbounded region equivalence relation.

(d) M^p *contains* $b_i < b_{i+1}$ *for* $1 \le i < |B|$.
(e) M^p *contains* $b_i = k$ *for* $-\kappa \le \pi(i) = k \le \kappa$ *and* $\rho(i) = 0$.
(f) M^p *contains* $b_i < k + 1$ *for* $-\kappa - 1 \le \pi(i) = k < \kappa$ *and* $\rho(i) > 0$.
(g) M^p *contains* $b_i > k$ *for* $-\kappa \le \pi(i) = k \le \kappa$ *and* $\rho(i) > 0$.
(h) M^p *contains* $b_i - b_j \lhd 1$ *for* $-\kappa \le \pi(j) = \pi(i) - 1 < \kappa - 1$, $\rho(i) \lhd \rho(j)$, *and*
    $\lhd \in \{<, =, >\}$.
3. $\mathrm{fgd}(M', M^p)$ *is* $\cong_\kappa^\eta$-*uniform, i.e., if* $P(\bar{r}) \in \mathrm{fgd}(M', M^p)$ *and* $\bar{r} \cong_\kappa^\eta \bar{s}$ *for* $m = \mathrm{arity}(P)$ *and* $\bar{r}, \bar{s} \in B^m$, *then* $P(\bar{s}) \in \mathrm{fgd}(M', M^p)$.[2]

As a result of these properties, any assignment β for the constants B defines an algebra uniform to our equivalence relation.

Lemma 31 ($\cong_\kappa^\eta$-Uniform Model Extraction). *Let* $(M'; N; U; B; k; \top)$ *be a stuck SCL(T) state that fulfills the* $\cong_\kappa^\eta$-*extraction-criterion and let* $\beta : B \to \mathbb{Q}$ *be a satisfying assignment for the* $\cong_\kappa^\eta$-*uniform trail extension* $M = M', M^p$. *Then there exists a* $\cong_\kappa^\eta$-*uniform algebra* $\mathcal{A}$ *satisfying* N *such that*

$$P^{\mathcal{A}} = \{\bar{s} \in \mathbb{R}^m \mid \exists \bar{t} \in B^m, \bar{s} \cong_\kappa^\eta \langle \beta(t_1), \ldots, \beta(t_m) \rangle \text{ and } P(\bar{t}) \in M\}$$

for all predicates P *of arity* m *in* N.

Proof. We have to prove that $\mathcal{A}$ satisfies all clauses $C \in N$ for all substitutions $\sigma : \mathrm{vars}(C) \to \mathbb{R}$. We do so by selecting one arbitrary substitution σ and by defining $Q = \{q_j \in (0, 1) \mid \exists q' \in \mathrm{codom}(\sigma) \cap [-\kappa, \kappa], \mathrm{fr}(q') = q_j \ne 0\}$, i.e., the set of fractional parts that occur in σ's codomain. Moreover, we assume that $q_1 < \ldots < q_n$ is the order of the elements in $Q = \{q_1, \ldots, q_n\}$. Since we chose B large enough, we can now create a substitution $\tau : \mathrm{codom}(\sigma) \to B$ such that $\tau(q') = b_i$ if:

1. $-\kappa \le \lfloor q' \rfloor < \kappa$, $\pi(i) = \lfloor q' \rfloor$, $\mathrm{fr}(q') = q_j \in Q$, and $\rho(i) = j$,
2. $-\kappa \le \lfloor q' \rfloor \le \kappa$, $\pi(i) = \lfloor q' \rfloor$, $\mathrm{fr}(q') = 0$, and $\rho(i) = 0$,
3. if q' is the j-th smallest element in $\mathrm{codom}(\sigma)$ that is smaller than $-\kappa$ and $\pi(i) = -\kappa - 1$, or
4. if q' is the j-th smallest element in $\mathrm{codom}(\sigma)$ that is larger than κ and $\pi(i) = \kappa$.

If we concatenate σ and τ, we get $M \models C \cdot \sigma \cdot \tau$ because $(M'; N; U; B; k; \top)$ is a stuck state (i.e., $M \models M' \models \mathrm{gnd}_B(N)$, Lemma 12). If we concatenate σ, τ, and β together, we get a $\cong_\kappa^\eta$-equivalent substitution $\sigma \cdot \tau \cdot \beta$ for all literals L in C, i.e., if $\mathrm{vars}(\bar{x}) = \mathrm{vars}(L)$, $\bar{x} \cdot \sigma = \bar{s}$ and $\bar{x} \cdot \sigma \cdot \tau \cdot \beta = \bar{r}$, then $\bar{s} \cong_\kappa^\eta \bar{r}$. The way we constructed $\mathcal{A}$ entails that $\mathcal{A} \models P(\bar{x}) \cdot \sigma$ if and only if $P(\bar{x}) \cdot \sigma \cdot \tau \in M$ because $\bar{x} \cdot \sigma \cong_\kappa^\eta \bar{x} \cdot \sigma \cdot \tau \cdot \beta$. Similarly, Corollary 28 entails that a theory atom $A \cdot \sigma$ is satisfied if and only if $A \cdot \sigma \cdot \tau \cdot \beta$ is satisfied. Hence, $\mathcal{A} \models C \cdot \sigma$ because $M \models C \cdot \sigma \cdot \tau$. □

If the rules of SCL(T) are applied in a way that all trail prefixes are explored, then SCL(T) is also guaranteed to visit a stuck state that fulfills the extraction criterion whenever there exists an algebra $\mathcal{A}$ that is uniform to our equivalence relation and satisfies N.

---

[2] $\bar{r} \cong_\kappa^\eta \bar{s}$ can be checked by comparing the atoms in M^p or by fixing a satisfying assignment for $M' \wedge M^p \wedge \mathrm{adiff}(B)$.

Lemma 32 ($\cong_\kappa^\eta$-Uniform Model Guarantee). *Let $\mathcal{A}$ be a $\cong_\kappa^\eta$-uniform alge-bra that satisfies N and let B be a sequence of constants that is large enough, i.e., $|B| \geq 2\kappa \cdot (\eta + 1) + 2\eta + 1$. Then any regular SCL(T) run starting in state $(\epsilon; N; U; B; 0; \top)$ (with $N \models_\mathcal{H} U$) will encounter a stuck state that satisfies the $\cong_\kappa^\eta$-extraction-criterion if SCL(T) explores all possible trail prefixes for B.*

Proof. We can construct a trail prefix M' for B that corresponds to a stuck state that satisfies the $\cong_\kappa^\eta$-extraction-criterion and from which we can extract $\mathcal{A}$. The trail prefix M' is constructed as follows: First construct a set of numbers $Q = \{q_0, \ldots, q_\eta\} \subseteq [0, 1)$ such that $q_0 = 0$ and $q_0 < \ldots < q_\eta$. Next we construct a set of numbers

$$\widehat{Q} = \{\widehat{q}_j^k \mid q_j \in Q, k \in \{-\kappa - 1, \ldots, \kappa\}, \text{ and } \widehat{q}_j^k = q_j + k\} \cup$$
$$\{\widehat{q}_j^\kappa \mid i \in \mathbb{N}, 2\kappa \cdot (\eta + 1) + \eta < i \leq |B|, j = i - 2\kappa \cdot (\eta + 1) + \eta + 1, \widehat{q}_j^\kappa = j + \kappa\}.$$

Each element in $\widehat{q}_j^k \in \widehat{Q}$ corresponds to one constant b_i. We denote this by an assignment $\beta : B \to \widehat{Q}$ such that $\beta(b_i) = \widehat{q}_j^k$ if $\pi(i) = k$ and $\rho(i) = j$. Now given these sets our trail prefix M' contains $P(\bar{s})/\text{comp}(P(\bar{s}))$ as a decision literal if and only if (i) P is a predicate in N, $m = \text{arity}(P)$, $\bar{s} \in B^m$, $\bar{r} \in \widehat{Q}^m$, (ii) if $s_t = b_i$, then $r_t = \beta(b_i)$, and (iii) $\bar{r} \in P^\mathcal{A}/\bar{r} \notin P^\mathcal{A}$. Moreover, we add to M' the following theory atoms as part of the first decision: we add $L \cdot \sigma$ to M' if there exists a grounding substitution σ for $|L| \in \text{bgd}(\text{atoms}(\text{gnd}_B(N)))$ such that $L \cdot \sigma \cdot \beta$ is satisfied.

The state $(M'; N; U; B; k; \top)$ (with $k = |\text{fgd}(M')|$) is a reachable stuck state because (i) all atoms $|L| \in \text{atoms}(\text{gnd}_B(N))$ are defined in M', (ii) $M' \wedge \text{adiff}(B)$ is satisfiable, e.g., by β, and (iii) $M' \wedge \text{adiff}(B) \models \text{gnd}_B(N)$ because for all $C \in N$, (iii.i) $\mathcal{A} \models C \cdot \sigma \cdot \beta$ and (iii.ii) $L \cdot \sigma \in C \cdot \sigma$ is in M' if and only if $\mathcal{A} \models L \cdot \sigma \cdot \beta$.

The state $(M'; N; U; B; k; \top)$ also has a $\cong_\kappa^\eta$-uniform trail extension $M' \wedge M^p$ because β by definition also satisfies the atoms in M^p and $\text{fgd}(M', M^p)$ is $\cong_\kappa^\eta$-uniform because the literals $\text{fgd}(M', M^p) \cdot \beta$ are $\cong_\kappa^\eta$-uniform. $\square$

The above lemma explains how we can construct conditions for clause sets N that guarantee that SCL(T) finds a satisfying algebra $\mathcal{A}$ for N (under certain fairness conditions). The condition just has to imply that N is satisfied by an algebra $\mathcal{A}$ that is uniform to our equivalence relation. In the case of BS(BD), we can prove this for all satisfiable clause sets N. This means SCL(T) can be turned into a decision procedure for BS(BD).

Lemma 33 (BS(BD) Uniform Satisfiability [24,25]). *If N is satisfiable, then it is satisfied by an $\cong_\kappa^\eta$-uniform algebra $\mathcal{A}$.*

Corollary 34 (SCL(T) Decides BS(BD)). *SCL(T) is a decision procedure for BS(BD) if (i) Restart is only applied to stuck states, (ii) Grow is only applied after a stuck state has been encountered for the current sequence of constants B, (iii) rules Grow, Restart, and Decide are operated in a fair way, such that no stuck state is visited more than once, and (iv) it explores all possible trail prefixes for some B with $|B| \geq 2\kappa \cdot (\eta + 1) + 2\eta + 1$.*

Example 35 (B too Small for Model Extraction). If our set of constants B is too small, then a stuck state might not imply an interpretation for all relevant $\cong^\eta_\kappa$-equivalence-classes. The same is true, if our constants are distributed unfairly over $\mathbb{Q}$, e.g., there exist no or not enough constants to represent an interval $[i, i+1)$ for $-\kappa \leq i, < \kappa$. Consider $B = [a, b]$ and a satisfiable BS(BD) clause set

$$N = \{\, 0 \leq x \wedge x < 1 \wedge -1 \leq y \wedge y < 0 \wedge x - y = 1 \| P(x, y),$$
$$0 \leq x \wedge x < 1 \wedge -1 \leq y \wedge y < 0 \wedge x - y \neq 1 \| \neg P(x, y)\}.$$

Starting from state $(\epsilon; N; \emptyset; B; 0; \top)$, a regular run can derive the following trail

$$M = [P(b, a)^{0 \leq x \wedge x < 1 \wedge -1 \leq y \wedge y < 0 \wedge x - y = 1 \| P(x, y) \cdot \{y \mapsto a, x \mapsto b\}}, 0 \leq b, b < 1,$$
$$-1 \leq a, a < 0, b - a = 1, P(a, a)^1, P(b, b)^2, P(a, b)^3]$$

The state $(M; N; \emptyset; B; 0; \top)$ is stuck and $M \models_\mathcal{H} \mathrm{gnd}_B(N)$. However, M does not satisfy the $\cong^\eta_\kappa$-extraction-criterion because B is too small. This makes sense because M does not define P for all $\cong^\eta_\kappa$-equivalence-classes, e.g., in all algebras $P(x, y)$ should be false for $-1 \leq y < 0, 0 \leq x < 1, x - y \neq 1$. We need at least one additional constant for each of the intervals $[-1, 0)$ and $[0, 1)$, and two for the intervals $(-\infty, -1)$ and $[1, \infty)$.

Example 36 (Successful BS(BD) model extraction). Consider $B = [a, b, c, d, e, f, g, h, i, j, k]$ and a satisfiable BS(BD) clause set $N = \{0 \leq x \wedge x < 1 \wedge -1 \leq y \wedge y < 0 \wedge x - y = 1 \| P(x, y), 0 \leq x \wedge x < 1 \wedge -1 \leq y \wedge y < 0 \wedge x - y \neq 1 \| \neg P(x, y)\}$. Starting from state $(\epsilon; N; \emptyset; B; 0; \top)$, a regular run can derive the trail $M = M', M''$, where M'' contains decisions $\neg P(x, y) \cdot \sigma$ for all groundings of $P(x, y)$ not defined in M' and

$$M' = [P(f, c)^{0 \leq x \wedge x < 1 \wedge -1 \leq y \wedge y < 0 \wedge x - y = 1 \| P(x, y) \cdot \{x \mapsto f, y \mapsto c\}},$$
$$0 \leq f, f < 1, -1 \leq c, c < 0, f - c = 1,$$
$$P(g, d)^{0 \leq x \wedge x < 1 \wedge -1 \leq y \wedge y < 0 \wedge x - y = 1 \| P(x, y) \cdot \{x \mapsto g, y \mapsto d\}},$$
$$0 \leq g, g < 1, -1 \leq d, d < 0, g - d = 1,$$
$$P(h, e)^{0 \leq x \wedge x < 1 \wedge -1 \leq y \wedge y < 0 \wedge x - y = 1 \| P(x, y) \cdot \{x \mapsto h, y \mapsto e\}},$$
$$0 \leq h, h < 1, -1 \leq e, e < 0, h - e = 1,$$
$$\neg P(f, d)^{0 \leq x \wedge x < 1 \wedge -1 \leq y \wedge y < 0 \wedge x - y \neq 1 \| \neg P(x, y) \cdot \{x \mapsto f, y \mapsto d\}}, f - d \neq 1,$$
$$\neg P(f, e)^{0 \leq x \wedge x < 1 \wedge -1 \leq y \wedge y < 0 \wedge x - y \neq 1 \| \neg P(x, y) \cdot \{x \mapsto f, y \mapsto e\}}, f - e \neq 1,$$
$$\neg P(g, c)^{0 \leq x \wedge x < 1 \wedge -1 \leq y \wedge y < 0 \wedge x - y \neq 1 \| \neg P(x, y) \cdot \{x \mapsto g, y \mapsto c\}}, g - c \neq 1,$$
$$\neg P(g, e)^{0 \leq x \wedge x < 1 \wedge -1 \leq y \wedge y < 0 \wedge x - y \neq 1 \| \neg P(x, y) \cdot \{x \mapsto g, y \mapsto e\}}, g - e \neq 1,$$
$$\neg P(h, c)^{0 \leq x \wedge x < 1 \wedge -1 \leq y \wedge y < 0 \wedge x - y \neq 1 \| \neg P(x, y) \cdot \{x \mapsto h, y \mapsto c\}}, h - c \neq 1,$$
$$\neg P(h, d)^{0 \leq x \wedge x < 1 \wedge -1 \leq y \wedge y < 0 \wedge x - y \neq 1 \| \neg P(x, y) \cdot \{x \mapsto h, y \mapsto d\}}, h - d \neq 1]$$

The state $(M; N; \emptyset; B; 0; \top)$ is stuck and $M \models_\mathcal{H} \mathrm{gnd}_B(N)$. Moreover, M satisfies the $\cong^\eta_\kappa$-extraction-criterion with the $\cong^\eta_\kappa$-uniform extension M^p such that:

$$M^p = [a < b, b < c, c < d, d < e, e < f, f < g, g < h, h < i, i < j, j < k,$$
$$a < -1, b < -1, c = -1, -1 < d, d < 0, -1 < e, e < 0, f = 0,$$
$$0 < g, g < 1, 0 < h, h < 1, i = 1, 1 < j, 1 < k,$$
$$h - e = 1, h - d > 1, g - d = 1, g - e < 1]$$

One satisfying assignment for M, M^p is $\beta = \{a \mapsto -1.7, b \mapsto -1.3, c \mapsto -1, d \mapsto -0.7, e \mapsto -0.3, f \mapsto 0, g \mapsto 0.3, h \mapsto 0.7, i \mapsto 1, j \mapsto 2, k \mapsto 3\}$ The extracted algebra $\mathcal{A}$ looks as follows:

$$
\begin{aligned}
P^{\mathcal{A}} &= \{(x,y) \in \mathbb{R}^2 \mid (x,y) \cong_\kappa^\eta (0.7, -0.3)\} \cup \{(x,y) \in \mathbb{R}^2 \mid (x,y) \cong_\kappa^\eta (0.3, -0.7)\} \\
&\quad \cup \{(x,y) \in \mathbb{R}^2 \mid (x,y) \cong_\kappa^\eta (0, -1)\} \\
&= \{(x,y) \in \mathbb{R}^2 \mid 0 \le x < 1, -1 \le y, y < 0, \mathrm{fr}(x) = \mathrm{fr}(y)\} \\
&\quad \cup \{(x,y) \in \mathbb{R}^2 \mid 0 \le x < 1, -1 \le y, y < 0, \mathrm{fr}(x) = \mathrm{fr}(y)\} \\
&\quad \cup \{(x,y) \in \mathbb{R}^2 \mid 0 \le x < 1, -1 \le y, y < 0, \mathrm{fr}(x) = \mathrm{fr}(y)\} \\
&= \{(x,y) \in \mathbb{R}^2 \mid 0 \le x < 1, -1 \le y, y < 0, x - y = 1\}
\end{aligned}
$$

Example 37 (Stuck State is not $\cong_\kappa^\eta$-Uniform). Consider almost the same run as in the previous example. The only difference is that M'' contains the decision $P(a, c)$. Then the state $(M; N; \emptyset; B; 0; \top)$ is reachable by a reasonable run, still stuck, $M \models_{\mathcal{H}} \mathrm{gnd}_B(N)$, and $\beta = \{a \mapsto -1.7, b \mapsto -1.3, c \mapsto -1, d \mapsto -0.7, e \mapsto -0.3, f \mapsto 0, g \mapsto 0.3, h \mapsto 0.7, i \mapsto 1, j \mapsto 2, k \mapsto 3\}$ is still a satisfying assignment for M, M^p. However, M does not satisfy the $\cong_\kappa^\eta$-extraction-criterion because the predicates in M are not uniformly defined. To be more precise, we have two different definitions for P and the equivalence class $\{(x,y) \in \mathbb{Q}^2 \mid x < -\kappa = -1, y = -\kappa = -1\}$, viz., $P(a, c), \neg P(b, c) \in M$ and $(a, c) \cong_\kappa^\eta (b, c)$.

It might seem like a reasonable idea to improve SCL(T) for BS(BD) by adding the $\cong_\kappa^\eta$-uniform trail extension M^p directly at the beginning to the trail. Intuitively, this will only remove stuck states that cannot fulfill the extraction criterion and we will still find a stuck state that satisfies the extraction criterion if there exists one. However, it is not always possible to get a resolution proof for unsatisfiability if we add the $\cong_\kappa^\eta$-uniform trail extension M^p greedily.

Example 38 (No resolution within extraction criterion). Consider the unsatisfiable BS(BD) clause set $N = \{0 < x \wedge x < 1 \wedge 0 < y \wedge y < 1 \wedge x - y < 0 \| P(y), 0 < x \wedge x < 1 \wedge 0 < y \wedge y < 1 \wedge x - y < 0 \| \neg P(x)\}$. The partition of constants defined in the $\cong_\kappa^\eta$-uniform trail extension M^p assigns only two constants a, b to the interval $(0, 1)$ because no clause contains more than two variables. It is however impossible to get a refutation proof for the unsatisfiability of the above two clauses if we only have two constants $a < b$ in the interval $(0, 1)$. If we add the $\cong_\kappa^\eta$-uniform trail extension M^p directly at the beginning of our regular SCL(T) run, then we must end up in a stuck state that contains the literals $P(b)$ and $\neg P(a)$ on the trail. This means that SCL(T) neither derives a clause $\Lambda \| \bot$, nor does it encounter a stuck state that has a uniform model.

5   SCL(T) Extensions and Discussion

We have presented the new calculus SCL(T) for pure clause sets of first-order logic modulo a background theory. The calculus is sound and refutationally complete. It does not generate redundant clauses. Moreover, it constitutes a decision procedure for certain decidable fragments of pure clause sets, such as BS(BD), and can even return an explicit satisfying algebra $\mathcal{A}$ in the case that the clause set is satisfiable.

There are further extensions to pure clause sets that still enable a refutationally complete calculus. In particular, first-order function symbols that do not range into a background theory sort and equality. The properties of the SCL(T) calculus rely on finite trails with respect to a fixed, finite set B of constants. By adding non-constant first-order function symbols trails will typically be infinite without further restrictions. Finite trails can, e.g., still be obtained by limiting nestings of function symbols in terms. Thus it seems to us that an extension to first-order function symbols that do not range into a background theory sort should be possible while keeping the properties of SCL(T). From an abstract point of view, also the addition of equality on the first-order side should be possible, because there exist complete procedures such as hierarchic superposition [1,4]. Then also foreground function symbols may range into a background theory sort, but the respective terms have to satisfy further conditions in order to preserve completeness. However, even in the pure first-order case there has not been a convincing solution so far of how to combine equational reasoning with explicit model building. One challenge is how to learn a clause from a conflict out of a partial model assumption that enjoys ordering restrictions on terms occurring in equations. If this can be sufficiently solved, the respective calculus should also be extendable to a hierarchic set up.

An efficient implementation of SCL(T) requires efficient algorithmic solutions to a number of concepts out of the theory. For fast model building an efficient implementation of Propagate is needed. This was our motivation for adding the all-different constraints on the constants, because they enable syntactic testing for complementary or defined literals. In addition, satisfiability of constraints needs to be tested. The trail behaves like a stack and it is ground. This fits perfectly the strengths of SMT-style satisfiability testing. Dealing with the non-domain constants out of the set B needs some care. They behave completely symmetric with respect to the instantiation of clauses in $(N \cup U)$. An easy way to break symmetry here is the addition of linear ordering constraints on these constants. If more is known about the specific fragment some clause set N belongs to, additional constraints with respect to the constraints or domain constants out of $(N \cup U)$ may be added as well. This is for example the case for the BS(BD) fragment. We could simply add the atoms of the $\cong_\kappa^\eta$-uniform trail extension M^p at the beginning to the trail. This would exclude many stuck states that cannot possible fulfill the extraction criterion and would therefore reduce the search space for SCL(T). Completeness would also be preserved because we either find a stuck state that satisfies the extraction criterion or the problem is unsatisfiable. Note, however, that we would not always get a refutation proof as a certificate of unsatisfiability.

If we add the $\cong_\kappa^\eta$-uniform trail extension M^p at the beginning to the trail, then all groundings of theory atoms can be automatically simplified to true or false. This means we could implement propagation for SCL(T) over BS(BD) by feeding a SAT solver with all groundings of clauses and using its propagation module. We might even reduce the search space of the SAT solver by replacing all ground literals $|L| = P(\bar{s})$ to $|L'| = P(\bar{r})$ such that $\bar{r}$ is the minimal element in the $\bar{s}$ equivalence class. This would guarantee that only $\cong_\kappa^\eta$-uniform literals are propagated. Conflict analysis would still need to be handled outside of the SAT solver so we can learn the much stronger non-ground clauses.

Checking whether a trail is $\cong_\kappa^\eta$-uniform (as required by Definition 30) can be done efficiently (in run-time $O(|M|\log(|M|))$). We just have to sort the foreground literals $|L| = P(\bar{s})$ first by predicate P and then by the smallest vector $\bar{r}$ (according to a lexicographic order over B) such that $\bar{s} \cong_\kappa^\eta \bar{r}$. The trail is $\cong_\kappa^\eta$-uniform if and only if no two neighbors $P(\bar{r})$, $\neg P(\bar{s})$ in the sorted list have $\bar{s} \cong_\kappa^\eta \bar{r}$. We could also add a new rule to the calculus that adds all $\cong_\kappa^\eta$-uniform instances of the same literal as soon as one has been derived.

Exploring all trail prefixes, as required by Theorem 25 and Corollary 34, requires book-keeping on visited stuck states and an efficient implementation of the rule Restart. The former can be done by actually learning new clauses that represent stuck states. Such clauses are not logical consequences out of N, so they have to be treated specially. In case of an application of Grow all these clauses and all the consequences thereof have to be updated. An easy solution would be to forget the clauses generated by stuck states. This can be efficiently implemented. Concerning the rule Restart, from the SAT world it is known that restarts do not have to be total [20], i.e., if a certain prefix of a trail will be reproduced after a restart, it can be left on the trail. It seems possible to extend this concept towards SCL(T).

As future work, we plan to implement SCL(T) and define extraction criteria for other (arithmetic) theories.

Acknowledgments. This work was funded by DFG grant 389792660 as part of TRR 248. We thank our reviewers for their valuable comments.

References

1. Bachmair, L., Ganzinger, H., Waldmann, U.: Refutational theorem proving for hierarchic first-order theories. Appl. Algebra Eng. Commun. Comput. (AAECC) **5**(3/4), 193–212 (1994). https://doi.org/10.1007/BF01190829
2. Baumgartner, P., Fuchs, A., Tinelli, C.: Lemma learning in the model evolution calculus. In: Hermann, M., Voronkov, A. (eds.) LPAR 2006. LNCS (LNAI), vol. 4246, pp. 572–586. Springer, Heidelberg (2006). https://doi.org/10.1007/11916277_39
3. Baumgartner, P., Fuchs, A., Tinelli, C.: (LIA) - model evolution with linear integer arithmetic constraints. In: Cervesato, I., Veith, H., Voronkov, A. (eds.) LPAR 2008. LNCS (LNAI), vol. 5330, pp. 258–273. Springer, Heidelberg (2008). https://doi.org/10.1007/978-3-540-89439-1_19
4. Baumgartner, P., Waldmann, U.: Hierarchic superposition revisited. In: Lutz, C., Sattler, U., Tinelli, C., Turhan, A.-Y., Wolter, F. (eds.) Description Logic, Theory Combination, and All That. LNCS, vol. 11560, pp. 15–56. Springer, Cham (2019). https://doi.org/10.1007/978-3-030-22102-7_2

5. Bjørner, N., Gurfinkel, A., McMillan, K., Rybalchenko, A.: Horn clause solvers for program verification. In: Beklemishev, L.D., Blass, A., Dershowitz, N., Finkbeiner, B., Schulte, W. (eds.) Fields of Logic and Computation II. LNCS, vol. 9300, pp. 24–51. Springer, Cham (2015). https://doi.org/10.1007/978-3-319-23534-9_2

6. Bromberger, M., Fiori, A., Weidenbach, C.: SCL with theory constraints. CoRR, abs/2003.04627 (2020)

7. de Moura, L., Bjørner, N.: Engineering DPLL(T) + saturation. In: Armando, A., Baumgartner, P., Dowek, G. (eds.) IJCAR 2008. LNCS (LNAI), vol. 5195, pp. 475–490. Springer, Heidelberg (2008). https://doi.org/10.1007/978-3-540-71070-7_40

8. de Moura, L., Jovanović, D.: A model-constructing satisfiability calculus. In: Giacobazzi, R., Berdine, J., Mastroeni, I. (eds.) VMCAI 2013. LNCS, vol. 7737, pp. 1–12. Springer, Heidelberg (2013). https://doi.org/10.1007/978-3-642-35873-9_1

9. Downey, P.J.: Undecidability of Presburger arithmetic with a single monadic predicate letter. Technical report, Center for Research in Computer Technology, Harvard University (1972)

10. Faqeh, R., et al.: Towards dynamic dependable systems through evidence-based continuous certification. In: Margaria, T., Steffen, B. (eds.) ISoLA 2020. LNCS, vol. 12477, pp. 416–439. Springer, Cham (2020). https://doi.org/10.1007/978-3-030-61470-6_25

11. Fiori, A., Weidenbach, C.: SCL clause learning from simple models. In: Fontaine, P. (ed.) CADE 2019. LNCS (LNAI), vol. 11716, pp. 233–249. Springer, Cham (2019). https://doi.org/10.1007/978-3-030-29436-6_14

12. Ge, Y., de Moura, L.: Complete instantiation for quantified formulas in satisfiabiliby modulo theories. In: Bouajjani, A., Maler, O. (eds.) CAV 2009. LNCS, vol. 5643, pp. 306–320. Springer, Heidelberg (2009). https://doi.org/10.1007/978-3-642-02658-4_25

13. Horbach, M., Voigt, M., Weidenbach, C.: The universal fragment of Presburger arithmetic with unary uninterpreted predicates is undecidable. CoRR, abs/1703.01212 (2017)

14. Bayardo Jr, R.J., Schrag, R.: Using CSP look-back techniques to solve real-world SAT instances. In: Kuipers, B., Webber, B.L. (eds.) Proceedings of the Fourteenth National Conference on Artificial Intelligence and Ninth Innovative Applications of Artificial Intelligence Conference, AAAI 1997, IAAI 1997, Providence, Rhode Island, USA, 27–31 July 1997, pp. 203–208 (1997)

15. Kovács, L., Voronkov, A.: First-order theorem proving and VAMPIRE. In: Sharygina, N., Veith, H. (eds.) CAV 2013. LNCS, vol. 8044, pp. 1–35. Springer, Heidelberg (2013). https://doi.org/10.1007/978-3-642-39799-8_1

16. Kruglov, E., Weidenbach, C.: Superposition decides the first-order logic fragment over ground theories. Math. Comput. Sci. **6**(4), 427–456 (2012). https://doi.org/10.1007/s11786-012-0135-4

17. Minsky, M.L.: Computation: Finite and Infinite Machines. Automatic Computation. Prentice-Hall, Englewood (1967)

18. Nieuwenhuis, R., Oliveras, A., Tinelli, C.: Solving SAT and SAT modulo theories: from an abstract Davis-Putnam-Logemann-Loveland procedure to DPLL(T). J. ACM **53**, 937–977 (2006)

19. Prevosto, V., Waldmann, U.: SPASS+T. In: Sutcliffe, G., Schmidt, R., Schulz, S. (eds.) ESCoR: FLoC 2006 Workshop on Empirically Successful Computerized Reasoning. CEUR Workshop Proceedings, Seattle, WA, USA, vol. 192, pp. 18–33 (2006)

20. Ramos, A., van der Tak, P., Heule, M.J.H.: Between restarts and backjumps. In: Sakallah, K.A., Simon, L. (eds.) SAT 2011. LNCS, vol. 6695, pp. 216–229. Springer, Heidelberg (2011). https://doi.org/10.1007/978-3-642-21581-0_18

21. Reynolds, A., Barbosa, H., Fontaine, P.: Revisiting enumerative instantiation. In: Beyer, D., Huisman, M. (eds.) TACAS 2018. LNCS, vol. 10806, pp. 112–131. Springer, Cham (2018). https://doi.org/10.1007/978-3-319-89963-3_7

22. Rümmer, P.: A constraint sequent calculus for first-order logic with linear integer arithmetic. In: Cervesato, I., Veith, H., Voronkov, A. (eds.) LPAR 2008. LNCS (LNAI), vol. 5330, pp. 274–289. Springer, Heidelberg (2008). https://doi.org/10.1007/978-3-540-89439-1_20

23. Silva, J.P.M., Sakallah, K.A.: GRASP - a new search algorithm for satisfiability. In: International Conference on Computer Aided Design, ICCAD, pp. 220–227. IEEE Computer Society Press (1996)

24. Voigt, M.: The Bernays–Schönfinkel–Ramsey fragment with bounded difference constraints over the reals is decidable. In: Dixon, C., Finger, M. (eds.) FroCoS 2017. LNCS (LNAI), vol. 10483, pp. 244–261. Springer, Cham (2017). https://doi.org/10.1007/978-3-319-66167-4_14

25. Voigt, M.: Decidable fragments of first-order logic and of first-order linear arithmetic with uninterpreted predicates. Ph.D. thesis, Saarland University, Saarbrücken, Germany (2019)

Incremental Search for Conflict and Unit Instances of Quantified Formulas with E-Matching

Jochen Hoenicke(✉) and Tanja Schindler(✉)

University of Freiburg, Freiburg im Breisgau, Germany
{hoenicke,schindle}@informatik.uni-freiburg.de

Abstract. We present a new method to find conflicting instances of quantified formulas in the context of SMT solving. Our method splits the search for such instances in two parts. In the first part, E-matching is used to find candidate instances of the quantified formulas. In principle, any existing incremental E-matching technique can be used. The incrementality avoids duplicating work for each small change of the E-graph. Together with the candidate instance, E-matching also provides an existing node in the E-graph corresponding to each term in this instance. In the second part, these nodes are used to evaluate the candidate instance, i.e., without creating new terms. The evaluation can be done in constant time per instance. Our method detects conflicting instances and unit-propagating instances (clauses that propagate new literals). This makes our method suitable for a tight integration with the DPLL($\mathcal{T}$) framework, very much in the style of an additional theory solver.

1 Introduction

Satisfiability Modulo Theories (SMT) solving is the problem of finding solutions for first-order formulas or proving unsatisfiability and has many applications, e. g., in software verification, scheduling, program synthesis. Many SMT solvers are based on the DPLL($\mathcal{T}$) framework, where a DPLL engine assigns truth values to ground literals, thereby creating a partial model. Specialized solver modules for each theory check the feasibility of the model or report conflicting literal assignments or new facts (ground literals) that are implied by the theory. Usually, these theory solvers handle only the quantifier-free fragment of the corresponding theory. A common approach to deal with quantified formulas is to add instances of the quantified formulas to the ground part of the problem in order to prove unsatisfiability. A challenge is to select those instances that are useful for the solving process, as adding too many formulas overloads the solver. Finding the most promising instances is an active topic of research [1,4,5,8,13–15].

In the context of the DPLL($\mathcal{T}$) framework, a conflicting instance that refutes the partial model provided by the DPLL engine is most useful [15]. Other useful

---

Partially supported by the German Research Council (DFG) under HO 5606/1-2.

F. Henglein et al. (Eds.): VMCAI 2021, LNCS 12597, pp. 534–555, 2021.
https://doi.org/10.1007/978-3-030-67067-2_24

instances are unit-propagating instances that show that a literal is implied by the partial model and allow the solver to assign the literal correctly. We present a new method for finding such conflicting or unit-propagating instances on the fly as the DPLL engine builds the partial model. This enables a tight integration of quantifier reasoning with the DPLL($\mathcal{T}$) framework.

The basic idea in DPLL($\mathcal{T}$) based solvers is to separate Boolean reasoning from theory reasoning. A DPLL engine searches for a solution of the Boolean core of the formula by guessing literals that should be true and propagating consequences from these guesses. The theory solvers guide the search by constantly checking if there is a model in the corresponding theory for the partial Boolean solution. If a theory solver finds a conflict, i.e., a subset of literals that together are unsatisfiable in the theory, then this is immediately reported to the DPLL engine in form of a lemma that states that one of the literals must be false. The DPLL engine backtracks decisions that lead to the conflict, and continues the search for a solution of the Boolean core augmented with the new lemma. This allows the DPLL engine to skip huge parts of the search space. Moreover, theory solvers can provide unit clauses that show that a literal must be true in the current context. This also reduces the search space considered by the DPLL engine, and has been shown to be effective for several quantifier-free logics [11].

We think that this approach is applicable for quantifier reasoning for the same reasons. Instead of adding many instances at a time, we consider a quantifier solver as one of the theory solvers in the DPLL($\mathcal{T}$) framework. That is, the quantifier solver actively participates in the search for a satisfying solution of a given problem by providing useful instances that guide the search in the right direction. A useful instance can be a conflicting instance that shows that the search took a wrong branch, or a unit-propagating instance that propagates a new fact. The core of our method is an incremental search for such conflicting and unit instances, that uses an incremental E-matching module. The incrementality is essential for the quantifier solver to find new instances without repeating the full search after each step in the solving process.

E-matching is the problem of finding ground terms that match a so-called *pattern*, i.e., a term that may contain variables. A term matches a pattern if it is equal, up to congruence, to the pattern instantiated with a suitable variable substitution. E-matching is used in many existing solvers as a heuristic to find potentially useful instances. The idea is to choose a set of patterns (a *multi-pattern*) for a quantified formula such that all variables are contained. An instance of a quantified formula is considered to be relevant if all patterns match for a common variable substitution. The success of E-matching based instantiation is strongly influenced by the choice of patterns. If the patterns are too restrictive, a relevant instance may not be found; if the patterns are too general, many irrelevant instances may be produced.

To illustrate E-matching based instantiation and its shortcoming, we consider the following example formula.

$$f(a, b) = a \wedge f(b, b) = b \wedge f(b, c) = c \wedge a = c \wedge b \neq c$$
$$\wedge \, (\, \forall x, y, z. \; f(x, y) \neq c \vee f(y, z) \neq c \vee f(x, z) = c \,)$$

A multi-pattern suitable for E-matching in the universally quantified subformula is $f(x, y), f(y, z)$. The E-matching engine matches each pattern with the terms in the ground part of the formula, to find values for x, y, and z, such that both instantiated patterns have an existing congruent term. One potential match yields the ground terms $f(b, c)$, $f(a, b)$ and the substitution $\{x \mapsto b, y \mapsto c, z \mapsto b\}$. This is a valid match: the instantiated second pattern $f(c, b)$ is congruent to $f(a, b)$ since $a = c$ is part of the ground formula. The instantiated clause $f(b, c) \neq c \vee f(c, b) \neq c \vee f(b, b) = c$ leads to a contradiction with the ground part and shows that the formula is unsatisfiable.

However, E-matching also finds a lot of instances that are not useful to show unsatisfiability. In the above example, also $\{x \mapsto a, y \mapsto b, z \mapsto b\}$ is matching the pattern. The corresponding instance is already satisfied as the last literal of the clause, $f(a, b) = c$, is already true. In total, E-matching finds five instances in this small example, of which three are already true, one is a conflict, and one derives some fact about the non-existing ground term $f(a, a)$. The main problem with producing irrelevant instances is that they can trigger new matches. This may even lead to so-called matching loops, e.g., if a new term from an instantiated formula matches the pattern again leading to increasingly larger variable substitutions.

E-matching is not only useful to find candidates for conflicting instances, it also provides congruent terms that can be used to evaluate the instances without any extra work. In the example above, $f(c, b) \neq c$ can be evaluated using the congruent term $f(a, b)$ for $f(c, b)$. This insight is the core of our method to find conflicting instances fast enough to be used as a DPLL($\mathcal{T}$) theory solver.

Our incremental search for conflicting and unit-propagating clauses is subdivided into two parts. First we search for candidate substitutions for quantified clauses by using E-matching for the quantified terms in the clause. We use the congruent terms provided by E-matching in the second part to evaluate the clause instance without actually building the instantiated terms. Only if the instance is found to be conflicting or unit-propagating, it is created. The approach of splitting this search into two parts has the advantage that the search for candidate substitutions using E-matching can be done incrementally [3] and does only little work each time a new ground literal is set or removed. The clause evaluation can be done literal by literal, which allows to not only detect conflicting instances, but also instances that propagate new literals.

We introduce the notation and basic definitions in Sect. 2. In Sect. 3, we give a brief overview of the DPLL($\mathcal{T}$) framework. We describe the congruence closure algorithm which is a decision procedure for the theory of equality, and outline E-matching based instantiation. In Sect. 4, we present our approach to find conflicting and unit-propagating instances of quantified formulas, and give theoretical results on correctness and completeness of the approach. Experimental evidence of the usefulness of our approach is given in Sect. 5. Finally, we mention related work in Sect. 6, and discuss future work in Sect. 7.

2   Notation and Basic Definitions

We assume standard sorted first-order logic with equality. A first-order *theory* is defined by its signature consisting of constant, function and predicate symbols, and a set of axioms for its interpreted symbols. We consider in the following mainly the theory of equality and uninterpreted functions T_E. The axioms of T_E establish reflexivity, symmetry and transitivity for the equality symbol $=$, and congruence for each uninterpreted function symbol.

A *term* is a variable, a constant, or the application of an n-ary function to n terms. An *atom* is the application of an n-ary predicate to n terms. A *literal* is an atom or its negation. A *clause* is a disjunction of literals. A term, literal or clause is *ground* if it does not contain variables.

In the following, we assume w.l.o.g. that every formula is in conjunctive normal form (CNF), i.e., it is a conjunction of clauses. We also assume that every variable occurring in the formula is universally quantified. The latter can be established by introducing Skolem variables or functions for existentially quantified variables [12]. Thus, the formula is a conjunction of clauses and each clause implicitly universally quantifies over its free variables.

We use the letters a, b, c to denote constant symbols, the letters f, g, h to denote uninterpreted function symbols, and the letters x, y, z to denote universally quantified variables. We use the letter t to denote ground terms and the letter p to denote terms that may contain free variables (patterns). We use the letter ℓ for literals, F and φ for formulas, and C for clauses. We use the symbol $\perp$ to denote the formula that is always false. We write $p[x_1, \ldots, x_n]$, $\ell[x_1, \ldots, x_n]$, $\varphi[x_1, \ldots, x_n]$, and $C[x_1, \ldots, x_n]$ for terms, literals, formulas, and clauses, respectively, containing at most the variables $x_1, \ldots, x_n$. For a formula F, we write T_F to denote the set of all terms occurring in F.

A *substitution* is a mapping from variables to terms, and it is a *ground* substitution if it maps all variables to ground terms. We write $\sigma = \{x_1 \mapsto t_1, \ldots, x_n \mapsto t_n\}$ for the substitution that maps variable x_i to term t_i for $i \in \{1, \ldots, n\}$. We also use the notation $p[x \mapsto t]$ to denote the term that results from replacing variable x in p with the term t.

3   Preliminaries

In this section, we outline standard methods in SMT solvers that are the basis for our approach, namely the DPLL(T) framework that separates Boolean reasoning from theory reasoning in SMT solvers, the congruence closure algorithm which is an efficient decision procedure for the quantifier-free fragment of the theory of equality T_E, and finally the technique of E-matching based instantiation which is a common approach to find useful instances of quantified formulas.

3.1 DPLL($\mathcal{T}$)

Many SMT solvers are based on the DPLL($\mathcal{T}$) framework. The basic idea is to separate Boolean reasoning from theory reasoning. The DPLL engine takes care of the propositional core of the CNF formula by assigning truth values to literals. In particular, it tries to satisfy each clause in the formula by assigning at least one literal to `true`. A clause where all literals are assigned to `false` is called a *conflict clause*. A clause where all but one literals are assigned to `false`, and this literal has not yet been assigned, is called a *unit clause*, and can be used to propagate this literal. If no unit clauses exist, the DPLL engine must make decisions on literals which may have to be backtracked if they lead to a conflict.

During the solving process, the currently assigned literals are passed to *theory solvers* that use specialized decision procedures. If a theory solver finds that the conjunction of literals is in conflict with the theory axioms, it returns a corresponding conflict clause (a subset of literals that are unsatisfiable) to the DPLL engine. The theory solver can also propagate literals that must be true in the theory under the current partial literal assignment by providing a unit clause. Conflict clauses may only contain existing literals, but theory solvers can create new literals that may be propagated by a unit clause to the DPLL engine or to other theories. In order to determine that a satisfying assignment has been found, a theory solver must also be able to provide a complete model.

The interaction between the DPLL engine and the theory solvers can happen in several stages. While it is enough to report any conflicts once all literals have been assigned, finding conflicts early and propagating literals implied by the theory during the search for a Boolean model can often help the DPLL engine to significantly reduce the search space [11]. However, theory reasoning comes with a certain cost, which is why it does not always make sense to compute all theory conflicts and propagations in each step of the solving process. Finding the right compromise between efficiency and completeness of theory propagation is the key in building an efficient solver.

3.2 Congruence Closure

The quantifier-free conjunctive fragment of the theory of equality $\mathcal{T}_E$ can be decided by computing the congruence closure for the equality relation on a graph representing the involved terms [10].

An *E-graph* is a graph with nodes (vertices) and two kind of edges. Figure 1 shows an example. Each node in the graph represents a term and for every term there is at most one node. If the term is a function application, it is labelled by the function symbol and solid edges point from the node to the arguments of the function application. Dashed edges, the so-called equality edges, represent equalities between these terms that were decided by the DPLL engine or that are propagated congruences. Let $\sim$ denote the transitive closure of all equality edges, i.e., $t_1 \sim t_2$ is true if and only if t_1 and t_2 are connected by a sequence of equalities. The connected components $[t]_= = \{t' \mid t \sim t'\}$ are called the congruence classes. There is an efficient algorithm based on union-find data

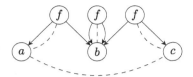

Fig. 1. E-graph for the formula $f(a, b) = a \wedge f(b, b) = b \wedge f(b, c) = c \wedge a = c$. Nodes represent terms, solid arrows between nodes symbolize function-argument relations, and dashed lines symbolize equality.

structures that builds the E-graph in $O(n \log n)$. The lookup whether $t_1 \sim t_2$ holds for two nodes t_1 and t_2 in the graph is in $O(1)$.

The congruence closure algorithm works incrementally in a DPLL setting. It starts with the empty E-graph that does not have any equality edge. When the DPLL engine decides or propagates an equality, the corresponding nodes are connected with an equality edge. If a disequality is decided, it is remembered for the corresponding pair of congruence classes (this information is updated whenever congruence classes are merged by a new equality edge).

Whenever congruence classes are merged, the congruence closure algorithm also propagates all implied *congruences*. For each pair of function application terms $f(t_1, \ldots, t_n)$ and $f(t'_1, \ldots, t'_n)$ on the same function symbol, the algorithm checks whether $t_i \sim t'_i$ holds for $1 \le i \le n$. If this is the case, the congruent function applications are connected by an equality edge. There are efficient data structures to quickly find the candidate application terms that may be affected by a previous merge of two congruence classes.

When a disequality is set between two terms with $t_1 \sim t_2$ or if two congruence classes are merged that already have a disequality between them, the congruence closure algorithm reports a conflict. This conflict can be explained by the disequality $t_1 \ne t_2$ and the path of equality edges between t_1 and t_2.

For terms t_1, t_2 existing as nodes in the E-graph, it can be determined in constant time (each node remembers its representative) whether the literals decided by the DPLL engine imply an equality $t_1 = t_2$. For literals $t_1 \ne t_2$, the algorithm can check if there a disequality set between the corresponding congruence classes. In that case the literals decided by the DPLL engine imply the disequality. However, not all implied disequalities can be found this way. For example, the literal $f(a, b) \ne f(b, a)$ implies $a \ne b$ but the congruence closure algorithm would not find this disequality.

3.3   E-Matching Based Instantiation

A common approach in SMT solvers to handle problems containing quantified formulas is to add instances of the quantified formulas to the ground part of the problem, and solve the resulting ground formula. A heuristic method to find instances that help the solving process is based on E-matching. It was first implemented in the Simplify theorem prover [5]. An incremental version has been presented for instance in [3].

E-matching is the problem of finding terms in the E-graph that match a given *pattern* (a term with free variables) up to congruence. The idea of E-matching based instantiation is that an instance $\varphi\sigma$ of a universally quantified formula $\forall x_1, \ldots, x_n.\ \varphi[x_1, \ldots, x_n]$ is useful to solve the problem if it contains enough terms that are congruent to terms in the current E-graph, as such an instance allows for deriving new information about existing terms. In order to find such instances, non-ground terms $p_1, \ldots, p_n$, a so-called *multi-pattern* (or trigger), from the formula φ are selected. They should contain all free variables of φ in order to extract a substitution from a match. The E-matching algorithm then searches for terms $t_1, \ldots, t_n$ in the E-graph, and a substitution σ, such that $t_1 \sim p_1\sigma, \ldots, t_n \sim p_n\sigma$ holds, where $\sim$ denotes the congruence closure of the equality edges of the E-graph.[1] We say that each t_i matches the pattern p_i. Here, t_i and $p_i\sigma$ need not be the same term, but congruent terms. In particular, t_i occurs explicitly in the E-graph, while $p_i\sigma$ does not necessarily occur there. For $p_i = f(p'_1, \ldots, p'_m)$, this means that the congruence class of t_i contains a term $f(t'_1, \ldots, t'_m)$ such that $t'_j \sim p'_j\sigma$ holds.

Example 1. Let $F : f(a) = b \wedge g(b) = c \wedge \forall x.\ g(f(x)) = d$. A useful pattern for E-matching is $p : g(f(x))$. Figure 2 shows the E-graph for the ground part, and how the pattern p is matched. The result of applying E-matching is $\sigma = \{x \mapsto a\}$ and the term t with $t \sim p\sigma$ is $g(b)$. Note that $p\sigma = g(f(a))$ does not exist in the E-graph.

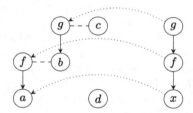

Fig. 2. E-matching for $F : f(a) = b \wedge g(b) = c \wedge \forall x.\ g(f(x)) = d$. The left part displays the E-graph for the ground part of F, the right part displays the pattern $g(f(x))$ for the quantified part. Solid arrows symbolize function-argument relations, dashed lines symbolize equality, and the dotted arrows display which terms in the E-graph match with which subterm of the pattern.

E-matching is usually used as a basis for a heuristic instantiation procedure. For a quantified formula φ and a corresponding multi-pattern $p_1, \ldots, p_n$, whenever matching terms $t_1, \ldots t_n$ and a substitution σ with $t_i \sim p_i\sigma$ are found, the instance $\varphi\sigma$ is added to the ground problem. One problem with E-matching is to

---

[1] From now on $\sim$ denotes the congruence closure of the equality edges in the E-graph and not the transitive closure as in the previous section. Note that this is also defined for $p\sigma$, if it does not exist in the E-graph.

choose the right multi-pattern. If the pattern is too strict, important instances may be missed. If the pattern is too loose, it creates too many irrelevant instances which may cause new matches. In general, E-matching cannot be used to show satisfiability for a quantified formula; although there are quantified formulas with patterns for which E-matching is complete.

4   Finding Conflict and Unit Instances

In this section we describe our algorithm to find conflict and unit instances for quantified clauses. We assume that the input formula was preprocessed into conjunctive normal form and that existential quantifiers were skolemized by introducing fresh constants or function symbols [12]. All variables occurring in clauses are universally quantified. Thus, a quantified clause always is of the form

$$\forall x_1, \ldots, x_n.\ \ell_1[x_1, \ldots, x_n] \vee \ldots \vee \ell_m[x_1, \ldots, x_n]$$

where $\ell_1, \ldots, \ell_m$ are literals containing at most the variables $x_1, \ldots, x_n$. We omit the universal quantifier and implicitly see all free variables in a clause as universally quantified.

The quantified clauses are handled by a separate quantifier theory. Given a quantified clause $C[x_1, \ldots, x_n]$, the theory searches for a ground substitution σ for $x_1, \ldots, x_n$ such that the resulting instance $C\sigma$ is in conflict with the current partial model, or leads to a propagation. We define such instances as follows.

Definition 1. *Let M be a (partial) literal assignment and let $C := \ell_1 \vee \ldots \vee \ell_m$ be the body of a quantified clause containing the free variables $x_1, \ldots, x_n$.*

1. *A ground instance $C\sigma$ for a substitution σ over $x_1 \ldots x_n$ is* conflicting *if $M \cup \{C\sigma\} \models_\mathcal{T} \bot$, or, equivalently, $M \models_\mathcal{T} \neg \ell_i \sigma$ for all $i \in \{1, \ldots, m\}$. (This definition follows [15].)*
2. *A ground instance $C\sigma$ is* unit-propagating *if there is an i such that $M \models_\mathcal{T} \neg \ell_j \sigma$ for all $j \neq i$.*

Note that this definition does not require a clause instance resulting from a conflicting or unit-propagating instance to be in conflict with the Boolean model, i.e., it is not a conflict or unit clause for the DPLL engine. Theory reasoning may be necessary to derive that the clause instance is unsatisfiable for the current partial assignment M. In particular, the literal instances do not always exist, and the definition of unit-propagating instances also allows new terms in $\ell_i \sigma$.

In the next section, we explain how to find conflicting and unit-propagating instances in the theory of equality $\mathcal{T}_E$. In Sect. 4.2, we then describe how the approach can be extended to the combination with linear arithmetic.

4.1   Finding Substitutions in the Theory of Equality

In the following we describe how to find conflicting and unit-propagating instances for quantified clauses in the theory of equality $\mathcal{T}_E$. As mentioned in the beginning of Sect. 4, the input formulas are preprocessed into conjunctive normal form. An uninterpreted predicate is treated as a function returning a Boolean and converted to an equality with the constant *true*. The preprocessor also applies destructive equality resolution (DER): clauses of the form $x \neq p \vee C$ where p does not contain x are replaced by the equivalent clause $C[x \mapsto p]$ where all occurrences of x are replaced by p. Also trivially false literals $x \neq x$ are removed from the clause. These formula simplifications are important for completeness as explained in Theorem 1 on page 14. From now on, let F be the preprocessed formula, and $C := C[x_1, \ldots, x_n]$ be a quantified clause in F with free variables $x_1, \ldots, x_n$.

Our approach to find conflicting and unit-propagating instances consists of three steps.

1. For each non-ground literal $p = p'$ or $p \neq p'$ in C, solve the E-matching problem for the multi-pattern p, p'. This finds ground substitutions σ for the variables in p, p' and congruent ground terms $t \sim p\sigma$, $t' \sim p'\sigma$.
2. Evaluate the equivalent literal $t = t'$ or $t \neq t'$ using information from the congruence closure theory solver.
3. Extract the common substitutions σ for all variables in C that are conflicting or unit-propagating.

We illustrate our approach with the help of the following example.

Example 2. We assume that the DPLL engine has already set the following literals to **true**.

$$M : f(a,b) = a, f(b,b) = b, f(b,c) = c, a = c$$

This literal assignment results in the E-graph displayed in Fig. 1. In the following we will show how to find conflicting and unit-propagating instances for the quantified clause

$$C : f(x,y) \neq c \vee f(y,z) \neq c \vee f(x,z) = c$$

with free variables x, y, z.

Step 1: Find Substitutions and Congruent Terms. The first step to find conflicting and unit-propagating instances for a quantified clause is to detect substitutions for which the value of the resulting instance in the current partial model can be determined without building the instance. This is the case if there exists a ground term $t \in T_F$ for each quantified term $p[x_1, \ldots, x_n] \in T_C$ such that t and $p[x_1, \ldots, x_n]$ are congruent under the substitution σ, i.e., $t \sim p[x_1, \ldots, x_n]\sigma$.

We search for such substitutions for each literal separately. In particular, for an equality or disequality literal in T_E, i.e., a literal ℓ with underlying atom $p[x_1, \ldots, x_n] = p'[x_1, \ldots, x_n]$, we search for a substitution σ such that there exist terms $t \in T_F$ and $t' \in T_F$ with $t \sim p[x_1, \ldots, x_n]\sigma$ and $t' \sim p'[x_1, \ldots, x_n]\sigma$. These substitutions can be found by applying E-matching on the multi-pattern $p[x_1, \ldots, x_n], p'[x_1, \ldots, x_n]$. If one of the two patterns p, p' is ground, then we use only the other as a pattern. The substitutions found by E-matching are then stored in a table, which we will refer to as *substitution table*, where each row stands for a substitution σ and also stores the terms $t, t' \in T_F$ with $t \sim p[x_1, \ldots, x_n]\sigma$ and $t' \sim p'[x_1, \ldots, x_n]\sigma$. If a variable appearing in the clause C does not appear in the literal ℓ, the substitution for this variable is irrelevant for the literal, and the column corresponding to the variable is filled with asterisks.

E-matching can be implemented to work incrementally, and therefore, the substitution tables can be built up incrementally as well.

Example 3. Consider again the literal assignment M and the quantified clause C from Example 2. After E-matching with the patterns $f(x, y)$, $f(y, z)$, and $f(x, z)$, respectively, the substitution tables for the literals look as follows.

$f(x,y) \neq c$			
x	y	z	congruent
a	b	$*$	$f(a,b), c$
b	b	$*$	$f(b,b), c$
b	c	$*$	$f(b,c), c$

$f(y,z) \neq c$			
x	y	z	congruent
$*$	a	b	$f(a,b), c$
$*$	b	b	$f(b,b), c$
$*$	b	c	$f(b,c), c$

$f(x,z) = c$			
x	y	z	congruent
a	$*$	b	$f(a,b), c$
b	$*$	b	$f(b,b), c$
b	$*$	c	$f(b,c), c$

Step 2: Evaluate Literal Instances. For each literal, we can now determine which value the literal instance resulting from a substitution would have in the current partial assignment. The value of a literal under a given substitution can be determined by checking equality or disequality for the congruent terms $t, t' \in T_F$ with $t \sim p\sigma$ and $t' \sim p'\sigma$. As mentioned in Sect. 3.2, the partial assignment for the theory of equality is represented by the E-graph, together with a set of disequality literals that are currently set to true by the DPLL engine.

If the literal is implied by the current partial assignment, the corresponding instance is irrelevant for the current state as the clause is already satisfied. If the negation of the literal is implied, it can lead to a conflicting or unit-propagating instance. If neither the literal nor its negation is implied, it is a possible candidate for unit-propagation. For an equality literal $\ell : p[x_1, \ldots, x_n] = p'[x_1, \ldots, x_n]$, the value $val_\sigma(\ell)$ under a substitution σ with congruent terms $t \sim p[x_1, \ldots, x_n]\sigma$ and $t' \sim p'[x_1, \ldots, x_n]\sigma$ is defined as follows.

$$val_\sigma(\ell) = \begin{cases} \texttt{irrel} & \text{if the congruence classes } [t]_= \text{ and } [t']_= \text{ are equal} \\ \texttt{false} & \text{if a disequality } t_1 \neq t_2 \text{ between terms } t_1 \in [t]_= \\ & \text{and } t_2 \in [t']_= \text{ is set} \\ \texttt{unit} & \text{otherwise} \end{cases}$$

For a disequality literal $\ell : p \neq p'$, the value $val_\sigma(\ell)$ is defined analogously with first and second case swapped.

We evaluate each row of the substitution table and get a *literal value table* where each row represents a substitution and the corresponding literal value. As in the substitution tables, a column full of asterisk indicates a variable that does not appear in the literal. We add a row full of asterisks in the end of the table that represents all substitutions where E-matching has not found congruent terms.

If all other literals evaluate to false under such a substitution, this substitution leads to a unit-propagating instance that propagates a literal on new terms. While it may sometimes be helpful to propagate these literals, it often leads to many unnecessary propagations and can even lead to matching loops. Therefore, we have an option to either mark this row as unit or as irrelevant depending on whether equalities on unknown terms should be propagated.

Example 4. The tables T_1, T_2, and T_3 below are the literal value tables corresponding to the substitution tables of $f(x, y) \neq c$, $f(y, z) \neq c$, and $f(x, z) = c$, respectively, from Example 3.

T_1

$x\ y\ z$	value
$a\ b\ *$	false
$b\ b\ *$	unit
$b\ c\ *$	false
$*\ *\ *$	unit/irrel

T_2

$x\ y\ z$	value
$*\ a\ b$	false
$*\ b\ b$	unit
$*\ b\ c$	false
$*\ *\ *$	unit/irrel

T_3

$x\ y\ z$	value
$a\ *\ b$	irrel
$b\ *\ b$	unit
$b\ *\ c$	irrel
$*\ *\ *$	unit/irrel

Step 3: Evaluate Clause Instances and Extract Substitutions. Once a table for each literal has been built, these tables are combined in order to determine the value of the clause instances under the substitutions found for the literals. As we are only interested in conflicting and unit-propagating instances, we consider substitutions where a literal instance has value irrel, or where two or more literals have value unit, to be irrelevant. Thus, we distinguish three values for the clause tables: false if all literals evaluate to false under a substitution, unit if all but one literal evaluate to false under a substitution and the remaining literal evaluates to unit, and irrel for all other cases.

The clause value tables are computed as follows. A new clause table starts with a row full of asterisks mapping to the value false, i.e., it looks as follows.

$x_1 \ldots x_n$	value
$* \ldots *$	false

Then for each row in the clause table and the next literal table, we check if they are compatible and combine them. Compatible means, for each variable the terms are currently congruent, or for one table the variable does not occur in the substitution, i.e., there is an asterisk in the corresponding column. If the rows are compatible, the substituted terms are combined by keeping the terms from the first table, except for the positions marked with an asterisk, where we use the terms from the second row. The values of the tables are combined according to the mapping

$$(x, \texttt{false}) \mapsto x$$
$$(\texttt{false}, x) \mapsto x$$
$$\text{else} \mapsto \texttt{irrel}$$

A row becoming irrelevant can be dropped. The clause table is combined with the literal table for each literal in the clause.

The result is a table that contains a row for each conflicting or unit-propagating instance with values `false` or `unit`, respectively, and a row full of asterisks with value `irrel`.

Example 5. We now combine the literal value tables from Example 4 step by step, i.e., in the first step we combine the default clause table T_0 with the table T_1 for $f(x, y) \neq c$, then we combine the result with the table T_2 for $f(y, z) \neq c$ and finally with T_3 for $f(x, z) = c$.

$T_0 + T_1$

x y z	value
a b *	false
b b *	unit
b c *	false
* * *	unit/irrel

$T_0 + T_1 + T_2$

x y z	value
a b b	unit
a b c	false
a b *	unit/irrel
b b c	unit
b c b	false
b c *	unit/irrel
* a b	unit/irrel
* b c	unit/irrel
* * *	irrel

$T_0 + T_1 + T_2 + T_3$

x y z	value
a b c	unit/irrel
b c b	unit
* * *	irrel

Note that the row for the substitution $\{x \mapsto b, y \mapsto c, z \mapsto b\}$ in $T_0 + T_1 + T_2$ and $T_0 + T_1 + T_2 + T_3$ results from combining $\{x \mapsto b, y \mapsto c, z \mapsto *\}$ from $T_0 + T_1$ with $\{x \mapsto *, y \mapsto a, z \mapsto b\}$ from T_2, which are compatible because $a \sim c$ holds.

The substitution $\sigma = \{x \mapsto b, y \mapsto c, z \mapsto b\}$ produces a unit-propagating instance for C containing the term $f(c, b)$ which is a new term, but congruent to the term $f(a, b)$ found for the literal $f(y, z) \neq c$. The substitution $\sigma = \{x \mapsto a, y \mapsto b, z \mapsto c\}$ also produces a unit-propagating instance for C, but this instance contains the new term $f(a, c)$ that is not congruent to any known term so far.

If we consider $M' : M, a \neq b$, the table T_3' for the literal $f(x, z) = c$ changes and so does the final clause table.

T_3'

x y z	value
a * b	irrel
b * b	false
b * c	irrel
* * *	unit/irrel

$T_0 + T_1 + T_2 + T_3'$

x y z	value
a b c	unit/irrel
b c b	false
* * *	irrel

The instance $C\sigma$ with $\sigma = \{x \mapsto b, y \mapsto c, z \mapsto b\}$ is conflicting for M'.

Instantiation. After computing the clause value tables, the conflicting instances are built. These instances often create new terms and literals, because with E-matching the term $p\sigma$ may not exist in the E-graph. However, in this case the solver for congruence closure can propagate these new literals to `false`.

The quantifier theory waits until all literals are propagated by the theory of equality and only then returns the instance as conflict clause.

If no conflicting instances are found, the unit-propagating instances are built. Again these may contain new terms and literals that the solver for congruence closure will propagate to `false`. Only when the instances become unit clauses, they will be returned by the quantifier theory solver.

Theoretical Results. The presented method is incomplete in the sense that it cannot detect all conflicting or unit-propagating instances for the theory of equality T_E. There are two reasons for the incompleteness:

1. The congruence closure algorithm does not propagate all implied disequalities. For example if $f(a) \neq f(b)$ is set, the disequality $a \neq b$ cannot be detected in the E-graph. Thus, when evaluating the literal $a = b$ it may incorrectly be classified as `unit` instead of `false`.
2. Some congruences cannot be found by E-matching because no congruent terms exist in the E-graph. In particular, the equality $(f(p_1, \ldots, p_n) = f(p'_1, \ldots, p'_n))\sigma$ holds if $p_i\sigma$ and $p'_i\sigma$ are congruent for $1 \leq i \leq n$, but there need not be congruent terms in the E-graph for $f(p_1, \ldots, p_n)\sigma$ and $f(p'_1, \ldots, p'_n)\sigma$.

The first reason can be avoided. Instead of just asking for the existence of a disequality edge between two terms, one could check if adding an equality between the terms and propagating all congruences leads to a conflict. However, this contradicts our main goal, which is to make the solver fast enough that it can find conflicting instances eagerly.

To understand the second reason, we investigate the cases in which an instance of a literal is conflicting, i.e., where $M \models_{T_E} \neg\ell\sigma$ holds. We distinguish four cases. In the first case, E-matching is sufficient to find the conflicting instance. The second to fourth cases can be avoided by preprocessing as explained later.

Lemma 1. *Let M be a consistent (partial) literal assignment, and let ℓ be a literal. Assume that all ground terms occurring in the literals in M and in the literal ℓ are present in the E-graph.*

If $M \models_{T_E} \neg\ell\sigma$ holds for a substitution σ, then

1. *the literal ℓ is an equality $p = p'$ or a disequality $p \neq p'$, there are terms t, t' in the E-graph with $t \sim p\sigma$ and $t' \sim p'\sigma$, and the corresponding disequality or equality between t and t' is implied by M, or*
2. *the literal ℓ is a disequality $x \neq p$, where p does not contain x, or*
3. *the literal ℓ is a disequality $x \neq x$, or*
4. *the literal ℓ is a disequality $f(p_1, \ldots, p_n) \neq f(p'_1, \ldots, p'_n)$ and for all corresponding subterms, $M \models_{T_E} (p_i = p'_i)\sigma$ holds.*

Proof. $M \models_{T_E} \neg\ell\sigma$ holds, iff $M \cup \{\ell\sigma\} \models_{T_E} \bot$. It is well-known that the congruence closure algorithm can find all ground conflicts. First, consider the case that $\ell : p = p'$ is an equality literal. The congruence closure algorithm would create new terms $p\sigma$, $p'\sigma$ and add an equality edge between them. Assume that case 1 does not apply. This means, $p\sigma$ or $p'\sigma$ are not congruent to an existing term; we assume w.l.o.g. that this holds for $p\sigma$. So before the equality literal $p\sigma = p'\sigma$ is considered, the node $p\sigma$ would not be equivalent to any other term in the E-graph and there would not be any function application on $p\sigma$. Hence, the step in the congruence algorithm that merges $p\sigma$ and $p'\sigma$ would not introduce any more congruences and it would only merge the fresh node $p\sigma$. Thus, any conflict found by the congruence closure algorithm for $M \cup \{\ell\sigma\}$ would already be present in M. We assumed that M is consistent, so this is a contradiction.

Let now $\ell : p \neq p'$ be a disequality literal. We assume that M is consistent, but $M \cup \{\ell\sigma\}$ is not. Hence, adding $p\sigma$ and $p'\sigma$ to the E-graph would derive an equality between these terms. If there is an equality between the new terms and some already existing terms, then we are in case 1. Otherwise, the equality can only follow by congruence, or $p\sigma$ and $p\sigma'$ are identical. If they are identical constants, the literal ℓ must be of form $x \neq y$ or $x \neq x$, as we assume that all ground terms are present in the E-graph. Hence, we are in case 2 or 3. Otherwise, both $p\sigma$ and $p'\sigma$ are function applications and their arguments are equal. Assume that we are not in case 4. Then either p or p' must be a variable, w.l.o.g. assume $p = x$. If we are not in case 2 or 3, then p' is a function application on a term that contains x. But then $\sigma(x) = p'(\sigma(x))$ must follow from M. This can only be the case if M contains an equality for a term congruent to $\sigma(x)$ or one of its parents. But then $\sigma(x)$ must have a congruent term t in the E-graph, so we were in case 1 all along. □

This lemma shows that the following preprocessing is sufficient to find all conflicting instances. Let $\mathcal{C}$ be a set of quantified clauses. We create a new set of preprocessed clauses $preprocess(\mathcal{C})$ by exhaustively applying the following rules on $\mathcal{C}$:

1. If there is a clause $C \in \mathcal{C}$ of the form $C : x \neq x \vee C'$, remove it and add the clause C' instead.
2. If there is a clause $C \in \mathcal{C}$ of the form $C : x \neq p \vee C'$ where p does not contain x, remove it and add $C'[x \mapsto p]$ instead (DER).
3. If there is a clause $C \in \mathcal{C}$ of the form $C : f(p_1, \ldots, p_n) \neq f(p'_1, \ldots, p'_n) \vee C'$, *copy* it and add the clause $p_1 \neq p'_1 \vee \cdots \vee p_n \neq p'_n \vee C'$.

Note that the third rule is sound because $f(p_1, \ldots, p_n) \neq f(p'_1, \ldots, p'_n)$ implies the disjunction $\bigvee p_i \neq p'_i$. The preprocessor must still keep the original clause, in case the literal is false due to an explicit disequality that can be found by E-matching.

After preprocessing, every conflict on a single clause instance can be found with E-matching:

Theorem 1. *Let M be a consistent (partial) literal assignment and $\mathcal{C}$ a set of quantified clauses. Let there be a clause $C \in \mathcal{C}$ and a substitution σ with $M \models_{T_E} \neg C\sigma$. Then there is a clause $C' \in preprocess(\mathcal{C})$, such that for each literal in C' of the form $p = p'$ (resp. $p \neq p'$) there are E-matching equivalent terms t, t' with $t \sim p\sigma$ and $t' \sim p'\sigma$ and $M \models_{T_E} \neg(t = t')$ (resp. $M \models_{T_E} \neg(t \neq t')$).*

4.2   Extension to Linear Arithmetic

The approach described in the previous section can be extended to formulas in other theories. In this section we consider the extension of our approach to linear arithmetic. Finding congruent terms in general is difficult and costly, in particular for literals containing terms that mix arithmetic and functions like, e.g., $f(g(x) + h(y))$. In the following, we describe some extensions that we think are useful and can still be treated with reasonable cost.

The first extension is to treat literals that contain arithmetic only at top level, i.e., literals of the form $c_0 + \sum c_i p_i[x_1, \ldots, x_n] = 0$ or $c_0 + \sum c_i p_i[x_1, \ldots, x_n] \leq 0$, where the p_i are terms of $\mathcal{T}_E$. In Step 1, we take the multi-pattern $p_1, p_2, \ldots$ to find congruent terms with E-matching. In Step 2, the value of the literal under a substitution σ with congruent terms $t_i \sim p_i[x_1, \ldots, x_n]$ can then be determined as follows. For $\ell : c_0 + \sum c_i p_i[x_1, \ldots, x_n] \leq 0$, we check if there exist any bounds on the term $c_0 + \sum c_i t_i$. If the term has an upper bound $u \leq 0$, then $val_\sigma(\ell) = \mathtt{true}$, if it has a lower bound $l > 0$, then $val_\sigma(\ell) = \mathtt{false}$, and $val_\sigma(\ell) = \mathtt{unit}$ otherwise. For $\ell : c_0 + \sum c_i p_i[x_1, \ldots, x_n] = 0$, if $c_0 + \sum c_i t_i$ has an upper bound u and a lower bound l, and $u = l = 0$, then $val_\sigma(\ell) = \mathtt{true}$. If it has a lower bound $l > 0$ or an upper bound $u < 0$, then $val_\sigma(\ell) = \mathtt{false}$, and $val_\sigma(\ell) = \mathtt{unit}$ otherwise. Our solver is based on the Simplex algorithm described in [7]. It uses the bound refinement method described there to propagate bounds that are implied by the current state of the tableau. While this is inherently incomplete, it is fast and the bounds are refined incrementally.

Another important extension is to treat arithmetical literals such as $x < t$. These literals occur frequently when reasoning about arrays, and fall into the decidable array property fragment [2]. In principle, any substitution for x can be evaluated using upper and lower bounds as above, but we restrict the substitutions to consider as follows. For a clause C containing arithmetical literals and other literals of the types above, we first build the partial clause value table by evaluating the other literals as described before. Then for each variable x in C, we collect a set R_x of relevant terms as follows:

1. $R_x := R_x \cup \{t \mid \sigma(x) = t$ for σ with partial clause value $\mathtt{false}$ or $\mathtt{unit}\}$.
2. If the clause contains a literal $x < t$ or $t < x$, then $R_x := R_x \cup \{t\}$.
3. If the clause contains a literal $x = t$, then $R_x := R_x \cup \{t+1, t-1\}$.
4. If the clause contains $x < y$ or $y < x$, then $R_x := R_x \cup R_y$.

This is inspired by [8]. Given those sets, the substitutions we consider for an arithmetical literal ℓ of form $x < t$, $t < x$ or $x = t$ are $\{\sigma_\ell = \{x \mapsto t\} \mid t \in R_x\}$, and for $\ell : x < y$ they are $\{\sigma_\ell = \{x \mapsto t, y \mapsto t'\} \mid t \in R_x, t' \in R_y\}$.

5   Implementation and Experiments

We implemented the presented method in the SMT solver SMTINTERPOL.[2] SMTINTERPOL is a DPLL($\mathcal{T}$)/CDCL based solver that supports the ground

---

[2] https://ultimate.informatik.uni-freiburg.de/smtinterpol/

fragments of the theory of equality, the theory of linear integer arithmetic, linear rational arithmetic, mixed linear integer-rational arithmetic, the theory of arrays with extensionality and constant arrays, and their combinations.

We implemented the quantifier support as a theory solver in the DPLL($\mathcal{T}$) framework. The DPLL engine informs all theory solvers about the literals that are currently set to true. Before each decision, all theory solvers search for conflicts and unit clauses in a *checkpoint*. If a theory solvers returns a new unit clause, it can be used to propagate new literals and thus avoid wrong decisions. Similarly, a conflict clause allows to backtrack immediately without doing further decisions. When the DPLL engine has assigned a truth value to all literals, a *final check* is performed where the theory solvers should check their model.

The solver for quantified formulas keeps a list of all quantified clauses and creates instances of them on the fly. The quantifier solver has two different settings to determine when to create new clauses. In the eager setting, it creates new clauses in the checkpoint before each decision of the DPLL engine, in the lazy setting, it only creates new clauses in the final check when all existing ground literals were decided by the DPLL engine. When our method finds a conflicting or unit-propagating instance, this instance is built. If the instance is a conflict in the sense that all literals are already set to false, it is returned immediately. If the instantiation creates new terms and literals, it will cause other theory solvers, in particular the congruence closure solver, to propagate congruences and truth values for the new literals. As soon as all but one literal in the instance are propagated to false, our quantifier solver can give the instantiated clause to the DPLL engine as a unit clause.

If our E-matching based procedure does not find any conflict or unit clauses in the final check, our new quantifier solver has to do more extensive checks to determine if the formula is satisfied. It checks the instances created from the substitution set described in [8] for formulas in the almost uninterpreted fragment. To ensure completeness it tries substitutions on "older" terms first in order to enumerate the terms in a systematic way, similarly to [13]. In particular this means that substitution with terms that occur in the input formula are preferred over terms that are created by the quantifier solver itself during the solving process. For terms with the same age, the final check prefers instances that are unit-propagating (and that were not found earlier, because they create new terms that are not equivalent to existing terms). If no such instances are found, any instance that is not yet satisfied is created, preferring substitutions that do not create new terms. This allows the solver to return "satisfiable" for formulas within the almost uninterpreted fragment when it has checked that all instances resulting from these substitution are satisfied. In case a problem contains literals outside the almost uninterpreted fragment, the solver will never return "satisfiable", but "unknown" if it cannot derive a conflict.

We implemented E-matching to find substitutions as described in Step 1 in Sect. 4 to work in an incremental way, similar to [3]. For each quantified clause, we choose as multi-pattern the set of all sub-terms occurring in the clause, i.e., the instantiation only creates a new term if there is an equivalent existing term.

It uses triggers within the solver for the theory of equality, that report new terms for sub-patterns as they are merged into the relevant congruence class, and cause the matching process to continue only then. As soon as the multi-pattern is matched, the substitution is saved. Any substitution found by E-matching is kept until a conflict is detected and the DPLL engine backtracks to a point where the pattern no longer matches.

To efficiently implement the substitution tables, the literal value tables and the clause value tables, we use directed acyclic word graphs (DAWGs). These are useful to quickly combine a clause value table with the next literal value table, especially in the presence of columns with asterisks.

In order to evaluate the usefulness of our algorithm, we compare our implementation against E-matching based instantiation. We tested four different settings: The settings "conflict/unit-eager" and "conflict/unit-lazy" use the presented algorithm to search for conflicting and unit-propagating instances. Both settings do not create new terms (up to congruence) and always prefer conflicting instances over unit-propagating instances. As the names suggest, the setting "conflict/unit-eager" runs our algorithm as described above in the checkpoint. The setting "conflict/unit-lazy" runs our algorithm in the final check, i.e., after a complete ground model has been built. The settings "E-matching-eager" and "E-matching-lazy" use our implementation of the E-matching algorithm in a more traditional way. They use the same multi-pattern as our presented algorithm, and build all instances where the multi-pattern was matched. This means that no new terms (up to congruence) are built in these settings. As above, the setting "E-matching-eager" searches for instances in the checkpoint while "E-matching-lazy" searches for instances in the final check.

We did two experiments to evaluate these algorithms [9]. First, we ran them on all SMT-LIB benchmarks in the logic UF on an AMD Ryzen Threadripper 3970X 32-Core CPU with 3.7 GHz, using 8 cores in total, and 15 GB RAM given to the solver. We set the timeout to 24 s. Second, we ran the UF division with the settings used for the SMT-COMP 2020[3] on the StarExec cluster[4] [16], including the same benchmark selection and the same scrambler with the same seed. The only difference was that we reduced the timeout to 10 min (instead of 20 min). The SMT-COMP benchmarks omit all benchmarks that were solved by all solvers in less than one second in the previous years and randomly selected 40 % of the remaining benchmarks. We also ran the solvers CVC4 version 1.8 and Z3 version 4.8.8 on the SMT-COMP benchmarks with the default settings. The results are summarized in Tables 1 and 2.

Table 1 shows that the settings that produce only conflict/unit instances solve more benchmarks than the settings that produce all E-matching instances. The difference is even more pronounced on the SMT-COMP benchmark set where easy benchmarks were removed. The difference between eager and lazy settings is only small, but in our experiments eager was slightly better. This shows that the additional overhead from doing conflict search before each decision is more than

---

[3] https://smt-comp.github.io/2020/
[4] https://www.starexec.org

compensated by the reduced search space. The evaluation also shows that our solver is not yet competitive with CVC4 and Z3. The simple E-matching strategy that requires all subterms to exists and the simple enumeration of terms by age as fallback strategy is no match to the more fine-tuned and diverse strategies in CVC4 and Z3.

Table 1. Number of benchmarks solved for each solver setting, with 24 s timeout (on all UF benchmarks) and with 10 min timeout (on the SMT-COMP 2020 UF selection). The settings "c/u" use our presented method to produce only conflict and unit-propagating instances. The setting "eager" produces all E-matching instances before every decision, "lazy" only when all literals were decided.

Solver	Setting	UF(all) 24 s timeout	UF(SMT-COMP) 10 min timeout
SMTINTERPOL	c/u-eager	2120/7668	211/2291
SMTINTERPOL	c/u-lazy	2105/7668	207/2291
SMTINTERPOL	eager	2011/7668	165/2291
SMTINTERPOL	lazy	1998/7668	161/2291
CVC4	–		514/2291
Z3	–		408/2291

In Table 2 we compare the number of instances produced by SMTINTERPOL in the different settings and by CVC4 and Z3. The numbers were obtained by dumping the statistics after the run. To make the numbers comparable, we only consider those benchmarks from the SMT-COMP benchmark set where all solvers in all settings could prove unsatisfiability. For SMTINTERPOL we also count the number of instances that were used in the final proof of unsatisfiability. The first apparent result is that only a fraction of the instances were needed. This shows the importance of choosing the right instances. The settings that produce only conflict/unit-propagating instances save a lot of instances that were not needed in the proof of unsatisfiability. Interestingly, CVC4 creates even fewer instances. Note that CVC4 also uses conflict based instantiation techniques. One reason that it needs even fewer instances than our approach might be that our enumeration strategy in the final check needs longer to find the right instances. Another reason is that CVC4 does not split large quantified formulas into several clauses (and thus needs only one instance where we may need one instance for each produced clause). The solver Z3, which does not use conflict based instantiation techniques, produces many more instances. The average is exaggerated due to one benchmark where it produces more than 5.7 million instances, but the median is also higher than in our conflict/unit-propagating settings.

For SMTINTERPOL we distinguish instances created by E-matching or by conflict/unit-propagation from instances created by the final enumeration step. This is depicted in the table as 588(230+358) denoting that 230 instances were

Table 2. Average and median number of instances created by the solvers on SMT-COMP 2020 benchmarks. For SMTINTERPOL also the average number of instances used in the proof of unsatisfiability is given. This statistic was generated for the 86 benchmarks that every solver could solve.

Solver	Setting	Avg. created instances	Median created instances	Avg. used instances
SMTINTERPOL	c/u-eager	588(230 + 358)	56	8(3 + 5)
SMTINTERPOL	c/u-lazy	545(195 + 351)	56	8(3 + 5)
SMTINTERPOL	eager	1455(1121 + 333)	195	8(3 + 5)
SMTINTERPOL	lazy	1450(1123 + 327)	217	8(3 + 5)
CVC4	–	216	14	?
Z3	–	83186	129	?

created by conflict/unit-propagation and 358 by the final enumeration. The results show that several necessary instances can only be found by enumeration, because they need to create new terms that are not equivalent to existing terms.

6   Related Work

Closest related to the presented approach is the work of Reynolds et al. [15]. The authors present a method to find conflicting substitutions for the theory of equality and show the effectiveness of their approach. For a quantified formula, they construct a set of equalities and disequalities such that a solution for the constraints in this set yields a conflicting substitution. While our method works only on clauses, their method works on general quantified formulas. The classification is done implicitly while constructing those constraint sets, but avoids introducing auxiliary functions. Some of the constructed equality constraints represent the problem of matching subterms of more complicated non-ground terms, but the algorithm does not use E-matching. The types of literals that pose a problem to our approach (i.e., congruences without congruent existing terms) cannot be detected by their method either. The authors also describe how the method can be used to find so-called constraint-inducing substitutions that produce instances that are not conflicting, but that can derive new information about existing terms. This is similar to our search for unit-propagating instances, but does not allow to find propagations on new terms. The main difference is that our approach is incremental and can therefore detect conflicting and unit-propagating instances early in the solving process.

Congruence closure with free variable (CCFV) [1] is a calculus for solving the so-called E-ground (dis)unification problem. Given a ground model, it tries to build a substitution for a quantified formula such that the ground model satisfies the corresponding instance, by decomposing the goal into smaller constraints. It can also be used to search for a conflicting substitution and can find all conflicting substitutions for the theory of equality, if the congruence closure propagates all disequalities. The method is not incremental, i.e., it needs to rerun completely if an equality or disequality literal is added.

A completely different approach to derive new facts from quantified clauses is the DPLL(Γ) calculus [4]. This approach combines the superposition calculus tightly with the DPLL($\mathcal{T}$) framework. Literals decided by the DPLL engine are used in the superposition solver to derive new quantified clauses. When the superposition solver finds a conflict, it can build by collecting all ground equalities used to derive the conflict. DPLL(Γ) can also propagate new ground literals using quantified clauses. While the approach is much more powerful and can even detect conflicts involving several clauses, this comes at the price of memory overhead. The superposition solver can propagate an arbitrary number of derived clauses when searching for conflicts. This is in contrast to the DPLL($\mathcal{T}$) framework where only a detected conflict triggers learning a new clause.

7   Conclusion and Future Work

We presented a new approach to find conflicting and unit-propagating instances of quantified formulas. The basic idea is to split this search in a part that searches for ground terms that are congruent to the quantified terms in a clause, and then evaluate the instances with the use of these terms before creating them. For the first part, we use E-matching, which can be implemented in an incremental way and avoids duplicating work when the E-graph changes. The evaluation can be done per literal such that the method can also detect instances that propagate literals on both known and new terms. The presented method has been implemented in the SMT solver SMTINTERPOL. We showed that by only producing conflicting and unit-propagating instances we can solve more benchmarks than by producing all instances found by E-matching. We also showed that the overhead to find these conflicting instances is small enough to run it in an eager setting before every decision. Therefore, we can tightly integrate quantifier reasoning in the DPLL($\mathcal{T}$) framework. We believe that the method can easily be implemented into other solvers using E-matching based instantiation, since E-matching can already report the equivalent terms needed for evaluating instances.

We also presented some extensions to the theory of linear arithmetic, and plan to extend the method further. For instance, with a solver for the theory of equality that supports *offset equalities* [6], literals such as $f(x) = g(x + 1)$ can easily be evaluated as described in Sect. 4.

The method is incomplete and must be complemented with a method that checks the model once all literals are assigned a truth value by the DPLL engine. This complementary method can have a strong influence on our presented method, in particular, if it creates many new terms. We plan to implement a version of model-based quantifier instantiation [8] in the future.

We also plan to implement a version of our method that does not create new literals for conflicting instances at all. Instead of creating the conflicting instance, it creates the clause with the existing equivalent literals enriched by the equality literals from the E-graph that were needed to prove the equivalence. Currently the quantifier solver has to wait for the congruence closure to prove that the conflicting instance is a conflict clause. We also expect that this approach keeps the E-graph small by not creating many congruent terms.

References

1. Barbosa, H., Fontaine, P., Reynolds, A.: Congruence closure with free variables. In: Legay, A., Margaria, T. (eds.) TACAS 2017, Part II. LNCS, vol. 10206, pp. 214–230. Springer, Heidelberg (2017). https://doi.org/10.1007/978-3-662-54580-5_13
2. Bradley, A.R., Manna, Z., Sipma, H.B.: What's decidable about arrays? In: Emerson, E.A., Namjoshi, K.S. (eds.) VMCAI 2006. LNCS, vol. 3855, pp. 427–442. Springer, Heidelberg (2005). https://doi.org/10.1007/11609773_28
3. de Moura, L., Bjørner, N.: Efficient E-matching for SMT solvers. In: Pfenning, F. (ed.) CADE 2007. LNCS (LNAI), vol. 4603, pp. 183–198. Springer, Heidelberg (2007). https://doi.org/10.1007/978-3-540-73595-3_13
4. de Moura, L., Bjørner, N.: Engineering DPLL(T) + Saturation. In: Armando, A., Baumgartner, P., Dowek, G. (eds.) IJCAR 2008. LNCS (LNAI), vol. 5195, pp. 475–490. Springer, Heidelberg (2008). https://doi.org/10.1007/978-3-540-71070-7_40
5. Detlefs, D., Nelson, G., Saxe, J.B.: Simplify: a theorem prover for program checking. J. ACM 52(3), 365–473 (2005)
6. Dutertre, B., de Moura, L.: The Yices SMT solver. Technical report, SRI International (2006). https://yices.csl.sri.com/papers/tool-paper.pdf
7. Dutertre, B., de Moura, L.: A fast linear-arithmetic solver for DPLL(T). In: Ball, T., Jones, R.B. (eds.) CAV 2006. LNCS, vol. 4144, pp. 81–94. Springer, Heidelberg (2006). https://doi.org/10.1007/11817963_11
8. Ge, Y., de Moura, L.: Complete instantiation for quantified formulas in satisfiability modulo theories. In: Bouajjani, A., Maler, O. (eds.) CAV 2009. LNCS, vol. 5643, pp. 306–320. Springer, Heidelberg (2009). https://doi.org/10.1007/978-3-642-02658-4_25
9. Hoenicke, J., Schindler, T.: Artifacts for incremental search for conflict and unit instances of quantified formulas with E-matching. Technical report, Zenodo (2021). https://doi.org/10.5281/zenodo.4277777
10. Nelson, G., Oppen, D.C.: Fast decision procedures based on congruence closure. J. ACM 27(2), 356–364 (1980)
11. Nieuwenhuis, R., Oliveras, A., Tinelli, C.: Solving SAT and SAT modulo theories: from an abstract Davis-Putnam-Logemann-Loveland procedure to DPLL(T). J. ACM 53(6), 937–977 (2006)
12. Nonnengart, A., Weidenbach, C.: Computing small clause normal forms. In: Robinson, J.A., Voronkov, A. (eds.) Handbook of Automated Reasoning (in 2 volumes), pp. 335–367. Elsevier and MIT Press, New York (2001)
13. Reynolds, A., Barbosa, H., Fontaine, P.: Revisiting enumerative instantiation. In: Beyer, D., Huisman, M. (eds.) TACAS 2018, Part II. LNCS, vol. 10806, pp. 112–131. Springer, Cham (2018). https://doi.org/10.1007/978-3-319-89963-3_7
14. Reynolds, A., King, T., Kuncak, V.: Solving quantified linear arithmetic by counterexample-guided instantiation. Form. Methods Syst. Des. 51(3), 500–532 (2017). https://doi.org/10.1007/s10703-017-0290-y

15. Reynolds, A., Tinelli, C., de Moura, L.M.: Finding conflicting instances of quantified formulas in SMT. In: Formal Methods in Computer-Aided Design, FMCAD 2014, Lausanne, Switzerland, 21–24 October 2014, pp. 195–202. IEEE (2014)
16. Stump, A., Sutcliffe, G., Tinelli, C.: StarExec: a cross-community infrastructure for logic solving. In: Demri, S., Kapur, D., Weidenbach, C. (eds.) IJCAR 2014. LNCS (LNAI), vol. 8562, pp. 367–373. Springer, Cham (2014). https://doi.org/10. 1007/978-3-319-08587-6_28

On Preprocessing
for Weighted MaxSAT

Tobias Paxian$^{(\boxtimes)}$, Pascal Raiola, and Bernd Becker

Albert-Ludwigs-Universität Freiburg,
Georges-Köhler-Allee 051, 79110 Freiburg im Breisgau, Germany
{paxiant,raiolap,becker}@informatik.uni-freiburg.de

Abstract. Modern competitive solvers employ various preprocessing techniques to efficiently tackle complex problems. This work introduces two preprocessing techniques to improve solving weighted partial MaxSAT problems: *Generalized Boolean Multilevel Optimization (GBMO)* and *Trimming MaxSAT (TrimMaxSAT)*.

GBMO refines and extends Boolean Multilevel Optimization (BMO), thereby splitting instances due to their distribution of weights into multiple less complex subproblems, which are solved one after the other to obtain the overall solution.

The second technique, TrimMaxSAT, finds unsatisfiable soft clauses and removes them from the instance. This reduces the complexity of the MaxSAT instance and works especially well in combination with GBMO. The proposed algorithm works incrementally in a binary search fashion, testing the satisfiability of every soft clause. Furthermore, as a by-product, typically an initial weight close to the maximum is found, which is in turn advantageous w.r.t. the size of e.g. the Dynamic Polynomial Watchdog (DPW) encoding.

Both techniques can be used by all MaxSAT solvers, though our focus lies on Pseudo Boolean constraint based MaxSAT solvers. Experimental results show the effectiveness of both techniques on a large set of benchmarks from a hardware security application and from the 2019 MaxSAT Evaluation. In particular for the hardest of the application benchmarks, the solver Pacose with GBMO and TrimMaxSAT performs best compared to the MaxSAT Evaluation solvers of 2019. For the benchmarks of the 2019 MaxSAT Evaluation, we show that with the proposed techniques the top solver combination solves significantly more instances.

1 Introduction

Preprocessing techniques play an increasingly important role in recent competitions for SAT, (D)QBF and MaxSAT [17,21,34]. Typically, time-intensive preprocessing techniques pay off with increasing problem complexity.

Almost all solvers of the MaxSAT Evaluation of 2019 use preprocessing techniques [10], e.g. stratification, at-most-one relations between soft clauses as well

This work is supported by DFG project "Algebraic Fault Attacks" (BE 1176/20-2).

F. Henglein et al. (Eds.): VMCAI 2021, LNCS 12597, pp. 556–577, 2021.
https://doi.org/10.1007/978-3-030-67067-2_25

as approaches based on Boolean Multilevel Optimization and many additional SAT based preprocessing techniques. There is even a stand-alone MaxSAT preprocessor, MaxPre [21].

Multi-Objective Combinatorial Optimization (MOCO) [15,16,32] problems are addressing multiple optimization problems with possibly conflicting purposes. Boolean Multilevel Optimization (BMO) [7,23] is the mapping of MOCO to MaxSAT solving.

This paper introduces *Generalized Boolean Multilevel Optimization (GBMO)*, which provides extended capabilities to split MaxSAT instances into subproblems with less soft clauses. These smaller instances are processed subsequently starting with the largest weights. We thereby reduce the complexity of the overall solving by solving multiple smaller subproblems.

The second technique, *TrimMaxSAT* uses similar techniques as backbone computing cf. [19,24,29], which is typically introduced as a search for all variables with an identical truth assignment in all solutions. In contrast to backbone computing we are looking only for the unsatisfiable core of soft clauses and instead of variables we are looking for always unsatisfiable soft clauses. Additionally, TrimMaxSAT finds a lower bound of the solution to the MaxSAT problem. The encoding size of Pseudo Boolean (PB) constraint based encodings like the Dynamic Polynomial Watchdog (DPW) [26] encoding can be significantly reduced if less soft clauses are used or the lower bound is closer to the MaxSAT solution.

The general workflow of the preprocessing techniques is illustrated in Fig. 1. At first, the list of weights is split into n sublists, with decreasing weight sizes, with sublist n containing the highest weights and sublist 1 the lowest. Then, the subproblems are processed subsequently starting with the highest weights. First, the soft clause set is reduced and the MaxSAT solver is called. After a solution to the subproblem is found, the solution is encoded with a PB-constraint and added to the hard clauses of the next MaxSAT problem, given by the instance with the next highest weights. At the end the result is printed.

In general, MaxSAT solvers follow different approaches with benefits on different kind of benchmarks. Approaches to solve MaxSAT, together with representative solvers are: PB-constraint based encoding (e.g. Pacose [27], QMaxSAT [22]), Branch-and-Bound (e.g. ahmaxsat [2]); UNSAT Core (RC2 [18], Maxino [3] and UWrMaxSAT [28]); Hitting Set (MaxHS [9]). This work focuses on PB-constraint based solvers, as we also use a PB-constraint encoding for the splitting technique (cf. Sect. 3). Nonetheless, the introduced splitting technique can also be used for non-PB-constraint based MaxSAT solvers. Furthermore, the proposed trimming technique (cf. Sect. 4) is especially useful for PB-constraint based solvers, reducing the size of the added encoding.

GBMO and TrimMaxSAT, the two preprocessing techniques introduced in this paper, reduce the size of the added encoding per solver call, especially for PB-constraint based solvers, and thus increase the feasibility.

This work evaluates solvers and benchmarks of the MaxSAT Evaluation 2019 and additional benchmarks from a hardware security application [30,31], where a collection of weighted partial MaxSAT instances was generated. These instances were chosen for the 2020 MaxSAT Evaluation [1]. In particular, this set contained several large instances with more than 1.2 million soft clauses, which are among the largest in comparison to instances from the MaxSAT Evaluations. These large instances are not feasibly solvable for most of the MaxSAT solvers of the Evaluation 2019, including our own MaxSAT solver Pacose [27]. In particular, our solver Pacose performs worst without the proposed techniques GBMO and TrimMaxSAT and best with them. For the Evaluation benchmark set, we show that all PB-constraint based solvers profit from GBMO and TrimMaxSAT.

We additionally investigate the top solver combination, where n solvers are run subsequently with a reduced timeout of $3600/n$ seconds each. In the last years (2017–2020), the top solver combination was always achieved for $n = 3$ and clearly outperformed the top solver. The top solver combination always included a PB-constraint based solver, which highlights the importance of investigating PB-constraint based solvers.

In this paper we tested our techniques on the benchmarks of the MaxSAT Evaluation 2019, where we were able to improve the top solver combination significantly, decreasing the distance to the Virtual Best Solver by 39%.

The remainder of the paper is structured as follows. In the next section preliminaries like SAT, weighted partial MaxSAT and Boolean Multilevel Optimization are introduced. In Sect. 3 the splitting algorithm GBMO is presented, and in Sect. 4 we describe TrimMaxSAT, our preprocessing technique to trim the MaxSAT instance. In Sect. 5 experimental results are provided. The paper concludes with Sect. 6.

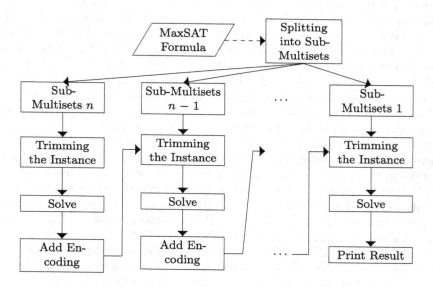

Fig. 1. General workflow of the combined preprocessing techniques.

2 Preliminaries

In this section we introduce the basic terminologies which will be used within this paper. We start with the foundations of SAT, MaxSAT and Pseudo Boolean (PB) Constraint based solvers, then we explain Boolean Multilevel Optimization (BMO) as introduced in [5,7,23].

2.1 SAT and MaxSAT

Boolean logic formulas are defined over a finite set of *Boolean variables* $x_1, \cdots x_n$ which can be assigned either *false* or *true*. A *literal* is either a Boolean variable x_i or its negation $\overline{x}_i$. Boolean formulas as used in this paper are given in *Conjunctive Normal Form (CNF)*. A CNF consists of conjunctions of *clauses*, which are disjunctions of *literals*. A *unit* clause contains only one literal. We use the notation that a CNF is a set of clauses. The satisfiability problem is solved by a *SAT solver*, which decides whether a Boolean formula φ given as CNF is satisfiable, i.e. whether there exists an assignment to the variables such that each clause of φ evaluates to *true*. If this is the case, a satisfying assignment, called *model* of φ is returned. *Incremental SAT solving* is an important technique used in modern SAT solvers, for growing formulas between iterative SAT solver calls. Thereby information collected about the formulas from previous solver calls is maintained and used in the subsequent solver calls.

MaxSAT is an optimization problem closely related to SAT, seeking for a *maximized* number of satisfied clauses. If we deal with *partial* MaxSAT, then the formula consists of two types of clauses: *soft* clauses $\mathbb{S} = \{s_1, \ldots s_m\}$ and *hard* clauses $\mathbb{H}$. For an optimal solution the number of satisfied soft clauses in $\mathbb{S}$ needs to be maximized, whereas all hard clauses in $\mathbb{H}$ have to be satisfied.

In the following we use *multisets*; in contrast to sets, multisets may contain multiple instances of the same element. We denote multisets with index M. For example if there are two soft clauses of weight 2, we write:

- $\{2,2\}_M$ for the respective multiset (used for GBMO) and
- $\{2\}$ for the regular set (used for classical BMO).

Weighted partial MaxSAT is another extension adding a multiset of positive integer weights $W = \{w_1, \ldots, w_m\}_M$ to the soft clauses, with w_i corresponding to s_i. The optimization goal is then to maximize the sum of weights for the satisfied soft clauses.

For brevity, in this paper MaxSAT is used as abbreviation for weighted partial MaxSAT, if not stated differently. For the sum of a multiset of weights W and any property $p : W \to \{true, false\}$ the following notations are used.

$$\sum W := \sum_{w \in W} w \text{ and } \sum_{p(w)} W := \sum_{w \in W \text{ and } p(w)=true} w \qquad (1)$$

When the set of hard clauses $\mathbb{H}$ is clear from context, for brevity we use the expression *MaxSAT(W_A)* to describe a MaxSAT solver call for the set of hard clauses $\mathbb{H}$ together with the soft clauses $S_A \subseteq \mathbb{S}$, in which the soft clauses correspond to the weights of the multiset W_A.

As already mentioned in the introduction, for the purpose of this paper PB-constraint based solvers, which use an iterative SAT based approach [36] as e.g. QMaxSAT and Pacose, are of special importance. In each incremental SAT solving call they force a higher weight to be satisfied as minimum. To do so, a *Pseudo-Boolean (PB) constraint* C of the form $\Sigma_j w_j \cdot r_j \geq M$, with Boolean variables r_j and positive integers w_j and M, is directly encoded into CNF. The soft clauses are directly connected to the PB-constraint network: r_j is true iff the soft clause $s_j \in \mathbb{S}$ is true. Naturally, w_j is the weight belonging to r_j and s_j. The MaxSAT problem can then be reduced to find a maximum value for M, such that C is still satisfied. More information on PB-constraints is e.g. found in [14]. For more information on the so-called relaxation literals r_j we refer to [27].

There are various methods and schemes for the encoding of PB-constraints. State-of-the-art iterative MaxSAT solvers use various and customized CNF encodings. For instance, the 2017 version of QMaxSAT [22] employs three different encodings: totalizer network [11], modulo totalizer network [25] and Warners adder network [33]. The 2018/2019 version only uses the mixed radix weighted totalizer [35]. Pacose uses the encodings Warners adder network [33] and Dynamic Polynomial Watchdog (DPW) [26].

PB-constraint based MaxSAT solvers have shown to be competitive in recent MaxSAT competitions[1]. As described in the introduction, the last years' (2017–2020) top solver combination always included a PB-constraint based solver. Still, large instances can be especially challenging for PB-constraint based solvers, therefore this work comprises a two-folded contribution to handle this issue.

2.2 Boolean Multilevel Optimization (BMO)

Boolean Multilevel Optimization problems address multiple objective functions with possibly conflicting goals. There are many works on solving multi-objective combinatorial optimization (MOCO) problems [15,16,32], of which the Boolean based formulation is BMO [5,7,23]. It is studied e.g. extensively in [23], which also introduces two extensions: BMO with upper bounds and partial BMO. BMO is introduced as an instance of Weighted MaxSAT with the following conditions: The instance consists of sets of clauses $C_1, C_2, \ldots, C_m$, where each set C_i contains exactly the clauses of one weight w_i. The sets are built and sorted in decreasing order due to their weight. For a BMO instance the following condition has to hold:

Definition 1 (Complete BMO). *An instance of Weighted MaxSAT is an instance of (complete) BMO iff:*

$$w_i > \sum_{1 \leq j < i} w_j \cdot |C_j| \ for \ i = 2, \ldots, m$$

---

[1] QMaxSAT 2nd solver 2017 and Pacose 3rd solver 2018, same number of solved instances as 2nd MaxHS.

If a MaxSAT instance was found to be a BMO instance, this information can be used to (amongst others) speed up the solving process. BMO techniques can be used with multiple different MaxSAT approaches, for example with UNSAT core based solvers, avoiding additional refinement steps and with PB-constraint based MaxSAT solvers, adding an encoding which guarantees the lower weight, as will be described later in further detail.

In our paper we describe in Sect. 3 a generalization of complete BMO and show on MaxSAT Benchmarks that this addition is useful.

Stratification [4, 6] is another related possibility of splitting the weight set. It restricts the set of clauses, sent to the SAT solver, at first to higher weights. As a result, unsatisfiability core based solvers tend to increase the resulting weight faster. However, this is not suited for PB-constraint based MaxSAT solvers and has other splitting rules. Therefore stratification is not discussed in further detail.

3   Generalized Boolean Multilevel Optimization (GBMO)

In this section we first (Sect. 3.1) define GBMO and prove that it can be used to split a given MaxSAT problem into smaller MaxSAT subproblems, which can be solved subsequently, also in cases where BMO is not applicable.

As an example, assuming each weight corresponds to one soft clause, with the original problem definition the weight combination $\{1, 1, 2, 2, 4, 14\}_M$ could not be split into subproblems as BMO only splits into subproblems with soft clauses of the same weight. With GBMO the multiset can be split into the subsets $\{1, 1\}_M$ $\{2, 2, 4\}_M$ $\{14\}_M$ and solved subsequently.

The proposed algorithm for performing the splitting is presented in Sect. 3.3 and uses a sufficient criterion, which is presented in Sect. 3.2.

3.1   GBMO – Definition and Correctness

Consider a MaxSAT problem, with an increasingly sorted multiset of weights of soft clauses. Then a *separation point* splits the multiset into a *left* multiset and a *right* multiset, if the sum of weights of the *left* multiset is non-strictly lower than any positive difference between the sums of any two subsets of the *right* multiset. This difference can equal the lowest weight of the right multiset (cf. Remark 1a).

We claim that with these generalized conditions an optimal solution to the original problem can be found by separately solving at first the *right* multiset and then solving a combination of the *left* multiset and an encoding ensuring the maximum found with the previous solving (of the *right* multiset).

Definition 2 (Generalized complete BMO (GBMO)). *Given a MaxSAT problem with weights W, with two partitions $W_L, W_R \subseteq W$. We say that W is separable and can be split into W_L and W_R, iff:*

- $\forall W_{R_1}, W_{R_2} \subseteq W_R$ with $\sum W_{R_1} > \sum W_{R_2}$:

$$\sum W_L \leq \sum W_{R_1} - \sum W_{R_2} \qquad (2)$$

We then say, that there is a splitting point *between W_L and W_R.*

Proposition 1. *Definition 2 generalizes complete BMO – formally: For every complete BMO instance as in Definition 1 with clause sets $C_1, \ldots, C_m$, corresponding weights $w_1, \ldots, w_m$ and the multiset W is defined to contain exactly one weight for each soft clause:*

For every i with $1 \le i < m$, there is a splitting point between the multisets $W_L = \{w \in W \mid w \le w_i\}_M$ and $W_R = \{w \in W \mid w > w_i\}_M$.

Proof. Given a BMO instance as in Definition 1 and define W_L and W_R as above. To prove that Definition 2 holds, multisets $W_{R_1}, W_{R_2} \subseteq W_R$ with $\sum W_{R_1} > \sum W_{R_2}$ are arbitrarily chosen.

Let k be chosen maximal (i.e. the highest weight w_k), such that

$$\{w \in W_{R_1} \mid w = w_k\}_M \ne \{w \in W_{R_2} \mid w = w_k\}_M$$

Then

$$\left| \sum_{w > w_k} W_{R_1} - \sum_{w > w_k} W_{R_2} \right| = 0$$

from which follows that

$$\left| \sum W_{R_1} - \sum W_{R_2} \right| = \left| \sum_{w = w_k} W_{R_1} - \sum_{w = w_k} W_{R_2} + \sum_{w < w_k} W_{R_1} - \sum_{w < w_k} W_{R_2} \right|$$

From the reverse triangle inequality ($\forall a, b \in \mathbb{R} : |a + b| \ge | \, |a| - |b| \, |$), it follows:

$$\left| \sum W_{R_1} - \sum W_{R_2} \right| \ge \left| \sum_{w = w_k} W_{R_1} - \sum_{w = w_k} W_{R_2} \right| - \left| \sum_{w < w_k} W_{R_1} - \sum_{w < w_k} W_{R_2} \right| \tag{3}$$

By choice of k:

$$\left| \sum_{w = w_k} W_{R_1} - \sum_{w = w_k} W_{R_2} \right| \ge w_k \tag{4}$$

Using $W_{R_1}, W_{R_2} \subseteq W_R$, the difference for weights $< w_k$ can be estimated:

$$\left| \sum_{w < w_k} W_{R_1} - \sum_{w < w_k} W_{R_2} \right| \le \sum_{w < w_k} W_R = \sum_{i < j < k} w_j \cdot |C_j|. \tag{5}$$

Inserting Eqs. 4 and 5 into Eq. 3 leads (with $\sum W_{R_1} > \sum W_{R_2}$) to:

$$\sum W_{R_1} - \sum W_{R_2} \ge w_k - \sum_{i < j < k} w_j \cdot |C_j| \tag{6}$$

By the Definition of a BMO instance, it also holds that

$$w_k > \sum_{1 \leq j < k} w_j \cdot |C_j| \tag{7}$$

After substituting w_k according to Eq. 7 in Eq. 6:

$$\sum W_{R_1} - \sum W_{R_2} > \sum_{1 \leq j < k} w_j \cdot |C_j| - \sum_{i < j < k} w_j \cdot |C_j| = \sum_{1 \leq j \leq i} w_j \cdot |C_j| = \sum W_L$$

proving that the criterion from Definition 2 holds. □

Remark 1. a. If $\sum W_L \leq \min(W_R)$ holds, we say that there is a *potential* splitting point between W_L and W_R. $\sum W_L \leq \min(W_R)$ follows from Eq. 2 for $W_{R_1} = \{\min(W_R)\}$ and $W_{R_2} = \emptyset$.

b. In Definition 2 it is sufficient to test Eq. 2 for disjoint W_{R_1} and W_{R_2}, since for every two non-disjoint subsets W'_{R_1} and W'_{R_2}, there exist the two disjoint subsets $W'_{R_1} \setminus (W'_{R_1} \cap W'_{R_2})$ and $W'_{R_2} \setminus (W'_{R_1} \cap W'_{R_2})$ with the same difference of their sums of weights.

c. While Definition 2 presents a general criterion for separability, the generality can lead in practice to trivial splitting points, in total hindering efficiency. To avoid splitting at such trivial splitting points, in the experiments we do not investigate splitting points where $W_L = \{1\}$ and $W_R = \{1, \dots\}$.

d. If for at least one pair W_{R_1} and W_{R_2}, it holds that $\sum W_L = \sum W_{R_1} - \sum W_{R_2}$, then it is only guaranteed that there is *an* optimal solution; not *every* optimal solution can be found, as some solutions might be blocked by adding an encoding for the optimal solution of W_R.

E.g. a MaxSAT problem with $W = \{1, 1, 2\}_M$ is separated into $W_L = \{1, 1\}_M$ and $W_R = \{2\}_M$, where the soft clauses associated with W_L are the unit clauses x_1 and the soft clause associated with W_R is the unit clause $\neg x_1$. If at first W_R is solved, the optimal solution assignment $x_1 = 0$ is found, but the other optimal solution assignment $x_1 = 1$ cannot be found.

Given a GBMO MaxSAT problem with a separable multiset of weights W as in Definition 2, we show in the following, that the optimal solution of the MaxSAT problem can be found by solving at first *MaxSAT(W_R)*, then fixing the found maximal weight and solving *MaxSAT(W_L)*.

Theorem 1. *Given a MaxSAT problem with a multiset of weights W, where W can be split into W_L and W_R as in Definition 2. Let W_R^* be a solution to MaxSAT(W_R).*

Then W_R^* can be used to find an optimal solution W^* to the initial MaxSAT problem, where also on the sub-multiset W_R, soft clauses with the same sum of weights are satisfied by both W_R^* and W^*, formally:

$$\exists W^* : \quad \sum W_R^* = \sum W_R \cap W^*$$

Remark 2. It is important to note, that the condition for a *potential* splitting point ($\sum W_L \leq \min(W_R)$) is not sufficient for separately solving the sub-multiset problems: As an example assume a weight multiset $\{50, 101, 102\}_M$ with a maximum weight of $50 + 101 = 151$ for the optimal solution. Even though for $W_L = \{50\}$ and $W_R = \{101, 102\}$ the condition $\sum W_L \leq \min(W_R)$ holds, solving *MaxSAT(W_R)* could lead to the solution 102. Since the soft clause of weight 102 cannot be satisfied together with the soft clause of weight 50, the solution would be falsely calculated to be of weight 102.

Proof (Proof of Theorem 1).

1. $\forall W^* : \sum W_R^* \geq \sum (W_R \cap W^*)$: Follows from the optimality of W_R^*.
2. $\exists W^* : \sum W_R^* \leq \sum (W_R \cap W^*)$ by Contradiction:
   Assume $\forall W^* : \sum W_R^* > \sum (W_R \cap W^*)$, then W_R^* is not an optimal solution (i.e. a candidate for W^*). Thus, for any optimal solution W^*: $\sum W^* > \sum W_R^*$. Also, because of Definition 2, Formula 2, the following holds:

$$\sum W_L \leq \sum W_R^* - \sum W_R \cap W^* \tag{8}$$

Additionally because $W \setminus W_R = W_L$ it holds that:

$$\sum W^* \leq \sum W_R \cap W^* + \sum W_L$$

All inequalities concatenated lead to a contradiction:

$$\sum W^* \leq \sum W_R \cap W^* + \sum W_L \overset{Eq.\,8}{\leq} \sum W_R^* < \sum W^*$$

$$\square$$

This shows that it is valid to solve the sub-multisets subsequently. The algorithm for the application of GBMO extracts at first all *potential* splitting points. Then, the main argument $\sum W_L \leq \sum W_{R_1} - \sum W_{R_2}$ has to be shown. Since any multiset W_R contains $2^{|W_R|}$ sub-multisets, the runtime to calculate $\sum W_L \leq \sum W_{R_1} - \sum W_{R_2}$ for all combinations of sub-multisets lies in $\mathcal{O}(2^{|W_R|})$ and tends to be infeasible for non-trivial W_R. Therefore we propose in Sect. 3.2 an efficiently computable necessary criterion, with which all of the potential non-trivial (cf. Remark 1.c) splitting points were found in the experiments.

3.2   Greatest Common Divisor

Many instances from the MaxSAT Evaluation and our hardware security application show certain patterns. Often, when iterating through a sorted multiset of weights W of a MaxSAT instance, the first weight of the next sub-multiset is the greatest common divisor (gcd) of all higher weights. It is noted, that the gcd of n integers can be calculated in only linear time [13]. The next theorem shows a sufficient condition for splitting the weight multiset W using the gcd. This easy-to-calculate sufficient condition will later be used for a test on a set of *potential* splitting points. Thus, we efficiently find several *actual* splitting points, so that the elaborate check of Definition 2 will only be performed on fewer *potential* splitting points.

Theorem 2. *Given a MaxSAT problem with weights W with two partitions $W_L, W_R \subseteq W$. Let g be the greatest common divisor of all weights in W_R and $\sum W_L \leq g$. Then W can be split into W_L and W_R.*

Proof. Given sub-multisets $W_{R_1}, W_{R_2} \subseteq W_R$ with $\sum W_{R_1} > \sum W_{R_2}$, it is to show, that the following equation holds (cf. Theorem 1):

$$\sum W_L \leq \sum W_{R_1} - \sum W_{R_2}.$$

For W_{R_1} and W_{R_2} there exist $k_1, k_2 \in \mathbb{N}$, so that $\sum W_{R_1} = k_1 \cdot g$ and $\sum W_{R_2} = k_2 \cdot g$. Thus:

$$\sum W_{R_1} - \sum W_{R_2} = k_1 \cdot g - k_2 \cdot g = (k_1 - k_2) \cdot g$$

Since $\sum W_{R_1} > \sum W_{R_2}$, it holds that $(k_1 - k_2) > 0$. Therefore:

$$(k_1 - k_2) \cdot g \geq g \geq \sum W_L$$

$\square$

Remark 3. For a MaxSAT problem as in Theorem 2, W_R^* can be calculated by dividing all weights of W_R through g and solving the problem with these smaller weights, leading potentially to a reduced encoding size.

3.3   Algorithm

The full algorithm works as follows:

1. Iterate over the sorted weights $\{w_1, \ldots, w_m\}_M$, from lowest weight w_1 to highest weight w_m. For each weight w_i the sum $w_i^{sum} = \sum_{j=1}^{i} w_j$ is calculated, building the multiset $W^{sum} = \{w_1^{sum}, \ldots, w_m^{sum}\}_M$.
2. Declare a *potential* splitting point if the sum of weights until that point is smaller than the next weight.
3. Iterate through all potential splitting points and check if it is an actual splitting point according to Theorem 2. If so, it is removed from the multiset of potential splitting points. If not, we have to check with the elaborate criterion in the next step.
4. Iterate again through the sub-multisets and check if the remaining potential splitting points fulfill the criteria from Definition 2. Due to the high cost, this only checks 10 million sub-multisets before aborting. If successful, an actual splitting point is found.
5. Start the solver call $MaxSAT(W_X)$ with W_X being the multiset with the highest weights, among all weight sub-multisets that have not been solved yet.

6. If there is another sub-multiset which has not been solved yet, take the soft clauses and the maximal weight solution from the previous MaxSAT call, generate a PB-constraint encoding out of these parameters and add these clauses to the set of hard clauses $\mathbb{H}$, then continue with Step 5. If all sub-multisets are processed continue with Step 7.

7. Iterate over all soft clauses W, check if they are satisfied in the model of the last MaxSAT solver call, accumulate the weights w_j of all satisfied soft clauses s_j and print the solution together with the model of the last MaxSAT solver call.

The splitting together with the approximation algorithm of Sect. 4 is visualized in Fig. 1 (p. 3). In the following, an example execution of the above described algorithm is explained in further depth.

Example 1. Given a multiset with 9 soft clauses, and sorted weights $W = \{w_1, \ldots, w_9\}_M = \{1, 1, 2, 5, 9, 14, 35, 35, 70\}_M$. Then the algorithm builds $W^{sum} = \{1, 2, 4, 9, 18, 32, 67, 102, 172\}_M$. Potential splitting points (Step 2) after w_3 and w_6 can be found, as $w_3^{sum} \leq w_4$ and $w_6^{sum} \leq w_7$. Criterion (Step 3): For the sub-multiset $\{w_4 - w_9\}_M$ the gcd is $1 < w_3^{sum}$ and thus not valid. For the third sub-multiset $\{w_7 - w_9\}_M$ the gcd is $35 > 32 = w_6^{sum}$ and thus a splitting point. Then for (Step 4) the algorithm builds the sum of each weight combinations of multiset $\{w_4 - w_6\}_M$, resulting in $Sums = \{0, 5, 9, 14, 19, 23, 28\}_M$. The minimal distance of two weight sums is $9 - 5 = 4$, thus we have a valid splitting point. Note that with weight 16 instead of 14 in the initial multiset W, this would not be an actual splitting point.

The three sub-multisets are then solved subsequently, starting with the highest weights. The solver call is $MaxSAT(w_7, w_8, w_9)$, followed by adding a PB encoding, which guarantees the just calculated maximum, to the hard clauses (Step 6). The next solver call (Step 5) is then $MaxSAT(w_4, w_5, w_6)$, followed by adding again an additional encoding (Step 6), ensuring the maximum. The last solver call $MaxSAT(w_1, w_2, w_3)$ is then performed and the solution is printed (Step 7).

As seen in the example, with the splitting technique many less complex MaxSAT solver calls are performed, instead of one potentially complex one. Especially for PB-constraint based solvers this turns out to be more efficient as demonstrated by the experimental results in Sect. 5.

4   Trimming the MaxSAT Instance (TrimMaxSAT)

In this chapter we describe TrimMaxSAT, a preprocessing *trimming* algorithm, which aims at reducing the size of a given MaxSAT instance, by incrementally testing the satisfiability of each soft clause (with respect to the hard clauses). If soft clauses are not satisfiable at all, they can be detected and removed. TrimMaxSAT uses similar techniques as backbone computing cf. [19, 24, 29], in contrast to backbone computing we are looking only for the unsatisfiable core of soft

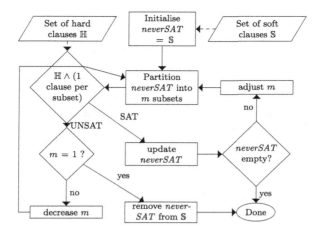

Fig. 2. TrimMaxSAT

clauses instead of variables and we are not checking the satisfiable core. This is especially beneficial if the MaxSAT instance is split as described in Sect. 3, since thereby the added encoding often forces a subset of the remaining soft clauses to be unsatisfiable. As a by-product, the algorithm generates partial solutions, which can be utilized to approximate the solution to the MaxSAT instance. More information on approximative MaxSAT solving, which is not the focus of this paper, is found e.g. in [12, 20].

4.1 Algorithm Overview

An overview of TrimMaxSAT is outlined in Fig. 2. The proposed algorithm maintains a set of clauses, which have never been satisfied (yet), called *neverSAT*. First, this set is initialized as the set of all soft clauses.

The algorithm starts a loop, where in each round at least m soft clauses of *neverSAT* are tested for satisfiability. The initialization of m is described later on in more detail.

At the beginning of each round, the set *neverSAT* is randomly partitioned into m sets of (nearly) equal size. Then, the algorithm performs an (incremental) SAT solver call to test, whether the hard clauses and at least one clause of each partition element can be satisfied together. If this is the case, all satisfied soft clauses are known to be satisfiable and can be removed from *neverSAT*. As a by-product a partial solution to the MaxSAT instance is found, which is stored, if it is higher than every previously calculated partial solution. After the trimming algorithm, the highest found solution can be handed to the MaxSAT solver, using this weight as a lower bound in the MaxSAT solving process.

If after a satisfiable SAT-solver call, the set *neverSAT* is empty, all soft clauses can be satisfied and the algorithm terminates without trimming the MaxSAT instance (but with a partial solution). If on the other hand *neverSAT* is not empty, i.e. there are still soft clauses which have not been satisfied yet, m is adjusted to satisfy other (potentially more) clauses with the next solver call.

If at one point the SAT solver call was unsatisfiable and $m > 1$, the test to satisfy m soft clauses at once was potentially too strong and m is decreased, so that the algorithm will test satisfying less soft clauses together.

Lastly, if the SAT solver call was unsatisfiable and $m = 1$, i.e. the set *neverSAT* was not really partitioned. Thus, no more clauses from *neverSAT* can be satisfied and thus all clauses in *neverSAT* can be removed from the MaxSAT instance without any impact on the solution.

In the following the algorithm is presented in more detail.

4.2   SAT-Encoding of the Soft Clause Partitioning

As described above, the algorithm utilizes a SAT solver to test, whether at least one clause per partition element for a given partition of *neverSAT* can be satisfied. To do so, a relaxation literal r_j (cf. Sect. 2.1, p. 5) is added to each soft clause and for every element in the partition one hard clause is added to the MaxSAT instance. This hard clause contains all negated relaxation literals of soft clauses in the corresponding partition element. Additionally every such hard clause contains the same new relaxation literal r'. By adding $\neg r'$ to the assumptions for the next solver call, we guarantee that this clause is satisfied if and only if at least one clause of the partition element is satisfied.

For the upcoming solver calls r' is added as a unit clause to the CNF, to remove all previously added soft clauses.

4.3   Candidate List for Partitioning

As described above, the algorithm divides in each round the set of all not (yet) satisfied soft clauses into partitions of varying size. To efficiently decide on the number of partition elements, the algorithm generates in every round a list containing only *reasonable* numbers of partition sizes m.

Not all positive numbers smaller than $n := |neverSAT|$ should be considered a *reasonable* candidate for m. Especially for big n, values close to n would result in highly similar partition elements (most partition elements contain only one clause). Therefore a list is created which contains only $\lfloor 2 \cdot \sqrt{n} \rfloor - 1$ elements, where the value m for the ith list-element is calculated with the following equation:

$$
m = \begin{cases} \lfloor n/i \rfloor, & \text{if } i < \sqrt{n} \\ \lfloor 2 \cdot \sqrt{n} \rfloor - i, & \text{otherwise} \end{cases}
$$

The element size of a given partition element specifies the number of soft clauses out of which at least one has to be satisfied. Clearly this number has to be a natural

Table 1. List for n = 25

i	m	el size
1	25	1
2	12	2.08
3	8	3.13
4	6	4.17
5	5	5
6	4	6.25
7	3	8.33
8	2	12.5
9	1	25

number. The elements of one partition should differ in size as little as possible, therefore only partition elements containing either $\lfloor n/m \rfloor$ or $\lceil n/m \rceil$ soft clauses are chosen. Exactly in the middle of the list the size m of the partition, i.e. the number of partition elements, and the element size, i.e. the number of soft clauses in a given partition subset, should be (almost) equal ($m \approx n/m \approx \sqrt{n}$).

The calculation of the candidate list is motivated by the argument that the minimal distance of at least 1 should hold for m and for the element size between any row of the list (cf. Table 1).

Example 2. In Table 1 a candidate list for $n = 25$ is presented. Choosing $i = 2$ would result in partition of size 12, i.e. 12 subsets of almost equal size: one with 3 elements soft clauses and 11 with 2 elements soft clauses.

4.4 Choosing a Candidate for Partition Size m

Choosing a candidate works similarly to a binary search on the candidate list described in Subsect. 4.3. A search variable $z \in (lb, 1)$ is introduced, where initially the lower bound lb of z equals 0. This search variable describes the current position in the candidate list of size l with $i = \lceil z \cdot l \rceil$.

The search starts at $z = 1/2$ (i.e. at the middle of the list), at which point the partition size m (nearly) equals the element size, $m = elementsize = \sqrt{n}$.

If it is possible to satisfy one soft clause of each partition element, the corresponding solver call returns `satisfiable`. In case of a `satisfiable` solver call we halve the difference of z to the lower bound lb. This means for the next calculation of i, $z = z - (z - lb)/2$. With the satisfiable solver call, the value of z is getting closer to 0, corresponding to position $i = 1$, in which each partition element contains one soft clause. If a `satisfiable` solver call satisfies all remaining soft clauses, which were not yet satisfied, then all soft clauses of the MaxSAT instance are determined to be satisfiable. Thus, the algorithm terminates in that case.

With an `unsatisfiable` solver call, the current value of z is set as a new lower bound ($lb = z$) and the difference of z to the lower bound is halved and z is increased by that value: $z = z + (1 - z)/2$. With an unsatisfiable solver call we're getting closer to the upper bound 1 for z, corresponding to the last element of the candidate list, which means forcing only one soft clause out of *neverSAT*. If that entails an unsatisfiable solver call, we can determine that no more soft clauses are satisfiable. In that case all remaining soft clauses from *neverSAT* can be removed from the MaxSAT instance and the algorithm terminates.

Lemma 1 (Termination). *The trimming algorithm is guaranteed to successfully terminate after a finite number of SAT solver calls.*

Proof. After every `satisfiable` solver call the (finite) set *neverSAT* shrinks and the algorithm terminates as soon as *neverSAT* is empty. Since *neverSAT* never grows, the number of `satisfiable` solver calls is finite.

With an `unsatisfiable` solver call, z is increased by $(1 - z)/2$. Thus, after a finite number of successive `unsatisfiable` solver calls, z reaches a value greater than $(l-1)/l$, where l is the size of the candidate list. Since $i = \lceil z \cdot l \rceil$, in this case $i = l$, thus the last element of the candidate list is chosen $(m = 1)$. As described above, if this call also returns unsatisfiable, the algorithm terminates.   □

5   Experimental Results

The presented methods have been evaluated on two benchmark sets: In Sect. 5.1 results on the new benchmark set, which is used by the hardware security application, are presented. Section 5.2 provides results on benchmarks from the MaxSAT Evaluation 2019. Note that these benchmarks contain two families of benchmarks (*spot5* and *max-realizability*) which are only separable with the new GBMO criterion.

The top six solvers from the Evaluation 2019 [10] and additionally QMaxSAT with the version of the MaxSAT 2017 Evaluation, are compared. QMaxSAT in the 2017 version uses different PB encodings and is therefore of special interest. The proposed techniques are implemented in C++. The solver Pacose20 was used with Glucose 4 [8] as back-end SAT solver. To show the vital impact of the proposed techniques on PB-constraint based solvers, we used our Pacose20 framework to simulate the solvers QMaxSAT18, QMaxSAT17 and the 2019 version Pacose19. The simulated solvers are denoted with a ∗.

Each experiment ran on one node (Intel Xeon E5-2650v2 core at 2.60 GHz, constrained to 8 GB of main memory, Ubuntu 18.04.3 in 64 bit mode) of our cluster. For TrimMaxSAT we used timeouts for each solver call and for the whole procedure, depending on the number of soft clauses for our experiments.

In the following we use cactus plots (Figs. 3a, b, 4 and 5a). The x-axes of the plots represent the number of solved instances and the y-axes the time needed to solve them. The first instances are always solved in only a few seconds, therefore we zoomed in on the part, where differences can be clearly seen.

5.1   Hardware Security Benchmarks

The benchmark set[2] was generated for a hardware security application. More details on the application are found in [30,31]. The instances vary in complexity, ranging from small benchmarks with only 47 soft clauses to very large benchmarks with more than 1.2 million soft clauses and nearly 30 million hard clauses. In our experiments, we used a timeout of 20 min, as with more time almost no additional instances are solved.

Figure 3a shows four variants of the Pacose20∗ solver only using DPW encoding: without any preprocessing technique *(P20∗)* the solver is able to solve 664 instances; with the trimming *(P20∗+T)* technique (cf. Sect. 4) 715 instances; with the GBMO *(P20∗+G)* technique (cf. Sect. 3) 770 instances; and with both techniques combined *(P20∗+T+G)* all 778 instances are solved, each in less than 183.5 s. The new trimming technique hereby removes 19.45 soft clauses with 9.5

---

[2] Available at the MaxSAT Evaluation 2020 [1].

solver calls, and if combined with GBMO it removes 20.8 soft clauses in 11.9 solver calls on average. The encoding is also getting remarkably smaller, as the following numbers of on average added clauses for commonly solved instances (solved by all internal techniques) show (numbers are given in millions (mil)): P20* 9.3mil, P20*+GBMO 3.9mil, P20*+T 2.3mil and P20*+T+G 0.7mil.

Figure 3b compares the 6 solvers of the MaxSAT Evaluation 2019 [1], together with the QMaxSAT version of 2017 and the proposed tpstrikepre-/ inprocessing preprocessing techniques *(P20*+T+G)*. Even if the "18" in the solver names might suggest otherwise, the solvers all participated in the MaxSAT Evaluation 2019. In this plot it can be seen that only two Evaluation solvers, namely *UWrMaxSAT* and *MaxHS* are able to solve all instances, and the PB-constraint based MaxSAT solvers (Pacose19 and QMaxSAT17/18), are the three solvers with the fewest solved instances. In contrast, if Pacose20* employs both preprocessing techniques *(P20*+T+G)*, the solver dominates the other solvers on the hardware security benchmark set. It is especially noteworthy, that *Pacose20*, the solving technique with the least amount of solvable instances (663, Fig. 3a) for this benchmark set, could be improved by using the proposed preprocessing techniques, so that in the end it could solve all instances (778) with the best solving times.

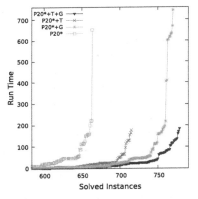

(a) Comparison of novel techniques.

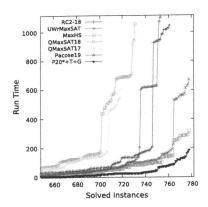

(b) Comparison of Evaluation solvers.

Fig. 3. Cacti plots on the hardware security benchmark set. Pacose (P) with Trim-MaxSAT (T) and GBMO (G) are abbreviated.

5.2   MaxSAT Evaluation Benchmarks

Many benchmarks from a wide range of applications are collected for the yearly MaxSAT Evaluations since 2006 when it first took place. For a thorough evaluation, we performed experiments on all benchmarks of all MaxSAT Evaluations (2006–2019). In total, 1 334 out of 15 168 unique instances could be separated, which equates around 8.79% of all instances. For comparison, here are the

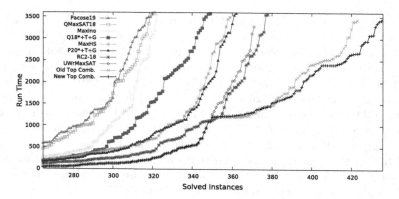

Fig. 4. Evaluation 2019 solvers, QMaxSAT (Q) and Pacose (P) with TrimMaxSAT (T) and GBMO (G) on our cluster. The rightmost curves are the top solver combinations.

numbers on how many instances were separable with the (BMO/GBMO) criteria in recent years, 2019 (16.55%/23.38%), 2018 (34.17%/43.50%) and 2017 (20.99%/25.16%) were separable. It is seen, that there are more separable instances in recent years. All weights of the benchmarks were maximally separable into 9 multisets. For completeness, variants of Pacose20* are compared on all 1 334 separable instances: $P20^*$ solves 1 161, $P20^*+GBMO$ solves 1 213 and $P20^*+T+G$ solves 1 215 instances if the timeout for TrimMaxSAT is set at 600 s. In the remainder of this section we focus on the benchmarks from the MaxSAT Evaluation 2019.

The proposed GBMO technique (cf. Sect. 3) is able to separate the instances from two benchmark families, which are not separable with the BMO criterion: *spot5* contains different weights inside each separated group of weights and *max-realizability* contains instances which are separable due to allowing $\sum W_L = \sum W_{R_1} - \sum W_{R_2}$ and it also contains different weights inside some of the groups of weights. The other instances which are separable due to the new GBMO criterion are widespread in many additional families.

In this section we compare the same 7 solvers from the MaxSAT Evaluation as in Sect. 5.1. Additionally we ran the PB-constraint based solvers QMaxSAT17*, QMaxSAT18* and Pacose19* with Glucose 4 (instead of Glucose 3) SAT solver and with assumptions, which is necessary to use GBMO and TrimMaxSAT. At the MaxSAT Evaluation 2019 there was an error[3] in the benchmarks of the *planning* family and therefore neither QMaxSAT nor Pacose were able to handle these 21 instances. In the * version all these instances can be handled and solved.

Last years' MaxSAT competitions have shown, that different benchmark families are better suited for different solver types. Therefore it is generally better to run solver combinations, i.e. to run n solvers subsequently for in total 3600 s (timeout of $3600/n$ seconds each), than to run only one solver alone for 3600 s. The best such combination is the *top solver combination*. Table 2 shows the top

---

[3] These instances had weights bigger than the top weight.

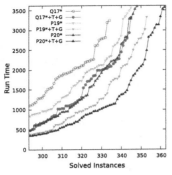

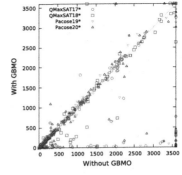

(a) Cacti with and without new techniques. (b) Scatter with and without GBMO.

Fig. 5. Evaluation 2019 comparison of solver. QMaxSAT (Q) and Pacose (P) with TrimMaxSAT (T) and GBMO (G) are abbreviated.

Table 2. Results of the MaxSAT Evaluations 2017–2020 (marked with E) and of experiments performed on our own cluster (marked with C). The respective number of solved instances of the virtual best solver (VBS), top solver (topS) and top solver combination (topC) are listed, followed by the names of the (always three) top solvers of the combination. Pacose (P), TrimMaxSAT (T) and GBMO (G) are shortened.

	Year	VBS	topS	topC	Solver1	Solver2	Solver3
E	2020	479	436	461	MaxHS	UWRMaxSAT	Pacose20
E	2019	459	380	429	MaxHS	UWRMaxSAT	QMaxSAT18
C	2019	456	378	423	MaxHS	UWRMaxSAT	QMaxSAT18
C	2019	456	378	436	MaxHS	UWRMaxSAT	P19/20*+T+G
E	2018	499	421	474	MaxHS	RC2-A	Pacose18
E	2017	650	538	607	MaxHS	Open-WBO-OLL	Open-WBO-LSU

solver combinations for the years 2017–2020 with at least one PB solver in each of them (always Solver3). As we focused on 2019 we included two rows (marked with C) with the results of the solvers on our cluster.

The virtual best solver (VBS), which contains the best overall results of all solvers (with full 3600 s timeout each), solves 456 instances on our cluster.

All top combinations (topC) are closer to the virtual best solver (VBS) than to the single top solver (topS). Without the techniques introduced in this paper, the old top combination has solved 423 instances on our cluster. Using the proposed techniques, the new top solver combination then includes Pacose*+TrimMaxSAT+GBMO (2019 or 2020) and solves 13 additional instances. In total, the distance (regarding the solved instances) to the VBS was decreased by 39% and the distance to the top solver was further increased by 29%.

Figure 4 shows results on the MaxSAT Evaluation 2019 benchmark set, which ran on our own cluster. Depicted are the 6 top solvers, the improved versions of Pacose20* and QMaxSAT18* (with TrimMaxSAT and GBMO) and results for the top solver combination before the techniques of this paper were used (*old top combination*) and the improved top solver combination with the techniques proposed in this paper (*new top combination*). It is seen, that the top solver combination is significantly improved.

Figure 5a and Table 3 show the pure impact of the proposed techniques. Especially noteworthy is the improvement of the PB-constraint based solvers. For clarity, in Fig. 5a QMaxSAT18* is omitted from the graphic, as the improvements of the solver were mostly in timing and also two instances because of Trim-MaxSAT. The graph would overlap with P19* and Q17*+T+G and therefore would hinder the figure's readability. For the other three solvers the improvement is clearly visible. Table 3 shows the significant improvement for all instances which are separable with GBMO. Three of the families in which almost all instances are separable are listed. Spot5 is of special interest because it contains different weights in each of the sub-multisets.

Figure 5b shows a scatter plot of the 4 PB-constraint based solvers with and without GBMO and all 586 instances from the weighted MaxSAT Evaluation 2019. Each dot represents one instance with both solving times of each solver with and without the GBMO technique. If it is solved faster with GBMO, the

Table 3. Results for the solvers of the MaxSAT Evaluation 19 on our cluster for all instances, which were separable, and for the families spot-5, haplotyping-pedigrees and shiftdesign for which GBMO had especially good results. We compared the combinations with GBMO (+G) and TrimMaxSAT (+T). The results are presented as in the MaxSAT Evaluation, at first the average solving times in seconds and in brackets the number of solved instances. QMaxSAT (Q) and Pacose (P) are shortened.

	total	GBMO	spot5	hap-ped	shiftd
	586	137	17	21	11
RC2-18	272.19 (378)	177.45 (115)	165.10 (6)	28.23 (21)	387.44 (10)
UWRMaxSAT	187.03 (371)	135.82 (118)	1125.38 (9)	26.74 (21)	442.50 (11)
MaxHS	269.01 (359)	243.63 (97)	1616.78 (4)	195.00 (19)	392.07 (4)
Maxino	214.31 (322)	161.37 (93)	3.29 (5)	8.54 (21)	780.78 (11)
Q18	327.73 (321)	175.03 (106)	384.56 (17)	78.60 (21)	346.05 (11)
P19	346.37 (319)	357.06 (97)	645.50 (13)	534.29 (18)	807.71 (8)
P19*	345.90 (345)	346.84 (100)	686.18 (13)	534.18 (18)	906.56 (9)
P19*+G	271.23 (354)	120.57 (110)	148.53 (17)	11.22 (21)	134.20 (11)
P19*+T+G	260.16 (353)	118.28 (110)	149.80 (17)	10.99 (21)	131.83 (11)
P20*	310.12 (348)	210.50 (97)	247.65 (17)	164.04 (11)	899.87 (9)
P20*+G	265.57 (360)	107.67 (110)	142.18 (17)	15.34 (21)	160.56 (11)
P20*+T+G	280.23 (362)	109.28 (110)	143.57 (17)	15.31 (21)	159.57 (11)
Q17*	345.46 (334)	348.48 (100)	807.23 (13)	546.48 (18)	900.69 (9)
Q17*+G	272.81 (345)	97.39 (110)	138.06 (17)	10.99 (21)	134.57 (11)
Q17*+T+G	274.18 (345)	97.80 (110)	140.29 (17)	10.77 (21)	131.81 (11)
Q18*	349.01 (347)	210.70 (109)	347.07 (17)	86.57 (21)	260.73 (10)
Q18*+G	304.55 (347)	106.40 (110)	139.57 (17)	9.42 (21)	168.43 (11)
Q18*+T+G	325.05 (349)	106.29 (110)	138.80 (17)	9.49 (21)	165.90 (11)

dot is in the lower right triangle, otherwise in the upper left triangle. Most dots are along the diagonal because these instances are not separable, or can be solved in only a few seconds with both variants. Some of the instances are solved slower due to the fact that using "$\leq$" instead of "$<$" in Eq. 2 (Page 6) can cross out possible solutions and therefore makes the instance in some cases harder to solve (cf. Remark 1d, Page 8). It is especially noteworthy that there are many instances solved in less than 500 s which were not solvable before.

In summary, all tested PB-constraint based solvers and the top solver combination can be significantly improved with the proposed techniques.

6   Conclusion and Outlook

Over the last years preprocessing techniques have played an increasing role in the development of solver technologies. This work investigated weighted partial MaxSAT problems and proposed

- a proven generalization of Boolean Multilevel Optimization (GBMO)
- different criteria to efficiently test whether splitting into subproblems is possible and
- a second preprocessing technique (TrimMaxSAT), which finds unsatisfiable soft clauses with incremental solver calls, to reduce the search space, especially for PB-constraint based MaxSAT solvers.

The impact of the proposed techniques is demonstrated on benchmarks from the MaxSAT Evaluation 2019, where the three PB-constraint based solvers improved performance and on a benchmark set from a hardware security application, where the proposed combination of preprocessing techniques outperforms all other state-of-the-art solvers. Additionally, we were able to significantly improve the top solver combination for the 2019 MaxSAT Evaluation.

In the future we plan to implement a greedy binary search for local optima based on the proposed trimming technique, to find better lower bounds for the solution. The additional information on how often soft clauses are solved will then be used to implement a more efficient encoding in terms of size.

References

1. MaxSAT evaluation (2006–2020). https://maxsat-evaluations.github.io
2. Abramé, A., Habet, D.: Local max-resolution in branch and bound solvers for Max-SAT. In: 2014 IEEE 26th International Conference on Tools with Artificial Intelligence, pp. 336–343. IEEE (2014)
3. Alviano, M., Dodaro, C., Ricca, F.: A MaxSAT algorithm using cardinality constraints of bounded size. In: Twenty-Fourth International Joint Conference on Artificial Intelligence (2015)
4. Ansótegui, C., Bonet, M.L., Gabàs, J., Levy, J.: Improving SAT-based weighted MaxSAT solvers. In: Milano, M. (ed.) CP 2012. LNCS, pp. 86–101. Springer, Heidelberg (2012). https://doi.org/10.1007/978-3-642-33558-7_9

5. Ansótegui, C., Bonet, M.L., Gabàs, J., Levy, J.: Improving WPM2 for (weighted) partial MaxSAT. In: Schulte, C. (ed.) CP 2013. LNCS, vol. 8124, pp. 117–132. Springer, Heidelberg (2013). https://doi.org/10.1007/978-3-642-40627-0_12
6. Ansótegui, C., Gabas, J.: WPm3: an (in) complete algorithm for weighted partial MaxSAT. Artif. Intel. **250**, 37–57 (2017)
7. Argelich, J., Lynce, I., Marques-Silva, J.: On solving Boolean multilevel optimization problems. In: Twenty-First International Joint Conference on Artificial Intelligence (2009)
8. Audemard, G., Simon, L.: On the glucose SAT solver. Int. J. Artif. Intel. Tools **27**(01), 1840001 (2018)
9. Bacchus, F.: MaxHS in the 2018 MaxSAT evaluation. MaxSAT Evaluation 2018, pp. 11, 12 (2018)
10. Bacchus, F., Järvisalo, M., Martins, R.: MaxSAT Evaluation 2019: Solver and Benchmark Descriptions. Department of Computer Science Report Series B, Department of Computer Science, University of Helsinki (2019)
11. Bailleux, O., Boufkhad, Y.: Efficient CNF encoding of Boolean cardinality constraints. In: Rossi, F. (ed.) CP 2003. LNCS, vol. 2833, pp. 108–122. Springer, Heidelberg (2003). https://doi.org/10.1007/978-3-540-45193-8_8
12. Berg, J., Demirović, E., Stuckey, P.J.: Core-boosted linear search for incomplete MaxSAT. In: Rousseau, L.-M., Stergiou, K. (eds.) CPAIOR 2019. LNCS, vol. 11494, pp. 39–56. Springer, Cham (2019). https://doi.org/10.1007/978-3-030-19212-9_3
13. Bradley, G.H.: Algorithm and bound for the greatest common divisor of n integers. Commun. ACM **13**(7), 433–436 (1970)
14. Eén, N., Sörensson, N.: Translating pseudo-Boolean constraints into SAT. J. Satisf. Boolean Model. Comput. **2**(1–4), 1–26 (2006)
15. Ehrgott, M., Gandibleux, X.: A survey and annotated bibliography of multiobjective combinatorial optimization. OR-Spektrum **22**(4), 425–460 (2000)
16. Ehrgott, M., Gandibleux, X., Przybylski, A.: Exact methods for multi-objective combinatorial optimisation. In: Greco, S., Ehrgott, M., Figueira, J.R. (eds.) Multiple Criteria Decision Analysis. ISORMS, vol. 233, pp. 817–850. Springer, New York (2016). https://doi.org/10.1007/978-1-4939-3094-4_19
17. Fazekas, K., Biere, A., Scholl, C.: Incremental inprocessing in SAT solving. In: Janota, M., Lynce, I. (eds.) SAT 2019. LNCS, vol. 11628, pp. 136–154. Springer, Cham (2019). https://doi.org/10.1007/978-3-030-24258-9_9
18. Ignatiev, A., Morgado, A., Marques-Silva, J.: RC2: a python-based MaxSAT solver. MaxSAT Evaluation 2018, p. 22 (2018)
19. Janota, M., Lynce, I., Marques-Silva, J.: Algorithms for computing backbones of propositional formulae. AI Commun. **28**(2), 161–177 (2015)
20. Joshi, S., Kumar, P., Martins, R., Rao, S.: Approximation strategies for incomplete MaxSAT. In: Hooker, J. (ed.) CP 2018. LNCS, vol. 11008, pp. 219–228. Springer, Cham (2018). https://doi.org/10.1007/978-3-319-98334-9_15
21. Korhonen, T., Berg, J., Saikko, P., Järvisalo, M.: MaxPre: an extended MaxSAT preprocessor. In: Gaspers, S., Walsh, T. (eds.) SAT 2017. LNCS, vol. 10491, pp. 449–456. Springer, Cham (2017). https://doi.org/10.1007/978-3-319-66263-3_28
22. Koshimura, M., Zhang, T., Fujita, H., Hasegawa, R.: QMaxSAT: a partial MaxSAT solver system description. J. Satisf. Boolean Model. Comput. **8**, 95–100 (2012)
23. Marques-Silva, J., Argelich, J., Graça, A., Lynce, I.: Boolean lexicographic optimization: algorithms & applications. Ann. Math. Artif. Intell. **62**(3–4), 317–343 (2011)

24. Marques-Silva, J., Janota, M., Lynce, I.: On computing backbones of propositional theories. In: ECAI, vol. 215, pp. 15–20 (2010)
25. Ogawa, T., Liu, Y., Hasegawa, R., Koshimura, M., Fujita, H.: Modulo based CNF encoding of cardinality constraints and its application to MaxSAT solvers. In: 2013 IEEE 25th International Conference on Tools with Artificial Intelligence (ICTAI), pp. 9–17. IEEE (2013)
26. Paxian, T., Reimer, S., Becker, B.: Dynamic polynomial watchdog encoding for solving weighted MaxSAT. In: Beyersdorff, O., Wintersteiger, C.M. (eds.) SAT 2018. LNCS, vol. 10929, pp. 37–53. Springer, Cham (2018). https://doi.org/10.1007/978-3-319-94144-8_3
27. Paxian, T., Reimer, S., Becker, B.: Pacose: an iterative SAT-based MaxSAT solver. MaxSAT Evaluation 2018, p. 20 (2018)
28. Piotrów, M.: UWrMaxSat-a new MiniSat+-based solver in MaxSAT evaluation 2019. MaxSAT Evaluation 2019, p. 11 (2019)
29. Previti, A., Järvisalo, M.: A preference-based approach to backbone computation with application to argumentation. In: Proceedings of the 33rd Annual ACM Symposium on Applied Computing, pp. 896–902 (2018)
30. Raiola, P., Paxian, T., Becker, B.: Partial (un-) weighted MaxSAT benchmarks: minimizing witnesses for security weaknesses in reconfigurable scan networks. MaxSAT Evaluation 2020, p. 44 (2020)
31. Raiola, P., Paxian, T., Becker, B.: Minimal witnesses for security weaknesses in reconfigurable scan networks. In: IEEE European Test Symposium, ETS, pp. 1–6. IEEE (2020)
32. Ulungu, E.L., Teghem, J.: Multi-objective combinatorial optimization problems: a survey. J. Multi-Crit. Decis. Anal. **3**(2), 83–104 (1994)
33. Warners, J.P.: A linear-time transformation of linear inequalities into conjunctive normal form. Inf. Process. Lett. **68**(2), 63–69 (1998)
34. Wimmer, R., Scholl, C., Becker, B.: The (D)QBF preprocessor HQSpre - underlying theory and its implementation. J. Satisf. Boolean Model. Comput. **11**(1), 3–52 (2019)
35. Zha, A., Uemura, N., Koshimura, M., Fujita, H.: Mixed radix weight totalizer encoding for pseudo-Boolean constraints. In: 2017 IEEE 29th International Conference on Tools with Artificial Intelligence (ICTAI), pp. 868–875. IEEE (2017)
36. Zhang, H., Shen, H., Manya, F.: Exact algorithms for MAX-SAT. Electr. Notes Theor. Comput. Sci. **86**(1), 190–203 (2003)

Compositional Satisfiability Solving
in Separation Logic

Quang Loc Le$^{(\boxtimes)}$

University College London, London, UK
`quang.le@ucl.ac.uk`

Abstract. We introduce a novel decision procedure to the satisfiability problem in array separation logic combined with general inductively defined predicates and arithmetic. Our proposal differentiates itself from existing works by solving satisfiability through compositional reasoning. First, following Fermat's method of infinite descent, it infers for every inductive definition a "base" that precisely characterises the satisfiability. It then utilises the base to derive such a base for any formula where these inductive predicates reside in. Especially, we identify an expressive decidable fragment for the compositionality. We have implemented the proposal in a tool and evaluated it over challenging problems. The experimental results show that the compositional satisfiability solving is efficient and our tool is effective and efficient when compared with existing solvers.

Keywords: Separation logic · Satisfiability · Regular proofs

1 Introduction

Satisfiability solvers are essential to symbolic analysis in checking code correctness. Such an analysis executes programs symbolically and constructs path conditions, those constraints on values stored in program variables and expressed in terms of input parameters, that reach a program point. A satisfiability solver is then utilized for discharging the path conditions to either detect and prune infeasible paths or to generate inputs that exercise a buggy path. So far, while techniques to satisfiability solving for heap-independent domains e.g., satisfiability modulo theories (SMT) [1], have been well developed, there have been a few works targeting heap-oriented logics. Heap-manipulating programs are often building-blocks of real-world applications (e.g., data structures like arrays and trees). Especially, heap-related bugs are the sources of the security vulnerabilities; for instance, memory leak, double free and use-after-free caused the vulnerabilities CVE-2020-12768, CVE-2019-3896 and CVE-2020-8649, respectively, found in the Linux kernel recently. Therefore, satisfiability solver that supports the symbolic execution over heap-manipulating programs is important.

Separation logic [16,36] formalism has been increasingly applied for reasoning about heap-based programs. Combining with general inductive definitions and

© Springer Nature Switzerland AG 2021
F. Henglein et al. (Eds.): VMCAI 2021, LNCS 12597, pp. 578–602, 2021.
https://doi.org/10.1007/978-3-030-67067-2_26

arithmetic, it can concisely and precisely represent constraints over unbounded and complex data structures (e.g., nested lists, AVL trees) [5, 10, 19, 23, 29–32]. The strength of the logic is the support for compositional reasoning through the separating conjunction operator, which allows reasoning about disjoint portions of heaps locally and independently. The compositional reasoning has been applied through the frame rule and automated using the bi-abduction technique [9, 19]. Implemented in Facebook's Infer [8], the compositional reasoning helps the verification scale up to millions of lines of code.

Our research question is whether the compositional reasoning introduced in [9] could be applied to a satisfiability solver or not. The satisfiability problem in separation logic was studied in [5] for inductive definitions with heap-only constraints and in [23] for those combining both heap and arithmetic (heap-independent) constraints. Given a formula, these works essentially compute a *base* that characterises its satisfiability precisely. In these works, a base generated for every formula is used to check the satisfiability of the formula itself. Yet another challenge is to develop a satisfiability solver that can derive a base for formula in a modular way: The base of a formula is defined by terms of the bases of its parts and a means of combining them.

In this paper, we present a satisfiability solver with the capability of the compositionality in *array separation logic* combined with general definitions of inductive predicates and arithmetic properties. We study a decidable fragment with *small heap model* property: The base of the formula is satisfied by those models, the interpretations of variables, where heaps are minimal and finite. Especially, the base is a separation logic formula without any inductive predicates. A base of a symbolic heap, a conjunctive formula, is inductively computed from the bases of its conjuncts. In this endeavour, the difficulty we face is to find a base for each inductive predicate defined with recursive definitions. To overcome this challenge, we develop an algorithm as an application of Fermat's method of infinite descent. The method of infinite descent is a standard approach to Diophantine equations. This method is typically applied in two ways:

1. To show that an equation P has no solution. Let n be a positive integer, suppose that whenever $P(n)$ holds, there exists a positive integer m such that $m < n$ and $P(m)$ holds. Then, $P(x)$ is false for all positive integers x.
2. To show that an equation P has a set of solutions. First, we need to hypothesize a simpler equation Q which satisfies the following two conditions:
   - $Q(a)$ and $P(a)$ hold for some natural number constant a,
   - and whenever $Q(n)$ and $P(n)$ hold, there exists a positive integer m such that $m < n$ and both $Q(m)$ and $P(m)$ hold.
   Then, P has the same set of solutions with Q.

The work in [21, 23] used the first application to show the unsatisfiability of a formula. Here, we apply the second approach to derive the base (like Q in the method of infinite descent) through a so-called regular unfolding tree that represents a set of all equisatisfiable solutions of a formula. The bases of inductive predicates are computed once and are independent of the contexts where they are used. Through compositionality, we hope that our proposal could help to improve the performance of those symbolic analyses (e.g., test case generation [29,31]) through the reuse of the bases to discharge hundreds of satisfiability problems over the same set of predicate definitions.

Contributions. Our primary contributions are summarised as follows.

- We propose a novel decision algorithm that can compositionally compute a base for checking the satisfiability of a separation logic formula.
- We show that our solver is more expressive than all existing works (without the separating implication). Alongside this, we describe a novel decision procedure for Presburger arithmetic that includes nested inductive definitions.
- We have implemented the proposal in a prototype solver, called S2S. Our experimental results on those benchmarks taken from SL-COMP 2019, a competition of separation logic solvers [37], and generated during the program verification show that S2S with compositional reasoning is effective and efficient.

Organization. The remainder of the paper is organized as follows. Section 2 illustrates our ideas and presents motivating examples. Section 3 describes the fragment of separation logic. Section 4 introduces regular unfolding trees, the intermediate structure constructed to represent all solutions of a formula. In Sect. 5, we present our solver and identify semantic conditions for decidability. We refer to the fragment satisfies these conditions as $\texttt{SLIDLIA}_{sem}$. The existing fragments presented in [3,5,14,18,21,23,39,41] are subsumed by $\texttt{SLIDLIA}_{sem}$ straightforwardly. Section 6 shows $\texttt{SLIDLIA}$, a novel syntactic decidable fragment of $\texttt{SLIDLIA}_{sem}$. Section 7 presents the implementation and evaluation. Section 8 discusses related work. Finally, Sect. 9 concludes.

2   Basic Concepts and Motivating Examples

In this section, we first informally explain how to apply Fermat's method of infinite descent to compute the bases for inductive predicates. Next, we elaborate on our ideas through two examples that are beyond the capability of existing works.

Generating Bases via Regular Unfolding Trees.
We show how to find a base, the "another simpler related equation" in the second application of the method of infinite descent, for an inductive predicate. We infer those bases through regular unfolding trees. Such a tree is a (possibly infinite) tree of formulas: the leaves are either base formulas - those without any inductive predicates - or nodes (called buds) which are linked back to inner nodes (called companions), the root of the tree is the formula being unfolded, and nodes are

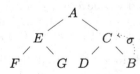

Fig. 1. A regular unfolding tree

companions), the root of the tree is the formula being unfolded, and nodes are connected to one or more children through predicate unfolding i.e., replacing an inductive predicate in the parents by its definition. Equivalently, an unfolding tree is a *regular* tree that is generated by a finite directed (cyclic) graph. Figure 1 shows an example of the regular unfolding tree, a tree with cycles through back-links. In the back-link between B and C, B is a bud, C is a companion and σ is a substitution between variables. B is linked back to C only when:

- There exist $P(\bar{x}) \in C$ and $P(\bar{y}) \in B$ s.t. $P(\bar{y})$ is in a formula unfolded from $P(\bar{x})$;
- And there exists B' such that B' is *equisatisfiable* with B, $B \Rightarrow B'$ and $B'\sigma \equiv C$.

The base of an inductive predicate is generated as the disjunction of the leaf bases of its regular unfolding tree. The most challenging task we have to solve is to compute bases for subtrees involving cycles. For such a subtree, we need to find a base formula that exactly characterises the set of solutions of the companion. In the following, we illustrate how to compute such a base for the subtree rooted by C in Fig. 1.

1. If the base leaf D is unsatisfiable, then we infer the base as `false`.
2. Otherwise, following the second application of infinite descent, we generate the base as a base formula that exactly characterises the satisfiability of $(D \vee B')$.

After that, the whole subtree rooted by the companion is replaced by the inferred base. The process which computes bases for subtrees involving cycles is applied repeatedly in a bottom-up manner until the tree does not contain any cycles. Then, the base of the root is the disjunctive set of satisfiable leaves of the final tree.

Comparing to the Base in [23]. Using regular unfolding trees, the work in [23] generates bases to check satisfiability without compositionality. The main difference between this work and ours is in inferring the bases for subtrees involving cycles in the second case above. To make a back-link with a bud B and a companion C, the algorithm in [23] finds a substitution σ and a formula B' for $B \Rightarrow B'$ and $B'\sigma \equiv C$. As it might over-approximate B, it might generate over-approximated bases. Since D is satisfiable, these bases are still complete when utilized to check the satisfiability of companion C and its ancestors. If, however, they are combined with some formula, the combined one might be over-approximated (as the frame rule says: $P(\bar{x}) \Rightarrow base$ implies $P(\bar{x}) * some\_formula \Rightarrow base * some\_formula$). Hence, the solver in [23] may produce false positives if it is for compositional solving. In contrast, ours ensures B' is equisatisfiable with B and the base generated exactly characterises the satisfiability of the predicate provided. Our solver is thus sound and complete for compositionality.

First Example. Let us consider the following satisfiability problem Δ_0:

$$\Delta_0 = \mathsf{odd}(x,y,m) * \mathsf{odd}(y,\mathsf{null},n) \wedge (\exists k.\ m + n = 2k + 1)$$

where $\text{odd}(x,y,m)$ is an inductive predicate representing singly-linked list segments with head pointer x, ending pointer y, and odd length m. Δ_0 is a symbolic heap. It is a conjunction of a spatial formula, $\text{odd}(x,y,m) * \text{odd}(y,\text{null},n)$, and a pure (heap-independent) formula, $\exists k.\ m + n = 2k + 1$. The spatial one specifies two connected list segments headed by x and y. The two lists are conjoined by the separating conjunction $*$ that tells us they lie on disjoint heap regions. The pure formula specifies that the sum of the lengths of the two lists, m and n, is an odd number.

The inductive predicate odd is mutually defined as follows.

$$\text{odd}(x,y,n) \equiv \exists x_1.\ x \mapsto \{x_1\} * \text{even}(x_1,y,n-1);$$
$$\text{even}(x,y,n) \equiv \text{emp} \wedge x = y \wedge n = 0 \vee \exists x_1. x \mapsto \{x_1\} * \text{odd}(x_1,y,n-1);$$

Here, each inductive definition is a disjunction of symbolic heaps. A symbolic heap may be existentially quantified. A heap formula is a conjunction of atomic predicates: emp to specify empty heap, points-to predicates (e.g., $x \mapsto \{x_1\}$ above) to assert a singleton heap, and occurrences of inductive predicates (e.g., $\text{even}(x_1,y,n-1)$ above).

Δ_0 is unsatisfiable. This problem is challenging for the existing solvers. It includes the arithmetic constraints which are beyond the fragments presented in Smallfoot [3], SLSAT [5], SPEN [13], Asterix [27] and Harrsh [17]. Due to the mutual recursion, it is beyond the capability of the algorithms presented in [14,18,39,41].

Δ_0 is in our decidable fragment. The proposed solver, S2S, proves its unsatisfiability through the following two phases. First, it computes for predicate odd a base that precisely characterises its satisfiability. Here, a base is a (possibly disjunctive) separation logic formula without any inductive predicate occurrences. Secondly, it derives a base Δ_0' for Δ_0 by replacing every occurrence of odd by the base inferred in the first phase. As Δ_0' does not contain any inductive predicates, satisfiability is decidable [21,28].

In this example, S2S infers the base for predicate $\text{odd}(x,y,n)$ as:

$$\{\ x \mapsto \{\_\} \wedge (\exists i.\ n = 2i + 1 \wedge i \geq 0)\ \} \text{ where } \_ \text{ denotes existential variables.}$$

After that, it replaces each occurrence of odd in Δ_0 with that base to obtain:

$$\Delta_0' \equiv x \mapsto \{\_\} * y \mapsto \{\_\} \wedge (\exists k.m+n=2k+1) \wedge (\exists i.m=2i+1 \wedge i \geq 0) \wedge (\exists i.n=2i+1 \wedge i \geq 0)$$

As Δ_0' is unsatisfiable (the unsatisfiable cores are underlined), so is Δ_0.

We now show how S2S infers the base for predicate $\text{odd}(x,y,n)$. It first generates the regular unfolding tree for $\text{odd}(x,y,n)$ in Fig. 2. In this tree, uppercase variables are existentially quantified, and the back-link is constructed based on the spatial (heap-dependent) projection of the formulas. Next, in a bottom-up manner, it finds a base for each subtree rooted by a companion and then replaces the whole subtree with that base. That base is a combination of its spatial part and its numeric part that are derived separately. For the subtree rooted by Δ_1 in Fig. 2, the spatial projection of the base is $x \mapsto \{\_\}$, the spatial

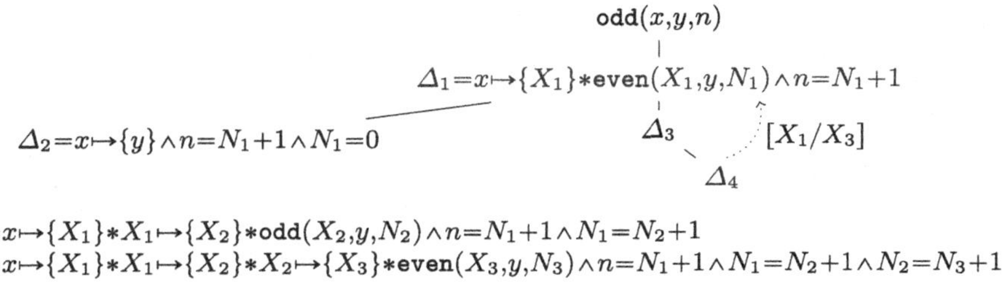

$$\text{odd}(x,y,n)$$

$$\Delta_1 = x \mapsto \{X_1\} * \text{even}(X_1, y, N_1) \wedge n = N_1 + 1$$

$$\Delta_2 = x \mapsto \{y\} \wedge n = N_1 + 1 \wedge N_1 = 0 \qquad \Delta_3 \qquad [X_1/X_3]$$

$$\Delta_4$$

$$\Delta_3 = x \mapsto \{X_1\} * X_1 \mapsto \{X_2\} * \text{odd}(X_2, y, N_2) \wedge n = N_1 + 1 \wedge N_1 = N_2 + 1$$
$$\Delta_4 = x \mapsto \{X_1\} * X_1 \mapsto \{X_2\} * X_2 \mapsto \{X_3\} * \text{even}(X_3, y, N_3) \wedge n = N_1 + 1 \wedge N_1 = N_2 + 1 \wedge N_2 = N_3 + 1$$

Fig. 2. Regular unfolding tree of $\text{odd}(x,y,n)$

formula of Δ_2. We, especially, show that the (infinite) set of all spatial formulas derived from this subtree is equisatisfiable with this base. The numeric projection of the base is equivalent to $\text{even}^N(N_1) \wedge n = N_1 + 1$ where $\text{even}^N(N_1)$ is defined from the ones of Δ_2 and Δ_4 as: $\text{even}^N(N_1) \equiv N_1 = 0 \vee \text{even}^N(N_3) \wedge N_1 = N_3 + 2$. Then, it derives for $\text{even}^N(N_1)$ an equivalent closed form, a Presburger formula, as : $\text{even}^N(N_1) \equiv \exists i.\ N_1 = 2i \wedge i \geq 0$. Finally, the base of $\text{odd}(x,y,n)$ is the base of Δ_1, the conjunction of its spatial and numeric projections, as $x \mapsto \{\_\} \wedge (\exists i.\ n = 2i + 1 \wedge i \geq 0)$.

Second Example. Let us consider the satisfiability problem in a fragment including the following nested lists whose data values are increasingly sorted.

$$\text{sllss}(x,y,mi,ma,n,n_0) \equiv \text{emp} \wedge x = y \wedge mi = ma \wedge n = n_0$$
$$\vee\ \exists u, mi_1, n_1. x \mapsto \{mi, u\} * \text{sllss}(u,y,mi_1,ma,n_1,n_0) \wedge x \neq y \wedge mi < mi_1 \wedge n = n_1 + 1$$
$$\text{nllss}(x,y,b,mi,ma,n,n_0) \equiv \text{emp} \wedge x = y \wedge mi = ma \wedge n = n_0$$
$$\vee\ \exists\ u, Z, m_1, m_2, n_1, n_2. x \mapsto \{mi, u, Z\} * \text{sllss}(Z,b,m_1,m_2,n_1,0) *$$
$$\text{nllss}(u,y,b,m_2,ma,n_2,n_0) \wedge x \neq y \wedge x \neq b \wedge mi < m_1 \wedge n = n_1 + n_2 + 1$$

Here, n and n_0 are parameters to capture the size (i.e., the number of heap cells) of the lists. nllss predicate contains nested length constraints that are beyond all existing decidable fragments. We show that nllss is in the decidable fragment, and can support compositional satisfiability solving. We compute the length constraints in arithmetic with addition and divisibility prior to transforming it into Presburger arithmetic. We show how to derive the bases for these predicates throughout the rest of the paper.

3   Array Separation Logic with Inductive Definitions

In this section, we first present the syntax and semantics of formulas in our work. After that, we show how to obtain spatial and numeric projections of formulas.

Definition 1 (Symbolic heap). *Terms t, (Presburger) pure formulas π, spatial formulas κ, symbolic heaps Δ and disjunctions Φ are given by the following grammar.*

$$\Phi ::= \Delta \mid \Phi \vee \Phi \qquad\qquad \Delta ::= \kappa \wedge \pi \mid \exists v.\ \Delta$$
$$\kappa ::= \texttt{emp} \mid v \mapsto \{t_1, .., t_N\} \mid P(\bar{v}) \mid array(t, t) \mid \kappa * \kappa \qquad \alpha ::= t{=}t \mid t{=}\texttt{null} \mid t{\leqslant}t$$
$$\pi ::= \texttt{true} \mid \alpha \mid \neg\pi \mid \pi \wedge \pi \mid \pi \vee \pi \qquad\qquad\qquad t ::= c \mid v \mid t{+}t \mid -t$$

where v ranges over an infinite set Var of variables, $\bar{t}$ over sequences of terms (either variables or null*) ($\bar{t}_i$ for its ith element), c over $\mathbb{Z}$, P over a finite set $\mathcal{P}$.*

The array predicate only records the bound of contiguous memory blocks, not their contents. Note that $t_1 \neq t_2$ is the short form for $\neg(t_1{=}t_2)$. $FV(\Phi)$ returns the free variables of Φ. We write $\Phi(\bar{v})$ to denote that $\bar{v} = FV(\Phi)$. $\Delta[t_1/v_2]$ denotes the formula obtained by substituting each term t_1 in Δ for the variable v_2. $\exists \bar{w}, v.\ \Delta \wedge v{=}x$ is normalised into $\exists \bar{w}.\ \Delta[x/v]$ and $\pi \wedge \pi$ is normalised into π.

Given a formula $\exists \bar{w}.\ P(\bar{v}) * v \mapsto \{\bar{t}\} * array(v_1, v_2) * \kappa \wedge x \diamond y \wedge \pi$ (where $\diamond \in \{=, \neq\}$), inductive predicate $P(\bar{v})$ (resp. $array(v_1, v_2)$) is called (heap) observable if there exists at least one variable in $\bar{v}$ (resp. $\{v_1, v_2\}$) that is quantifier-free (i.e., $x \diamond y \wedge \pi$ implies that $\bar{v} \setminus \bar{w} \neq \emptyset$); $v \mapsto \{\bar{t}\}$ is called (heap) observable if v is quantifier-free (i.e., $x \diamond y \wedge \pi$ implies that $v \notin \bar{w}$). Finally, $x \diamond y$ is observable if both x and y are quantifier-free (i.e., $x \diamond y \wedge \pi$ implies that $\{x; y\} \cap \bar{w} = \emptyset$). If a predicate is not observable, it is unobservable. $\overline{\Delta}$ is a formula obtained by replacing every $v \mapsto \{\bar{t}\} \in \Delta$ by $v \mapsto \{\_\}$.

Φ is a *base* formula if it does not contain any occurrence of inductive predicates. Otherwise, it is an *inductive* formula. We use B to denote a conjunctive base formula.

A definition of an inductive predicate is a disjunction as $P(\bar{v}) \equiv \Phi$. In each disjunct of Φ (called a definition rule), all variables which are not formal parameters are existentially quantified. We use $\texttt{base}^{\mathcal{P}}(P(\bar{v}))$ to denote the base of $P(\bar{v})$.

Semantics. Concrete heap models assume a set *Loc* of locations (heap addresses), such that $Loc \subseteq \mathbb{Z}$ and $\texttt{null} \notin \mathbb{Z}$. The semantics is given by a satisfaction relation: $s,h \models \Phi$ is valid if the stack $s \in Stacks$ and heap $h \in Heaps$ satisfies the formula Φ. Stack and heap abstractions are defined (assume that every points-to predicate has at most N fields):

$$Heaps \overset{\text{def}}{=} Loc \rightharpoonup_{fin} \mathbb{Z}^N \qquad\qquad Stacks \overset{\text{def}}{=} Var \to \mathbb{Z}$$

Suppose that $dom(f)$ is the domain of function f, $h_1 \# h_2$ denotes disjoint heaps h_1 and h_2, and $h_1 \cdot h_2$ denotes the union of two disjoint heaps. If s is a stack, $v \in Var$ and $\alpha \in \mathbb{Z}$, we write $s[v \mapsto \alpha] = s$ if $v \in dom(s)$ and $s[v \mapsto \alpha] = s \cup \{(v, \alpha)\}$ if $v \notin dom(s)$. The interpretation of an inductive predicate $P(\bar{v})$, denoted by $[\![P(\bar{v})]\!]$, is based on the least fixed point semantics (cf. [23]). Then, the semantics is shown below.

$$
\begin{array}{llll}
s,h \models \texttt{emp} & \texttt{iff} & dom(h){=}\varnothing & s,h \models \texttt{true} \quad \texttt{iff} \quad \text{always} \\
s,h \models v{\mapsto}\{v_1,..,v_N\} & \texttt{iff} & dom(h){=}\{s(v)\} \text{ and } h(s(v)){=}(s(v_1),..,s(v_N)) \\
s,h \models array(t_1,t_2) & \texttt{iff} & s(t_1){\leqslant}s(t_2) \text{ and } dom(h){=}\{s(t_1),...,s(t_2)\} \\
s,h \models \texttt{P}(\bar{v}) & \texttt{iff} & (h,s(\bar{v}_1),..,s(\bar{v}_k)) \in [\![\texttt{P}(\bar{v})]\!] \\
s,h \models \kappa_1 * \kappa_2 & \texttt{iff} & \exists h_1,h_2.\ h_1\#h_2, h{=}h_1.\ h_2 \text{ s.t. } s,h_1 \models \kappa_1 \text{ and } s,h_2 \models \kappa_2 \\
s,h \models \kappa \wedge \pi & \texttt{iff} & s,h \models \kappa \text{ and } s \models \pi \\
s,h \models \exists v.\ \Delta & \texttt{iff} & \exists \alpha.\ s[v{\mapsto}\alpha], h \models \Delta \\
s,h \models \Phi_1 \vee \Phi_2 & \texttt{iff} & s,h \models \Phi_1 \text{ or } s,h \models \Phi_2
\end{array}
$$

Semantics of pure formulas is omitted, for simplicity.

Projections [23,39]. For every variable $v \in Var$, if it appears in a spatial formula then it is a *spatial* variable. Otherwise, it is a *numeric* variable. $\bar{x}^S$ (resp. $\bar{x}^N$) is a sequence of variables similar to $\bar{x}$ excluding numeric (resp. spatial) variables. $|\bar{x}^S|$ is a sequence of variables obtained by replacing every spatial variable in $\bar{x}$ with a fresh existential one.

For each inductive predicate $\texttt{P}(\bar{t}) \equiv \Phi$, we assume the inductive symbol $\texttt{P}^S$ and predicate $\texttt{P}^S(\bar{t}^S)$ for its spatial projection that satisfy $\texttt{P}^S(\bar{t}^S) \equiv \Phi^S$. Similarly, we presume the inductive symbol $\texttt{P}^N$ and predicate $\texttt{P}^N(\bar{t}^N)$ for its numeric projection that satisfy $\texttt{P}^N(\bar{t}^N) \equiv \Phi^N$. Given pure conjunction π, we can rewrite it as $\pi \equiv \alpha \wedge \beta \wedge \gamma$ where $FV(\alpha) \subseteq FV(\pi)^S$ and there does not exist another $\alpha' \in \pi$ such that $\alpha \in \alpha'$, $FV(\beta) \subseteq FV(\pi)^N$ and there does not exist another $\beta' \in \pi$ such that $\beta \in \beta'$, and γ is the conjunction of the remaining constraints. In the following, we define the two projections.

Definition 2. *The spatial projection* $(\Phi)^S$ *is defined inductively as follows.*

$$
\begin{array}{llll}
(\Delta_1 \vee \Delta_2)^S & \equiv (\Delta_1)^S \vee (\Delta_2)^S & (\texttt{P}(\bar{v}))^S & \equiv \texttt{P}^S(\bar{v}^S) \\
(\exists \bar{v}.\Delta)^S & \equiv \exists \bar{v}^S.(\Delta)^S & (x{\mapsto}\{\bar{v}\})^S & \equiv x{\mapsto}\{|\bar{v}^S|\} \\
(\kappa \wedge \alpha \wedge \beta \wedge \gamma)^S & \equiv (\kappa)^S \wedge \alpha & (array(v_1,v_2))^S & \equiv array(v_1,v_2) \\
(\kappa_1 * \kappa_2)^S & \equiv (\kappa_1)^S * (\kappa_2)^S & (\texttt{emp})^S & \equiv \texttt{emp}
\end{array}
$$

Similarly, the numeric projection $(\Phi)^N$ *is defined inductively as follows.*

$$
\begin{array}{llll}
(\Delta_1 \vee \Delta_2)^N & \equiv (\Delta_1)^N \vee (\Delta_2)^N & (\kappa_1 * \kappa_2)^N \equiv (\kappa_1)^N \wedge (\kappa_2)^N \\
(\exists \bar{v} \cdot \Delta)^N & \equiv \exists \bar{v}^N \cdot (\Delta)^N & (\texttt{P}(\bar{v}))^N \equiv \texttt{P}^N(\bar{v}^N) \\
(\kappa \wedge \alpha \wedge \beta \wedge \gamma)^N & \equiv (\kappa)^N \wedge \beta & (x{\mapsto}\{\bar{v}\})^N \equiv (array(v_1,v_2))^N \equiv (\texttt{emp})^N \equiv \texttt{true}
\end{array}
$$

Definition 3 (Closed form). *Any numeric project* $\texttt{P}^N(\bar{v}^N)$ *of an definition is called Presburger-definable if there exists a Presburger formula* π *such that for any stack s, we have: $s \models \texttt{P}^N(\bar{v}^N)$ iff $s \models \pi$. We call π is the closed formula of the projection.*

We use function *Pres* to map every Presburger-definable projection into its closed form.

Example 1. The numeric projection of predicate *sllss* in Sect. 2 is:

$$\texttt{sllss}^{\texttt{N}}(mi,ma,n,n_0) \equiv mi{=}ma{\wedge}n{=}n_0$$
$$\vee\ \exists mi_1, n_1.\texttt{sllss}^{\texttt{N}}(mi_1,ma,n_1,n_0){\wedge}mi < mi_1{\wedge}n = n_1{+}1$$

This numeric predicate is in the decidable fragment DPI [39] and its closed form is $Pres(\texttt{sllss}^{\texttt{N}}(mi,ma,n,n_0)) \equiv mi \leqslant ma{\wedge}n \geqslant n_0$.   □

4   Regular Unfolding Trees

Given an inductive predicate with spatial and pure constraints, its regular unfolding tree is generated based on the spatial projection and the base is collected for the spatial and arithmetic projections, separately. In this section, we first introduce regular unfolding trees (Subsect. 4.1). After that, we present an algorithm to construct the trees where back-links are generated based on the spatial projection of formulas (Subsect. 4.2). We also discuss the properties of the trees that are foundations for correctness.

4.1   Data Structure

A regular unfolding tree $\mathcal{T}$ is a tuple $(V, E, \mathcal{C})$ where

- V is a finite set of nodes each of which is a symbolic heap Δ.
- E is a set of labeled and directed edges $(\Delta, L, \Delta') \in E$ where Δ' is derived from unfolding an inductive predicate in Δ and L is a label to record which disjunct rule of the definition has been used. Given $\texttt{P}(\bar{v}){\equiv}\bigvee_{i=1}^{n} \exists \bar{w}_i.\Delta_i$ and a node $\texttt{e} \equiv \Delta * \texttt{P}(\bar{t})$ where $\texttt{P}(\bar{t})$ is chosen for unfolding, then new n nodes $\texttt{e}_i \equiv \Delta * (\exists \bar{w}_i.\Delta_i)[\bar{t}/\bar{v}]$ and new n edges $(\texttt{e}, (\texttt{P}(\bar{t}), \exists \bar{w}_i.\Delta_i)[\bar{t}/\bar{v}], \texttt{e}_i)$ are created.
- $\mathcal{C}$ is a back-link (partial) function. In a back-link $\mathcal{C}(\Delta_c{\rightarrow}\Delta_b, \sigma)$, the leaf node Δ_b is linked back to an ancestor Δ_c when the following two conditions hold. First, there exist $\texttt{P}(\bar{x}) \in \Delta_c$ and $\texttt{P}(\bar{y}) \in \Delta_b$ such that $\texttt{P}(\bar{y})$ is in a subformula unfolded from $\texttt{P}(\bar{x})$. Secondly, there exists Δ_b' s.t. $\Delta_b^S \Rightarrow \Delta_b'^S$, $\Delta_b'^S$ is equisatisfiable with Δ_b^S, and $\Delta_b'^S\sigma \equiv \Delta_c^S$. In such a back-link, Δ_b is a *bud*, and Δ_c is a *companion*.

A leaf node is marked as *open* or *closed*. It is marked as closed when it is either a base formula, unsatisfiable or a bud in a back-link. Otherwise, it is marked as open and may be chosen to reduce into multiple open nodes through predicate unfolding. $\texttt{base}^{\mathcal{P}}(\Delta)$ denotes the set of satisfiable base formulas of the subtree rooted by node Δ.

4.2   Generating Regular Unfolding Trees

Regular unfolding trees are generated via procedure $\omega\texttt{-SAT}$, described in Algorithm 1. Given a formula Δ_0, $\omega\texttt{-SAT}$ creates an initial tree with one open node Δ_0. Then, it iteratively applies the following procedures until all leaf nodes are marked as closed.

Algorithm 1: Procedure ω-SAT

input : Δ_0
output: $\mathcal{T}$
1 $\mathcal{T} \leftarrow \{\Delta_0\}$;   /* initialize */
2 **while true do**
3 $\quad$ $\mathcal{T} \leftarrow base\_eval(\mathcal{T})$;   /* eval bases */
4 $\quad$ $\mathcal{T} \leftarrow link\_back(\mathcal{T})$;   /* generate back-link */
5 $\quad$ $(\text{is\_exists}, \Delta_i) \leftarrow \text{choose\_bfs}(\mathcal{T})$;   /* open leaf for unfolding */
6 $\quad$ **if** *not* is_exists **then**
7 $\quad$ $\quad$ | return $\mathcal{T}$;
8 $\quad$ **else**
9 $\quad$ $\quad$ | $\mathcal{T} \leftarrow \text{unfold}(\Delta_i)$;
10
11 **end**

---

1. Leaf Node Evaluation via procedure *base_eval* (line 3). It checks satisfiability for every *base* leaf node and marks them *closed* accordingly.
2. Back-link Construction via procedure *link_back* (line 4). It attempts to link an open leaf node with an ancestor via some equisatisfiability and substitution principles.
3. Reduction. It chooses an occurrence of inductive predicates in an open leaf node (line 5) to unfold (a.k.a. instantiate - line 9) in a breadth-first manner.

base_eval makes use of the following procedure eXPure to discharge a base formula. eXPure transforms a separation logic formula to a formula in first-order logic. Given a base formula $B \equiv \exists \bar{w}.\ *_{i=1}^{n}\ array(v_i, t_i) * *_{i=1}^{m} x_i \mapsto \{\bar{y}_i\} \wedge \pi$, eXPure works as follows. If $\pi \Rightarrow \bigvee_{1 \leqslant i \leqslant n} v_i = \text{null} \vee t_i = \text{null} \vee \bigvee_{1 \leqslant i \leqslant m} x_i = \text{null}$, then $\pi_B = \text{eXPure}(B) \stackrel{\text{def}}{=} \text{false}$. Otherwise,

$$\pi_B = \text{eXPure}(B) \stackrel{\text{def}}{=} \exists\ \bar{w}.\ \bigwedge_{1 \leqslant i \leqslant n} v_i \leqslant t_i \wedge \bigwedge_{1 \leqslant i < j \leqslant n} (t_i < v_j) \vee (t_j < v_i) \wedge$$
$$\bigwedge_{1 \leqslant i \leqslant n, 1 \leqslant j \leqslant m} (x_j < v_j) \vee (t_i < x_j) \wedge \bigwedge \{ x_i \neq x_j \mid i, j \in \{1...m\} \text{ and } i \neq j\} \wedge \pi$$

Lemma 1. *For any stack s and base formula B, $s \models \text{eXPure}(B)$ iff $\exists h.\ s, h \models B$.*

The procedure *link_back* was designed based on the spatial part of the formulas. As we show that satisfiability in (dis)equalities relies only on quantifier-free variables, existentially quantified heaps could be discarded. Particularly, a leaf node Δ_b, say $\Delta_b \equiv \exists \bar{w}.\ \Delta_{b_1} * \Delta_{b_2} * \kappa_d$, is linked back to an internal node Δ_c only when:

1. every heap predicates in $(\exists \bar{w}.\ \Delta_{b_2})^S$ are unobservable; and
2. κ_d contains duplicate inductive predicate occurrences. Given $\Delta_{b_1} \equiv \kappa_{b_1} \wedge \pi_{b_1}$, for every inductive predicate $P(\bar{v})$ in κ_d, there exists a substitution σ over a subset of existentially quantified variables of $\bar{v}$ such that $(P(\bar{v}))^S \sigma$ is in $(\kappa_{b_1})^S$; and

3. there exists a substitution $\sigma_c \equiv [t_1/v_1, .., t_n/v_n]$ where v_i, t_i ($i \in \{1...n\}$) are existentially quantified such that $\overline{(\Delta_c)^S} \equiv (\exists \bar{w}.\ \overline{(\Delta_{b_1})^S})\sigma_c$.

Properties of ω-SAT over Spatial Projection. We now show some properties of ω-SAT over fragment SHID, a fragment of array separation logic with spatial-only definitions of inductive predicates. These properties are fundamental for compositionality.

Definition 4. (Fragment SHID). *Every inductive symbol* $P_i \in \mathcal{P}$ *in* SHID *is defined as:* $P_i(\bar{v}_i) \equiv \bigvee_{j=1}^{m}(\exists \bar{w}_{i_j}.\ \kappa_{i_j} \wedge \pi_{i_j})$ *where* π_{i_j} *($1 \leqslant j \leqslant m$) are (dis)equalities.*

For every back-link with a companion Δ_c and a bud Δ_b, if Δ_b is *satisfiable* then every formula derived from unfolding Δ_b is of the form $B * B_r$ and there exists a substitution σ such that $B\sigma$ is a leaf node of the subtree rooted by Δ_c and B_r is unobservable.

Proposition 1 (Completeness). *For any* s, h *and a back-link with a companion* Δ_c *and a bud* Δ_b, *if* $s, h \models \Delta_b$, *then* $\exists B \in \mathrm{base}^{\mathcal{P}}(\Delta_c)$ *and* $\exists s' \subseteq s, h' \subseteq h$ *s.t.* $s', h' \models B$.

We show the small model property of the bases generated.

Lemma 2 (Small Model). *For any* s, h *and base satisfiable formula* $B * B_r$ *where* B_r *is unobservable, if* $s, h \models B$, *then* $\exists s' \supseteq s, h' \supseteq h$. $s', h' \models B * B_r$.

ω-SAT with link_back always terminates over SHID as the numbers of both definitions in the system and quantifier-free variables in a formula are finite.

Proposition 2 (Termination). ω-SAT *terminates in* SHID.

An unfolding tree is a cyclic proof only when every leaf nodes are either unsatisfiable or linked back. A cyclic proof is generated as a witness for unsatisfiability.

Proposition 3 (Soundness). *If* Δ *has a cyclic proof,* Δ *is unsatisfiable.*

Example 2. We illustrate ω-SAT over shape-only singly-linked list sll and nested lists nll, the spatial projections of the ones in Sect. 2, without arithmetic properties.

$$\mathrm{sll}(x,y) \equiv \mathrm{emp} \wedge x{=}y \ \vee \ \exists u.x{\mapsto}\{\_,u\}{*}\mathrm{sll}(u,y){\wedge}x{\neq}y$$
$$\mathrm{nll}(x,y,b) \equiv \mathrm{emp} \wedge x{=}y \ \vee \ \exists\, u,Z.x{\mapsto}\{\_,u,Z\} * \mathrm{sll}(Z,b) * \mathrm{nll}(u,y,b){\wedge}x{\neq}y{\wedge}x{\neq}b$$

Figure 3a shows unfolding tree for sll. This tree is constructed as follows. Starting from $\Delta_{s_0} \equiv \mathrm{sll}(x,y)$, ω-SAT unfolds the inductive symbol to obtain B_{s_1} and Δ_{s_2}.

$$B_{s_1} \equiv \mathrm{emp} \wedge x{=}y \qquad\qquad \Delta_{s_2} \equiv \exists u_1.x{\mapsto}\{\_,u_1\}{*}\mathrm{sll}(u_1,y){\wedge}x{\neq}y$$

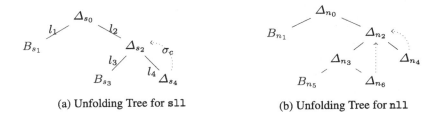

(a) Unfolding Tree for $\mathtt{sll}$ (b) Unfolding Tree for $\mathtt{nll}$

Fig. 3. Regular unfolding trees

with two new edges whose the labels are as follows.

$$l_1 \equiv (\mathtt{sll}(x,y), \mathtt{emp} \wedge x{=}y) \qquad l_2 \equiv (\mathtt{sll}(x,y), \exists u_1.x{\mapsto}\{\_,u_1\}*\mathtt{sll}(u_1,y)\wedge x{\neq}y)$$

ω-SAT evaluates B_{s_1} as satisfiability and marks it as closed. For Δ_{s_2}, ω-SAT unfolds the inductive predicate to obtain $B_{s_3} \equiv x{\mapsto}\{\_,y\}\wedge x{\neq}y$ and the following Δ_{s_4}.

$$\Delta_{s_4} \equiv \exists u_1,u_2.x{\mapsto}\{\_,u_1\}*u_1{\mapsto}\{\_,u_2\}*\mathtt{sll}(u_2,y)\wedge x{\neq}y\wedge u_1{\neq}y$$

The two new edges have the following labels.

$$l_3 \equiv (\mathtt{sll}(u_1,y), \mathtt{emp} \wedge x{=}y) \qquad l_4 \equiv (\mathtt{sll}(u_1,y), \exists u_2.u_1{\mapsto}\{\_,u_2\}*\mathtt{sll}(u_2,y)\wedge u_1{\neq}y)$$

Δ_{s_4} is linked back to Δ_{s_2} and marked as closed since Δ_{s_4} could be rearranged as: $\Delta_{s_4} \equiv \exists u_1,u_2.\Delta_{b_1} * \Delta_{b_2}$ where $\Delta_{b_1} \equiv x{\mapsto}\{\_,u_1\}*\mathtt{sll}(u_2,y)\wedge x{\neq}y$ and $\Delta_{b_2} \equiv u_1{\mapsto}\{\_,u_2\}\wedge u_1{\neq}y$ s.t. (i) $\exists u_1,u_2.\Delta_{b_2}$ is unobservable and (ii) $\overline{\Delta_{s_2}} \equiv (\exists u_1,u_2.\overline{\Delta_{b_1}})\sigma_c$ where $\sigma_c \equiv [u_1/u_2]$. That means, if Δ_{s_4} had been kept unfolding, its sub-tree would have included an infinite set of base formulas each of which has the same observable heap with B_{s_3} i.e., of the form $x{\mapsto}\{\_,\_\}\wedge x{\neq}y*B_r$ where B_r is unobservable. Obviously, models satisfying B_{s_3} are the smallest and have finite heap domains. Since all leave nodes are marked as closed, ω-SAT terminates.

Similarly, Fig. 3b shows the unfolding tree for $\mathtt{nll}$ whose details are as follows.
$\Delta_{n_0} \equiv \mathtt{nll}(x,y,b)$, $B_{n_1} \equiv \mathtt{emp} \wedge x{=}y$, $B_{n_5} \equiv x{\mapsto}\{\_,y,b\}\wedge x{\neq}y\wedge x{\neq}b$
$\Delta_{n_2} \equiv \exists u_1,Z_1.x{\mapsto}\{\_,u_1,Z_1\} * \mathtt{sll}(Z_1,b) * \mathtt{nll}(u_1,y,b)\wedge x{\neq}y\wedge x{\neq}b$

$\Delta_{n_3} \equiv \exists u_1.x{\mapsto}\{\_,u_1,b\} * \mathtt{nll}(u_1,y,b)\wedge x{\neq}y\wedge x{\neq}b$
$\Delta_{n_4} \equiv \exists u_1,Z_1,Z_2.x{\mapsto}\{\_,u_1,Z_1\} * Z1{\mapsto}\{\_,Z_2\} * \mathtt{sll}(Z_2,b) * \mathtt{nll}(u_1,y,b)$
$\qquad\qquad \wedge x{\neq}y\wedge x{\neq}b\wedge Z_1{\neq}b$
$\Delta_{n_6} \equiv \exists u_1,u_2,Z_2.x{\mapsto}\{\_,u_1,b\} * u_1{\mapsto}\{\_,u_2,Z_2\} * \mathtt{sll}(Z_2,b)*\mathtt{nll}(u_2,y,b)$
$\qquad\qquad \wedge x{\neq}y\wedge x{\neq}b\wedge u_1{\neq}y\wedge u_1{\neq}b$

5 Compositional Satisfiability Solver

$\mathtt{S2S}$ compositionally discharges a formula as follows. First, it computes for every inductive predicate $\mathtt{P}(\bar{t})$ a base, denoted as $\mathtt{base}^{\mathcal{P}}(\mathtt{P}(\bar{t}))$ - a set of *satisfiable* base

---

Algorithm 2: Deriving Bases.

---

    input : $\mathcal{P}$
    output: base$^{\mathcal{P}}$
1 **foreach** $\mathtt{P_i}(\bar{t}_i) \in \mathcal{P}$ **do**
2      $(V, E, \mathcal{C}) \leftarrow \omega\text{-}\mathsf{SAT}(\mathtt{P_i}(\bar{t}_i))$;   `/* reduction tree */`
3   **repeat**
4          $\mathcal{C}(\Delta_c {\rightarrow} \Delta_b, \sigma) \leftarrow$ out-most cycle of $(V, E, \mathcal{C})$;
5          $\Psi^S \leftarrow \varnothing$;
6          $\alpha \leftarrow \bigvee\{\Delta^N_{b_i}\}$;   `/* arithmetic of sat buds */`
7   **foreach** $\Delta^S_{\mathsf{sat}} \in \mathcal{C}(\Delta_c {\rightarrow} \Delta_b, \sigma)$ **do**
8              $\Psi^S \leftarrow \Psi^S \cup \{\Delta^S_{\mathsf{sat}}\}$;   `/* spatial of sat leaf bases */`
9              $\alpha \leftarrow \alpha \vee \Delta^N_{\mathsf{sat}}$;   `/* arithmetic of sat leaf bases */`
10   **end**
11   **if** $\Psi^S = \varnothing$ **then**
12          $\Delta_c \leftarrow \mathsf{false}$;   `/* unsat - cyclic proofs */`
13   **if** Δ^N_c *contains one inductive predicate* **then**
14          $\beta \leftarrow Pres(\Delta^N_c)$;   `/* `$\Delta^N_c \equiv \alpha$` */`
15   **else**
16          $\beta \leftarrow Pres(\alpha)$;
17        $\Delta_c \leftarrow \bigvee\{B \wedge \beta \mid B \in \Psi^S\}$;
18   **until** *no more cycles*;
19   base$^{\mathcal{P}}((\mathtt{P_i}(\bar{t}_i))) \leftarrow \{\Delta^{noncyc}_{\mathsf{sat}} \mid \Delta^{noncyc}_{\mathsf{sat}} \text{ is sat}\}$;   `/* sat leaf nodes */`
20 **end**
21 **return** base$^{\mathcal{P}}$;

---

formulae, that precisely charaterises its satisfiability. If this set is empty, then $\mathtt{P}(\bar{t}) \equiv \mathtt{false}$. After that, to discharge formula Δ it replaces every occurrence of inductive predicates with the corresponding base to obtain a disjunctive base formula, denoted by base$^{\mathcal{P}}(\Delta)$, before using procedure eXPure to transform this base formula into π_B in first-order logic. Finally, π_B could be discharged efficiently by using an SMT solver.

In the rest of this section, we first present the algorithm to collect the bases (Subsect. 5.1). After that, we identify five semantic conditions for decidability and compositionality (Subsect. 5.2). Finally, we show a syntactic decidable fragment, an extension of SHID, where the satisfiability solving can be compositional (Subsect. 5.3).

5.1 Computing Bases

Algorithm 2 describes how to infer bases for inductive predicates. In intuition, for each inductive predicate, it first computes a regular unfolding tree where cycles are generated based on the spatial projection of buds and companions. After that, for every cycle, it infers bases for the spatial projection and closed form for the numeric projection separately. Finally, it conjoins the two bases. In particular, it first generates an unfolding tree at line 2. (We assume that all subtrees whose leaf nodes are either unsatisfiable or linked back are eliminated afterward.) At line 4, out−most cycle in each path is the one which has the farthest companion from the root. At line 6, it collects numeric parts of all buds (each cycle has one companion and one or more buds). Next, for each cycle, it collects the spatial projection and numeric projection of all *satisfiable* leaf nodes (lines 7–9). If spatial projection of all base leaf nodes is unsatisfiable, it returns unsatisfiable (line 12). Every base formula generated by the cycle is equisatisfiable with one of those in the set of all spatial bases collected. For the numeric, it computes the closed form of satisfiable instances (lines 13–16). (Recall that *Pres* is the function that maps numeric projection of each inductive definition in the decidable fragment to a Presburger formula.) Note that if the numeric companion Δ_c^N is an occurrence of an inductive predicate, it computes the closed form using a more precise on-the-fly definition ($\Delta_c^N \equiv \alpha$ at line 14). Finally, at line 17, it replaces the companion with the combined base. This process of computing bases for cycles is repeated in such a bottom-up manner until the tree does not contain any cycles. Finally, it collects all the satisfiable leaf nodes of the tree.

Example 3. For the inductive predicates in Example 3, the base computed for the cycle of sll is $(B_{s_3})^S = \exists Y.\ x \mapsto \{\_,Y\} \wedge x \neq y$ and the base of generated for sll is a disjunctive set of the two satisfiable base leaf nodes: $\mathtt{base}^{\mathcal{P}}(\mathtt{sll}(x,y)) \equiv \{B_{s_1}; (B_{s_3})^S\}$. Similarly, the base computed for nll is: $\mathtt{base}^{\mathcal{P}}(\mathtt{nll}(x,y,b)) \equiv \{B_{n_1}; (B_{n_5})^S\}$. □

5.2   Decidability and Compositionality

We state the five conditions for a fragment of inductive predicates such that Algorithm 2 is terminating, and the generated bases are both sound and complete. First, the following condition ensures the separation of the spatial and numeric projections such that there is no over-approximation of the two projections. Suppose that the pure formula π of a definition rule in SLIDLIA$_{\mathtt{sem}}$ is $\pi \equiv \alpha \wedge \beta \wedge \gamma$ where α is the spatial constraint, β is the arithmetic constraint and γ is the mixing constraint between the two domains.

C1. γ *is* true. We note that if all inductive definitions of P($\bar{t}$) in a fragment satisfy **C1**, then such γ of any formula derived from unfolding P($\bar{v}$) is also true.
   For the termination of ω-SAT at line 2, we need the following condition.

C2. α in every definition rule in SLIDLIA$_{\mathtt{sem}}$ is a conjunction of (dis)equalities.
   The completeness further requires the three following conditions.

– Every back-link generated for the spatial projection is (sound and) complete when combined with pure bases. Recall that a bud is of the form $\Delta_b \equiv \exists \bar{v}.(\kappa_{b_1} \wedge \alpha_{b_1} \wedge \beta_{b_1}) * (\kappa_{b_2} \wedge \alpha_{b_2} \wedge \beta_{b_2}) * \kappa_d$ where $\kappa_{b_2} \wedge \alpha_{b_2} \wedge \beta_{b_2}$ is unobservable and κ_d is the duplicate conjunction. As ω-SAT always returns the observable part, unlike in SHID, discarding $(\kappa_{b_2} \wedge \alpha_{b_2} \wedge \beta_{b_2} * \kappa_d)^S$ may make the combined bases incomplete; that is $(\Delta_b)^S$ is unsatisfiable while $(\Delta_b)^N$ is satisfiable.

The completeness is retained only when: For any s, we have   if $s \models (\Delta_b)^N$, then $\exists\, s',\, h'.\ s',\!h' \models (\Delta_b)^S$. As ω-SAT always returns the observable part, the following condition is equivalent.

C3. For any s, h, we have: if $s, h \models (\Delta_{b_1})^S$, then $\exists\, s',\, h'.\ s',\!h' \models (\Delta_b)^S$.

- **C4.** *If the system of inductive definitions contains arithmetic constraints, each cycle in the regular unfolding tree derived for an inductive definition contains at most one satisfiable spatial projection leaf node* (line 8). This condition forbids the over-approximation of the combination at line 17.

- **C5.** *Numeric projection of every inductive predicate (at line 16) or on-the-fly numeric predicate (at line 14) is Presburger-definable* i.e., the numeric predicate is in a decidable fragment like DPI [39]. This ensures that the numeric base computed is equivalent to the numeric constraints of the whole subtree.

Suppose Algorithm 2 infers a base $B^S \wedge \pi$ for subtree involving a cycle and $B*B_r$ is a base leaf of the subtree. By Lemma 2, for every v where $s(v) \in dom(h' \backslash h)$, v is existentially quantified. Hence, the heaps in $h' \setminus h$ could not be accessed by the outer scope of B_r. As so, for any formula Δ, $B * B_r * \Delta$ is equisatisfiable with $(B^S \wedge \pi) * \Delta$. Therefore, satisfiability could be performed modularly via the inferred base $B^S \wedge \pi$.

Theorem 1 (Composition). *For any stack s, heap h and Δ, we have:*

- *(if) if $s, h \models \mathtt{base}^{\mathcal{P}}(\Delta)$, then $\exists s', h'.\ s', h' \models \Delta$.*
- *(only if) if $s, h \models \Delta$, then $\exists s', h'.\ s', h' \models \mathtt{base}^{\mathcal{P}}(\Delta)$.*

Motivating Example Revisited. We show how to compute the bases of predicate $\mathtt{sllss}(x,y,mi,ma,n,n_0)$ in the second motivating example. In the definition of this predicate, x, y are spatial variables and mi, ma, n and n_0 are numeric variables. **C1** and **C2** hold straightforwardly for this definition.

At line 2, ω-SAT constructs a reduction tree whose shape is similar to the tree in Fig. 3a. Its respective nodes are as follows. $\Delta_{ss_0} \equiv \mathtt{sllss}(x,y,mi,ma,n,n_0)$

$B_{ss_1} \equiv \mathtt{emp} \wedge x=y \wedge mi=ma \wedge n=n_0$

$\Delta_{ss_2} \equiv \exists u_1,m_1,n_1.\, x \mapsto \{mi,u_1\} * \mathtt{sllss}(u_1,y,m_1,ma,n_1,n_0) \wedge x \neq y \wedge mi < m_1 \wedge n = n_1 + 1$

$B_{ss_3} \equiv x \mapsto \{mi,y\} \wedge x \neq y \wedge mi < ma \wedge n = n_0 + 1$

$\Delta_{ss_4} \equiv \exists u_1,u_2,m_1,m_2,n_1,n_2.\, x \mapsto \{mi,u_1\} * u_1 \mapsto \{m_1,u_2\} * \mathtt{sllss}(u_2,y,m_2,ma,n_2,n_0)$
$\qquad \wedge x \neq y \wedge u_1 \neq y \wedge mi < m_1 \wedge m_1 < m_2 \wedge n = n_1 + 1 \wedge n_1 = n_2 + 1$

In Δ_{ss_4}, $\Delta_{b_1}^S \equiv x \mapsto \{mi,u_1\} * \mathtt{sllss}^S(u_2,y)$, $\kappa_d \equiv \mathtt{emp}$ and the spatial projection of the unobservable is $\Delta_{b_2}^S \equiv u_1 \mapsto \{m_1,u_2\} \wedge u_1 \neq y$. As $\overline{\Delta_{b_2}^S}$ is separate from $\overline{\Delta_{b_1}^S}$, **C3** holds. And as the cycle in the reduction tree has only one base B_{ss_3}, **C4** holds. As shown in the preceding subsection, its numeric projection is in DPI and is thus Presburger-definable: $Pres(\mathtt{sllss}^N(mi,ma,n,n_0)) \equiv mi \leqslant ma \wedge n \geqslant n_0$. Thus, **C5** holds. Moreover, the base for the cycle of the tree is computed as $B_{22} \equiv (B_{ss_3})^S \wedge Pres((\Delta_{ss_3})^N \vee (\Delta_{ss_4})^N)$,

$B_{22} \equiv (B_{ss_3})^S \wedge Pres((\varDelta_{ss_2})^N)$

$\equiv \exists Y.x \mapsto \{mi,Y\} \wedge x \neq y \wedge Pres(\exists m_1, n_1.\mathtt{sllss}^N(m_1,ma,n_1,n_0) \wedge mi < m_1 \wedge n = n_1+1)$

$\equiv \exists Y, m_1, n_1.x \mapsto \{mi,Y\} \wedge x \neq y \wedge (m_1 \leqslant ma \wedge n_1 \geqslant n_0 \wedge mi < m_1 \wedge n = n_1+1)$

Finally, the base computed for $\mathtt{sllss}$ is: $\mathtt{base}^{\mathcal{P}}(\mathtt{sllss}(x,y,mi,ma,n,n_0)) \equiv \{B_{ss_1}; B_{22}\}$.

The remaining question is syntactic decidable fragments where the satisfiability is compositional. $\mathtt{SHID}$ satisfies the five conditions for compositionality straightforwardly. As definitions of inductive predicates in [3,14,18,21,23,39,41] satisfy these five conditions, satisfiability is compositional in these fragments. The next subsection shows a new decidable fragment.

5.3 Compositionality with Small-Model Arithmetic Properties

We study fragment $\mathtt{SHIDe}$ that is an extension of $\mathtt{SHID}$ with small-model arithmetic pure properties (e.g., sortedness) where every inductive predicate also has small models w.r.t. satisfiability. Given a predicate $\mathtt{P_i}(\bar{v}_i)$, if two parameters $v, t \in \bar{v}_i$ define a small-model pure property then in every instantiation unfolded from $\mathtt{P_i}(\bar{v}_i)$, the constraints over v, t is: $\exists w_1, ..., w_n.v \diamond w_1 \wedge w_1 \diamond w_2 \wedge ... \wedge w_n \diamond t$ (where $\diamond \in \{=, \geqslant, \leqslant\}$).

Definition 5. ($\mathtt{SHIDe}$). *Given every definition* $\mathtt{P_i}(\bar{v}_i) \equiv \bigvee_{j=1}^{m} (\exists \bar{w}_{i_j}. \ \kappa_{i_j} \wedge \pi_{i_j})$ *in* $\mathtt{SHID}$, π_{i_j} *($1 \leqslant j \leqslant m$) may contain* $\diamond$ *operators over parameters of inductive predicate* $\mathtt{P_i}$ *such that for any* s, h *if* $s, h \models \mathtt{P_i}(\bar{v}_i)$, $\forall l_1 \in dom(h).\exists l_2 \in dom(h)$ *s.t.* $h(l_1) = (...,l_2,...,l_{j_1},..)$, $h(l_2) = (...,l_{j_2},...)$ *and* $l_{j_1} \diamond l_{j_2}$ *holds where* l_{j_1} *and* l_{j_2} *are the* j^{th} *components.*

Example 4. We define linked lists being sorted as follows.

$\mathtt{sllso}(x,y,mi,ma) \equiv \mathtt{emp} \wedge x=y \wedge ma=mi$
$\vee \ \exists u,mi_1.x \mapsto \{mi,u\} * \mathtt{sllso}(u,y,mi_1,ma) \wedge x \neq y \wedge mi < mi_1$

For any formula B unfolded from $\mathtt{sllso}(x,y,mi,ma)$, in case B has an empty heap, $mi=ma$. Otherwise, $mi<ma$. Hence, the base that includes one with the empty heap and another with *one* singleton heap is sufficient to characterise the satisfiability of $\mathtt{sllso}(x,y,mi,ma)$. Particularly, to compute base for $\mathtt{sllso}(x,y,mi,ma)$, ω-$\mathtt{SAT}$ constructs for it a cyclic reduction tree that has the same structure as the tree of $\mathtt{sll}(x,y)$ (in Example 3). $\square$

Obviously, ω-$\mathtt{SAT}$ terminates to compute bases for a definition in $\mathtt{SHIDe}$ that is a combination of a definition in $\mathtt{SHID}$ with the small-model pure properties.

6 Decidable Fragment $\mathtt{SLIDLIA}$

We define a syntactic fragment, called $\mathtt{SLIDLIA}$ (Subsect. 6.1). The decidability and compositionality of $\mathtt{SLIDLIA}$ rely on the decidability of its numeric inductive predicates. In Subsect. 6.2, we show that $\mathtt{AID}$ - Arithmetic with Inductive Definitions, the fragment including these numeric projections, is indeed decidable.

6.1 Predicate Definition

A predicate in SLIDLIA with one pair of numeric parameters is defined as:

$$P(r,F,\bar{B},v_s,v_t) \equiv emp \wedge r = F \wedge v_s = v_t$$
$$\vee \; \exists X_{tl}, \bar{Z}, v_s', \bar{Z}_s. r \mapsto \{\bar{p}\} * \kappa' * P(X_{tl}, F, \bar{B}, v_s', v_t) \wedge \alpha \wedge \beta$$

where r is called the root parameter, F the target parameter, $\bar{B}$ the border parameters, v_s, v_t is a pair of parameters to capture a pure property, $r \mapsto \{\bar{p}\} * \kappa'$ the matrix of the heaps. r, F and $\bar{B}$ are spatial variables and v_s, v_t are numeric variables. Moreover, this definition is constrained by the following five conditions.

Y1. $\{X_{tl}\} \cup \bar{Z} \subseteq \bar{p} \subseteq \{X_{tl}\} \cup \bar{Z} \cup \bar{B}$.

Y2. $\kappa' := Q(R,U,\bar{Y},S,T) \mid \kappa' * \kappa' \mid emp$ where $Q \not\equiv P$, $R \in \bar{Z}$ and for any $Q_1(R_1,...) \in \kappa'$ and $Q_2(R_2,...) \in \kappa'$ then $R_1 \not\equiv R_2$, $U \in \bar{Z} \cup \bar{B} \cup \{r, X_{tl}, \mathtt{null}\}$, $\bar{Y} \subseteq \bar{B} \cup \{r, X_{tl}, \mathtt{null}\}$, and $S \in \bar{Z}_s$ and $T \in \bar{Z}_s \cup \{v_s'\}$.

Y3. α is a conjunction of (dis)equalities and $FV(\alpha) \subseteq \{r, F, \mathtt{null}\} \cup \bar{B}$.

Y4. β is of the one of the following forms:

- $\beta \equiv \beta' \wedge v_s = v_s' + c_1 z + c_2$ where $c_1, c_2 \in \mathbb{Z}$, $FV(\beta') \subseteq \bar{Z}_s$, and $z \in \bar{Z}_s$.
- $\beta \equiv \beta' \wedge v_s \diamond v_s' + c_1$ where $c_1 \in \mathbb{Z}$, $\diamond \in \{=, \geqslant, \leqslant\}$, $FV(\beta') \subseteq \bar{Z}_s$.

Y5. There is no mutual recursion.

The extension to multiple pairs of numeric parameters is straightforward. SLIDLIA is subsumes the decidable fragments presented in [3,13,14,18,21,23]. SLIDLIA $\subset$ SLIDLIA$_{sem}$ because **Y3** and **Y4** imply **C1**; **Y3** ensures **C2**; **Y2** implies **C3**; **Y1** and **Y2** imply **C4**. We show **C5** in the next subsection. SLIDLIA includes sllss, nllss (shown in Sect. 2), skip-lists, nested lists.

6.2 Decidability of Fragment AID

We show a procedure to compute the closed form of the numeric projections of definitions in SLIDLIA. Recap that the numeric projection of a definition is of the form:

$$P^N(v_s,v_t) \equiv v_s = v_t \; \vee \; \exists v_s', \bar{z}. \bigwedge_{i=0}^{n} P_i^N(S_i,T_i) \wedge P^N(v_s',v_t) \wedge \beta' \wedge \beta_0$$

where $\beta_0 \equiv v_s \diamond v_s' + c$ or $\beta_0 \equiv v_s = v_s' + c_1 m + c_2$, $\diamond \in \{\geqslant, \leqslant\}$, $\bigwedge_{i=0}^{n} P_i^N(S_i,T_i) \equiv \mathbf{true}$ when $n=0$, $S_i, T_i \in \bar{z}$, and $FV(\beta') \subseteq \bar{z}$.

As definitions in SLIDLIA do not allow mutual recursion (condition **Y5**), the computation of the closed form of these numeric definitions can be performed in a bottom-up manner: the closed forms of all pred $P_i^N(S_i,T_i)$ are computed before the computation of the closed formula of pred $P^N(v_s,v_t)$. The computation of the closed formula is based on the two forms of β_0 above. First, we show the computation for the first form.

Lemma 3. *Given any numeric projection in the following form*

$$P^N(v_s,v_t) \equiv v_s = v_t \; \vee \; \exists v_s', \bar{z}. P^N(v_s',v_t) \wedge \beta'(\bar{z}) \wedge v_s \diamond v_s' + c$$

where $\diamond \in \{=, \geqslant, \leqslant\}$, and $c \in \mathbb{Z}$. Then, we have:

$$P^N(v_s,v_t) \equiv v_s - v_t \vee \exists \bar{z}, k. \beta'(\bar{z}) \wedge v_s - v_t \diamond ck \wedge k \geqslant 1$$

The computation for the second form of β_0 is based on the arithmetic of addition and divisibility [2,4,24]. Authors in [2,24] show that the formulas of the form $\exists \bar{v}. \bigwedge_{i=1}^{K} f_i(\bar{v}) \mid g_i(\bar{v})$ are decidable, where f_i, g_i are linear functions over $\bar{v} \equiv \{v_1, .., v_n\}$ and the symbol $\mid$ means that each f_i is an integer divisor of g_i when both are interpreted over $\mathbb{N}^n$. Recently, authors in [4] presented a decision procedure for an extension with universally quantified formulas. They proposed to eliminate the quantifiers and transform the formulas in the language $\langle +, \mid, 0, 1 \rangle$ into Presburger arithmetic.

Proposition 4. ([4]). *The following formula is Presburger-definable:*

$$Q z Q_1 x_1 ... Q_n x_n . \bigvee_{i=1}^{N} (\bigwedge_{j=1}^{M_i} h_{ij}(z) \mid f_{ij}(\bar{x}, z) \wedge \bigwedge_{j=1}^{M_i} h'_{ij}(z) \big/ g_{ij}(\bar{x}, z) \wedge \pi(\bar{x}, z))$$

where Q, $Q_1, .., Q_n \in \{\exists, \forall\}$, π is quantifier-free, f, f', h, g are linear functions.

Secondly, we show that the closed form for the second form of β_0 is in the arithmetic of addition and divisibility.

Lemma 4 (Nested Quantitative Property). *Given a numeric projection of the form:*

$$\text{P}^{\text{N}}(v_s, v_t) \equiv v_s = v_t \ \vee \ \exists v'_s, \bar{z}. \text{P}^{\text{N}}(v'_s, v_t) \wedge \beta' \wedge v_s = v'_s + c_1 z + c_0$$

where $FV(\beta) \subseteq \bar{z}$ and $z \in \bar{z}$, $c_0, c_1 \in \mathbb{Z}$. Then, $\text{P}^{\text{N}}(v_s, v_t) \equiv \exists \bar{z}. \beta'(\bar{z}) \wedge c_1 z + c_0 \mid v_s - v_t$.

By Proposition 4, $\exists \bar{z}. \beta(\bar{z}) \wedge c_1 z + c_0 \mid v_s - v_t$ is Presburger-definable. Hence, Lemma 3, Lemma 4 and Theorem 4 imply that $\text{P}^{\text{N}}(v_s, v_t)$ is Presburger-definable.

Theorem 2. *Numeric projections of definitions in* SLIDLIA *is Presburger-definable.*

7   Implementation and Evaluation

We have implemented a prototype tool, called S2S, using OCaml for the satisfiability problems. We made use of Z3 [11] as a back-end SMT solver for the arithmetic.

S2S gives a precise answer to those problems in a fragment that satisfies the five conditions in Sect. 5.2. For those that are beyond these conditions, S2S infers over-approximated bases to check their unsatisfiability. In particular, if **C1.** or **C2.** is violated, i.e., formulas with pointer arithmetic constraints, S2S discards these constraints. For efficiency, checking the satisfiability of buds to comply with **C3.** can be ignored. If **C4.** or **C5.** is violated, i.e., an arithmetically inductive definition is beyond the decidable fragment AID, S2S computes for it an over-approximated closed form using the technique described in [21]. In intuition, for each definition, it first generates a set of Horn clauses to capture the least fixed point set of its values. After that, it uses the fixed point analysis in [34,40] to solve these clauses.

To demonstrate the efficiency, we have evaluated S2S on two sets of satisfiability benchmarks. The first one includes those generated by the program verifier S2 [19,22] (Subsect. 7.1), and the second one consists of those taken from the recent competition for separation logic solvers SL-COMP 2019 [37,38] (Subsect. 7.2). All experiments were performed on a machine with Intel Core i7-6700 3.4 GHz and 8 GB RAM. If a solver runs longer than 600 s, we terminate it and mark the result as unknown.

Table 1. Satisfiability solving with/without compositional reasoning

Data Structure (pure properties)	#query	#unsat	#sat	without		with	
				#Z3	Time	#Z3	Time
Singly llist (size)	666	75	591	3,173	1.01	762	0.40
Sorted llist (size, sorted)	217	21	196	796	0.55	336	0.36
Doubly llist (size)	452	50	402	1,803	0.79	552	0.46
Heap trees (size, maxelem)	386	38	348	3,732	6.03	865	2.61
AVL (height, size)	881	64	817	9,051	23.06	2,026	10.85
RBT (size, blackheight, color)	1,741	217	1,524	3,491,730	74,158	1,767	2.81
rose-tree (size)	25	8	17	300	0.34	153	0.25
	4,368	473	3,895	3,510,585	74,189.78	6,461	17.74

7.1   Efficiency of Compositional Solving

In this section, we present experiments over satisfiability problems with and without compositional reasoning. These problems come from the symbolic execution of the heap-based verification tool [19]. Each test suit consists of a high number of test problems over the same set of inductive predicates. Then we run S2S over the suite in two settings. For the first one, S2S generates bases for each input without reusing the bases inferred for inductive definitions. For the second one, S2S generates bases for each test by reusing the bases of inductive definitions.

The experimental results are shown in Table 1. The first column shows the names of inductive predicates and pure properties that includes cyclic linked-list, sorted singly-linked list, doubly-linked list, AVL trees, red-black tree, and rose trees. Pure properties in each data structure include size properties (number of allocated objects), sortedness, the maximal element of heaps, the height of trees, and color (red or black). The next column captures the number of satisfiability problems sent to the solver for the verification of each program. The next two columns describe the number of unsat and sat queries, respectively. The remaining four columns are divided into two groups corresponding to the runs without and with composition. For each group, we report the number of Z3 invocations in the first column and the time taken in seconds in the second column. In the last row, we sum the values of all the measurements of all data structures.

The results show that S2S with the compositional reasoning is much more efficient. In all experiments, the compositional solving helps to discharge the queries quickly with small numbers of Z3 invocations. To sum up, S2S with the compositional reasoning took as 0.024% (17.74 s/74,189.78 s) in time and 0.184% (6,461/3,510,585) in the numbers of Z3 invocations as without the compositional reasoning. The experimental results of red-black trees, AVL with height and size properties, especially, confirm the great advantage of the compositional reasoning. On average, S2S with the compositional reasoning took 0.0028 s to discharge one satisfiability problem.

7.2   Experiments on SL-COMP 2019 Benchmarks

We have compared S2S against the state-of-the-art solvers like Asterix [28], SLSAT [5], SPEN [13], S2SAT$_{SL}$ [23], and Harrsh [17]. We have conducted the comparisons over *all* three satisfiability divisions of the competition: *qf_shls_sat*, *qf_shid_sat*, and *qf_shidlia_sat*. All test problems are in our decidable fragments. For each division, we report the number of correct outputs and time (in minutes and seconds) taken by each tool. We note that as Asterix supported hardwired singly-linked lists only, it is unable to handle the problems in *qf_shid_sat*, and *qf_shidlia_sat*. Similarly, as SPEN, SLSAT and Harrsh have not supported arithmetic, *qf_shidlia_sat* is beyond their interests.

We report the results in Table 2. In this table, the first column presents the name of the tools. The remaining columns show the results of three divisions each of which includes three columns: the number of correct satisfiability results (sat), the number of correct unsatisfiability results (unsat), and the time (*m* is for minutes and *s* for seconds) taken, respectively, by each tool. - means the solver has not supported these benchmarks in the corresponding division yet. In the third row, the number between "(..)" reports the total number of tests in a column.

Table 2. Experimental Results on SL-COMP benchmarks

Tool	*qf_shls_sat*			*qf_shid_sat*			*qf_shidlia_sat*		
	sat (55)	unsat (55)	Time (110)	sat (81)	unsat (18)	Time (99)	sat (15)	unsat (18)	Time (33)
Asterix [28]	55	55	0.56s	-	-	-	-	-	-
SPEN [13]	55	55	16.60s	-	-	-	-	-	-
S2SAT$_{SL}$ [23]	55	55	36.61s	50	12	382m	13	8	120m6s
Harrsh [17]	55	55	11m7.41s	55	18	274m56s	-	-	-
SLSAT [5]	54	54	36m22s	57	18	218m51s	-	-	-
S2S	55	55	1.18s	56	18	237m55s	15	18	10.07s

The first group shows the results of division *qf_shls_sat*. Each test problem, generated randomly by Asterix's authors [27], contains 10–20 pointer-typed variables pointing to singly-linked lists. In this division, all tools performed pretty well. In particular, Asterix performed the best, S2S was the second, and SPEN was the third. Asterix and S2S decided all tests correctly in a short time. SLSAT was timeout in 3 test problems. We note that as the definition of the singly-linked list was hardwired syntactically in Asterix, in contrast to S2S, Asterix would save the parsing time for this definition in these 110 tests.

The second group reports the results for division *qf_shid_sat* targeting general inductive definitions. It includes 40 challenging tests (succ-circuit[01..20] and succ-rec[01..20]), generated by SLSAT's authors [5], each of which requires a brute-force search of 2^n values. SLSAT, S2S, and Harrsh performed pretty well in this division. SLSAT performed the best; it was either timeout or stack overflow at only 24 problems: succ-circuit[07..20] and succ-rec[11..20]. Note that, in SL-COMP 2019 [37], S2S was implemented together with an under-approximate technique and outperformed other tools; it discharged all problems in this division correctly in a super short time.

The third group, whose tests were contributed by the authors of [14, 23, 41], describes the results of division *qf_shidlia_sat* targeting the combination of linearly compositional inductive predicates and pure properties. While S2SAT$_{SL}$ could handle 21/33 tests in 120 min, S2S reported correctly for all tests within 10.07 s.

S2SAT$_{SL}$ also base on cyclic proofs. It did not support compositionality. Instead of reusing the bases, it constructed cyclic proofs for every input. Its termination thus relies on not only those definitions of inductive predicates but also the arithmetical constraints in the input. For instance, S2SAT$_{SL}$ could not handle $\Delta_{01} \equiv \texttt{els}(x,n) \wedge n = 320001$ and $\Delta_{02} \equiv \texttt{els}(x,n) \wedge n = 320000$ in which els predicate represents lists with an even number of elements and n captures the length. If we increased the timeout to a large enough number, S2SAT$_{SL}$ would manage the second test successfully but would not terminate for the first one. In contrast, S2S first inferred for $\texttt{els}(x,n)$ the base as $\texttt{base}^{\mathcal{P}}(\texttt{els}(x,n)) \equiv \{\texttt{emp} \wedge x = \texttt{null} \wedge n = 0, \exists k.\ x \mapsto \{\_\} \wedge n = 2k \wedge k > 0\}$. After that, to decide Δ_{01}, it replaced this base into Δ_{01} and found that both disjuncts are unsatisfiable. It thus decided Δ_{01} as unsatisfiable. For Δ_{02}, after replacing the base into Δ_{02}, it found that the second disjunct was satisfiable. Hence, it concluded Δ_{02} is satisfiable.

8   Related Work

The "base" was first introduced for shape-only predicates by Brotherston *et al.* [5] and then extended for the combination of shape and arithmetic properties by Le *et al.* [23]. While the former computes the base based on a fixed point algorithm, the latter makes use of cyclic proofs. However, these works did not discuss compositionality. Unlike [5] and [23], this work presents a compositional reasoning as well as the most expressive syntactic decidable fragments. Our proposal is a generation of the work presented in [23]: It returns all equisatisfiable solutions of a formula. The proposed decidable fragment, SHIDe, is slightly extended from the one on general inductive definitions introduced in [5] and [23]. A crucial contribution of our work is to show that we can apply compositional reasoning into this fragment for efficiency.

The authors in [21] propose a cyclic proof system for the combination of heap structures and universally pure constraints. In another direction, work in [39] presents a decision procedure for a fragment where every predicate has two spatial base pairs, and their pure projections are Presburger-definable. Recently, authors in [23] extended the cyclic proof system in [21] for decidable fragments that subsume the ones presented in both [21] and [39]. They also identify *semantic* conditions for decidable fragments with arithmetic constraints. Our focus complements [23] as we target compositional satisfiability solving. The authors in [6,7] studied satisfiability for array separation logic. However, these works did not consider inductive predicates like ours. Nevertheless, developing a cyclic proof system to reason about the contents of array predicates might be future work; for example, by reducing array theory into string constraints [20].

The idea of small models of heap structures and data has been discussed in the literature: in separation logic [3,15,18] and other logics [25,26]. However, unlike ours, the works in separation logic mainly focused on the entailment problem. Berdine *et al.* present pioneering results for lists and binary trees [3]. They show that a singly-linked list has the small model property; every singly-linked list predicate can be precisely characterised by those heap models of size zero or two. Recently, this fragment was extended with some small-model pure properties in [18]. Our proposal infers small models for compositionality in a fragment, far beyond the lists and trees, including array separation logic with general inductive predicates and small-model pure properties.

Other related works include those satisfiability solvers presented in [14,17,32, 33,41]. The authors in [17] present a decision procedure based on heap automata. [14,41] present a graph-based technique with predicates that are beyond the singly-linked lists. These works support compositional predicates and one-hole trees with sortedness, size, and balancedness. However, they have supported neither mutually recursive definitions nor nested lists like ours. Our work closely relates to the satisfiability solver for STRAND logic [25]. In [25], the authors discussed satisfiability-preserving embedding that helps to enumerate a finite number of minimal models. Similar to this work, given a formula, our procedure derives for it a base with the minimal model property that precisely characterises its satisfiability. Unlike this work, while our solver works compositionally, STRAND did not support the compositionality.

Those works in [12,35] complement our work. While these works supported the separating implication, they did not consider inductive definitions like ours. Finally, the work in [39] discusses a solver for arithmetic with inductive definitions. This work proposes to infer for each numerically inductive predicate a closed-form, an equivalent formula in Presburger arithmetic. We here extend the decidable fragment in [39] with nested list predicates.

9   Conclusion

We have presented a novel satisfiability solver in a fragment of array separation logic combined with inductive definitions and arithmetic properties. Our proposal differentiates itself from existing works on the compositional reasoning via the base inference. Furthermore, we have shown that satisfiability solving can be compositional in the current fragments. We have implemented the proposal into S2S and evaluated it over the two sets of non-trivial benchmarks: taken from the SL-COMP 2019 and generated from the verification of complex-pointer programs. The experimental results show that S2S is effective and efficient. and is promising for being used in a verification system.

Acknowledgments. The author was partially supported by the UK's Engineering and Physical Sciences Research Council (EPSRC): Grant number EP/R006865/1.

References

1. Barrett, C., Kroening, D., Melham, T.: Problem solving for the 21st century: efficient solver for satisfiability modulo theories. In: Knowledge Transfer Report, Technical report 3. London Mathematical Society and Smith Institute for Industrial Mathematics and System Engineering, June 2014
2. Bel'tyukov, A.P.: Decidability of the universal theory of natural numbers with addition and divisibility. J. Sov. Math. **14**(5), 1436–1444 (1980)
3. Berdine, J., Calcagno, C., O'Hearn, P.W.: A decidable fragment of separation logic. In: Lodaya, K., Mahajan, M. (eds.) FSTTCS 2004. LNCS, vol. 3328, pp. 97–109. Springer, Heidelberg (2004). https://doi.org/10.1007/978-3-540-30538-5_9
4. Bozga, M., Iosif, R.: On decidability within the arithmetic of addition and divisibility. In: Sassone, V. (ed.) FoSSaCS 2005. LNCS, vol. 3441, pp. 425–439. Springer, Heidelberg (2005). https://doi.org/10.1007/978-3-540-31982-5_27
5. Brotherston, J., Fuhs, C., Gorogiannis, N., Pérez, J.N.: A decision procedure for satisfiability in separation logic with inductive predicates. In: Proceedings of CSL-LICS. ACM (2014)
6. Brotherston, J., Gorogiannis, N., Kanovich, M.: Biabduction (and related problems) in array separation logic. In: de Moura, L. (ed.) CADE 2017. LNCS (LNAI), vol. 10395, pp. 472–490. Springer, Cham (2017). https://doi.org/10.1007/978-3-319-63046-5_29
7. Brotherston, J., Kanovich, M.: On the complexity of pointer arithmetic in separation logic. In: Ryu, S. (ed.) APLAS 2018. LNCS, vol. 11275, pp. 329–349. Springer, Cham (2018). https://doi.org/10.1007/978-3-030-02768-1_18
8. Calcagno, C., et al.: Moving fast with software verification. In: Havelund, K., Holzmann, G., Joshi, R. (eds.) NFM 2015. LNCS, vol. 9058, pp. 3–11. Springer, Cham (2015). https://doi.org/10.1007/978-3-319-17524-9_1
9. Calcagno, C., Distefano, D., O'Hearn, P.W., Yang, H.: Compositional shape analysis by means of bi-abduction. J. ACM **58**(6), 26 (2011)
10. Chin, W.-N., Gherghina, C., Voicu, R., Le, Q.L., Craciun, F., Qin, S.: A specialization calculus for pruning disjunctive predicates to support verification. In: Gopalakrishnan, G., Qadeer, S. (eds.) CAV 2011. LNCS, vol. 6806, pp. 293–309. Springer, Heidelberg (2011). https://doi.org/10.1007/978-3-642-22110-1_23
11. de Moura, L., Bjørner, N.: Z3: an efficient SMT solver. In: Ramakrishnan, C.R., Rehof, J. (eds.) TACAS 2008. LNCS, vol. 4963, pp. 337–340. Springer, Heidelberg (2008). https://doi.org/10.1007/978-3-540-78800-3_24
12. Echenim, M., Iosif, R., Peltier, N.: The Bernays-Schönfinkel-Ramsey class of separation logic on arbitrary domains. In: Bojańczyk, M., Simpson, A. (eds.) FoSSaCS 2019. LNCS, vol. 11425, pp. 242–259. Springer, Cham (2019). https://doi.org/10.1007/978-3-030-17127-8_14

13. Enea, C., Lengál, O., Sighireanu, M., Vojnar, T.: Compositional entailment checking for a fragment of separation logic. Formal Meth. Syst. Des. **51**(3), 575–607 (2017). https://doi.org/10.1007/s10703-017-0289-4
14. Gu, X., Chen, T., Wu, Z.: A complete decision procedure for linearly compositional separation logic with data constraints. In: Olivetti, N., Tiwari, A. (eds.) IJCAR 2016. LNCS (LNAI), vol. 9706, pp. 532–549. Springer, Cham (2016). https://doi.org/10.1007/978-3-319-40229-1_36
15. Iosif, R., Rogalewicz, A., Vojnar, T.: Deciding entailments in inductive separation logic with tree automata. In: Cassez, F., Raskin, J.-F. (eds.) ATVA 2014. LNCS, vol. 8837, pp. 201–218. Springer, Cham (2014). https://doi.org/10.1007/978-3-319-11936-6_15
16. Ishtiaq, S.S., O'Hearn, P.W.: Bi as an assertion language for mutable data structures. SIGPLAN Not. **36**(3), 14–26 (2001)
17. Jansen, C., Katelaan, J., Matheja, C., Noll, T., Zuleger, F.: Unified reasoning about robustness properties of symbolic-heap separation logic. In: Yang, H. (ed.) ESOP 2017. LNCS, vol. 10201, pp. 611–638. Springer, Heidelberg (2017). https://doi.org/10.1007/978-3-662-54434-1_23
18. Katelaan, J., Jovanović, D., Weissenbacher, G.: A separation logic with data: small models and automation. In: Galmiche, D., Schulz, S., Sebastiani, R. (eds.) IJCAR 2018. LNCS (LNAI), vol. 10900, pp. 455–471. Springer, Cham (2018). https://doi.org/10.1007/978-3-319-94205-6_30
19. Le, Q.L., Gherghina, C., Qin, S., Chin, W.-N.: Shape analysis via second-order biabduction. In: Biere, A., Bloem, R. (eds.) CAV 2014. LNCS, vol. 8559, pp. 52–68. Springer, Cham (2014). https://doi.org/10.1007/978-3-319-08867-9_4
20. Le, Q.L., He, M.: A decision procedure for string logic with quadratic equations, regular expressions and length constraints. In: Ryu, S. (ed.) APLAS 2018. LNCS, vol. 11275, pp. 350–372. Springer, Cham (2018). https://doi.org/10.1007/978-3-030-02768-1_19
21. Le, Q.L., Sun, J., Chin, W.-N.: Satisfiability modulo heap-based programs. In: Chaudhuri, S., Farzan, A. (eds.) CAV 2016. LNCS, vol. 9779, pp. 382–404. Springer, Cham (2016). https://doi.org/10.1007/978-3-319-41528-4_21
22. Le, Q.L., Sun, J., Qin, S.: Frame inference for inductive entailment proofs in separation logic. In: Beyer, D., Huisman, M. (eds.) TACAS 2018. LNCS, vol. 10805, pp. 41–60. Springer, Cham (2018). https://doi.org/10.1007/978-3-319-89960-2_3
23. Le, Q.L., Tatsuta, M., Sun, J., Chin, W.-N.: A decidable fragment in separation logic with inductive predicates and arithmetic. In: Majumdar, R., Kunčak, V. (eds.) CAV 2017. LNCS, vol. 10427, pp. 495–517. Springer, Cham (2017). https://doi.org/10.1007/978-3-319-63390-9_26
24. Lipshitz, L.: The diophantine problem for addition and divisibility. Trans. Am. Math. Soc. **235**, 271–283 (1978)
25. Madhusudan, P., Parlato, G., Qiu, X.: Decidable logics combining heap structures and data. In: Proceedings of the 38th Annual Symposium on Principles of Programming Languages, POPL 2011, New York, NY, USA, 2011, pp. 611–622. ACM (2011)
26. McPeak, S., Necula, G.C.: Data structure specifications via local equality axioms. In: Etessami, K., Rajamani, S.K. (eds.) CAV 2005. LNCS, vol. 3576, pp. 476–490. Springer, Heidelberg (2005). https://doi.org/10.1007/11513988_47
27. Pére, J.A.N., Rybalchenko, A.: Separation logic + superposition calculus = heap theorem prover. In: Proceedings of the 32nd ACM SIGPLAN Conference on Programming Language Design and Implementation, PLDI 2011, New York, NY, USA, 2011, pp. 556–566. Association for Computing Machinery (2011)

28. Navarro Pérez, J.A., Rybalchenko, A.: Separation logic modulo theories. In: Shan, C. (ed.) APLAS 2013. LNCS, vol. 8301, pp. 90–106. Springer, Cham (2013). https://doi.org/10.1007/978-3-319-03542-0_7

29. Pham, L.H., Le, Q.L., Phan, Q.-S., Sun, J.: Concolic testing heap-manipulating programs. In: ter Beek, M.H., McIver, A., Oliveira, J.N. (eds.) FM 2019. LNCS, vol. 11800, pp. 442–461. Springer, Cham (2019). https://doi.org/10.1007/978-3-030-30942-8_27

30. Pham, L.H., Le, Q.L., Phan, Q.-S., Sun, J., Qin, S.: Testing heap-based programs with java starfinder. In: Proceedings of the 40th International Conference on Software Engineering: Companion Proceedings, ICSE 2018, New York, NY, USA, 2018, pp. 268–269. ACM (2018)

31. Pham, L.H., Le, Q.L., Phan Q.-S., Sun, J., Qin, S.: Enhancing symbolic execution of heap-based programs with separation logic for test input generation. In: Proceeding of ATVA (2019)

32. Piskac, R., Wies, T., Zufferey, D.: Automating separation logic with trees and data. In: Biere, A., Bloem, R. (eds.) CAV 2014. LNCS, vol. 8559, pp. 711–728. Springer, Cham (2014). https://doi.org/10.1007/978-3-319-08867-9_47

33. Piskac, R., Wies, T., Zufferey, D.: GRASShopper - complete heap verification with mixed specifications. In: Ábrahám, E., Havelund, K. (eds.) TACAS 2014. LNCS, vol. 8413, pp. 124–139. Springer, Heidelberg (2014). https://doi.org/10.1007/978-3-642-54862-8_9

34. Popeea, C., Chin, W.-N.: Inferring disjunctive postconditions. In: ASIAN, pp. 331–345 (2006)

35. Reynolds, A., Iosif, R., Serban, C.: Reasoning in the Bernays-Schönfinkel-Ramsey fragment of separation logic. In: Bouajjani, A., Monniaux, D. (eds.) VMCAI 2017. LNCS, vol. 10145, pp. 462–482. Springer, Cham (2017). https://doi.org/10.1007/978-3-319-52234-0_25

36. Reynolds, J.C.: Separation logic: a logic for shared mutable data structures. In: Proceedings 17th Annual IEEE Symposium on Logic in Computer Science, pp. 55–74 (2002)

37. Sighireanu, M., Gorogiannis, N., Iosif, R.: SL-COMP 2019. https://www.irif.fr/sighirea/sl-comp/19/index.html. Accessed 15 Nov 2020

38. Sighireanu, M., et al.: SL-COMP: competition of solvers for separation logic. In: Tools and Algorithms for the Construction and Analysis of Systems - 25 Years of TACAS: TOOLympics, Held as Part of ETAPS 2019, Prague, Czech Republic, April 6–11, 2019, Proceedings, Part III, pp. 116–132 (2019)

39. Tatsuta, M., Le, Q.L., Chin, W.-N.: Decision procedure for separation logic with inductive definitions and Presburger arithmetic. In: Igarashi, A. (ed.) APLAS 2016. LNCS, vol. 10017, pp. 423–443. Springer, Cham (2016). https://doi.org/10.1007/978-3-319-47958-3_22

40. Trinh, M.-T., Le, Q.L., David, C., Chin, W.-N.: Bi-abduction with pure properties for specification inference. In: Shan, C. (ed.) APLAS 2013. LNCS, vol. 8301, pp. 107–123. Springer, Cham (2013). https://doi.org/10.1007/978-3-319-03542-0_8

41. Xu, Z., Chen, T., Wu, Z.: Satisfiability of compositional separation logic with tree predicates and data constraints. In: de Moura, L. (ed.) CADE 2017. LNCS (LNAI), vol. 10395, pp. 509–527. Springer, Cham (2017). https://doi.org/10.1007/978-3-319-63046-5_31

Author Index

Printed in the United States
by Baker & Taylor Publisher Services